Praise for *Inside Active Directory*

Praise for the First Edition

"Trust me on this one...if you're an Active Directory engineer or architect, this is the book you need. It's the companion that's going to help you keep your job if you're up in the middle of the night trying to understand how something works or why it's not working. It's truly an amazing book."

—*Scott Rachui, MCSE and Senior Active Directory Engineer, author of* MCSE Exchange Server 5.5 for Dummies

"This is the best book on Windows 2000 that I have read and one of the best computer books I have ever read. The most unique quality is the excellent explanation of how to use scripting to maximize your results and minimize your effort. This book is especially well suited to the enterprise audience that has to deploy many servers (100+) and not just 1–10. If you have even a small bit of programming experience, you will really appreciate the in-depth explanations of Windows 2000 under the covers."

—*Eric Chipko*

"Wow!! I love this book. I'd trade all my books covering Active Directory for this book in a second. The material is covered at a depth that I haven't seen in any other book—and I've looked at most of them. The material is presented in a straightforward manner that doesn't put you to sleep. An NT4 administrator could easily read this book and become an expert at Active Directory. I especially appreciated the chapter on Active Directory security."

—*Brian Arkills, author of* LDAP Directories Explained

Praise for the Second Edition

"If you are committed and really desire to know what makes Active Directory tick—and with it the backbone of the latest, and greatest, generation of Windows Network Operating Systems—then there is no better guide to get you there than this book. *Inside Active Directory* has no equal in the breadth, depth, and scope of its value to a technical practitioner."

—*Rick Kingslan, Microsoft MVP, Directory Services*

"Kouti and Seitsonen provide excellent coverage of topics a lot of people have difficulty understanding and setting up properly. This book supplies you with sound background theory so you can understand these concepts and at the same time gives just the right amount of detail to actually accomplish what you are trying to do."

—*Harold McFarland, Editor,* Readers Preference Reviews

"The style of this book is very appealing. It gives sufficient detail for the experienced administrator and explains what is happening 'behind the scenes' at each step, which is extremely helpful when problems arise. An excellent read and an essential component for any skilled administrator!"

—*Jeff Dunkelberger, Solutions Architect*

"An outstanding refresh of an already great book, *Inside Active Directory, Second Edition,* should be in the toolbox of any serious Active Directory administrator, architect, or developer. *Inside Active Directory* is one of the five books I refer to on a weekly basis. Thanks to the authors for all their hard work and dedication."

—*Joe Richards, Microsoft MVP, Windows Server/Active Directory*

Inside Active Directory

Second Edition

Microsoft Windows Server System Series

Books in the **Microsoft Windows Server System Series** are written and reviewed by the world's leading technical authorities on Microsoft Windows technologies, including principal members of Microsoft's Windows and Server Development Teams. The goal of the series is to provide reliable information that enables administrators, developers, and IT professionals to architect, build, deploy, and manage solutions using the Microsoft Windows Server System. The contents and code of each book are tested against, and comply with, commercially available code. This series should be an invaluable resource for any IT professional or student working in today's Windows environment.

TITLES IN THE SERIES

Paul Bertucci, *Microsoft SQL Server High Availability,* 0-672-32625-6 (Sams)

Peter Blackburn and William R. Vaughn, *Hitchhiker's Guide to SQL Server 2000 Reporting Services,* 0-321-26828-8 (Addison-Wesley)

William Boswell, *Learning Exchange Server 2003,* 0-321-22874-X (Addison-Wesley)

Roberta Bragg, *Windows Server 2003 Security,* 0-321-30501-9 (Addison-Wesley)

Eric L. Brown, *SQL Server 2005 Distilled,* 0-321-34979-2 (Addison-Wesley)

Bill English, Olga Londer, Shawn Shell, Todd Bleeker, and Stephen Cawood, *Microsoft Content Management Server 2002: A Complete Guide,* 0-321-19444-6 (Addison-Wesley)

John C. Hancock and Roger Toren, *Practical Business Intelligence with SQL Server 2005,* 0-321-35698-5 (Addison-Wesley)

Don Jones, *Managing Windows® with VBScript and WMI,* 0-321-21334-3 (Addison-Wesley)

Sakari Kouti and Mika Seitsonen, *Inside Active Directory, Second Edition: A System Administrator's Guide,* 0-321-22848-0 (Addison-Wesley)

Jason Nadrowski and Stacy Draper, *SharePoint 2003 Advanced Concepts,* 0-321-33661-5 (Addison-Wesley)

Shyam Pather, *Microsoft SQL Server 2000 Notification Services,* 0-672-32664-7 (Sams)

Jeffrey R. Shapiro and Marcin Policht, *Building High Availability Windows Server™ 2003 Solutions,* 0-321-22878-2 (Addison-Wesley)

Buck Woody, *Administrator's Guide to SQL Server 2005,* 0-321-39797-5 (Addison-Wesley)

For more information please go to www.awprofessional.com/msserverseries

Inside Active Directory

A System Administrator's Guide

Second Edition

Sakari Kouti

Mika Seitsonen

Addison-Wesley

Boston • San Francisco • New York • Toronto • Montreal
London • Munich • Paris • Madrid
Capetown • Sydney • Tokyo • Singapore • Mexico City

The publisher offers discounts on this book when ordered in quantity for bulk purchases and special sales. For more information, please contact:

U.S. Corporate and Government Sales
(800) 382-3419
corpsales@pearsontechgroup.com

For sales outside of the U.S., please contact:

International Sales
international@pearsoned.com

Visit Addison-Wesley on the Web: www.awprofessional.com

Library of Congress Cataloging-in-Publication Data

Kouti, Sakari.
Inside Active Directory : a system administrator's guide / Sakari Kouti,
Mika Seitsonen.—2nd ed.
p. cm. — (Microsoft Windows server system series)
Includes bibliographical references and index.
ISBN 0-321-22848-0 (pbk. : alk. paper)
1. Microsoft Windows (Computer file). 2. Operating systems (Computers)
3. Directory services (Computer network technology) I. Seitsonen, Mika.
II. Title. III. Series

QA76.O63K678 2005
005.265—dc22

2004008402

ISBN 0-321-22848-0
Text printed on recycled paper
3 4 5 6 7 8 9 10 11—CRS—09080706
Third printing, August 2006

As the first edition, about AD2000,
was dedicated to my first son, Miika, born in 2000,
this second edition, about AD2003,
is dedicated to my second son, Mikke, born in 2003.

—Sakari

For my daughter, Rosanna

—Mika

Contents

Preface

During the seven years that Windows NT was sold before Active Directory shipped as part of Windows 2000 (and consequently, as part of Windows Server 2003), administrators didn't need to learn practically anything new, at least about the core operating system features. User and group management, domains and domain models, and resource management had been the same in all Windows NT versions.

With the introduction of Active Directory, that all changed. There is a huge difference in managing Windows networks over the old NT administration model. Therefore, Active Directory will require quite a lot of study on the part of NT professionals.

Despite some administrative wizards in the user interface and the new Microsoft Management Console (MMC) administration interface, implementing and administering Active Directory requires probably more learning, testing, piloting, and planning than Windows NT required.

About This Book

This book is an implementer's and administrator's guide to Active Directory. Throughout the book, you will learn the workings, architecture, administration, and planning of Active Directory. Depending on your needs, however, you don't have to read this book from cover to cover, as we describe later in this preface.

The first version of Active Directory was included in Windows 2000 (AD2000, as we call it), and the second version is included in Windows Server 2003 (AD2003, as we call it). The first edition of this book covered AD2000, and this second edition covers primarily AD2003, but secondarily also AD2000.

The following list evaluates the appropriateness of this book for a number of potential audiences.

- *A current NT professional.* You are the target audience for this book. However, you may want to browse relatively quickly through any introductory pages that we have in the beginning of many chapters.
- *A current NetWare or UNIX professional.* Prior knowledge of Windows NT is not required to successfully learn from this book. Your earlier networking skills will most likely enable you to pick up each topic quite readily. However, you probably shouldn't skip any introductory topics.
- *A network operating systems novice.* Because we tend to start each chapter with the very basics, at least in theory you can use this book to effectively learn Active Directory. Obviously, you need to invest more time reading than an experienced IT professional. You should also have a test PC that you can use to try out the different tasks and experiments that the book describes.
- *A current Windows 2000/Windows Server 2003 professional.* Even if you are already familiar with Active Directory, we trust that you will learn more than a few things from this book.
- *A developer.* This book is an administrator's guide and not a programmer's guide. However, the book contains more architectural topics than the average book for an administrator, so you may find this book valuable to you in addition to a programmer's guide.

For all target audiences, it is possible that you are not interested in all the advanced topics in this book, so you are free to skip any of them.

We believe that this book has the following strengths.

- We present well-thought-out diagrams that help you easily comprehend the various key concepts and other topics related to Active Directory.
- At worst, a book just shows screen shots and shortly explains what is already evident from the user interface or the online Help. In contrast, this book contains thorough and accurate information on the topics it covers.
- We claim that this book contains very few errors.
- Even though this book is not a reference guide, we present many extensive reference tables.
- If you install Active Directory on a test PC, you can try out most of the tasks and experiments described in this book, whether they are written to be walkthroughs or not.

We have divided the book into three parts.

- *Part I: Background Skills* (Chapters 1 and 2) gives the big picture of Active Directory so you can successfully plan and implement an Active Directory network. This part also discusses the installation of Active Directory.
- *Part II: Core Skills* (Chapters 3 through 7) describes the concepts, planning, and administration of both the physical and the logical structure of Active Directory. The topics presented in this part include user and group management, access control, and Group Policy. Even though Part III covers advanced skills, most chapters in this part discuss related advanced topics.
- *Part III: Advanced Skills* (Chapters 8 through 11) looks at advanced techniques, including the schema and scripting. Along with these topics, we also uncover many aspects of Active Directory architecture. You can probably live without the information in these chapters, but by reading them, you can greatly deepen your knowledge and understanding of Active Directory and make use of it when implementing and administering Active Directory networks.

We'll now present a short summary of each chapter. Mika wrote Chapter 2 and Chapter 7, and Sakari wrote the remaining chapters.

Chapter 1: Active Directory: The Big Picture

Before going into detail, we give you a general picture of Active Directory. After you learn the concepts introduced in this chapter, you can skip freely some later chapters that you might not be interested in. However, we encourage you to browse through the table of contents of any such chapter to make sure that you are not going to unintentionally miss anything important.

Chapter 2: Active Directory Installation

In this chapter, we explain how to install Active Directory. We also describe the post-installation tasks, as well as how to automate and troubleshoot installation.

Chapter 3: Managing OUs, Users, and Groups

Once you have an Active Directory domain up and running, one obvious task is to create a user account for each user and plan how to enhance user administration by using groups and organizational units (OUs). This chapter looks at managing OUs, users, contacts, groups, and computer objects, and covers some related topics.

Chapter 4: Securing Active Directory

Active Directory has an access control mechanism that enables you to define who can read or modify what information in Active Directory. In this chapter, we explain the concepts and architecture of access control, as well as how to manage permissions in various scenarios.

Chapter 5: Sites and Replication

For Active Directory to work efficiently when your network spans multiple geographic locations, you must plan and implement the physical structure and define it in Active Directory itself. In this chapter, we describe the concepts, management, and advanced topics of the physical structure. Some of the content is also relevant for a company with just one site.

Chapter 6: Domains and Forests

Active Directory has several levels of hierarchies that you can use to implement an effective logical structure for your company network. In this chapter, we discuss whether you should use one or many domains and one or many forests, and how you should plan and manage that logical structure. We also revisit the physical structure, because it somewhat overlaps with the logical structure. In addition, we explain the anatomy of LDAP searches.

Chapter 7: Group Policy

Active Directory has an extensive management architecture called "Group Policy." You can use Group Policy to manage various aspects of Active Directory objects—for example, user desktop and server security settings. Some of the largest changes to Active Directory day-to-day management come in the form of Group Policy tools. In addition to these tools, you learn the architecture, inheritance, and processing of Group Policy in this chapter.

Chapter 8: Active Directory Schema

This chapter examines the Active Directory data model and how it is enforced by the rules of the schema. After reading this chapter, you'll better understand how Active Directory works behind the scenes, and you'll also gain knowledge that you can use if you are going to extend the schema.

Chapter 9: Extending the Schema

One of Active Directory's advantages over Windows NT is that you can extend the Active Directory schema, either to accommodate directory-enabled applications or for some administrative purpose. In this chapter, we explain the considerations for extensions and describe the process itself.

Chapter 10: Administration Scripts: Concepts

By downloading scripts from the Internet or writing your own scripts and executing them, you can greatly enhance and automate administration. In this chapter, we explain how to get started with technologies such as Windows Script Host (WSH), VBScript, and Active Directory Service Interfaces (ADSI).

Chapter 11: Administration Scripts: Examples

In this chapter, we present over 50 sample scripts along with their explanations. Outputs of many of the scripts provide some architectural information about Active Directory, and you can run those scripts without understanding what they do on each line. Therefore, you can use these scripts not only for various administrative tasks, but also to gain more knowledge about Active Directory. This chapter also introduces some additional scripting concepts, such as ActiveX Data Objects (ADO), between the sample scripts.

About the Authors

Both authors of this book are Finnish. Even though Finland is a small country, you may be familiar with something that came from here—for example, the Linux operating system, Nokia cell phones, and the IRC protocol for Internet chatting.

Sakari has worked with microcomputers for 22 years and with PC networks for 18 years. The last 15 years, he has instructed courses on network operating systems, such as LAN Manager, NetWare, Windows NT, Windows 2000, and Windows Server 2003. Because he has always enjoyed learning new technologies thoroughly and explaining and teaching them to others, it was quite natural for Sakari to write first technical articles and later this book. While still a student back in the 1980s, Sakari worked part-time as a programmer, which helped him write the scripting chapters in this book.

Mika's network experience also spans 15 years. After spending 5 years in implementing networks, he became a network trainer. Consequently, Mika shares Sakari's background in continually learning new technologies and passing that information on to others. Mika has been eager to achieve Microsoft certifications, and as a result, he has achieved Windows 2000 and Windows Server 2003 MCSEs (Microsoft Certified Systems Engineer), among the first people in the world to do so. Mika was awarded MVP, Directory Services in July 2004.

This book has a companion Web site: `http://www.kouti.com/`. This site contains all the sample scripts presented in the book as downloadable files, as well as some other tables and files relating to the book contents.

Acknowledgments

Because roughly 80 percent of the book's content is unchanged from the first edition, the first-edition acknowledgments still apply.

We would like to thank Gary Clarke of Addison-Wesley, who originally hired us to write the first edition of this book. We would also like to thank Rebecca Bence, Jenie Pak, Michael Slaughter, and Stephane Thomas from Addison-Wesley, who cooperated with us during the preparation of the first edition, and Stephane Thomas and Ebony Haight during the second edition. Ebony had a hard time trying to convince us that there are such things as deadlines in the publishing business.

We thank the entire production team of the first edition for their cooperation and assistance (including Joan M. Flaherty, Tyrrell Albaugh, Amy Fleischer, Nicole LeClerc, and Kathy Glidden), and the team of the second edition (including Debby English, Julie Nahil, and Kathy Glidden).

We are deeply grateful to our Addison-Wesley reviewers of the first edition, Jeff Dunkelberger, Scott Lewandowski, and Erik Olson, who read the manuscript and gave us valuable feedback. Our special thanks go to Keith Walls for his great reviews. We are equally grateful to the second-edition reviewers, Brian Arkills, Jeff Dunkelberger, James Edelen, Rick Kingslan, Harold McFarland, and Joe Richards, for their thorough and observant reviews.

Our thanks also go to Pertti Pellonpoika and our other colleagues at Sovelto for their comments and discussions that helped in creating this book. We acknowledge Sovelto as a fine training organization and as a working environment that stimulates learning.

Andreas Luther and Richard Ault of Microsoft answered many of our questions, for which we are grateful. For the second edition, we received help also from Microsoft's Nathan Muggli and Rob Kochman.

Sakari would like to personally thank Dina Ralston, who hired him to write some articles for *Windows NT Magazine* (now called *Windows & .NET Magazine*) and serve as a member of the magazine's editorial review board. This started the series of events that led to writing this book. Sakari would also like to thank Reino Korpela, who taught Sakari about computers at school back in 1977 and who later gave him his first summer job in microcomputers in 1982; Ilkka Liedes, who hired him in 1986 to work with personal computers and who soon after assigned him his first project with PC networks; and Risto Linturi, who hired him in 1989 to instruct courses on PC operating systems and network operating systems. And finally, Sakari would like to express special thanks to Satu. His first son, Miika, was born 12 months before the first-edition manuscript deadline, and Satu took care of Miika so that Sakari could concentrate (well, mostly anyway) on writing and finishing the book. Later, their second son, Mikke, was born just before the work for the second edition started.

Mika first and foremost thanks Sakari for asking him to join this project, which Mika considers yet another great learning experience. Mika also appreciates his wonderful fiancée, Päivi, for having the patience for Mika's book writing, which seemed to always be on the to-do list. Mika's thanks are also due to Peter Ting, and Simo EW and Marjatta Laine, who have given him great confidence and advice for the walk of life. Mika would also like to thank Professor Markku Tuominen from the Lappeenranta University of Technology for planting the seed for continuous learning.

Sakari Kouti
Espoo, Finland

Mika Seitsonen
Tervakoski, Finland
April 2004

PART I

Background Skills

CHAPTER 1

Active Directory: The Big Picture

In this chapter we introduce the major concepts, definitions, building blocks, and features of Active Directory. This overview provides a frame of reference so that as you read the later chapters, you can see where each topic fits into the big picture. Topics in this chapter include

- A brief introduction and history, including a noninclusive list of differences between Active Directory in Windows Server 2003 (AD2003) and Windows 2000 (AD2000), and a brief comparison of Active Directory to Windows NT and to Novell's NDS (Novell Directory Services)
- Basic building blocks, such as domains, domain controllers (DCs), trust relationships, organizational units (OUs), groups, objects, sites, replication, and the global catalog (GC)
- Active Directory hierarchies: OU trees, which are built of organizational units, domain trees; and forests
- An explanation of the way Active Directory uses the Domain Name System (DNS) and its dynamic updates, Group Policy, access control with inheritance, and delegation
- Architecture, including the data model, the schema, container and leaf objects, partitions, object naming, X.500, the Lightweight Directory Access Protocol (LDAP), programmatic access, the Kerberos authentication protocol, and public key infrastructure (PKI)
- Other features of interest, such as virtual containers and publishing
- Active Directory's limitations

The presentation of these topics is brief because we address most of them in depth in later chapters. We discuss the following topics, however, only in this chapter: a comparison of Active Directory to Windows NT and NDS, object naming, X.500, the Kerberos protocol, PKI, and Active Directory's limitations.

Introduction to Active Directory

Active Directory is a *directory service* and, like any directory service, its ultimate purpose is to store information about users, resources, and other network entities, and to provide that information to anyone or anything that has access to the directory, according to access permissions. This information helps administrators to manage the network and users to find people and resources.

Active Directory replaces the user account database and domain models that were used in Windows NT. It also adds a wealth of features that qualify it as a directory service, rather than a simple user account database.

Even though Active Directory has a database of information, it is not a relational database like SQL Server. As all directory services, Active Directory has been optimized for storing relatively static information, and for providing scalable and distributed access to that information. The information in Active Directory is represented as *objects* that you create for each user, group, and computer. There are also objects for contact people, printers, shared folders, application services, other resources, and configuration information.

A Brief Description

We can describe Active Directory from three points of view. From each point, we view one of the three "faces" of Active Directory:

- *The Windows NT face.* Administrators can create user accounts to control how each user can use the network. Users log on using these accounts and act according to the settings that administrators have specified (such as having to change the password every month).
- *The enterprise services face.* Active Directory provides a scalable and hierarchical infrastructure for managing enterprise-sized distributed networks. For example, administration of various parts can be delegated to lower levels. If desired or necessary, the head

office administrators can set policies that affect desktops of some or every satellite office.

- *The directory face.* An organization can store its address book of users and customers, as well as other relevant information about anything they want. For example, it can use Active Directory to search users by name or printers by features. Because permissions specify granular access to the information, the organization can choose which attributes of which objects various types of employees can see.

We can also characterize Active Directory by three types of users.

- *Administrators* manage and configure the network, including the user accounts, services, and devices. They do this by creating specific objects and storing appropriate configuration and other information in them. All administration can be done through Active Directory, and doing so should result in efficient administration, as well as a secure and consistent network environment.
- *Users* log on to Active Directory (i.e., "to the network") using a password or a smart card, and then use the configured resources and possibly search for people, resources, or other useful information. If permitted, users can also modify information in Active Directory. Active Directory group policies can provide users with certain desktop settings and restrictions, as well as offer company applications for them to use. Group policies are applied during logon and periodically refreshed afterward.
- *Applications, services, and computing devices* can read their configuration information from Active Directory and act accordingly. They can also write information to Active Directory, if so programmed. Consequently, we can talk about *directory-enabled applications (DEAs)* and *directory-enabled networking (DEN)*. In addition to configuration information, an application (for example, a faxing application) can use the Active Directory in ways it would use an address book. The server services of client-server applications (using such technologies as RPC, WinSock, and COM) may publish their connection points in Active Directory for users and client applications to find them.

In general, the information in Active Directory falls into one of two categories.

- Certain information in certain objects is *significant* (as we call it), which means that it affects how some aspects of Windows work. For example, significant information controls when and how network users can log on or which services they can use.
- The remaining information is *informational* (e.g., Jack's postal address). It may be interesting and useful to people or directory-enabled applications, but Windows doesn't use this information itself. Consequently, informational data doesn't have the controlling aspect of significant information.

Given these definitions, informational information can still control users' lives, even though Windows doesn't use that information. For example, a device to control the main door of a company could use Active Directory to store information such as the access codes. In this example, when a user types a key code at the door, the device can check Active Directory for approval of the code and open the door only if the code is verified.

NOTE We use the terms *significant* and *informational* to help you understand the two categories of information that Active Directory contains. You can use the categories as a reference, but it is not important to try to place each piece of information into one of the categories.

Finally, Active Directory has the following technical features:

- The information in Active Directory is highly available because identical information is on several servers (called *domain controllers*). As administrators design the network, they can choose the location of each server. This provides both fault tolerance and, in the case of a geographically dispersed network, scalability and proximity of information.
- A change in one domain controller is guaranteed to reach the other domain controllers, even though this will take a while. Consequently, some domain controllers may be out-of-date at any given time. This concept is called *loose consistency.* Inside a local area network (LAN), each change in one domain controller should reach any other domain controller within a minute (or up to 20 minutes with Windows 2000 domain controllers).
- Because all changes (are likely to) need to be copied to several domain controllers, both in the same building as well as perhaps

to offices located on other continents, the information put in Active Directory should be "globally" useful and relatively static, and each piece should not be very large. If an organization needs to store information that doesn't fit these criteria, it should consider storing that information somewhere else, such as the SQL Server or file system. With Windows Server 2003 domain controllers, the organization could also use Active Directory application partitions, because they enable you to specify on which domain controller(s) the information will reside.

- Hierarchies and permissions allow distributed management of the data. Network administrators can delegate tasks so that assisting administrators and even end users can maintain part of the information. Also, Active Directory is one of the foundations of the Windows 2000 and later security model.
- Permissions allow control over which users will see what information.
- Optimization for a high number of reads.
- The information is highly typed, which means that Active Directory enforces rules for the structure and content of the information.
- Distributed security allows companies to build intranets and extranets and to use distributed applications in this environment.
- Allowance of standards-based read and write access using the LDAP protocol. Additionally, LDAP allows effective searches on the information in Active Directory.

The First Look at Active Directory

Figure 1.1 and Figure 1.2 show two basic views of Active Directory. The screen shot in Figure 1.1 shows an administrator's view of the objects for users, groups, and contacts. The screen shot in Figure 1.2 shows the view an end user sees when she opens My Network Places. In this case, the two views show exactly the same objects, but this may not be the case every time.

NOTE The view in Figure 1.2 is available only in Windows 2000, not in Windows XP or Windows Server 2003. In these later versions, the end user is not meant to browse the OU structure. You can, however, enable browsing in the later versions by copying a file from Windows 2000. This is explained in Chapter 3.

Figure 1.1 An administrator can create a tree of folders, like the tree in the left pane. Each folder may contain user, group, and contact objects, among others. Note that this figure shows only a small part of Active Directory's contents.

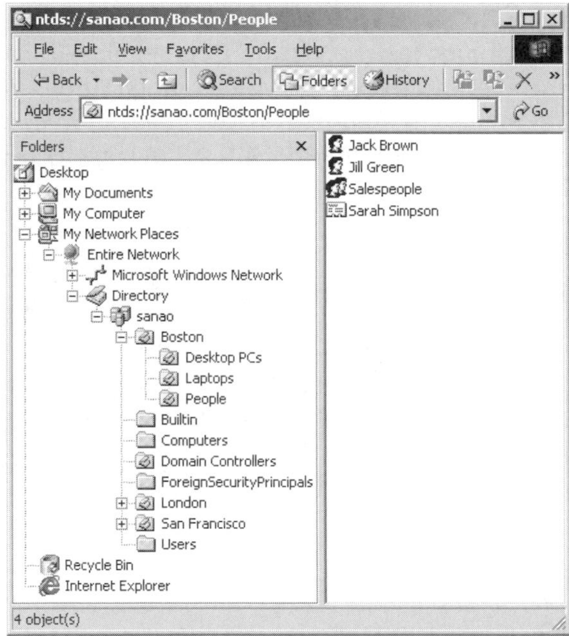

Figure 1.2 An end user of Windows 2000 (but not of newer versions) can open My Network Places to see part of the directory tree in Active Directory.

NOTE As Figure 1.1 and Figure 1.2 show, the administrator's and end user's views of the directory are quite similar. In practice, however, end users typically use a search user interface instead of a navigation tree (see the Note on page 7 about the Windows versions).

History

Windows Server 2003 and Active Directory are the latest in a long line of Microsoft operating systems and network operating systems (NOS). In this section, we review Microsoft's previous NOS products, explore the history of directories, including some products from other vendors, and look at the development of Windows 2000/Windows Server 2003.

Previous Microsoft Network Operating Systems

Microsoft's first network operating system was MS-NET, which was used in the 1980s with Microsoft's disk operating system (MS-DOS). Microsoft's next NOS was LAN Manager, which first shipped in 1988 to be used with Operating System/2 (OS/2) version 1.1. OS/2 was developed jointly by Microsoft and IBM. With either MS-NET plus MS-DOS or LAN Manager plus OS/2, there was a separate NOS and an operating system, but the subsequent version, Windows NT, integrated the two. Microsoft and IBM had agreed that IBM would develop OS/2 version 2 while Microsoft would simultaneously work on OS/2 version 3. Microsoft started this development in early 1989.

In parallel with developing OS/2 version 3, Microsoft had already developed the "DOS-based" Windows beginning in the early 1980s. It hadn't been especially popular, until 1990, when the launch of Windows 3.0 was a huge success. This encouraged Microsoft to change the user and programming interfaces of the OS/2 version it was developing from OS/2 Presentation Manager to Windows and to change the product name from OS/2 to Windows NT. Understandably, the cooperation between Microsoft and IBM ended, so Microsoft became the sole owner and developer of Windows NT. Since 1993, Microsoft has published the following versions of Windows NT:

- 1993: Windows NT 3.1
- 1994: Windows NT 3.5
- 1995: Windows NT 3.51

- 1996: Windows NT 4.0
- 1997: Windows NT 4.0 Service Pack 3
- 1998: Windows NT 4.0 Service Pack 4

Although not truly new versions, the two service packs are in the list because they brought a number of new features to Windows NT. For a few years there was no new version of Windows NT because Microsoft focused all its efforts on the next major version of its operating system, Windows 2000.

Finally, Windows 2000 shipped in the beginning of 2000 and started gradually to gain momentum. Three service packs were also released, before Windows Server 2003 shipped in March 2003. In June 2003, Windows 2000 Service Pack 4 was released.

The History of Directories

Telephone directories as well as other directories and catalogs on paper existed long before any computer systems. Now in the computer era, we have new kinds of directories, including

- *E-mail systems* such as Lotus (currently owned by IBM) Notes, Novell GroupWise, and Microsoft Exchange 5.5 (later Exchange versions use Active Directory). Each has a directory of the e-mail users of the system and the contact people outside the organization.
- Practically all *network operating systems* have had some kind of directory to contain the usernames and passwords of the users of that network. Examples are Microsoft LAN Manager and Windows NT with their user account databases, as well as Novell NetWare 3 with its Bindery.
- There have been also *real directory services in network operating systems.* The most notable are StreetTalk and NDS. Banyan started selling StreetTalk for its VINES network operating system in the 1980s, and Novell shipped NDS with NetWare 4.0 in 1993.
- *Internet directories* are offered by companies such as Yahoo, Switchboard, Bigfoot, WhitePages.com, VeriSign, and WhoWhere. If you open the Windows Address Book, you will see some of these companies.

All the directories listed (short of NDS) concentrate on storing contact information about users or information that allows users to log on. However, a directory doesn't have to be only for these purposes.

For example, Active Directory allows storing information about practically anything, although its foremost use is to store information about people.

Directory standards—the most important being X.500 and LDAP—are part of directory history. X.500 is an international standard for directories and LDAP is a popular protocol for accessing directories. (We will discuss both standards at the end of this chapter.) The following chronology indicates the major milestones in the history of directories.

- 1988: The first version of X.500 was finalized.
- 1992: Developers from the University of Michigan released the first LDAP software.
- 1993: The first version of LDAP (LDAPv1) was published as RFC (Request For Comments) 1487.
- 1995: LDAPv2 was published as RFC 1777 (and other RFCs).
- 1996: About 40 companies, including Microsoft, Netscape, and Novell, announced that they would support LDAP in their directory services products.
- 1997: LDAPv3 was published as RFC 2251 (and others).
- 1998: Netscape shipped the first commercial LDAPv3 server, called iPlanet.
- 2000: Microsoft shipped Active Directory as part of the Windows 2000 product (we call it AD2000 in this book).
- 2003: Microsoft shipped the second version of Active Directory, shipped as part of the Windows Server 2003 product (we call it AD2003 in this book).

The History of Windows 2000

The development of Windows NT's successor, code-named Windows "Cairo," started early in the 1990s, even though Windows NT wasn't published until 1993. Cairo's roots might be in the keynote speech of the Comdex trade show in 1990. In that speech Microsoft's Bill Gates introduced a vision called "information at your fingertips," and demonstrated some of its possible technologies accompanied by music and themes from the TV series *Twin Peaks*.

In 1991 the project for Cairo was launched, and Jim Allchin was appointed to be the project lead. Before joining Microsoft, Allchin was a technology officer at Banyan, the maker of StreetTalk. Allchin was a suitable choice for the Cairo project because he was a professor-type guy who could understand and develop new technologies that many people in the industry or at Microsoft couldn't even imagine.

Originally Cairo was planned to contain, among other things, an object-oriented file system, a distributed file system, and Kerberos security. The last two features made it to Windows 2000 (and consequently to Windows Server 2003), but the object-oriented file system did not. A directory service was also part of the picture, but at that time X.500 was too complex and resource-intensive to be used in personal computers. Only some years later, when the lighter LDAP was born, could Microsoft start incorporating it into Cairo.

Cairo was a parallel project to Windows NT development. The two had separate project teams; however, some Cairo technologies were used already in Windows NT. Also, over the years, the definition of Cairo evolved, and at some point it began to refer to a vision of a future Windows version instead of a specific forthcoming product.

In 1996 Microsoft demonstrated Cairo technologies to the public and named the forthcoming product "Windows NT 5.0." Although it was anticipated that Windows NT 5.0 would ship in 1997, a few more years passed before the launch.

In 1998 Microsoft renamed Windows NT 5.0 as "Windows 2000" for at least two reasons. People often called Windows NT simply "NT," which was a trademark of Northern Telecom (currently Nortel Networks). However, Microsoft does own the trademark "Windows." Also, Microsoft was planning to consolidate all Windows versions to the NT platform, in which case the designation "NT" would no longer be needed.

Windows 2000 had quite a long beta-testing phase, as the following chronology illustrates:

- 1996: Technology preview to run on Windows NT 4.0
- 1997: Windows NT 5.0 beta 1
- 1998: Windows NT 5.0 beta 2
- 1999: Windows 2000 beta 3
- 2000: Windows 2000

The main new feature of Windows 2000 was its directory service (Active Directory). When Microsoft launched Windows NT 4.0 in 1996, its marketing actually renamed Windows NT domain models to "directory services," but the change was in the name only, not in the features.

Because Novell NDS shipped in 1993 and Windows 2000 shipped in 2000, Microsoft could be considered to be seven years behind Novell.

However, in its first version, Active Directory was mostly an enterprise-class directory service, but of course it could benefit from some maturing. An advantage over Novell, however, is that Microsoft got a fresh start to build its directory service for the needs of the current intranet and Internet era. The only old burden Microsoft carries is the old Windows NT domain concept, which introduces some rigidity to Active Directory.

The History of Windows Server 2003

The necessary maturation of Active Directory mentioned in the previous paragraph materialized quite well, when Windows Server 2003 shipped.

The next Windows version after Windows 2000 had the code name "Whistler." It referred to both the workstation and server versions, and since 1993 these two had been launched side by side. This policy changed when the workstation version of Whistler was launched as Windows XP in the fall of 2001. After that, it took over a year and half before the corresponding server version shipped as Windows Server 2003.

Windows Server 2003 contains "everything" that Windows XP contains, and because the former is a little newer, it is understandably slightly more current than Windows XP. In regard to Active Directory, AD2003 is not substantially different from AD2000. The three years of development brought "only" more maturity, as the next section describes.

The product name of Windows Server 2003 changed a few times before it was launched in 2003 (Windows 2002, Windows .NET Server, Windows .NET Server 2003, and Windows Server 2003). ".NET" was in the name to promote the .NET concept, but because .NET didn't start to gain momentum very fast, Microsoft dropped ".NET" from the name so that slow adoption of .NET wouldn't lead to slow adoption of Windows Server 2003. Another reason for dropping ".NET" was probably the confusion it was causing.

Back in the 1990s, Microsoft at first missed the fast and massive proliferation of the Internet. However, they soon made extra efforts to get on par with the market, and they succeeded quite well. A similar situation occurred at the beginning of the millennium, when Microsoft first missed the increased need for security. Again, they made extra efforts to fix this.

During the development of Windows Server 2003, Microsoft made intense efforts to enhance the security of this new Windows operating system. The entire company took two months to focus strictly on security training, coding practices, and reengineering many of the product's features. The effort was remarkable, when you consider that the product was already late and they were already taking heat in the press not only for security weaknesses in Internet Information Server (IIS) 5 and Windows 2000, but also for the ongoing delays.

In retrospect, this was an excellent decision, but it must have not been an easy one at the time. This effort has manifested itself in many improvements in the product, as well as in Microsoft's general stance regarding security and its enhanced respect in security circles. Actually, one of the largest sponsors (and often a very active participant) of the various security conferences and hacker-attended events is none other than Microsoft, which only a few years ago was derided anytime the mere concept of security was mentioned. All this is a remarkable turnaround. Security is now integral to every aspect of the product.

Microsoft has also launched an "SD3" approach to deliver secure computing: (a) secure by design—a massive change in how Microsoft creates software; (b) secure by default—turning off features by default and giving guidance to users who balance between security and functionality; and (c) secure in deployment—giving new tools to make it easier to maintain security.

AD2003 Compared to AD2000

One of the design goals of AD2003 was that AD2000 skills, the existing structure, and design principles must be valid also in AD2003. Other goals were better security, better scalability in a large environment, better manageability, and better monitoring. Another goal was to minimize the number of design decisions that could not be changed afterward.

In this section we briefly list and describe many of the new features of AD2003 over AD2000. We assume here that you know AD2000 pretty well, and if you don't, you may want to skip to the next section. Note that this list is by no means exhaustive.

Deployment

- *Install from media*. When you install an additional domain controller to a domain, you can load the initial contents of the Active Directory database from a backup, such as CD-R disk. After this, only the latest changes need to be replicated from other domain controllers. When you are installing domain controllers to remote locations in a large forest, this can save hours of replication.

- *Functional levels.* In AD2000, your domains were in either mixed mode or native mode. In AD2003, your domains are on one of the domain functional levels: Windows 2000 mixed, Windows 2000 native, Windows Server 2003 interim, or Windows Server 2003. In AD2000, there were no modes for the forest, but in AD2003, your forest has one of the forest functional levels: Windows 2000, Windows Server 2003 interim, or Windows Server 2003. Some new features of AD2003 are available regardless of either the domain or forest functional level, but others require rising to a certain level. We list which features each level provides in Table 2.2 and Table 2.3 in Chapter 2.
- *ADMTv2*: The Active Directory Migration Tool (ADMT) is a tool to migrate users, groups, and computer objects from NT domains to Active Directory or from Active Directory to Active Directory, either interforest or intraforest. Windows Server 2003 includes version 2 of ADMT. It enables you to migrate user passwords along with the users, and version 2 also has some 20 other enhancements over version 1. ADMTv2 does not require the target forest to be AD2003; you can use the new version also when migrating to a Windows 2000 forest, provided that the target domain is in Windows 2000 native mode.

Domain Management

- *Users and Computers snap-in enhancements.* The new features include drag-and-drop moving of objects, showing effective permissions, showing the inheritance parent, editing multiple objects, saving queries, and restoring default permissions.
- *DS commands.* DSAdd and five other commands enable you to add, delete, modify, read, and query Active Directory objects from the command line.
- *Directory quotas.* You can set quotas for how many objects certain security principals may create or own on a given directory partition.
- *The `lastLogonTimestamp` attribute.* This attribute is replicated among domain controllers, so it enables easier tracking of when user or computer accounts have logged on than the non-replicating `lastLogon` attribute.
- *Basic and query-based authorization groups.* You can use Authorization Manager (AzMan.msc) to create these new types of

application groups. A basic group contains other application groups or normal Windows users or groups as members. A query-based group's membership is determined dynamically based on an LDAP filter. Windows doesn't use application groups, but you could have applications that use these new group types for authorization and role-based administration.

Replication

- *Linked value replication (LVR).* In AD2000, each multivalued attribute was replicated in one chunk (i.e., all values together). The area this affected most was group membership management, where the following three drawbacks existed: (a) there was a 5,000-member maximum; (b) when one member was added to a group, all the thousands of members needed to be replicated, not just the new one; and (c) if the membership was modified on two domain controllers within replication latency (for example, five minutes), only one of the changes was kept and the other was lost. In AD2003, each value is replicated independently, so these three problems are eliminated.
- *Improved inter-site topology generator (ISTG).* The ISTG in AD2000 could automatically create a replication topology for a forest of a maximum of 200 sites (depending also on the hardware and the number of domains). In AD2003, the algorithms are much more efficient, so the maximum is at least thousands of sites. As of this writing, Microsoft's testing is still in progress to find out when the maximum is finally reached.
- *Global catalog replication improvements.*
- *Bridgehead server load balancing.* Instead of having just one bridgehead server per partition, per site, and per protocol (RPC or SMTP), all domain controllers on a site can act as bridgehead servers. This is beneficial especially in a branch office scenario, where a large number of sites communicate with one hub site.
- *New compression algorithm.* The new algorithm to compress intersite replication data gives about a 20 percent CPU performance improvement, but has a little worse compression ratio. Since the modern wide area network (WAN) links are usually quite fast, this trade-off is not a problem.
- *Application partitions.* The query and access control features of Active Directory make it an excellent place to store application data. In AD2000, however, a limitation was that there were only

two scopes of replication (in addition to the global catalog). The data was replicated either to all domain controllers in the domain or to all domain controllers in the forest. You can create application partitions on Windows Server 2003 domain controllers, and for each application partition, you can specify on which domain controller(s) the replica of the partition should reside.

Global Catalog

- *Universal group membership caching*. Normally, when a user logged on in AD2000, the domain controller that was processing the logon needed to contact a global catalog server to find out the universal groups that the user was a member of. In AD2003, the domain controller caches this information during the first logon of each user and subsequently updates the information every eight hours. This relieves the domain controller from having a constant connection to a global catalog server, which in turn means that the number of global catalog servers can be reduced. With this change, global catalog servers are mostly needed for applications, such as Exchange, but not that much for logons.
- *No GC full sync*. In AD2000, if the schema was modified so that a new attribute was added to the partial attribute set (PAS), meaning that it would be part of the global catalog, a full sync occurred with all the global catalog servers of the forest. In other words, all global catalog information needed to be replicated again to each global catalog server. This could cause gigabytes of replication in a large network. In AD2003, only the values of the added attribute are replicated.

Forest Management

- *DC rename*. In AD2003, you can rename domain controllers. You can do this either with the Control Panel or the NetDom command.
- *Domain rename*. In AD2003, you can rename any domain in the forest (NetBIOS and/or DNS name). You can also restructure the domains with this feature, except that the forest root domain is always the same. During the rename process, the forest is temporarily offline, and you may need to reinstall applications, such as Exchange. Domain rename is not recommended as a routine operation. Use it only if you really need to and with great caution.

- *Forest trusts*. You can create a forest trust among the root domains of two forests. Whereas an external trust enables access from one domain to another, a forest trust enables access from any domain in one forest to any domain in another forest. The owners of each forest have several ways to limit the access from the foreign forest, either per domain and/or per server (selective authentication, SID filtering, and name suffix routing). Two other benefits are that (a) authentication from one forest to another uses Kerberos instead of the older Windows NT/LAN Manager (NTLM) authentication, and (b) a user of one forest can log on to a workstation in another forest, and she can use her user principal name (UPN) (such as `jill.green@sanao.com`) in the process.
- *DNS zones in application partitions*. If Active Directory–integrated zones are used, they are stored in application partitions, enabling better control of what zone information to replicate where.
- *Lingering object detection and removal*. Lingering objects may occur when a once-deleted object reappears in the forest. This could happen, for example, when a domain controller that was offline over 60 days is brought back online. In AD2003, such objects don't replicate to other domain controllers (by default), and you can remove lingering objects with the RepAdmin tool.
- *Restoring deleted objects*. AD2003 enables you to restore deleted objects. For example, you can restore a deleted user object and its old security ID (SID). Unfortunately, you cannot restore most of the other user attributes, so you still need backups. You can restore a deleted object with LDP but not with the Users and Computers snap-in.

Security

- *Signed and encrypted LDAP traffic between admin tools and domain controllers*.
- *Thirty new security settings in Group Policy*. Windows 2000 with SP4 has 115; Windows Server 2003 has 145.
- *Domain password policy*. By default, you must use complex passwords that are at least seven characters long.
- *SMB Signing and Secure Channel Signing*. These reduce the vulnerability for "man in the middle" attacks but at the same time may affect the ability of earlier Windows clients to authenticate and use network resources.

- *Auditing of Active Directory access*. By default, this is on, although only a few items are logged.
- *Domain controller security log maximum size*. This is 128MB, whereas on a member server it is 16MB.
- *Enhanced ACL Editor*. The new version shows where a permission is inherited from. It also contains the Effective Permissions tab.
- *Constrained delegation for computers*. This option allows delegated Kerberos authentication to run only selected services on a computer rather than running all services.
- *Kerberos key distribution center (KDC) key version numbers*. Kerberos keys are changed when a user changes her password. The old keys are stored for a period of time. Version numbering makes it more efficient to locate the correct key for decrypting encrypted communications. Version numbers are constructed from the update logon timestamp attribute when a user changes her password. They are also used for compliance with RFC 1510.
- *Permission compatibility level*. By default, when you run DCPromo, "Permissions compatible only with Windows 2000 or Windows Server 2003 servers" is selected, which clears Everyone and Anonymous Logon from the group Pre-Windows 2000 Compatible Access.
- *Service accounts*. Most services run with the Local Service or Network Service account, instead of the more privileged System account.
- *LDAP connections over Transport Layer Security (TLS) (RFC 2830)*.
- *Digest authentication for LDAP connections*. This feature uses DIGEST-MD5 SASL (RFC 2829).

Group Policy

- *GPMC*. Group Policy Management Console (GPMC) is a new snap-in to manage all aspects of Group Policy, except the management of the actual settings (which is performed with the traditional GPO Editor). GPMC has an enhanced user interface to manage a number of Group Policy objects (GPOs), their inheritance, permissions, application, backup, and so on. GPMC also enables analyzing and simulating the combined effect of multiple policies. In addition, GPMC is scriptable and comes with 32 sample scripts. You must download GPMC separately from Microsoft's Web site.

- *WMI filters*. You can use Windows Management Instrumentation (WMI) filters to specify where a given GPO should apply. A traditional example is to limit the scope of an application-installing GPO to only workstations that have at least 4GB of free disk space.

Directory Database

- *Single Instance Storage (SIS)*. Different Active Directory objects contain a lot of identical permission entries because of inheritance and schema defaults. SIS enables storing identical information only once, which can reduce the size of the directory database some 40 percent (if you upgrade a Windows 2000 server, you must perform an offline defragmentation of the database to gain this).
- *Manual trigger of online defragmentation.*

Schema

- *InetOrgPerson objects*. RFC 2798 defines the inetOrgPerson class, which is the normal user objects class in many directory products other than Active Directory. In AD2003, you can use inetOrgPerson objects just as you use user objects, which makes interoperability with other products, or migrating from another product, easier.
- *InetOrgPerson objects can be converted to user objects and vice versa.*
- *Use of the `userPassword` attribute for storing inetOrgPerson and user passwords.* By default, the `unicodePwd` attribute is used.
- *Schema defunct and reuse*: In AD2003, you can reuse more freely the names and identifiers (such as `lDAPDisplayName` and `attributeID`) of deactivated schema classes and attributes.
- *Dynamic objects*. In AD2003, you can create objects with a predetermined time to live (TTL), to store temporary data. After the TTL has elapsed, the object is automatically removed.
- *Dynamically linked auxiliary classes*. Such classes can be dynamically linked to directory objects rather than a whole class. Consequently, the attributes listed in the dynamically linked auxiliary class are valid in the affected directory objects.

Active Directory Compared to Windows NT

Table 1.1 lists some technical changes from Windows NT to Active Directory. If you are not familiar with Windows NT, you probably will want to skip this table. We explain each item later in the chapter.

Table 1.1 Windows NT versus Active Directory

Feature	Windows NT*	Active Directory
Group types	Only security groups	Security groups and distribution groups
Group scopes	Global and local groups	Global, universal, and domain local groups (and local groups in member servers and workstations)
Group nesting (one group a member of another)	Global groups may be members of local groups	Free nesting within each scope
Trust relationships	Intransitive, one way (although you can create one trust to either direction)	Transitive, two way (or bidirectional)
Replication type	Single master from PDC to BDC(s)	Multimaster from any domain controller to another, except in some special cases
Replication in WAN	Needs to replicate the same data multiple times over a WAN link (to different BDCs)	Replicates the data only once over a given WAN link
Replication amount	Whole object at a time	Only changed properties of an object
Replication amount for a new user account	About 1KB	At least about 4KB (however, this may be compressed up to over 10:1 when replicated between sites)
Member server may be changed to domain controller without reinstalling	No	Yes

(continued)

* When we refer to Windows NT without a version number, we mean the latest version, 4.0. However, in most cases the information also applies to earlier versions.

Table 1.1 Windows NT versus Active Directory *(cont.)*

Feature	Windows NT*	Active Directory
Per–domain controller administration privileges	No	Some
Object hierarchy	No	In folders called organizational units (and in other container objects)
Delegation of administration	Only per domain (also some "delegation" with operator privileges)	Per OU, per object, or per attribute (and also operator privileges)
Policies	System Policy (some 70 settings)	Group Policy (some 1,000 settings)
Extensible schema	No	Yes, may add new object classes and properties
User object projects	About 32	Over 200 (in the base schema)
TCP/IP	May be used	Must be used
NetBIOS	Always present	May be used if needed for downward compatibility
Database	SAM, part of the registry	Extensible Storage Engine (ESE), developed from the Jet database
Authentication	NTLM	Kerberos (also NTLM supported)

Active Directory Compared to NDS

Some differences between NDS and Active Directory are listed in Table 1.2. If you are familiar with NDS, you can use the table to relate your knowledge to Active Directory. If you are not familiar with NDS, you will probably want to skip this table.

NOTE Despite the plus and minus column, the purpose of Table 1.2 is not to be a competitive comparison of all pros and cons. It is included merely to help you learn Active Directory on the basis of your existing NDS knowledge.

Table 1.2 NDS Compared to Active Directory

Feature	NDS	Active Directory	Active Directory versus NDS*
Group types	One type, can be used for security and distribution	Security groups and distribution groups	+
Group scopes	One scope, about the same as universal in Active Directory	Global, universal, and domain local groups	+
Group nesting	No	Free nesting within each scope	+
Replication type	Multimaster	Multimaster, except some special cases	
Replication criteria	Time, which must be synchronized for all servers	Update sequence numbers (still time must be synchronized to be within five minutes)	+
Site	No (WAN replication not so effective)	Yes (allows effective WAN replication)	+
A server can host replicas of multiple partitions	Yes	No	–
Per-server administration privileges	Yes	Some	–
Object hierarchy	Yes, one big OU tree	Yes, a domain tree or forest and a separate OU tree in each domain; in AD2003 also a group of forests linked with forest trusts	*(continued)*

* A plus sign (+) indicates that Active Directory has an advantage over NDS. A minus sign (–) indicates that Active Directory is at a disadvantage compared to NDS. If neither sign appears in the column, the feature is not, in our opinion, better or worse; it is just different.

Table 1.2 NDS Compared to Active Directory *(cont.)*

Feature	NDS	Active Directory	Active Directory versus NDS*
Can give permissions to OUs for other objects	Yes	No	–
Country, Locality, Organization object types	Yes	Exist in the schema but are not used	
May merge trees	Yes	No	–
Partitions	OU tree–based; may be split and merged	Domains; changing is difficult or impossible	–
Partition is also administrative boundary	No	Yes	–
Global catalog	Catalog Services starting from NetWare 5; that version has drawbacks compared to Active Directory	Yes	+
Delegation of administration	Per OU, per object, or per attribute	Per OU, per object, or per attribute	
Policies	Z.E.N.works add-on	Group Policy	
Administration tools	One "big" tool for the whole directory (NwAdmin)	Several "small" tools for various aspects of the directory (MMC snap-ins)	
Extensible schema	Yes	Yes	
TCP/IP	May be used	Must be used	
LDAP support	Through a gateway	Native	+
Alias objects	Yes	No; however, the functionality is rarely needed	

Table 1.2 NDS Compared to Active Directory *(cont.)*

Feature	NDS	Active Directory	Active Directory versus NDS*
Security equivalence	Yes	No	
RDN and current context	Yes	Not in the relative sense, but the object-naming attribute is also called RDN	
Tree visibility to end users	Visible, which is somewhat distracting to users	Mostly invisible, which should result in easier use	+
Typeless naming of objects	Yes	No, although canonical names get close	

Table 1.2 mainly covers the legacy NDS version that was shipping with NetWare 4, although NetWare 5 is also mentioned once. Since NDS is continually developed, much of this information does not apply to the newest NDS versions.

NOTE As of this writing, a newer version of NDS eDirectory (formerly called NDS 8) is shipping. One of its new features is native LDAP support.

A Sample Company

Throughout this book, we use Sanao Corporation as our sample company. Its registered DNS name is `sanao.com`. Depending on our demonstrational needs, we may present slightly different Sanao Corporations in different chapters. Thus, Sanao Corporation may have just one domain in one example and three domains in another example.

Basic Building Blocks

Active Directory has a number of building blocks, beginning with *domains,* which you create by installing *domain controller* servers. Domains have *trust relationships* between them. Active Directory information must be *replicated* between domain controllers, whether they are located in the same or different *sites.* You can organize the objects in Active Directory in *organizational units.* Figure 1.3 shows the logical and physical structure of Active Directory.

The following sections introduce these basic building blocks of Active Directory. In addition, they briefly explain how you can use different kinds of *groups* to help in administration and how the *global catalog* knows every object in your Active Directory.

Domain Controllers

When you install Active Directory on a Windows 2000 or Windows Server 2003 server computer, you *promote* it to a *domain controller.* Usually you perform this installation right after you install Windows itself by running a utility called DCPromo.

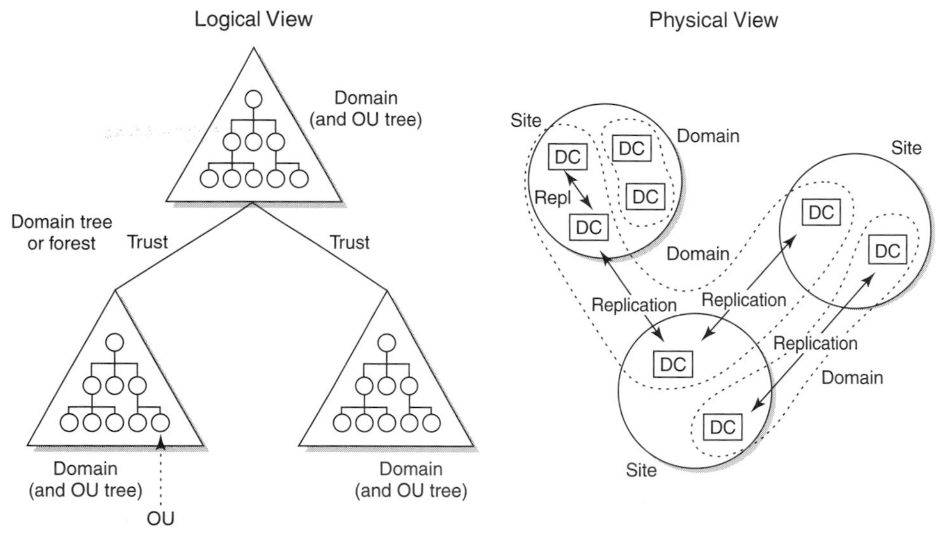

Figure 1.3 Active Directory has a logical and a physical structure, which are mostly independent from each other. "DC" stands for "domain controller."

During the Active Directory installation, you have the option to create a new domain or to join the server to an existing domain. Each domain controller belongs to exactly one domain (as does every member server and workstation that is joined to a domain).

Domains

A *domain* is maintained by one or (preferably) more domain controllers. The domain controllers of one domain may reside in one or more physical locations. An organization may choose to have one or more domains. Each domain is three things at the same time.

- *A unit of replication.* When you add a user or another object to an Active Directory server (i.e., a domain controller), that object is replicated to all other domain controllers in that domain. The outcome is that all the domain controllers in one domain contain the same Active Directory information (except when there has just been a change that hasn't yet reached the other domain controllers).
- *Part of the DNS namespace.* Therefore, each domain has a DNS name, such as `sales.sanao.com`. In other words, each Active Directory domain is also a DNS domain.
- *An administrative unit.* The people who create a domain usually have control over its domain controllers and Active Directory information. The groups Domain Admins, Account Operators, and Administrators have various administrative rights to the domain controllers of the domain and permissions to Active Directory information of the domain, and these rights and permissions are domainwide. A domain also acts as a security policy boundary, so there are some security settings (password policy, account lockout policy, and Kerberos policy) that affect the whole domain.

IF YOU KNOW NT Like Windows NT, Active Directory uses domains and trusts between the domains as basic building blocks. However, both of these basic items include new features in Active Directory.

Trust Relationships

If an organization has more than one domain, its domains might be totally separate (that is, each in a separate Active Directory forest). More likely, though, they are connected with trust relationships.

The advantage of having trusts between domains is that you can give a user or group in one domain permission to access a resource in another domain. Thus, if a user needs to access the resources in two domains, there is no need to make two user accounts for him or her. Another benefit is that groups can have members from other domains. Consequently, trusts also enable centralized administration from one domain to another.

Normal trusts between Active Directory domains are *transitive* and *two way* (or *bidirectional*). Transitive trusts allow access to go across domains ("trans" means "across" or "through"); that is, if you have a trust between domains A and B, and another one between domains B and C, you can give a user from domain A access to a resource in domain C, even though there is no direct trust between A and C. The trust in this case goes through domain B. Transitive trusts greatly reduce the number of necessary trusts because there is no need to explicitly define a trust between every pair of domains.

A two-way trust is a trust that works both ways. Not only can you give users in domain A access to resources in domain C, but you can also give users in domain C access to resources in domain A.

IF YOU KNOW NT Trusts in Windows NT are neither transitive nor two way (although you could create two one-way trusts to look like one two-way trust). This architecture often required a large number of trusts and complex domain models. Each domain with user accounts needed to be trusted by all other domains. For this reason, it usually made sense to have the user accounts in one or few domains to keep the number of trusts smaller than they would be without this arrangement. This, in turn, led to two tiers of domains: First-tier domains contained user accounts and second-tier domains were created for resources. There are no tiers in Active Directory; everything is symmetrical and you can have user accounts in any domain.

Figure 1.4a shows six Windows NT domains in a *complete trust* domain model. All six domains contain user accounts. Because the trusts are one way and intransitive, there must be two of them between each pair of domains (symbolized with two-headed arrows). In other words, each domain must have one trust with each of the five other domains. This makes 6 × 5 = 30 trusts, or 15 lines. (Actually, if you have six circles on paper, 15 is the maximum number of lines that you can draw between them.) Figure 1.4b shows six Active Directory domains in a domain tree. Because these trusts are transitive and two way, you need only five trusts,

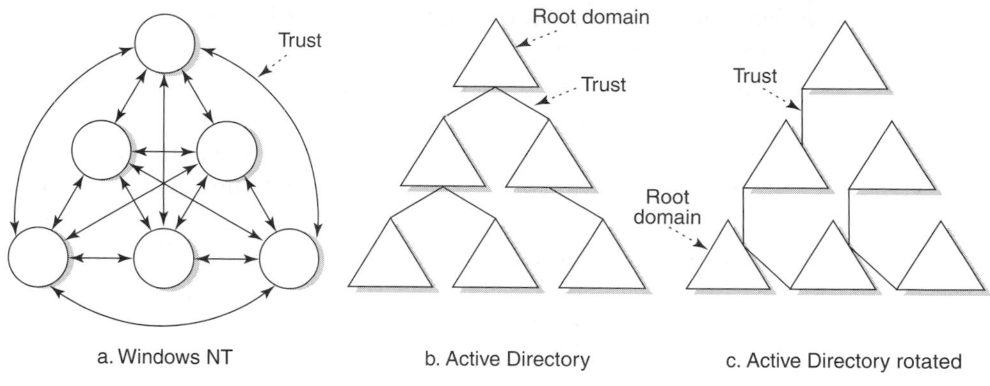

Figure 1.4 Two-way and transitive trusts streamline the structure of domain relationships.

or five lines (the minimum number to connect the six triangles on paper), to establish the same functionality as in Figure 1.4a. Finally, Figure 1.4c shows Active Directory rotated to emphasize that, unlike Windows NT, Active Directory doesn't have first-tier and second-tier domains. The users in all Active Directory domains are equal, and all of them can access the resources in all domains (with proper permissions, of course). Thus, an Active Directory domain tree (and forest) is comparable to a Windows NT complete trust model, with far fewer trusts. The formula for Windows NT is n x (n – 1), while for Active Directory it is just n – 1.

Organizational Units and Other Objects

An administrator using Active Directory creates a user object for each user, a printer object for each shared printer, and so on. Other object types include computer, group, and shared folder. The administrator does not create all objects—some are created automatically by Active Directory or some other software, especially during installation.

You can create organizational units in Active Directory domains just as you create folders in a file system. You can store objects in different OUs just as you store files in different folders in a file system. This way, you can store them in logical groupings in a tree structure, which is especially useful if you have many objects.

In addition to this logical grouping of objects, you can use OUs for the following purposes.

- You can delegate the administration of each OU (including users and other objects there) to a different administrator. For example, in a geographically dispersed network, perhaps covering several time zones, it is probably easier to give the local administrators permission to create user objects, reset forgotten passwords, and so on. Delegation of administration is implemented with permissions.
- You can control how end users see, read, and modify the objects and their properties in each OU by specifying various permissions to users to access the OU contents.
- You can assign different group policies to the users and computers in each OU.

NOTE You can assign permissions (to read, write, create, and so on) per object, not just per OU. However, this is usually impractical and a better choice is to stick to the per-OU permissions.

Unfortunately you cannot assign permissions to OUs. This means that if you have an OU that contains 30 users, you probably need to create a security group and put those users in this group in order to give them permissions for specific folders or other resources.

IF YOU KNOW NDS In NDS you can give permissions to OUs, so there is no need to create a group to correspond to each OU.

You should create OUs to match administrative units. They are usually physical locations, object types (e.g., users in one OU and printers in another), or the organizational structure. In the last case, for example, the top-level OUs could be Human Resources, Finance, and Marketing. Below the top-level OUs created with one criterion, you can create second-level OUs (and below) based on another criterion.

Groups

You can use groups in Active Directory for at least two purposes. It is easier and more efficient to give access permissions to groups than it is to give them to a large number of individual users or computers. You can also use groups as e-mail distribution lists, given that your e-mail application can read the lists from Active Directory. This leads to two *group types:*

- *Distribution groups* can be used as distribution lists in Active Directory–capable e-mail applications and for any other Active Directory–capable application. For example, an application could control the doors of your company and let only people in a certain distribution group go through a certain door. This may sound like a security-related function, but the point is that there is an application that uses this distribution group for something, but Windows doesn't use the group for anything.
- *Security groups* are everything that distribution groups are. Additionally, you can assign Windows access permissions to a security group, while you cannot do so to a distribution group. That is, a security group can be given permissions for various parts of the operating system, such as Active Directory or a file system.

NOTE Windows uses only security groups; it does not use distribution groups.

Every group, whether a distribution or a security group, has a defined scope. There are three *group scopes:*

- Global
- Universal
- Domain local

The group scope defines how a group can be used across domain boundaries. Depending on its scope, the group may be valid in other domains, so that it can be assigned as a member of a group in another domain, or assigned permissions for resources in that domain. The scope also dictates whether the group can have members from other domains.

In addition, the group scope determines which group can be a member of which other group. A global group can be a member of a universal group and a universal group can be a member of a domain local group. Also, a global group can be a member of a domain local group. The remaining combinations are not possible, such as a universal group being a member of a global group. Figure 1.5 illustrates the possible memberships and permissions assignments for global and domain local security groups.

Instead of giving permissions for resources directly to users or computers, you can put them in groups and give the access permissions to

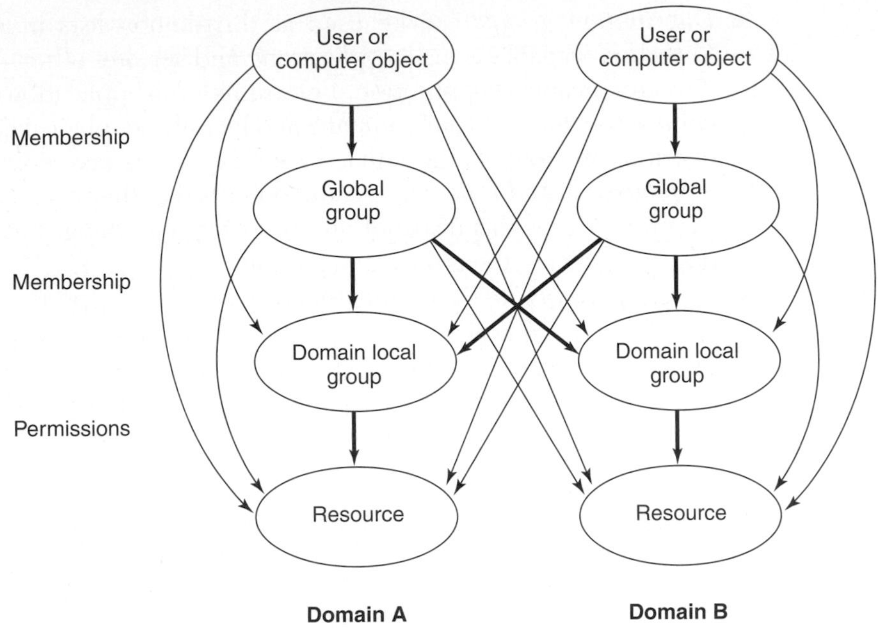

Figure 1.5 Grouping users and computers and assigning permissions to the groups facilitates access control.

these groups. This approach greatly facilitates permission management. As Figure 1.5 indicates, a global group can be used in another domain, and a domain local group can take members from other domains, but not vice versa. Figure 1.5 also shows the recommended path, which the thicker line represents. You will normally save time and energy in administration if you follow the recommended path and avoid the others.

In addition to *nesting* groups of the different scopes that we have described, you can freely nest groups of the same scope. For example, group A can be a member of group B, which is a member of group C, which is a member of group D, and so on. You shouldn't nest more than a few groups, however, because you would quickly lose track of who is a member of which group. However, being able to nest groups should help you create a selection of groups, the members of which can be easily managed.

The easiest strategy for group usage is to use only universal groups because they have no membership limitations and they can be given permissions to any resource in any domain. However, there is a penalty attached to them when you have both multiple domains and multiple sites. The members of universal groups are stored in the global catalog, which contains some information about every object in the entire Active Directory. The more you use these groups, the more replication traffic there is between sites, and the slower user logons become.

IF YOU KNOW NT The groups in Windows NT correspond to security groups in Active Directory. Windows NT's old global and local groups are about the same as global and domain local groups in Active Directory. Universal groups and free group nesting are new features. Another new feature is that a domain local group can now be used in the member servers and workstations of the domain.

IF YOU KNOW NDS NDS has only one type of group, and it does not allow nesting.

Sites

Administrators create *sites* as areas with "good connectivity." Typically, each LAN would be a site, and the WAN connections between these sites (i.e., LANs) would be called *site links*. Technically, you define a site as one or more TCP/IP subnets.

Why do we need sites? They help Active Directory to understand what the world and physical network is like. When Active Directory knows which servers are on the same site, it knows whether there is a fast or slow communications link between any two servers. For slow links (i.e., intersite), domain controllers compress the replicated data, but for fast links (i.e., intrasite LANs), they save processor cycles and send the data uncompressed. You can also define for each site link a cost parameter that determines the route Active Directory will use to replicate between multiple sites.

NOTE The cost parameter determines only which domain controllers will communicate when replicating. It doesn't affect the physical IP routing (unless some router vendor makes a router that would understand the costs of Active Directory site links).

Based on this information, Active Directory and Windows 2000 and later use sites mainly for the following purposes:

- Active Directory can decide how to replicate information efficiently between domain controllers. If the domain controllers are not on the same site, Active Directory uses several optimization techniques in replication.
- Active Directory clients find the closest logon servers (i.e., domain controllers) based on sites.
- The Distributed File System (DFS) of Windows 2000 and later can use site information to make intelligent decisions about which server a user is directed to when she requests a file.
- The File Replication Service (FRS) of Windows 2000 and later uses sites to know how to replicate SYSVOL and other folders that you assign to be replicated.
- An administrator using Active Directory can assign group policies to sites.
- Active Directory–aware applications may use site information for their own purposes.

NOTE In addition to the site functions listed, knowledge about the physical network can be used when users locate printers. When a user queries Active Directory for a printer, if the option is enabled, she will be offered printers first from her TCP/IP subnet. If she wants, she can search for printers from other locations also.

Replication

Each piece of Active Directory information should reside on more than one domain controller. This setup provides fault tolerance against a server failure. Another benefit is load balancing when many workstations are accessing Active Directory simultaneously. The third advantage is proximity of information—when a domain controller is placed on the same site with users and Active Directory information is replicated to that domain controller, workstations get the information from a local server instead of across a WAN link.

For the information to reside and stay current on several domain controllers, changes must be *replicated* from one server to another. In other words, the information is kept up-to-date by periodically copying the changes in one domain controller across the network to the other domain controllers of that domain.

NOTE Not all Active Directory information is replicated. For example, each domain controller tracks when a user last logged on using that domain controller. This information is part of the user objects, but it is a nonreplicating property. Also, the Active Directory database contains indexes of the properties that are marked (either in the base configuration or by an administrator) to be indexed. Each domain controller builds these indexes locally.

Remember that domains are units of replication, but sites tell when and how to replicate. Inside a site, domain controllers initiate replication after having waited 15 seconds or 5 minutes after a change (in Windows Server 2003 and Windows 2000, respectively). In this case, they use direct remote procedure call (RPC) connections.

When you add more than one domain controller to a site, Active Directory builds a certain replication topology. If there were ten domain controllers, a bad topology would be one long chain. This would mean that domain controller A would replicate to B (one hop), which would replicate to C (a second hop), which would replicate to D (a third hop), and so on until domain controller J (a total of nine hops). The chain would be so long that replicating changes from A to J would take too much time and J would fall behind. In addition, a long chain is not as fault tolerant. For these reasons, Active Directory takes care that the replication chain is on the average no more than three hops from one domain controller to another. Active Directory achieves this by arranging the domain controllers in a ring topology and adding shortcuts across the ring (unless you turn off the shortcut creation).

Between sites, Active Directory compresses the replicated data. The replication takes place by default every 3 hours, but an administrator can change that to another interval (e.g., once an hour or every 30 minutes), down to a minimum of every 15 minutes. Alternatively, if an organization has good WAN links, it can choose to use intrasite delays (15 seconds or 5 minutes) also in intrasite replication. RPC is usually used, as in the intrasite case, but you can also choose SMTP messaging (automated e-mail).

The SMTP option uses the Intersite Messaging service, which is part of Windows 2000 and Windows Server 2003. However, you can use

SMTP instead of RPC to replicate only the enterprise forest information between domains, or application partitions (explained later in this chapter). Normal domain replication must always use RPC.

Active Directory uses *multimaster* replication. This means that you can make changes, such as adding users, to any domain controller (of the appropriate domain). Your changes are then replicated to all other domain controllers in the same domain. Windows NT used *single-master* replication, which allowed changes to only one server, the *primary domain controller (PDC)*. These changes were then replicated to other domain controllers, called *backup domain controllers (BDCs)*. This made making changes sometimes a bit difficult, especially in WAN environments and failure situations. If the PDC was on a remote site, to make any changes, you had to communicate with it over a WAN link, and if the PDC or the WAN link was down, changes were not possible.

Active Directory replicates only changed properties, not entire user accounts as in Windows NT. Unlike Novell NDS, Active Directory replication does not rely on synchronized time in different servers to determine what to replicate. Instead, Active Directory uses *update sequence numbers (USNs)* and version numbers.

NOTE There is a time synchronization service under Active Directory. It is needed mainly because the Kerberos authentication protocol requires the workstation clock to be within 5 minutes (by default) of the server clock, and the server clocks within 5 minutes each other. Successful Kerberos authentication ensures, among other things, that domain controller–to–domain controller replication is possible.

WARNING Failure to keep the domain controllers within 5 minutes of each other can have disastrous consequences. Users may get locked out of a domain controller, and only forestwide Enterprise Admins can fix the situation, not domainwide Domain Admins.

Although normal Active Directory replication is multimaster, all domain controllers are not equal. There are two forestwide and three domainwide roles, which are held by only one (per forest or per domain) domain controller at a time.

The five roles are called *operations masters,* or *flexible single-master operations (FSMOs)*. As the name implies, they work in a single-master fashion, meaning that a particular domain controller is needed for a particular operation.

The two forestwide roles are

- Schema master
- Domain naming master

The three domainwide roles are

- RID master (where "RID" stands for "relative identifier")
- PDC master (or PDC emulator)
- Infrastructure master

Describing the functions of these operations masters is not feasible in this introductory chapter. We address them in Chapter 5.

Global Catalog

In a large network with many domains and sites, it is not appropriate for all Active Directory information to replicate to all sites. This raises the possibility that only part of the information needed is at the same site as the user. Without some mechanism to tie these domains together, if that user searched the Active Directory for other users or for resources such as printers, the user's query would travel from site to site across many WAN links to collect all the requested information, which is not efficient. Also, if the result were a list of 1,000 user names, it would be slow to transfer back to the user who performed the search.

To avoid such time-consuming and costly steps, the *global catalog* helps to do all searches in your entire enterprise forest locally, which should dramatically increase their efficiency. The global catalog contains some basic information about every object in the whole Active Directory forest. It contains properties that are likely to be used in search operations, such as a user's first and last name.

One of the global catalog properties is the distinguished name of each object. It specifies the domain name and complete path to the object, which makes it easy to locate the object. To read properties that are not in the global catalog, your workstation must contact a domain controller of the domain where the object is; the distinguished name will be needed in this location process.

Out of the box, the global catalog contains 151 of all 1,070 properties (or 138 of 863 in AD2000). If you want, you can define additional properties to be included in the global catalog.

Administrators designate which domain controllers host a copy of the global catalog. After that, replication of the global catalog occurs with the normal replication of the Active Directory, so any changes will be replicated as soon as any other changes. By contrast, the Catalog Services in NetWare 5 use a separate process to copy the information to the catalog, perhaps once a day.

Information in the global catalog is subject to the same per-object and per-property permissions as normal domain data. Additionally, the global catalog is read-only.

Normally, there should be at least one global catalog server on each site, but sometimes it is better to leave some sites without a global catalog server, in which case the users of those sites have to read the information in the global catalog over a WAN link. Alternatively, those users do not use the global catalog at all, as we explain in Chapter 6.

Hierarchies

Depending on the size of the network, an administrator will probably build some kind of structure and hierarchy into Active Directory. The five models from the simplest and smallest to the largest are as follows:

- Single domain with no OU structure
- OU tree in a single domain
- Domain tree (with an OU tree in each domain)
- Forest of domain trees (with an OU tree in each domain)
- Multiple forests

As you might guess, a small company with centralized administration might choose a simple model with just one domain and no OU tree, whereas a large enterprise with decentralized administration would do better with a multidomain forest model.

The following sections introduce these five models and discuss the situations in which they would be most appropriate. These sections also summarize some concepts introduced earlier in this chapter.

NOTE In Chapter 6 we discuss this topic further and give additional considerations for which model to select.

Single Domain with No OU Structure

The first model, one domain with no OU structure (see Figure 1.6), is suitable for small companies with centralized administration. They could either put all users and groups in the predefined Users container, or they could actually create a couple of OUs. However, we still call this a "no structure" model because there are not enough OUs to talk about an OU tree.

In this model, one company could even be in several locations, as long as the company's WAN links could handle the amount of replication (which depends on the size of the Active Directory database and the frequency of changes). In single-domain environments, the whole database is replicated automatically to all domain controllers on all sites.

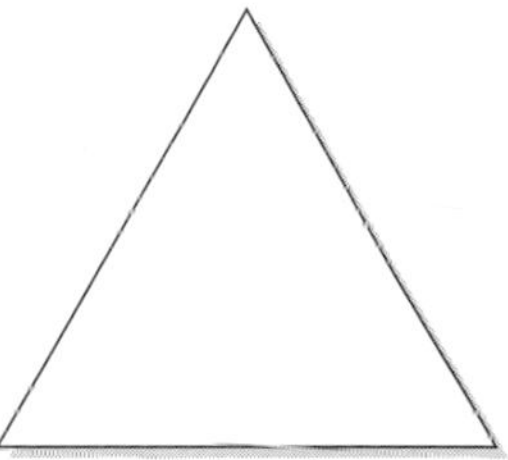

Figure 1.6 The simplest form of hierarchy is no hierarchy, such as this single domain with no internal structure. Active Directory domains are usually represented with triangles.

IF YOU KNOW NT One domain with no OUs in Active Directory is quite similar to one domain in Windows NT. If you currently have just one domain, chances are that you will have one domain with Active Directory.

Fortunately, Active Directory also has some improvement over Windows NT. There should be less data to be replicated, because you will replicate only the changed properties, not entire user accounts. On the other hand, you will have more information in your Active Directory to replicate than you had in Windows NT. You can store more information about each user, such as fax numbers, addresses, and so on, in Active Directory. In addition, you are not limited to storing just users and groups: Active Directory can host information about printers, services, applications, and other resources or data.

In Active Directory, you can assign some administrative *privileges* for domain controllers even on a per-server basis. This helps if you have three remote sites with one domain controller and one administrator on each. You can allow each site administrator to "log on locally" via the server keyboard and perform some administrative tasks on his or her "own" domain controller, and at the same time you can disallow these privileges on the domain controllers of the other sites. For example, you could create a group called London Local Administrators and give this group the right to log on locally, as well as other appropriate user rights.

Unfortunately, you cannot assign all privileges this way. For example, the right to share folders or format hard disks is always assigned per domain, applying to no or all domain controllers.

IF YOU KNOW NT In Windows NT, the administrative privileges apply to all domain controllers in a domain.

OU Tree in a Single Domain

As explained earlier, administrators create OUs to group objects, delegate administration, control what users can see and modify, and assign group policies. When you create a number of OUs for any of these reasons, you get an OU tree, which is our second model. Because our first model had no hierarchy, this second model is the first level of hierarchy. Figure 1.7 shows an OU tree inside a domain.

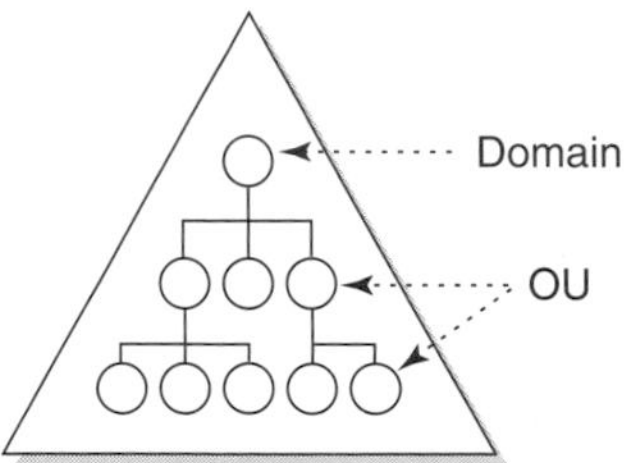

Figure 1.7 The first level of hierarchy is a tree of OUs inside a domain. When you place users and other objects in this tree, you can delegate their administration on a per-OU basis.

NOTE The top object in an OU tree is not an OU, but rather the same domain that we represent with a triangle. We draw it as part of the tree to get a complete tree. See Figure 1.7 for an example.

An administrator should have a specific reason to create each OU, and he should not just create them because it feels nice. Obviously, a tree's naming and structure should be logical. Also, the tree should be no larger or deeper than necessary.

End users of Windows 2000 will see the OU tree if they open My Network Places and double-click Entire Network and then Directory. Otherwise, they don't usually see the tree. Users of later versions of Windows, such as Windows XP, don't see the OU tree at all (unless they copy a file from Windows 2000, as explained in Chapter 3).

Because a domain is a unit of replication and there is just one domain in this model, all information is replicated to all domain controllers on all sites (as in the previous model). This is a good thing if your WAN links can handle the resulting (compressed) amount of replication of all the changes. If not, you should evaluate using multiple domains, so that you would have one of the remaining two models, a domain tree or a forest.

IF YOU KNOW NT When you migrate from Windows NT 4.0 or 3.51 to Active Directory, you might elect to use a single domain with an OU tree, even if you currently run a master domain model with several resource domains. With Windows NT, resource domains were created to decentralize administration, but given the per-OU and (limited) per-server administration capabilities of Windows 2000, you might achieve the same goal with just one domain. Therefore, you might no longer need separate resource domains.

Domain Trees

When it becomes impractical to replicate everything to everywhere, you need to create several domains. You will most likely organize them as a *domain tree.* Because domains are more independent than OUs inside a domain, this also means a step toward decentralization in the administrative model.

For example, password and lockout policies are domainwide and can be different in each domain, but not in each OU. Similarly, each domain has groups called Administrators and Server Operators, who can share folders on domain controllers and format their hard disks. If you want to give someone these privileges for domain controller A but not for domain controller B, these two domain controllers must be in different domains.

When you create several domains and put them in one tree, you get a model like the tree in Figure 1.8. The first domain you create becomes the *root domain* of its tree. When you place each subsequent domain in the tree, you select some existing domain as the *parent domain* for it. A transitive and bidirectional trust is automatically established between a domain and its parent.

The trust relationships make all the domains in the tree one big happy family. As stated earlier, you can give any user in any domain permissions for any resource or object in any domain, either directly or via group memberships. The domains in a tree also share a common schema (explained later in the chapter) and global catalog.

If the domain tree grows large, the path from one subdomain to another can become quite long. In this case, you can create extra unidirectional *shortcut trusts* between distant domains. They speed up authentication from one domain to another.

Each domain in the tree has its own OU tree, which is totally separate from all others. By contrast, in NDS all OUs form one big tree.

With a domain tree (and a forest), your organization needs to agree on who will own and maintain the root domain. You might consider

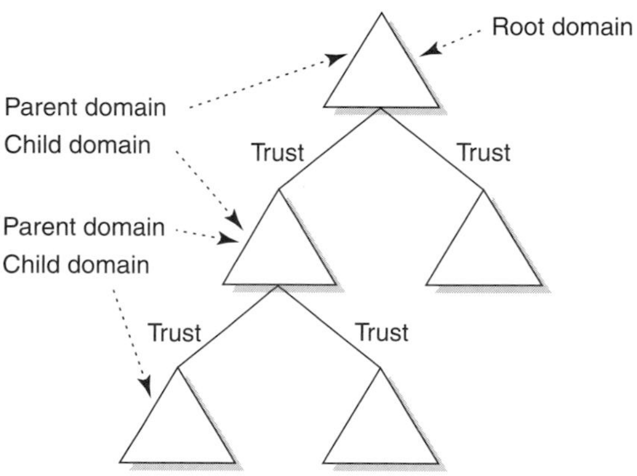

Figure 1.8 Whereas an OU tree is the lower-level hierarchy, a domain tree, such as the one in this figure (or a forest), is the higher-level hierarchy. Each domain has a transitive trust to its parent domain. The top domain with no parents is the root domain.

implementing your business units as second-level domains below the root domain. These units would have their independent OU structures and possibly some child domains. Because you may not want higher-level domains to change often, an even better choice might be to base them on continents and locations.

Domain Names

Every Active Directory domain must match a DNS domain so that Active Directory domains use DNS names. The root domain of our sample company's Active Directory domain tree is called `sanao.com` and the two next-level Active Directory child domains are `sales.sanao.com` and `rd.sanao.com`.

Each of these domains also has an LDAP name, such as `DC=rd, DC=sanao, DC=com`. (More on LDAP later in this chapter.)

The DNS namespace of a domain tree is *contiguous*. You create a child's domain name by prepending a part to the parent's domain name, as Figure 1.9 shows.

- `Sanao.com` is the registered DNS name of our sample company, so it is the root domain name in this example.
- When we add "sales," we get `sales.sanao.com`.
- When we add "largecust," we get `largecust.sales.sanao.com`.

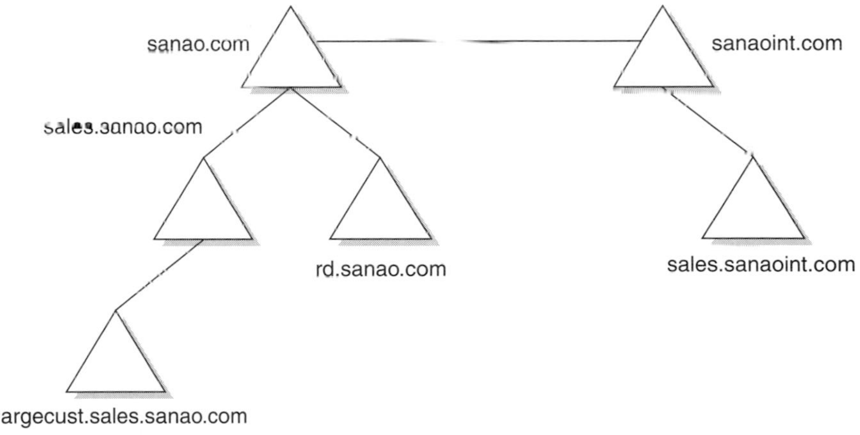

Figure 1.9 Active Directory domains use DNS names. The Active Directory domains in a tree must have a contiguous namespace. If this is not the case, you must have a forest with more than one domain tree. Here `sanao.com` is one tree and `sanaoint.com` is another tree.

If the namespace is not contiguous, the domains cannot be in the same tree, but they can be in the same forest. In addition to the preceding example, you could have another domain tree with the two domains `sales.sanaoint.com` and `sanaoint.com`. The two trees would be in the same forest.

Surprisingly, the DNS names of workstations, member servers, and domain controllers don't have to be in the same DNS domain as the Active Directory domain they belong to. Therefore, computer `ws1.eastcost.sanao.com` can be a member of the `sales.sanao.com` Active Directory domain. This arrangement is not recommended, however, because it is normally more difficult to use and maintain.

Forest of Domain Trees

If you must or want to use more than one DNS name on the top level, such as `sanao.com` and `sanaoint.com` in our previous example, you will end up with more than one domain tree, and thus have a *forest.* Remember, all domain trees in the forest have contiguous DNS namespaces.

There are only two differences between a domain tree and a forest of several domain trees.

- The DNS namespace is not contiguous in a forest.
- When you perform a search on objects of a subtree, the search's scope includes just one domain tree at a time. (For more information on this subject, see Chapter 6.)

As with a single domain tree, a forest of domain trees has the transitive and two-way trusts for access permissions and group assignments, as well as a common schema and global catalog. Figure 1.10 shows a forest of domain trees.

The layout in Figure 1.10 of a two-tree forest gives the impression that the root domains of both trees are on one level. This is true only from the DNS naming point of view. From the administrative point of view, the root domain of the second tree is below the root domain of the first tree, as Figure 1.11 illustrates. Only the first domain of the forest (*forest root domain*) contains such groups as Enterprise Admins and Schema Admins, which give control to forestwide administration.

If independent business units have their own domain trees in a forest, they are no more independent than if they had child domains

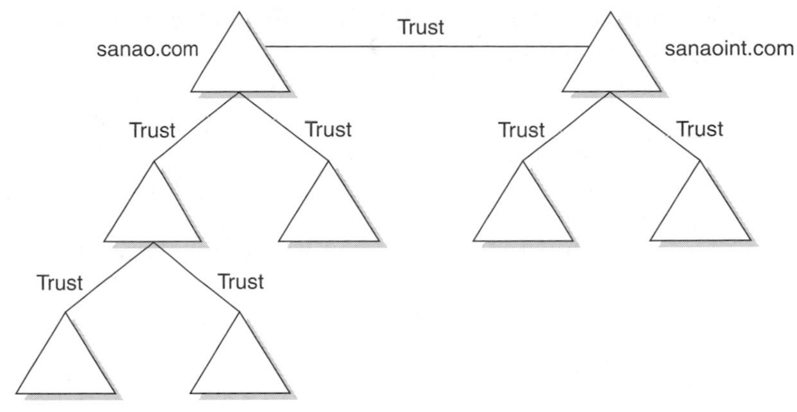

Figure 1.10 A forest of domain trees. The main difference between one domain tree and a forest is that the domain DNS names in a forest are not contiguous.

right below the root domain of the first domain tree (i.e., the forest root domain).

As Figure 1.11 shows, the second domain tree is not on par with the first one. However, the problem is that now it looks as if there is just one domain tree rather than a forest of two domain trees. The only slight difference between Figure 1.8 (single domain tree) and Figure 1.11 is that the intertree trust (called a *tree root trust*) is drawn on the sides of the

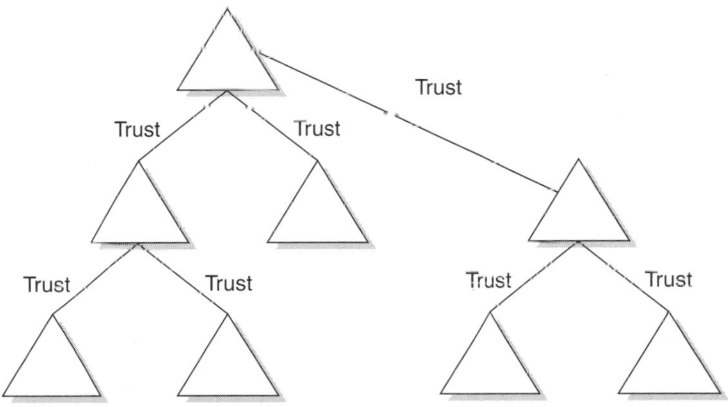

Figure 1.11 These two domain trees are not equal, as they may seem to be in Figure 1.10. However, placing one tree lower in the figure, as shown here, might incorrectly make it look like a branch of the first tree.

two top triangles instead of starting from the bottom of the first triangle and ending at the top of the other.

NOTE Figure 1.10, with the two domain trees drawn on the same level, is the normal way to represent a forest.

Even though in this section we call only this fourth model a forest, you would of course have a forest even when you have just one domain with just one domain controller. From here on, we use the term "forest" whether one or several domain trees are in that forest, unless we specifically need to address a single domain tree. After all, there are only two differences between them, as described in the beginning of this subsection.

Multiple Forests

The most decentralized model is to have multiple forests. Each forest is totally independent of each other, but the cooperation between forests requires extra work compared to the single-forest models. The multiple-forest model can be used after company mergers and acquisitions, and perhaps also when an organization has quite independent divisions.

In AD2000, you could create Windows NT–like external trusts among two domains in two forests. In AD2003 (in the Windows Server 2003 forest functional level), you can create *forest trusts* between the root domains of the two forests. Whereas an external trust enables access from one domain to another, a forest trust enables access from any domain in one forest to any domain in another forest. However, the owners of each forest have several ways to limit the access from the foreign forest, either per domain and/or per server. The methods are called selective authentication, SID filtering, and name suffix routing, and they are explained in Chapter 6.

In addition to the forestwide nature of forest trusts, they offer two other benefits over external trusts.

- Authentication from one forest to another uses Kerberos instead of the older NTLM authentication.
- A user of one forest can log on to a workstation in another forest, and she can use her UPN (such as `jill.green@sanao.com`) in the process.

Even though Figure 1.10 illustrates a forest with two domain trees, the same figure can also illustrate two forests with a forest trust in between.

DNS Integration

Active Directory has a close relationship with DNS, the naming system used for the Internet and many intranets. Active Directory uses DNS for two related purposes: naming domains and computers and locating servers and (Active Directory) services. Therefore, to use Active Directory, the DNS service must be running on the network. The foremost choice is to use the DNS service included in Windows 2000 or later. Another possibility for companies is to continue using their existing DNS infrastructure.

The most common existing DNS product is the Berkeley Internet Name Domain service, or BIND, which runs on UNIX. For BIND to work with Active Directory, the former must support a feature called *service location* (or *SRV*) *records* to be able to locate services and not just computers. Your life will also be easier if it supports dynamic updates of DNS information. BIND version 8.2.1 and later fulfill both requirements.

The best choice is probably to use the Windows 2000 or later DNS service. It naturally supports service records and dynamic updates. Also, you can store the DNS information (i.e., *zone*) in Active Directory instead of a text file. This allows secure updates. If you select this option, only authenticated domain members can perform dynamic DNS updates.

Another benefit of storing the information in Active Directory is multimaster replication—traditional DNS uses single-master replication. In multimaster replication, any domain controller that has the DNS service installed and running can serve as the primary DNS server. Consequently, the dynamic DNS updates that client computers perform do not depend on only one server. In addition, hardly any configuration is needed for the replication.

If a UNIX-based DNS service is used with Active Directory, it is best to stick to the standard character set of A through Z, 0 through 9, and the dash. With the DNS service included in Windows 2000 or later, you may use the Unicode character set, which offers you a much broader selection of characters. However, to ensure interoperability with various systems, even with Windows 2000 or later, it may be wise to use the basic character set.

NOTE Even if your organization chooses to use Windows 2000 or later DNS for Active Directory services, you can continue to use a UNIX-based DNS implementation as your main DNS service.

Locating Computers and Services

The job of a DNS service is to know which computer name or service name corresponds to which IP address and to tell this information to anyone who asks for it.

To be able to communicate with a server called `dc1.sanao.com`, a workstation first needs to request that server's IP address from a DNS server. The answer looks something like this: 192.168.15.14.

For a user to be able to log on to Active Directory, the workstation needs an IP address of any domain controller in that domain. Therefore, the workstation doesn't query the DNS for a particular server name, but rather for a specific service name. The process may involve several queries, and because the site information is also used, the workstation can find a domain controller on its own site, or secondarily, a domain controller on the closest site.

When querying a service name, DNS might return the IP addresses of more than one server, along with some priority and weight information. This way, the workstation can choose the best server among those that offer the desired service.

Dynamic DNS Updates

The DNS service in Windows 2000 and later supports dynamic DNS updates, as defined in RFC 2136 (Request For Comments, meaning an "Internet standard"). It relieves the administrator from manually adding and editing the DNS records for computers and services.

NOTE Quite a few Web sites contain RFC documents for you to read and download. The "original" RFC site is `http://www.ietf.org/rfc`.

Each workstation and server has an IP address, which is either configured statically in the computer or retrieved from a Dynamic Host

Configuration Protocol (DHCP) server at startup. As each Windows 2000 and later computer boots up, it automatically registers this IP address with the dynamic DNS. For earlier versions, you can configure the DHCP server to do the registration. Domain controllers also register the necessary service names so that other computers can find Active Directory services.

IF YOU KNOW NT Dynamic DNS will obsolete Windows Internet Naming Service (WINS) eventually. However, this will not happen until organizations eliminate existing legacy Windows computers and applications. Until all machines are Windows 2000 or later, these companies will be forced to use WINS or some other form of NetBIOS name resolution.

Security and Policies

Active Directory is part of the trusted computing base of Windows 2000 and later. This means that information in Active Directory is protected, as are the files in the Windows NTFS file system. Anyone who wants to access information in Active Directory or the file system must be authenticated, usually with a username and password, and then be subject to discretionary access control.

Access Control

There is a *security descriptor (SD)* attached to each object in Active Directory. Both OUs and objects inside OUs have security descriptors. A security descriptor contains the owner of the object, the *discretionary access control list (DACL)*, and the *system access control list (SACL)*. The DACL contains a list of *access control entries (ACEs)*, which define who can access the object and in what way (read, write, and so on). If necessary, you can set read and write access on individual properties, such as a certain user's last name or fax number.

You assign permissions to *security principals*. They are users (and inetOrgPersons), security groups, computer objects, and well-known security principals.

You can give someone any of three *standard permissions* for an OU object. Each of the standard permissions maps to a set of *special permissions*. Usually the standard permissions are enough, but if necessary, you can go to a more detailed level and use the special permissions. Figures 1.12 and 1.13 show the lists of the permission options for an OU object, although in the latter figure all the special permissions don't fit in the window. Note that in Figure 1.12 the first three permissions (Full Control, Read, and Write) are standard permissions, but the remaining ones in the list are special permissions.

IF YOU KNOW NT Active Directory permissions and old NTFS permissions in Windows NT are very similar because both use SDs, DACLs, and ACEs. However, there are three major differences. First, Active Directory uses a different inheritance model (which is explained in the next section). Second, you can set permissions on individual properties. And third, the user interface in Active Directory enables you to deny individual permissions—in Windows NT you can only deny all access.

IF YOU KNOW NT Actually, the first and third changes (inheritance and allow/deny individual permissions) are also true for NTFS in Windows 2000 and later.

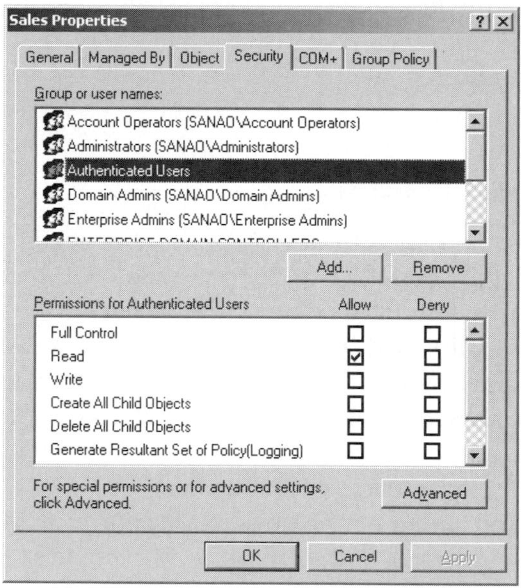

Figure 1.12 For every Active Directory object, you can define who can access it and in what way.

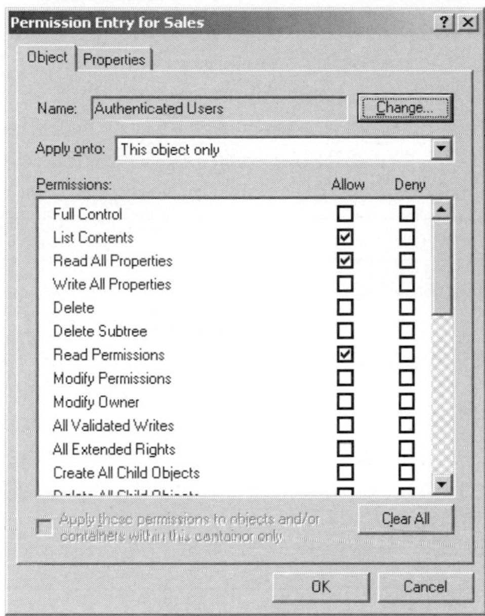

Figure 1.13 If necessary, you can select special permissions to fine-tune the level of access to an object in Active Directory.

Inheritance

Active Directory uses *static inheritance* for object permissions. The word "inheritance" means that when you add permissions for some OU or other container, you can specify that those new permissions apply also to the child objects. You can choose to which type of children they apply and whether the permissions apply only to immediate children or to the whole tree beneath the object. Also, for each object, you can choose whether it will allow inheriting permissions from above.

Static inheritance means that Active Directory copies the new permissions to the access control list of each appropriate child object. This copying takes some processor power, as well as space in the Active Directory database, but the advantage is that when the objects are later accessed, Active Directory doesn't need to walk up the tree to check for inheritable permissions.

Windows Server 2003 domain controllers save disk space because they store identical inherited permissions only once. The technology used is called Single Instance Storage.

IF YOU KNOW NDS NDS uses dynamic inheritance, which has exactly the opposite pros and cons of Active Directory. That is, it doesn't take any processing power when applying the permissions, but when objects are later accessed, NDS needs to walk up the tree to check for inheritable permissions. Also, disk space is saved because there are no copied permissions in the child objects.

IF YOU KNOW NT Active Directory has a couple of significant improvements over Windows NT NTFS. First, when you apply new permissions to child objects, these permissions won't completely replace the old permissions; they just add new ACEs to the list. Second, the new ACEs carry a flag, which indicates that they are inherited. This way, both people and machines recognize which permissions are inherited and which are assigned directly to an object.

NOTE If you add a permission that affects a thousand objects, only the security descriptor of the one parent object needs to be replicated to the other domain controllers. When they receive a new inheritable permission, they will copy it locally to the child objects.

Delegation of Administration

Because you can set access control by the OU, by the object, and even by the property, you can delegate administration of all or part of your OU tree. For example, if you create three OUs, different administrators can manage users and other objects in each of them. You can also set permissions so that a certain user can edit the e-mail and postal addresses of all users, but can do nothing else.

The Delegation of Control wizard helps in delegation. Ultimately the wizard just assigns permissions, so you can do the same delegation with the dialog boxes shown in Figures 1.12 and 1.13. The wizard interface, however, may be less intimidating, especially in the beginning of the learning process.

Group Policy

You can use *Group Policy* to centrally manage users' working environment and workstations. Group Policy also affects servers, and administrators use it to define, apply, and enforce the following:

- Automated application installation (either forced or optional)
- Forced registry settings to users or computers
- Security settings
- Logon/logoff scripts and startup/shutdown scripts
- Folder redirection of the Start Menu, Desktop, My Documents, and Application Data folders so that they can be located on a network server instead of the normal user profile folder
- Some settings for Remote Installation Services (RIS)

Part of the Group Policy settings affect computers, and the remaining settings affect users. You store the settings in *Group Policy objects*, or *GPOs*, that you create for chosen sites, domains, and OUs. The locations of the user objects and computer objects determine which GPOs apply to each user and computer. Figure 1.14 shows the contents of a Group Policy object.

IF YOU KNOW NT Group Policy replaces System Policy and user rights. However, Group Policy includes additional settings.

Several GPOs may affect a user and a computer simultaneously. There could be one GPO assigned to the site, one to the domain, one to an upper-level OU, and yet another to the lower-level OU where the user or computer object resides. A nearer GPO in this chain overrides

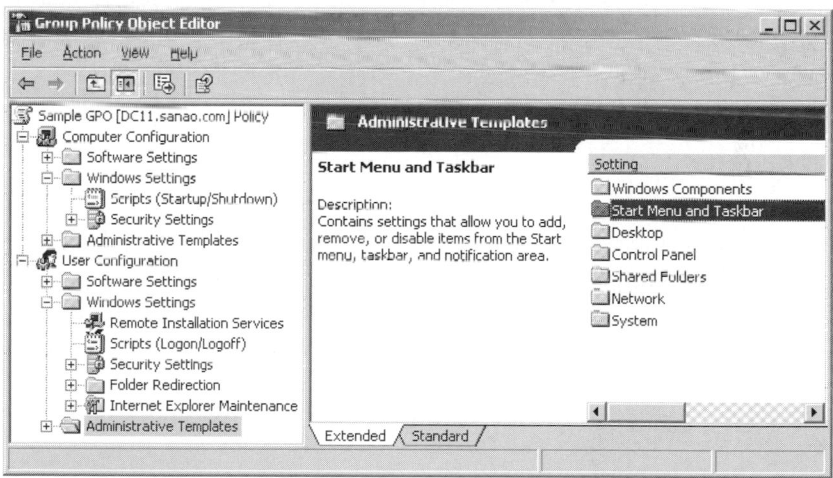

Figure 1.14 There are Group Policy settings for both computers and users. However, you can disable either.

settings in a farther GPO, unless you have blocked this inheritance. You can also force inheritance on the upper level, which takes precedence over blocking.

Despite the name, you cannot assign GPOs directly to groups, nor can you assign GPOs to individual users or computers. You can get the same result, however, by giving the read and apply permissions for a GPO only to some of the users or computers in an OU where the GPO applies.

AD2003 contains a new feature called WMI filters. They enable you to assign GPOs dynamically based on certain criteria. A typical example is to apply a GPO only to those workstations that have at least 10GB of free disk space. WMI filters use the WMI query language (WQL), and the filter for the preceding example is (assuming here that a gigabyte is a billion bytes) as follows:

```
Select * from Win32_LogicalDisk where FreeSpace >
    10000000000
```

Because group policies may contain hundreds of settings, it may be tedious to set them correctly manually. Fortunately, at least for the security settings, you can avoid this burden somewhat by using *security templates,* which are predefined text files that list the appropriate choice of settings (e.g., for a "secure workstation").

See also the discussion of a new tool, Group Policy Management Console, in the "AD2003 Compared to AD2000" section earlier in this chapter.

Architecture

This section introduces the Active Directory data model and other architecture-related issues. The schema, object naming, X.500, and LDAP are covered, as well as the physical architecture, Kerberos, public key infrastructure, and programmatic access to Active Directory.

Data Model

Active Directory stores information about users, resources, and other network entities. The stored information is represented as objects, so there is an object for each user, computer, printer, and so on.

Objects of the same type belong to the same *class,* such as (again) `user`, `computer`, and `printQueue`. Out of the box, Active Directory supports 191 classes (or 142 in AD2000). However, if you use the basic administrative tool, the Users and Computers snap-in, you can directly create objects in only 9 of the classes.

Every class defines a set of *mandatory* and *optional properties* that the objects belonging to the class must or may have, respectively. A property is often called an *attribute.* Out of the box, Active Directory has a total of 1,070 properties (or 863 in AD2000) and the `user` class uses 257 of them (or 207 in AD2000). Fortunately, you don't need to enter data in all of the properties when you create a user account. Examples of `user` properties are `sn` (surname) and `homePhone`.

In Chapter 3, we list about 60 `user` properties that you can set with the Users and Computers snap-in. In Chapter 11, we present a script that lists all properties of a given class.

Figure 1.15 shows the relationship between a class and an object of that class.

The Users and Computers snap-in doesn't always seem to match the underlying data model. For example, you cannot create a user account using the snap-in unless you enter a "User logon name." However, the corresponding property (called `userPrincipalName`) is actually optional, not mandatory.

Each property uses one of 23 *syntaxes,* such as integer 14, string "abc," or time 04/26/2000 2:59:01 PM. The property may be *single-valued* (having just one value), such as `homePhone`, or *multivalued* (having a list of values), such as `otherHomePhone`. Because Active Directory is also a database, some of the properties are indexed, as in any decent database implementation. Searching for objects is faster if the search criteria use an indexed property.

The Schema

The *schema* is a set of rules that dictate which object classes a directory can contain, the object relationships, and the possible content of each object. This is true for Active Directory, as well as other directory services. In other words, the schema governs the structure and content of Active Directory. For example, the schema states which object classes, attributes, and syntaxes your Active Directory can contain. It specifies the mandatory and optional attributes of each class and indicates whether an attribute is indexed. In addition, it defines which attributes are replicated to the global catalog.

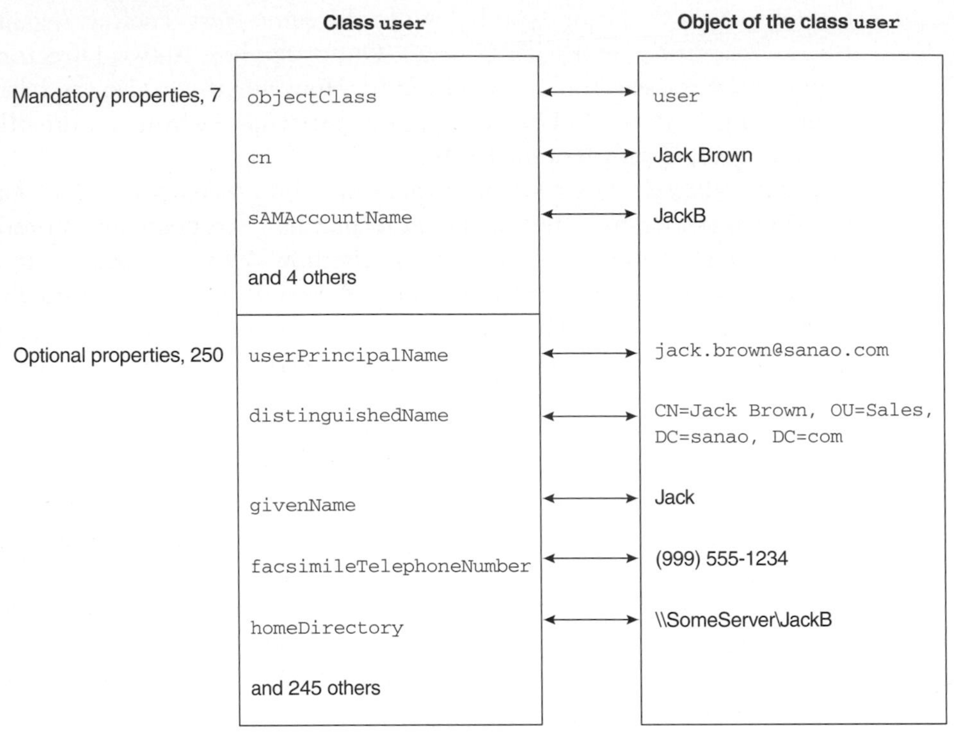

Figure 1.15 The class `user` defines 7 mandatory and 250 optional properties. Each user object must have a value for all mandatory properties and it may have a value for any optional property.

Classes can *inherit* from one another. For example, there is a class called `person` that has, among other attributes, `sn` (surname) and `telephoneNumber`. Another class, `organizationalPerson`, inherits all attributes in `person`, and adds `title` and `facsimile TelephoneNumber`. Finally, the class `user` inherits all attributes in `organizationalPerson` and adds attributes such as `home Directory` and `badPwdCount`.

In addition to the inheritance chain, the `user` class gets a number of attributes from the *auxiliary* classes `mailRecipient` and `securityPrincipal`.

NOTE You may wonder about the strange names of some attributes. Many of them come from the X.500 standard (discussed a little later in this chapter).

Extending the Schema

When you create a forest, it uses the base schema that Microsoft has defined as a default for all installations. Microsoft chose to store the Active Directory schema as objects in Active Directory itself. You may thus query the schema to find out what it supports. You (or your applications) can also extend the schema—that is, you can create new classes or attributes or add new attributes to existing classes. When creating classes, you would probably use the class inheritance described in the preceding section.

Adding attributes such as `userSalaryInformation` allows the use of *directory-enabled applications* in areas such as messaging or human resource management. For example, Exchange 2000 and later use Active Directory and extend the schema for its purposes.

In a global network, the organization must agree on the centralized administration of the schema. For example, the Australian administrators cannot just install their own directory-enabled application, such as a human-resources application, and the Canadians install some other directory-enabled application. Because the schema is common for the whole forest, only those who belong to the Schema Admins security group are able to extend the schema.

Schema changes require careful planning and testing because many of the changes have implications for the whole enterprise, and they are sometimes irreversible (at least without reinstalling the forest). Fortunately, Active Directory has many restrictions and guarding mechanisms to prevent disastrous changes.

Container and Leaf Objects

Objects of some classes are *container objects,* which means that they can contain other objects, just as folders can contain files. The rest are *leaf objects.* They cannot contain other objects, any more than files can contain other files. We call these two types of classes *container classes* and *leaf classes.*

One obvious example of a container class is `organizational-Unit` and an example of a leaf class is `contact`. However, there are many others: A total of 67 classes of Active Directory's base schema are container classes and 124 are leaf classes (56 and 86 in AD2000).

A class that seems to be a leaf class in the user interface could actually be a container class under the hood. An example of this is the `user` class. `User` objects may contain `nTFRSSubscriptions` and `class-Store` objects, so the `user` class is actually a container class.

NOTE In addition to referring to a type of class, the words "container" and "leaf" can also refer to two specific classes. One of the 67 container classes is a class called `container` and one of the 124 leaf classes is a class called `leaf`.

NOTE The X.500 standard defines such container classes as `country`, `locality`, and `organization`, but Active Directory doesn't normally use them.

Partitions

As mentioned earlier, an Active Directory domain is a unit of replication. A unit of replication is called a *partition,* or sometimes a *naming context* (*NC*). This means that a domain is a partition. However, domain is not the only type of partition. Every domain controller holds a copy of the following three partitions:

- The *domain partition,* where users, groups, OUs, and such reside
- The *schema partition,* where schema classes and attributes reside
- The *configuration partition,* where information on the forest structure resides, such as the sites and domains

Information in the first partition (i.e., users, groups, and so on) is replicated among the domain controllers of one domain, whereas the schema and configuration partitions are replicated among all domain controllers in the forest. A copy of a partition in a given domain controller is called a *replica.*

In addition to the three partitions just listed, a Windows Server 2003 domain controller may hold copies of *application partitions.* An application partition can contain objects other than security principals (users, groups, computer objects). Replicas of an application partition can reside in any combination of the forest's domain controllers, without any relevance to domain boundaries. By default, an AD2003 forest contains a ForestDnsZones application partition and a Domain DnsZones application partition to correspond to each domain in the forest.

The domain controllers that are designated as global catalog servers hold a partial copy of all other domain partitions of the forest. A partial copy contains all objects, but it contains only those attributes that are part of the global catalog.

Figure 1.16 shows the partitions of one sample forest (without the DNS zone partitions or any other application partitions). The two rightmost partitions exist in every domain controller, whereas the `sales.sanao.com` and `sanao.com` partitions exist only in the domain controllers of the corresponding domain.

You can manage the two leftmost partitions using the Users and Computers snap-in. Most of the configuration partition you manage with the Sites and Services snap-in, and the schema partition (at least partly) with the Schema Manager snap-in.

Naming Objects

Just as each file in the file system needs a name, each object in Active Directory needs a name. Actually, there are quite a few names for an object in Active Directory, as Table 1.3 shows.

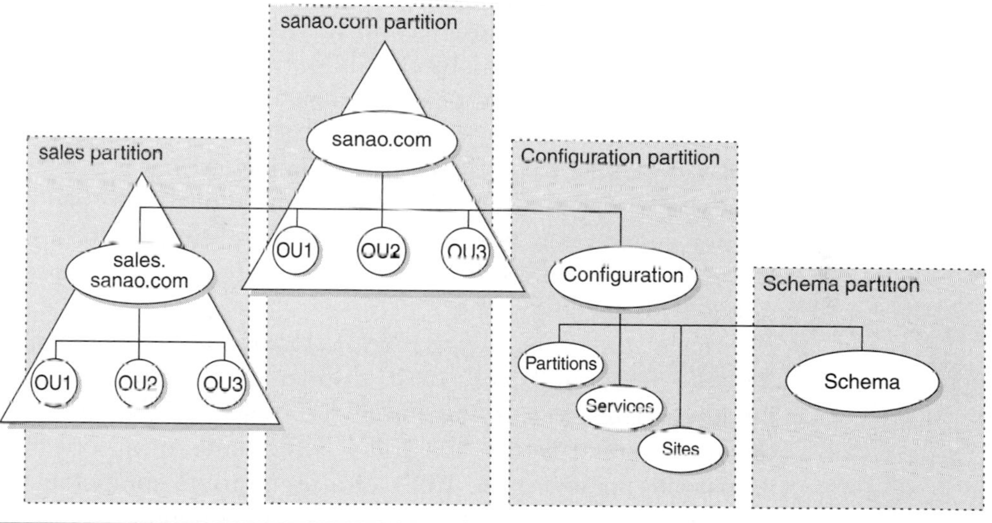

Figure 1.16 Every configuration, schema, and child domain is an independent partition, but together they form a logical tree, where each one is a child to some other partition.

Table 1.3 Syntaxes of Active Directory Names

Type	Example
LDAP distinguished name (DN)	`CN=Jack Brown, OU=Sales, DC=sanao, DC=com`
LDAP relative distinguished name (RDN)	`Jack Brown`
Common name (CN)	`Jack Brown`
Canonical name, two versions	`DC=com/DC=sanao/OU=Sales/CN=Jack Brown` or `sanao.com/Sales/Jack Brown`
User principal name (UPN)	`Jack.Brown@sanao.com`
Downlevel name (SAM name)	`SANAO\JackB`

Using the examples in Table 1.3, the following is a brief discussion of each naming syntax.

- *Distinguished name (DN).* Because every object resides in an OU tree, which in turn resides in a domain tree, a distinguished name specifies the path to the object in both trees. `CN=Jack Brown, OU=Sales` specifies the object's name and location inside one domain's OU tree, and `DC=sanao, DC=com` identifies the domain. Each component of the name has a naming attribute prefix. CN stands for common name, OU for organizational unit, and DC for domain component. There are also the prefixes C (country), O (organization), and L (locality), but they are usually not used in Active Directory.
- *Relative distinguished name (RDN).* This is the first component (i.e., the "least significant") of the distinguished name, and it must be unique among its *sibling objects* (i.e., objects in the same container). In other words, the RDN is the name of an object in its parent container. The RDN of a user, group, computer, and almost all other objects is the same as its common name. The RDN of an OU is the same as its OU attribute, and the RDN of a domain is the same as its DC attribute. CN, OU, and DC are also called *naming attributes.* Our example in Table 1.3 shows just `Jack Brown`, but with some utilities, you may need to include the prefix, such as `CN=Jack Brown`.

- *Common name (CN).* Our sample names are for a user object; therefore, the object has a common name, which is the same as its RDN.
- *Canonical name.* This is an alternative format (or actually two formats) for a distinguished name. The first format uses slashes as separators where a distinguished name uses commas. Also, as we go through the name from left to right, the first format lists the name components from top to bottom, while a distinguished name lists them from bottom to top. The second format is quite similar to a Web page's Uniform Resource Locator (URL), such as `www.microsoft.com/windowsserver2003`.
- *User principal name (UPN).* You can define a UPN for each user, who then uses it to log on and to enter in other places that require a username. Because a UPN looks like an e-mail address, it should be easy for users to remember and type.
- *Downlevel (SAM) name.* Each user (and some other objects such as groups and computers) must have a downlevel name, which is similar to the user account names in Windows NT. The downlevel name can also be used for logon and in many other places where a username is required. Depending on the place, the user types either "SANAO\JackB" or just "JackB."

NOTE All Active Directory objects have a DN, an RDN, and a canonical name, but objects of only some classes have a UPN or downlevel name. For example, a user object *may* have a UPN (an optional attribute) and *must* have a downlevel name (a mandatory attribute). A CN exists for most object classes.

NOTE None of the names are case-sensitive.

Fortunately, you don't have to type all of these long names every time you want to access an object. For example, the GUI relieves end users from typing names other than sometimes UPNs and downlevel names. Also, administrators can survive without typing the names, at least as long as they use the graphical MMC snap-ins shipping with Windows 2000 and later. However, if they start using the utilities in the Support Tools package (included in the Windows 2000 and Windows Server 2003 CD) or the Resource Kit (sold separately), they need to learn to type those long names (mostly the distinguished names).

The X.500 Standards

"X.500" refers to a series of international standards that define the features and aspects of a directory service, including its information model, functional model, namespace, and authentication framework. Table 1.4 lists some of these standards.

The standards were prepared collaboratively by the International Organization for Standardization/International Electrotechnical Commission (ISO/IEC) (`http://www.iso.ch/`) and the International Telecommunication Union, Telecommunications Standardization Sector (ITU-T) (`http://www.itu.int/`).

ITU-T is one of the United Nations organizations and it publishes standards, called Recommendations, in series designated by letters. The X series, including X.500, concerns "data networks and open system communications." The V series concerns "data communication over the telephone network." If you have used a V.34 modem, you have been using a device that conforms to one of these recommendations.

ITU-T traditionally approves new recommendations in a World Telecommunication Standardization Conference held every four years. The first version of X.500 appeared in 1988 and is often called X.500 (88). Similarly, the next two versions are X.500 (93) and X.500 (96).

The Active Directory data model (classes and so on) is derived from the X.500 data model, and Active Directory implements many X.500 features. Examples are a subset of the 1993 version of Directory Access Protocol (DAP), Directory System Protocol (DSP), and Directory Information Shadowing Protocol (DISP). However, Active Directory is not a full X.500 directory service. Microsoft has stripped away more complex and unnecessary features. Also, Active Directory uses LDAP, which makes some difference.

X.500 is also referred to as an "OSI directory service," where "OSI" stands for "Open Systems Interconnection." OSI hasn't had a particularly good reputation in the telecommunications area. OSI protocols and other OSI standards have been considered slow, complex, and resource-intensive. For these reasons, most of them have not been widely adopted. LDAP made X.500 viable by taking the best parts of it and streamlining it.

The bad reputation is also true for DAP, which we just mentioned. X.500 clients use it to access directory information on directory servers (also called *Directory System Agents*, or *DSAs*). DAP and other X.500 protocols run over ISO/OSI transport protocols, so there are two

Table 1.4 X.500 Standards

ITU-T Recommendation	ISO/IEC Standard	Name
X.500 (2/2001)	9594-1:2001	The Directory: Overview of concepts, models, and services
X.501 (2/2001)	9594-2:2001	The Directory: Models
X.509 (3/2000)	9594-8:2001	The Directory: Public-key and attribute certificate frameworks (previously Authentication framework)
X.511 (2/2001)	9594-3:2001	The Directory: Abstract service definition
X.518 (2/2001)	9594-4:2001	The Directory: Procedures for distributed operation
X.519 (2/2001)	9594-5:2001	The Directory: Protocol specifications
X.520 (2/2001)	9594-6:2001	The Directory: Selected attribute types
X.521 (2/2001)	9594-7:2001	The Directory: Selected object classes
X.525 (2/2001)	9594-9:2001	The Directory: Replication
X.530 (2/2001)	9594-10:2001	The Directory: Use of systems management for administration of the Directory
X.583 (12/1997)		The Directory: Protocol Implementation Conformance Statement (PICS) proforma for the Directory Access Protocol
X.584 (12/1997)		The Directory: Protocol Implementation Conformance Statement (PICS) proforma for the Directory System Protocol
X.585 (12/1997)		The Directory: Protocol Implementation Conformance Statement (PICS) proforma for the Directory Operational Binding Management Protocol
X.586 (12/1997)		The Directory: Protocol Implementation Conformance Statement (PICS) proforma for the Directory Information Shadowing Protocol

protocols with bad reputations that run on top of each other. For these reasons, a lightweight version of DAP (LDAP) was developed.

LDAP

The Lightweight Directory Access Protocol (LDAP) is a simplified version of the more complex DAP, and it runs on the more popular and light TCP/IP, rather than ISO/OSI. Clients can use LDAP to connect to and be authenticated to directories and to search and modify information in them either over the Internet or inside an organization. Active Directory is also a directory, and Windows 2000 and later clients access Active Directory using LDAP. This includes also the network traffic that various administrative tools generate. In other words, clients "talk LDAP" when they read or write information to Active Directory domain controllers.

NOTE Although in the next section we list the other access methods, we want to emphasize that almost all access to Active Directory takes place with LDAP.

LDAP version 1 was published as RFC 1487 in 1993 and was made obsolete by LDAP version 2 (LDAPv2), RFC 1777, in 1995. The next year about 40 companies, including Microsoft, Netscape, and Novell, announced that they would support LDAP in their directory services products. Finally, in 1997 LDAP version 3 (LDAPv3) was published as RFC 2251.

As of this writing, RFC 1777 already has a "historical" status and RFC 2251 has a "proposed" status. However, you shouldn't worry that they don't carry an actual "standard" status. They are still widely supported, and many other Internet technologies still have a "proposed" status. For example, RFC 977, which defines the NNTP protocol to be used to distribute news articles (or discussions and junk ads in practice) on Internet news areas and query news servers, has been on the "proposed" status list since 1986, and yet tens of millions of people use it every day.

NOTE When people wanted a lighter version of DAP back in 1993, the average PC was dramatically slower than it is nowadays. Compared to the other services that Windows 2000 or later is running, DAP would be a piece of cake with the current microcomputers. However, LDAP has already taken over DAP, so it is *probably* too late for a DAP era.

LDAPv3 Specifications

Although we earlier indicated just one RFC number per LDAP version, a number of specifications actually make up each LDAP version. To give you an idea of the kind of things the LDAP specification family includes, Table 1.5 and Table 1.6 list them for LDAPv3. Table 1.5 lists the core specifications. When the first six of them (RFCs 2251–56) were published in 1997, authentication was not included yet. It was introduced later in RFCs 2829 and 2830, and finally RFC 3377 ties these all together. Table 1.6 lists the remaining specifications. If you quickly browse through the two tables, you will get an idea of what kind of work has been done and is being done with LDAP.

About half of the RFCs in Table 1.6 carry a "proposed" status and the remaining ones are "informational." Informational RFCs are not on the normal RFC standards track. Some other standards organization or vendor has perhaps developed them, but they are published as RFCs because they may be of general interest or may be recommended for use on the Internet.

Active Directory supports LDAPv2 and LDAPv3. Each domain controller is an LDAPv3 directory server, but it can also communicate with LDAPv2 clients.

Table 1.5 LDAPv3 Core Specifications

RFC Number	Date	Title
RFC 2251	12/1997	Lightweight Directory Access Protocol (v3)
RFC 2252	12/1997	Lightweight Directory Access Protocol (v3): Attribute Syntax Definitions
RFC 2253	12/1997	Lightweight Directory Access Protocol (v3): UTF-8 String Representation of Distinguished Names
RFC 2254	12/1997	The String Representation of LDAP Search Filters
RFC 2255	12/1997	The LDAP URL Format
RFC 2256	12/1997	A Summary of the X.500(96) User Schema for use with LDAPv3
RFC 2829	5/2000	Authentication Methods for LDAP
RFC 2830	5/2000	Lightweight Directory Access Protocol (v3): Extension for Transport Layer Security
RFC 3377	9/2002	Lightweight Directory Access Protocol (v3): Technical Specification

Table 1.6 Other LDAPv3 Specifications

Number	Category	Date	Title
1823	Informational	8/1995	The LDAP Application Program Interface
2164	Proposed	1/1998	Use of an X.500/LDAP directory to support MIXER address mapping
2247	Proposed	1/1998	Using Domains in LDAP/X.500 Distinguished Names
2589	Proposed	5/1999	Lightweight Directory Access Protocol (v3): Extensions for Dynamic Directory Services
2596	Proposed	5/1999	Use of Language Codes in LDAP
2696	Informational	9/1999	LDAP Control Extension for Simple Paged Results Manipulation
2713	Informational	10/1999	Schema for Representing Java(tm) Objects in an LDAP Directory
2714	Informational	10/1999	Schema for Representing CORBA Object References in an LDAP Directory
2739	Proposed	1/2000	Calendar Attributes for vCard and LDAP
2798	Informational	4/2000	Definition of the inetOrgPerson LDAP Object Class
2820	Informational	5/2000	Access Control Requirements for LDAP
2849	Proposed	6/2000	The LDAP Data Interchange Format (LDIF) - Technical Specification
2891	Proposed	8/2000	LDAP Control Extension for Server Side Sorting of Search Results
2926	Informational	9/2000	Conversion of LDAP Schemas to and from SLP Templates
2927	Informational	9/2000	MIME Directory Profile for LDAP Schema
3045	Informational	1/2001	Storing Vendor Information in the LDAP root DSE
3062	Proposed	2/2001	LDAP Password Modify Extended Operation

Table 1.6 Other LDAPv3 Specifications *(cont.)*

Number	Category	Date	Title
3112	Informational	5/2001	LDAP Authentication Password Schema
3296	Proposed	7/2002	Named Subordinate References in Lightweight Directory Access Protocol (LDAP) Directories
3384	Informational	10/2002	Lightweight Directory Access Protocol (version 3) Replication Requirements
3671	Proposed	12/2003	Collective Attributes in the Lightweight Directory Access Protocol (LDAP)
3672	Proposed	12/2003	Subentries in the Lightweight Directory Access Protocol (LDAP)
3673	Proposed	12/2003	Lightweight Directory Access Protocol version 3 (LDAPv3): All Operational Attributes
3674	Proposed	12/2003	Feature Discovery in Lightweight Directory Access Protocol (LDAP)
3687	Proposed	2/2004	Lightweight Directory Access Protocol (LDAP) and X.500 Component Matching Rules
3698	Proposed	2/2004	Lightweight Directory Access Protocol (LDAP): Additional Matching Rules
3703	Proposed	2/2004	Policy Core Lightweight Directory Access Protocol (LDAP) Schema
3712	Informational	2/2004	Lightweight Directory Access Protocol (LDAP): Schema for Printer Services
3727	Proposed	2/2004	ASN.1 Module Definition for the LDAP and X.500 Component Matching Rules

Each application protocol over TCP/IP must use a port number. LDAP's port number is by default 389. Web browsing would use by default port 80, and DNS lookups, port 53.

LDAPv3 Operations

RFC 2251 defines 11 LDAPv3 operations, which are described in Table 1.7.

Table 1.7 LDAPv3 Operations

Operation	Description
Bind	This operation connects* and authenticates (perhaps anonymously) the client to a directory server.
Unbind	This operation terminates a session to a directory server.
Unsolicited Notification	This is an advisory message that a directory server sends to the client in the event of an extraordinary event (i.e., an error). This message is not a response to any client request.
Search	This operation retrieves the selected attributes of one or more directory objects. You can either do a genuine search on some criteria or just "search" with a certain distinguished name. The latter case is actually a normal read, because you exactly specify the object to read.
Modify	This operation applies a list of modifications to a given directory object.
Add	This operation adds a given object to the directory, with the included attribute values.
Delete	This operation deletes a given object from the directory.
Modify DN	This operation renames a given object or moves a given subtree to a new location.
Compare	This operation compares a given object and a given attribute value. For example, you could ask if Jack's phone number is "555-1234." The LDAP server would answer either yes or no.
Abandon	This operation abandons a designated previous operation.
Extended	This operation allows extending existing operations and adding operations.

* Although in the table we say that the operations do this and that, to be exact, they just send a request to a server. Insufficient permissions, some other restrictions, or an error condition will prevent the server from fulfilling the request.

A client can send most requests either *synchronously* or *asynchronously*. The former choice means that the client application won't do anything else while it waits for a response; the latter choice indicates just the opposite situation.

One of the ways DAP was lightened to become LDAP was by the exclusion of Read or Move operations. They were unnecessary because the Search and Modify DN operations provide the functionality.

Physical Architecture

In X.500 a directory server is called a *Directory System Agent (DSA)*, and each Active Directory domain controller is also a DSA. In Windows 2000 and Windows Server 2003, the DSA feature "lives" in a process called LSASS.EXE (Local Security Authority Subsystem), and there is a file, NTDSA.DLL (NT Directory System Agent), that implements most of the functionality. Figure 1.17 shows NTDSA.DLL, as well as the other physical components of a domain controller.

NOTE Obviously the files NTDSA.DLL and ESENT.DLL reside also on disk (permanent storage), but in Figure 1.17 we have drawn them in RAM. In this context, they are only meaningful when they are loaded in RAM and their functions are executed there.

Whenever Active Directory modifies some information, it does so through *transactions*. This means that the requested Modify operation is atomic—that is, it either completes in full or it is not applied at all. Each transaction is first written to a transaction log, and if this succeeds, the information is also stored in the actual database (NTDS.DIT). This protects the database from corruption, and any decent database product, such as SQL Server, uses a similar technique. Generally, directory information is mostly searched and read; the transaction logs are needed only when the information is modified.

The Extensible Storage Engine (ESE) handles the storage files, and the DB layer above it handles the database tables on a logical level. Active Directory uses only two database tables, while a typical customer-tracking application uses tens of tables, created perhaps in SQL Server. The *object table* contains the information of all Active Directory objects, and the *link table* implements the object relationships. You can think of the object table as a large Excel spreadsheet, where each row corresponds to one object and each column corresponds to one attribute.

ESE uses the Indexed Sequential Access Method (ISAM) technology, which Microsoft called Jet previously. Microsoft uses an ISAM table manager in Access, Exchange, WINS, and FRS, among others.

The DB layer handles data using a flat model; in other words, there is no hierarchy. The Directory System Agent (DSA) above it creates the hierarchical namespace where OUs and other containers form a tree of objects. You could also call the DSA a directory layer.

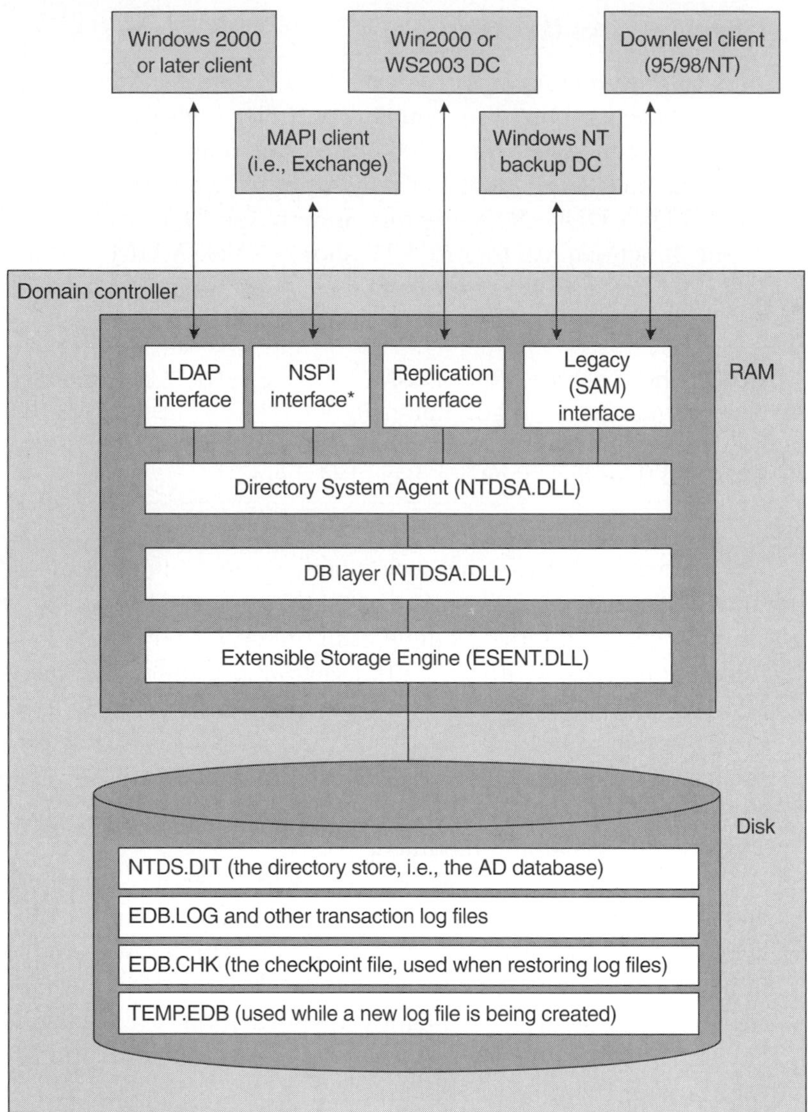

* The NSPI interface is available in global catalog servers that have been rebooted after the global catalog promotion.

Figure 1.17 Each Active Directory domain controller has NTDS.DIT and other files on disk that contain Active Directory information. Through a selection of interfaces, the DSA component offers this information to others who need it.

Most of the directory access takes place using the LDAP protocol. Normal Windows 2000 and later clients use it, as do other LDAP clients.

ADSI

Whether you write simple administration scripts with VBScript or applications with C/C++, you will use *Active Directory Service Interfaces (ADSI)* to programmatically access Active Directory. ADSI is a strategic API for Microsoft: Most Active Directory management utilities included in Windows 2000 and Windows Server 2003 use ADSI.

NOTE C programmers could also use the low-level LDAP C API instead of ADSI, but Microsoft recommends using ADSI.

ADSI is implemented as *Component Object Model (COM)* objects. COM is Microsoft's programming technology that allows, among other things, binary program components to interact.

ADSI can be used with other LDAP directories besides Active Directory and, using different providers, with Internet Information Server, NetWare, and Windows NT.

Figure 1.18 illustrates the principle of ADSI.

As LDAP does as a protocol, ADSI as an interface includes operations for authentication, creating and deleting objects in Active Directory, and for reading and writing information in object attributes.

The following five-line VBScript script will give you an idea of what a simple ADSI script might look like. The sample script lists names and descriptions of all users that exist in the Users container.

```
Set objCont = GetObject("LDAP://CN=Users,DC=sanao,DC=com")
objCont.Filter = Array("user")
For Each objChild In objCont
  WScript.Echo objChild.Name & vbTab & objChild.Description
Next
```

Use Notepad to save the lines with the filename Users.vbs. Start the command prompt and change to the folder where you saved the file. Then type "cscript users.vbs" (without quotes) and press Enter.

If you have only the default objects in the Users container, the first lines of the output you get should look like the following (the first line is

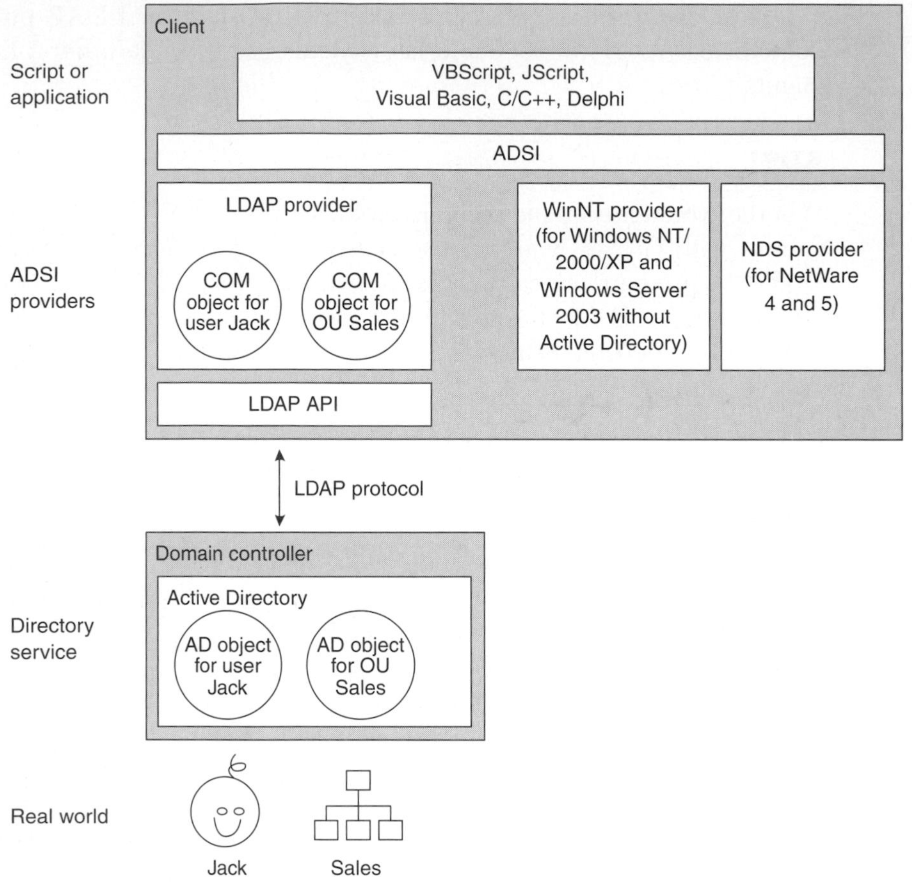

Figure 1.18 Active Directory objects abstract real-world users and resources. ADSI COM objects in turn abstract Active Directory objects. When your script manipulates the COM objects, it eventually affects the corresponding Active Directory objects.

the command line and the output of the Administrator and Guest lines are wrapped to fit on this page):

```
C:\MyTests>cscript users.vbs
CN=Administrator        Built-in account for administering
                        the computer/domain
CN=Guest        Built-in account for guest access to the
                computer/domain
CN=krbtgt       Key Distribution Center Service Account
```

When searching a number of objects using some search criteria, you can use *ActiveX Data Objects (ADO)*. ADO is a general Microsoft database interface on top of ADSI, among other data providers, so you can make simultaneous queries for information from more than one data source—for example, in Active Directory and SQL Server or an Oracle database.

NOTE The WinNT provider is not just for Windows NT. You use it to manage users and groups in Windows 2000/XP workstations and Windows 2000/Server 2003 member servers. You also use the WinNT provider when you manage file shares and so on, on any Windows 2000/Server 2003 computer, including domain controllers.

Kerberos Authentication

Active Directory uses Kerberos version 5 (RFC 1510) as its primary authentication method instead of Windows NT/LAN Manager (NTLM), which was used in Windows NT.

Kerberos is based on tickets. When a workstation starts up or a user logs on, the workstation contacts a Kerberos *key distribution center (KDC)*, which is a service running on all domain controllers. The KDC returns a *ticket-granting ticket (TGT)*, which the workstation caches for later use. The user needs the TGT when she wants to start a session with some server. In this case, her workstation acquires a *session ticket* from the KDC for that server. Figure 1.19 illustrates the computers and the tickets.

Kerberos has three advantages over NTLM that are worth mentioning.

- *Faster session authentication.* When a client connects to a member server in a domain (such as server B operating as a file server in Figure 1.19), the client offers its session key. The key has enough information for authentication, so the server does not need to contact its domain controller to check the user's validity. This speeds up client connections, especially when many clients are accessing one server.
- *Impersonation.* If a client makes a request to a server (server B in Figure 1.19), and in order to fulfill it the server makes a request to another server (server C in Figure 1.19), the first server can impersonate the client to the second server. That is, it gets the

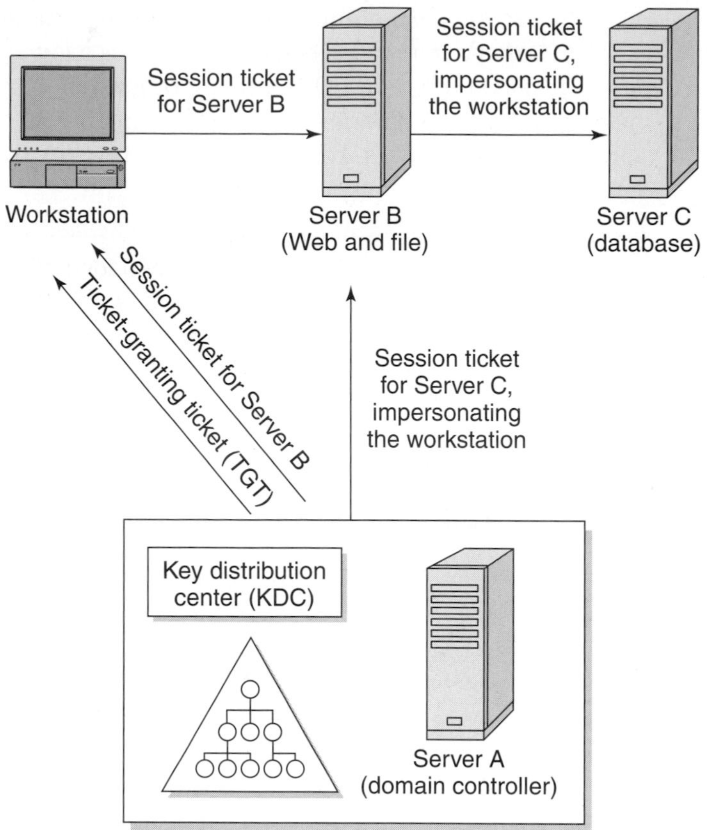

Figure 1.19 A Kerberos key distribution center (KDC) issues ticket-granting tickets (TGT) and session tickets to users, workstations, and servers for authentication.

data using the client's credentials, not using some fixed account for all users.

- *Mutual authentication.* Not only does the server know that it is talking to the correct client, but it is also possible for the client to know that it is communicating with the correct server.

NOTE Active Directory still supports NTLM for downlevel clients and when authenticating from one forest to another through an external trust.

Public Key Infrastructure

Active Directory and Windows 2000 and later support *public key technology.* In other words, they can use X.509 version 3 certificates with private/public-key pairs. This is referred to as *public key infrastructure (PKI).* You can choose to buy certificates from a commercial *certificate authority (CA)*—for example, VeriSign—or you can create certificates yourself using the Certificate Services included in Windows 2000 and Windows Server 2003. In either case, the certificates may be stored in Active Directory, so you and your users can use them for the following purposes:

- File encryption with Encrypting File System (EFS)
- E-mail encryption
- Web browser traffic encryption (i.e., HTTPS)
- TCP/IP traffic encryption (i.e., IPSec)
- Logon and authentication
- Use of digitally signed drivers and system files (AuthentiCode)

Windows 2000 and later also support *smart cards,* which could be described as "credit cards with processor and memory." They are a very secure place to store users' private keys. You can use a smart card and a personal identification number (PIN) for logon instead of a traditional username and password, which increases logon security dramatically.

If you have an extranet for customers and business partners, you can create user accounts for them and store their public keys in your Active Directory. They can then authenticate to your network using their own private keys and gain access to resources you have assigned to them.

Windows Server 2003 introduces editable certificate templates, but they are available only in the Enterprise Edition.

Other Features

Active Directory has many features—far too many to delve into in this introductory chapter, but we will mention two more that we haven't already covered. You can create virtual containers for external directories, and you can publish certain services in Active Directory. Also in this section, we will say a few words about special considerations that Active Directory adds when connecting your network to the Internet, and we'll list the current limitations in Active Directory.

Virtual Containers

You can make another LDAP directory look like part of your Active Directory by creating a *virtual container.* To make this happen, you create an external cross-reference and define three things:

- The common name for the cross-reference object
- The DNS name of the server holding a copy of the foreign directory
- The DN of the "starting point" in the foreign directory

Publishing

Publishing is making information available in Active Directory so users can find it. The information can be interesting by itself, such as another user's phone number, or it can be a reference to something interesting, such as a printer, a shared folder, or an application service.

Whenever a user or printer object is created, publishing happens automatically at the same time. When developing applications, however, you can choose what to publish in Active Directory and what to store elsewhere—for example, in the file system or database.

As you know, the information in Active Directory is replicated to all domain controllers in a domain. For this reason, it pays to put in Active Directory information that doesn't change often and that is of interest to a large number of people. For example, a printer object is static, but a print job is not. Application partitions, which were introduced in Windows Server 2003, allow for more flexibility when storing data in Active Directory, because with those partitions, you can freely select the domain controllers where a replica of a given application partition exists. Another option is to use Active Directory Application Mode (ADAM), as explained in Chapter 9.

The following application information is probably well suited for storage in Active Directory.

- *Application configuration.* This information would help provide consistent settings to all users in your company. Alternatively, an application such as Microsoft Internet Security and Acceleration (ISA) Server can store its configuration in Active Directory and provide a centralized configuration for several servers.

- *Connection points for client-server applications.* With connection points, a client can find server services and connect to them, whether they are provided with the RPC, WinSock, or COM technology. The client doesn't need to know the name or address of the server computer beforehand, because the client can find this information in Active Directory. The connection points are standard Active Directory objects, and they can be separate for end users and administrators. (To be exact, COM-based services advertise themselves a little differently. They use the class store instead of connection point objects.)
- *Application data.* If the data is of interest to a number of people, and suitable for an Active Directory object-attribute structure, that data could be stored in Active Directory instead of the file system.

We mentioned the term "directory-enabled application" (or DEA) when we covered extending the schema. If an application is using any of the three items in the previous list, it will also have to be directory enabled.

Connecting to the Internet

Windows 2000 and later and Active Directory use pretty much the same TCP/IP protocols in an internal network that are being used on the public Internet. If you connect your network to the Internet, you may need to install a firewall to control what information (such as computer names) is displayed on the Internet as well as to control incoming and outgoing traffic.

IF YOU KNOW NT Windows NT networks are based on NetBIOS names and NetBIOS communications. A small or medium-sized company using Windows NT could easily get some sort of protection for its network by filtering the NetBIOS ports 137 through 139 in its Internet router. A firewall, however, is still highly recommended.

Outside the firewall is a *demilitarized zone (DMZ)*. The servers in this zone are made visible to the Internet, even though there is usually another firewall between the DMZ and the Internet. Figure 1.20 shows the two firewalls and the servers.

NOTE In practice there are several ways to implement firewalls, but in this context we are interested only in what is and is not visible to the Internet (e.g., certain services on the DMZ are visible, but the internal network is not).

There are separate DNS zones (DNS information database) for the outside world and internal use. This means that people on the Internet don't see the same computer and domain names and IP addresses that the company employees see.

Because the servers in the DMZ are made visible to the Internet, Internet users can see `www.sanao.com` and send e-mail to `some.one@sanao.com`. Note that the Internet service provider could also host any of the three servers on its own network.

There are no Active Directory servers (i.e., domain controllers) outside the inner firewall, so they should be safe from hackers and crackers.

There are three ways to pick up the Active Directory forest name that is in use internally (see Figure 1.20).

- Use the same DNS name (e.g., `sanao.com`) internally and externally. This choice is logical, because the employees can use the same domain name whether they are accessing resources from the internal network or the Internet. However, it may be confusing for both administrators and users to comprehend and remember which resources are on the internal Web servers and which are on the servers for the public Internet.
- Use different DNS names internally and externally. In Figure 1.20 we have `sanao.org`, but you could have something else, such as `sanaoint.com` or `sanao.local`. Unless you use the "local" top-level domain, you should register the internal name with a registration authority (a company or an organization that issues registered DNS names—for more information, visit the Internet Corporation for Assigned Names and Numbers at `http://www.icann.org/`).
- Use internally a DNS name that is delegated from the external name (e.g., `corp.sanao.com`).

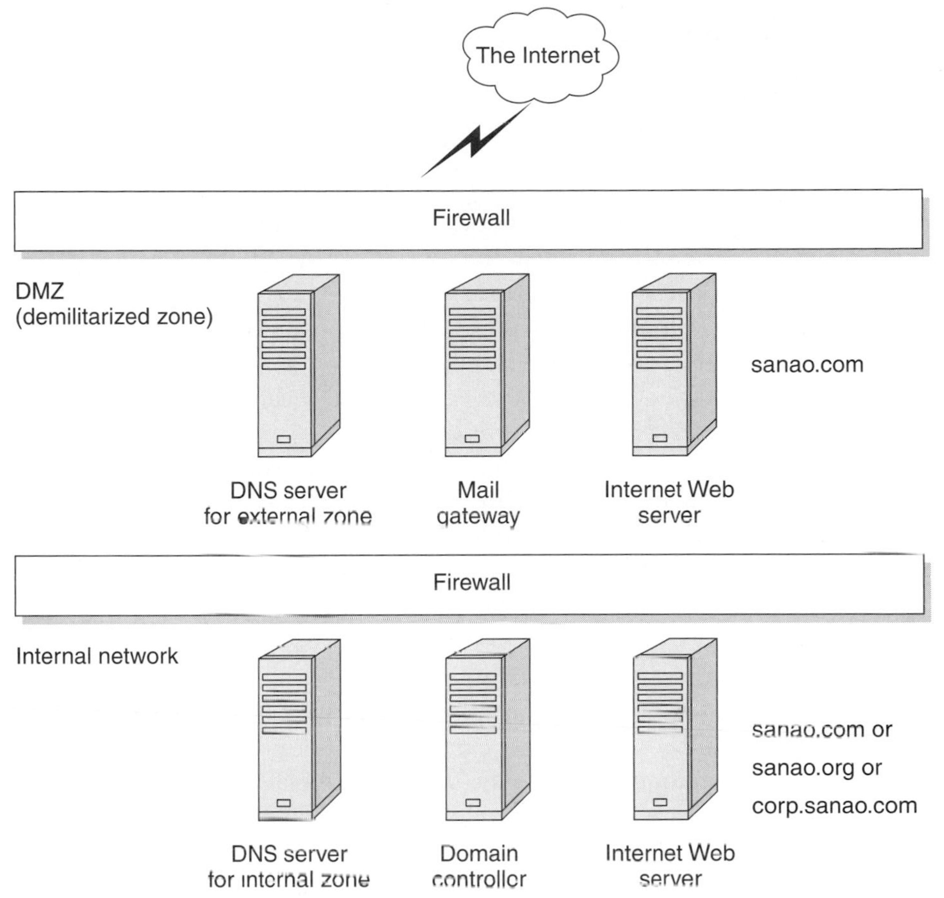

Figure 1.20 An organization that has an Internet presence usually has a DNS server, a mail gateway, and a Web server that are accessible from the Internet. Here they are placed on the DMZ between the two firewalls. Note that there are no Active Directory servers (i.e., domain controllers) in this zone.

Active Directory's Current Limitations

This chapter has introduced Active Directory's features and concepts. In the real world, nothing is perfect. So, to give you a full picture, we must address some of Active Directory's limitations and shortcomings. We mentioned some of them earlier in this chapter, so this section serves also as a summary and indicates what is expected to appear in Active Directory in the next versions over the next few years.

No Forest Changes

Active Directory offers many choices, but it does not always allow you to change them after installation. Thus, you must make some things right the first time.

A domain can join a forest only when you create the domain—you cannot join it afterward. In AD2000, you cannot rename a domain or move it to another place in the forest, but in AD2003 you can (if the forest functional level is Windows Server 2003). Even in AD2000, however, removing a domain is possible. If the domain to be removed has child domains, they are also removed.

In addition in AD2000, you cannot rename a domain controller, although you can demote it to a member server, rename it, and promote it again to a domain controller. In AD2003, you can rename a domain controller if the domain functional level is Windows Server 2003. A higher functional level enables more new features, but it also prohibits domain controllers that are running older versions of Windows. For more information, see the "Domain and Forest Functional Levels" section in Chapter 2.

You cannot merge two forests.

The partition concept is not transparent, because it is tied to domains. For example, you cannot split a domain into two partitions or merge two domains into one—you cannot change partition boundaries. This difficulty is somewhat relieved by the fact that you can move objects from one domain to another. However, even if you remove all objects from a domain, you cannot eliminate the domain without eliminating its child domains (except quite laboriously with the new domain rename feature: Move the domain to a location where it has no child domains).

IF YOU KNOW NDS In Novell NDS you can freely create (split) and merge partitions to control what to replicate to which locations (although you cannot differentiate local and remote replication).

Because research and development are constantly under way, future versions of Active Directory will probably not have many of the current limitations.

Domain Nature

An Active Directory domain is three things at the same time that you could claim shouldn't have anything to do with each other:

- A partition (i.e., a replication unit)
- Part of the DNS namespace, so that an Active Directory domain must match a DNS domain
- An administrative unit and a security policy boundary

This means that when you choose your domain structure and boundaries, even though the three are independent, you must consider all three at the same time and make them coincide. Fortunately, these three planning criteria often match quite easily.

IF YOU KNOW NDS In NDS, partitions and administrative units are independent.

Other Limitations

The two preceding sections, as well as this one, list Active Directory's shortcomings when it is compared to NDS. This is not to say that NDS is better. Active Directory also has many advantages over NDS. It is not useful, however, to focus on them here.

One NDS server can host replicas of multiple partitions, which gives flexibility in placing various parts of directory information on various servers. An Active Directory server (that is, a domain controller) can host only one domain (although it can host multiple application partitions). If you have 20 small branch offices, and each office has one server with its own domain, Active Directory does not allow you to place replicas of those directory databases in one server in your main office. Instead, you need 20 extra servers (one for each domain) to host the replicas. On the other hand, if you put those branch offices in the headquarters domain, they would unnecessarily replicate all the user and object information from the headquarters and other offices. One thing you can do, however, is create a common domain for the 20 branch offices. This way, you avoid having 20 domains or the need to replicate all headquarters users to the branch offices.

As mentioned previously, you cannot give permissions to OUs. This means that if you have 30 users in an OU, you probably need to create a group and put the same 30 users in it to be able to give them permissions for certain folders or objects.

Some Differences from NDS

Active Directory is missing two features which are not necessary, so we obviously don't consider this a shortcoming. We mention them here so that you can see other possibilities.

In NDS you can move around the directory tree using the workstation command line (command CX), and your current location is called the *current context.* If you refer to an object with a relative path (*relative distinguished name,* or *RDN* in NDS), this path depends on your current context, as a relative filename depends on your current directory (i.e., ..\SomeFolder\SomeFile). Active Directory does not have the concept of current context. It does have the concept of RDN, but Active Directory RDN is always relative to the parent object name.

Unlike NDS, Active Directory does not support creating *alias objects.* An alias object would point to another object—this way, a user could refer to an object either directly or through its alias. The need for alias objects in Active Directory is not great, however. Extensive search capability, UPNs, shared folder objects, and other techniques are used instead.

The Next Version of Active Directory

As of this writing (in March 2004), Microsoft expects to ship the next version of Active Directory around 2007. It is part of a future Windows Server product that is currently code-named "Longhorn."

Microsoft is also expected to ship Windows Server 2003 Release 2 (R2) in 2005. R2 would contain Windows Server 2003 with Service Pack 1 and the additional feature packs that can currently be downloaded separately. These include Active Directory Application Mode (ADAM), Automated Deployment Services (ADS), DSML Services for Windows, Group Policy Management Console (GPMC), Identity Integration Feature Pack (IIFP), Services for NetWare 5.02 SP2, Shadow Copy Client, Software Update Services (SUS) 2.0, Windows Rights Management Services (RMS) and client, Windows SharePoint Services (WSS), and Windows System Resource Manager (WSRM).

Conclusion

This chapter introduced the concepts on which Active Directory is based and the features it offers. Understanding of these elements now forms the base of your knowledge of Active Directory. The next chapter explains the Active Directory installation process. You will soon have your server up and running so you can start exploring Active Directory.

CHAPTER 2

Active Directory Installation

Many phases of installing Windows 2000 and Windows Server 2003 have been automated so well that they are usually quite easy to set up, even for a person who is not technologically skilled. The installation is separated into two parts: installing the operating system and installing Active Directory. We have decided not to cover the first part (operating system installation) in this book. Instead, you can look for more information in the online Help. If you are installing Windows 2000/Server 2003 for the first time, the same help documentation is also available on the Microsoft Web site at `http://www.microsoft.com/windows2000/techinfo/proddoc` or `http://www.microsoft.com/windowsserver2003/proddoc`. The files in the SETUPTXT (Windows 2000) or DOCS (Windows Server 2003) subfolder of the installation CD are also worth looking at. In addition, you can find an extensive collection of links to Windows Server 2003 documentation on `http://go.microsoft.com/fwlink/?LinkID-19793`.

TIP You can install and use Windows Server 2003 Help on your Windows XP computer. Select Start, Help and Support. Click Options on the toolbar. Click "Install and share Windows Help". Click "Install Help content from a CD or disk image". Locate the Windows Server 2003 setup CD with Browse, and click Find. Select the Help, and click Install. The Help .chm files are copied to the C:\WINDOWS\Help folder on your computer. You can then use the command Switch to switch from one operating system's Help content to another.

IF YOU KNOW NT When you installed Windows NT, you had to know whether to install it as a stand-alone server or as a primary or backup domain controller. After setup, the only way to change the role between stand-alone server and domain controller was to reinstall the operating system. This has changed with Windows 2000. Now you install the computer as a stand-alone or member server and promote it to a domain controller afterward if you wish.

We include here a few tips that you should be aware of after installing Windows Server 2003.

- Windows Server 2003 includes a new system component called Internet Explorer Enhanced Security Configuration (IEESC). As the name implies, the IEESC raises IE security levels, which is generally a good thing since users should not browse the Internet from a server. However, IEESC brings along at least one issue related also to Active Directory management. When you are using Group Policy Management Console, you must add about:security_mmc.exe to the IE Trusted zone in order to use all the functionality in reports. In your test environment, you could remove IEESC with Add/Remove Windows Components.
- Windows Server 2003 also enables analyzing shutdown or restart reasons afterward through a shutdown event tracking feature, which you see when shutting down or restarting the computer. In a lab environment, you can disable this feature with gpedit.msc. Locate Local Computer Policy\Computer Configuration\Administrative Templates\System\Display Shutdown Event Tracker, double-click the setting, select Disabled, and click OK.
- Microsoft finally changed the NTFS permissions on the root folder of the system drive. You should be aware of this and the change in the default share permissions (Everyone: Read), which was first introduced in Windows XP Service Pack 1 and is now also included in Windows Server 2003.
- You have basically two options for remotely administering another Windows Server 2003 computer with the GUI. You can install the administrative tools into your own computer by running adminpak.msi (from the i386 folder on the setup CD or from the %windir%\system32 folder of a Windows Server 2003 computer). Alternatively, you can enable the Remote Desktop on a Windows Server 2003 from the System Properties, and use Remote Desktop Connection (Start, Run, mstsc) or the Remote Desktops MMC snap-in on administrative tools.

NOTE In Windows 2000 servers, you had to install Terminal Server in Remote Administration mode in order to access it with a Terminal Services client.

TIP You can easily enable Remote Desktop remotely from the command prompt with the wmic command. Open Windows Server 2003 Help and Support Center, use wmic as the keyword for the search, and open the first hit (Managing systems with WMIC: WMI Command-line) under Help Topics. Use the first command using the RDTOGGLE alias under "Examples for using Terminal Server aliases".

For the purpose of studying Active Directory with this book, you could use the values in Table 2.1 when installing a test server.

NOTE You cannot promote Windows Server 2003 Web Edition to a domain controller.

Table 2.1 Sample Configuration for Windows 2000/2003 Server

Feature	Value
Server version	Windows 2000: Server or Advanced Server Windows Server 2003: Standard Edition or Enterprise Edition Evaluation, retail, or Volume Licensing license
System partition	8GB, formatted as NTFS
Regional and language options	According to your preferences
Licensing mode	Per seat
Computer name	LONSANAO1
Administrator password	Complex and long enough (setup suggests using at least a six-character complex password; seven-character passwords are enforced on AD2003 domains by default)
Date and Time Settings	According to your location
IP address	Static—10.0.100.1
Subnet mask	255.255.255.0
Workgroup	SANAO

TIP You can access the command prompt during the Windows 2000/Server 2003 setup GUI phase by pressing Shift+F10. By pressing Shift+F11, you can see what the setup is actually doing.

This chapter is divided into the following sections.

- Windows 2000 Active Directory introduced the concept of domain modes—mixed and native, depending on the version of supported domain controllers and functionality. The "Domain and Forest Functional Levels" section discusses this concept, which has been taken further in Windows Server 2003.
- The "Installing Active Directory" section discusses a number of far-reaching decisions related to Active Directory and DNS designs. Using the sample configuration described in this chapter, you might consider installing Active Directory on a test computer first. Although Windows Server 2003 introduces new options for changing the Active Directory structure afterward, such as renaming domain controllers and domains, it is always better to get it right the first time. For Windows 2000, changes in domain structure design are not possible without demoting domain controllers first and then promoting them again. We also discuss the new technique of installing additional domain controllers from removable media in this section.
- After the installation, there are numerous actions you can take, including verifying the success of the installation process. We discuss these actions in the "After Active Directory Installation" section.
- The "Automating Active Directory Installation" section briefly introduces automating the installation of Active Directory.
- The "Problems with Active Directory Installation" section presents some scenarios you might come across when implementing Active Directory. The most common recovery tools are also introduced.
- The "Uninstalling Active Directory" section provides you with the information you need to uninstall Active Directory.

Domain and Forest Functional Levels

When Windows 2000 was introduced, it was important for it to coexist in earlier Windows NT 4.0 networks, especially for those domains that were upgraded. Thus, Windows 2000 Active Directory (AD2000) domains have two modes: mixed mode and native mode. A mixed mode AD2000 domain contains either both Windows NT 4.0 and Windows 2000 domain controllers, or only Windows 2000 domain controllers. In addition, Windows NT 4.0 backup domain controllers may still be added into it. AD2000 is in mixed mode after Active Directory installation. By upgrading all domain controllers in a domain to Windows 2000 and changing the domain mode to native mode (with Active Directory Users and Computers, or Domains and Trusts), you can start using all the features, such as universal security groups and group nesting, provided by native mode. On the other hand, changing a domain to native mode stops providing replication to NT 4.0 backup domain controllers, prevents installation of new Windows NT 4.0 backup domain controllers to the domain, and removes the option to roll back an unsuccessful upgrade from a Windows NT 4.0 domain to Windows 2000 Active Directory.

Windows Server 2003 Active Directory (AD2003) takes this concept one step further by introducing domain and forest functional levels. Having just two modes is no longer enough, since three versions of domain controllers (Windows NT 4.0, Windows 2000, and Windows Server 2003) can exist in the same domain or forest, all with different capabilities. In order to be backward compatible, all AD2003 domains start at the Windows 2000 mixed functional level, which means that not all the features are available until changing modes. Windows Server 2003 domain controllers have new features, but when those domain controllers interact with earlier domain controllers, they act as if they were of the same version.

The term for moving from one level to another has been changed. You no longer change the mode but rather raise the functional level with either Active Directory Users and Computers, or Domains and Trusts. See Figure 2.1 for an example of how to raise the domain functional level. We go through these management tasks later in this chapter after we have installed Active Directory.

In addition to Windows 2000 mixed- and native-level domains, an AD2003 domain can be set to the Windows Server 2003 interim level when a Windows NT 4.0 domain is upgraded to Windows Server 2003

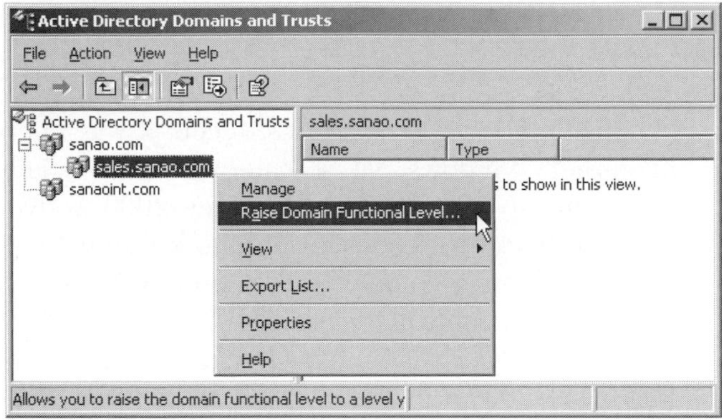

Figure 2.1 You can raise the domain functional level with Active Directory Domains and Trusts (displayed here) or Active Directory Users and Computers.

by upgrading the existing PDC to Windows Server 2003. No Windows 2000 domain controllers can be introduced into an AD2003 interim functional-level domain. A domain on the AD2003 interim level is the same in functionality as a Windows 2000 mixed-level domain.

The highest domain functional level is Windows Server 2003. An AD2003 domain on this level has all the functionality of Windows 2000 mixed and native levels and more. Table 2.2 lists the different domain

Table 2.2 Domain Functional Levels

Domain Functional Level	Features Supported	Domain Controllers Supported
Windows 2000 mixed	Universal distribution groups	Windows NT 4.0
	Group nesting for distribution groups	Windows 2000
	Group nesting for adding global groups as members of a domain local group or local group on member servers and workstations	Windows Server 2003
	Installation of additional DC from media; only for Windows Server 2003 domain controllers	
	Renaming a domain controller with System Properties; only for Windows Server 2003 domain controllers	

Table 2.2 Domain Functional Levels (*cont.*)

Domain Functional Level	Features Supported	Domain Controllers Supported
	No global catalog (GC) full synchronization after attributes are added to a GC partial attribute set (PAS); only for Windows Server 2003 domain controllers Application directory partitions; primarily for storing DNS records; only for Windows Server 2003 domain controllers InetOrgPerson object class for user accounts; can be managed only with Windows Server 2003 domain controllers Six command-line tools (`%windir%\system32\ds*.exe`) for managing AD objects; only for Windows Server 2003 domain controllers Signed and encrypted LDAP traffic between admin tools and domain controllers; only for Windows Server 2003 domain controllers Universal group membership caching; enables user logon without connection to a global catalog server; only for Windows Server 2003 domain controllers Directory quotas; enables setting a quota of objects that a user can own in a directory partition; quotas are only enforced by Windows Server 2003 domain controllers on originating updates; can be managed only with Windows Server 2003 domain controllers WMI providers for replication and trust health monitoring; only for Windows Server 2003 domain controllers Active Directory Users and Computers user interface enhancements over Windows 2000; drag-and-drop; ACL Editor improvements, including show effective permissions and show inheritance parent; selection of multiple objects;	

(continued)

Table 2.2 Domain Functional Levels (*cont.*)

Domain Functional Level	Features Supported	Domain Controllers Supported
	saved queries; restore default permissions for AD objects Improved object picker (component to select users, contacts, groups, and computers) over Windows 2000; easier to locate objects in large networks; search can be narrowed down to a specific OU	
Windows Server 2003 interim	Same as Windows 2000 mixed	Windows NT 4.0 Windows Server 2003
Windows 2000 native	Same as Windows 2000 mixed, plus Universal security and distribution groups Group nesting for both security and distribution groups Group conversions (e.g., universal to global); the conversions must go "through" universal—for example, global > universal > domain local The scope of domain local groups becomes domainwide; they can be assigned permissions to resources on member servers, and they can become members of local groups in member servers and workstations Requirement for global catalog connection when ordinary users log on Remote Access permissions of an individual user can be set with Remote Access Policy instead of just Allow or Deny SID history; enables use of permissions on resources set for accounts prior to their moving from one domain to another—in other words, does not require setting permissions for new security principals; conversions also between security and distribution groups.	Windows 2000 Windows Server 2003

Table 2.2 Domain Functional Levels (*cont.*)

Domain Functional Level	Features Supported	Domain Controllers Supported
Windows Server 2003	Same as Windows 2000 native, plus Renaming DC with the NETDOM /COMPUTERNAME command; more reliable than renaming a DC from System Properties `lastLogonTimestamp` attribute; enables tracking when user accounts have been used for logging in to the network because it is replicated to all DCs within the domain Redirecting new user and computer accounts with the commands `redirusr` and `redircmp` to a given container/OU instead of using the default Users and Computers containers Use of `userPassword` attribute for storing inetOrgPerson and user passwords; by default, `unicodePwd` attribute is used Storage of authorization policies by Authorization Manager; the authorization policies can be used to assign permissions in applications based on user roles Constrained delegation for computers; option to allow delegated authentication to run only selected services on a computer rather than running all services Kerberos KDC key version numbers; Kerberos keys are changed when user changes her password. Old keys are stored for a period of time. Version numbering makes it more efficient to locate the correct key for decrypting encrypted communications. Version numbers are constructed from the update logon timestamp attribute when a user changes her password. Also used for compliance with RFC 1510. Selective authentication cross-forest; option to limit the servers in a trusting forest that are available for authentication for security principals from a trusted forest	Windows Server 2003

functional levels and the features and domain controllers each level supports.

Certain AD2003 features, such as forest trust, affect and also place requirements on the whole forest and all domain controllers in it. Thus, AD2003 also introduces the forest functional level, with three alternatives: Windows 2000, Windows Server 2003 interim, and Windows Server 2003. The Windows Server 2003 forest functional level is available only after all domains have been raised to the Windows Server 2003 functional level. Forest functional levels and their features are listed in Table 2.3.

Table 2.3 Forest Functional Levels and Supported Features and Domain Controllers

Forest Functional Level	Features Supported	Domain Controllers Supported
Windows 2000	Global catalog replication improvements (if both replication partners are Windows Server 2003)	Windows NT 4.0 Windows 2000 Windows Server 2003
Windows Server 2003 interim	Same as Windows 2000, plus Linked value replication (LVR); only group membership changes are replicated instead of the whole group Improved inter-site topology generator (ISTG); less complicated algorithm improves scalability	Windows NT 4.0 Windows Server 2003
Windows Server 2003	Same as Windows 2000, plus Forest trust; trust between forest root domains, transitive between all domains in forests connected with the trust Domain rename; using \VALUEADD\MSFT\MGMT\DOMREN\RENDOM.EXE on the setup CD. For more information, see `http://go.microsoft.com/fwlink/?LinkId=5585` Bridgehead load balancing Schema defunct; enables schema redefinitions by deactivating previously added classes and attributes	Windows Server 2003

Table 2.3 Forest Functional Levels and Supported Features and Domain Controllers (*cont.*)

Forest Functional Level	Features Supported	Domain Controllers Supported
	Dynamic objects of the `dynamicObject` class; per RFC 2589, objects have a TTL (time to live); can be stored only on domain partitions; Windows Server 2003 DCs support storing on application partition, irrespective of domain or forest functionality	
	Conversion of an inetOrgPerson object instance into a User object instance and vice versa; inetOrgPerson is a subclass of the User class	
	Create instances of the new group types basic and query based; used by the role-based Authorization Manager	
	Dynamic auxiliary classes; auxiliary class(es) can be dynamically linked to certain objects rather than the whole class	

WARNING Changing domain or forest functional levels are one-way operations, and they cannot be reversed!

Installing Active Directory

The installation of Active Directory is completely separate from the Windows 2000/Server 2003 setup. It is usually started with the command DCPROMO. Alternatively, you could start it from the Configure Your Server (for Windows 2000) or Manage Your Server (for Windows Server 2003) window that is displayed when an administrator logs on to the computer.

TIP If you have checked "Don't display this page at logon", you can access Configure Your Server and Manage Your Server from Start, Administrative Tools.

When Active Directory is installed onto a computer, the computer is promoted to a domain controller. The same command, DCPROMO, can be used to uninstall Active Directory—that is, to demote the computer to a stand-alone or member server.

IF YOU KNOW NT It was important to select the server role right the first time when installing Windows NT because you *could not* change the roles of stand-alone/member server and domain controller after installation.

Requirements and Recommendations

In order to install Active Directory, you must have the following:

- A computer running Windows Server 2003, Standard, Enterprise, or Datacenter Edition (or Windows 2000 Server, Advanced Server, or Datacenter Server).
- A partition or volume formatted as NTFS, because the SYSVOL folder needs NTFS.
- Adequate disk space (200MB for the Active Directory database and 50MB for the Active Directory log files). Table 2.4 illustrates the minimum disk space requirements per Microsoft recommendation.

TIP An installation of Active Directory with default objects takes 42MB of disk space, with the database itself taking 10MB. In order to estimate the space requirement for the Active Directory database in your environment, you might want to use Active Directory Sizer, which comes

Table 2.4 Minimum Disk Space Requirements for Different AD2003 Domain Controllers per Microsoft recommendations

Component	Minimum Disk Space Requirement
Operating system	1.5–2GB
Database NTDS.DIT	0.4GB per 1,000 users
Transaction log files	500MB
SYSVOL	500MB
Global catalog	Domain controller requirement for the domain hosting the GC + sum of domain controller requirements for other domains / 2

with the Windows 2000 Resource Kit Supplement 1 in the apps\adsizer folder. You can also download the Sizer from `http://www.microsoft.com/windows2000/techinfo/planning/activedirectory/adsizer.asp`.

- Required permissions—you must be a member of the local Administrators group of a computer in order to create a new forest, a member of the Enterprise Admins group in order to create a new domain in an existing forest, or a member of the Domain Admins group in order to install additional domain controllers in an existing domain.
- TCP/IP settings configured either with DHCP or manually.
- A DNS server that supports service location (SRV) resource records. Alternatively, you can allow the Installation Wizard to create and configure a DNS server for Active Directory.

The following features are also recommended for the DNS service:

- Support for the dynamic update protocol (RFC 2136), because it reduces administrative effort considerably.

NOTE Depending on its location in the AD hierarchy, the Netlogon service running on a domain controller may register over 20 service location (SRV) records on DNS. In addition, every Windows 2000/XP/Server 2003 and DHCP server may also register records dynamically. You can see the records a DC registers in the file %windir%\system32\config\netlogon.dns.

- Support for incremental zone transfers (RFC 1995). Only new or updated resource records are replicated between DNS servers.

TIP You can find the RFC Internet standards at `http://www.rfc-editor.org/`.

TIP A working TCP/IP stack must be available when the Active Directory Installation Wizard is running. Although the wizard will start, it won't complete. You might come across this situation when you install a laptop with the network cable disconnected. To get around this problem, you can install the Microsoft Loopback Adapter, which is a virtual network adapter installable using the Hardware Wizard. Alternatively, see Microsoft Knowledge Base (KB) article 239924 for instructions on disabling technology known as "Media Sense," Windows 2000's/Server 2003's ability to detect network connection status.

If you do not want to install your own DNS server, you must define the IP address of an existing DNS server. If you are using a BIND DNS server, you should use at least version 8.1.2.

Creating Domains, Trees, and Forests

As mentioned, installing Active Directory is initiated with the DCPROMO command, which starts the Active Directory Installation Wizard. Although only a few steps are involved in using the Installation Wizard, the decisions that you make during those few steps can have far-reaching consequences, especially in Windows 2000.

Before Installation

Before you install Active Directory, you must choose the Active Directory domain name. The domain name should conform to DNS standards, and it could even be the same name that you or your company is known by on the Internet. If possible, select a name that represents your entire organization, because an Active Directory tree can accommodate only one DNS root name. If one DNS root name cannot be used (for example, if your company has acquired another company with a strong DNS identity), you can join two domains to form a forest. If both companies have already implemented separate Active Directory forests, they can be joined with AD2003 forest trust.

If your network is connected to the Internet and you are not using firewalls or proxy servers, the root domain name must be unique in the Internet DNS namespace. You can ensure its uniqueness by registering your root domain name with an Internet domain name registering authority. We recommend the registration also in order to ensure that no name conflict would arise should there ever be an application requiring your Active Directory to be connected to the Internet.

NOTE Currently, there are no applications requiring a company's Active Directory DNS records to be available from the Internet. However, a company might have an Active Directory forest set up for some kind of extranet or Internet application. Another, more suitable solution for such a scenario might be Active Directory Application Mode (ADAM). For more information, see `http://www.microsoft.com/windowsserver2003/adam`.

In addition, if the connection to the Internet exists, your DNS naming scheme must conform to the Internet's domain-naming rules. For additional information, see RFCs 1034, 1035, 1036, and 2052.

As you will notice while learning Active Directory, thorough knowledge of DNS is essential. Active Directory and DNS are tightly integrated.

Next, you must decide where in the Active Directory namespace to locate your new domain controller. Your options include

- A new forest
- A new child domain in an existing tree
- A new domain tree in an existing forest
- A new domain controller for an existing domain

If you are installing your first Windows 2000/Windows Server 2003 domain controller, the domain becomes a forest root domain (FRD) and forms a new Active Directory forest.

At the latest, after installing the first DC, you should also decide the number of domain controllers. As a rule of thumb, the "Designing and Deploying Directory and Security Services" book in the Microsoft Windows Server 2003 Deployment Kit recommends one domain controller per 5,000 users. Even for the smallest domain, it is wise to install at least two DCs to provide fault tolerance.

The Installation Process

The flowchart in Figure 2.2 shows the steps you need to perform to install a new domain controller in the preferred position in your Active Directory structure.

The common steps for most options include the following:

- Define the DNS name of the domain. The name consists of domain labels separated by periods. The domain labels can contain letters, numbers, and hyphens. It cannot contain spaces or the following characters: `!"#$()*+,'/:;<=>?@[\]^`{|}~`. The DNS name must be unique in the network. An example of a DNS name is `sanao.com`.

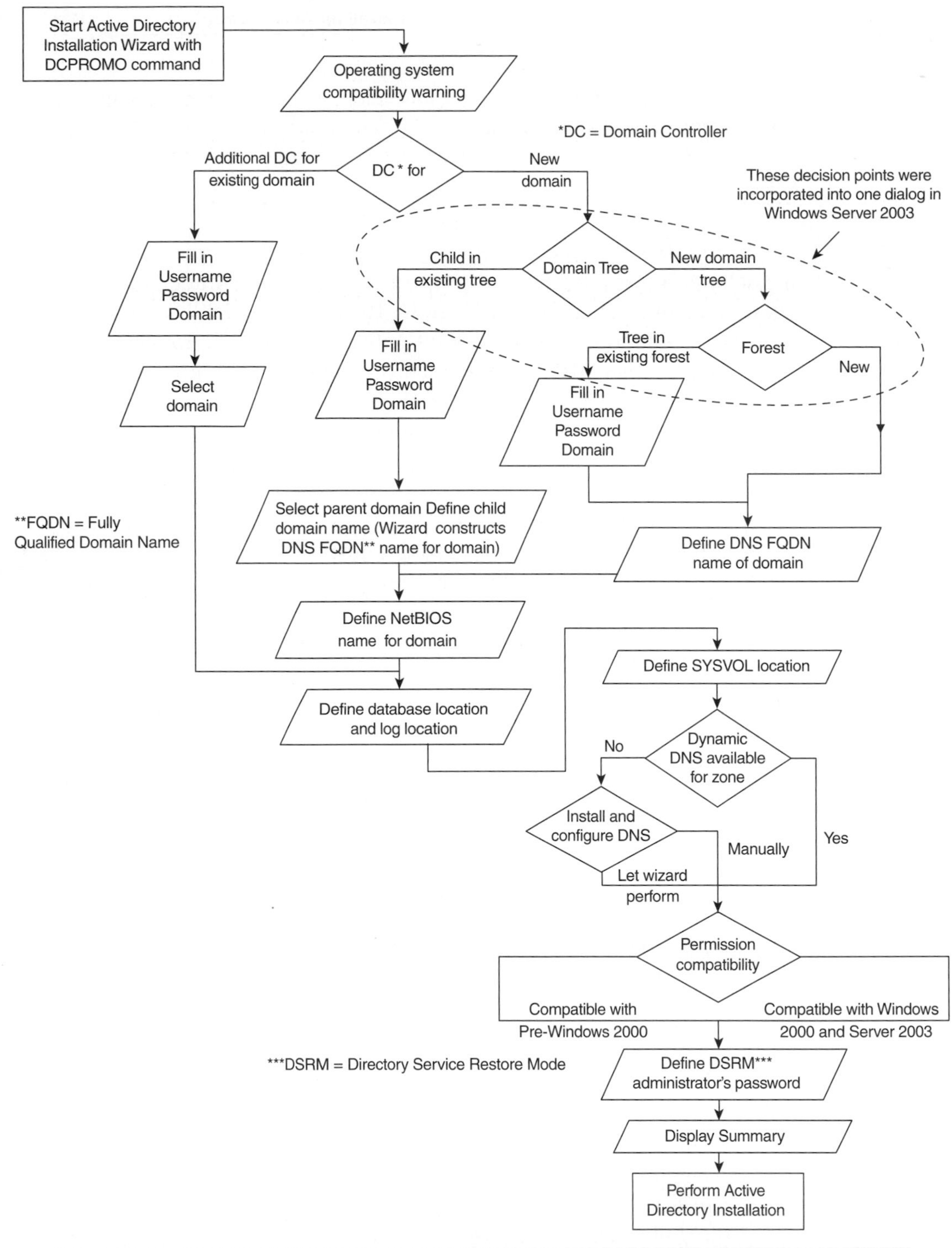

Figure 2.2 Using the Active Directory Installation Wizard, an administrator goes through these steps to define Active Directory settings.

- Define the NetBIOS name of the domain to be used by the clients of an earlier Windows version. If a domain with that same name already exists in your network, the wizard suggests you use that name suffixed by a sequence number starting from zero. An example of a NetBIOS name is SANAO.

NOTE The maximum length of a DNS domain name is 64 characters or 155 bytes. The 64-character limit is usually reached earlier unless you use Unicode characters, which can take three bytes per character. The maximum number allowed in the user interface is 64 characters. The maximum length of a NetBIOS name is 15 characters.

- Define the location for the database that stores Active Directory. The default location is %systemroot%\NTDS.
- Define the location for the log files. The log files temporarily store the changes to Active Directory. To optimize performance, place the database and log files on separate physical disks. The default location is %systemroot%\NTDS.
- Define the location for System Volume (SYSVOL). The shared system volume is a folder tree that stores Group Policies and some other files. SYSVOL is replicated among domain controllers. SYSVOL must be located on a partition or volume formatted as NTFS. The default location is %systemroot%\SYSVOL.

TIP You should locate all Active Directory files on a physical drive that does not contain the system volume. This increases security by reducing the likelihood of disk space attacks.

- Define the password for the administrator in *Directory Services Restore Mode (DSRM)*. You can access the restore mode from the startup screen by pressing F8. Because Active Directory will not be running in this option, another administrator user account (along with the password) is stored in the registry.

TIP You can reset the DSRM password using the Windows 2000 SP2 (or later) utility setpwd. The utility does not ask you to confirm the password, and thus you have to be extra careful when using it. In Windows Server 2003, start NTDSUTIL and use the `Set DSRM Password` command. Both of these methods work only while Active Directory is running—that is, they cannot be used while you are in DSRM.

- Decide whether to weaken the permissions—that is, whether there is need for anonymous logon to access Active Directory. This is the case if, for example, users are accessing the network through NT 4.0 RAS servers. If you decide to weaken the permissions, the Everyone (and Anonymous Logon in Windows Server 2003) group is added to the Builtin group Pre-Windows 2000 Compatible Access. This group has permission to read any attribute of any user object in Active Directory. Thus, you should consider the security implications twice before enabling this option. Windows 2000 installation defaults to the less secure option (compatible with pre–Windows 2000 servers), whereas Windows Server 2003 installation defaults to the more secure option (compatible only with Windows 2000 and Windows Server 2003). Table 2.5 lists the membership of the Pre-Windows 2000 Compatible Access group.

NOTE The membership of the Pre-Windows 2000 Compatible Access group is obviously per domain, and as such, it only appears when you are installing the first domain controller for a new domain.

TIP If you want to remove the Everyone group after installation, use the Active Directory Users and Computers snap-in. In order to add the Everyone group into the Pre-Windows 2000 Compatible Access group on a Windows 2000 domain controller, use the following command:

```
net localgroup "Pre-Windows 2000 Compatible Access"
/add everyone.
```

On a Windows Server 2003 domain controller, you can also use Active Directory Users and Computers to add the Anonymous

Table 2.5 Membership of Pre-Windows 2000 Compatible Access in Windows 2000/ Server 2003

Group	Permissions Compatible with Pre–Windows 2000 Server Operating Systems	Permissions Compatible Only with Windows Server 2003 Operating Systems
Windows 2000	Everyone	–
Windows Server 2003	Anonymous Logon Authenticated Users Everyone	Authenticated Users

Logon and Everyone groups into the Pre-Windows 2000 Compatible Access group.

In addition to the steps you perform, certain events take place behind the scenes.

- First, the Active Directory Installation Wizard ensures that a previous installation or removal of Active Directory has not taken place without the computer having first been restarted, that the Installation Wizard is not already running, and that an installation or removal operation of Active Directory is not already in progress.
- Next, the Installation Wizard verifies the existence of a properly configured TCP/IP stack. If the TCP/IP protocol is not installed or configured properly, the wizard will stop and enable you to install and configure it. The same applies in Windows Server 2003 if you have defined a static IP address and have omitted the IP address of the DNS server.
- Next, the wizard verifies the operation of the DNS service. In Windows 2000, if the DNS client is not running on the first domain controller, if its DNS server IP address is improperly configured, or if the DNS cannot be found, you might see the following message: "The wizard cannot contact the DNS server that handles the name 'sanao.com' to determine if it supports dynamic update. Confirm your DNS configuration, or install and configure a DNS server on this computer." After this message is displayed and you have clicked OK, you choose whether to install and configure the DNS service yourself or to let the wizard do it. The analysis and especially the display of its results have been improved in Windows Server 2003. An unsuccessful check results in the window displayed in Figure 2.3.
- The wizard checks that the DNS name is unique in the forest. The wizard will not continue without a valid name. Similarly, after you have entered the NetBIOS name, its uniqueness is verified within your network. If the name already exists, the Installation Wizard suggests a name for you suffixed with the number zero.
- The wizard verifies the user's credentials. The account used to create new domains must have the appropriate access privileges. By default, only members of the local Administrators group can create a new forest, and only members of the Enterprise Admins group can add new domains to an existing forest. In order to install additional domain controllers into an existing domain, your account must belong to the Domain Admins group.

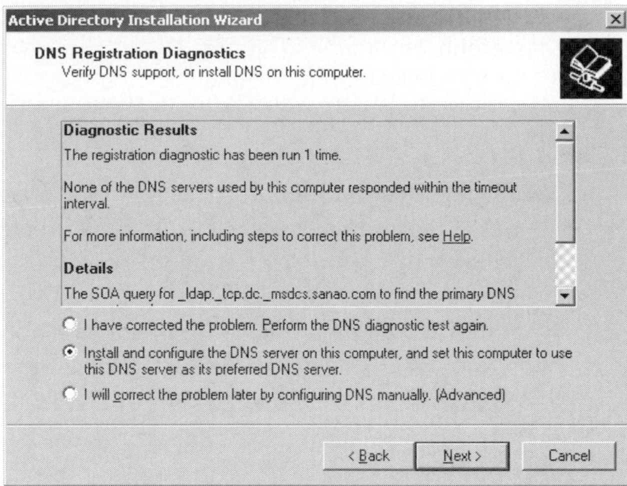

Figure 2.3 DNS diagnostics have been improved in Windows Server 2003. Also, the results are shown in more detail during the installation process.

The actual installation starts after you've completed all steps in the Installation Wizard and accepted the settings displayed on the Summary screen shown in Figure 2.4.

There are a number of steps included in the creation of Active Directory. These steps differ significantly depending on the role of the

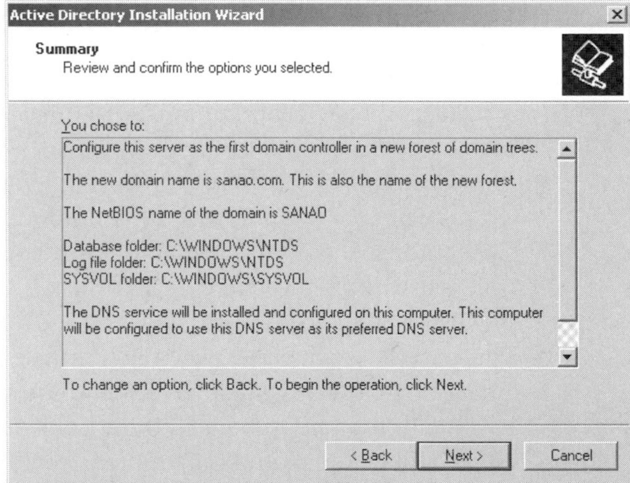

Figure 2.4 The Active Directory Installation Wizard lets you review the settings before it starts the promotion.

new domain controller. Table 2.6 lists the common steps for promoting the Windows Server 2003 domain controller for a new forest—that is, for creating a new forest.

TIP See Chapter 2, "Active Directory Data Storage of Windows 2000 Server Distributed Systems Guide," in the Windows Server 2000 Resource Kit (`http://www.microsoft.com/resources/documentation/windows/2000/server/reskit/en-us/distsys/part1/dsgch02.mspx`) for very detailed information on the installation process in various scenarios.

Table 2.6 Steps during Active Directory Installation

Step	Notes
Stop service NETLOGON.	Nobody can log on to the domain using this computer.
Create the System Volume C:\WINDOWS\SYSVOL.	
Prepare for system volume replication using the root C:\WINDOWS\SYSVOL.	
Copy the initial Directory Service database file C:\WINDOWS\system32\ntds.dit to C:\WINDOWS\NTDS\ntds.dit.	
Install the Directory Service.	Default Active Directory objects are created on the new domain controller.
Configure service RPCLOCATOR.	RPCLocator allows distributed applications to use the Microsoft RPC name service. RPCLocator manages the RPC name service database.
Configure service NETLOGON.	Netlogon runs the domain controller locator, creates secure channels between clients and domain controllers, registers DNS SRV records, and supports NT 4 replication protocol.
Set the LSA policy information from policy (null).	

(continued)

Table 2.6 Steps during Active Directory Installation (*cont.*)

Step	Notes
Configure service kdc to start automatically.	Kerberos Key Distribution Center (KDC) service generates session keys and grants service tickets for mutual client-server authentication.
Configure service IsmServ to start automatically.	Intersite Messaging service allows the sending and receiving of replication messages between domain controllers in different sites.
Configure service TrkSvr to start automatically.	Distributed Link Tracking Server service stores information so that files moved among NTFS volumes within a domain can be tracked for each volume in the domain. In Windows Server 2003, Distributed Link Client is started instead.
Configure service w32time to start automatically.	Windows Time service synchronizes the computer clock with an external source as well as among the computers in Active Directory.
Set the computer's DNS computer name root to `sanao.com`.	
Set security on the domain controller and Directory Service files and registry keys.	NTFS and registry ACLs are updated.

While the Installation Wizard configures Active Directory, it displays its progress in a window, as shown in Figure 2.5.

To work with our sample company, Sanao, as you progress through this book, create a new forest with the settings in Table 2.7.

Installing Additional Domain Controllers

In order to increase fault tolerance, it's a good idea to have at least two domain controllers per domain. Another reason to have additional domain controllers is to accommodate low-bandwidth links in network topology by placing a domain controller in a location close to the user to facilitate authentication or searches. Sometimes the WAN link connecting the branch office to the main location can be slow or unreliable. In order to save replication over a slow connection, AD2000 domain controllers had to be installed in the main office and then

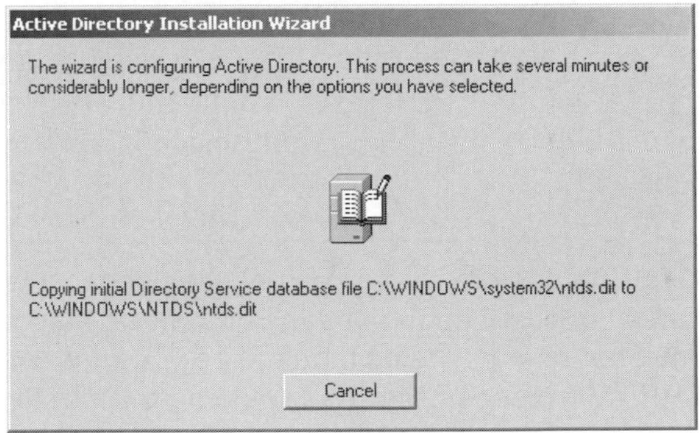

Figure 2.5 Default database creation is one of the very first steps in installing Active Directory.

shipped to the remote location. AD2003 introduces a new option to install additional domain controllers by facilitating system state backup. The technique is called *install from media,* in which you take a system state backup on an existing Windows Server 2003 domain controller. You store this backup on removable media such as a CD or DVD, which is then delivered to the location where you wish to install a new domain controller. Although the new domain controller still has to be synchronized online with up-to-date AD information on an ongoing

Table 2.7 Sample Configuration Used in This Book

Setting	Value
Type of domain	New forest (i.e., a new domain in a new tree in a new forest)
Complete DNS name	`sanao.com`
NetBIOS name	`SANAO`
Location of database and log files	C:\WINDOWS\NTDS (C:\WINNT\NTDS for Windows 2000)
Location of SYSVOL folder	C:\WINDOWS\SYSVOL (C:\WINNT\SYSVOL for Windows 2000)
Permissions	Use the default "Permissions compatible only with Windows 2000 or Windows Server 2003 operating systems". For Windows 2000, do *not* use the default, but use "Permissions compatible only with Windows 2000 servers" instead.

basis, and the necessary DNS records have to be created, there is no need to replicate the bulk of the AD database over a slow or unreliable link. In addition, a network connection is required for checking the permissions to install an additional domain controller, as displayed in Figure 2.6.

NOTE Install from media can only be used for installing additional Windows Server 2003 domain controllers; that is, the first domain controller for each domain has to be installed using the normal DCPROMO process. The source domain controller must also be Windows Server 2003.

The steps for installing additional domain controllers from media are as follows:

1. Using the Windows Server 2003 backup tool, take a system state backup of an existing domain controller onto removable media such as a CD or DVD. (Alternatively, you can first create the backup files on disk and copy them to removable media).

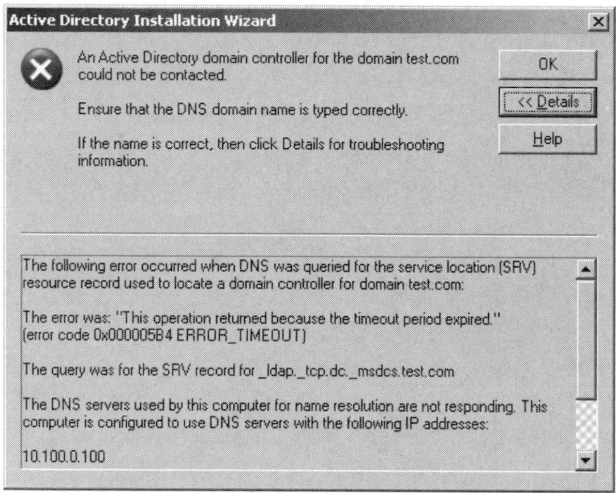

Figure 2.6 When you install an additional domain controller from transferred system state files, a network connection is still required to check necessary permissions, to replicate recent changes, and to update DNS records. In this case, the permission check could not be accomplished, because the DNS server could not be contacted.

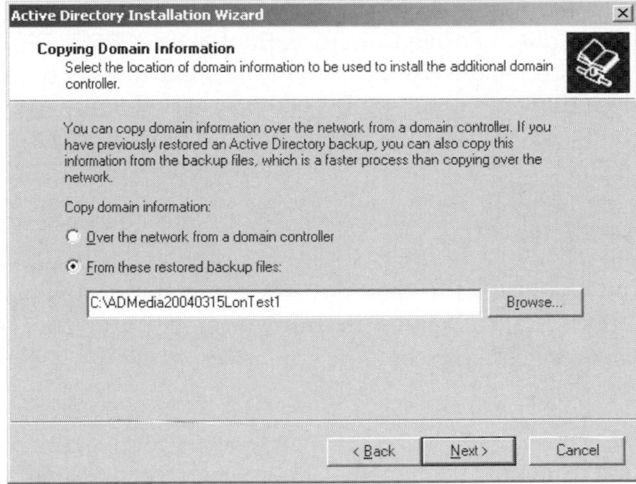

Figure 2.7 Using `dcpromo /adv`, you have the option to use the files from the restored system state backup.

TIP Instead of "surfing" in the Start menu (Start, All Programs, Accessories, System Tools, Backup), you can start the backup tool by typing "ntbackup" into the Run dialog.

---

2. Deliver the media to the new location.
3. Using the Windows Server 2003 backup tool, restore the system state to an alternate location. You may have to catalog a backup file (use Catalog in the Tools menu) in order to locate your transferred backup file.
4. Promote the new server to a domain controller using the `dcpromo /adv` command. The phases of the Installation Wizard are the same as in normally promoting an additional domain controller except for the dialog shown in Figure 2.7. In this dialog, you have the option to use the files restored from the system state. Alternatively, you can replicate the database over the network, which would result in the same behavior as if you did not use the `/adv` parameter when starting DCPROMO.

TIP You can considerably reduce the amount being backed up as the system state by clicking Advanced after you click Start Backup. Unselect "Automatically backup System Protected Files with the

System State". In addition, the system state on a DC consists of five directories: Active Directory, Boot Files, COM+ Registration Database, Registry, and SYSVOL. You may restore the system state to an alternate location on the source DC and only transfer Active Directory, Registry, and SYSVOL to a new DC before starting DCPROMO.

After the promotion is complete, the system state backup files on the new domain controller should be automatically deleted, the metadata for the new domain controller is replicated to other domain controllers, changes to the directory after the backup was created are replicated to the new domain controller, and DNS records are being created.

NOTE Install from media can be used for installing additional global catalog servers as well. If this is the case, the source domain controller must be a global catalog server. If the source DC was a GC, you are being asked during the running of DCPROMO whether you want to configure the new DC as a GC as well.

After Active Directory Installation

After the Active Directory installation is complete, you have to restart your computer. The first time that an administrator logs on to the first domain controller in a new forest, dcphelp.exe runs and you see a command prompt flash briefly. Dcphelp adds 56 display specifier objects for all 23 non-English locales that are supported by Windows 2000/Server 2003. This is accomplished by the csvde import of %SystemRoot%\system32\mui\dispspec\dcpromo.csv. You should not interrupt the dcphelp process, because this might prevent some of the objects from being created in `CN=DisplaySpecifiers,CN=Configuration,DC=forest,DC=name` and consequently users in non-English locales from seeing everything correctly in the GUI. You can see the steps that dcphelp takes in %Windir%\Debug\dcpromohelp.log.

TIP If dcphelp was unsuccessful, see KB article 308592 for further instructions.

Now you will have to determine if everything went well.

Verifying the Installation

You can verify that the Active Directory installation was successful by checking that the following items are present.

- The database file ntds.dit is stored in %Systemroot%\NTDS.
- The shared system volume is located in %Systemroot%\SYSVOL.
- A site called Default-First-Site-Name has been created. You can check this with the Active Directory Sites and Services snap-in in the Administrative Tools. This only applies to the first domain controller of the forest.
- The first domain controller in the forest is a GC server. You can verify this by checking the properties of Sites, Default-First-Site-Name, Servers, Yourserver, NTDS Settings in Active Directory Sites and Services.
- The Domain Controllers OU and default containers Builtin, Computers, ForeignSecurityPrincipals, and Users have been created in Active Directory. Check this with the Active Directory Users and Computers snap-in.
- Group Policies Default Domain Policy and Default Domain Controllers Policy have been created and linked to the domain and Domain Controllers OU, respectively. Check this with the Active Directory Users and Computers snap-in.
- Five new shortcuts for MMC snap-ins have been created in the Start menu under Administrative Tools: Active Directory Domains and Trusts, Active Directory Sites and Services, Active Directory Users and Computers, Domain Security Policy, and Domain Controller Security Policy.

NOTE When a Windows Server 2003 computer is promoted to a domain controller, Local Security Policy is removed from Administrative Tools. You can still access it using secpol.msc.

- Display specifiers have been added by dcphelp. Check that the last line of the %Windir%\Debug\Csv.log file states "The command has completed successfully."
- If you are installing additional domain controllers into your forest, you should check that they are replicating without errors. Use the Support Tools command `repadmin /replsum` in order to analyze the replication.

NOTE The parameter `/replsum` is new for the Windows Server 2003 version of Support Tools. Unfortunately, you can only install Windows Server 2003 Support Tools to Windows XP or newer. You can use the `/showreps` parameter in Windows 2000.

The database file and the shared SYSVOL may be located elsewhere if you used locations different from the defaults provided during the installation.

In addition, you may want to check the Active Directory installation log files DCPROMO.LOG and dcpromoui.log, which are stored in the %Systemroot%\Debug folder.

NOTE If you run DCPROMO several times—for example, when testing promotion—the DCPROMO.LOG file is appended, whereas the older dcpromoui.log file is saved with a new name with a sequence number—for example, dcpromoui001.log.

To ensure that the DNS service location (SRV) resource records were created during the promotion, make sure you see them in the %Systemroot%\system32\config\netlogon.dns file. You can copy them from this file to an alternative DNS server that doesn't support dynamic updates. However, if you're using Windows 2000/Server 2003, you should see the SRV resource records within the MMC, as displayed in Figure 2.8. If you cannot see the records, you can try restarting the Netlogon service (Start, Administrative Tools, Services) and refreshing DNS thereafter. Another place you might want to check is the IP address of the DNS server that your DNS client (resolver) uses.

TIP An alternative way of restarting the Netlogon service on command prompt is to use the command `net stop netlogon & net start netlogon`.

Ensuring Compatibility with Earlier Clients

Windows Server 2003 increases the security in many ways over previous Windows versions. Two such improvements, SMB Signing and Secure Channel Signing, reduce the vulnerability for "man in the middle"

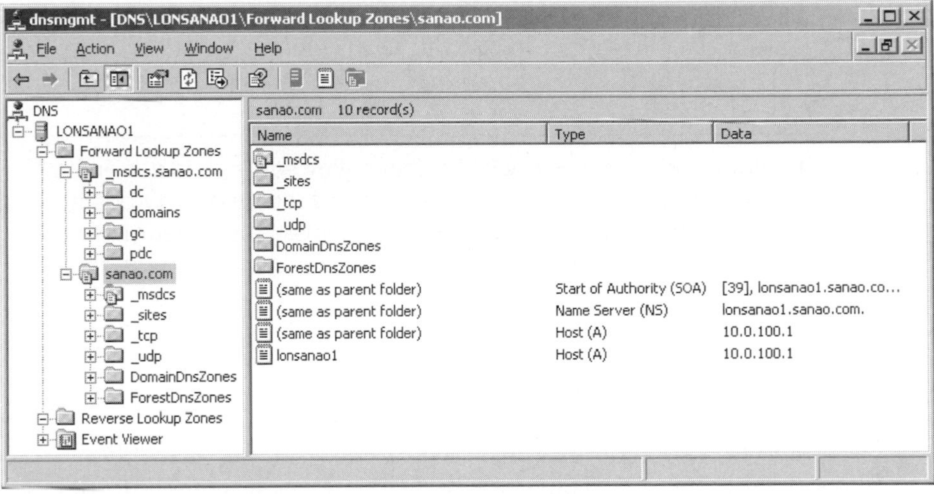

Figure 2.8 A Windows Server 2003 DNS snap-in after Active Directory has been installed.

attacks but at the same time may affect the ability of earlier Windows clients to authenticate and use network resources as well as Samba servers in your Windows domain. The settings for these improvements are defined in the Default Domain Controllers Policy, both under Computer Configuration\Windows Settings\Security Settings\Local Policies \Security Options:

- Domain member: Digitally encrypt or sign secure channel data (always)
- Microsoft network server: Digitally sign communications (always); for SMB Signing

The Secure Channel Signing requirement affects computers running Windows NT 4.0 prior to Service Pack 4. Secure channels are used by Windows NT–based machines for communications between domain members and domain controllers as well as between domain controllers that have trust relationships.

The SMB Signing requirement affects clients running LAN Manager, Windows for Workgroups, Windows 95 without directory services client, Windows NT 4.0 prior to Service Pack 3, and devices (including Pocket PC 2002 and previous versions) based on the Windows CE .NET version 4.1 or earlier.

If you have these older clients, you have two options: You can either upgrade the clients or remove the requirements from the Active Directory domain by disabling the aforementioned settings.

TIP Unchecking the box "Define this policy setting" is not enough, since these settings are also defined in the local security policy. Thus, you should leave the check box checked and select Disabled. The group policy inheritance will then take care of overwriting the local setting.

Configuring Time Service

Members (including domain controllers) of an AD2000/2003 forest use the Windows Time service to synchronize computer clocks. The correct time is synchronized through Active Directory starting from the PDC of the forest root domain and ending with the Windows 2000 Professional workstation on the lowermost domain in the domain hierarchy. Thus, it is necessary to configure the clock of this DC to be synchronized. You can use the following commands in order to configure the PDC to synchronize its time from an external time source:

```
C:\>w32tm /config /syncfromflags:manual /manualpeerlist:
  timekeeper.isi.edu, clock.isc.org
C:\>w32tm /config /update
```

TIP You can find a public NTP server list from `http://www.ntp.org`.

The Time service uses the Network Time Protocol (NTP), and thus you may have to open its port (UDP 123) in your firewall in order to get it working.

In order to resynchronize the time of your computer, you have two alternative commands:

```
net stop w32time & net start w32time
```

or:

```
w32tm /resync
```

DNS-Related Tasks

A working DNS service including both servers and clients is the cornerstone of an Active Directory network. The scope of this book doesn't allow for a thorough discussion of DNS, but we will walk you through the basic steps in order to get the DNS up and running.

TIP You can learn more about DNS service in the book *DNS on Windows Server 2003,* by Cricket Liu, Matt Larson, and Robbie Allen (O'Reilly, 2003, `http://www.oreilly.com/catalog/dnswinsvr/`).

Removing the DNS Root Domain and Configuring a Forwarding Address

If your computer doesn't have an IP address, when you started the Active Directory installation the Windows 2000 Active Directory Installation Wizard assumed that you were not connected to the Internet or that you were using a network address translation (NAT) and possibly a firewall. As a result, the wizard created a zone for a DNS root domain (.). If you later connect your computer to the Internet through your company or an ISP, you might want to remove the root domain from the Forward Lookup Zones in order to enable external name resolution for the clients. You do this by starting the DNS snap-in from Administrative Tools. Then double-click Forward Lookup Zones and delete the root zone. Restart the snap-in or click the computer icon and refresh by pressing F5. This enables you to configure your DNS server as a *forwarder*—that is, it forwards the DNS queries that it cannot answer by itself to another defined name server. To configure the IP address of the DNS server to which you want to forward the queries, go to the Forwarders tab in DNS Server Properties.

TIP The Windows Server 2003 Active Directory Installation Wizard does not create the root zone in any circumstances. Consequently, there is no need to remove it. However, depending on your firewall and name resolution configuration, you might have to add it in both versions (Windows 2000 and Server 2003).

The Windows Server 2003 DNS service introduces two new features for finer-grade name resolution. The first of them is called *conditional forwarding*. It enables you to configure forwarding per domain or even per record. Conditional forwarding is most useful when you are configuring DNS name resolution between two Active Directory forests. The other feature is called *stub zones*, where only the records for name servers in those zones are replicated via zone transfers. See Windows Server 2003 online Help and Support for more information on these features.

Creating a Forward Lookup Zone and Enabling Dynamic Updates

If you decided not to let the Active Directory Installation Wizard install and configure the DNS service, you must first install the DNS service and then configure a Forward Lookup Zone for the DNS service. You can install the service from the Control Panel by selecting Add/Remove Programs, Add/Remove Windows Components, Networking. Perform the following steps to create the Forward Lookup Zone. (The steps are for Windows Server 2003. However, they are very similar in Windows 2000.)

1. Start the DNS service snap-in from the Start menu if it isn't already running.
2. Double-click your computer icon.
3. Double-click Forward Lookup Zones.
4. Right-click Forward Lookup Zones and select New Zone from the context menu. Click Next.
5. Select Primary zone and check "Store the zone in Active Directory (available only if the DNS server is a domain controller)." If you do not check the latter, the zone file is stored in %windir%\System32\Dns and replicated to other DNS servers with zone transfers (that you must manually configure). A zone stored in Active Directory is replicated automatically through Active Directory replication. Click Next.
6. If you checked the "Store the zone in Active Directory" check box in the previous step, you must select the replication scope. Use the default for now. We will provide more information in a later section, "Managing DNS Replication." Click Next.
7. Type the name for the zone. It is probably the same as your Active Directory forest root (i.e., `sanao.com`). Then click Next.
8. Specify that the zone allows only secure dynamic updates. You should not select "Nonsecure and secure" in the "Dynamic

updates" field unless you have good reasons for doing so. Click Next and finally click Finish.

9. Enter the command `ipconfig /registerdns` on the command line in order to register the host (A) record.
10. Restart the Netlogon service (Start, Administrative Tools, Services, or enter the following command: `net stop netlogon & net start netlogon`).

Creating a Reverse Lookup Zone and Enabling Dynamic Updates

In order to test the DNS service with either its own monitoring tool or the DNS diagnostics tool, nslookup, you should first configure a Reverse Lookup Zone for the computers in the same IP subnet as the server resides in for the DNS service. Perform the following steps to create the Reverse Lookup Zone:

1. Start the DNS service snap-in from the Start menu if it isn't already running.
2. Double-click your computer icon.
3. Double-click Reverse Lookup Zones.
4. Right-click Reverse Lookup Zones and select New Zone from the context menu. Click Next.
5. Select Primary zone and check "Store the zone in Active Directory (available only if the DNS server is a domain controller)." Click Next.
6. If you checked the "Store the zone in Active Directory" check box in the previous step, you must select the replication scope. Use the default for now. We will provide more information in a later section, "Managing DNS Replication." Click Next.
7. Type the first three octets of your network ID (for example, 10.0.10), and then click Next.
8. Specify that the zone allows only secure dynamic updates. You should not select "Nonsecure and secure" in the "Dynamic updates" field unless you have good reasons for doing so. Click Next and finally click Finish.
9. Enter the command `ipconfig /registerdns` on the command line to register the pointer (PTR) record for the domain computer in the Reverse Lookup Zone.

When you start nslookup in the interactive mode, the first thing it does is try to find the name corresponding to the IP address of the DNS server used. If you do not create the Reverse Lookup Zone or if the DNS computer does not have its record there, you'll see an error like the following:

```
C:\>nslookup
DNS request timed out.
    timeout was 2 seconds.
*** Can't find server name for address 10.0.10.100: Timed
out
Default Server:  UnKnown
Address:  10.0.10.100
```

However, nslookup (and Active Directory, too) would work OK even without the Reverse Lookup Zone.

Storing DNS Zones in Active Directory

Other tasks that you might want to perform after installing Active Directory include configuring a DNS zone as Active Directory–integrated. If you let the Active Directory Installation Wizard install and configure the DNS service, the zone would already be Active Directory–integrated—that is, records would be stored in Active Directory and also replicated within it. Active Directory–integrated zones also support Secure Dynamic updates per RFCs 2078 and 2137. This means that permissions defined for records stored in Active Directory are checked before updates are possible. You can change a zone to only allow secure dynamic updates by selecting Secure only in the "Dynamic updates" field of the zone properties.

Application Partitions

AD2003 introduces a new directory partition or naming context called application partitions. Application partitions are sometimes also referred to as program partitions or non-domain-naming contexts (NDNCs). They make it possible to configure replication topology and latency differently from the means (three naming contexts—domain, configuration, and schema—and the global catalog) introduced in AD2000. Application partitions act like domains; they are containers of objects. However, they can be replicated to any domain controller in a forest. They cannot contain security principals, nor can they be replicated to the global catalog.

In AD2000, there was a problem in replicating the forestwide DNS records (especially records for global catalog servers and GUIDs for all domain controllers located in the _msdcs subdomain of the forest root domain) to all domain controllers running the DNS service in the forest. This was because the forestwide records were stored in the system container of the domain partition. Thus, if a DNS zone was stored in Active Directory (aka Active Directory–integrated), all domain controllers only within that domain would replicate the zone and records within it. In order to ensure the availability of these important records in geographically diverse networks, you had to separate the _msdcs subdomain into its own zone and configure it as a secondary zone on DNS servers in child domains.

AD2003 fixes these problems by creating two application partitions for DNS: ForestDnsZones, which is replicated to all domain controllers running the DNS service in a forest, and DomainDnsZones, which is replicated to all domain controllers running the DNS service in a domain. By default, if the forest root domain DNS zone is stored in Active Directory, the _msdcs.forest.name zone containing forestwide DNS records is stored in the ForestDnsZones partition, and the domain zone in the DomainDnsZones partition.

NOTE If you use Manage Your Server to configure the first server in your network and let it install Active Directory, another application partition, `DC=TAPI3Directory,DC=yourdomain,DC=com` with `OU=Dynamic`, is created automatically. This partition is used by some Telephony API (TAPI) applications for locating the nearest Internet Locator Service (ILS) server. Such an application is H.323 IP telephony. You can use the tapicfg command for configuring TAPI application partitions.

Managing application partitions requires you to know the replication architecture in greater depth. Thus, we will discuss application partitions in depth, as well as managing them, in Chapter 6.

Managing DNS Replication

When you create a new DNS zone and store it in Active Directory, you have the option to define its replication scope, as displayed in Figure 2.9.

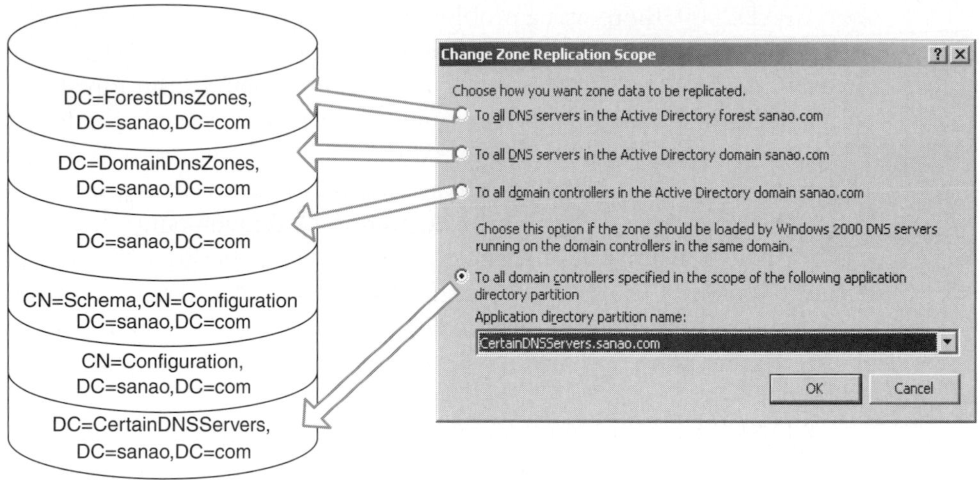

Figure 2.9 DNS zones can be stored in different Active Directory partitions and are consequently replicated to the appropriate domain controllers.

You can ensure the creation of the application partition by checking the DNS event log. Figure 2.10 displays an event that is created when a ForestDnsZones partition is created.

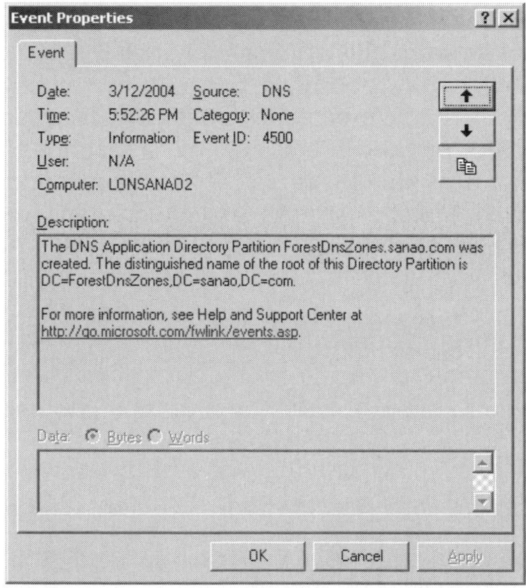

Figure 2.10 Creation of default application partitions for DNS is recorded in the DNS event log.

Managing Functional Levels

AD2000 stores the domain mode in the `nTMixedDomain` attribute of the domain. The value 1 indicates mixed mode, and the value 0 indicates native mode. When you change a Windows 2000 domain from mixed to native mode, the system does not check to see whether there still are Windows NT 4.0 BDCs. If there were any, they would be dropped out of the forest. Thus, the administrator must be certain that no NT 4.0 BDCs exist when making the change, since there is no way to reverse the change.

AD2003 stores the functional level in a new attribute, `msDS-Behavior-Version`. This attribute exists for the domain controller, domain, and forest, as displayed in Table 2.8. You can use, for example, the ADSI Edit or LDP support tools to view the values for the attribute.

TIP You can also see the forest root domain functional level and forest functional levels in the `rootDSE` object.

The value of the attribute is increased by the product version so that Windows 2000 is represented with the value 0, Windows Server 2003 interim with the value 1, and Windows Server 2003 with the value 2. The absence of a value in the NTDS Settings object indicates that the

Table 2.8 Storage of Functional Levels in the `msDS-Behavior-Version` Attribute in AD2003

Object	Location of the Object	Example
Domain controller	NTDS Settings of domain controller (`nTDSDSA` class)	`CN=NTDS Settings, CN=LONSANAO1,CN=Servers, CN=Default-First-Site-Name,CN=Sites, CN=Configuration, DC=sanao,DC=com`
Domain	Domain object (`domainDNS` class)	`DC=sanao,DC=com`
Forest	Partitions container (`crossRefContainer` class)	`CN=Partitions, CN=Configuration, DC=sanao,DC=com`

domain controller is running Windows 2000. The NTDS Settings object doesn't exist for NT 4.0 BDCs.

After the first domain controller has been installed and the forest created, the domain is in the Windows 2000 mixed functional level and the forest is in the Windows 2000 functional level. If you want to raise the domain functional level, you can use Active Directory Users and Computers or Active Directory Domains and Trusts. Only Active Directory Domains and Trusts can be used to raise the forest functional level.

Raising the forest to the Windows Server 2003 functional level ensures the absence of NT 4.0 BDCs by checking the value of the `nTMixedDomain` attribute to verify that it has a value of 0 in every domain of the forest. Raising the domain level to Windows Server 2003 doesn't perform this type of check and thus behaves similarly to changing the domain mode in Windows 2000. Figure 2.11 displays these attributes for a newly created Windows Server 2003 domain, `sanao.com`.

Raising the forest functional level automatically raises all domain functional levels that have not been raised to the forest level, assuming all domain controllers in the forest are running Windows Server 2003. This means that when you raise the forest functional level to Windows

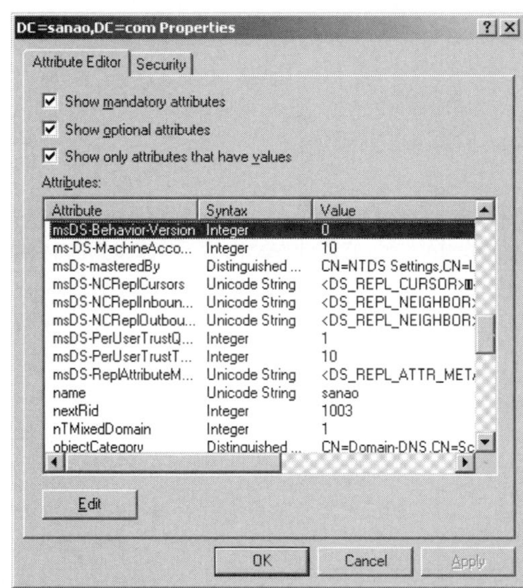

Figure 2.11 Attributes `msDS-Behavior-Version` and `nTMixedDomain` as displayed in ADSI Edit

Server 2003, all Windows 2000 native-level domains are also raised to the Windows Server 2003 domain functional level.

NOTE In order to raise the forest functionality, you must be a member of Enterprise Admins, and to raise the domain functionality, you must be a member of Domain Admins or Enterprise Admins.

Installing Additional Tools

There are at least three packages of tools you might want to install after the Active Directory promotion. The first of them, Support Tools, is most valuable when you are exploring Active Directory under the surface. Some tools in the Support Tools package, such as adsiedit.msc and repadmin.exe, are used extensively in this book. You can install Support Tools using \SUPPORT\TOOLS\SUPTOOLS.MSI on the installation CD. The second package is obvious: the Resource Kit tools. You can download them from Microsoft at `http://www.microsoft.com/reskits/`. Another tool well worth downloading and installing is the Group Policy Management Console (GPMC), which we will discuss in depth in Chapter 7.

You should also consider the security implications of installing the additional tools on domain controllers. The other option would be to install them on an administration workstation.

Changing Folder Locations

After you have installed your domain controllers, it might become necessary to move Active Directory–related folders and the files they contain. Changing the location of the SYSVOL folder is rather complicated to do without reinstalling Active Directory. However, moving the database folder and the log file folder (%SystemRoot%\NTDS by default for both) is possible to accomplish by starting the computer in Directory Services Restore Mode and using the `ntdsutil - files` command.

TIP Active Directory defragments the database online. However, the online defragmentation does not reduce the size of the database if you have created a large number of objects and subsequently removed them. You can use the `ntdsutil, files, compact` command in Directory Services Restore Mode in order to reduce the size that the Active Directory database takes.

TIP For detailed instructions on moving the database, log files, or SYSVOL after you have installed Active Directory, see the Active Directory Operations Guide at `http://go.microsoft.com/fwlink/?LinkId=18545`.

Other Post-Installation Tasks

You may want to download and read the document "Best Practice Guide for Securing Active Directory Installations" on the Microsoft Web site, for information on turning off unnecessary services and changing security settings.

Users and Computers are two default containers created during AD installation. You might want to change these to OUs or, alternatively, redirect new user and computer accounts when they are created. After you have installed several domain controllers, you may want to transfer master operation roles. We will discuss these tasks in the chapters to follow.

Automating Active Directory Installation

Just like the Windows 2000/Server 2003 operating system installation, the Active Directory installation can be automated. So far, there are no tools to create an answer file for Active Directory installation. It is reasonably simple, however, and you can use the following example as a template and modify the files with a text editor (Notepad, for example).

Let's say you want to create a new Active Directory forest with the root domain called `sanao.com`. You assume Windows 2000/Server 2003 has been installed with default settings. Here are the contents of a sample answer file for Active Directory installation on the first domain controller:

```
[DCInstall]
AutoConfigDNS = Yes
ConfirmGc = Yes
CreateOrJoin = Create
DatabasePath = %SYSTEMROOT%\ntds
DNSOnNetwork = No
DomainNetbiosName = sanao
```

```
LogPath = %SYSTEMROOT%\ntds
NewDomain = Forest
NewDomainDNSName = sanao.com
RebootOnSuccess = Yes
ReplicaOrNewDomain = Domain
SafeModeAdminPassword = r7rg/&HW92
SysVolPath = %SYSTEMROOT%\sysvol
SiteName = London
TreeOrChild = Tree
```

You start automated Active Directory installation with a command switch /answer—for example, `DCPROMO /answer:c:\dcpromo.txt`. Alternatively, you could include the preceding lines in the Windows 2000/Server 2003 answer file in order to automate installation of Windows 2000/Server 2003 and, subsequently, Active Directory.

TIP For further information on using answer files to automate Active Directory installation, read ref.chm inside the cabinet file DEPLOY.CAB in the \SUPPORT\TOOLS folder of the Windows Server 2003 setup CD.

TIP You can use an answer file also when using install from media in order to automate Active Directory installation.

TIP Windows 2000 answer files are slightly different from those for Windows Server 2003. See KB article 223757 for examples. The previously mentioned ref.chm contains the section "Changes in Answer Files," which documents the differences.

Problems with Active Directory Installation

The most common problems with Active Directory are related to name resolution (that is, DNS). These include the inability to find a parent domain, problems with simple DNS queries, and so on.

You can try to sort out the name-resolution problems by testing the DNS service with the DNS snap-in or nslookup. To use the snap-in, open it from the Start menu, right-click your server, and select Properties. You can test the operation of the service by checking the Simple

Query and Recursive Query box and clicking Test Now. Alternatively, you can check whether the DNS service replies to queries by using the command-line tool nslookup, as follows:

1. Start the command prompt by clicking the Start button, selecting Run, cmd, and then pressing Enter.
2. At the command prompt, type "nslookup" (without quotes) and press Enter.
3. Type "set type=SRV" (without quotes) and press Enter. This filters the SRV-type records only.
4. Type "_ldap._tcp.Active_Directory_Domain_Name" (without quotes) and press Enter.
5. You should see a response that looks like this:

```
C:\>nslookup
Default Server:  lonsanao1.sanao.com
Address:  10.0.10.100
> set type=srv
> _ldap._tcp.sanao.com
Server:  lonsanao1.sanao.com
Address:  10.0.10.100
_ldap._tcp.sanao.com       SRV service location:
          priority        = 0
          weight          = 100
          port            = 389
          svr hostname    = lonsanao1.sanao.com
lonsanao1.sanao.com         internet address = 10.0.10.100
```

TIP Other tools for DNS diagnostics include the Windows Server 2003 Support Tool utilities DCDiag, NetDiag, and especially DNSLint with its HTML output. And if you want to delve deeper, you can download the Windows version of dig from `http://www.isc.org/index.pl?/sw/bind/` and a utility using it from `http://www.washington.edu/computing/support/windows/UWdomains/dnsTool.htm`. This URL is case-sensitive!

Recovery Options

Windows 2000/Server 2003 includes a number of recovery options. We briefly discuss the most important of them in the following sections. For further information on recovery, see the Windows 2000 online Help or Windows Server 2003 Technical Reference.

You can access the Startup options menu by pressing F8 after the BIOS has finished its diagnostics when the screen goes blank. If you see the Windows Server 2003 logo, you missed the timing. In Windows 2000, a message for accessing the Startup options menu is shown at the bottom of the screen.

Startup Options

Safe Mode is familiar to everyone who has used Windows 95, 98, or XP. It enables you to start a computer with minimal drivers and services (7 of them in Windows Server 2003) loaded. However, while in Safe Mode, you cannot administer Active Directory, because not all necessary services are started. Safe Mode with Networking starts 17 services and consequently enables restricted administration of Active Directory.

NOTE The DNS server service is not started in Safe Mode with Networking.

If a newly installed driver causes Windows 2000/Server 2003 to stop working, the Last Known Good option might be the cure. Table 2.9 presents the various startup options and their uses.

TIP Windows XP introduced the Roll Back Driver option, which you can use to retain the previous version of the driver. You can access this option in Windows Server 2003 from the Driver tab after you have successfully started the computer in Safe Mode.

NOTE Windows XP introduced System Restore for restoring the system to an earlier state. This functionality is not available in Windows Server 2003.

Table 2.9 Windows 2000/Server 2003 Startup Options

Option	Purpose
Safe Mode	Starts the computer using basic files and drivers only, without networking. The drivers and files used are for mouse, monitor, keyboard, mass storage, base video, and default system services. A boot log file is also saved/appended.
Safe Mode with Networking	Starts the computer using basic files and drivers only (Safe Mode), but includes network support. Does not support PCMCIA networking. A boot log file is also saved.
Safe Mode with Command Prompt	Starts the computer using basic files and drivers only, without networking, and displays only the command prompt. A boot log file is also saved/appended.
Enable Boot Logging	Creates a boot log of devices and services that are loading. The log is saved to a file named Ntbtlog.txt in the %systemroot% directory.
Enable VGA Mode	Starts the computer using the basic VGA (video) driver. This mode is useful when a newly installed driver for your video card is preventing the computer from starting properly. The basic video driver is always used when you start the computer in any Safe Mode.
Last Known Good Configuration	Starts the computer using the settings (registry information) that Windows saved at the successful startup. Use only in cases of incorrect configuration, since it does not solve problems caused by corrupted or missing drivers or files. Note: When you use Last Known Good Configuration, any system setting changes made after the last successful startup are lost.
Directory Services Restore Mode	Starts a domain controller without Active Directory. You must know the Restore Mode administrator password that you defined during Active Directory installation. This option is only for Windows 2000/Server 2003 domain controllers.
Debugging Mode	Starts the computer while sending debug information through a serial cable to another computer.

Directory Services Restore Mode

It might be necessary to either recover some portion of Active Directory from backup or defragment the Active Directory database. In these situations, the computer must be running without Active Directory. Directory Services Restore Mode fulfills this functionality.

TIP See the Windows Server 2003 online Help for information on restoring Active Directory, with the keywords "restore System State data," ntdsutil.

Recovery Console

The Recovery Console is a utility that many Windows NT administrators looked forward to for a long time. The Recovery Console enables you to start Windows 2000/Server 2003 into a command-line console where certain operations, such as replacing damaged files or disabling services, are possible. Earlier this kind of functionality existed only with third-party products such as ERD Commander from Sysinternals (`http://www.sysinternals.com/`).

Table 2.10 lists the console commands and their purposes. Most file- or folder related commands work only in the system directories of the Windows installation, removable media, the root folder of any hard disk partition, or the local installation sources. Most commands are restricted versions of the equivalent Windows 2000/Server 2003 or earlier commands.

NOTE There are restrictions on file operation commands. You may only be able to access Windows or Cmdcons folders, removable media, the root directory of any disk partition, and the local installation files.

Installing and Starting the Recovery Console

You can install the Recovery Console using the `WINNT32 /CMDCONS` command. The installation takes over 8MB (6MB for Windows 2000) of disk space from the system partition (i.e., the partition where the necessary files to load the operating system are stored). After you've installed the Recovery Console, it appears on the Windows 2000/Server 2003 boot-up menu. From there, you can start it anytime you boot up the computer.

Table 2.10 Windows 2000/Server 2003 Recovery Console Commands

Command	Purpose
ATTRIB	Changes file or folder (directory) attributes.
BATCH	Executes commands specified in a text file.
BOOTCFG (new for Windows Server 2003)	Configures startup options. You can rebuild the boot.ini file based on the scan results of Windows installations on your disk.
CD/CHDIR	Changes the current folder or displays its name. Use quotation marks around a folder name that contains spaces. `CD ..` only works with a space between CD and the dots.
CHKDSK	Checks a disk and displays a status report. Requires the AUTOCHK.EXE file.
CLS	Clears the screen.
COPY	Copies a single file to a new location. Doesn't support wildcards. Compressed files from installation source are extracted automatically.
DEL/DELETE	Deletes one or more files.
DIR	Lists files and folders, also with various attributes such as hidden and system.
DISABLE	Disables a specified Windows system service or driver. Displays the old start type before resetting it to disabled.
DISKPART	Used for managing disk partitions. If you start it without parameters, displays a similar partition-management interface to the one used during setup.
ENABLE	Enables a specified Windows system service or driver. Displays the old start type before resetting it to enabled.
EXIT	Exits the recovery console and restarts the computer.
EXPAND	Extracts a file from a compressed cabinet (.cab) file. Works only if the system was booted from the original installation media. Doesn't support wildcards.
FIXBOOT	Writes a new boot sector onto the system partition. Supports only the Intel platform.
FIXMBR	Repairs the MBR of the disk from where the system starts booting (boot partition).
FORMAT	Formats a partition or volume with FAT, FAT32, or NTFS.
HELP	Displays a list of the Recovery Console commands.

Table 2.10 Windows 2000/Server 2003 Recovery Console Commands (*cont.*)

Command	Purpose
LISTSVC	Lists all available services and drivers and their startup status.
LOGON	Lists available Windows 2000/Server 2003 installations and requests the password for the local administrator.
MAP	Lists active mappings between drive letters and physical devices. Displays ARC paths (that are used in BOOT.INI) with the Arc parameter.
MD/MKDIR	Creates a folder (directory).
MORE	Displays the contents of a text file.
RD/RMDIR	Removes a folder (directory).
REN/RENAME	Renames a single file.
SET	Displays and sets Recovery Console environment variables—e.g., AllowAllPaths. Disabled by default. You can enable it with Group Policy.
SYSTEMROOT	Sets the current directory to systemroot.
TYPE	Displays the contents of a text file.

NOTE In Windows Server 2003, when installing the Recovery Console, you have an option to download latest system files from Windows Update to be included in the Recovery Console.

Alternatively, you can use the setup floppy disks (only for Windows 2000) or the Windows 2000/Server 2003 setup CD to boot up the computer and select Repair instead of Install. On the next screen, if you are using Windows 2000, you have the option to use the traditional ERD process (by pressing Enter) or to start the Recovery Console (C). In Windows Server 2003, the Recovery Console (R) option is available already on the first screen, and there is no option for the ERD process.

IF YOU KNOW NT The Recovery Console was first introduced in Windows 2000. You can also use it to try to repair NT 4.0, although this is not supported.

NOTE The Windows Server 2003 setup CD no longer contains the setup floppy disks. In order to start Windows Server 2003 from a floppy disk, you have to create an MS-DOS startup disk that contains CD drivers. See KB article 810562 for more information.

Using the Recovery Console

After the Recovery Console starts, it scans the hard disk for existing Windows 2000/Server 2003 installations. You select from a list the installation that you want to repair, after which you have to type the local administrator's password. Then you can start using the commands that were listed in Table 2.10. You can finish the Recovery Console and restart the computer by typing "EXIT".

TIP The Recovery Console uses the same administrator account stored on the registry as Directory Services Restore Mode. Thus, you can reset both passwords at the same time. See the section "The Installation Process" earlier in this chapter.

TIP The administrator password for the Recovery Console can be disabled by configuring Computer Configuration\Windows Settings\Security Settings\Local Policies\Security Options\Recovery console: Allow automatic administrative logon. We recommend that you not change the default, which is to ask for the password—that is, the setting is disabled.

NOTE The Recovery Console does not use country settings in Windows 2000—that is, the keyboard layout configuration is set to U.S. (English). In Windows Server 2003, you can select the keyboard layout when the Recovery Console starts (and prior to typing the password).

Automated System Recovery

Automated System Recovery (ASR) was first introduced in Windows XP. It enables you to start your Windows Server 2003 computer if all attempts fail by restoring system state data, system services, and all disks associated with the operating system components. ASR uses a floppy disk to store disk configuration. You can create an ASR backup with the Windows Server 2003 Backup application. In order to restore the system, press F2 when starting the computer with the setup CD.

Uninstalling Active Directory

There are situations in which you might want to uninstall Active Directory. For example, a software developer might have created an application that updates the schema. In Windows 2000, you cannot remove added attributes or classes from an Active Directory schema; you can only disable them. Thus, it might become necessary to uninstall Active Directory from a computer to clean up the schema, after which you can reinstall Active Directory. Another situation would be if you have been experimenting with Active Directory and you want to install the computer to an existing domain.

The requirements for Active Directory removal are:

- You must be a member of Domain Admins in order to remove replica domain controllers in a domain, and a member of Enterprise Admins in order to remove domains from a forest, or relevant permissions must have been delegated.
- No application partitions exist in the domain.

Uninstalling Active Directory couldn't be much easier. You start by demoting a domain controller into a stand-alone/member server with the DCPROMO command. If the domain controller in question is also a GC server and other domain controllers will remain in the forest, you should ensure that some other domain controller is defined as a GC server. Otherwise, the users might not be able to log on to a domain.

Next, you are asked whether the domain controller in question is the last domain controller in a domain. If this is the case, the computer becomes a stand-alone server and the domain no longer exists. If it isn't, it will be demoted to a member server. Next, you are asked how the possible application partitions are handled. Finally, you must enter the appropriate credentials in order to be able to complete the removal and finally define a new password for the local administrator.

TIP Use the Help and Support Center with the keywords "Application directory partitions and domain controller demotion" for more information on removing application partitions.

As Figure 2.12 shows, a number of things happen when Active Directory is removed from the last domain controller in a domain.

- Member computers in the domain cannot log on to the domain, nor can they access any services in it.
- All user, group, computer, and other objects are removed.
- All cryptographic keys are deleted. Thus, they should be exported with the Certificate Export Wizard before the uninstallation continues.

TIP Search the Windows 2000 online Help or Windows Server 2003 Help and Support with the keywords "certificate export" for further instructions on exporting certificates along with private keys.

- All encrypted data should be decrypted, although it is possible to access the data if the keys were exported.
- DNS subdomains and SRV records are deleted upon restarting the computer. If the computer is the last domain of the

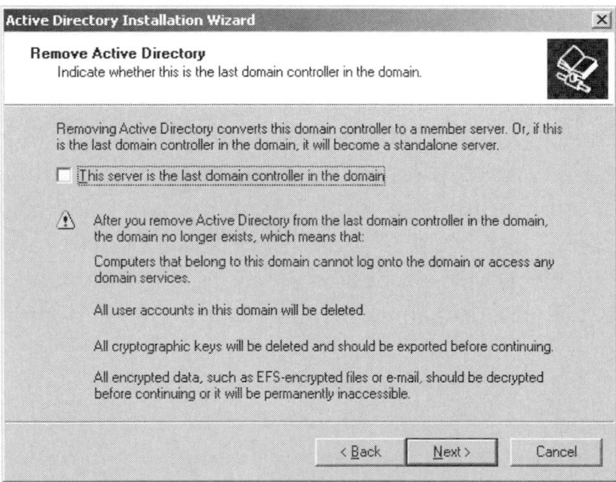

Figure 2.12 Removing Active Directory has a number of consequences.

Active Directory root domain, the Forward Lookup Zone is also removed.

WARNING Make sure that if you select "This server is the last domain controller in the domain" for the server you are going to demote, the server really is the last one in the domain. Otherwise, you will end up with a major problem because data in Active Directory will become inconsistent with the actual situation.

Windows Server 2003 introduces forced removal of Active Directory. You can start it by using the `dcpromo /forceremoval` command. AD is removed even without network connection to other domain controllers, and the forced removal ignores service failures. After AD is removed, the computer becomes a stand-alone server. You should then remove the metadata for this server in the Active Directory. This technique is also available in Windows 2000 Service Pack 4.

TIP See "delete extinct server metadata" in the online Help and KB article 216498 for removing the metadata of an unrecoverable domain controller from Active Directory. See also the section "Transferring Operations Master Roles" in Chapter 5.

Automating Active Directory Uninstallation

Uninstalling Active Directory can be automated in the same way Active Directory installation can be automated. Obviously, the answer file differs because there are not so many questions to be answered and the questions are somewhat different.

Here's a sample answer file called DCUNINST.TXT for uninstalling Active Directory:

```
[DCInstall]
AdministratorPassword=#%UD(8992
IsLastDCInDomain=Yes
Password=&63trG##/>
RebootOnSuccess=Yes
UserName=Administrator
```

This file can be used with the command `dcpromo /answer: c:\dcuninst.txt`.

Conclusion

In this chapter, you have learned how to promote Windows 2000/2003 Server to a domain controller. Now you have at least a small Active Directory network up and running, so you are ready to explore various aspects of Active Directory. Chapter 3 begins this exploration with the management of OUs, users, and groups, which make up the core content of Active Directory.

PART II

Core Skills

CHAPTER 3

Managing OUs, Users, and Groups

The most visible part of Active Directory administration is managing objects with the Users and Computers snap-in. This snap-in enables you to create organizational units (OUs) to set up an OU tree in a domain. You also use this snap-in to populate the OU tree by creating objects of the following eight classes in the OUs you want:

- Users (or alternatively, inetOrgPersons, new in AD2003)
- Contacts
- Computers
- Groups
- MSMQ queue aliases (new in AD2003)
- Shared folders
- Printers

This chapter covers managing OUs and the first five classes in the list. We will proceed as follows:

- First, we describe the contents of your Active Directory domain right after installation.
- Second, we explore how to manage OUs and objects of each of the five other classes (i.e., users, inetOrgPersons, contacts, computers, and groups).
- Finally, we discuss some additional features of the Users and Computers snap-in, and we discuss or list additional tools for managing objects.

This chapter focuses on the Users and Computers snap-in. If you have to create many objects, other tools you can use include DSAdd (new in AD2003), LDIFDE, CSVDE, scripting, or some Resource Kit tools. DSAdd we cover at the end of this chapter; the other tools we just list there, but cover later in the book.

NOTE Behind the scenes, a domain object can contain objects of 35 classes (23 in AD2000), and an OU can contain objects of 59 classes (35 in AD2000). However, with the Users and Computers snap-in, you can normally create and see objects of only the nine classes just listed.

NOTE MSMQ Queue Alias is listed as an alternative when you create new objects in the Users and Computers snap-in. You can, however, create and use such objects only if you first install Microsoft Message Queuing 3.0 (MSMQ). Because such aliases (corresponding to the `msMQ-Custom-Recipient` class) reside in the directory, they help applications to locate message queues. Further discussion of the topic is outside the scope of this book. Also, we don't mention MSMQ queue aliases later in this chapter, even though they would appear in some lists, and so on.

Active Directory after Installation

After you have created your first domain by installing Active Directory on a server (i.e., promoting it to a domain controller), there are certain users, computers, groups, and containers already in place (see Figure 3.1). You see these objects with the Users and Computers snap-in, which you start by clicking the Start button and selecting Administrative Tools, Active Directory Users and Computers.

TIP Another way to start the Users and Computers snap-in is to click the Start button, select Run, type `dsa.msc`, and press Enter.

You will see the following predefined objects in the snap-in:

- Five containers, one of which is an OU
- Some user objects (or user accounts)
- Some group objects (sometimes referred to as group accounts)
- One computer object (or computer account) for your domain controller

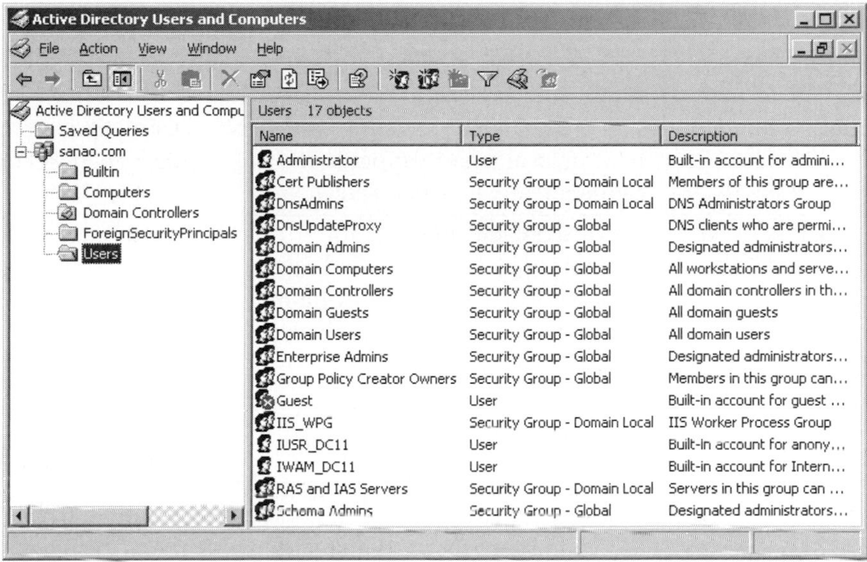

Figure 3.1 A newly installed domain (`sanao.com` in the figure), which is the root domain of a forest

NOTE Active Directory contains only objects. Users, groups, and computers, however, are often called *accounts* instead of objects. You could also argue that an account is something that can authenticate (user or computer), so a group is not an account, but "just" a group of accounts.

NOTE If you upgrade a Windows NT domain, you will see the users, groups, and computers of that domain in Active Directory.

Predefined OUs and Other Containers

The objects in a domain should reside in containers instead of at the domain level, just as files on disk should reside in folders instead of in the root folder. Accordingly, the predefined objects are stored in containers below the domain level. Table 3.1 describes the five predefined containers. Because they have extra system-flags protection, you cannot rename, move, or delete them—they are always there (unless you redirect some of them, as explained a little later in the section "Redirecting the Users and Computers Containers to OUs").

Table 3.1 The Predefined Containers in Active Directory

Container	OU	Purpose	Possible Contents
Builtin	No	This is a container for the predefined built-in local security groups (you cannot create them yourself).	Computer, group, user, inetOrgPerson
Computers	No	This is a default container for computer objects corresponding to Windows NT/2000/XP workstations and member servers in this domain.	Computer, contact, group, printer, user, inetOrgPerson, shared folder
Domain Controllers	Yes	This is a default container for computer objects corresponding to domain controllers of this domain.	Computer, contact, group, OU, printer, user, inetOrgPerson, shared folder
Foreign Security Principals	No	This is a container for placeholders that represent group members from domains external to the forest. This includes well-known security principals, such as Authenticated Users, if they are members of some group in the domain.* Objects in this container are visible only when the snap-in's Advanced Features are turned on.	Computer, contact group, printer, user, inetOrgPerson, shared folder
Users	No	This is a default container for users and groups.	Computer, contact, group, printer, user, inetOrgPerson, shared folder

* We discuss well-known security principals in Chapter 4 and foreign security principals in Chapter 6.

NOTE In Table 3.1, the Possible Contents column lists the object types (that is, classes) that you can create in the corresponding container using the Users and Computers snap-in. With an "under-the-hood" tool, such as ADSI Edit, you could create other types of objects. However, there is no need to use the predefined containers for anything but what is described in the table.

You shouldn't use the Builtin container for anything, even though it is possible to create computers, groups, and users in it. Likewise, you could create users in the Computers container or computers in the Users container, but there is no point in doing so. Putting such things together is comparable to placing your cookbooks and music CDs on the same shelf. It is possible, but why do it?

If you want, you can keep your users in the Users container and computers in the Computers container. If you do so, however, you can neither create OUs in them nor assign Group Policy for them, because these containers are not OUs. If you have more than 20 users, for example, and you want to delegate some administration, you will probably end up creating new OUs for your users and computers (i.e., outside the Users or Computers containers). We will come back to this issue in the "Administering OUs" section later in this chapter.

The Domain Controllers container is an OU, and therefore you can create OUs in it and assign Group Policy(ies) for it. This OU already has a Default Domain Controllers Policy Group Policy object (GPO) assigned, which affects the security and other settings of your domain controllers. You are likely to keep the computer objects for your domain controllers in this container and other OUs that you create below it.

Why These Containers?

It may seem that the way these predefined containers were chosen is odd. Why are most of them not OUs? Some explanation is given by the fact that these containers ease the upgrade from Windows NT to Active Directory. During the upgrade process, the old user accounts and groups are migrated to the Users container, old workstation and member server accounts are migrated to the Computers container, and old domain controller accounts are migrated to the Domain Controllers container.

In addition to migration, the default Users and Computers containers are also used whenever users, groups, and computers are created using downlevel tools. Such tools are Windows NT User Manager and Server Manager, Net commands (Net User, Net Group, Net Localgroup, Net Computer), Windows Support Tools NetDom Add command without the /OU switch, and any tool that uses the old Windows NT APIs to create these objects. Also, when a Windows NT/2000/XP workstation joins a domain and there is no precreated computer account, the account will be created in the default Computers container.

In Windows NT, built-in local groups were internally stored separately from other groups, users, and computer accounts. This separation was brought over to Active Directory in the form of the Builtin container.

So why are these three containers not OUs? One explanation could be that this way you are intentionally discouraged from using them in the long run and you must create new OUs instead.

Redirecting the Users and Computers Containers to OUs

If your domain is on the Windows Server 2003 functional level, you can redirect the predefined Users container and the Computers container to OUs you have created. After the redirection, these new OUs will be the default containers for users, groups, and computers. For example, you can create the Employees OU and the Workstations OU, and then perform the redirection using the following commands:

```
redirusr OU=Employees,DC=Sanao,DC=com
redircmp OU=Workstations,DC=Sanao,DC=com
```

During the redirection, the system-flags protection is moved from the old default containers to the new ones. Therefore, you could rename or delete the old containers.

The predefined Users container and Computers container don't allow you to apply group policies to them, but if you perform the redirection to a normal OU, you can apply group policies. On the other hand, if your users and computers are already in normal OUs and you don't use any tools that would create new users or computers in the default containers, there is not much advantage in the redirection.

For more information, see the Microsoft Knowledge Base article 324949 at `http://www.microsoft.com`.

Predefined Users

Two user objects are always present: Administrator and Guest. You cannot delete either of them, but you can rename them at will. Renaming Administrator offers some extra protection because a potential network intruder would need to guess the new name in addition to the password. However, if you have a large network and many administrative personnel, it may be confusing for the Administrator account to have a different name.

NOTE The default permissions of Active Directory allow any user of the forest to see the names of administrative accounts, so renaming them is really minimal "protection." You can think of it as adding a small extra hurdle in a potential intruder's path. If you chose permissions compatible with pre–Windows 2000 servers, anonymous users can also see this information.

Active Directory has predefined user accounts besides Administrator and Guest, depending on what services are installed. Table 3.2 lists the typical predefined user accounts in Active Directory.

If you enable the Guest account, be careful about the permissions you give to it or the Everyone group (and in AD2000 also to the Domain Users or Users groups). After all, anyone who "walks in the door" can use the Guest account. There are two ways to use the Guest account.

Table 3.2 The Predefined User Accounts in Active Directory

Name	Present	Description
Administrator	Always (although could be renamed); cannot be disabled in AD2000 but can be disabled in AD2003	The only user account you can use when you log on for the first time. The Administrator account of the first domain in a forest has the widest possible administrative permissions on Active Directory and the domain controllers in the same forest. You can create other user accounts with permissions as wide. The Administrator accounts of the later domains in a forest have the widest possible administrative permissions for their own domains.
Guest	Always (although could be renamed); disabled by default	If someone doesn't have a user account, he can use the Guest account (if the account is enabled). (See the discussion in the text.)
IUSR-_*servername*	One for each domain controller that has IIS installed	If IIS allows anonymous access (e.g., by Web browsers), anonymous users use permissions of this user account.
IWAM-_*servername*	One for each domain controller that has IIS installed	IWAM stands for IIS Web Application Manager. The IISWAM. OutofProcess Pool component (part of IIS) uses this user account. *(continued)*

Table 3.2 The Predefined User Accounts in Active Directory *(cont.)*

Name	Present	Description
krbtgt	Always; disabled by default; hidden by default; cannot be enabled or renamed	The Kerberos key distribution center (KDC) uses this account. "Krbtgt" is part of the KDC's service principal name (SPN). Also, a symmetric key is derived from the password of krbtgt, and this key is used to encrypt and decrypt TGTs. Only the KDC knows this password and it changes the password periodically.
TsInternetUser	For Windows 2000 Terminal Services	When an optional Internet Connector license is enabled, Terminal Services clients are not prompted with a logon dialog box. Instead, they are logged on automatically with the TsInternetUser account.

- If your workstation is a member of a domain of the forest where the Guest account is enabled (in some of its domains), you just type "guest" in the logon dialog box, select the correct domain, and start using the workstation and the network.
- If your workstation is in a workgroup or in a different forest from the one in which the Guest account is enabled (in some of its domains), you first need to log on with some other user account. When you connect to the resources of the domain where the Guest account is enabled, you are granted access based on that Guest account's permissions. You never type "guest" anywhere—you just use "Jack," for example. When the server doesn't recognize "Jack," it switches to use "Guest" automatically. The catch is that if there is another Jack, who most likely uses a different password, you are denied access. The server just thinks that someone is trying to crack Jack's account and doesn't use Guest at all.

Predefined Groups

Active Directory includes predefined security groups. Some of them reside in the Builtin container and the rest reside in the Users container, as follows:

- *Builtin:* Built-in local security groups
- *Users:* Mostly global security groups

The primary purpose of most of these predefined groups is to be the means by which administrative rights and permissions are assigned. To be anything more than an end user in the network, a user needs one or more of the following types of permission or rights:

- User rights, such as permission to change the system time or log on locally. These rights are controlled with Group Policy settings and/or local policy settings. There are also some fixed rights. For example, only members of the Administrators group can format hard drives, and you cannot give this right to anyone else.
- Administrative permissions (i.e., the ability to create, delete, change, and so on) for Active Directory objects.
- Administrative permissions for registry keys.
- Administrative permissions for folders and files.
- Administrative permissions for other resources (printers, for example).

Most of the predefined groups have specific administrative rights or permissions associated with them, so you can give some users the appropriate rights and permissions by adding their names to the corresponding groups. Instead of worrying about all of the items in the list individually, it is far easier to just put Jack in the Account Operators group and Jill in the DNS Admins group, for example. They will get suitable permissions in one package.

Sticking just to "predefined" doesn't get you through life, though—at least not with Active Directory. You often need to assign individual rights and permissions, probably not using the predefined groups. But that's another story for another chapter (Chapter 4, to be exact).

Figure 3.2 shows the relationship among the groups in the Builtin and Users containers in an Active Directory domain. It also shows the corresponding relationships that existed in Windows NT.

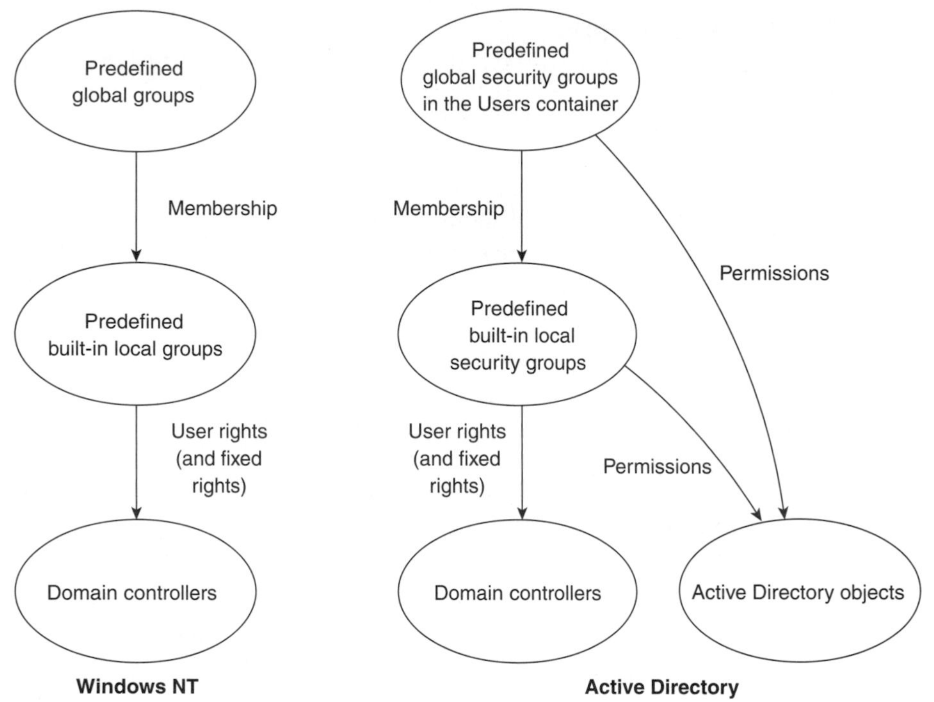

Figure 3.2 In Windows NT, the only meaning of predefined global groups (Domain Admins, Domain Users, and Domain Guests) was that they were members of some built-in local groups, which in turn had rights to administer the system. This is true also for Active Directory, but in addition both group categories have certain direct permissions to Active Directory objects.

NOTE In addition to the permissions and rights shown in Figure 3.2, built-in local (security) groups have permissions for system files and registry keys.

NOTE In Windows NT it was easy to make a user of another domain an administrator in a local domain. It only required making him a member of the Administrators group in the local domain. Because of the difference in how global groups get permissions, as illustrated in Figure 3.2, this is more difficult in Active Directory. If you make the foreign user a member of Administrators in Active Directory, he won't get the permissions of Domain Admins, so he will be only a partial administrator. You cannot make him a member of Domain Admins, because that group accepts members only from the same domain. Note that this note only applies to the administrative privileges for the domain account database and domain controllers. It doesn't apply to the administrative privileges for any member servers or workstations.

Predefined Built-in Local Security Groups

Table 3.3 describes the predefined groups in the Builtin container. You cannot delete, rename, or move any of them, because of their system-flags

Table 3.3 The Predefined Built-in Local Security Groups

Name	Predefined Members	Abilities*
Administrators	Administrator, Domain Admins, Enterprise Admins	By default, members of this group have almost total control of the domain controllers of the domain, including formatting hard drives and all the rights that the following four "operators" have. For Active Directory, this group has by default "Full Control except Delete Subtree or Delete All Child Objects" permission for almost all objects in the domain.
Account Operators	None	By default, members of this group can create, delete, and manage user, inetOrgPerson, group, and computer objects in the Active Directory domain, except in the Domain Controllers OU. Account operators can log on locally to domain controllers of the domain and shut them down. In Windows 2000, Account Operators can modify their own account and the accounts of other account operators. However, they cannot modify administrator accounts. Starting with Windows 2000 SP4 and Windows Server 2003, Account Operators cannot modify account operators. For more information, see the "AdminSDHolder Object" section in Chapter 4. *(continued)*

* See also Tables 4.44 through 4.47 in Chapter 4 for the lists of specific rights of these built-in groups.

Table 3.3 The Predefined Built-in Local Security Groups (*cont.*)

Name	Predefined Members	Abilities*
Server Operators	None	In the domain controllers of the domain, members of this group can create, delete, and manage file shares and printers, and start, stop, and configure services. Also in the domain controllers, they can log on locally, back up and restore files, change computer time, and shut down the domain controller either locally or remotely. Note that the list here is descriptive, but not quite exhaustive.
Backup Operators	None	By default, members of this group can back up and restore files and folders in the domain controllers of the domain, even if the member user doesn't have permissions for those files and folders. They can also log on locally on the domain controllers of the domain and shut the domain controllers down.
Print Operators	None	Members of this group can create, delete, manage, and share printers in the domain controllers of the domain, and by default they can create, delete, and manage printer objects in the Active Directory domain. They can also log on locally on the domain controllers of the domain and shut the domain controllers down.
Users	Domain Users, Authenticated Users, Interactive	By default, this group has no user rights or permissions. You can just ignore this group.** If you want to give permissions to all forest users, you can use Authenticated Users. You can also create groups such as SanaoUsers or SanaoBostonUsers and use them instead of the predefined Users group.

** Note that being able to ignore the Users group refers to the Users group in Active Directory, which is visible only on domain controllers. Each member server and workstation has a separate Users group, and each of them has some permissions for the corresponding local computer. Therefore, that latter Users group you probably need to use when managing permissions of the workstations and member servers in your organization.

Table 3.3 The Predefined Built-in Local Security Groups (*cont.*)

Name	Predefined Members	Abilities*
Guests	Guest, Domain Guests, IUSR-*_servername*, IWAM_*servername* (in AD2000)	By default, this group has no rights or permissions. You can just ignore this group.
Pre-Windows 2000 Compatible Access	Everyone*** and Anonymous Logon, if you selected "Permissions compatible with pre-Windows 2000 server operating systems" when you installed the domain; otherwise, Authenticated Users (the latter is the default)	By default, this group has permission to see all the objects in a domain and all the properties of all users, inetOrgPersons, and groups. Everyone/Anonymous need these permissions if you have certain server services (e.g., Remote Access Service) running on Windows NT servers in your Active Directory domain.
Replicator	None	Windows NT servers and workstations use this group for the Directory Replicator service.
Remote Desktop Users	None	Members of this group are allowed to use the Remote Desktop connection.
Network Configuration Operators	None	Members of this group can modify the local TCP/IP settings and some other network settings of the domain controllers. For a complete list, see Microsoft Knowledge Base article 297938.
Performance Monitor Users	None	Members of this group can use the Performance console, or perform similar monitoring with another tool.
Performance Log Users	Network Service	Members of this group can use the Performance Logs and Alerts console, or perform similar monitoring with another tool. *(continued)*

*** This refers to the well-known security principal Everyone.

Table 3.3 The Predefined Built-in Local Security Groups (*cont.*)

Name	Predefined Members	Abilities*
Incoming Forest Trust Builders	None	This group appears only in the forest root domain. The members can create incoming, one-way trusts to the forest.
Windows Authorization Access Group	Enterprise Domain Controllers	Members of this group can read the constructed `tokenGroupsGlobalAndUniversal` (TGGAU) attribute on user, inetOrgPerson, group, and computer objects. TGGAU contains a list of the object's global and universal group memberships, and an application can use this information, for example, to make decisions about users that are not logged on. The Pre-Windows 2000 Compatible Access group can also read TGGAU, but if the application is not in that group, you could use the Windows Authorization Access Group instead. For more information, see Microsoft Knowledge Base article 331951.
Terminal Server License Servers	None	This group is used for Terminal Server licensing.

protection. Note that each group in the table is always present in all domains. They have rights and/or permissions to their local domain only, and those rights/permissions apply only on the domain controllers. For example, the Remote Desktop Users group members can use the remote desktop of the domain controllers of the domain in question.

NOTE In the next chapter, we describe in more detail the default user rights and default Active Directory permissions of the groups in Table 3.3.

Predefined Groups in the Users Container

The remaining predefined groups are in the Users container. They are mostly global security groups, but there are also some domain local security groups. Table 3.4 describes the predefined groups in the Users container of a domain.

NOTE When you install the first domain of the forest, Enterprise Admins and Schema Admins are global groups. When you later change this domain to the Windows 2000 native or Windows Server 2003 functional level (as discussed in Chapter 2), those groups will change to universal groups, which allows them to have members from other domains.

Table 3.4 The Predefined Groups in the Users Container

Name	Predefined Members	Description
Enterprise Admins	Administrator of the first domain of the forest	Members of this group can administer all the domains in the enterprise. By default, this group is a member of Administrators in all domains of the forest. Enterprise Admins has Full Control to practically all objects in all domains of the forest. In addition, membership in this group is necessary to create child domains or sites. This group appears only in the first domain of the forest (that is, the forest root domain.)
Schema Admins	Administrator of the first domain of the forest	Members of this group can modify the schema of the forest. This group appears only in the first domain of the forest (that is, the forest root domain.)
Domain Admins	Administrator	Members of this group can administer this domain. By default, this group is a member of Administrators in this domain and all joined workstations/member servers. Domain Admins has Full Control to most objects of the domain.
Group Policy Creator Owners	Administrator	Members of this group can create Group Policy objects if they also have appropriate permissions for the OU for which they are creating the GPO. In addition, they can manage the GPOs they have created. *(continued)*

Table 3.4 The Predefined Groups in the Users Container *(cont.)*

Name	Predefined Members	Description
Domain Users	Every user account of the same domain	By default, this group has no rights or permissions. You can use it if you need to give permissions to all users of the domain.
Domain Guests	Guest	By default, this group has no rights or permissions. You probably don't need this group.
Domain Controllers	Each domain controller of the same domain	By default, this group has no rights or permissions. You can use it if you need to give permissions to all domain controllers of the domain.
Domain Computers	Each workstation and member server of the same domain	By default, this group has no rights or permissions. You can use it if you need to give permissions to all workstations and member servers of the domain.
Cert Publishers	Each computer that is running an enterprise certificate authority	By default, this group has permission to read and write the `userCertificate` property of the users and computers in the domain. Therefore, members of this group can publish certificates for users and computers.
DnsUpdate Proxy	None	DHCP servers may dynamically register DNS resource records on behalf of DHCP clients. In this case, the DHCP servers become the owners of those records. This is a problem if the client or some other DHCP server later wants to start maintaining those records. By placing the computer objects of the DHCP servers as members in this group, the servers won't become record owners, so the problem described here is resolved. This group is missing if there is no DNS service in the domain.
IIS_WPG	None	The IIS_WPG group (worker process group) appears with Internet Information Services (IIS) 6.0, and it is used for the needs of IIS.

Table 3.4 The Predefined Groups in the Users Container *(cont.)*

Name	Predefined Members	Description
DnsAdmins	None	Members of this group can administer the DNS service. This group is missing if there is no DNS service in the domain.
RAS and IAS Servers	Each computer that is running the Routing and Remote Access Services (RRAS)	By default, this group has permission to read Logon Information, Remote Access Information, Group Membership, and Account Restrictions of all users of the domain. RRAS servers need those permissions.

By default, Domain Admins is a member of the Administrators group of all workstations and member servers. Similarly, Domain Users is a member of the Users group of those computers.

Figure 3.3 illustrates the memberships of some predefined users, global groups, and built-in local groups that are listed in Tables 3.2 through 3.4.

In Chapter 4, we discuss the well-known security principals. Many of them are like groups, and you can assign permissions to them. They are not real groups, however, because the operating system, not a network administrator, controls their "membership."

Well-known security principals include Authenticated Users and Everyone, which you already saw as group members in Table 3.3 and

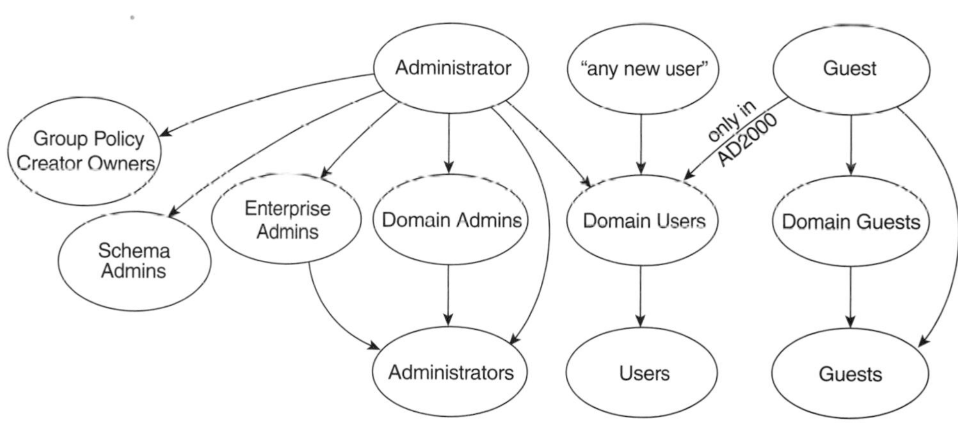

Figure 3.3 The predefined users and groups have several predefined memberships. In addition, any new user is a member of Domain Users.

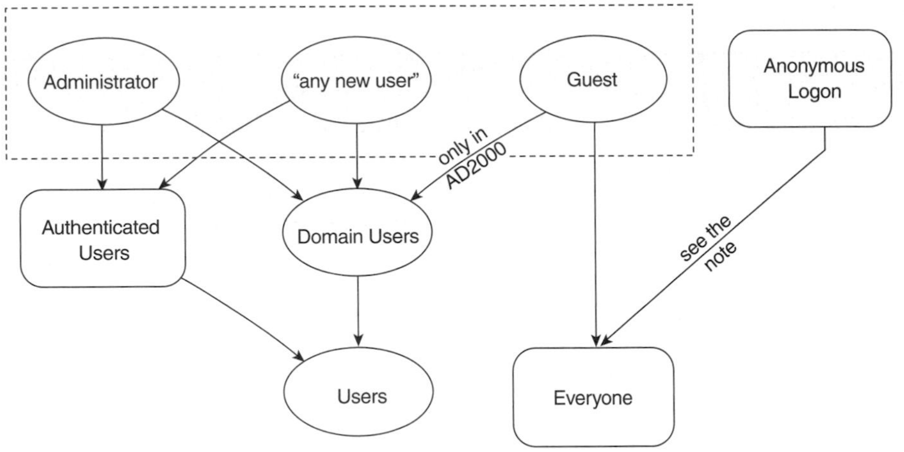

Figure 3.4 The well-known security principals Authenticated Users, Everyone, and Anonymous Logon can be seen as part of the membership hierarchy. However, their "membership" is controlled by the operating system, not by a network administrator.

Table 3.4. Therefore, we have included Figure 3.4 to illustrate those memberships here, even though the remaining discussion is in the next chapter.

NOTE In AD2000, Anonymous Logon is a "member" of Everyone. In AD2003, the security was tightened, and the "membership" is true only if you enable the security policy "Network access: Let Everyone permissions apply to anonymous users." This policy is located in Computer Configuration, Windows Settings, Security Settings, Local Policies, Security Options. See Chapter 7 for more information on policies.

Figure 3.4 reveals the memberships for the various end-user groups. Table 3.5 lists the end users (users of the group's domain, users of the whole forest, and so on) that are members of each user group.

Typically, an administrator uses Authenticated Users to assign permissions to all users of a forest and Domain Users to assign permissions only to the users of one domain.

Predefined Computer Objects

In the beginning, there is just one computer object. It is for your first (and at that point, only) domain controller in the Domain Controllers container.

Table 3.5 End-User Memberships

Group	Type	All Users in Group's Domain	All Forest Users	Guest	Anonymous
Everyone	Well-known	X	X	X	(see the Note)
Users	Built-in local	X	X	only in AD2000	
Authenticated Users	Well-known	X	X		
Domain Users	Global	X		only in AD2000	

Administering OUs

As you know, it is more efficient to organize your disk files in folders than to keep them in the root directory of a disk. Similarly, you are usually better off when you store Active Directory users, groups, and other objects in "folders" called OUs (organizational units). These OUs form an OU tree (also referred to as a domain structure) inside your domain. Figure 3.5 illustrates this.

NOTE In Figure 3.5, the uppermost circle (the root of the tree) is not an OU but rather the domain object that represents the domain (the triangle). We could drop the domain object out of the image, but it's more natural to have the tree as a whole. Also, in many ways the domain object behaves like an OU, so you can think of it as part of the tree.

Features of OUs

Besides providing a logical structure through the OU tree, OUs offer the following benefits.

- An OU is a Group Policy target, so you can assign a different Group Policy to each OU.

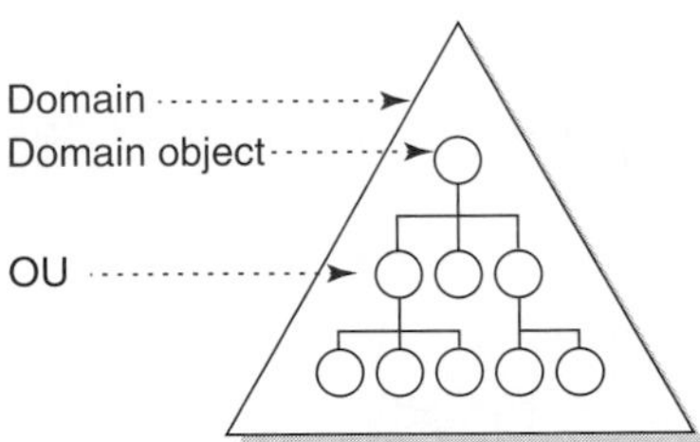

Figure 3.5 OUs inside a domain form an OU tree.

- If you want to delegate administration of some Active Directory objects, the most convenient way to do so is to put them in one OU and delegate administration of that OU. You could delegate administration of even single users and other objects, but the outcome would be difficult to manage. If you stick to only per-OU permissions, it is easier for you to track what you are doing.
- Using per-OU permissions, you can control object visibility—that is, which objects and object properties various users may see.

Unfortunately, even though you can assign permissions *for* OUs, you cannot assign permissions *to* OUs. In other words, you cannot define that all users in a certain OU get access to a certain folder or other resource. This will probably result in extra work for you, because you need to create a security group and put all the users in this group to give them access.

IF YOU KNOW NDS In NDS you can give permissions to OUs, so there is no need to create a group to correspond to each OU.

NOTE In Active Directory, OUs are not related to partitioning the directory database. They are purely logical units inside a domain. The domain in turn is the partition unit.

If there are several domains in your forest, each has a totally independent OU tree. The OU tree of an upper domain does not "continue" to a tree in a lower domain. However, if you have a Windows 2000 workstation and look at the tree by selecting My Network Places, Entire Network, Directory, you will see the child domains as siblings of the first-level OUs, as Figure 3.6 illustrates. Windows XP or Windows Server 2003 doesn't show Directory in My Network Places.

TIP Although it is not supported by Microsoft, you can enable the OU browsing of Windows 2000 also in Windows XP. Just copy the file DSFolder.dll from Windows 2000 to the System32 folder of Windows XP and register it with the command `regsvr32 dsfolder.dll`.

IF YOU KNOW NDS In NDS, all OUs form one big tree.

OUs are created primarily for administrators' use—end users don't usually see OUs. For example, when an end user performs a search operation for other people in Active Directory (by clicking the Start button and selecting Search), the user doesn't see the found users' OUs at all, and he couldn't even if he wanted to. For example, if there is a Jack Brown in OU Sales and another Jack Brown in OU Production, the person doing the search cannot tell the difference between them from the search dialog box. This is also true if a user is searching for a certain printer.

On the other hand, if the user has a Windows 2000 workstation and selects My Network Places, Entire Network, Directory, he will be able to browse the OU tree and see which user or printer is in which OU.

It is a matter of opinion whether hiding the OU tree from users is a good or bad thing.

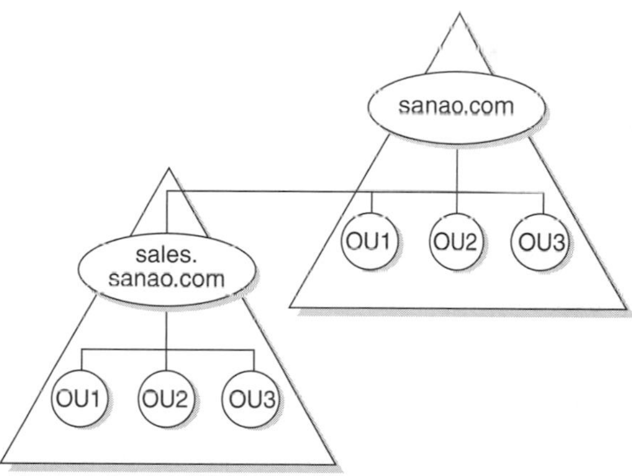

Figure 3.6 The Sales domain is a child of the Sanao domain. If you look at the tree via My Network Places of Windows 2000, you will see Sales as a sibling of the first-level OUs of Sanao.

Managing OUs

Managing OUs includes the following tasks:

- Creating OUs
- Setting OU properties
- Moving, renaming, and deleting OUs
- Setting Group Policy, checking the Resultant Set of Policy (RSoP), assigning a COM+ partition set, assigning permissions, and delegating administrative tasks

In this chapter, we focus on the first three items in the list. The last item is discussed in later chapters as follows: Group Policy and RSoP, see Chapter 7; permissions and delegating, see Chapter 4; and COM+ partition sets, see Windows Server 2003 Help and Support Center.

As you read on, we encourage you to try these management tasks in your domain. You cannot do any irreversible harm to your domain.

Creating OUs

Creating an OU is as easy as creating a disk folder. Just follow these steps:

1. Launch the Users and Computers snap-in.
2. Right-click the parent OU you want (or the domain object) and choose New, Organizational Unit.
3. Type in the name you want and press Enter.

IF YOU KNOW NDS Unfortunately, the Insert key doesn't do the trick here as it does with the NwAdmin software for NDS.

The maximum number of characters in an OU's name is 64, which is usually more than enough. After all, it is best to use short (but descriptive) names. The OU name is a Unicode character string, so at least in theory you could have some Gurmukhi characters in an OU name. You could also put all the possible punctuation characters in an OU name, but this would make your life harder if every now and then you had to type the distinguished name of such an OU.

Setting OU Properties

After you have created an OU, you can set its properties by right-clicking the OU and choosing Properties. The dialog box in Figure 3.7 will appear.

Table 3.6 lists the property choices. None of them affects the way Windows works. They just provide information for human beings.

Table 3.6 shows the property LDAP names, which you will need if you use certain Resource Kit utilities or scripting, or if you set per-property permissions. One of the properties in the table is indexed, and five are part of the global catalog. Indexing makes searches faster, and the global catalog makes reading properties faster if you have multiple domains and sites.

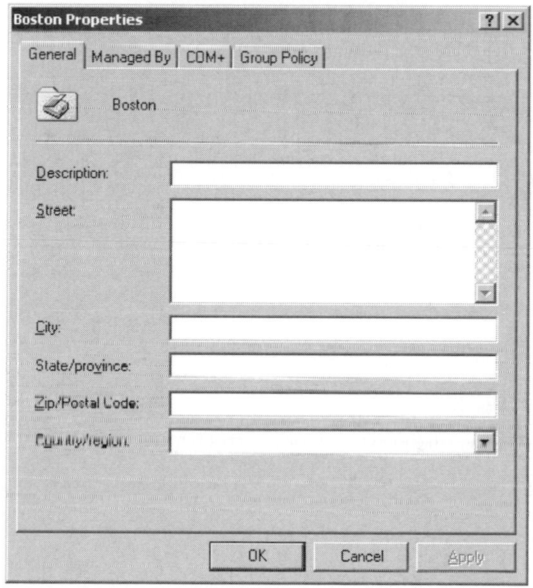

Figure 3.7 Some of the properties that you can enter for an OU include address-related information.

NOTE When you set properties for an OU, if you add a user in the Managed By tab as the "manager" of an OU, that user doesn't get any permissions for the OU. This setting is purely informational. The other fields on that tab are the manager's properties, not the OU's.

Table 3.6 Properties of an OU Object

Property	LDAP Name*	Syntax	Indexed	In GC
Description	`description`	Text (1,024)**		X
Street	`street` (Street-Address)	Text (1,024) (Each new line takes two characters.)		X
City	`l` (Locality-Name)	Text (128)	X	X
State/province	`st` (State-Or-Province-Name)	Text (128)		X
Zip/Postal Code	`postalCode`	Text (40)		
Country/region***	`co` (Text-Country)	Text (128)		
	`c` (Country-Name)	Text (3)		X
	`countryCode`	Integer		
Managed By	`managedBy`	DN**** (You select a user or contact from a list.)		

* In addition to the LDAP name, each property has a common name. It is included in parentheses if it is different from the LDAP name.

** If the syntax is Text (i.e., a string of Unicode characters), we indicate also the maximum number of characters in the property (e.g., 1,024).

*** Country/region is stored in three properties: `co` contains the country's name (e.g., UNITED STATES), `c` contains the country's abbreviation (e.g., US), and `countryCode` contains the numeric ISO country code (e.g., 840).

**** DN = distinguished name.

NOTE Behind the scenes, the base schema lists 123 possible properties for an OU (104 in AD2000). Most of them are not used, so it doesn't matter that you can set only a few of them using the Users and Computers snap-in.

If you have Advanced Features turned on in the Users and Computers snap-in, you will see also the Security and Object tabs in the properties dialog box. The information in the former tab is discussed in Chapter 4, and the information in the latter tab is discussed in Chapter 5.

Moving, Renaming, and Deleting OUs in a Tree

You may find that your original OU tree is no longer optimal as a result of either insufficient planning or changed circumstances. If you need to rearrange your OU tree, you can easily move, rename, and delete OUs.

To move an OU inside a domain, either (a) drag it to a new location with the mouse, (b) use cut/paste with the keyboard or mouse, or (c) right-click the OU, select Move, and then choose the destination from the OU tree that opens up and click OK.

Note that not all of the OU's group policies and permissions move with it.

- Group policies and permissions that are assigned for the object being moved move with the object.
- Group policies and permissions that are inherited from above do not move with the object being moved. Instead, the OU will inherit new ones in its new location.

You can move several sibling OUs at once. Select them in the right-hand pane of the snap-in by using the Shift and/or Ctrl keys. Then proceed as previously described.

NOTE If you want to move an OU to another domain in your forest, you need to use another tool, such as the Support Tools command-line tool MoveTree. It is discussed further in Chapter 6.

You can rename an OU either by right-clicking the OU and selecting Rename or by selecting the OU and pressing F2. After you type the new name, press Enter.

Similarly, you delete an OU by right-clicking it and selecting Delete or by selecting the OU and pressing the Delete key. If the OU being deleted contains other objects, you are prompted to accept deleting them, too.

Planning OUs

Even though "OU" stands for "organizational unit," you don't necessarily create OUs to match the organizational units of your company. You create OUs for administrative units, physical locations, and object types (e.g., an OU for users, an OU for printers, and so on), or you can create OUs based on corporate structure.

OU trees are like folder trees on disk: There isn't just one "right" way to create them. When planning your OUs, keep in mind the following aspects of OUs:

- OUs are purely logical entities: They are not related to physical partitions or replication.
- OUs are for delegation of administration.
- OUs are for Group Policy (including application publishing and assignment).
- OUs are for controlling object visibility.
- OUs are easy to reorganize. However, reorganizing them may confuse some users if they have learned a certain structure.
- Each OU should have a specific need and purpose to exist.
- There is no practical limit on how deep the OU tree can be. However, keep in mind the previous bullet about a specific purpose for each OU.
- OUs are mainly administrative units; typically users do not see them (although Windows 2000 users can if they want).

If you have more than one domain, you might want the OU trees in all domains to be planned according to similar principles.

The aforesaid suggests that you should create OUs based on how administration is organized in your organization. The three typical scenarios are the following:

- Geographical: If Boston has its own administrators and London has its own, you should probably create the Boston and London OUs.
- Object type: If some people administer users and others administer printers, you should probably create the Employees and Printers OUs, for example.
- Organization: If the Sales department has its own administrators and Production has its own, you should probably create the Sales and Production OUs.

It is also quite possible that more than one of these three divisions are used in your organization. In this case, you should create one level based on one division and another level based on another division. For example, your top-level OUs could be based on geography, and second-level OUs based on object type.

Administering Users, InetOrgPersons, and Contacts

The traditional reason for creating user accounts is to give your users a means to log on to the network. The properties of a user's account control the user's access to the network, and the properties can define some network services for the user in question. Examples of these properties are the password, the account expiration date, a requirement for a smart card logon, and the network path of the user's home folder.

Directory services such as Active Directory have brought a second aspect to user accounts. At this point, we tend to refer to them as "user objects" instead of "accounts." In addition to being a means of access to the network and its services, a user object can store additional information about the user. Some of this information is meant for other human beings—for example, the user's fax number, title, or Web home page address. As a container of such "contact" properties, a user object can function much like an address book entry. A user object can also include properties for use by directory-enabled applications (e.g., Exchange e-mail, a faxing application, personnel-management software, and so on).

In addition to user objects, you can create *contact objects*. Typically you create a user object for each employee of your organization and a contact object for each person outside your organization whose contact information you want to store. A contact object can contain a subset of the properties that a user object can contain, as you can see in Figure 3.8 and Table 3.7.

The Users and Computers snap in shows the properties of a contact and user object in a number of tabs in the properties dialog box, as shown in Figure 3.8.

Table 3.7 lists the tabs shown in Figure 3.8, except for the tabs Remote control, Terminal Services Profile, Environment, and Sessions, which are related to Terminal Services. (We don't cover them in this book about Active Directory.) Table 3.7 introduces the terms *significant properties* and *informational properties* and shows that a user object can contain both types of properties, but a contact object can contain only the latter.

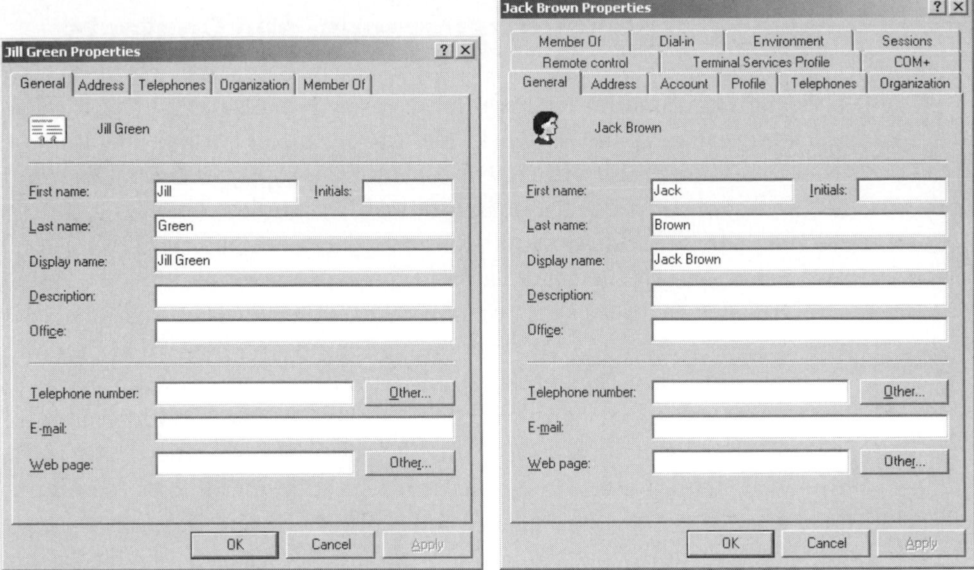

Figure 3.8 Contact object properties on the left are shown in five tabs. User object on the right has the same five tabs of a contact object and eight additional tabs. The five tabs that appear in both screen shots (General, Address, Telephones, Organization, and Member Of) contain the same properties except that the Member Of tab contains a Primary Group setting only for user objects.

The Users and Computers snap-in contains tabs for user and/or contact objects that are not shown in Figure 3.8.

- The Published Certificates tab is visible only when you turn on Advanced Features from the View menu.
- Turning on Advanced Features also makes the Object and Security tabs visible. Because they are common to all object types, we don't include them in this discussion of user and contact objects.
- Applications can add tabs. For example, if you install Exchange 2000, it will add some tabs, such as Exchange General and Exchange Features.

To summarize the functions for user objects (and to add a couple of functions):

Table 3.7 The Nature of User and Contact Objects

Tab Name	User Object	Contact Object	Category*
Account	X		*Significant properties:* Properties that control user access to the network or define network services for the user
Profile	X		
Published Certificates	X		
COM+	X		
Member Of**	X		
Dial-in	X		
General	X	X	*Informational properties* Properties that contain information for human beings or are meant for some applications to use
Address	X	X	
Telephones	X	X	
Organization	X	X	
Member Of	X	X	

* The terms "significant properties" and "informational properties" are not official. They are introduced in this book to distinguish these two types of properties.

** The Member Of tab is shown twice because it has two natures: security and distribution list. The first nature applies only to user objects, but the second nature applies to both user and contact objects.

- A user object is an account that a user can log on with (using the corresponding significant properties).
- A user object is a placeholder for a collection of informational properties.
- A user object is a *security principal*. This means that you can give permissions to the user for resources and assign security group memberships to the user.
- The location of a user object in Active Directory dictates which group policies apply to the corresponding user.

A contact object (actually, the person who corresponds to the object) can never log on to the network. Also, a contact object is not a security principal, so it cannot have any permissions. Of course, even if a contact object had permissions, no one would be able to use them, because a contact object cannot be used to log on.

The third type of people is the inetOrgPerson object, which is new to AD2003. An inetOrgPerson object is identical to a user object in practically every way. For more information, see the "Creating InetOrg Persons" section a little later in this chapter.

When you start to manage users and contacts, your tasks will include some or all of the following.

- Create users, inetOrgPersons, and contacts.
- Set user, inetOrgPerson, and contact properties.
- Copy users and inetOrgPersons, and move, rename, and delete users, inetOrgPerson, and contacts.
- Assign Group Policy and permissions, and delegate administration.

The next sections cover the first three items, but as mentioned earlier, the last item will be discussed in later chapters (Chapter 7 and Chapter 4).

If you want to try the management tasks discussed in this section, create a test OU where you can create test users.

Creating Users

When you choose to create a user with the Users and Computers snap-in, you use a three-page wizard to do so. Figure 3.9 shows the first page

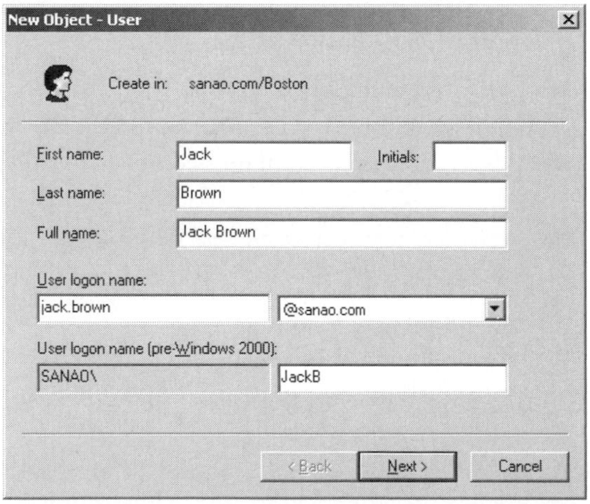

Figure 3.9 On the first page of the user creation wizard, you enter the various names of the new user.

of the wizard, where you enter the various names of the new user. Figure 3.10 shows the second page of the wizard, where you can specify a password and some password settings. For example, you can require that a new user change her password at first logon so that only the user knows it and only she can legitimately log on with that account. Alternatively, you can specify that the user cannot change the password. This capability is useful, for example, when several users use the same account. With this setting, you can prevent any of the users from changing the common password. The third page of the wizard displays a summary of what you have selected.

Table 3.8 describes the different name properties shown in the first page of the user creation wizard. All the name properties in the table are Unicode strings, and all, except Initials, are indexed and part of the global catalog.

WARNING Experience with Windows NT shows that using even common European characters, such as ä, in names may cause problems. Even though they are supported in principle, many command-line and graphical utilities can't handle them.

In addition to the name properties in Table 3.8, each object has a distinguished name and a canonical name (see Chapter 1). Furthermore,

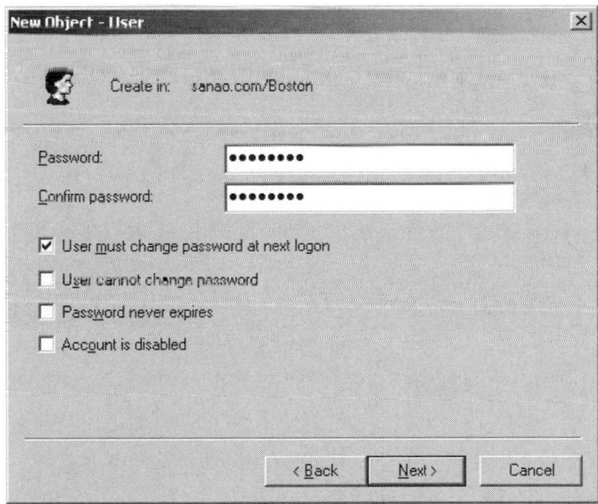

Figure 3.10 On the second page of the user creation wizard, you can specify a password and the way it will be used.

Table 3.8 Name Properties of a User Object

Property	LDAP Name	Maximum Length (Characters)	Required	Unique	Description
First name	`givenName`	64		No	Purely informational.
Initials*	`initials`	6		No	Purely informational.
Last name	`sn` (Surname)	64		No	Purely informational.
Full name	`name` (RDN) and `cn` (CommonName)	64	X	Within OU	This becomes the object's common name in the OU tree. The wizard suggests "firstname initials. lastname".**
Display name	`displayName`	256		No	Purely informational, initially the same as Full name. You can change it later independent of Full name.

* The user creation wizard treats Initials as the middle-name initial and not the first- and last-name initials (for example, "JB" for "Jack Brown").

** You can modify the forest configuration so that the default full name is "lastname, firstname" instead of the normal "firstname lastname." We explain how to do this in Table 9.8 in Chapter 9.

Table 3.8 Name Properties of a User Object (*cont.*)

Property	LDAP Name	Maximum Length (Characters)	Required	Unique	Description
User logon name	`userPrincipalName`	1,024	X	Within forest	User can log on using this name on a Windows 2000 or later computer. This name is often the same as the user's e-mail address.
User logon name (pre-Windows 2000)	`sAMAccountName`	256 (schema rule), 20 (SAM rule)***	X	Within domain	User can log on using this name on any old or new Windows machine. Despite its label, this name can be used throughout Windows 2000 and later. This name also becomes the name of the user's profile folder when she logs on for the first time.

*** The maximum length of the `sAMAccountName` property is 256 characters in regard to schema rules. On properties that relate to Windows NT compatibility, however, Active Directory enforces SAM rules also. Consequently, the actual maximum length is 20 characters.

there are two name properties in the base schema that the snap-in doesn't display: the middle name and the generation qualifier (Jr., Sr., III, and so on).

In most cases, you create one user object for each network user. However, some situations call for a second user account.

- If a user is an administrator, he might have two user accounts: one with normal privileges for everyday use and another one with administrative privileges. It is safer if he uses the latter account only when performing administrative tasks.
- If a user needs to use several forests and there is no explicit trust between them, she needs a user account in each forest.
- If a user accesses the network with a mobile device through the Mobile Information Server, he may have a second account with fewer rights and permissions for this mobile access than his normal account has.
- If a user has a stand-alone server or workstation that is in a workgroup instead of a domain, he will need a *local* user account in that machine. Active Directory user accounts cannot be used when the computer hasn't joined a domain.

UPN Suffixes

User logon names consist of two parts: the actual user name (e.g., `jack.brown`) and a *UPN suffix* (e.g., `@sanao.com`). For the first part you can enter any text, but for the second part you must choose the UPN suffix from a fixed list. By default, the list contains the name of the domain (e.g., `sales.sanao.com`) and the name of the root domain (e.g., `sanao.com`).

An enterprise administrator of a forest can add UPN suffixes to the list using the Domains and Trusts snap-in (click the Start button and then select Administrative Tools, Active Directory Domains and Trusts). Once the snap-in has started, the enterprise administrator right-clicks the uppermost line of the left pane (i.e., Active Directory Domains and Trusts) and selects Properties. The dialog box that appears enables the administrator to define additional UPN suffixes.

If the root domain is `corp.sanao.com`, for example, the administrator can add a UPN suffix `sanao.com`, so the users in the forest can have logon names such as `jack.brown@sanao.com` instead of `jack.brown@corp.sanao.com`.

Creating InetOrgPersons

AD2003 includes a new object type (that is, object class), inetOrgPerson, which is identical to the user object type in practically every way. InetOrgPerson was defined in RFC 2798 to represent a standard network user, and many other directory services use it for this purpose. Therefore, inetOrgPerson was brought along to Active Directory so that it would be easier to interoperate with these other products or to migrate them to Active Directory.

Although inetOrgPerson should be identical to user, Microsoft recommends that you test it with your applications that would use Active Directory as an authentication method, and your other projected usage scenarios, before you actually start using inetOrgPerson objects.

If inetOrgPerson objects are not needed in your forest, you can modify the forest schema so that InetOrgPerson doesn't appear in the New context menu of the Users and Computers snap-in. You would need to change the `defaultHidingValue` property of the `inetOrgPerson` schema class definition to TRUE. This setting affects all administrators of the forest, unless they use some other tool to create objects. For more information, see Chapter 9 or Microsoft Knowledge Base article 311555 at `http://www.microsoft.com`.

Creating Contacts

To create a contact, you use the contact creation wizard in the Users and Computers snap-in. The wizard has only one page, which is shown in Figure 3.11. A contact object is like an address book entry for e-mail and other applications, and it contains only informational properties. It usually represents a person who is not working for your company, and a contact cannot log on to your network. Therefore, you don't specify a logon name for a contact object. The "Full name" entry becomes the common name of the object in the OU tree.

Setting User, InetOrgPerson, and Contact Properties

You can define more than 50 settings for each user and more than 30 settings for each contact. Behind the scenes, a user object can have 257 properties (207 in AD2000) and a contact object can have 165 properties (138 in AD2000). Fortunately, the only *required* properties are a few names (which we mentioned in our discussion of creating users).

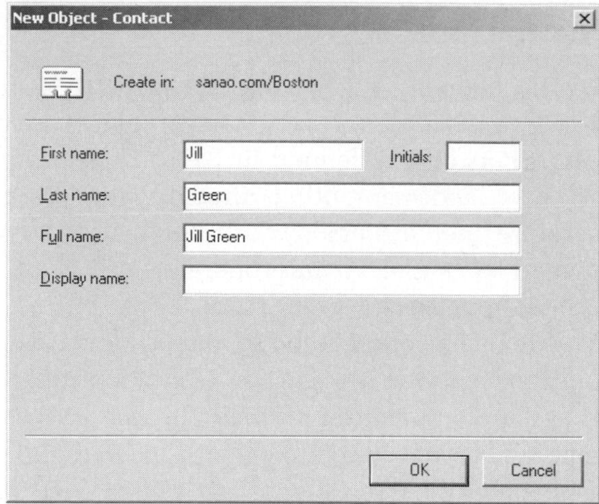

Figure 3.11 When you create a contact, you don't specify logon names. Also, there is no second page, which would have the password settings (i.e., significant properties) that you saw when creating a user object.

NOTE Although we mention exact counts here and in many other places, you don't have to know the exact numbers. We use exact counts because it is simply easier to express "165 properties" than "well over 150 properties." It is not always possible to be precise, however. We say that you can define "more than 50" settings. In this case, there is more than one way to count the settings in the user interface.

Of the many possible settings, the major significant properties of a user object are set in the Account, Profile, and Dial-in tabs. The major informational properties of user and contact objects are set in the General, Address, Telephones, and Organization tabs. The Member Of tab is covered in the "Administering Groups" section of this chapter.

NOTE Windows provides context-sensitive help for each of the settings. In addition, many of the setting names are self-explanatory.

Significant Properties of a User Object: The Account Tab

Figure 3.12 shows the contents of the Account tab, which sets significant properties of a user. It includes settings that control how and when the

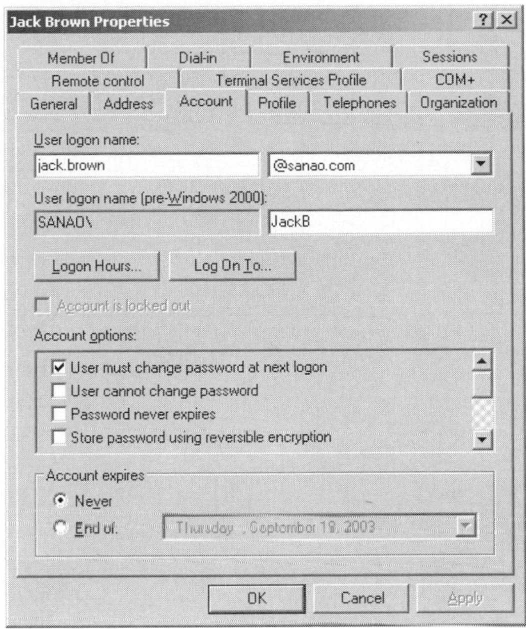

Figure 3.12 The Account tab of the user Jack Brown

user can log on, as well as a few settings that control passwords. Table 3.9 lists other settings, except the 11 yes/no check boxes, which appear in Table 3.10.

NOTE Because Logon Hours is internally stored as GMT/UTC, an administrator who looks at a user's settings will see the hours as local to the administrator's time zone, regardless of where that is. For example, if a Boston administrator allows a user in Boston to log on between 8:00 AM and 3:00 PM, an administrator in Belgium (6 hours ahead of Boston) who checks that user's setting for logon hours would see times between 2:00 PM and 9:00 PM. There are no adjustments for daylight saving time, however. This is good because this way the allowed logon hours won't change twice a year, when daylight saving time and standard time start.

Table 3.10 lists the yes/no settings in the Account tab. You cannot set the first setting—you can only clear it. The other ten settings you can either set or clear. Eight of the 11 settings are stored in a property called `userAccountControl` so that one bit represents each setting.

Table 3.9 Significant Properties of a User Object: The Account Tab

Property/ Setting	LDAP Name	Syntax	Description
User logon name	`userPrincipal-Name`	Text (1,024)	User can log on using this name on a Windows 2000 or later computer. This name is often the same as the user's e-mail address.
User logon name (pre-Windows 2000)	`sAMAccount-Name`	Text (256 [schema rule], 20 [SAM rule])*	User can log on using this name on any old or new Windows machine. Despite its label, this name can be used throughout Windows 2000 and later. Also, this name becomes the name of the user's profile folder when she logs on to each Windows NT/2000/XP/Server 2003 computer for the first time.
Logon Hours**	`logonHours`	(Binary)	Weekdays and hours in one-hour increments during which the user is allowed to log on.
Log On To/Logon Workstations	`user-Workstations`	Text (1,024)	A list of computer NetBIOS names that the user is allowed to log on to.
Account options	`userAccount-Control`	Yes/No	These 11 settings are described in Table 3.10.
Account expires	`account-Expires`	Date	The date after which the user account is no longer usable (although it doesn't vanish then). You can use this for temporary users.

* If the syntax is Text (i.e., a string of Unicode characters), we indicate also the maximum number of characters in the property (e.g., 256).

** The Logon Hours property is set and shown in local time but internally stored as GMT/UTC. The amount of time zone correction is taken from the local computer configuration.

The setting "Account is locked out" is stored in the `lockoutTime` property, the setting "User must change password at next logon" is stored in the `pwdLastSet` property, and the setting "User cannot change password" is determined by permissions. You can learn more about the way settings are stored in Chapter 11.

Table 3.10 Significant Properties of a User Object: The Account Options

Setting	Description
Account is locked out	If someone tries to log on and enters a wrong password too many times, the account is locked either for a specified time or until the administrator unlocks it. You define the acceptable number of wrong attempts and associated time periods using Group Policy.
User must change password at next logon	After you assign a password to a user, it is a good practice to require the user to change it as soon as he logs on. Then you won't know it anymore.
User cannot change password	This is useful, for example, if several users use one account. You can use this setting to prevent them from changing the password.
Password never expires	You can force users to change their passwords periodically (e.g., every 30 days), but then use this setting to exempt some users from this policy. This is useful, for example, when defining passwords for service accounts. In that case, there is no human being to change the password every month.
Store password using reversible encryption	Normally Active Directory stores passwords using irreversible encryption, meaning that the user's clear-text password cannot be calculated (except through a special "dictionary attack"). You must enable this setting if the corresponding user is using a Macintosh workstation or if she wants to use IIS digest authentication to be able to pass a firewall.
Account is disabled	If a user is away a long time, you can "freeze" the user's account for that time but still not delete it.
Smart card is required for interactive logon	Self-explanatory.

(continued)

Table 3.10 Significant Properties of a User Object: The Account Options *(cont.)*

Setting	Description
Account is trusted for delegation	This setting is described in Chapter 4 in the "Impersonation and Delegation" section. Note that when the domain is on the Windows Server 2003 functional level, this setting appears on the Delegation tab, and that tab is only visible for accounts that have been assigned service principal names.)
Account is sensitive and cannot be delegated	This setting is described in Chapter 4 in the "Impersonation and Delegation" section.
Use DES encryption types for this account	This setting causes Windows 2000 and later to use Kerberos DES-CBC-MD5 instead of the default RSADSI RC4-HMAC for this user account. The setting affects how Kerberos ticket-granting tickets (TGTs) are encrypted. Data Encryption Standard (DES) is used to encrypt both the ticket and the key of the initial TGT, and DES is also used to encrypt the key of the forwarded TGT. However, RSA is used to encrypt the ticket of the forwarded TGT.
Do not require Kerberos preauthentication	Normally Windows 2000 and later use preauthentication with Kerberos authentication, but it is not compatible with all implementations of Kerberos. Consequently, you must not require preauthentication if the corresponding user account is going to use such an implementation. Selecting this option may expose the user account to denial-of-service attacks.

There is one password setting that is not visible in the Users and Computers snap-in. You could type the following command on the command line when sitting at a domain controller:

```
NET USER JackB /PasswordReq:No
```

This command relieves JackB from having a password. For example, even though other users of the domain would be required to use at least a six-character password, he would not. Note that you must use the pre–Windows 2000 name of the user in this command.

Even though this command relieves Jack from having a password, he cannot clear his password—an administrator must do this. If Jack later changes his password to "abcdef," he cannot change it back to empty.

You can see the current setting for Jack using the following command:

```
NET USER JackB
```

NOTE The minimum length of a password for domain users is set using Group Policy, which is discussed in Chapter 7.

Microsoft has prepared a long and thorough online document called Account Passwords and Policies, which you can access at the address `http://www.microsoft.com/technet/prodtechnol/windowsserver2003/technologies/security/bpactlck.mspx`.

Significant Properties of a User Object: The Profile Tab

Figure 3.13 shows the contents of the Profile tab. The Profile tab is not about control as the Account tab is—it's about providing services to users. Table 3.11 lists the Profile tab's four significant properties. They all may contain an "unlimited" number of Unicode characters.

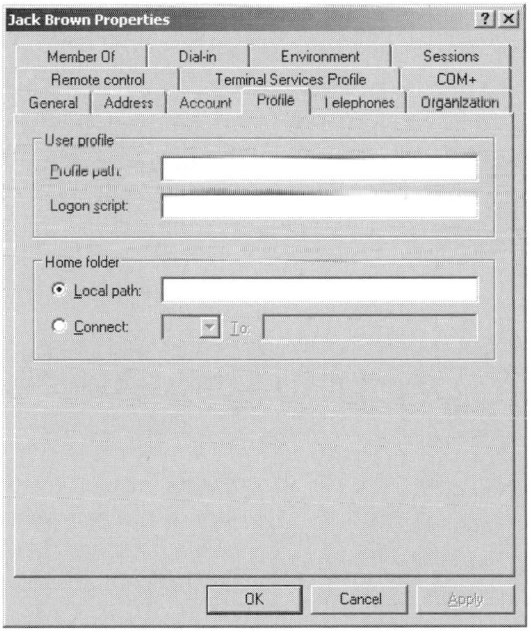

Figure 3.13 The Profile tab of the user Jack Brown

Table 3.11 Significant Properties of a User Object: The Profile Tab

Property	LDAP Name	Description
Profile path	`profilePath`	This specifies a Uniform Naming Convention (UNC) name, such as \\Server\Prof$\JackB, to be the network folder where the user's roaming profile is stored. This way, Jack's roaming profile is downloaded to whichever Windows NT/2000/XP workstation he logs on to, and it is uploaded back to the server when he logs off. The dollar sign ($) in the `Prof$` sharename makes it invisible so that users don't browse it.
Logon script	`scriptPath`	This field is the old (i.e., Windows NT) way to define a logon script for a user. The new way (i.e., Active Directory) is to use Group Policy. An example of this path is Logon.Bat. The name is relative to the UNC path *anydomaincontroller*\Netlogon.
Home folder: Local path/To	`homeDirectory`	You can assign each user a private or shared folder on some server. The To field defines the path—for example, \\Server\Users\JackB. If possible, the snap-in creates the folder for you. It also gives Administrators and the user Full Control. The snap-in doesn't, however, remove the inherited permissions, so it is quite possible that the Users group will have Read permission for the new home folder. A home folder is an alternative to the My Documents folder, which you can also store on a server using Group Policy. When saving documents, newer applications usually default to *`My Documents`*, whereas some may use the `%homedrive%` and `%homepath%` environment variables. The "Local path" field defines a path such as D:\JackB, but that path exists on only one local machine.
Home folder: Connect	`homeDrive`	A drive letter that connects (or maps) to the user's home folder.

You may use the `%username%` environment variable in the "Profile path" and "Home folder: To" fields. Its value will be the user's logon name (pre–Windows 2000)—that is, his "downlevel logon name." For example, the path \\Server\Prof$\%username% actually means \\Server\Prof$\JackB. This variable is handy when you edit several users at once. At that time, for example, you will be able to set the home folder for several users at once.

Significant Properties of a User Object: The Dial-in Tab

The settings in the Dial-in tab define whether the user may use dial-in or virtual private network (VPN) connections, and if so, in what way. These significant properties apply more to managing communication settings than to managing user settings. Therefore, this tab is outside the scope of this book. The screen shot in Figure 3.14 is provided here for reference.

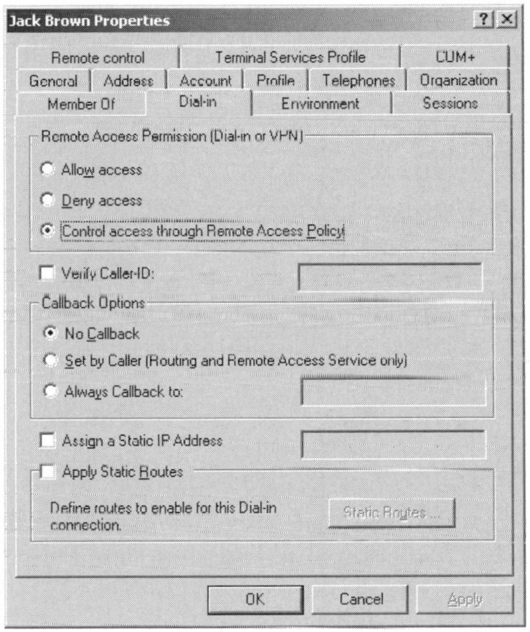

Figure 3.14 The Dial-in tab defines whether the user may use dial-in or VPN connections.

Informational Properties of Users and Contacts

As previously stated, the informational properties don't affect the network user (unless you create a query-based group with the Authorization Manager snap-in and base that group on some otherwise informational property). They provide information for other people and for applications that use them. Consequently, these two criteria dictate how you use each of the informational properties. We cannot tell you here the rules to use each informational property, but we can offer a few general guidelines.

If you or any of your users are not interested in these properties, and if you don't have applications to take advantage of them, you can simply leave all the informational properties blank.

Except for Country/region and Manager, both of which you select from a list, you edit all the informational properties in text fields that have very little format checking. These fields have no stringent requirements for acceptable entries. This means that you could fill in the property fields with just about anything, such as your favorite recipes or the hair color of each user, even though the property label indicates a phone number.

Although you have free rein in determining informational properties, the following are some guidelines to keep in mind.

- Use each property consistently. Ideally, you have a written document that describes which properties are in use in your company and in what format the information should be entered.
- Some of the properties can be used in search operations. Here, consistency is especially important.
- Some of the properties can be used in query-based groups. Here, consistency is even more important.
- By default, each user can see all of his or her properties. Each user can also change those properties that are categorized as Personal Information and Web Information (together consisting of 43 properties, and the same number in AD2000).
- By default, every logged-on user can see certain properties of all other users. These properties are categorized as General Information, Public Information, Personal Information, and Web Information, and they consist of a total of 93 properties (89 in AD2000).

NOTE The information categories mentioned here (Personal Information, General Information, and so on) are used in the management of permissions. Therefore, they are covered in detail in the next chapter, which deals with securing Active Directory. Unfortunately, the categories are quite different from the tabs in user properties. For example, General Information doesn't have anything to do with the General tab.

Table 3.12 lists the properties in the four tabs containing informational properties. We don't include screen shots, because they would show just a number of text boxes.

Table 3.12 Informational Properties of User and Contact Objects

Property	LDAP Name	Syntax (Characters)	Index	GC	Comments
General Tab					
First name	`givenName`	Text (64)	X	X	
Initials	`initials`	Text (6)			Even though the creation wizard treats this as a middle-name initial, you can enter "JB" for an existing Jack Brown.
Last name	`sn` (Surname)	Text (64)	X	X	
Display name	`displayName`	Text (256)	X	X	This is not the common name (`cn`) you see in the OU tree. The user's display name is shown in the Computer Locked dialog box, for example.
Description	`description`	Text (1,024)		X	
Office	`physical-Delivery-OfficeName`	Text (128)	X		
Telephone number	`telephone-Number`	Text (64)		X	This is the primary office phone number.

(continued)

Table 3.12 Informational Properties of User and Contact Objects *(cont.)*

Property	LDAP Name	Syntax (Characters)	Index	GC	Comments
Phone Number (Others)	`other-Telephone`	Text (64)			These are the other office phone numbers.
E-mail	`mail`	Text (256)	X	X	
Web page	`wWWHomePage`	Text (2048)			`http://something`, `ftp://something`, `file://something`.
Web Page Address (Others)	`url`	Text			A list of multiple values.
Address Tab					
Street	`street-Address`	Text (1,024)			
P.O. Box	`post-OfficeBox`	Text (40)			
City	`l` (Locality-Name)	Text (128)	X	X	
State/province	`st` (State-Or-Province-Name)	Text (128)		X	
Zip/Postal Code	`postalCode`	Text (40)			
Country/region	`co` (Text-Country)	Text (128)			For example, "UNITED STATES."
	`c` (Country-Name)	Text (3)		X	For example, "US."
	`countryCode`	Integer			For example, "840."
Telephones Tab					
Home	`homePhone`	Text (64)		X	

Table 3.12 Informational Properties of User and Contact Objects *(cont.)*

Property	LDAP Name	Syntax (Characters)	Index	GC	Comments
Home Phone Number (Others)	`otherHome-Phone`	Text (64)			A list of multiple values.
Pager	`pager`	Text (64)			
Pager Number (Others)	`otherPager`	Text (64)			A list of multiple values.
Mobile	`mobile`	Text (64)			
Mobile Number (Others)	`otherMobile`	Text (64)			A list of multiple values.
Fax	`facsimile-Telephone-Number`	Text (64)			
Fax Number (Others)	`other-Facsimile-Telephone-Number`	Text (64)			A list of multiple values.
IP phone	`ipPhone`	Text (64)		X	
IP Phone Number (Others)	`other-IpPhone`	Text		X	A list of multiple values.
Notes	`info`	Text (1,024)			
Organization Tab					
Title	`title`	Text (64)			
Department	`department`	Text (64)			
Company	`company`	Text (64)			
Manager	`manager`	DN; you select a user or contact from a list		X	Setting this doesn't give the manager any permissions.

(continued)

Table 3.12 Informational Properties of User and Contact Objects *(cont.)*

Property	LDAP Name	Syntax (Characters)	Index	GC	Comments
Direct reports	`directReports`	DN			This property is read-only in the snap-in. If you set Jill to be Jack's manager, Jack will appear in the direct reports of Jill.

The "Country/region" field has a fixed set of options from which you choose. The result is stored in three properties, as described in the table.

Editing Multiple Users

The Windows Server 2003 version of the Users and Computers snap-in enables you to edit multiple objects at the same time. Typically, you would use this feature for user objects (or possibly for inetOrgPerson objects). For other object types, you can edit only the description text.

As you see in Figure 3.15, you can edit quite a few properties for multiple users simultaneously.

Other Operations to Manage Users, InetOrgPersons, and Contacts

After you have created a number of users and contacts (and possibly inetOrgPersons) and packed them full of properties, you are ready to perform other operations. Open the context menu by right-clicking with your mouse or press a shortcut key to manipulate existing users and contacts in the following ways:

- Copy (only users and inetOrgPersons, not contacts)
- Move
- Rename
- Delete
- Disable an account (only users and inetOrgPersons, not contacts)

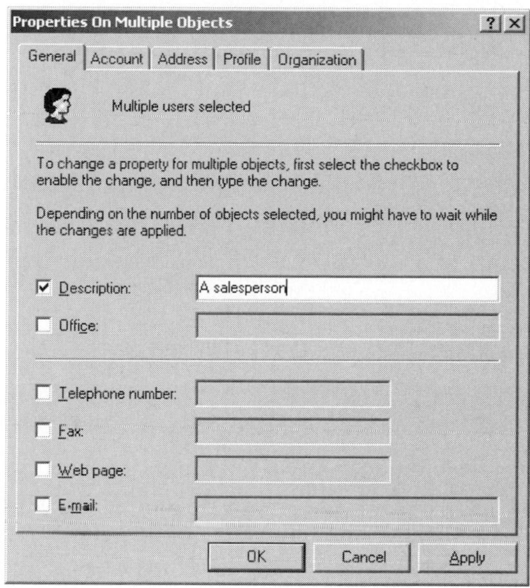

Figure 3.15 You can edit quite a few properties for multiple users simultaneously.

- Reset a password (only users and inetOrgPersons, not contacts)
- Open a home page
- Send e-mail

Copying Users and InetOrgPersons

You can copy an existing user or inetOrgPerson to create a new one. You do this by right-clicking the object and then selecting Copy. This launches a wizard similar to the one that enables you to create users from scratch. For brevity, we only talk here about users, because inetOrgPersons behave identically.

Copying a user saves time if the new user will have many of the same properties as an existing one. When you copy the user, by default 33 properties of the existing user are copied to the new one. However, only 20 of these properties are visible in the Users and Computers snap-in. Table 3.13 lists these properties, as well as some other categories.

The remaining 13 properties may have values to copy if you have set them programmatically with ADSI Edit or with some other means. However, it's not likely that you have done so.

Obviously, several properties (e.g., names and phone numbers) are personal and therefore not meaningful to copy. On the other hand, there are properties that would be nice to copy, but which are by default not included in the 33 copied properties. Table 3.13 lists five such properties.

If you anticipate needing to create several similar user objects, you can create user templates. A user template is a normal user object that represents a typical user of some department. When you need a new

Table 3.13 Properties That Are Copied When Users Are Copied

Category	Properties
Copied and visible in the snap-in (20 properties)	`accountExpires`, `c` (Country/region)*, `co` (Country/region), `company`, `countryCode` (Country/region), `department`, `homeDirectory`, `homeDrive`, `l` (City), `logonHours`, `manager`, `memberOf`, `postalCode` (Zip/Postal Code), `postOfficeBox`, `primaryGroupID`, `profilePath`, `scriptPath` (Logon script), `st` (State/province), `userAccountControl` (Account options), and `user Workstations` (Logon Workstations)
Copied but not visible in the snap-in (13 properties)	`Assistant`, `codePage`, `division`, `employeeType`, `localeID`, `logonWorkstation`, `maxStorage`, `otherLoginWorkstations`, `postalAddress`, `preferredOU`, `showInAddressBook`, `showInAdvancedViewOnly`, and `street`
Not copied but visible in the snap-in and would be nice to be copied (5 properties)	`description`, `facsimileTelephone Number` (Fax), `otherFacsimile TelephoneNumber` (Fax Number (Others)), `physicalDelivery OfficeName` (Office), and `street Address` (Street)

* We have included in parentheses the property names that you see in the Users and Computers snap-in if those names are quite different from the LDAP names in the table.

user for that department, you can copy the user template to be the new user and modify it as necessary.

The copied properties are defined in the schema. You can add attributes (e.g., `streetAddress`) to the list, as Chapter 9 will explain.

Moving Users, InetOrgPersons, and Contacts

Every now and then you may want to move some users, inetOrgPersons, or contacts from one OU to another. You move them within a domain either (a) by dragging the object to a new location with the mouse, (b) by using cut/paste with the keyboard or mouse, or (c) by right-clicking the object, selecting Move, and then choosing the destination from the OU tree that opens up and clicking OK. Note that

- Permissions that are assigned for the object being moved move with the object.
- Group policies (regarding users and inetOrgPersons) and permissions that are inherited by the object from above do not move with the object being moved. Instead, the moved object inherits the new group policies and permissions in its new location.

You can move several sibling objects at once. Select them in the right-hand pane of the snap-in by using the Shift and/or Ctrl keys. Then proceed as usual.

It is possible to move objects to another domain in your forest. To do so, you need to use another tool, such as the Support Tools command-line tool MoveTree, which is discussed in Chapter 6.

Renaming Users, InetOrgPersons, and Contacts

You can rename a user, inetOrgPerson, or contact by right-clicking the object and selecting Rename or by selecting the object and pressing F2. A third way is to click an already selected object. After you type the new name, press Enter. Because these objects have many names, you have a chance to change one or all of the names in a dialog box, as Figures 3.16 and 3.17 show.

After you rename a user, the old name still appears in the following properties: E-mail, Web page, Profile path, Logon script (if using personal), and Home folder. Also, the corresponding physical folders, as well as the local copy of the user's profile (i.e., C:\Documents and

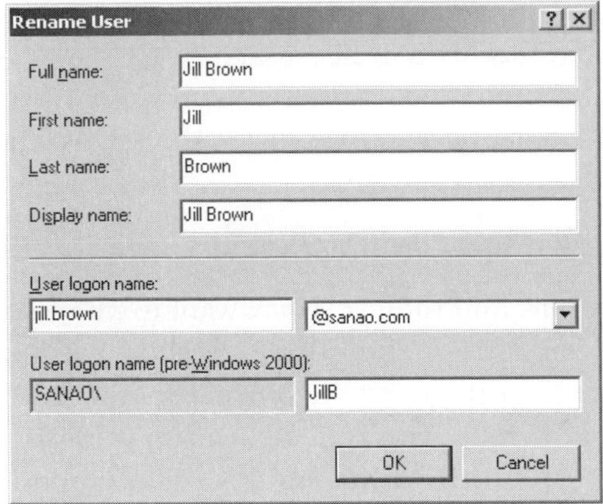

Figure 3.16 When you rename a user or an inetOrgPerson, you are prompted with a dialog box that enables you to change a number of names at once. The first field, Full name, refers to the common name of the object.

Settings*username*), will keep the old name. If you want all of these to reflect the new name, you must change each of them manually.

Deleting Users, InetOrgPersons, and Contacts

You delete an object by right-clicking it and selecting Delete or by selecting the object and pressing the Delete key. As a safety mechanism, you need to confirm the delete but you cannot undo it.

Figure 3.17 When you rename a contact, you are prompted with a dialog box that enables you to change a number of names at once. The first field, Full name, refers to the common name of the object.

A user object or an inetOrgPerson object is a security principal: It may have security group memberships and permissions for resources. Each security principal has a security ID (SID), which is the identifier to be used in these assignments. A SID is a long number and a SID is never reused. If you delete a user object and then re-create it, it will have a new SID, so the new user has none of the memberships or permissions of the old user. You must assign memberships and permissions specifically to the new user.

Disabling User or InetOrgPerson Accounts

The context menu for a user object or an inetOrgPerson object contains an operation called "Disable Account." It has the same effect as the "Account is disabled" check box in the Account tab of the properties dialog box. This operation is usually used for a limited time. For example, if someone is out of the company for six months, you could freeze his user account but still not delete it.

When you see a red *X* icon on the account, it is already disabled. In this case the context menu has an operation called "Enable Account."

Resetting User or InetOrgPerson Passwords

You will never see your users' or inetOrgPersons' passwords, but you can change them using the "Reset Password" operation in the context menu. The most obvious reason to do this is because a user has forgotten his password.

Opening Home Pages of Users, InetOrgPersons, and Contacts

If someone has a home page, and the corresponding property is defined in his object, you can open the home page in a browser using the "Open home page" operation in the context menu.

Sending E-mail to Users, InetOrgPersons, and Contacts

If someone has an e-mail address, and the corresponding property is defined in her object, you can send her e-mail with the "Send mail" operation in the context menu.

Administering Computer Objects

Just as Active Directory has a user object for each network user, it has a computer object for each computer in the domain. However, this applies "only" to Windows Server 2003, Windows XP, Windows 2000, and Windows NT computers. Other workstations (e.g., Windows 95 and 98 and non-Microsoft operating systems) that are not using the NT-based integrated security cannot have a computer object.

IF YOU KNOW NDS NDS allows a broader range of workstation types than does Active Directory, which means that you can manage more types of workstations with the help of the directory service.

Also, computer objects are used only for computers that join a domain. If a stand-alone server or workstation will be in a workgroup instead of a domain, it will not be assigned a computer object in Active Directory.

You could categorize computer object properties as either significant or informational, just as we did with user objects. However, the distinction among computer objects is not as clear as it is among user objects, so we don't use these terms with computer objects in this book (short of a couple of exceptions).

The purposes of computer objects are as follows:

- As inherited from the very first version of Windows NT back in 1993, a computer account ties the workstation or server to the Windows NT/2000/XP/Server 2003 security model.
- A computer object is a placeholder for properties that help you when you are remotely installing and managing workstations.
- A computer object is a placeholder for properties that are purely informational.
- A computer object is a security principal. This means that just as with a user, you can give permissions for resources and assign security group memberships to the computer.
- The location of a computer object in Active Directory dictates which group policies apply to the corresponding computer.

Computer objects are treated slightly differently, depending on whether they are for domain controllers or for workstations and member servers. Table 3.14 compares the two.

Table 3.14 Comparing Domain Controllers and Other Computer Objects

Feature	Domain Controller	Workstation and Member Server
Creation of the object	Automatically while installing Active Directory on the server (using DCPromo).	• Semiautomatically while joining the computer to the domain. • Manually with (a) the Users and Computers snap-in, (b) the DSAdd Computer command, (c) the NetDom tool (part of the Support Tools), or (d) using a script.
Default container of the object	Domain Controllers.	Computers.
Use of the default location	Probably yes.	Probably not (place the computer objects in OUs instead).
Computer GUID	You cannot set this property.	You may set this property, which helps when using Remote Installation Services and signifies a managed computer.

When you start to manage computer objects, your tasks will include the following:

- Create computer objects.
- Set computer object properties.
- Move, rename, disable, reset, and delete computer objects.
- Assign Group Policy and permissions, and delegate administrative tasks.

In this chapter, we focus on the first three items in the list. The last item is discussed in later chapters. If you want to try the management tasks discussed in this section, you can create some test computer objects in your test OU. To test all the features, however, you will need some test workstations.

Creating Computer Objects

As Table 3.14 in the previous section implies, computer objects are created in three ways.

- A computer object for a domain controller is created automatically in the Domain Controllers OU when you install Active Directory on that server by running the Active Directory Installation Wizard (i.e., DCPromo).
- When you join a stand-alone server or workstation to a domain, either during computer installation or afterward, you have the option to create the computer object. An object created in this way goes to the Computers container.
- You precreate the computer object manually using one of the four ways listed in Table 3.14. The Users and Computers snap-in way—the graphical choice—is explained next. The DSAdd Computer command is introduced at the end of this chapter.

NOTE The second and third items in the list require appropriate permissions or user rights, which are explained in Chapter 4. In short, any forest user can by default join ten workstations to a domain.

You can store the computer objects either in the Computers container or in various OUs in the domain. The latter option allows different OU-based group policies for different computers.

When you right-click the appropriate target OU and select New, Computer, you will launch a three-page or four-page creation wizard, the first page of which you see in Figure 3.18. Here you specify the name for the object, the downlevel name for the computer, and the user or group who can later join the computer to the domain. If the joining computer is running Windows NT, you must select the "pre-Windows 2000" check box. If the joining computer will be a Windows NT backup domain controller, you must select the "backup domain controller" check box.

Figure 3.19 shows the second page of the creation wizard. If you use Windows 2000, the pages beyond the first one will appear only if you have installed Remote Installation Services (RIS) to install Windows 2000 Professional computers.

Figure 3.18 When you create a computer object, on the first page of the creation wizard you are prompted to specify the name for the object, the downlevel name for the computer, and the user or group who can later join the computer to the domain.

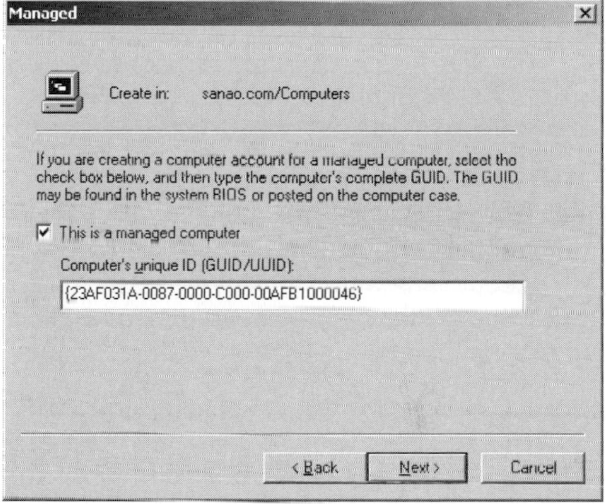

Figure 3.19 On the second page of the creation wizard you can specify that this is a "managed computer" (to indicate that you will use Remote Installation Services, or RIS, "prestaging" for this computer) and enter the computer's GUID.

NOTE Whether you get the additional wizard pages in Windows 2000 or not depends on which computer you are sitting at. For example, if there are two domain controllers in your domain (DC1 and DC2) and you have installed RIS on DC2, you will see the two additional pages if you are sitting at DC2 or any workstation. However, if you are sitting at DC1, you won't see the pages.

Computer manufacturers assign a unique GUID to each computer they sell. If you enter this GUID into Active Directory, it will help RIS to match a certain computer system to a certain computer object.

After you have bought a computer and turned it on for the first time to install Windows 2000 or Windows XP onto it, the RIS service sends the computer's GUID to a RIS server. This way, RIS can locate the correct computer object in Active Directory.

If you selected the "This is a managed computer" option on the wizard's second page, you will see a third page, which is shown in Figure 3.20. The last page displays the summary of your selections, and we don't show this screen.

NOTE The computer GUID shown in Figure 3.19 is not the same as the GUID that each Active Directory object has. Chapter 8 offers more in-depth treatment of object GUIDs.

NOTE You cannot specify the computer GUID or RIS server name for an existing computer object using the Users and Computers snap-in if you didn't specify "managed computer" when you first created the object. To edit properties directly, you need to use ADSI Edit or some other means. The aforementioned information is stored in the properties `netboot-GUID` and `netbootMachineFilePath`.

A computer object has several names, which are listed in Table 3.15.

Setting Computer Object Properties

The Users and Computers snap-in shows you about 15 computer object properties, and you can set about 8 of them. Behind the scenes, a computer object may have 280 properties (228 in AD2000.)

Table 3.16 lists the properties in five tabs. We discuss a sixth tab, Member Of, later in this chapter in the "Administering Groups"

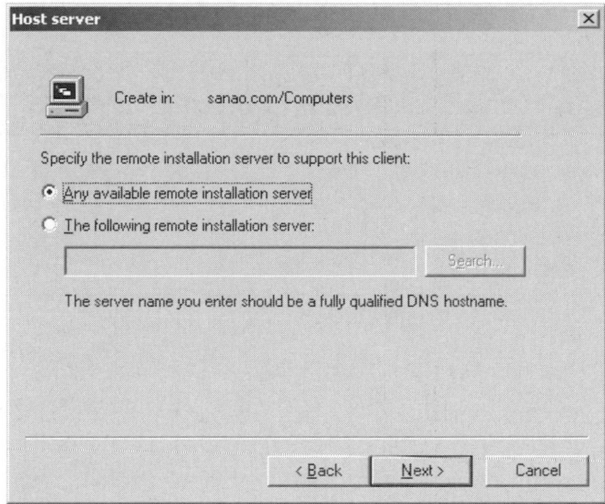

Figure 3.20 If you selected the "This is a managed computer" option in the creation wizard's second page (Figure 3.19), you will see a third page that enables you to specify a certain remote installation server. You can use this for load balancing, so that certain client computers (identified by the GUID) install Windows 2000 or Windows XP from a certain server.

section, and a seventh tab, Delegation, in Chapter 4. An eighth tab, Dial-in, relates to managing communication settings, so we don't cover it in this book about Active Directory. We don't include screen shots, because they would show just a number of text boxes. Many of the setting names are self-explanatory. Note that Windows Server 2003 also provides context-sensitive help for each of the settings.

Other Operations to Manage Computer Objects

Other operations you can do to manipulate computer objects are move, delete, disable, and reset. You can also rename computers or start computer management to manage the computer corresponding to the object.

Moving Computer Objects

If you need to move a computer object from one OU to another, you do it in the same way you move users. When you are moving a computer within a domain, either (a) drag it to a new location with the mouse, (b) use cut/paste with the keyboard or mouse, or (c) right-click the

Table 3.15 Name Properties of a Computer Object

Property	LDAP Name	Maximum Length	Required	Unique	Comments
Computer name	`name` (RDN) and `cn` (Common-Name)	64	X	Within OU	This becomes the object common name in the tree.
DNS name	`dNSHostName`	2048		In the world	The target computer updates this property automatically.
Computer name (pre-Windows 2000)	`sAMAccount-Name`	256 (schema rule), 20 (SAM rule)	X	Within the enterprise	This is the downlevel name of the computer, which is also the same as the computer NetBIOS name. Internally, Active Directory stores a dollar sign ($) at the end of the name.

computer, select Move, and then choose the destination from the OU tree that opens up and click OK. Between domains in a forest you use another tool, such as the Support Tools command-line tool MoveTree, which is discussed in Chapter 6.

You can move several sibling objects at once by selecting them in the right-hand pane of the snap-in by using the Shift and/or the Ctrl key.

When you move computer objects

- Permissions that are assigned for the object being moved move with the object.
- Group policies and permissions that are inherited from above do not move with the object being moved. Instead, the moved object inherits the policies and permissions from its new location.

Table 3.16 Properties of a Computer Object

Property	LDAP Name	Syntax*	Index	GC	Comments
General Tab					
Computer name (pre-Windows 2000)	`sAMAccount-Name`	Text (256 [schema rule], 20 [SAM rule])	X	X	This is the downlevel name of the computer, which is also the same as the computer NetBIOS name. Internally, Active Directory stores a dollar sign ($) at the end of the name.
DNS name	`dNSHostName`	Text (2048)		X	
Role	`userAccount-Control`	Two choices	X	X	Bit 0x2000 indicates a "Domain controller"; bit 0x1000 indicates a "Workstation or server".
Description	`description`	Text (1024)		X	
Trust computer for delegation	`userAccount-Control`	Yes/no	X	X	This setting is described in Chapter 4 in the "Impersonation and Delegation" section. Note that when the domain is on the Windows Server 2003 functional level, this setting appears on the Delegation tab. *(continued)*

* If the syntax is Text (i.e., a string of Unicode characters), we indicate also the maximum number of characters in the property (e.g., 1,024).

Table 3.16 Properties of a Computer Object *(cont.)*

Property	LDAP Name	Syntax*	Index	GC	Comments
Operating System Tab					
Name	`operating-System`	Text			A read-only text such as "Windows Server 2003."
Version	`operating-System-Version`	Text			A read-only text to indicate the normal version, such as "5.2" (Windows 2000 is "5.0", Windows XP is "5.1", and Windows Server 2003 is "5.2"), and the more precise version (i.e., build number), such as "3790."
Service Pack	`operating-System-ServicePack`	Text			A read-only text to indicate whether or not you have installed any service packs on the machine, such as "Service Pack 1."
Location Tab					
Location	`location`	Text (1,024)	X	X	

Table 3.16 Properties of a Computer Object (*cont.*)

Property	LDAP Name	Syntax*	Index	GC	Comments
Managed By Tab					
Managed By	`managedBy`	DN; you select a user or contact from a list			The user or contact you select gets no permissions for the computer. This setting is purely informational. The other fields on the tab are the manager's properties. Note that this setting is not related to the "This is a managed computer" check box that you saw in the creation wizard.
Remote Install Tab**					
Computer's unique ID	`netbootGUID`	Binary (text in the user interface)	X	X	Same as the computer's GUID. It helps when using RIS, and it signifies a managed computer.
Remote Installation server	`netboot-Machine-FilePath`	Text		X	This property specifies the DNS name of the selected installation server.
Server Settings	N/A	N/A	N/A	N/A	This button takes you to the properties of the server object.

** The Remote Install tab is present only if you created the object for a "managed computer" by checking the box on the second page of the creation wizard. If you are using Windows 2000, the tab is present only when you are sitting at the correct computer, as explained in the preceding section, "Creating Computer Objects."

Deleting Computer Objects

You delete an object by right-clicking it and selecting Delete or by selecting the object and pressing the Delete key. Because there is no Undo option, a safety mechanism asks you to confirm the deletion.

A computer object is a security principal like a user object. Therefore, if you delete a computer object and then re-create it, the new object doesn't have the memberships or permissions of the old one.

If you delete a computer object, the corresponding computer is no longer part of the domain. Therefore, no one can log on to the computer using a domain user account.

Disabling Computer Accounts

You can disable the computer account by right-clicking the computer object and selecting Disable Account. Doing so will prevent users sitting at that computer from logging on using a domain user account.

You cannot disable a domain controller.

Resetting Computer Accounts

When a Windows NT/2000/XP/Server 2003 computer that is a member of a domain starts, the computer logs on to the domain using the computer account and some password known to the machine. After this, a user sitting at the computer can enter his username and password to log on to the domain.

The aforementioned machine logon sets up a *secure channel,* which enables the member computer to communicate with a domain controller to exchange user and password information. For example, if the computer account password stored in the local computer (called *LSA secret*) doesn't match the one stored in Active Directory, authentication to the domain is not possible, and the user will receive an error such as the one shown in Figure 3.21.

An administrator can solve the problem by using the Reset Account context menu item on the corresponding computer object. Resetting a computer account resets its password to the initial value, which is "computername$" (without quotes). In addition, the member computer must be joined to a workgroup and then joined to the domain again.

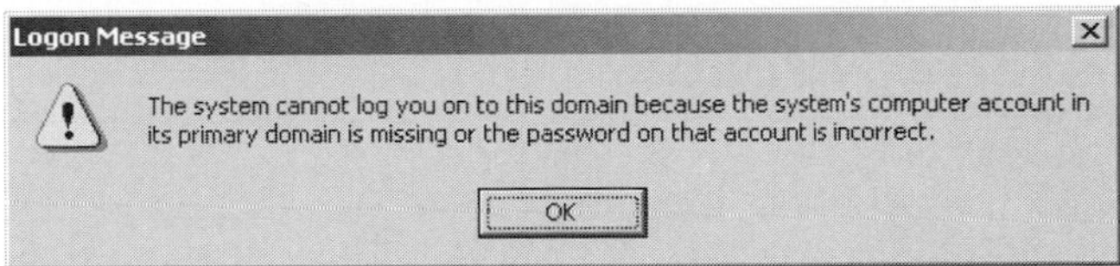

Figure 3.21 If the member computer cannot establish a secure channel with a domain controller, the user receives an error message such as the one shown here and is not able to log on using a domain user account.

NOTE You can reset a computer account also with the DSMod Computer command and -reset option. In addition, Support Tools includes two command-line utilities, NetDom and NLTest, which you can use to reset computer accounts, among other things.

Managing Computers

When you right-click the computer object and select Manage, the Computer Management snap-in starts and sets the focus to the corresponding computer. This way you can manage its system tools, storage, server applications, and services.

Renaming Computers

You rename a Windows 2000/XP workstation or a Windows 2000/Server 2003 member server using the Control Panel of that computer. Select System, then the Computer Name tab, and finally the Change button. Once you enter a new name and click OK, you are prompted for the name of a domain user who has permission to change the name of the workstation or member server, as well as that user's password.

This operation renames the computer (i.e., the NetBIOS name and DNS name) and changes the common name and the pre–Windows 2000 name of the computer object.

Renaming domain controllers was discussed in Chapter 2.

Administering Groups

Managing users, inetOrgPersons, contacts, and computer objects is usually much more effective when you treat them in groups than when you treat them individually. Whether you need to send e-mail or assign permissions for a printer, you most often want the target to be several users instead of just one. When you need the same group again, the fact that you already have it created will save you work. Of course, there is no laborsaving benefit if you create a group and then use it only once.

Groups are extremely handy and you really cannot manage a network without them. However, you use them mainly for assigning permissions and group policies. Specifically, you cannot use groups for the following purposes:

- Setting properties of several users, inetOrgPersons, contacts, or computer objects, or applying properties for them
- Moving or deleting several users, inetOrgPersons, contacts, or computer objects

In addition to administrators, end users can use Active Directory groups, usually as distribution lists. Table 3.17 describes in more detail the purposes for which you can use groups.

NOTE Because inetOrgPerson objects behave identically to user objects, each time we discuss users in this "Administering Groups" section, that discussion applies also to inetOrgPersons. For brevity, we don't show inetOrgPersons separately.

Group Types

You can create two types of groups in Active Directory: *security groups* and *distribution groups*. Both types can have users, inetOrgPersons, contacts, and computer objects as members. In addition, AD2003 introduces new basic and query-based application groups. The Windows operating system, however, doesn't currently use them. We explained these new application groups briefly in Chapter 1.

NOTE AD2003 allows any object type to be a group member. You don't need such a feature in normal user administration, but a directory-enabled application could use it.

Table 3.17 illustrates that security groups have two natures, but distribution groups have only one. Thus, distribution groups have a subset of security group features.

Table 3.17 The Nature of Security and Distribution Groups

Nature	Security	Distribution	Purpose
Security nature Group is a security principal, which Windows uses to determine permissions.	X		Assign permissions, and possibly audit settings, for folders, files, and Active Directory objects.
			Assign group policies (not directly, but by assigning permissions for a certain Group Policy only to some group).
			Other miscellaneous use, such as check the group membership in a logon script and then apply some commands, in case the user was in that group.
Application nature Group is available to directory-enabled applications. Windows doesn't use it, but any application may use it.	X	X	Send e-mail (i.e., the group operates as a distribution list).
			When using a directory-enabled application, use the group for whatever purpose the application needs.

NOTE Even though labeled "application nature," an application could use the distribution feature also for some security use. For example, you could have an application that controls the doors of your company. The application could open a certain door for a user if he is a member of a certain distribution group. This Note is related to Table 3.17.

IF YOU KNOW NT Security groups are the traditional groups that existed in Windows NT. Distribution groups were introduced with Active Directory.

As Table 3.17 indicates, a security group has all the features of a distribution group, and it can also be used for assigning permissions. This leads to the following question: Why do we use distribution groups at all, if they are less capable? The reason is that they are a little "cheaper" than security groups in terms of the logon process.

When a user logs on to the network or accesses the resources of a server for the first time, Windows builds an *access token* for that user. An access token is a list in RAM that contains the user's identity and the groups that the user belongs to. But it doesn't contain any distribution groups. Because distribution groups are not needed when determining access, they are not needed in the access tokens. This, in turn, leads to a somewhat faster logon process and a smaller access token in memory. Of course, you probably won't notice the difference in a small network.

NOTE Access tokens are discussed in more detail in Chapter 4.

On the other hand, as long as you don't have any directory-enabled applications, you cannot use distribution groups, even though you can create them. Remember that Windows doesn't use them. This means that it's quite possible that you need to create only security groups, even though they are a little more "expensive."

Figure 3.22 summarizes the features of the two group types.

NOTE A contact is never able to log on, so it never gets an access token, and it cannot access resources. Therefore, it is not part of the security nature of groups, even though it can be a member of a security group.

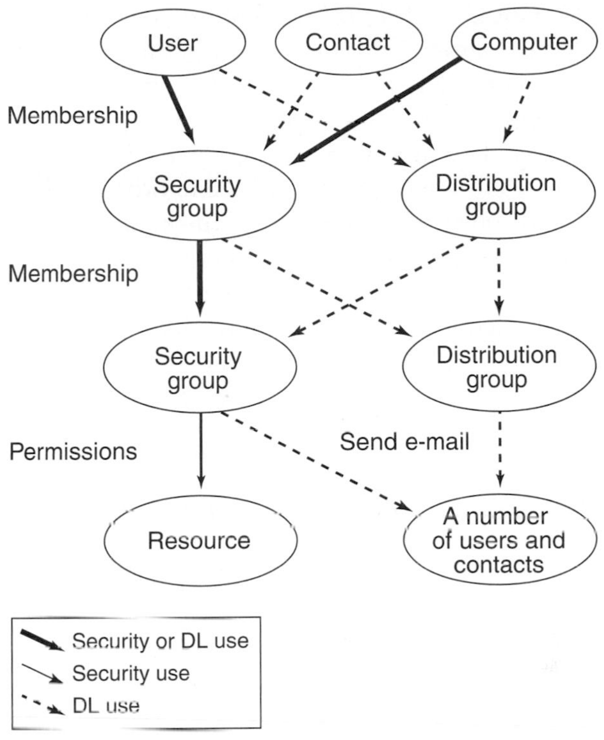

Figure 3.22 The solid lines in this figure represent the security nature of groups. All lines except the thin solid line in the lower-left corner represent the application nature of groups.

NOTE Figure 3.22 shows groups as members of other groups. Depending on the domain functional level and group scopes (discussed in the next section), not all groups can be members of all other groups.

Group Scopes

In addition to the two group types (security and distribution), groups are divided into three scopes: *global groups, universal groups,* and *domain local groups.* The group scope indicates if the group can accept members from other domains and if it can be used in other domains.

Group scopes are not very important if you have only one domain. In that case, you can do just fine with only universal groups, unless you anticipate having several domains at some later time.

Group nesting means that groups can be members of other groups; that is, a group is inside another group. Group scopes and nesting behave differently depending on the domain functional level. Regarding group functionality, the four levels fall in two categories. The first category could be called "Windows NT compatible" (including the levels Windows 2000 mixed and Windows Server 2003 interim), and the other category could be called "pure Active Directory" (including the levels Windows 2000 native and Windows Server 2003).

We will first explain the Windows NT–compatible case. Even if you have already raised your domain functional level and/or plan to use only "pure Active Directory," you should read the section about mixed mode. In this section we explain many principles of how to use groups in administration, regardless of the domain functional level.

Group Scopes in Windows NT–Compatible Functional Levels

Distribution groups in Windows NT–compatible functional levels work just like distribution groups in pure Active Directory levels. Consequently, we'll discuss distribution groups in the next section, which is about pure Active Directory levels.

NOTE Contact objects don't quite follow the containment rules that we will present from this point on. A global group can have user and computer object members only from its own domain, but it can have contact object members also from other domains.

Security groups in Windows NT–compatible functional levels work like the groups in Windows NT. You can have global and domain local security groups, but you can't have universal security groups.

You cannot freely nest security groups in Windows NT–compatible functional levels, but you can put global groups as members into domain local groups, as Figure 3.23 illustrates.

NOTE We don't include contact objects in the figures from now on because we are concentrating on the security nature of the groups.

In the one-domain case in Figure 3.23, you can draw an arrow from any circle to any other, as long as you move downward. In the two-domain case, only the two upper circles are visible in the other domain, and only the two lower circles accept arrows from the other domain.

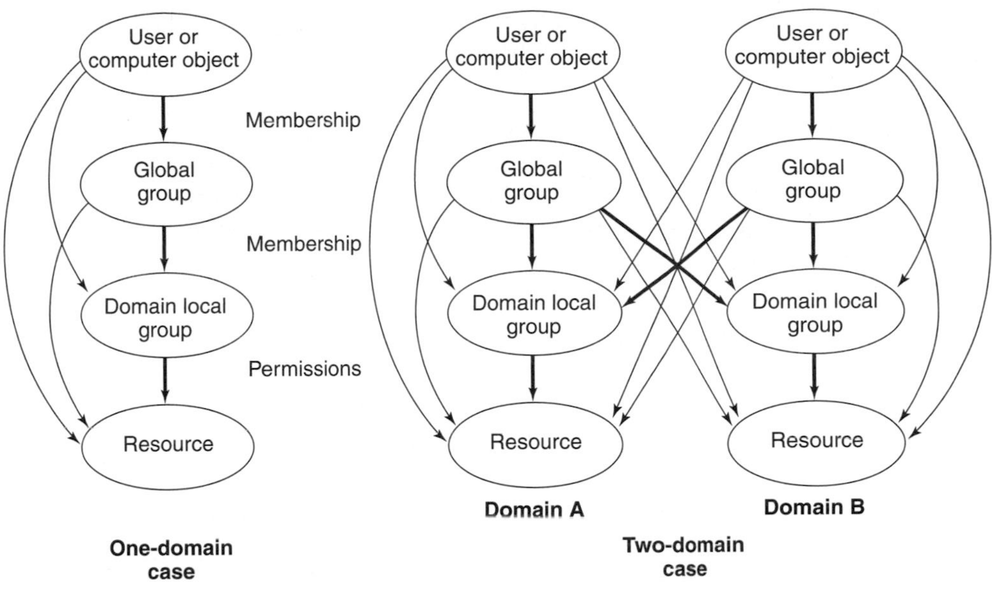

Figure 3.23 In Windows NT–compatible domain functional levels you can put users and computer objects in global groups, put global groups in domain local groups, and then give permissions to domain local groups. This preferred arrangement is indicated in the image by thick lines. You can also use the shortcuts indicated by the thin lines.

Remember that normal trust relationships in Active Directory are bidirectional. In the case of two domains, domain A trusts domain B and vice versa. Consequently, a domain A global group can be a member of a domain B domain local group, and a domain B global group can be a member of a domain A domain local group. In other words, if you looked at Figure 3.23 in a mirror, you would see a similar figure.

Because Figure 3.23 has quite a few arrows, to simplify the two-domain case, Figure 3.24 shows only the preferred (thick) arrows.

The thin lines (shortcuts) are less desirable for the following reasons:

- By giving permissions to one group instead of 200 users, you get dramatically shorter permission lists. This saves disk space, speeds up permission evaluation, and is easier to manage. For example, when your organization hires a new employee, she will get all the needed permissions when you add her to a few groups. The worse alternative would be to go through all server folders and add permissions to this new user.

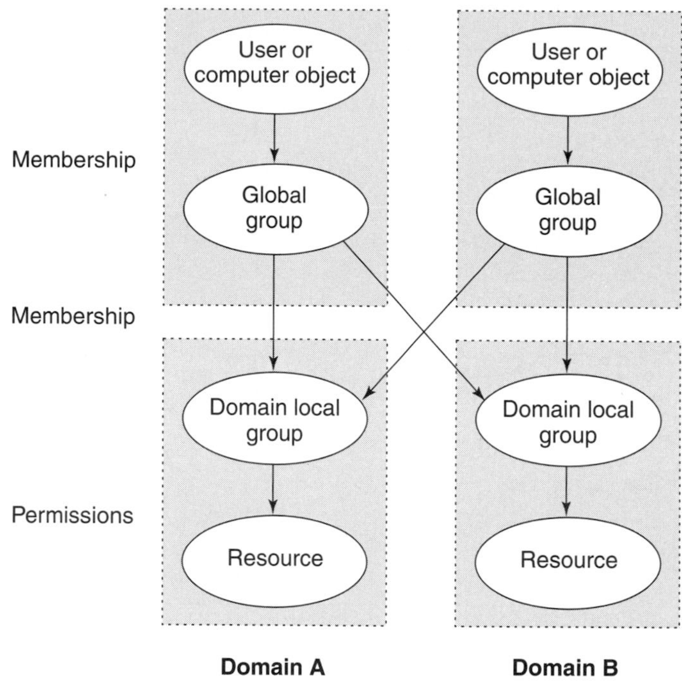

Figure 3.24 Global groups are usually associated with people (and computer objects). Domain local groups are resource oriented. The dotted boxes symbolize this division.

- You should use global groups to group users (and computer objects). These groups are also a level of isolation. If the user list changes, the groups stay the same, and therefore hide the changes from the lower levels. This is especially valuable in a multidomain situation. If one domain gets a new user, the administrators in other domains don't have to do anything, because they already have the appropriate global groups as members in the appropriate domain local groups.
- You should use domain local groups for resource-oriented purposes. You often create a domain local group either for one resource or for a certain type of resource, such as all color printers. This way, if a new group of users needs access to all the color printers, you can just make this group a member of the rColorPrintersPrint domain local group, instead of giving permissions for 17 color printers individually.

NOTE The first *r* in the rColorPrintersPrint domain local group name indicates that it is a resource-oriented group. *Print* indicates that this group has the print permission for the corresponding printers. You can use these kinds of naming conventions at will.

NOTE A domain local group is valid only in the local domain. You can use such a group to assign permissions for an Active Directory object, but when that object is replicated to global catalog servers that are members of other domains, your Allow or Deny permissions are not valid there. If a user subsequently queried this object using one of those "foreign" global catalog servers, she might get access you did not intend (because a Deny permission is not in effect). Therefore, Microsoft recommends that you shouldn't use domain local groups to assign permissions for Active Directory objects in a multidomain forest. Typically, the term *resource* you see in the figures on these pages refers to a shared folder or printer on a server, instead of an Active Directory object.

Example of Group Usage

We present in this section a basic example of group usage. We want to limit the number of people who can print on the color printers in our domain, so we perform the following steps.

1. When we deployed Active Directory, we established certain global groups to group the users in our domain. We put the users in groups based on the organizational structure (oMarketing and oFinance), as well as functional categories (fAssistants and fManagers). Note that we cannot use OUs for anything here.
2. Now we create a new local group, rColorPrintersPrint, and give that group permission to print to each color printer. We have three color printers and we have to assign the Print permission for each printer individually.
3. As the final step, we assign appropriate global groups as members of the rColorPrintersPrint group. We want everyone in the marketing department and all managers to be able to print in color.

Figure 3.25 illustrates the result.

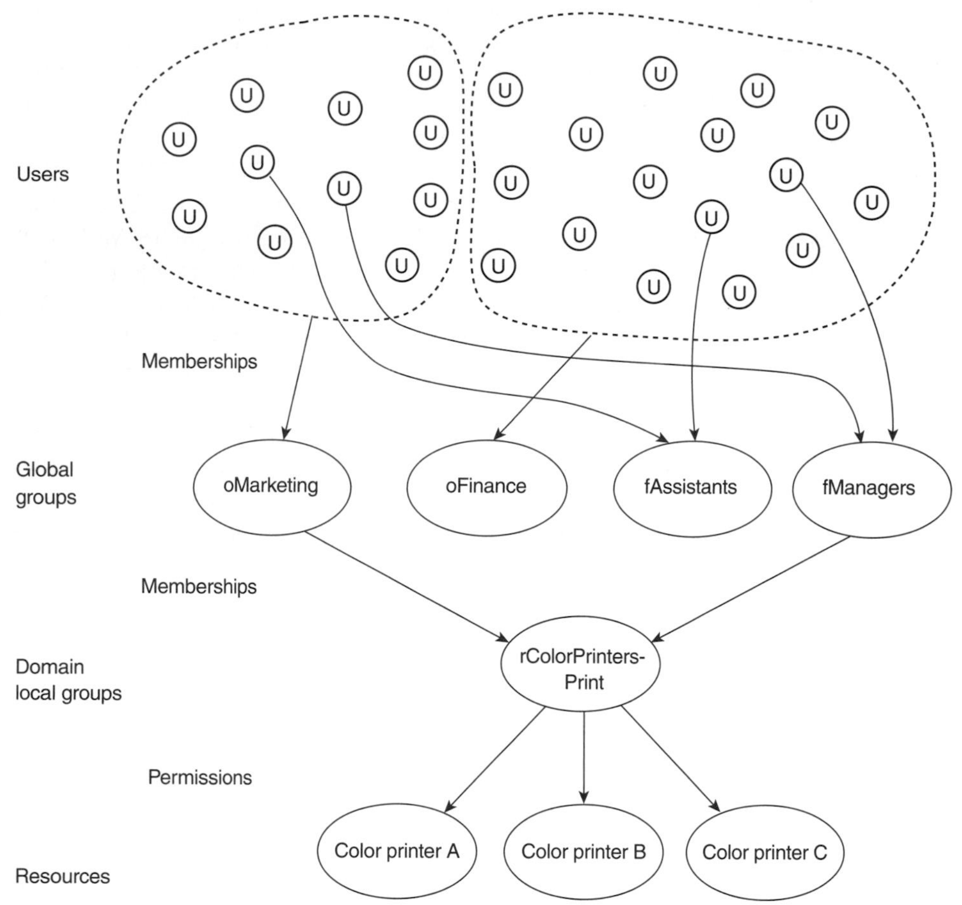

Figure 3.25 We have grouped our users into global groups, so we don't need to handle individual users. We give the actual Print permission to a domain local group and then assign appropriate global groups as members of this domain local group.

NOTE If a workstation or member server, instead of a domain controller, handles one of the color printers, the domain local group cannot be used while we are still in one of the Windows NT–compatible functional levels. Once we raise the level to one of the pure Active Directory levels, we can start using domain local groups in workstations and member servers.

If you have only one domain and you feel that you don't need two levels of groups, you may skip either level. Either you can make users (and computer objects) members of domain local groups, or you can give permissions directly to global groups.

The domain local group in Figure 3.25 may seem unnecessary. However, imagine that you have 17 color printers and, along with marketing personnel and managers, you want to allow assistants to print to them. With the domain local group you can do this quickly: You only need to put fAssistants as a member in rColorPrintersPrint. Without the domain local group, you would need to open the properties dialog box of 17 printers in quite a few servers and assign permissions to fAssistants individually in each dialog box.

See also the "Efficient Group Nesting" section later in this chapter and the associated Figure 3.38.

Group Scopes in Pure Active Directory Functional Levels

In the pure Active Directory functional levels, you can have any of the three group scopes in either of the two group types—that is, there are six possible combinations. Unlike in the Windows NT–compatible functional levels, now you can have universal security groups.

Security groups and distribution groups now work the same way with each other. Therefore, we don't need to make a distinction between them, and we don't discuss them separately here.

In the Windows NT–compatible functional levels, global groups are the upper level and domain local groups are the lower level. In the pure Active Directory functional levels, universal groups are a third level between the two earlier levels. A group from a higher level can be a member in a group from a lower level, as Figure 3.26 illustrates.

NOTE Figure 3.27, Figure 3.28, and Figure 3.29 are more complex than earlier images. To be as clear as possible, we don't show users and computer objects on the top or resources on the bottom in those three figures. You can still imagine them to be there.

Deciding how to use all these groups in the pure Active Directory functional levels is more complicated than in the Windows NT–compatible functional levels. We delve into this discussion in the

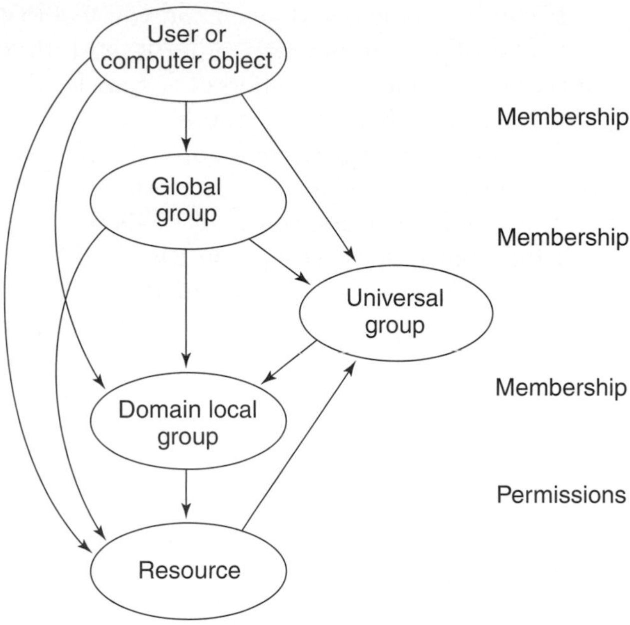

Figure 3.26 In the pure Active Directory functional levels, you have three levels of groups. Any upper-level object can be a member of any lower-level object. This figure illustrates the situation in one domain.

"Planning Groups" section later in the chapter. We'll just mention the three basic strategies here:

- Forget universal groups and use only global and domain local groups, as described in the preceding section about the Windows NT–compatible functional levels.
- Use only universal groups.
- Use all three levels (and pray that you know what is going on in Active Directory). If you have several domains and sites, you will probably need all three levels.

NOTE Because there are now three possible strategies for using groups, Figure 3.26 does not indicate (with thick lines) a preferred path.

Figure 3.27 introduces a second domain. It illustrates that global groups cannot accept members from other domains (except contacts),

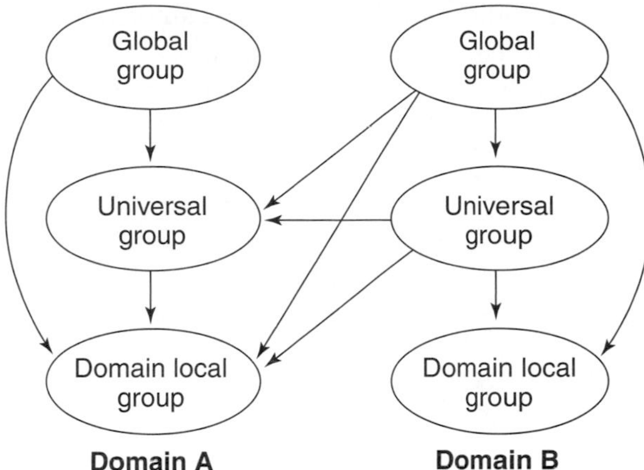

Figure 3.27 When crossing domain boundaries, global groups cannot accept members from other domains, and domain local groups cannot be used in other domains. Universal groups, however, have no such restrictions.

and domain local groups cannot be used in other domains, but universal groups don't have either of these restrictions.

NOTE As you may remember from the Windows NT–compatible section, the arrows between domains should be symmetrical. To keep Figure 3.27 uncluttered, we do not show the arrows from domain A to domain B.

If one of the domains in Figure 3.27 were in one of the Windows NT–compatible functional levels and the other were in one of the pure Active Directory functional levels, the image would still be accurate. Obviously, one of the domains couldn't have universal security groups, but after having removed that, all the remaining arrows would be valid. For example, if domain A were in the Windows 2000 mixed functional level and domain B were in the Windows Server 2003 functional level, the domain local groups in domain A would accept both global and universal groups as members from domain B.

The figures so far have shown only one group of each scope in each domain. In reality, you will have many groups of each scope. In the pure Active Directory functional levels, you can freely nest groups of the same scope. Global group A can be a member of global group B, which is a member of global group C, which is a member of global group D, and so on. In other words, any group can be a member of any other group of the same scope in the same domain.

Building on Figure 3.27, Figure 3.28 shows five groups of each scope in each domain.

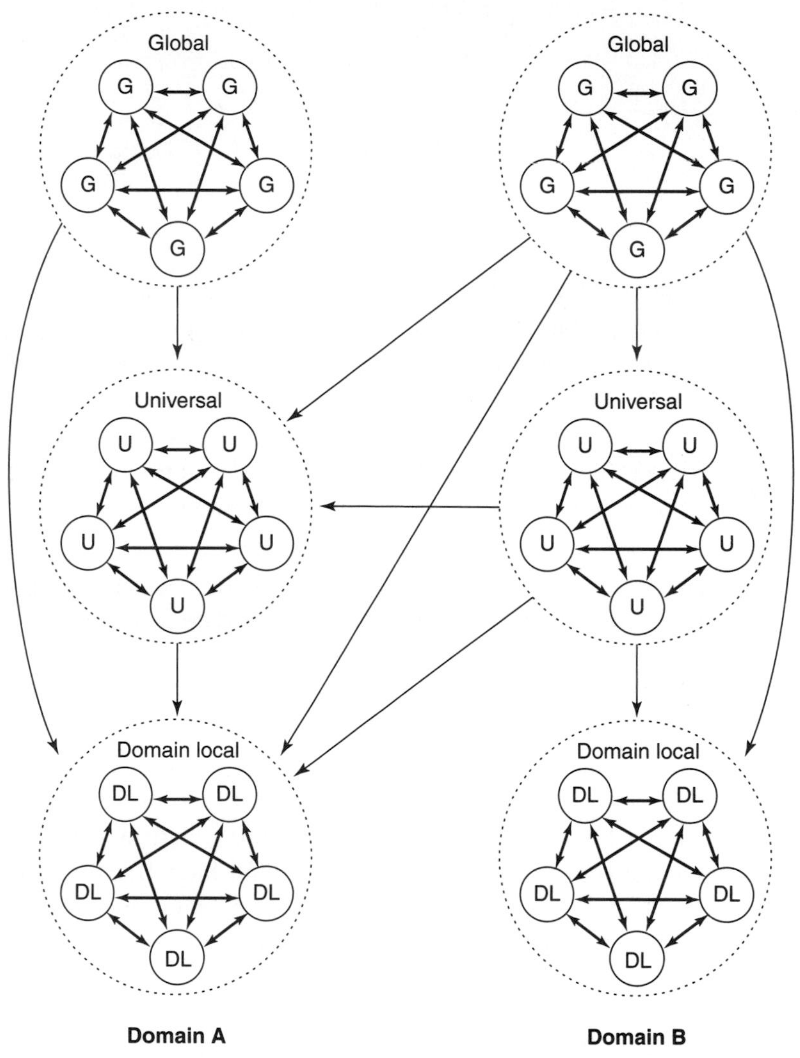

Figure 3.28 Within each scope in each domain, any group can be a member of any other group. From one scope or domain to another, groups that can be a member of other groups are indicated with an arrow.

NOTE In Figure 3.28, the arrow from the global groups in domain A to the universal groups in domain A symbolizes that any of the upper five groups can be a member of any of the lower five groups. An actual representation would have 25 arrows, but we use just one. These 25 arrows would be needed 14 times, between each scope of groups in each domain. To give you a clear image, we use only 10 arrows instead of 350.

NOTE Again, in Figure 3.28, arrows from domain A to domain B were left out to make the image clear.

Built-in Local Groups

The last aspect of group scopes concerns the built-in local security groups (Administrators, Account Operators, and so on) that reside in the Builtin container. Technically, they belong to a different "domain"—the Builtin domain—therefore, you cannot nest domain local groups with built-in local security groups or vice versa. Figure 3.29 illustrates this concept.

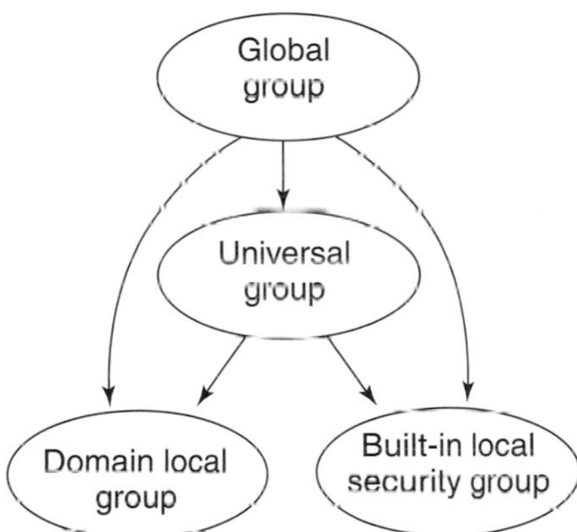

Figure 3.29 Built-in local security groups belong technically to a different "domain." Therefore, you cannot nest them with domain local groups.

Managing Groups

Now you are ready to create and manage groups. Before you implement the groups in your production environment, you should first read the "Planning Groups" section of this chapter.

Managing groups includes the following tasks:

- Creating groups of different types and scopes
- Changing the type or scope of a group
- Managing group memberships
- Setting the primary group of a user
- Setting group properties
- Moving, renaming, and deleting groups
- Sending e-mail to groups

When you create and manage groups, we suggest that you visualize your groups in the way that we have presented groups in the figures in this book. Having a clear visual image of them in your head, or even on paper, will help. The user interface of the Users and Computers snap-in doesn't indicate graphically that you should put users in global groups, global groups (perhaps) in universal groups, and so on.

Creating Groups

You create groups with the Users and Computers snap-in just as you create any other object. Right-click the target OU and select New, Group. Figure 3.30 is a screen shot of the dialog box that appears. Because you cannot assign permissions to an OU, the first group you create is probably a global security group with the same name as the OU. When you add each user of the OU to this group, you can give him or her permissions with the help of this group.

Table 3.18 describes the two names shown in Figure 3.30.

NOTE Distribution groups are created for directory-enabled applications. It is unlikely that those applications use the pre–Windows 2000 name. However, you must define it for every distribution group.

Many of the dialog boxes in the Users and Computers snap-in give no hint of the scope or type of existing groups. Therefore, you might consider adding your own hint—for example, add "gs" to the name, with "g" standing for "global" and "s" standing for "security" group. With

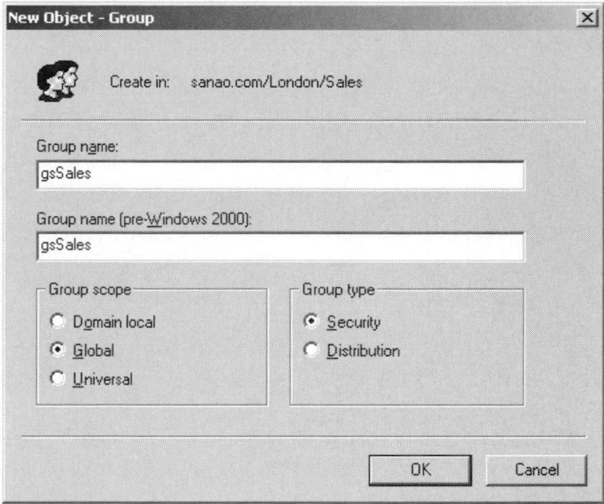

Figure 3.30 When you create a group, the first dialog box that appears calls for naming the group and assigning its scope and type. The first group is likely to have the same name as the OU.

Table 3.18 Name Properties of a Group Object

Property	LDAP Name	Maximum Length	Required	Unique	Description
Group name	`name` (RDN) and `cn` (Common-Name)	64	X	Within OU	This becomes the object common name in the tree.
Group name (pre-Windows 2000)	`sAMAccount-Name`	256	X	Within domain	This name appears on non–Active Directory computers and software, such as the old User Manager. Despite its label, this name can be used throughout Windows 2000 and later.

domain local groups, you could use "l" instead of "d" to not confuse them with distribution groups.

You could also use letters to indicate whether the group was created by organization, by functionality, by resource, or by some other criteria. Table 3.19 gives some suggestions on how to use these symbol letters.

In addition to making names more descriptive, these symbols sort similar groups sequentially when the user interface is using an alphabetical list.

Table 3.19 presents examples of letters that indicate scope and type, such as "gs," and letters that indicate logical grouping, such as "o." Of course, you can use both types, but be aware that confusion can arise if you use too many identifiers like these.

Changing Group Type or Scope

The Windows NT–compatible functional levels don't enable you to change group type or scope. Raising the functional level to either pure Active Directory alternative (Windows 2000 native or Windows Server 2003) enables these changes, with two restrictions (see Figure 3.31).

Table 3.19 Symbol Letters for Group Names

Letter(s)	Examples	Meaning
gs	gsSales	Global security groups.
us	usSAPUsers	Universal security groups.
ls	lsSAPUse lsColorPrint	Domain local security groups. The first group has permissions to use SAP software, and the second group has permissions to print in color.
o	oDirectSales oChannelSales	Groups created according to the organizational structure (which don't match OUs).
ou	ouSales	Groups created to match OUs.
f	fSalesmen fAssistants	Groups created according to function (for example, salesmen from all OUs).
r	rSAPUse rColorPrint	Groups created for resources. Because these are usually domain local groups, this example has the same group names as the "ls" example.

Figure 3.31 You can change a group scope to and from a universal group, but you can't change scope directly from a domain local group to a global group or vice versa.

- If the new type or scope would lead to an illegal situation in terms of memberships, the change is obviously forbidden. For example, if your domain local group has other domain local groups as members, you cannot change it to a universal group. Universal groups cannot have domain local groups as members.
- You cannot change a domain local group to a global group or vice versa, except via a universal group.
- In a multidomain forest, you cannot change a universal group to a domain local group, unless you perform the change with a domain controller that is a global catalog server. Consequently, if none of the domain's domain controllers is a global catalog server, you cannot perform the change at all.

Managing Group Memberships

Each user, contact, computer, and group is a "member" of only one OU. At the same time, each can be a member of several groups, because a group membership is just a group property; it is not part of the tree structure.

A user's or computer's new group membership becomes effective in each server or workstation when the user or computer authenticates to that server or workstation the next time. This typically takes place when the user logs on or the computer is restarted, but it also takes place if the user creates a connection to a server where there was no existing connection.

The Users and Computers snap-in allows you to manage group membership in three ways:

- The Members tab of the group
- The Member Of tab of the (incoming) member
- The "Add to a group" function

You cannot drag objects over groups to become members of them.

WARNING If you have an AD2000 forest or an AD2003 forest running on the Windows 2000 functional level, you should take into account the following warning: If you delegate group management to assistant administrators, you should advise them to modify group memberships only on one domain controller (perhaps the PDC emulator). All members of a group are stored in one multivalued property. If that member list is modified on two domain controllers simultaneously (within replication latency), one of the two changes will be lost.

WARNING You could give users the permission to "Add/Remove self as member" of some group. For the reason and scenarios given in the previous warning, some changes could be lost, and the risk would be quite great if all users could modify membership themselves.

NOTE Because all members of a group are stored in one multivalued property, there is a limit of 5,000 members in one group. The limit doesn't apply in the Windows Server 2003 (or Windows Server 2003 interim) forest functional level.

The Members Tab of the Group

The first way to manage groups is through the Members tab. When you right-click a group, select Properties, and then click the Members tab, you'll see a list of the members of the group, as Figure 3.32 shows.

As you would guess, you remove members by selecting them and clicking the Remove button.

To add members to a list, click Add. Another dialog box opens, where you can enter the objects to be added as members (see Figure 3.33). In the "From this location" field choose the domain or folder (or Entire Directory).

After you have typed the new member names in the text box, you can check whether they are valid with the Check Names button. If you want to type several names, you must separate them with semicolons. If more than one object matches the name you typed, clicking OK or Check Names brings up the dialog box in Figure 3.34.

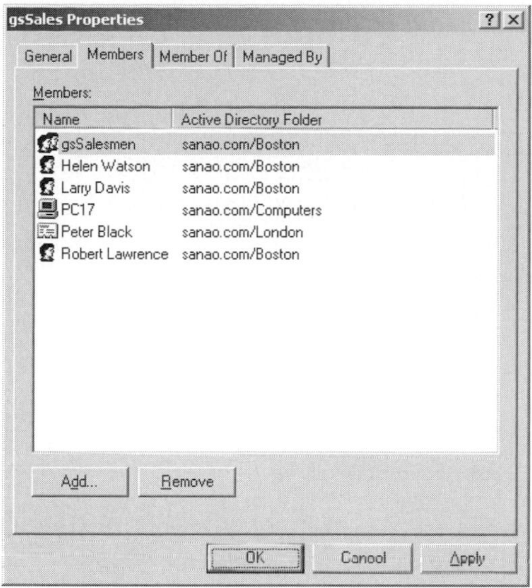

Figure 3.32 The gsSales group currently has users, contacts, computers, and other groups as members.

NOTE When you added group members, Windows 2000 showed by default a list of possible members. Windows Server 2003 doesn't show this, because in a large domain it is time consuming. You can display the list, however, by clicking Advanced in the dialog box shown in Figure 3.33 and then clicking Find Now in the dialog box that opens.

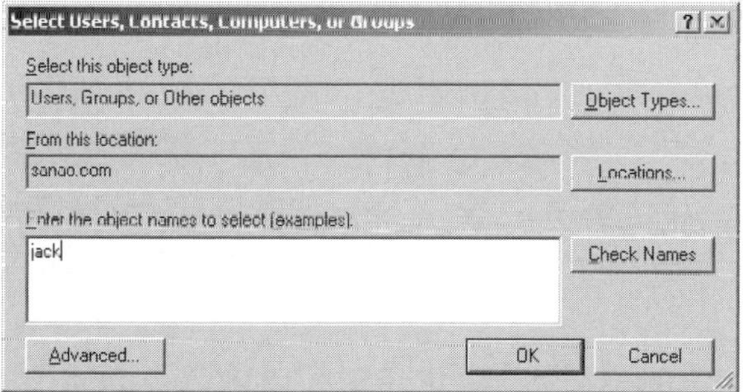

Figure 3.33 To enter new members for a group, first choose the domain or folder (or Entire Directory) in the "From this location" field and then enter the names, using semicolons as separators. If you want, you can click Check Names before clicking OK.

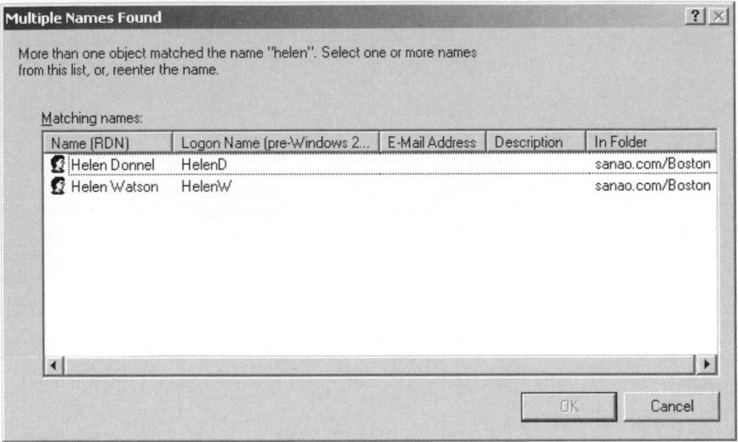

Figure 3.34 If you type a name that matches several objects, you are prompted to select the name you intended.

The Member Of Tab of the Incoming Member

User, contact, computer, and group objects have a Member Of tab, which shows the groups that the object belongs to. If you have several domains in the forest, however, from other domains the tab shows just universal groups.

The Members Of tab and consequent dialog boxes work in the same way as the Members tab and consequent dialog boxes.

Add to a Group Function

The context menu of each user and contact (accessed with a right-click) has an "Add to a group" option. When you select this menu item, you can choose the group in which to place the selected object or objects.

In Windows 2000, the "Add to a group" option is a menu item also for each OU. In this case, you can make all users and contacts in the OU members of the group. If the OU has child OUs, you can choose for each one whether to include users and contacts in them as well.

Setting a User's Primary Group

Each user and computer object's Member Of tab includes a setting for a *primary group*. You probably won't need this setting, because it is used only by the POSIX subsystem (i.e., when running a kind of UNIX application in Windows) or by Apple Macintosh workstations.

The default primary group of a user is Domain Users, and the default primary group of a computer is Domain Computers. If needed, you can change this setting to some other global or universal security group.

You cannot remove an object from its primary group. Therefore, if you want to move a user out of Domain Users, you first must change that user's primary group to something else.

NOTE The primary group of a user is not stored in the `members` property of the group, but rather in the `primaryGroupID` property of the user. Consequently, the 5,000-member maximum of the Windows 2000 forest functional level doesn't apply to primary groups, which means that you could have 100,000 users (or more) in your domain and they could all be members of Domain Users.

Setting Group Properties

Behind the scenes a group object may, by default, have 132 properties (107 in AD2000). The user interface displays only a few of them, as shown in Figure 3.35.

Figure 3.35 There are not many properties that you can set for a group object.

Table 3.20 lists the properties of group objects that are visible in the Users and Computers snap-in other than group type, scope, and members, which we discussed in the previous sections. The settings are mostly self-explanatory. Note that Windows Server 2003 also provides context-sensitive help for each of the settings.

Table 3.20 Properties of a Group Object

Property	LDAP Name	Syntax*	Index	GC	Comments
General Tab					
Description	`description`	Text (1,024)		X	
Group name (pre-Windows 2000)	`sAMAccount-Name`	Text (256)	X	X	This name appears on non–Active Directory computers and software, such as the old User Manager. Despite its label, this name can be used throughout Windows 2000 and later.
E-Mail	`mail`	Text (256)	X	X	
Comments	`info`	Text (1,024)			
Managed By Tab					
Managed By	`managedBy`	DN** you select a user or contact from a list			The user or contact you select doesn't get permission for the group. This setting is purely informational. The other fields on the tab are the manager's properties.

* In the Syntax column, Text (256) means a text field with a maximum of 256 Unicode characters.

** DN = distinguished name.

Table 3.20 Properties of a Group Object (*cont.*)

Property	LDAP Name	Syntax*	Index	GC	Comments
Manager can update membership list	nTSecurity-Descriptor	N/A		X	The Windows Server 2003 version of the Users and Computers snap-in contains this new check box. If you check this setting, the manager gets permission to modify the `member` property of the group.

Moving Groups

You move groups between OUs just as you move other objects. When moving a group within a domain, either (a) drag it to a new location with the mouse, (b) use cut/paste with the keyboard or mouse, or (c) right-click the group, select Move, and then choose the destination from the OU tree that opens up and click OK. To move groups between domains in your forest, you use another tool, such as the Support Tools command-line tool MoveTree. It is discussed in Chapter 6.

You move several sibling objects at once by selecting them in the right-hand pane of the snap-in and using the Shift and/or Ctrl key.

When you move groups

- Permissions that are assigned for the object being moved move with the object.
- Permissions that are inherited from above do not move with the object being moved. Instead, the object inherits new permissions in its new location.

Renaming Groups

You rename a group either by right-clicking it and selecting Rename or by selecting the group and pressing F2. After you type the new name, press

Enter. Because groups also have a pre–Windows 2000 name, a dialog box appears that gives you a chance to change that name, too.

Deleting Groups

You delete a group by right-clicking it and selecting Delete or by selecting the group and pressing the Delete key. Because there is no Undo, as a safety mechanism, you must confirm that you want to delete the group.

Like a user, a group is a security principal. Therefore, if you delete and then re-create it, the new object doesn't have the memberships or permissions of the old one.

Sending E-mail to Groups

If the group has an e-mail address defined, you can send it e-mail with the "Send mail" operation in the context menu. Naturally, you need an e-mail application for this feature to work.

Planning Groups

Now you know group mechanics and properties, so you can use this knowledge to decide what the best way is to use groups effectively for a specific network in terms of manageability, administrative burden, and cost to network efficiency.

Planning groups involves deciding on group names, types, and scopes.

- It often pays to use letters in group names that indicate the kind of group it is, as explained earlier in this chapter.
- As explained earlier, because of access tokens, you should use distribution groups when you don't need the security feature but intend just to use the group with some directory-enabled application.
- This section concentrates on group scopes and describes three strategies for using them.

Before we discuss the three strategies, we need to study universal groups a little more.

Universal Groups Revisited

Recall that universal groups don't have the limitations of global or domain local groups. This prompts the following question: Why not use only the most feasible (i.e., universal) groups? Actually, Microsoft originally planned Active Directory to have only universal groups, not global or domain local groups. But the universal groups introduce extra cost, so Microsoft brought along the other two scopes.

Universal groups are more expensive in two ways. The first is related to the global catalog and the second is related to access tokens. Table 3.21 explains both.

The outcome of the rightmost column in Table 3.21 is that if you have only one domain, neither cost in the table is an issue, so you can use universal groups with confidence.

The reason to have universal group members in the global catalog is to provide an efficient means to effectively implement groups in a WAN environment with multiple sites. The global catalog takes care that the

Table 3.21 The Extra Costs Related to Universal Groups

Cost	Explanation	Is an Issue
Global catalog	All membership information of universal groups is replicated to the global catalog. This means that every time the members change, this information has to be replicated to all sites of the enterprise throughout the world (provided that they all have a global catalog server). To minimize changes, have only groups as members of universal groups. This way, changes in membership don't occur as often as when users are members.	If you have both multiple domains and multiple sites
Access tokens	Global and domain local groups come only from the applicable domain into the user's access tokens. Universal groups, however, come to the user's access tokens from all domains of the enterprise forest. Thus, using universal groups leads to larger access tokens (consuming some memory) and to slower logon times.	If you have multiple domains and a fairly large number of groups

membership information is present on all sites (provided each site has a global catalog server). Therefore, checking a user's membership (needed to determine his access to resources) doesn't require crossing WAN links to other sites.

NOTE If you test universal groups, you may run into the following "problem" (only in AD2000): You create a test universal group on a domain controller that is not a global catalog server. Then you test the new group and find out that it doesn't work (yet). The reason is that because the universal group membership is read from a global catalog server, it doesn't work until the group and the membership information have been replicated to the global catalog server, where your domain controller reads this information. You may even be sitting at a domain controller that contains this information, but still it must be read from elsewhere.

To summarize, we can make two claims that may sound contradictory at first:

- Universal groups are suitable for small networks.
- Universal groups are suitable for large networks.

The rationale behind the two claims comes from the three benefits of universal groups.

- *For small networks:* Cost is not an issue, and universal groups are easy to learn because there is only one scope with free nesting.
- *For large networks:* Universal groups provide an effective way to create groups with members from multiple sites.
- *For large networks:* Only universal groups have the scope to take members from different domains and to be assigned permissions for resources in different domains (see Figure 3.36).

The first benefit (for small networks) means that you would use only universal groups. The other two benefits (for large networks) mean that you would use universal groups occasionally in addition to global and domain local groups.

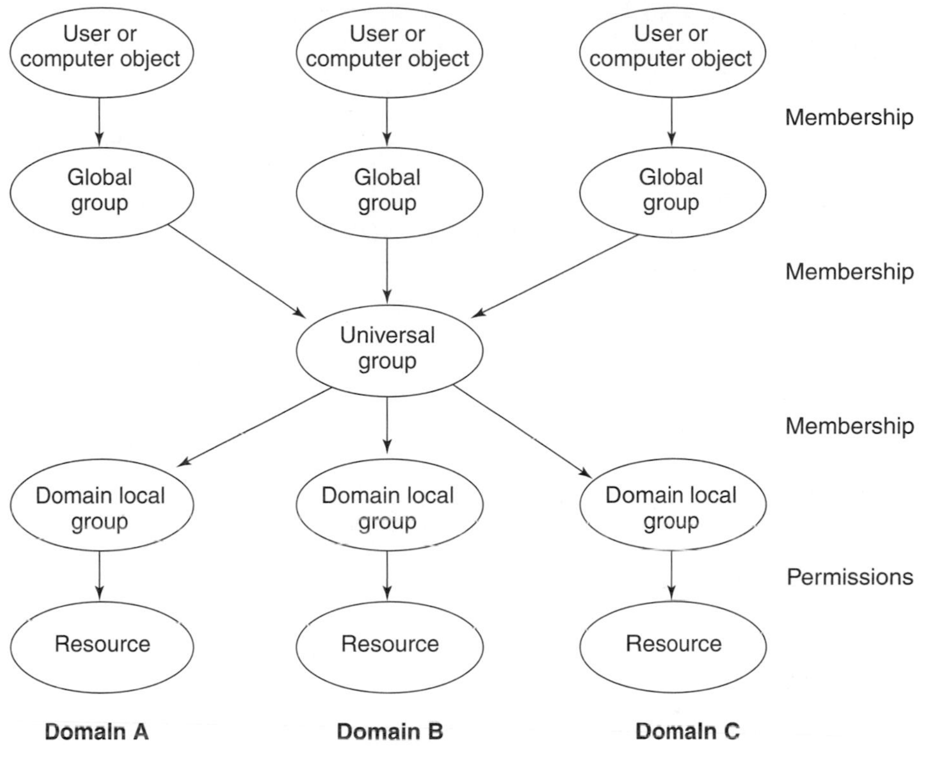

Figure 3.36 If you need a group that can have members from different domains and that can be given permissions for resources in different domains, your only choice is a universal group.

NOTE If you removed the universal group from Figure 3.36, you could achieve the same networking result. It would be very cumbersome to do so, however. You would need 9 (3 x 3) direct memberships from the global groups to the domain local groups. Or, with 17 domains, you would need 289 (17 x 17) direct memberships.

Three Group Strategies

There are three basic approaches to organizing groups according to scope, as Figure 3.37 illustrates.

- *Use only global and domain local groups (strategy A).* If you feel comfortable with the two levels of groups that global and domain

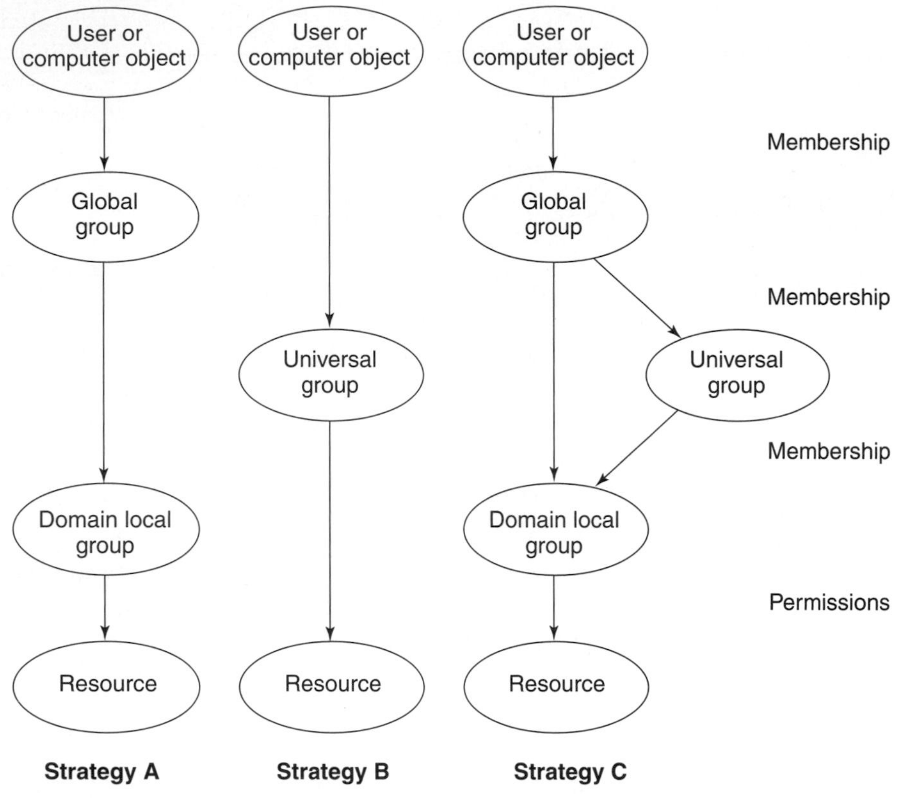

Figure 3.37 Depending on your network's size and needs, you can choose one of three group scope use strategies.

local groups provide (most likely from earlier Windows NT experience), you could use this as your group strategy. You have either just one domain or maybe a few of them.

- *Use only universal groups (strategy B).* If you have only one domain and you don't want to learn and think about different group scopes or levels, you will do fine with using just universal groups. You can use one level of groups between users and resources, without group nesting. Or you can put some groups in other groups to have a little nesting. Whether or not you develop logical levels for your groups is your choice. Of course, there are always some predefined global and local groups.
- *Use all three scopes (strategy C).* If you have multiple domains (and perhaps sites), you probably need all three group scopes. You'll mostly use global and domain local groups because they

don't have the extra "cost." In this strategy, you use universal groups only when you need a group with members from different domains (perhaps in different sites) and when you want to assign permissions for resources in different domains.

We have a few final comments about group usage before we move on to the next section.

- Don't get carried away with group nesting. If you have more than three levels, you might lose track of your group hierarchy. Too much nesting could easily confuse, rather than simplify, network administration.
- You might want to create a group containing only one person. Active Directory doesn't have a role object class as Novell NDS has, but you could use groups in this sense. Usually one person at a time holds a role, so the group has only one member. For example, if some user is taking care of backups this month, you could put her in a group and give that group the appropriate permissions. When someone else takes over the role, you change the group membership by removing the first user and adding the new user.

Efficient Group Nesting

Group nesting in pure Active Directory functional levels is relatively free. The only restrictions are—as explained earlier in this chapter—that (a) you cannot put "lower" groups as members in "upper" groups, such as putting a universal group in a global group, and (b) based on group scopes, only some memberships are allowed across domain boundaries. Consequently, you can do almost whatever you want with group nesting.

We cannot present all the various scenarios here, but we present one efficient and systematic use of nesting. It uses the following steps (illustrated in Figure 3.38).

1. We put each user in one global group that is based on the smallest (necessary) organizational unit (not to be confused with the OUs of Active Directory). We denote these groups with "o1".
2. We put each user in one global group that is based on the smallest (necessary) location unit. We denote these groups with "L1" (where uppercase is more distinguishable than lowercase).

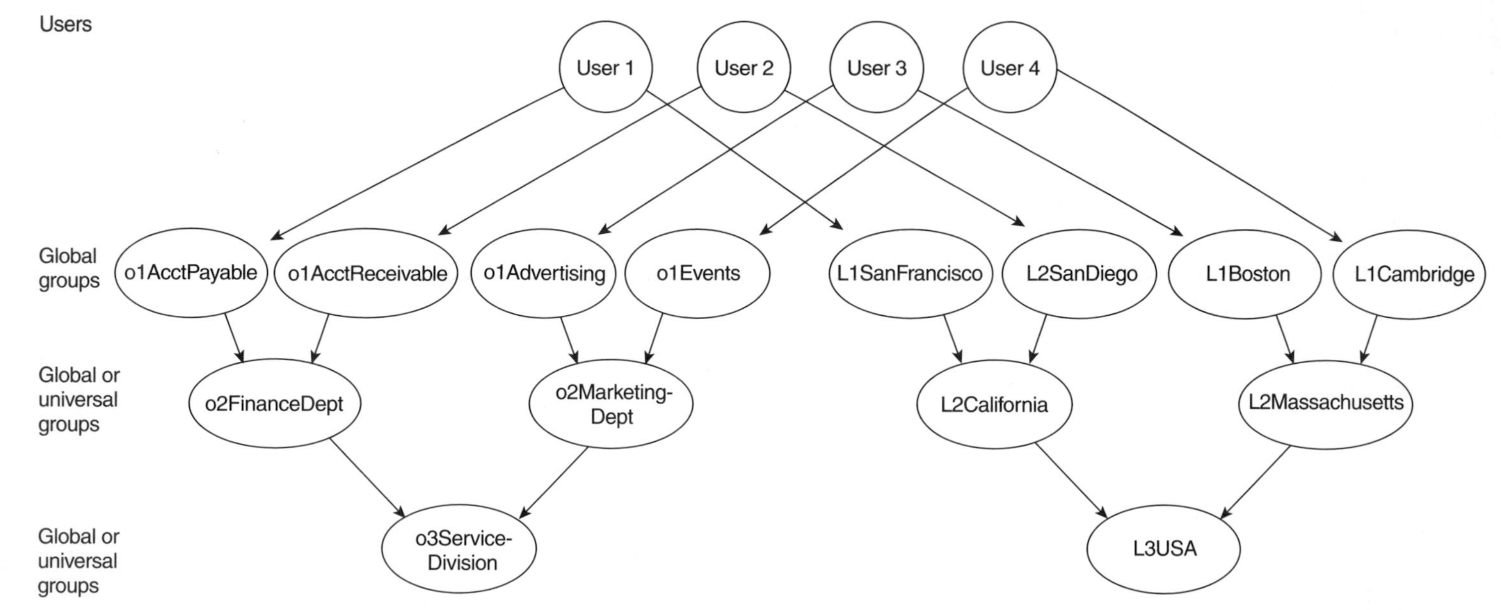

Figure 3.38 You can develop a systematic group nesting approach by assigning each user to one small organizational group and to one small geographical group. Then you assign these groups to larger groups, and those to even larger groups.

3. We nest the smallest organization groups into larger ones, denoted with "o2", and similarly the smallest location groups into larger ones, denoted with "L2".
4. As the fourth step, we nest the o2 groups into o3 groups, and L2 groups into L3 groups.

This approach deserves the following comments:

- You need to put each user in only a minimal number of groups (two in this case).
- In addition to this systematic model, you may need to put users in some other groups, such as in the functional groups illustrated in Figure 3.25.
- If you implement the scenario in a single domain, you can do with just global groups.
- If you have several domains, either your organizational or geographical group division does not match your domain division. Consequently, some of your group memberships must cross domain boundaries, and consequently, some of the o2, o3, L2, or L3 groups must be universal instead of global. It is most likely that all the members of each o1 and L1 group are in a single domain, so all o1 and L1 groups can be local.
- In the unlikely event that, for example, the members of o1AcctPayable are in two domains, you must make that group universal. You must also make intermediate global groups, one in each domain, because due to excessive replication, users should not be directly in universal groups. You could call those intermediate global groups o0AcctPayableDomA and o0AcctPayableDomB. Note that these intermediate groups are not shown in Figure 3.38.
- It is quite possible that either the organizational or geographical group structure more or less matches your OU structure. The group structure, however, has nothing to do per se with the OU structure. Also, the groups' locations in the OU tree don't affect how they work.
- If your OU structure matches the geographical structure, for example, you can place each geographical group in the corresponding OU. This way the person who was delegated the administration of the Boston OU, for example, can manage both the Boston users and the L1Boston group. And the person who is responsible for the Massachusetts OU can put L1Boston and L1Cambridge into L2Massachusetts.

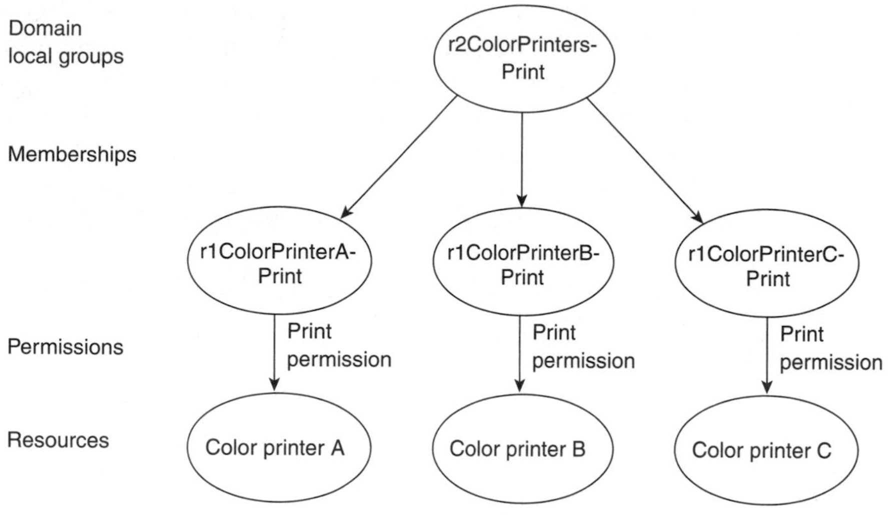

Figure 3.39 To simplify permission management, you can create a domain local group (or a local group in a member server) for each color printer and then assign a larger color printer group to each per-printer group.

- If you have no use for one of the largest groups in Figure 3.38, such as L3USA, you can obviously choose not to create it at all.

If you feel you have the need, you can also nest the resource-oriented (domain local) groups. For example, you can create a group for each color printer and then a larger group to cover several color printers. See Figure 3.39 for an illustration.

Tips on Tools

We use the Users and Computers snap-in often, as a main tool, and there are some helpful tips that we haven't yet covered. In addition, the snap-in is not the only tool available to manage Active Directory objects. Before we conclude this chapter, we'll say a few words about the Users and Computers snap-in, as well as about other means to manage objects.

The Users and Computers Snap-In

We have been using the Users and Computers snap-in throughout the chapter. Here we'll briefly fill in some last few holes.

Choosing a Domain

You can connect to another domain by right-clicking the uppermost line of the left pane (Active Directory Users and Computers . . .), selecting Connect to Domain, and then specifying a new domain either by typing its name or selecting it from a list.

Choosing a Domain Controller

Sometimes you want to communicate with a certain domain controller. You can choose one by right-clicking the uppermost line of the left pane (Active Directory Users and Computers . . .), selecting Connect to Domain Controller, and then selecting a new domain controller from a list or typing in a new domain controller's name in the dialog box shown in Figure 3.40.

Finding Objects and Information

The context menu of the domain object and each OU has a Find item. You can use it to find objects that match certain criteria.

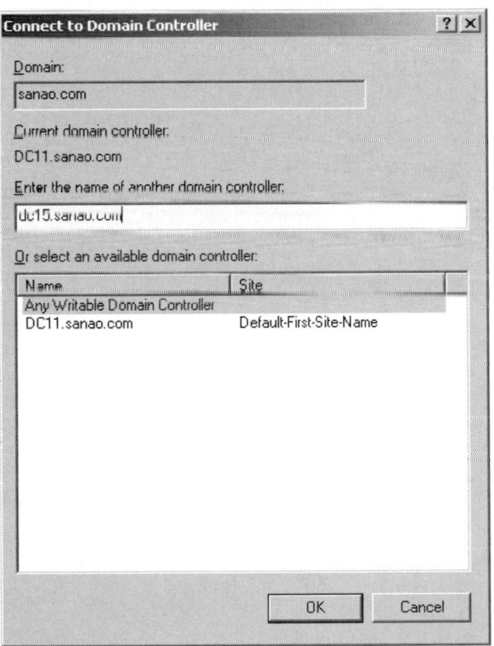

Figure 3.40 You can specify a domain controller to communicate with in the Connect to Domain Controller dialog box.

Windows Server 2003 includes a new Find feature called Common Queries. It enables you to find things such as all disabled user accounts or user accounts that haven't logged on for two months.

See also the "Search Tools" section in Chapter 6.

Filter Options

The View menu of the snap-in includes Filter Options. This feature enables you to specify the objects you want to see when you browse various container objects. (For more information about finding and filtering objects, see Chapter 6.)

Saved Queries

The Windows Server 2003 version of the Users and Computers snap-in includes a new feature called saved queries. You see the Saved Queries folder in the left-hand pane of the snap-in and—as the name implies—you can store there queries for later use. For example, you can define a query that displays all users of the domain that don't have a home folder property set.

As you can see in Figure 3.41, when you create a new query, you can specify a name for it, the starting point ("Query root"), whether to include subcontainers, and finally, the actual query. The query string is shown as an LDAP query string, but when you define it (by clicking Define Query),

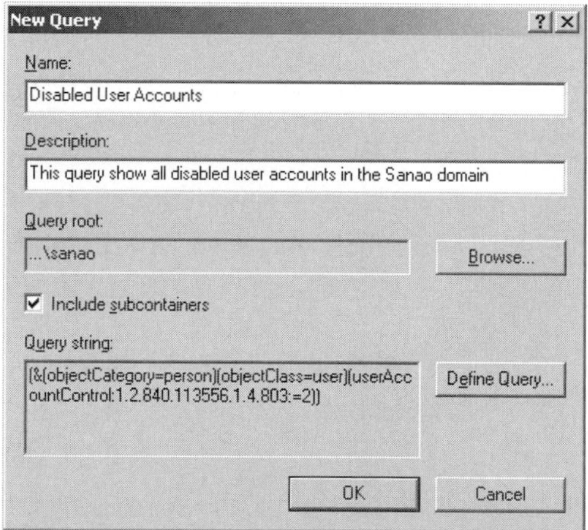

Figure 3.41 You can create and save often-used queries in the Saved Queries folder of the Users and Computers snap-in.

you have a myriad of user-friendly alternatives to specify the query that suits your needs. Or you can also directly type an LDAP query string, if you first learn how to form them in Chapter 6.

Viewing Advanced Features

The View menu of the snap-in includes Advanced Features. If you turn on those features, the user interface will make the following adaptations:

- Each object will show additional tabs in the property pages. We discuss the Security tab in Chapter 4 and the information in the Object tab in Chapter 5.
- You will see additional containers and objects. The System container includes miscellaneous domain-specific objects, such as the Group Policy containers. The LostAndFound container includes objects that lost their parent container due to a replication conflict. This is explained in Chapter 5. The Program Data container includes things such as Authorization Manager data that defines query-based groups. Finally, the NTDS Quotas container includes quota specifications if certain security principals have a certain maximum of how many directory objects they may own (see Chapter 4.)

DSAdd and Other Command-Line Tools

Windows Server 2003 includes a number of handy new command-line tools to search, display, add, modify, move, and delete objects. You can add computers, contacts, groups, OUs, users, and quota specifications. For other operations, the object type selection is wider, and you can search, move, or delete any object types. Figure 3.42 shows the help for the DSAdd command. In addition to the help provided from the command line, the Help and Support Center includes the help for the commands.

Figure 3.43 shows an example of how to create a user account with the DSAdd command. Note that the switches to specify first name, last name, and so on are not LDAP names or display names of the properties.

You can use the output of one command as input for another command. This is called *piping*. For example, you can list all users in a certain OU and add them as members in a certain group, as shown in Figure 3.44.

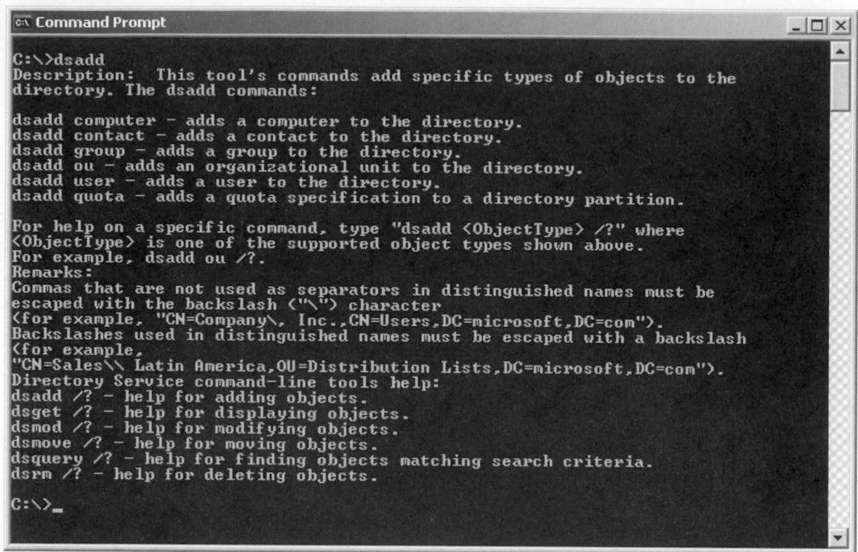

Figure 3.42 The DSAdd command enables you to add objects of six different types. There are also other commands to search, display, modify, move, and delete objects.

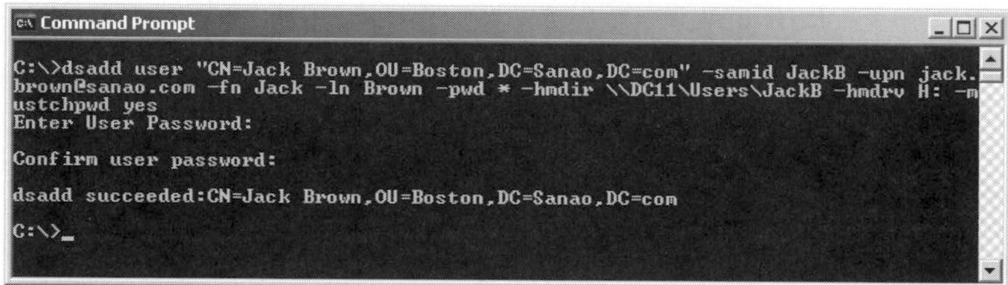

Figure 3.43 With the DSAdd command, you can create users from the command line and set many properties for them.

Figure 3.44 You can use one command to list all users of an OU (DSQuery) and then use this list as input for another command (DSMod).

Alternative Means to Manage Users and Other Objects

In addition to the Users and Computers snap-in, you have the following means available to you to manage users and other objects:

- *ADSI Edit:* This tool is part of Windows Support Tools. While the Users and Computers snap-in shows only some objects and some of their properties, ADSI Edit shows everything. It is not practical for everyday administration, but occasionally you might need it. We use ADSI Edit in quite a few places in later chapters.
- *LDIFDE and CSVDE:* These two tools are part of the operating system. They enable you to import and export objects between Active Directory and a text file. We explain how to use them in Chapter 6.
- *Net commands:* The operating system includes about 20 Net commands that were inherited from Windows NT, which inherited them from LAN Manager. You can create batch files with them to automate administration, but they don't understand the directory structure of Active Directory. You can get a list of these commands by typing "NET HELP" (without quotes), and you can get help with an individual command by typing "NET HELP *command.*"
- *WSH scripts:* You can download scripts from the Internet or write scripts that will do "anything," including managing Active Directory objects. Chapter 10 and Chapter 11 provide further information.

Conclusion

At this point you should have a pretty good understanding of users, computers, and groups in Active Directory and how to manage them. Later chapters address designing Active Directory and give practical examples of how to use the objects discussed in this chapter.

This chapter focused mainly on one tool: the Users and Computers snap-in. Later chapters introduce some Windows Support Tools and Resource Kit tools, and explain how to use scripting in user and group management.

This chapter assumed that you have full control over all objects in Active Directory. The next chapter explains how to control access and administrative rights to Active Directory by assigning permissions and user rights.

CHAPTER 4

Securing Active Directory

The previous chapter's discussion of managing OUs, users, and groups in Active Directory assumes that you always have a right to do what you want. In fact, Active Directory has access control features that facilitate the management of access to various elements in the directory. In this chapter we examine how Active Directory's access control works.

First we briefly review Windows security in general. Then we give some background for Active Directory access control. After that we move to the main topic, which is how permissions work to protect each Active Directory object.

You have three ways to manage permissions, and we describe each of them in separate sections of the chapter:

- You can manage the permissions manually. In our explanation, we don't just describe how to manage permissions, we also explore the permission mechanisms behind the administrative user interface.
- You can use the Delegation of Control wizard.
- You can accept the default permissions, which we list in a number of tables.

After we describe the mechanisms and user interface, we introduce scenarios to illustrate the kinds of permissions you can use in different practical situations and the way to implement these permissions.

As a final step to discussing permissions, we delve into the underlying architecture. This information is normally presented only to programmers, but administrators can also benefit from it.

At the end of the chapter we introduce *user rights*. They don't control access to individual objects—they control access to the system as a whole.

As a security-related topic, we discuss in Chapter 6 how to secure trusts between forests (using SID filtering, selective authentication, and name suffix routing). In Chapter 6 we also stress the importance of the physical security of domain controllers.

Introduction to Windows Security

From the very beginning, Windows NT, and consequently Windows 2000, Windows XP, and Windows Server 2003, were designed with security in mind. Windows 2000 and later enhance the security features of Windows NT and introduce new security technologies to accommodate the needs of the current intranet and Internet era. Securing data so that only those who are supposed to see it do see it is a major concern of businesses. Windows 2000 and later have "AAA" security as a result of the following features:

- *Authentication* checks the user's identity when he starts to use the network. A user tells who he is by typing a logon name and proves this by typing the correct password. Alternatively, a user can be required to insert a smart card in a reader and type a personal identification number (PIN). Authentication may be *interactive* when it takes place in the computer that the user is sitting at. Otherwise, a *network* authentication occurs when the target resource is in a different computer from the one the user is using. There are various underlying authentication protocols, such as Kerberos version 5 and Windows NT/LAN Manager (NTLM).
- *Authorization* protects the objects and resources in the network. This process determines whether the user has permission to read, modify, create, or delete a certain object or resource.
- *Auditing* enables administrators to log the usage of objects and resources. This allows administrators to see who has been gaining access to each object and what he has been doing with it.

This chapter focuses on authorization with respect to objects in Active Directory. We also briefly discuss auditing.

Some other features of Windows 2000 (and later) security include the following.

- Windows 2000 and later support *single sign-on,* which means that a user must enter her logon name and password only once, and then she can use objects and resources in different servers and workstations, even in different domains.
- *Public key infrastructure (PKI)* provides data protection by encrypting the data on disk (Encrypting File System, or EFS) and on the wire (SSL and IPSec) so that unauthorized users on a

network cannot read the data. PKI also allows digital signing of documents and software components to ensure they are not tampered with. Another application of PKI is to authenticate users who have digital certificates.

- An administrator can assign and enforce the security settings he chooses to a number of workstations and servers by using *Group Policy* and *security templates*. He can also analyze whether the current security settings of those computers are acceptable. (See Chapter 7 for more information about Group Policy.)

Whether you are administering or simply using a Windows network, you must have appropriate rights and permissions to do the things you need to do. Table 4.1 lists the typical areas of rights and permissions.

Merely putting people in the correct security groups often gives them all the rights and permissions they need. Unfortunately, there are cases that require setting them manually. Therefore, Table 4.1 mentions which utility you can use in each case to control the rights and permissions.

Table 4.1 Rights and Permissions Needed to Administer and Use Windows Servers

Rights or Permissions	Explanation	Utility to Control
User rights	Control systemwide things such as who can back up the system, log on locally to a computer, or change computer time	Group Policy Management Console, Group Policy Object Editor, or the Local Security Policy snap-in (SecPol.msc)
Permissions for Active Directory objects	Control who can create, delete, or modify Active Directory objects, or even just see their names and properties	The Users and Computers snap-in, the Sites and Services snap-in, and others
Permissions for registry keys	Control querying and setting values in the registry (which includes most of the computer and application settings)	Registry Editor (RegEdit.Exe)
Permissions for folders, files, and shares	Control the use and modification of files	Folder and file properties in Windows Explorer or any folder window

(continued)

Table 4.1 Rights and Permissions Needed to Administer and Use Windows Servers *(cont.)*

Rights or Permissions	Explanation	Utility to Control
Permissions for other resources (e.g., printers)	Control the usage and administration of the corresponding resources	Printer properties in the Printers and Faxes folder
Permissions for services	Control service-related operations such as who can start and stop a service or change its configuration	Group Policy Management Console, Group Policy Object Editor, or the Security Configuration and Analysis snap-in

NOTE User rights may override permissions. For example, if a user has the right to make backups, she can do so even though she doesn't have permission to read the files she is backing up.

NOTE The utilities mentioned are the typical ones, but there may be other choices. Also, you can control rights and permissions with scripting.

NOTE Table 4.1 lists rights and permissions that you can assign to users and groups (the latter is usually preferable). In addition, a number of security settings affect the whole computer and are not user- or group-specific. For example, you can disable the Ctrl-Alt-Delete requirement for logon if you don't need the protection it offers against malicious password-capturing programs.

Background for Active Directory Access Control

When any user tries to access any Active Directory object, the system first checks if that user has permission for the access he requested. Depending on the result, the user is either granted or denied access.

Active Directory permissions are used to control access to Active Directory. Administrators obviously need permission to create users and other objects, as well as modify existing objects. End users need permission to read the properties of their own objects and perhaps modify some of those properties. They also benefit from being able to see other users' e-mail addresses, fax numbers, and so on.

Between a full-powered administrator and an ordinary end user, there may be various levels of assistant administrators with partial administrative permissions and rights. There may also be a person who is otherwise an end user, but who can modify some information, such as the address information of all the users in her department.

In the previous chapter about OUs, users, and groups, you operated with full access. In this chapter you will learn and study what the world looks like when access is controlled and limited.

Controlling Access

The permissions that determine who can access an object and in which way (read, modify, create, delete, and so on) are stored as a property (called `nTSecurityDescriptor`) in every Active Directory object. That property also identifies the *owner* of the object.

The permissions are defined as a list of individual permission entries. It is up to the owner to specify appropriate permissions for the objects she owns. One of the permissions the owner can give to someone else is Modify Permissions. As the name implies, this allows the other party (in addition to the owner) to modify the permission list. Figure 4.1 illustrates these concepts.

NOTE A developer could create an object without an access control list. In that case, everyone would have full access to the object. In reality, however, there is always an access control list. If (and when) the list exists but is empty, no one has access to the object.

`NTSecurityDescriptor` is part of the global catalog. This means that when users search for other users or resources, they can search only on the properties that they are allowed to read, and they are shown only the objects and properties they are allowed to read.

Security Principals

You assign permissions to *security principals,* which are users (and inetOrgPerson objects), computer objects, security groups, and well-known security principals. Figure 4.2 shows them on the left. You cannot

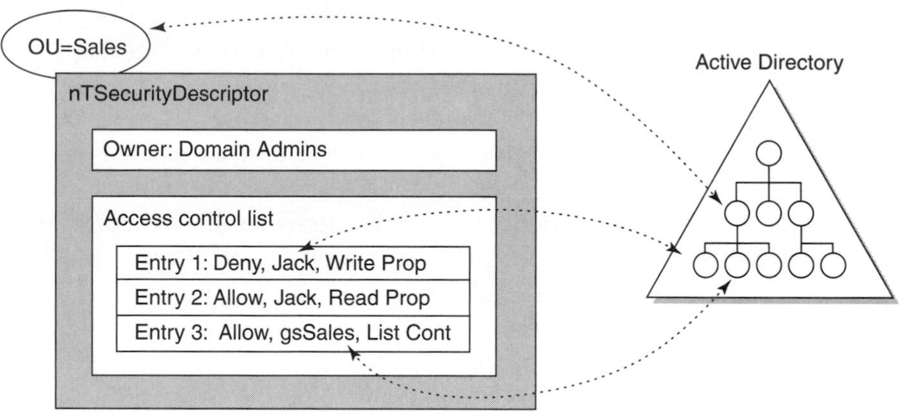

Figure 4.1 Each Active Directory object contains the `nTSecurityDescriptor` property, which identifies the owner of the object and specifies the permissions given to various users and groups. These users and groups are also objects in Active Directory.

give permissions to OUs; however, we include it (unattached) in Figure 4.2 in anticipation of Microsoft making this possible in the future. You can give permissions for any Active Directory object, as shown on the right side of Figure 4.2.

IF YOU KNOW NDS In Active Directory, only the four types on the left side of Figure 4.2 can have permissions for objects and resources, while in NDS any directory object can have permissions for objects and resources.

As Figure 4.2 shows, you can assign user Jack permissions for group gsSales, group gsSales permissions for user Jack, user Jack permissions for user Jill, or user Jill permissions for user Jack.

NOTE Remember that the best choice is to assign permissions to domain local groups, the second best choice is to use global or universal groups, and the last choice is to assign permissions directly to users.

No matter which type of security principal gets the permissions, it's always the logged-on user (or a background process running under some

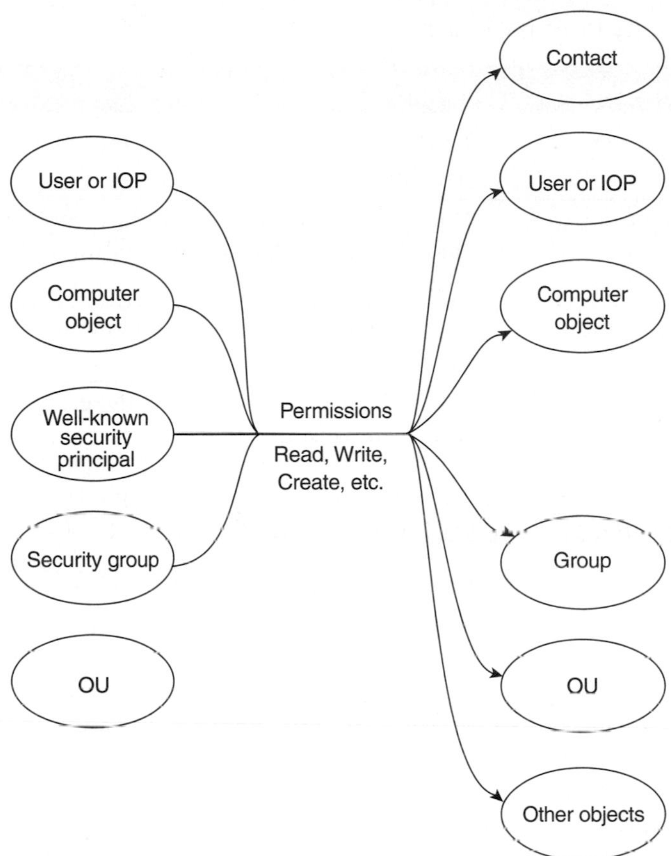

Figure 4.2 You can give permissions to four different security principals, shown on the left side of the image, and you can give them for any Active Directory object, like those shown on the right side of the image. IOP stands for inetOrgPerson.

user account) who is actually using them. Table 4.2 lists when a user can leverage the permissions given to one of the four security principal types.

IF YOU KNOW NDS There is no concept of security equivalence in Active Directory.

Table 4.2 Security Principal Types

Security Principal Type	When a User Can Leverage
User or inetOrgPerson	Obviously, when the user (or inetOrgPerson) is the user himself
Computer object	When the process is using the local System account (more on this in the "Access Control Architecture" section)
Well-known security principal (e.g., Interactive)	When the user meets the condition (e.g., when he is an interactive user)
Security group	When the user is a member of the group, either directly or via other groups

Well-Known Security Principals

The term *well-known security principal* refers to fixed accounts that are somewhat like users or groups. However, you cannot delete or rename them. Actually, you don't even see them in the list of users and groups (except in the dialog boxes where you give permissions).

A well-known security principal may include a number of users, but you cannot designate who these "members" are. For example, whether a user is a "member" of Interactive depends on the circumstances—he is a "member" if he is sitting at the computer where the resource being accessed resides. Table 4.3 explains Interactive and the other well-known security principals.

Well-known security principals are referred to as *special identities* in the Help and Support Center. The reason for well-known security principals to exist is that they allow administrators to assign permissions to these special identities, so that appropriate users can use those permissions. You can also think of well-known security principals as "dynamic groups," because their "member" lists are dynamically determined. Do not confuse them, however, with query-based groups, which were introduced in Windows Server 2003 and explained briefly in Chapter 1. The member list of query-based groups is actually also dynamically determined.

The number of these "dynamic groups" was increased in Windows Server 2003, compared to Windows 2000 (which in turn was increased, compared to Windows NT). This indicates that future versions of Windows may introduce even more of them, such as "Those-who-authenticated-using-a-smart-card."

Table 4.3 Well-Known Security Principals

Security Principal	Explanation
Anonymous Logon	This account represents anyone who just came to the network and started accessing a server without a username (if anonymous logon is allowed). This is sometimes referred to as *null session.* Note that Windows clients don't let users choose whether or not to use a username. This choice depends on the operation (most operations use the username, but some operations use a null session) and is made automatically in the background.
Authenticated Users	This account includes anyone* who has been authenticated by a valid username and, usually, a valid password. This includes all users who have a valid user account in the forest. It also includes all users of any trusted external domain/forest if the corresponding trust uses domainwide/ forestwide authentication. However, the Guest account is not included.
Batch	This account includes anyone who did the authentication using a special Batch logon type (e.g., the task scheduler jobs).
Creator Owner	Permissions given to Creator Owner are inherited by child objects so that the owner of each existing and new child object (usually the one who created the child object) gets permissions for the child object. If you later change some Creator Owner permissions, the change will affect the existing objects as well. Also, if the owner changes, the new owner will get these permissions. (For more information, see the "Creator Owner" section later in this chapter.)
Creator Group	This choice is the same as the preceding one, except that instead of the owner himself, his primary group is used.
Dialup	This account includes anyone who logged on (or authenticated) using a dial-up or virtual private network (VPN) connection.
Enterprise Domain Controllers	This account includes the Active Directory domain controllers of the forest.
Everyone	In Windows Server 2003, this account includes Authenticated Users and Guest. In earlier versions, it also includes Anonymous Logon. See Figure 3.4.

(*continued*)

* Here "anyone" could mean either a real user (person) or some process in the computer.

Table 4.3 Well-Known Security Principals *(cont.)*

Security Principal	Explanation
Interactive	This account includes anyone who authenticated from the same (local) computer. In other words, the user must be sitting at the keyboard of the computer where the resource is. This account also includes a remote desktop connection.
Network	This account includes anyone whose authentication request came from some other computer.
Proxy	Not used.
Restricted	Reserved for future use.
Self (or Principal Self)	This account is a placeholder for the object itself. Giving Self some permission for Jack is the same as giving Jack that permission for Jack. Using Self is especially helpful when giving some permission to all users in an OU for themselves (i.e., giving the permission for the OU and specifying that it is inherited by all child user objects).
Service	This account includes anyone who did the authentication using a special Service logon type. Examples of this are the services running in a computer.
System (or LocalSystem)	This is a fixed account that services in Windows run with, unless they are assigned to use some other account (see also the "Access Control Architecture" section). The System account does not have a password, and it has permissions to quite a few files and Active Directory objects, as well as over 20 user rights.
Terminal Server User	This account includes users who logged on using Terminal Services version 4.0 application compatibility mode.
This Organization**	This Organization represents users who did not authenticate across a trust with selective authentication enabled. In other words, it represents Authenticated Users of the local forest and of trusted forests when selective authentication is not used on the trust. See also Other Organization.

** Introduced in Windows Server 2003

Table 4.3 Well-Known Security Principals (*cont.*)

Security Principal	Explanation
Other Organization**	Other Organization is present in the authorization data if the authentication request comes across a trust where selective authentication is enabled. The presence triggers the authenticating domain controller to check if the Allowed to Authenticate permission is granted. If not, the access is denied and an authentication firewall error is displayed. If the permission is granted, the authentication succeeds, and Other Organization becomes effective (by becoming part of the access token). Consequently, if you assign permissions to Other Organization, users from other forests (with selective authentication enabled) who are allowed to authenticate receive those permissions. For more information about selective authentication, see Chapter 6.
Local Service**	This fixed account has many fewer permissions than the System account (no default permissions to Active Directory and only three user rights, plus those assigned to normal users). Therefore, some Windows Server 2003 services that don't need the wide permissions of the System account use Local Service instead. Local Service has no password, but it has its own subkey (S-1-5-19) under HKEY_USERS in the registry. Local Service is not valid in other computers in the network.
Network Service**	The description of Local Service applies to Network Service, with two exceptions: (a) The registry key is S-1-5-20, and (b) like the System account, Network Service presents the computer's credentials to remote computers, so you can assign permissions using the corresponding computer account.
NTLM Authentication**	This account includes users who authenticated using NTLM authentication. In short, NTLM is used when Kerberos cannot be used, and this happens most commonly when a Windows NT computer is involved or when an external trust is used.

(continued)

** Introduced in Windows Server 2003

Table 4.3 Well-Known Security Principals *(cont.)*

Security Principal	Explanation
SChannel Authentication**	This account includes users who authenticated using secure channel authentication (using a PKI certificate) of IIS. The secure protocol is either Secure Sockets Layer (SSL), Transport Layer Security (TLS), or Private Communications Technology (PCT).
Digest Authentication**	This account includes users who authenticated using digest authentication, which is one of the available IIS authentication methods for HTTP communications (starting with Windows XP and Windows Server 2003). Digest authentication can also be used with Simple Authentication Security Layer (SASL)-based communications.
Remote Interactive Logon**	This account includes users who logged on using the remote desktop connection.

** Introduced in Windows Server 2003

NOTE You shouldn't use the System account to run third-party services in domain controllers, because that account has so many rights to Active Directory. It is safer to use some other account, such as Network Service or Local Service. In member servers and workstations, the System account doesn't have rights to Active Directory, but it is still better to use other accounts for running services.

IF YOU KNOW NT In Windows NT it was quite common to run services with the System account. If you got into this habit, now is a good time to get out of it.

NOTE You cannot extend the list of well-known security principals. They are preprogrammed into Windows.

NOTE Microsoft provides four authentication packages with Windows XP and Windows Server 2003 (Kerberos, NTLM, SChannel, and Digest), and a fifth one called Negotiate, which is used to select among Kerberos or NTLM. Of the four actual packages, three have a corresponding well-known security principal (described in Table 4.3), but for some reason Kerberos does not.

You can put a well-known security principal as a member in a domain local or built-in group, using either the Users and Computers snap-in or a command such as the following:

```
NET LOCALGROUP "Print Operators" Interactive /ADD
```

This command would put Interactive as a member in the Print Operators built-in group, allowing any locally logged-on user to create a print queue, for example.

NOTE You can put Interactive in a domain local or built-in group, or assign permissions to Interactive. However, Active Directory in Windows 2000 doesn't honor either of these settings—that is, a user logged on at a domain controller cannot use those permissions to access Active Directory. For example, if Interactive is a member of Print Operators, a user who is logged on at a domain controller cannot create a printer object. However, he can create a printer (i.e., print queue) because it is outside Active Directory. In Windows Server 2003, Active Directory does honor the settings.

Managing Active Directory Permissions

To manage permissions in your Active Directory, you can use the following means (in order of preference):

- *Default settings.* If you can cope with per-domain permissions, and you don't need per-OU (or even more granular) permissions, you will probably do fine with the default permissions. All you need to do is put users in appropriate, predefined administrative groups, such as Account Operators.
- *Wizard.* Use the Delegation of Control wizard to give additional permissions that the defaults won't cover.
- *ACL Editor.* Turn on Advanced Features in the Users and Computers snap-in and start using the Security tab (i.e., ACL Editor) to assign permissions manually.

In this chapter we discuss the three choices in just the opposite order. First we explore ACL Editor and the mechanisms behind it. Then we talk about the Delegation of Control wizard. Last, we list the default permissions for various Active Directory objects. The reason for the opposite order is that if you want to understand the Delegation of Control wizard or the defaults, you need to understand the permissions mechanisms. Those in turn can best be explained with the manual user interface, so we start with it.

Remember that to be able to manage permissions for some object, you need to either be the owner of that object or have Modify Permissions permission for it.

When you start to use ACL Editor, we recommend you proceed in the following order:

- Don't change anything.
- Don't click OK or Apply.
- Learn how the permissions work.
- Learn some more.
- First use a small test network.
- When you finally start making changes in the production network, explore the results after each change.

If you make unwanted changes, permissions may become either too loose or too tight. The former case is a security risk if someone accidentally or deliberately makes use of the excess permissions. The latter case may result in a loss of some functionality.

To correct the wrong permissions, you first need to discover the problem and then know which permissions to restore. To determine the latter, you can see what kind of permissions other similar objects have and proceed on the assumption that those permissions are appropriate to restore. You could also use security templates to restore the defaults, as discussed in Chapter 7.

NOTE If you remove all administrative permissions for an object (usually by blocking inheritance to it and removing some permission entries), the owner of the object can restore the permissions.

Permission Concepts

Before we look at the user interface for permission management, we'll introduce a few concepts.

- By *special permissions* we mean individual "atomic" permissions. A *standard permission* is a group of special permissions; that is, one standard permission maps to a group of special permissions. The goal is to define standard permissions so that you seldom need to assign individual special permissions. This is analogous to file and folder permissions; however, the distinction between standard and special permissions is not as clear in the case of Active Directory as in the case of files and folders.

- Permission may be for access to the whole object *(object permissions)*, or it may be for access to one or several of the properties of the object *(property permissions)*.
- Permissions can be *inherited* (or propagate) so that a permission assigned in an upper level affects all the lower levels.

IF YOU KNOW NT Active Directory permissions are in many ways similar to the old NTFS permissions in Windows NT because both build on security descriptors, owners, DACLs, and ACEs. However, there are three major differences. First, Active Directory uses a different inheritance model, which is explained later in this chapter. Second, in Active Directory you can set permissions on individual properties. Third, the user interface in Active directory enables you to deny individual permissions, rather than deny everything as you must in Windows NT.

NOTE When you change any permissions, they take effect immediately after the change has replicated to the user's target domain controller. The user doesn't need to log off and log on again for the changes to take effect.

Table 4.4 shows an overview of standard and special permissions, as well as object and property permissions.

With these few basic concepts in mind, we turn to the user interface for permissions management.

Anatomy of ACL Editor Dialog Boxes

You can assign permissions via four dialog boxes. You may not need to use them all, however.

- *Dialog box A:* A view of standard and some special permissions for an object and standard permissions for its properties (that is, property sets) ("Basic")

Table 4.4 Overview of Permissions

	Standard Permissions	Special Permissions
Object Permissions	Full Control, Read, Write (each of which maps to several special permissions)	Eleven individual permissions for any object class (e.g., List Contents, Delete Subtree, and Modify Owner) and two more for parent classes (Create All Child Objects and Delete All Child Objects); also numerous individual permissions for one object class (e.g., Manage Replication Topology for domain or Reset Password for user)
Property Permissions	Read or Write permission for a property set (i.e., a certain group of properties)	Read or Write permission for an individual property

- *Dialog box B:* A view of individual permission entries, either standard or special ("Advanced")
- *Dialog box C:* A view of special permissions for an object
- *Dialog box D:* A view of standard permissions (that is, for property sets) and special permissions (that is, for individual properties) for object properties

Figure 4.3 illustrates how these four dialog boxes cover standard and special permissions for objects and properties.

The four dialog boxes may seem a little complicated at first. After all, you have to select Advanced Features and click the Advanced button to see them. To help you understand the dialog boxes, we discuss each one and show a screen shot of it in the sections that follow.

We'll mention the inheritance features here, but we'll study them in more detail a little later in the "Inheritance" section.

Dialog Box A

Dialog box A is shown in Figure 4.4. Table 4.5 describes its elements.

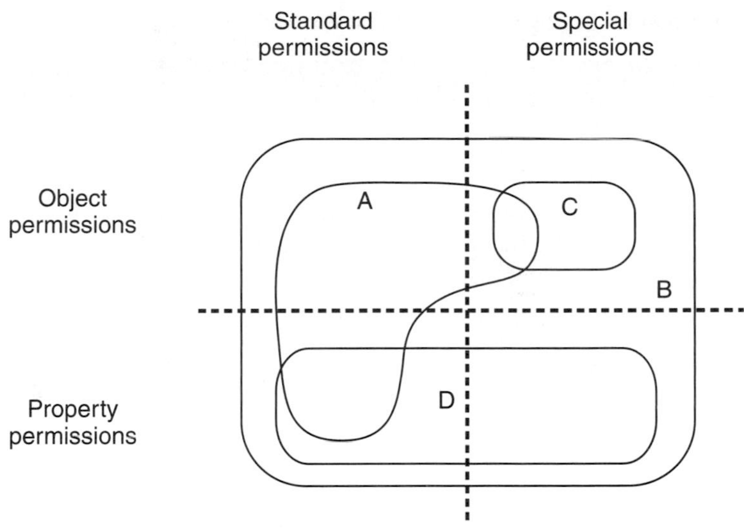

Figure 4.3 The four dialog boxes of ACL Editor (A, B, C, and D) cover standard and special permissions, as well as object and property permissions in different ways.

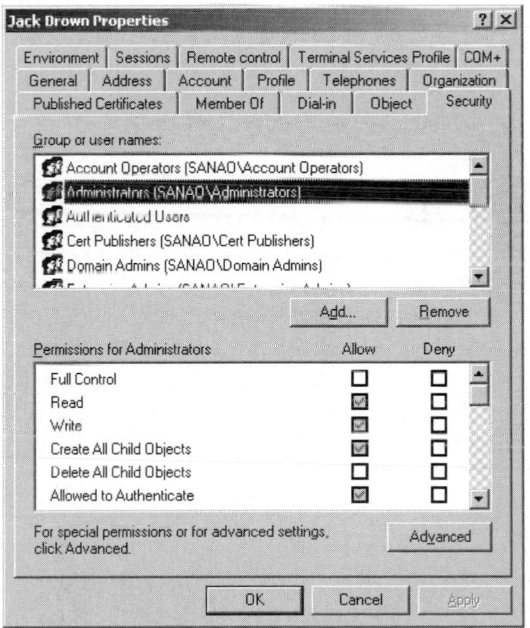

Figure 4.4 Dialog box A ("Basic") shows standard and some special permissions for an object and standard permissions for its properties (that is, for property sets).

Table 4.5 Elements of Dialog Box A ("Basic")

Element	Description
Title bar	Indicates that you are looking at permissions for Jack Brown.
Group or user names	Shows all the names (i.e., security principals) that have some permissions for Jack Brown. Each name appears just once on the list. Using the corresponding buttons, you can add and remove names from the list.
Permissions for <the selected group or user>	Lists the standard permissions and some special permissions that this class of object may have and standard permissions that its properties may have (that is, property sets.) (The check marks indicate which permissions the selected name is granted or denied. Obviously, you can check and uncheck the Allow and Deny boxes to change the permissions of the selected name. If a check box is grayed out, it means that the permission in question was inherited from an upper level—you cannot change the setting here. A check box is grayed out also when you don't have a permission to modify the permissions. The lowermost check box is Special Permissions. It is checked, if the permissions include something that cannot be shown in the preceding lines.
Advanced button	Clicking the Advanced button takes you to dialog box B. This button is not related to any name on the list, but it applies to the target object as a whole (i.e., Jack Brown).

WARNING There are two cases where dialog box A adds check marks (and consequently permissions) automatically. First, if you add a name to the list, it gets a number of check marks right away (to correspond to the Read permission and applying to "this object only"). Second, if you check the Read box, for example, a number of other boxes get checked automatically. If you now clear that Read box, the other boxes won't clear. Unfortunately, there is no Clear All button. Before you click OK or Apply, be sure that only the appropriate boxes have check marks.

WARNING In some cases there are additional permissions present, even though the dialog box doesn't show the Special Permissions box checked, so you cannot be sure that the information dialog box A shows is always accurate.

WARNING Some of the permissions are passed on to child objects by inheritance and some are not. Dialog box A may look exactly the same for both cases, so you cannot tell the difference without opening dialog box B.

Dialog Box B

Figure 4.5 shows dialog box B. The box displays a list of entries to indicate who has permissions, the type of permissions, whether the permission was inherited from above (and from where), and whether each applies to the target object and/or child objects. Table 4.6 describes the elements in this box.

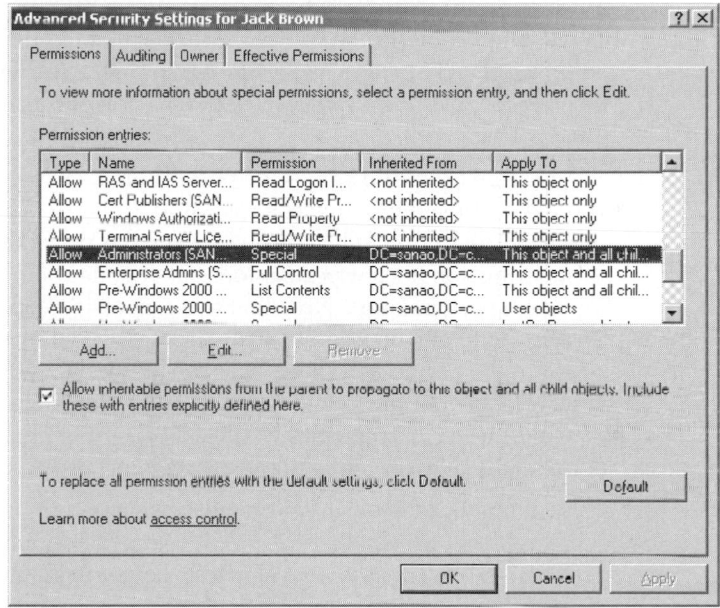

Figure 4.5 Dialog box B ("Advanced") shows the individual permission entries as either standard or special permissions. However, the text might display just "Special" without further information.

Table 4.6 Elements of Dialog Box B ("Advanced")

Element	Description
Permission entries	There is one line for each entry. (You may be familiar with the term *access control entry [ACE]* from Windows NT. A "permission entry" here is the same as an ACE.) Note that sometimes one entry is multiplied to several entries (and consequently lines in the dialog box). This takes place if you check a combination of permissions that Active Directory cannot store in a single entry. For example, if Jack has Full Control and you modify this single entry by removing one property permission (using dialog box D), Jack will have at least 50 permission entries after that. They list all other permissions, except the one removed property permission.
Type column	This column is either Allow or Deny, depending on whether you are giving or prohibiting the associated permission(s).
Name column	This column contains the security principal that has the permission(s). The same name can appear on the list several times to cover all the different permission elements this security principal has.
Permission column	This column briefly describes the permission(s) given with this entry. If it displays just "Special" or "Read Property," you need to click the Edit button (which is replaced by the View button if you have permission to view permissions but not edit them) to see the actual permission(s). Note that one permission entry may correspond to one or several permissions. In the latter case, however, the permissions must have such characteristics that Active Directory can store them in a single permission entry. For example, Read All Properties, Write All Properties, and Read Permissions all three fit in a single permission entry.
Inherited From column	This column displays whether the permission entry is inherited and, if so, from which object above. You cannot edit inherited permissions (except on the level where they were granted). Or actually, you can edit an inherited permission entry to include more permissions, but this results in the creation of a new entry.
Apply To column	This column shows the scope of the permission(s). (For more information, see the "Inheritance" section later in this chapter.)
Allow inheritable permissions . . .	This check box dictates whether this object can inherit permissions from upper levels (in which case it can also pass them on to lower levels).

Table 4.6 Elements of Dialog Box B ("Advanced") (*cont.*)

Element	Description
Buttons	The Add and Remove buttons enable you to add and remove entries. Clicking the Add or View/Edit button takes you to dialog box C (although with the Add button you must first specify who will get the permissions.) Note that unlike the Advanced button in dialog box A, the View/Edit button is related to the selected entry. If you don't have a permission to modify the permissions, you see the View button instead of the Edit button. The default button will obviously restore the same default permissions for this object that existed right after the object was created. Clicking the Default button has a funny-looking side effect: All inherited permission entries disappear from the list. When you reopen the dialog box, however, the inherited permissions are back in place.

WARNING If you click OK or Apply in dialog box B, your changes are saved, even if you subsequently click Cancel in dialog box A.

TIP You can sort the entries by any column by clicking that column header. When you sort by the Name column, you can make sure that you see all the entries of a given security principal.

Dialog Box C

Figure 4.6 shows dialog box C, which displays the special permissions for an object. Table 4.7 describes the elements in this dialog box.

Dialog Box D

Figure 4.7 shows dialog box D. The elements (fields) in dialog box D are the same as in dialog box C. The difference is that instead of special object permissions, the list contains standard and special permissions for object properties. (We'll study the list in the "Permissions for Object Properties" section later in this chapter.) In the visible area of the list in Figure 4.7, Public Information, Remote Access Information, and Web Information are standard permissions (that is, property sets), and the remaining items are special permissions (that is, individual properties.)

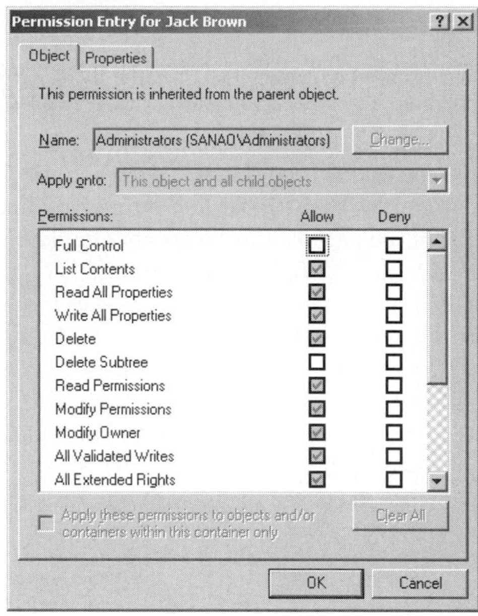

Figure 4.6 Dialog box C shows the special permissions for an object.

Table 4.7 Elements of Dialog Box C

Element	Description
Name/ Change	The "Name" field shows which security principal has the permission(s) shown in the dialog box. If you need to change the owner of this (these) permission(s), you can click the Change button. Note, however, that the original security principal loses its permission(s), and the change you make applies to the selected permission entry only.
Apply onto	This field determines the scope of the permission(s). See the "Inheritance" section later in this chapter.
Permissions	This field lists all the special object permissions that this class of object can have. The check marks indicate the current permissions, and if the box is grayed out, the permission is inherited and you cannot change it here. The check boxes are also grayed out if you don't have a permission to modify the permissions.

Table 4.7 Elements of Dialog Box C (*cont.*)

Element	Description
Apply these permissions . . .	If the “Apply onto” field defines that the permissions apply to children also, then by default they apply to the whole object tree beneath. By checking this box, you limit the scope to the first level only.
Clear All	Clicking this button clears all the check boxes.

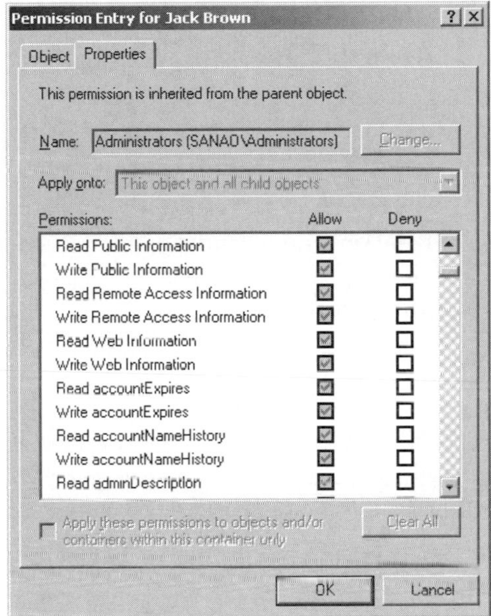

Figure 4.7 Dialog box D shows the standard and special permissions for object properties.

Summary of the Dialog Boxes

As a summary, Table 4.8 lists how dialog boxes A, C, and D show the various standard/special and object/property permissions. Also, this time we have divided special object permissions into three categories. We don’t include dialog box B, because it shows all permissions that are specified for an object and its properties.

Table 4.8 Permissions for a User Object by Categories

Type	For	Permissions	A	C**	D**
Standard	Objects	Full Control, Read, Write	X		
Special	Objects	Eleven individual permissions for any object class (such as List Contents, Delete Subtree, and Modify Owner) and two more for container classes (Create All Child Objects and Delete All Child Objects)	(X)*	X	
Special	Objects	"Extended rights" (e.g., Manage Replication Topology for domain objects or Reset Password for user objects)	X	X	
Special	Objects	Create or delete objects of a certain class		X	
Standard	Properties	Read or Write permission for a property set (i.e., a certain group of properties)	X		X
Special	Properties	Read or Write permission for an individual property			X

* Of the 13 first special object permissions, dialog box A shows only two (Create/Delete All Child Objects). Consequently, we have put the X in parentheses.

** In addition to the X marks in the table, dialog box C shows Full Control and dialog box D contains Read/Write All Properties.

Standard and Special Object Permissions

As Table 4.8 indicates, in addition to standard object permissions there are three categories of special object permissions:

- Thirteen (or 11) individual permissions
- Extended rights
- Create/delete objects of a certain class

We suggested earlier that you first try to use standard permissions, and only if they are not enough, use the more granular special permissions. Even though the "basic" dialog box A already shows some special permissions, you should keep in mind that dialog box A shows only an

Table 4.9 Dialog Box A Permissions for a User Object by Category

Type	For	Permissions	Comments
Standard	Objects	Full Control Read Write	You'll see these three permissions for practically any object class.
Special	Objects	Create All Child Objects Delete All Child Objects	You'll see these two permissions for any container object class. Note that user and computer objects are internally containers, but a contact is not.
Special	Objects	Allowed to Authenticate Change Password Receive As Reset Password Send As	These listed extended rights are for user objects (and computer objects).
Standard	Properties	Read/Write General Information and so on	These permissions are for user objects (and maybe also for some others).

approximation of permissions, while dialog boxes B, C, and D describe them accurately. Therefore, if you start to define special permissions, it is a good idea to switch to use dialog boxes B, C, and D.

In this section we delve into the permissions that you see on the lists of the dialog boxes and the relationship between standard and special permissions, or among dialog boxes.

We start by categorizing dialog box A permissions for a user object. Remember that each object class may have a slightly different list (see Table 4.9).

The seven special object permissions listed in Table 4.9 exist in dialog boxes A and C.

Standard Object Permissions

There are three standard object permissions: Full Control, Read, and Write. You see them in dialog box A and each of them maps to a number of special permissions that you see in dialog box C. Table 4.10 lists these mappings.

Table 4.10 Dialog Box A Permission Mappings to Dialog Box C

Special Permission	Full Control*	Read	Write
List Contents	X	X	
List Object**	X		
Read All Properties	X	X	
Write All Properties	X		X
Delete	X		
Delete Subtree	X		
Read Permissions	X	X	
Modify Permissions	X		
Modify Owner	X		
All Validated Writes	X		X
All Extended Rights	X		
Create All Child Objects	X		
Delete All Child Objects	X		

* Dialog box C contains Full Control also. It is not a special permission: It shows on the list as a shortcut to quickly give all permissions.

** By default, the List Object functionality is not enabled and the permission is not visible in dialog box C.

When you check some permissions in dialog box A, you will see the corresponding permissions checked in dialog box C. Likewise, if in dialog box C you check a combination that matches a permission in dialog box A, you will see that permission checked when you go back to dialog box A.

NOTE Some check boxes automatically check others outside Table 4.10. For example, checking All Extended Rights autochecks Change Password. The autochecked permissions are actually a subset of the first checked permission.

Thirteen (or 11) Individual Permissions

This category of special object permissions doesn't have a name, but each time you see 13 or 11 in this chapter, it most likely refers to this category. Each of the 13 permissions corresponds to one bit in the Access-Mask field of a permission entry. This set of 13 permissions may apply to any Active Directory object except two (Create/Delete All Child Objects) that apply only to container objects.

Table 4.11 lists the same permissions as Table 4.10, but now we include an explanation of each permission.

Table 4.11 Special Object Permissions for Any Object Class

Special Permission	Explanation
List Contents	The right to list names of the immediate children of this object but not their properties or even types (i.e., classes).
List Object	By default, this functionality is not enabled and the permission is not visible in the list of dialog box C. If you add this permission programmatically, however, it will show in dialog box B. You can enable the functionality and make the permission visible in dialog box C (see the explanation of this permission in the text).
Read All Properties*	The permission to read all properties (except the owner and permissions) of the object.
Write All Properties	The permission to write to all properties (except the owner and permissions) of the object.
Delete	The permission to delete the object.
Delete Subtree	The permission to delete a subtree as one operation. However, this only works if the user also has the Delete permission for the root object of the subtree.
Read Permissions	The permission to see the owner and permissions for the object but not its auditing settings.
Modify Permissions	The permission to modify the permissions for the object.
Modify Owner	The permission to take ownership of the object and, starting with Windows Server 2003, to give the ownership to someone else. However, giving the ownership is not possible unless the person performing the operation also has the "Restore files and directories" user right.

(continued)

* You could claim that some of the permissions in the table, such as Read All Properties and Write All Properties, are for properties, not for the object. Also, permissions and owner are technically stored in one property, so being able to modify them is actually being able to modify a property. However, we count them all as object permissions.

Table 4.11 Special Object Permissions for Any Object Class *(cont.)*

Special Permission	Explanation
All Validated Writes	The permission to perform any validated write. Active Directory can validate that writes to certain properties are of the correct syntax. Examples of such properties are the DNS host name and service principal name.
All Extended Rights	As the name implies, this permission is equal to all extended rights.
Create All Child Objects	The permission to create child objects for the object.
Delete All Child Objects	The permission to delete immediate child objects of the object.

Enabling and Using the List Object Permission

The three visible "read" permissions (i.e., List Contents, Read All Properties, and Read Permissions) are usually enough to cover various read-related scenarios. The fourth (normally invisible) "read" permission is List Object.

To enable the List Object functionality and make the permission visible in dialog box C, you must modify the `dSHeuristics` property (using ADSI Edit, for example) of the object `CN=Directory Service, CN=Windows NT, CN=Services, CN=Configuration, DC=sanao, DC=com`. The property uses string syntax and by default the value is not set. Each character in the value corresponds to one setting, so that "0" indicates a default setting and "1" indicates the alternate setting. The third character from the left controls the List Object functionality. In other words, to enable it, you must write "001" (without quotes) into the `dSHeuristics` property.

NOTE If `dSHeuristics` already contains a value, you should only change the third character from "0" to "1." If the first character of the property is "1," the first/last name functionality of Ambiguous Name Resolution (ANR) is suppressed, and if the second character is "1," the last/first name functionality is suppressed. For more information on ANR, see Chapter 8.

While the List Contents permission allows viewing of all immediate child objects, using List Object allows hiding some of them. If someone doesn't have List Contents permission to the parent object, List Object can be used to grant him permission to see the existence of individual child objects. That user sees only those child objects for which he has the List Object permission and the remaining child objects are invisible to him.

NOTE For the List Object permission to work, you must grant it also for the parent object. Obviously, this permission must not propagate to the child objects, or otherwise they would all be visible. Either block the inheritance in the child objects, or define the parent object permission to be for "this object only."

The List Object Permission Peculiarity

In a prerelease version of Windows 2000, the standard permission Read corresponded to four special permissions: List Contents, List Object, Read All Properties, and Read Permissions. In the final release, however, Microsoft dropped List Object, so Read now corresponds to three special permissions.

Quite a few Active Directory default permission entries are still based on the old definition of Read, so with the new definition, those entries actually are "standard permission Read + special permission List Object." This will show in the following ways in the dialog boxes (when the List Object functionality is disabled):

- *Dialog box A:* Read and Special Permissions
- *Dialog box B:* Special
- *Dialog box C:* List Contents, Read All Properties, and Read Permissions

---

NOTE Dialog box C's display of the "standard permission Read + special permission List Object" entry is incorrect, or incomplete, because it doesn't include List Object (unless you have enabled the functionality with the `dSHeuristics` property).

Consider the following example. When you create a new group object, Authenticated Users gets Read + List Object default permissions for the group, and this shows in dialog boxes A, B, and C as just listed. If you next give Jack a Read permission for the group, the permission will, of course, show as Read in dialog boxes A and B. In dialog box C, however, Jack's permission (i.e., Read) maps to the same three permissions

(List Contents, Read All Properties, and Read Permissions) as the default permission (i.e., Read + List Object) seems to map. The fact that the latter contains a fourth permission is invisible.

When the List Object functionality is disabled, the Read standard permission corresponds to the aforementioned three special permissions. If you enable the functionality, Read now corresponds to the four special permissions—that is, to List Object also. Consequently, if you now grant someone the Read standard permission, she will get four special permissions instead of three.

NOTE This peculiarity in the user interface doesn't hurt your permission management by causing any wrong permissions. After all, since List Object is invisible by default, it is also inactive. It is just a slight inconvenience that instead of seeing Read in dialog boxes A and B, you see Read + Special Permissions or Special.

Extended Rights

AD2003 defines 52 extended rights out of the box (39 in AD2000.) Each of them has a corresponding Active Directory object to define it (as discussed in more detail in the "Access Control Architecture" section). A directory-enabled application can create its own extended rights and use them as it wishes (see the "Permissions in Applications" section later in this chapter.)

Extended rights apply to one or more object classes, and consequently you will see a different list of these permissions in different object classes. Table 4.12 describes the five extended rights that apply to user objects in AD2003 (the same five apply also to computer and inetOrgPerson objects.)

Table 4.13 lists the extended rights that apply to each class in AD2003 (excluding the `user` class).

Contact or shared folder objects have no extended rights of their own.

NOTE Shared folders have, of course, share permissions and folder permissions, but those are outside Active Directory.

We won't try to describe the meaning of the permissions in Table 4.13, because each of them relates to a certain service or function. To

Table 4.12 Extended Rights for User Objects

Special Permission	Explanation
Change Password	Allows the password to be changed if the old password is known. In other words, the user can change her own password.
Reset Password	Allows a new password to be set even if the old password is not known. In other words, an administrator can change a user's forgotten password.
Allowed to Authenticate	This permission is used, if you choose selective authentication, when setting up a forest trust between two forests or an external trust between two domains. For more information, see Chapter 6.
Receive As	Not used by Windows 2000 or Windows Server 2003 operating system (but used by Exchange 2000 and later).
Send As	Not used by Windows 2000 or Windows Server 2003 operating system (but used by Exchange 2000 and later).

Table 4.13 Extended Rights for Other Classes

Object Class	Exists As	Extended Rights
`computer`	Trivial	Validated write to DNS host name, Validated write to service principal name (and the ones listed in Table 4.12)
`group`	Trivial	Add/Remove self as member, Send To
`domainDNS`	`DC=sanao, DC=com`	Add GUID, Change PDC, Add/Remove Replica In Domain, Create Inbound Forest Trust, Enable Per User Reversibly Encrypted Password, Migrate SID History, Unexpire Password, Update Password Not Required Bit

(continued)

Table 4.13 Extended Rights for Other Classes *(cont.)*

Object Class	Exists As	Extended Rights
domainDNS, organizationalUnit	DC=sanao, DC=com and trivial	Generate Resultant Set of Policy (Logging), Generate Resultant Set of Policy (Planning)
dMD	CN=Schema, CN=Configuration, DC=sanao, DC=com	Change Schema Master, Update Schema Cache
dMD, configuration, domainDNS	Two previous (DC=sanao and CN=Schema), and CN=Configuration, DC=sanao, DC=com	Replicating Directory Changes, Manage Replication Topology, Replication Synchronization, Replicating Directory Changes All, Monitor Active Directory Replication, Reanimate Tombstones
addressBookContainer	Doesn't exist by default	Open Address List
crossRefContainer	CN=Partitions, CN=Configuration, DC=sanao, DC=com	Change Domain Master, Execute Forest Update Script
groupPolicyContainer	CN={31B2...}, CN=Policies, CN=System, DC=sanao, DC=com	Apply Group Policy
infrastructure-Update	CN=Infrastructure, DC=sanao, DC=com	Change Infrastructure Master
msDS-QuotaContainer	CN=NTDS Quotas in each partition root except the schema partition	Query Self Quota
mSMQConfiguration	Doesn't exist by default	Peek Computer Journal, Peek Dead Letter, Receive Computer Journal, Receive Dead Letter
msMQ-Group, mSMQQueue	Doesn't exist by default	Send Message
mSMQQueue	Doesn't exist by default	Peek Message, Receive Message, Receive Journal

Table 4.13 Extended Rights for Other Classes (*cont.*)

Object Class	Exists As	Extended Rights
nTDSDSA	CN=NTDS Settings	Abandon Replication (only in AD2000), Allocate Rids, Do Garbage Collection, Check Stale Phantoms, Recalculate Hierarchy, Recalculate Security Inheritance, Refresh Group Cache for Logons
pKICertificateTemplate	Doesn't exist by default	Enroll
rIDManager	CN=RID Manager$, CN=System, DC=sanao, DC=com	Change Rid Master
samServer	CN=Server, CN=System, DC=sanao, DC=com	Domain Administer Server, Enumerate Entire SAM Domain
site	Trivial	Open Connector Queue

understand the meaning of the permission, you must be familiar with that service or function. Also, the permission names are more or less self-explanatory.

Create/Delete Objects of a Certain Class

In addition to giving permission to create and delete child objects of any class, you can give the permission for each applicable object class separately. For example, you could give permission to create just user objects.

Permissions for Object Properties

In addition to object permissions, you can control who can read and write Active Directory information on a per-property basis.

The permission list in dialog box D (i.e., the Properties tab in Advanced, View/Edit) has the following types of permissions, although the second one may not be present with all object classes:

- Read/Write all properties
- Read/Write various property sets (i.e., groups of properties)
- Read/Write individual properties

The first item on the list (Read/Write all) is actually one of the special object permissions. We will discuss the other two, permissions for property sets and individual properties, in the following subsections.

NOTE Technically, object permissions and owner are stored in one property. However, even if you have write permission to all properties, you cannot modify permissions or owner.

Permissions for Property Sets

In addition to extended rights, property sets are defined in corresponding Active Directory objects. Table 4.14 lists the 12 property sets that exist in AD2003 (10 in AD2000) out of the box. The table also lists the classes to which each property set applies and the common name of each corresponding object.

As mentioned earlier, each property set includes a number of properties. For example, giving the permission Read Public Information is equivalent to giving Read permissions for 34 corresponding properties.

Of the 12 property sets in Table 4.14, you cannot use the following, at all or partly:

- *Phone and Mail Options.* This property set doesn't include any properties, so checking it has no meaning.
- *Group Membership.* In AD2000, this property set included one property (`member`) and it gave permission to add and modify members. However, this property set applies only to users and users cannot have members, so you could not use that property set in AD2000. It didn't give permission to make the user a member in a group. Once we told Microsoft about this bug, they promised that it would be fixed in AD2003. They added the `memberOf` property to this property set, which in theory would allow the user's membership to be modified. However, `memberOf` is a backlink property (see Chapter 8), which doesn't allow modifications, even if there were permissions. Therefore, the Group Membership property set still doesn't work for writes, and it seems that the only way to delegate group membership administration is to allow

Table 4.14 Base Schema Property Sets

Property Set	Object Common Name	User*	Computer	Contact	Group	Domain
Phone and Mail Options	Email-Information	X			X	
General Information	General-Information	X				
Group Membership	Membership	X				
Personal Information	Personal-Information	X	X	X		
Public Information	Public-Information	X	X			
Remote Access Information	RAS-Information	X				
Account Restrictions	User-Account-Restrictions	X	X			
Logon Information	User-Logon	X				
Web Information	Web-Information	X		X		
Domain Password & Lockout Policies	Domain-Password					X
DNS Host Name Attributes	DNS-Host-Name-Attributes		X			
Other Domain Parameters (for use by SAM)	Domain-Other-Parameters					X

* Whenever a property set applies to user objects, it also applies to inetOrgPerson objects.

the user to write to the `member` attribute of the appropriate groups. You can still use that property set for reads.

- *Domain Password & Lockout Policies.* In AD2000, this property set applies to the class `domain`, which is an abstract class that cannot have objects in the directory. (The domain objects that you do see are of the class `domainDNS`.) Consequently, this property set was never visible in ACL Editor. In AD2003, this property set applies also to the class `domainDNS`, which is the normal visible domain object in the Users and Computers snap-in, and therefore you can now use it. The properties that belong to this property set can be found in the Default Domain Policy Group Policy object (GPO). A nonadmin person, however, can probably not access this GPO using the Group Policy Object Editor. He could use the old NT4 User Manager to set minimum password length, for example, if he also has permission to write to the "Other Domain Parameters (for use by SAM)" property set. Most likely, there is no need for others than domain administrators to specify values for properties included in Domain Password & Lockout Policies, which means that you wouldn't need this property set.

The three property sets of Table 4.14 that are not used with user objects are the following (along with their properties):

- *Domain Password & Lockout Policies*: `lockOutObservationWindow`, `lockoutDuration`, `lockoutThreshold`, `maxPwdage`, `minPwdAge`, `minPwdLength`, `pwdHistoryLength`, and `pwdProperties`
- *Other Domain Parameters (for use by SAM)*: `domainReplica`, `forceLogoff`, `modifiedCount`, `oEMInformation`, `serverRole`, `serverState`, and `uASCompat`
- *DNS Host Name Attributes*: `dNSHostName` and `msDS-AdditionalDnsHostName`

The following seven tables (Tables 4.15 through 4.21) list the properties that are included in each of the remaining property sets. The tables have the following three columns:

- *Snap-in Tab:* Because the property sets are quite user oriented, we list in which tab of a user object you can see the corresponding property when using the Users and Computers snap-in. "N/A" (not applicable) indicates the properties that are not visible in the snap-in. As you will notice, the property sets have nothing in common with the tabs of the snap-in.

- *Snap-in Name:* The field name you see in that tab.
- *LDAP Name:* The attribute name that you use with ADSI and LDAP. If the attribute common name is quite different from the LDAP name, we include the common name in parentheses.

Table 4.15 lists the properties that are included in the General Information property set.

Table 4.16 lists the properties that are included in the Personal Information property set.

Table 4.15 Property Sets: General Information

Snap-in Tab	Snap-in Name	LDAP Name
General	Display name	`displayName`
Member Of	Primary group	`primaryGroupID`
Account	User logon name (pre-Windows 2000)	`sAMAccountName`
N/A	N/A	`adminDescription`, `codePage`, `countryCode`, `objectSid`, `sAMAccountType`, `sDRightsEffective`, `showInAdvancedViewOnly`, `sIDHistory`, `uid`, `comment` (`User Comment`)*

* The last property, `comment`, is not the same as Comments in the Telephones tab.

Table 4.16 Property Sets: Personal Information

Snap-in Tab	Snap-in Name	LDAP Name
General	Office	`physicalDeliveryOfficeName`
General	Telephone number	`telephoneNumber`
General	Phone Number (Others)	`otherTelephone` (Phone-Office-Other)
Address	Street	`streetAddress` (Address)

(continued)

Table 4.16 Property Sets: Personal Information *(cont.)*

Snap-in Tab	Snap-in Name	LDAP Name
Address	P.O. Box	postOfficeBox
Address	City	l (Locality-Name)
Address	State/province	st (State-Or-Province-Name)
Address	Zip/Postal Code	postalCode
Address	Country/region	c (Country-Name)
Telephones	Home	homePhone (Phone-Home-Primary)
Telephones	Home Phone (Others)	otherHomePhone (Phone-Home-Other)
Telephones	Pager	pager (Phone-Pager-Primary)
Telephones	Pager Number (Others)	otherPager (Phone-Pager-Other)
Telephones	Mobile	mobile (Phone-Mobile-Primary)
Telephones	Mobile Number (Others)	otherMobile (Phone-Mobile-Other)
Telephones	Fax	facsimileTelephoneNumber
Telephones	Fax Number (Others)	otherFacsimileTelephoneNumber (Phone-Fax-Other)
Telephones	IP phone	ipPhone (Phone-Ip-Primary)
Telephones	IP Phone Number (Others)	otherIpPhone (Phone-Ip-Other)
Telephones	Notes	info (Comment)
Published Certificates	List of X509 certificates published for the user account	userCertificate (X509-Cert)
N/A	N/A	assistant, homePostalAddress (Address-Home), internationalISDNNumber, mSMQDigests, mSMQSignCertificates, personalTitle, postalAddress, preferredDeliveryMethod, primaryInternationalISDNNumber (Phone-ISDN-Primary), primaryTelexNumber (Telex-Primary),

Table 4.16 Property Sets: Personal Information *(cont.)*

Snap-in Tab	Snap-in Name	LDAP Name
NA	NA	registeredAddress, street (Street-Address), teletexTerminalIdentifier, telexNumber, thumbnailPhoto (Picture), userCert, userSharedFolder, userSharedFolderOther, userSMIMECertificate, x121Address

NOTE The Personal Information property set includes all properties of the Address and Telephones tabs, except for the case described in the following warning.

WARNING The Country/region information is stored in three properties: co contains the country's name (e.g., UNITED STATES), c contains the country's abbreviation (e.g., US), and countryCode contains the numeric ISO country code (e.g., 840). Unfortunately, these three properties belong to three different property sets (Public Information, Personal Information, and General Information, respectively.) If you grant someone permission to write to the Personal Information property set, he can use the Users and Computers snap-in to modify the country/region of the affected users, but only one of the three properties gets updated. The remaining two will still store the old value and, consequently, be out of sync.

Table 4.17 lists the properties that are included in the Public Information property set.

NOTE The Public Information property set includes all properties of the Organization tab.

Table 4.18 lists the properties that are included in the Remote Access Information property set.

Table 4.19 lists the properties that are included in the Account Restrictions property set.

Table 4.20 lists the properties that are included in the Logon Information property set.

Table 4.17 Property Sets: Public Information

Snap-in Tab	Snap-in Name	LDAP Name
General	N/A	cn (Common-Name)
General	N/A	name (RDN)
General	First name	givenName
General	Initials	initials
General	Last name	sn (Surname)
General	Description	description
General	E-mail	mail (E-mail-Addresses)
Account	User logon name	userPrincipalName
Organization	Title	title
Organization	Department	department
Organization	Company	company
Organization	Manager	manager
Organization	Direct reports	directReports (Reports)
Object	Object class	objectClass
N/A	N/A	allowedAttributes, allowedAttributesEffective, allowedChildClasses, allowedChildClassesEffective, altSecurityIdentities, co (Text-Country), displayNamePrintable, distinguishedName (Obj-Dist-Name), division, legacyExchangeDN, notes (Additional-Information), o (Organization-Name), objectCategory, objectGUID, otherMailbox, ou (Organizational-Unit-Name), proxyAddresses, servicePrincipalName, showInAddressBook, systemFlags, msDS-AllowedToDelegateTo, msDS-Approx-Immed-Subordinates, msDS-Auxiliary-Classes

Table 4.18 Property Sets: Remote Access Information

LDAP Name
msNPAllowDialin, msNPCallingStationID, msRADIUSCallbackNumber, msRADIUSFramedIPAddress, msRADIUSFramedRoute, msRADIUSServiceType, tokenGroups, tokenGroupsGlobalAndUniversal, tokenGroupsNoGCAcceptable

Table 4.19 Property Sets: Account Restrictions

Snap-in Tab	Snap-in Name	LDAP Name
Account	Account options	userAccountControl
Account	Account expires	accountExpires
N/A	N/A	pwdLastSet, userParameters, msDS-User-Account-Control-Computed

Table 4.20 Property Sets: Logon Information

Snap-in Tab	Snap-in Name	LDAP Name
Account	Logon Hours	logonHours
Account	Log On To/Logon Workstations	userWorkstations
Profile	Profile path	profilePath
Profile	Logon script	scriptPath
Profile	Home folder: Local path/To	homeDirectory
Profile	Home folder: Connect	homeDrive
N/A	N/A	badPwdCount, lastLogoff, lastLogon, logonCount, logonWorkstation, lastLogonTimestamp

Table 4.21 Property Sets: Web Information

Snap-in Tab	Snap-in Name	LDAP Name
General	Web page	`wWWHomePage`
General	Web Page Address (Others)	`url` (WWW-Page-Other)

Table 4.21 lists the properties that are included in the Web Information property set.

If you have write permission for only some of the properties, the Users and Computers snap-in displays those properties as editable, while other properties are grayed out. A possible outcome is illustrated in Figure 4.8.

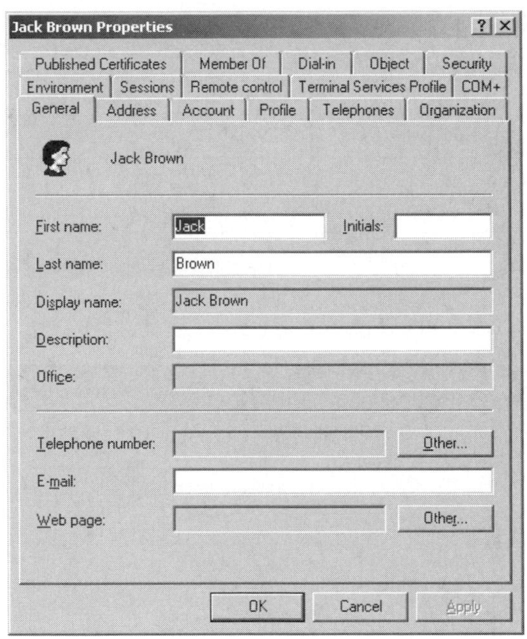

Figure 4.8 If you have write permission for only some of the properties (such as for the Public Information property set in this example), the Users and Computers snap-in displays those properties as editable (white background), while other properties are grayed out.

Permissions for Individual Properties

Dialog box D shows a list of properties from which you select read and write permissions for individual properties. Normally only some of the properties of a given class are visible in the dialog box. For user objects, you see about 120 properties of the 257 possible properties (65 of 207 in AD2000).

Each property in the list is shown using one of two names:

- *Display name (such as First Name).* A display name is used if one is specified for the property in the container, such as `CN=409, CN=DisplaySpecifiers, CN=Configuration, DC=sanao, DC=com`. Display names are explained in Chapter 9.
- *LDAP name (such as `givenName`).* An LDAP name is used if there is no display name for the property.

NOTE The display name is often the same as the descriptive name that you see in the user property pages of the Users and Computers snap-in, but it can also be different. For example, the display name could be E-Mail Address, while the descriptive name is E-mail.

You may find the default list of properties to be unsatisfactory for you. For example, there are First Name and E-Mail Address (Others) in the list, but Last Name and the ordinary E-mail are missing (as was the case already in AD2000). Also, the default list contains many, many properties (such as `userSharedFolder`) that are not visible in the Users and Computers snap-in.

You can modify the property list by editing the file DSSec.Dat, which is in the Winnt\System32 folder. The file is about 12,000 lines of text—it lists the attributes of each class that should be filtered out of the list in dialog box D.

NOTE You must edit DSSec.Dat on the computer that you use to run the Users and Computers snap-in and ACL Editor.

The following lines show some of the contents of DSSec.Dat (although not consecutive lines):

```
[user]
aCSPolicyName=7
```

```
dSCorePropagationData=7
mail=7
mhsORAddress=7
ou=7
siteObjectBL=7
sn=7
```

The header line in brackets (`[user]`) specifies the LDAP name of the class, and each subsequent line gives an LDAP name of the property to be filtered out. You have the following choices to specify values:

- *Property=7:* The property is not included in dialog box D.
- *Property=6:* "Read property" is included.
- *Property=5:* "Write property" is included.
- *Property=0:* Both "Read property" and "Write property" are included.
- *The property is not included in DSSec.Dat:* Both "Read property" and "Write property" are included in dialog box D.

If you want to give permission to read or write e-mail address or last name properties individually, perform the following steps:

1. Make a backup copy of the file DSSec.Dat.
2. Open the file and locate the line `[user]`.
3. After that header line, locate the line `mail=7`. Either remove the line or change the value to 0.
4. After that header line, locate the line `sn=7`. Either remove the line or change the value to 0.
5. Restart the Users and Computers snap-in. Now you should see E-Mail Address and Last Name in dialog box D.

Most of the classes in the file have the following line after the class header:

```
@=7
```

This line specifies that the corresponding class shouldn't be visible in the ACL Editor list of possible "Apply onto" classes. By default, 120 classes are invisible and 71 are visible (only 22 are visible in AD2000).

If you modify DSSec.Dat to your needs once, you can copy the new version to the other workstations and servers on which you are going to run the Users and Computers snap-in and ACL Editor.

NOTE Compared to AD2000, Microsoft added 49 new classes to AD2003 and 50 new properties for the `user` class. None of these new classes and properties are filtered out in DSSec.Dat, even though they are mostly not interesting to permission administrators.

Renaming Objects

There is no single Rename permission in Active Directory. Instead, you have permission to rename an object if you have permission to write to certain of its properties.

Recall from Chapter 1 that the name of the object in its parent container is its RDN. Depending on the object class, the RDN is exactly the same as the CN, OU, or DC property (or one of the more rare alternatives). Consequently, if you want to rename an object, you must have write permission to both its RDN property and this other property, such as CN. Also, if you have the Write All Properties permission, you can rename an object.

Giving permission to write to all properties is easy, but giving permission to write to only the CN and RDN properties (to be able to rename an object) is slightly trickier. We explain the process and use contact objects as an example. Contact objects use CN as their naming property, so to rename them, you must be able to write to the CN and RDN properties.

Remember that all properties have an LDAP name and some properties also have a display name. Table 4.22 lists both of these names for the CN and RDN properties.

The ACL Editor dialog box D for contact objects has a "Write name" line and a "Write Name" line. The former line corresponds to RDN and the latter corresponds to CN. You must allow writing to both properties, so you must check the Allow boxes on both lines.

Table 4.22 Names of Object-Naming Properties

Naming Property	Display Name	LDAP Name
CN	Name	`cn`
RDN	N/A	`name`

NOTE If you rename a contact object with ADSI Edit, you only need permission to write to the CN and RDN properties. If you use the Users and Computers snap-in, you also need permission to write to the First Name and Last Name properties. Or when renaming contacts, you must clear the first and last name from the Rename dialog box.

The preceding example applies to user objects, too.

Permissions in Applications

Application developers can write applications that add extended rights to Active Directory. If your company develops or buys such applications, you may see additional permissions not listed in the previous section. For example, an application could add a new "Can decide own salary" permission, which would apply to user objects. Windows 2000 and later wouldn't use this permission for anything, but the application in question could make use of it.

If the application adds properties to the schema of a forest, those properties will be visible in dialog box D. It is also possible to create new property sets. (For an example of creating a property set, see Chapter 9.)

Applications can launch the four permission dialog boxes (A, B, C, and D), so you may see them as part of some application on your system.

Inheritance

Active Directory uses *static inheritance* for permissions. The word "inheritance" means that when you add permissions for some OU or other container, you can specify that these new permissions apply also to the child objects—that is, the children inherit the permissions from the parent object. You can choose to which types of children the permissions apply and whether they apply only to immediate children or to the whole tree beneath the object.

Static inheritance means that Active Directory copies the permissions to the access control list of each appropriate child object. This takes some processor power while copying, as well as space in the Active Directory database, but the advantage is that when the objects are later accessed, Active Directory only has to check the permissions of the object itself. With *dynamic inheritance,* each opening of an object requires checking the permissions of that object and all its parent objects.

IF YOU KNOW NDS While Active Directory uses static inheritance, NDS uses dynamic inheritance.

IF YOU KNOW NT Active Directory has two significant improvements over Windows NT NTFS. First, when you apply new permissions to child objects in Active Directory, these permissions won't completely replace the old permissions (as was the case with Windows NT's "Copy to subdirectories" option)—they just add ACEs to the list. Second, the new ACEs carry a flag that indicates they are inherited. This way, both humans and machines will recognize which permissions are inherited and which are assigned directly to an object.

NOTE If you add a permission that affects a thousand objects, only the security descriptor of the one parent object needs to be replicated to the other domain controllers. When the other domain controllers receive a new inheritable permission, they copy it locally to the child objects.

You can control inheritance in two ways.

- You can choose per object whether or not an object will inherit permissions. If you choose that the object declines to inherit, there is no way to force inheritance from the upper level.
- When you add permissions, you can choose whether they apply also to child objects and, if so, to which type of children. You can apply the permissions only to immediate children or to the whole OU tree subordinate to the object.

IF YOU KNOW NDS Active Directory has no inheritance filters. An object inherits either all or nothing.

Choosing If a Child Allows Inheritance

At the bottom of dialog box B (Figure 4.5), there is a check box with the text "Allow inheritable permissions from parent to propagate to this object and all child objects. Include these with entries explicitly defined here." The default is checked—that is, inheritance is on for that object. If you clear the check box to turn inheritance off, you have to select

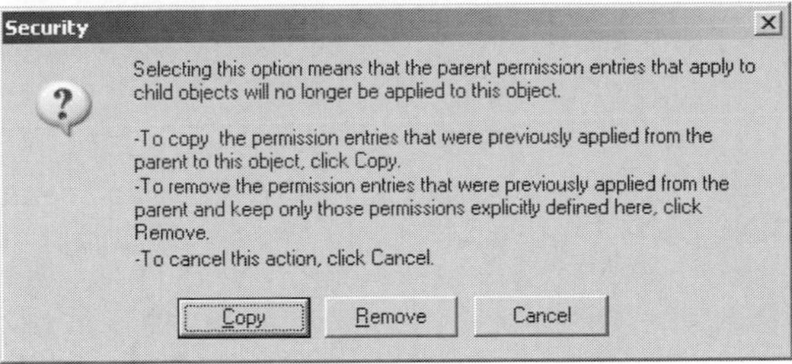

Figure 4.9 If you clear the "Allow inheritable permissions . . ." check box, you have to select whether to copy or remove the permissions that were previously inherited.

whether to copy or remove the permissions that were previously inherited, as shown in Figure 4.9.

Normally it's best to click Copy. Then it is easy to browse through the list to remove unnecessary permissions. If you click Remove, you must remember to add administrative permissions for someone before you click OK or Apply. If you select Copy, in Windows Server 2003 you will probably see the warning message displayed in Figure 4.10 (if you are operating on a container object). You can usually dismiss it by clicking Yes, but you should also read the "Permission Performance" section later in this chapter.

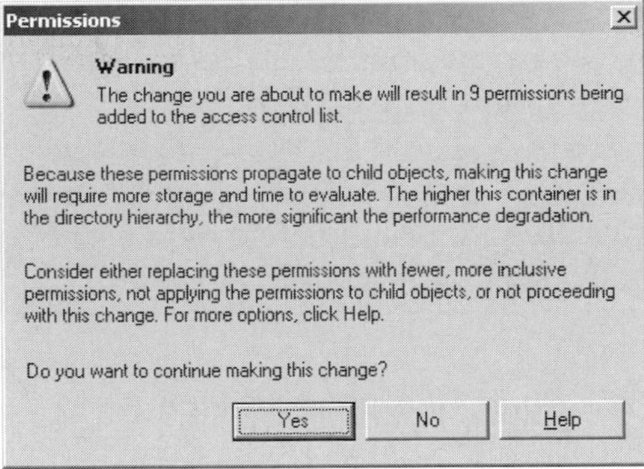

Figure 4.10 If you click Copy when disabling inheritance, in Windows Server 2003 you will probably get a warning message about the possible performance impact. You can usually click Yes, but read the "Permission Performance" section later in this chapter.

NOTE If the result of the Remove is that no one has administrative permissions, the owner of the object can still restore the permissions.

If you deny inheritance to an object, the permissions above that object in the hierarchy won't pass on to children below that object either.

If you stop inheritance and click Copy and then allow inheritance again, you'll see all the inherited permission entries twice: once for the copy created when you stopped inheritance and once for the permission that is now inherited again.

Choosing If a Parent Wants a Child to Inherit

Each time you define a permission entry for an object, you also decide if it will affect children (provided, of course, that the children allow it to affect them). You have four choices for the scope of the entry (in parentheses is the text that you see in the user interface).

- It will affect the object only ("This object only").
- It will affect the children only ("Child objects only").
- It will affect both the object and children ("This object and all child objects").
- It will affect one type of child only (e.g., "User objects").

NOTE When setting permissions for a user object, for example, you could choose inheritance of permissions by about 70 child classes, such as Site Link object or Printer object. However, none of those classes can be a child of a user, so choosing them has no meaning.

By default, inheritance in the last three cases is for the whole tree beneath. If you want to limit the inheritance to the immediate children only, you can check the "Apply these permissions to objects and/or containers within this container only" box.

Figure 4.11 illustrates the inheritance choices.

When you add permissions in dialog box A, they default to "This object only." Also, you cannot see or control inheritance in that dialog box. When you add permissions in dialog box B, the default is "This object and all child objects."

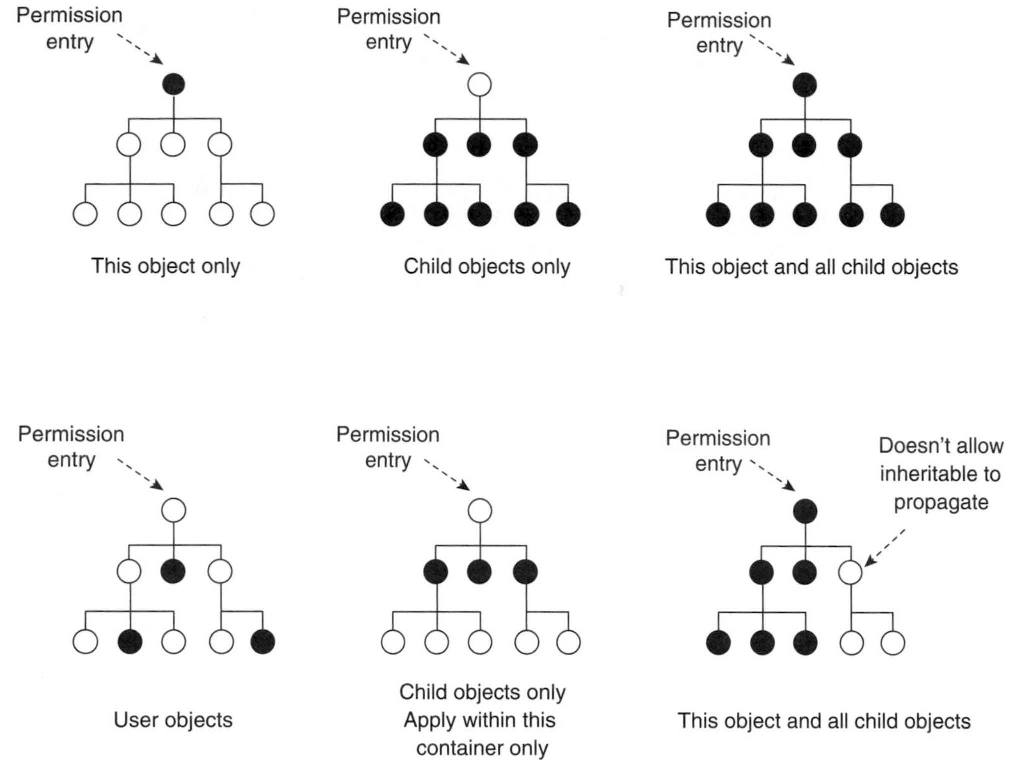

Figure 4.11 Various inheritance options enable you to define which objects (filled circles) inherit a permission entry.

Ownership

Each Active Directory object has an owner. She can always control the permissions for her object. That is, she can decide who can access that object and in what way. Of course, anyone who has the Modify Permissions permission can control permissions, too.

By default, the owner is the user who created the object. However, if the creator is a member of Domain Admins, that group is the owner. In AD2000, if the creator was not a member of Domain Admins, but was a member of Administrators, then Administrators was the owner. In AD2003 in a similar case, the creator is the owner, not Administrators.

You may take ownership of an object if either of the following is true:

- You have the Modify Owner permission (which is also part of Full Control).
- You have the user right to "Take ownership of files or other objects," which by default the Administrators group has.

NOTE It is possible that different domain controllers have different settings for user rights. If this is the case, whether you can take ownership or not depends on which domain controller you are connected to.

- When a normal user changes ownership of an object, he becomes the new owner (i.e., he "takes ownership"), but an administrator can choose whether he or the group Administrators becomes the new owner (see Figure 4.12).

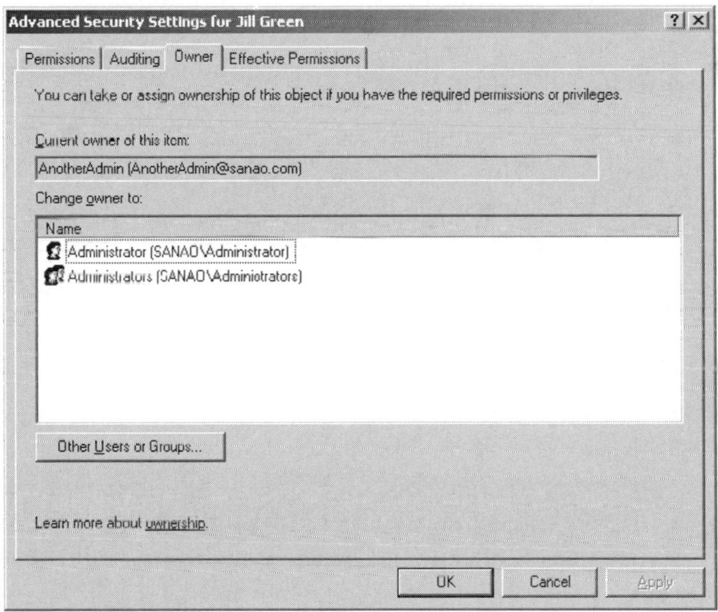

Figure 4.12 An administrator can choose whether to take ownership himself or to give it to the group Administrators.

In Windows 2000, giving the ownership to someone else was not possible (except for an administrator to the group Administrators). This ensured that an administrator could not take ownership from some user, access the object, and then give the ownership back before the original owner notices anything.

Starting with Windows Server 2003, it is possible to give the ownership to someone else. This requires not only the Modify Owner permission, but also the "Restore files and directories" user right. You give the ownership by clicking the Other Users or Groups button of Figure 4.12, then selecting the new owner, and finally clicking OK or Apply.

Creator Owner

One of the well-known security principals is Creator Owner. If you assign permissions to this security principal, those permissions will be inherited in a special way. That is, any present or future owner of a present or future child object can use those permissions on that child object. Figure 4.13 illustrates the following example:

- First you assign the Write All Properties permission to Creator Owner for `OU=Sales, DC=sanao, DC=com`.
- If you specify that the permission should apply to "This object only" or "This object and all child objects," Active Directory will change that to "Child objects only." However, you could specify that the permissions apply only to some objects, such as users, or only to immediate children.
- Now Jack creates a user called `CN=Helen, OU=Sales, DC=sanao, DC=com`. Jack is not an administrator, so he becomes the owner of Helen.
- The Creator Owner entry that was created three steps earlier will cause two inherited permission entries for the Helen object. The first entry is the Write All Properties permission to Jack, applying to "This object only." The second entry is the Write All Properties permission to Creator Owner, applying to "Child objects only."

If the ownership changes, the new owner will get the Creator Owner permissions and the old owner will lose them.

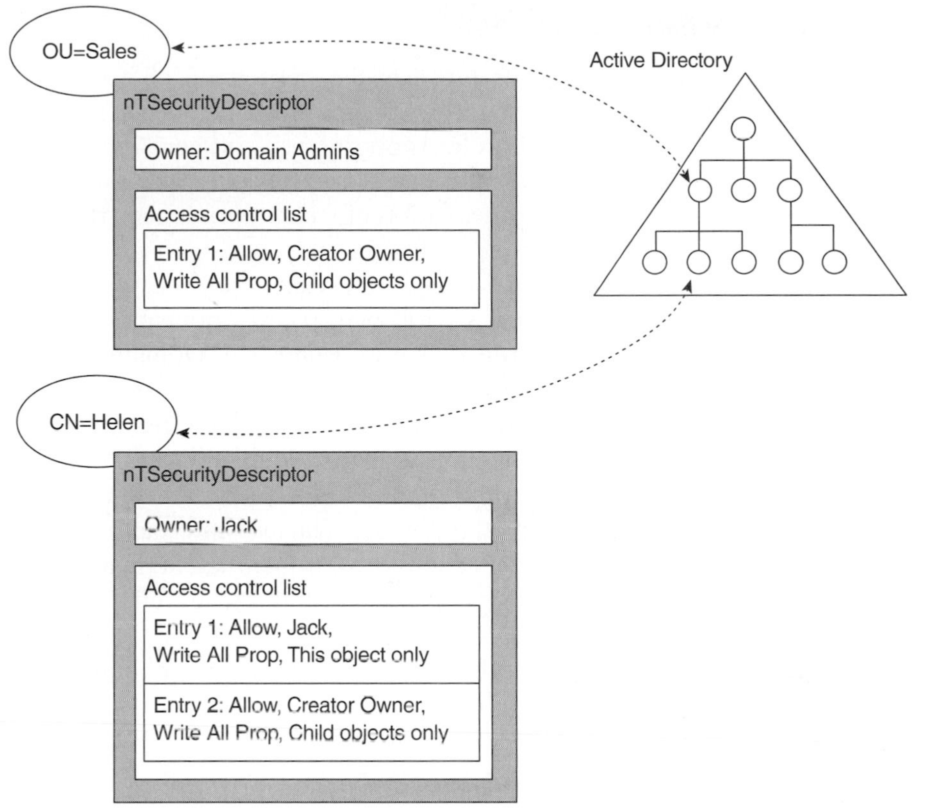

Figure 4.13 Permissions given to Creator Owner (for `OU=Sales`) cause two inherited permission entries to appear for child objects (`CN=Helen`).

How Permissions Accumulate

Active Directory permissions are cumulative. For a given user, Windows sums up all the permissions granted to him directly, permissions granted to the groups he belongs to (either directly or indirectly), and permissions granted to the well-known security principals (those "dynamic groups") that apply to him.

For a target object, Windows sums up permissions assigned for that object, as well as all the permissions that affect the object by inheritance. The exception to this normal rule of accumulation is the set of Deny permissions. They usually take precedence over Allow permissions, as described in the following section.

Effective Permissions

The Effective Permissions tab lists the permission choices visible in ACL Editor dialog boxes C and D (that is, the 11/13 special permissions, extended rights, permissions for property sets, and permissions for individual properties). When you specify a security principal (such as a user or group), you see an approximation of which permissions that security principal has.

The list of permissions is only an approximation, because the calculation doesn't take into account the following security principals: Anonymous Logon, Batch, Creator Group, Dialup, Enterprise Domain Controllers, Interactive, Network, Proxy, Restricted, Remote, Service, System, Terminal Server User, Other Organization, and This Organization. Most notably, this exclusion list contains Interactive and Network, which means that if permissions are granted for all local users or network users, these permissions are not included in the list. The user interface doesn't allow you to select Interactive, for example, to be included in the calculation.

Because group memberships are essential when effective permissions are determined, the person performing the query must have permission to read group memberships. By default, all authenticated users have such permission for other users.

Deny Permissions and the Ordering of Permission Entries

When someone tries to access an Active Directory object (or another protected object such as a file on disk), a Windows component called the security reference monitor (SRM) evaluates whether the requested access should be allowed or denied. As the SRM performs its duty, it steps through the list of permission entries, starting from the beginning. As soon as it finds enough entries to determine that the access should be denied or allowed, it stops walking the list and returns the result. This means that the order of the permission entries dictates what the effective permissions actually are.

The preferred order of the entries in the list is as follows:

1. Noninherited Deny entries
2. Noninherited Allow entries
3. Inherited Deny entries
4. Inherited Allow entries

Consequently, Deny permissions take precedence over Allow permissions, except that inherited Deny permissions don't take precedence over noninherited Allow permissions.

As an exception, when an application adds permission entries, it can sometimes deviate from the preferred order. For example, Exchange purposely disorders permission entries to get "unusual" results. This way, it hides membership of groups from all but account operators.

You can use Deny entries for two main purposes.

- You can allow certain permissions to a broad set of users (i.e., a group) and then exclude a narrower set of users (i.e., another group or an individual user) from getting those permissions.
- You can allow "almost all permissions." For example, if you need to allow writing almost all properties, you can "allow all" in one permission entry and then "deny one or two" in another entry.

If you tried to implement the latter scenario without Deny entries, you might get quite a few permission entries. For example, if you first give Write All Properties to Jack and then deselect one of the properties, ACL Editor would generate 119 Write Property entries and 9 property set entries. In Windows Server 2003, however, you would get a warning message before the generation, shown in Figure 4.14. If you click Yes, the result is shown in Figure 4.15.

Using Deny entries for either of the aforementioned purposes leads to a smaller number of permission entries than not using Deny entries. This has the following two advantages:

- Permission management is easier.
- Performance is better because Active Directory has fewer entries to evaluate (see the next section, about permission performance).

Figure 4.16 shows how to allow "all but one property." The fifth entry on the list grants Jack permission to write to any property, but the first entry denies writing to one of the properties. Deny entries are ordered to be the first in the list. That way, they (except the inherited Deny entries) override any Allow entries when the permissions are evaluated.

NOTE You can sort the entries freely in the user interface by clicking any of the column headers. This doesn't affect the internal storage order, which dictates the actual effect of the permission entries (that is, usually Deny permissions override Allow permissions).

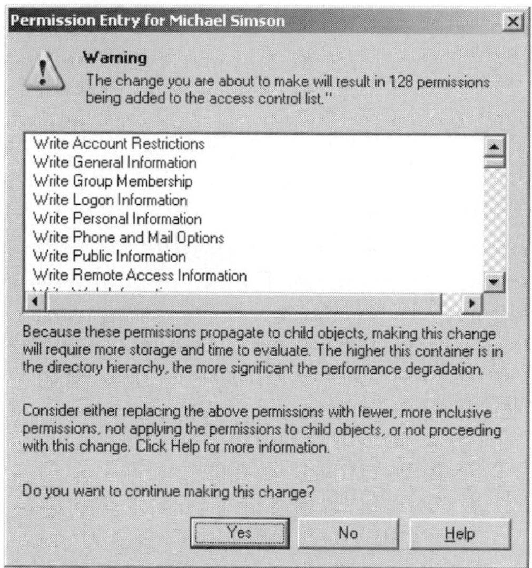

Figure 4.14 Deselecting a permission for one property generates a separate permission entry for all remaining properties.

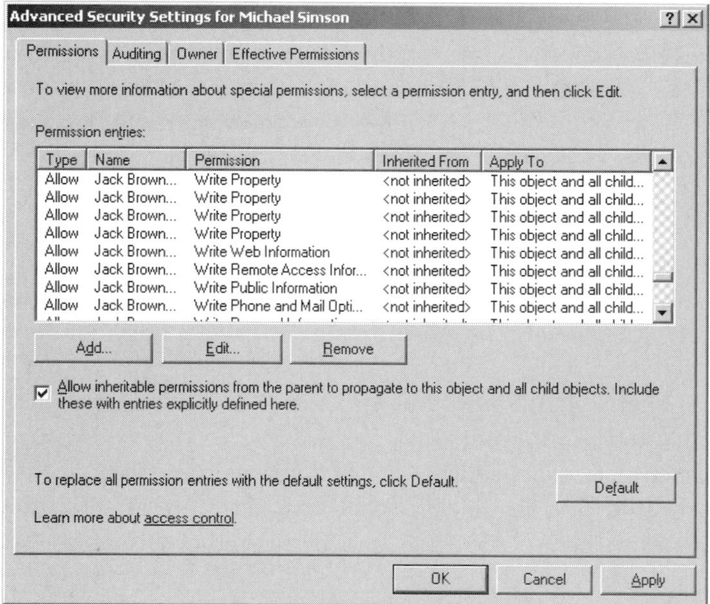

Figure 4.15 Deselecting a permission for one property generates a separate permission entry for all remaining property sets and properties.

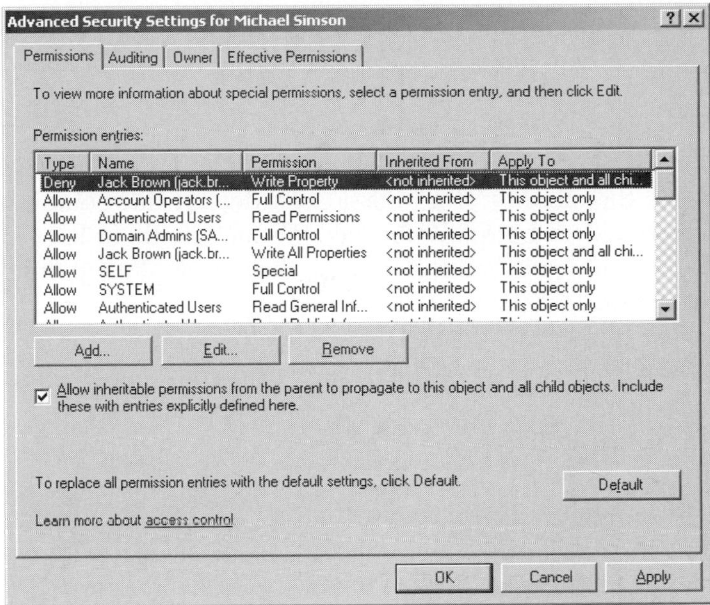

Figure 4.16 The better way to deny permission to a single property is to use a Deny permission entry. The first entry in the figure overrides the fifth entry.

NOTE Remember that inherited Deny permissions are weaker than noninherited Allow permissions. Consequently, if you assign a Deny permission that is inherited to child objects, you must evaluate what kind of noninherited Allow permissions the child objects currently have or will have in the future. Otherwise, your Deny permission scenario might not work as wanted. Evaluating future permissions is obviously not easy, but at least you should take into account the default noninherited permissions that each new objects gets at creation time.

Permission Performance

You should avoid having a large number of permission entries for an object. Having fewer entries has three advantages.

- The directory database requires less space.
- Accessing Active Directory is faster because it needs to evaluate fewer entries when determining whether to allow access to a user.

- Accessing Active Directory is faster because more objects fit in the domain controller cache, so fewer objects need to be read from disk.

Microsoft Knowledge Base article Q271876 lists several ways to reduce the number of permission entries. At this point in the chapter, they should all be quite obvious. We include them here (although expressed a little differently) because they nicely sum up this discussion of permissions.

We listed the 13 (or 11) individual permissions earlier in this chapter. Any combination of them can be stored in one 32-bit number and, consequently, in a single permission entry. This includes the standard permissions Full Control, Read, and Write, as well as any custom combination you select.

The number of permission entries will be larger if you specify certain properties, child object types, or extended rights instead of just granting permissions to all of them.

- When granting read and/or write permission to all properties, you can cover all properties with one permission entry (along with the other 11 or 9 individual permissions). If this is not viable, using a property set is better than using individual properties (if there is a property set to match your need).
- Similarly, granting create and/or delete permission to all child objects fits in one permission entry. If you need to specify three object types, that will take three permission entries.
- Each individual extended right requires one permission entry, while All Extended Rights is just one entry.

If a permission entry is passed on to child objects by inheritance, it will need space and slow down the permission evaluation of those objects also. Therefore, you should avoid inheritance of a large number of permission entries in a large OU tree. (The "Access Control Architecture" section later in this chapter offers more background information about what a single permission entry can store.)

NOTE It is easy to monitor the number of permission entries, because they all show on separate lines in ACL Editor dialog box B.

DSACLS

Windows Support Tools includes a command-line tool, DSACLS, that allows you to display and modify permission entries. You can list the permission entries of an object using a command such as the following:

```
dsacls ou=boston,dc=sanao,dc=com
```

That object would probably contain about 18 permission entries. The output of the first three entries would look like the following:

```
Access list:
Effective Permissions on this object are:
Allow SANAO\Domain Admins                   FULL CONTROL
Allow NT AUTHORITY\ENTERPRISE DOMAIN        SPECIAL ACCESS
  CONTROLLERS                               READ PERMISSONS
                                            LIST CONTENTS
                                            READ PROPERTY
                                            LIST OBJECT
Allow NT AUTHORITY\Authenticated Users      SPECIAL ACCESS
                                            READ PERMISSONS
                                            LIST CONTENTS
                                            READ PROPERTY
                                            LIST OBJECT
Allow NT AUTHORITY\SYSTEM                   FULL CONTROL
```

Note that in the second and third permission entries, SPECIAL ACCESS is the heading and the following four lines list the individual permissions of that entry.

NOTE In Chapter 11 we present some scripts that list detailed information about permission entries, either on the command line or in Excel. You can also check two other permission-related command-line tools in Support Tools: ACLDiag and SDCheck. ACLDiag enables you to check if a given object's permissions include any of the Delegation of Control wizard's common tasks (discussed later in the chapter) or if the permissions include the schema defaults (also discussed later in the chapter). SDCheck lists an object's permissions on a given domain controller, which enables you to compare object permissions in different domain controllers to verify that they are replicated correctly.

AdminSDHolder Object

Active Directory contains a mechanism to protect the user accounts and groups that are members of administrative groups. Also, the administrative groups are protected, not just their members. Every hour, the domain controller that holds the PDC master role in the domain checks that the permission lists and inheritance setting of these user accounts and groups are identical to the permission list and inheritance setting of a special AdminSDHolder object. The PDC master modifies any differing permission list, so that it will be again identical to the permission list of AdminSDHolder.

Users and groups that are protected with this mechanism are identified with the `adminCount` attribute value of 1. The PDC master sets this attribute value during its hourly check for all new users and groups that have become members of protected groups during the last hour. You can list all the affected objects to a file, using a command such as the following:

```
ldifde -f prot.txt -d DC=sanao,DC=com -r (adminCount=1) -l dn
```

In AD2000, the protected groups are Enterprise Admins, Schema Admins, Domain Admins, and Administrators. AD2003 extends the list (as does Windows 2000 SP4) by adding Account Operators, Server Operators, Print Operators, Backup Operators, and Replicator. In addition, Administrator, the Domain Controllers group (but not its members), and krbtgt are protected. Consequently, account operators can no longer modify their own accounts or the accounts of other account operators.

If a user is removed from a protected group, the hourly permission check (and the possible restoration) that the PDC master performs stops applying to the user object. The PDC master does not restore the old permission entries that existed perhaps six months earlier, before the user was added to the protected group. You must manually specify any permission or inheritance settings you want after the removal from the group. In addition, the `adminCount` attribute is probably not cleared automatically, so you might want to do that manually. It does not seem to hurt to still have that attribute value set, but it's better to clear it.

If you want to restore the schema default permissions and reenable the permission inheritance, you can use the following two commands, respectively (the options S and P must be uppercase):

```
dsacls "CN=Jack Brown,OU=Boston,DC=sanao,DC=com" /S
dsacls "CN=Jack Brown,OU=Boston,DC=sanao,DC=com" /P:N
```

NOTE In addition to direct members of the listed protected groups, any indirect members are affected by the protection mechanism. Distribution groups are not normally valid in security-related mechanisms, but here they are also included. The reason is that they could be converted to security groups. However, you cannot see these memberships using the command `WhoAmI /Groups`, because that command only takes into account the security groups.

The AdminSDHolder object resides in the System container of the domain. By default, this object doesn't allow inheritance, and its permission list is somewhat stricter than those in normal user accounts. This way, a lower-level administrator cannot make unwanted changes on the most powerful administrative user accounts.

You can modify the permission list of AdminSDHolder, which will reflect the permission lists of the administrative user accounts in a while. However, we don't recommend you do so. If the graphical ACL Editor doesn't include some extended right, for example, you can use the DSACLS command to grant that right.

User accounts and groups that are protected do not inherit permissions from their containers. For example, if a "normal" user in some OU is a member of Print Operators, her user account won't inherit any permissions from the OU level. If this is a problem, you can read Microsoft Knowledge Base article 817433 for considerations and more information.

Delegation of Control Wizard

The previous section explains how to control permissions manually with ACL Editor dialog boxes, which we designated A, B, C, and D, as well as the permission mechanisms behind them. In this section we introduce an alternative user interface, the Delegation of Control wizard. The Delegation of Control wizard is a shortcut to assigning permissions. With it you can quickly assign permissions for some typical cases, but naturally the wizard offers only a small subset of possibilities, compared to ACL Editor.

As mentioned earlier, Microsoft recommends using the wizard as the primary tool for managing permissions and delegating administrative tasks because it is easier to learn than ACL Editor and it is straightforward to use. However, if you are comfortable with ACL Editor, there is no reason why you shouldn't use it.

You can also first use the wizard to get things approximately right and then fine-tune the permissions with ACL Editor.

In short, "delegation" means that you give someone else permission to make changes to some of the objects in an Active Directory domain. Because you can do this either manually or using the wizard, we discuss the various delegation scenarios in a separate section, "Usage Scenarios for Active Directory Permissions." There we introduce a number of delegation scenarios and how to implement them using either the wizard or ACL Editor.

Common Tasks

When you use the wizard, the target for delegation is normally either at the OU or domain level. Consequently, you start the wizard by right-clicking an OU or domain object (or another container, such as Users) and selecting Delegate Control. You can use the wizard to delegate either "common" or "custom" tasks. With the first option, you have to define only the following:

- Which group, or perhaps user, will get the permissions.
- Which of the predefined common tasks you want to select. An OU has 11 predefined tasks (six in AD2000) and a domain has two. AD2003 also adds nine predefined tasks for containers of the `container` class, such as the Users container.

The screen shots in Figure 4.17 and Figure 4.18 illustrate these two selections.

Two characteristics are common to all common tasks:

- The resulting permissions apply to the whole tree beneath, not just one object or one level.
- The wizard doesn't stop inheritance—that is, it doesn't create an independent tree.

Table 4.23 lists the permissions that result from delegating each common task.

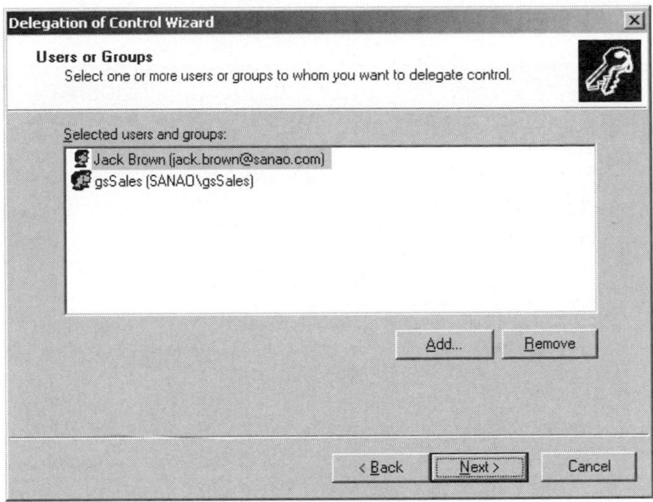

Figure 4.17 Your first task with the Delegation of Control wizard is to choose which users or groups will get the permissions.

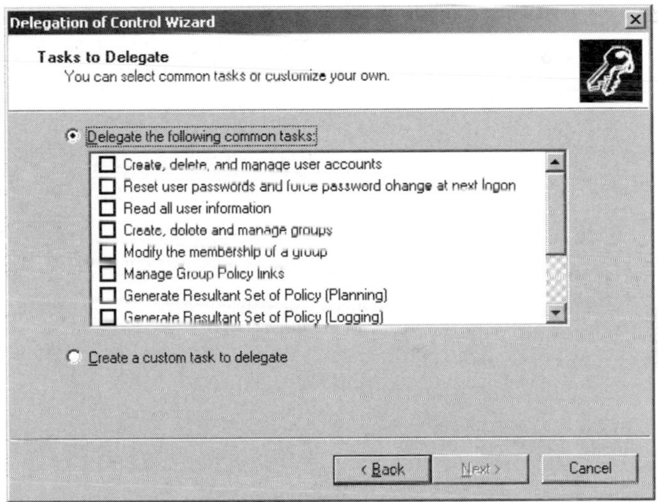

Figure 4.18 The Delegation of Control wizard offers 11 predefined common tasks for an OU. If one (or more) of them is right for you, you don't need to specify anything else.

Table 4.23 Delegation of Control Wizard Common Tasks

Present For	Common Task	Resulting Permission Entries	Apply To
OUs, containers	Create, delete, and manage user accounts*	Create/Delete User Objects	This object and all child objects
		Full Control	User objects
OUs, containers	Reset user passwords and force password change at next logon*	Reset Password	User objects
		Read/Write `pwdLastSet`	User objects
OUs, containers	Read all user information*	Read All Properties	User objects
OUs, containers	Create, delete, and manage groups	Create/Delete Group Objects	This object and all child objects
		Full Control	Group objects
OUs, containers	Modify the membership of a group	Read/Write Members	Group objects
OUs	Generate Resultant Set of Policy (Planning)	Generate Resultant Set of Policy (Planning)	This object and all child objects
OUs	Generate Resultant Set of Policy (Planning)	Generate Resultant Set of Policy (Planning)	This object and all child objects
Containers	Create, delete, and manage WMI Filters	Create/Delete `msWMI-Som` Objects	This object and all child objects
		Full Control	`msWMI-Som` objects
Domains	Join a computer to the domain	Create Computer Objects	This object and all child objects

* There is an identical common task for inetOrgPersons, but to save space, we don't list it separately.

Table 4.23 Delegation of Control Wizard Common Tasks *(cont.)*

Present For	Common Task	Resulting Permission Entries	Apply To
OUs, domains, sites	Manage Group Policy links	Read/Write `gPLink`	This object and all child objects
		Read/Write `gPOptions`	This object and all child objects

WARNING If you delegate group management to some assistant administrators in AD2000 or AD2003 in the Windows 2000 mixed or Windows 2000 native forest functional level, it's a good idea to advise them to modify group memberships on only one domain controller (e.g., the PDC emulator). All members of a group are stored in one multivalued property. If that member list is modified on two domain controllers simultaneously (within replication latency), one of the two changes will be lost. When the forest functional level is raised to Windows Server 2003 (or Windows Server 2003 interim), each member is replicated separately, and there is no risk of losing modifications.

Customizing the List of Common Tasks

The list of common tasks is defined in the file DelegWiz.Inf, which is in the Winnt\Inf folder. The file is about 190 lines of text—it lists three features of each common task:

- For which container classes the common task is available
- The descriptive text of the common task
- Which permissions are granted if the common task is delegated

The file syntax is relatively straightforward, and once you have finished reading this chapter, you should be able to modify the file to your needs. The following lines show the definition of the first common task that was described in Table 4.23:

```
[template1]
AppliesToClasses=domainDns,organizationalUnit,container

Description = "Create, delete, and manage user accounts"

ObjectTypes = SCOPE, user

[template1.SCOPE]
user=CC,DC

[template1.user]
@=GA
```

The first two lines after the `[template1]` section heading are easy to interpret.

- The `AppliesToClasses` line lists the classes for which the template is present.
- The `Description` line includes the descriptive text of the common task.

NOTE The `AppliesToClasses` line in the sample does *not* specify that the common task would be present for domain objects. Microsoft has specified `domainDns` on the line, while the LDAP name of the domain class is `domainDNS`. This small difference in uppercase/lowercase causes the common task (as well as eight others in the default DelegWiz.Inf) not to be present for domain objects.

The remaining lines specify the permissions that this common task induces and these lines are slightly trickier.

- The `ObjectTypes` line lists the permission entries (two, in this case): `SCOPE` indicates that the first entry will apply to "this object and all child objects" and `user` indicates the class to which the second entry will apply.
- The `user=CC,DC` line means "create children, delete children, where children are user objects."
- On the `@=GA` line, `GA` stands for "Generic All" (which is the same as Full Control) and `@` indicates that the permission entry should

apply to the class listed on the ObjectTypes line. In other words, the line defines that the delegate gets Full Control to user objects.

The acronyms CC, DC, and GA are defined in Security Descriptor Definition Language (SDDL). See Chapter 9 for more information on SDDL and Chapter 11 for more information on Generic All.

Next, we show an example of how to add new common tasks. The sample task enables the delegate to unlock locked user accounts. The possible lock state is stored in the lockoutTime property of each user, as (again) explained in Chapter 11.

```
[template14]
AppliesToClasses=organizationalUnit

Description = "Unlock locked user accounts"

ObjectTypes = user

[template14.user]
lockoutTime=RP,WP
```

In addition to inserting the preceding lines in DelegWiz.Inf, you must add the template name (template14) at the beginning of the file on the Templates line.

NOTE You must edit DelegWiz.Inf on the computer that you use to run the Delegation of Control wizard.

Custom Tasks

An alternative to selecting from the list of common tasks is creating a custom task. Again, you start by right-clicking the target object and selecting Delegate Control. Then you perform the following steps:

1. In the first screen, select the group, or perhaps user, that will get the permissions (see Figure 4.17).
2. In the second screen, select "Create a custom task to delegate" (see Figure 4.18).

3. Select that the resulting permissions will apply to all objects (in the tree below) or that they will apply to certain object types from a list of 71 object types (see Figure 4.19).
4. Select the permissions to grant (see Figure 4.20).

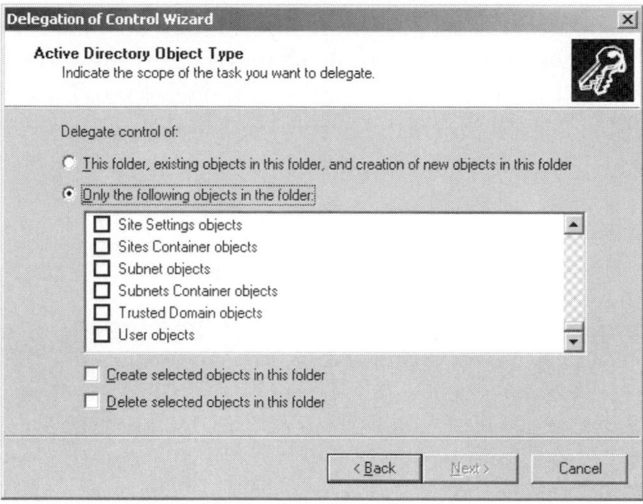

Figure 4.19 When you create custom tasks to delegate, you must select to which objects the resulting permissions will apply or that they apply to all object types.

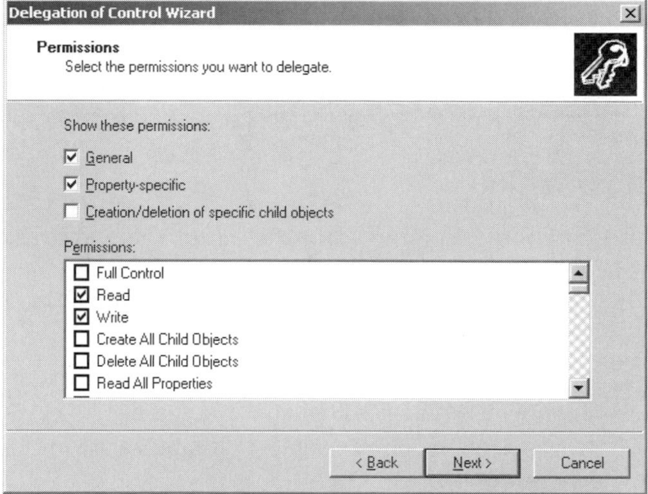

Figure 4.20 As the last step of custom task delegation, you select the permissions to grant.

NOTE DSSec.Dat, which we discussed earlier in the section on per-property permissions, affects also the classes and properties that are visible in the Delegation of Control wizard.

NOTE The list in Figure 4.20 is different for different object types (classes) that you selected in the previous step.

Note that the dialog box to customize permissions to delegate does not include most of the "11/13" special object permissions (List Contents, Delete Subtree, and so on) that appear in dialog boxes A, B, C, and D.

As with common tasks, delegation of permissions with custom tasks always applies to the whole tree. Also, the wizard doesn't stop inheritance in this branch of the tree.

Clearly, creating custom tasks with the Delegation of Control wizard doesn't give you any capability that dialog boxes A, B, C, and D do not offer. The wizard's main benefit (as with any wizard) is the step-by-step user interface, which is a great help when you are performing tasks you are not accustomed to.

After the wizard has completed, you can check which permissions were actually granted by opening dialog box B of ACL Editor. It may be educational to see the outcome. Also, you can check that everything happened as you wished.

DSRevoke

You cannot see or delete existing permissions with the Delegation of Control wizard, so to cover this, Microsoft released the DSRevoke command-line tool in November 2003. You can download the .exe file and an accompanying Word document at `http://www.microsoft.com`.

Two sample commands follow. The latter command asks for verification before removing any permissions.

```
dsrevoke /report /root:OU=Boston,DC=sanao,DC=com Sanao\Jack
dsrevoke /remove /root:OU=Boston,DC=sanao,DC=com Sanao\Jack
```

NOTE DSRevoke shows and removes permissions of only the domain object and OU objects. Consequently, you can use DSRevoke sensibly only if you have refrained from granting permissions for objects other than the domain and OUs.

Default Permissions for Objects

We said earlier that it's preferable to use Active Directory default permissions unless you specifically need something different. For this reason, you should know what the defaults are and where they come from.

Sources of Default Permissions

The predefined objects in Active Directory (such as the Users container or Domain Admins group) have the default permissions that Microsoft decided would be most appropriate. Any new objects that are created in your forest after the installation will have default permissions from the following two sources:

- *Inherited permissions.* New objects (except Group Policy containers) allow inheritance, so any inheritable permissions from the parent object apply to them.
- *Class-specific defaults from the schema.* The schema contains definitions for all object types (i.e., classes). Part of that definition is the default access control list for a new object. In addition, you can restore these defaults to an existing object with the `dsacls /S` command.

Because Active Directory permissions accumulate, the effect of both sources is combined. Members of administrative groups are an exception to the sources listed here, as described in the AdminSDHolder section earlier in this chapter.

Common Features of Default Permissions

The default permissions for objects that are visible in the Users and Computers snap-in when Advanced Features are not turned on have some features in common.

- Almost all objects allow inheritance. The only exceptions are in AD2003 the predefined objects Administrators, Print Operators, Backup Operators, Replicator, Server Operators, Account Operators, Administrator, Domain Controllers, Schema Admins, Enterprise Admins, and Domain Admins, and in AD2000 the predefined objects Enterprise Admins, Schema Admins, Domain Admins, and Administrator.

- The only objects that add default inheritable permission entries are the domain object and Builtin container. All other objects have "This object only" permission entries by default (except that they will naturally pass on what was inherited from the domain object).
- The only object that has any Deny entries is Guest. It denies permission to change the password from Everyone and (redundantly) Self.
- Authenticated Users (i.e., all users of the forest and trusted external domains) have Read + List Object permission for all other objects except Guest, new users, and new inetOrgPerson objects. In AD2000 exceptions are also Administrators, Backup Operators, and krbtgt. For new users and inetOrgPerson objects, Authenticated Users has permission to Read Permissions as well as to read General, Personal, Web, and Public Information. In addition, Authenticated Users is by default a member of the Pre-Windows 2000 Compatible Access group, which in turn has Read + List Object permission for all users, inetOrgPerson objects, and groups of the domain (by inheritance from the domain object).

NOTE The last item on the list of common features of default permissions means that, by default, all users can see who the members of Schema Admins and Enterprise Admins are, which is probably not desired. It also means that all users can see all the properties and permissions of all other users and groups.

Pre-Windows 2000 Compatible Access

One of the well-known security principals is Pre-Windows 2000 Compatible Access. By default, this group has permission to see the existence of most of the objects in a domain and permission to see the properties of all users, inetOrgPerson objects, and groups in a domain. Everyone/Anonymous need these permissions if you have certain server services (e.g., Remote Access Service) running on Windows NT servers in your Active Directory domain.

The member list of Pre-Windows 2000 Compatible Access was determined when you installed Active Directory to create a new domain and chose the option for Permission.

- If you selected "Permissions compatible with pre-Windows 2000 server operating systems," Everyone and Anonymous Logon will be members.

- If you selected "Permissions compatible only with Windows 2000 or Windows Server 2003 operating systems," Authenticated Users will be a member.

Remember that Everyone includes all authenticated users and Guest.

If you want to change the choice you made at the time of installation, you can modify the membership accordingly. Use either the Users and Computers snap-in or a command such as one of the following:

```
NET LOCALGROUP "Pre-Windows 2000 Compatible Access" Everyone /ADD
NET LOCALGROUP "Pre-Windows 2000 Compatible Access" Everyone /DELETE
```

Listing Default Permissions

You can use ACL Editor anytime to see what the permissions are for any object. Some other means are DSACLS, ACLDiag, and SDCheck, described earlier in this chapter, and the VBS scripts shown in Chapter 11.

To give you an overview of the default permissions, we include Tables 4.24 through 4.32, which list the default permission entries for the following predefined and new objects:

- Domain object (Table 4.24 and Table 4.25)
- Users container and Computers container (Table 4.26)
- Domain Controllers OU (Table 4.27)
- First domain controller in Domain Controllers OU and workstation in Computers container (Table 4.28)
- New OU in domain (Table 4.29)
- New contact or new shared folder in new OU (Table 4.30)
- New group in new OU (Table 4.31)
- New user and new inetOrgPerson in new OU (Table 4.32)

However, we have dropped a few redundant permission entries to keep the tables shorter and clearer. Also, we don't list any inherited permission entries in Tables 4.25 through 4.32, because they are identical to the ones in Table 4.24. There is a more comprehensive Excel table of default permissions on the Web at `http://www.kouti.com/`, for both AD2000 and AD2003.

We have divided the domain object permission entries in two tables. The first table (Table 4.24) lists the inheritable permission entries. They affect all objects that allow inheritance and that are of applicable type.

Table 4.25 lists the domain object permission entries for "This object only."

Table 4.24 Inheritable Default Permissions for the Domain Object

Security Principal	Permissions	Apply To
Administrators	Full Control except Delete All Child Objects and Delete Subtree	
Enterprise Admins	Full Control	
Pre-Windows 2000 Compatible Access	List Contents	
Pre-Windows 2000 Compatible Access	Read, List Object	Group
Pre-Windows 2000 Compatible Access	Read, List Object	User
Pre-Windows 2000 Compatible Access	Read, List Object	inetOrgPerson
Enterprise Domain Controllers	Read tokenGroups	User
Enterprise Domain Controllers	Read tokenGroups	Group
Enterprise Domain Controllers	Read tokenGroups	Computer

Table 4.25 Noninheritable Default Permissions for the Domain Object

Security Principal	Permissions
Everyone	Read All Properties
Enterprise Domain Controllers	Replicating Directory Changes
Enterprise Domain Controllers	Replication Synchronization
Enterprise Domain Controllers	Manage Replication Topology
Enterprise Domain Controllers	Read, List Object
Administrators	Replicating Directory Changes
Administrators	Replication Synchronization
Administrators	Manage Replication Topology
Administrators	Replicating Directory Changes All
Authenticated Users	Read, List Object
Authenticated Users	Update Password Not Required Bit
Authenticated Users	Unexpire Password
Authenticated Users	Enable Per User Reversibly Encrypted Password

(continued)

Table 4.25 Noninheritable Default Permissions for the Domain Object (*cont.*)

Security Principal	Permissions
Domain Admins	Full Control except Delete, Delete Subtree, and Delete All Child Objects
LocalSystem	Full Control
Pre-Windows 2000 Compatible Access	Read All Properties, Read Permissions
Domain Controllers	Replicating Directory Changes All
Incoming Forest Trust Builders	Create Inbound Forest Trust

Table 4.26 Default Permissions for the Users and Computers Containers

Security Principal	Permissions
LocalSystem	Full Control
Domain Admins	Full Control except Delete and Delete Subtree
Account Operators	Create/Delete Computer Objects*
Account Operators	Create/Delete User Objects
Account Operators	Create/Delete inetOrgPerson Objects
Account Operators	Create/Delete Group Objects
Print Operators	Create/Delete Printer Objects
Authenticated Users	Read, List Object

* This permission is only for the Computers container, not for the Users container.

Table 4.27 Default Permissions for the Domain Controllers OU

Security Principal	Permissions
Authenticated Users	Read, List Object
Domain Admins	Full Control except Delete, Delete Subtree, and Delete All Child Objects
Enterprise Domain Controllers	Read, List Object
LocalSystem	Full Control

Table 4.28 lists the default permissions for the first domain controller in your forest. The same default permissions apply also to workstations that you add in the Computers container, with the difference described in the table note.

Table 4.28 Default Permissions for the First Domain Controller in the Domain Controllers OU

Security Principal	Permissions
Domain Admins	Full Control
Account Operators*	Full Control
LocalSystem	Full Control
Authenticated Users	Read, List Object
Everyone	Change Password
Self	Create/Delete All Child Objects
Print Operators	Create/Delete Printer Objects
Cert Publishers	Read/Write userCertificate
Self	Validated write to service principal name
Self	Read/Write Personal Information
Self	Validated write to DNS Host Name Attributes
Windows Authorization Access Group	Read tokenGroupsGlobalAndUniversal
Jack*,**	Read, List Object, Delete, Delete Subtree, All Extended Rights
Jack*,**	Write Account Restrictions
Jack*,**	Write Computer name (pre-Windows 2000)
Jack*,**	Write Logon Information***
Jack*,**	Write Description
Jack*,**	Write Display Name
Jack*,**	Validated write to DNS Host Name Attributes
Jack*,**	Validated write to service principal name

* This permission is only for the Computers container, not for the domain controller.

** These entries contain the security principal that you allow to install the corresponding workstation.

*** Note that the Logon Information property set does not apply to computer objects, so it is listed here in vain.

Table 4.29 Default Permissions for a New OU in a Domain

Security Principal	Permissions
LocalSystem	Full Control
Domain Admins	Full Control
Account Operators	Create/Delete Computer Objects
Account Operators	Create/Delete User Objects
Account Operators	Create/Delete inetOrgPerson Objects
Account Operators	Create/Delete Group Objects
Print Operators	Create/Delete Printer Objects
Enterprise Domain Controllers	Read, List Object
Authenticated Users	Read, List Object

Table 4.30 Default Permissions for a New Contact or a New Shared Folder in a New OU

Security Principal	Permissions
Domain Admins	Full Control
LocalSystem	Full Control
Authenticated Users	Read, List Object

Table 4.31 Default Permissions for a New Group in a New OU

Security Principal	Permissions
Domain Admins	Full Control
LocalSystem	Full Control
Authenticated Users	Read, List Object
Account Operators	Full Control
Self	Read, List Object
Windows Authorization Access Group	Read tokenGroupsGlobalAndUniversal
Authenticated Users	Send To

NOTE Even though Administrators is not on the permission list, remember that they have most permissions to every object by inheritance. However, if you block inheritance to some OU and you don't copy Administrators' inherited permissions there, they cannot manage shared folder objects in that OU.

Table 4.32 Default Permissions for a New User and New InetOrgPerson in a New OU

Security Principal	Permissions
Domain Admins	Full Control
LocalSystem	Full Control
Account Operators	Full Control
Self	Read, List Object
Self	Change Password
Self	Send As
Self	Receive As
Self	Read/Write Personal Information
Self	Read/Write Phone and Mail Options
Self	Read/Write Web Information
RAS and IAS Servers	Read Remote Access Information
RAS and IAS Servers	Read Account Restrictions
RAS and IAS Servers	Read Group Membership
RAS and IAS Servers	Read Logon Information
Authenticated Users	Read Permissions
Authenticated Users	Read General Information
Authenticated Users	Read Personal Information
Authenticated Users	Read Web Information
Authenticated Users	Read Public Information
Everyone	Change Password
Windows Authorization Access Group	Read tokenGroupsGlobalAndUniversal
Terminal Server License Servers	Read/Write terminalServer
Cert Publishers	Read/Write userCertificate

NOTE Phone and Mail Options doesn't map to any properties, so that permission is meaningless.

NOTE There are three delete permissions: Delete, Delete Subtree, and Delete All Child Objects. Many of the tables mention "Full Control except Delete . . ." Note that there were various combinations of two or three delete permissions.

Where Security Principals Have Permissions

The preceding tables list for each target object which security principals have permissions for them. Table 4.33 takes a different perspective and shows where some of the most typical security principals (in the column headers) have permissions. It serves as a brief summary and helps you see what it means to be a person such as a domain administrator or an account operator.

Changing Default ACLs

The default access control list for each type of new object is part of the class definitions in the schema. If some of the defaults don't meet your needs, you can change them.

In Chapter 8 we explain how the `defaultSecurityDescriptor` property specifies the default for each class using Security Descriptor Definition Language (SDDL). In Chapter 9 we explain how you can modify the class definitions.

You can list all default security descriptors with the following command (replacing `dc=sanao,dc=com` for your forest name):

```
ldifde -f defaults.txt -d cn=schema,cn=configuration,
dc=sanao,dc=com -r (objectCategory=classSchema) -l
defaultSecurityDescriptor
```

NOTE The command is shown on several lines because of wrapping, but it is one command. Note also that there is no space after the comma at the end of the first line.

Table 4.33 Permissions of Typical Security Principals

Target	Account Operators	Administrators	Authenticated Users	Domain Admins
Domain object, Builtin		Four replication extended rights, Full Control except two deletes	Read, List Object, three password extended rights	Full Control except three deletes
Domain controllers (OU)		Full Control except two deletes	Read, List Object	Full Control except three deletes
Computers (container), Users (container), new OU	Create/Delete User, InetOrgPerson, Group, Computer (last one not in Users)	Full Control except two deletes	Read, List Object	Full Control except two deletes (in Computers and Users), Full Control (in new OU)
First DC		Full Control except two deletes	Read, List Object	Full Control
Users (group), Guests, Group Policy Creator Owners, Cert Publishers, RAS and IAS Servers, Domain Users, Domain Guests, Domain Computers, DnsAdmins, DnsUpdateProxy, Incoming Forest Trust Builders, Network Configuration Operators, Performance Log Users, Performance Monitor Users,	Full Control	Full Control except two deletes	Read, List Object, Send To	Full Control

(*continued*)

Table 4.33 Permissions of Typical Security Principals (*cont.*)

Target	Account Operators	Administrators	Authenticated Users	Domain Admins
Pre-Windows 2000 Compatible Access, Remote Desktop Users, Terminal Server License Servers, Windows Authorization Access Group, and new group	Full Control	Full Control except two deletes	Read, List Object, Send To	Full Control
New user, new inetOrgPerson	Full Control	Full Control except two deletes	Read General, Public, Personal, and Web Information, Read Permissions	Full Control
Enterprise Admins, Schema Admins, Domain Admins, Administrators, Server Operators, Account Operators, Print Operators, Backup Operators, Administrator, krbtgt, Replicator, Domain Controllers (group) (also, these don't allow inheritance)		Full Control except Delete Subtree	Read, List Object	Full Control except two deletes
New computer	Full Control	Full Control except two deletes	Read, List Object	Full Control
New contact, new shared folder		Full Control except two deletes	Read, List Object	Full Control

Usage Scenarios for Active Directory Permissions

Generally speaking, you can have two goals when you modify Active Directory permissions:

- *To allow changes to be made.* You give someone permission(s) (i.e., delegate) to make certain changes so that he can manage some objects or properties in the objects.
- *To allow properties to be seen.* You give some end user permission(s) to see certain properties in certain objects, which allows her to use the corresponding information.

For both goals, we describe scenarios and their implementation. However, almost all scenarios relate to the first goal.

In addition to using default permissions, you have two ways to delegate administration:

- Use the Delegation of Control wizard.
- Assign permissions manually with ACL Editor.

You can use the methods independently or you can combine them. You can first use the Delegation of Control wizard to set some permissions and then adjust the permissions by hand with ACL Editor.

General Practices

Before we get to the actual scenarios, we list some general practices.

- It is usually best to assign permissions to a group instead of an individual user. This is true even if only one user would be a member of that group. For example, if you want to give someone permissions to manage the Sales OU, you could create a group called gsSalesAdministrator, give it the permissions, and assign that one user as a member. This group would act as a role. It is more self-documenting to use this role in the permission lists instead of a username. Also, if the role owner changes, it is easy to put a new user in the group.
- If you delegate the administration of an OU to some role group, you might want to create that group in some OU other than the one being delegated. This makes sure that the assistant administrator cannot put other people in that group or accidentally delete it.

- Microsoft recommends that you establish comprehensive security groups and assign permissions to the groups before creating users.
- You can delegate administration of some groups to the managers of those groups.
- Remember that someone should have full control for every object.
- Because you cannot force inheritance, as soon as you give someone permission to modify permissions, he can block your access to that object. This is also true for any OU or other object that someone else has created. Fortunately, you can still take ownership and then restore your own permissions.

For additional reading, you can download two Microsoft documents on AD2003 security at `http://www.microsoft.com`: (a) a 150-page document, Best Practice Guide for Securing Windows Server Active Directory Installations, published in January 2004, and (b) a 209-page document, Best Practices for Delegating Active Directory Administration, published in November 2003. The latter document also has an accompanying 225-page appendix that lists and documents in numerous tables numerous security-related items, such as all extended rights.

Delegation Scenarios (to Make Changes)

Because you can set permissions per OU, per object, and even per property, you may delegate administration of all or part of your OU tree. This means that you give total or partial control of all or some objects in all or some of your OUs to an assistant administrator(s). Such delegation can have the following benefits:

- It reduces your workload.
- Often people who are close to end users and resources have more information about them and are thus better able to manage them.
- End users probably get better service when they can turn to someone who is near them (and in the same time zone, if your network spans time zones).

When delegating, you need to implement proper naming and other standards as well as give enough information about the task, the technology, and the company policies to whomever you delegate something to.

To make the possibilities clear, we offer several scenarios of delegation, followed by an example of each.

- *Scenario A: Delegating an OU Tree with Possible Blocking.* An assistant administrator gets total control over some OU and the whole tree beneath it. He could block you out (or maybe he did already).
- *Scenario B: Delegating an OU Tree without Blocking.* An assistant administrator gets total control over some OU and the whole tree beneath it. She cannot block you out.
- *Scenario C: Delegating Administration of Group Policy.* Even if you delegate the administration of an OU to an assistant administrator, he cannot create or manage group policies. Assigning permission to create or manage group policies is a separate task.
- *Scenario D: Delegating Administration of Certain Objects (Such As Users).* An assistant administrator gets total control over some object type, either in one OU or in the whole domain. For example, he could be responsible for managing user objects or printers.
- *Scenario E: Delegating Control over Noninformational Aspects.* An assistant administrator gets control over some noninformational aspects of users or other objects. For example, she could manage the members of some group or reset user passwords when needed.
- *Scenario F: Delegating Cross-Object Permissions to Carry Out a Function.* Some support people manage users' workstations. They may need cross-object type permissions to carry out their job functions, possibly for computer objects and group policies.
- *Scenario G: Delegating Administration of Informational Properties.* An assistant administrator gets partial control over user objects. For example, a secretary maintains some informational properties, such as address and organization information (e.g., title), for the employees of her department.
- *Scenario H: Delegating Permission to a User's Own Informational Properties.* A user (or several users) is given a permission to maintain all or most of his informational properties. You don't want to give him permission to modify any significant properties.

Scenario A: Delegating an OU Tree with Possible Blocking

In this scenario you want to give an assistant administrator total control over an OU, including any objects beneath it (i.e., the whole OU tree). With total control, he could remove any permissions that you had for the OU—that is, he could block you out.

First, create a group such as gsSalesAdministrator and assign the appropriate user as a member of this group. He would become an "OU administrator." If you want to control gsSalesAdministrator and the user object of the OU administrator, you can create these two objects outside the OU being delegated.

Then, use the Delegation of Control wizard on the OU to create a "custom task to delegate," select "This folder, . . ." as the target, and specify Full Control.

An alternative way to accomplish the same goal is to use ACL Editor to create the following permission entry for the OU object:

- Allow / gsSalesAdministrator / Full Control / This object and all child objects

After these steps, the OU administrator should use ACL Editor to perform one or more of the following steps, depending on how independent he wants to be (because you gave him Full Control, you cannot control the level of independence anymore):

- *Take ownership of the OU.* When the assistant administrator takes ownership of the OU, the domain administrators can no longer control permissions for it (unless the assistant administrator lets them have Full Control).
- *Disallow inheritable permissions from parent.* The assistant administrator stops inheritance from the parent container. When ACL Editor asks whether to Copy or Remove the previously inherited permissions, the OU administrator should choose Copy and go on to the next step.
- *Remove unnecessary administrative permissions.* Because the OU administrator didn't remove permissions in the previous step, Enterprise Admins, Domain Admins, Administrators, and Account Operators probably still have various administrative permissions for the OU. The OU administrator should evaluate them and remove unnecessary permissions.

NOTE The OU administrator might want to keep some permissions that were inherited and remove some permissions that were directly assigned for the OU object. Therefore, he cannot simply choose Remove when he is disallowing inheritance.

WARNING By default, when a new user object is created, Domain Admins and Account Operators get Full Control for that object. This is defined in the base schema and it will happen even if the OU administrator disallows inheritance and removes all "unnecessary" administrative permissions.

If the OU administrator wants to be really independent and wants to disallow even the automatic permissions of Domain Admins and Account Operators (see the Warning), he has two options.

- Talk to the people who manage the enterprise forest to modify the base schema, so that Domain Admins and Account Operators wouldn't get Full Control by default to new user objects (as well as many other object types). (We explain default permissions in Chapter 8 and modification of the schema in Chapter 9.) If a change is made, it affects all OUs in all domains of the forest, not just the one OU being delegated.
- Modify the permissions of each new object after its creation.

Neither of the proposed solutions is very practical, so the OU administrator probably has to accept that he cannot be completely independent.

NOTE By default, members of the Administrators group can take ownership of any object. Therefore, you can take the OU back from the OU administrator by taking the ownership, giving yourself Full Control, and removing the administrative permissions of the OU administrator.

The OU administrator cannot create Group Policy objects for his OU because GPOs are stored outside the OU. However, he can create links to existing GPOs.

Scenario B: Delegating an OU Tree without Blocking

This scenario is similar to scenario A in that you want to delegate the administration of an OU tree to an assistant administrator. The difference is that this time you don't want him to block you out. Therefore, you don't want to let him take ownership of the OU object or give permission to Modify Permissions. To achieve your goal, you use ACL Editor to create the following permission entries:

- Allow / gsSalesAdministrator / Full Control / Child objects only
- Allow / gsSalesAdministrator / all permissions except Delete, Modify Permissions, and Modify Owner / This object only

---

NOTE Even though the assistant administrator cannot block you out of the base OU, he can create a sub-OU and block you out of there. He can also block your access to any other child object so that, for example, you cannot manage some user account in that OU. If that happens, remember that you can make yourself the owner of that object, after which you can give yourself permissions for it.

Scenario C: Delegating Administration of Group Policy

Even if an assistant administrator has Full Control for an OU, he cannot create Group Policy objects for it. You can change this by delegating the administration of GPOs using one of the following three methods:

- *Put the assistant administrator as a member in the Group Policy Creator Owners group.* This way, he can create GPOs for those OUs for which he has the Write Property permission for the `gPLink` property. Most likely he will have this permission only for the OU that was delegated to him. Note that because Group Policy Creator Owners is a global group, it can have members only from the local domain.
- *Use the Group Policy Management Console (GPMC) to grant the assistant administrator a permission to create GPOs.* GPMC is discussed in Chapter 7.
- *Create a GPO for the OU and assign administrative permissions to the assistant administrator for that GPO.* To do this, select Properties in the OU context menu, select the Group Policy tab, and click the New button. Once you have given the GPO a name and pressed Enter, click the Properties button, select the Security tab, and give the assistant administrator the appropriate permissions (as discussed in the next list). Note that if GPMC is installed, the process is slightly different, as explained in Chapter 7.

The first option, making the assistant administrator a member of the Group Policy Creator Owners group, is probably easier if you don't want to control how many (and which) GPOs he creates. If you choose the third option, creating a GPO and assigning the assistant administrator permissions for that GPO, you can give permissions to him in one of three ways:

- *Full Control.* The assistant administrator could manage the GPO, he could manage the permissions for the GPO, and the GPO would apply to him (given that his user account would reside in the scope of the GPO).
- *Read, Write, Create All Child Objects, and Delete All Child Objects.* The assistant administrator can see the contents of the GPO and modify them, but he cannot modify permissions for the GPO. In addition, the GPO does not apply to him (see Figure 4.21). This alternative is equal to the "Edit settings" permission in GPMC.
- *Full Control except Apply Group Policy.* If the preceding alternative is not enough for the assistant administrator, you can also grant him the additional permissions Delete, Modify Permissions, and Modify Owner. This alternative is equal to the "Edit, delete, and modify security" permission in GPMC. Note that to be precise, this alternative is approximately "Full Control except Apply Group Policy," but not quite.

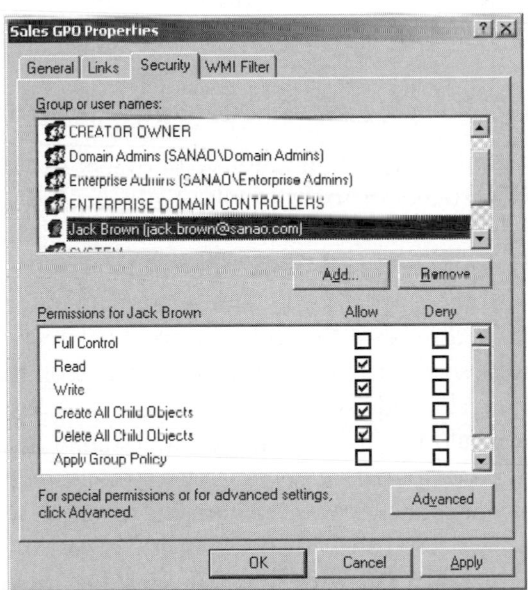

Figure 4.21 To give an assistant administrator (Jack) permission to edit the settings of a GPO, grant him the permissions Read, Write, Create, and Delete.

NOTE You can select any of the three options for giving permissions in dialog box A of ACL Editor.

Scenario D: Delegating Administration of Certain Objects (Such As Users)

In this scenario, an assistant administrator gets total control over some object type, either in one OU or in the whole domain. For example, if you want to delegate administration of user objects in some OU tree to gsSalesUserAdmins, create the following permission entries for the OU:

- Allow / gsSalesUserAdmins / Create/Delete User Objects / This object and all child objects
- Allow / gsSalesUserAdmins / Full Control / User objects

Delegation of administration of user and group objects is one of the common tasks in the Delegation of Control wizard, but you can also do this with ACL Editor. If the delegation is to cover the whole domain, you can just make the assistant administrator a member of Account Operators (if it doesn't hurt that this way he will get permissions for computer and group objects, too).

Scenario E: Control over Noninformational Aspects

In this scenario, an assistant administrator gets control over some noninformational aspects of users or other objects. For example, she could manage the members of some group or reset user passwords when needed. Both tasks are on the list of common tasks of the Delegation of Control wizard.

When we discussed the Delegation of Control wizard earlier in this chapter, we also showed how to add a new task on the list of its common tasks: unlock a locked user account.

If you would like to delegate administration of some "normal" noninformational properties, you can follow the instructions in scenario G, which explains the task for informational properties.

Scenario F: Cross-Object Permissions to Carry Out a Function

In this scenario, some support people need cross-object permissions to carry out some function. For example, they manage users' workstations and thus need permissions for computer objects and group policies. We have covered this, because in scenario C we explained how to delegate Group Policy administration and in scenario D we explained how to delegate administration of a certain object type.

Another example is the need to manage home folders. You would need the following permission entries for the base OU:

- Allow / gsHomeFolderAdmins / Write Property (Home Folder) / User objects
- Allow / gsHomeFolderAdmins / Write Property (Home Drive) / User objects

In addition, you would need to give Full Control to the folder on disk where the home folders would reside. This way, the home folder administrators could create home folders and give permissions to users for the folders.

NOTE You cannot delegate the permission to share folders. Only Administrators and Server Operators (and Power Users in member servers and workstations) can share folders.

Scenario G: Administering Informational Properties

You can store address book information and other informational properties in Active Directory. It is often easiest to delegate administration of at least some of these properties to non-IT personnel such as a secretary or an assistant, whose task would be to maintain this information for the employees of his department. The permission entries that you create to delegate this task resemble the following:

- Allow / gsInfoAdmins / Write Property (Fax Number) / User objects

You could also consider using a property set, such as Public Information, instead of individual properties if you find a set that suits your needs.

Scenario H: User's Own Informational Properties

In this scenario, you give a user (or several users) permission to maintain all or most of her informational properties. You don't want to give her permission to modify any significant properties, such as the logon name or password expiration settings.

Any user can modify her Personal Information and Web Information (Phone and Mail Options is also on the list of permission entries, but it doesn't map to any properties). Personal Information includes all properties of the Address and Telephones tabs (except for the Country/region information—see the Warning next to Table 4.16), so the user might already have all the permissions she needs.

If you need to add permissions, you would create the following permission entry for the base OU specifying the appropriate property:

- Allow / Self / Write Property / User objects

By using the well-known security principal Self, you can get the job done quite easily. An alternative would be much more tedious. You would have to assign Jack permissions for Jack, Jill permissions for Jill, Sarah permissions for Sarah, and so on for all the remaining users.

NOTE You can use Self nicely with OUs but not sensibly with groups.

User Scenarios (to See Properties)

End users can see by default the properties included in the General Information, Public Information, Personal Information, and Web Information property sets of other users in the forest. Consequently, you probably don't need to add Read Property permissions to and for them. However, if the need arises—for example, when your organization adds user properties to the schema and wants other users to see them—you can use an almost similar permission entry as in the delegation scenarios:

- Allow / Authenticated Users / Read Property / User objects

If your organization has added some properties to the schema, you may have also created a property set for them. Obviously, you can use this property set in the permission entry shown here.

Auditing Active Directory Access

If you want to see who has done what in Active Directory, you can use auditing. You may do it for both security and troubleshooting. Enabling auditing consists of two operations:

- A. Adding appropriate auditing entries, which you do in almost the same way as you create permission entries
- B. Turning on auditing for all or some domain controllers

In AD2000 and in AD2003 that was upgraded from AD2000, the domain object (as well as the root objects of schema and configuration partitions) has by default an auditing entry that applies to the domain object and all child objects. The entry specifies that all modifications made by anyone (i.e., the well-known security principal Everyone) be logged. This would mean that all modifications to Active Directory would be logged. However, this doesn't happen, because by default auditing is not turned on for any domain controller (or any other computer).

In AD2003 that was installed from scratch, the domain object also has by default some auditing entries. The inheritable ones, however, are only two that define that writing to `gPLink` or `gPOptions` of an OU should be logged. On the other hand, auditing is already turned on in the Default Domain Controller Policy.

The meaning of the two preceding paragraphs is that, depending on the forest version, either requirement A or B is filled, but not both. Therefore, depending on your forest version, you must modify the defaults if you want Active Directory use to be logged.

Adding Auditing Entries

There is no wizard for adding auditing entries, so your only option is to use ACL Editor dialog boxes B, C, and D. (Dialog box A is not useful in this case, except that you need to use its Advanced button to get to dialog box B.) In dialog box B you select the Auditing tab. Clicking Add or View/Edit takes you to dialog boxes C and D.

NOTE The "Allow inheritable permissions . . ." check box in the Permissions tab works independently from the "Allow inheritable auditing entries . . ." check box in the Auditing tab.

Although we call the three dialog boxes by the same names as the dialog boxes for permissions, they are slightly different. The difference is that with permissions you have Allow and Deny entries, but with auditing you have Success and Fail entries. An All entry means both Success and Fail. The list of possible permissions (Delete, Delete Subtree, and so on) is the same in both types of dialog boxes.

Figure 4.22 shows dialog box B with some auditing entries.

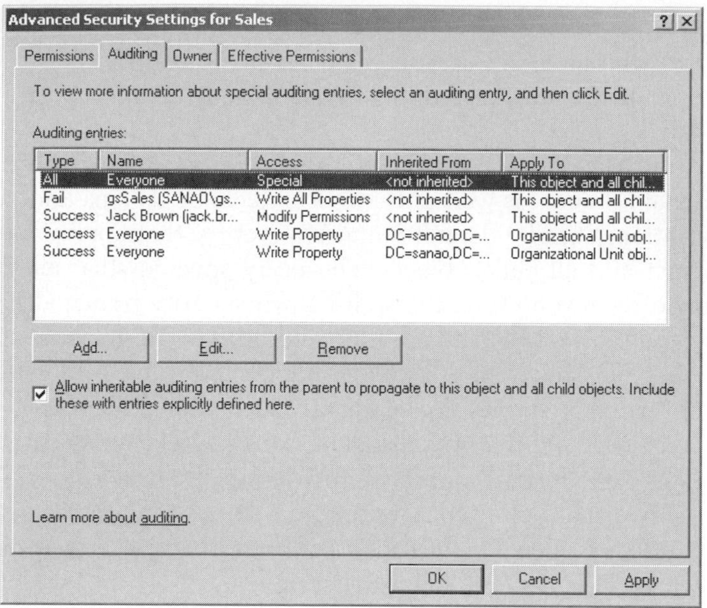

Figure 4.22 In ACL Editor's dialog box B, you can add entries to audit successful access to an object, failed access, or both.

Success and Fail entries cause Active Directory to generate an audit record each time an object is accessed successfully or unsuccessfully, respectively. Different entries define whose access and what kind of access are logged.

Turning On Auditing

If you want Active Directory to generate audit records, you must have auditing turned on. That setting could be different for every computer, but because you can access Active Directory objects using any domain controller, it makes sense to have auditing on for all domain controllers of a domain, if any. Remember that in a from-scratch installed forest, auditing is on by default.

If auditing is not already on, the easiest way to enable it is to edit the Domain Controller Security Policy. You do this by clicking the Start button and selecting Administrative Tools, Domain Controller Security Policy. This opens a security settings editor. In the left pane, navigate to Security Settings, Local Policies, Audit Policy. The resulting screen, shown in Figure 4.23, offers a list of policy options in the right pane.

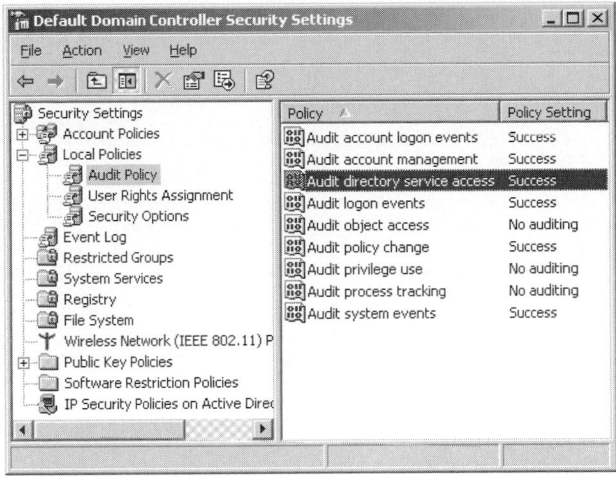

Figure 4.23 To audit Active Directory access, you must have auditing on. In that case, there is Success, Failure, or both enabled in the "Audit directory service access" policy.

Here you double-click "Audit directory service access," and then check Success, Failure, or both.

If you modify the setting, it will eventually affect all domain controllers of the domain. The File Replication Service replicates the change to other domain controllers, and each of them refreshes the security policy settings every five minutes.

NOTE In addition to the Audit Policy node in the left pane of Figure 4.23, there is an Event Log node three lines below it. Event Log contains the log file settings, such as the maximum size for each log file.

NOTE Audit policy is part of Group Policy, which is a complex mechanism to control computer and user settings. In addition to this brief introduction, we discuss the subject a little more in the "User Rights" section at the end of this chapter. Also, Chapter 7 is dedicated to Group Policy.

Viewing Audit Records

Audit records that Active Directory generates are stored in a C:\Windows\System32\Config\SecEvent.Evt file on each domain controller. You can view them using the Event Viewer snap-in. One way to launch it is to

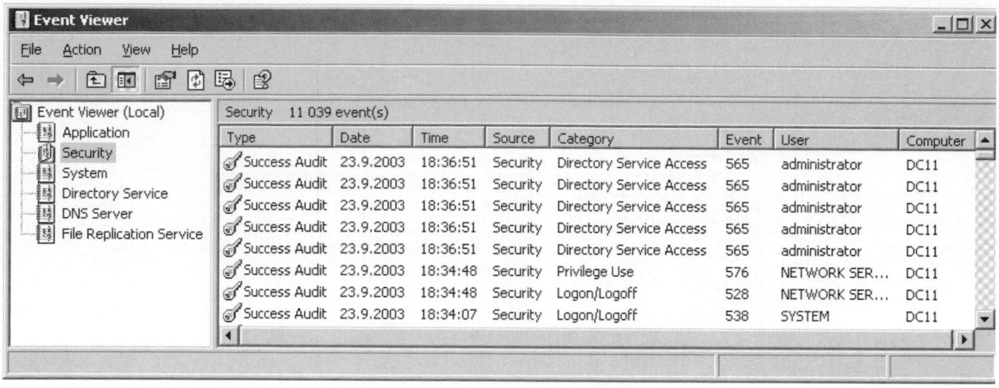

Figure 4.24 In the Event Viewer, audit records are shown under Security.

click the Start button and select Administrative Tools, Event Viewer. When you select Security in the left pane, you see audit records that have been recorded on the local computer. You can see the audits recorded on another computer by right-clicking "Event Viewer (Local)" and selecting a new server name. Figure 4.24 shows some sample records.

NOTE Each domain controller generates audit records only for events that were originally performed on that domain controller. For example, an administrator (perhaps sitting at a workstation) connected to DC1 creates a user, and that user is replicated to DC2. Only DC1 will have corresponding audit records.

NOTE When you create a user with the Users and Computers snap-in, the snap-in performs several operations, so there will be several audit records.

In addition to the header information shown in Figure 4.24, you can see a detailed description of each record. The following lines show a description of a record that was generated when Administrator modified the Initials property of Herbert.

```
Event Type:        Success Audit
     Object Server:       DS
Event Source:      Security
Event Category:    Directory Service Access
Event ID:          566
```

```
Date:               9/23/2003
Time:               3:07:27PM
User:               SANAO\administrator
Computer:           DC11
Description:
Object Operation:
      Object Server:          DS
      Operation Type:         Object Access
      Object Type:            contact
      Object Name:            CN=Herbert Clinton,OU=Boston,
                              DC=sanao,DC=com
      Handle ID:              -
      Primary User Name:      DC11$
      Primary Domain:         SANAO
      Primary Logon ID:       (0x0,0x3E7)
      Client User Name:       administrator
      Client Domain:          SANAO
      Client Logon ID:        (0x0,0x47B7B)
      Accesses:               Write Property

      Properties:
      Write Property
            Public Information
                  initials
      contact

      Additional Info:
      Additional Info2:
      Access Mask:              0x20
```

In the preceding lines, "Client User Name" specifies the user who requested the operation, and "Primary User Name" specifies the user who actually performed the operation (by impersonation, as explained in the next section).

Access Control Architecture

Now that you know how Active Directory permissions work in practice, we take a further look "under the hood" in this section. Knowing the architecture of access control will help you understand better how permissions work in Active Directory. The basic elements are as follows:

- Each process runs in the *security context* of some user account; that is, the process is using the rights and permissions of that account.
- *SIDs* and *access tokens* help to identify each user and the security context of a process.
- Access to each object is controlled by a *security descriptor.* It contains, among other fields, a *discretionary access control list (DACL),* which in turn contains a number of *access control entries (ACEs).*
- Some ACEs are linked to *extended rights* and *property sets,* each ACE being linked to one extended right or property set.

Processes and User Accounts

Each process in a Windows NT/2000/XP/Server 2003 computer runs with some user account (see Figure 4.25). In technical terms, the process runs in the *security context* of the account. Most of the processes that correspond to the user's applications run naturally with his account. Many of the background processes, including *services.exe,* run under a special account called *System,* or *LocalSystem.* Some background processes also run under LOCAL_SERVICE and NETWORK_SERVICE.

NOTE Services in Windows NT/2000/XP/Server 2003 can run in their own process, or several services can run in one process. Either way, all services run in the background—you don't see any windows for them onscreen.

A user may start an application with the Run As feature (see Help and Support for instructions), in which case she assigns some other user account for the application process. Services usually run with the System account, but you can define also for them that they run with some Active Directory user account.

The System account is a local "built-in" user account. It is not recognized outside that computer and thus cannot have rights outside that computer. If you want it to access something in the outside world, you can give the appropriate permissions to the computer object corresponding to that computer. The local System account can then use the permissions assigned to that computer object.

Because each user account can have different rights and permissions, each process in a computer can have different rights and permissions.

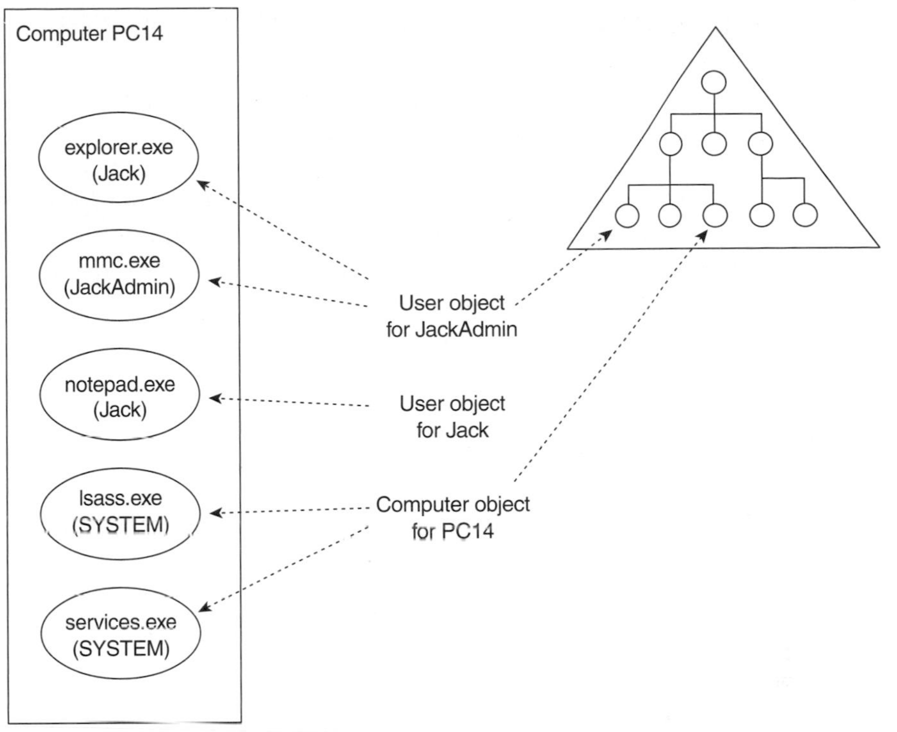

Figure 4.25 Each process in a computer runs with a user account and thus is using the rights and permissions of that account. An Active Directory computer object represents the local System account.

Often, background services (running in the background processes) have more rights and permissions than the person sitting at the computer. Also, the user can start some programs (such as administrative utilities) with more rights and permissions using the Run As feature if she has an administrative account and password.

Impersonation and Delegation

A process that is serving others can *impersonate* them. This means that when a serving process starts doing work for a client process, a thread in the serving process first switches to use the security context of the client. This way, the access check (for authorization) is done against the originating client's rights and permissions, not the powerful rights and permissions of the serving process.

When impersonating a client that is on a different computer than the server, the serving process and the resource being accessed must reside in the same computer. In other words, impersonation can take place only on two computers at the most.

Delegation takes authentication a step further, because now the target of access can be on a separate server, adding a third computer. A typical example is a configuration of a workstation with a Web browser, a Web server, and a database server. The Web browser requests a page from the Web server. In order to construct the page, the Web server needs to get some information from the database server. Because the Web server can make the query to the database with the (delegated) identity of the workstation user, every user can see on his Web page just the database information to which he has legitimate access.

IF YOU KNOW NT Windows NT supported impersonation but not delegation. The Kerberos authentication protocol in Windows 2000 and later allows support of delegation as well. The preceding three-computer scenario is possible if all three are running Windows 2000 or later.

As Figure 4.26 shows, administrators can control if delegation is possible by using the following settings in the user and computer objects:

- *User account of the client.* The setting "Account is sensitive and cannot be delegated" must not be checked (as is the case by default).
- *Service account of the first service.* If the service is running as LocalSystem, the corresponding computer object must have the setting "Trust computer for delegation" checked (as is the case by default with domain controllers). If the service is running as some other user account, that account must have the setting "Account is trusted for delegation" checked. Note that when the domain is on the Windows Server 2003 functional level, this "trust for delegation" setting appears on the Delegation tab of the computer and user accounts, and that tab is only visible for accounts that have been assigned service principal names (SPNs). As a new feature in AD2003, the Delegation tab also allows specifying the services that the delegation applies to (previously it was for all services).

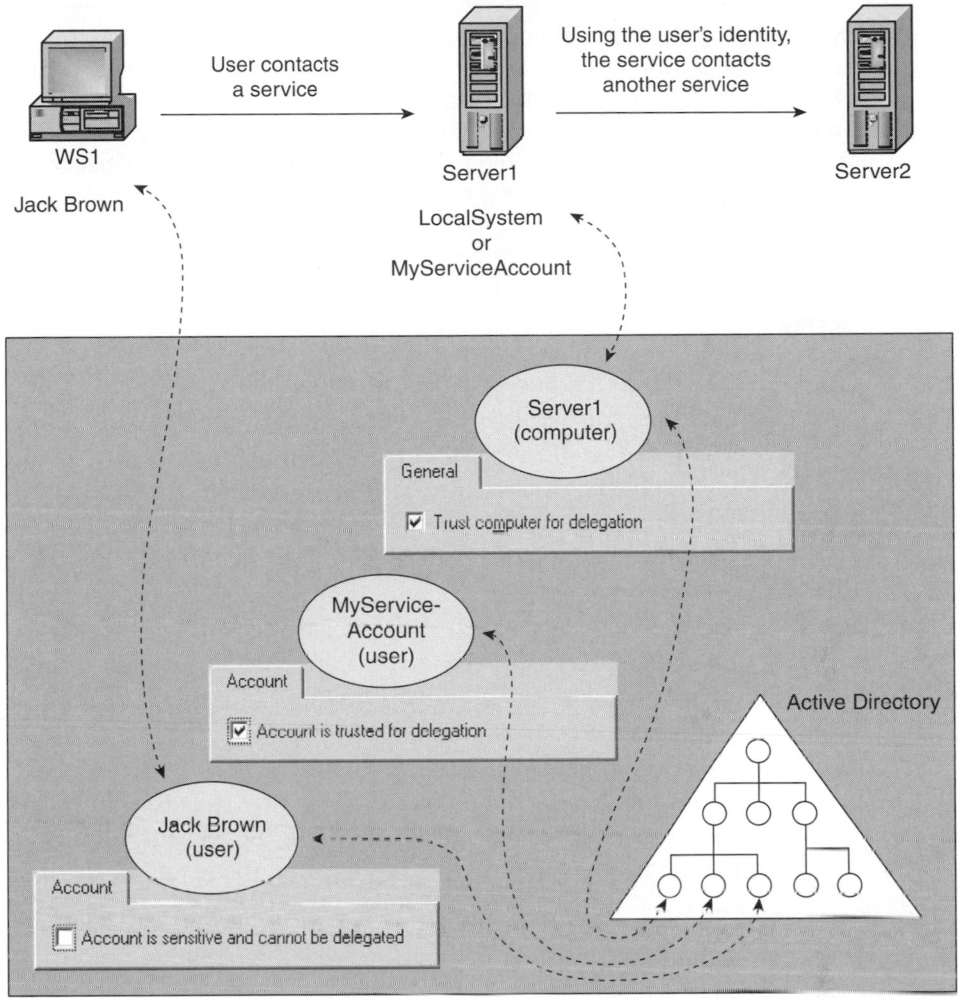

Figure 4.26 The service can run as either some user account or LocalSystem. Depending on the choice, the user account or the computer account must have the setting "Account is trusted for delegation"/"Trust computer for delegation" (respectively) checked. Or if the domain is running on the Windows Server 2003 functional level, there is a similar setting on the Delegation tab. The client's user account must not have the "Account is sensitive and cannot be delegated" setting checked.

NOTE By default, domain controllers are trusted for delegation. If you enable delegation also for a member server, all the present and future services in that computer that use LocalSystem can start impersonating clients when accessing services in other servers. Therefore, it is safer to enable delegation only for a specific user account rather than the computer. A service that would need delegation would run as that user account.

SIDs

Windows NT/2000/XP/Server 2003 identifies each security principal with a unique *security ID (SID)*. Thus every user, computer object, security group, and well-known security principal has a SID.

In the first three cases, the SID is stored in the `objectSid` property in each object. In the fourth case, the SIDs are "well known," meaning that the values are fixed. Well-known security principals are listed as objects in `CN=WellKnown Security Principals, CN=Configuration, DC=`<*forest_name*> and each of those objects contains an `objectSid` property to store the corresponding well-known SID.

All access control in both Active Directory and the NTFS file system, as well as other security areas, is based on the fact that those who will access secured objects are identified with SIDs.

SIDs are internally stored as binary structures, but they are usually represented as strings that start with an *S* followed by a string of numbers. A SID of a user account could look like the following:

```
S-1-5-21-1718597718-1078345429-1030254238-1207
```

We can break down the string into the parts listed in Table 4.34.

If you are a programmer and want to explore the binary structure of a SID, you can go to `http://msdn.microsoft.com/library` and search `AllocateAndInitializeSid`.

Table 4.35 lists the six options for the identifier authority.

NOTE Values 0 through 4 are universal well-known SID authorities. In theory they are meaningful also in operating systems other than Windows NT/2000/XP/Server 2003, if those operating systems only used the same security model.

Table 4.36 lists the SIDs in the "NT Authority" category.

Table 4.34 Parts of a SID

Part	Description
1	Revision level. It doesn't change very often, because it has been the same the whole decade (i.e., for all Windows NT and later versions).
5	Identifier authority. There are six options defined (see Table 4.35). However, there is plenty of room for more: The 48 bits of this part allow 281,474,976,710,656 choices.
21	A subauthority identifier. "21" indicates that this is a normal SID for some account in some domain.
1718597718-1078345429-1030254238	These three 32-bit numbers (a total of 96 bits) identify the domain. When a domain is installed, the installation process creates these numbers to be *statistically unique* (based on installation time and domain name). This should ensure that there are no two identical domain SIDs in the world.
1207	*Relative ID (RID)*, a 32-bit number. For predefined users and groups, the RID is predefined (its value being less than 1000). For every user, group, and computer object that you create, Active Directory assigns a RID, starting from 1000. It never uses the same RID twice, so if you create a Jack, delete Jack, and then create a new Jack, the latter Jack gets a new RID and thus a different SID.

Table 4.35 Identifier Authorities

Value	Name	Comments
0	Null SID Authority	You don't need this.
1	World SID Authority	Contains the "group" Everyone (S-1-1-0).
2	Local SID Authority	You don't need this.
3	Creator SID Authority	Contains the "groups" Creator Owner, Creator Group, Creator Owner Server, and Creator Group Server (S-1-3-0 through S-1-3-3).
4	Nonunique Authority	You don't need this.
5	NT Authority	Contains all other well-known security principals (S-1-5-x), users, groups, and so on (see Table 4.36).

Table 4.36 NT Authority SIDs

SID	Description
S-1-5-1 . . . 20	Seventeen well-known security principals (Dialup, Network, Batch, Interactive, Service, Anonymous Logon, Proxy, Enterprise Domain Controllers, Self, Authenticated Users, Restricted, Terminal Server User, Remote Interactive Logon, This Organization, System, Local Service, and Network Service)*.
S-1-5-21-x-x-x-x	Normal SID for some account in some domain. This includes three predefined user accounts (Administrator, Guest, and krbtgt) and ten predefined global groups (Domain Admins, Domain Users, Domain Guests, Domain Computers, Domain Controllers, Cert Publishers, Schema Admins, Enterprise Admins, Group Policy Creator Owners, and RAS and IAS Servers).
S-1-5-32-x	SIDs for the "BUILTIN domain" (and located in the Builtin container of a normal domain), also called *aliases*** (Administrators, Users, Guests, Power Users, Account Operators, Server Operators, Print Operators, Backup Operators, Replicator, Pre-Windows 2000 Compatible Access, Remote Desktop Users, Network Configuration Operators, Incoming Forest Trust Builders, Performance Monitor Users, Performance Log Users, Windows Authorization Access Group, and Terminal Server License Servers). Power Users is not in Active Directory but is in member server and workstation local user databases.
S-1-5-64-x	SIDs for "security package IDs" (NTLM Authentication, SChannel Authentication, and Digest Authentication).
S-1-5-1000	SID for Other Organization.

* The meanings of the well-known security principals are explained in Table 4.3 in the "Well-Known Security Principals" section earlier in this chapter.

** Aliases in the BUILTIN domain also use well-known SIDs. However, in this book we call them groups instead of well-known security principals. You can assign members to them, after all.

As you can see in Table 4.36, the built-in groups, such as Administrators, use the same SID in all domains. However, ACL Editor shows them belonging to different domains. Therefore, if you assign SANAO\-Administrators some permissions for any object in the schema or configuration partitions and then check the result on a DC of another domain, it would seem that the permissions were assigned to a group such as

SALES\Administrators. It would look as if the permissions were not for the same trustee, when in reality the SID is S-1-5-32-544 on both domain controllers.

You can inspect different SIDs with the Windows Support Tools utility GetSID. At the command prompt, type the following:

```
GETSID \\MYSERVER "Domain Admins" \\MYSERVER "Domain Admins"
```

The utility will print the SID of Domain Admins onscreen. You need to type everything twice, because GetSID wants to compare two accounts on two servers.

Access Tokens

Each time a user or background process authenticates itself to some computer (e.g., when a user logs on), Windows NT/2000/XP/Server 2003 in that target computer builds an access token for that user for that session. An access token contains the following:

- SID for the user account
- SIDs for the groups the user is a member of (either directly or via other groups), including any well-known security principals, such as Interactive, the user dynamically "is a member of"
- List of the user rights held by the user or his groups
- Default permissions (default DACL) for newly created objects
- Owner SID—that is, the default owner for newly created objects (it must be one of the user or group SIDs in this access token)
- Primary group SID—that is, the default primary group for newly created objects (it must be one of the group SIDs in this access token)
- Access token source, which is an eight-character string that distinguishes sources such as Session Manager, LAN Manager, and RPC Server
- Indication of whether the access token is a normal ("primary") or impersonation access token

An access token describes the security context of a process. Especially the first three items identify "who" this process is and which rights it has. When the process tries to perform various operations in the computer, Windows uses access token information to determine whether to allow or disallow each operation.

Each process has a *primary access token.* When a thread in a serving process impersonates a client, it has another access token called an *impersonation token,* or sometimes a *client access token.*

An access token is either built or copied. As mentioned previously, the access token is built during logon or authentication to a new server. If the user then starts new processes without specifying a different username, the access token of the starting process is copied more or less identically to the new process.

You may know that changes in group memberships are not effective until the user in question logs off and then logs on again. The reason is that the access token with the group information is generated only at logon time or when authenticating to a new server.

You can see the basic access token information (user, groups, and privileges) with the command WhoAmI. Figure 4.27 shows an example of the command output when the user LocalAdmin executes the command. The output is taken from Windows 2000 because the Windows Server 2003 version of WhoAmI displays much wider text lines, which look quite ugly in a screen shot. If you test the command, you can redirect the output to a text file (using >) and then open it in Notepad.

```
C:\WINNT\System32\cmd.exe

C:\>whoami /all
[User]      = "SANAO\localadmin"  S-1-5-21-1547161642-1606980848-842925246-1112

[Group  1] = "SANAO\Domain Users"  S-1-5-21-1547161642-1606980848-842925246-513
[Group  2] = "Everyone"  S-1-1-0
[Group  3] = "BUILTIN\Administrators"  S-1-5-32-544
[Group  4] = "BUILTIN\Users"  S-1-5-32-545
[Group  5] = "BUILTIN\Pre-Windows 2000 Compatible Access"  S-1-5-32-554
[Group  6] = "LOCAL"  S-1-2-0
[Group  7] = "NT AUTHORITY\INTERACTIVE"  S-1-5-4
[Group  8] = "NT AUTHORITY\Authenticated Users"  S-1-5-11

(X) SeChangeNotifyPrivilege           = Bypass traverse checking
(O) SeSecurityPrivilege               = Manage auditing and security log
(O) SeBackupPrivilege                 = Back up files and directories
(O) SeRestorePrivilege                = Restore files and directories
(O) SeSystemtimePrivilege             = Change the system time
(O) SeShutdownPrivilege               = Shut down the system
(O) SeRemoteShutdownPrivilege         = Force shutdown from a remote system
(O) SeDebugPrivilege                  = Debug programs
(O) SeSystemEnvironmentPrivilege      = Modify firmware environment values
(O) SeSystemProfilePrivilege          = Profile system performance
(O) SeProfileSingleProcessPrivilege   = Profile single process
(O) SeIncreaseBasePriorityPrivilege   = Increase scheduling priority
(X) SeLoadDriverPrivilege             = Load and unload device drivers
(O) SeCreatePagefilePrivilege         = Create a pagefile
(O) SeIncreaseQuotaPrivilege          = Increase quotas
(X) SeUndockPrivilege                 = Remove computer from docking station
(O) gation                  = Enable computer and user accounts to be trusted for
 delegation
(O) SeMachineAccountPrivilege         = Add workstations to domain

C:\>_
```

Figure 4.27 WhoAmI allows the logged-on user to see her username, groups, and privileges, along with SIDs. The screen shot is taken from Windows 2000 because its output fits better on a book page.

NOTE Sometimes the Windows 2000 version of WhoAmI displays only some of the desired results. For example, it may display the username and the first three groups and then quit. The Windows Server 2003 version seems to work.

Security Descriptors

Each object in Active Directory is protected with a *security descriptor*, which describes who is allowed to access the object and in what way. A security descriptor contains the *owner* of the object, the *discretionary access control list (DACL)*, and the *system access control list (SACL)*. DACLs and SACLs in turn contain a number of *access control entries (ACEs)* (see Figure 4.28). ACEs are the permission and auditing entries that you have seen throughout this chapter that determine which users

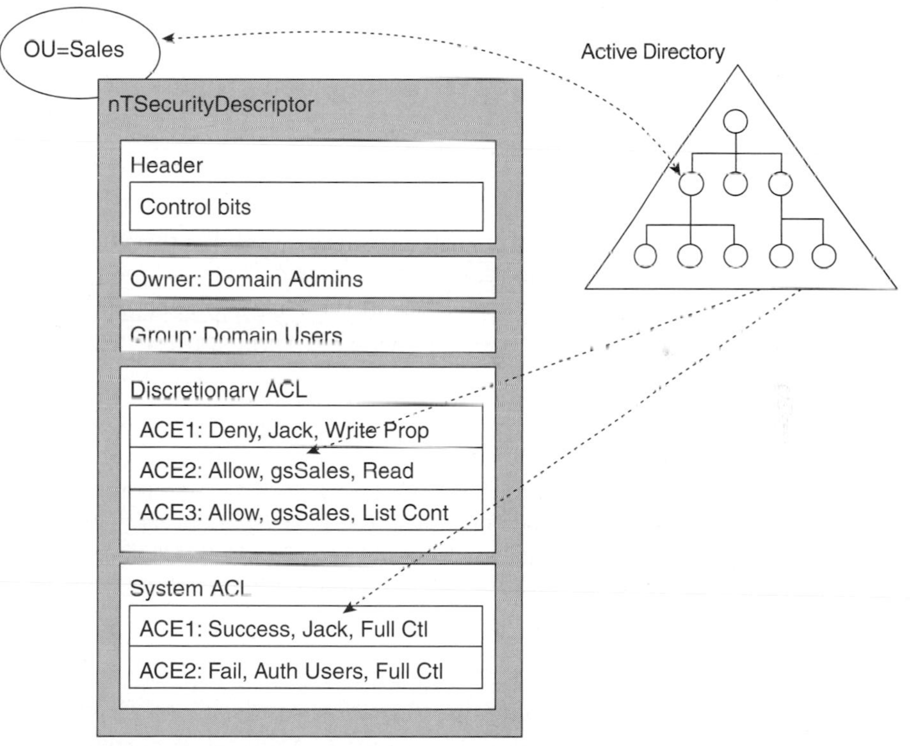

Figure 4.28 Each Active Directory object has an `nTSecurityDescriptor` attribute, which is where the security descriptor is stored. The discretionary ACL and the system ACL contain ACEs.

Table 4.37 Parts of a Security Descriptor

Part	Description
Header	Contains, among others, the flags `SE_DACL_PROTECTED` and `SE_SACL_PROTECTED`. Setting the former flag prevents this object from inheriting permission entries. Setting the latter flag does the same for auditing entries.
Owner	Owner of the object. This identity can control permissions for the object.
Group	Primary group of the owner. Active Directory doesn't use this information.
Discretionary ACL	Contains ACEs, and each ACE is one permission entry. ACEs in a DACL determine who may access the object and in what way. Some of the ACEs may be inherited from above, and some are assigned directly to the object.
System ACL	Contains ACEs, and each ACE is one auditing entry. ACEs in a SACL determine whose usage, and what kind, will be recorded in the audit log. Some of the ACEs may be inherited from above, and some are assigned directly to the object.

and groups may access the object and in what way or whose usage is recorded in the audit log, respectively. A DACL contains permission entries and a SACL contains auditing entries.

The security descriptor is stored with each object in the attribute `nTSecurityDescriptor`. Table 4.37 describes most parts of a security descriptor.

NOTE As you read about the contents and settings of a security descriptor, you will notice that they correspond to various check boxes and settings in the user interface. If the correspondence is obvious, we don't expressly describe it.

ACE Contents

Because most access control information resides in ACEs, we describe each ACE field and its possible values in Tables 4.38 through 4.42. We start with a summary table (Table 4.38).

Table 4.38 Fields of an ACE

Field	Description
Trustee	The security principal to which this entry applies.
AccessMask	A 32-bit number (bitfield), each bit of which represents one permission mostly corresponding to special object permissions of the user interface (see Table 4.39).
AceFlags	A 32-bit number (bitfield) whose bits represent mostly different inheritance options (see Table 4.40).
AceType	A 32-bit number that indicates if this is an Allow, Deny, or auditing entry (see Table 4.42).
Flags	A 32-bit number (bitfield) whose two first bits tell whether ObjectType or InheritedObjectType are present (i.e., not empty) (see Table 4.41).
ObjectType	If the ACE applies to only one object class, property, property set, or extended right, this field identifies which one.
InheritedObjectType	If only one child object class can inherit the ACE, this field identifies which one.

The AccessMask, AceFlags, and Flags fields consist of bits, and each bit has some meaning (although perhaps not all 32 bits have assigned meanings). The idea of these *bitfields* is that you can pack several on/off settings into one field, each of them in one bit.

Tables 4.39 through 4.42 list the meanings of the bits. The hexadecimal values in the tables indicate in which bit each setting is. For example, a hex value 4 in binary is 0100. It is thus the third bit from the right (the rightmost bit is called the *least significant* bit).

TIP You can try different values with Calculator. For example, choose the Scientific view, select Hex, enter "80," click Bin, and notice that the display shows "1000 0000" (with the space if you have Digit grouping on).

NOTE The AceType field, described in Table 4.42, isn't a bitfield. It's just one of six possible values.

Table 4.39 ACE AccessMask Bits

Name	Hex	Permission in User Interface
ADS_RIGHT_DS_CREATE_CHILD	1	Create All Child Objects, Create *certain* Objects
ADS_RIGHT_DS_DELETE_CHILD	2	Delete All Child Objects, Delete *certain* Objects
ADS_RIGHT_ACTRL_DS_LIST	4	List Contents
ADS_RIGHT_DS_SELF	8	All Validated Writes, Validated write to service principal name, and so on
ADS_RIGHT_DS_READ_PROP	10	Read All Properties, Read *property set*, Read *property*
ADS_RIGHT_DS_WRITE_PROP	20	Write All Properties, Write *property set*, Write *property*
ADS_RIGHT_DS_DELETE_TREE	40	Delete Subtree
ADS_RIGHT_DS_LIST_OBJECT	80	List Object (normally not visible in the UI)
ADS_RIGHT_DS_CONTROL_ACCESS	100	All Extended Rights, Change Password, Receive As, and so on
ADS_RIGHT_DELETE	10000	Delete
ADS_RIGHT_READ_CONTROL	20000	Read Permissions
ADS_RIGHT_WRITE_DAC	40000	Modify Permissions
ADS_RIGHT_WRITE_OWNER	80000	Modify Owner

Table 4.40 ACE AceFlags Bits

Name	Hex	Explanation
ADS_ACEFLAG_INHERIT_ACE	2	Child objects can inherit this ACE.
ADS_ACEFLAG_NO_PROPAGATE_INHERIT_ACE	4	Only immediate child objects can inherit this ACE.
ADS_ACEFLAG_INHERIT_ONLY_ACE	8	This ACE doesn't apply to the object itself. The ACE is only for inheritance for children.

Table 4.40 ACE AceFlags Bits (*cont.*)

Name	Hex	Explanation
ADS_ACEFLAG_INHERITED_ACE	10	The system sets this flag if the ACE was inherited instead of assigned directly to the object.
ADS_ACEFLAG_SUCCESSFUL_ACCESS	40	If this flag is set in SACL, the system generates audit messages for successful accesses.
ADS_ACEFLAG_FAILED_ACCESS	80	If this flag is set in SACL, the system generates audit messages for failed access attempts.

Table 4.41 ACE Flags Bits

Name	Hex	Explanation
ADS_FLAG_OBJECT_TYPE_PRESENT	1	The ObjectType field is not empty.
ADS_FLAG_INHERITED_OBJECT_TYPE_PRESENT	2	The InheritedObjectType field is not empty.

Table 4.42 ACE AceType Bits

Name	Value	Explanation
ADS_ACETYPE_ACCESS_ALLOWED	0	This ACE allows access. ObjectType and InheritedObjectType are both empty, so this ACE isn't for a particular object class, property, property set, or extended right.
ADS_ACETYPE_ACCESS_DENIED	1	Same as previous, except this ACE denies access.
ADS_ACETYPE_SYSTEM_AUDIT	2	Same as previous, except this is an auditing ACE.

(*continued*)

Table 4.42 ACE AceType Bits (*cont.*)

Name	Value	Explanation
`ADS_ACETYPE_ACCESS_ALLOWED_OBJECT`	5	This ACE allows access. Either ObjectType is not empty (so this ACE is for some particular object class, property, property set, or extended right) or InheritedObjectType is not empty (so this ACE will be inherited to certain object types).
`ADS_ACETYPE_ACCESS_DENIED_OBJECT`	6	Same as previous, except this ACE denies access.
`ADS_ACETYPE_SYSTEM_AUDIT_OBJECT`	7	Same as previous, except this is an auditing ACE.

ObjectType Field

Many ACEs apply to only one object class, property, property set, or extended right. In this case, the ObjectType field contains a *globally unique identifier (GUID)*, which identifies the target. A GUID is a 128-bit number that is usually represented as a series of 32 hexadecimal characters with some delimiting dashes and curly braces. For example, the `schemaIDGUID` for the user objects class looks like the following:

```
{BF967ABA-0DE6-11D0-A285-00AA003049E2}
```

NOTE Active Directory identifies each object with an `objectGUID` property. It is not used in this context.

A GUID can be represented in several binary formats. If you are a programmer and want to explore them, you can go to `http://msdn.microsoft.com/library` and search "eFormat Enumeration."

Table 4.43 lists the four cases: object class, property, property set, and extended right. It mentions which property the ObjectType GUID refers to and in which object this property resides. It also gives an example of each case (see also Figure 4.29).

Table 4.43 How the ObjectType Field Identifies a Permission Target

Target	Property to Refer	In Object	Example
Object class	schemaIDGUID	Some classSchema object	If a DS_CREATE_CHILD ACE applies only to user objects (i.e., Create User Objects), ObjectType field contains the schemaIDGUID of the user class.
Property	schemaIDGUID	Some attributeSchema object	If someone has permission to read only the Zip/Postal Code of some user, the ObjectType field of the ACE contains the schemaIDGUID of the postalCode attribute.
Property set	rightsGuid	Some controlAccessRight object	If someone has permission to read only the Personal Information of some user, the ObjectType field of the ACE contains the rightsGuid of the Personal-Information control access right.
Extended right	rightsGuid	Some controlAccessRight object	If someone has permission to Reset Password of some user, the ObjectType field contains the rightsGuid of the User-Force-Change-Password control access right. Also, a permission ADS_RIGHT_DS_CONTROL_ACCESS must be included in the AccessMask.

Table 4.43 mentions controlAccessRight objects. There is one object for each property set and one for each extended right, so with either permission type, the corresponding ACE needs to be linked to one of these objects. They are stored in the configuration partition of Active Directory under the CN=Extended-Rights container.

Adding Extended Rights

Active Directory contains a number of extended rights, such as Change Password, Reset Password, Receive As, and Send As. Software developers may add extended rights to be used with their applications. To be exact, they can write an installation program that adds these extended rights objects (`controlAccessRight` objects) once their customer runs it.

The new extended rights appear automatically in the permission user interfaces of the relevant objects.

Windows 2000 or Windows Server 2003 does not use the new extended rights for anything; they are only for the purposes of the application whose installation program created them.

In Chapter 9 we present a detailed example of how to create a new property set. You can use that example also to create a new extended right if you make one modification: You must use the value "256" for the `validAccesses` property. That value corresponds to `ADS_RIGHT_DS_CONTROL_ACCESS`, which you saw in Table 4.39, AccessMask bits.

Property Sets

Some property sets are General Information and Personal Information. Developers may add property sets just like extended rights (Chapter 9 shows how to do this). Typically, a common installation program creates a property set and the properties it contains, and the installation program is included with the application that will use these new properties and property set(s). Many of the base schema properties already exist in some set, and each property can belong to only one property set. Consequently, in AD2000 you probably didn't create any property sets for base schema properties. In AD2003, however, you can remove base schema properties from base property sets and put them in self-defined property sets. If you have the energy, you can create your own more logical property sets in place of the base sets.

WARNING Be very careful if you modify the predefined property sets, and make sure you know what you are doing. If you break a property set that Windows or Exchange uses, for example, you are probably in trouble. Also, you are out of Microsoft support in this case.

A property belongs to a property set if the `attributeSecurityGUID` property of the corresponding `attributeSchema` object contains the same GUID as the `rightsGuid` property of the `controlAccessRight` object corresponding to the property set. When an ACE applies to only one object class, property, property set, or extended right, the GUID in the ObjectType field links the ACE to the appropriate target. The target is either a certain class or attribute object or a `controlAccessRight` object corresponding to a property set or extended right. In Figure 4.29, the Postal-Code property belongs to the Personal-Information property set because of the `attributeSecurityGUID` link.

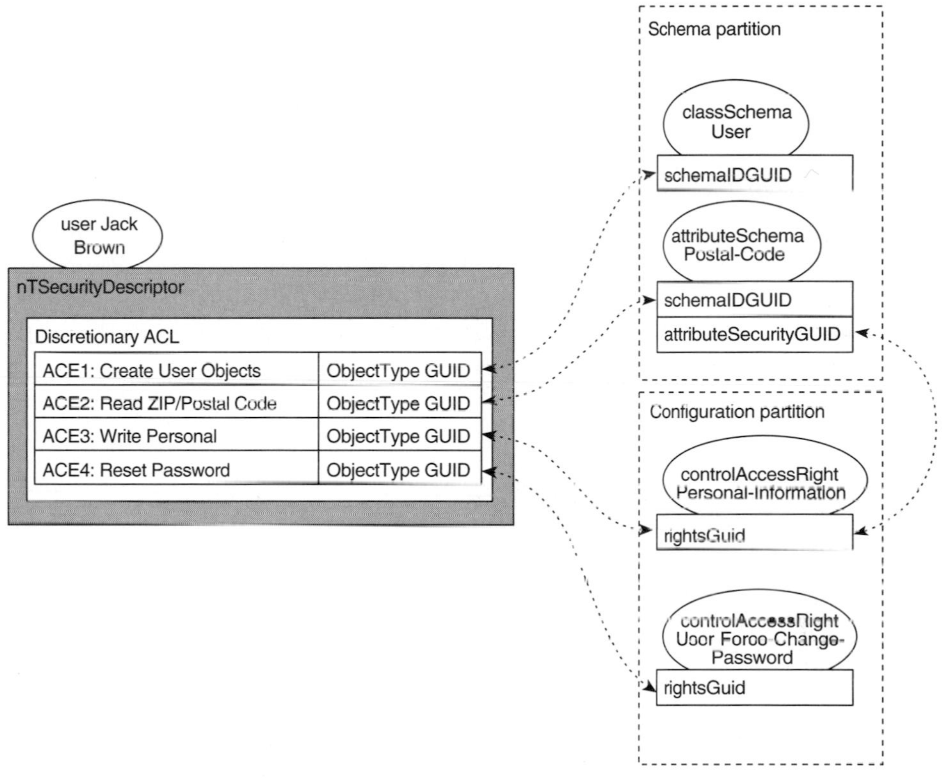

Figure 4.29 The arrows in the image represent matching GUIDs. For example, ACE2 applies only to one property, Postal-Code, and this is denoted by including Postal-Code's `schemaIDGUID` in ACE2. In addition, the rightmost arrow between `attributeSecurityGUID` and `rightsGuid` defines that the Postal-Code property belongs to the Personal Information property set. (This rightmost arrow is part of the base schema that Microsoft has defined. It's not part of the security settings that you would define.

NOTE One hundred thirty-six properties (i.e., `attributeSchema` objects) of the base schema belong to some property set. In addition, ten properties have `attributeSecurityGUID` defined to a value that doesn't match to any property set.

This concludes our discussion about access control architecture and access control. In Chapter 11, we will present a few scripts that you can use to list or manage ACEs. Even if you are not interested in scripting, we recommend that you read that section and try out the scripts that list ACEs without changing anything. Doing so will deepen your knowledge of the access control architecture.

Single Instance Storage

Different Active Directory objects contain a lot of identical permission entries because of inheritance and schema defaults. Single Instance Storage (SIS) enables storing identical security descriptors only once, which can reduce the size of the directory database some 40 percent. If you upgrade a domain controller from Windows 2000 server, you must perform an offline defragmentation of the database to gain the saving in space.

Domain Controller Access

The emphasis in this chapter is on the access permissions of Active Directory. There are also other Windows 2000 and/or Windows Server 2003 features that can help you secure your Active Directory. We list them here and then discuss the first one in the list in more detail:

- *Directory object quotas* help you regulate how many objects various users can create, which protects from a denial-of-service attack or an unintentional mass creation of objects.
- *LDAP query policies* enable you to set certain maximums for the resources a domain controller may use when answering LDAP queries of LDAP clients. Again, this can be used to prevent denial-of-service attacks. For more information, see Microsoft Knowledge Base article 315071.
- *IP deny lists* enable you to block individual IP addresses or ranges of IP addresses from accessing domain controllers. The feature

exists as a menu item in the Windows 2000 version of NTDSUtil, but is removed from the Windows Server 2003 version. For more information, see Microsoft Knowledge Base article 314976.

- *Anonymous access* is disabled by default in Windows Server 2003 domain controllers and enabled in Windows 2000 domain controllers. For more information, see Microsoft Knowledge Base article 326690.
- *LDAP over SSL* (or LDAPS) can be used so that domain controller communication is encrypted on the wire. For more information, see Microsoft Knowledge Base article 247078. In addition, the Windows Server 2003 version of Administrative Tools (that is, Admin Pak) uses LDAPS.
- *SMB signing and secure channel signing* are enabled by default in Windows Server 2003 domain controllers. For more information, see the "Security Settings" section in Chapter 7.

Directory Object Quotas

A denial-of-service attack can be performed by creating a huge number of objects in Active Directory. This could also happen unintentionally because of a bug in an application or a human error. To protect from such incidences, you can set quotas on how many directory objects a given security principal (user, inetOrgPerson, computer) can own in a given partition. (This includes domain and application partitions and the configuration partition, but the schema partition doesn't support quotas.) The object's creator becomes its owner, but as you know, the ownership can be transferred.

Windows 2000 doesn't understand or enforce directory object quotas, so for the quotas to be effective, all domain controllers that host the corresponding partition should be running Windows Server 2003. Also, quotas are enforced only on originating updates and not when a replicated update is applied. See Chapter 5 for information on originating and replicated updates.

Setting Directory Object Quotas

You can set a default quota for the partition and individual quotas for users, inetOrgPersons, computers, and security groups. If there is a quota for both a user and one or more groups she is a member of, the largest quota is used. If an individual quota is not assigned (either directly or through group membership), the quota of the partition is used. By default, the partition quota is unlimited. Members of Domain Admins and Enterprise Admins are not subject to quota control.

You would use the DS commands to manage quotas. The first of the following commands sets Jack's quota to 15 owned objects in the Sanao domain. The second command raises his quota to 18 objects, and the third command sets the default quota for the partition.

```
dsadd quota -part DC=sanao,DC=com -acct jack.brown@sanao.com
    -qlimit 15
dsmod quota "CN=SANAO_JackB,CN=NTDS Quotas,DC=sanao,DC=com"
    -qlimit 18
dsmod partition DC=sanao,DC=com -qdefault 500
```

As you can see from the second command, the quota definition created in the first command exists in the `CN=NTDS Settings` container and has the name `<domain>_<pre-windows2000name>`. You could actually specify the quota object's name in the DSAdd command, but the default name is probably quite OK.

NOTE If a user is able to create new users, he can create more objects than his quota would allow him to. He could first create a hundred users and then, depending on the permission delegation, he could use these users to create more objects.

Viewing Directory Object Quotas

You can view individual quota entries, effective quota limits, and the current quota usage with DS commands. An effective quota limit sums up the effect if a user is in a group that has a higher quota, and if none of the quota entries apply, the effective limit equals the partition default.

The following command (wrapped on two lines) displays the effective quota limit along with the current usage:

```
dsget user "CN=jack brown,OU=boston,DC=sanao,DC=com"
    -part DC=sanao,DC=com -qlimit -qused
```

However, it seems that a higher quota that is gained through group membership shows in the DSGet command only after the user has once logged on. It also seems that the command displays the quota and usage only when issued on a domain controller.

To see the effective quota and the current usage for all users in a domain, use the following command:

```
dsquery user domainroot |
    dsget user -part DC=sanao,DC=com -qlimit -qused -dn
```

The following command displays the individual quota limit of Jack (as has been defined in his quota object):

```
dsget quota "CN=SANAO_JackB,CN=NTDS Quotas,DC=sanao,DC=com"
    -qlimit
```

If you want to see the individual quota limit but don't know the name of the quota object, you can use the DSQuery command and pipe the output to the input of DSGet. The resulting command is:

```
dsquery quota domainroot -acct sanao\jackb | dsget quota
    -qlimit
```

To get a list of all quota entries that are at least ten objects, you can specify a filter in the DSQuery command, pipe the result to DSGet, and specify that you want the name (acct) and quota limit (qlimit) displayed.

```
dsquery quota domainroot -qlimit ">=10" | dsget quota -acct
    -qlimit
```

User's Own Quota and Usage

The `CN=NTDS Quotas` object contains two constructed attributes, `msDS-QuotaEffective` and `msDS-QuotaUsed`, which display a different result for each user—that is, her own effective quota limit and current usage. Normal users have very limited permissions for this object: just an extended right, Query Self Quota, which allows them to view these two values. Therefore, the ways to view the values are also limited, and an ADSI script, for example, doesn't work.

One way to view the values is to use ADFind, made by Joe Richards (see `http://www.joeware.net`), and create a batch file with the following line (wrapped on two lines here):

```
adfind -b "CN=NTDS Quotas,DC=sanao,DC=com"
      -s Base msDS-QuotaEffective msDS-QuotaUsed
```

If you add a second line that contains `pause`, the user can see the result even when the command is launched from the graphical user interface.

Tombstone Quotas

As explained in Chapter 5, when an object is deleted, most of its attributes are stripped, and what is left, is called a tombstone. This tombstone exists by default for 60 days, so that knowledge of the deletion can be replicated to all domain controllers (even if one of them were offline for 55 days). It is possible to have the tombstones counted with a lower weight, when the user's quota usage is determined.

By default, the tombstone weight is 100, which means that they are as "expensive" as normal objects. To set the weight to 50 percent, for example, you would use the following command:

```
dsmod partition DC=sanao,DC=com -qtmbstnwt 50
```

Now that Windows Server 2003 requires by default complex passwords, the option in the preceding command makes you wonder if complex command options also are required nowadays.

The `CN=NTDS Quotas` contains a constructed multivalued attribute, `msDS-TopQuotaUsage`, which seems to contain those ten security principals that own the most objects. When viewed with LDP, they are sorted in descending order, but when viewed with ADSI Edit, they appear in random order. Each value looks like the following. Now that the tombstone weight is 50 percent, we have the formula "213 + 50% x 7 = 217.

```
<MS_DS_TOP_QUOTA_USAGE>
     <partitionDN> DC=sanao,DC=com </partitionDN>
     <ownerSID> S-1-5-21-546331233-4068841660-521421359-512
         </ownerSID>
     <quotaUsed> 217 </quotaUsed>
     <tombstonedCount> 7 </tombstonedCount>
     <liveCount> 213 </liveCount>
</MS_DS_TOP_QUOTA_USAGE>
```

User Rights

Permissions are properties relating to (and attached to) objects such as files, folders, and Active Directory objects. User rights are assignments relating to the system as a whole. An example of this is the right to change a computer's clock setting.

As with permissions, it is best to assign user rights to groups instead of individual users. Also, you might not want to change the user rights of a predefined group such as Backup Operators, but instead create a new group and assign it the needed rights. For example, if your goal is to assign some users rights that they might need to use a certain computer (e.g., "log on locally" and "change the time"), you could create a Users-OfThisComputer group and then assign the two corresponding user rights (and perhaps some others) to that group. Any user that you put in this group obviously gets the rights you want her to get.

User Rights Categories

There are 39 user rights (34 in Windows 2000) that you can assign to security principals.

NOTE Of the four security principal types (users, security groups, well-known security principals, and computer objects), computer objects do not need user rights. Each computer object corresponds to the local System account of the computer, and those accounts have all the user rights they need anyway.

Some of the rights can be called "logon rights" and some can be called "privileges." We categorize them as follows:

- Five logon rights
- Five deny logon "rights" to correspond to each logon right
- Nineteen "normal" privileges (i.e., you might actually need these)
- Ten advanced privileges (i.e., you probably won't need these)

In addition to these settable rights, there are some fixed user rights. For example, the right to format hard drives is built into the Windows NT/2000/XP/Server 2003 program code, so you cannot assign that right to any user or group. If you are a member of Administrators, you can format hard drives. For example, Server Operators cannot format hard drivers of Windows Server 2003 domain controllers.

In the subsequent sections, we list the user rights and which groups have them by default for a domain controller. There are also some user rights with the special users TsInternetUser, IURS_server, and IWAM_server, but we don't list them, because they are related to specific services and not to Active Directory in general.

For a member server or workstation, the defaults are somewhat different from those of a domain controller. One reason for this is that those computers have the group Power Users instead of Server Operators, Print Operators, and Account Operators.

The names of the rights are partly self-explanatory. Also, the Windows Server 2003 Help system has a description of each, so we don't repeat those descriptions here. Next to each right, we mention in parentheses the application programming interface (API) name for the user right. You may need the API name with some Resource Kit utilities (NTRights and ShowPriv).

Logon Rights

Each time an authentication occurs, it is one of five types: Interactive, Network, Terminal Service, Batch, or Service. The five logon rights define who can authenticate using which logon type. Table 4.44 lists these logon rights and their "deny" counterparts and the groups to which they are assigned.

The "deny logon" rights override the "allow logon" rights. Therefore, you can allow something to a broader set of users (i.e., a group) and then, if needed, exclude some of the rights from a narrower set of users (i.e., another group or individual user).

The first two logon rights in Table 4.44 have, by default, different assignments for a workstation and a member server. They are as follows:

- *Access this computer from the network:* Administrators, Power Users, Backup Operators, Users, Everyone
- *Allow log on locally:* Administrators, Power Users, Backup Operators, Users, Guest

---

WARNING Typically you don't want end users or guests to be able to log on at the keyboard of your member servers. To prevent them from doing so, remove Users and Guest from the "Allow log on locally" list.

Table 4.44 Logon Rights: Default Assignments for Domain Controllers

Logon Right	Admin*	SO	AO	PO	BO	AU	EO
Access this computer from the network (SeNetworkLogonRight)	X					X	X
Allow log on locally (SeInteractive-LogonRight)	X	X	X	X	X		
Allow log on through Terminal Services (SeRemoteInteractiveLogonRight)	X						
Log on as a batch job (SeBatchLogon-Right)							
Log on as a service (SeServiceLogon-Right)							
Deny access to this computer from the network (SeDenyNetworkLogonRight)							
Deny log on locally (SeDeny-InteractiveLogonRight)							
Deny log on through Terminal Services (SeDenyRemoteInteractive-LogonRight)							
Deny log on as a batch job (SeDeny-BatchLogonRight)							

* Admin = Administrators, SO = Server Operators, AO = Account Operators, PO = Print Operators, BO = Backup Operators, AU = Authenticated Users, and EO = Everyone

Normal Privileges

This category includes the privileges that you might need at some point when administering Windows networks. Table 4.45 lists the 19 normal privileges along with their default assignments.

NOTE We mentioned that there are some fixed rights, such as the right to format hard drives. "Take ownership of files or other objects" is listed in Table 4.45 as a user right that can be assigned. In addition, Administrators have that user right as a fixed right for objects outside Active Directory (such as files). In other words, even if you remove that right from Administrators, they still can take ownership of elements such as files and registry keys. However, they cannot take ownership of Active Directory objects anymore.

Table 4.45 Normal Privileges: Default Assignments for Domain Controllers

Logon Right	Admin*	SO	AO	PO	BO	AU	EO
Deny log on as a service (`SeDeny-ServiceLogonRight`)							
Add workstations to domain** (`SeMachineAccountPrivilege`)						X	
Back up files and directories (`SeBackupPrivilege`)	X	X			X		
Bypass traverse checking (`SeChangeNotifyPrivilege`)***	X					X	X
Change the system time (`SeSystemtimePrivilege`)	X	X					
Create a pagefile (`SeCreate-PagefilePrivilege`)	X						
Create global objects (`SeCreate-GlobalPrivilege`)	X****						
Enable computer and user accounts to be trusted for delegation (`SeEnableDelegationPrivilege`)	X						
Force shutdown from a remote system (`SeRemoteShutdownPrivilege`)	X	X					
Increase scheduling priority (`Se-IncreaseBasePriorityPrivilege`)	X						
Load and unload device drivers (`SeLoadDriverPrivilege`)	X			X			
Manage auditing and security log (`SeSecurityPrivilege`)	X						
Modify firmware environment values (`SeSystemEnvironmentPrivilege`)	X						

* Admin = Administrators, SO = Server Operators, AO = Account Operators, PO = Print Operators, BO = Backup Operators, AU = Authenticated Users, and EO = Everyone.

** This rights assignment means that, by default, any user of the forest can add workstations and member servers to this domain—up to ten computers per user. This ten-computer limit is stored in the `ms-DS-Machine AccountQuota` property of each domain object. If the need arises, a domain administrator can change the value using a tool such as ADSI Edit.

*** This right has "ChangeNotify" in the API name because the same privilege is required to receive notifications of changes to files or directories.

**** Also, the well-known security principal Service has this privilege, but we don't have room for any more columns.

Table 4.45 Normal Privileges: Default Assignments for Domain Controllers (*cont.*)

Logon Right	Admin*	SO	AO	PO	BO	AU	EO
Perform volume maintenance tasks (`SeManageVolumePrivilege`)	X						
Profile single process (`SeProfile-SingleProcessPrivilege`)	X						
Profile system performance (`SeSystemProfilePrivilege`)	X						
Remove computer from docking station (`SeUndockPrivilege`)	X						
Restore files and directories (`SeRestorePrivilege`)	X	X			X		
Shut down the system (`SeShutdownPrivilege`)	X	X		X	X		
Take ownership of files or other objects (`SeTakeOwnershipPrivilege`)	X						

Advanced Privileges

Table 4.46 lists the advanced user rights. By "advanced" we mean that you probably don't need to modify them or care about them.

Fixed Rights

Table 4.47 lists some rights that are built into Windows 2000 and Windows Server 2003. The assignments are fixed, so you cannot modify them. There are also other operations an administrator can perform that a normal user cannot, so the list is not exhaustive. Those other operations are scattered throughout the operating system, and listing them doesn't serve the purpose of this Active Directory book.

NOTE Because the rights in Table 4.47 are assigned only by the membership of certain groups, you cannot assign them to different domain controllers in one domain. For example, if you have a domain that has one domain controller in Boston and another domain controller in London, anyone who can format a hard drive in the Boston domain controller is allowed to do it also in the London domain controller.

Table 4.46 Advanced Privileges: Default Assignments for Domain Controllers

Privilege	Admin*	Svc	Net Svc	Local Svc
Act as part of the operating system (SeTcbPrivilege)**				
Create a token object (SeCreateTokenPrivilege)				
Create permanent shared objects (SeCreatePermanentPrivilege)				
Debug programs (SeDebugPrivilege)	X			
Generate security audits (SeAuditPrivilege)			X	X
Impersonate a client after authentication (SeImpersonatePrivilege)	X	X		
Adjust memory quotas for a process (SeIncreaseQuotaPrivilege)	X		X	X
Lock pages in memory (SeLockMemoryPrivilege)				
Replace a process-level token (SeAssignPrimaryTokenPrivilege)			X	X
Synchronize directory service data (SeSyncAgentPrivilege)				

* Admin = Administrators, Svc = Service, Net Svc = Network Service, and Local Svc = Local Service

** Tcb = trusted computer base

Table 4.47 Some Fixed Rights Assignments for Domain Controllers

Fixed Right	Admin*	SO	AO	PO	BO	AU
Assign user rights	X					
Unlock a locked computer	X					
Format hard drives	X					
Run CHKDSK	X					
Take ownership of files or other objects, excluding Active Directory objects	X					

* Admin = Administrators, SO = Server Operators, AO = Account Operators, PO = Print Operators, BO = Backup Operators, and AU = Authenticated Users

Table 4.47 Some Fixed Rights Assignments for Domain Controllers (*cont.*)

Fixed Right	Admin*	SO	AO	PO	BO	AU
Share folders and delete shares	X	X				
Create, manage, delete, and share printers	X	X		X		
Stop and start services	X	X				
Configure services	X	X				

* Admin = Administrators, SO = Server Operators, AO = Account Operators, PO = Print Operators, BO = Backup Operators, and AU = Authenticated Users

Active Directory Permissions Instead of Rights

Having certain Active Directory permissions is effectively equivalent to having the following rights:

- *Fixed right:* Assign user rights (see Table 4.47)
- *User right:* Add workstations to domain (see Table 4.45)

Assign User Rights

If you have a Write permission to some Group Policy object, you can modify the user rights assignments that it contains, and the outcome is very similar to the "Assign user rights" fixed right. The two are not quite equal, however, because the Write permission doesn't allow using the NTRights command, which we describe shortly.

Add Workstations to Domain

Having the permissions Create Computer Objects and Delete Computer Objects for the Computers container is equal to having the "Add workstations to domain" user right (except for the ten-computer limit). Assigning these two permissions to a group such as gsWorkstationInstallers allows its members to join workstations and member servers to that domain.

The two permissions can also be assigned for any OU in the domain. In this case the joining process is a little different: The workstation installer must create the computer account in the appropriate OU before joining the workstation.

Applying User Rights

User rights are applied using the Group Policy infrastructure and/or local security policy. Both are described in Chapter 7, so we don't go into the details in this chapter. This section, however, provides a brief introduction.

Brief Introduction to Group Policy

Group Policy affects a computer depending on where the corresponding computer object is located in Active Directory. The computer object of each domain controller is by default in an OU called Domain Controllers. To that OU is linked a Group Policy object called Default Domain Controllers Policy. By default, the settings in that object affect every domain controller of that domain.

The computer object of each member server and workstation is by default in a container called Computers. It is not possible to link any Group Policy to this container, so what affects those computers by default is a GPO called Default Domain Policy. It is linked to the domain object.

If you place computer objects in some other OUs or you create new Group Policy objects, the defaults might no longer be in use. For example, you can create the OUs Boston and London and then move all Boston domain controller objects to the Boston OU and all London domain controller objects to the London OU. This way, you can assign different user rights for the domain controllers of Boston and London.

NOTE If different GPOs apply to different domain controllers of the same domain, those domain controllers will have different user right assignments. This is a good thing when you control the right to log on locally, but it is a bad thing when you control the right to take ownership. It is not logical that your ability to take ownership of Active Directory objects depends on which domain controller you are connected to.

By default, the settings in a GPO linked to an object higher in the tree also affect objects on a lower level. Therefore, the settings defined in the Default Domain Policy also affect domain controllers unless the Default Domain Controllers Policy has conflicting settings, in which case the latter settings prevail.

Any Group Policy setting overrides the corresponding setting in the local security policy. However, the settings that are "not defined" in Group Policy can be set in the local security policy.

Group Policy settings are applied to a computer when it starts and afterward to a domain controller by default every 5 minutes. With member servers and workstations, that default interval is 90 minutes, give or take 30 minutes.

Modifying User Rights for Domain Controllers

In this subsection we briefly describe the basic choices for modifying user rights for domain controllers. Because we are sticking to the basics, you would modify only the Default Domain Controllers Policy GPO. The most common ways to modify domain controller user rights (i.e., that GPO) are the following:

- *Edit the Default Domain Controllers Policy.* Right-click the Domain Controllers OU (in the Users and Computers snap-in), select Properties, select the Group Policy tab, select Default Domain Controllers Policy, and click Edit. This opens the Group Policy Object Editor. In the left pane, navigate to Computer Configuration, Windows Settings, Security Settings, Local Policies, User Rights Assignment.
- *Edit the Domain Controller Security Policy directly.* Click the Start button and select Administrative Tools, Domain Controller Security Policy. This opens a "subset" of the Group Policy Object Editor. In the left pane, navigate to Security Settings, Local Policies, User Rights Assignment.
- *Use the Resource Kit command NTRights.* For example, if you want to assign the right to log on locally to all users (not for a production network but perhaps for a test network), you use the following command:

```
ntrights +r SeInteractiveLogonRight -u Users
```

Figure 4.30 shows the contents of the Default Domain Controller Security Settings. In the left pane, User Rights Assignment is selected. The right pane shows the current user rights assignments for domain controllers. Note the exception to the default configuration: "Allow log on locally" is assigned also to the group Users (just for testing purposes—this is not good for a production network). Some policy settings

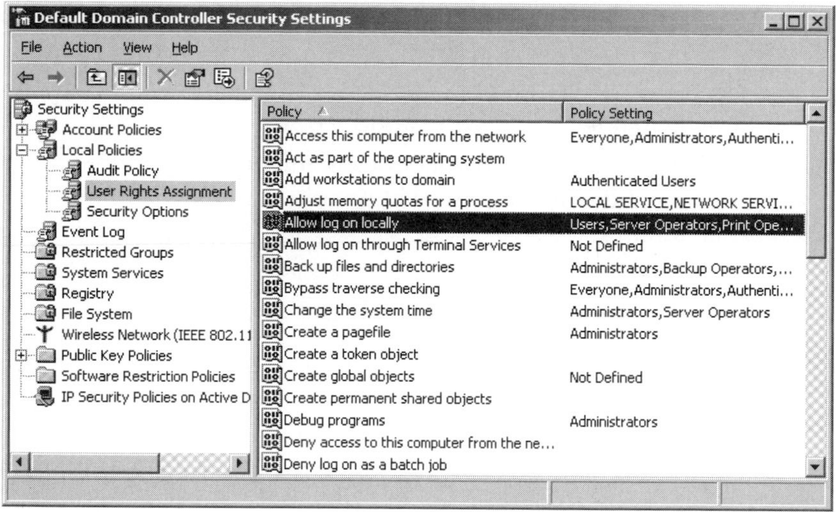

Figure 4.30 This figure shows some default user rights assignments for domain controllers, with one exception. The right to "Allow log on locally" is assigned also to Users.

are "Not defined", which means that those settings can be taken from the lower-priority local security policy. Some policy settings are deliberately empty, which means that no one has the right, and it cannot be granted to anyone in the local security policy.

The five user rights that are "Not defined" are the same five that are new to Windows Server 2003.

Modifying User Rights for Member Servers and Workstations

Still sticking to the basics, the following are two strategies for modifying user rights for member servers and workstations:

- *Modify the Default Domain Policy GPO*. This affects all workstations and member servers in the domain (and also domain controllers, regarding those settings that are "not defined" in the Default Domain Controllers Policy GPO).
- *Modify local security settings*. This affects only one computer.

To modify the Default Domain Policy GPO, you have the following two basic choices:

- *Edit the Default Domain Policy.* Right-click the domain object, select Properties, select the Group Policy tab, select Default Domain Policy, and click Edit. This opens the Group Policy Object Editor. In the left pane, navigate to Computer Configuration, Windows Settings, Security Settings, Local Policies, User Rights Assignment.
- *Edit the Domain Security Policy.* Click the Start button and select Administrative Tools, Domain Security Policy. This opens a "subset" of the Group Policy Object Editor. In the left pane, navigate to Security Settings, Local Policies, User Rights Assignment.

To modify local security settings, again you have two basic choices:

- *Edit the Local Security Policy.* Click the Start button and select Administrative Tools, Local Security Policy. This opens a "subset" of the Group Policy Object Editor. In the left pane, navigate to Security Settings, Local Policies, User Rights Assignment.
- *Use the Resource Kit command NTRights.* For example, if you want to assign the right to change system time to all users, you use the following command:

```
ntrights +r SeSystemTimePrivilege -u Users -m \\PC17
```

If you don't include the machine's name, the command will apply to the local computer.

Conclusion

In this chapter you learned how to control access to Active Directory objects by assigning permissions to them. With this information, along with the information presented in the previous chapter about managing users and other objects, you now have the knowledge and the skills to plan and administer the contents of Active Directory.

In the next two chapters we will explain the physical and logical structure of Active Directory. These structures make up the infrastructure that hosts Active Directory's contents.

CHAPTER 5

Sites and Replication

This chapter describes how Active Directory can keep identical information on several domain controllers by replicating a change of information in one domain controller to the other appropriate domain controllers. We also cover some other aspects of the physical communication between domain controllers.

To help Active Directory in its task, you must describe your physical network to it, such as which LANs you have and what kind of WAN links are between the LANs. You will do this by creating appropriate site objects and other objects in Active Directory.

We have divided the chapter into three sections.

- We start by introducing the concepts of the Active Directory physical structure. As we explain the terms and features, we try to keep the discussion at an introductory level. Regardless of the size of your network, you should read this section.
- The second section explains the administrative user interface and the various management tasks you should or may do. It covers setting things up step by step and administering the physical structure of an established network.
- In the third section we return to topics discussed in the first two sections, but this time we cover them in detail. As a result, this section contains information that not all readers will need. Here we describe such things as the replication process and the formation of replication topologies in different cases. The information in this advanced section explains the architecture of replication, which you can use when diagnosing replication problems. Also, if you plan replication for a large network, you should read this section.

There are also some replication-related topics in Chapter 6. In that chapter, we discuss Active Directory network traffic, which includes replication traffic. Also in Chapter 6, as we discuss planning domains and forests, we cover some physical aspects, such as how to place domain controllers on different sites.

Concepts of the Physical Structure

Most of this book is about the logical aspects of Active Directory. In this chapter, however, it is time to get physical. Here we talk about *sites, replication, replicas, partitions, domain controllers,* and the *global catalog.* These elements make up the physical structure of Active Directory.

The logical and physical structures of Active Directory are independent of each other for the most part. However, as you may remember from Chapter 1, a domain is part of both structures. On the logical side, a domain is an administrative and security policy boundary, and part of the DNS namespace. On the physical side, a domain is the replication unit, or partition. In LDAP terminology, partitions are called *naming contexts (NCs).*

Why Replication?

Each section of Active Directory information resides in at least one domain controller. However, there should be redundancy—that is, all information should reside in more than one domain controller. The major time- and money-saving reasons for this are as follows:

- Fault tolerance. If one domain controller fails, the information is available from other domain controllers, which store the same information. Note that as with fault tolerance in general, redundancy with Active Directory doesn't eliminate the need to make backups.
- *Load balancing.* When many workstations are accessing Active Directory, the information they are requesting is retrieved faster when there is more than one domain controller to provide it.
- *Proximity of information.* Workstations get the information from a local domain controller instead of across a slow WAN link.

Nature of Active Directory Replication

Active Directory is a *loosely consistent* database. The information in different domain controllers is not necessarily consistent (the same) at any given time. However, when there are no changes for a while, the information will tend toward consistency—that is, all the domain controllers of one domain will have the same information. This is called *convergence.*

For the information to be the same in several domain controllers, any changes must be *replicated* from one domain controller to another. Active Directory notices if an object is created, deleted, or moved/renamed, or if an attribute is added, changed, or deleted. All these operations are consequently replicated from the originating domain controller to the other appropriate domain controllers. This causes replication traffic in LANs in physical locations and in WAN links between physical locations.

There are two trade-offs associated with replication.

- *High replication load versus latency.* The more frequently you replicate changed information, the greater load this puts on domain controllers and the network. On the other hand, the less frequently you replicate, the older the information will be in some domain controllers. In any case, there is always *latency;* that is, the changed information is not instantly available in all domain controllers.
- *Replication in WAN versus user access in WAN.* If the information source is in Boston and the consumer is in London, either the information needs to be replicated to London or the consumer needs to access it across a WAN link from Boston. An administrator makes this choice by either placing a remote domain controller in London or not. The decision must be made separately for each domain, because each domain contains different information.

These trade-offs are affected by how often the information is changed and how often it is read. If the information rarely changes, latency is not much of an issue. If that were the case, it would also be easier to put a domain controller in London, because few changes mean little replication. Also, if the London personnel read the information frequently, it would pay to put a domain controller there, so that the information is replicated once over the WAN link instead of several people reading it all the time over that link.

NOTE We return to the topic of how to place domain controllers in Chapter 6. In that chapter we also explain the number of bytes that replication (and clients accessing domain controllers) puts on network traffic.

Active Directory mostly uses *multimaster* replication. This means that you can make changes (e.g., you can add users) to any domain controller of the domain, and then your changes are replicated to other domain controllers in the same domain.

As a contrast, with Windows NT you could make changes to only one server, which was called a *primary domain controller (PDC)*. The changes were replicated to all other servers, which were called *backup domain controllers (BDCs)*. The Windows NT approach (i.e., *single-master* replication) was a little more difficult than the Active Directory approach, especially in WAN environments and failure situations because you always had to communicate with the PDC when making a change.

If you have Windows NT backup domain controllers in an Active Directory domain, they will need to replicate the part of Active Directory information that is recognized by or compatible with the Windows NT world. The backup domain controllers use downlevel replication to get this information.

In addition to replicating information among Windows 2000 or later domain controllers, it is possible to synchronize objects in disparate systems, such as Novell NDS and Microsoft Exchange 5.5. The Windows 2000 Server CD includes Active Directory Connector (ADC), which enables you to synchronize Active Directory with Exchange 5.5. Microsoft Services for NetWare version 5 (SFNW5) includes the Microsoft Directory Synchronization Services (MSDSS) component, which enables you to synchronize between Novell NDS and Active Directory.

Another option is Microsoft Identity Integration Server (MIIS), which was formerly Microsoft Metadirectory Services (MMS). It enables you to use Active Directory to manage identity information stored in heterogeneous directory services. MIIS comes in two versions:

- Identity Integration Feature Pack for Microsoft Server Active Directory (IIFP) is included in the Windows Server 2003, Enterprise Edition, license. IIFP enables synchronizing user objects of one forest to contact objects of another forest. It also enables synchronizing users, groups, and Exchange 2000/2003 global address lists among forests, and synchronizing identity information between Active Directory and Active Directory Application Mode (ADAM).
- MIIS, Enterprise Edition, costs $25,000 US per processor. It supports Active Directory, ADAM, Windows NT 4 domains, attribute-value pair text files, comma-separated-value files, delimited text files, Directory Services Markup Language (DSML) 2.0,

Exchange 5.5, Exchange 5.5 Bridgehead, Exchange 2000 and Exchange 2003 Global Address List (GAL) synchronization, fixed-width text files, LDIF files, Lotus Notes/Domino 4.6/5.0, Novell NDS, eDirectory, DirXML, Sun/iPlanet/Netscape directory 4.x/5.x (with "changelog" support), Microsoft SQL Server 2000, SQL Server 7.0, Oracle 8i/9i, Informix, dBase, and ODBC and OLE DB support via SQL Server Data Transformation Services.

Partitions and Replicas

When we talk about replication, we also need to talk about *partitions* and *replicas*. Partitions are the units of replication; that is, they dictate what is replicated to which domain controllers. Replicas are the identical copies of a given partition in different domain controllers.

NOTE Remember that replicas of a partition are truly identical only when there have been no changes for a while. Otherwise, some replicas may have recent changes that haven't yet replicated to all other replicas of the same partition.

The vast majority of Active Directory information is in per-domain domain partitions. That is, most information is replicated among the domain controllers of one domain. There are also two forestwide partitions called *schema* and *configuration*. We often call them *enterprise partitions*. Their information is replicated among all the domain controllers of the forest.

A new partition type introduced in Windows Server 2003 is *application partitions*. It is created by an administrator (using the NTDSUtil command) or an application. Any domain controllers (that are running Windows Server 2003) of the forest can host a given application partition, regardless of domain boundaries. An application partition can be used for (reasonably) any purpose that an application wants. By default, there is the ForestDnsZones application partition for each forest and the DomainDnsZones application partition for each domain.

Table 5.1 describes the four kinds of partitions in Active Directory. A domain partition has full replicas in normal domain controllers and partial replicas in global catalog servers.

We mention in Table 5.1 that the global catalog is using partial replicas, because it contains only some of the attributes. Of the 1,070 attributes in the AD2003 base schema, 151 are included in the global catalog

Table 5.1 Active Directory Partition Types

Partition Name	Number	Domain Controller Used to Modify	Contains
Schema partition	One per forest	Schema master	The schema—the definitions of the classes and attributes supported in the forest
Configuration partition	One per forest	Any DC in the forest (some information, however, requires the domain naming master)	Knowledge about sites, partitions, extended rights, and some other per-forest information
Application partition	Any number	Any DC in the forest that hosts the corresponding partition	Data of the application that created the partition; cannot contain any security principals, such as users, security groups, or computer objects
Domain partition (full replica)	One per domain	Any DC of the corresponding domain	Per-domain objects such as users, OUs, and groups
Domain partition (partial replica for global catalog)		Replica is read-only; it is replicated from other domain partitions	Some attributes of every object in the corresponding domain partition

(138 of 863 in AD2000). We don't list them here, but in Chapter 11 we present a script that can list them for you.

Table 5.2 shows an example of the replicas of an enterprise forest that has three domains and five domain controllers. We don't show any application partitions in the table, but any number of application partitions could reside on any domain controller.

The example in Table 5.2 has five partitions:

- One schema partition (one for the forest)
- One configuration partition (one for the forest)
- Three domain partitions (one for each domain)

As you can see in Table 5.2, every domain controller has a replica of at least three partitions (schema, configuration, and its own domain). Those that we have designated as global catalog servers (DC1 and DC4) also have partial replicas of all other domain partitions.

You can see too that in the sample forest there are 15 full replicas (3 x *number of domain controllers*) and four partial replicas ([*number of domains* – 1] x *number of global catalog servers*). Again, we don't count any possible application partitions.

NOTE As discussed in Chapter 1, a domain controller cannot host full replicas of other domains. You must have separate server computers (i.e., domain controllers) to host full replicas of different domains.

Table 5.2 shows which replicas of which partitions are on which domain controllers. Figure 5.1 shows two domain partitions and configuration and schema partitions drawn in the logical namespace. We don't show any application partitions in Figure 5.1, but we discuss them in more detail in Chapter 6.

Overview of the Replication Process

Unlike Windows NT, Active Directory replicates only changed properties, not entire user accounts or other objects. This has two advantages.

- There is less data to be replicated.
- Replication conflicts are less frequent. If someone changes Jack's phone number in a Boston domain controller and someone else changes his fax number in a London domain controller, there is

Table 5.2 Replicas of an Active Directory Sample Forest

	DC1 + GC (in domain A)	DC2 (in domain A)	DC3 (in domain B)	DC4 + GC (in domain C)	DC5 (in domain C)
Schema partition	Full replica	Full replica	Full replica	Full replica	Full replica
Configuration partition	Full replica	Full replica	Full replica	Full replica	Full replica
Domain partition of domain A	Full replica	Full replica		Partial replica	
Domain partition of domain B	Partial replica		Full replica	Partial replica	
Domain partition of domain C	Partial replica			Full replica	Full replica

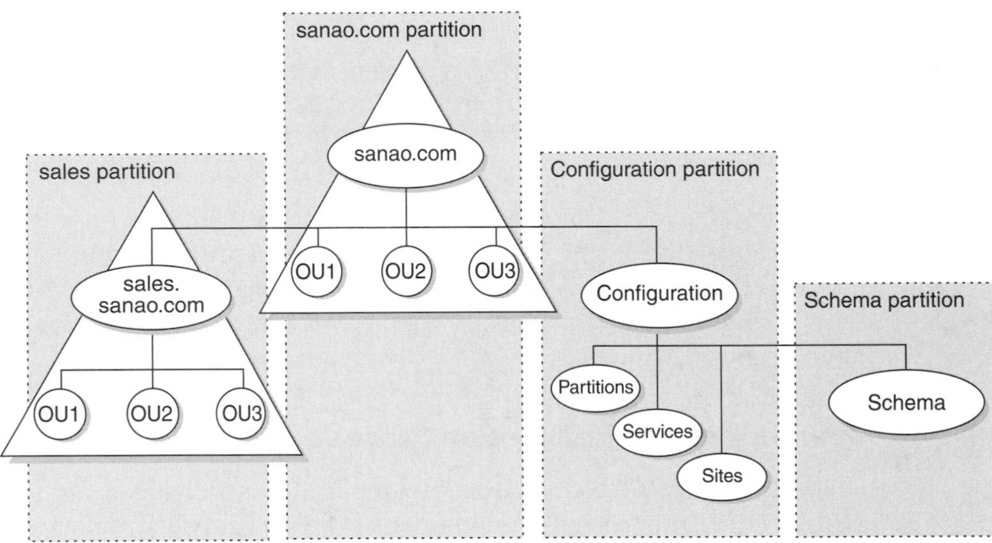

Figure 5.1 Every configuration, schema, and child domain is an independent partition, but together they form a logical tree where each partition is a child to another one.

no conflict. Even though the changes are for the same object, they are for different properties.

Unlike Novell NDS, Active Directory replication does not rely on synchronized time among servers. Instead, Active Directory uses *update sequence numbers (USNs)* and version numbers to determine what to replicate.

However, Windows 2000 and later have a time service to synchronize time on all computers in a forest. The primary reason for this service is that the Kerberos authentication protocol requires the clocks in different computers to be approximately synchronized (within 5 minutes, by default). Also, Active Directory uses timestamps of changes in conflict resolution. One type of conflict is a situation where the same property of the same object has been changed in two domain controllers. If the time of the two domain controllers is not synchronized, regardless of time service, the "wrong" change could prevail, or win the conflict.

Consider the following example. Someone changes Jack's phone number in a Boston domain controller and then someone else changes it 10 seconds later in a London domain controller. The clock of the Boston domain controller is 15 seconds fast, so even if the change there were older, it would eventually prevail because the clock would indicate that it's the more recent change. Is this bad? No, because if two administrators change Jack's phone number to different values in Boston and London almost simultaneously, it only means that you haven't organized administration very well in your forest. There really isn't a sensible way to tell which phone number should be saved in that case.

The important thing is that the result is consistent, and with Active Directory replication, the same change prevails in every domain controller, even though it could be 10 seconds older than some other change. The timestamps of both conflicting changes are replicated with the change, so each domain controller will pick the same winner, whether the times were synchronized or not.

You may wonder how USNs and version numbers work in the replication process. The short answer is that they automatically work so that they get the job done. The long, detailed answer is in an advanced section, "The Replication Process," later in this chapter.

Overview of Replication Topologies

When you have more than one domain controller, Active Directory automatically builds a certain replication topology. That topology dictates from which domain controller (or controllers) every other domain controller will get the changes.

The component that creates the topology is the *Knowledge Consistency Checker (KCC)*. It wakes up every 15 minutes in each domain controller to check if there are changes in the selection of domain controllers or in any replication objects that would require changes in the replication topology.

The intrasite replication topology is by default a bidirectional ring. For example, with four domain controllers, A replicates to B, B to C, C to D, and D to A, and it's the same in the opposite direction. Figure 5.2 shows a ring with eight domain controllers.

As the number of domain controllers increases, the KCCs add shortcut connections to the ring to prevent the chain from becoming too long. The shortcut connections take care that the path between any two domain controllers (which replicate the same partition) is almost never more than three hops. Because the replication latency from one domain controller to another is 15 seconds in AD2003 (or 5 minutes in AD2000), a maximum of three hops means a maximum of 45 seconds (or 15 minutes in Windows 2000) before the change is replicated to all appropriate domain controllers in a site. The exact delays are explained in the "Change Notification" section later in this chapter.

A bidirectional replica ring exists for each separate partition. However, if all the domain controllers host all replicas, there is only one ring in practice. Therefore, the illustration in Figure 5.2 is accurate only when there is only one domain and all domain controllers host the same application partitions (most likely, ForestDnsZones and DomainDnsZones).

The intersite replication topology is based on *bridgehead servers*. They are the only domain controllers that replicate to and from other sites. A bridgehead server collects all changes on its site in the partitions it is responsible for, and then replicates the changes to bridgehead servers on other appropriate sites. Those bridgehead servers in turn replicate the changes further on their sites. This way, any change needs to travel a WAN link only once.

In most cases the automatically generated intrasite topology is fine, and there is no need to adjust it manually, not to mention create the topology manually from the ground up. This applies also to the intersite topology with two exceptions: First, you must provide background information for Active Directory (and this requires planning), and second, there are cases where you might create at least some of the intersite connections manually.

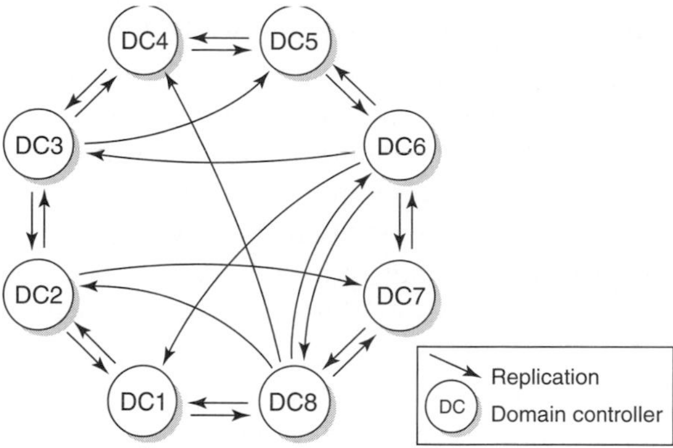

Figure 5.2 An intrasite replication topology forms a bidirectional ring, with possible shortcut connections to prevent chains from becoming too long.

Sites

Active Directory can replicate more efficiently if it knows which domain controllers are connected with a fast network (usually a LAN) and which are connected over a slower network (usually a WAN link). You can describe this to Active Directory by creating appropriate site objects and other objects in Active Directory.

In addition to Active Directory replication, sites serve a number of other uses.

- Active Directory clients find logon servers (i.e., domain controllers) based on sites. They will use a domain controller on the same site, but if none is available, they will use a domain controller on the closest site.
- Windows 2000 and later Distributed File System (DFS) uses site information to decide which server sends the user the files she requested.
- Windows 2000 and later File Replication Service (FRS) uses site information to know how to replicate files and folders in SYSVOL and other folders. FRS also uses the replication topology created by the KCCs to get the necessary files and folders replicated.
- You may assign group policies to sites, in which case they by default apply to all users and computers on that site.
- Active Directory–aware applications may use site information for their own purposes.

Each site corresponds to one or more TCP/IP subnets. For example, one site could correspond to subnet 10.0.14.0/23 and another to subnet 10.0.17.0/24, or one site could correspond to both subnets.

The main function of subnets in Active Directory is to serve as building blocks to sites and to operate as a link to the physical IP network. In addition, once you have described the subnets to Active Directory by creating appropriate subnet objects, you can enable users to find the printers closest to them using this subnet-based location information.

NOTE If you want to test intersite replication in a small test network, you can place domain controllers on different sites, even though they are physically in the same subnet. However, this doesn't work for a production network. In that case, you need correct subnet information because it determines on which site the client computers are assumed to be.

When you plan whether to have a site for a certain office or not, you can use the following considerations.

- There is no exact speed that indicates a network is fast or slow. If you have a T-1 or a 2Mbps link to some office, you could decide that the link is fast enough for the office not to be a separate site. Or you could decide the link is too slow and you need to create a new site for that office. The latter choice is more likely.
- Active Directory employs various techniques to use bandwidth sparingly when communicating among sites. One technique is data compression, and we list the other techniques in the next section. Consequently, speed is not the only criterion in your decision to create a separate site. If the link is fast but expensive, unreliable, or congested, you should create a separate site for the corresponding office.
- Most uses for sites that we list require that there is (or will be) at least one server at the physical location for which the site is being created. For example, DFS cannot offer files from a local server unless there is a local server. However, one of the items, assigning group policies, doesn't require an on-site server.
- If you create a site for an office, the domain controllers that replicate intersite (i.e., the bridgehead servers) need to use some CPU power to compress data and you will have a few more objects to manage. You also need to watch that these bridgehead servers are

operational. Beyond these considerations, adding an extra site doesn't cost anything.

- If you create a site for an office or a neighboring building on a campus area, the replication latency to that office or building will be longer. If this is not tolerable, you can shorten the latency and even enable change notifications, in which case the intersite replication latency is as short as intrasite replication latency. The procedure is explained in an advanced section, "Using Change Notifications in Intersite Replication," later in this chapter.
- Inside a site, all domain controllers should be able to communicate freely with all others; you cannot (reasonably) limit this. If a firewall or some other aspect of the physical network doesn't allow free communication, you should create several sites, even though these domain controllers would be in the same LAN. For more information, see the 82-page Microsoft white paper called Active Directory in Networks Segmented by Firewalls and available at `http://www.microsoft.com`.
- If you have many domain controllers (e.g., more than 20) in a physical location, you will have quite a large replica ring with numerous shortcuts. You may consider creating several sites for that physical location, as long as you have several IP subnets there.

Each domain controller of every domain in a forest belongs to some site. If you don't create sites, all domain controllers go to a site called Default-First-Site-Name. On the other hand, if you create sites to match the physical locations of your network, the number and distribution of domain controllers would be arranged something like Table 5.3, and the layout would look something like Figure 5.3.

Table 5.3 Number of Domain Controllers in Each Domain and Site of a Forest

	Boston	San Francisco	London
`sanao.com`	3 DCs	Simulated*	1 DC
`sales.sanao.com`	2 DCs	1 DC	1 DC
`rd.sanao.com`	Simulated*	2 DCs	Simulated*

* There is no domain controller (DC) of the corresponding domain on the corresponding site. A DC from the closest site registers itself in DNS to appear on the "empty" site, so clients on that site can find a DC.

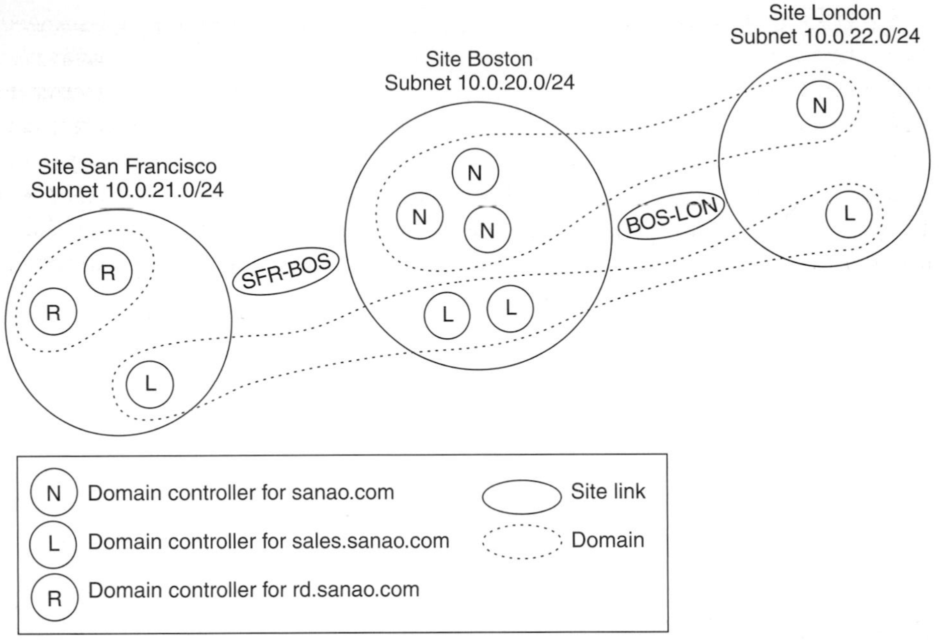

Figure 5.3 Each domain controller is on an Active Directory site, which usually matches a physical site. For example, you could create in Active Directory the London site for your London office.

Sanao Corporation, our sample company, has headquarters in Boston and offices in San Francisco and London. In addition to the root domain, there are two child domains (Sales and RD). There are five domain controllers in Boston, three in San Francisco, and two in London.

Three cells in Table 5.3 are marked Simulated. There is no domain controller of the corresponding domain on the corresponding site. However, a domain controller from some other site (the closest possible) is pretending to be there by having registered the appropriate DNS service records. This way, a client can always easily find a domain controller for logons and other similar domain communication. For example, there could be a workstation of the RD domain in London. When that client needs logon services, it can find a domain controller for this, even though that server is located in San Francisco. The domain controller in San Francisco is said to *cover* the London site.

You can control site coverage by using registry parameters located in `HKEY_LOCAL_MACHINE`, `SYSTEM`, `CurrentControlSet`, `Services`, `Netlogon`, `Parameters`. To stop a domain controller from covering other sites, you should set the AutoSiteCoverage parameter (of type REG_DWORD) to 0. To add a specific site to be covered by a domain controller, add the site name in the SiteCoverage parameter (of type REG_MULTI_SZ). For more information on these parameters, see the Registry Reference included in the Resource Kit. The reference is also available on the Internet at http://technet.microsoft.com, in the location TechNet Home, Products & Technologies, Windows Server 2003, Product Documentation, Windows Server 2003 Deployment Kit, Windows Server 2003 Resource Kit Registry Reference.

Links between sites are called *site links.* Site links represent networks, so each site link may correspond to one WAN link between two sites or to a network that connects several sites. Examples of the latter case are a frame relay, an ATM, or another kind of "cloud" network (meaning that you either don't know or don't care which route the network packets take to reach another site).

Overview of Intrasite and Intersite Replication

As mentioned, intrasite and intersite replication processes are different. Table 5.4 compares their features.

By default, replication is *transitive.* This means that domain controller B can pass on to domain controller C the changes it received from domain controller A. Domain controller A and domain controller C don't need to communicate directly. This is an advantage even in intrasite replication, but it pays off especially in intersite replication. The data needs to be replicated only once to the next city, and from the bridgehead server on the destination city it then spreads locally to other domain controllers.

Windows Server 2003 contains a new compression algorithm for intersite replication that gives about 20 percent CPU performance improvement but has a little worse compression ratio. Since the modern WAN links are usually quite fast, this trade-off is not a problem. The algorithm is backward compatible with Windows 2000, and you could also revert to the old one via a registry setting. Microsoft recommends that to save the CPU on bridgehead servers, you use the new algorithm and only revert to the old one if your WAN link speed is 64Kbps or lower.

Change Notification

As mentioned in Table 5.4, intrasite replication uses the "notify and pull" method, which works as follows:

Table 5.4 Comparison of Intrasite and Intersite Replication

Feature	Intrasite	Intersite
Transport protocol	RPC (Remote Procedure Call)	RPC (although called IP) or SMTP. The latter can be used only for the two enterprisepartitions (schema, configuration), application partitions, and the global catalog but not for the normal domain partitions.
Default topology	Ring (with possible shortcuts)	Minimum cost spanning tree.
Connections	Between any two domain controllers on the site	Between bridgehead servers on each site.
Approximate latency	By default, 15 seconds (or 5 minutes in AD2000) from one domain controller to the next (hop), almost always a maximum of 45 seconds (or 15 minutes in AD2000) from any domain controller to any other domain controller	By default, 3 hours from one site to the next, but you could change it to, for example, every 15 minutes or once a day.
Replication model	Notify and pull (via RPC), and pull with a schedule as a backup mechanism	Either pull with a schedule (via RPC) or store and forward (via SMTP).
Compression	No	Yes, compresses down to between 10 percent and 15 percent (or even less). However, if there is less than 32KB of data to be replicated, there is no compression.

1. A domain controller has some new changes, which either originated on that domain controller or were replicated from another domain controller.
2. After waiting the *initial notification delay* of 15 seconds (by default in AD2003, or 5 minutes by default in AD2000) of the first change, the domain controller sends a *change notification* to the domain controllers that are its direct replication partners (to that direction) on the same site. We can call them the source

domain controller and the target domain controllers, respectively. To be exact, the change notifications are sent only to those replication partners that are interested in the corresponding partition. If the change is in some user object (i.e., the domain partition), the change notification is not sent to partners that replicate only the enterprise partitions from that source domain controller.

3. Each target domain controller requests the changes from the source domain controller, which sends the changes to the target. However, if other replication requests are already pending, the source domain controller puts the new request in a queue and sends the changes to the target only after the earlier requests have been served. Pull replication, which Active Directory uses, is more efficient than the alternative, push replication. With the latter option, it would be difficult to know exactly which updates the target is missing, and—most likely—much information would be replicated in vain, because that information would be on the target already.

If the change notifications were sent to all targets at the same time, they would "attack" the source simultaneously, causing a load peak. Therefore, the source domain controller actually sends the change notifications at slightly different times, waiting a period of the *subsequent notification delay* for each subsequent domain controller.

Change Notification Delay

The default values for the initial notification delay and the subsequent notification delay are 15 seconds/3 seconds or 5 minutes/30 seconds, depending on the notifying (source) domain controller version.

The default values are 15 seconds and 3 seconds in the following source domain controllers:

- A Windows Server 2003 domain controller installed from scratch (not upgraded)
- A Windows Server 2003 domain controller upgraded from Windows NT 4
- A Windows Server 2003 domain controller upgraded from Windows 2000, with the default initial notification delay being in effect during the upgrade and the forest functional level being Windows Server 2003

On the other hand, the old default values 5 minutes and 30 seconds are used in the following source domain controllers:

- A Windows 2000 domain controller
- A Windows Server 2003 domain controller upgraded from Windows 2000, with the forest functional level being Windows 2000

In the preceding third bullet, if a nondefault initial notification delay was in effect when the domain controller was upgraded from Windows 2000 to Windows Server 2003, that nondefault value is retained.

You can modify the default value of the two delays either per source domain controller or in AD2003 also per partition. If both are modified, the per-source domain controller values take precedence.

- *Per source domain controller*. You do this by modifying the registry of the corresponding source domain controller. The two `DWORD` parameters are `Replicator notify pause after modify (secs)` and `Replicator notify pause between DSAs (secs)`, and you need to store them under the key `HKEY_LOCAL_MACHINE`, `SYSTEM`, `CurrentControlSet`, `Services`, `NTDS`, `Parameters`.
- *Per partition*. You do this by modifying the cross-reference object of the corresponding partition in the Partitions container (see Chapter 6 for more information on cross-reference objects). The two `Integer` properties are `msDS-Replication-Notify-First-DSA-Delay` and `msDS-Replication-Notify-Subsequent-DSA-Delay`.

Scheduled Replication

While intrasite replication is based on notifications, intersite replication is based on schedules. A target domain controller requests changes from the source domain controller according to a schedule.

By default, the schedule specifies that the target will request changes every 3 hours, day and night. Administrators can change the schedule either per site link or per server-to-server connection and specify the allowed hours and weekdays to request changes, as well as how often in these specified time periods the requests should be made. An example schedule would be once an hour between 1:00 AM and 7:00 AM. Certain weekdays can also be specified, but typically replication occurs at least daily.

Increasing the frequency from 3 hours has the effect of consuming more bandwidth; if we had 40KB to replicate every 15 minutes, the compression would be less efficient than if we combined the data into a 480KB chunk to be replicated every 3 hours. The obvious benefit of a higher frequency is that changes get to other sites sooner.

NOTE You can enable change notification also for intersite replication. We explain this in the "Using Change Notifications in Intersite Replication" section later in this chapter.

NOTE Intrasite replication uses change notification as the primary method. However, in case a notification is lost, there is a schedule-based replication as a backup mechanism. Each target domain controller requests changes from the source by default once an hour.

Site Link Bridges

It is possible to combine two or more site links as a *site link bridge.* You need to do this only in rare cases (e.g., when your WAN is not fully routed). You will probably never need site link bridges—in this introductory section we mention them only so that when you see them in the administrative interface, you will recognize them and know that you probably don't need them.

Urgent Replication

Active Directory may use three urgency levels for replication, as described in Table 5.5. Urgent replication is used for certain important events.

NOTE Because the `lastLogon` property is never replicated from one domain controller to another, you will get different dates and times, depending on where you read that property. On the other hand, if the `lastLogon` property were replicated, it would create large amounts of replication traffic, mostly in vain.

Like normal replication, urgent replication is based on change notifications, except that the source domain controller sends the notification immediately instead of waiting 15 seconds or 5 minutes.

Table 5.5 Urgency Levels of Active Directory Replication

Urgency Level	Timetable	Examples of Events
Normal replication	After waiting the initial notification delay (by default either 15 seconds or 5 minutes) from the first change for intrasite, or according to a schedule (e.g., every 3 hours) for intersite	Almost all changes
Urgent replication	Immediately for intrasite; by default not used for intersite (i.e., normal intersite schedule is used)	Replicating a newly locked-out user object
No replication	Never replicated	`lastLogon` and `lastLogoff` properties of user objects

If you enable change notification on a per–site link basis or per–server-to-server-connection basis for intersite replication, you will get urgent replication also between sites.

The following events trigger an urgent replication between domain controllers.

- The account lockout policy of the domain is changed.
- The domain password policy of the domain is changed.
- A domain controller computer account password is changed.
- A Local Security Authority (LSA) secret is changed. (An LSA secret is used by secure channels, trust relationships, and service passwords.)
- The RID master state is changed.
- A user or computer account (i.e., object) is locked out as a result of too many failed logon attempts with a wrong password. In this case the account lockout is urgently replicated first to the PDC master of the domain, which is the first domain controller to perform the actual lockout (because a failed authentication is always retried at the PDC master). Next, the account lockout is urgently replicated to all other possible domain controllers of the domain. The possible ones are the ones that exist on the following sites: (a) the site of the original DC receiving the failed logon attempt, (b) the site of the PDC master, and (c) all sites that are reached from

the first two sites with a change notification–enabled site link or connection.

If the domain is in mixed mode when urgently replicating to Windows NT backup domain controllers, two items from the preceding list still apply: lockout and LSA secret. There is also one new event.

- An interdomain trust password is changed. Each trusting domain has an account in the trusted domain, and the password for that account is automatically changed once a week (by default).

Password changes are not urgently replicated. However, the domain controller that receives a request to modify a password immediately updates the password at the PDC master, regardless of any site link information or change notification settings. After this, the new password is normally replicated to all other domain controllers of the domain. If a user tries to access other servers immediately after changing her password, Active Directory can still allow the access by retrying the authentication at the PDC master, where the new password was immediately stored. The process is called PDC chaining.

Nonreplicating Properties

As mentioned in Table 5.5, some properties are not replicated at all. There are 55 such properties in the base schema (39 in AD2000):

```
badPasswordTime                    badPwdCount
bridgeheadServerListBL             directReports
distinguishedName                  dSCorePropagationData
frsComputerReferenceBL             fRSMemberReferenceBL
isPrivilegeHolder                  lastLogoff
lastLogon                          logonCount
managedObjects                     masteredBy
memberOf                           modifiedCount
msCOM-PartitionSetLink             msCOM-UserLink
msDS-Cached-Membership             msDS-Cached-Membership-Time-Stamp
msDS-ExecuteScriptPassword         msDs-masteredBy
msDS-MembersForAzRoleBL            msDS-NonMembersBL
msDS-ObjectReferenceBL             msDS-OperationsForAzRoleBL
msDS-OperationsForAzTaskBL         msDS-ReplicationEpoch
msDS-RetiredReplNCSignatures       msDS-TasksForAzRoleBL
msDS-TasksForAzTaskBL              netbootSCPBL
```

```
nonSecurityMemberBL
ownerBL
partialAttributeSet
prefixMap
replPropertyMetaData
repsFrom
rIDNextRID
schemaUpdate
serverState
subRefs
uSNCreateduSNLastObjRem
whenChanged
objectGUID
partialAttributeDeletionList
pekList
queryPolicyBL
replUpToDateVector
repsTo
rIDPreviousAllocationPool
serverReferenceBL
siteObjectBL
uSNChanged
```

You can use the scripts presented in Chapter 11 to list nonreplicating properties, global catalog properties, or other such properties. You can also find this information (regarding the base schema) in the tables at `http://www.kouti.com`.

NOTE In addition to nonreplicating properties, the directory database of a domain controller (i.e., the NTDS.DIT file) contains other information that is not replicated. One large portion of such information consists of the database indexes that are created locally on each domain controller instead of being replicated across the network.

Last Logon Timestamp

The old `lastLogon` attribute is not replicated among domain controllers, but AD2003 introduces a new attribute, `lastLogonTimestamp`, which is replicated. Using the new attribute, you don't have to scan all the domain controllers for the latest logon time—you can read the value from any domain controller. However, to avoid excessive replication, this new attribute is updated only if 14 days (by default) has passed since the last update (*update interval*). Therefore, it is an indication of whether a user has logged on "this month," but not whether she logged on today after lunch. Like `lastLogon`, the value of the `lastLogonTimeStamp` attribute is a 64-bit large integer.

If you want to adjust the balance between replication traffic and the accuracy of the last logon information, you can change the default 14-day update interval by setting the number of days in the `msDS-LogonTimeSyncInterval` attribute of the domain object. The schema specifies a minimum of 0, and samsrv.dll specifies a fixed maximum of

100,000 days. In this range, the different values and their effects are as follows:

- Value does not exist: The update interval is the default 14 days.
- Value is 0 (zero): The `lastLogonTimestamp` attribute is not updated at all; in other words, this feature is disabled.
- Value is 1 through 5 (days): The update interval is the specified value.
- Value is over 5 (days): The update interval is the specified value minus a random number between 0 through 5 (this random number causes updates to spread more evenly over time).

Global Catalog

In a large forest with many sites and domains, not all Active Directory information is normally replicated to all sites. This means that only part of the information is on the site where the user is. Consequently, if there were no global catalog, if that user searched Active Directory for other users or resources such as printers, her query would need to travel from site to site across many WAN links, which is not efficient. Also, if the result of the search were a list of 1,000 user names, it would take a long time for the result to transfer back to the user who performed the search.

The global catalog (GC) enables you to perform all searches from the closest GC server (usually local to your site), and the search would cover all objects in all domains of your enterprise forest. You don't need to contact a domain controller of each domain, which should make the search dramatically more efficient. The global catalog includes all the objects of a forest but only part of their properties. In other words, the global catalog contains a partial replica of all domain partitions in the forest.

The global catalog includes especially properties that are likely to be used in search operations, such as a user's first and last name. The Active Directory base schema defines 1,070 properties, and by default 151 of them are in the global catalog (or 863/138 in AD2000).

Originally, only the first domain controller of your forest is a global catalog server. Your responsibility is to assign additional domain controllers to serve also the GC function. As a rule of thumb, each site should have (at least) one global catalog server. This allows users on all sites to search locally. Some applications may also have additional requirements for GC service. For example, Exchange 2000/2003 designers and Microsoft suggest that a GC server exist for every four Exchange servers or for every 10,000 users. These applications should be considered when you are designing your Active Directory environment, to ensure that enough domain controllers also act as GC servers.

Overview of Operations Masters

Although Active Directory replication is mostly multimaster, there are five cases in which a special single-master role is attached to only one domain controller in a domain or the enterprise forest. These five roles are called *operations masters.* The old name was *flexible single-master operation,* and you may see *FSMO* (pronounced "fizmo") in a few places in the user interface and various documents. Table 5.6 describes the five roles.

The first domain controller in a forest will get the two forestwide roles, and the first domain controller in each domain will get the three

Table 5.6 Operations Masters

Role	Number	Main Functions
Schema master	One per forest	When an administrator changes the schema (which he probably does rarely), this operations master performs the actual change.
Domain naming master	One per forest	When an administrator adds domains to or deletes domains from a forest, or he adds or removes cross-references to domains in external directories (which he probably does rarely), this operations master performs the actual additions or deletions.
RID master	One per domain	This operations master gives a number of RIDs to other domain controllers, so that the latter can use them for SIDs when creating security principals such as users and security groups.
PDC master (or PDC emulator)	One per domain	This operations master acts as a primary domain controller for any pre–Windows 2000 servers and workstations. It also serves as a center for password changes, account lockout, and time synchronization for Windows Server 2003/XP/2000 computers.
Infrastructure master	One per domain	This operations master maintains references to objects in other domains, such as group members, in case the target objects get moved or renamed.

domainwide roles. The first domain controller in the forest is also a global catalog server.

In a multidomain forest, the infrastructure master shouldn't be in a computer that is also a global catalog server, so for a root domain you should change the default configuration by transferring one of those roles to another domain controller.

Managing the Physical Structure

You describe your physical network for Active Directory by creating and configuring a number of objects in the configuration partition of your enterprise forest. The tool you use for this is the Sites and Services snap-in. In the following sections, we describe the objects and the snap-in, as well as the various tasks you may need to perform. If you have only one physical location, you might not need to do anything. However, we do list some tasks even for a single-site case in the "Setting Up a Single Site" section.

Active Directory Objects for Sites and Replication

There are ten types of objects that you can use to define the physical structure and four types of container objects that help in building the object tree. Figure 5.4 shows these as an object tree. Table 5.7 briefly describes each object in Figure 5.4.

NOTE Figure 5.4 shows object names, not types. For example, an object called NTDS Settings is actually of type Domain Controller Settings (meaning class `nTDSDSA`). Also, because object names IP and SMTP are the same type, there are 11, not 10, solid-line objects in the figure.

The Big Picture of Objects

We mentioned earlier that sites have functions besides controlling replication. If we focus only on this main function, and simplify things a bit, we can make the following related claims.

- Connection objects affect directly how, when, and where replication takes place.

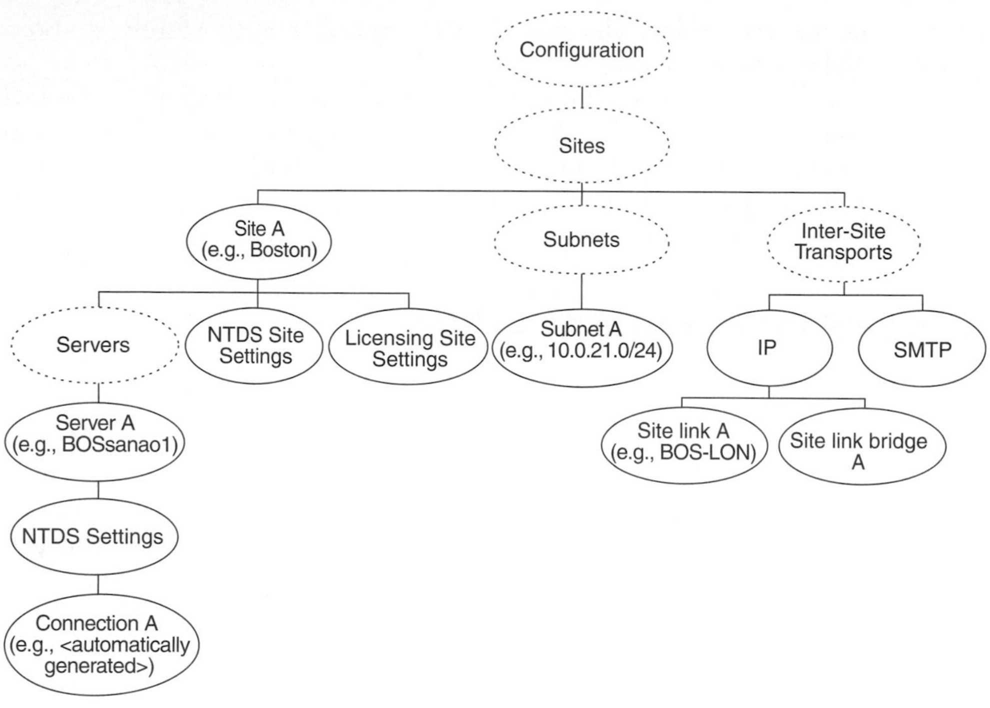

Figure 5.4 The solid line around an object indicates that the object is defining the physical structure of Active Directory. The objects with dotted lines are containers for other objects—they don't have meaningful properties. An *A* in an object's name (e.g., Site A) indicates that there may be more than one such object (e.g., Site A, Site B, and so on). In those cases, we also include a sample name, such as Boston.

Table 5.7 Active Directory Objects for Sites and Replication

Name	Type (and Class)	Number	Description
Boston*	Site (`site`)	1 per site	Enables you to divide your network into "islands" of fast connections and place each server on some "island."
NTDS Site Settings	Site Settings (`nTDSSite-Settings`)	1 per site	Contains some site properties. You probably don't need to modify them, however.

* These names correspond to items in Figure 5.4. Of course, the names of objects change according to each physical setup.

Table 5.7 Active Directory Objects for Sites and Replication (*cont.*)

Name	Type (and Class)	Number	Description
Licensing Site Settings	Licensing Site Settings (`licensing-SiteSettings`)	1 per site	Defines the licensing computer for the licensing service. You probably don't need to modify the setting, however.
BOSsanao1*	Server (`server`)	1 per server	Enables you to define on which "island" the server is located, so various services will know what is local and what is not.
NTDS Settings	Domain Controller Settings (`nTDSDSA`)	1 per domain controller	The existence of this object symbolizes that the server is a domain controller. It also contains some domain controller settings.
<automatically generated>*	Connection (`nTDS-Connection`)	1 per DC-to-DC replication link for each direction	Each domain controller has one connection object for every other domain controller it will replicate from. The object defines how and when replication occurs.
10.0.21.0/24*	Subnet (`subnet`)	1 per IP subnet	Enables you to describe the subnets of which a site consists and to which site a new server belongs.
IP	Inter-Site Transport (`interSite-Transport`)	1	Hosts all RPC over IP-based intersite links and site link bridges and contains some settings.
SMTP	Inter-Site Transport (`interSite-Transport`)	1	Hosts all SMTP-based intersite links and site link bridges and contains some settings.
BOS-LON*	Site Link (`siteLink`)	1 per link between sites	Enables you to define which and what kind of WAN links you have between your sites.
Whatever	Site Link Bridge (`siteLink-Bridge`)	1 per collection of site links	Needed only in some special cases.

- All other object types only exist to affect which and what kind of connection objects exist. Either they give hints to the KCCs that create the connection objects, or they enable you to create the connection objects you want under certain NTDS Settings objects for certain domain controllers.

Figure 5.5 illustrates these claims.

NOTE NTDS stands for "NT Directory Service." Windows 2000 was called Windows NT 5.0 until it was renamed in 1998.

NOTE There is no arrow from the Licensing Site Settings object because it is the only one that doesn't affect replication.

The aforementioned claims and consequently the diagram in Figure 5.5 are something of a simplification of the ways things work in reality. Next we show the object relationships (almost) without simplification.

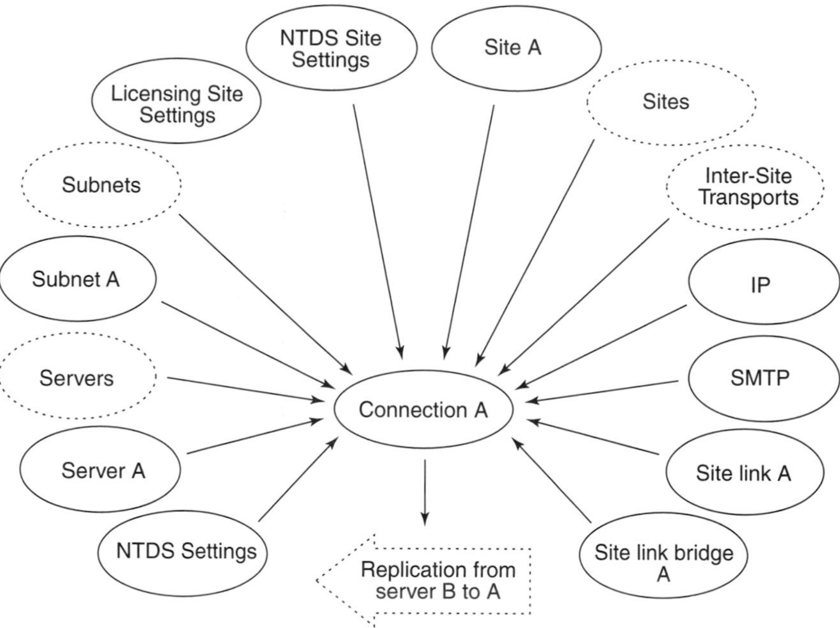

Figure 5.5 If we simplify things, connection objects dictate how, when, and where replication takes place. All other objects exist just to affect which and what kind of connection objects exist.

The solid-line objects in Figure 5.4 and Figure 5.5 have properties that link them to other objects or control the replication topology and process. Figure 5.6 shows these relationships and functions and gives the big picture of the objects that define the physical structure of Active Directory.

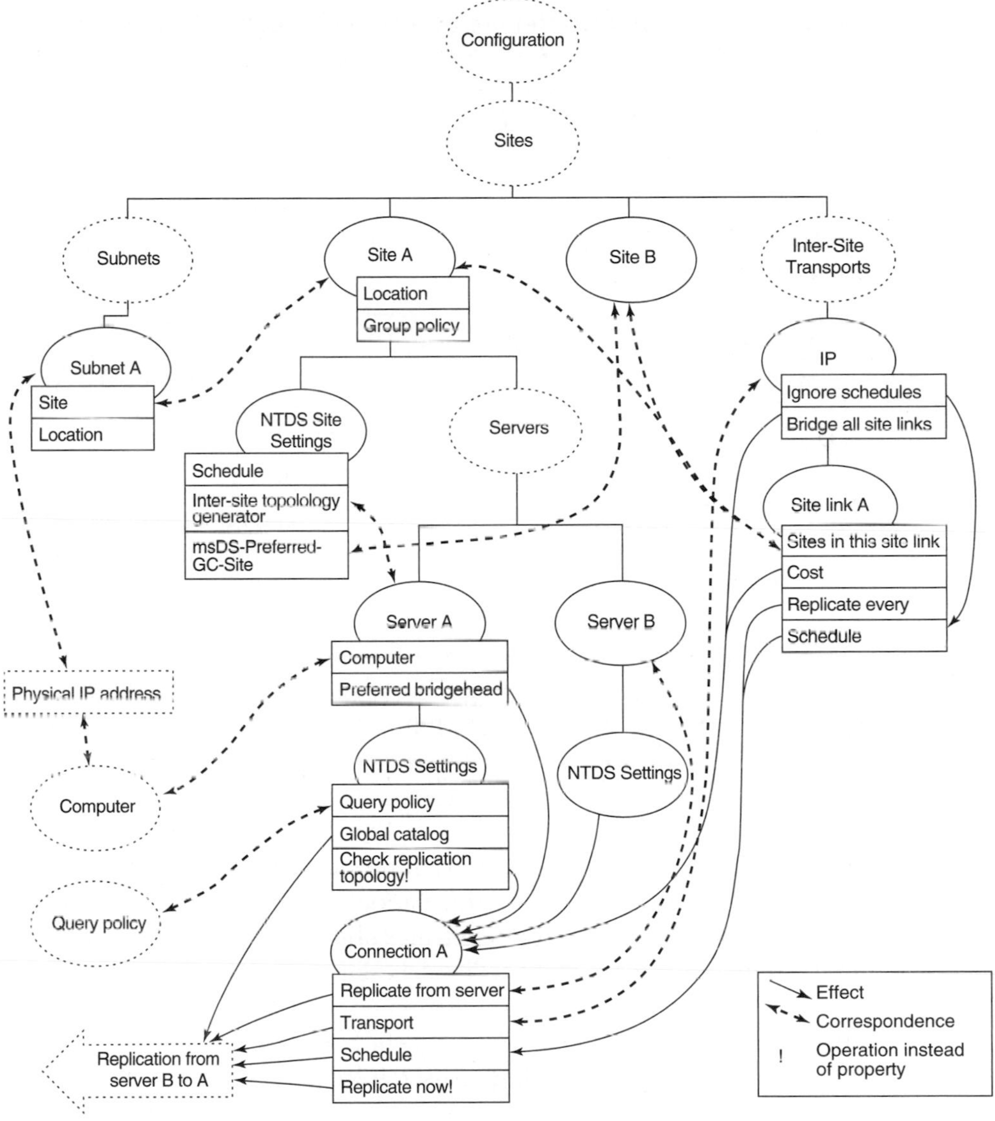

Figure 5.6 The big picture of the objects that define the physical structure of Active Directory as well as their relationships.

NOTE In Figure 5.6, the solid-line arrows (to represent an effect) that point to the connection object reflect how the other objects affect the automatically created connection objects. If you created some of the connection objects manually, these arrows wouldn't apply to them.

NOTE When you create intersite connection objects, all arrows in Figure 5.6 apply. When you create intrasite connection objects, the arrows from the IP and site link objects, as well as those from the Preferred Bridgehead property, don't apply.

Figure 5.6 shows 8 of the 11 solid-line objects of Figure 5.4. We dropped the following three objects to make the figure a little more focused and clear:

- *SMTP.* It is mostly analogous to IP.
- *License Site Settings.* They are used for the awkward License Logging service. It is much easier to turn off the service and manage client access licenses by hand. Or in Windows Server 2003, the service is already turned off by default.
- *Site link bridges.* They are part of advanced topics and, consequently, we discuss them later in the "Creating and Managing Site Link Bridges" section.

There is actually one arrow missing from Figure 5.6. We could have drawn one from the Schedule property of NTDS Site Settings to the Schedule property of the connection object. We give a reason for this omission along with Figure 5.7, which shows a subset of the big picture that focuses on an automatically created (by a KCC) connection object.

As Figure 5.7 illustrates, when a KCC determines which intersite connection objects to create and what properties to use for them, it uses (among others) two pieces of information: the selection of domain controllers (represented by NTDS Settings objects) and the selection of site links (along with their costs). The schedule and "Replicate every" frequency of the site link object are combined to be the schedule of the connection object. If the connection object is for intrasite replication, the schedule in NTDS Site Settings is used instead of the one in the site link.

NOTE The schedule in NTDS Site Settings is by default once an hour. As explained earlier, it is only a backup mechanism in case a notification gets lost. Normally the 15-second/5-minute delay of change notifications dictates the intrasite replication latency.

The Sites and Services Snap-In

You open the Sites and Services snap-in by clicking the Start button and selecting Administrative Tools, Active Directory Sites and Services. Alternatively, you can click the Start button, select Run, type "dssite.msc", and press Enter. A fully configured forest of our sample company Sanao Corporation could look like the one in Figure 5.8.

You use the Sites and Services snap-in in pretty much the same way you use the Users and Computers snap-in to view, create, and manipulate objects. By default, the Sites and Services snap-in connects to "Any Writable Domain Controller." If you happen to sit at a domain controller, it will be that target. On the other hand, if you are at a workstation, the target is whatever domain controller your workstation has found. In either case, you can select a specific target by right-clicking the first node in the tree (Active Directory Sites and Services), selecting Connect to

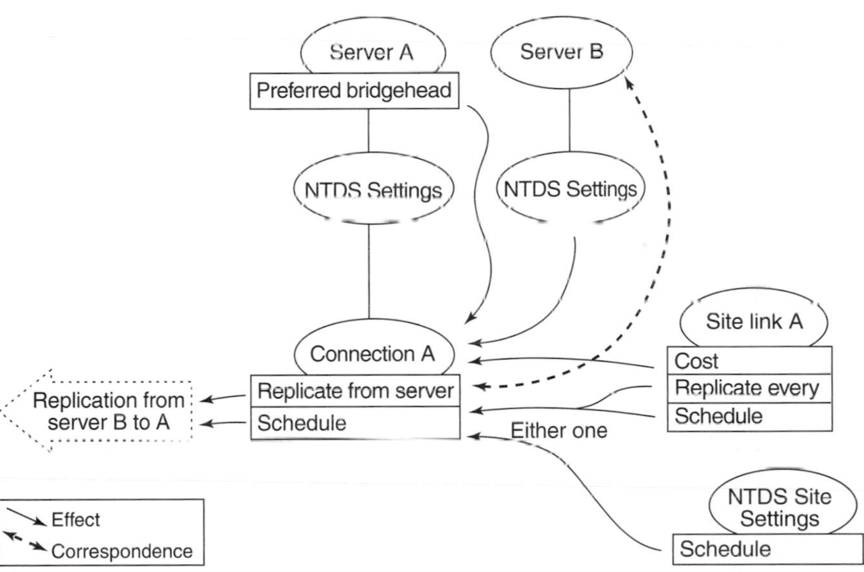

Figure 5.7 When a KCC determines which intersite connection objects to create and what properties to use for them, it uses a number of other objects as its information source. For intrasite connection objects, NTDS Site Settings properties are used instead of site link properties.

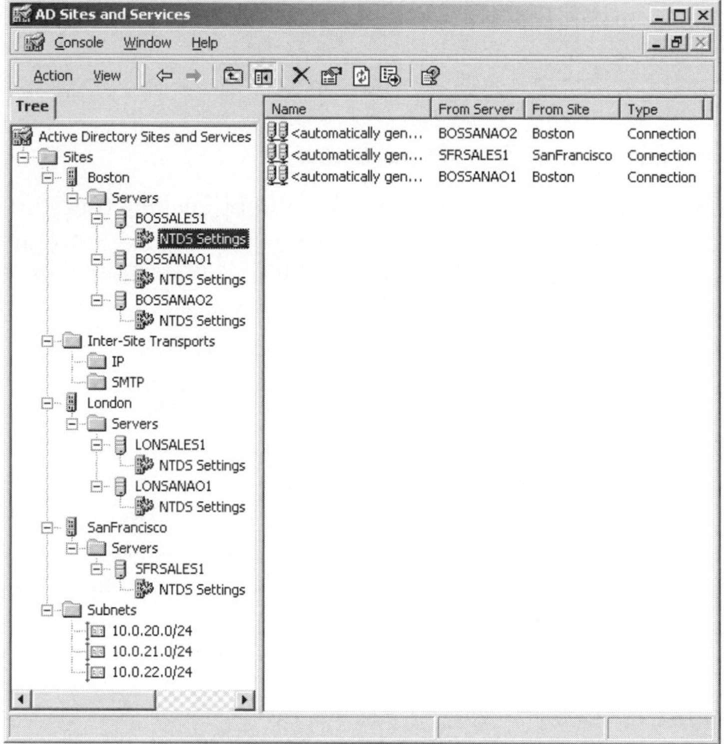

Figure 5.8 Here are the physical structure objects of Sanao Corporation. Compared to the preceding big picture, you can see six of eight objects. Site link and NTDS Site Settings are not visible, because you can't see the leaf objects of different containers at the same time.

Domain Controller, and then selecting the target you want. You will see the currently selected domain controller in brackets in the first node in the tree.

NOTE You can create and modify replication objects using any domain controller of the forest. However, there would be the normal replication delay before any change would be replicated to other domain controllers. Consequently, it is often necessary to specify a certain domain controller as the snap-in target and also to change the target to various domain controllers to check if they already know about the change.

As an alternative to changing the target of the snap-in (see the corresponding Note), you could take the following steps:

1. Modify objects on the domain controller you already have as the target.
2. Initiate immediate replication of those objects to the domain controller that needs them.
3. Initiate immediate checking of replication topology on the latter domain controller, which generates some changes on the connection objects.
4. Initiate immediate replication back to your target domain controller.
5. Refresh the view.

These steps illustrate that because replication includes delays and several domain controllers, it takes quite a few mouse clicks to test things. When applying settings in production, you can either take the same steps to make sure that the result is what you wanted, or you can just perform step 1 and trust that in a while Active Directory will react as you want it to.

Because the name of the snap-in is "Sites and Services," you might wonder where the services are. You can access the Services node by right-clicking the first node in the tree (Active Directory Sites and Services) and selecting View, Show Services Node. However, the objects in the Services node don't have anything to do with the physical structure of Active Directory.

Test Environment

Using just one computer, you can test-drive many of the things described in this chapter. That computer will be the first and only domain controller in your enterprise forest. If you also have a second computer available, you can test-drive even more things. Depending on what you want to test, you can promote the second computer to the following roles:

- Another domain controller in the same domain
- A domain controller in a child domain
- A member server in the domain
- A domain controller in another forest

The last two items are actually not related to this chapter, but we mention them here for completeness.

An even better option is to use VMware Workstation or Microsoft Virtual PC. Either one enables you to have several servers and workstations in one computer.

Tasks in Managing the Physical Structure

In this section we introduce the tasks you may or must do when managing the physical structure of Active Directory. We divide the tasks as follows:

- Setting up a single site
- Setting up multiple sites
- Administering sites

If your network spans multiple geographical locations, you should create and configure the appropriate Active Directory objects to model the physical network. On the other hand, if your entire network is in a single location and on a single LAN, everything happens fairly automatically. Setting up the physical structure of Active Directory is much easier in the latter case.

Only Enterprise Admins can perform forestwide operations such as creating new sites and child domains. Per-domain administrators can perform domainwide operations such as adding a domain controller or initiating immediate domain replication from one domain controller to another.

Tables 5.8 through 5.12 in the following sections list the tasks. The tables include references to pages in the later sections where we describe each task in more detail.

Setting Up a Single Site

As mentioned, to set up a single site everything is quite automatic. About all you need to do is to install the domain controllers for the domains you want. (To review installation, see Chapter 2.) After you install domain controllers, you might need to perform only the three tasks in Table 5.8.

Setting Up Multiple Sites

To set up the physical structure for a multisite Active Directory network, you must first perform the tasks to set up a single site. Obviously, there are a number of additional tasks, which Table 5.9 and Table 5.10 list in their typical order.

Table 5.8 Tasks for Setting Up a Single Site

Task	Background	See Page
Perhaps assign some additional domain controllers as global catalog servers.	The first domain controller you install in the enterprise forest automatically becomes a global catalog server. In a large environment, you may want more than one of them. In a one-domain forest, you should promote all domain controllers to be global catalog servers.	417
Change the infra-structure master role or the first global catalog server of the root domain to another domain controller if the forest contains several domains.	The first domain controller of a forest is both an infrastructure master and a global catalog server. However, these two roles shouldn't be in the same domain controller (unless you have only one domain in the forest or all domain controllers in the domain are global catalog servers).	417 or 503
In some cases, adjust the replication topology by creating appropriate connection objects.	The replication topology is created and maintained automatically.	461 in the "Advanced Topics" section

NOTE Table 5.9 and Table 5.10 assume that the physical network is up and running. To "create a subnet" just means that you need to create a certain Active Directory object. You must already have sufficient routers configured for the correct physical subnets and operational WAN links between the routers.

First, let's do a couple of simple things with your default site, which is probably your main site, and your default IP site link.

After performing the tasks in Table 5.9, your main site is configured. Of course, it takes the normal replication delay from 15 seconds up for these changes to replicate to all domain controllers in the site.

Table 5.9 Tasks for the Default Site and Site Link

Task	Background	See Page
Rename Default-First-Site-Name to something else, such as "Boston."	When you install a new forest, a site called Default-First-Site-Name is created by default. All domain controllers that you install will first belong to this site (until you create additional sites and define their subnets). Because you will have several sites, this first site should have a descriptive name.	410
Create a subnet or subnets for this default site and associate this site with each of the subnets.	Each site should be assigned the correct subnets. This way, additional domain controllers that you install will belong to the appropriate site straight away. This also helps clients find a domain controller for logon and other needs.	412
Define the replication schedule and cost for DEFAULTIPSITELINK.	DEFAULTIPSITELINK is the only site link at this point. You'll probably start using it soon, so it's good to set the schedule now. The cost is relative to costs in other site links; you only need to set the cost if you will have other site links.	422 and 448

NOTE If at this point your forest already has domain controllers in multiple physical locations, they all belong to one site anyway. The consequence is that they replicate using the intrasite replication mechanisms. Similarly, if you now install new domain controllers, they will go to your main (and only) site.

Next you perform the steps in Table 5.10 for each additional physical location (for which you have decided to create a site).

The tasks in Table 5.9 and Table 5.10 are more or less the normal things that you need to do when setting up the physical structure of Active Directory. In addition, there are a couple of tasks that we consider "advanced" that we list in Table 5.11 and discuss later in the "Advanced Topics" section.

Table 5.10 Tasks for Additional Sites and Site Links

Task	Background	See Page
Create a new site, such as "London." Select that it will use DEFAULTIPSITELINK.	Each site must use at least one site link. You can select just the default link at this point. When you create another link, you can attach this site to the new link at that time.	413
Create a subnet or subnets for the newly created site and associate this site with each of the subnets.	Each site should be assigned the correct subnets. This way, additional domain controllers that you install will belong to the appropriate site straight away. This helps clients find a domain controller for logon and other needs.	412
Perhaps create a site link and select sites that will use it. Set the schedule and cost of this site link.	Depending on your physical WAN and domain structure, you may want site links in addition to to create DEFAULTIPSITELINK. The site links are either RPC- ("normal") or SMTP-based.	422 (normal), 468 (SMTP)
Install new domain controllers for the new site and move the ones from your main site that belong here.	For the replication to work efficiently, each domain controller object must belong to the correct site.	414
Select the global catalog servers for the site.	Each site should usually contain at least one global catalog server. They must be assigned manually (except for the first one in a forest).	417

Table 5.11 Advanced Tasks for Setting Up Multiple Sites

Task	Background	See Page
If your TCP/IP network is not fully routed or your AD2000 network has well over 100 sites, you may need to create site link bridges.	By default, all site links are bridged together. Sometimes you need to break this and create site link bridges for site links manually.	457

(continued)

Table 5.11 Advanced Tasks for Setting Up Multiple Sites (*cont.*)

Task	Background	See Page
Adjust the replication topology by creating appropriate connection objects and assigning preferred bridgehead servers.	The replication topology is created and maintained automatically (based on the sites and site links you have created). If you are not happy with the default, you can make changes manually. A bridgehead server is the domain controller that will replicate to and from other sites.	451 and 461

Administering Sites

After you have set up your site or sites, you can perform the administrative tasks listed in Table 5.12.

If there are changes in your network, in addition to performing the administrative tasks listed in Table 5.12, you must revisit the earlier tasks of setting things up. For example, if you upgrade a WAN link to use a greater speed, you may want to modify some site link costs.

Using the Default-First-Site-Name Site

When you install a new forest, a site called Default-First-Site-Name is created automatically. Until you create more sites, all domain controllers

Table 5.12 Tasks for Administering Sites

Task	Background	See Page
Change some operations master role to another domain controller, especially if the previous one fails.	Although Active Directory replication is mostly multimaster, there are five cases in which a special single-master role is attached to only one domain controller in a domain or the enterprise forest. These five roles are called "operations masters."	503
Use the Replicate Now option to initiate immediate replication.	Occasionally, you may not want to wait for the automatic replication to take place. You can select the Replicate Now menu option to initiate immediate replication from one domain controller to another.	416

Table 5.12 Tasks for Administering Sites (*cont.*)

Task	Background	See Page
Use the Check Replication Topology option to initiate an immediate replication topology check.	The KCCs check every 15 minutes (by default) if the replication topology is still optimal. If you change domain controllers, site links, or other background information that affects replication, you can wake up the KCC to perform this check immediately by selecting Check Replication Topology from the menu.	416
Remove a domain controller.	There are obviously instances when you want to take a domain controller offline or remove it permanently.	426
Monitor replication.	You can use various tools to monitor and diagnose replication.	429

that you install belong to this site. If you will have several sites, this first site should have a descriptive name, so you will want to rename it. If this will be your only site, you may leave the name unchanged. You rename the site as you would rename any other object by pressing F2 or right-clicking the object and selecting Rename. Figure 5.9 shows our sample company Sanao in a phase where the first site is not yet renamed to Boston and the other two sites for San Francisco and London are missing.

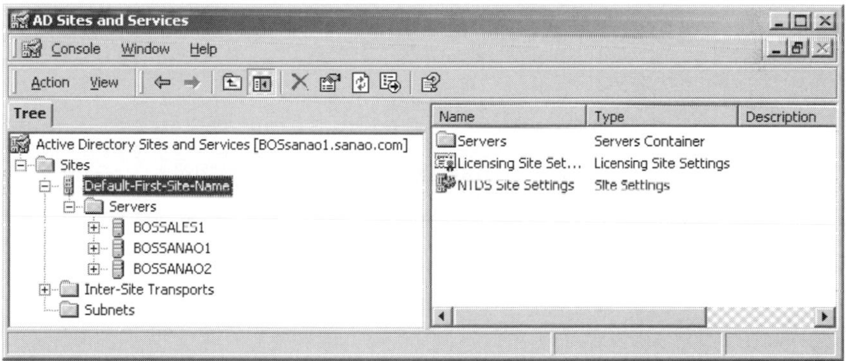

Figure 5.9 Default-First-Site-Name is waiting to be renamed to Boston. We include the location in the domain controller names, so the three installed domain controller names start with "BOS."

After you have created other sites, you can actually move all your domain controllers to them and then delete the Default-First-Site-Name site. However, you gain nothing by doing it this way—it is easier simply to rename the site.

Creating and Managing Subnet Objects

Each site consists of one or more subnets. One of the administrator's tasks is to create an object for each subnet and attach it to the appropriate site object. Figure 5.10 shows the creation of a subnet object.

Once the site's subnet infrastructure is in place, it makes installing domain controllers easier. When you promote a server to a domain controller, it will know by its IP address to which subnet, and thus to which site, it belongs. Otherwise, the domain controller would go to the site of its source domain controller and you might need to move it to the correct site manually. The source domain controller is the domain controller that is contacted by the server being promoted. The latter must be able to communicate with an existing forest during the promotion process.

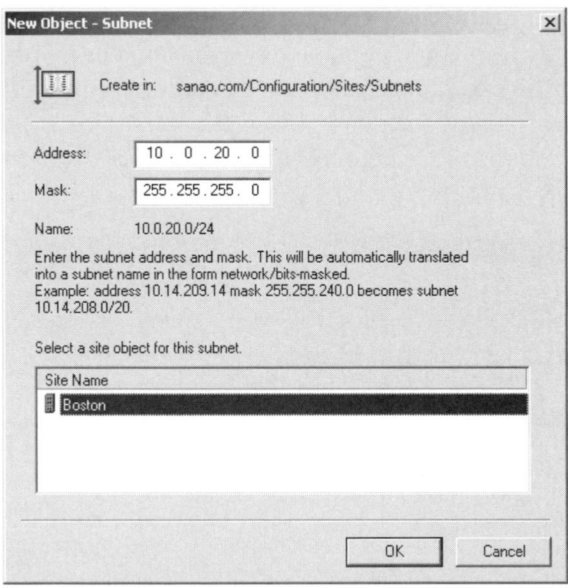

Figure 5.10 When creating a subnet object, you must select its site. Our sample company Sanao uses the address 10.0.20.0 for its Boston headquarters.

After you have created a subnet, you can make the following changes:

- *Rename a subnet.* When you rename a subnet, such as 10.0.20.0/24, you actually change either the network address or mask of the subnet.
- *Change the site.* You can select a new site for the subnet if needed.
- *Delete a subnet.*
- *Set the description and location texts.* The location text helps users to locate printers.
- *Change permissions, auditing entries, or ownership of the object.* In practice, you don't do this, because the default permissions are fine.

Creating and Managing Site Objects

You define a site for Active Directory by creating an object for the site, as Figure 5.11 illustrates.

If you create a site before you create its site link or links, you must select DEFAULTIPSITELINK. Later when you create the correct site link or links, you can attach them to this site.

If the site link or links for the new site already exist(s), you can select one of them when creating the site object. If you want to attach several site links to the new site, you need to attach the other site links after you have created the site object.

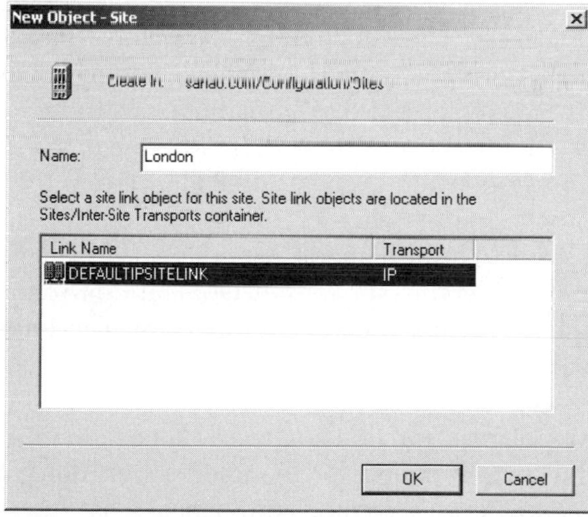

Figure 5.11 To create a site object, enter a name for it and select the site link to use.

You can also choose to have the site use DEFAULTIPSITELINK permanently.

Other operations you can perform on sites are as follows:

- *Rename a site.* A site name is purely informational, so renaming it doesn't affect anything. Remember, though, that other software may use Active Directory sites.
- *Delete a site.* Before you delete a site, move all its domain controllers to other sites. Otherwise, those server objects will be deleted with the site object, in which event your forest won't have information on all its domain controllers anymore.
- *Set the description and location texts.*
- *Assign Group Policy*. This is discussed in Chapter 7.
- *Change permissions, auditing entries, or ownership of the object.* You can usually get by without doing this, because the default permissions are fine.
- *Set the replication schedule in NTDS Site Settings.* Intrasite replication is notification based (with a default delay of 15 seconds/ 5 minutes), so this schedule is used only as a backup mechanism in case a notification message gets lost. If you think you'll lose sleep worrying about lost notifications, you could change this backup schedule from 60 minutes to a lower value, such as 30 or 15 minutes.

Moving and Managing Server Objects

Each domain controller in an Active Directory forest is represented by a server object, which contains an NTDS Settings object. As mentioned earlier, the server object may already belong to the appropriate site or you may need to move it there. The location of the server objects tells Active Directory which domain controllers are on the same site so it can decide, for example, whether to use intrasite or intersite replication mechanisms and how to build the replication topology.

The object type is Server, not Domain Controller, because it could also represent member servers of the forest. This enables you to define, for example, on which sites the member servers that are running your DFS services will reside.

Server objects for domain controllers contain an NTDS Settings object, but server objects for member servers don't. Server objects for domain controllers are created automatically, but server objects for member servers must be created manually (only if you need to define a location of a member server).

NOTE In this chapter we often refer to a domain controller object (or just domain controller) when we mean the server object that corresponds to a domain controller. This occurs most of the time, actually, because we don't talk much about member servers.

Figure 5.12 shows the Sanao configuration after the London site has been created but before the two corresponding domain controller objects were moved there. Subnet 10.0.22.0 is for London, but you don't need the subnet when you move domain controllers.

NOTE Because of replication latency, it may take a while until you can see a moved server in the new site.

Now that the London site exists and the subnet 10.0.22.0 has been defined for it, any new domain controller that is using a corresponding IP address (10.0.22.x) will appear in the London site right after it has been promoted.

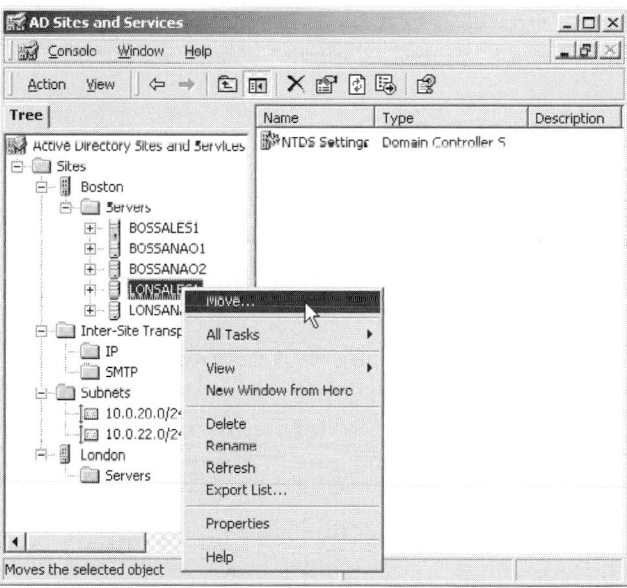

Figure 5.12 The London site was just created, so the two "LON" domain controllers are still under the Boston site object. Now we move them to the correct location, the London site.

In addition to moving domain controller objects between locations, you can perform the following operations on the server objects:

- *Delete a server object.* We discuss this operation in the "Removing Domain Controllers" section.
- *Set the description text.* This text is purely informational.
- *Set a domain controller as a preferred bridgehead.* This setting causes the domain controller to be used (along with other possible preferred bridgehead servers) to communicate with domain controllers on other sites. We discuss the topic later in this chapter in the "Intersite Replication Topologies" section.
- *Change the computer object associated with a server object.* You could use this operation when you have created a server object for a member server.
- *Change permissions, auditing entries, or ownership of the object.* You probably won't perform any of these operations, because the default permissions are fine.

NOTE You cannot rename a domain controller until the domain is running on the Windows Server 2003 functional level.

Managing NTDS Settings

As mentioned earlier, every server object corresponding to a domain controller contains an NTDS Settings child object. This child object hosts the domain controller–specific properties, which control replication to that domain controller. The existence of the NTDS Settings object also indicates that the corresponding server is a domain controller.

The NTDS Settings object in turn contains connection objects that dictate where the domain controller pulls its replication data from. The KCCs in each domain controller create connection objects automatically when building up the replication topology. You can also create and manage the connection objects manually, which we discuss in the "Intersite Replication Topologies" section later in the chapter.

The associated operations are as follows:

- *Check the replication topology.* If you make changes that could affect the optimal replication topology, such as when you add domain controllers or change site links, either you can wait up to

15 minutes for the KCC to wake up or you can initiate the check immediately by right-clicking NTDS Settings and selecting Check Replication Topology. For intersite topologies, this function takes effect only if the corresponding domain controller is an *inter-site topology generator.*

- *Replicate now.* If you don't want to wait 15 seconds/5 minutes for the intrasite replication to take place (or longer for the intersite replication), you can right-click a connection object and select Replicate Now.
- *Set the description text for NTDS Settings.* This text is purely informational.
- *Set the query policy.* Query policies enable administrators to set certain maximums for the resources a domain controller may use when answering LDAP queries of LDAP clients. The maximums can be used to prevent denial-of-service attacks, for example. The NTDSUtil tool allows definition of the default policy values. You can also programmatically (using ADSI) create query policy objects and then select one of them for a certain domain controller or site. The Windows 2000 Resource Kit includes a script, ModifyLDAP.vbs, that enables you to create and manage query policies. Because query policies are related to the LDAP protocol and not the physical structure of Active Directory, we don't cover them here.
- *Set a domain controller to be a global catalog server.*

Figures 5.13 through 5.16 show how to use an NTDS Settings object and the connection objects in it.

NOTE You can check the replication topology for BOSsanao1 even though your Sites and Services snap-in is connected to BOSsanao2. This will adjust the connection objects of BOSsanao1 immediately. However, these adjustments won't show until they have replicated from BOSsanao1 to BOSsanao2 and you have selected Refresh.

Promoting a Domain Controller to Be a Global Catalog Server

If you implement Active Directory in a new remote office, you will probably have at least one domain controller there, and at least one of the domain controllers might be a global catalog server.

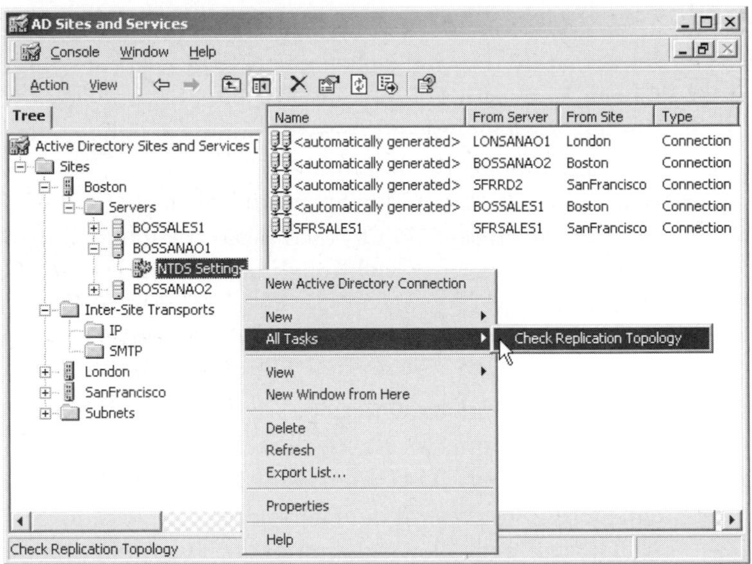

Figure 5.13 You can manually check if the automatically generated connection objects are still optimal. In addition, the KCC performs the check automatically every 15 minutes.

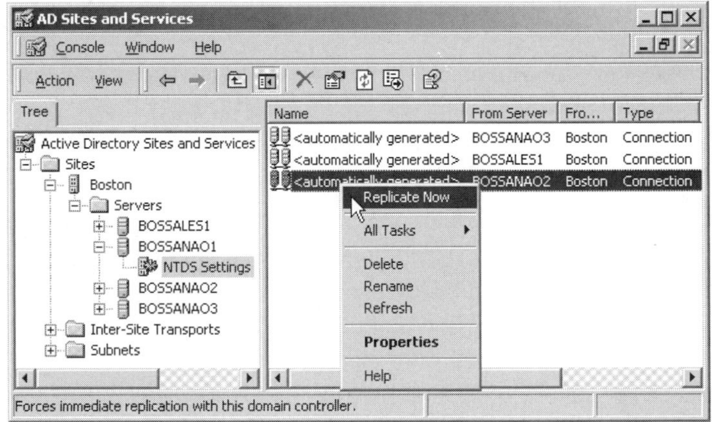

Figure 5.14 If you don't want to wait 15 seconds/5 minutes for the automatic intrasite replication from BOSSANAO2 to BOSSANAO1, you can start it immediately.

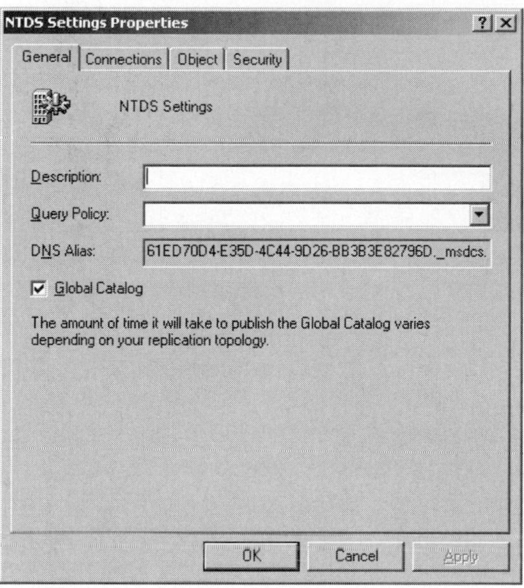

Figure 5.15 NTDS Settings properties include an indication of whether or not the corresponding domain controller is a global catalog server. The Connections tab (in the Windows Server 2003 version of the snap-in) lists the domain controllers this domain controller replicates from and to.

If you have a large multidomain forest and a lot of objects in Active Directory, you may want to perform the implementation in steps. You can first install a domain controller to the remote office, let it replicate the domain partition, and let the local administrators get acquainted with the new environment.

After a few days, or perhaps a week, when you can see that everything is OK, you can set the domain controller to be a global catalog server also. If there was 500MB to replicate for the domain partition, the global catalog might now need another 500MB.

In a single-domain forest, all domain controllers should also be global catalog servers, and you can perform the global catalog server promotion right away with no impact in each domain controller.

When you check Global Catalog in the NTDS Settings properties and click OK or Apply, the corresponding domain controller starts replicating in the partial replicas of other domains in the forest (depending on the schedule settings). It doesn't yet advertise itself to be a global catalog server.

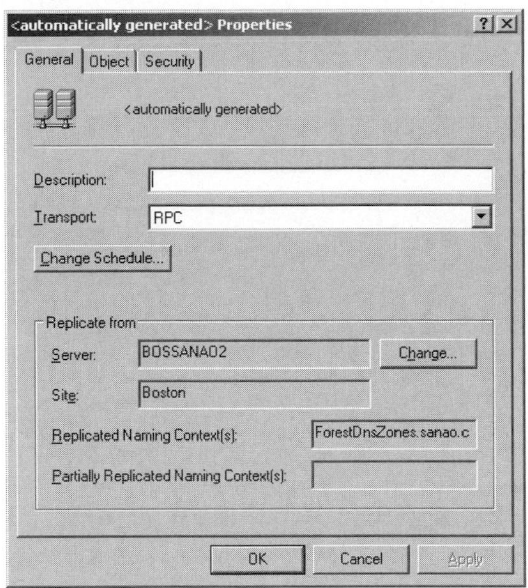

Figure 5.16 The property page of a connection object defines where to replicate from and what to replicate. "Replicated Naming Context(s): ForestDnsZones.sanao.com, DomainDnsZones.sanao.com, sanao.com" means that this domain controller replicates the domain partition (or naming context) and the two DNS application partitions from BOSsanao2. Note that because the text box is quite narrow, you see only the beginning of the three-partition list. In addition, the connection object is used to replicate the schema and configuration partitions, even though this isn't indicated on the property page.

By default, advertising starts when the domain controller has received a partial replica of all other domains that have a domain controller on the same site. Advertising means that the domain controller dynamically registers the appropriate SRV records in DNS. The domain controller also opens the global catalog TCP port 3268 (for normal LDAP traffic) and TCP port 3269 (for SSL traffic). Consequently, clients can start using its services.

Once the global catalog promotion is complete and the advertising starts, the advertising doesn't stop, even if there is to be a new domain that the global catalog server doesn't have yet. You can check to see if a domain controller is a global catalog server (i.e., the promotion is complete) in the following ways.

- There is a registry entry `Global Catalog Promotion Complete` with the value "1" in the key `HKEY_LOCAL_MACHINE`, `SYSTEM`, `CurrentControlSet`, `Services`, `NTDS`, `Parameters`.
- The `rootDSE` object contains an attribute `isGlobalCatalogReady` with the value TRUE. You can see this by starting the LDP utility, opening the Connection menu, selecting Connect, typing the domain controller name, and clicking OK. The attribute should now be visible in the right-hand pane. (In addition, Chapter 11 contains a script to display the `rootDSE` attributes.)
- Go to the command prompt and enter a command such as `repadmin /showreps dc1`. If the promotion is complete, the second line from the beginning ("DC Options") contains "`IS_GC`."
- Go to the command prompt and enter a command such as `nltest /dsgetdc:sanao /server:dc1`. You should see eight lines of information about the domain controller. If the promotion is complete, the last line (`Flags`) contains "`GC`."

NOTE LDP, RepAdmin, and NLTest are included in Windows Support Tools.

If the global catalog server is supposed to be used for NSPI calls (for Outlook/Exchange), you must reboot the server after it has started advertising as a global catalog server. The reboot activates the NSPI interface on the server.

If you uncheck Global Catalog in the NTDS Settings properties and click OK or Apply, the KCC in the corresponding domain controller starts tearing down the partial replicas of that domain controller. In AD2003, the KCC performs this teardown as fast as it can. In AD2000, the KCC removes 500 objects every 15 minutes as long as there are objects to remove. At this pace, the KCC removes 2,000 objects in an hour, or 48,000 objects in 24 hours. Depending on the number of objects in your forest, it may take a while for the KCC to complete its mission.

If during the teardown process you recheck the domain controller to be a global catalog server again, the KCC is not allowed to add partial replicas that are currently being removed. Consequently, only when the last partial replica has been removed can the last partial replica be added again and the domain controller start advertising itself as a global catalog server.

Creating and Managing Site Links

A site link connects two or more sites. As you create each site, you must associate it with at least one site link. As Figure 5.17 shows, site link objects reside under Inter-Site Transports in either the IP or SMTP container, depending on whether they apply to RPC or SMTP replication, respectively.

If you have only two sites, you don't need more than one site link: DEFAULTIPSITELINK. If you have a few sites, say three or four, you may still do fine with no additional site links. This is true if the network among the sites is like a cloud or a mesh (e.g., a frame relay network). That is, it doesn't matter which route the packets take as they travel from one site to another.

Knowing which site links to create requires familiarity with the intersite topologies of Active Directory. We address topologies and planning site links in the advanced section of this chapter.

You usually create site links in the IP container. The process to create STMP site links is similar, but there are some special considerations. We discuss SMTP site links later in the "Configuring SMTP Replication" section.

Besides the descriptive text and the list of sites, a site link has three properties you can set: cost, replication interval, and schedule (see Figure 5.18).

- Cost is a number between 1 and 99,999 (or 32,767 in AD2000), with the default being 100. It doesn't represent actual money—it

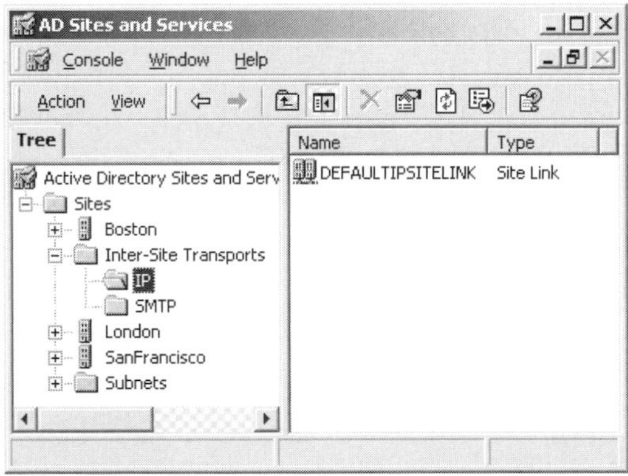

Figure 5.17 The first site link is the predefined DEFAULTIPSITELINK. As you need them, you can create more site links in the containers IP and SMTP.

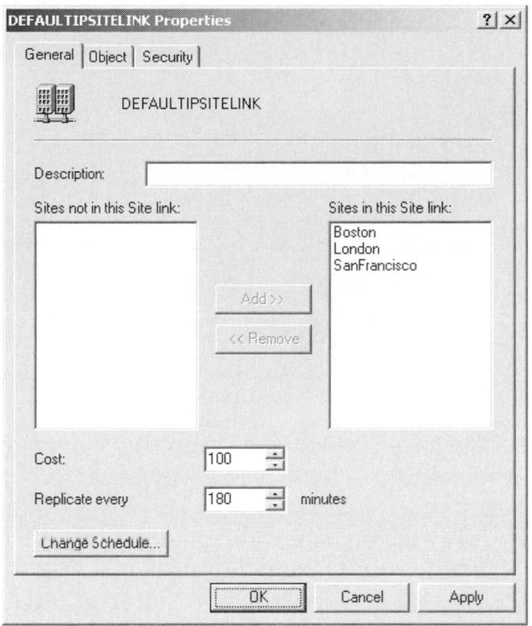

Figure 5.18 All three sites of Sanao use DEFAULTIPSITELINK first. The default relative cost is 100 and default replication interval is 180 minutes, or 3 hours.

is just a number that Active Directory compares with costs in other site links. When building the intersite replication topology, Active Directory favors site links with lower cost over links with higher cost. Because a site link's cost is relative to the costs of other site links, the cost doesn't matter when you have only one site link. We discuss assignment of costs in the "Site Link Costs" section later in this chapter.

- The "Replicate every" field indicates the replication interval in minutes. By default, intersite replication takes place every 3 hours (180 minutes). The possible range is 15 to 10,080 minutes (1 week).
- The Change Schedule button enables you to list the weekdays and hours when this site link is available—that is, when replication can occur using the interval indicated in the "Replicate every" property field. By default, a site link is always available. Figure 5.19 shows the dialog box that appears when you click the Change Schedule button.

As illustrated in Figure 5.6, the replication properties of a site link object don't affect replication directly. Instead, they act as a template for

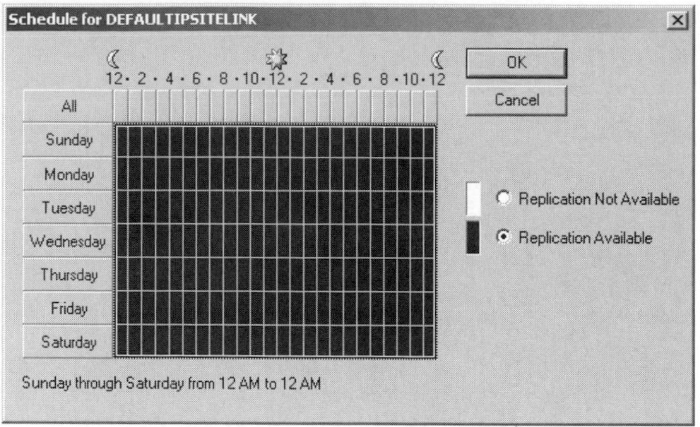

Figure 5.19 The schedule for a site link indicates the hours and days of the week that the site link is available. By default, it is always available.

automatically generated connection objects. When a connection object is generated, the effect of the site link's interval and availability properties is combined. For example, if the interval for a site link is 30 minutes and the link is available from 5:00 PM to 7:00 AM daily, the resulting connection object's schedule will be "twice per hour, but only from 5:00 PM to 7:00 AM."

The IP and SMTP containers have two check boxes that affect all site link objects under the corresponding container (see Figure 5.20).

If you check the "Ignore schedules" box, replication will be always available to the corresponding protocol, using the interval specified in the "Replicate every" field. SMTP ignores schedules by default. The "Bridge all site links" check box is discussed in the advanced section "Intersite Replication Topologies"—for now, don't touch it.

Managing Licensing Computers

Each site can have one server designated as a licensing computer. By default, it is the first domain controller on the site, but you can change the role to another server. The licensing computer does not have to be a domain controller. Figure 5.21 shows one of the property pages of the Licensing Site Settings object.

A licensing computer stores licensing information in three files in the %Systemroot%\System32 folder (often C:\Winnt\System32). The file LLS\LlsUser.LLS (user and usage information) is always present. Files CPL.CFG (purchase history) and LLS\LlsMap.LLS (license groups) are

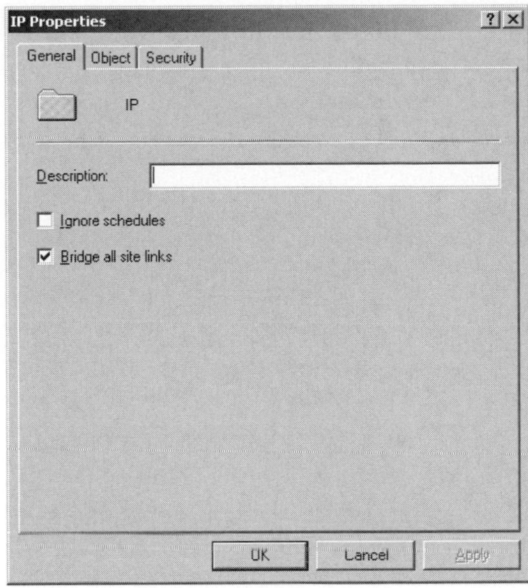

Figure 5.20 The IP and SMTP containers have two settings that affect all the site links under the corresponding container.

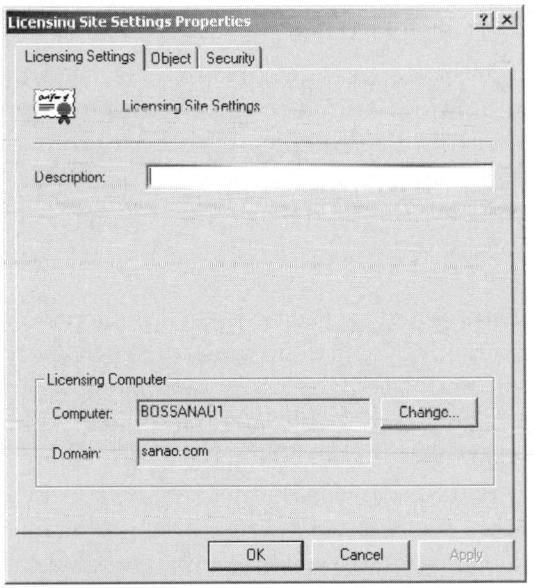

Figure 5.21 Each site object has Licensing Site Settings as a child object, which enables you to select the licensing computer for the site.

present depending on the licensing configuration and group mappings you selected. If you want to move the information in these files to the new server when you change a licensing computer, you need to do the following:

1. Change the licensing computer to be a new server.
2. Stop the License Logging service on the new server.
3. Copy the three files from the old server to the new server to the same locations as on the old server.
4. Start the License Logging service on the new server.

NOTE The level of sophistication (or rather, the lack of it) of the Windows 2000/Windows Server 2003 License Logging service and the administrative user interface is about the same as that contained in Windows NT.

Removing Domain Controllers

From time to time, you may want to take a domain controller offline, either temporarily or permanently. It is best to do this in a planned and organized way.

First, consider how the downtime of the domain controller will affect your network. This obviously depends on the current functions of the domain controller, the length of the downtime, your network size, your network configuration, and so on.

The domain controller may offer the following Active Directory–related services:

- *Normal domain services.* Even if the target domain controller is a plain domain controller with no special services, it should offer logon and LDAP services (among others) to network clients. Each domain probably has other domain controllers to offer these services as well, but the one you are taking offline might be the only one close to some users.
- *Global catalog server.* If the target domain controller is a global catalog server, will you have enough global catalog servers (in suitable locations) if you remove this one?
- *Operations master roles.* If the target domain controller holds some operations master roles, depending on the roles and length

of the downtime, you should perhaps transfer the roles to another domain controller(s). If you demote the domain controller by running DCPromo, the roles will be transferred automatically. However, Microsoft recommends that you do not rely on this automatic role transfer feature. When you transfer the role manually before demotion, you can choose which domain controller will take the role. We discuss the five operations master roles, including the impact of the downtime of each, in the "Managing Operations Masters" section later in this chapter.

- *Bridgehead server.* The target domain controller may be a bridgehead server, meaning that intersite replication goes through that domain controller. If you haven't assigned preferred bridgehead servers, Active Directory will select a new bridgehead server if the original goes offline.

NOTE Remember to check whether the target domain controller hosts any services that are not related to Active Directory, such as normal file services, Web services, and application services.

Once you have made sure that you can take the domain controller offline without undesirable consequences, you can do so with the following instructions. (Remember that "temporary" tends to become "permanent.")

- Shut down the domain controller and do whatever maintenance you need to do. This is probably OK for a short downtime. Note, however, that your domain controller doesn't replicate any changes to other domain controllers before shutdown. Therefore, if you can't get the domain controller back online for any reason, you lose the recent changes to Active Directory (the ones that weren't replicated). You can reduce the risk if you use the Replicate Now function just before shutting down. Because that operation initiates only incoming replication, you must select some other domain controller of the same domain for which you perform the Replicate Now operation.
- If the downtime extends to days or you cannot get the domain controller online at all, you can delete the corresponding NTDS Settings object. This way, the KCCs will know that this domain controller doesn't exist and they will adapt the replication topology accordingly. Note, however, that even if you don't delete the NTDS Settings, the other domain controllers will notice that one

is missing and they will create temporary connections to bypass the missing domain controller. It is not possible to delete the NTDS Settings object while the domain controller is still online. If you bring the domain controller back online, it will re-create the NTDS Settings object and things will get back to normal. Even though you could delete the NTDS Settings object manually, Microsoft Knowledge Base article Q216498 ("How to Remove Data in the Active Directory after an Unsuccessful Domain Controller Demotion") describes the steps to delete the object using the NTDSUtil command-line tool. The advantage of using NTDSUtil is that it performs a more complete cleanup of obsolete objects and DNS records.

- If you are permanently removing a domain controller, you must first demote it to a member server (or to a stand-alone server, if it is the last domain controller in the domain) by running DCPromo. This will delete the NTDS Settings object automatically and has the benefit of replicating all the recent changes out from the domain controller. The process also automatically transfers any operations master roles (but not global catalogs) to other domain controllers, if you did not do that manually already. After you have shut the server down permanently, you can delete the corresponding server and computer objects.

NOTE The server object and NTDS Settings object will be re-created if you restart the corresponding domain controller. However, once you delete the computer object, it's difficult, if not impossible, to get the domain controller back into your domain (except by reinstalling it or by authoritatively restoring the computer object from a backup).

NOTE If you delete the computer object for a running domain controller, it cannot replicate with other domain controllers anymore. Note that even though it is isolated from the rest of the domain, it may still accept changes and logons from workstations, which don't suspect that there is anything wrong. If you add a workstation to the domain, it may create its object in this isolated domain controller and you will be in trouble, because you now have two versions of your domain.

When you demote a domain controller to a member server, the corresponding computer object is moved from Domain Controllers (or whatever container it was in) to the Computers container (or to the redirected container if `redircmp` has been used; see Chapter 3) and the membership of the object is changed from the Domain Controllers group to Domain Computers. If you change a member server from a domain to a workgroup, the corresponding computer object will be disabled, but not deleted. You may delete it if you wish.

Monitoring and Diagnosing the Physical Structure

A number of tools help you monitor and diagnose the physical structure of Active Directory. The *Distributed Systems Guide* of the Windows 2000 Server Resource Kit contains about 200 pages about monitoring and diagnosing Active Directory. You can use it as a source of information and for detailed instructions on how to solve a certain problem or use a certain tool. As of this writing, a Windows Server 2003 version was not yet published, but by the time you read this book, that new Resource Kit should also be out.

Table 5.13 lists the names of the tools, along with brief descriptions.

Table 5.13 Tools to Diagnose Replication

Tool	Type	Description
Sites and Services	Snap-in	We described this tool earlier in this chapter.
Replication Monitor* (ReplMon.exe)	Graphical	A feature-rich but not very polished tool to show and log various aspects of the physical structure.
Event Viewer	Snap-in	One of the Windows 2000 and later logs is Directory Service. Event sources NTDS Replication and NTDS KCC generate information, warnings, or error messages related to replication.
Performance Monitor	Snap-in	The NTDS performance object includes more than 100 counters. The names of quite a few start with *DRA* (Directory Replication Agent). You can use them, for example, to show a graph over time of replicated incoming and outgoing bytes.

(continued)

* These tools are included in Windows Support Tools, which you need to install separately from the Windows installation CD.

Table 5.13 Tools to Diagnose Replication *(cont.)*

Tool	Type	Description
Network Monitor (NetMon.exe)	Graphical	You can use Network Monitor to capture and analyze network packets (called frames). The version included in Windows 2000 and Windows Server 2003 has some restrictions. For example, you can capture only packets that are sent to or from the local computer (including multicasts and broadcasts). The full version is included in Microsoft Systems Management Server (SMS).
Registry Editor (RegEdit, in Win2000 also RegEdt32.exe)	Graphical	You can use Registry Editor to specify some settings or to check existing settings.
RepAdmin.exe*	Command	Includes about 36 command-line switches (or 20 in the Windows 2000 version) that enable you to show replication data or manage replication.
DCDiag.exe*	Command	Tests to see if all is OK in one domain controller or all domain controllers of a site or forest.
NetDiag.exe*	Command	Performs a number of network connectivity tests and is also able to fix minor problems.
NLTest.exe*	Command	Includes over 30 command-line switches that enable you to show, as well as manage, domain and replication-related information.
DSAStat.exe*	Command	Compares replicas on different domain controllers and detects differences; also lists counts of objects of each class. A sample command is `dsastat /s:dc1;dc2`.
NTDSUtil.exe	Command	Biased to managing the directory database, although it has other functions too. One function related to this chapter is to remove the Active Directory objects of a selected domain controller or partition. You could use the former function if your demotion process would be interrupted for some reason, leaving some unnecessary objects still in Active Directory.

Table 5.13 Tools to Diagnose Replication (*cont.*)

Tool	Type	Description
Microsoft Operations Manager (MOM)	Bought separately	Installs a monitoring agent in each domain controller and then monitors how the servers are performing; contains also some artificial intelligence to detect and identify certain typical errors.

TIP The contents of the *Distributed Systems Guide* of the Windows 2000 Server Resource Kit are available on Microsoft's Web site (`http://www.microsoft.com/`), so you can point your Web browser there and perform a search using words that relate to your problem.

Windows Server 2003 includes a new replication latency event that reveals as a summary if replication from some domain controller seems not to work. It is event ID 1864 in the Directory Service event log, and it is logged if the domain controller hasn't received replication information from some domain controller in more than 24 hours. The event description shows how many domain controllers have not replicated to the local domain controller during:

- The past 24 hours
- The past week
- The past month
- The past two months
- The tombstone lifetime (60 days by default)

If this event ID appears in the log, you can use the following methods A and B to resolve which domain controllers don't replicate.

Does Replication Work—Method A

You can use the following command to verify that replication works throughout the forest (requires the Windows Server 2003 version of RepAdmin):

```
repadmin /replsum /bysrc /bydest /sort:delta
```

The first lines of the output might look like the following:

```
Source DC       largest delta  fails/total  %%  error
 LONSANAO1    02d.11h:39m:17s   43 /  82  100  (8524) The DSA operation...
 SFRSALES1        13h:52m:09s    7 /   9  100  (8524) The DSA operation...
 LONSALES2             18m:31s    0 /  17    0
 LONSALES3             18m:30s    0 /   9    0
 SFRRD2                18m:30s    0 /   9    0
```

In the output, the "largest delta" column reveals that with the first two domain controllers, the replication delay is more than it should be, based on the replication configuration, such as the replication interval in your site links. Also, the "fails" count should be 0 for all domain controllers.

If there are errors, you can next use the following command:

```
repadmin /showrepl * /csv >dcpairs.txt
```

This command lists all the communicating DC pairs (per direction) of the forest, where each such pair corresponds to one connection object. With each pair, the command shows the number of failures, last failure time, last success time, and last failure error code. You can import this information into a spreadsheet program, such as Excel, and sort on the last success time, to locate any problems you might have.

Does Replication Work—Method B

Another RepAdmin command you can use is the following:

```
repadmin /showvector /latency dc=sanao,dc=com
```

It shows the last time that the local domain controller was able to replicate with the other domain controllers that host a given partition (either directly or transitively via other domain controllers). The `/latency` option causes it to sort the output based on time. The output looks like the following:

```
Boston\LONsanao2    @ USN  312883 @ Time 2004-01-24 23:05:13
Boston\LONsanao1    @ USN   61503 @ Time 2004-01-27 11:48:17
Boston\BOSsanao2    @ USN  723422 @ Time 2004-01-27 12:54:42
Boston\BOSsanao3    @ USN  192323 @ Time 2004-01-27 13:07:11
Boston\BOSsanao1    @ USN  319342 @ Time 2004-01-27 13:09:52
```

The preceding command works also with the Windows Server 2003 version of RepAdmin, but the new version includes a new (replacing) option:

```
repadmin /showutdvec /latency * dc=sanao,dc=com
```

It shows the same output as the previous command, but this time for a number of domain controllers. The asterisk (*) specifies all domain controllers, but you can also name one, or all that start with "bos" by typing "bos*" (without quotes).

Replication Permissions

To be able to use the Replicate Now feature, a person must have the Replication Synchronization extended right for the root object of each partition (i.e., schema, configuration, domain, and any application partitions for normal domain controllers, and also the remaining domains for global catalog servers). Consequently, because in AD2003 there are two DNS application partitions, you must grant the Replication Synchronization right for five different objects until that person can use Replicate Now. You can use the ACL Editor to assign this permission to appropriate administrators, as explained in Chapter 4. The easiest way to locate all necessary objects is to use ADSI Edit and launch the ACL Editor from there.

To be able to get replication status, a person must have the Manage Replication Topology extended right. All the information in the previous paragraph applies also to this permission.

Advanced Topics

We have postponed the discussion of the advanced topics until this section. One obvious reason is that this way you could learn the easier skills and concepts before delving into the finer aspects of replication. The other reason is that an administrator could install and use Active Directory quite well without this information, at least if his network doesn't span multiple sites. The subjects covered here are as follows:

- Intrasite and intersite replication topologies
- Configuring SMTP replication

- The replication process
- Time synchronization
- Managing operations masters

Even though you may not need this in-depth knowledge when you first use Active Directory, eventually you will probably encounter situations that require it. An administrator who has a deep understanding of the network's physical structure is equipped for troubleshooting and solving the problems that arise.

Intrasite Replication Topologies

As mentioned earlier, Knowledge Consistency Checkers (KCCs) automatically create topologies for both intrasite and intersite replication. When determining the optimal topology, KCCs base their decisions on replication objects such as sites, site links, and domain controllers (or to be exact, the NTDS Settings objects). If there are changes in these objects, the KCCs automatically make the necessary alterations. They also monitor replication for problems that would necessitate temporary or permanent changes in the topology.

Replication Ring

An automatically created intrasite replication topology forms a bidirectional ring, as Figure 5.22 shows.

Each domain controller establishes an inbound *replication partnership* with two other domain controllers. For example, in Figure 5.22 DC1 will pull replication data from DC2 and DC5.

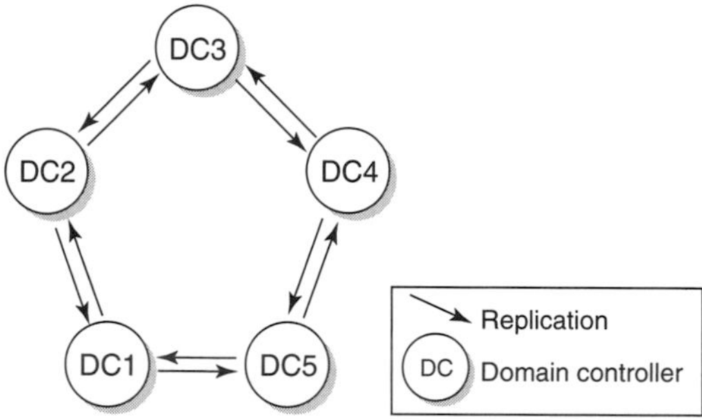

Figure 5.22 An intrasite replication topology forms a bidirectional ring.

The order of the domain controllers in the ring is determined by the `objectGUID` property of the NTDS Settings object under their corresponding domain controller objects. The domain controllers are sorted in ascending order and the ones with the smallest and largest GUIDs close the ring.

Drawing the Replication Ring

It is beneficial to know the order of domain controllers in your replication ring when you diagnose replication problems or use the Replicate Now function to get some changes faster to other domain controllers. Therefore, you may want to document the ring order on each site of your network. If you install five domain controllers and call them DC1, DC2, DC3, DC4, and DC5, they probably won't be in consecutive order in the ring. Figure 5.22 assumes that the GUIDs happen to be in the same order as the server names.

Chapter 11 presents a short script that lists the GUIDs. The list helps you to document your topology.

Another way to get the GUID list is to use the DNS management snap-in, with some manual work. Select Forward Lookup Zones, open `_msdcs` in "your forest name," and you will see a list of GUIDs, each corresponding to one of your domain controllers. Export the list to a text file by right-clicking `_msdcs` with your mouse. Next, edit the file to extract the lines that belong to the site you are interested in. Before you can sort the GUIDs to help you in drawing the ring, you must edit each GUID. When you see a GUID represented with dashes, the byte order is different from the actual binary format. Therefore, you need to swap bytes of the first three parts of the GUID, but not the last two. You change bytes 1, 2, 3, 4 to 4, 3, 2, 1, so if you start with "752d5592-07dc-11d3-a61f-4000f006f0d0," you will get "92552d75-de07-d311-a61f-4000f006f0d0." Now you can sort the GUIDs "alphabetically" and draw your ring.

Connection Objects

As you learned earlier, each domain controller object (i.e., NTDS Settings) hosts a connection object for each inbound replication partner—that is, the partners it pulls data from—as Figure 5.23 illustrates.

The KCCs add, delete, and possibly modify the connection objects automatically. However, they don't delete or modify any connection objects that you created. If you delete an automatically created connection object, a KCC may soon re-create it, if it determines that it is needed

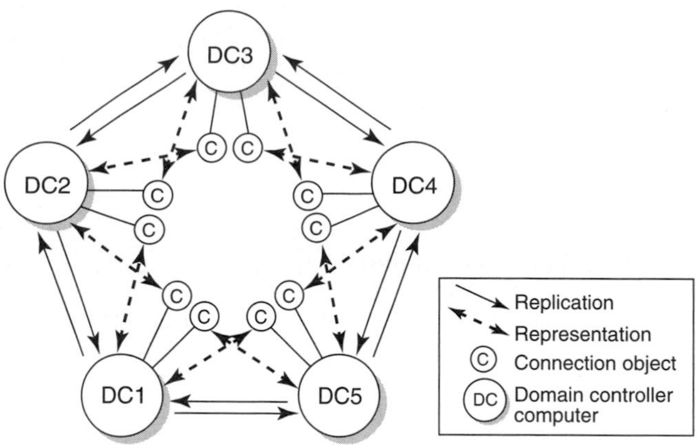

Figure 5.23 Each domain controller object (i.e., NTDS Settings) has a connection object for each inbound partner. Thus, in a bidirectional ring there are two connection objects in each domain controller object.

anyway. If you manually modify an automatically created connection object, you have the option to change it to be administered manually.

NOTE Each connection object has an `options` property, which determines the "owner" of the object. If the least significant bit of `options` is 1, the object is maintained automatically by the KCC; if it is 0, you will maintain the object manually.

Intrasite replication should work just fine with the automatic topology, so we explain the process of creating connection objects with the discussion of intersite replication.

As the Ring Grows

When you add a domain controller, its place in the ring is determined by its GUID. It kind of "squeezes" in between its two new neighbors.

The KCCs take care that there are almost never more than three hops between any two domain controllers in the intrasite replication topology. Because the replication delay with one hop is 15 seconds or 5 minutes, a three-hop maximum means that a change to an Active Directory object will reach all domain controllers in the site in 45 seconds or 15 minutes. See the "Change Notification Delay" section earlier in this chapter.

NOTE Remember that the 15-second or 5-minute delay may actually be slightly longer. When the domain controller with changes notifies its replication partners, it adds 3 or 30 seconds for each partner after the first one. Consequently, the 45-second or 15-minute delay may also be slightly longer.

The largest ring that has three hops at most between any two domain controllers has seven domain controllers. When a ring has eight or more domain controllers, the KCCs add shortcut connections to the basic ring. Otherwise, the greatest "distance" would be four hops or more. In an eight-DC ring, each domain controller has a third (shortcut) inbound connection, and the starting point is chosen randomly regardless of GUIDs. Figure 5.24 shows a ring topology of eight domain controllers.

The exact logic for a KCC to add shortcut connections goes as follows:

1. The KCC knows the number of domain controllers in the ring.
2. Based on this number, the KCC calculates the minimum number of connections that each domain controller must have to get a topology, where the path between any two domain controllers is three hops at the most.
3. If the local domain controller has fewer than this number of connections, the KCC chooses random source domain controllers from the ring and creates connections from them to achieve this minimum number of connections.

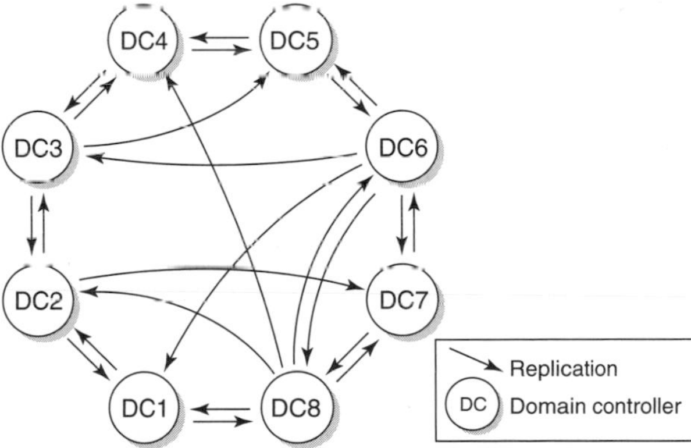

Figure 5.24 When the replica ring grows to at least eight domain controllers, it must have shortcut connections to maintain the three-hop maximum.

NOTE The exact logic of creating shortcut connections means that the KCCs only approximate the three-hop maximum. The minimum number of connections that is calculated in step 2 assumes that those connections will exist between domain controllers in the optimal way. However, in step 3 the connections are created randomly. Therefore, in rare cases of a large ring, the maximum number of hops could be four, resulting in a 1-minute or 20-minute replication latency.

The KCCs run independently in each domain controller and they don't negotiate with each other when building the topology. But because they base their decisions on the same information (the replication objects and the ordering of GUIDs) and use the same algorithms, they cooperate to build a common topology.

NOTE The number of connection objects per domain controller can be larger than described here, which might happen if there are some DNS problems or other connectivity problems in the network. If a domain controller cannot contact some of its replication partners, it will create temporary connection objects to bypass the failed connection.

In Transition

The independence of the KCCs means that each one will change its part of the topology at a slightly different time from the next one. By default, a KCC wakes up 5 minutes after a domain controller boots up and every 15 minutes thereafter.

A new domain controller will add its connection objects right away. The existing domain controllers accommodate the change, as the KCC in each one happens to wake up on its own schedule. Consequently, it may take 15 minutes or longer before the topology shown in Figures 5.22 through 5.24 is actually completed.

When a replication object such as a domain controller object is created or changed in a domain controller, it needs to be replicated to other domain controllers, just as any ordinary Active Directory object does. Also, it may take 45 seconds/15 minutes for this change to reach all domain controllers in the site. Therefore, if some KCCs check the replication topology during this period, they will find outdated information on which to base their decisions.

The new topology should be applied throughout the site in 16 minutes/a half hour—that is, after 45 seconds/15 minutes (for replication latency) plus 15 minutes (for any KCC to wake up). Of course, it will take yet another 45 seconds/15 minutes until the changes any KCC made are replicated back to other domain controllers. Finally, after 17 minutes/45 minutes the replication objects of the site should be consistent again.

NOTE Remember that a KCC picks a random starting point for a shortcut connection. Therefore, if you delete a shortcut connection object and then initiate Check Replication Topology, the new connection object you get will probably be for a different source domain controller. There is no harm done if you try this out.

Several Partitions

All that we have said so far about intrasite replication rings assumes that the domain controllers are part of the same domain and they all host the replicas of the same application partitions. The situation is a little different when there are several domains or only some of the domain controllers host replicas of a given application partition. This is because each replication partition has its own independent replication topology. When you think about it, it is actually quite obvious, because the whole idea of a partition is to be the unit of replication.

For example, if there are two domains on a site, there are the following replica rings (with possible shortcut connections) on that site:

- The domain controllers of domain A create a replica ring for domain A.
- The domain controllers of domain B create a replica ring for domain B.
- All domain controllers on the site create one large replica ring for the schema and configuration partitions. These two partitions use a common topology, because every domain controller of an enterprise forest has a replica of each of these partitions.
- The domain controllers that host a given application partition create a replica ring for that partition. Most likely, there are three such partitions (and consequently three replica rings): ForestDnsZones, DomainDnsZones for domain A, and DomainDnsZones for domain B. For example, consider Figure 5.22 a couple of pages back. If DC1, DC3, and DC5 would host ForestDnsZones, but DC2 and DC4 would not, DC1, DC3, and DC5 would create a three-DC replica ring for that partition, in addition to the one shown in Figure 5.22.

In addition, the global catalog must be replicated across domains, obviously using the computers that are assigned to be global catalog servers.

NOTE Because each application partition may exist on a “random” selection of domain controllers, showing those replica rings would make the figures quite messy. Therefore, we show the replication topologies of “only” the domain partitions and the enterprise partitions (schema and configuration).

Figure 5.25 shows how replication topologies for multiple partitions build up. By *domain replication* we mean the replication of a domain partition between domain controllers of that domain. *Enterprise replication* means the replication of schema and configuration partitions. This figure does not show global catalog replication or application partition replication.

NOTE To make the figure less crowded, we use bidirectional arrows instead of the unidirectional arrows in previous figures.

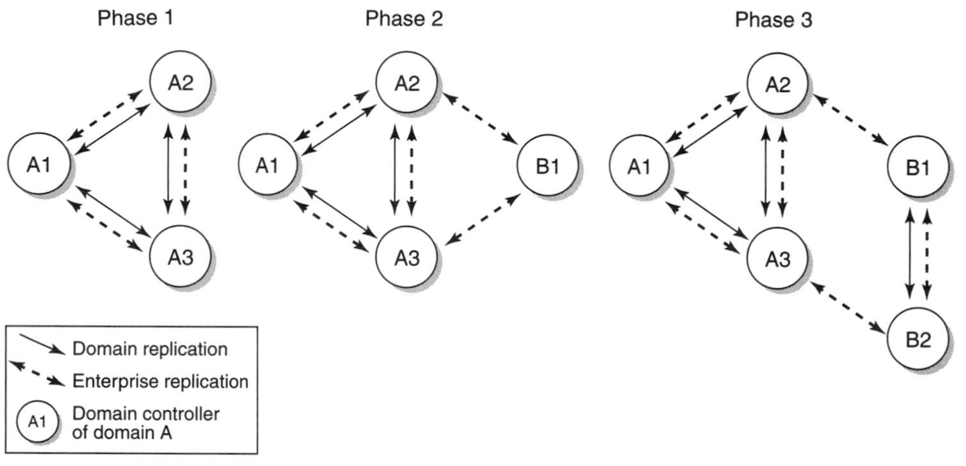

Figure 5.25 Domains A and B have their own replication topologies. Schema and configuration partitions use a common topology, shown with the “enterprise replication” arrows. In phase 1 we have only domain A. In phase 2 we add the first domain controller for domain B, and in phase 3 we add a second domain controller for domain B.

In phase 1 we have three domain controllers, all of which belong to domain A. Both the domain partition and the two enterprise partitions replicate with a simple replication ring.

Next, in phase 2 we add the first domain controller for domain B. This, of course, doesn't incur any changes to domain A's topology, but the enterprise replication ring accommodates this new domain controller. Note that the enterprise connection between A2 and A3 is not removed. Because that connection is needed for the domain A ring, the same connection can be used for the enterprise replication as well.

NOTE Even though each partition has an independent topology, the enterprise topology mostly follows a domain topology while "traveling" in that domain. That is, a domain replication connection is never alone; it always has an enterprise replication connection running parallel to it.

Finally, in phase 3 we add a second domain controller for domain B. Again, this doesn't affect domain A's ring, but the enterprise ring gets one additional member. Domain B also gets a small "ring" as B1 and B2 replicate from each other. This time the old connection between A3 and B1 is removed. It would have been used only for enterprise replication, which didn't need that connection anymore.

Figure 5.26 shows the several partitions of Sanao Corporation's Boston site, again without global catalog or application partition replication.

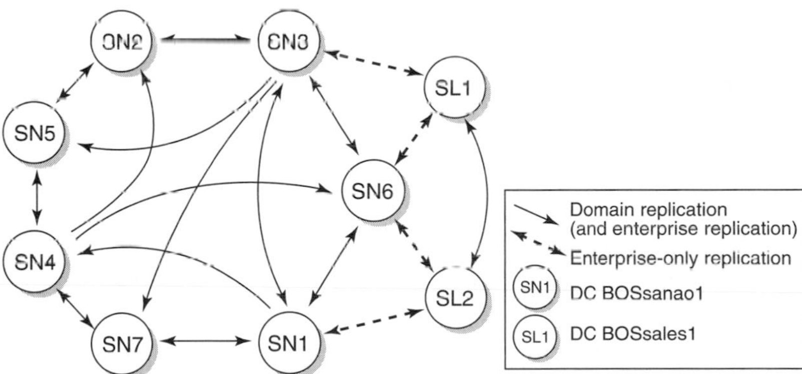

Figure 5.26 The seven domain controllers in `sanao.com` make up one ring, and the two in `sales.sanao.com` another. Together they build a nine-DC enterprise ring. In that ring BOSsanao6 is between BOSsales1 and BOSsales2 because of the GUID order of their NTDS Settings objects.

NOTE Starting with Figure 5.26 we simplified the diagrams. Because a domain connection always has an enterprise connection by its side, we show the latter connections only when they exist alone.

Global Catalog Replication

Each domain controller that is a global catalog server must host all the objects of all the domains in the enterprise. That domain controller has by nature the objects of its own domain. Although global catalog servers host all objects of the forest, they host only part of the properties (those that are part of the global catalog) of the objects in the other domains. A global catalog server must get the objects of other domains by global catalog replication. The corresponding replicas are called *partial replicas* and, obviously, only some of the properties need to be replicated to them. Figure 5.27 shows the replicas and replication of the global catalog in Sanao Corporation's forest. Figure 5.28 shows how global catalog replication fits in the replication topology.

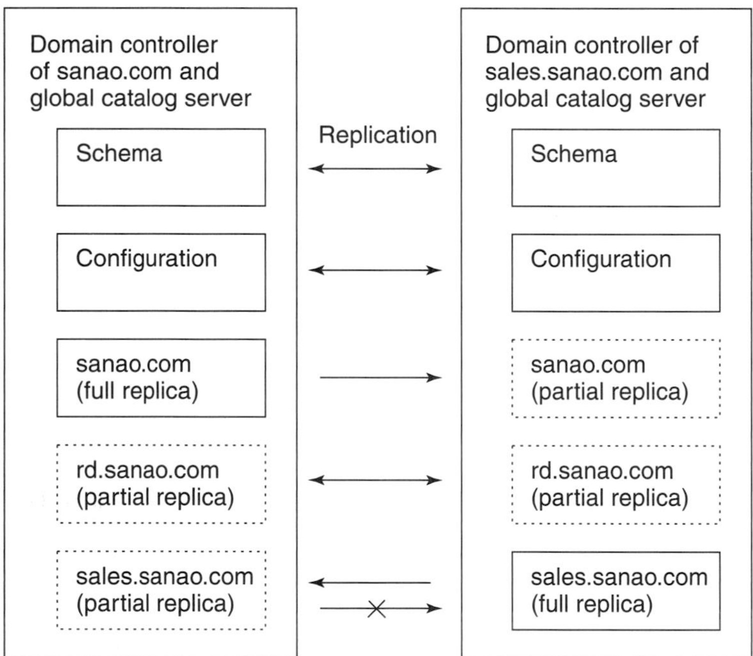

Figure 5.27 A normal (full) domain replica can be a source for the global catalog (partial replica) but not vice versa. Also, partial replicas (the ones in the global catalog) can be sources for each other.

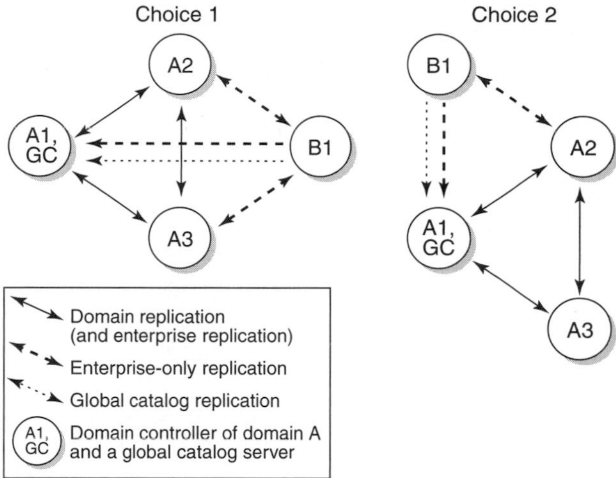

Figure 5.28 Global catalog replication takes place from B1 to A1, and in this case it is unidirectional. It must be this way because B1 is the sole domain controller in domain B and A1 is the only global catalog server in the enterprise forest. Whether the forest uses choice 1 or 2 depends on B1's location in the enterprise replication ring.

Global catalog replication from a full-domain replica is one-way, such as from B1 to A1 in Figure 5.28. Just as with domain replication, a global catalog replication partnership doesn't exist alone. It always has an enterprise replication partnership by its side.

Figure 5.29 shows the global catalog replication of Sanao Corporation's Boston site.

Intersite Replication Topologies

Now that we have described the intrasite topologies, we are ready to examine the intersite case. Intersite topologies are like intrasite topologies in that KCCs automatically create intersite topologies based on replication objects. The resulting topology, however, is a spanning tree instead of a ring. While in the intrasite case the replication objects are created automatically, in the intersite case administrators must plan what objects (excluding the connection objects) to have as well as create them manually. Also, it is more likely in the intersite case that administrators would create all or part of the topology (i.e., the connection objects) manually.

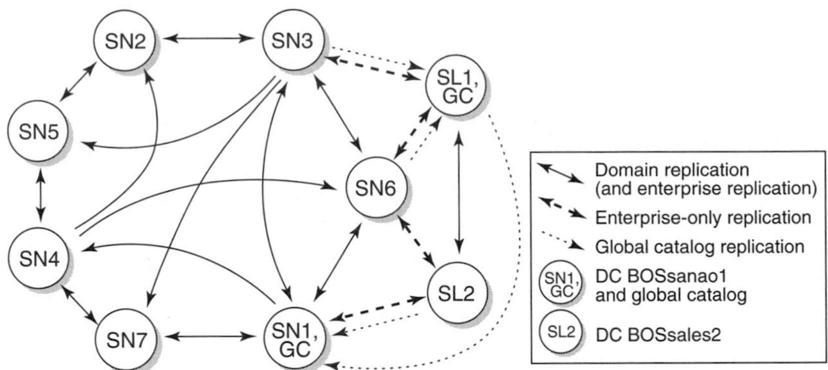

Figure 5.29 Sanao Corporation has two global catalog servers in Boston, which happen to be domain controllers in different domains. The two servers get their cross-domain data mainly via existing connections. Only the connection from BOSsales1 to BOSsanao1 is new, compared to the topology in Figure 5.26.

We start by explaining the "operator" that is responsible for creating the topology.

Inter-Site Topology Generator

The first domain controller on each site becomes the *inter-site topology generator (ISTG)* for that site. It means that the KCC in that machine is responsible for managing the incoming intersite connections for all domain controllers on its site.

When building an intrasite topology, it is possible that a number of independent KCCs are operating and still producing a single, agreed-upon topology (based on the GUID ordering). In an intersite topology, however, a single KCC must be responsible for the whole site; therefore, the ISTG is designated.

There is one ISTG on each site. If the original ISTG becomes unavailable, another domain controller automatically assumes that role. The change is easy because no data has to be transferred from the old ISTG to the new one.

The Sites and Services snap-in doesn't allow you to control which domain controller has the role, but you can see the current owner in the property page of the NTDS Site Settings object under each site object. You can change the ISTG role to another domain controller by modifying the `interSiteTopologyGenerator` property of the NTDS Site Settings object, using ADSI Edit, for example. However, there should be no need to change the role manually, unless you have such a large network that you want to change the role to a domain controller, which must have ample CPU power to perform the calculations needed to determine the optimal topology.

Site Links and the Topology

The automatic intersite topology generation has the following two phases:

1. You create appropriate site link objects and possibly specify some other settings (e.g., in the IP container object) to give Active Directory hints for the kind of topology it should create.
2. Based on the information from the previous phase, the ISTG on each site creates the incoming connection objects for the domain controllers on its site. These connection objects make up the intersite topology of the forest.

The two phases may overlap. After all, each KCC wakes up every 15 minutes to check if any changes to the topology are necessary.

Next we examine which routes Active Directory uses between sites in an intersite topology. Our samples require only one domain controller on each site and only one domain in the forest. Compare the two cases in Figure 5.30. In case A there is one site link among three sites, and in case B there are two site links.

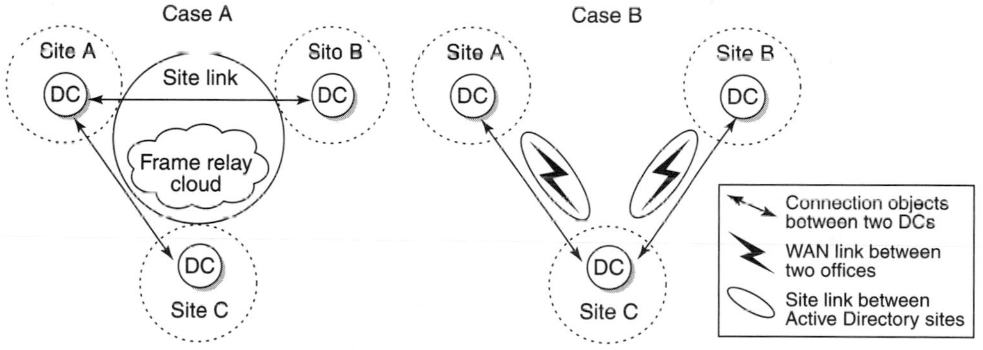

Figure 5.30 When Active Directory site links are created according to the physical network, they ensure that connections between domain controllers use the physical network efficiently.

NOTE Remember that site link objects represent connections between sites, and the resulting connection objects represent connections between domain controllers.

Case A's network has a cloudlike WAN. It doesn't matter whether domain controllers on sites A and B or on sites B and C communicate. Consequently, we create only one site link object to connect all three Active Directory sites and thus let the ISTGs freely decide which connections to create. Case B has a physical WAN link between offices A and C and another physical WAN link between offices B and C. To ensure that the connections between domain controllers match the physical WAN links, we must create the site links to match the WAN links.

NOTE Active Directory cannot sense the physical WAN topology. You must describe it using correct site links.

Figure 5.31 presents case C, where the site links are not optimal. Site links between sites A and B and between sites A and C cause corresponding connections between the domain controllers. In this case, if we create Jack Brown in the domain controller on site B, that object will be replicated first to the domain controller on site A. However, the network packets will travel through the router in office C. Finally, Jack Brown is replicated from site A to site C, meaning that the object travels again in the wire between offices A and C, although now in the opposite direction. Obviously, this setup is not efficient.

Figure 5.32 illustrates case D. Now there are two consecutive site links from site A to C to B. The difference between case C (in Figure 5.31)

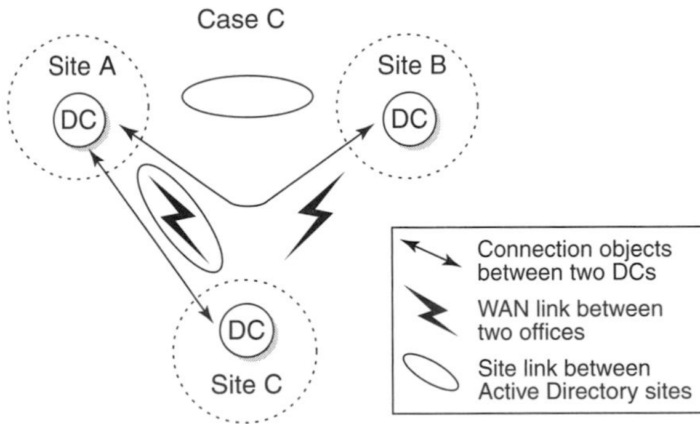

Figure 5.31 Poorly selected site links result in inefficient intersite replication.

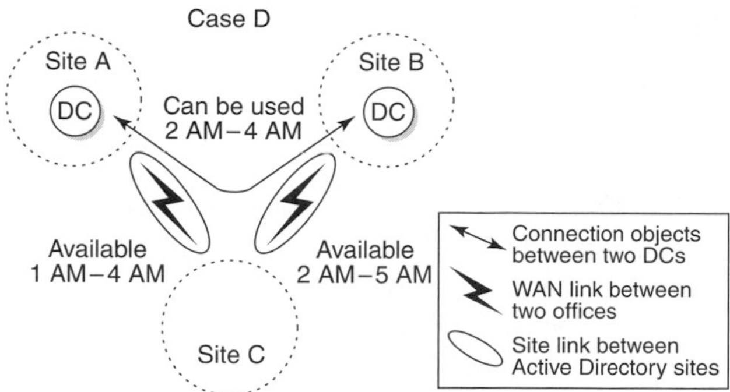

Figure 5.32 By default, all site links are bridged together, which allows two domain controllers to create a connection over several consecutive site links.

and case D (in Figure 5.32) is that in case D the domain doesn't have a domain controller on site C. Consequently, the domain controllers on sites A and B must communicate directly. This is possible because two things are true:

- The two consecutive site links are bridged. This is not shown in this figure, but as you saw earlier in this chapter, the IP container by default contains the setting "Bridge all site links." This is sometimes expressed with the words "by default site links are transitive." If you remove the default setting, you may need to create site link bridge objects, as discussed later in this chapter.
- The schedules of the two site links overlap so that there is a common time window between 2:00 AM and 4:00 AM every day.

If the two site links have different replication intervals, the longer one is used.

NOTE The cost of site links doesn't matter in cases A, B, C, and D. The cost is meaningful only if there are several alternative routes from which Active Directory can choose.

NOTE If the topology is somehow broken—for example, there is a site that is not connected to others with a site link—you would log event 1311, which you would see using the Event Viewer. Microsoft Knowledge Base article 307593 explains how you can use the `repadmin /showism` command to troubleshoot this.

Site Link Costs

If there are multiple routes between sites, the site link cost is used to determine which route to use. Lower cost is favored over higher cost, as Figure 5.33 illustrates. In this sample there are three site links, which means that there are two possible routes between any two sites in the sample network. The site link between sites B and C has the highest cost (700), so the other two links will be used.

Site link costs are cumulative. The ISTGs on each site build a minimum-cost spanning tree topology among sites. In a large network with many site links the possible accumulation plays a role when the ISTGs calculate the minimum cost tree.

Site link cost is between 1 and 99,999 (or 32,767 in AD2000). The number doesn't represent actual money; it is just a number that Active Directory compares with costs in other site links. Because it is relative to the costs of other site links, you can think of it as representing the priority of a site link. If a network has more than a couple of Active Directory site links, it is a good idea to establish a standard that specifies the cost to use for each kind of WAN link. You should consider at least the following criteria:

- *Link speed.* A link that transmits at 56Kbps or at 64Kbps (i.e., 64,000bps) could correspond to a cost of 32,000; a link that transmits at 128Kbps could correspond to a cost of 16,000; and so on. In this proportional model you would divide 2 billion by the link speed. Consequently, a link that transmits at 2Mbps would mean a cost of 1,000, and a T-3 speed (45Mbps) would mean a cost of about 50.

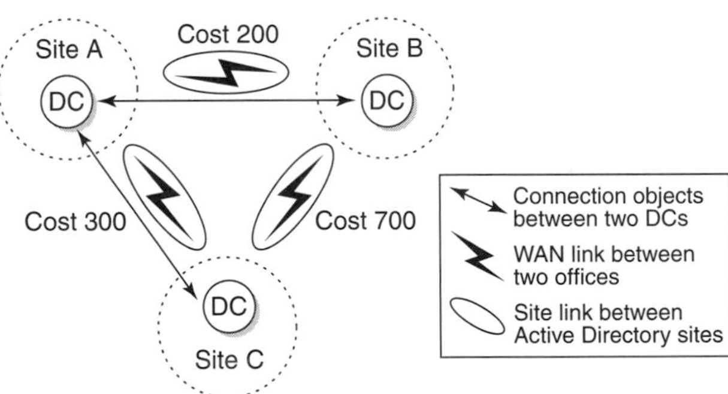

Figure 5.33 When multiple routes are available, the ISTGs choose the route with the lowest cost.

- *Type of link or network.* Instead of a mathematical approach to link speed, you could use simple categories, such as a cost of 100 for company backbone links, a cost of 500 for fast domestic leased lines, a cost of 1,000 for international leased lines, and a cost of 5,000 for dial-up lines.
- *Monetary cost.* If you have a link that transmits at 64Kbps on a leased line or at 64Kbps on an ISDN dial-up line, the latter should have a higher cost. You need to pay the phone company for each minute the ISDN line is open, so it would be wise to specify a lower cost (and consequently, a higher priority) for the leased line.

In addition to these items, link availability, reliability, and latency may affect the costs you choose.

NOTE The cost doesn't affect directly which route the replication packets take. The cost affects only which domain controllers will communicate. It is then up to the routers and other physical routing topology of the network to determine the actual route of the packets.

Cost is not meaningful if there are no domain controllers (of the same partition) between the two endpoint domain controllers. Consider Figure 5.34. When the two domain controllers on sites B and C replicate, they might use the WAN link B–C or the two WAN links B–A and A–C. You cannot specify the route with Active Directory, nor will you know which one was chosen.

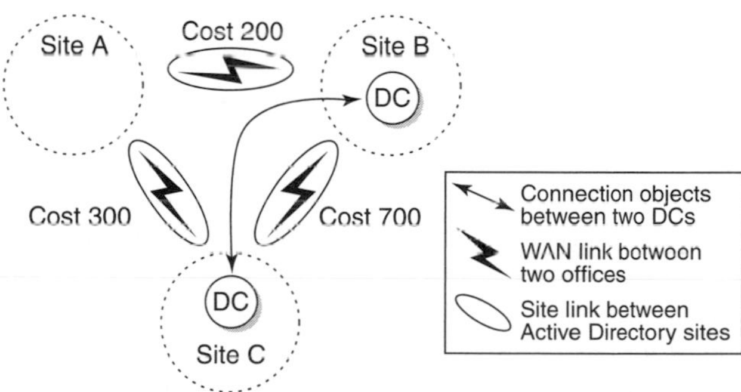

Figure 5.34 With Active Directory site links, you cannot specify which routes the network packets will take when there are no domain controllers between the endpoint domain controllers.

Intersite Topology of One Domain

Now that you know how the routes between sites are chosen, we are ready to add several domain controllers per site to give the full picture of the replication topology of one domain. We naturally want to replicate any change in Active Directory data only once from site to site. That is why only one domain controller at each end of the link is doing the intersite replication. These domain controllers are called *bridgehead servers*. As ISTGs create the intersite topology, they choose which domain controllers will be the bridgehead servers and create the appropriate connection objects for them. Figure 5.35 shows how one domain (`sanao.com`) replicates among three sites. To simplify the figure, we have fewer domain controllers on each site than in the examples of intrasite replication. Also to simplify, we assume that all domain controllers host the same application partitions.

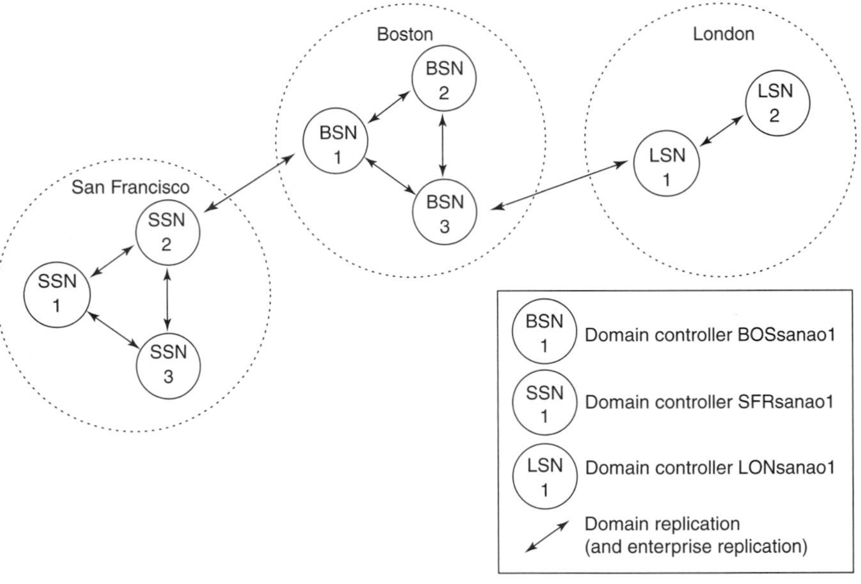

Figure 5.35 In this one-domain sample of `sanao.com`, for each pair of linked sites there is one domain controller at each end to replicate all changes in and out, to and from that site. As with intrasite replication, enterprise replication topology follows the topology of the only domain in the forest.

NOTE In AD2000, only one domain controller per site per partition was a bridgehead server. In Figure 5.35, this would mean that BOSsanao3 was the bridgehead server for both the San Francisco and London sites. In AD2003, however, BOSsanao1 is the bridgehead server for San Francisco, but BOSsanao3 is the bridgehead server for London.

Preferred Bridgehead Servers

Instead of letting the ISTG choose bridgehead servers, you can designate the domain controller you want to be the *preferred bridgehead server*. The ISTG will use this domain controller as the bridgehead as long as it is up and running.

You can also designate more than one domain controller per site to be preferred bridgehead servers. If all the (or the only) preferred bridgehead servers fail, intersite replication is no longer possible.

You should designate one or multiple preferred bridgehead servers if you know that they are better suited for intersite replication than just any domain controller that the ISTG happens to choose. Two typical scenarios are the following.

- If you have a large environment with many changes to replicate, the domain controllers you designated as preferred could have the processing power to do the compression used in intersite replication.
- If your site has a firewall and only one domain controller can pass the firewall to the outside world, you obviously need to designate this domain controller to be the preferred bridgehead server.

In addition, Microsoft recommends that a PDC master not be a bridgehead server, and you can ensure this by designating other domain controllers(s) to be bridgehead server(s). You do the designation per protocol, as Figure 5.36 shows.

NOTE If you designate any preferred bridgeheads for the site, the ISTG cannot choose freely anymore. Make sure that your preferred bridgehead server list contains such domain controllers that all partitions are covered, including any application partitions. The exception is partitions that have replicas only on the local site, because obviously there is no need to replicate them.

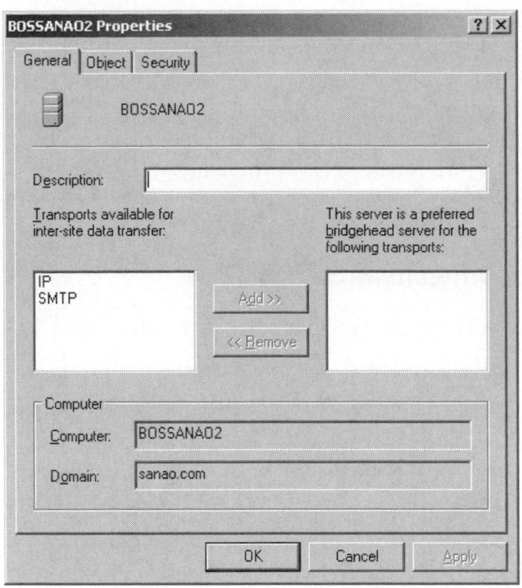

Figure 5.36 Server object properties enable you to assign that domain controller as a preferred bridgehead server on either RPC over IP (shown as "IP") or SMTP protocols, or both.

Managing Bridgehead Server Failures

If an automatically selected bridgehead server fails, the ISTG will create a fail-over connection automatically. It will do this after at least two hours after the first replication failure and after at least two consecutive failures. If the ISTG cannot find a new appropriate domain controller for the connection object (one that has the correct partition and that is on the correct site), it will log an event, which you can see using the Event Viewer. Obviously, in this case the intersite replication of the partition or partitions that the failed bridgehead server handled is not possible until the problem has been resolved.

The ISTG responds the same way when you have more than one preferred bridgehead server and one of them fails. If the last preferred bridgehead server fails, the ISTG cannot create a replacing connection. It is up to you to fix the problem by taking one of the following steps.

- For the site in question, add a new preferred bridgehead server that is capable of replicating the partition(s) that lost their bridgehead. If that includes a domain partition, you must select a domain controller of that domain.

- Remove all preferred bridgehead designations from the site in question. This way, the ISTG can pick a bridgehead server. Of course, if only the failed domain controller would be able to pass the firewall, this option wouldn't fix replication.

Once you have performed one of the operations on some domain controller on the site that has lost one of its bridgehead servers, the change will replicate to all domain controllers on that site. Consequently, the ISTG will know about the fix and it will create a new connection object. However, that connection object is only for incoming replication, which means that the other affected sites won't learn about the change you made. Therefore, you need to perform the same fix (add or remove preferred bridgehead servers) on some domain controller on other sites as well (all or some or no other sites, as the Note describes).

NOTE The change you made is part of the configuration partition, which is part of the enterprise replication. Depending on your domain and site configuration, the change may replicate to other sites using other bridgehead servers that are still functional.

Intersite Topologies of Several Partitions

As with the intrasite replication of several partitions, each intersite partition has an independent replication topology. Different domains have totally separate replication topologies, and the enterprise replication topology follows the domain topologies whenever possible. When there is no domain connection to use (i.e., no intradomain or no global catalog connection), the enterprise replication topology will have a connection created just for it. This means that bridgehead servers must be established per partition also. That is, each domain in a given site that needs to replicate from (and to) other sites will have its own bridgehead server. Figure 5.37 shows the intersite replication topologies for two domains. To make room in the figure, we do not include the domain controller names. Figure 5.38 shows the intersite topologies with enterprise replication.

NOTE Even though both Boston and San Francisco have three domain controllers for `sanao.com` and two for `sales.sanao.com`, the two sites have different enterprise replication rings. This is because the GUID order happens to result in two different rings.

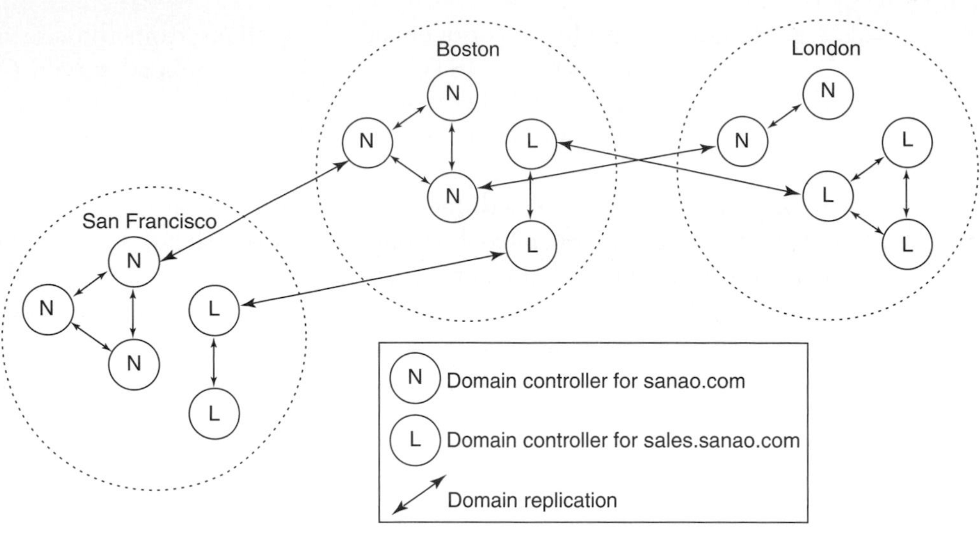

Figure 5.37 Different domains have totally different replication topologies. They also have their own bridgehead servers.

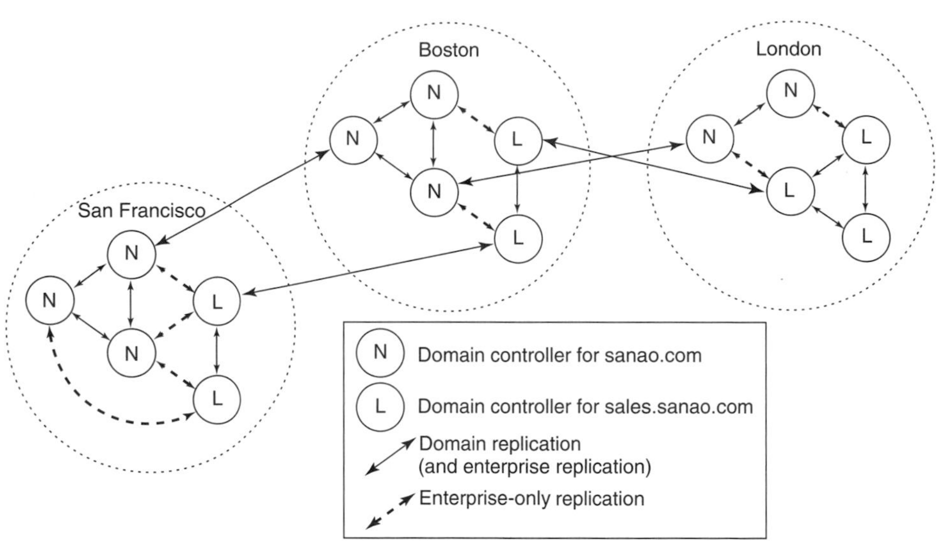

Figure 5.38 The enterprise replication topology consists of one ring in each site and the intersite connections. There are no enterprise-only connections between sites, however, because there already are enough domain connections, including enterprise replication.

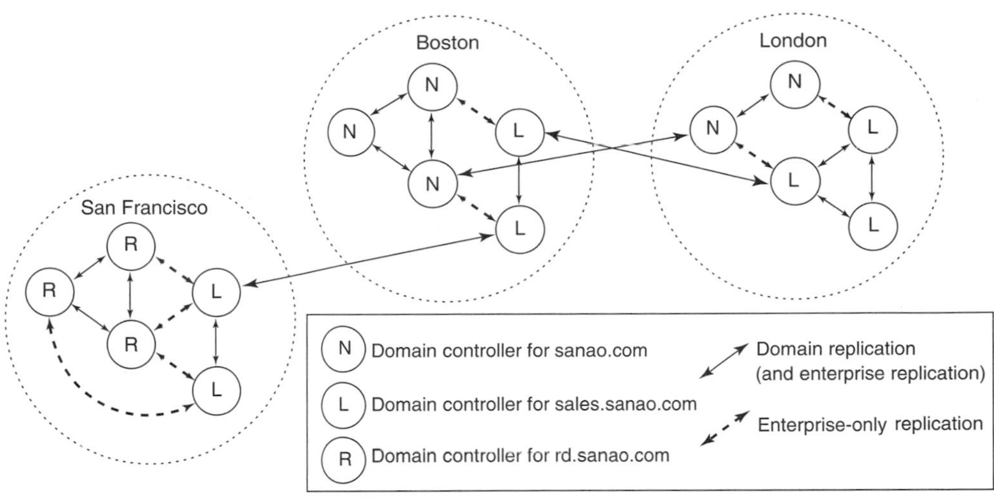

Figure 5.39 Because `rd.sanao.com` has domain controllers only in San Francisco, it doesn't replicate to other sites. The only domain link to San Francisco is of `sales.sanao.com`, so that connection will be used for enterprise replication to and from that site.

In the previous example, both domains had controllers in all three sites. If we transform the three `sanao.com` domain controllers in San Francisco to a new domain, `rd.sanao.com`, it will naturally have some implication on the topologies. The effect is shown in Figure 5.39.

Intersite Global Catalog Replication

The last aspect of intersite replication to describe is the global catalog replication. Figure 5.40 and Figure 5.41 show our sample topology with the global catalog replication.

In our first case (Figure 5.37 and Figure 5.38) there were two domains, and both had domain controllers in all three sites. This means that all domain information was present in all sites. Consequently, it is easy to have a global catalog server on each site, because all global catalog replication can take place locally. Figure 5.40 illustrates this case with global catalog replication added.

NOTE One enterprise replication arrow in San Francisco is one-way. The other direction is included in the global catalog replication arrow. Remember that all arrows are actually one-way. We are just using one two-way arrow instead of two one-way arrows to simplify the figure.

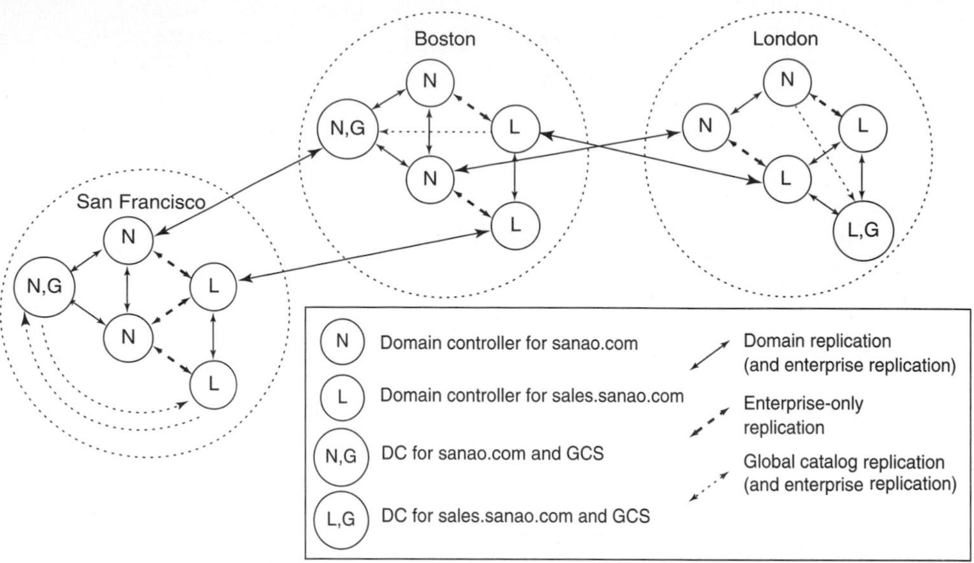

Figure 5.40 Because both domains (`sanao.com` and `sales.sanao.com`) have controllers in all three domains, global catalog replication doesn't increase traffic in any WAN links. In this scenario, that replication is always local to a site.

Our other enterprise case in Figure 5.39 introduced the domain `rd.sanao.com` in San Francisco. In that scenario the domains were not present on all sites, and therefore, part of global catalog replication takes place intersite. This is illustrated in Figure 5.41.

NOTE It is purely coincidental that there is one global catalog server in each domain in Figure 5.41.

The basic rule for global catalog servers is to have at least one in each site. In a large environment, however, you might decide not to comply with this basic convention because the global catalog servers might generate more traffic on the WAN links than they can take. After all, AD2003 includes universal group membership caching, which means that global catalog servers are not permanently needed for logons. For more information on this feature, see Chapter 6.

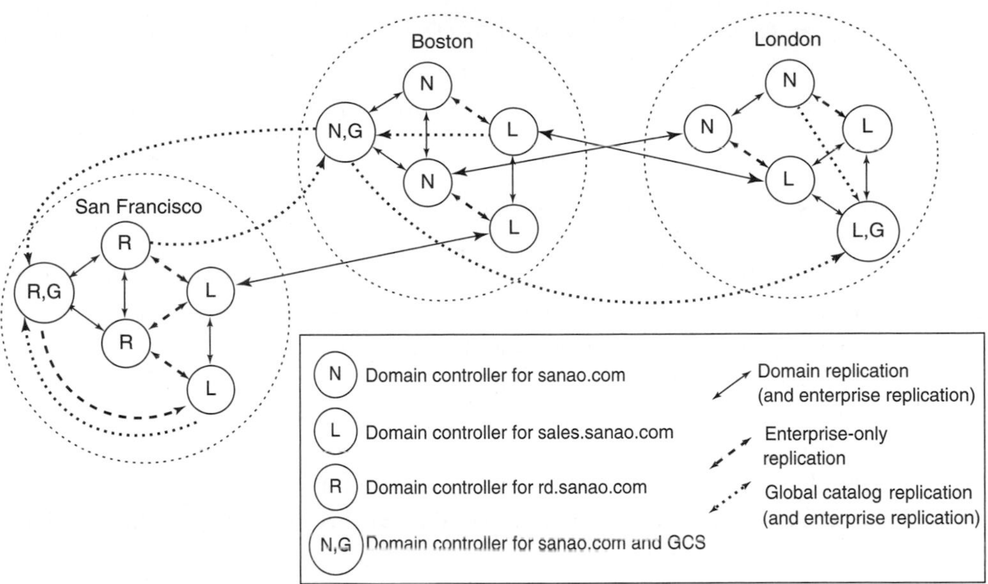

Figure 5.41 Each global catalog server needs to get the partial replica of two other domains. This often comes from another site, thus increasing WAN traffic. Because the partial replica of `rd.sanao.com` is in the Boston global catalog server, it can be the source of this information for the London global catalog server. This connection is one-way, because the Boston global catalog server can read `sales.sanao.com` intrasite.

Creating and Managing Site Link Bridges

Remember that a site link is an object that symbolizes a physical link between two or more sites. A *site link bridge* object symbolizes two or more site links together that use the same protocol (RPC over IP or SMTP).

NOTE We explained earlier that there are bridgehead servers at the ends (or edges) of site links. However, don't confuse them with site link bridges.

Site links (including their cost) and site link bridges both give the ISTGs hints about how to create connection objects when building an intersite replication topology. You have three ways to create your intersite topology:

- *Create site links* and let the ISTGs manage the connection objects based on them (as discussed so far).
- *Create site link bridges* (in addition to creating site links) to give additional hints to the ISTGs about which connection objects to create.
- *Create connection objects* manually.

The first choice in the list is by far the most common. Site link bridges are necessary only in some complex scenarios. Also, you don't usually need to create connection objects manually.

We mentioned earlier that there is a "Bridge all site links" check box in the properties of the IP and SMTP container objects. By default, that setting is on for both protocols, so all the site links in your forest are bridged together (i.e., they are transitive) for a given protocol. You don't see a site link bridge object to symbolize this; there is just the check box setting.

Instead of one large automatic site link bridge, you could create several smaller ones. This happens as follows:

1. Turn off site link transitiveness by clearing the aforementioned check box.
2. Create the appropriate site link bridge objects manually in the IP or SMTP containers.

NOTE Even if you turn off automatic bridging, you might need only a few, if any, site link bridge objects.

NOTE If you turn off automatic bridging and don't create the necessary site link bridges, an ISTG could no longer include some domain controllers in the replication topology. Consequently, it would log event 1311, which you would see using the Event Viewer. Microsoft Knowledge Base article 307593 explains how you can use the `repadmin /showism` command to troubleshoot this.

Any network described by site links and site link bridges can also be described by site links alone, as Figure 5.42 illustrates. The figure assumes that automatic bridging of all site links is off. The goal is to get the domain controllers on sites A and B to communicate.

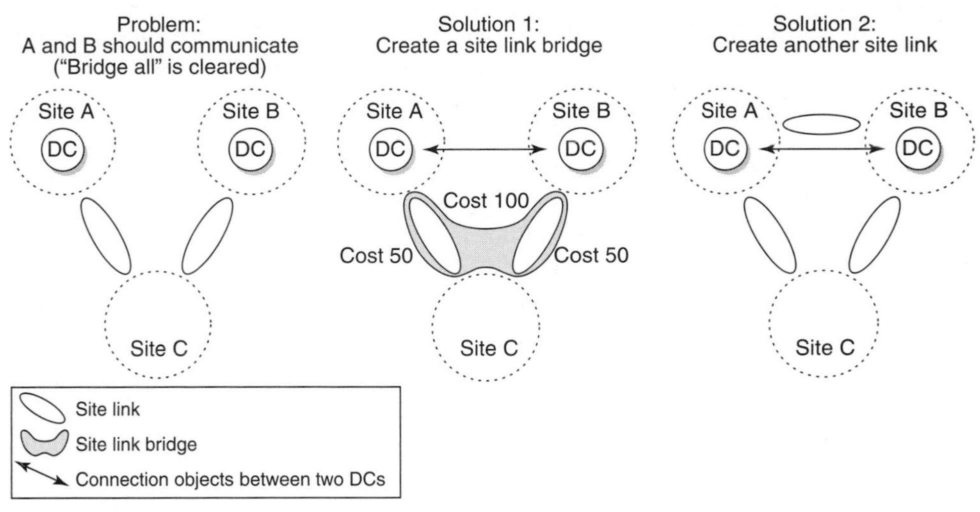

Figure 5.42 A site link bridge "chains" two or more site links so that two domain controllers can communicate over this chain. However, the same result can be achieved by creating a new site link. The cost of a site link bridge is the sum of the site link costs.

Solution 1 is to create a site link bridge. It joins the two site links into one, using as the cost the cumulative cost of the two site links. Each site link in a bridge must have a common site with another site link in that bridge.

Solution 2 is to simply create a third site link. This makes sites A and B adjacent, so no bridging (i.e., transitiveness) is necessary. Microsoft has more than 100 site links in their corporate Active Directory network and they don't need any site link bridges.

NOTE As the number of site links increases, solution 2 may become more complicated. Depending on the topology and placement of domain controllers, you might need to create many site links to replace one site link bridge and consequently you would have to manage the cost and schedule of each site link separately.

We haven't still answered the ultimate question: Automatic bridging of all site links is the easiest choice, so why turn it off? The answer is that in a large network there would be so many permutations in possible routes (including the cumulative costs) that it might take too much CPU power on the ISTG to calculate the optimal topology.

"Too much" is a highly relative expression. Microsoft says in Knowledge Base article Q244368 (which applies to Windows 2000) that you can "Bridge all site links" as long as the following is true:

```
(1 + number of domains) * number of sites^2 <= 100,000
```

According to this formula, if you have just one domain, the limit would be about 220 sites; with two domains, it would be about 180 sites. Because of the aforementioned relativity, this formula is more like a rule of thumb. Server speed and network topology will affect the exact results. Also, if the ISTG calculates the topology every 15 minutes, there is no exact number of seconds or minutes it would be allowed to spend.

The algorithms that calculate the topology are much more efficient in Windows Server 2003. While the limit in Windows 2000 was about 200 sites, in Windows Server 2003 it is at least 3,000 sites. Microsoft's current thinking, as of this writing, is that the new algorithm scales up to 5,000 sites. Therefore, with the new environment, you are not likely to need manual site link bridges.

If you have a large network, performing the following steps will show you how much time the calculation takes:

1. Find out the current ISTG of a site by looking it up in the NTDS Site Settings object.
2. Select Check Replication Topology on the NTDS Settings object of the ISTG and time the result. Another way is to use the Performance snap-in (in Administrative Tools) to draw a graph of the ISTG's CPU usage and see if the CPU is fully utilized for 3 minutes, for example, recurring every 15 minutes. This would (most likely) indicate that it takes 3 minutes for the ISTG to perform its calculations. Yet a third way is to modify the ISTG's registry. In the key `HKEY_LOCAL_MACHINE`, `System`, `CurrentControlSet`, `Services`, `NTDS`, `Diagnostics` change the value `1 Knowledge Consistency Checker` to 3 or greater. This causes the KCC to log events 1009 and 1013 in the Directory Service event log, to indicate the start and end of each calculation period.

If the ISTG would take too much CPU even after automatic bridging was disabled, Knowledge Base article Q244368 presents a script that triggers the topology generation process. You can schedule the script to run during off-peak hours to avoid overloading the ISTG domain controller during business hours.

A typical scenario for a large network is a hub-spoke topology with headquarters and 500 branch offices. All replication takes place between headquarters and some branch office, so there is no need to calculate routes and costs from one branch office to another. Disabling automatic bridging would greatly save the CPU on ISTGs. Also, in this case you would probably not need manual site link bridges either.

Creating and Managing Connection Objects

As you know, the KCCs create and manage connection objects automatically, and this normally produces the best results. If you aren't happy with the resulting topology, the solution is not to create connection objects manually, but to modify the background information, such as site links or site link properties. You can also check that there are no errors in network connectivity, including DNS services. Nevertheless, the following are reasons to create connection objects manually.

- You would have so many (thousands) sites and site links that even without automatic site link bridging, it would take the ISTGs too long to calculate the topology. In this case, you would probably create the connection objects programmatically using an ADSI script. You can get such scripts, as well as detailed planning and deployment information, from the Branch Office Guide at `http://www.microsoft.com/` (use the Search feature to locate the correct pages). There is a Windows 2000 version of the guide, and by the time you read this, there should be also a Windows Server 2003 version.
- Later in this chapter we explain that each operations master should have a standby domain controller ready to take over the role in case of a failure. There should be a direct replication connection from the operations master to the standby, which you can ensure by creating the connection object manually.
- Sometimes you might want fewer than three hops between two servers on a site with many domain controllers.
- You might want to replicate temporarily from a certain server to another. You could create a connection object, initiate replication, and then delete the connection object.

NOTE Site links and site link settings (such as cost and schedule) don't affect manually created connection objects. You assign all the properties (most important, the schedule) yourself.

You start creating a connection object by locating the NTDS Settings object of the receiving end's domain controller. When you right-click the latter object, you can select New Active Directory Connection from the context menu. Next you choose the source domain controller in a dialog box, as shown in Figure 5.43.

When you click OK, the next screen appears, and you can type a name for the object, which is probably the same as the source domain controller name (in this example, SFRsales1). We don't show that screen, because it contains only the text field for the name.

The properties and schedule dialog boxes for a connection object are shown in Figure 5.44 and Figure 5.45, respectively. The other property you can set besides the schedule is the transport to be used. Table 5.14 lists the transport choices.

The two lowermost text fields in Figure 5.44 indicate which partitions (or naming contexts) are replicated fully or partially, respectively,

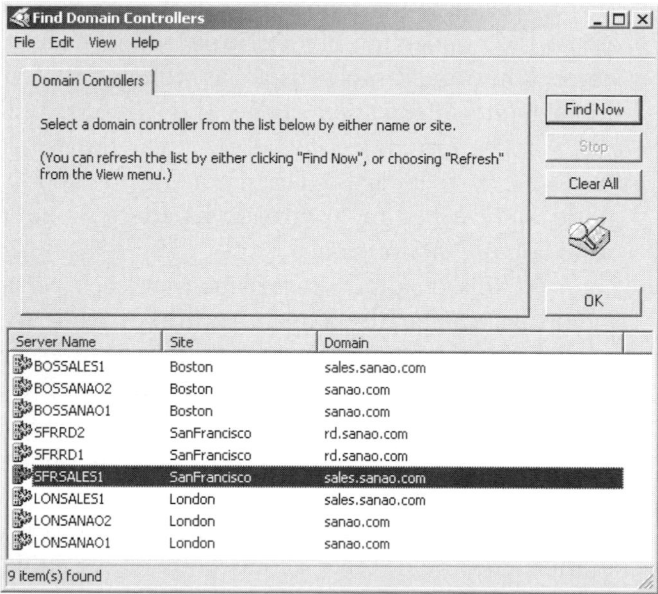

Figure 5.43 When you create a connection object manually, you choose the source domain controller from a list.

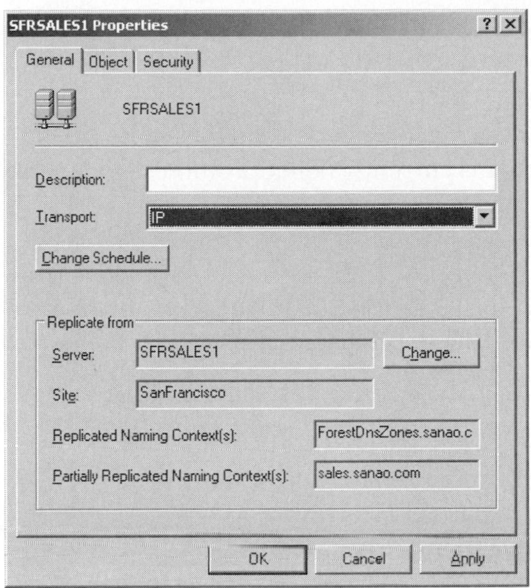

Figure 5.44 When you create an intersite connection object, the RPC protocol is called IP. The other protocol option is SMTP. The two lowermost fields tell you which partitions are replicated fully or partially, respectively, over this connection.

over the corresponding connection. The upper of these text fields may contain any of the following entries:

- ForestDnsZones
- DomainDnsZones
- The domain controller's own domain (if the source and destination domain controllers are in the same domain)
- Any application partition that exists on both the source and the destination domain controller

In addition to the four listed items, the configuration and schema partitions are always replicated. If none of the four listed items apply, the upper text field shows just "<Enterprise Configuration only>" to indicate the replication of the configuration and schema partitions.

The lowermost text field in Figure 5.44 (partial replication) indicates global catalog replication. It may contain the following text:

- "All other domains," if the source and destination domain controllers both are global catalog servers

- The name of the source domain, if the destination domain controller is a global catalog server, but the source domain controller is not
- The names of several domains (but not all), if the global catalog server is currently being promoted or demoted
- Empty

NOTE If you choose the SMTP transport, there are some special considerations, which are discussed a little later in the "Configuring SMTP Replication" section.

Table 5.14 Transport Protocols for Replication

Display Name	Protocol	Can Be Used
RPC	RPC over IP (same as next)	Intrasite, for any data
IP	RPC over IP (same as previous)	Intersite, for any data
SMTP	SMTP over IP	Intersite, for schema and configuration partitions, application partitions, and the global catalog; not for domain data

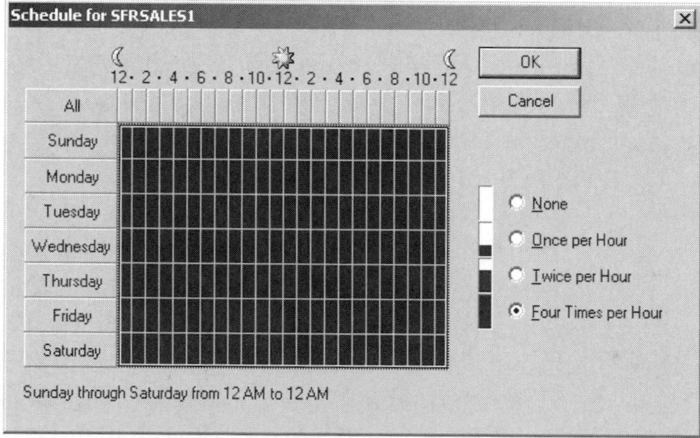

Figure 5.45 Manually created connection objects don't use the interval/availability settings pair. Instead, you define the schedule directly with the weekly grid.

If the need arises, you can change the source for a connection object in its properties dialog box. You should also rename the object to match the new source domain controller.

If you delete a manually created connection object, you can either create something else for a replacement or let the KCCs determine whether some new connections are needed.

Windows Server 2003 Resource Kit includes an Active Directory Load Balancing (ADLB) command-line tool that helps in distributing the bridgehead server load when many branch offices replicate from a central hub site. ADLB both distributes connection objects among hub domain controllers and staggers the replication schedule to make it occur at different times to different branch sites. For more information on ADLB, see the Branch Office Guide from Microsoft.

Reciprocal Replication

If your replication takes place over a dial-up link, you can make use of *reciprocal replication.* When the link is open, you can replicate changes in both directions during one call, which will help you save money on your phone bills. Also, it is possible that the branch office can call the headquarters, but not vice versa. In this case, you must use reciprocal replication. The order of events is the following:

1. The branch office dials up to the headquarters.
2. The branch office bridgehead server requests and receives any changes in the headquarters bridgehead server.
3. The branch office bridgehead server sends a change notification to the headquarters bridgehead server.
4. The headquarters bridgehead server requests and receives any changes in the branch office bridgehead server.

You would define reciprocal replication by modifying the `options` property of the corresponding site link object (or alternatively, of the manually created connection object). The easiest tool for this is ADSI Edit. First, locate the correct site link object in the configuration partition. Then open the properties of that site link and select to view the `options` property.

Reciprocal replication is defined in the second bit from the right. If the `options` property has no existing value, you can just set it to a decimal value of 2. If there is already a value (most likely to be 1), you must add 2 to that existing value and set the result as the new value of the property.

NOTE Adding the two values together is, in this case, equivalent to doing a "bitwise OR" operation on them. If the reciprocal replication bit was already on, the "bitwise OR" operation produces the correct result, but adding 2 does not. In the latter case, you obviously would not change the value at all.

NOTE You must modify the property on a headquarters domain controller. If you modified it on a branch office domain controller, the change would never replicate to the headquarters if the headquarters could not dial up to the branch office.

Using Change Notifications in Intersite Replication

As mentioned earlier, change notification is used by default in intrasite replication, but you can enable it also for intersite replication. You might do this in the following cases.

- You want urgent replication to take place also intersite.
- You have a high-speed WAN and you want to achieve the same low-latency replication as what you have intrasite.

The initial notification delay was changed from 5 minutes to 15 seconds in Windows Server 2003. Depending on your WAN, this new value may be too fast, so you might want to adjust the delay to be somewhat longer, as explained in the "Change Notification Delay" section earlier in this chapter. The same delay is used for intrasite replication and for intersite replication where change notifications are enabled. Therefore, you must find a value that is fast enough for intrasite and long enough for intersite.

To define change notifications on a site link, modify the same `options` property that we just described with reciprocal replication. The difference is that you set the first bit from the right instead of the second. A value of 1 means "use change notifications," a value of 2 means "use reciprocal," and a value of 3 means "use both."

The two settings end up in the `options` property of the automatically generated connection objects. In those objects the second bit from the right means "use reciprocal," and the third bit from the right means "use change notifications." You could also use these bits manually if you create connection objects manually.

NOTE If there are several bridged site links in a chain between two domain controllers, all of their `options` properties are "anded" together. In other words, if even one of the site links in the chain doesn't have either bit set, the corresponding setting is not used.

Table 5.15 lists the two bits of site links, and Table 5.16 the three bits of connection objects.

Site Options

In addition to site link objects and connection objects, a third replication object, NTDS Site Settings, may contain the `options` property. Table 5.17 describes the five bits that you can use to control connection object creation on the corresponding site, and a sixth one to enable universal group membership caching.

Table 5.15 Options Property Bits of Site Links

Bit from Right	Hex Value	Description
1	1	Setting this bit causes change notifications to be used.
2	2	Setting this bit causes reciprocal replication to be used.

Table 5.16 Options Property Bits of Connection Objects

Bit from Right	Hex Value	Description
1	1	A value of 1 means that the connection object is maintained automatically by the KCC. A value of 0 means that an administrator manually maintains the object.
2	2	Setting this bit causes reciprocal replication to be used.
3	4	Setting this bit causes change notifications to be used.

Table 5.17 Options Property Bits of NTDS Site Settings

Bit from Right	Hex Value	Description
1	1	Setting this bit disables the automatic intrasite topology generation by the KCCs.
2	2	Setting this bit disables the cleanup of outdated replication connections.
3	4	Setting this bit disables the automatic generation of shortcut connections in the site's replication ring. Consequently, the three-hop maximum is not maintained.
4	8	Setting this bit disables the detection of failed replication links and the generation of temporary bypass connections.
5	10	Setting this bit disables the automatic intersite topology generation by the ISTG.
6	20	Setting this bit enables universal group membership caching.
7	40	Setting this bit forces the KCCs to operate in Windows Server 2003 behavior mode.
8	80	Setting this bit forces the KCCs to use the Windows 2000 ISTG election algorithm.
9	100	Setting this bit prevents the KCCs from randomly picking a bridgehead server at connection-creation time.
10	200	Setting this bit allows the KCCs to use replication schedule hashing, which causes the replication to occur at different times with different partner sites.
11	400	Setting this bit enables creation of static fail-over connections, which leads to redundant topology.

Configuring SMTP Replication

As mentioned previously, you can use Simple Mail Transfer Protocol (SMTP) to replicate the schema and configuration partitions and application partitions, as well as to replicate global catalog information among domain controllers in different domains. But you cannot use it to replicate normal domain partitions among domain controllers in one domain. SMTP can only be used for intersite replication.

The reason for the limitation with SMTP replication is that intra-domain replication must be somewhat synchronized with the File Replication Service (FRS), because the latter is used to replicate group policies. While SMTP replication is asynchronous, FRS doesn't yet support asynchronous replication.

SMTP replication encrypts the replicated data. Therefore, for it to work, you need to set up Certificate Services (included in Windows 2000 and later) as well as install and configure an enterprise *certificate authority (CA)*.

Just as with RPC over IP replication, you can create SMTP site links (and perhaps site link bridges) and let the ISTGs create the appropriate connection objects. Or you can create the SMTP connection objects manually.

To route replication requests and responses between domain controllers, the SMTP replication uses two services that are included in Windows 2000 and later: the Intersite Messaging (ISM) service and the SMTP service. The latter service is shown as an IIS component. SMTP replication ignores the availability schedules of site links and uses only the interval settings (i.e., the "Replicate every" fields).

Reasons to use SMTP replication are as follows.

- You have sites where there is no direct connection from any other site.
- Your replication traffic goes over the public Internet, so you can make use of encryption by using the SMTP choice. However, you can also get encryption by using IPsec with normal RPC over IP replication.
- You have unreliable WAN links. If the network is reliable, you can use RPC even though the network would be slow.

If you need to replicate domain partitions to some site, you must always use RPC. Once you use RPC for this, you should use RPC also for enterprise and global catalog replication.

Microsoft's Web site (`http://www.microsoft.com/`) contains a document called "Step-by-Step Guide to Setting up ISM-SMTP Replication." If you point your Web browser to the Microsoft site and perform a search using the document's title, you'll be able to access procedural information on setting up SMTP replication (and Certificate Services) on Windows 2000. By the time you read this, there will probably be a corresponding document for Windows Server 2003.

The Replication Process

Now that you have learned how replication topologies are built, it's time to examine how the data flows along the paths in the topology.

To be efficient, the Active Directory replication process must have the functions listed in Table 5.18.

NOTE For this replication process section, it doesn't make any difference whether the replication is intrasite or intersite.

Table 5.18 Functions of the Active Directory Replication Process

Function	Mechanisms
Because Active Directory replicates individual changed properties and those changes may initiate in any domain controller, there must be a way to identify new and changed objects and properties in each domain controller.	Update sequence numbers
Each domain controller replicates the changes from one or more replication partners. They need to know what new changes the partner has in order to be able to retrieve them.	High-watermark vectors
There may be multiple paths in the replication topology from one domain controller to another. *Propagation dampening* prevents a change from replicating endlessly or replicating several times to the same domain controller.	Up-to-date vectors
When changed properties are replicated, the receiving domain controller must determine for each property whether it should keep the property value just received or the property value already in the local database. Also, in a multimaster replication system it is possible that someone changes a property in some domain controller, and before the change has replicated to some other domain controller, someone changes the same property there. This leads to a *collision* (or conflict), which must be resolved.	Version numbers and timestamps
When an object is deleted, the deletion must be replicated to other domain controllers.	Tombstones

Background

Before we address the five mechanisms in Table 5.18, we need to lay some foundation. We can divide the replication process into the following four steps:

1. A user or an application makes a change to an object or property in a domain controller (domain controller A). This is called an *originating update* and it is stored in the directory database of domain controller A.
2. Domain controller A sends a notification about the change to its outbound replication partner(s) (including domain controller B). This step is skipped in the schedule-based intersite replication.
3. Domain controller B sends a request for updates to domain controller A.
4. Domain controller B receives the change, which is called a *replicated update* (in contrast to an *originating update*), and stores it in its directory database. A replicated update can also correspond to a number of originating updates that originate even from different domain controllers.

Because Active Directory replication is transitive, after domain controller B has stored the change, it may replicate it to domain controller C, which may replicate it to domain controller D, and so on.

There can be four types of originating updates:

- Creating an object
- Deleting an object
- Moving or renaming an object
- Adding some properties to an object, or changing or deleting the properties of an object

Domain controllers and their databases are identified in the replication operations with two GUIDs:

- *Server GUID.* This GUID identifies a domain controller and it is the `objectGUID` property of the NTDS Settings object under the corresponding server object. This is the same GUID that is used to set the order of domain controllers in a replication ring.
- *Database GUID.* This GUID identifies the directory database of a domain controller. It is the `invocationId` property of the

NTDS Settings object. The database GUID is originally the same as the server GUID, but when you do a directory database restore, the database GUID changes. This way, you can differentiate an after-restore database from the original database.

Active Directory treats updates to the database as transactions. The entire update operation is either committed as a whole to the database, or it is rejected. This prevents corruption of the database.

Update Sequence Numbers

Each domain controller has an independent 64-bit counter called the *update sequence number (USN).* Whenever a transaction for either an originating update or a replicated update is committed (not aborted) to the database of a domain controller, the domain controller increments its USN by one and stores the new value with the committed change.

Storing the current USN with each change yields an order of the changes—an implied relative "timestamp" that lets other domain controllers request changes that were made after a certain "time." Having USNs in the domain controllers relieves them and you from maintaining an exact time for all your domain controllers. You don't lose or duplicate changes even if the times of two domain controllers disagree by a significant amount.

If the replication was interrupted or a domain controller was down for a while, with the help of USNs it will know where it stopped, and replication can continue from that point.

If the USNs run out, you need to reinstall your forest. However, with 64 bits you can do 100 changes per second, and still your USNs would last for more than 5 billion years. Microsoft has promised an upgrade that solves this forest-reinstallation problem before then.

Each Active Directory object has six USN properties, two of which are used in this context.

- `uSNCreated` contains the current USN from the time of the object creation. Applications can use `uSNCreated` to request any new objects, but this property is not used by replication.
- `uSNChanged` contains the current USN from the time of the latest change to the object (excluding changes to nonreplicating properties). This value is the same as the largest local USN of the object's properties (discussed shortly). We can use `uSNChanged` to request new changes to any object.

Both these attributes are indexed in the database for fast access and comparison. They are also in the global catalog.

In addition to the two per-object USNs, Active Directory stores two USNs for each property, as well as three other pieces of identifying information:

- *Originating USN.* This is the USN that was stored with the property at the time of the originating update on the originating domain controller.
- *Local USN.* This number is based on the current USN of the local domain controller. Local and originating USNs are the same in the database of the originating domain controller.
- *Version number.* This is a 32-bit number that starts at 1 and is incremented by 1 with each originating update to the property, but not with a replicated update. Unlike a USN, the version number is not domain controller–specific; it follows its property wherever it will be replicated. The version number indicates the number of times a property is changed during its lifetime. However, if you change the property simultaneously on two domain controllers, one of those changes is eventually left out of the count (and also, because of a collision, the corresponding change is lost).
- *Timestamp.* This is a 64-bit time value in GMT/UTC (Greenwich Mean Time/Coordinated Universal Time) for each property change.
- *Originating domain controller.* This is the database GUID of the domain controller where the update was originated.

The local USN never leaves the local domain controller. The other four values together form a *stamp* that follows the property value when it is replicated to other domain controllers. These values can be used when resolving conflicts, as explained a little later.

Replication Metadata

The originating USN, local USN, version number, timestamp, and originating domain controller values are called *replication metadata* and they are stored in binary format in the `replPropertyMetaData` property of each object. If you add their sizes plus 4 bytes to identify the property they relate to, you will notice that they create a 48-byte overhead on disk for each property.

To see the values for a given object, you can use a command such as the following:

```
repadmin /showmeta "ou=sales,dc=sanao,dc=com"
```

This produces output such as the following:

```
8 entries.
Loc.USN Originating DC   Org.USN  Org.Time/Date       Ver Attribute
======= =============== ========= =============       === =========
  20489     Boston\DC11     20489 2003-10-28 13:35:35   1 objectClass
  20489     Boston\DC11     20489 2003-10-28 13:35:35   1 ou
  57494     Boston\DC11     57494 2004-01-29 15:24:15   1 description
  20489     Boston\DC11     20489 2003-10-28 13:35:35   1 instanceType
  20489     Boston\DC11     20489 2003-10-28 13:35:35   1 whenCreated
  20489     Boston\DC11     20489 2003-10-28 13:35:35   1 nTSecurityDescriptor
  20489     Boston\DC11     20489 2003-10-28 13:35:35   1 name
  20489     Boston\DC11     20489 2003-10-28 13:35:35   1 objectCategory
```

The description attribute was entered on January 29 at 3:24 PM. The remaining seven attributes were created when the object was created, on October 28.

Another choice is to start the graphical ReplMon, add a domain controller to the list, and select Show Attribute Meta-Data for Active Directory Object.

`ReplPropertyMetaData`, `uSNCreated`, and `uSNChanged` are not replicated to other domain controllers. However, the four values in `replPropertyMetaData` are transferred with the property value, so that data means a 40-byte overhead for each property on the wire.

NOTE The transfer overhead is 8 bytes smaller than the storage overhead because the local USN is not transferred.

NOTE Active Directory doesn't keep track of the newness or changes of nonreplicating properties. Consequently, the "repl" properties, or a property such as `lastLogon`, won't get USNs or timestamps, nor will they advance the `uSNChanged` property of the corresponding object.

AD2003 has a new attribute, `msDS-ReplAttributeMetaData`, which contains the same metadata, but this time in XML format. This multivalued attribute contains one value for each of the attributes listed in the metadata. The Sales OU in the preceding example contains eight attributes, so there are eight values in its `msDS-ReplAttributeMetaData`. The one for the `description` attribute is the following (compare it to the preceding RepAdmin output to get the picture):

```
<DS_REPL_ATTR_META_DATA>
    <pszAttributeName>description</pszAttributeName>
    <dwVersion>1</dwVersion>
    <ftimeLastOriginatingChange>
        2004-01-29T20:24:15Z</ftimeLastOriginatingChange>
    <uuidLastOriginatingDsaInvocationID>
        61ed70d4-e35d-4c44-9d26-bb3b3e82796d
    </uuidLastOriginatingDsaInvocationID>
    <usnOriginatingChange>57494</usnOriginatingChange>
    <usnLocalChange>57494</usnLocalChange>
    <pszLastOriginatingDsaDN>
        CN=NTDS Settings,CN=DC11,CN=Servers,CN=Boston,
            CN=Sites,CN=Configuration,DC=sanao,DC=com
    </pszLastOriginatingDsaDN>
</DS_REPL_ATTR_META_DATA>
```

The Z after the date/time indicates that the time is in UTC/GMT. We added some extra line breaks and indentation to fit the data on the book page.

Viewing Changes

You can view changes that have just replicated or are about to replicate using the `repadmin /showchanges` command. The former case is based on a cookie file that records the current status. When you reissue the command, you get a list of changes that occurred since running the command the previous time. For example, first run the following command:

```
repadmin /showchanges dc1 dc=sanao,dc=com /cookie:mycookie.txt
```

Next, make a couple of changes on DC1, such as modifying Herbert's phone number and Jack's title. Issue the preceding command again, and you get the following result:

```
Using cookie from file mycookie.txt (324 bytes)

==== SOURCE DC: dc1 ====
```

```
Objects returned: 2
(0) modify CN=Herbert Hanson,OU=Boston,DC=sanao,DC=com
    1> objectGUID: 6bb6b913-3f88-46cb-b223-450de4e057dc
    1> telephoneNumber: 555-1234
    1> instanceType: 0x4 = ( IT_WRITE )
(1) modify CN=Jack Brown,OU=Boston,DC=sanao,DC=com
    1> objectGUID: be40f6ab-8cfe-46fb-b775-432343bc2ab8
    1> title: Big Boss
    1> instanceType: 0x4 = ( IT_WRITE )
New cookie written to file mycookie.txt (324 bytes)
```

The latter case—changes that are about to replicate—uses another variation of `repadmin /showchanges`. This time you need to specify the source domain controller's GUID, so you first type `repadmin /showreps`. In the resulting output, you locate the appropriate partition (such as `DC=sanao,DC=com`), and under that partition, the correct domain controller (such as DC5). Next to DC5, there is a line such as `DC object GUID: c6b3872f-516f-4e6b-a5d4-6f4483714924`. Now you have enough information to type the final command, as follows (wrapped here on two lines):

```
repadmin /showchanges dc1 c6b3872f-516f-4e6b-a5d4-6f4483714924
    dc=sanao,dc=com
```

TIP You can use the copy/paste feature of Cmd.exe instead of typing the GUID.

Among other things, the output displays changes from DC5 to DC1 that have yet to replicate. The following lines show part of the output.

```
==== SOURCE DC: c6b3872f-516f-4e6b-a5d4-
     6f4483714924._msdcs.sanao.com ====

Objects returned: 1
(0) add CN=Jack Brown,OU=Boston,DC=sanao,DC=com
    1> parentGUID: <16 byte blob>
    1> objectGUID: be40f6ab-8cfe-46fb-b775-432343bc2ab8
    4> objectClass: top; person; organizationalPerson; user
    1> sn: Brown
    1> givenName: Jack
    1> instanceType: 0x4 = ( IT_WRITE )
```

USN and Version Number Example

Tables 5.19 through 5.22 show how USNs and version numbers work when you are creating objects and modifying properties. Table 5.19 shows the data when you create a new user on DC1. If the USN on DC1 were 22,113, it would be advanced to 22,114.

NOTE The example in Table 5.19 is simplified. In reality, when you create a new user, she gets at least 30 properties and the USN counter advances two to five steps. This is because whether you use the snap-in or an ADSI script, behind the scenes there are multiple transactions. These transactions update also properties that you didn't specifically set.

The user that was created on DC1 is next replicated to DC2. The current USN of DC2 is 31,331, so it advances to 31,332. Table 5.20 shows the outcome.

Table 5.21 shows the next step: the change of Sam's home directory on DC2. Because some time has elapsed from the operation in Table 5.20, the USN of DC2 has advanced to 32,522. With the change of the home directory, it advances to 32,523.

The last step, shown in Table 5.22, is to replicate the changed property back to DC1. The current USN of DC1 is 23,776, so now it advances to 23,777.

Table 5.19 A Newly Created Object on DC1

Property	Value	Local USN	Originating DC	Originating USN	Version	Timestamp
`uSNCreated`	**22114***					
`uSNChanged`	**22114**					
`name`	**Sam Brown**	**22114**	**DB GUID of DC1**	**22114**	**1**	**UT**
`givenName`	**Sam**	**22114**	**DB GUID of DC1**	**22114**	**1**	**UT**
`homeDirectory`	**\\Srv1\Users\Sam**	**22114**	**DB GUID of DC1**	**22114**	**1**	**UT**

* Bold indicates changed data.

Table 5.20 A Replicated Object on DC2

Property	Value	Local USN	Originating DC	Originating USN	Version	Timestamp
uSNCreated	**31332***					
uSNChanged	**31332**					
name	*Sam Brown***	**31332**	*DB GUID of DC1*	*22114*	*1*	*UT*
givenName	*Sam*	**31332**	*DB GUID of DC1*	*22114*	*1*	*UT*
homeDirectory	*\\Srv1\Users\Sam*	**31332**	*DB GUID of DC1*	*22114*	*1*	*UT*

*Bold indicates changed data.

** Italics indicate that the data is new to this domain controller, but it is identical to the data in its replication source.

Table 5.21 A Change to a Property on DC2

Property	Value	Local USN	Originating DC	Originating USN	Version	Timestamp
uSNCreated	31332					
uSNChanged	**32523***					
name	Sam Brown	31332	DB GUID of DC1	22114	1	UT
givenName	Sam	31332	DB GUID of DC1	22114	1	UT
homeDirectory	**\\Srv2\Users\Sam**	**32523**	**DB GUID of DC2**	**32523**	**2**	**UT**

* Bold indicates changed data.

NOTE The properties `cn`, `ou`, `dc`, `l`, `o`, and `c` are treated differently in replication. Depending on the object class, one of these properties is the "naming attribute" of the object. Because the value is the same as the `name` property (i.e., RDN), it is sufficient to replicate only the `name` property. If you look at the metadata of a naming attribute, such as `cn`, you will notice that the originating DC and originating USN are always the same as the local ones, indicating that the value was generated locally instead of by replication.

Table 5.22 A Changed Property Replicated Back to DC1

Property	Value	Local USN	Originating DC	Originating USN	Version	Timestamp
`uSNCreated`	22114					
`uSNChanged`	**23777***					
`name`	Sam Brown	22114	DB GUID of DC1	22114	1	UT
`givenName`	Sam	22114	DB GUID of DC1	22114	1	UT
`homeDirectory`	*\\Srv2\ Users\Sam***	**23777**	*DB GUID of DC2*	*32523*	*2*	*UT*

* Bold indicates changed data.

** Italics indicate that the data is new to this domain controller, but it is identical to the data in its replication source.

Now that you are familiar with the basic mechanics of USNs, we move on to examine how a domain controller knows what changes to replicate.

High-Watermark Vectors

Each domain controller maintains one high-watermark vector for each partition for which it contains a replica. Consequently, a domain controller that is not a global catalog server has high-watermark vectors for its domain partition, for the schema partition, for the configuration partition, and one for each of its application partitions.

A high-watermark vector is a table that stores the highest replicated USN of each incoming replication partner of the corresponding partition. In other words, the table has rows at most for the same domain controllers that the owner has connection objects for. If a connection object is used to replicate only some partitions, the corresponding domain controller appears in the high-watermark vectors of only those partitions. Table 5.23 is a high-watermark vector of DC1.

Each high-watermark vector is stored in the nonreplicating `repsFrom` property of the corresponding partition's root object. That property stores other information also.

With the help of the high-watermark vector, a domain controller can detect and request recent changes from its replication partner. When a

Table 5.23 The High-Watermark Vector of DC1

Incoming Replication Partner	Highest Replicated USN from the Partner
Database GUID of DC2	25882
Database GUID of DC5	6577
Database GUID of DC9	18183

domain controller requests changes from its partner, it sends the following information in the request:

- The naming context (partition) for which the changes are requested.
- The maximum number of objects requested.
- The maximum number of values requested.
- An indication of whether or not to send parents.
- The highest replicated USN of the partner (taken from the vector). This tells the partner which changes the receiving end already has, so the partner will send only the new changes (i.e., the ones with the USN greater than requested, provided that propagation dampening doesn't kick in).
- An up-to-date vector, which takes care of propagation dampening.

The partner (or source domain controller) returns the following information:

- The source DC's server GUID
- The source DC's database GUID
- A number of object-update entries, which all contain the GUID for the object and a list of one or more property-update entries
- The largest `uSNChanged` so the destination can update its high-watermark vector
- An indication of whether or not there was more data, if the maximum number of objects or values didn't prevent sending it
- If there is no more data, an up-to-date vector from the source DC

Up-to-Date Vectors

Like a high-watermark vector, an up-to-date vector is a table that a domain controller has for each of its partitions (see Table 5.24). Instead

Table 5.24 The Up-to-Date Vector of DC1

Domain Controller	Highest Originating USN from the DC
Database GUID of DC2	25882
Database GUID of DC3	19234
Database GUID of DC5	6577
Database GUID of DC7	32904
Database GUID of DC9	18180

of replication partners, these vectors contain entries (i.e., highest USNs) for each domain controller from which the owner has ever received originating updates.

In Windows Server 2003, an up-to-date vector also contains the time when the local domain controller last completed a full replication cycle with each source domain controller. This information enables easy detection of domain controllers that are not replicating, either because of communication problems or because they are offline. This feature is used when logging the 1864 error and with the `/showvector` and `/showutdvec` RepAdmin options. See the "Monitoring and Diagnosing the Physical Structure" section earlier in this chapter.

NOTE Actually, the table has entries for all domain controllers of the forest (current and removed), but only the ones just mentioned have any practical meaning.

The highest USNs in the table are originating USNs, not replicated USNs. Each highest originating USN in the table states that all changes from the corresponding domain controller with a USN less than or equal to the one in the table have been received by the domain controller that owns the table.

Each up-to-date vector is stored in the nonreplicating `replUpToDateVector` property of the corresponding partition's root object.

With the help of up-to-date vectors, domain controllers can filter out changes that the other party has already received from another domain controller. That is, the vectors provide propagation dampening, which prevents a change from replicating endlessly or from replicating several times to one domain controller.

The next example (Tables 5.25 through 5.29) describes propagation dampening step by step. We have a minimal network with three domain controllers: DC1, DC2, and DC3. They are all replication partners of each other. We will demonstrate how a change made to DC2 propagates to DC1. With each step, we show the contents of the high-watermark vector and up-to-date vector of DC1, as well as the USNs of all three domain controllers.

Table 5.25 shows the initial state.

Now an administrator changes some user's home directory on DC2. This causes the USN of DC2 to advance by one to 8,023, as shown in Table 5.26.

DC1 will get a notification about the change from DC2, so it will request any changes greater than 8,022 (its high-watermark vector for DC2) from there. DC1 also sends its complete up-to-date vector to DC2. It contains USN 8,022 for DC2, so DC2 doesn't filter out the change. Consequently, DC2 will return the new home directory to DC1. Getting and storing this change advances the USN of DC1 to 9,916.

DC2 also returns its last changed USN (8,023), which DC1 uses to update the DC2 entry of its high-watermark vector, and an up-to-date

Table 5.25 USN of Each DC and Vectors of DC1: Initial State

DC	Current USN
DC1	9915
DC2	8022
DC3	12331

DC	High-Watermark Vector	Up-to-Date Vector
DC2	8022	8022
DC3	12331	12320

Table 5.26 USN of Each DC and Vectors of DC1: Step 1

DC	Current USN
DC1	9915
DC2	**8023***
DC3	12331

DC	High-Watermark Vector	Up-to-Date Vector
DC2	8022	8022
DC3	12331	12320

* Bold indicates a changed value.

vector, which DC1 uses to update the DC2 entry of its up-to-date vector. Table 5.27 shows the resulting vectors.

Next, the same change is replicated from DC2 to DC3. Obviously, this doesn't change the vectors of DC1, but the USN of DC3 advances, as Table 5.28 shows.

Now DC3 has a new change, which it presents (or notifies) to DC1. The latter sends a request to DC3 asking for any changes newer than 12,331. This would return the changed home directory (12,332) again to DC1 if there weren't the up-to-date vector.

In the request, DC1 sent its complete up-to-date vector, which states that changes originated in DC2 already reside in DC1 up to 8,023. As you remember, there is an originating USN stored with each property (in this case, 8,023 with the new home directory). Therefore, DC3 realizes that DC1 already knows about the new home directory and filters it out. The result is that DC3 returns no objects or properties to DC1, but it does return its last changed USN. DC1 uses this information to update its high-watermark vector, as shown in Table 5.29.

Table 5.27 USN of Each DC and Vectors of DC1: Step 2

DC	Current USN
DC1	**9916***
DC2	8023
DC3	12331

DC	High-Watermark Vector	Up-to-Date Vector
DC2	**8023**	**8023**
DC3	**12331**	**12320**

* Bold indicates a changed value.

Table 5.28 USN of Each DC and Vectors of DC1: Step 3

DC	Current USN
DC1	9916
DC2	8023
DC3	**12332***

DC	High-Watermark Vector	Up-to-Date Vector
DC2	8023	8023
DC3	12331	12320

* Bold indicates a changed value.

Table 5.29 USN of Each DC and Vectors of DC1: Step 4

DC	Current USN
DC1	9916
DC2	8023
DC3	12332

DC	High-Watermark Vector	Up-to-Date Vector
DC2	8023	8023
DC3	**12332***	12320

* Bold indicates a changed value.

TIP You can see the up-to-date vector of a given domain controller and partition using the RepAdmin command (included in Support Tools) with the `/showvector` option, or in the Windows Server 2003 version of the tool also with the `/showutdvec` option.

Collisions

In a multimaster replication system, it is possible that people or applications make changes on different domain controllers that, once they are replicated, are clearly in conflict. There are two steps to minimizing the number of these collisions.

- Active Directory narrows the possibility of collisions, because it keeps track of changes on a per-property basis. Therefore, changing two properties of one object in two domain controllers doesn't create a collision. If the forest is on the Windows Server 2003 interim or Windows Server 2003 functional level, Active Directory also keeps track of changes of linked multivalued attributes (such as group members) on a per-value basis.
- You, the administrator, should organize and delegate administration in such a way that several people are not likely to change the same properties to different values (almost) simultaneously.

When a changed property (or value) is replicated to another domain controller, Active Directory must choose whether to keep the replicated property or the one already on the destination. As seems natural, the property being replicated wins almost always. However, the exact logic is as follows:

- If the version numbers are different, let the larger one win, otherwise . . .
- If the timestamps are different, let the later one win, otherwise . . .
- Let the one win that was originated on the domain controller with a higher database GUID

We can call the three values combined a *stamp* and express the three-step logic in only three words: larger stamp wins.

It is highly unlikely that Active Directory would need to use the third value on the list, but it must have some unambiguous way to determine the winner in every possible situation. If you're playing with the first two options, you will have three scenarios:

- *A normal change* (incoming version number is larger). The property was changed only once in only one domain controller. Consequently, the property being replicated has a larger version number (+1) and it will propagate to every domain controller.
- *A collision* (equal version numbers). The same property was changed on two domain controllers. Consequently, both changes have the same version number. Active Directory will use the timestamp to determine the winner.
- *A peculiarity* (incoming version number is smaller). For example, an administrator could change a user's phone number twice on DC1: first accidentally to a wrong value and then to the correct one. This would advance the version number by two, so if a little later the phone number were changed on DC2, that latter change would lose, because its version number was incremented only by one.

NOTE The last scenario means that a later change may lose even if clocks are synchronized. However, this shouldn't be a problem in practice.

WARNING If you have an AD2000 forest or an AD2003 forest running on the Windows 2000 functional level, you should take into account the following warning: Because group memberships are stored as multivalued lists, changing the member list of one group on two domain controllers within the replication cycle (i.e., replication delay between these two domain controllers) would result in one of the changes being destroyed.

In addition to the property value conflict just discussed, there are two other types of collisions. Table 5.30 describes how Active Directory handles the three kinds of collisions that could occur. They are possible in domain and configuration partitions, and application partitions, but not in the schema partition—the schema partition is updated in a single-master fashion (as discussed later in the "Managing Operations Masters" section).

NOTE In the name conflict case in Table 5.30, the given name, surname, display name, user principal name, or pre–Windows 2000 name (SAM name) won't change. This means that two users will end up having the same UPN and SAM name. It is up to the administrator to rename them as well for one of the users.

Table 5.30 How Active Directory Handles Collisions

Collision Type	Example	Resolution
Property value conflict	Someone changes a property in DC1, and before the change has replicated to DC2, someone changes the same property there. This collision is detected when the local version number is the same as the replicated one, and the two values are different.	If timestamps are different, use the later timestamp; otherwise, use the one with a higher database GUID.
Creation or move under a deleted container	Someone creates a user in OU1 on DC1 and someone deletes OU1 on DC2.	OU1 will be deleted and the user will be moved to the LostAndFound container of the domain or to LostAndFoundConfig if the change was made to the configuration partition.
Sibling object name conflict	Two users with identical common names are created on two domain controllers at the same time. Two users could also be moved or renamed to be the same.	The user that has a larger stamp (i.e., usually was created a little later) will get the printable representation of its GUID appended to its common name (and consequently its DN and canonical name).

NOTE Even though schema updates are made in a single-master fashion, they could still conflict with other changes. If you add a class or property and then create an object based on them, the new object might reach some domain controller before the knowledge of the schema modification does. If this happens, the destination domain controller aborts processing the current replication data and writes a "schema mismatch" message to the event log. Then it resyncs the schema from the source domain controller and requests again the normal replication data. This time everything should go fine.

If the conflicting name of the last case in Table 5.30 was originally "Jack Brown," after the append operation it will be something like "Jack Brown*CNF: 507c75a0-28f9-48cb-7c33-cb946d109184." The asterisk (*) represents a reserved character (000A hex) normally seen as a white box. Because of the reserved character, this automatic name can never conflict with anything that you have created.

NOTE Because the second byte of the special character, 0A hex, is traditionally interpreted as a linefeed, it may cause a headache with some tools, such as CSVDE and LDIFDE.

Remember that the most important feature of conflict resolution is consistency. After things cool down, each domain controller has reached the same state and the same change has won everywhere. It really doesn't matter whether another change that lost was made two seconds earlier or later, perhaps in another town.

Tombstones

When an object is deleted, there must be something left to replicate to other domain controllers so that they will learn about the deleted object. This is why Active Directory doesn't immediately delete an object, but instead turns it into a tombstone. The following changes are made to an object when it is "deleted."

- The `isDeleted` property is set to true.
- An internal property, When-Deleted (this property has no LDAP name), is set to the time of the `isDeleted` property's timestamp.
- The `nTSecurityDescriptor` is set to a special value.
- The common name is changed to something like "Jack Brown* DEL: 507c75a0-28f9-48cb-7c33-cb946d109184." As with conflicts,

the asterisk (*) represents a reserved character (000A hex), so this name can never conflict with anything that you have created.

- The object is moved to the Deleted Objects container (which is a hidden container residing in all partitions).
- If the object is deleted on a Windows Server 2003 domain controller, the object's original location is stored in the `lastKnownParent` attribute.
- Most of the properties are stripped, leaving just a few that Active Directory needs.
- The following 29 attributes (or 24 in AD2000) may exist in a tombstone:

```
attributeID                         distinguishedName
attributeSyntax                     objectClass
dNReferenceUpdate                   objectGUID
governsID                           objectSid
groupType                           oMSyntax
instanceType                        name
lDAPDisplayName                     replPropertyMetaData
legacyExchangeDN                    sAMAccountName
msDS-AdditionalSamAccountName       subClassOf
msDS-Auxiliary-Classes              systemFlags
msDS-Entry-Time-To-Die              uid
msDS-IntId                          userAccountControl
mSMQOwnerID                         uSNChanged
nCName                              uSNCreated
nTSecurityDescriptor
```

This tombstone is replicated to other domain controllers and consequently the original object is "deleted" from them also. After this, it takes quite a while before the tombstone object is actually deleted from the database of each domain controller. This time is called *tombstone lifetime,* and the default value is 60 days. Microsoft recommends that you never change the value; in normal networks it shouldn't be a problem that deleted objects (i.e., tombstones) reserve space in directory databases for a couple of extra months.

NOTE If you ignore Microsoft's recommendation and change this value, you do so by modifying the `tombstoneLifetime` property of `CN=Directory Service, CN=Windows NT, CN=Services, CN=Configuration, DC=sanao, DC=com`.

There is a *garbage collector* task that runs on each domain controller. It wakes up by default every 12 hours to check if there are tombstones to delete from the database. The deletion criterion is that the internal When-Deleted property of the tombstone must be at least 60 days older than the current time.

Once a tombstone is deleted, its space can be reused for other objects. However, the database size doesn't shrink unless you do an offline defragmentation. You would do that in Directory Services Restore Mode, as explained in the Resource Kit documentation. The operation is normally unnecessary, but if you have removed a large number of objects and want to recover the disk space, you can perform it.

In Chapter 6 we describe the LDAP search that you can use to list the tombstones. Next to that example, we also show how to restore deleted objects from a tombstone (which is possible starting with Windows Server 2003). This restore feature is no replacement for normal backups, because you can restore only those attributes that were preserved in the tombstone.

Tombstone Lifetime Dependencies and Lingering Objects

After the tombstone lifetime has elapsed, and the garbage collector has deleted the tombstone, the corresponding object must not be reintroduced into the forest in any way. This might leave the directory in an inconsistent state; some domain controllers would contain the object and some wouldn't. This causes three dependencies of the tombstone lifetime, which must be obeyed.

- The tombstone's lifetime must not be shorter than the worst-case replication latency. If it were, the tombstone might be deleted before it had replicated to every appropriate domain controller.
- The tombstone lifetime is the maximum age of a backup. If you restored a backup that was older than the tombstone lifetime, you would also restore objects that were intentionally deleted after the backup was taken. For this reason, the Windows backup utility doesn't allow restoring directory databases that are older than the tombstone lifetime.
- A domain controller must not be offline and/or unreachable longer than the tombstone lifetime. If this were the case, that domain controller would not know about the object deletions, and when you brought it back online (or you fixed an error that had prevented replication for three months), it would restore the

unwanted deleted objects. Such objects are called *lingering objects* or *zombies*.

Using Strict Replication Consistency to Protect from Lingering Objects

Windows 2000 SP3 and Windows Server 2003 include a new registry setting that controls whether the corresponding domain controller uses strict or loose replication consistency. Newly installed (not upgraded) Windows Server 2003 domain controllers have by default the strict setting, and other domain controllers have by default the loose setting. This `REG_DWORD` value, `Strict Replication Consistency`, is stored in the key `HKEY_LOCAL_MACHINE`, `SYSTEM`, `CurrentControlSet`, `Services`, `NTDS`, `Parameters`.

The strict or loose replication consistency setting specifies how a domain controller behaves when it is about to receive updates from another domain controller to an object that doesn't exist in its local database. Such a situation must mean that the corresponding object in the other domain controller is a lingering object, and the process is called *lingering object detection*. The detection process also performs some other checks, such as whether the `whenCreated` timestamp is different on the source and the destination.

There are two possible modes:

- *Loose replication consistency*. To solve the dilemma of receiving updates to a nonexisting object, the destination domain controller requests the entire object from the source domain controller (i.e., not just the changed attributes). Then, it re-creates the object it doesn't have, so the once-deleted object appears in the forest again. This is usually unwanted behavior.
- *Strict replication consistency*. After detecting a lingering object in the source domain controller, the destination domain controller puts the source domain controller in quarantine (or actually, the partition in question). The quarantine is removed when the lingering object is deleted or when the destination domain controller is changed to use loose replication consistency.

NOTE You can remove the possible lingering objects with the `repadmin /removelingeringobjects` command. You can also use the /ADVISORY_MODE option to see if there are any lingering objects. To see the syntax, type repadmin /experthelp.

Time Since the Last Replication Check to Protect from Lingering Objects

Independent of lingering object detection—and independent of the strict/loose consistency setting—Windows Server 2003 always quarantines a source domain controller's partition (i.e., source replica) if replication has not succeeded for more than a tombstone lifetime. If you consequently use the Replicate Now operation of the Sites and Services snap-in, you will get the error "cannot replicate because the time since the last replication has exceeded the tombstone lifetime." You would also probably get an error with the event ID 2042 in your event log.

To recover from this error, first delete any lingering objects with repadmin /removelingeringobjects. Next, if DC2 did quarantine DC1, force the replication with a command such as the following:

```
repadmin /repl DC2 DC1 DC=sanao,DC=com /force
```

This fixes the problem for one partition, but when you try Replicate Now again, you may get the same error, but this time referring to the next partition. At worst, you must issue the command also for the configuration and schema partitions, ForestDnsZones and DomainDnsZones, for any other application partitions, and in the case of a global catalog server, for each other domain in the forest.

The protection described here can be turned off via the registry. The value is HKEY_LOCAL_MACHINE, System, CurrentControlSet, Services, NTDS, Parameters, Allow Replication With Divergent and Corrupt Partner : REG_DWORD : 1. However, using this setting is dangerous, because you might get lingering objects into your forest uncontrolled (not that it is any better to get them in a controlled way).

One scenario for using the registry setting is if you have VMware or Virtual PC images of test domain controllers, and you store them for several months before reusing them. Another option is to increase the tombstone lifetime for such a test forest (see the instructions earlier in this section). It is quite likely that you won't need to garbage collect tombstones in your test forest, so you could easily set their lifetime to five years, for example. Consequently, even after having stored them for four years, you would not run into the protection problem described here.

Time Synchronization

As explained with the replication process, Active Directory replication uses timestamps only when resolving collisions. Therefore, time synchronization between domain controllers is not needed to determine what objects/attributes get replicated or which attribute value is preserved.

Synchronized time between various computers in a forest is more crucial for the Kerberos authentication protocol. The clocks of two computers must not vary by default more than five minutes for Kerberos to work. This ensures among other things that domain controller–to–domain controller replication is possible.

WARNING Failure to keep the domain controllers within five minutes of each other can have disastrous consequences. Users may get locked out of a domain controller, and only forestwide Enterprise Admins can fix the situation, not domainwide Domain Admins.

There can be also other needs for synchronized time. Managing a network with many computers, starting batches at the right times, and diagnosing the events in such an environment is easier when the time in all computers is synchronized. A third need for synchronized time in your network arises if your organization uses applications that rely on synchronized time.

A service included in Windows 2000 and later takes care of time synchronization. The internal name for the service is *W32Time* and the display name is *Windows Time*. This service lives in the process svchost.exe (or services.exe in Windows 2000) and it is implemented in the file w32time.dll.

The W32Time service in Windows 2000 uses Simple Network Time Protocol (SNTP), defined in RFC 1769. Windows Server 2003 and Windows XP use a more accurate and sophisticated Network Time Protocol (NTP), which is defined in RFC 1305. Both NTP and SNTP use UDP port 123, so you must open this port in your routers and firewalls if you want NTP/SNTP packets to pass them.

Time Convergence Hierarchy

W32Time uses the treelike hierarchy that is already in place in a forest.

- Each workstation and member server gets the time from a domain controller in its own domain (the same domain controller that the client is using anyway for authentication and other domain functions).

- Each domain controller gets the time from any domain controller in its parent domain (where it prefers the PDC master) or the domain controller that owns the PDC master role in its own domain.
- Each PDC master gets the time from any domain controller in its parent domain (where it prefers the PDC master).

When we get up to the root domain of the forest, the PDC master there is authoritative for the whole forest. For this domain controller you have three options.

- Maintain time manually.
- Install some hardware that tracks the correct time, such as a card that gets the time from the atomic clock of a Global Positioning System (GPS) satellite.
- Set the domain controller to get the time using the NTP/SNTP protocol from some host on the Internet. For a list of sources, see Microsoft Knowledge Base Article 262680, or visit either the National Institute of Standards and Technology (NIST) Web site (`http://www.boulder.nist.gov/timefreq/service/its.htm`) or the US Naval Observatory Web site (`http://tycho.usno.navy.mil/ntp.html`).

Controlling the Time Service

You can control the time service, for example, to set the external time source. You have two commands for time service operations: NET TIME and W32TM. To get help for these, you can type either of the following commands:

```
NET TIME /HELP
W32TM /?
```

To set the PDC master of the forest root domain to use two external hosts as time sources, you can use commands like the following (the first one changes the configuration; the last two cause the change to take effect):

```
NET TIME /SETSNTP:"tick.usno.navy.mil tock.usno.navy.mil"
NET STOP W32TIME
NET START W32TIME
```

To set the computer time based on another computer time, you can use the following command:

```
NET TIME \\someotherserver /SET /YES
```

The latter command is normally not necessary, because the time is synchronized automatically throughout the forest. You can achieve the two preceding tasks also with the W32TM command, as follows (A sets the external sources, B causes the change to take effect, and C resynchronizes a workstation's clock):

```
A: w32tm /config /syncfromflags:manual
    /manualpeerlist:"tick.usno.navy.mil tock.usno.navy.mil"
B: w32tm /config /update
C: w32tm /resync
```

Monitoring the Time Service

In addition to checking if there are any W32Time errors in the System event log, you can use the following command to perform some monitoring of the service:

```
w32tm /monitor
```

The output would look like the following:

```
dc2.sanao.com [10.0.20.22]:
    ICMP: 13ms delay.
    NTP: -0.0461954s offset from dc1.sanao.com
        RefID: dc1.sanao.com [10.0.20.21]
dc1.sanao.com *** PDC *** [10.0.20.21]:
    ICMP: 0ms delay.
    NTP: +0.0000000s offset from dc1.sanao.com
        RefID: tick.usno.navy.mil [192.5.41.40]
```

The command lists the domain controllers of the default domain. The ICMP line shows how "near" each time source is to the workstation where the command is issued, the NTP line shows the current offset of the time source's clock to its time source, and the RefID line shows where the domain controller synchronizes its time from.

To see the time offset of the local computer and a given time server (from either the local forest or an external one), you can type a command such as this (followed by its output):

```
C:\>w32tm /stripchart /computer:tick.usno.navy.mil
Tracking tick.usno.navy.mil [192.5.41.40].
The current time is 1.2.2004 22:12:28 (local time).
22:12:28 d:+00.3805142s o:-00.0053861s  [      *      ]
22:12:31 d:+00.3704998s o:-00.0026064s  [      *      ]
22:12:33 d:+00.3604854s o:+00.0044388s  [      *      ]
```

The command displays the delay and offset to the specified NTP server, by default every two seconds, until you press Ctrl-C.

There are some registry settings that control the Windows Time service and store the external time source name or IP address. The settings are stored in HKEY_LOCAL_MACHINE, SYSTEM, CurrentControlSet, Services, W32Time. You can display them with the following commands:

```
w32tm /dumpreg /subkey:Parameters
w32tm /dumpreg /subkey:Config
```

You can control the same settings also with group policies (Computer Configuration - Administrative Templates - System - Windows Time Service).

Managing Operations Masters

Active Directory uses single-master replication or operation in five special cases where a multimaster approach would be prone to conflicts or extremely difficult to implement. In this section we explain the functions of each of these operations masters, also called flexible single-master operation (FSMO) roles.

Two of the roles are forestwide and three are domainwide. This leads to a simple formula for the number of operation master roles in your forest:

```
number of roles = 2 + (3 x number of domains)
```

Note that any role can be independently placed, so a given domain controller may hold from zero to five roles at a time.

The two forestwide roles are as follows:

- Schema master
- Domain naming master

The three domainwide roles are as follows:

- RID master
- PDC master (or PDC emulator)
- Infrastructure master (or infrastructure daemon)

In the next five subsections we describe the functions of each of the operations masters. After that we discuss the placement considerations and how to transfer or seize any of the roles to another domain controller, perhaps as a response to an operations master failure.

Schema Master

If you ever change the base schema of your forest, you make all changes to the domain controller that is holding the forestwide schema master role. These changes to the schema partition are then replicated to every other domain controller in the forest.

Domain Naming Master

The following changes are made to the forestwide domain naming master:

- Adding a domain to the forest or removing a domain from a forest
- Adding an application partition or removing an application partition
- A number of changes to the Partitions container when domain rename is performed in AD2003
- Adding or removing a cross-reference to a domain in an external directory

RID Master

As you know, every time a new security principal (i.e., user, computer, security group, trusting domain) is created in some domain, that security principal gets a security ID (SID). You also know that this SID consists of a domain part and a unique relative ID (RID).

Each domain controller has a pool of RIDs to issue to security principals that are created in that domain controller. With Windows 2000 pre-SP4, when the amount of free RIDs falls below 100, the domain controller retrieves 500 new RIDs from the per-domain RID master. This means that every domain controller should always have between

100 and 600 RIDs available. With Windows 2000 SP4 and Windows Server 2003, new RIDs are retrieved earlier, at the level of 250 free RIDs, which offers better resiliency if the RID master was offline for a while.

In rare cases when the pace of creating new security principals is high, the default RID block size of 500 new RIDs might not be enough. Microsoft Knowledge Base article 316201 explains how you can modify the default value and how it slightly increases the risk that the billion RIDs of a domain might run out (which would prevent you from ever creating new security principals in that domain anymore).

TIP If you are interested in how the RID pool information is stored in `CN=RID Manager$, CN=System, DC=<yourdomain>` and `CN=RID Set, CN=dcname, OU=Domain Controllers, DC=<yourdomain>`, you can read Microsoft Knowledge Base article 305475.

A RID master is also used when you move an object from one domain to another. It removes the object from the first domain and puts it in the second domain. If you move an Active Directory object between domains with MoveTree, you must initiate the move on the RID master of the source domain. With this requirement, Active Directory makes sure that two administrators cannot move the same object to two domains simultaneously. Such a conflict would lead to two identical objects being in the forest, both using the same GUID. This would be an illegal situation.

PDC Master

The per-domain PDC master has functions for both pre–Windows 2000 computers and for a pure Windows 2000 and later network. The former case includes the following functions.

- Pre–Windows 2000 computers, such as Windows NT backup domain controllers (BDCs), member servers, and workstations, expect to find a primary domain controller (PDC) in their domain. The PDC master fills this need. For example, when any change is made from a downlevel computer to a user object, such as a user changing her password, this is written first to the PDC (master). After that, each Windows NT BDC will replicate the change from the PDC.

- The old browser service (for building up the Network Neighborhood for users) needs a *domain master browser* to exchange computer lists between IP subnets. The PDC master also emulates this function, which is natural, because in old networks the PDC was always the same computer as the domain master browser.

The PDC master is used in the following ways for Windows 2000 and later computers.

- When a user changes his password on any domain controller, the change is pushed by the Netlogon service to the PDC master on a best-effort basis (not part of replication). This is beneficial if the user immediately tries to access some other server and his new password hasn't yet been replicated to every domain controller. If the authenticating domain controller notices that the user's password doesn't match, it can check with the PDC master to see if there is a new password for the user. The changed password is also normally replicated to other domain controllers.
- All user and computer account lockouts are processed on the PDC master. This way, both the setting of lockouts and the releasing of lockouts happens instantly without a replication delay.
- The PDC master of each domain is the preferred time server over the other domain controllers (as discussed in the "Time Synchronization" section earlier in this chapter).

As you can see, Windows 2000 and later clients use the PDC master only indirectly via a domain controller.

The push of passwords to the PDC master can be disabled between sites with the following registry setting (where the value 1 means true):

```
HKEY_LOCAL_MACHINE\SYSTEM\CurrentControlSet\Services\
   Netlogon\Parameters
   AvoidPdcOnWan : REG_DWORD : 1
```

Infrastructure Master

When an object references another object, such as when a group references its member, and the referenced object is not in the directory database of the domain controller (because the two objects are in different domains), a special record called a *phantom* is needed in the directory database to represent the referenced object. A phantom contains two or three identifiers of the referenced object: the GUID, the distinguished name (DN), and if the referenced object is a security principal, a SID.

The GUID never changes, but the DN will change if the object is moved or renamed. The SID will change if the object is moved from one domain to another. Consequently, the DN and SID in the phantom must be updated in these cases. The per-domain infrastructure master of the referencing object's domain is responsible for updating the phantom after a move or renaming operation. It must also replicate changed phantoms to other domain controllers in the domain. The infrastructure master performs its duty by periodically scanning its directory database for references to objects that are not in its database (because they are in other domains of the forest) and by contacting a global catalog server to check if these references are still valid.

For example, the group `CN=gsSales, OU=Salesmen, DC=sales, DC=sanao, DC=com` has a member from a different domain: `CN=Jack Brown, OU=Boston, DC=sanao, DC=com`. If Jack were moved from the Boston OU to the London OU, his new DN would be `CN=Jack Brown, OU=London, DC=sanao, DC=com`. The infrastructure master in the Sales domain would update the reference (i.e., the phantom) accordingly.

Global catalog servers don't need phantoms, and consequently they don't create or update them. A global catalog server contains all objects of the forest, so it will never find references where the target wouldn't be in its database.

NOTE Don't confuse phantoms with tombstones (i.e., objects marked as deleted), zombies (i.e., lingering objects), or foreign security principals (references to objects outside the forest).

Operations Master Placement

As you know, the two forestwide roles go by default to the first domain controller of the forest and the three domainwide roles go to the first domain controller of each domain.

In a small forest you may settle for the default configuration, but in a large forest you probably need to make some changes. Table 5.31 describes the different scenarios as incremental steps. Table 5.32 describes the role placement in a multidomain forest.

Table 5.31 Placement Rules for Operations Masters

Number of Domains, DCs	Other Conditions	Placement
One domain, one DC	Any	All five roles are in the only DC.
One domain, several DCs	Small to medium domain	All five roles are in the first DC (the default). You can call it an *operations master domain controller (OMDC)*.
	A large domain with more load	You could select a more powerful computer as the OMDC than the original OMDC might be (i.e., transfer all five roles there). The load on the schema, domain naming, and infrastructure masters is zero or next to zero. The RID master may experience some load and the PDC emulator is subject to a heavy load (depending on the number of users and workstations).
	Multiple sites	You should select an OMDC that can be accessed from any site reliably and with a decently fast connection.
	Even more load	If you feel that all five roles are too much for one DC, you can transfer the PDC emulator role to another DC. That new DC should also be accessible from any site, because the downlevel clients communicate directly with it.
Several domains	Any	See Table 5.32.

Table 5.32 Placement Rules for Operations Masters in a Multidomain Forest

Roles	Placement
Schema and domain naming masters	You should keep these two roles in the same domain controller—this way, you will have one less special DC to look after. You have the most control over the roles when they are in the root domain. The domain naming master must be on a domain controller that is a global catalog server, if the forest functional level is Windows 2000. Otherwise, the domain naming master may be in a non-GC domain controller.

Table 5.32 Placement Rules for Operations Masters in a Multidomain Forest *(cont.)*

Roles	Placement
RID and PDC masters (in each domain)	You can apply the instructions from Table 5.31; that is, keep these two roles in the same domain controller, unless a heavy load would make you separate them.
Infrastructure master (in each domain)	This role must not be on a global catalog server. If it is, the domain controller doesn't need (or contain) any phantoms, so it won't notice when the cross-domain references are out-of-date and need updating. This would hurt the other domain controllers in the domain (the ones that are not global catalog servers), because no one would send them updated phantoms. You would see an error about this in the event log (see Figure 5.46). The infrastructure master should have a good network connection to a global catalog server, preferably in the same site. As an exception, if all the domain controllers of the domain are global catalog servers, the infrastructure master can be on any of them, because the infrastructure master is actually not needed for anything anymore.

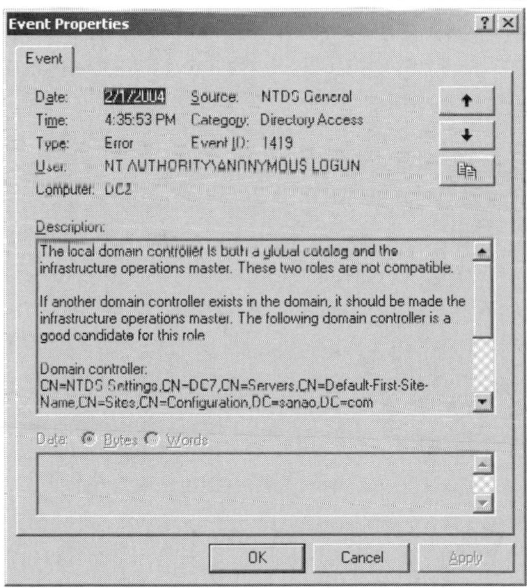

Figure 5.46 If the infrastructure master role is in a domain controller that is also a global catalog server, an error message is logged. You can see this error using the Event Viewer.

NOTE In most of the cases in Table 5.31, all five operations master roles are in the same domain controller. You are not forced to use this configuration, but it is simpler to manage, especially when responding to operations master failures (covered in a later section).

NOTE Remember to review your operations master placement if you make changes in your forest that might affect this placement.

In addition to selecting the placement of the operations masters, you should designate standby OMDCs. You can prepare for a possible failure of the original OMDC by using the following guidelines.

- Designate a standby for each OMDC in your forest. A standby is another domain controller on the same site (and naturally in the same domain, for the domainwide roles).
- If you want to prepare for a sitewide disaster, designate a second standby off-site. It should have a reasonably fast and reliable communication link to the primary site.
- Each standby for the roles schema master, domain naming master, and RID master should have a connection object for its primary OMDC to directly replicate from there. If there is an automatically created connection object, you cannot rely on it being there tomorrow; the KCC may have changed the replication topology. Therefore, you should create the needed connection objects manually. This way, the standby OMDC's Active Directory data is as current as possible at the time of the primary OMDC's failure. The requirement in this bullet doesn't apply to the roles PDC emulator and infrastructure master, because they don't carry any vital configuration information that should be transferred to the new role owner.
- If some child domain has only one domain controller, you don't need to install a second domain controller just to get a standby for that domain (although otherwise it is a good idea to have at least two domain controllers in each domain).
- If you have a domain of Windows 2000 mixed functional level with Windows NT BDCs, it is better to have the standby PDC emulator in the same site as the PDC emulator. This way, the Windows NT BDCs don't have to perform a full sync (i.e., replicating the whole domain partition) if the standby PDC emulator ever needs to replace the original one.

- The standby should be capable for the role. For example, because the domain naming master must be on a global catalog server (if the forest is on the Windows 2000 functional level), the standby should already be a global catalog server so that you don't have to promote it in a hurry when the original role owner has failed.

We will discuss in the subsequent "Managing Operations Master Failures" subsection what to do in case of a failure of an OMDC.

Transferring Operations Master Roles

You could change a role to another domain controller to respond to a failure or just to put it in a better place. The former case requires a drastic operation, called *seizing a role.* In this situation, before seizing an operations master role to another domain controller, you must understand failures (see the next section). The latter case, called *transferring a role,* is not a drastic or difficult operation, because it happens in cooperation with the old role owner.

Under the hood, the current owner of each role is identified by an `fSMORoleOwner` property in a certain object of Active Directory. This property points to the NTDS Settings object of the domain controller that owns the role.

You can see and transfer each role with some graphical MMC snap-in, so you need the `fSMORoleOwner` property only if you are writing ADSI scripts. We give an example of this in Chapter 11.

Table 5.33 lists the graphical snap-in, as well as the object that contains the `fSMORoleOwner` property for each role.

WARNING If you transfer one of the first three roles in Table 5.33, you must not restore the domain controller that used to have the role from a backup, where it still holds the role. If you do so, you could corrupt your enterprise forest or one domain.

Another way to see the current role owners is to use the NTDSUtil command-line utility. You can use the following command (all as one line):

```
Ntdsutil roles Connections "Connect to server myserver" Quit
    "select Operation Target" "List roles for connected server"
    Quit Quit Quit
```

Table 5.33 How to See or Transfer the Role Owner

Role	Graphical Snap-In	Object That Contains `fSMORoleOwner`
Schema master	Schema Manager, right-click the snap-in root in the left pane and select Operations Master	`CN=Schema, CN=Configuration,` *`<my forest>`*
Domain naming master	Domains and Trusts, right-click the snap-in root in the left pane and select Operations Master	`CN=Partitions, CN=Configuration,` *`<my forest>`*
RID master	Users and Computers, right-click the domain and select Operations Masters	`CN=RID Manager$, CN=System,` *`<my domain>`*
PDC master (or PDC emulator)	Same as for RID master	*`<my domain>`*
Infrastructure master	Same as for RID master	`CN=Infrastructure,` *`<my domain>`*

NOTE You must type a real server name instead of "myserver."

Alternatively, you can use just the following command:

```
Ntdsutil
```

Once you see the utility prompt (`ntdsutil:`), you type one word or part at a time of the command just listed (`roles`, `connections`, and so on) and press Enter after each command. You can also abbreviate each word, as long as the abbreviation is unambiguous. Instead of `roles` and `connections`, you would type only `ro` and `co`.

Managing Operations Master Failures

If a failure does occur, an operations master role is not seized automatically. Instead, you need to do this manually after you consider the following.

- Most of the failures won't affect users (see Table 5.34)—at least not anytime soon. Therefore, it is often best to fix the original OMDC to get it back online.
- It is, of course, possible that the failure is not in the OMDC itself, but in the network connection to it. Consequently, you don't want to seize the role to another domain controller, but rather you want to fix the network connection.
- If after a failure you seize the role of the schema master, domain naming master, or RID master to the standby, you must make absolutely sure that the original OMDC never gets back online. Otherwise, you might end up with two competing masters, which could corrupt your forest or corresponding domain. In other words, if the original OMDC just seems not to answer, don't automatically seize any of the three roles. First, consider if you really want to seize the role, and then if you do, turn off the original OMDC, disconnect it from the network, and format or destroy its hard disk. Also make sure that you don't later restore the original role to the original domain controller from a backup.
- The other two roles, PDC master and infrastructure master, you can seize to a standby without fear of drastic consequences. Also, if you later get the original OMDC back online, you can restore the roles to it.

NOTE Because seizing the schema master, domain naming master, or RID master role is quite drastic, the graphical snap-ins listed in Table 5.33 refuse to do it. Instead, you must use NTDSUtil.

Table 5.34 lists what happens if an OMDC fails.

Figure 5.47 shows the error message that appears when the RIDs run out. In addition, you will get events 16645 and 16651 in the System event log.

The outcome of Table 5.34 is that, of the five roles, you could consider the PDC master to be some kind of a single point of failure. However, in case of a failure, you can rather easily assign a new domain controller to take care of the role.

You can run DCDiag to verify that each operations master is operational.

Table 5.34 Impact of Different Operations Master Failures

Role	Failure Affects Users	Impact of a Failure
Schema master	No	Schema administrators cannot make changes to the schema.
Domain naming master	No	Administrators cannot add or remove domains or application partitions, or manage cross-references to external directories. Also, the domain rename procedure is not available.
RID master	No	Because every DC has 100–600 RIDs in its pool at any time, an administrator starts to notice the failure of the RID master after he has created that number of security principal objects (such as users) on the same domain controller.
PDC master	Yes	Pre–Windows 2000 BDCs don't have a master to replicate from; pre–Windows 2000 clients cannot change their passwords or see Network Neighborhood changes in other sites. If Windows 2000 or later clients change their passwords, they cannot immediately access other servers with the new password. Until replication completes, they must use the old password. The network time may not get synchronized among domain controllers.
Infrastructure master	No	If an administrator in some other domain moves or renames objects that are referenced by objects in this domain (such as users in other domains as members of groups in this domain), those references won't get updated to reflect the move or rename operation.

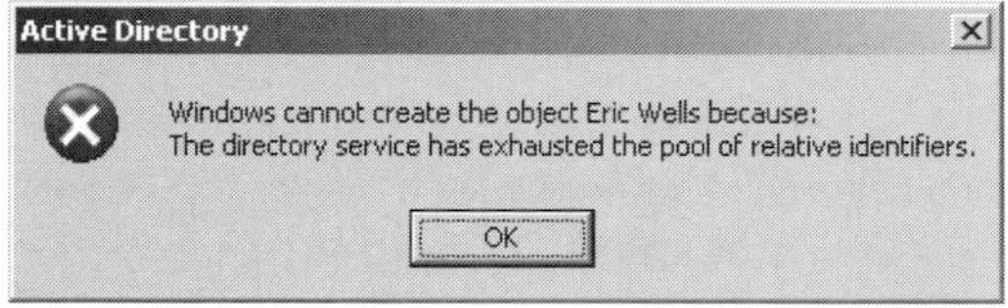

Figure 5.47 If a domain controller runs out of RIDs, perhaps because of a RID master failure, it doesn't allow you to create security principal objects anymore. If you try to create a user or a group with the Users and Computers snap-in, you will get this error message.

Seizing Operations Master Roles

You can seize the PDC master and infrastructure master roles using the Users and Computers snap-in, as described in Table 5.33. These two roles do not include any vital domain or forest configuration information, so you don't need to worry about the new role owners being up-to-date before the seize operation. If you anticipate that the current role owner will be unavailable for an unacceptably long time, you can go ahead and seize the role(s). If the original role owner later becomes available again, you can transfer the role(s) back.

The remaining three roles (i.e., schema master, domain naming master, and RID master) do carry vital configuration information, so you should make sure that the new role owner is as up-to-date as possible before you seize the role using the command-line tool NTDSUtil. Remember also that these three roles are not constantly needed, so you shouldn't seize the role at all if there is a chance that the original role owner will later become available.

Obviously, if the current role owner has failed, there is nothing you can do anymore to make its configuration information up-to-date in other domain controllers. Of course, because most of this configuration information changes infrequently, it is quite possible that the information is already up-to-date in other domain controllers. What you can do is locate the domain controller with the information being closest to up-to-date (even if not quite up-to-date). If your standby OMDC has a connection object to replicate directly from the original OMDC (as instructed earlier in this section), the information in the standby is probably the closest of any candidate domain controllers to being up to date.

NOTE It doesn't matter if the new schema master or domain naming master role owner is not up-to-date before the seize operation, as long as it is the closest of all candidates to being up-to-date. If the failed role owner had information that even the best candidate doesn't have, that missing information cannot corrupt the domain or forest. After all, there is no one alive that would know about that information.

NOTE The preceding note does not apply to RID masters. A RID master may have issued RIDs to other domain controllers, even though the state of the RID master has not yet been replicated to them. Fortunately, RID master state changes are replicated using urgent replication, which should minimize the risk of domain corruption in case of a RID master failure. By default, however, urgent replication takes place only intra-site, so it helps only if there is another domain controller of the same domain on the same site as the failed RID master.

To locate the best candidate for the new role owner, you can use the RepAdmin command with the `/showvector` option, or also the `/showutdvec` option in the Windows Server 2003 version of the tool. Either option displays the up-to-date vector of a given domain controller for a given partition. The latter option can also display the vector of several domain controllers at once, which can help in this case. For example, the domain naming master of the `sanao.com` forest was DC2 until it failed an hour ago. Because the hard drive failed completely, and you don't have a backup of it on tape, you decide to seize the role to another DC. The forest had four DCs, so you are left with DC1, DC3, and DC4. These are the three candidates that you must evaluate.

With the first option, you type the following three commands:

```
repadmin /showvector cn=configuration,dc=sanao,dc=com dc1.sanao.com
repadmin /showvector cn=configuration,dc=sanao,dc=com dc3.sanao.com
repadmin /showvector cn=configuration,dc=sanao,dc=com dc4.sanao.com
```

With the latter option, you type just one command:

```
repadmin /showutdvec * cn=configuration,dc=sanao,dc=com
```

Each of the three commands displays output such as the following, or the last command displays the lines three times, once for each target domain controller. The time is shown only in the Windows Server 2003 version of the tool:

```
Default-First-Site-Name\DC1     @ USN 15108  @ Time 2004-01-27 14:32:28
Default-First-Site-Name\DC2     @ USN  6792  @ Time 2004-01-27 13:45:11
Default-First-Site-Name\DC3     @ USN 12193  @ Time 2004-01-27 14:35:08
Default-First-Site-Name\DC4     @ USN  9733  @ Time 2004-01-27 14:39:51
```

To find out which DC has the latest information originated in DC2 (the failed role owner), compare the DC2 line of each of the three outputs. If your designated standby has the largest USN (as it should), seize the role to that DC. If another DC has the largest USN, seize the role to that DC instead, or wait until normal replication brings your designated standby up-to-date and make it the role owner after all. You can also use the Replicate Now function so that you don't have to wait so long.

If the new role owner should be DC3, seize the role with the following command (all as one line):

```
Ntdsutil roles Connections "Connect to server dc3.sanao.com" Quit
    "seize domain naming master" Quit Quit
```

Alternatively, you can use this command:

```
Ntdsutil
```

Once you see the utility prompt (`ntdsutil:`), you type one word or part at a time of the command just listed (`roles`, `connections`, and so on) and press Enter after each command.

Conclusion

After finishing this long chapter, you should have a good understanding of and be well equipped to manage the physical structure of your Active Directory network. You know what the automatically generated replication topology is for intrasite and intersite replication and what configuration information to enter for this automatic topology to be optimal. You are familiar with the replication process, so you can diagnose a failure efficiently. Finally, you know how to set up and manage the special domain controllers in your network, the global catalog servers, the bridgehead servers, and the operations masters. Once you read Chapter 6, which covers the logical structure, you are ready to roll.

CHAPTER 6

Domains and Forests

The previous chapter covered replication and the physical structure of Active Directory. We continue the same theme in the beginning of this chapter; when we talk about domains and forests, we also have to talk about domain controller and global catalog placement. This in turn requires that we first examine how much network traffic Active Directory causes.

After we have established the placement of various servers, we examine whether these servers should belong to one or several domains and to one or several forests. We continue this topic by discussing forest structures, such as the forest root domain (FRD), and trust relationships among domains and forests.

After addressing the aforementioned design issues, we move on to managing forests. This includes managing various trusts, moving objects in a forest, managing groups and permissions, examining referrals and cross-references, and delegating domain installation.

In the last section we explain how to use different tools to perform searches in a forest. Within this discussion, we explain many LDAP concepts and techniques.

Domain Controller Placement

A major design issue in Active Directory is the placement of domain controllers and, consequently, the directory information. To help us determine these locations, we will first examine the amount of Active Directory's network traffic.

Active Directory Network Traffic

Microsoft has measured how much data traffic Active Directory generates for the following traffic types:

- Windows 2000 client logon traffic
- Active Directory replication traffic (with AD2000)
- LDAP client traffic

In this section we present the summary numbers of the first and third traffic types as well as some derived numbers of the second type. If you want to read the full 140-page description of all the numbers, you can refer to the book *Building Enterprise Active Directory Services—Notes from the Field,* by Microsoft Press. You can get numbers also with a tool that Microsoft has written called Active Directory Sizer (ADSizer), which you can download from `http://www.microsoft.com/windows2000`. The tool asks you to enter information about users and other objects you have, how often people log on, how often administrators make changes, and so on.

NOTE As of this writing, there are no numbers for ADSizer later than for Windows 2000. Those Windows 2000 numbers, however, are a good indication for Windows Server 2003, too. Also, the numbers from the Microsoft Press book presented here should roughly apply also to Windows XP and Windows Server 2003, so it pays off to include them in the book.

Once you have entered the requested information, ADSizer estimates the number of domain controllers along with their hardware requirements, the domain database size, the global catalog size, network traffic, and some other information. Unfortunately, we cannot show screen shots of ADSizer, because its license strictly forbids publishing any results the tool has given.

NOTE Even though ADSizer can give you the numbers, you are better off if you have some background in Active Directory replication traffic. Therefore, this section deserves its space in this book.

Windows 2000 Client Logon Traffic

The logon process has two phases:

1. When a typical Windows 2000 workstation boots up, it generates about 70KB of network traffic. About 12KB of this goes toward obtaining Kerberos tickets, and 28KB goes toward an LDAP query for domain controller LDAP functionality and Group Policy query and download.
2. Next, a workstation user logs on to her workstation interactively, which typically generates about 85KB of network traffic. About 28KB of this goes toward exchanging Kerberos tickets, and 38KB goes toward querying and downloading group policies.

These numbers add up to a total of about 155KB of network traffic, whereas with Windows 95/98 the number was about 50KB. Most of the traffic is exchanged with a domain controller, but a small amount is exchanged with DNS and other servers.

The following factors affect the exact amount of the traffic.

- Each group that the user belongs to adds roughly 600 bytes to the interactive logon traffic. This is due to the Kerberos ticket growth because the tickets include more group SIDs. If you have put the user in 100 universal groups, this means about 60KB of extra traffic. However, if you are using domain local groups instead, only the groups of the home domain are included in the tickets.
- Each Group Policy object (GPO) that affects the computer or user adds perhaps 3KB. Note that even if the same GPO affects the computer and the user, both add their own 3KB. The exact number depends on the GPO size, so 3KB is just a rough estimate. After startup and logon, group policies are refreshed by default every 90 minutes. This causes more traffic, especially if there are changes in the group policies.
- Using a roaming profile adds easily several hundred kilobytes of traffic. When a user logs on, the workstation needs to check if there are changes in the server-based copy of the profile and, obviously, download any changes. During logoff there is likely to be even more traffic, when all changes to the local profile are uploaded back to the server.
- If folder redirection is used so that some user files are on the server, this naturally causes traffic every time the user accesses

those files (except that client-side caching probably saves from transferring some bytes between the client and the server). If offline folders are used also, the user can read files locally from the workstation, but any changes need to be written to the server. These traffic types are not tied to logon time.

- If a startup and/or logon script is executed, it adds some traffic, especially if it launches some programs from the domain controller disk to be run in the workstation.

Most communication of the last three items on the list is not necessarily with a domain controller, but it may be with any designated file server.

Because the numbers presented in this subsection are per workstation and user, you can easily scale them up to the number of workstations and users that are (concurrently) booting up and logging on.

Active Directory Replication Traffic

Microsoft has measured the actual replication traffic of AD2000 for different numbers of objects in different cases. From these "raw data" tables, we have derived the number of bytes each new object adds to the number of bytes that need replication and how many bytes you need to add as a base number.

In other words, we show you the two parameters (A and B) of the following linear function:

```
Y = A x X + B
```

You may have seen this formula in school. The following formula shows the same thing, this time expressed with our replication terms:

```
Amount = Number-of-bytes-per-object x Number-of-objects +
    Base-number-of-bytes
```

The fancy mathematical term for what we just did is *(linear) regression analysis*. There is a mathematical algorithm to find out the most representative line for the data set we had. However, we were more interested in finding out the practically representative parameters than the mathematically representative parameters, so we sought them manually.

NOTE Setting aside the mathematical approach, there is no single right answer for what the parameters should be. Determining which line best represents some nonlinear data set is to some degree a matter of taste. Therefore, our numbers are a good estimation, but you should not take them as the absolute and only truth.

Table 6.1 shows the results for five replication types and four object types. The rightmost column of the table gives the margin of error when you use this linear formula instead of Microsoft's detailed tables. The numbers without parentheses indicate the replication bytes caused by creating each new object with just mandatory attributes (i.e., parameter A). The numbers in parentheses indicate the base number (i.e., parameter B).

NOTE Even though Table 6.1 shows the same numbers for all group scopes, the numbers for universal groups are a couple of percentage points higher in the case of global catalog replication.

As you can see in Table 6.1, the margin of error in the two intrasite cases is really small. This means that the intrasite replication of Active Directory is quite linear and you can easily calculate the total numbers (except for the effect of additional attributes).

Table 6.1 Replication Traffic Amounts When Creating New Objects

Replication Type	User	Security Group	Volume	Printer	Margin of Error (%)
Intrasite domain	3,985 (2,097)	2,087 (2,137)	1,747 (2,134)	3,519 (1,958)	0 to +2
Intrasite GC	3,017 (2,177)	2,087 (2,259)	1,808 (2,196)	2,637 (2,095)	–1 to +1
Intersite domain	256 (8,260)	180 (8,112)	180 (7,476)	192 (8,058)	–1 to +14
Intersite GC	210 (8,114)	180 (8,132)	153 (8,048)	192 (8,090)	0 to +5
Intersite GC with SMTP	408 (29,350)	357 (25,168)	314 (24,780)	372 (25,418)	0 to +24

NOTE Now that the numbers contain only the mandatory attributes, the difference between domain replication (full) and global catalog replication (partial) is small or even nonexistent. In real life when you are using additional attributes, the domain numbers are likely to increase more than the global catalog numbers, thereby increasing the difference.

NOTE Even though we say that the numbers in Table 6.1 include only the mandatory attributes, this is not quite true. When you create a user with ADSI and specify only the mandatory attributes, some other attributes also get a value (`accountExpires`, `codePage`, `countryCode`, and `pwdLastSet`). This explains why the domain numbers are larger than the global catalog numbers, even though all seven mandatory attributes are part of the global catalog.

The three intersite cases in Table 6.1 are using compression, so the per-object numbers are mostly less than a tenth of the intrasite numbers. However, the base numbers in parentheses are larger because initiating intersite replication takes more bytes. There is no notification of changes, which would specify the changed partition, so the receiving domain controller has to check all three partitions (or more, in the case of a global catalog server).

Using SMTP instead of direct RPC doubles the numbers. SMTP packs bytes less efficiently for transportation, and SMTP headers need to be added and they cannot be compressed.

Compression in the three intersite cases introduces nonlinearity, which increases our margins of error. The first error comes from the fact that compression takes place only if there is more than 32KB of data to be replicated.

We have picked up the formula parameters from the data that is above the compression threshold, so any results we calculate will represent the compressed traffic quite well. With small object counts without compression, however, the correct numbers could be two to four times larger than the ones that our formula produces. Fortunately, this involves only a few tens of kilobytes in this case.

The compression threshold is between 10 and 20 objects for all other cases, except for users and intersite domain replication, where the threshold is right after five users.

The intersite margins of error shown in Table 6.1 (+14, +5, and +24) are from above the compression threshold. Above this threshold, the formula produces the largest errors around 100 objects. The reason for this is that the proportional savings from compression are the biggest when adding the first tens of objects after the compression has started.

NOTE The compression threshold also means that replicating 100 objects may take fewer bytes than replicating 10 objects.

In addition to the numbers in Table 6.1, we present some other results.

When adding ten-character Unicode string attributes to existing user objects and replicating them intrasite, we can derive the following formula from the Microsoft numbers:

```
Amount = 2250 B + Number-of-users x (290 B +
    Number-of-attributes x 92 B)
```

The margin of error is ±3 percent, so the results are quite accurate. You can see that each ten-character string (2 bytes per Unicode character) takes about 90 bytes when replicated. If you add the ten-character attributes when you create user objects, you can use the same 90 bytes as an estimated value per attribute.

The group numbers in Table 6.1 don't include members. We derived the following formula to take the members into account (noncompressed intrasite replication):

```
Amount = 2137 B + Number-of-groups x (2087 B +
    Number-of-members x 165 B)
```

The margin of error is again quite small, between –1 and +4 percent. The formula means that replication of each group member takes 165 bytes.

NOTE As you know, all members of a group are stored in one multivalued attribute. Therefore, if you add one member to the existing 3,000 members, in AD2000 all 3,001 get replicated.

In domain replication, members are replicated for both global and universal groups, but in global catalog replication, members are replicated only for universal groups.

Replicating password changes intersite is less efficient than replicating normal string attributes. Active Directory encrypts a password before storing it to the directory database, and this encrypted data doesn't compress as well as normal average data. Each password takes almost a kilobyte to replicate intersite.

When using Active Directory–integrated zones in DNS servers, the DNS record changes are part of Active Directory replication. Each host record (i.e., A record) takes about 120 bytes to replicate intersite in addition to approximately 10KB as a base number.

Replication of the schema and configuration partitions shouldn't add many bytes, because you probably do not add schema objects, domains, or sites often. When you do make some of these changes, each new object takes roughly a few hundred bytes to be replicated intersite to all domain controllers of the forest.

LDAP Client Traffic

As you know, clients access Active Directory information using the LDAP protocol. The reasons for access may be queries and other reads or administration and other modifications. The users who cause this traffic may be administrators, end users, directory-enabled applications, or network devices that use Active Directory.

Microsoft tested LDAP traffic using the native LDAP C API, ADSI, user tools such as Windows Address Book, and administrative MMC snap-ins. Here is a brief summary of Microsoft's findings:

- Connecting and authenticating (using the SSPI interface) with LDAP takes about 7KB, with ADSI about 10KB, and with a snap-in about 29KB. An anonymous bind with LDAP takes only 124 bytes.
- Obviously, the traffic increases when the client is retrieving more properties of an object. Retrieving all properties (using the property list "*") of a large number of objects can cause excessive amounts of traffic, so you should avoid it.
- Searching many OUs doesn't increase the traffic, because the search is executed inside a single server anyway.
- Modifying objects with native LDAP causes the least amount of traffic. However, using ADSI causes roughly only one and one-half times more traffic, and using a snap-in causes only three times more traffic.
- Reading from the global catalog causes about the same amount of traffic as reading the same information from a normal LDAP port.
- LDAP traffic can be tuned, for example, to set a certain page size. This and similar settings are explained in Chapter 11.

Determining the Placement of Directory Information

Part of Active Directory planning is to determine what directory information to store in each location of your enterprise network.

You may recall from the previous chapter that the replicas of the configuration and schema partitions reside on every domain controller of a forest, whereas the replicas of any given domain reside only on the domain controllers of that domain. And application partitions of AD2003 reside on any designated domain controllers. You also know that some domain controllers are designated as global catalog servers, in which case they contain a partial replica of every other domain of their forest.

Now we examine the choices you have in placing the domain controllers, which is the same thing as placing Active Directory information. We will discuss three topics:

- Looking at all sites and domains together
- Looking at a single site and domain
- Looking at global catalog server placement

The first section introduces the playing field on a somewhat abstract level. In the second section, we discuss how to make the actual selections about domain controller placement. The third section continues the placement discussion, now concentrating on global catalog servers.

NOTE Our discussion doesn't cover application partitions. It is purely a per-application decision which domain controllers should host a given application partition. If the following general discussion suggests that you shouldn't place a domain controller in London, for example, but you have an application that would benefit from an application partition in London, you should obviously place a domain controller in London.

Looking at All Sites and Domains Together

In this section we present and compare three general scenarios, each of which uses three sites: Boston, San Francisco, and London. The scenarios are as follows:

- One domain that has domain controllers on each site
- Three domains that all have domain controllers on only one site
- Three domains that all have domain controllers on each site

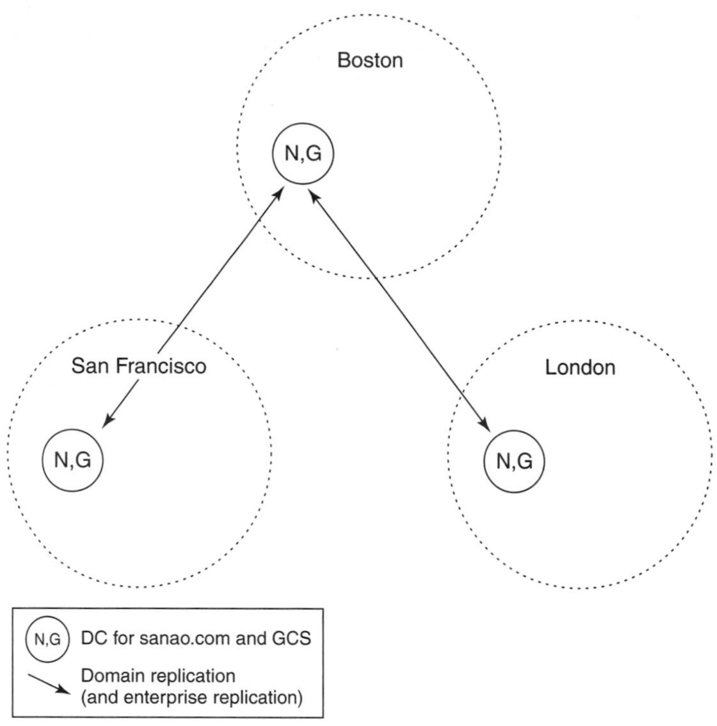

Figure 6.1 In this first scenario there is only one domain and this domain has domain controllers on each site.

When there is only one domain, as Figure 6.1 shows, all Active Directory information is stored in each domain controller and must be replicated to every site. This involves the maximum possible amount of replication among sites. However, for users it also means that all directory information is local to them (the best possible proximity of information).

Figure 6.2 shows the second scenario. The only replication necessary to be replicated among sites is replication of the enterprise information, meaning the configuration and schema partitions. Because we have placed a global catalog server on each site, we also need to replicate those attributes of the domain partition objects that are part of the global catalog.

Setting aside the effect of the global catalog, the scenario in Figure 6.2 requires the minimum amount of replication and offers the worst possible proximity of information. The users would always need to access information in other domains over a WAN link. If we dropped two global catalog servers, the amount of replication would be even less and the proximity of information would be even worse.

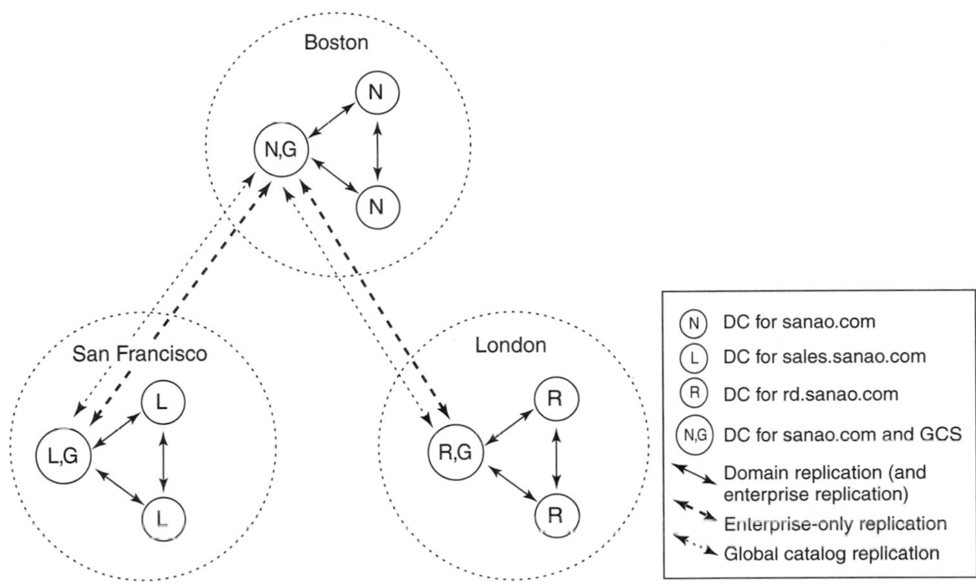

Figure 6.2 In this second scenario there are three domains and each of them has domain controllers on only one site.

NOTE Whether not having proximity of information is a drawback depends on whether the users ever need to access information from other domains.

Figure 6.3 shows a scenario where the domain controllers of each domain are distributed on all sites. This third scenario is actually equivalent to the first scenario with regard to the amount of replication and proximity of information. Therefore, having three domains instead of one brings no savings in replication. Three perhaps independent divisions can now have their own domains, but they also need to buy their own domain controllers on each site.

NOTE The second and third scenarios (see Figure 6.2 and Figure 6.3) represent the two extreme cases of a multidomain forest. In practice, your solution is likely to fall between the two; that is, some of your domains would have all domain controllers on one site, and others would have domain controllers on several but probably not all sites.

Next we examine the placement of a domain controller from the viewpoint of a single site and a single domain.

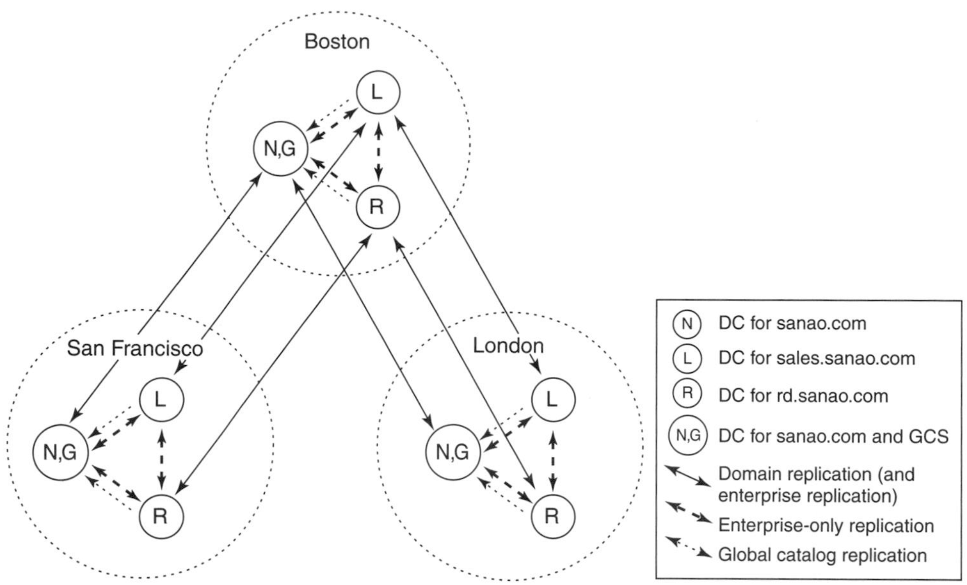

Figure 6.3 In this third scenario there are three domains and each of them has domain controllers on each site.

Looking at a Single Site and Domain

When placing directory information, you naturally would like to give your users local access to the information they need. On the other hand, you don't want excessive replication over WAN links.

Having learned the elementary numbers earlier in this chapter, now you should decide if it is better to put a domain controller (and perhaps also a global catalog server) on a remote site, causing replication over the WAN link, or not to put one on a remote site, causing logon and other traffic over the WAN link.

NOTE When evaluating whether or not to put a domain controller on a remote site, you cannot simply calculate which approach causes less traffic and choose it. Client traffic usually occurs when a user is sitting at a workstation waiting for a transaction to complete, whereas replication takes place "backstage" and can be scheduled to off-peak hours.

Let's consider the London site from the previous section as an example. As we suggested earlier, the least replication occurs in the first of the following cases and the most replication occurs in the last of them:

- We don't place domain controllers of any American domains in London and we don't have a global catalog server there.
- We designate a global catalog server to reside in London (which is normally wise).
- We put a domain controller for some American domain in London.

The exact amount of replication traffic depends also on how you plan sites and domains, and on the size of the domain and the frequency of changes.

The amount of client traffic (logon and other LDAP traffic) depends only on the number of clients and how and how often they use Active Directory and features such as group policies and roaming profiles.

This leads to a (quite obvious) conclusion: With a small number of clients, it is better not to place a domain controller on a remote site, but with a large number of clients it probably pays off to place a domain controller on a remote site.

We are not going to give more precise numbers or exact rules, because so many variables affect the final traffic numbers. Besides, you can use the ADSizer tool to calculate numbers for various scenarios. You must also remember that your decisions will be only partly based on numbers, because intuition plays an important role too. Microsoft states in the Windows Server 2003 Deployment Kit that at least a location that has more than 100 users should have its own domain controller.

However, we give the following (some also quite obvious) additional considerations:

- The need for an on-site domain controller is probably greater when there are users of that domain on that site, because the users need the logon services. If users are just making LDAP queries to get Active Directory information about foreign domains, they can live better without an on-site domain controller for that domain.
- If you place a domain controller on a remote site, that computer contains all the directory information of that domain, including users' passwords. Consequently, you should see to the physical security of that domain controller in the new site. Physical access to any domain controller enables an attacker to corrupt your entire forest.
- If you place a domain controller on a remote site, you also need to plan who will manage it and how, either locally or remotely.
- If you choose not to place a domain controller on-site, you need to make sure that the users of that site don't suffer too much. You

should give them a WAN link that is decent enough (in both speed and reliability) to use for logons and other access. You could have a hub site that contains domain controllers for the branch sites to use.
- A global catalog server is always a domain controller, so if a global catalog server is needed on some site, that site must have at least one domain controller.

If you decide to place a domain controller on a remote site to serve users there, you have one more decision to make, with the following two options:

- Do not create a new domain, which means that you have to replicate an existing domain over the WAN (this is what we have been mainly discussing in this section).
- Create a new domain for the site, so that only the schema, the configuration, and possibly the global catalog need to be replicated. (We will return to this option later in this chapter.)

We have mentioned the global catalog a couple of times. Now we will seriously consider global catalog placement.

Looking at Global Catalog Server Placement

A global catalog server must be contacted in the following cases.

- A user queries something from the global catalog, for example, by using the Start menu (click the Start button and select Search).
- A user or computer logs on and the computer is a member of a domain that is on the "Windows 2000 native" domain functional level, and the authenticating domain controller is running Windows 2000. In this case the authenticating domain controller needs to contact a global catalog server to find memberships of any universal security groups to be included in the access token. If the authenticating domain controller were running Windows Server 2003, it could cache the universal group memberships, so a constant connection to a global catalog server wouldn't be required. We discuss this two sections later.
- A user uses his user principal name (UPN) to log on or to perform some other operation, such as changing a password. If the domain part of the UPN is not the user's domain, the mapping to a correct user account must be resolved from the global catalog information.

- An organization uses Exchange 2000 or later, which uses the Active Directory global catalog for its global address list.
- An organization uses another global catalog–requiring application, such as MSMQ (Microsoft Message Queue) or an application that uses DCOM (Distributed COM).

If you don't want the traffic to take place over a WAN link in some of these cases, because of either speed or reliability, you must place a global catalog server on a remote site.

Universal group membership caching, which is available in Windows Server 2003 domain controllers, removes the need to contact a global catalog server during a normal logon (consequent to the first logon in a given location). This leads to the following three specific reasons to place a global catalog server on a remote site:

- There is an application on the remote site that requires a fast (that is, local) connection to a global catalog server. This corresponds to the last two items of the preceding five-item list.
- Microsoft recommends that if there are more than 100 users on the site, it should have a global catalog server.
- The remote site doesn't have a 100 percent reliable WAN link to a site with a global catalog server, and a large number of roaming users visit the remote site (which means that there will be a lot of first-time logons).

The following are additional considerations for placing global catalog servers.

- You can place a global catalog server on more sites than what the previous list suggests, or you could place a global catalog server on every site. However, this increases replication to the site, and one of the domain controllers on that site needs to be powerful enough to host the global catalog.
- The directory database of a global catalog server is larger than the database in a normal domain controller. For this reason, you must be sure there is adequate hardware in any domain controller that you assign to be a global catalog server.
- Universal group members are stored in the global catalog. To avoid excessive replication, put users and computers as members in universal groups only via global groups. Be careful with the amount of global catalog replication—for example, refrain from adding many new attributes to the global catalog.

- If the increase in replication or database size is more than you are willing to accept, given your WAN links and server hardware, you should leave some sites without a global catalog server. However, make sure that there is adequate service (speed and reliability) for that site also.
- In 2001, Microsoft had 166 Active Directory sites in its corporate network, and 165 of them had a global catalog server.
- If there is only one domain in your forest, make all domain controllers global catalog servers. In the one-domain case, this doesn't add replication, nor will it increase the size of the database, but it will maximize the availability of global catalog servers.
- If you already have a global catalog server on some site, having several global catalog servers on the same site doesn't add intersite replication. Once the data gets to the first global catalog server on the site, it will replicate intrasite to other global catalog servers.

NOTE Combining the first and last listed considerations for placement of global catalog servers can lead to an interesting claim. If there should normally be a global catalog server on each site, and once there is one, there could easily be several, we could claim that you could easily make all the domain controllers of your forest global catalog servers. However, if this were the case, all your domain controllers might need more hardware, so we don't make that claim. Also, if there were many domain controllers (say, over 20) on a site, it would be impractical (because of extra replication) to promote them all to global catalog servers.

Disabling the Requirement for a Global Catalog Server During Logon

With Windows 2000 domain controllers, if it becomes a problem that a site doesn't contain a global catalog server, and one cannot be contacted across a WAN link, you can add the following registry key on the domain controllers on that site:

```
HKEY_LOCAL_MACHINE\System\CurrentControlSet\Control\Lsa\
    IgnoreGCFailures
```

With this setting, users logging on may not be recognized as members of the correct universal groups. If one of these groups were denied access to some resource, the members of that group could still access the resource.

You can use this method also with Windows Server 2003 domain controllers, but the preferred method is universal group membership caching, which is discussed next.

Universal Group Membership Caching

Normally, when a user logged on in AD2000, the domain controller that was processing the logon needed to contact a global catalog server to find out the universal groups that the user was a member of. In AD2003, the domain controller can cache this information indefinitely during the first logon of each user, and subsequently update the information every eight hours. This relieves the domain controller from having a constant connection to a global catalog server, which in turn means that the number of global catalog servers can be reduced. With this change, global catalog servers are mostly needed for applications, such as Exchange, but not that much for logons.

You enable universal group membership caching in the NTDS Site Settings properties. After you have clicked the corresponding check box, you could also specify from which site the caching occurs. Normally you can just use <Default>, in which case Active Directory determines the closest site to use.

Designing Domains and Forests

When you design the structure of your Active Directory, you must choose whether to use one or multiple domains, and one or multiple forests. If you select a multidomain forest, you must plan the structure of the forest, choose a root domain, and possibly create shortcut trust relationships to optimize authentication.

Single or Multiple Domains and Forests

Recall the four Active Directory hierarchies that we introduced in Chapter 1:

- One domain with no structure
- OU tree in one domain
- Domain tree
- Forest of domain trees

In this chapter we adjust the list a bit. Because we discussed OUs in Chapter 3, we don't need to differentiate the first two hierarchies for the purposes of this chapter. In both cases we just have a domain, which may or may not have an OU tree. Also, apart from DNS names and some search capabilities, the last two items in the list are the same, so we consolidate them as well. When we add one new item, we get the following list of possibilities:

- A single domain (with or without an OU tree)
- Multiple domains in a single forest (with one or several domain trees)
- Multiple forests

These three options lead to two questions: Will you have a single or multiple domains, and in the latter case, will you have a single or multiple forests? You must select one of the three options as the structure for your Active Directory. In making your choice, you must weigh conflicting benefits and costs, so you must know your priorities. Table 6.2 contains a summary of the differences among the three options.

Note that the three last items in Table 6.2 (policies, administration, and replication) make a difference when you are choosing one or multiple domains. Similarly, the four first items (number of schemas, configurations, global catalogs, and complete trust areas) make a difference when choosing one or multiple forests.

Single or Multiple Domains

Microsoft recommends that you use only one domain, unless you can specifically justify each additional domain. In this section we explain what it means to have multiple domains in your organization. We also list the costs related to additional domains. Remember that we already have discussed domains in several chapters. You may wish to review the following subjects in the cited chapters:

- Active Directory building blocks and hierarchies in Chapter 1
- The logical aspects of a domain (the OU tree and other objects of a domain) in Chapter 3
- The physical aspects of a domain (managing domain controllers and operations master roles) in Chapter 5
- Placement of domain controllers earlier in this chapter

Table 6.2 Per-Domain and Per-Forest Features

Feature	Single Domain	Multiple Domains in a Single Forest	Multiple Forests
Number of schemas	1	1	1 per forest
Number of forest configurations	1	1	1 per forest
Number of global catalogs	1	1	1 per forest
Number of complete trust areas	1	1	1 per forest*
Global catalog placement	Can be in every DC without extra cost	Evaluate which DCs should host the GC	Evaluate which DCs should host the GC
Universal groups	No benefit but no cost	Benefits in certain cases, extra cost in all cases	Depends on whether there is one or several domains in each forest
Number of password, account lockout, and Kerberos policies	1	1 per domain	1 per domain
Units of administration	1	1 per domain	1 per domain
Units of replication	1	1 per domain	1 per domain

*If two forests are running on the Windows Server 2003 functional level, you can create a forest trust between them. Depending on how you configure the forest trust, it can combine the complete trust areas of the two forests into one. We present more information on the topic in the "Forest Trusts" section later in this chapter.

You already know that a domain is a unit of administration, unit of policy, and unit of replication. If you need more than one of any of these units, you obviously need multiple domains.

Multiple Domains Because of Units of Administration

A domain is an administrative unit in two senses.

- Administrative groups (most notably Domain Admins, Administrators, and Account Operators) have, by default, wide permissions to Active Directory objects in their own domain. It is possible but cumbersome to change the defaults. Consequently, if some part of your organization must have autonomous control over part of the objects, and they want to be isolated so that "outsider" Domain Admins and so on are not able to get there, you should create a separate domain for them. Note, however, that this does not protect from rogue domain administrators from other domains. If some domain administrators in the forest are not highly trusted, a separate forest should probably be deployed.
- Outside Active Directory, there are a number of fixed rights that Administrators and/or Server Operators have for all domain controllers of a domain. These rights include formatting hard drives, sharing folders, creating and sharing printers, as well as starting and configuring services. If you want someone to have these rights on London domain controllers, but not on Boston domain controllers, those domain controllers must be in different domains.

Also, geopolitical boundaries or legislation in some countries may prohibit administration in a foreign country.

Multiple Domains Because of Units of Policy

Group Policy includes some policies that apply only per domain. They are visible also in per-OU GPOs, but they come into play only when set in a per-domain GPO. These policies include all settings in Computer Configuration, Windows Settings, Security Settings, Account Policies, which contains the following policy branches:

- *Password Policy.* For example, if you require a longer password for some users than others, those two kinds of users must be in different domains.
- *Account Lockout Policy.* These settings enable you to specify that too many wrong passwords entered for a user in a given time will

lock that account for a specified amount of time. This way, for example, a potential intruder can guess someone's password only three times, and then wait 15 minutes.

- *Kerberos Policy.* These settings enable you to specify how long Kerberos tickets are valid. By default, a ticket-granting ticket (TGT) is valid for 10 hours.

In addition, the following settings in Computer Configuration, Windows Settings, Security Settings, Local Policies, Security Options apply per domain:

- Automatically log off users when logon time expires (Windows 2000)
- Network security: Force logoff when logon hours expire (Windows Server 2003)
- Rename administrator account
- Rename guest account

Multiple Domains Because of Units of Replication

Because a domain is a directory partition, it is a unit of replication: Each object that is created in a domain is replicated to all domain controllers in that domain. When you have more changes in directory information than it is feasible to replicate to every domain controller, you must create additional domains. This includes the following cases:

- *Too many changes (or WAN links that are too slow).* You have more changes than you want to replicate everywhere or to a certain location. Either you feel that you don't want to spend WAN bandwidth to replicate objects to places where they are not needed, or you simply don't have enough (free) bandwidth. The reasons for this are that the link is too slow, it is unavailable part of the day, or more important traffic needs to use that link. Microsoft has presented a rough estimate that even with links as slow as 56Kbps, you could have 100,000 users in a single domain.
- *Too many objects.* Even though a single domain can host at least 100 million objects, you don't want all domain controllers to be powerful enough to store all the objects in your forest.

- *Cost by usage.* You have to pay for certain WAN links by usage. As you know, replicated data is compressed and you can optimize replication. For example, you can schedule it to occur only once a day and use reciprocal replication (i.e., once a link is open, replicate to both directions). However, by creating a separate domain, you may reduce traffic even more, and thereby lower monetary cost.
- *SMTP.* You don't have a direct connection to a site, but it can be reached with SMTP mail. Because SMTP replication is possible only between domains (i.e., schema, configuration, and global catalog replication), you must create a separate domain for that site.

Multiple Domains Because of Existing Windows NT Domains

Another reason to have multiple domains is that your existing Windows NT network has multiple domains, and you upgrade those domains to Active Directory *in place.* This leads to having exactly the same domains in Active Directory that you had in Windows NT.

This selection of domains might not be ideal for your organization in the long run, but it is a mandatory intermediate stage when you are performing this kind of upgrade. If your ideal forest includes fewer domains—perhaps just one—you can later consolidate domains on your path toward this ideal structure. In a large network, however, it could take a year or two to reach the ultimate goal.

Although we don't address migration strategies in this book, we want to mention an alternative to in-place upgrade. You can create an empty new forest with ideal domains and then migrate existing users, groups, and so on to this new forest.

Nonreasons to Create Multiple Domains

With Windows NT you needed to create several domains if there were too many user and computer accounts for one domain. The limit was about 40,000 users, or 26,000 users with computer accounts. This is not a concern with Active Directory, because even one domain can host at least 100 million objects, given that the server hardware is capable.

With Windows NT the only way to delegate administration of some users and groups to another administrator was to create another domain. With Active Directory, per-OU permissions allow delegation in a single domain.

Branch Office Environment

As a special case, if you have a large number of branch offices, you can get detailed planning and deployment information from the Branch Office Guide at `http://www.microsoft.com/` (use the Search feature to locate the correct pages). The guide also includes scripts to automate the deployment process.

The basic approach in a branch office environment is to have a domain for the headquarters and another domain common to all branch offices. Or in a large environment, there might be several domains for the headquarters and a new child domain for every 100 branch offices.

Costs of Additional Domains

Each additional domain introduces the following costs:

- *Additional domain controllers.* Because a domain controller can host only one domain, you need new domain controller computers (including Windows server licenses) for the new domain. Fault tolerance requires at least two domain controllers per domain. If the domain is present on several sites (most likely because of user needs), you must have more domain controllers accordingly.
- *More interdomain communications.* The more domains there are, the more likely it is that a user accessing a resource and the resource are in different domains. In this case, the user's workstation must communicate with domain controllers in both domains. In addition, if the two domains don't have a direct trust relationship, the user's workstation must communicate with a domain controller in each domain along the trust path between the two end domains. This is how the Kerberos authentication protocol implements transitive trusts. Figure 6.4 illustrates the process. This item can be costly because the more often interdomain authentication is needed, the more likely it is that some domain on the trust path is sometimes unavailable to some user.
- *Increased risk of having to move users and groups among domains.* As users and groups are scattered in more domains, the possibility increases that in case of reorganization or a job change you must move some of those objects, or users' computer objects, to other domains. This is somewhat more laborious to administrators and somewhat less transparent to the users than moving objects inside a domain. In the case of groups, the group scope is also significant

in cross-domain moves—universal groups are easier to move than global or domain local groups. (We return to this subject later in this chapter.)

- *Duplicate administration.* Each domain must be administered independently, which may mean unnecessary extra work. For example, group policies must be established, OU trees must be created, and bridgehead servers must be managed separately for each domain.

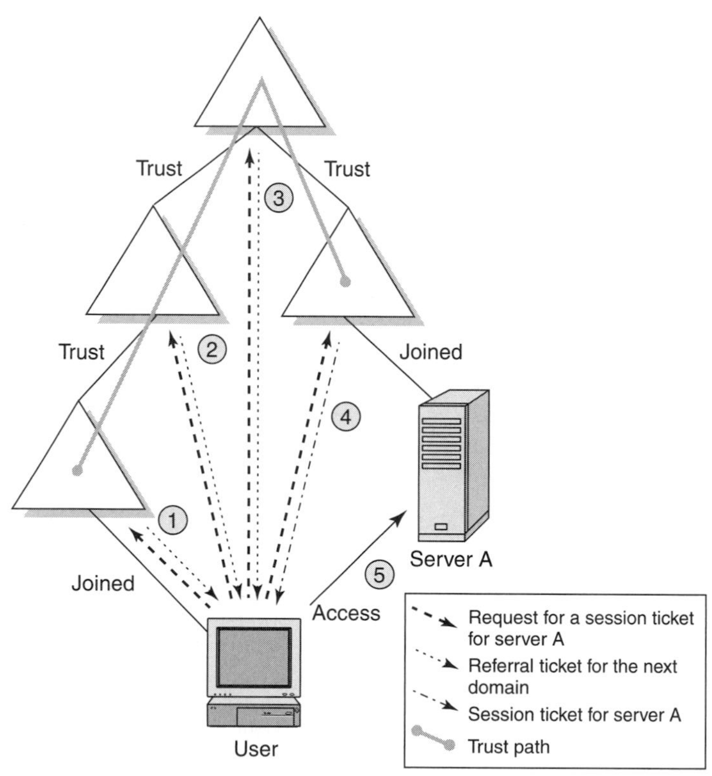

Figure 6.4 When a user accesses a server in a different domain, authentication is carried out with the Kerberos protocol and transitive trusts. The user's home domain returns a referral ticket for the next domain along the trust path. A domain controller in that domain returns another referral ticket, until the target server's domain is reached. A domain controller in this final domain returns a session ticket for the target server, and this allows the user to access the server. Fortunately, each machine on the path caches Kerberos tickets, so the next time, the process will be quicker.

Single or Multiple Forests

If you choose to have multiple domains, you must decide whether to have a single or multiple forests. Again, multiple forests incur additional costs, so you should create only one forest unless you can specifically justify multiple forests.

The following four forest features must be considered when you are choosing either a single or multiple forests. These four features are possible reasons to create multiple forests and they also represent costs if you do have multiple forests.

- A forest has a common schema.
- A forest has a common enterprise configuration.
- A forest has a common global catalog.
- A forest is an area of complete trust.

Even though we can treat these four features separately, they have one thing in common: The likelihood that an organization will implement multiple forests is greater if that organization has autonomous administration groups that don't trust each other. Consequently, each administration group wants to have its own forest. By "don't trust" we are not suggesting that the IT personnel are an especially suspicious kind of people. It is merely a question of the organization having quite independent divisions, and the upper management of each division not allowing administration from foreign divisions. Alternatively, there are multiple organizations that form a partnership.

There are three variations in the singleness or multipleness of forests:

- All divisions put up a single common forest (see Figure 6.5).
- One or some divisions opt to be left out of the common forest (see Figure 6.6).
- All divisions put up their own forests (see Figure 6.7).

If the organization ends up having multiple forests, they probably want to interact with each other. We discuss this in the "Trusts between Forests" section later in this chapter.

NOTE All four costs affect administrators, but only multiple global catalogs affect end users.

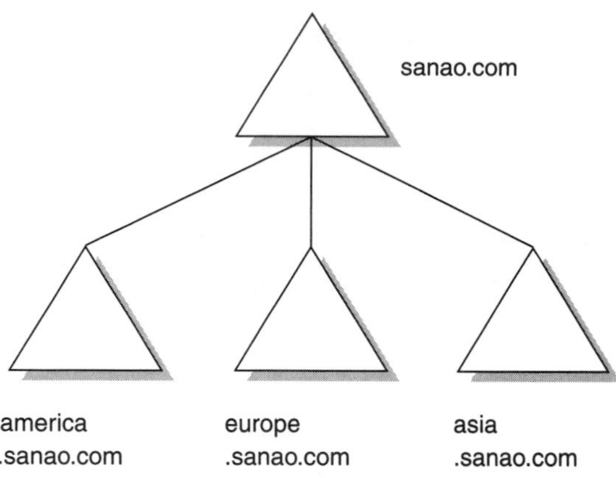

Figure 6.5 The preferred choice is that all divisions of an organization form a single forest. Only if there is a specific reason should multiple forests be created. Note that the three child domains (america, europe, and asia) are geographically oriented, and they do not represent the divisions.

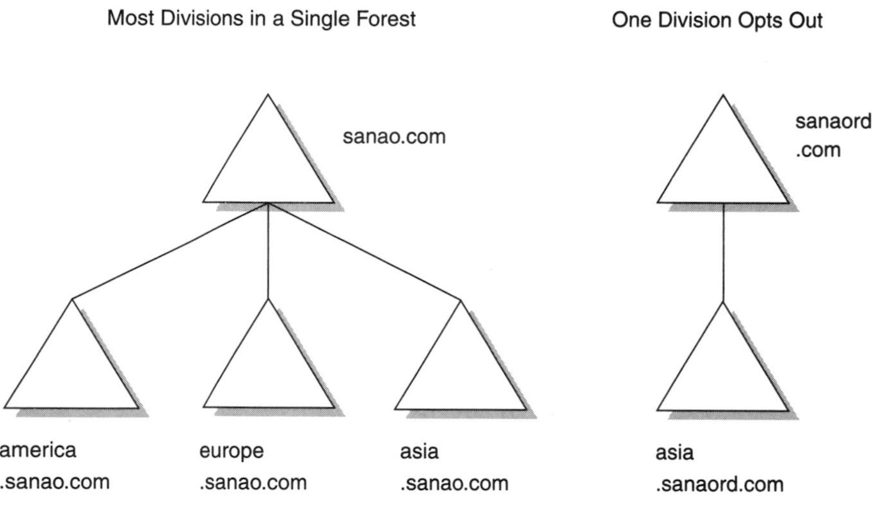

Figure 6.6 In this scenario, the R&D division of Sanao Corporation wants isolation from the rest of the corporation, so it has created its own forest.

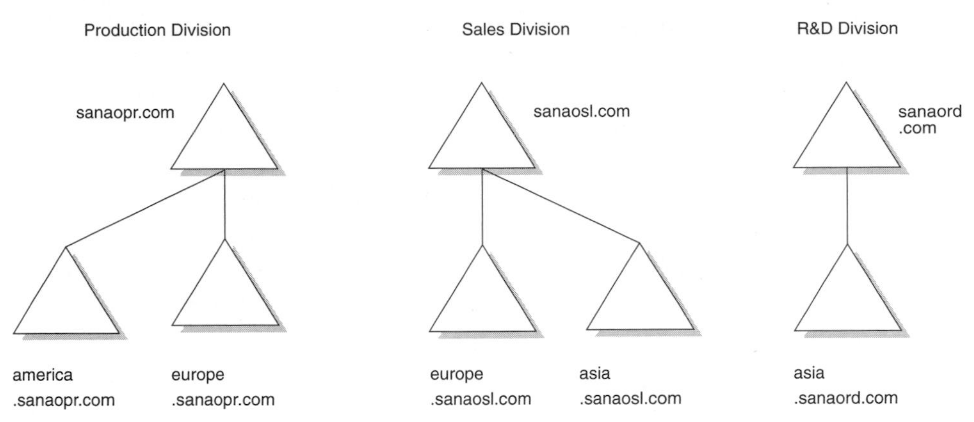

Figure 6.7 In this scenario, Sanao Corporation has such independent divisions that they all have created their own forests.

WARNING Administrators of child domains and domain controllers must be highly trusted also in the traditional sense of "trust." There are several ways (which we don't describe in this book) for a child domain administrator to gain system privileges and modify the forest configuration, which modifications subsequently replicate to all other domain controllers of the forest. Such privileges can also be gained by anyone who has a suitable boot diskette and physical access to one of the domain controllers. If part of the organization feels that another part (either their premises or administrators) is not worth this trust, those parts should deploy separate forests. This way, they are protected from the aforesaid risks, and they can also use the protections described in the "Trusts between Forests" section later in this chapter.

Number of Schemas

Someone should "own" the schema; there should be a single person or group to decide which schema changes are allowed as well as to coordinate and implement the changes. If the schema owner cannot be agreed on, there must be multiple schemas and, consequently, multiple forests. Also, if part of the organization wants to have control over the schema, it must create its own forest.

Another schema-related reason for multiple forests is a need to have multiple different schemas. This requirement should be quite rare in a production network. Classes and attributes that are added to the schema have several names and numeric identifiers that ensure their uniqueness. Therefore, a single schema (and forest) can host all schema extensions that applications from various vendors might need. However, you must have a separate forest to test any applications that require schema changes.

Multiple schemas can be slightly costly because they may require duplicate administrative work. If a change is necessary to multiple forests, it must be applied to each forest separately. If there is a setup program to take care of this, the amount of administrative work is probably tolerable.

Number of Forest Configurations

Similar to the schema management, there should be a person who is responsible for the forest configuration. He or she would be called the forest owner, and it would be best that he or she would own the schema also. The forest configuration includes definitions of the sites and site links in the forest and domains, as well as some other enterprisewide configuration information. The forest owner also approves each new domain to be added to the forest. The forest owner is responsible for all these changes in terms of both political decision making and administrative power.

Again, if part of the organization wants to maintain autonomous control over this information, it must create its own forest.

Sites and site links must be created and managed separately for each forest, which results in duplicate administrative work. You must consider all the circumstances to decide if the costs are worth the benefits.

Number of Global Catalogs

The global catalog is used mainly for four purposes:

- Searches
- Applications, such as Exchange, MSMQ (Microsoft Message Queue) or an application that uses DCOM (Distributed COM)
- User principal names (UPNs)
- Universal groups

When end users use Windows to search for something from the "Entire Network," they actually search from the global catalog. It would be confusing for users if the Entire Network included only part of the Active Directory objects in the enterprise's network. Thus, there should normally be only one forest. On the other hand, if a service provider maintained Active Directory networks for separate companies, separate global catalogs would probably be acceptable.

In addition to searches, the global catalog is used in two ways for user logons and authentications to servers: locating the user object via a UPN and checking memberships of universal groups. (UPN is called "user logon name" in the Users and Computers snap-in.)

A UPN, such as `jack.brown@sanao.com`, has a *UPN suffix*, such as `sanao.com`. This UPN suffix may be different from the user's domain name. For example, Jack's user object could be in the domain `domestic.sales.sanao.com` and still he could have the aforementioned UPN. This has two advantages: The name is easier to remember, and if the user's domain changes, his UPN doesn't have to change.

The UPN is a property of a user object, and the property is stored in the global catalog. Whenever someone enters "jack.brown@sanao.com" as a logon name, Active Directory can query the global catalog to locate the actual domain of the user object as well as the user object. Now, if there were two forests and two global catalogs and the user were sitting at a computer in a different forest from the user object, a UPN wouldn't work if there were an external trust between the forests. If there were a forest trust, however, the UPN would work and the user could log on.

NOTE Smart card logons rely on UPNs, so whenever a smart card is used to log on from a different forest, a default UPN must be used.

During a user logon or authentication to a server, memberships in universal groups are checked from the global catalog.

Complete Trust Area

A forest is a complete trust area and, therefore, a forest is the following:

- A scope of security principals (users, computers, and groups)
- A scope of Authenticated Users
- A scope of Enterprise Admins

NOTE In addition to the three listed complete trust consequences, one characteristic of a forest is that trust relationships inside a forest are "unlocked doors without guards." By contrast, trust relationships between forests can be controlled and secured in various ways, as described in the "Trusts between Forests" section later in this chapter. This may constitute reason enough for multiple forests.

The domains of each forest form a complete trust area. Any user or computer in the forest can be a member of any group (in accordance with the group scope), and any of the three can be assigned permissions to any object or resource in the forest. If this complete trust setup is not acceptable, multiple forests must be used.

Because a forest is a complete trust area, Authenticated Users includes all users of the forest and, by default, Authenticated Users has permission to read most objects in all domains of the forest. Therefore, all users of a forest can see practically all objects in the forest and read most or all properties of most of the objects. If you want to hide the objects in one domain from the users of other domains, consider putting that domain in a separate forest.

An alternative approach to creating a separate forest is to modify the default permissions so that the objects in a domain become hidden from the users in other domains in the same forest. However, this approach is somewhat laborious and more prone to errors than putting the domains in separate forests. Authenticated Users has a "Read + List Object" permission entry for the domain object. Phase 1 is not laborious or error-prone: You can use the Change button in ACL Editor to replace Authenticated Users for Domain Users in this entry, which causes only the local domain users to be able to browse the domain's objects and to see their properties (see Figure 6.8).

In AD2003, the Pre-Windows 2000 Compatible Access group includes Authenticated Users (depending on how you installed the domain; see Chapter 3), and Pre-Windows 2000 Compatible Access also has quite a few permissions to see objects and their properties. Therefore, you should not just change Authenticated Users for Domain Users, but also remove Authenticated Users from Pre-Windows 2000 Compatible Access, or remove the permissions of the latter.

In phase 2 the process becomes laborious and error-prone. The permission change from Authenticated Users to Domain Users (see Figure 6.8) prevents users from other domains from navigating into the domain. However, savvy outside users can still see the objects in the domain by specifying names such as `CN=Users, DC=sales, DC=sanao, DC=com` or using tools such as LDP (Ldp.exe), which is included in Support Tools. Therefore, to really hide all the objects in the domain, you should replace Authenticated Users for Domain Users in all the objects of the domain (and remember to do this also for each new object). If medium security is enough, you can modify the permissions of only the top-level containers in the domain and hope that outsiders don't figure out any object names at lower levels.

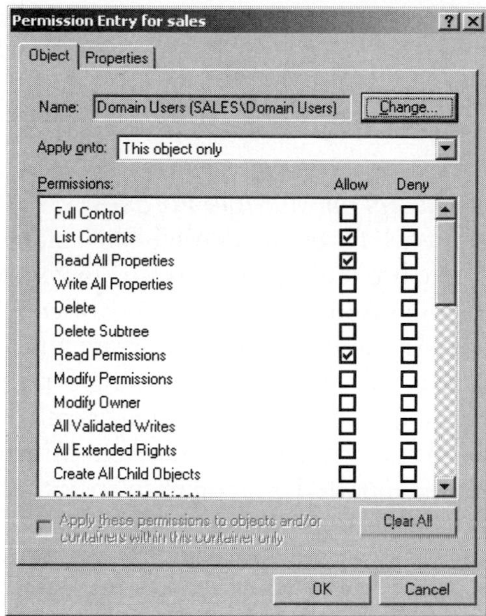

Figure 6.8 Authenticated Users has a "Read + List Object" permission entry for each domain object. You can use the Change button in ACL Editor to assign this entry to Domain Users instead of Authenticated Users. This limits access to the objects of the domain to only the local domain users.

NOTE If you plan to use the security modifications described here, you should first test them thoroughly in your environment.

The root domain of a forest includes the group Enterprise Admins, and that group is a member of Administrators in each domain. Also, Enterprise Admins has Full Control for the domain object, which also applies to all child objects (that allow inheritance). Therefore, Enterprise Admins has almost the widest possible permissions and rights to all objects in the domain as well as to its domain controllers.

If you want to block Enterprise Admins out of a domain, you can just remove the group from Administrators, and remove that one aforementioned permission entry. It is not necessary to put the domain in a separate forest to achieve this kind of independence (given, of course, that you highly trust the enterprise administrators). However, blocking Enterprise Admins out of a domain is probably not a good idea. If there is a problem in the domain or in the forest, Enterprise Admins would need access to this domain. Also, maybe the only member in Enterprise Admins is the forest owner, and he or she is highly trusted anyway, so there is no need for the blocking.

Other Reasons for Multiple Forests

Because Active Directory doesn't allow merging forests, an organization may have to use multiple forests for "historical" reasons. If independent divisions built Active Directory networks before any central coordination, those divisions have to be separate forests (until there is a version of Active Directory that allows merging forests). Also, company acquisitions, mergers, and partnerships may result in a multiforest network.

Some large organizations may split off Exchange in a separate forest so it can be supported by a separate operations group. Exchange security is tightly coupled with Active Directory, and it tends to assume Exchange administrators are also domain administrators. Consequently, you can only protect a forest from a rogue Exchange administrator if that Exchange is in a separate forest. This is actually the recommended deployment for a large decentralized company with a centralized mail system.

Other Costs of Additional Forests

In addition to the four main reasons for a single or multiple forests, there are the following miscellaneous costs.

- Administrators cannot move user accounts and other objects between forests (as they can between domains in a forest). However, they can clone objects between forests. The latter option doesn't preserve user passwords or maintain object GUIDs.
- Between AD2000 domains in two different forests, only NTLM, not Kerberos, authentication is used. However, between AD2003 forests connected by a forest trust, Kerberos is used.
- Exchange 2000 and later use Active Directory's global catalog as its global address list. If there are multiple forests and consequently multiple global catalogs, users of one forest cannot browse potential recipients from other forests. One Exchange organization can operate only in a single forest and only one Exchange organization can operate in a single forest.

Forest Planning Considerations

When you plan a forest for your organization, you must know three topics:

- The three faces of a forest
- How to add shortcut trusts to optimize authentication
- How to choose the root domain

The Three Faces of a Forest

You can look at the structure of the domains in a forest from three viewpoints (see Figure 6.9).

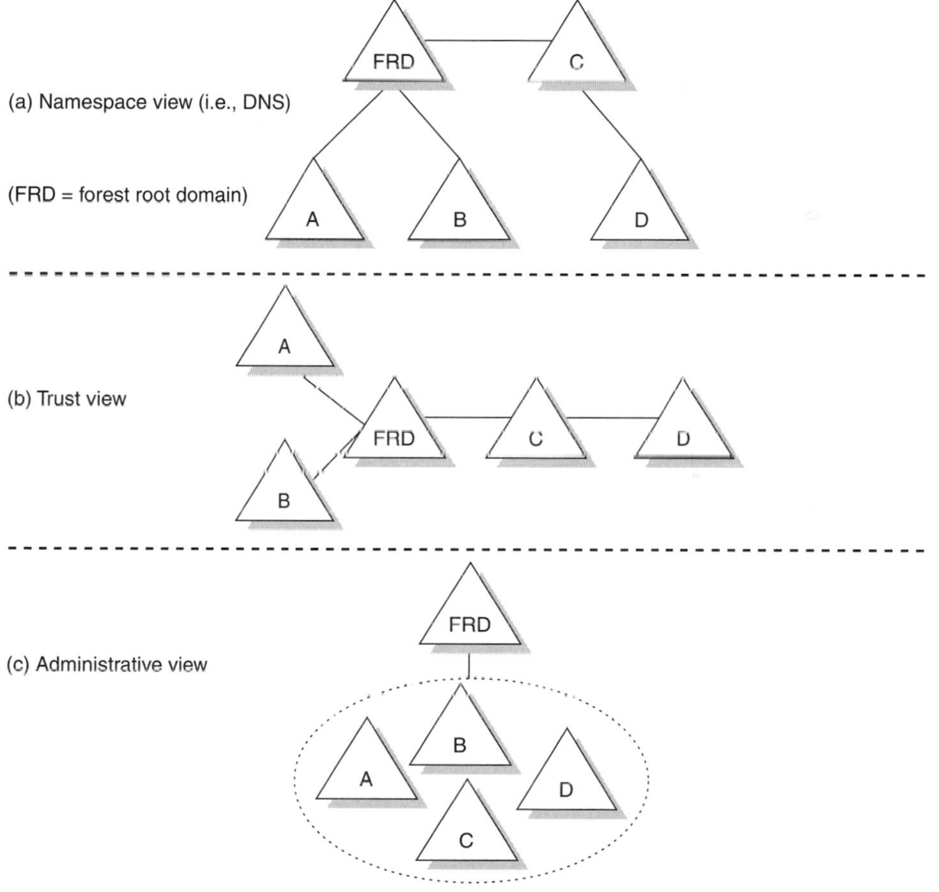

Figure 6.9 Three views of a forest: (a) namespace view, (b) trust view, and (c) administrative view

As Figure 6.9 illustrates, the three faces of a forest are as follows:

- *Namespace view.* This is the traditional view from which forests are presented. Each domain tree (two in Figure 6.9) in the forest has a root domain, and the first of them is also the forest root domain. The domains in this view are arranged according to the DNS namespace. This view also dictates how the search scopes are determined (as explained later in this chapter).
- *Trust view.* If we think only of the trust relationships among the domains, we can forget the traditional levels, where a child domain is on a lower level than its parent. All that matters are the trust paths between various domain pairs. As you saw in Figure 6.4, the user's workstation must contact each domain on the trust path to the target domain where the accessed resource resides. The longer this trust path is, the longer it takes to authenticate. In addition, the authentication speed depends on the speed of the workstation's connection to each domain controller on the path. The forest root domain is the central station of this authentication traffic.
- *Administrative view.* The structure of the domains in a forest has no administrative meaning. In this view you can think of the domains (except the forest root domain) as just a bunch of domains. Group policies or permissions don't inherit from one domain to another. Administrators from parent domains don't get permissions or rights to child domains, and administrators from child domains can be managerial superiors to administrators from parent domains. The forest root domain is special because it contains Enterprise Admins and Schema Admins, and anyone who controls the forest root domain can control these two groups.

NOTE If domain C in Figure 6.9 were not a separate domain tree, but merely a child domain in the first tree, the namespace view would be different. The trust view and administrative view would still look exactly the same.

Shortcut Trusts

To speed up users' authentication from one domain to another, administrators can add shortcut trusts between domains in the same forest. Like the old Windows NT trusts, shortcut trusts are one-way. Unlike the old Windows NT trusts, shortcut trusts are transitive.

Shortcut trusts not only make interdomain authentications faster, but they can also improve fault tolerance. Without shortcut trusts, if the user's workstation cannot contact a domain (i.e., a domain controller of that domain) along the trust part to the target domain, the authentication fails. However, if there is a shortcut trust between the user's domain and the resource domain, the missing domain is bypassed and the authentication succeeds. If the communication failure also prevents part or all of the DNS name resolution, this bypassing mechanism probably will not work.

Shortcut trusts don't cost anything other than the few minutes' work that it takes administrators to create one. Therefore, consider creating a shortcut trust between each pair of domains in which users from one domain relatively frequently access resources in the other domain, and where a normal parent-child trust does not already exist as part of the forest structure. If there are only a few domains in the forest, you can even create all possible shortcut trusts without using energy to consider whether they are needed or not. There are no drawbacks to this approach.

Figure 6.10 illustrates a five-domain forest (using two views), where users of domain D quite frequently access resources in domain B.

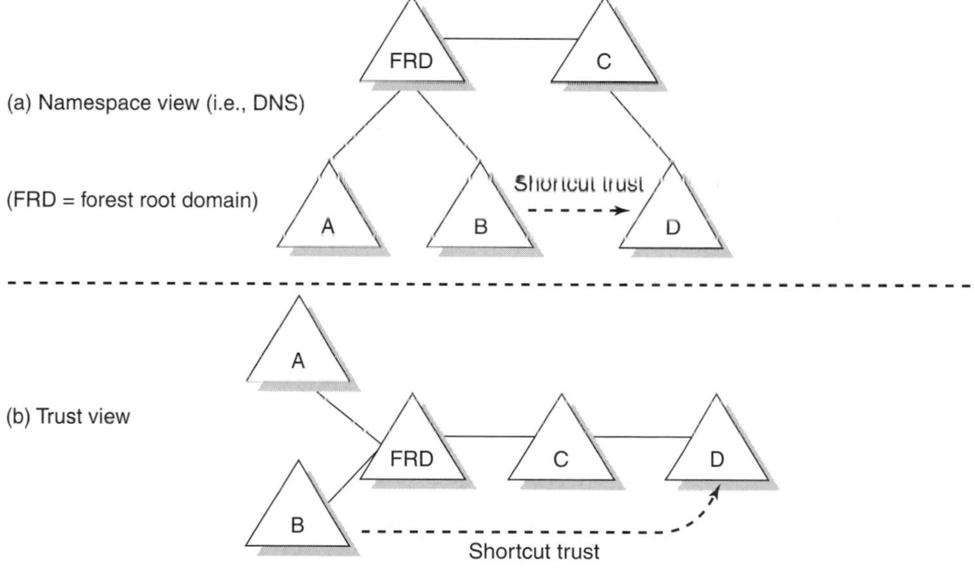

Figure 6.10 If users in domain D quite frequently access resources in domain B, it pays to create a shortcut trust in the opposite direction. Without the shortcut trust, each authentication would need to go via domain C and the forest root domain.

Therefore, administrators have created a shortcut trust in the opposite direction—in other words, from domain B to domain D. Figure 6.11 illustrates a four-domain forest where all possible shortcut trusts are created.

NOTE Because shortcut trusts are transitive, creating one trust helps users only in the subsequent domains. All users of the forest can use this new shortcut when it makes the trust path shorter to a target domain.

The Forest Root Domain

If you decide to have multiple domains in a forest, one of those domains is the forest root domain. In addition, if there are multiple domain trees in the forest, each consequent domain tree has a root domain.

Only the forest root domain contains the groups Enterprise Admins and Schema Admins, so members of Domain Admins and Administrators

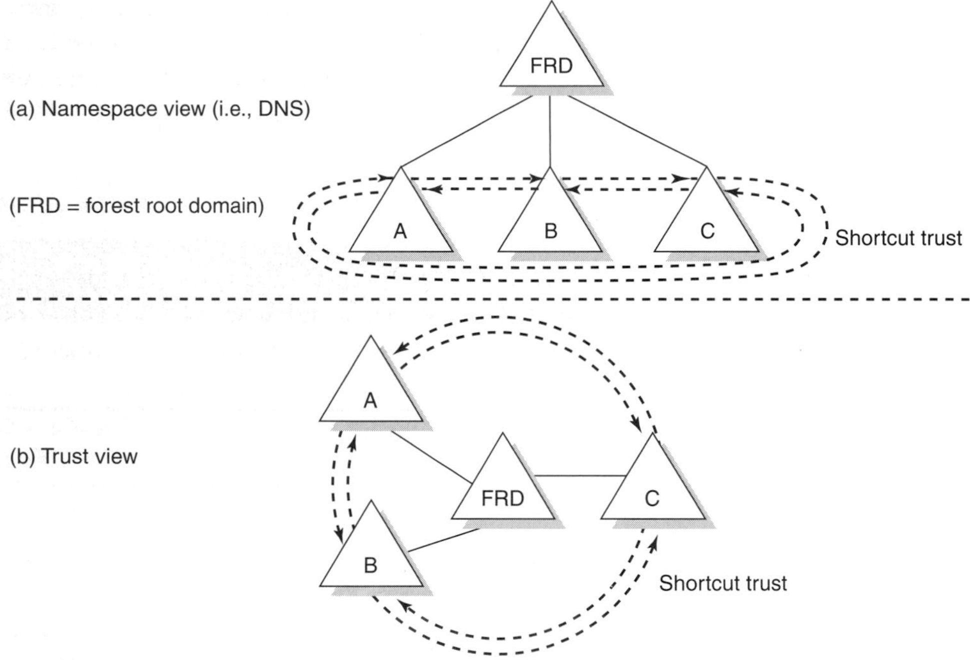

Figure 6.11 Because it takes only 15 minutes to create the six (i.e., all possible) shortcut trusts in this figure, it is probably not worth trying to find out which ones are actually needed.

in that domain can control the members of the two former forestwide groups.

Selecting a forest root domain is a permanent choice. It is the first domain you create in a forest, and after you create it you cannot transfer the root "role" to any other domain. You cannot create a new domain above the forest root domain; you can create only child domains. Also, you cannot delete the forest root domain (unless it is the last domain in the forest being removed).

WARNING You cannot reinstall a forest root domain to an existing forest. Consequently, if all domain controllers of the forest root domain fail, and there is no backup to restore them, you have to install all domains in the forest from scratch. Obviously, you want to avoid this.

The following are two requirements for the forest root domain.

- *The forest root domain should be well monitored and maintained.* The organization cannot afford to lose the forest root domain. That domain contains Enterprise Admins and Schema Admins, and probably the schema master and domain naming master as well.
- *The forest root domain should be easily accessible.* The forest root domain is the central station for interdomain authentications, even though not all interdomain authentications must travel through the forest root domain (it depends on the trust paths and shortcut trusts). Consequently, all parts of the network should be connected to the forest root domain by a reliable and relatively fast link.

The forest root domain can be either "empty" or nonempty. In the latter case, it can contain 30,000 users, for example. We must use quotation marks with the word "empty" because even though we wouldn't create hundreds of users, computers, or other objects in the forest root domain, it would still contain all the predefined objects of any domain. Figure 6.12 illustrates the two choices.

An "Empty" Forest Root Domain

On the left side of Figure 6.12, one of the three child domains would have had to be chosen to be the forest root unless the organization had created an "empty" domain for this purpose. In an organization with

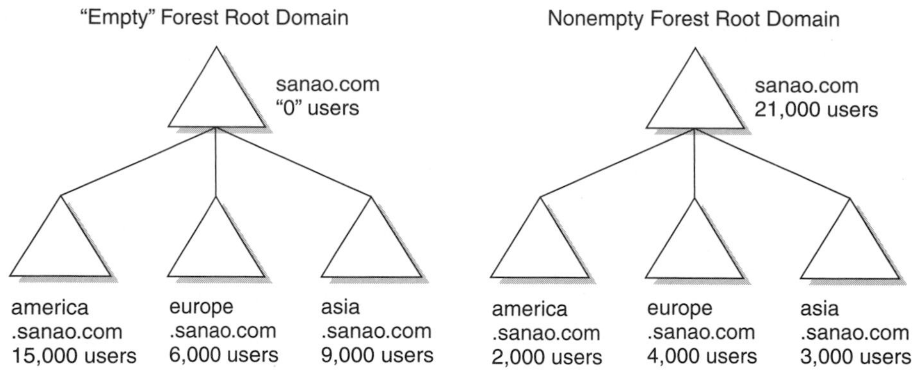

Figure 6.12 The forest root domain can be either "empty," in which case all users and other objects are created in child domains (or in other trees), or the forest root domain can contain most of the users in the organization.

relatively independent divisions and decentralized IT administration, it is difficult to raise any division domain above others, so the model with an "empty" forest root domain suits such an organization well (given that the organization didn't opt for multiple forests).

Using this approach, the three divisions of Figure 6.12 would have to create and manage a fourth domain and buy domain controllers for it. They would have to establish a committee or team to be responsible for the forest root domain, the schema, and the configuration of the forest. This approach would offer the following benefits for the organization.

- *Never obsolete.* An "empty" FRD never becomes obsolete. If `europe.sanao.com` on the left side of Figure 6.12 were chosen to be the FRD, and two years later the organization decided to sell all European functions, the organization would still have to use `europe` as the FRD.
- *Light to replicate.* An "empty" FRD is light and easy to replicate to various locations of the network (given that appropriate domain controllers are bought and installed).
- *Ownership easily transferred.* You may want to assign the ownership of the forest root domain (and consequently, the forest) to a different IT team or outsource it. This is easier with an empty root that doesn't contain a lot of objects and resources.
- *More controlled admin power.* With an "empty" FRD and separate division domains, the administrators of any division domain cannot control the membership of Enterprise Admins or Schema

Admins. In other words, the organization can isolate the forest administration (with required permissions and rights) from domain administration. This also means fewer accidental wrong changes to the forest configuration.

Because of the listed benefits, Microsoft considers it a best practice to have an empty forest root domain. Even if you need only one domain, you could have an empty root above your main domain. This could make a possible future restructuring or merger easier. The downsides, however, for having an empty root with a single child domain are that (a) it is more complex than having just one domain, (b) more server hardware and licenses are needed, and (c) more work is needed in deploying, managing, and troubleshooting the forest.

The forest root domain could contain some objects in addition to the predefined objects that exist in any domain. For example, the user accounts for enterprise administrators or schema administrators, as well as some other administrative accounts, would most likely reside in the forest root domain.

NOTE You can set a strict password policy for the forest root domain so that passwords of enterprise administrators are required to be longer than in other domains and fewer wrong passwords are tolerated before an account locks up.

A Nonempty Forest Root Domain

On the right side of Figure 6.12, one organization has most of its employees in the headquarters office (assumed to be in North America) and it has centralized IT administration. It is convenient for this organization to have a forest root domain that contains all the headquarters users. The other three domains contain fewer users in South America, Europe, and Asia.

In this scenario, the domain administrators of the main domain also control the forest by controlling the membership of Enterprise Admins and Schema Admins. Therefore, the number of domain administrators in that domain should be limited, and user administration, as well as other normal domain administration, should be structured so that various OUs are delegated to various OU administrators.

WARNING Only members of Administrators can share folders, format hard disks, and perform some other such tasks on domain controllers.

As you assign people to this group so that they can perform these tasks on the domain controllers of the main domain, those same people get permission to modify the membership of Enterprise Admins and Schema Admins as well. Unless this is what you want, you should remove Administrators from the permission lists of Enterprise Admins and Schema Admins.

If the users in Europe, Asia, or South America access a foreign domain, it is most likely the main domain in headquarters. However, if a user in Europe sometimes accesses the Asia domain, the authentication needs to travel via the headquarters domain in North America. Placing a domain controller of the headquarters domain in Europe shortens the transmission path, but it results in replicating all the changes in the 21,000 North American users to Europe.

Another way to make authentication from Europe to Asia faster is to create a shortcut trust from Asia to Europe. This solution doesn't require extra hardware or replication traffic. As long as there are only a few domains, it is probably the best choice. If there are 17 domains in the Asia branch of the domain tree and another 17 in the Europe branch, the administrators can (but they shouldn't) create 578 ($2 \times 17 \times 17$) shortcut trusts to directly cover all cases when a user in some of the European or Asian domains accesses a resource in the other continent. However, because shortcut trusts are transitive, creating just two shortcut trusts on the top level (from the top domain of the Europe branch to the top domain of the Asia branch and vice versa) bypasses the need to communicate with North America.

Various Roots

There are actually quite a few different roots related to Active Directory:

- *Forest root domain.* This was explained in the preceding paragraphs.
- *Tree root domain.* This is the root domain of each domain tree in a forest.
- `RootDSE`. This concept is part of the LDAPv3 specification. `RootDSE` is the root of the directory information tree and it is referred to with an empty distinguished name. Despite its name, `rootDSE` doesn't operate as a root in the sense that you could browse any tree beneath it. `RootDSE` is a virtual object that contains 22 properties (or 19 if the server is running Windows 2000). The purpose of these properties (and, consequently, of

`rootDSE`) is to provide the basic information of an LDAP server to an LDAP client. When the client connects to a server, the former can ask the latter such things as the name of the forest and the domain the server is part of, which LDAP controls and authentication mechanisms the server supports, and whether or not the server contains the global catalog.

- *DNS root.* In our sample name `sanao.com`, "sanao" is a *second-level domain (SLD)*, and "com" is a *top-level domain (TLD)*. Above `com` and other top-level domains, such as `org`, `gov`, and `edu`, is the root of the DNS namespace. This DNS root is denoted with a single dot (.).
- *Root of an OU tree.* Each domain can have an OU tree, and the root for this tree is the domain object of the domain.

Trusts between Forests

You can create two types of trusts between forests: (a) external trusts that existed already in AD2000 and that are between two domains of two forests, and (b) forest trusts that are new to AD2003 and that are between the forest root domains of two forests. This way, a forest trust connects two entire forests together, not just two domains as an external trust does.

NOTE Another way to provide some access for the resources in a forest to users external to the forest is to use PKI. You can give those users PKI certificates and then map the certificates to user accounts in your forest.

Name Resolution between Forests

If you want to connect two forests with a trust, an obvious requirement is that their computers must be able to resolve computer and service names of each other. Even though we don't cover DNS in this book, we briefly describe your alternatives. The first two are new to Windows Server 2003 DNS service, compared to the Windows 2000 version.

- *Conditional forwarding.* This option means that you specify per DNS server that if a certain DNS domain is queried, the server should forward the query to a specific other server (where the latter is either a Windows or another DNS server). For example, the DNS server DC2 (part of the `sanao.com` forest) knows that whenever `sanaoeurope.com` is queried, it should forward the query to DC6 (which is part of the `sanaoeurope.com` forest). Conditional forwarding requires that the name being queried must be on the same or a higher level than the local DNS zone. For example, the DNS server DC2 (part of the `sanao.com` forest) would never forward queries for `rd.sanao.com`, because the latter domain is on a lower level, and consequently, conditional forwarding does not work. It is easy to configure firewalls for conditional forwarding, because you know exactly which DNS servers would communicate with which others. Two downsides are, however, that you must configure each server separately, and whenever new name servers are added to the target domain, you must modify your conditional forwarding configuration.

- *Stub zone*. A stub zone is a copy of the zone, containing only a few records of the zone: the start of authority (SOA) record, the name server (NS) records, and possibly glue records, which are of the type host (A) record. Based on this information, the correct DNS server can be contacted and the name resolved. Stub zones have three advantages: (a) You can store them in Active Directory, so that they are replicated automatically; (b) if a new name server is added to the target zone, this information is automatically configured in the stub zone; and (c) the target name can be on the same, lower, or higher level than the source zone. Possible drawbacks are that zone transfers must be allowed on the target zone, and firewalls may block some queries, because you may not have prepared for all server-to-server combinations that will communicate.
- *Secondary zone*. Here you create a standard secondary zone of the foreign zone on the local DNS server. The advantage of this option is that it works also with non-Windows Server 2003 DNS servers (either older Windows or UNIX, etc.). On the other hand, there is more data to replicate (the entire zone), and zone transfers must be allowed on the target zone.

External Trusts

The first type of trusts between forests, *external trusts,* is unidirectional and nontransitive (i.e., Windows NT–like). Consequently, you must manually create a trust relationship between each pair of domains (in the correct direction) where cross-domain resource access is needed. For example, if users in domain A need access to resources in domain B, domain B must trust domain A (of course, proper permissions must be assigned also). Figure 6.13 illustrates external trusts.

NOTE Between forests with external trusts, authentication takes place with NTLM instead of Kerberos.

Creating an outgoing external trust from a domain to a domain in an external forest makes the users of the target domain part of the Authenticated Users of the source domain (unless selective authentication is used, as discussed later). Consequently, those external users can see practically all objects in the source domain. However, note that because external trusts are not transitive, the external users cannot see the objects in the other domains of the forest. Figure 6.14 illustrates this concept.

AD2003 brings two new features to external trusts: SID filtering and selective authentication (although SID filtering is also available for Windows NT 4.0 and Windows 2000 as part of a Security Roll-up package). We dedicate a section to each feature, and they appear after the next section, on forest trusts.

Forest Trusts

Like external trusts, forest trusts are between two forests. Forest trusts are handy when, for example, two companies merge, one company acquires

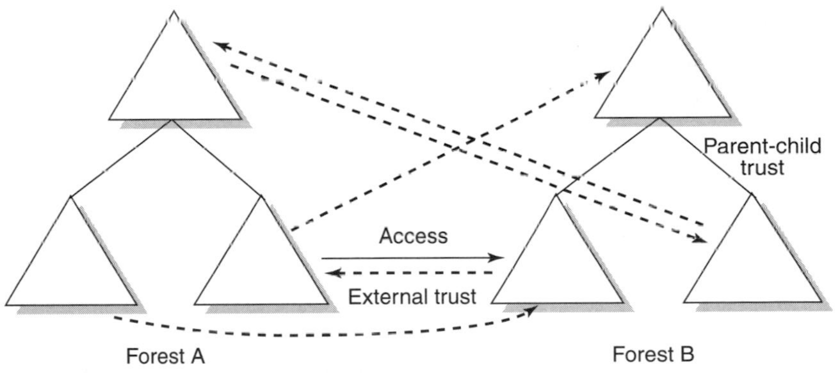

Figure 6.13 Interforest access from one domain to another requires an external trust in the opposite direction of the required access. With two three-domain forests, there could be 18 trusts between different domain pairs, but this figure contains "only" 5.

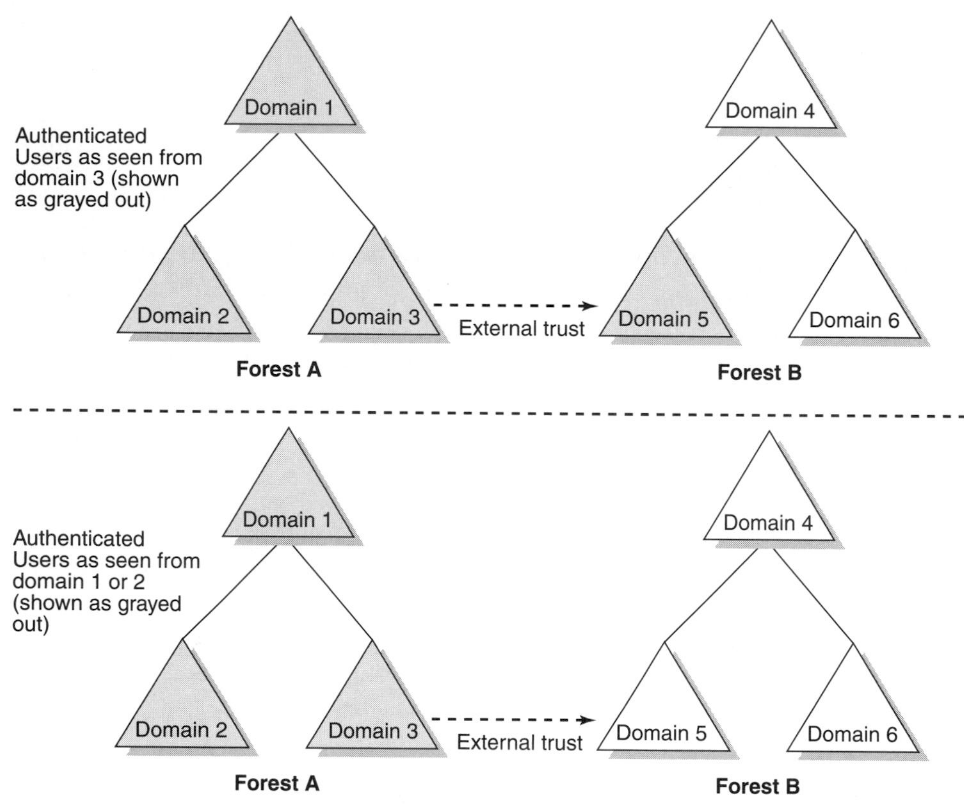

Figure 6.14 Each outgoing external trust enlarges the scope of Authenticated Users. Because external trusts are not transitive, however, the enlarged scope applies only to the trusting domain (domain 3 in the figure). The figure applies if the trust doesn't use selective authentication.

another, or an organization has individual divisions. A requirement of forest trusts is that both forests must be running on the Windows Server 2003 forest functional level.

Forest trusts have the following benefits over external trusts:

- Forest trusts are transitive. Consequently, a forest trust allows assigning group memberships and/or permissions between any two domains in different forests, not just between the forest root domains where the trust actually resides. Note, however, that if SID filtering is used, it disables half of this transitiveness. We explain this later in the "SID Filtering" section. Also, the transitiveness of forest trusts does not apply to "forest chains." That is, if forest A trusts forest B, and forest B trusts forest C, there is no implicit trust from forest A to forest C. If you need forest A to trust forest C, you must create an explicit one-way forest trust between the two.

- Forest trusts allow a user from the trusted forest to log on to a computer in the trusting forest. This is always possible if the logging-on user specifies her logon name in the user principal name (UPN) format, such as `jill.green@sanao.com`. However, if the user enters her pre-Windows 2000 logon name (that is, the SAM name), only the forest root domain of the trusted forest is available in the drop-down list. Therefore, users of child domains cannot log on this way. A third option, new to Windows Server 2003 (and not present in Windows XP with SP1 or Windows 2000 with SP4), is to enter a name such as `sanao\jill`. This new option works for user accounts of both the trusted forest root domain and its child domains.
- Forests trusts use Kerberos authentication between forests.

You can grant permissions to the users, global groups, and universal groups of the trusted forest for the resources in the trusting forest. You can also assign all three as members in domain local and local groups of the trusting forest.

NOTE A universal group cannot have members from another forest. Therefore, you must assign the members (foreign users, global groups and universal groups) separately to each local group in the trusting forest.

A forest trust can combine two forests into one "complete trust area," so that Authenticated Users includes all users of both forests, and any user of either forest can have permissions to any resource in either forest. There are three methods, however, to limit this widest possible trust and make a trust to a foreign forest more secure: (a) selective authentication, (b) SID filtering, and (c) name suffix routing. All three can limit how resources in the local forest can be accessed from the foreign forest. We describe the methods in the following three sections.

Selective Authentication

Each trust between forests uses one of two authentication modes. A forest trust uses either forestwide or selective authentication, and an external trust uses either domainwide or selective authentication. Whether a two-way trust uses forestwide/domainwide or selective authentication is chosen separately for each direction.

With forestwide/domainwide authentication, any user of the foreign forest/domain can authenticate to any server in the local forest/domain. Then, after authentication, normal access permissions specify what the user can do on the server. In addition, any such foreign user belongs to Authenticated Users in the local forest/domain (and consequently by default gets quite a few permissions, such as seeing most objects of the forest and their properties, and being a member of the Users group in each computer and domain).

Using selective authentication, you control which users or groups of the foreign forest/domain can authenticate to which servers in the local forest/domain. You do this with the extended right (or permission) Allowed to Authenticate, which is visible in each computer object. For example, if you want Jack from `sanaoeurope.com` to be able to authenticate to the server Srv02, which resides in the `sanao.com` forest, you must grant Jack the Allowed to Authenticate permission for Srv02's computer object.

NOTE You grant the Allowed to Authenticate permission for the computer object of the server, where the to-be-accessed resource resides. You do not need to grant the permission for any authenticating domain controllers (unless the resource resides on a domain controller).

If the user does not have the required permission, she will get an error that the server is not accessible and "The machine you are logging onto is protected by an authentication firewall. The specified account is not allowed to authenticate to the machine."

If the two forests/domains belong to the same organization, it is normally most convenient to use forestwide/domainwide authentication. Conversely, if they belong to different organizations, selective authentication is probably more appropriate. Also, if the trust is heavily and widely used, forestwide/domainwide authentication is better than selective authentication.

TIP If you need to grant the authentication permission for a number of servers or workstations, and those computer objects are in the same OU without any other computer objects, you can use permission inheritance. Grant the permission for the OU where the objects reside and specify that the permission will inherit to computer objects.

SID Filtering

SID filtering prevents one type of Elevation of Privilege attack from the foreign forest (or Windows NT domain) to the local forest. After giving a brief background, we explain the threat, countermeasure, and impact, as well as how to control SID filtering.

Microsoft security bulletin MS02-001 discusses the issue, at the address `http://www.microsoft.com/technet/security/bulletin/ms02-001.asp`.

Background of SIDs and SID History

As explained in Chapter 4, each user account and other security principal has a security ID (SID) to identify it for security purposes, such as for group memberships and for permissions in ACLs. A SID consists of a domain part (that is the same for all security principals in the domain) and a relative ID (RID). The resulting SID is unique in the forest, and it is also extremely likely that it is unique in the world.

Each user account can also have a SID history property, which is used for migration scenarios. When a user is migrated to another domain (or forest), she will get a new SID, the domain part of which matches the new domain. Her old SID, however, can be retained in the SID history property, which is later used in all her authentications. This way, she retains her permissions and group memberships that existed in the previous domain. SID history is meant to be a temporary solution after the migration, and once the user's new identity (with the new SID) has all the necessary permissions and group memberships, her SID history property may be deleted.

The Possible Attack

If someone could present a false SID during authentication, he could gain practically any administrative or other permissions, so he would perform an Elevation of Privilege attack. Even an administrator cannot (well, never say never) counterfeit his normal primary SID. He could, however, add a false SID to the SID history property of a user account.

Because counterfeiting SIDs requires administrative privileges, it should not be a problem in a single forest, where forest administrators and domain administrators must be highly trusted anyway. When there are two forests, however, and a forest trust or an external trust connects them, counterfeiting SIDs—that is, SID spoofing—becomes a risk that must be considered. You do not necessarily trust highly the administrators of the other forest, especially if it belongs to a different organization.

The SID spoofing risk also applies to a scenario where a domain of your forest has an external trust to a Windows NT domain.

The foreign administrator who is breaking into the local forest could place in his SID history a SID that is an enterprise administrator, for example, in the local forest.

The Countermeasure

To remove the risk of SID spoofing, you can use SID filtering. When an authentication request comes from the foreign forest/domain to the local forest/domain, SID filtering at the local end removes all SIDs that do not match the domain part of the trusted domain (where the request is received from). This effectively disables the functionality of SID history across this trust.

The Impact

SID filtering is often quite OK, and there is no harm done (except for the intruder's purposes). However, using SID filtering prevents using the following three things across the trust where it is enabled:

- *SID history does not work.* This only hurts if the trusted domain contains user accounts that would need to access resources across the trust, and the access requires a SID from the SID history. If this scenario applies to you, you should consider granting new permissions and assign new group memberships to the new identities of the migrated users. After this, you wouldn't need the SID history anymore, so you could enable SID filtering.
- *A forest trust is only half-transitive.* As illustrated in Figure 6.15, in the trusted forest, there is no transitivity. For example, if `sanaoeurope.com` trusts `sanao.com`, a user from `rd.sanao.com` cannot access `sanaoeurope.com`. If you disable SID filtering, the access is possible again. Note that in the trusting forest, there is normal transitivity all the time. For example, if `sanao.com` trusts `sanaoeurope.com`, a user from `sanaoeurope.com` can access `rd.sanao.com` regardless of SID filtering.
- *Universal groups don't necessarily work.* If a universal group resides in the same domain as the user (in the trusted domain of the trust), it works, and it can have permissions in the trusting forest/domain. However, if the universal group is in another domain of the trusted forest, its SID won't match the trusted domain, so SID filtering will remove it.

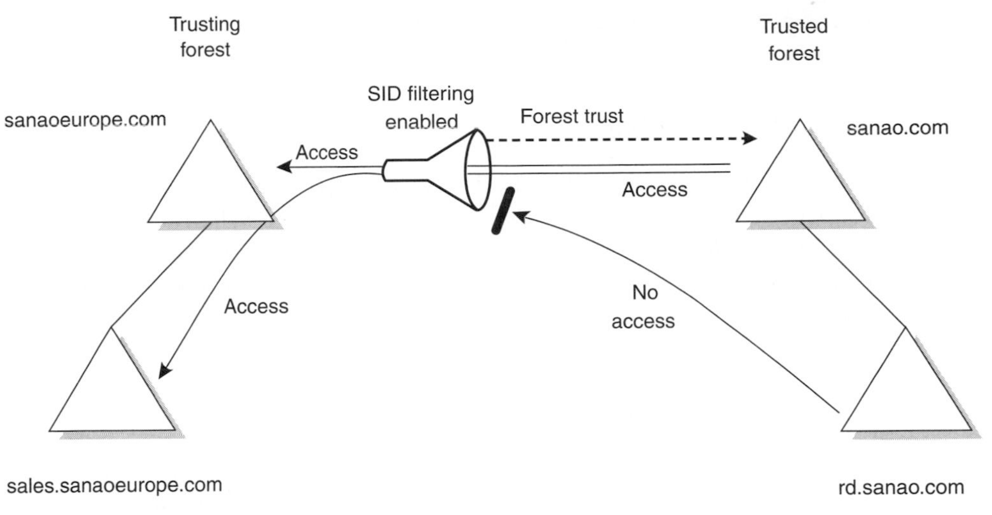

Figure 6.15 When SID filtering is enabled on a forest trust, only the users from the forest root domain can access the trusting forest. They can, however, access any domain in the trusting forest.

Of the three listed problems, losing half of the forest trust's transitivity is most likely to be a problem for you. However, it is only a problem with a multidomain forest, and obviously, it does not hurt you if there is only one domain in the trusted foreign forest.

Controlling SID Filtering

Depending on how you create a forest trust or an external trust, SID filtering is probably turned on by default, and if so, you get a notification stating this. After creating the trust, you can check whether SID filtering is enabled or disabled using a command such as the following (NetDom is part of Windows Support Tools):

```
netdom trust sanao.com /domain:sanaoeurope.com /quarantine
```

In the preceding command, `sanao.com` is the trusting domain and `sanaoeurope.com` is the trusted domain. The following two commands would enable and disable SID filtering, respectively:

```
netdom trust sanao.com /domain:sanaoeurope.com
    /quarantine:yes
```

```
netdom trust sanao.com /domain:sanaoeurope.com
    /quarantine:no
```

Name Suffix Routing

The previous two securing methods (selective authentication and SID filtering) apply to both external trusts and forest trusts, but name suffix routing is a feature of forest trusts only. You can use this feature both to block unwanted access to your local forest and to ensure legitimate access with the foreign forest.

Blocking Unwanted Access

With name suffix routing, you can specify which domains of the trusted (foreign) forest are valid when their users and groups access the resources in the trusting (local) forest. In other words, if you are an administrator of the trusting forest, you can block out some domains of the trusted forest so that their users and groups have no access to your forest.

When a domain of the trusted forest is blocked out, its users cannot remotely access the resources of the trusting forest. Nor can they log on to the workstations of the trusting forest. If permissions were granted to a group in the blocked domain for a resource in the trusting forest, those permissions are not valid either. However, if a user in a valid domain is a member of a group in a blocked domain, and that group is a member in a valid domain, permissions granted to the latter group are valid in the trusting forest.

Name suffix routing uses the term *unique name suffix*. Each forest has the following unique name suffixes (see also Figure 6.18 some pages later):

- The forest name (`sanao.com` in Figure 6.18)
- Any domain tree names of the forest (`sanaoint.com` in Figure 6.18)
- Any UPN suffixes specified in the forest configuration (using the Domains and Trusts snap-in, for example)

If the trusted forest contains more than one unique name suffix, you are prompted at trust-creation time to select which ones to route and which ones to block. You can later modify the settings in the trust properties, as Figure 6.16 illustrates.

NOTE If you have added individual UPN suffixes to users using a script, for example, those UPN suffixes are not part of the forest configuration, and therefore they will not be visible in the list shown in Figure 6.16.

You could think of unique name suffixes as the top-level name suffixes. They may have subordinate name suffixes, or child domains in practice. When routing of the parent name suffix is enabled, the child name suffixes are routed as well. This is why the names in Figure 6.16 have an asterisk, such as `*.sanaoint.com`. However, you can enable/disable child names (i.e., domains) individually, as shown in Figure 6.17. Because `rd.sanao.com` is individually disabled, `sanao.com` displays "Exceptions" in Figure 6.16.

By default, all nonconflicting names that exist when a forest trust is created will be routed. If you later add new domains or UPN suffixes in the trusted domain, you must manually (well, if appropriate) enable those new name suffixes. `Sanao.net` in Figure 6.16 is such a new name suffix (a UPN suffix that was just created).

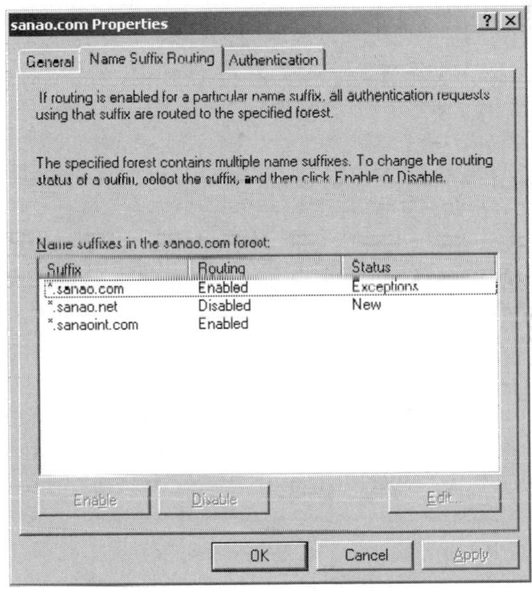

Figure 6.16 You can select the parts of a foreign forest from where users can access your local forest. All three names on the list are unique name suffixes of the `sanao.com` forest. `Sanao.net` was just added in that forest, so next you would need to enable it to be routed.

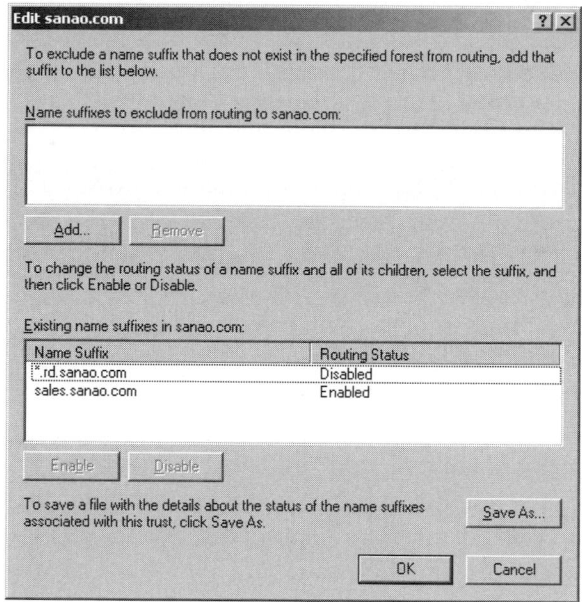

Figure 6.17 You can individually enable or disable each name suffix that exists in a unique (or top-level) name suffix.

NOTE If you block out `rd.sanao.com`, for example, and a user in that domain has the UPN suffix `sanao.com`, which is not blocked out, she still cannot access your local forest.

Ensuring Legitimate Access

Name suffix routing (that is, nonblocked) is essential to connecting two forests with a forest trust so that users of one forest can access the resources and log on to the other forest. Usually, this works fine without any special steps, but if there are naming conflicts in one of the following three areas, the routing of the conflicting name is disabled:

- *Conflicting DNS names of domains or UPN suffixes.* A conflict will occur if the two names are identical or if one is subordinate to the other (such as `sanao.com` and `corp.sanao.com`).
- *Conflicting NetBIOS names of domains.* Because NetBIOS names are not hierarchical, there may be a BOSTON domain in two forests, for example.

- *Conflicting domain parts of SIDs*. This can only happen if you have cloned domain controllers without using SysPrep or if you are extremely, extremely unlucky to have identical SIDs in two domains by accident.

In each listed conflicting case, access from inside the local forest is not affected, but access from outside the local forest is disabled.

Consider this example. A basic conflict occurs between two forests. You create a forest trust between forest A and forest B, and both forests have a domain with an identical DNS or NetBIOS name. If you need routing from the conflicting domain, your only option is to start renaming domains (which is possible in Windows Server 2003).

A more "advanced" conflict occurs between three forests. You already have a forest trust from forest A to forest B, and then you create another forest trust from forest A to forest C. At this point you notice that forest B and forest C contain a domain with an identical DNS or NetBIOS name. The users of the conflicting domain in forest C cannot access forest A, because the new trust loses the competition. The users in the conflicting domain of forest B, however, can still access forest A, so they were not hurt by adding the new trust.

In the preceding three-forest example, you can rename domains again to remove the conflict. Or if you realize that the conflicting domain users of forest B don't actually need to access forest A, but the ones in forest C do need to, you can disable the former name routing (from forest B) and then enable the latter name routing (from forest C). If the conflict is in a DNS name, you can use the Domains and Trusts snap-in and the screens shown in Figure 6.16 and Figure 6.17. If the conflict is in the NetBIOS name, however, you must use the `NetDom Trust` command (from Windows Support Tools).

You can type a command such as the following:

```
netdom trust sanaoeurope.com /namesuffixes:sanao.com
```

The command will produce output such as the following:

```
   Name, Type, Status, Notes
1. *.sanao.net, Name Suffix, Enabled
2. *.sanaoint.com, Name Suffix, Enabled
3. *.rd.sanao.com, Domain disabling exclusion
4. *.sanao.com, Name Suffix, Enabled
5. marketing.sanaoint.com, Domain DNS name, Enabled
```

```
6. MARKETING, Domain NetBIOS name, Enabled,
   For marketing.sanaoint.com
7. s-1-5-21-1200319115-1906473553-800657386, Domain SID,
   Enabled, For marketing.sanaoint.com
8. sanaoint.com, Domain DNS name, Enabled
9. SANAOINT, Domain NetBIOS name, Enabled, For sanaoint.com
10. s-1-5-21-818466588-1802320308-899519789, Domain SID,
    Enabled, For sanaoint.com
11. sales.sanao.com, Domain DNS name, Enabled
12. SALES, Domain NetBIOS name, Enabled, For sales.sanao.com
13. s-1-5-21-1021733379-1578890251-243955535, Domain SID,
    Enabled, For sales.sanao.com
14. rd.sanao.com, Domain DNS name, Admin-Disabled,
      Has matching or superior exclusion record
15. RD, Domain NetBIOS name, Admin-Disabled, For rd.sanao.
    com, Has matching or superior exclusion record
16. s-1-5-21-1770414764-1998507016-1550387488, Domain
    SID, Admin-Disabled, For rd.sanao.com, Has matching or
    superior exclusion record
17. sanao.com, Domain DNS name, Enabled
18. SANAO, Domain NetBIOS name, Enabled, For sanao.com
19. s-1-5-21-632508713-469933409-1151220268, Domain SID,
    Enabled, For sanao.com
```

The list contains all names that you saw in Figure 6.16 and Figure 6.17. It also contains the NetBIOS names and SIDs of each Active Directory domain. If you now want to disable or enable a certain name routing, you use the `ToggleSuffix` option of the `NetDom Trust` command and specify a number from the preceding list.

Managing Domains and Forests

Now that you are familiar with forest structures, we are ready to examine how to manage various tasks in a forest. We discussed single-domain management in earlier chapters, so here we focus on a multidomain forest.

Managing Trusts

Table 6.3 lists the trust types, some of which we have discussed earlier in this chapter. One of the first two trust types (parent-child or tree root) is created automatically each time a new domain is installed in a forest. The trust relationships of the remaining types (shortcut, external, forest, and non-Windows) must be created manually, typically using the Domains and Trusts snap-in. If a trust does not seem to work, an administrator can verify and reset it.

Trusted Domain Objects

Trusts are represented by `trustedDomain` objects, which reside in the System container of each domain. The properties of these objects describe the type and features of the trust, as conveyed in Table 6.3.

Table 6.3 Trust Types

Trust Type	Explicit	Direction	Transitiveness	Purpose*
Parent-child	No	Two-way	Transitive	To create the forest structure and make it a complete trust area; this trust is between a parent and child domain.
Tree root	No	Two-way	Transitive	To create the forest structure and make it a complete trust area; this trust is between a tree root domain and the forest root domain.
Shortcut	Yes	One-way or two-way**	Transitive (except for domains above the trust-partner domains)	To make a trust path shorter between two domains in the same forest.

(continued)

* The general purpose of any trust relationship is to enable administrators and resource owners to give a user or group of one domain permissions to access a resource in another without creating a duplicate user account in the other domain. This column describes the specific purposes of each trust type that are based on this general purpose.

** A two-way trust is the same as two one-way trusts in opposite directions. Consequently, if you first create a one-way trust and then later create another one-way trust in the opposite direction, you end up having a two-way trust.

Table 6.3 Trust Types (*cont.*)

Trust Type	Explicit	Direction	Transitiveness	Purpose*
External	Yes	One-way or two-way**	Nontransitive	To be able to assign group memberships and/or permissions between two domains in different forests or between an Active Directory domain and a Windows NT domain.
Forest	Yes	One-way or two-way**	Transitive (although can be limited with selective authentication, SID filtering, and/or name suffix routing)	To combine two forests more tightly than with external trusts; a forest trust allows group memberships and/or permissions between any two domains in different forests, not just between the forest root domains where the trust actually resides.
Realm***	Yes	One-way or two-way**	Transitive or nontransitive	To be able to give access to Windows users for resources in non-Windows Kerberos realms and vice versa; you can think of a Kerberos realm as a kind of Windows domain.

*** This was called "Non-Windows Kerberos Realm trust" in AD2000.

However, the actual `trustType` property of the object specifies a type for each trust that differs a bit from those in Table 6.3:

- *Value 1: Downlevel trust.* This trust is with a Windows NT domain (being external).

- *Value 2: Uplevel (Windows 2000 or later) trust.* This trust is with an Active Directory domain (being parent-child, root domain, shortcut, external, or forest).
- *Value 3: MIT.* This trust is with a (non-Windows) MIT Kerberos version 5 realm.
- *Value 4: DCE.* This trust is with a DCE realm. DCE refers to Open Group's Distributed Computing Environment specification. This trust type is mainly theoretical, and it is not even present in the Platform SDK header files (except as a comment line).

An "uplevel" trust (value 2) can be of any type listed in Table 6.3, except the last one (non-Windows). Downlevel trusts (value 1) can be only external, and MIT trusts (value 3) can be only non-Windows trusts.

The other meaningful properties of `trustedDomain` objects are the following:

- `trustPartner`: For Active Directory domains, this is the DNS name of the partner domain. For Windows NT trusted domains, this is the NetBIOS name of the partner domain. For non-Windows trusted domains, this is the name of the partner Kerberos realm.
- `flatName`: For Windows trusted domains, this is the NetBIOS name of the partner domain. For non-Windows trusted domains, this is the name of the partner domain or it is NULL.
- `trustDirection`: 0 = disabled, 1 = incoming (i.e., trusting domain), 2 = outgoing (i.e., trusted domain), 3 = both directions.
- `trustAttributes`: (hexadecimal values in AD2003) 1 = the trust is nontransitive; 2 = the trust is valid only for Windows 2000 (and newer) computers; 4 = the domain is quarantined (that is, SID filtering is enabled); 8 = the trust is a forest trust; 10 = the trust is a cross-organization trust (that is, selective authentication is being used); 20 = the trust is internal to the forest; 40 = the trust is a forest trust where EnableSIDHistory is on (see the corresponding NetDom option in Help and Support).
- `trustAttributes`: (hexadecimal values in AD2000) 1 = the trust is nontransitive; 2 = the trust is valid only for Windows 2000 (and newer) computers; 40 0000 = the trust is to the parent domain; 80 0000 = the trust is to another tree root domain in the forest.

Viewing Trusts

There are several ways to view the trusts of a domain. The primary way is to use the Domains and Trusts snap-in. You can also use the NLTest or NetDom command-line tool from Support Tools or view the actual `trustedDomain` objects using the Users and Computers snap-in, LDP, or ADSI Edit (the last two being from Support Tools).

Figure 6.18 shows a sample of the hierarchy of domains that you see when you launch the Domains and Trusts snap-in. Figure 6.19 shows the list of trusts that you see when you right-click a domain, select Properties, and select the Trusts tab. When you select a trust and click Properties (or Edit in Windows 2000), you see the trust properties, as shown in Figure 6.20.

You can see the same trust properties of Figure 6.20 (and also the Object and Security tabs) with the Users and Computers snap-in. Turn on Advanced Features and locate the Trusted Domain objects in the System container. Then right-click any of those objects and select Properties.

NLTest lists the trusts of the domain of a certain domain controller when you type the following command:

```
nltest /trusted_domains /server:sanaodc1.sanao.com
```

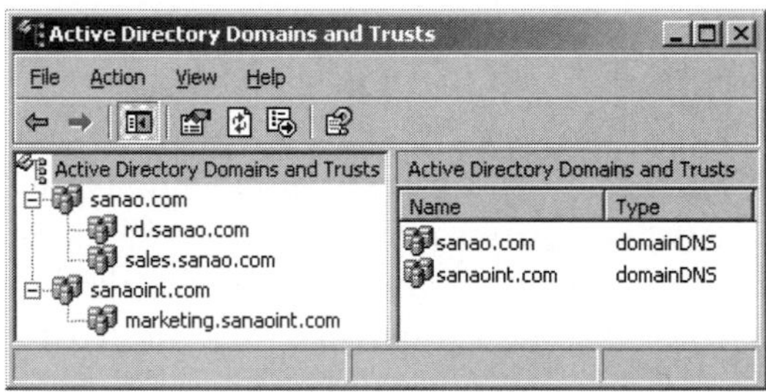

Figure 6.18 The Domains and Trusts snap-in displays the domains of a forest and enables you to manage them and their trusts.

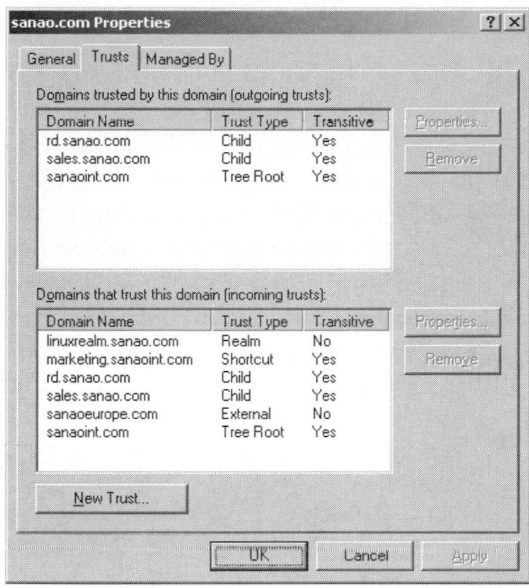

Figure 6.19 The Trusts tab of the domain properties lists both trusted and trusting domains of that domain. Domains with a two-way trust appear in both lists. The screen shot includes most of the trust types listed in Table 6.3.

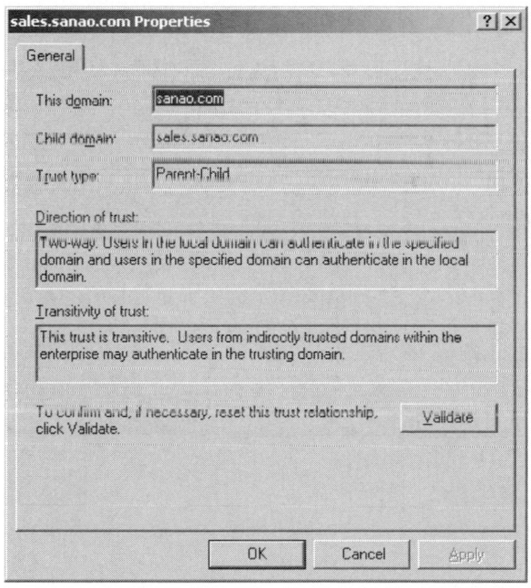

Figure 6.20 The properties of a trust viewed in the Domains and Trusts snap-in. If you view the same properties with the Users and Computers snap-in, you see also the Object and Security tabs.

With the trusts shown in Figure 6.19 the output would be this:

```
List of domain trusts:
    0: SALES sales.sanao.com (NT 5) (Forest: 6) (Direct
       Outbound) (Direct Inbound) ( Attr: 0x20 )
    1: RD rd.sanao.com (NT 5) (Forest: 6) (Direct
       Outbound) (Direct Inbound) ( Attr: 0x20 )
    2: SANAOINT sanaoint.com (NT 5) (Forest Tree Root)
       (Direct Outbound) (Direct Inbound) ( Attr: 0x20 )
    3: SANAOEUROPE sanaoeurope.com (NT 5) (Direct Inbound)
    4: linuxrealm.sanao.com (MIT) (Direct Inbound)
       ( Attr: non-trans )
    5: MARKETING marketing.sanaoint.com (NT 5) (Forest: 2)
       (Direct Inbound) ( Attr: 0x20 )
    6: SANAO sanao.com (NT 5) (Forest Tree Root) (Primary
       Domain) (Native)
The command completed successfully
```

For each trust, the output shows a trust index (domain controller–specific), the NetBIOS and DNS names of the trusted domain, and the contents of the `trustType` property ("NT 5" means "uplevel" trust—that is, Windows 2000 or later). The other flags of SALES indicate that its parent domain is index number 6 (i.e., SANAO), and the trust is both incoming and outgoing (i.e., two way). The flags of SANAO indicate that it is a tree root domain, it is the domain of the target server (`sanaodc1.sanao.com`), and it is running in (at least) Windows 2000 native mode.

NOTE The information about native mode is shown only for the domain of the target domain controller. In other words, SALES could also be a Windows 2000 native mode (or later) domain, but NLTest doesn't show it.

To list the direct trusts of `sanao.com` using NetDom, you would type the following:

```
netdom query trust /d:sanao.com /direct
```

With the trusts shown in Figure 6.19, the output would be this:

```
Direction Trusted\Trusting domain                  Trust type
========= =======================                  ==========
<->       sales.sanao.com                          Direct
<->       rd.sanao.com                             Direct
<->       sanaoint.com                             Direct
<-        hr.sanao.com                             Direct
<-        marketing.sanaoint.com                   Direct
 ->       linuxrealm.sanao.com                     Non-Windows
The command completed successfully.
```

Validating Trusts

You can validate (or verify) a trust by clicking the Validate button shown in Figure 6.20 (or the Verify button in Windows 2000). The outgoing part of the trust (if one exists) will be validated in any case. If the trust is two-way or incoming, you are prompted whether you want to validate (also) the incoming part of the trust. If so, you must provide an administrative account name and password of the partner domain. Without these credentials, the incoming part cannot be validated.

If everything is OK with the trust, you see either one of the dialog boxes shown in Figure 6.21. If there is a problem with the trust, you get a warning like the one in Figure 6.22 or Figure 6.23. With the latter warning, you have the option of trying to reset the trust passwords. If you choose this, and the repair attempt is successful, you get the dialog box shown in Figure 6.24.

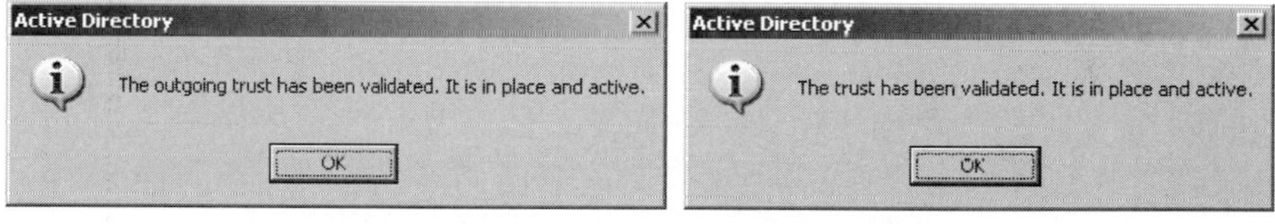

Figure 6.21 Normally, everything is OK with a trust, so you receive an OK message as a result of the validation of the trust. If you chose not to validate the incoming part of the trust (when prompted), only the outgoing part is validated (the left-hand dialog box). If you chose to validate also the incoming trust or the trust contains only the outgoing part, the entire trust is validated (the right-hand dialog box).

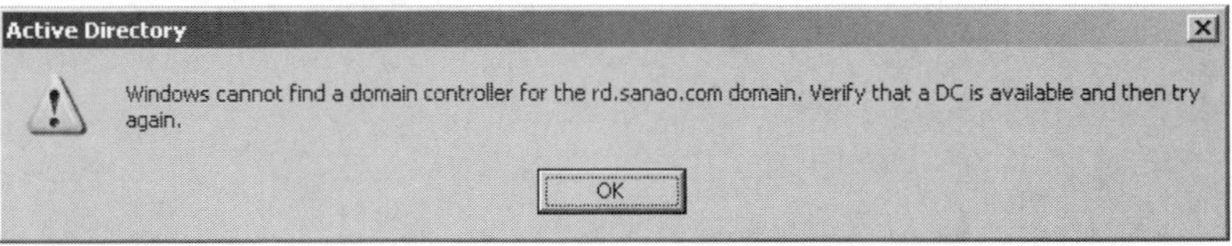

Figure 6.22 If the server cannot contact a domain controller of the partner domain of the trust, it displays an error message.

A trust is between two domains, and you could claim that a domain is just an abstract thing in the network. The domain controllers are the real thing there. Consequently, it is possible to check only if a trust works between a domain controller in the trusting domain and a domain controller in the trusted domain. These connections between domain controllers that make up the trusts between domains are called *secure channels.* In other words, a trust is between two domains, but a secure channel is between two domain controllers.

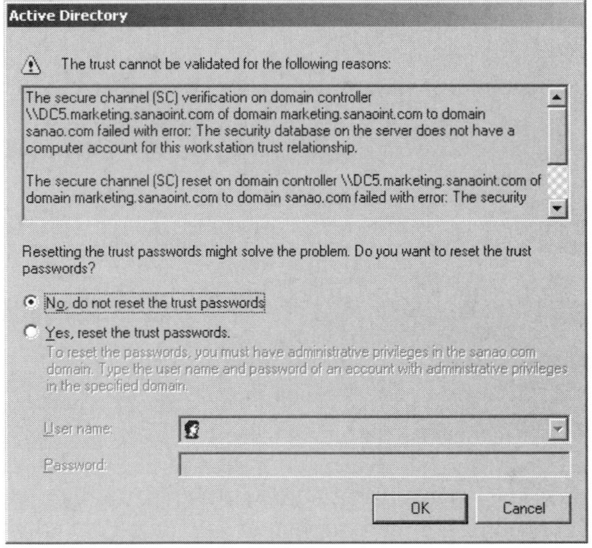

Figure 6.23 If there is an error in the secure channel making up the trust, the snap-in displays this and gives you the option of trying to reset the trust password.

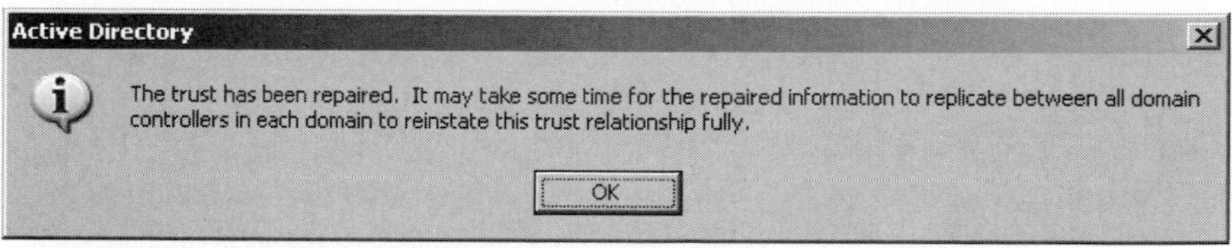

Figure 6.24 If the repair attempt of the trust is successful, you get the confirmation message shown here. Otherwise you get the message "The trust cannot be repaired because . . ."

NOTE There is also a secure channel from each Windows NT/2000/XP/Server 2003 workstation and server that has joined a domain to a domain controller in the domain that the computer has joined. In addition, there are secure channels between the domain controllers of the same domain. However, in this discussion of trusts, we are only talking about the interdomain secure channels.

Just as there is a computer account for each computer that is a member of the domain, there is also an "interdomain trust account" for each trusting domain. Both these account types have a dollar sign ($) as the last character of their SAM account name. The interdomain trust accounts reside in the `CN=Users` container of the trusted domain, and their SAM account names are those such as RD$, SALES$, and SANAO EUROPE$. A trust password (see Figure 6.23) refers to the password of this account. Resetting a trust refers to resetting the password of this account.

There are three command-line tools that you can use to verify trusts: NLTest, NetDom, and DCDiag. All three are part of Support Tools. We show a sample of each, but you can see more command-line options and examples in the Support Tools help.

To verify the trust from Sales to Sanao using NetDom, you would type the following:

```
netdom trust sales.sanao.com /domain:sanao.com /verify
    /ud:administrator /pd:*
```

NOTE The command appears on two lines because of wrapping, but it is one command.

The `ud` option specifies the username for the domain specified with the `domain` option and `pd` defines its password. Because of the asterisk (*), the user is prompted to enter a password. If there is a problem with the trust, you can try to reset it by replacing the `verify` option of the preceding command with the `reset` option.

WARNING It is possible that the `reset` option won't work in the Windows 2000 version of the tool. If the target of the secure channel of the local domain controller is offline, the preceding `NetDom /verify` command displays this message: "The network path was not found. The command failed to complete successfully." If you next try `NetDom /reset`, you may get the same error message, and your secure channel won't reset to a working target. In this case, try using NLTest instead.

To query, verify, and reset a trust from a domain controller in `sales.sanao.com` to the domain `sanao.com` using NLTest, you would type the following:

```
nltest /server:dc2.sales.sanao.com /sc_query:sanao.com
nltest /server:dc2.sales.sanao.com /sc_verify:sanao.com
nltest /server:dc2.sales.sanao.com /sc_reset:sanao.com
```

In addition to querying, verifying, or resetting the trust (or secure channel, to be exact), all three commands would show to which domain controller in `sanao.com` dc2's secure channel is connected.

WARNING The preceding `sc_query` command may show "success" for a secure channel, even though the target domain controller is offline. Therefore, if you think there is something wrong, you should use `sc_verify`, and you can always run the `sc_reset` command as well. Resetting a secure channel doesn't cause any harm, such as a disruption to the network services of users.

The last sample command uses DCDiag:

```
dcdiag /v /s:dc2.sales.sanao.com
    /test:outboundsecurechannels /testdomain:sanao
    /nositerestriction
```

NOTE The command appears on two lines because of wrapping, but it is one command.

The `v` option stands for "verbose"—it causes DCDiag to display more output. DCDiag tests all domain controllers of the source domain, and `nositerestriction` specifies that domain controllers from all sites should be checked. If the current target of the secure channel is offline, this DCDiag command should reset the secure channel so that it is established to a working domain controller. If this doesn't happen, you can use NLTest to reset the secure channel manually.

Creating Explicit Trusts

Explicit trusts include shortcut, external, realm, and forest trusts. You can create any of them with the New Trust Wizard. It asks you the necessary information, creates the trust, and validates it.

The selection of wizard pages—and consequently the information you must enter—depends on which type of trust you are creating and also on your selections on previous wizard pages. For example, shortcut trusts are always transitive, so the wizard doesn't ask you this. Table 6.4 lists which wizard pages appear in which case.

For example, you want to speed up the authentication between `rd.sanao.com` and `sales.sanao.com` in the forest presented in Figure 6.18. To achieve this, you need a two-way shortcut trust between the two domains. You open the properties of `rd.sanao.com`, select the Trusts tab, and launch the wizard by clicking New Trust (see Figure 6.19). You must provide the following information for the wizard:

- *The name of the target domain, forest, or realm with which the trust is to be created* (see Figure 6.25). In this example the target domain is `sales.sanao.com`.
- *The trust direction: two-way, incoming, or outgoing* (see Figure 6.26). In this example you create a two-way trust. If the `rd` users would frequently access the `sales` domain, but not vice versa, a one-way trust would be enough. The direction should be opposite to the access—that is, from `sales` to `rd`. When seen from `sales`, this one-way trust would be outgoing, and when seen from `rd`, it would be incoming. `Sales` would be the trusting domain, and `rd` would be the trusted domain. If you feel that it is hard to remember which way this goes—that is, which domain is trusting and which is "trusted by," to speed up the authentication to a certain direction—don't worry, you are not alone. To help you remember, you can take "ed" from "trusted" and "ing" from

Table 6.4 New Trust Wizard Pages That Appear in Different Cases

Page	Shortcut	External	Realm	Forest
The name of the target domain, forest, or realm	Yes	Yes	Yes	Yes
External or forest trust	No	Yes*	No	Yes*
Realm trust yes/no	No	No	Yes	No
Nontransitive or transitive	No	No	Yes	No
Two-way, incoming, or outgoing	Yes	Yes	Yes	Yes
Created for this domain only or at both ends	Yes	Yes	No	Yes
Admin name and password for the other domain	Yes**	Yes**	No	Yes**
Domainwide or selective authentication (local domain)	No	Yes	No	No
Domainwide or selective authentication (other domain)	No	Yes**	No	No
Forestwide or selective authentication (local forest)	No	No	No	Yes
Forestwide or selective authentication (other forest)	No	No	No	Yes**
Trust password	Yes***	Yes***	Yes	Yes***
Confirm outgoing trust	Yes****	Yes****	No	Yes****
Confirm incoming trust	Yes****	Yes****	No	Yes****
Routed name suffixes selection	No	No	No	Yes*****

* Appears if the trust is being created between the forest root domains of two forests and if both forests are on the Windows Server 2003 forest functional level (if the forest functional level is lower, the trust type will be external).

** Appears if you selected that the trust is to be created at both ends.

*** Appears if you selected that the trust is to be created for "this domain only."

**** You can perform confirmation if the trust is created at both ends.

***** Appears for local forest and/or other forest if the corresponding forest contains multiple names (i.e., multiple trees and/or additional UPN suffixes).

"trusting." "Ed" is like a username, so the trusted domain contains the user who will access, and "ing" is like "thing," so the trusting domain contains the thing (i.e., the resource) the user will access.

- *Whether the trust is to be created only for the local domain or also for the partner domain* (see Figure 6.27). Before a trust can be used, it must be established at both ends. If you select in the wizard "This domain only," you or someone else must later create the trust at the other end. In this case, you must now specify a password, and the same password must be used when the other end is created. It is easier to create the trust for both ends now, but the catch is that you must know and enter an administrative user account and password for the other domain.

Note that you didn't specify the trust type (shortcut) in the wizard. Because both ends of the new trust are domains in the same forest, the wizard knew it must be a shortcut trust.

The corresponding graphical trust-creation tool of Windows 2000 doesn't allow creating a two-way trust at once or a trust for both ends at once. Therefore, to get a two-way shortcut trust with that version, you must create the trust four times (two directions times two ends).

Creating an external trust is very similar to creating a shortcut trust. The additional step is that you can choose between domain and selective authentication (described earlier in this chapter). If the other end is a Windows NT domain, the user interface is slightly different, because you would use the User Manager tool of Windows NT. Also, if a Windows NT domain should trust an Active Directory domain, it is better to establish the trust first at the Active Directory end. This way, the Windows NT domain can verify the trust right away, and you will see a pop-up message stating this.

After creating an external trust (or a forest trust), you should check and possibly set the state of SID filtering. We showed the commands earlier in this chapter in the "SID Filtering" section.

In turn, creating a forest trust is very similar to creating an external trust. The two differences are that the alternative to selective authentication is forest authentication (the users of the other forest can authenticate anywhere in the local forest), and you can select which name suffixes are routed between the forests. Both topics were described earlier in this chapter.

If the target name is "not a valid Windows domain name," the wizard assumes it is a Kerberos V5 realm. You are given a chance to correct the name, if you just mistyped it, but otherwise the wizard will continue to

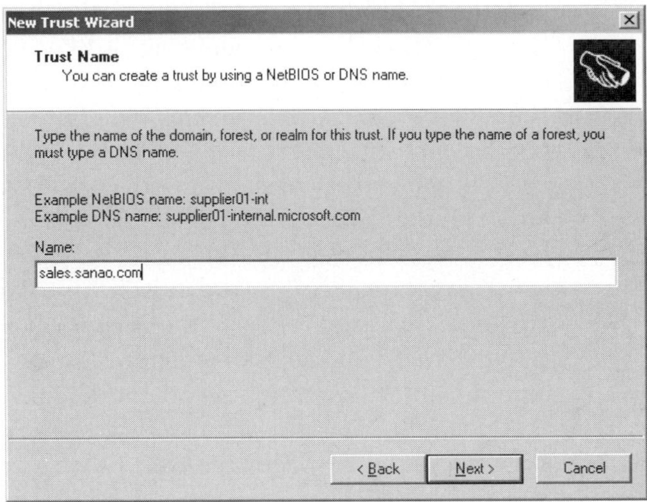

Figure 6.25 When creating a trust with the New Trust Wizard, you must enter the name of the target domain, forest, or realm.

create a realm trust. You can create such a trust only for the local domain and not for the other end, so you must always specify a trust password, and you cannot confirm the trust right away (see Table 6.4). You can also specify whether the trust will be transitive or not.

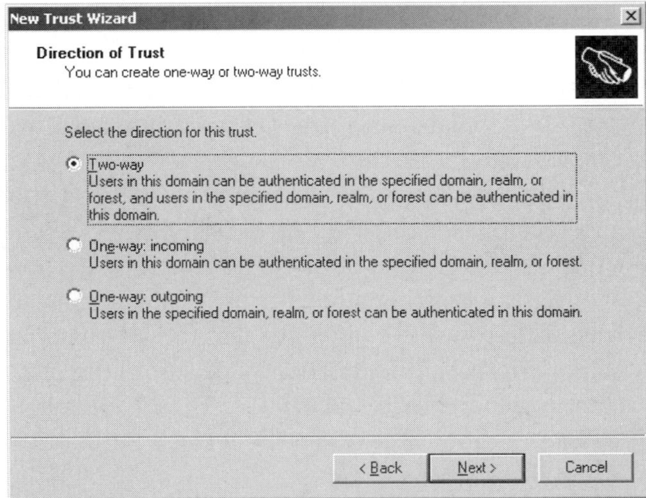

Figure 6.26 When creating a trust, you must specify its direction.

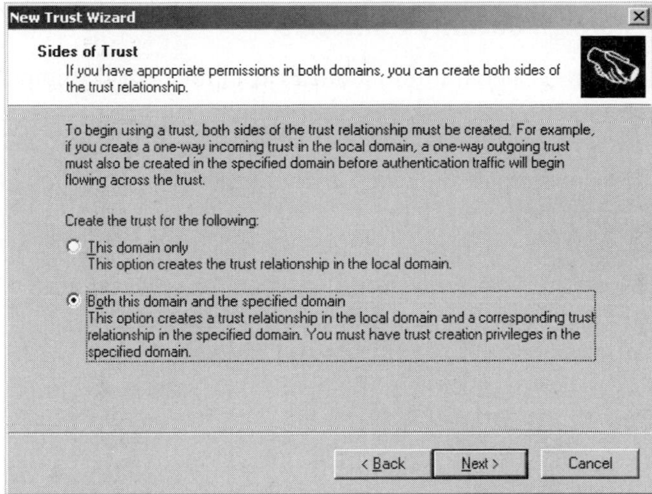

Figure 6.27 The New Trust Wizard allows you to create the trust for both ends at the same time. However, to be able to create the trust also for the other end, you must know an administrative user account and a password for that domain.

In addition to the Domains and Trusts snap-in, you can establish trusts with NetDom. To create the shortcut trust from `rd` to `sales`, you would issue the following command:

```
netdom trust rd.sanao.com /d:sales.sanao.com /ADD
```

NOTE You can add the option `/twoway` to the preceding command to create a two-way shortcut trust.

To create a realm trust between `sanao.com` and `linuxrealm.sanao.com`, with the trust password "abc", you would use the following command (at the Active Directory end):

```
netdom trust /d:linuxrealm.sanao.com sanao.com /ADD
    /PT:abc /REALM /TwoWay
```

NOTE The command appears on two lines because of wrapping, but it is one command.

Foreign Security Principals

There is a container called ForeignSecurityPrincipals in each domain. It contains placeholders that represent group members from domains external to the forest. There are placeholders also for well-known security principals such as Authenticated Users, if they are members of some group in the domain.

When you add to a group a member from an external forest, the corresponding placeholder is automatically added to ForeignSecurity Principals. The name of this `foreignSecurityPrincipal` object is the security ID (SID) of the object it refers to. If you remove the external member from the group, the corresponding `foreignSecurity Principal` object is not deleted.

Objects in ForeignSecurityPrincipals are visible only when Advanced Features of the Users and Computers snap-in are turned on. However, the container is always visible.

Moving Objects in a Forest

The Users and Computers snap-in and the DsMove command allow you to move objects inside a domain. If you need to move user, group, or computer objects to another domain in a forest, or between forests, you should use the Active Directory Migration Tool (ADMT). Version 2 of the tool is available on the Windows Server 2003 CD, in the folder I386\ADMT. ADMT allows you to migrate the aforementioned object types and perform some other migration-related tasks, such as migrating trusts and translating users' roaming profiles.

If you need to move other types of objects, such as contacts, you must use the command-line tool MoveTree, which is part of Windows Support Tools. MoveTree, however, works also for user and group objects (but not for computer objects). In this section we explain MoveTree.

You can also use other migration tools to move and/or copy users and other objects between domains. You can buy a commercial tool such as NetIQ Domain Migration Administrator (`http://www.netiq.com/products/dma/default.asp`), FastLane Migrator (`http://www.quest.com/fastlane/Migrator/index.asp`), or BindView bv-Admin Migration Solutions (`http://www.bindview.com/Products/DirAdminMig/Migration/index.cfm`).

MoveTree Features

The MoveTree tool has the following features:

- MoveTree moves objects from one domain to another in a single forest.
- MoveTree moves a container (along with its contents) or an individual object.
- Each object that is a security principal has a SID. Because SIDs are domain-specific, the SID must change when the object is moved to another domain. During the move, MoveTree adds the object's SID in the old domain to the `sIDHistory` property of the object in the new domain. This way, the moved user (or other security principal) maintains all group memberships and permissions in the forest.
- MoveTree maintains users' passwords.
- MoveTree maintains objects' GUIDs.
- MoveTree maintains the Group Policy links of the moved objects. However, this means that after the move, users and computers access their group policies from another domain, which is slower. To restore the earlier performance, you can (and should) re-create similar group policies for the new domain and remove the links from the old ones.
- If a move operation is interrupted, the not-yet-moved objects are left in a special container in the LostAndFound container of the source domain. This *orphan* container has the same name as the GUID of the container that was being moved.
- The source domain controller of the move operation must be the RID master of the source domain.

MoveTree Limitations

MoveTree has some limitations, although only the first three in the following list are actual drawbacks. The remaining limitations in the following list are more or less obvious.

- MoveTree can move only empty (i.e., containing no members) global and domain local groups. However, it can move nonempty universal groups without problems. We discuss these options in the next section.

- MoveTree can move only users that are not members of any global or domain local groups. However, it can move members of universal groups.
- MoveTree cannot move computer objects. You should use ADMT (or possibly NetDom) instead. To be specific, MoveTree will move computer objects, but the corresponding workstations or member servers won't know about the move, so they cannot build a secure channel to the domain. Consequently, they can no longer use any domain user accounts. In effect, they are cut out of the domain.
- MoveTree requires the target domain to be on the Windows 2000 native functional level or higher. Otherwise, the SID history feature wouldn't work.
- MoveTree moves only Active Directory objects. Profiles, policies, logon scripts, and other file-based information outside Active Directory are not moved.
- MoveTree cannot move the computer objects of domain controllers or any of their child objects.
- MoveTree doesn't move system objects—that is, objects whose class schema object's `systemOnly` property value is True.
- MoveTree cannot move objects in the containers Builtin, ForeignSecurityPrincipals, System, and LostAndFound.
- MoveTree cannot move objects that would have a name conflict or another conflict in the target domain. This includes duplicate names and accounts that do not conform to the password restrictions of the target domain.

Moving Groups

As stated in the previous list, MoveTree can move global and domain local groups only if they don't have members. Therefore, you must take special steps to be able to move these groups. You have two options to move global groups.

- Convert any global groups to be moved to universal groups, and then convert them back to global groups after the move. This approach is relatively easy, although because universal group members are stored in the global catalog, converting the groups will cause a peak in your global catalog replication.
- Document the members of each global group, remove the members, move the groups, and then add the same members back. The easiest way to document the members of a group is to issue the

command `NET GROUP MyGGroup >Members.txt`. This command lists all the members and writes them to the Members.txt file. To get the members back to the group in the latter option, you can use two batch files. The first file you get by renaming Members.txt to Members.bat and modifying it a little. The resulting file is shown in Figure 6.28. The other file, AddMember.bat, is called from Members.bat, and it is shown in Figure 6.29.

Because domain local groups are by nature used for resources in one domain, you shouldn't need to move them to other domains. However, if necessary, you can move them by using one of the options presented here for global groups.

Using MoveTree

MoveTree has four main options:

- `/check` causes MoveTree to perform a trial run to check if the requested move operation is possible. After the trial run, you can check the text file movetree.chk to see if there is anything to prevent the actual move.
- `/start` causes MoveTree to perform a trial run to check if the requested move operation is possible, and if so, to perform the actual move.

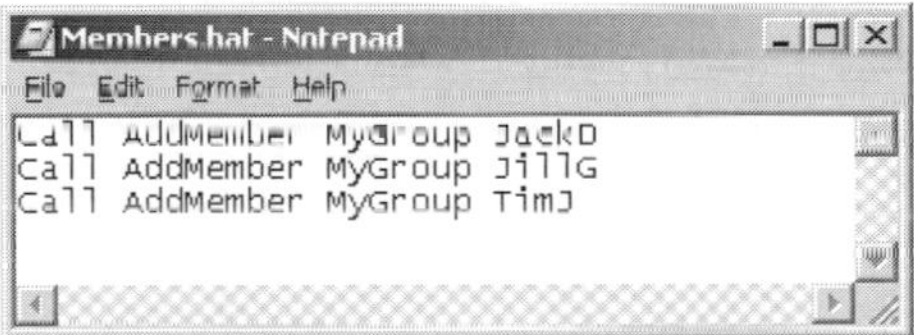

```
Call AddMember MyGroup JackD
Call AddMember MyGroup JillG
Call AddMember MyGroup TimJ
```

Figure 6.28 You can add a number of members back to a group with a batch file that calls another batch file for each member to be added.

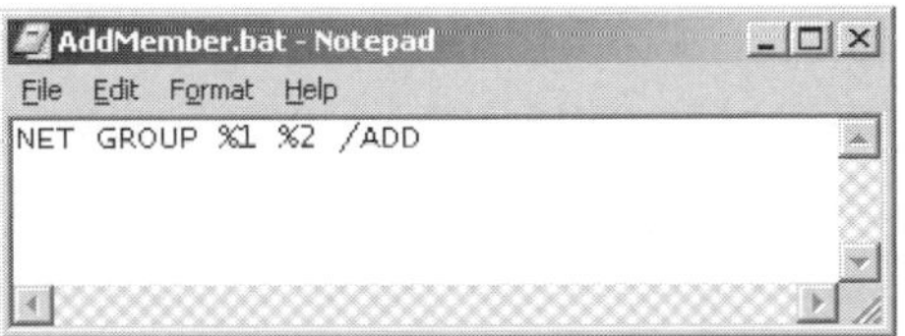

```
NET GROUP %1 %2 /ADD
```

Figure 6.29 This command adds the given user (`%2` command-line parameter) to the given group (`%1` command-line parameter).

- `/startnocheck` causes MoveTree to perform the actual move without a trial run.
- `/continue` causes MoveTree to continue a move that was interrupted because of a network fault or the target domain controller becoming unavailable.

In addition to one of the aforementioned main options, you must specify the source and destination domain controllers, as well as source and destination object distinguished names. However, with the `continue` option, the source DN is optional. You can also specify an administrative username and password with the `/u` and `/p` options, if your logon credentials are not powerful enough. The following command moves the OU Salesmen from `sanao.com` to `sales.sanao.com` and renames the OU to SalesRep:

```
movetree /start /s sanaodc1.sanao.com /d
    salesdc2.sales.sanao.com /sdn
    ou=salesmen,dc=sanao,dc=com /ddn
    ou=SalesRep,dc=sales,dc=sanao,dc=com
```

NOTE The command appears on several lines because of wrapping, but it is one command.

SanaoDC1 must be the RID master of `sanao.com` for the move operation to succeed. If there are no errors, you see the following output:

```
MOVETREE PRE-CHECK FINISHED.
MOVETREE IS READY TO START THE MOVE OPERATION.

MOVETREE FINISHED SUCCESSFULLY.
```

If the move operation is not possible, you are prompted to read the movetree.chk file and correct any problems.

Managing Groups and Permissions in a Forest

In a multidomain forest, users of one domain often need permissions in another domain. These permissions can be assigned either directly or via group memberships.

Predefined Administrative Groups in a Forest

We explained the predefined administrative groups (Enterprise Admins, Domain Admins, and Administrators) in Chapter 3 and their default permissions in Chapter 4. Here we revisit the topic by showing the default memberships of these groups in a multidomain forest.

Figure 6.30 illustrates the roles of different administrators in a forest and their default memberships. Enterprise Admins from the forest root domain is a member of Administrators in each domain of the forest.

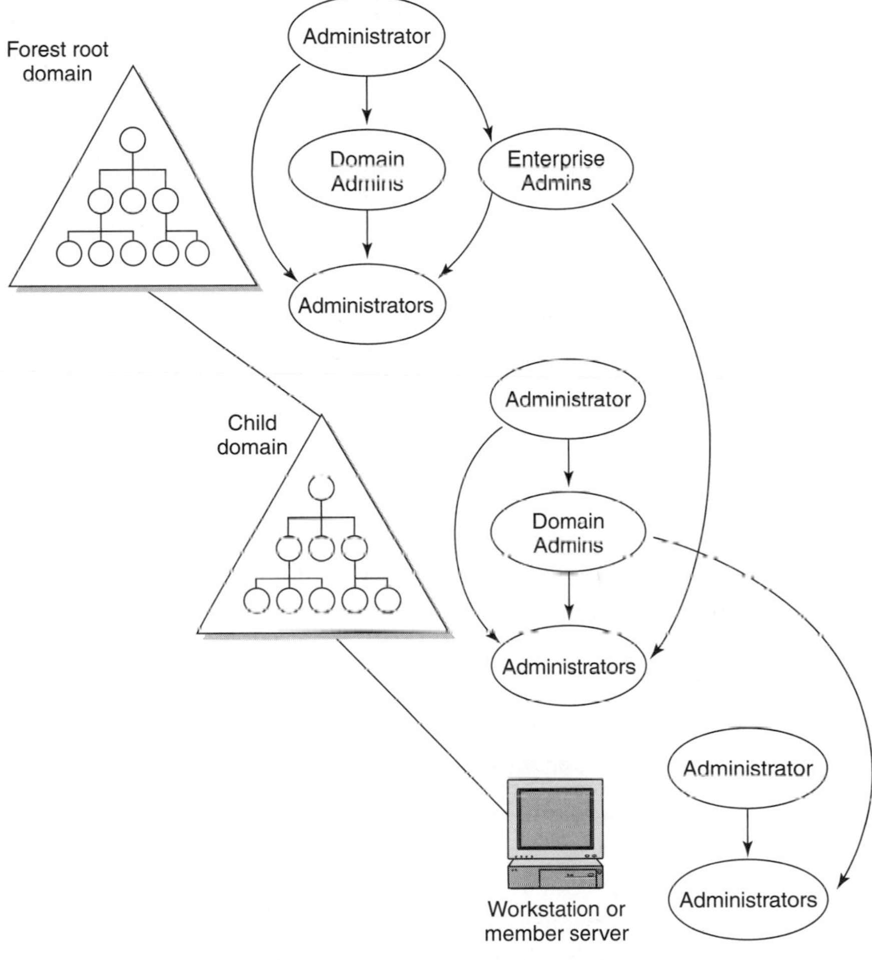

Figure 6.30 Enterprise Admins from the forest root domain is a member of Administrators in each domain of the forest.

Consequently, Enterprise Admins gets quite a few permissions and rights in all domains. However, Enterprise Admins is not a member of Domain Admins in any domain. Consequently, Enterprise Admins doesn't get permissions or rights that are assigned directly to Domain Admins.

In addition to its memberships, Enterprise Admins has direct permissions for Active Directory objects. For example, Enterprise Admins has Full Control for each domain object, and that permission is for "this object and all child objects." Consequently, Enterprise Admins has effective full-control permissions for all objects in each domain, except for the few exceptions that don't allow inheritance.

If Enterprise Admins should be blocked out from some child domain, the child domain administrators should do two things:

- Remove Enterprise Admins from the Administrators group.
- Remove the Enterprise Admins' permission entry from the domain object.

Predefined User Groups in a Forest

Recall that Table 3.5 in Chapter 3 shows that if you give permissions to Domain Users, only the users of the local domain can use those permissions. If you give permissions to Authenticated Users, all users of the forest can use them.

Figure 3.3 and Figure 3.4 in Chapter 3 illustrate the default memberships of the various predefined groups, such as Domain Users and Users. Those figures describe the memberships in a single-domain forest, but the figures also apply to a multidomain forest. There are no predefined interdomain end-user memberships that would add anything to these figures.

Group Member and Permission Assignments in a Forest

When assigning members to a group or assigning permissions, you can select the domain or OU from which the potential members or permission holders can be selected. You can also choose Entire Directory, in which case the list is retrieved from the global catalog. This is illustrated in Figure 6.31. In each case the list shows only those objects that are possible for that case. For example, when you are assigning permissions, the list doesn't contain contacts or distribution groups, and the list never contains domain local groups from other domains.

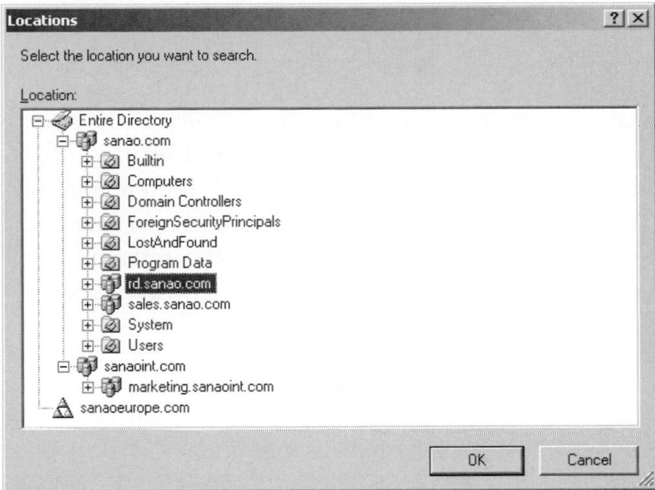

Figure 6.31 When selecting members or permission holders, you can choose the domain or OU from which to select them. If you choose Entire Directory, you will get a list of all candidate objects from the whole forest. `Sanaoint.com` is another tree in the forest, and `sanaoeurope.com` is another forest to which there is a forest trust from the local forest.

Referrals and Cross-References

Because a directory is normally divided into partitions (or naming contexts), a single directory server (that is, domain controller) doesn't necessarily contain all directory information. In the case of Active Directory, this is true when there are multiple domains in a forest, or if there is one domain in the forest but some domain controllers contain application partitions. On the other hand, even in a single-domain Active Directory forest, there are three partitions: schema, configuration, and the domain (plus a couple of application partitions for DNS zones).

When an LDAP client requests an object or objects from an LDAP server (in the case of Active Directory, a domain controller), the client includes the distinguished name of a *base object* in the request (see the "LDAP Searches" section later in this chapter). If the server doesn't contain the partition where the base object should be, the server returns an LDAP *referral* to the client. For example, the client is connected to a domain controller of the Sales domain but requests a user object that resides in the Sanao domain.

A referral points the client to another server (or multiple equal servers), which should contain the base object that the client requested. If this is not the case, the referred server sends another referral to the client, pointing it to yet another server(s). It is up to the client to *chase* these referrals—that is, to request the base object from the referred server. If referral chasing is turned on in a Windows 2000 or later computer, the operation takes place in the WLDAP32.DLL component of the operating system. Otherwise, the referral "error" is returned to the calling application, which can decide whether or not to chase the referral.

NOTE LDAP search operations may span partition boundaries. This concept is close to referrals, but we discuss it in the "Continuation References" section later in this chapter.

Cross-Reference Objects

Referrals are based on cross-references, which are forestwide configuration information residing in every domain controller. Cross-references are *internal,* when the referred partition is in the same forest, or *external,* when the reference points outside the forest. An external cross-reference could point to another Active Directory forest or a non–Active Directory LDAP directory.

Cross-references are stored in `crossRef` objects, which reside in the `CN=Partitions` container of the configuration partition. There is a `crossRef` object for each partition of the forest (i.e., schema, configuration, all domains, and all application partitions). These internal cross-references are created automatically when the forest or each subsequent domain is installed, or when an application partition is created. In addition, administrators can create external cross-references to partitions outside the forest. Because all domain controllers of a forest host the configuration partition, they all have the knowledge of all partitions of the forest as well as any external cross-references that are defined. Figure 6.32 shows the automatically created (i.e., internal) `crossRef` objects of the `sanao.com` forest. That forest has two trees (`sanao.com` and `sanaoint.com`) and three child domains in those trees: `rd.sanao.com`, `sales.sanao.com`, and `marketing.sanaoint.com`.

A `crossRef` object has seven properties that are worth mentioning. Table 6.5 describes the first six and Table 6.6 describes the last one, the `systemFlags` property.

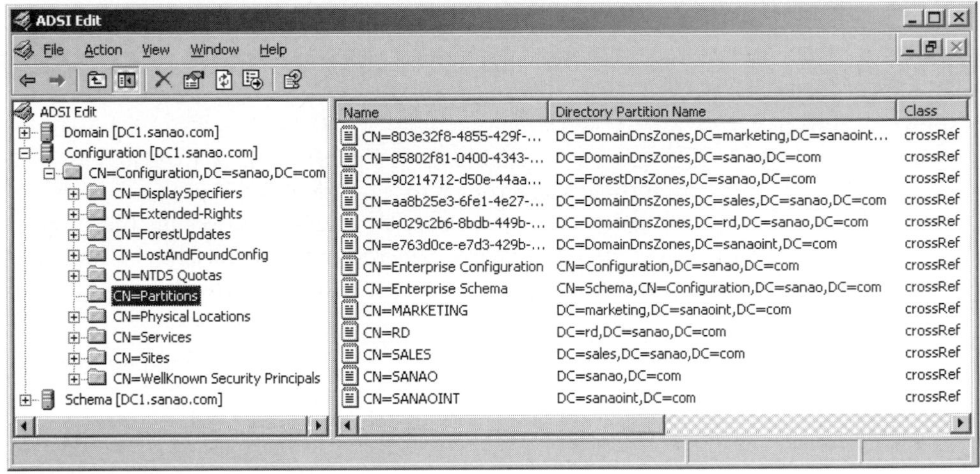

Figure 6.32 The `CN=Partitions` container includes a `crossRef` object for each partition of the forest.

Table 6.5 Properties of Cross-Reference Objects

Property	Sample Value (Sales)	Description
`dnsRoot`	`sales.sanao.com`	This property specifies where the referred partition resides. It is the DNS name of either the corresponding domain or a specific server. When the client receives this DNS name in the referral, the client can query a DNS server to find out the IP address to connect to.
`nCName`	`DC=sales, DC=sanao, DC=com`	This property specifies the distinguished name of the referenced partition (or naming context). The `nCName` properties of all internal cross-reference objects together define the directory structure of the forest. *(continued)*

Table 6.5 Properties of Cross-Reference Objects *(cont.)*

Property	Sample Value (Sales)	Description
`trustParent`	`CN=SANAO, CN=Partitions, CN=Configuration, DC=sanao, DC=com`	If the corresponding partition is an Active Directory domain other than a forest or tree root domain, this property specifies the `crossRef` object corresponding to the parent domain.
`rootTrust`	<not defined>	If the corresponding partition is an Active Directory tree root domain other than the forest root domain, this property specifies the `crossRef` object corresponding to the forest root domain (comparable to a parent domain).
`superiorDNSRoot`	<not defined>	If you want to define a *superior reference* for a forest, add it as a distinguished name to this property of the `crossRef` object that corresponds to the forest root domain. A superior reference is used (if defined in this property) when the base object of the request doesn't match a partition known to the server. The purpose is to serve as a "last resort" access point to requests that otherwise cannot be resolved. Normally, an Active Directory forest doesn't have a superior reference defined. It is always external to the forest.

Table 6.5 Properties of Cross-Reference Objects *(cont.)*

Property	Sample Value (Sales)	Description
`msDS-NC-Replica-Locations`	<not defined>	If the corresponding partition is an application partition, this property lists the domain controllers (as DNs to their NTDS Settings objects) where the partition resides.
`systemFlags`	3	See Table 6.6.

NOTE If the `systemFlags` property is not defined for an object, it is equal to both bits having the value "0."

Creating External Cross-References

Members of Enterprise Admins and Domain Admins of the forest root domain can create external cross-references by creating appropriate `crossRef` objects. This allows end users to access the corresponding external directories without needing to specify the correct external server name or IP address.

Table 6.6 `SystemFlags` Property Bits of Cross-Reference Objects

Bit from Right	Hex Value	Description
1	1	The value "1" indicates an internal cross-reference; the corresponding partition is in this forest. The value "0" indicates an external cross-reference; the corresponding partition is outside this forest.
2	2	The value "1" indicates that the partition represents a domain. Consequently, the cross-reference objects for the schema and configuration partitions have the value "0" in this bit.
3	4	The value "1" indicates an application partition.

NOTE A trust to an external Active Directory forest doesn't need a `crossRef` object. Any necessary referrals can be generated based on the information registered in DNS.

Although we describe seven `crossRef` properties in Table 6.5 and Table 6.6, only two must be defined with external cross-references: `nCName` and `dnsRoot`. The administrator enters the distinguished name of the external partition in the former property and the DNS name of the server that hosts it in the latter property. In addition, a descriptive `cn` must be defined as for any new object.

The partition name referenced by an external cross-reference may or may not be contiguous to the forest namespace. An example of a cross-reference with a noncontiguous partition name results when an administrator of the `sanao.com` forest adds a `crossRef` object for `microsoft.com`. In this case, the administrator could define `nCName` to be `DC=microsoft, DC=com` and `dnsRoot` to be `ldap.microsoft.com`. If a user subsequently queries that external noncontiguous name (i.e., `DC=microsoft, DC=com`) or some of its child objects, her workstation would be referred to contact `ldap.microsoft.com`.

While cross-references with noncontiguous names typically refer to directories outside the organization, cross-references with contiguous names probably refer to partitions and servers that are internal to the organization. For example, Sanao Corporation could have calendar information in a Linux-based LDAP server, and they want that data to appear under `sanao.com/Sales`. Therefore, an administrator creates a `crossRef` object and defines `nCName` to be `CN=calendar, OU=sales, DC=sanao, DC=com` and `dnsRoot` to be `calendar server.boston.sanao.com`. As long as the Sales OU exists in the forest and the Linux server is configured to serve the correct distinguished name (`CN=calendar, OU=sales, DC=sanao, DC=com`), clients should be able to contact and use the calendar server.

Managing Application Partitions

The query and access control features of Active Directory make it an excellent place to store application data. In AD2000, however, a limitation was that there were only two scopes of replication (in addition to the global catalog). The data was replicated either to all domain controllers in the domain or to all domain controllers in the forest. You can create application partitions on Windows Server 2003 domain controllers, and for each application partition, you can specify on which domain controller(s) the replica of the partition should reside.

The primary means to create and manage application partitions is that the application that will use a given application partition also creates that partition, as well as replicas on appropriate domain controllers. The alternative means is to use the NTDSUtil command, and its `Domain management` submenu. For the exact commands, refer to Microsoft Knowledge Base article 322669.

Delegating Domain Installation

Only members of Enterprise Admins (and members of Domain Admins of the forest root domain) can install domains to a forest. This is easy if the first domain controller of each domain resides in the headquarters. If this is not the case, the aforementioned administrators, or root administrators, have four options to get the child domains created.

- They can travel to the locations of each new domain to run DCPromo on the first domain controller of each domain.
- They can use Terminal Services on the incoming domain's first domain controller. This enables the root administrators to perform the domain creation (i.e., to run DCPromo) without leaving the headquarters.
- They can install the first domain controller (or others as well) in the headquarters and then ship them to appropriate locations.
- They can delegate the child domain installation.

Because in the first three options the root administrators personally perform the actual domain installation, those options are more suitable for an organization with centralized administration. The fourth option, delegation, may be appropriate for organizations with decentralized administration. We first list the summary steps of the fourth option and then describe the process in more detail.

1. A root administrator modifies the permissions of certain objects in the schema and configuration partitions.
2. A parent domain administrator modifies the permissions of each (incoming) parent domain.
3. A root administrator precreates a cross-reference object for each child domain using the NTDSUtil command-line tool.

4. A root administrator modifies the permissions of each cross-reference object.
5. A root administrator ensures that the DNS name of the incoming domain controller can be resolved to an IP address.
6. An incoming administrator of each incoming child domain runs DCPromo to install his child domain.

NOTE Before step 6, the creator should wait until all changes of steps 1 through 4 have replicated to the domain controller that his new domain controller will communicate with (i.e., "the source domain controller") during the promotion. This domain controller can be found by capturing the network packets of the early promotion process using Network Monitor (included in Windows server).

Step 1 is performed only once, and steps 3 through 6 are performed once for each new child domain. Step 2 is performed once for each parent domain that will get child domains installed by delegation.

Table 6.7 Permission Modifications for Delegating Child Domain Installation

Object	Trustee	Permission	Apply To*	Purpose
Schema and Configuration container objects	Domain Creators	Read	This+Ch	To be able to replicate the schema and configuration partitions to the incoming domain controller
	Domain Creators	Replicating Directory Changes	This	
	Domain Creators	Replicating Directory Changes All	This	
	Domain Creators	Replication Synchronization	This	
	Domain Creators	Monitor Active Directory Replication	This	
	Domain Creators	Manage Replication Topology	This	

* "This" means "This object only," "Ch" means "Child objects only," and "This+Ch" means "This object and child objects."

Table 6.7 Permission Modifications for Delegating Child Domain Installation (*cont.*)

Object	Trustee	Permission	Apply To*	Purpose
The Servers container under the object site object for the site where the server object will appear (based on IP address)	Domain Creators	Read	This+Ch	To be able to create a server object and the NTDS Settings for the incoming domain controller
	Domain Creators	Create All Child Objects	This+Ch	
	Creator Owner	Full Control	Ch	
The computer object for the server being promoted (if not a stand-alone server)	Domain Creators	Full Control	This+Ch	To be able to move the object and modify its status to be a DC
`CN=System` container in the parent domain	Domain Creators	Read	This	To be able to create a `trustedDomain` object for the incoming child domain
	Domain Creators	Create All Child Objects	This	
	Creator Owner	Full Control	Ch	
Cross-reference object for the child domain**	Domain Creators	Full Control	N/A	To be able to access the cross-reference object

** A root administrator creates this object with NTDSUtil, as explained in the text. Consequently, the permissions described in this table can be assigned only after the creation of the object.

We list the required permission modifications in Table 6.7 (i.e., steps 1, 2, and 4). As always in permission management, you shouldn't assign permissions directly to any user, but to a group instead. Our sample group is "Domain Creators." It is most natural to create this group in the forest root domain. It could be a global group; if you want to assign members from other domains, however, you must make it a universal group. In addition, we assign Full Control for some objects to the well-known security principal Creator Owner. As explained in Chapter 4, the result is that the one who created the object (and became the owner) gets Full Control for it.

When a root administrator creates the cross-reference object for the incoming child domain, he must specify the child domain's name and the name of its first domain controller. He would use the NTDSUtil command, as demonstrated on the following lines, entering the text in bold.

```
C:\>ntdsutil
ntdsutil: domain management
domain management: connections
server connections: connect to server dc1.sanao.com
Binding to dc1.sanao.com ...
Connected to dc1.sanao.com using credentials of locally
logged on user
server connections: quit
domain management: list
Found 7 Naming Context(s)
0 - CN=Configuration,DC=sanao,DC=com
1 - DC=sanao,DC=com
2 - CN=Schema,CN=Configuration,DC=sanao,DC=com
3 - DC=DomainDnsZones,DC=sanao,DC=com
4 - DC=ForestDnsZones,DC=sanao,DC=com
5 - DC=sales,DC=sanao,DC=com
6 - DC=DomainDnsZones,DC=sales,DC=sanao,DC=com
domain management: precreate dc=RD,dc=sanao,dc=com
     dc6.rd.sanao.com
adding object
CN=rd,cn=Partitions,CN=Configuration,DC=sanao,DC=com
domain management: quit
ntdsutil: quit
Disconnecting from dc1.sanao.com ...
```

NOTE You can abbreviate each command word, as long as the abbreviation is unambiguous. For example, type `do ma` instead of `domain management`.

NOTE The domain name in the preceding `precreate` command (i.e., "RD") must be in uppercase letters.

NOTE All domain creations (i.e., cross-reference object creations) take place on the domain naming master. If you connect with NTDSUtil to a domain controller other than the domain naming master, that domain controller refers your `precreate` command to the domain naming master.

A cross-reference object created this way contains an extra property that is not listed in Table 6.5. This new property is `Enabled` and it has a value of FALSE, meaning that the corresponding partition doesn't exist yet.

NOTE `Enabled` is an LDAP name, but unlike other LDAP names, it starts with an uppercase letter.

The incoming domain controller must have a DNS host record so that its name (such as `dc6.rd.sanao.com`) can be resolved to an IP address (such as 10.10.1.28). The primary DNS suffix (such as `rd.sanao.com`) must be set in a dialog box that opens when you click the Start button and select Control Panel, System, Computer Name, Change, More. Of course, the computer name (such as dc6) must also be set to match the name in the `precreate` command. The new name and DNS suffix can be registered to the DNS service with the following command:

```
IPCONFIG /REGISTERDNS
```

At this point you should be able to "ping" `dc6.rd.sanao.com` from other computers in the forest. If this is not the case, the DCPromo process will fail.

If the DNS service allows only secure updates, the DNS name registration is not possible unless the incoming domain controller first joins some domain in the forest, most logically the parent domain. In this case, the computer `dc6.rd.sanao.com` must be a member of the Active Directory domain `sanao.com`. This is not possible unless you clear the setting "Change primary DNS suffix when domain membership changes" in the same dialog box where you set the primary DNS suffix. This, in turn, is not possible unless you add the child domain name in the `msDS-AllowedDNSSuffixes` property of the parent domain object, using a tool such as ADSI Edit.

Once a root administrator has assigned Full Control for the new cross-reference object to Domain Creators (see Table 6.7), a member of this group can start the promotion process by running DCPromo. When asked for credentials, the domain creator enters a name such as JackB and an appropriate password and domain name. Root administrators can assign various members to this group as necessary, and they can remove members from the group when they are no longer necessary.

If you intend to use this delegation technique, you should first test it in a lab environment to make sure it works for your environment as you like.

Delegating Domain Controller Installation

By default, members of Domain Admins can install new domain controllers to their domain. If they need domain controllers in remote locations, they can—as root administrators can when delegating domain installation—to travel, to use Terminal Services, to ship computers, or to use delegation. We explain the last option here.

NOTE Microsoft highly recommends that domain controller installation not be delegated, unless absolutely required.

We use a sample group, DC Installers, to be the target of the delegation. Because that group will get some permissions for the schema and configuration partitions, it is logical to create this group in the forest root domain. The person who will perform the domain controller installation needs a user account in the forest, most logically in the domain where the domain controller will appear. We use Jack as our sample installer. This scenario requires DC Installers to be a universal group.

The delegation process consists of the following steps:

1. A root administrator modifies the permissions of certain objects in the schema and configuration partitions.
2. A domain administrator modifies the permissions of the domain object.
3. A domain administrator assigns Jack the user right to log on locally on domain controllers. He can also type the `gpupdate` command, so that Jack doesn't have to wait five minutes for his new right.
4. Jack installs Windows 2000 or Windows Server 2003 on the incoming domain controller computer and joins the computer as a member server in the domain. This way, he can be authenticated with a domain account (which is required) when he later performs the DCPromo process.
5. Jack makes his domain account a member of the local Administrators group of the member server.
6. A domain administrator modifies the permissions of the computer object of the incoming domain controller.

7. A domain administrator defines the computer object to have the setting "Trust this computer for delegation to any service."
8. A domain administrator moves the computer object from `CN=Computers` to `OU=Domain Controllers`.
9. Jack (using his domain account) runs DCPromo to promote the member server to a domain controller.

NOTE Before step 9, Jack should wait until all changes of steps 1 through 8 have replicated to the domain controller that his new domain controller will communicate with ("source domain controller") during the promotion.

Step 1 is performed only once per forest; steps 2 and 3 are performed one time for the domain. The remaining steps are performed once for each new domain controller. Table 6.8 lists the required permission modifications (i.e., steps 1, 2, and 6).

Table 6.8 Permission Modifications for Delegating Domain Controller Installation

Object	Trustee	Permission	Apply To*	Purpose
Schema and Configuration container objects and the domain object	DC Installers	Read	This+Ch	To be able to replicate the schema, configuration, and domain partitions to the incoming domain controller
	DC Installers	Add/Remove Replica In Domain**	This	
	DC Installers	Replicating Directory Changes	This	
	DC Installers	Replicating Directory Changes All	This	
	DC Installers	Replication Synchronization	This	
	DC Installers	Monitor Active Directory Replication	This	

(continued)

* "This" means "This object only," "Ch" means "Child objects only," and "This+Ch" means "This object and child objects."

** This permission can and should be assigned only to the domain object.

Table 6.8 Permission Modifications for Delegating Domain Controller Installation (*cont.*)

Object	Trustee	Permission	Apply To*	Purpose
	DC Installers	Manage Replication Topology	This	
The Servers container under the site object for the site where the server object will appear (based on IP address)	DC Installers	Read	This+Ch	To be able to create a server object and the NTDS Settings object for the incoming domain controller
	DC Installers	Create All Child Objects	This+Ch	
	Creator Owner	Full Control	Ch	
The Domain Controllers OU	DC Installers	Create All Child Objects	This	To be able to move the computer object in this OU
Computer object for the incoming domain controller***	DC Installers	Read and Write	This+Ch	

*** You should assign these permissions to the computer object of the member server. During the promotion process, the object will be converted to the domain controller object.

LDAP and Searches

Active Directory access takes place using LDAP, so obviously any Active Directory searches must be LDAP searches. We first explain the mechanics of LDAP searches and then show how to implement them using different tools.

LDAP Searches

One of the LDAP operations listed in Table 1.7 (in Chapter 1) is search. This operation retrieves the selected properties of one or more objects that meet the given criteria.

When an LDAP client sends a search request to an LDAP server, the client includes eight parameters in the search that specify what is to be searched and what is to be returned. Table 6.9 describes the four main parameters (`baseObject`, `scope`, `filter`, and `attributes`). The remaining four parameters—`derefAliases`, `sizeLimit`, `time`

Table 6.9 The Main Parameters of an LDAP Search

Parameter	Example	Description
Base object	`DC=sanao,DC=com`	This parameter is the distinguished name of the *base object* of the query. The base object is also called the *root object,* because the scope of the query is from this object downward.
Scope	`SubTree`	This parameter defines which objects are evaluated to see if they pass the filter. `Base` means that the query targets only the base object itself. If the base object doesn't pass the filter, no objects are returned. `OneLevel` means that the query targets only the immediate children of the base object (which itself is excluded). `SubTree` means that the whole tree beneath the base object is evaluated. By default, even with the `SubTree` option, the scope of the query doesn't cross partition (naming context) boundaries, such as from a parent domain to a child domain.
Filter	`(&(object Category=person) (sn=a*))`	This parameter specifies the criteria that each object must meet to be included in the search result set. This example filter includes users and contacts whose last name starts with *A*. We elaborate on LDAP filters later in this chapter.
Property List	`distinguished Name, givenName, sn`	This parameter lists the property LDAP names* that are to be returned for each matching object in the result set of the search.

* The properties in the Filter and Property List parameters are usually identified by their LDAP names. Another way to identify properties is to use their object identifiers (OIDs), which are explained in Chapter 8. The OID of sn is 2.5.4.4, so `(sn=a*)` would change to `(2.5.4.4=a*)`.

Limit, and typesOnly—are described in Table 11.8 in Chapter 11. You might need that information when you use scripts to perform searches. (Note that Table 11.8 also includes some other options. They are implemented using extended LDAP controls, which are discussed later in this chapter.)

NOTE LDAP searches are also called LDAP queries.

Figure 6.33 illustrates the Scope parameter, described in Table 6.9.

Property Lists

You can specify the property list of an LDAP search in the following ways.

- The property list contains a comma-separated list of LDAP names (or OIDs) of the properties that are to be included in the search results.
- The property list is empty or *, in which case all nonconstructed properties are returned. Constructed properties are explained in Chapter 8.
- The property list explicitly contains a constructed property—for example, canonicalName. If you are using the LDP tool, the constructed property must be the only property in the list.
- The property list contains *, canonicalName, for example. This list retrieves all nonconstructed properties and canonicalName. However, this form does not seem to work with the LDP tool.

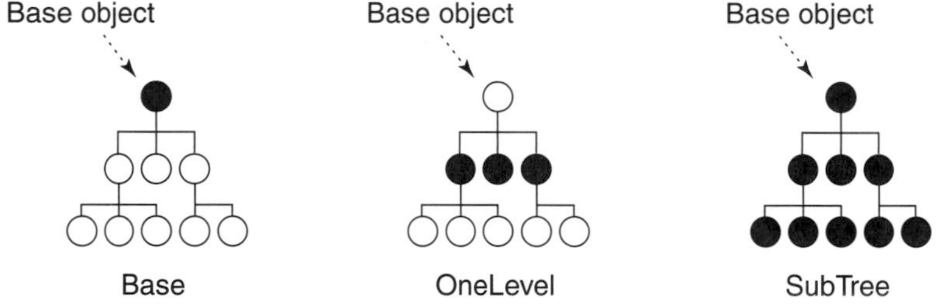

Figure 6.33 The Scope parameter of an LDAP search operation specifies which objects are evaluated to see if they pass the LDAP search filter.

- The property list is `1.1`, in which case no properties are returned. `1.1` is an imaginary OID. It doesn't correspond to any property; therefore, no properties are returned.
- The property list is `"otherHomePhone;range=0-2"`, for example. This form returns the first three values of the multivalued property `otherHomePhone`. To request the next three values, you would use the list `"otherHomePhone;range=3-5"`. Note that when using ranges, you must include the quotes.

LDAP Search Filters

An LDAP search filter is a text string that sets the criteria that an object must meet to be included in the search results. All conditions in the filter inspect whether certain properties in an object have certain values. These properties must be nonconstructed, so you cannot include constructed properties in the filter. Here's an example of a simple filter:

```
(sn=a*)
```

Properties are usually identified by their LDAP names. For an object to pass this filter, the first character of the object's last name (surname) must be "A" or "a." Almost all properties of the base schema that use string syntax are case-insensitive, so uppercase and lowercase *a* are equal in the filter. The only exceptions are the 13 properties that use the syntax "Printable string." The wildcard character (*) specifies that the remaining characters (zero, one, or several) can be any characters.

If we want to include only certain types of objects, we use the `objectClass` and/or `objectCategory` properties. For example:

```
(objectCategory=person)
```

It is usually better to use `objectCategory` because it is an indexed attribute, while `objectClass` is not. If you are searching among thousands of objects, using indexed attributes is more efficient. Using either property may actually include several types of objects.

- Several object classes may use a common object category. For example, both users and contacts belong to the category `person`. Consequently, `(objectCategory=person)` includes both users and contacts.

- Using an object class in the filter includes the child classes of that class. For example, in the schema `computer` is a child class of `user`, so `(objectClass=user)` includes both users and computers. If we wanted only users, we could use the two conditions together. The resulting filter would be this:

```
(&(objectCategory=person)(objectClass=user))
```

NOTE An LDAP search requires that a filter be present. If you want to include all objects, you can use the filter `(objectClass=*)`.

NOTE Object classes, child classes, categories, and property syntaxes are explained in more detail in Chapter 8.

Filters can be combined to create more complex filters. The sample filter presented in Table 6.9 is as follows:

```
(&(objectCategory=person)(sn=a*))
```

This filter includes two conditions. The ampersand character (&) at the beginning stands for "AND," so both conditions must be true.

Table 6.10 describes the various filter elements that you can use.

Because parentheses and asterisks have special meanings in the search filter, you must use an *escape sequence* instead of them if any value should contain one of these characters. An escape sequence consists of a backslash (\) and the ASCII value of the character in hexadecimal form. Table 6.11 lists these escape sequences. In addition to the values in the table, any bytes can be expressed with the corresponding hexadecimal escape sequence. For example, to include the byte E2 (hex), you can use the escape sequence "\E2."

As you can see, Table 6.10 includes "greater/less than or equal to," but not just "greater/less than." You can achieve the same result by using the fact that "greater than or equal to" is the opposite of "less than." For example, if you needed to specify "salary less than 30,000," the following filter would be illegal:

```
(salary<30000)
```

Table 6.10 LDAP Search Filters

Type	Format	Examples	True If
Presence	`(prop=*)`	`(sn=*)`	The `sn` property (i.e., last name) exists.
Equality	`(prop=value)`	`(sn=brown)`	The last name is Brown, brown, BROWN, or some other permutation of the same letters in uppercase/lowercase.
Substrings	`(prop=[initial]*[any]*[final]`	`(sn=a*)`	The last name starts with "A" or "a."
		`(sn=*son)`	The last name ends with "son" (or some uppercase/lowercase permutation).
		`(sn=*z*)`	The last name contains "z" or "Z."
		`(sn=a*z*son)`	The last name starts with "a," contains "z," and ends with "son" (or some uppercase/lowercase permutation).
Greater than or equal to	`(prop>=value)`	`(sn>=x)`	The last name starts with "x" or a later letter.
		`(salary>=30000)`	The salary is at least 30,000. This property is not part of the base schema, so this filter is meaningful only if such a property is added to the schema.
Less than or equal to	`(prop<=value)`	`(sn<=d)`	The last name starts with "a," "b," or "c," or it is "D" (or "d").
Approximate	`(prop~=value)`	`(sn~=bruwn)`	The last name is about "bruwn." Note that the exact logic of this filter type is implementation-specific, and Active Directory doesn't support this filter type at all.
And	`(&(filter A)(filter B))`	`(&(objectCategory=person)(sn=a*))`	The object is a user, contact, inetOrgPerson, person, or organizationalPerson, and the last name starts with "A" or "a."

(continued)

Table 6.10 LDAP Search Filters (*cont.*)

<table>
<tr><th>Type</th><th>Format</th><th>Examples</th><th>True If</th></tr>
<tr><td>Or</td><td><code>(|(filter A)(filter B))</code></td><td><code>(|(sn=a*)(k*))</code></td><td>The last name starts with “A,” “a,” “K,” or “k.”</td></tr>
<tr><td rowspan="2">Not</td><td rowspan="2"><code>(!(filter))</code></td><td><code>(!(sn=k*))</code></td><td>The last name does not start with “K” or “k.”</td></tr>
<tr><td><code>(&(!(sn=*))(object-category=person))</code></td><td>The object is a user, contact, inetOrgPerson, person, or organizationalPerson, and the last name is missing.</td></tr>
<tr><td>Extensible</td><td><code>(prop:ruleOID:=value)</code></td><td></td><td>Active Directory supports two extensible matching rules, which are explained in the “Specifying Values” section.</td></tr>
</table>

Therefore, you must use the following filter instead:

```
(&(!(salary>=30000))(salary=*))
```

The first part of this filter reads “salary not greater than or equal to 30,000.” The second part specifies that the salary property must exist. Otherwise, in addition to the correct objects, objects would be included that don’t have a salary defined at all (which may or may not be what you want).

Table 6.11 The Escape Sequences in LDAP Search Filters

Character	Escape Sequence
(	\28
)	\29
*	\2A
\	\5C

Specifying Values

Table 6.10 shows how you can use normal strings and integers in the search filter comparison values. Next we expand the topic by explaining how to specify values using various syntaxes:

- *Boolean.* Possible values are TRUE and FALSE. A sample filter is `(showInAdvancedViewOnly=TRUE)`.
- *Integer.* Possible values are integers in a decimal form. Hexadecimal values are not accepted. A sample filter is `(salary=30000)`.
- *Unicode string (or directory string).* This is the most common string syntax, and you specify the values as you have seen in the examples so far. A sample filter is `(sn=Brown*)`.
- *Octet string.* An `octet string` is binary data, so the value must be defined using escape sequences. For example, a three-byte (24-bit) value "E277BD" would be expressed as `\E2w\BD`. Note that "77" is the ASCII code of "w," so we use "w" instead of `\77`. For example, to list all properties that belong to the General Information property set (see Table 4.15 and Figure 4.29 in Chapter 4), you would use the filter `(attributeSecurityGuid=\42\2f\ba\59\a2\79\d0\11\90\20\00\c0\4f\c2\d3\cf)`. Some of the escape sequences in this filter could be changed to letters, such as the first `\42` to uppercase "B." However, doing so would make the filter look even more ugly. The 16 bytes in the filter are the `rightsGuid` of the corresponding property set converted to a binary GUID representation. (The section "List Binary GUIDs.vbs" in Chapter 11 sheds more light on this messy topic.)
- *DN (or distinguished name or DN String).* The entire DN value must be supplied and the wildcard (*) is not allowed. For example, to list all objects (in practice, group objects) where Jack is a member, you would use the filter `(member=cn=jack brown, ou=boston, dc=sanao, dc=com)`. Note that technically `objectCategory` uses the `DN` syntax. However, it enables you to use LDAP display names such as `(objectCategory=person)`.
- *OID string.* The entire OID value must be supplied and the wildcard (*) is not allowed. As with the `DN` syntax, you can use the LDAP display name instead of the OID value.
- *Generalized time string.* The form of the value in a filter is either "YYYYMMDDHHMMSS.0Z" or "YYYYMMDDHHMMSS.0[+/-]

HHMM." The "Z" in the former form means "no time differential"; that is, the time is in GMT/UTC time. The latter form includes a time zone differential to GMT/UTC. For example, Finland is 2 hours ahead of GMT/UTC. If you wanted to list objects that were created on or after February 26, 2001, 3:20 PM (local time), you would use the filter `(whenCreated>=20010226152000.0+0200)`. The same filter using the GMT/UTC time would be `(whenCreated>=20010226132000.0Z)`.

- *UTC time string.* The principles described for the Generalized time string apply also to this syntax. However, the forms of the values are either "YYMMDDHHMMSSZ" or "YYMMDDHHMMSS[+/-]HHMM." As you see, the year is expressed with two digits and there are no tenths of a second. Also, the seconds value (SS) is optional.

NOTE The description for the `Integer` syntax applies also to the syntaxes `Enumeration` and `Large integer` (or `INTEGER8`). The description for the `Octet string` syntax applies also to the syntaxes `NT security descriptor`, `SID string`, `Access point DN`, `Presentation address`, `Replica link`, `DN with Unicode string`, `DN with binary` (or `DN with octet string`), and `OR name`.

Active Directory supports two extensible matching rules: a bitwise AND and a bitwise OR. The general format of an extensible matching rule is as follows:

```
(property:ruleOID:=value)
```

The rule OID for bitwise AND is 1.2.840.113556.1.4.803, and the rule OID for bitwise OR is 1.2.840.113556.1.4.804. Therefore, to do a bitwise AND, you would use a filter, as follows:

```
(property:1.2.840.113556.1.4.803:=value)
```

In a sample scenario, you would need to list all global security groups. The group scope and type are both stored in a single `groupType` property that is using the `Integer` syntax. Figure 11.8 in Chapter 11 shows that a global group is denoted by the value "2," and a security group is denoted by the value "8000 0000" (hex). In bitwise arithmetic, we add these two values to get "8000 0002" (hex). Then we must convert this to a decimal to be able to use it in an LDAP filter. Using Windows Calculator, for example, we get "2,147,483,650." The resulting filter is as follows:

```
(groupType=2147483650)
```

We didn't need the rule OID yet in the preceding example. Next, we want to list all global groups, whether they are security or distribution groups. This means that we need to study only one bit in `groupType`, which requires use of the AND operators. The resulting filter is as follows:

```
(groupType:1.2.840.113556.1.4.803:=2)
```

Multidomain Searches

Normal LDAP searches are limited to one partition (naming context), which means that you get objects of only one domain at a time. You have two options to direct a search to multiple partitions: either turn on *referral chasing* or use the global catalog.

- *Referral chasing.* This is a special LDAP feature that allows a search to travel to other partitions to find more objects. Normally, this means extending the search to child domains. In a large network, the LDAP client might need to communicate with servers all over the world to be able to fulfill the query. Consequently, the global catalog option is usually much more effective.
- *The global catalog.* Normal LDAP searches use the standard LDAP port 389, but if you direct the search to the port 3268, you perform a global catalog search. Because every global catalog server stores the whole global catalog (and these global catalog servers are usually located on each site), you can usually perform a global catalog search without communicating with domain controllers on remote sites. When searching the global catalog, you can also use a nonexistent object as the base object. For example, if you specify an empty distinguished name, or `dc=com`, your search covers both `sanao.com` and `sanaoint.com` if they are part of your forest. If you're using the referral chasing approach, you cannot reach both these domain trees in one query. Figures 6.34, 6.37, 6.42, and 6.43 are examples of searching the global catalog.

We further discuss both options in Chapter 11.

Continuation References

We explained in the "Referrals and Cross-References" section that if an LDAP server doesn't contain the partition where the base object specified in an LDAP request should be, the server will return a referral that points the client to another server. A slightly different case is when the client performs an LDAP search and the base object *is* found on the server, but the server is unable to search all the objects in the scope. In this case, the server returns the matching objects residing in its partition, as well as *continuation references* to subordinate partitions.

For example, a client that is connected to `dc1.sanao.com` wants to find all users with the last name of Brown. The client specifies the starting point of the search (i.e., the base object) to be `DC=sanao, DC=com` and the scope to be `SubTree`. The steps of the process are as follows:

1. The client sends a query to `dc1.sanao.com` for the base object `DC=sanao, DC=com` and the scope `SubTree`.
2. `Dc1.sanao.com` returns the two Browns that exist in `sanao.com`. The server also returns continuation references to all immediate child partitions of `sanao.com`. There is one child domain, `sales.sanao.com`, and the configuration partition, so the server returns two LDAP URLs: `ldap://sales.sanao.com/DC=sales, DC=sanao, DC=com` and `ldap://sanao.com/CN=Configuration, DC=sanao, DC=com`.
3. The client queries DNS and learns that `dc1.sales.sanao.com` serves `sales.sanao.com`. The client connects and authenticates to this server.
4. The client sends a query to `dc1.sales.sanao.com` for the base object `DC=sales, DC=sanao, DC=com` and the scope `SubTree`.
5. `Dc1.sales.sanao.com` returns the only Brown that exists in `sales.sanao.com`. There are no more child domains, so the server doesn't return continuation references.
6. The client sends a query to `dc1.sanao.com` for the base object `CN=Configuration, DC=sanao, DC=com` and the scope `SubTree`.
7. There are no Browns in the configuration partition, so `dc1.sanao.com` returns only the continuation reference for the schema partition—that is, an LDAP URL `ldap://sanao.com/CN=Schema, CN=Configuration, DC=sanao, DC=com`.

8. The client sends a query to `dc1.sanao.com` for the base object `CN=Schema, CN=Configuration, DC=sanao, DC=com` and the scope `SubTree`.
9. There are no Browns in the schema partition either (nor are there any child partitions), so `dc1.sanao.com` returns an empty LDAP search result.

The term "continuation reference" is used in the LDAP RFC 2251. Microsoft documentation uses the term "subordinate reference" instead.

Search Tools

Windows 2000 and later include a number of tools that enable you to perform searches in various ways:

- *The Find dialog box.* End users can access this tool in Windows 2000 by opening My Network Places and selecting Entire Network, Directory, and then selecting Find in the context menu of any visible domain tree, or in Windows XP by opening My Network Places and clicking Search Active Directory in the task pane. Administrators can access the same tool in the Users and Computers snap-in by selecting Find in the context menu of any container. The Find dialog box provides a graphical interface for performing searches, as shown in Figure 6.34. If you select Entire Directory as the target for the query, you will actually use the global catalog. If you select Custom Search, Advanced, you can enter LDAP filters (called LDAP queries here).
- *ADSI Edit.* This tool enables you to enter an LDAP filter, which specifies the objects that you see in the right-hand pane of the tool. To target the query to a domain partition, right-click Domain in the left-hand pane and select New, Query. This opens a dialog box (shown in Figure 6.35) that enables you to define the query. When you click OK, you get the list shown in Figure 6.36.
- *The Users and Computers snap-in.* The View menu of the snap-in includes an item called Filter Options that enables you to specify which objects to show when you browse various container objects. If you select the custom filter type and the Advanced tab, you can enter an LDAP filter.
- *Saved Queries.* The Windows Server 2003 version of the Users and Computers snap-in contains a new feature called saved queries. This feature is discussed in Chapter 3, and it is very

similar to the LDAP filter feature of ADSI Edit (described two bullets back).

- *LDIFDE.* This tool allows importing and exporting objects between Active Directory and a text file using LDIF format. LDIFDE stands for "LDIF Directory Exchange," and LDIF stands for "LDAP Data Interchange Format." LDIF is defined in RFC 2849. When exporting data, you can specify as command-line arguments the base object, scope, LDAP filter, and list of properties to be exported. However, you cannot turn on referral chasing. See the example later in this section of how to export (i.e., search) objects with LDIFDE.
- *LDP.* This tool deserves a longer description, so we dedicate the next section to it.
- *Scripts.* Using scripts to perform searches is explained in Chapter 11.

TIP The command to open the Find dialog box is `rundll32 dsquery.dll,OpenQueryWindow` (where the last word is case-sensitive). You can put this command in a batch file or Start menu item, to make it easier to access the Find dialog box.

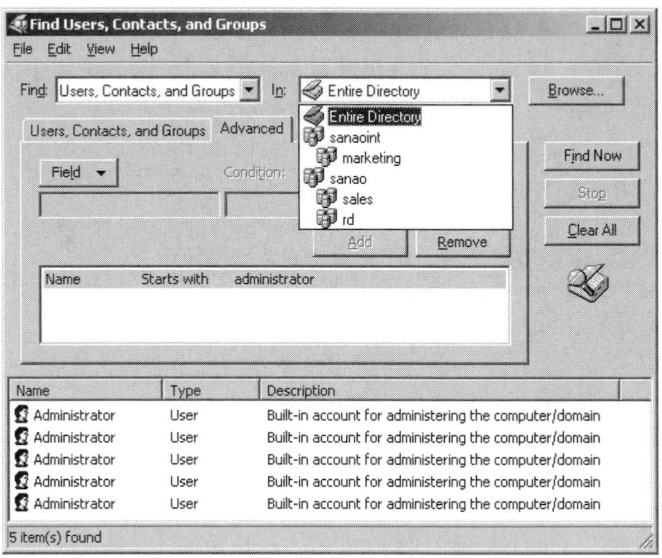

Figure 6.34 This search is directed to Entire Directory, meaning the global catalog. Therefore, the Administrator accounts of all five domains in the forest are found. If you click Browse in the upper-right corner, you can target the search to an individual OU instead of a domain.

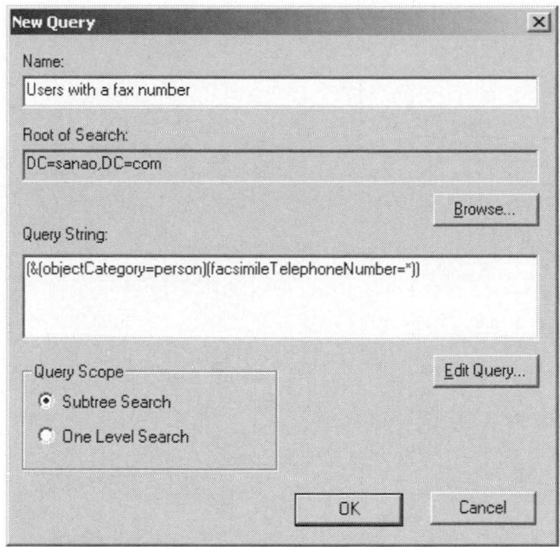

Figure 6.35 ADSI Edit enables you to enter an LDAP filter that specifies the objects to include in the right-hand pane.

Figure 6.37 illustrates an example of how to export (i.e., search) objects with LDIFDE. We have issued an LDIFDE command three times, with slight modifications each time. In each command we use the verbose mode (/v) to see the names of the exported objects ("entries" in LDAP terminology) and direct the output to the file Output.txt. In each command, we want to list all objects that have the common name Administrator. The first command is a normal LDAP query, so we get

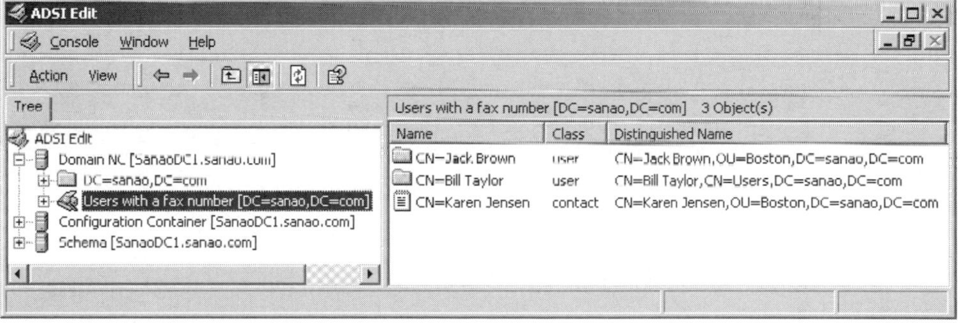

Figure 6.36 By using an LDAP filter, you can select objects that meet certain criteria to be listed in the right-hand pane. These objects can reside in different containers, so you effectively remove the tree structure in this view.

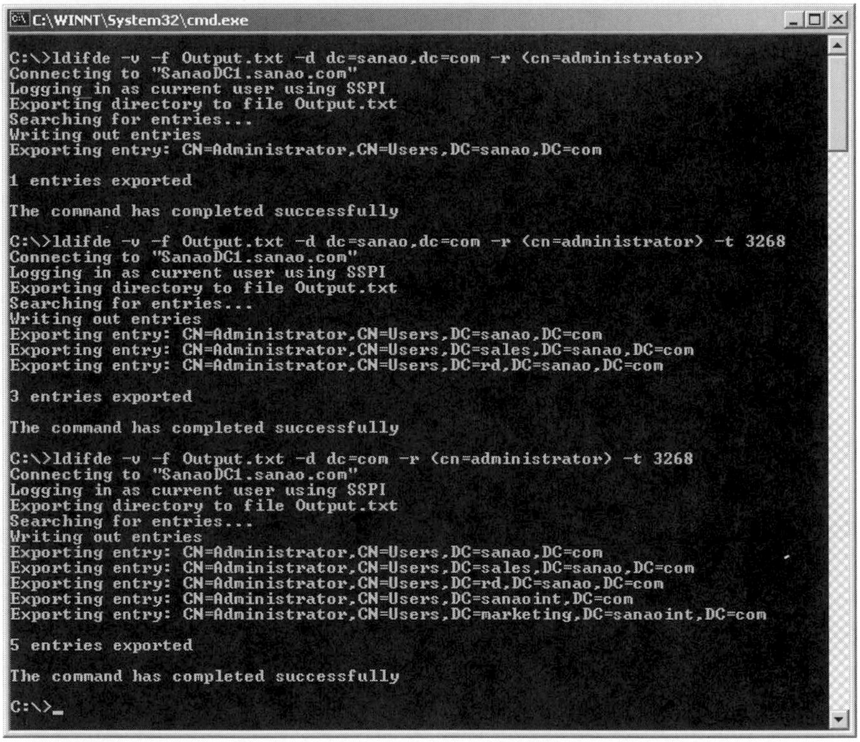

```
C:\WINNT\System32\cmd.exe

C:\>ldifde -v -f Output.txt -d dc=sanao,dc=com -r (cn=administrator)
Connecting to "SanaoDC1.sanao.com"
Logging in as current user using SSPI
Exporting directory to file Output.txt
Searching for entries...
Writing out entries
Exporting entry: CN=Administrator,CN=Users,DC=sanao,DC=com

1 entries exported

The command has completed successfully

C:\>ldifde -v -f Output.txt -d dc=sanao,dc=com -r (cn=administrator) -t 3268
Connecting to "SanaoDC1.sanao.com"
Logging in as current user using SSPI
Exporting directory to file Output.txt
Searching for entries...
Writing out entries
Exporting entry: CN=Administrator,CN=Users,DC=sanao,DC=com
Exporting entry: CN=Administrator,CN=Users,DC=sales,DC=sanao,DC=com
Exporting entry: CN=Administrator,CN=Users,DC=rd,DC=sanao,DC=com

3 entries exported

The command has completed successfully

C:\>ldifde -v -f Output.txt -d dc=com -r (cn=administrator) -t 3268
Connecting to "SanaoDC1.sanao.com"
Logging in as current user using SSPI
Exporting directory to file Output.txt
Searching for entries...
Writing out entries
Exporting entry: CN=Administrator,CN=Users,DC=sanao,DC=com
Exporting entry: CN=Administrator,CN=Users,DC=sales,DC=sanao,DC=com
Exporting entry: CN=Administrator,CN=Users,DC=rd,DC=sanao,DC=com
Exporting entry: CN=Administrator,CN=Users,DC=sanaoint,DC=com
Exporting entry: CN=Administrator,CN=Users,DC=marketing,DC=sanaoint,DC=com

5 entries exported

The command has completed successfully

C:\>_
```

Figure 6.37 Depending on the options used with LDIFDE, the tool returns a different number of objects. In this figure, the command was issued three times, with slight modifications each time.

the only Administrator in our domain. The second query is directed to the global catalog (-t 3268), so we get these users from all three domains that exist in `sanao.com` or its child domains. The third query is also directed to the global catalog, but now we use `dc=com` as the base object. Consequently, we get all five Administrator users, not only from `sanao.com`, but also from `sanaoint.com`.

The LDP Tool

Support Tools includes LDP (Ldp.exe), which is a versatile although not very polished tool to access most of the LDAP features. LDP uses the native LDAP C API instead of ADSI, as do most of the other administrative tools of Windows 2000 and Windows Server 2003.

When you launch LDP (click the Start button and select Run, type LDP, and then press Enter), you see only an empty window. Performing the following steps gets you started:

1. Select Connect in the Connection menu. This enables you to type the DNS name of the server that you want to communicate with. If you leave the server name empty, you will connect to the local server. You can also specify the port number, but it is usually the standard LDAP port 389.
2. When you click OK, LDP establishes a TCP session with the given LDAP server, queries the `rootDSE` information, and displays this information in the right-hand pane. That pane also displays all other output as you continue to use the tool. The Connection menu includes the Save and Print functions, which enable you to transfer the generated output to a text file or to paper. You can also use Copy/Paste with Ctrl-C/Ctrl-V.
3. So far you have connected anonymously. When you select Bind in the Connection menu, you can type the username, password, and domain to authenticate with.
4. When you click OK, LDP binds to the previously specified server using the given credentials. You should see the text "Authenticated as dn:'administrator'" (or whatever your username is) in the right pane.

At this point you are connected and have proved your identity, which allows you to perform any LDAP operations that you have permissions for. You have two paths to choose from. You can either open a tree that you can navigate or perform various LDAP operations listed in the Browse menu (Add, Delete, Modify, Modify DN, Search, Compare, and so on). We'll briefly explain the tree navigation option and the Search operation.

To open a navigation tree, select Tree in the View menu, and then enter the distinguished name of the base object to navigate from. If you entered "dc=sanao,dc=com," you would get a tree like the one in Figure 6.38. The right-hand pane displays all the (nonconstructed) properties of the base object. The number in front of the property indicates the number of values the property has. All properties that are visible in Figure 6.38 show "1>", so they all have only a single value.

To clear the output in the right-hand pane, press Ctrl-N.

As you double-click any child object, the properties of that object are displayed and the children of that child are listed in the tree.

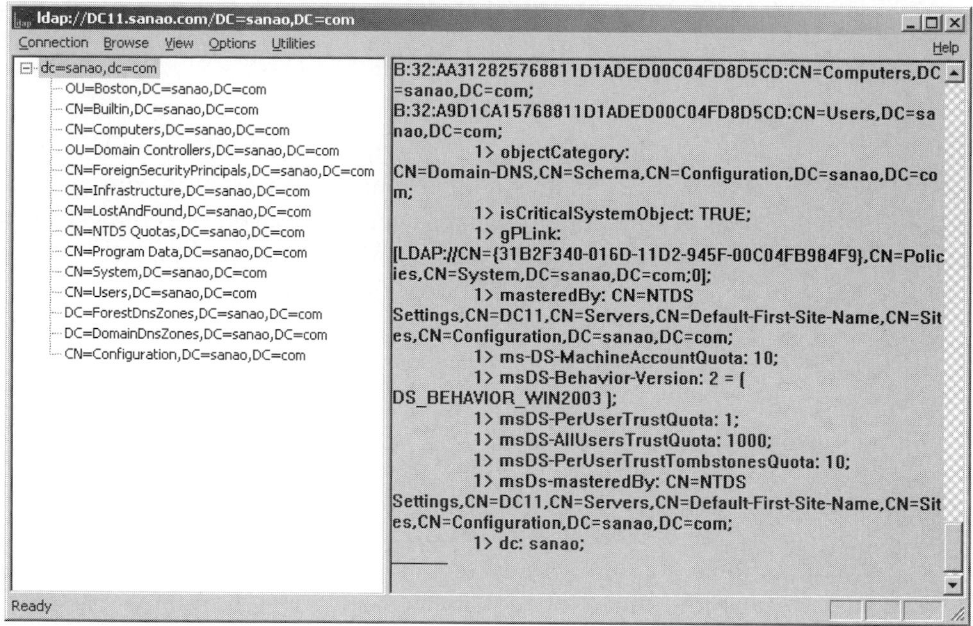

Figure 6.38 LDP enables you to specify a starting point (`dc=sanao, dc=com` here) from which to navigate the tree and to see all the properties of each object.

You initiate a search operation by selecting Search in the Browse menu. The dialog box that opens is shown in Figure 6.39. If you click Options, the dialog box shown in Figure 6.40 appears. These two dialog boxes enable you to specify the search parameters, as described earlier in this section when we discussed LDAP searches in general.

When you perform the search specified in Figure 6.39 and Figure 6.40, you get the result shown in Figure 6.41. In other words, the only object matching the query is the Administrator of `sanao.com`. If you

Figure 6.39 When performing an LDAP search, you must specify the base object, the search filter, and the scope of the search.

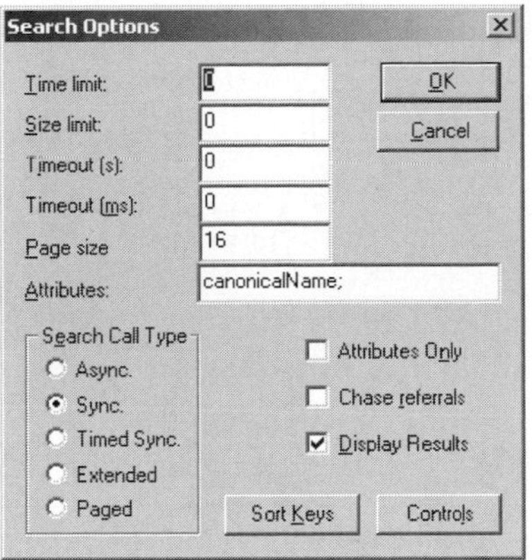

Figure 6.40 In addition to the basic parameters of the preceding figure, you may need to modify other search options, most often the list of properties (i.e., attributes) to be returned.

select "Chase referrals" and rerun the query, it covers the child domains also, so you get three Administrator users instead of just one. This is illustrated in Figure 6.42.

If you want to reach all domain trees of the forest, you must switch to using the global catalog. First disconnect the current connection, and then establish a new connection, this time using the port 3268. Bind again using the same credentials as you used in the first connection. When you perform the query specified in Figure 6.39 and Figure 6.40, you get three Administrator users as in Figure 6.42, even though you didn't turn on referral chasing. If you next change the base DN to be just

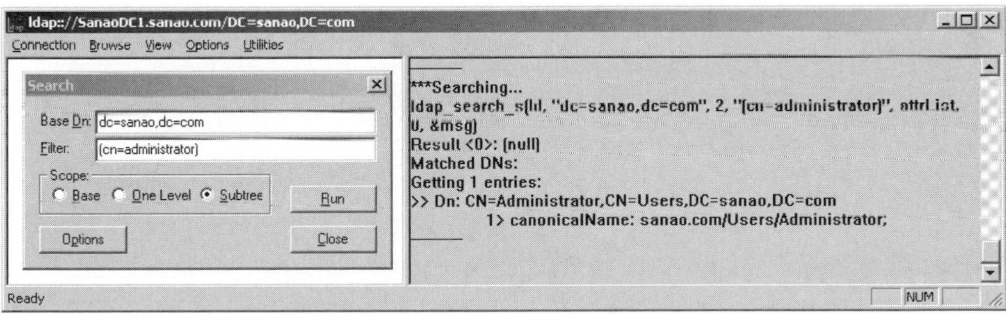

Figure 6.41 A normal LDAP query covers only one domain, so you get only one Administrator.

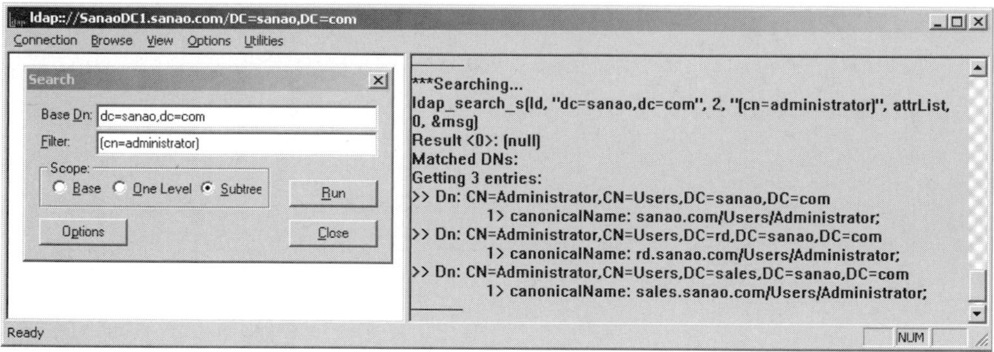

Figure 6.42 When referral chasing is turned on, or when the global catalog is queried, all child domains are also covered, so you get three Administrator users.

dc=com or an empty string, you get all Administrator users from all domain trees, as shown in Figure 6.43.

Extended LDAP Controls

The LDAP specification allows vendors to extend existing operations and add new operations. Here we talk about the former case. RootDSE includes two properties, supportedControl and supported Capabilities, that list the extended controls that Active Directory supports. We list these controls in Table 6.12, along with a short

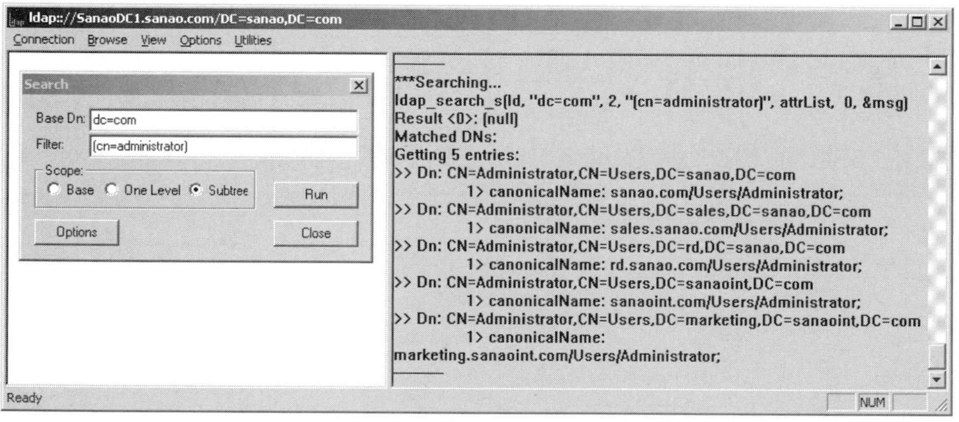

Figure 6.43 When searching the global catalog, you can specify nonexistent base objects, such as dc=com or an empty string. This means that you can search sanao.com and sanaoint.com at the same time.

Table 6.12 Extended LDAP Controls of Active Directory

Control	Description
1.2.840.113556.1.4.319	Paging search results. This control allows the client to request the results in chunks, instead of all objects at once.
1.2.840.113556.1.4.417	Show deleted object. This control allows listing the tombstones.
1.2.840.113556.1.4.473	Sorting search results. This control allows the client to request that the results be sorted.
1.2.840.113556.1.4.474	Server response sort. A server can respond to the client that initiated a sort request using the previous control.
1.2.840.113556.1.4.521	Cross-domain move. This control allows an object to be moved from one domain to another in a forest.
1.2.840.113556.1.4.528	Server notification. The client can register to be notified when changes are made to objects in Active Directory.
1.2.840.113556.1.4.529	Return extended distinguished names. This control makes the server return a special form of the distinguished name that includes the GUID of the object. This name never changes even though the object was moved or renamed.
1.2.840.113556.1.4.619	Server lazy commit. The server commits a modify operation to the client before the modify is actually written to disk, so the client doesn't have to wait as long.
1.2.840.113556.1.4.800	Windows 2000 supported capabilities. This control indicates that the responding server is a Windows 2000 server and it has all the capabilities of Active Directory. This control is a kind of version number for the directory service.
1.2.840.113556.1.4.801	Server security descriptor operations. This control allows the client to pass flags to the server to control security descriptor behaviors.
1.2.840.113556.1.4.805	Tree delete. This control allows a client to request deletion of a container including the whole tree beneath it (inside a single partition).
1.2.840.113556.1.4.841	Directory synchronization. This control allows the client to search and retrieve the latest changes from the directory.
1.2.840.113556.1.4.970	Search statistics. This client-side control retrieves search statistics. For more information, see the Microsoft online article "Creating More Efficient Microsoft Active Directory-Enabled Applications" at `http://www.microsoft.com`. *(continued)*

Table 6.12 Extended LDAP Controls of Active Directory *(cont.)*

Control	Description
1.2.840.113556.1.4.1338	Verify distinguished name server. If an object was recently added, and you want another object to refer to it by its DN, the DC that you are using might not yet be aware of the new object. This control allows you to specify the global catalog server that should know the new object.
1.2.840.113556.1.4.1339	Do not generate referrals. This control tells the server not to return referrals, so the search is limited to one partition only.
1.2.840.113556.1.4.1340	Server search operations. This control allows the client to pass flags to the server to control search behaviors. A flag with the value 1 is the same as the previous control (Do not generate referrals). A flag with the value 2 allows nonexistent search base objects, such as `dc=com`.
1.2.840.113556.1.4.1413	Server permissive modify. This control modifies the behavior of an extended LDAP modify request so that no error is returned if a nonexistent property is trying to be deleted, or if a property is added that already exists, as long as the old and new values are the same.
1.2.840.113556.1.4.1504	Attribute-scoped query (ASQ). This control enables performing a search on objects that are listed as DNs in an attribute. For example, the `member` attribute of a group contains the group members. Using this control, you can direct the search to these group members. For more information, see an online article at `http://msdn.microsoft.com`.
2.16.840.1.113730.3.4.9	VLV request. This control is used to perform a virtual list view (VLV) request on a server.
2.16.840.1.113730.3.4.10	VLV response. This control returns VLV data from the server to the requesting workstation.

description. Developers may need to use these controls frequently, but administrators need them only occasionally, if at all.

Virtual List View

Virtual List View (VLV) is a new feature in Windows Server 2003 (and Windows XP) and a very useful LDAP control. VLV provides a means for a client to retrieve information from an LDAP server in a table format and to browse this information. You can test VLV with the LDP tool, where the Browse menu contains the Virtual List View menu item.

Like the paged control, VLV allows you to segment large responses, and like the sort control, VLV allows you to return the responses in a certain order. By default, VLV sorts the results on the `cn` attribute, but you can use the Sort Keys feature of LDP to specify another attribute. In addition, you can specify where to start the responses from. For example, an e-mail client application could use VLV to list a limited number of contacts starting with a specific contact.

Listing Deleted Objects

As an example of extended controls, we explain how to list the deleted objects (i.e., tombstones) of a domain. This requires the use of the corresponding control 1.2.840.113556.1.4.417.

After you have connected and bound to a server LDP, you perform a search with the following parameters:

- The base object is the domain (such as `dc=sanao, dc=com`).
- The search filter is `(isDeleted=*)`.
- The scope is `SubTree`.
- The list of attributes should be `1.1` if you want to list just the names of the objects.
- The search call type is Extended.

In addition, you must click the Controls button in the Search Options dialog box. This opens the Controls dialog box that enables you to add the control 1.2.840.113556.1.4.417 as an active control. Type this long number in the Object Identifier field, make sure that the control type is Server, and then click "Check in". You don't need to specify a value. The resulting screen is shown in Figure 6.44. Alternatively, in the Windows Server 2003 version of LDP, you can just select "Return deleted objects" in the "Load Predefined" list. This fills in the correct OID. Either way, click OK a couple of times to get back to the Search dialog box, and then click Run. Figure 6.45 contains the resulting output.

Restoring a Deleted Object

Windows Server 2003 allows you to restore a deleted object from a tombstone. An obvious requirement is that the tombstone must still exist, which means that the tombstone lifetime must not have elapsed yet. A limitation

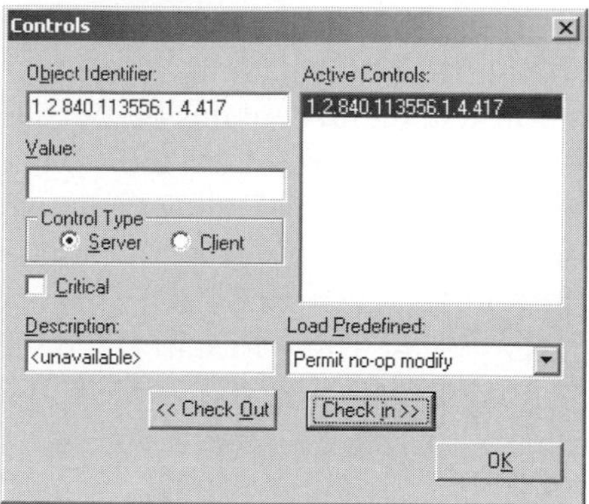

Figure 6.44 You can add extended controls to perform operations that are not part of the basic LDAPv3 functionality. This control enables you to list the deleted objects of a domain.

is that the attributes that were deleted when the object was deleted (and converted to a tombstone) cannot be restored; they are gone forever. If you restore a container object, its child objects are not automatically restored. Consequently, this feature is no replacement for a "good ol' backup."

To restore a deleted object, you must be a member of Domain Admins and there must be at least one Windows Server 2003 domain controller. You can also delegate this capability by granting the Reanimate Tombstone extended right to a user or a group for the partition root object, such as the domain object. In addition, the delegate must have permission to modify the relative distinguished name (RDN), any mandatory attributes, and any appropriate optional attributes. He or she

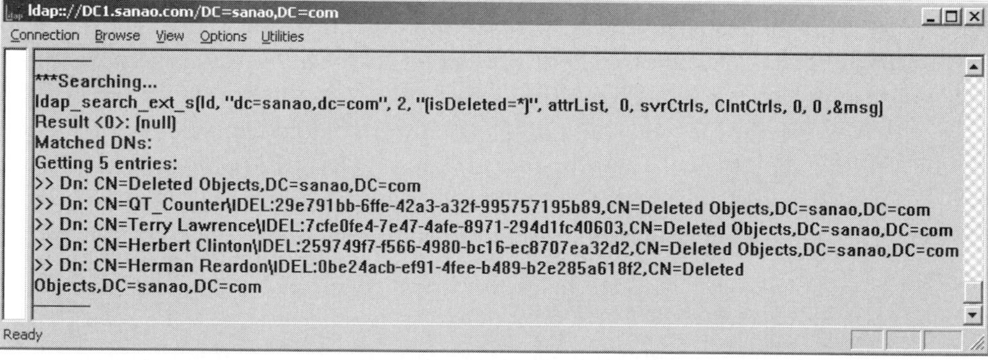

Figure 6.45 Deleted objects (i.e., tombstones) have special names and they are stored in a hidden container, Deleted Objects.

must also have permission to create child objects of the appropriate class in the container where the object is restored.

You perform the restoration with an extended synchronous LDAP modify call (`ldap_modify_ext_s`), in which you must include the following elements:

- Modify the distinguished name so that the RDN is normal again (no GUID or special characters) and the new parent container is something other than `CN=Deleted Objects`.
- Remove the `isDeleted` attribute.
- Provide a value for any mandatory attributes that did not exist in the tombstone.

The restore operation is meant to be used in application programs, but you can try it with LDP, using the following steps:

- Create a test OU and then delete it.
- Get a list of deleted objects, as explained in the previous section. In the attribute list, you can use `lastKnownParent` instead of 1.1. If the object was deleted in Windows Server 2003, that attribute shows where the object existed before deletion.
- Copy the distinguished name of your test OU to the Clipboard.
- Then, select Modify in the Browse menu and paste the distinguished name in the Dn field.
- Fill the Entry List as illustrated in Figure 6.46 (but instead of Sales, use your test OU's name).

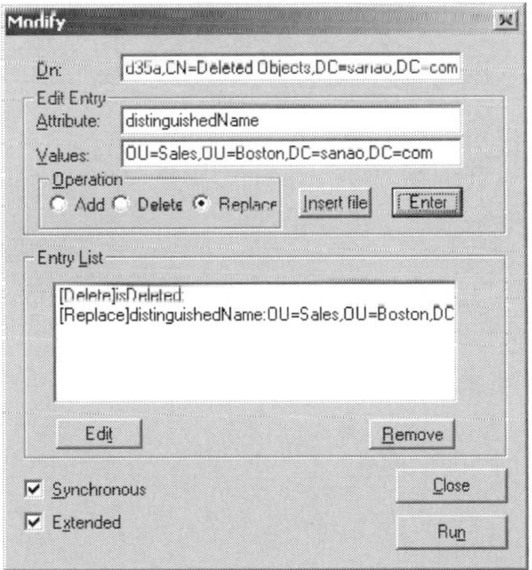

Figure 6.46 You can restore a deleted object from a tombstone.

- Check Extended.
- Click Run.

If the restored object is a user object, it is disabled initially.

LDAP Data Interchange Format

LDAP Data Interchange Format (LDIF) is a text file format that is defined in RFC 2849. The most typical use of LDIF files with Active Directory is to export and import directory information to and from a text file using the LDIFDE command-line tool.

There are two slightly different types of LDIF files, which are used for the following purposes:

- The file describes the content of the directory—that is, one or several objects along with their property values.
- The file describes changes to the directory—that is, one or several modifications to be performed on directory entries. This type of file is created when information is exported with LDIFDE, and this is also the file type that you could import back to the directory.

LDIF Files to Describe Content

The following lines illustrate a sample of the first case (i.e., a content-describing file):

```
dn: CN=Jack Brown, OU=Boston, DC=sanao, DC=com
objectClass: user
givenName: Jack
sn: Brown
# This is a comment line
otherHomePhone: 123 123
otherHomePhone: 321 321
description: Here is a description
 for Jack
thumbnailPhoto:: xyzxyz==

dn: CN=Jill Green, OU=Boston, DC=sanao, DC=com
objectClass: user
givenName: Jill
```

(etc.)

The sample requires the following comments:

- The contents of an object are on consecutive lines, starting with the DN property. There is an empty line between objects.
- Each property/value pair is on a separate line (to contain the property LDAP name, a colon, and the value).
- Apart from the DN property in the first line of each object, the remaining properties of an object can be in any order.
- Multiple values of a property are on separate lines (see the `otherHomePhone` property).
- A line may be folded to continue on the next line by adding one space in the beginning of the subsequent line(s) (see the `description` property).
- An empty value can be denoted by including only the property LDAP name and a colon (e.g., `sn:`).
- A line that starts with a pound sign (#) is a comment line.
- Binary values are encoded using base64, in which case there are two colons after the property LDAP name (see the `thumbnailPhoto` property). Also, other values that contain "unsafe" characters, such as the European characters é, ö, and ä, are encoded with base64. Safe characters are the ones with an ASCII code between 1 and 127, except carriage return (code 0D) and linefeed (code 0A). In addition, the first character must not be a space, a colon (:), or a less-than sign (<), to be safe. The given name of Björn Borg, the famous tennis player from the 1970s, is "QmrDtnJu" (without quotes) when expressed in base64.

NOTE When importing information with LDIFDE, you can have the line `givenName: Björn`, but when exporting, LDIFDE will generate the line `givenName: QmrDtnJu`.

Base64 Encoding

Base64 encoding works as follows.

1. The value to be encoded is divided into three-byte sections (i.e., 24 bits each).
2. Each 24-bit section is divided into four 6-bit values (i.e., from 0 to 63).

3. Each 6-bit value is mapped to one of the following 64 characters: uppercase alphabets A through Z, lowercase alphabets a through z, numbers 0 through 9, plus sign (+), or slash (/).

This results in a string of basic alphabets, numbers, and possibly some plus signs and slashes. If the number of bytes in the original value is not a multiple of three, the encoded value will have one or two equals signs (=) at the end, so the number of characters is always a multiple of four.

LDIF Files to Describe Changes

The previous discussion of content-describing LDIF files applies also to LDIF files that describe changes to the directory. As a new element, the latter files contain extra lines that specify the operations to perform.

An LDAP client can manipulate objects in an LDAP server using four operations: add, delete, modify DN, and modify (see Table 1.7 in Chapter 1). These four operations are referred to in an LDIF file when defining the changes to be applied to a directory. Table 6.13 lists the choices, along with a sample file of the first three. Compared to content-describing LDIF files, there is one extra line in each sample: "change type: something."

The fourth choice, Modify, has three further choices. Table 6.14 lists them, showing a sample file of each. Compared to content-describing LDIF files, there are now the following three extra lines:

- `changetype: modify`
- `add:`, `delete:`, or `replace:`, along with the property LDAP name
- A hyphen (-) to end the block of lines that add/delete/replace started

You can perform several Modify operations on one object. In this case the DN and changetype appear only once. The following example adds a phone number for Jack and deletes his office property:

```
dn: CN=Jack Brown, OU=Boston, DC=sanao, DC=com
changetype: modify
add: otherHomePhone
otherHomePhone: 123 456
-
delete: physicalDeliveryOfficeName
-
```

Table 6.13 LDIF Operations

Operation	Sample File

Add object	`dn: CN=Jack Brown, OU=Boston, DC=sanao, DC=com`
	`changetype: add`
	`objectClass: user`
	`givenName: Jack`*

Delete object	`dn: CN=Jack Brown, OU=Boston, DC=sanao, DC=com` `changetype: delete`

Modify object DN (i.e., rename and/or move)	`dn: CN=Jack Brown, OU=Boston, DC=sanao, DC=com`
	`changetype: moddn`
	`newrdn: CN=John Brown`**
	`deleteoldrdn: 1`***
	`newsuperior: OU=London, DC=sanao, DC=com`****

Modify object	See Table 6.14.

* In addition, mandatory properties, which Active Directory does not automatically fill, must be specified, and other optional properties may be defined (each on a separate line). For a user object, `sAMAccountName`, `userAccountControl`, and `userPrincipalName` should be specified, and in Windows 2000, `sAMAccountName` must be specified.

** This line must be present even if the RDN stays the same (e.g., from `CN=Jack Brown` to `CN=Jack Brown`).

*** Active Directory requires that this value always be 1 (i.e., True); you are not allowed to leave the old name present in the directory. This line must be right after the newrdn line.

**** If this line is omitted, the object is not moved, but only renamed. If present, this line must be right after the deleteoldrdn line.

This section is not an exhaustive description of LDIF files. For example, you can include extended LDAP controls in LDIF files, which we don't cover here. For more information, refer to RFC 2849.

Setting user passwords with LDIF files requires special handling. See Microsoft Knowledge Base article Q263991 for more information.

Table 6.14 LDIF Modify Operations

Operation	Sample File
Add a property or additional value(s)	dn: CN=Jack Brown, OU=Boston, DC=sanao, DC=com changetype: modify add: otherHomePhone otherHomePhone: 123 456 -
Delete a property or individual value(s)	dn: CN=Jack Brown, OU=Boston, DC=sanao, DC=com changetype: modify delete: otherHomePhone otherHomePhone: 123 456* -
Replace all existing value(s) with new value(s)	dn: CN=Jack Brown, OU=Boston, DC=sanao, DC=com changetype: modify replace: otherHomePhone otherHomePhone: 123 457 -

* This line specifies the value of a multivalued property that must be deleted. If this line is omitted, all the values are deleted and the property becomes "<not set>." Multiple values can be specified, each on a separate line.

Conclusion

In this chapter you have learned the logical structure of Active Directory, and you've also learned which aspects to consider when you plan the optimal Active Directory structure for your organization. This chapter, along with the three previous chapters, covered the management of Active Directory content and structure. These topics are what we consider the core skills of Active Directory: planning, deploying, and administering. There is one more to come, however, as we explain Group Policy in the next chapter.

CHAPTER 7

Group Policy

Group Policy Concepts

Microsoft's *IntelliMirror* initiative groups various technologies to help administrators manage user environments efficiently and consequently reduce the *total cost of ownership (TCO)*. In order to achieve the lower TCO, these technologies, of which Group Policy (GP) is one, enable centrally administering users' data, applications, and settings. *Change and Configuration Management (CCM)* includes IntelliMirror coupled with workstations installed with Windows 2000/Server 2003 Remote Installation Services (RIS). A user's Windows 2000/XP Professional computer can literally break apart, and with CCM, an administrator can install a new computer within minutes. When the user starts the computer and logs on for the first time, he will receive the centrally stored previous settings together with administrator-assigned settings and applications. When data is stored centrally, it will also be still available to the user.

NOTE The Windows Server 2003 RIS Service also supports installing server operating systems—that is, Windows 2000 Server and Windows Server 2003. A better solution for bulk installation of Windows Server 2003 systems is called *Automated Deployment Services* (ADS), which is one of the Windows Server 2003 *Feature Packs*. You can download the feature packs from `http://www.microsoft.com/windowsserver2003/downloads/featurepacks`.

Group Policy doesn't only make users' lives easier. It also gives administrators an efficient and pervasive tool to manage logon scripts, security settings such as password policies, and user interface restrictions. Administrators can even deploy applications and maintain them with Group Policy. Thus, Group Policy can be considered as the primary management infrastructure of Active Directory networks.

The term "Group Policy" is a bit misleading. Although it implies a direct relationship with user or computer groups, there is actually no such relationship. Rather, the term "Group Policy" refers to *a group of policy settings*. And to complicate matters more, you can control the effect of these Group Policy settings by filtering them with permissions defined for security groups. Thus, Group Policy is loosely related to security groups. However, the term "Policy Group" or "Group of Policies" might have been a better choice by Microsoft.

Group Policy facilitates both centralized and decentralized management of machine and user settings. In the former method, the policy settings are stored in *Group Policy objects (GPOs)* within Active Directory. If Active Directory is not available, or if you want to apply a specific setting on a particular computer, you might want to configure the *Local Computer Policy* that exists in every Windows 2000/XP/Server 2003 computer. Used in this decentralized manner without Active Directory, the policies contain fewer settings and are more difficult to manage.

In addition to Group Policy, System Policies introduced in Windows NT 4.0 can still be used to control individual Windows 2000/XP/Server 2003 workstations or servers if these computers are members of a Windows NT 4.0 domain.

Used with Active Directory, GPOs are identified with 128-bit globally unique identifiers (GUIDs). GPOs can be associated with a site, a domain, or an OU and are stored at domain partition(s). Settings defined in these GPOs are processed by so-called *client-side extensions (CSE)* based on the location of user and computer objects in the Active Directory structure. Thus, in order to deploy Group Policy effectively, you must take Group Policy into consideration in the planning stage of Active Directory deployment.

NOTE Sometimes the terms "local" and "nonlocal" are used to refer to the Local Computer Policies available in every Windows 2000/XP/Server 2003 computer and to Group Policy objects stored in Active Directory.

Group Policy settings are divided into computer and user categories. These settings are processed in various stages, the most obvious being when the computer starts up or when a user logs on. They are also processed periodically, and the processing can be initiated manually.

In order to process the settings, Group Policy has client-side and server-side components. The client-side extensions interpret and process the settings that are read either from the local machine or from Active Directory. The server-side components take care of securing, storing, and replicating the GPOs.

NOTE Group Policy has been developed as an extensible platform. Thus, an independent software vendor (ISV) can extend the functionality of Group Policy by incorporating its own server-side and client-side components. See `http://www.autoprof.com` for two such products: Policy Maker Professional and Policy Maker Software Update.

The management of group policies can be divided into several main tasks: creating Group Policy objects, managing Group Policy links, and configuring Group Policy settings. You can accomplish most tasks with two built-in tools: the Group Policy tab of an Active Directory container and an MMC snap-in called the Group Policy Object Editor (GPOE) (or Group Policy in Windows 2000).

Troubleshooting Windows 2000 group policies was difficult because of the lack of appropriate tools. There were few command-line tools in the Windows 2000 Resource Kit. Windows XP includes an improved version of one of these tools and a graphical Resultant Set of Policy (RSoP) tool (rsop.msc).

Windows Server 2003 brings along a welcome improvement for Group Policy management called *Group Policy Management Console* (GPMC). GPMC groups together all of the GP management functionality except managing individual settings. In addition, it introduces some new functions, such as reporting, backup and restore for individual GPOs, and scripting GPO management tasks. GPMC is one of the Windows Server 2003 Feature Packs. You can use GPMC to manage GPOs also in Windows 2000 Active Directory. The computer into which you want to install GPMC must be running either Windows Server 2003 or Windows XP (with Service Pack 1 and .NET Framework). Windows 2000 domain controllers must be running at least Service Pack 2, although Service Pack 3 is recommended.

TIP GPMC SP1 is available in English, French, German, Spanish, Chinese, and Japanese. If you want to install it into a Windows XP system that runs a different language version, you should first install XP Service Pack 2. It includes a Post-SP1 hotfix that is included in the GPMC setup for the six languages. Otherwise, see Microsoft Knowledge Base (KB) article 326469.

In addition to making it easier to deploy, manage, and troubleshoot Group Policy, GPMC helps you learn and understand Group Policy architecture better because of its intuitive user interface. Thus, we recommend that you download and install it in order to learn the topics introduced in this chapter and Group Policy in general.

You don't have to start using all Group Policy settings (almost 1,000 of them) at the same time that you deploy your Active Directory. However, when you install an Active Directory domain, two GPOs are created in the new domain. The Default Domain Policy is linked to the domain, and the Default Domain Controllers Policy is linked to the Domain Controllers OU. The Default Domain Policy contains security settings such as minimum password length and complexity requirement, whereas the Default Domain Controllers Policy contains primarily user right assignments such as allowing members of certain groups to log on locally on domain controllers.

NOTE When you start using GPMC for Group Policy management in an AD2000 domain that was created prior to Windows 2000 SP4, you will receive a warning when opening the Default Domain Policy or the Default Domain Controllers Policy or any GPO created prior to Service Pack 4 installation. This is due to a slight mismatch in permissions between the GPO components in the Active Directory and the file system. GPMC suggests fixing the permissions, which you should allow it to perform.

Tools for Managing Group Policies

Tools available for GP management in every Windows 2000/Server 2003 Active Directory system are the Group Policy (Object Editor) snap-in and the property pages of the Active Directory Users and Computers snap-in (for GPOs linked to a domain or to OUs) and the Active Directory Sites and Services snap-in (for GPOs linked to a site). By default, the Active Directory management snap-ins open with the Group Policy extension, which enables you to manage Group Policy objects. To access group policies, you right-click any container that a group policy is linked to or to which you intend to link a GPO. Select Properties and open the Group Policy tab. Figure 7.1 shows the Group Policy tab for the Domain Controllers OU.

The property pages of Active Directory Users and Computers and Active Directory Sites and Services for managing group policies are available until you install GPMC. After you have installed GPMC, only a button for opening it remains in the Group Policy tab, as displayed in Figure 7.2. You can also open GPMC from the Start menu (under Administrative Tools) or by typing "gpmc.msc" into the Run dialog.

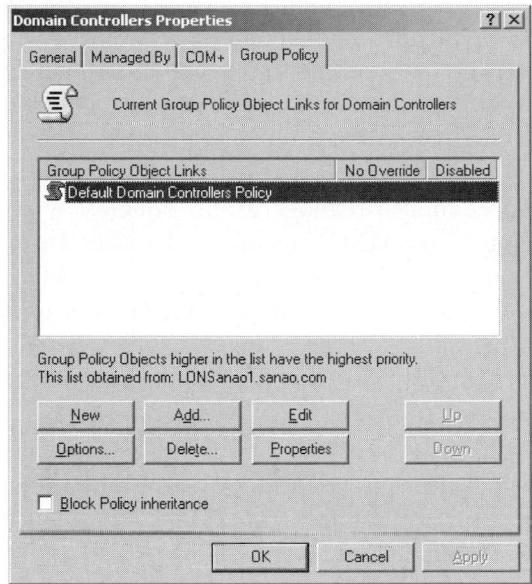

Figure 7.1 Group Policy tab for the Domain Controllers OU

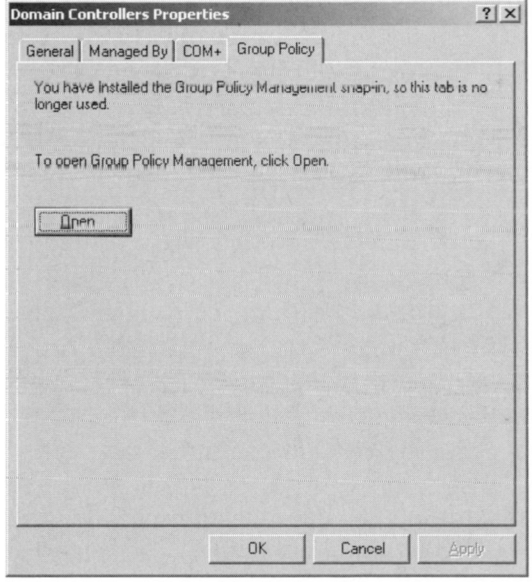

Figure 7.2 Group Policy tab for the Domain Controllers OU after GPMC has been installed

NOTE If you have the Group Policy tab open when installing GPMC, the Group Policy tab seems to disappear completely. It appears again when you restart Active Directory Users and Computers or Active Directory Sites and Services.

You can also manage group policies by accessing them directly by creating a new MMC console and adding the Group Policy snap-in into it. Then you can browse for the desired GPO. This method enables you to only manage the settings of GPOs unless you add other snap-ins to your console.

The Group Policy dialog box (without GPMC) can be used to perform most Group Policy management tasks, including

- Creating and deleting Group Policy objects
- Linking and unlinking GPOs
- Enabling and disabling links
- Enabling or disabling either the computer side or the user side of settings
- Controlling inheritance
- Managing permissions

You can delegate certain Group Policy tasks, such as linking GPOs to an OU, with the Delegation of Control wizard or ACL Editor. You use ACL Editor to set permissions on GPOs in order to filter them from affecting members of certain groups.

GPMC integrates the functionality of these tools and adds the following operations to this list:

- Reporting GPO settings and storing the report in HTML or XML format
- Backing up, restoring, copying, and importing individual GPOs
- Searching GPOs
- All aspects of delegating Group Policy management
- Analyzing Group Policy processing
- Scripting GPO management tasks

In addition, the intuitive interface of GPMC makes it easy to accomplish all GPO management from one window. GPMC is displayed in Figure 7.3.

Individual group policy settings are configured with the Group Policy MMC snap-in, which is displayed in Figure 7.4. The snap-in has been

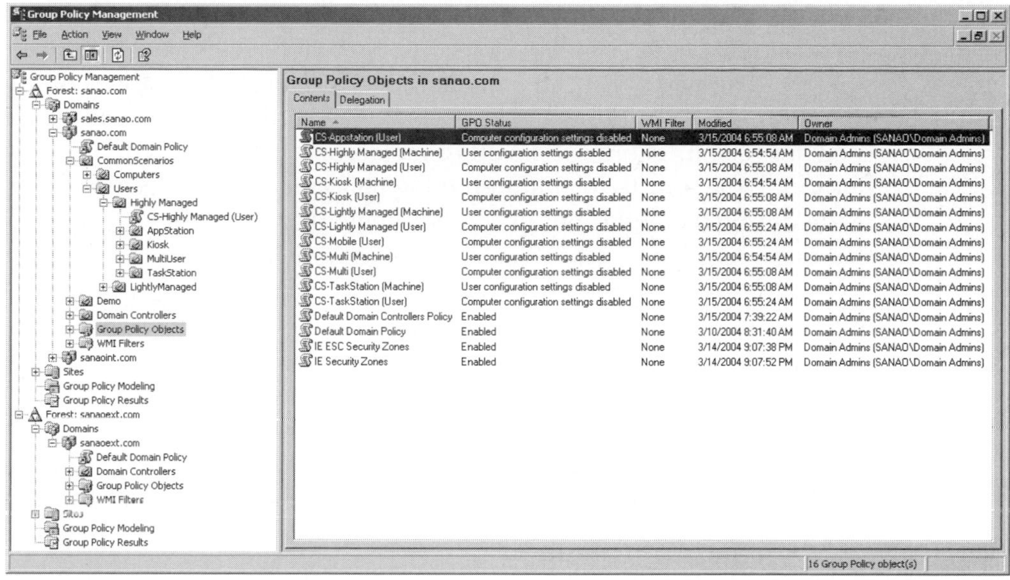

Figure 7.3 Group Policy Management Console touts an intuitive user interface.

renamed the Group Policy Object Editor in Windows Server 2003 in order to distinguish it from the Group Policy Management Console snap-in. You can access the Group Policy (Object Editor) snap-in from the property pages of Active Directory Users and Computers or Active Directory Sites and Services, or from GPMC.

NOTE In the Windows XP and Windows Server 2003 Group Policy (Object Editor) snap-ins, there is no need to open the properties and the Explain tab of an individual administrative template setting, since the description is displayed in the Extended tab.

NT 4.0 System Policy Compared to Windows 2000/XP/Server 2003 Group Policy

Windows NT 4.0 had a feature called System Policy. Group Policy retains the functionality of the NT 4.0 System Policy, but with vast improvements. Group Policy also contains new functionalities that were previously found via various management tools or that were not at all there in NT 4.0.

In NT 4.0 networks, System Policy was primarily used to restrict users' actions on their workstations. The System Policies were by default stored in one binary file, ntconfig.pol, that was most often stored in the Netlogon share on domain controllers. The settings were read when users logged on. There was no other means to process the System Policy but to ask the user to log off and to log on again. The changes could be made during the night, but in a larger network it was difficult to ensure that every user had been subjected to the new policy set.

Another major problem with NT System Policy was *registry tattooing*. This means that a System Policy–initiated change in a registry setting could be removed only by making another change in the same setting. Thus, it could be difficult to ensure a consistent state of one specific setting through a number of workstations or servers.

Table 7.1 lists the major differences between NT 4.0 System Policy and Group Policy in newer Windows operating systems.

Table 7.1 NT 4.0 System Policy Compared to Group Policy

Feature	System Policy	Group Policy
Purpose	Restricting users' desktops	Efficient management and control of users' desktops and settings; part of IntelliMirror
Number of registry settings	72	More than 450 (Windows 2000) More than 780 (Windows XP) More than 800 (Windows Server 2003)
Number of security settings	N/A	More than 100 (Windows 2000) More than 130 (Windows XP) More than 140 (Windows Server 2003)
Scope	Domain	Site, domain, OU
Focus	Computer, user, global group	Filtering with permissions given for groups Filtering with WMI filters (Windows Server 2003 Active Directory)
Security	Share and NTFS permissions on shared folder Netlogon	Active Directory, registry, and NTFS permissions

Table 7.1 NT 4.0 System Policy Compared to Group Policy *(cont.)*

Feature	System Policy	Group Policy
Registry tattooing	Yes	No (for registry settings defined in administrative templates)
Settings are processed	At logon	When the computer starts or the user logs on, when the computer is shut down or the user logs off, automatically at adjustable periodic intervals, manually with the command SECEDIT (Windows 2000) or GPUPDATE (Windows XP/ Server 2003)

Group Policy Contents

By default, there are at least 115 security-related settings, 97 registry-based computer settings, and 359 registry-based user settings that you can configure through Group Policy. These figures are for Windows 2000 (with Service Pack 4). Table 7.2 lists the number of settings for Windows XP (with Service Pack 1) and Server 2003.

NOTE The numbers in the table have been counted by individual rows of settings in the details pane of the Group Policy Object Editor. Some settings have several values in them—for example, in a Windows Server 2003 GPO, Computer Configuration\Administrative Templates\System\Windows Time Service\Global Configuration Settings has 15 individual values that you can define.

Table 7.2 Number of Group Policy Settings in Various Windows Versions

Setting Type	Windows 2000 SP4	Windows XP SP1	Windows Server 2003
Computer security settings	115	136	145
Registry-based settings for computer	97	316	340
Registry-based settings for user	359	467	468

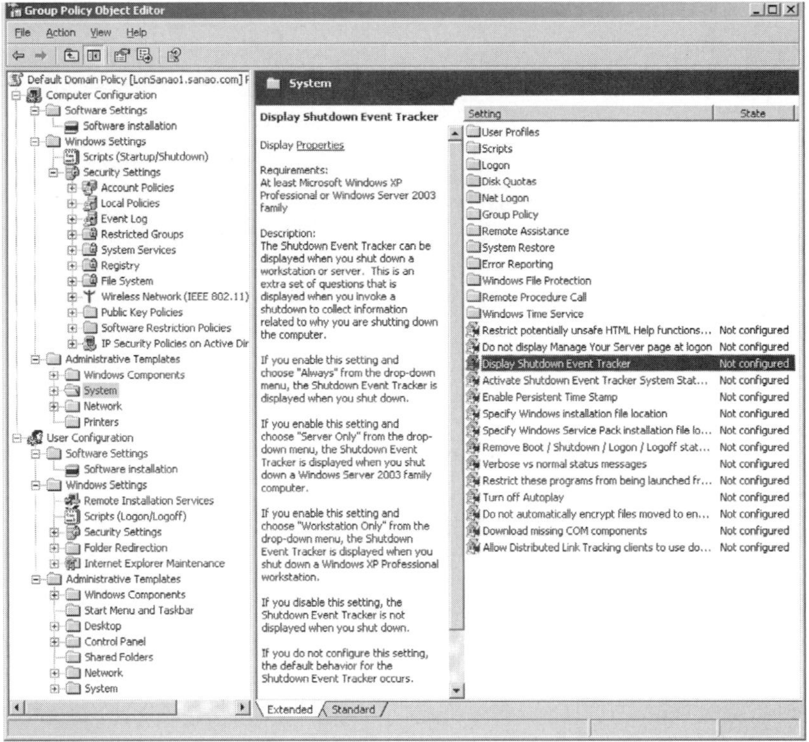

Figure 7.4 Default Domain Policy GPO opened with the Group Policy snap-in

Figure 7.4 shows a Default Domain Policy GPO opened for editing so that all major categories are visible. We discuss each category in this section.

Table 7.3 describes the three main categories. All three exist for both computers and users.

Computer versus User

You can define policy settings separately for computers and users. Some settings make sense when applied to computers, and others make sense when applied to users. For example, you'll usually want to specify security settings appropriate to individual computers.

A computer's settings are processed when the computer starts and at periodic intervals afterward. When a user logs on, the user policy settings are processed. There is one exception to this rule, and you may want to use it if certain user settings must be the same, no matter who logs on to the computer. For example, although a user who belongs to

Table 7.3 Summary of Group Policy Contents

Category	Purpose	Available for Computer	Available for User
Software settings	Installing, upgrading, and removing applications	Yes	Yes
Windows settings	Defining scripts and security settings; for users, some other settings (see next columns)	Startup and shutdown scripts, numerous security settings, software restriction policies	Logon and logoff scripts, few security settings, Internet Explorer settings, RIS settings, folder redirection, software restriction policies
Administrative templates	Defining registry settings centrally	Yes	Yes

the Administrators group is assigned a certain set of applications, we do not want those applications to be installed when the user logs on to domain controllers. We describe this exception, called *loopback processing*, in greater detail later in this chapter.

NOTE There are few settings that can be defined for both computer and user. If the same setting conflicts, the computer policy usually wins.

Software Settings

Previous operating system versions of Windows (NT, 9*x*, and ME) offer no centralized way to manage software applications. Active Directory together with Group Policy provides a method to centrally define which applications are available or installed to which users or computers. You can manage the whole software application life cycle from installation through upgrades and patches to removal with Group Policy application management. You can define the following policies with software settings:

- *Application deployment.* Application shortcuts appear either in Add/ Remove Programs in the Control Panel or in users' Start menus when their computers start or they log on to their workstations. A service introduced in Windows 2000 called Windows Installer installs the applications unless they are legacy (i.e., installed with setup routines).

- *Patches and upgrades for existing packages.* An application that was deployed with Group Policy can be *redeployed.* Redeployment could take place if, for example, few files required by the application were updated. Larger modifications such as new versions of the application can also be deployed with Group Policy as upgrades. Upgrades can be optional or mandated. You may want to use the mandated upgrade if, for example, you want to ensure the version compatibility of saved application files when the storage format has changed.
- *Application removal.* Applications that were deployed with Group Policy can also be removed with Group Policy.

Group Policy–managed application deployment settings are not processed periodically, but rather take place only when users log on or log off, or a computer starts. This makes sense when you think about the possibility of an administrator removing a word-processing application in the middle of a user's typing a letter with that application.

Group Policy might not be the optimal deployment solution in larger environments or if alternative software deployment methods have been developed in-house. This is a result of shortcomings of the management, such as the limited reporting/logging it provides and the lack of scheduling. Thus, system/enterprise management software such as Microsoft's Systems Management Server (SMS) 2003 might be more applicable in these scenarios. SMS application management also takes different network connections and bandwidths into consideration. In addition, SMS provides asset management through its inventory functionality.

We discuss the use of Group Policy for software management later in this chapter in the "Software Management with Group Policy" section.

Scripts

When you administer a large number of Windows 2000/XP/Server 2003 computers, especially servers, scripting is very convenient. This is also true of workstation administration and logon scripts. You can still use legacy batch files, but de facto scripting in Active Directory networks uses VBScript or JScript scripts, which are interpreted with Windows Script Host (WSH). Scripts are run hidden by default.

Scripts for stand-alone workstations and servers can be defined in the Local Computer Policy. You can access the Local Computer Policy with a built-in MMC console called gpedit.msc. Alternatively, you can define scripts with an MMC console with the Group Policy snap-in added and targeted to Local Computer.

IF YOU KNOW NT User logoff scripts as well as computer startup and shutdown scripts are new to Windows 2000/XP/Server 2003.

IF YOU KNOW NT You can still define logon scripts in the user settings in Windows 2000/Server 2003 Active Directory and store them in the Netlogon share of the domain controllers. However, defining a logon script with Group Policy per OU is recommended because this offers more functionality. It is also better to use only one method rather than both.

TIP You can find a lot of sample scripts at `http://www.microsoft.com/technet/scriptcenter.`

Security Settings

Security settings can easily be controlled centrally with Group Policy. In addition to configuring various security settings manually for different GPOs, you may want to use the *Security Configuration Toolset* (SCTS). It consists of the secedit command and two MMC snap-ins: Security Templates, and Security Configuration and Analysis. Microsoft has created a number of sample configurations for different configurations and environments. These configurations are stored in *security templates*, which are stored as text-based files with the extension .inf in %systemroot%\security\templates. Windows Server 2003 comes with nine security templates. Although security templates are text files, modifying them with a text editor such as Notepad can quickly become too complicated, especially when configuring permissions. The Security Templates snap-in is the tool for modifying them. It is not available in the Start menu by default, and as a result, you would have to create your own MMC console and add this snap-in into it. If you want to start with an empty configuration with all settings undefined, you can create a new template. Later, you could import the settings into one or more GPOs.

TIP You can import the settings of a security template into a GPO with the Group Policy Object Editor. Right-click the Computer Configuration\Windows Settings\Security Settings node of the GPO and select Import Policy.

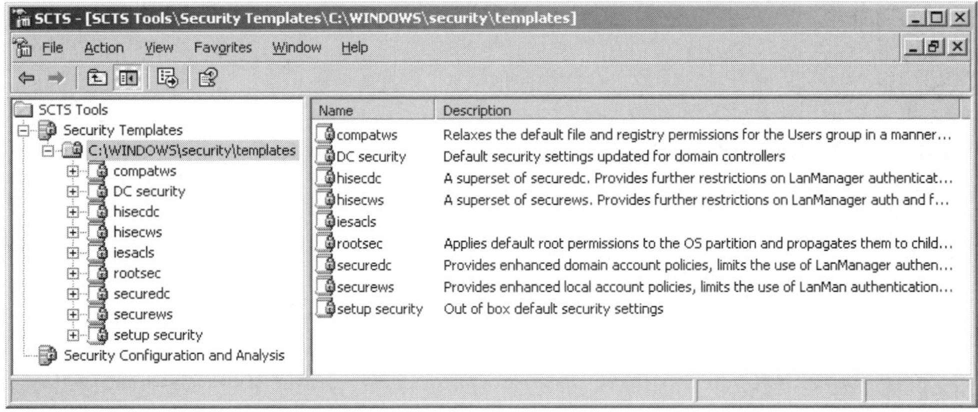

Figure 7.5 You can create your own SCTS console by adding the Security Templates and Security Configuration and Analysis snap-ins into it. Windows Server 2003 ships with nine security templates.

Alternatively, you can analyze your computer with the Security Configuration and Analysis snap-in and compare its security settings to those defined in one of the templates. And if you want, you can configure the security settings based on a template with the same snap-in. You can also perform analysis and configuration from the command line with the secedit command. Figure 7.5 illustrates a manually created SCTS console with the two snap-ins.

IF YOU KNOW NT The Security Configuration Toolset was ported to Windows NT 4.0 in Service Pack 4. You can find the tools in the Security Configuration Manager (SCM) subfolder on the Service Pack 4 (or later) CD or at `ftp://ftp.microsoft.com/bussys/winnt/winnt-public/tools/scm/`.

TIP You should download the Windows Server 2003 Security Guide from Microsoft Web site. It contains the appropriate settings for three different scenarios as well as the security templates for servers in different roles in these scenarios.

Account Policies

Account policies include password, account lockout, and Kerberos policies. When defined in Active Directory–stored GPOs, these policies are effective only at the domain level (i.e., they must be defined in GPOs linked to the domain), although they appear on GPOs linked to other container types (site and OU) as well. These settings can also be defined in the Local Computer Policy for stand-alone and domain member workstations and servers. If the workstation or server is a member of a domain, and the same setting in Active Directory–stored GPOs has no other value configured, the policy defined in the Local Computer Policy can remain in effect. The Local Computer Policy does not have Kerberos policies.

TIP In addition to password, account lockout, and Kerberos policies, three other security options also apply only when defined in GPOs linked to the domain. These are renaming administrator and guest accounts and automatically logging off users when their logon times expire. See Knowledge Base article 259576 for more information.

In Windows 2000, a password complexity requirement is one policy option in the password policies, and in Windows Server 2003, the complexity requirement is on by default. A complexity requirement means that users' passwords must contain characters from three of the following five categories:

- English uppercase characters (A through Z)
- English lowercase characters (a through z)
- Base 10 digits (0 through 9)
- Nonalphabetic characters (for example, !, $, #, %)
- Unicode characters

In addition, the password may not contain the user's account or full name.

IF YOU KNOW NT In Windows NT 4.0 you had to either install passfilt.dll from Service Pack 2 or newer and make registry changes manually or install Passprop.exe from the Resource Kit to force complex passwords.

Local Policies

Local policies include Audit Policy, User Rights Assignment, and Security Options. There are nine types of events to be audited, and you can define whether successful or failed events are logged into the security log. There are 36 user rights in Windows 2000 and 39 in Windows Server 2003, including change system time and allow logon locally. (We discuss user rights in detail in Chapter 4.)

Windows Server 2003 is the first Windows operating system that has some security auditing turned on by default. In the Default Domain Controllers Policy, the following categories are set to audit successful events:

- Audit account logon events
- Audit account management
- Audit directory service access
- Audit logon events
- Audit policy change
- Audit system events

In member and stand-alone servers, only account logon and logon events are set to audit successful events. In production networks, you might also want to collect failures to accomplish these tasks. Thus, we recommend that you change the auditing settings in the Default Domain Controllers Policy.

NOTE Windows Server 2003 introduces more granular operation-based auditing for object access. For example, by collecting object access events, you can see whether data was written to the file and by which application. Operation-based audits are logged with event ID 567 in the security log.

In Windows 2000, auditing is defined not to collect any events for successes or failures in the Default Domain Controllers Policy. Thus, turning auditing on only on the domain level would leave no trails for logon attempts with incorrect passwords on domain controller security logs unless you change the Default Domain Controllers Policy too.

NOTE To collect security events for file and folder access, as well as specify "Audit object access," you must also define which user or group and what type of action you want to audit in the system access control list (SACL) of the file or folder. You can access the SACL from the Audit tab in the file or folder properties' Security tab. The same applies for "Audit directory service access." You should first enable auditing in a GPO, and then configure the user or group and type of actions to be audited in the SACL of the Active Directory object.

The importance of security in Windows operating systems can also be seen in the number of security options, which has grown from 40 in Windows 2000 to 67 in Windows Server 2003. At the same time, the security options have been grouped into categories. Some of these options were available in Windows NT System Policies or directly with changing registry settings, but most are new. For example, you can set the LAN Manager authentication level so that the more secure NTLMv2 authentication is required. You must remember that defining this level carries implications for clients connecting to the computers that are controlled by this policy (i.e., Windows 9*x* and NT with SP3 and lower cannot connect if NTLMv2 is required).

Similar implications are caused for Windows 95 and Windows NT 4.0 SP3 or earlier clients by two default settings for Windows Server 2003 domain controllers. These settings are also in the security options:

- Domain member: Digitally encrypt or sign secure channel data (always)
- Microsoft network server: Digitally sign communications (always)

NOTE Windows NT 4.0 SP3 actually supports SMB signing, but it does not support encrypting or signing secure channel data.

When you install the first domain controller for a new Windows Server 2003 domain, you will receive a warning regarding these settings and their effect of earlier clients not being able to connect. You can either relax these settings by disabling them in the Default Domain Controllers Policy or alternatively install the Active Directory client extension on the legacy client computers. See the following note.

NOTE One option to enable NTLMv2 and SMB signing in Windows 9*x* and NT computers is to install the Active Directory client extension. For Windows 9*x*, it is available on the Windows 2000 distribution CD. For Windows NT, you can find the client on the Microsoft site at `http://www.microsoft.com/windows2000/server/evaluation/news/bulletins/adextension.asp`.

NOTE Windows Server 2003 online Help includes information on security settings. If you are using Windows 2000, see the Windows Group Policy Reference in the Windows 2000 Server Resource Kit for more information on security settings.

Some other security options are the ability to prevent users from installing unsigned drivers, the ability to rename administrator and guest accounts, and the ability to define the action that takes place when a smart card that was used for logon is removed (either locking the computer or logging off the current user).

NOTE When the security log fills, Microsoft recommends using the audit log setting "Shut down system immediately if unable to log security audits" in Security Options, rather than "Shut down the computer when the security audit log is full" in Event Log Settings. The former causes the system to halt with the blue screen message "STOP: C0000244 {Audit Failed} An attempt to generate a security audit failed." The latter setting has been removed from Windows XP and Windows Server 2003.

IF YOU KNOW NT NT has seven event categories for auditing. The new categories in Windows 2000/XP/Server 2003 are "Audit account logon events" and "Audit directory service access." The former can be used to log on events where the computer was used to validate/authenticate a user (e.g., on a domain controller). The latter is similar to "Audit object access," in which the access of registry keys or NTFS files or folders was audited. With "Audit directory service access," you can audit the access to Active Directory objects as defined in their SACL. In NT, there were 10 basic and 17 advanced user rights. Most security options are new in Windows 2000/XP/Server 2003.

Event Log

You can define various settings for application, security, and system logs. For example, you can restrict guest access to these logs, define their maximum sizes, and define how full logs are handled. By default, event log policies are not defined in the Default Domain and Default Domain Controllers policies. The Local Computer Policy does not have Event Log Policy. Instead, these settings are defined in the properties of the event logs during the setup.

NOTE The default maximum log file sizes have finally been increased to 16MB for Windows Server 2003 (from 512KB in earlier versions). In addition, the default security log size for domain controllers is 128MB.

Restricted Groups

You may want to control the membership of some groups, which the Restricted Groups policies enable you to do. You can either add members to a certain group or define the set of group(s) to which a certain group belongs. If you leave the "Members of this group" list empty, it means that the group should have no members. If you leave the "This group is a member of" list empty, of course, you do not indicate which groups the group belongs to. By default, this policy is not defined in the Default Domain and Default Domain Controllers policies. The Local Computer Policy does not have Restricted Groups Policy.

NOTE Starting with Windows 2000 SP4 and Windows XP SP2, you can add domain local groups to the local groups of computers.

System Services

You can set the default state (Automatic, Manual, or Disabled) of services upon startup. You can also define permissions, such as start, stop, and pause, for all system services. By default, this policy is not defined in the Default Domain and Default Domain Controllers policies. The Local Computer Policy does not have System Services Policy.

NOTE If you define the startup status of a certain service as Automatic and stop the service, it will not be started automatically during the periodic refresh of Group Policy, but rather upon the next startup of the system.

NOTE In this category only those services appear that are installed on the system on which you are administering the GPO.

Registry

You can define the permissions and audit settings for registry keys. By default, this policy is not defined in the Default Domain and Default

Domain Controllers policies. The Local Computer Policy does not have Registry Policy.

File System

The File System Policy enables you to define the permissions and audit settings for file system objects such as files and folders. By default, this policy is not defined in the Default Domain and Default Domain Controllers policies. The Local Computer Policy does not have File System Policy.

Wireless Network (IEEE 802.11)

Wireless networks are becoming ubiquitous these days. Windows Server 2003 brings along the ability to set the most common WLAN settings, such as whether ad hoc computer-to-computer networks are allowed, and the encryption and authentication settings for preferred networks. Obviously, WLAN settings are not defined in the Default Domain Policy or the Default Domain Controllers Policy, since they are specific to a company or a location. The Local Computer Policy does not have Wireless Network (IEEE 802.11) Policies.

NOTE Wireless Network Policies are new to Windows Server 2003.

Public Key Policies

The Encrypted Data Recovery Agents setting enables you to add certificates for users who should be able to decrypt files or folders encrypted by other users, in case these files are needed while users are away (for example, on vacation). By default, the domain administrator account has the necessary certificate added to this policy to be able to recover all other domain users' files. If you delete this policy, no files can be encrypted with Encrypting File System (EFS). For stand-alone Windows 2000 computers, the local administrator has the ability to recover the files encrypted on that computer. This feature was removed in Windows XP—that is, recovery agent is not required. If a certification authority (CA) does not exist in the network, the key pairs and certificates required for EFS are generated automatically by the operating system. This is the only public key policy available on the Local Computer Policy.

With Automatic Certificate Request Settings, you can define types of certificates that computers can automatically request. With this setting, an administrator could, for example, define computers in a certain OU to request an IPSec certificate in order to use IPSec encryption later for securing data communication between computers. Windows Server 2003 also enables automatic deployment of certificates to users. This could be useful, for example, when deploying smart cards.

NOTE You must have Windows Server 2003, Enterprise Edition, as the CA in order to deploy user certificates automatically.

Trusted Root Certification Authorities are authorities that are automatically trusted when, for example, a user opens a Web page that requires a secured communication link. With this policy, you can specify that a group of computer and user resources residing in an OU trust certain CAs.

The Enterprise Trust policy, an extension of the Trusted Root Certification Authorities, enables you to add certificate trust lists (CTLs), which are signed lists of Trusted Root CAs.

With the exception of the data recovery agent policy, these policies are not defined in the Default Domain and Default Domain Controllers policies.

Software Restriction Policies

Introduced in Windows XP, software restrictions enable allowing users to run certain applications or prohibiting them from doing so. You can either allow running all applications except those defined in software restriction policies (also known as SAFER) rules, or you can prohibit running any application other than those that are explicitly allowed.

You can define unrestricted/disallowed applications with four different types of rules:

- *Hash rule.* A hash is automatically calculated for a selected file.
- *Certificate rule.* The certificate for a trusted software publisher is assigned.
- *Path rule.* The path to the file, directory, or registry key is defined. Registry key paths are enclosed in percentage signs.
- *Internet zone rule.* Software is installed by Windows Installer from different Internet Explorer security zones.

NOTE By default, certificate rules are not turned on. To turn on certificate rules, type “regedit” into the Run dialog and then click OK. Locate and then click the registry key `HKLM\SOFTWARE\Policies\Microsoft\Windows\Safer\CodeIdentifiers`. In the details pane, double-click AuthenticodeEnabled, and then change the value data from 0 to 1.

If several rules apply to the selected software, the rules are applied in the order shown in this list, with the hash rule having the highest priority. Also, if two path rules are applied to the same object, the more specific rule takes precedence. And finally, if two rules with different security levels apply to the application, the more conservative rule takes precedence.

In addition to defining which applications a user can use, you can use software restriction policies to define which group can select trusted publishers. Available groups include end users, local computer administrators, and enterprise administrators. Also, you can exempt the policies from applying to administrators.

NOTE In a Windows Server 2003 Terminal Server environment, software restriction policies are a useful substitution for the Windows 2000 Terminal Server Application Security Tool that was available in the Windows 2000 Resource Kit.

NOTE In Windows XP (and SP1) you have to restart the computer for SAFERs to take effect.

By default, SAFER policy is not defined in the Local Computer Policy or in the Default Domain and Default Domain Controllers policies.

IP Security Policies

IP Security (IPSec) enables authenticated and/or encrypted data communication between computers. By default, there are three IPSec policies defined in each domain or Local Computer Policy, with a lot of settings for each. However, none of the IPSec policies is assigned, and as a result, none of them is in effect. You should use the predefined ones only as samples and create IPSec policies with settings applicable to your own environment.

Administrative Templates

The Administrative Templates section contains registry-based settings. If you are familiar with Windows NT, you already know the principle. The configurable settings are defined in template files. These templates, which have the extension .adm, define which options are available for you to change in the graphical UI (Group Policy snap-in or System Policy Editor) and how the selected settings modify the registry. You can leave a setting undefined, or you can select Enabled or Disabled. In some policies, you might also have to define the value (i.e., not only Enabled or Disabled), as illustrated in Figure 7.6. If you select Enabled or Disabled, the setting is written to a .pol file according to the value

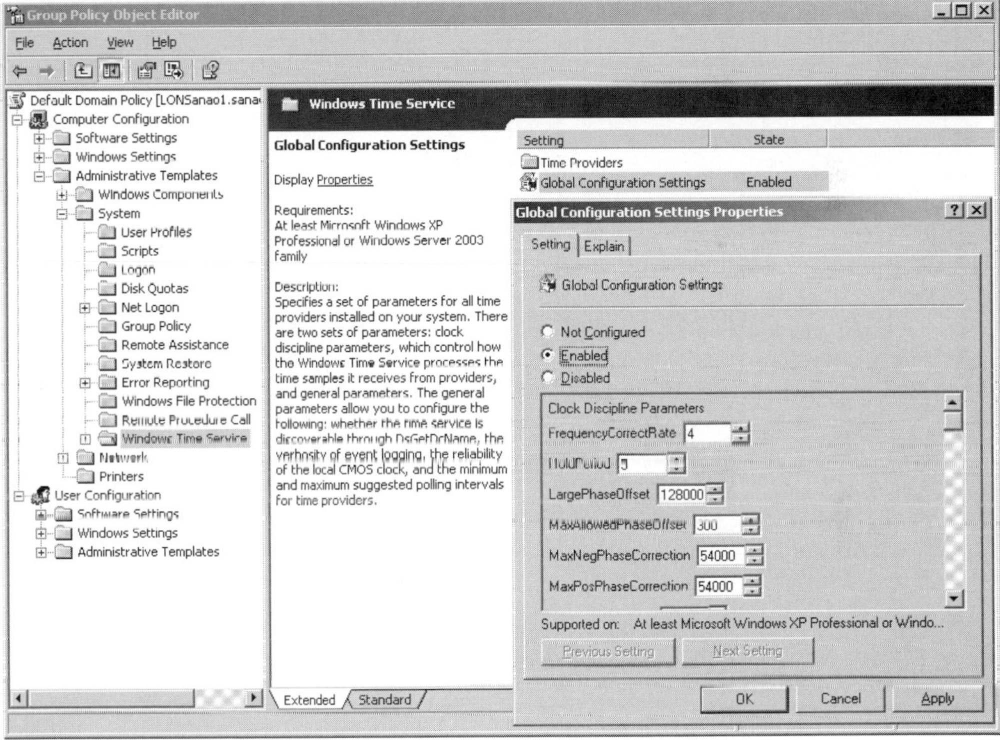

Figure 7.6 Defining the settings for administrative templates can be more complex than simply selecting Enabled or Disabled. You can see more information about the settings and their effect on the Explain tab. In Windows XP and Server 2003, you already see the same information in the Extended tab of the Group Policy Object Editor.

defined in the template. The setting in the registry is configured according to the .pol file when Group Policy CSE processes the GPO.

The templates are Unicode-based text files that are stored in %SystemRoot%\inf. By default, three templates (conf.adm, inetres.adm, and system.adm) are loaded in Windows 2000 and five (conf.adm, inetres.adm, system.adm, wmplayer.adm, and wuau.adm) in Windows Server 2003. If you want to add more templates, right-click Administrative Templates in either the Computer or User configuration and click Add/Remove Templates. Figure 7.7 illustrates the templates that are loaded by default as well as the templates that come with Windows Server 2003 and are located in %SystemRoot%\inf. Table 7.4 lists these templates and their purpose as well as whether they can be used with Group Policy.

NOTE The same templates are used for both Computer and User configurations.

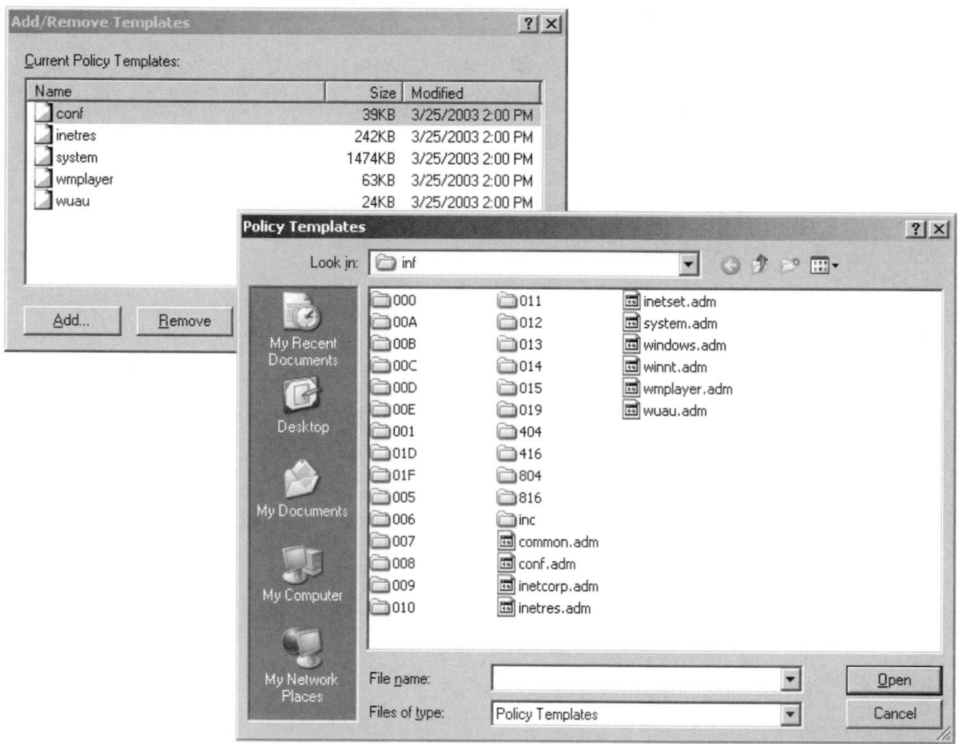

Figure 7.7 By default, five templates are loaded in Windows Server 2003. You can add more by right-clicking Administrative Templates and selecting Add/Remove Templates.

Table 7.4 Default Template Files in %SystemRoot%\inf

File	Contents	Note
AER_1003.adm	Settings for error reporting	Only available in Windows 2000 SP3 and SP4
common.adm	Settings for Windows NT	Cannot be used with Group Policy; not available in Windows XP
conf.adm	Settings for NetMeeting	—
inetcorp.adm	IEAK settings for previous versions of Internet Explorer	Cannot be used with Group Policy
inetres.adm	Settings for Internet Explorer	—
inetset.adm	IEAK settings for previous versions of Internet Explorer	Cannot be used with Group Policy
system.adm	All other settings apart from IE and NetMeeting	By far the largest template file, with the most settings
windows.adm	Settings for Windows 9*x*	Cannot be used with Group Policy; not available in Windows XP
winnt.adm	Settings for Windows NT	Cannot be used with Group Policy; not available in Windows XP
wmp.adm (wmplayer in Windows XP and Windows Server 2003)	Settings for Windows Media Player	—
wuau.adm	Settings for Windows Update Automatic Update client	Available in Windows 2000 SP3 (or newer), XP SP1 (or newer), and Windows Server 2003 (or newer)

TIP You can download the Group Policy Settings Reference for Windows Server 2003 Excel spreadsheet from the Microsoft Web site. The spreadsheet includes all settings included in the five .adm files (system.adm, inetres.adm, conf.adm, wmplayer.adm, and wuau.adm). Alternatively, you can create the spreadsheet yourself with the Resource Kit tool ADM File Parser, which we will discuss later in this chapter.

TIP Windows Server 2003 Resource Kit Tools include inetesc.adm for configuring Internet Explorer Enhanced Security Configuration (IEESC).

TIP If you are administering Internet Explorer settings—for example, security zones—with Windows Server 2003 that has Internet Explorer Enhanced Security Configuration enabled (as it is by default; you can change this from Add/Remove Windows components), the resulting GPOs are not compatible with computers that do not have IEESC. Thus, you will have to create another GPO with IEESC uninstalled, or you will have to configure the GPO from Windows XP or Windows 2000.

As the number of settings in the administrative templates has grown, the size of the .adm files has increased accordingly. Table 7.5 illustrates the growth. Since the total size of the five default .adm files in Windows Server 2003 is 1.8MB, the replication of the file system portion of each new GPO by the File Replication System (FRS) could be one reason not to test new group policies in production networks with congested WAN connections.

We are not going to list all the different administrative template categories. Instead, we have included Table 7.6, which lists the new categories that were introduced in Windows XP and Windows Server 2003.

Table 7.5 Number of Settings and Size (in Kilobytes) of Default Template Files in Different Windows Versions*

File	Windows 2000 SP4	Windows XP SP1	Windows Server 2003
AER_1003.adm	30 (34)	N/A	N/A
common.adm	20 (30)	N/A	20 (30)
conf.adm	34 (34)	33 (39)	34 (40)
inetcorp.adm	7 (7)	7 (7)	7 (7)
inetres.adm	91 (110)	93 (242)	94 (243)
inetset.adm	16 (18)	17 (19)	17 (19)
system.adm	352 (737)	556 (1,344)	596 (1,475)
windows.adm	39 (18)	N/A	39 (18)
winnt.adm	56 (25)	N/A	56 (25)
wmp.adm (wmplayer in Windows XP and Windows Server 2003)	5 (4)	8 (34)	19 (64)
wuau.adm	4 (25)	2 (19)	4 (25)

* The number of settings was determined with the Windows Server 2003 Resource Kit tool ADM File Parser.

NOTE Most of the new settings require at least Windows XP or Windows Server 2003 as the target for the GPO in order to apply. You can see the requirement for the target computer for each setting in the Extended tab of the Group Policy Object Editor in Windows XP and Server 2003.

Table 7.6 New Administrative Template Categories in Administrative Template Files Included with Windows XP and Windows Server 2003

Category	Windows XP	Windows Server 2003	Description
Computer Configuration			
Windows Components\ Application Compatibility		X	Control running 16-bit applications and application compatibility features
Windows Components\ Internet Information Server		X	Control the ability to install IIS
Windows Components\ Terminal Services	X	X	Some 40 settings for controlling most of Terminal Services functionality
Windows Components\ Windows Messenger	X	X	Control whether user can use Windows Messenger and whether it starts upon logon
Windows Components\ Windows Media Digital Rights Management		X	Control Digital Rights Management access, Internet/ intranet access for license acquisition and security upgrades
Windows Components\ Windows Update	X	X	Control frequency, scheduling restarts, and source of Windows Updates (for Windows Update Services—WUS service) *(continued)*

Table 7.6 New Administrative Template Categories in Administrative Template Files Included with Windows XP and Windows Server 2003 *(cont.)*

Category	Windows XP	Windows Server 2003	Description
System\Scripts	X	X	Control the way computer startup and shutdown scripts are processed; located in System\Logon in Windows 2000
System\Netlogon	X	X	Control the behavior of various settings related to Netlogon service. Also for setting DC locator DNS records in Branch Office scenario*
System\Remote Assistance	X	X	Control offering and soliciting remote assistance
System\System Restore	X	X	Control user's ability to configure system restore or switch system restore off completely
System\Error Reporting	X	X	Control options available when application errors occur; settings were in aer1033.adm in Windows 2000 SP4
System\Windows Time Service	X	X	Settings for NTP client and server
System\Network\DNS Client	X	X	13 settings for controlling DNS client behavior—for example, setting to update records in top-level domain DNS zones; only DNS suffix can be set in Windows 2000 in System\DNS Client
System\Network\Network Connections	X	X	Settings for Internet Connection Firewall, QoS, SNMP

* Read more in the Branch Office Deployment Guide, which you can download from the Microsoft Web site.

Table 7.6 New Administrative Template Categories in Administrative Template Files Included with Windows XP and Windows Server 2003 (*cont.*)

Category	Windows XP	Windows Server 2003	Description
User Configuration			
Windows Components\Application Compatibility	X	X	Control access to 16-bit applications
Windows Components\Help and Support Center	X	X	Control displaying dynamically updated "Did you know" content on the home page of Help and Support Center
Windows Components\Terminal Services	X	X	Control user-specific Terminal Server settings such as time limits for connections and level of remote control
Windows Components\Windows Messenger	X	X	Exactly the same settings as for the computer configuration
Windows Components\Windows Media Player	X	X	Control user interface, playback, and networking settings of Media Player
Shared Folders	X	X	Controls users' ability to publish shared folders and DFS roots to Active Directory
System\User Profiles	X	X	Control profile size and directories excluded in roaming profiles; located in System\Logon/Logoff in Windows 2000
System\Scripts	X	X	Control processing logon and logoff scripts; located in System\Logon/Logoff in Windows 2000

(*continued*)

Table 7.6 New Administrative Template Categories in Administrative Template Files Included with Windows XP and Windows Server 2003 *(cont.)*

Category	Windows XP	Windows Server 2003	Description
System\Ctrl+Alt+Del Options	X	X	Remove buttons from Windows Security dialog box; located in System\Logon/Logoff in Windows 2000
System\Logon	X	X	Control running programs at user logon; located in System\Logon/Logoff in Windows 2000
System\Power Management	X	X	Control prompting user for password on resume from hibernate/suspend

NOTE At the time of writing, Windows XP SP2 is nearing completion. The largest new categories it introduces for Group Policy are the capability to control Internet Communication Settings and the renamed Windows Firewall (previously Internet Connection Firewall). In the SP2 Release Candidate 2 version, there were 75 new computer settings and 21 new user settings in the system.adm, compared with Windows Server 2003.

In Windows NT 4.0, the settings specified in the System Policy templates were modifying registry values under many locations in the registry. Removing a changed setting was problematic because you had to use another policy or registry editor to do this. As a result, starting with Windows 2000, all registry-based settings that are modified with Group Policy are grouped under four keys. The preferred locations are `HKEY_CURRENT_USER\Software\Policies` and `HKEY_LOCAL_MACHINE\Software\Policies`. In addition, `HKEY_CURRENT_USER\Software\Microsoft\Windows\CurrentVersion\Policies` and `HKEY_LOCAL_MACHINE\Software\Microsoft\Windows\CurrentVersion\Policies` can be used. The policy settings that are defined in the default .adm files and that modify registry values in these four locations are called *true policies*, *true settings*, or *policy settings that can be fully managed*.

If the existing 800 registry-based settings do not include the settings that you want to control, you can always create your own .adm files. Try to stick to those settings that are stored under the previously mentioned keys. To use a value that is defined somewhere else in the registry, you have to create a new .adm file or modify an existing one. We recommend creating a completely new one so that it is easy to distinguish between the originals and your own templates.

Applications that are developed for Windows 2000 or newer operating systems may also contain their own .adm files. For example, the Microsoft Office 2003 Resource Kit includes 12 .adm files for individual Office applications, totaling 1,053 settings.

TIP You can learn more about the administrative template file format in the Platform SDK on the Microsoft Web site. Use these words (administrative template file format) as keywords when searching the Microsoft Web site.

In Windows 2000, a value that is stored outside the previously mentioned four registry keys is called a *preference*. By default, preferences are not displayed in the Group Policy snap-in. This is to discourage administrators from using Group Policy to configure settings outside the keys defined for the purpose. In Windows XP/Server 2003, preferences are called *Windows NT 4.0 system policy settings*.

In order to see the preferences in Windows 2000, you must right-click Administrative Templates, select View, and deselect Show Policies Only. In Windows XP/Server 2003, you accomplish the same by right-clicking Administrative Templates, selecting View, and then selecting Filtering. Clear the check box "Only show policy settings that can be fully managed". You can distinguish preferences from true policies because preference (or Windows NT 4.0 system policy settings in Windows XP/Server 2003) icons have a red dot instead of the blue dot that appears on policy settings.

TIP You can also deselect Show Policies Only from the View menu of the Group Policy snap-in in Windows 2000 while any of the administrative template nodes are selected. The same applies for accessing Filtering in Windows XP/Server 2003.

As an example, Figure 7.8 illustrates the contents of a template file with which you can configure a setting to prevent a computer from taking

ParticipationinBrowserElections.adm - Notepad

File Edit Format View Help

```
CLASS MACHINE

CATEGORY  !!Network
   CATEGORY !!Browser

      POLICY !!MaintainServerList
         KEYNAME "System\CurrentControlSet\Services\Browser\Parameters"
            #if version >= 4
               SUPPORTED !!SUPPORTED_Win2k
            #endif

            EXPLAIN !!ParticipateElection_Explain
            PART !!MaintainServerList                    DROPDOWNLIST
               VALUENAME "MaintainServerList"
                  ITEMLIST
                     NAME !!MaintainNo VALUE "No"
                     NAME !!MaintainYes VALUE "Yes"
                     NAME !!MaintainAuto VALUE "Auto"
                  END ITEMLIST
            END PART
      END POLICY

   END CATEGORY    ; Browser
END CATEGORY    ; Network

[strings]
Browser="Browser"
MaintainAuto="Auto"
MaintainNo="No"
MaintainServerList="Participation in browser elections."
MaintainYes="Yes"
Network="Network"
ParticipateElection_Explain="Defines participation in browser elections.
Value No prevents computer from participating as a browser.\n\nIf set to
Auto or Yes, the browser service starts automatically."
SUPPORTED_Win2k="At least Microsoft Windows 2000"
```

Figure 7.8 The contents of a user-defined template with which you can prevent a computer from taking part in browser elections

part in browser elections. This could be desirable if you have Windows XP/Server 2003 computers that you do not want to become so-called master browsers, thus causing them unnecessary load. This could happen if your domain controllers are still Windows 2000. A Windows XP/Server 2003 computer wins the master browser election based on an operating system version criterion. The NetBIOS Browser service maintains a list of computers with shared resources so that users can browse them through My Network Places (or Network Neighborhood in NT).

TIP Another way to centrally manage your own settings with Active Directory is to use security options. You can accomplish this by modifying the sceregvl.inf file that is used by the Security Templates and Security Settings node of the Group Policy Object Editor. See KB article 214752 for more information.

When you add this template to Administrative Templates, a new node called Browser is created under Computer Configuration\Administrative Templates\Network, as you can see in Figure 7.9.

TIP You can use the Windows 2000 Resource Kit tools browmon or browstat to see the current browser status.

TIP You can centrally prevent administrators from seeing and using preferences by enabling the Enforce Show Policies Only setting, which you can locate under User Configuration\Administrative Templates\System\Group Policy.

You can use Unicode characters in Windows 2000/XP/Server 2003 Group Policy templates. To edit Unicode files, you have to use an editor, such as Notepad, that supports them.

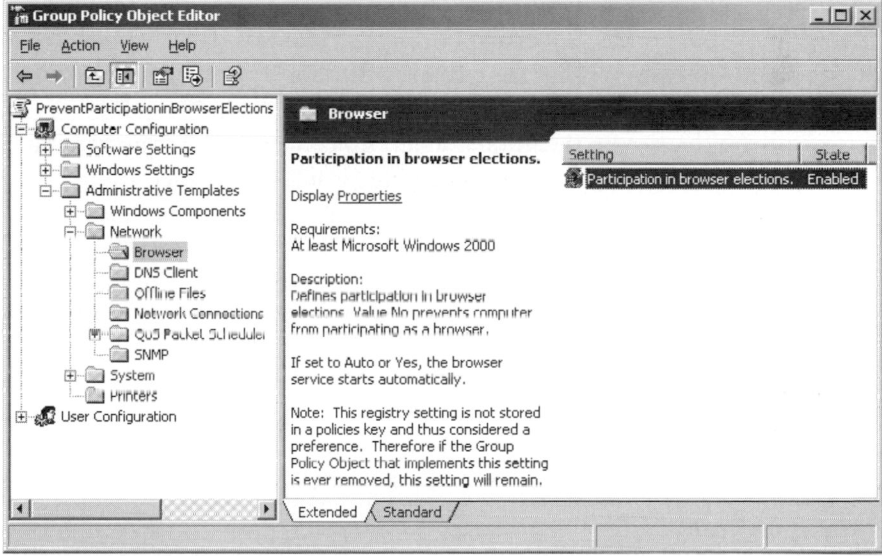

Figure 7.9 You can see the sample preference "Participation in browser elections" created with ParticipationinBrowserElections.adm with the Group Policy snap-in after clicking Filtering in the View menu and clearing "Only show policy settings that can be fully managed" (or deselecting Show Policies Only in the View menu in Windows 2000). You can use the same dialog for filtering settings that apply to different versions of the operating system or its integrated components, such as Internet Explorer and Media Player.

WARNING Using Edit for modifying and saving an .adm file causes the Group Policy Object Editor to crash when loading the administrative template.

TIP Some third-party administrative template editors exist. You can try ADM Template Editor from `http://www.sysprosoft.com.`

Other Policies

There are three other categories of policies that you can define for users: folder redirection, remote installation services, and Internet Explorer maintenance.

Folder Redirection

The user profile contains certain subfolders that would be better stored on the server rather than in the local profile (%SystemDrive%\Documents and Settings\User). When the data in these folders is physically on the server, it can be backed up centrally. One way to achieve this is to use roaming profiles. Roaming profiles introduce their own problems, such as replicating temporary Internet Explorer files, which can be a large number of files. This would cause delays for users logging on or off their computers, because these files have to be copied from or to a file server.

TIP You might want to deploy a new feature of Windows Server 2003, Shadow Copies of Shared Folders, in order to ease (but not to replace) backup. See Windows Server 2003 online Help for more.

Folder redirection in Windows 2000/Server 2003 Active Directory enables you to redirect certain folders from the user profile to a file server. The folders that you can redirect include the following:

- Application Data
- Desktop
- My Documents

- My Pictures (separately from My Documents only in Windows 2000)
- Start Menu

You can define each of these folders to be stored on different UNC paths. And with advanced settings, users in different security groups can have their folders stored in different network locations, according to the security group(s) to which they belong (see Figure 7.10). If a user belongs to at least two groups for which the redirection has been defined, the first redirection with a matching group remains in effect. There are no Up/Down buttons for rearranging the redirections, so you have to create them in the correct order.

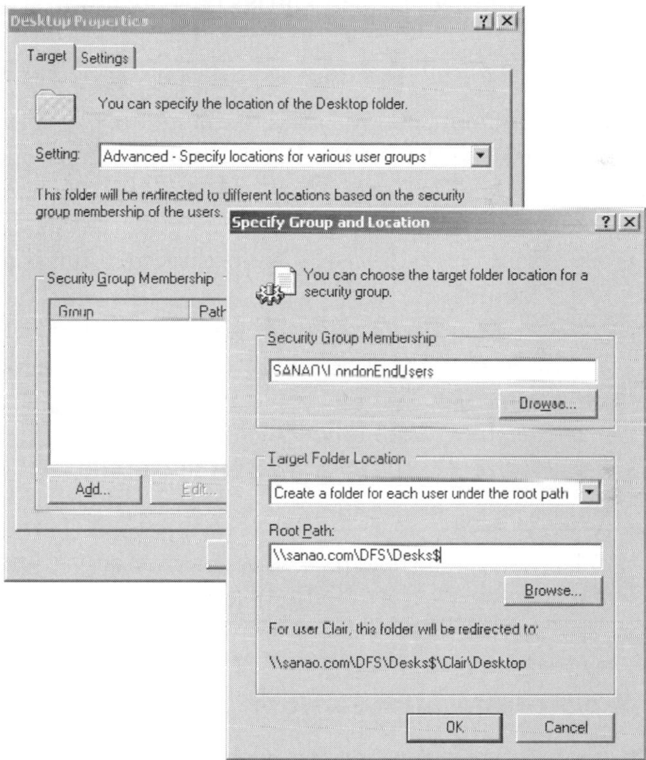

Figure 7.10 With advanced folder redirection, you can redirect certain users' profile subfolders into different network locations based on those users' security group membership.

The steps to perform folder redirection are as follows.

1. Determine which folders to redirect based on the policy at logon time.
2. The desired redirected location is determined and access is verified.
3. If the folder does not exist, it is created and NTFS permissions are set. If the folder exists, NTFS permissions and ownership are checked.
4. If desired, the contents are moved.

TIP Ensure that you change the default share permissions from Everyone Read to something appropriate in your environment. The change from Everyone Full Control to Everyone Read was first introduced in Windows XP SP1 and is consequently in Windows Server 2003, too.

In Windows 2000, you had to define the target folder manually. Windows Server 2003 Folder Redirection has four options for the target location:

- Redirect to the user's home directory; this is only available for My Documents.
- Create a folder for each user under the root path; this appends %username% followed by the redirected folder to the path specified.
- Redirect to the following location.
- Redirect to the local user profile location.

NOTE There are problems involved in redirecting Application Data. Thus, you should avoid redirecting it.

Remote Installation Services

Remote Installation Services (RIS) is one way to deploy the Windows 2000/XP/Server 2003 operating systems. In addition to adding and configuring RIS, the operation of RIS requires Active Directory, DHCP, and DNS services. RIS can be used to deploy the operating system only or the operating system with applications already installed.

With four "Choice Screen" settings, the user can be allowed or denied permission to make certain choices during the installation. One example is to restrict the user from seeing the Custom Setup choice when he starts installing Windows XP with RIS into a new computer.

Internet Explorer Maintenance

Internet Explorer maintenance enables administrators to centralize the configuration of users' Internet Explorer browsers, such as the contents of Favorites or proxy or security zone settings. In earlier Windows networks, the Internet Explorer Administration Kit (IEAK) was used to accomplish the same task. Even in Windows 2000/Server 2003 networks, the IEAK still has its role in creating Internet Explorer installation packages.

As an exception to all other categories, IE maintenance enables you to set the initial configuration only once when the GPO is processed for the first time. The settings in all other categories are processed periodically thereafter. You can use this initial configuration by right-clicking Internet Explorer Maintenance and selecting Preference Mode. In preference mode, there are two additional sets of settings available under Advanced: Corporate Settings and Internet Settings.

Group Policy Objects and Links

In this section we explain the common pool of Group Policy objects (GPOs) in a domain. You may choose to link one or several of these GPOs to each OU (as well as the domain or the site), so that a number of GPOs may affect a given computer or user. We also examine how to control GPO inheritance and priorities.

Group Policy Objects

Group policies are stored and edited in virtual Group Policy objects. Two kinds of GPOs exist: local and nonlocal. Every Windows 2000/XP/ Server 2003–based computer has one local group policy called the Local Computer Policy. Nonlocal GPOs are Active Directory–based, and stored in the domain container and in the shared SYSVOL folder. The GPOs are identified by GUIDs, which are also used in the replication process. You can locate the GUID of a GPO by clicking Properties on the Group Policy tab (see Figure 7.11).

Figure 7.11 The General tab of the Default Domain Policy Properties dialog box displays the GUID for a GPO. The GUIDs for the Default Domain Policy and the Default Domain Controllers Policy GPOs are the same in all Active Directory networks.

Because the Group Policy extension in the Active Directory Users and Computers and Active Directory Sites and Services snap-ins does not contain all information for GPOs, you can use either ADSI Edit or LDP to see additional information. Figure 7.12 displays all defined properties of the Default Domain Policy GPO with the LDP tool. You can find the instructions for opening this view in Chapter 6.

The components of the GPOs reside in Active Directory and the file system and are illustrated in Figure 7.13. The component that resides in Active Directory is called the Group Policy container (GPC). The actual class in the schema is called Group-Policy-Container, with the LDAP display name `groupPolicyContainer`. Table 7.7 lists the most important properties of a GPC.

TIP The Policies container that contains GPCs in the Active Directory Users and Computers snap-in is not visible by default. To make it visible, select View, Advanced Features, and then locate System, Policies under

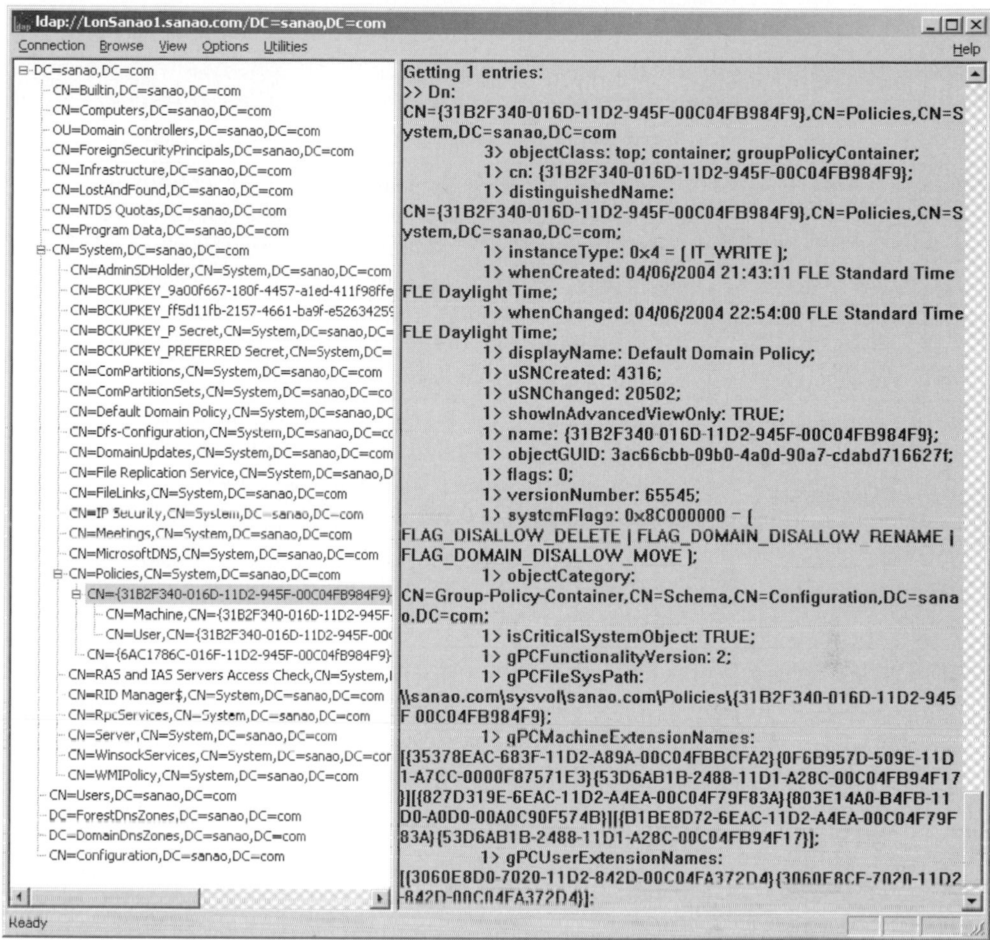

Figure 7.12 Default Domain Policy as displayed in the Windows 2000/Server 2003 Support Tool LDP.

your domain object. However, you may want to use the LDP tool for displaying the attributes of a GPC.

In addition to these properties, all GPCs contain two subcontainers, Machine and User, which an independent software vendor (ISV) can extend in order to use Active Directory to store policies for its applications.

Table 7.7 Important Properties of a Group Policy Container

Property	Description
`displayName`	The name that is displayed in the user interface.
`Flags`	Indicates whether the computer or user sections are disabled. If both are enabled, the value for this property is 0. If Disable User Configuration Settings is checked in the policy's properties, this property has the value 1, and if Disable Computer Configuration Settings is checked in the policy's properties, this property has the value 2. The value 3 means that both are disabled.
`versionNumber`	The version of the GPC. It is compared with the version number in a GPT component, the gpt.ini file, by client extensions in order to determine whether the components of a GPO are in sync.
`gPCFunctionality Version`	The version of the MMC Group Policy extension that created this GPC. For Windows 2000/Windows Server 2003, this value is 2.
`gPCFileSysPath`	The Distributed File System (DFS) path for the file system–based component of the GPO.
`gPCMachine ExtensionNames`	A bracket-separated ([]) list of GUIDs for client-side extensions that have computer settings defined in this GPO. Within each entry there are two or more GUIDs delimited with braces ({}). The first GUID in each entry contains the CSE that processes the GPO and applies them to the client. The other GUIDs identify MMC snap-ins and their extensions that are used to manage the settings for this CSE. If Disable Computer Configuration Settings is checked in the policy's properties, this property has no value.
`gPCUserExtension Names`	The same as `gPCMachineExtensionNames` for those client-side extensions that have user settings defined in this GPO. If Disable User Configuration Settings is checked in the policy's properties, this property has no value.
`gPCWQLFilter`	A reference to the linked WMI filter that is stored in `CN=SOM,CN=WMIPolicy,CN=System,DC=<domain>`.

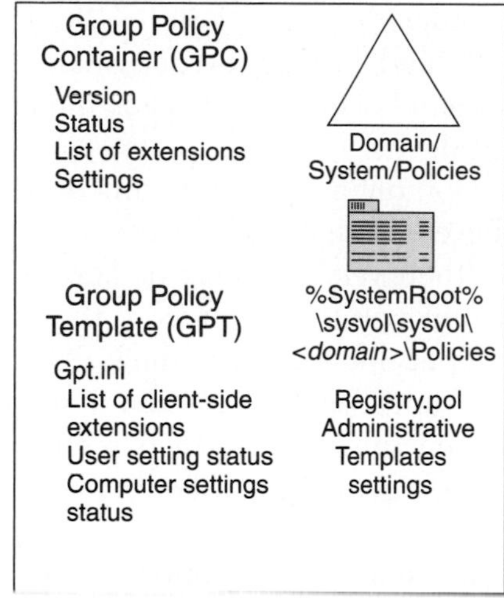

Figure 7.13 Components of a Group Policy object

```
{31B2F340-016D-11D2-945F-00C04FB984F9}
  Adm
  MACHINE
    Applications
    Microsoft
      Windows NT
        SecEdit
    Scripts
      Shutdown
      Startup
  USER
    Applications
    Documents & Settings
    Microsoft
      IEAK
      RemoteInstall
    Scripts
      Logoff
      Logon
```

Figure 7.14 A sample Group Policy template folder structure

The Group Policy template (GPT) is a folder structure stored in the %SystemRoot%\sysvol\sysvol\<*domain*>\Policies folder of domain controllers. It contains information about applications managed with Group Policy, security settings, scripts, and Administrative Template–based policy settings. Figure 7.14 displays a GPT folder structure for a sample GPO under \\sanao.com\sysvol\sanao.com\Policies\{31B2F340-016D-11D2-945F-00C04FB984F9}.

NOTE You should always manage GPOs through the virtual objects. For example, directly manipulating SYSVOL gets you in trouble sooner rather than later.

The GPT contains a file called GPT.INI in the root of an individual policy folder. For the Active Directory–based GPOs, GPT.INI contains only the version number. In Windows Server 2003, for new GPOs it also contains the following line:

```
displayname=name of the GPO
```

The version numbers for the GPT and the GPC are used by the client components to determine whether the settings in a GPO have changed and also to check that the GPT and the GPC are in sync. This is to ensure reliable processing of the Group Policy. If the version numbers do not match, the GPO is not processed.

Because the settings in either Computer Configuration or User Configuration are read based on the event that takes place (e.g., the computer starts or the user logs on), their versions must be kept separate. This is in order for the client extensions to determine if there has been a change in the settings of the applicable section of the GPO. This is achieved through revision numbers kept separately for computer and user sections. You can see the revision numbers of each section by checking the properties of the GPO. See Figure 7.11 earlier in this chapter for an example.

Version numbers are coded as a decimal representation of a 4-byte hexadecimal number, the upper two bytes of which contain the GPO user settings version and the lower two bytes contain the computer settings version. The version number of 65545 in Figure 7.12 equals 10009 hexadecimal, thus giving a user settings revision of 1 and a computer settings revision of 9. You can ensure this in Figure 7.11.

The version number is 0 for a new GPO. For the default GPOs (Default Domain Policy and Default Domain Controllers Policy), the version number is 1 because one change has occurred in the computer section (it being the change in security settings that were all stored at the same time).

Empty subfolders Machine and User are created when you create a new GPO. In Windows 2000, when you open a new GPO for editing, three default .adm files (conf.adm, inetres.adm, and system.adm) are copied from %Systemroot%\inf into the Adm folder. In Windows Server 2003, five default .adm files (conf.adm, inetres.adm, system.adm, wmplayer.adm, and wuau.adm) are copied already at the time the GPO is created. In addition, the file admfiles.ini, listing these .adm files, is also created in Windows Server 2003.

TIP You can use the setting User Configuration\Administrative Templates\System\Group Policy\Disable automatic update of ADM files, to prevent the system from loading the most recently revised copies of the .adm template files from the %Systemroot%\inf folder on the computer that you use for editing the GPO.

The files Machine\Registry.pol and Computer\Registry.pol store all registry-based settings that you define in the Administrative Templates. The file Machine\Registry.pol is created when you make the first change to any setting in the Administrative Templates under Computer Configuration. The file User\Registry.pol is created similarly after the first change in any user administrative template setting.

IF YOU KNOW NT Registry policy files (registry.pol) in Windows 2000/XP/Server 2003 are text files (although without straightforward syntax), whereas in Windows NT they were binary files.

The subfolders Machine\Scripts\Shutdown and Machine\Scripts\Startup are created when you click the Windows Settings node under Computer Configuration. As the name implies, these folders are used to store the computer startup and shutdown scripts. The folders User\Scripts\Logoff, User\Scripts\Logon, and User\Documents & Settings are created when you click the Windows Settings node under User Configuration. The script folders again store user-specific scripts, whereas Folder Redirection settings are stored in Documents and Settings. These settings are stored in a text file called fpdeploy.ini.

Machine\Microsoft\Windows NT\SecEdit contains the file GptTmpl.inf, which stores security settings. This subfolder tree and file is created when you click Security Settings in the Group Policy snap-in. User\Microsoft\IEAK is created when you open the Internet Explorer Maintenance node in the MMC console, and it stores Internet Explorer settings in various files and subfolders in a similar manner to IEAK. User\Microsoft\RemoteInstall stores RIS settings in a text file called oscfilter.ini.

Finally, the Applications subfolder under both the User and Computer folders contains the files required for application deployment with Group Policy. These include the application assignment scripts using the filename format {GUID}.aas.

If a third-party software developer wants to use Group Policy to store the application settings as policies, they can use the registry.pol file for registry settings. They may also create subfolders under the Machine and User folders in a manner similar to the way Microsoft stores RIS and IE settings. For example, Autoprof's Policy Maker uses these folders to store its settings in XML files.

By default, an Active Directory domain contains two GPOs—namely, the Default Domain Policy and the Default Domain Controllers Policy. By default, there is no GPO associated with the first site of a new Active Directory forest: Default-First-Site-Name.

Local Computer Policy

You can use the Local Computer Policy to define settings for a Windows 2000/XP/Server 2003 computer that is not a member of a domain. It is stored in the %SystemRoot%\SYSTEM32\GroupPolicy folder. The file gpt.ini in this folder contains information as a subset of the attributes of a GPC object's information, as illustrated in Table 7.8.

The subfolders for the Local Computer Policy are almost similar to the Active Directory–based GPOs apart from the folders for application deployment, which is not available without Active Directory. In addition, the security settings are stored in %SystemRoot%\security\Database\secedit.sdb.

TIP The Group Policy folder is hidden by default. In order to see it, you must check the Windows Explorer setting in the Tools menu, Folder Options, View, Show hidden files and folders. In addition, the Group Policy folder is created in Windows Server 2003 only after you first open it with gpedit.msc.

TIP If you do not have Active Directory yet and you want to use the same Local Computer Policies for several Windows 2000/XP/Server 2003 computers, you can define the settings for one of the computers and then copy the contents of %SystemRoot%\system32\GroupPolicy to other computers.

NOTE You can use the Local Computer Policy to define settings also for computers that are members of an Active Directory domain. You just have to remember that if the same setting with a different value in Active Directory–stored GPOs applies to a computer or a user, it will override the setting stored in the Local Computer Policy.

NOTE The settings that are defined in an Active Directory–based GPO and are in effect on a Windows Server 2003 computer are disabled in the Local Computer Policy. This is also indicated with a domain-resembling icon in the beginning of the setting row.

Table 7.8 The Rows of a gpt.ini File of Local Computer Policy

Row	Description
`Options`	Indicates whether the computer or user sections are disabled. If both are enabled, the value for this property is 0. If Disable User Configuration Settings is checked in the policy's properties, this property has the value 1, and if Disable Computer Configuration Settings is checked in the policy's properties, this property has the value 2. The value 3 means that both are disabled.
`Version`	The version number of the local policy. Version numbers are constructed in the same way as those for Active Directory–based GPOs. We discussed this a bit earlier.
`gPCFunctionality Version`	The version of the MMC Group Policy extension that created this GPC. For Windows 2000/Windows Server 2003, this value is 2.
`gPCMachine ExtensionNames`	A bracket-separated ([]) list of GUIDs for client-side extensions that have computer settings defined in the Local Computer Policy. Within each entry there are two or more GUIDs delimited with braces ({}). The first GUID in each entry contains the CSE that processes the Local Computer Policy and applies them to the client. The other GUIDs identify MMC snap-ins and their extensions that are used to manage the settings for this CSE. If Disable Computer Configuration Settings is checked in the policy's properties, this row does not exist.
`gPCUser ExtensionNames`	The same as `gPCMachineExtensionNames` for those client-side extensions that have user settings defined in the Local Computer Policy. If Disable User Configuration Settings is checked in the policy's properties, this row does not exist.

Group Policy Links

A Group Policy object is associated with an Active Directory container by a link. You can link GPOs to three types of Active Directory container objects: sites, domains, and OUs. You cannot link a GPO to the default containers (Builtin, Computers, and Users), because they are not OUs.

TIP See Chapter 3 and KB article 324949 for instructions for redirecting the Users and Computers containers.

As Figure 7.15 shows, a GPO can be linked to several containers. Alternatively, a container can be associated with several GPOs. In the latter case, you can define the priority of the GPOs by clicking the Up and Down buttons in the Group Policy dialog box. The links in the list are read from bottom to top (i.e., the first link is read last), and as a result settings in the GPO that this link associates remain in effect should the same setting with a different value be defined in another GPO lower in the list.

If you don't have GPMC, you have to see the individual site, domain, or OU in order to see linked GPOs. GPMC illustrates linked GPOs clearly.

NOTE The maximum number of GPOs applied to any user or computer is 999. You should be at least a little bit worried about your OU/Group Policy plan if you are getting afraid of exceeding that number.

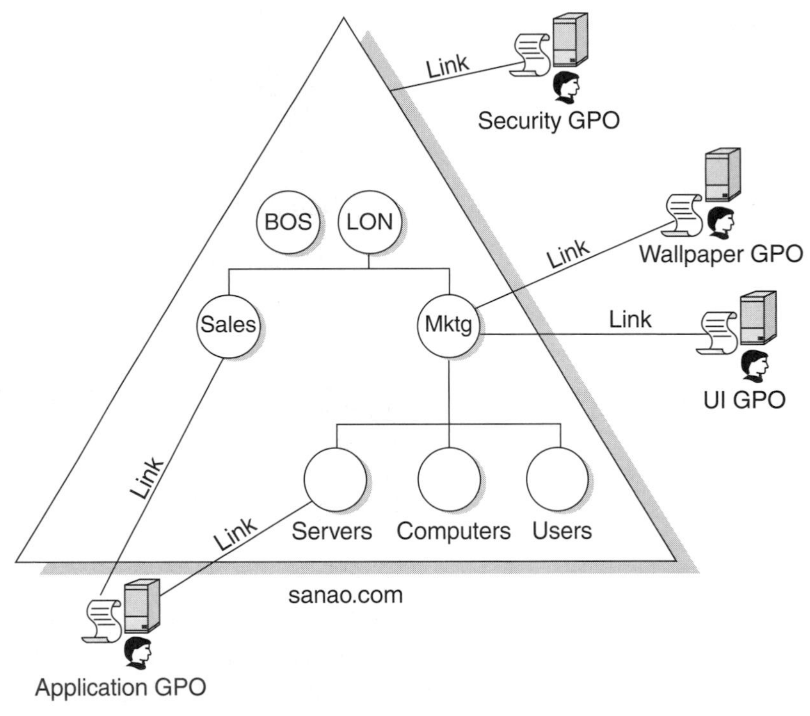

Figure 7.15 You can link a GPO (Application GPO) to several containers, or several GPOs to one container (Mktg).

Scope of Group Policies

Group policies can be defined on site, domain, and OU levels. This is sometimes referred to as *Scope of Management* (SOM). As also mentioned earlier, they cannot be set on container objects such as computers and users. However, the policies that affect the parent container (in this case, domain) also affect the objects in the child containers. Figure 7.16 illustrates GPOs linked to different containers.

GPMC displays this very clearly on the Scope tab of a GPO, as illustrated in Figure 7.17.

TIP GPMC does not display other forests, domains, or even your own site by default. In order to display other forests, you can right-click the top node, Group Policy Management, and select Add Forest. To access other domains and site(s), you can right-click the Domains or Sites node and select Show Domains or Show Sites.

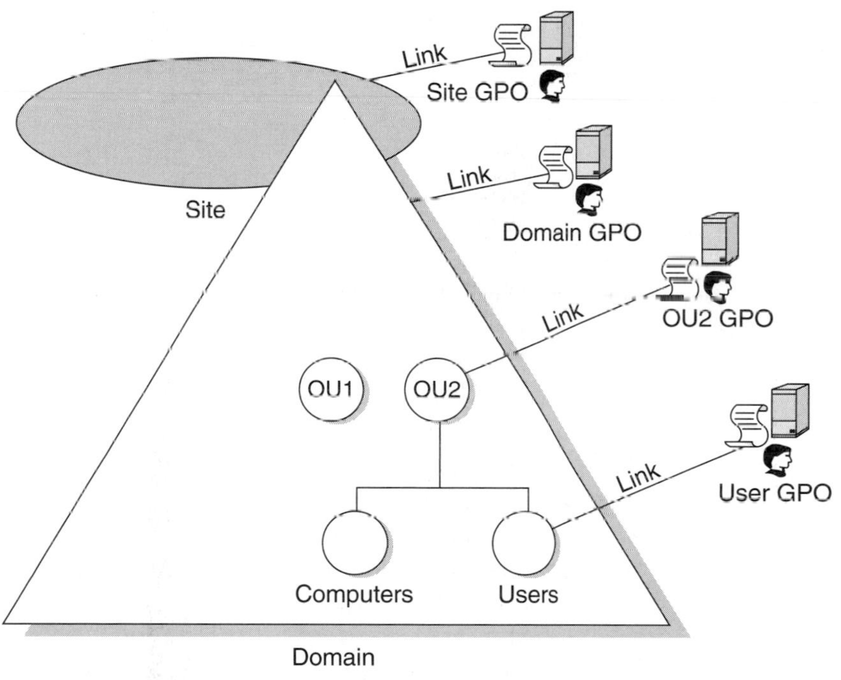

Figure 7.16 GPOs that contain policies for computer and user objects can be associated with sites, domains, and OUs.

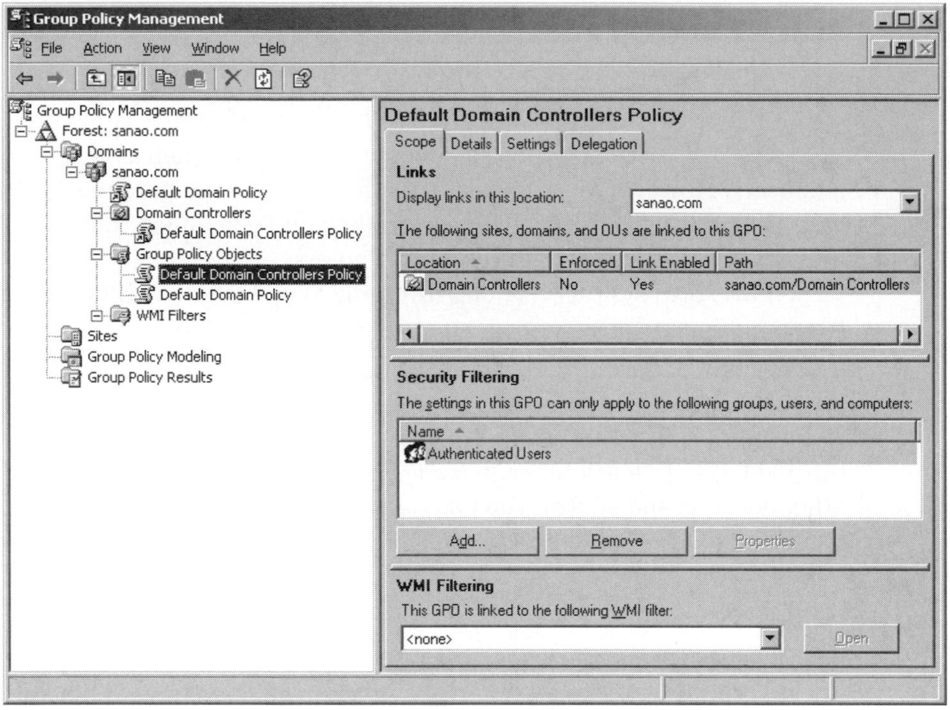

Figure 7.17 GPMC shows the scope of a GPO.

Inheritance

By default, Group Policy settings are inherited from the parent container down the tree to the objects in the child containers. The path through the tree is based on the user or computer object's location. If there are conflicting settings, the nearest setting usually remains in effect. Consider the example illustrated in Figure 7.18.

In the case illustrated in Figure 7.18, three GPOs are linked to three containers.

- A GPO that contains security settings is linked to a domain. Such settings could include the maximum password age and the minimum number of characters in the password.
- An administrative template GPO that contains a setting for common wallpaper is linked to the LON (London) OU. Thus, all users in London would have similar wallpaper on their desktops.

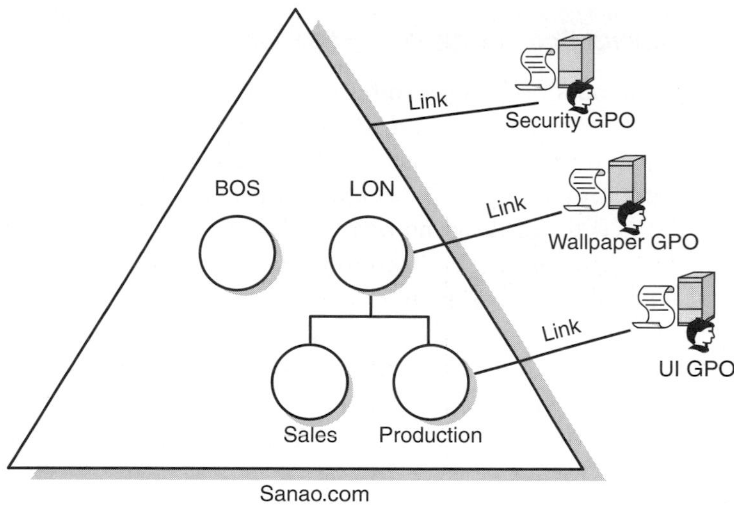

Figure 7.18 A sample domain, `sanao.com`, with three linked GPOs

- An administrative template that contains some user interface modifications is linked to the Production OU. For example, the Documents menu could be removed from the Start menu.

NOTE You have to use Active Desktop settings in order to set the wallpaper with Group Policy.

All user and computer objects in the `sanao.com` domain receive the same security settings. User and computer objects in the LON OU and the OUs below it receive the same wallpaper. In addition, user objects in the Production OU receive the same user interface restrictions.

NOTE GPOs do not span over domain boundaries. The only way to have a GPO apply to several domains is to use a GPO linked to a site. Theoretically, it is possible to link a GPO from one domain to containers in another. However, you should not do so—it can slow the logon process dramatically because the client computer has to access a domain controller from the source domain for the GPC and the GPT.

Solving Conflicting Policy Settings

Some policy settings can have conflicting settings on different GPOs. As we mentioned earlier, in these cases the setting in effect closest to the object wins. Another sample situation is where the same setting exists for both user and computer categories. If, for example, the setting was defined for prohibiting user configuration of offline files for both computer and user, the computer configuration would take precedence, as displayed in Figure 7.19. The same figure illustrates well how the Explain tab for each administrative template setting has a wealth of information, including information on processing conflict situations. In Windows XP and Server 2003, you can see the same information in the left side of the Extended tab of the Group Policy Object Editor.

Blocking Inheritance

You may want to block inheritance from group policies linked to parent containers. In this case, the policies set in GPOs linked to the parent containers do not affect objects on this container or its children. By

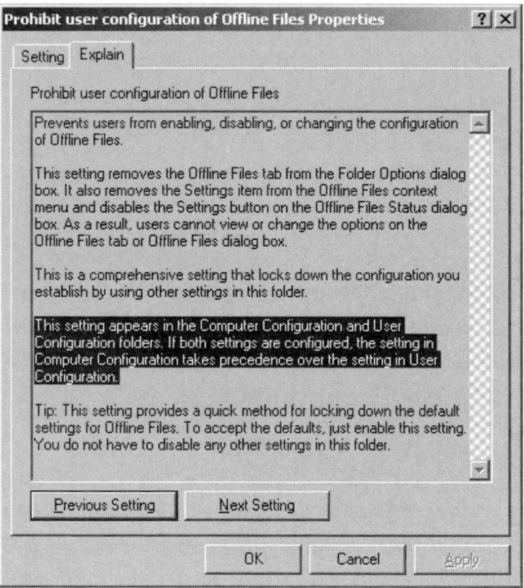

Figure 7.19 This sample setting can be defined for both user and computer. Usually the setting defined for computer wins in this kind of situation. For a different result, see the "Prohibit 'Make available Offline' for these files and folders" setting.

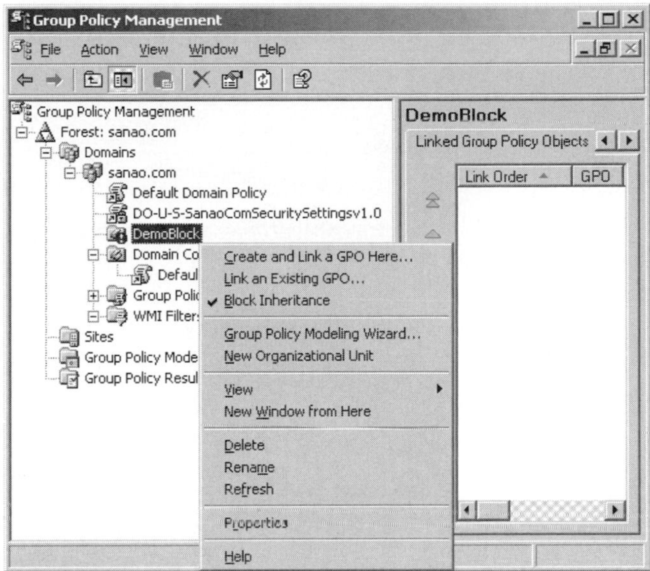

Figure 7.20 GPMC displays Block Policy inheritance with an exclamation mark in a blue circle. Blocking is done with the shortcut menu.

blocking, you cannot define specific policies to be blocked. In other words, it is all or nothing. In Figure 7.20 the administrator for an OU called DemoBlock has blocked inheritance with GPMC.

If you have not deployed GPMC, you block policy inheritance in the properties of an AD container object. The mouse pointer in Figure 7.21 indicates the "Block Policy inheritance" setting.

Enforcing Group Policy

To override blocking or to ensure that a conflicting setting from higher in the hierarchy remains in effect, a domain administrator may want to enforce that the settings in a given GPO linked to the domain apply to every object within the domain, regardless of whether inheritance has been blocked by another, lower-level administrator. With GPMC installed, you can enforce a GPO by right-clicking its link and selecting Enforced or by right-clicking the link on the Scope tab. An enforced GPO is displayed with a small lock over the GPO icon, as illustrated in Figure 7.20 for the GPO DO-U-S-SanaoComSecuritySettingsv1.0.

If you haven't installed GPMC, you check No Override for the GPO link. You can either double-click the No Override column or click

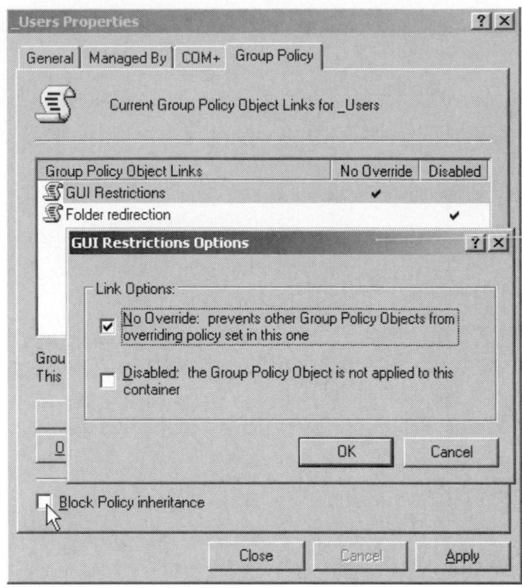

Figure 7.21 Block Policy inheritance is done on the Group Policy tab per Active Directory container. If you click Options and check No Override, you force settings in a linked GPO to affect all user and computer objects in child containers.

Options and select No Override from the Options dialog box, as displayed in Figure 7.21. The third way to define this setting is to right-click the GPO link and select No Override.

Filtering Group Policies with Groups

Finally, we get to create a relationship between Group Policy and security groups. The relationship comes through the fact that certain permissions are required for the policies to have an effect on objects in a container.

In order to be affected by settings in a GPO, a User or Computer account needs to have Read and Apply Group Policy permissions for the given GPO. By default, the Authenticated Users security group has these permissions for all new GPOs. This is illustrated in Figure 7.22.

In GPMC, the Scope tab of a GPO has a Security Filtering section that displays the objects that the GPO applies to. This is illustrated in Figure 7.17 earlier in this chapter. To see the permissions with ACL Editor, you can access the Security tab for a GPO by clicking Properties in

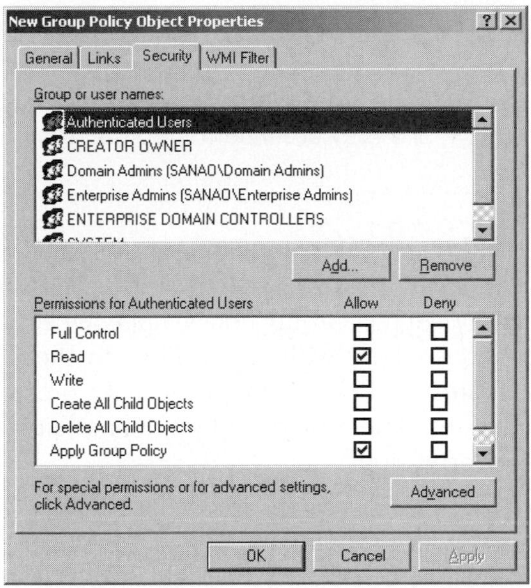

Figure 7.22 Default permissions for a GPO include the Read and Apply Group Policy permissions to Authenticated Users.

the Group Policy dialog box without GPMC, or after it has been installed by clicking Advanced on the Delegation tab of a GPO or a GPO link.

TIP You must use ACL Editor in order to deny the Apply Group Policy permission with GPMC installed since GPMC does not have this option available otherwise.

Domain Admins, Enterprise Admins, and System have all permissions except All Extended Rights and Apply Group Policy for all GPOs. Enterprise Domain Controllers has Read permission for all GPOs. Because the members of these groups are also members of Authenticated Users, the settings defined in GPOs also affect them. If you do not want group policies to affect users in these groups, you have two options:

- You can remove the Apply Group Policy permission from these groups by checking the Deny column.
- You can remove the Apply Group Policy permission from Authenticated Users, create another group to which you would like to give Read and Apply Group Policy permissions for this GPO, and assign appropriate users as members in that new group.

NOTE To be exact, Enterprise Domain Controllers has three ACEs defined on `CN=Policies, CN=System,DC=<domain>`. The command `dsacls` shows these as SPECIAL ACCESS for tokenGroups READ PROPERTY, and they are inherited to the group, user, and inetOrgPerson objects.

In addition to the permissions just mentioned, the well-known security principal Creator Owner has all permissions except All Extended Rights and Apply Group Policy, applying to child objects only. These permissions (along with permissions to the GPO itself) allow anyone who creates a GPO to administer it. In order to be able to access the GPO in List Object mode, all predefined permissions also include List Object permission.

NOTE Although security filtering is a useful method for manipulating the inheritance of the GPOs, you should use it with caution. Otherwise, you might cause some settings to apply to users or computers that they should never apply to.

Filtering Group Policies with WMI

In AD2000 Group Policy infrastructure is static because GPOs are applied rigidly according to the location of user and computer objects within the Active Directory hierarchy.

For certain policies it might be beneficial to be able to filter the effect only for those computers that meet some functional specification or criteria, such as the amount of available memory or disk space, or the existence of a certain peripheral or hotfix. WMI filters, which are available in Windows Server 2003 Active Directory, fulfill this need, consequently making Group Policy somewhat more dynamic.

Windows Management Instrumentation (WMI) is the standard interface for retrieving, defining, and monitoring almost all Windows settings. Microsoft first incorporated WMI into Windows 2000, and you can install it to earlier operating system versions. As the name implies, WMI filters make use of WMI. They do it in the form of WMI Query Language (WQL) queries. If you are familiar with SQL query syntax, you are off to a good start with WQL. We'll show you an example of how to construct a simple WQL query to locate the computers with a certain DVD-ROM drive model.

NOTE Although Windows 2000 includes WMI, always keep in mind that only Windows XP and newer operating systems support WMI filters!

1. First, start `WBEMTEST` (Windows Management Instrumentation Tester) from the command line or the Run dialog. You can then click Connect and type "root\cimv2" into the Namespace field.
2. Click Connect again, and you should have all buttons available.
3. In order to enumerate the available WMI classes, click the Enum Classes button. Leave the "Enter superclass name" field empty, select Recursive, and click OK. You should see over 800 classes being listed in Windows XP/Server 2003.
4. Double-click the class that you want to use. For this example, double-click Win32_CDROMDrive. The Object Editor for the class opens.
5. In order to see the existing objects for the class, click the Instances button.
6. Double-click the row for your CD-ROM drive. You can see the properties for the existing drive. Let's select the value of the property Caption being "TOSHIBA DVD-ROM SD-C2612" as our criterion.
7. The resulting WQL query would be as follows:

```
SELECT * FROM Win32_CDROMDrive WHERE Caption="TOSHIBA
DVD-ROM SD-C2612"
```

8. Now, let's try out the query and see whether it works. Close all open WBEMTEST dialogs except the first one (with the title Windows Management Instrumentation Tester) and click Query.
9. Type the query and click Apply. If you don't get any errors, your query is probably ready to be used in the WMI filter. If you see your CD-ROM drive in the results, then this query would evaluate to true on your computer, and if this WMI filter were linked to a certain GPO, the settings in that GPO would apply to your computer. See the "Managing WMI Filters" section later in this chapter for more information on managing WMI filters.

The number of WMI classes varies depending on the operating system version, and the applications and services installed. Windows 2000 contains fewer than 600, Windows XP almost 900, and Windows Server 2003 some 850 classes in the cimv2 namespace. In Windows Server 2003, you get another 63 classes by adding WMI Windows Installer Provider from Management and Monitoring Tools in Add/Remove Windows Components. You have to add WMI Windows Installer Provider to Windows Server 2003 in order to use several Windows Installer classes, including Win32_Product, with which you can obtain information on applications that are installed on the computer.

Although Windows 2000 has integrated WMI, the WMI filters are ignored by Windows 2000 computers. Consequently, if you have a mixed environment with Windows 2000 Professional and Windows XP workstations, and you want certain settings to apply only to Windows XP computers, you have to be innovative. The easiest way is to use separate OUs for Windows 2000 and Windows XP computers, and to create and link different GPOs for these OUs.

We have included here a few sample WQL queries that you can follow when creating your own queries.

To include those computers that have at least 300MB of free space available on the NTFS volume mapped to drive letter C, use this query:

```
SELECT * FROM Win32_LogicalDisk WHERE Win32_DeviceID = "C:"
AND Freespace > 314572800 AND FileSystem = "NTFS"
```

To list those computers with a 3Com network card capable of IPSec processing, use this query:

```
SELECT * FROM Win32_NetworkAdapter WHERE Name LIKE
"%3CR990%"
```

To list those computers that have the IIS service running, use this query:

```
SELECT * FROM Win32_Service WHERE Name="W3SVC" AND
Started="TRUE"
```

TIP You can learn more about Windows Management Instrumentation in the book *Understanding Windows Management Instrumentation (WMI) Scripting*, by Alain Lissoir (Digital Press, 2003, `http://www.lissware.net/`)

Although you should keep Group Policy in mind while planning the OU structure in order to avoid using excessive security group and WMI filtering (or any other way to alter the default behavior of Group Policy inheritance), you have three options in a larger environment where AD management has been delegated. In such an environment, you often design the top-level OUs defined per geographical area or functional divisions. Different kinds of workstations and servers might be on the fourth or fifth layer of the OU hierarchy. You can create a GPO and link it to several lower-level OUs. This solution represents the challenge of maintaining the GPO links. The second option is to use WMI filters, but they might slow down the GPO processing or your environment might include Windows 2000 computers that do not support WMI filters. The third option is to link the GPO into an OU higher in the OU tree and use security group filtering by including the necessary users or computers in groups and assigning the Apply Group Policy permission to these groups. This option might become easier to manage in the long run. For example, you can automatically assign computers into groups based on the operating system.

Processing Group Policy

Workstations and servers apply group policies by processing them at startup/logon time and periodically thereafter. You can also trigger this processing manually if you want to test a certain setting or if you want to get policies to apply immediately.

Processing Basics

Group policies are processed when certain events occur, the most obvious being when the computer starts and when the user logs on. The Local Computer Policy is processed first, and then the Active Directory tree is processed, starting from the site, going to the domain, and then moving to the OUs where the computer or user object is located. Table 7.9 lists the different events, along with their actions, that cause Group Policy processing to start.

TIP An acronym to remember the sequence of GPO processing is LSDOU: *L* for Local Computer Policy, *S* for GPO(s) linked to the site, *D* for GPO(s) linked to the domain, and finally GPO(s) linked to the OU(s).

NOTE Changes that you make to the Local Computer Policy are implemented immediately unless they conflict with an Active Directory–based setting that overrides the change. The immediate processing is a result of the fact that changing a setting in the Local Computer Policy triggers the Group Policy processing to start.

NOTE The location of any of the groups that a user or computer is a member of does not have any effect on the GPO processing.

Table 7.9 Processing Group Policies

Event	What Gets Applied	Based On
Computer starts	Computer settings	Location of computer object
User logs on	User settings	Location of user object (with the exception of loopback processing)
User logs off	Logoff scripts	Location of user object
Computer shuts down	Shutdown scripts	Location of computer object
Periodic refresh for computers	Computer settings	Location of computer object
Periodic refresh for users	User settings	Location of user object
Change in the Local Computer Policy	The effective settings from the Local Computer Policy or Active Directory–based GPOs	Location of computer and user objects
Windows 2000: `SECEDIT/ REFRESHPOLICY` command	`MACHINE_POLICY`; Computer settings `USER_POLICY`; User settings	Location of computer object Location of user object
Windows XP/Server 2003: `GPUPDATE` command	User and computer settings	Locations of user and computer objects

Windows XP Fast Logon Optimization

By default, group policies are processed synchronously for Windows 2000 and Windows Server 2003, which means that computer policy is completed before the Ctrl-Alt-Delete dialog box is presented, and user policy is completed before the shell (i.e., Windows Explorer) becomes active so the user can start using it.

TIP In Windows 2000 you can change the synchronous processing behavior with the "Apply Group Policy for computers asynchronously during startup" and "Apply Group Policy for users asynchronously during logon" settings under Computer Configuration\Administrative Templates\System\Group Policy.

In order to speed up the logon process, Windows XP does not wait for the network to be fully initialized at startup and logon. Both computer and user GPOs are processed asynchronously in the background as the network becomes available. There are two scenarios in which this *fast logon optimization* does not take place during logon:

- When a user logs on to a computer for the first time (in other words, she does not yet have cached credentials)
- When a user has a roaming user profile or a home directory, or synchronous logon scripts

The side effect of fast logon optimization is that even three logons may be required for changes to take effect. This would be the case for advanced folder redirection. Also, if you define a roaming user profile, home directory, or logon script in the user account properties, two logons may be required before these settings work for the user. In order to ensure that all policies are processed at computer startup and user logons, you can turn off fast logon optimization with the Computer Configuration\Administrative Templates\System\Logon\"Always wait for the network at computer startup and logon" setting. Fast logon optimization does not apply to Windows Server 2003.

TIP In Windows XP and Server 2003, you can force the next foreground policy processing to be done synchronously with the `GPUPDATE /SYNC` command.

Processing Group Policy Periodically

Most group policies are processed periodically in the background. Two exceptions are folder redirection and software deployment. These two policies only take place when the computer starts or the user logs on.

The periodic processing helps to distribute the centrally defined policies for users and computers without the need for users to restart their computers or to log off and log back on again. Usually, the settings in GPOs are reapplied only if the GPOs have changed. You can use the "Process even if the Group Policy objects have not changed" option to reapply settings for certain CSEs even if there is no change in the GPO. This could be the case if you doubt that a user somehow managed to change the settings.

TIP You can disable background processing by enabling the policy Computer Configuration\Administrative Templates\System\Group Policy\"Disable background refresh of Group Policy".

The default processing interval for domain controllers is 5 minutes. It can be modified in Computer Configuration\Administrative Templates\System\Group Policy\Group Policy refresh interval for domain controllers. For computers and users, the default interval is 90 minutes with a 0–30 minute offset (i.e., between 90 and 120 minutes). The random offset prevents all clients from refreshing their policies simultaneously.

NOTE You cannot specify a time for Group Policy background processing.

NOTE Security settings are processed periodically every 16 hours (960 minutes) even if there are no changes in the GPOs. The registry `REG_DWORD` value (in minutes) for setting the period is `HKEY_LOCAL_MACHINE\SOFTWARE\Microsoft\Windows NT\CurrentVersion\Winlogon\GPExtensions\{827D319E-6EAC-11D2-A4EA-00C04F79F83A}\MaxNoGPOListChangesInterval`.

Manual Refresh of Group Policy

You can refresh Group Policy manually with the following commands: Windows 2000:

`SECEDIT /REFRESHPOLICY MACHINE_POLICY` for machine settings and `SECEDIT /REFRESHPOLICY USER_POLICY` for user settings.

Windows XP/Server 2003:

`GPUPDATE /Target:{Computer | User}` by default both computer and user policies are refreshed.

Starting Group Policy processing manually would be useful if, for example, you wanted to implement a certain policy immediately without waiting through the refresh policy interval. You can ensure that the policies defined in the GPOs are reapplied even if there are no changes in the GPOs by using the `/ENFORCE` (Windows 2000) or `/FORCE` (Windows XP/Server 2003) parameters at the end of the command.

TIP The GPUPDATE parameter `/LOGOFF` causes the user to log off if there are client-side extensions that do not process in the background, such as software installation or folder redirection for a user. The parameter `/BOOT` has a similar effect for settings such as the assigned software installation for a computer.

TIP Checking the "Logon using dial-up connection" check box in the logon screen forces the update of user and machine policies. You may want to do this if there is no connection to a domain controller at logon, since policies are not updated otherwise.

Slow Link Processing

There is no point in processing certain policies over a slow connection. Consider, for example, a user dialing in with his cellular phone to check e-mail. If you have set up a software installation policy to upgrade users' e-mail applications, it would take a long time for the upgraded package to be loaded over the slow connection. Thus, certain Group Policy extensions are not processed if a slow link is detected.

On the other hand, it is a security problem if the security settings are not processed over the slow connection. Table 7.10 lists the default status of slow link processing, as well as whether or not the behavior can be changed.

Slow link detection is accomplished with consecutive ICMP pings that are sent to the authenticating domain controller. If the response from any

Table 7.10 Slow Link Processing Options

Extension	Processed When Slow Link Is Detected	Behavior Can Be Modified to Allow Processing over Slow Link
Security settings	Yes	No
Administrative templates (Group Policy option is called "Registry processing")	Yes	No
Software installation	No	Yes
Remote installation	Not applicable, because it only takes place when a new computer is installed. It would not make much sense to even try to install Windows 2000/XP/Server 2003 over a slow-speed connection because of the amount of data to be transferred.	
Scripts	No	Yes
EFS recovery	Yes	No
IPSec	Yes	No
Disk quota	No	Yes
Folder redirection	No	Yes
Internet Explorer Maintenance	No	Yes
Wireless	Yes	Yes
Software Restriction Policy	Yes	No

of the pings is less than 10 milliseconds (ms), the link is considered to be fast. Otherwise, the link speed is calculated with the following formula:

```
link speed = 16000/(average ping for 2048 byte packet)
```

You can manually try out the connection speed with this command:

```
C:\>ping -l 2048 lonsanao1.sanao.com
Pinging lonsanao1.sanao.com [10.10.0.11] with 2048 bytes of
data:
Reply from 10.10.0.11: bytes=2048 time=108ms TTL=127
Reply from 10.10.0.11: bytes=2048 time=105ms TTL=127
Reply from 10.10.0.11: bytes=2048 time=107ms TTL=127
Reply from 10.10.0.11: bytes=2048 time=109ms TTL=127
Ping statistics for 10.10.0.11:
    Packets: Sent = 4, Received = 4, Lost = 0 (0% loss),
Approximate round trip times in milli-seconds:
    Minimum = 105ms, Maximum = 109ms, Average = 107ms
```

Thus, the estimated link speed is 16000/107=150Kbps, and the link would be considered slow. The threshold round-trip time for a fast link (default 500Kbps) is 32 ms.

NOTE In order for the calculation to be successful, the ping (i.e., ICMP echo) must be allowed to pass through the firewall if there is one between the client and the domain controller. If ICMP is not allowed, only those settings that are processed regardless of the speed of the connection are processed. If ICMP is not permitted, you may disable the slow link detection. This solution has its side effects since all links are then considered fast, and consequently all policies are applied, including application deployment and folder redirection.

Loopback Processing

By default, a user obtains settings that are the result of Group Policy processing based on the location of the user object. Sometimes you may want to configure users' settings based on the location of the computer object—for example, for software installation. A user could be assigned certain applications by specifying them in a Group Policy object linked to an OU in which the user object is located. However, when the user logs on to a server computer, you may not want all applications to be installed onto that server. The feature you use to modify the default behavior is called *loopback processing*. It is defined in Computer Configuration\Administrative Templates\System\Group Policy\User Group Policy loopback processing. Two modes of operation are available:

- Replace mode
- Merge mode

In replace mode, the user settings defined in the computer's GPOs replace the settings that the user would have normally received. In merge mode, the user settings defined in GPOs that affect the user object are processed first, and then the user settings defined in GPOs that affect the computer object are processed. Thus, the settings defined in the GPOs that affect the computer object have higher priority if settings come into conflict.

NOTE You will see similar behavior to the loopback processing mode when logging on to a Windows Server 2003, Windows XP SP1 or newer, or Windows 2000 SP4 or newer computer across the forest trust. In other words, you will receive user settings according to the location of the computer object in the other forest. See the "Registry-Based Settings for Group Policy Processing" section at the end of this chapter for changing this behavior.

Group Policy Processing in Detail

Let's walk through the Group Policy processing in detail when a computer is started and a user logs on to that computer.

1. The user starts her computer. If her computer's IP information is configured to be assigned dynamically, a DHCP server is contacted to obtain this information. Otherwise, the information is retrieved from the registry.
2. The computer locates a domain controller with a DNS name query. It then creates a secure channel with one of the domain controllers in its site.
3. The computer determines its location from the Active Directory configuration container based on its IP address. If it has already done so, the information is cached in the registry from where it is retrieved. The registry key is `HKLM\System\CurrentControlSet\Services\Netlogon\Parameters\DynamicSiteName`.

4. The computer Group Policy processing starts. First the network connection speed to the domain controller is determined in order to decide whether the link is considered slow.
5. The computer executes the `GetGPOList` application programming interface (API) call to the domain controller. This call is used to determine which GPOs apply to the computer object. The applicable GPOs are determined based on the computer object's location in the Active Directory hierarchy.

NOTE If you move a computer object to a new OU, the change will not have an effect on Group Policy immediately, since the location of user and computer objects is cached on the client for 30 minutes. You can log off or restart if you don't want to wait.

---

6. Once the list is obtained, the version information and GPO options are studied in order to determine which GPOs must be processed. The GPOs are sorted by priority. The value of the `gPCFileSysPath` of the applicable GPOs is obtained in order to determine the location of the GPTs.

NOTE GPTs are accessed through automatically created domain-based DFS (Distributed File System) roots—for example, \\sanao.com\sysvol\sanao.com\Policies\{31B2F340-016D-11D2-945F-00C04FB984F9}.

---

7. The client-side extensions (CSEs) process the policies defined in the local Group Policy and the GPTs. The user sees at least two dialog boxes with "Applying computer settings" and "Applying security policy" messages. In addition, software may be installed. A number of registry settings affect the processing. For example, if the loopback processing mode is defined for a GPO, it sets `HKEY_LOCAL_MACHINE\Software\Policies\Microsoft\Windows\System\UserPolicyMode` to 1 for merge mode and 2 for replace mode. This forces the processing to be altered when the user logs on.
8. The time for the next Group Policy refresh is determined—for example, 92 minutes.
9. The user sees the logon screen. She types her username and password.

10. The user is authenticated by a domain controller with Kerberos authentication.
11. If the authentication is successful, the user profile type and location are determined.
12. The user Group Policy processing starts. First, the network connection speed to the domain controller is determined in order to decide whether the link is considered slow.
13. The `GetGPOList` call is executed again. This time the applicable GPOs are determined based on the user object's location in the Active Directory hierarchy unless the loopback processing mode is set in the registry.
14. Once the list is obtained, the version information and GPO options are studied in order to determine which GPOs must be processed. The GPOs are sorted by priority.
15. The value of the `gPCFileSysPath` of the applicable GPOs is obtained in order to determine the location of the GPT.
16. The CSEs process the policies defined in the local Group Policy and the GPTs. The user sees at least two dialog boxes with "Loading your personal settings" and "Applying your personal settings" messages. In addition, software may be installed at this stage. The message "Installing managed software . . ." is displayed for the user.
17. The user's profile is loaded. The default user shell (usually Windows Explorer) is started, and the user may start using the computer.

Determining Effective Group Policies

Windows XP introduced a handy tool for determining effective policies called Resultant Set of Policy (RSoP). The tool is in the form of an MMC snap-in and can be started with rsop.msc. You can see the result of processing group policies in Figure 7.23.

NOTE Windows 2000 does not incorporate any tool for properly determining the effective policies. The Windows Server 2000 Resource Kit contains a command-line tool, Group Policy Results (gpresult.exe). This tool was integrated into Windows XP with some improvements over the Windows 2000 Resource Kit version.

Windows XP and Windows Server 2003 also incorporate RSoP functionality into the online Help. We will discuss these tools in depth later in the "Group Policy Analysis" section of this chapter.

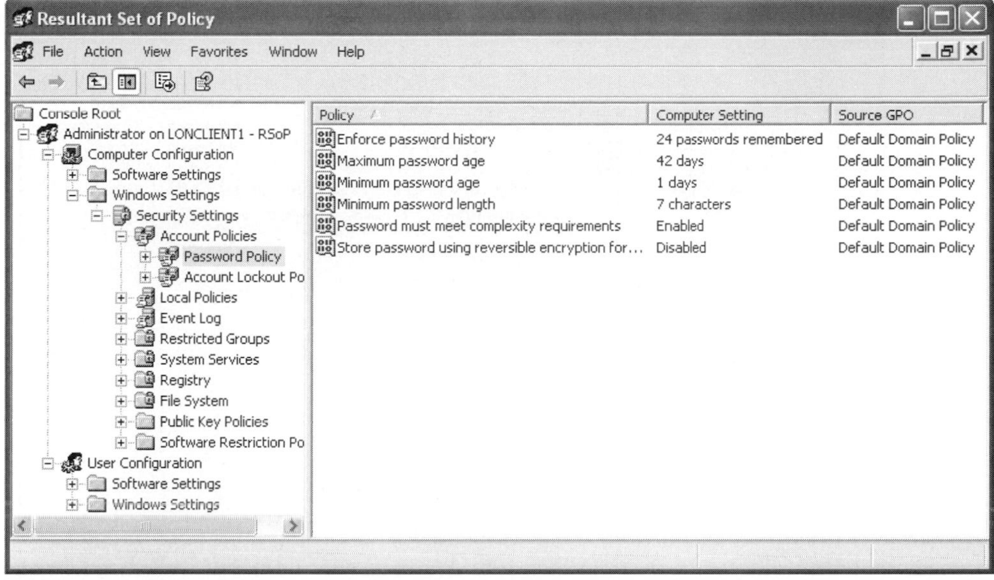

Figure 7.23 The Resultant Set of Policy MMC snap-in (rsop.msc) is available in every Windows XP/Server 2003 computer.

Determining Effective Group Policy Security Settings in Windows 2000

Modifying and determining effective policies for the security settings was easy on Windows 2000. On domain controller computers, there are shortcuts for accessing security policies for all default levels (i.e., Domain, Domain Controller, and Local). To see the effective security settings, click the Start button, and then select Programs, Administrative Tools, Local Security Policy. For example, to change the maximum tolerance for computer clock synchronization for Kerberos authentication, go to Account Policies, Kerberos Policy, as shown in Figure 7.24. As you can see, this setting has not been defined for the Local Computer Policy. However, because the account policies are effective only when defined at the domain level, the setting 5 minutes must come from the Default Domain Policy or some other policy linked to the domain.

Because user rights can be assigned to several users and groups, the Local Policy Setting and the Effective Policy Setting are displayed slightly differently in Windows 2000, as in the dialog box shown in Figure 7.25.

In this case, the right to change the system time has been given to the Administrators and Power Users groups in the Local Computer Policy. We

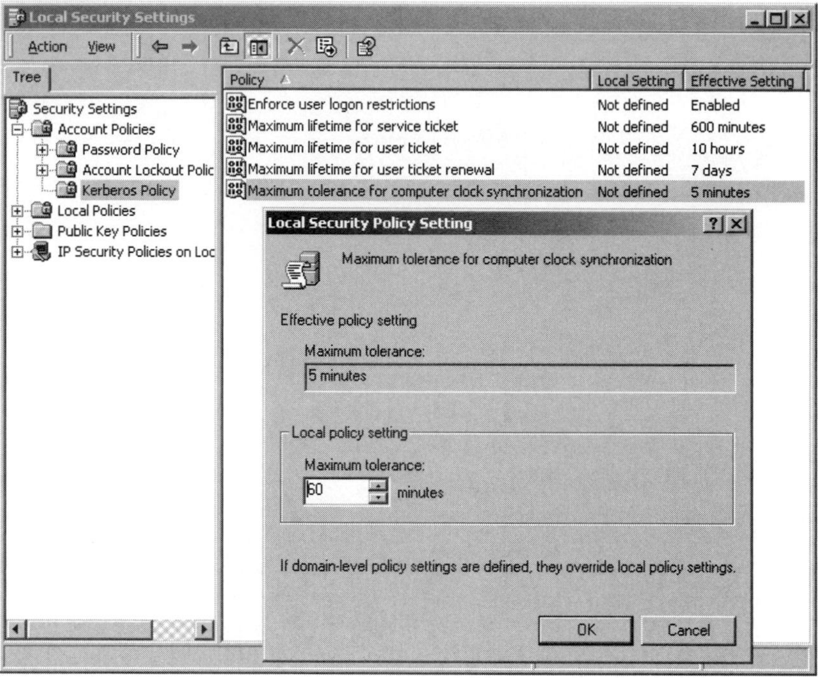

Figure 7.24 Clicking the Start button and selecting Programs, Administrative Tools, Local Security Policy enables you to see the effective security settings in Windows 2000.

took the screen shot in Figure 7.25 from a domain controller, which by default does not have a Power Users group, although it had one prior to becoming a domain controller. In addition, the setting has been overridden by the group policies inherited from the Active Directory–based GPOs. The Server Operators group currently has the right to change the system time, and if you go and see the default GPOs, you will find that Administrators and Server Operators have been given this right in the Default Domain Controllers Policy GPO.

TIP When you want to see whether certain security settings are in effect after you have changed something and refreshed the policy with the secedit command, you can refresh the displayed effective settings in the Local Security Policy console by right-clicking Security Settings and clicking Reload. This tip is useful only in Windows 2000 since Windows XP and Windows Server 2003 do not show the effective settings in a way similar to Windows 2000.

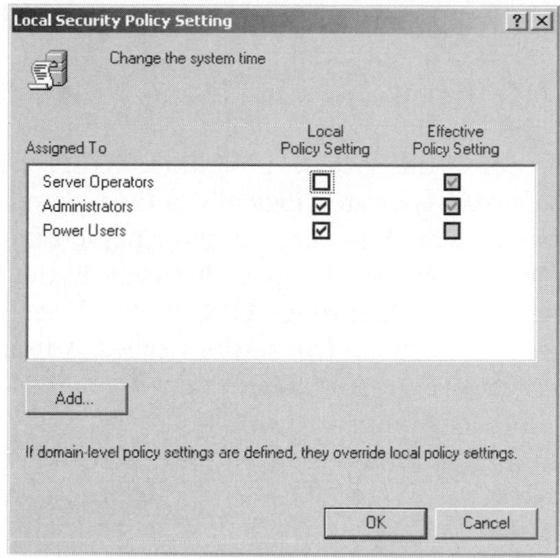

Figure 7.25 When you open the Local Computer Policy for editing in Windows 2000, you can see the user rights settings defined in the Local Computer Policy as well as the effective setting. The Effective Policy Setting may be different from the Local Policy Setting because of the settings defined in Active Directory–based GPOs.

TIP If you want to display only those Administrative Templates policies that have been configured, right-click Administrative Templates, select View, Filtering, and check "Only show configured policy settings" (or select View, Show Configured Policies Only in Windows 2000). You may have to click Administrative Templates first in order to see the View option in the context menu.

TIP You can create views similar to the restricted ones in built-in Security consoles in any stand-alone MMC snap-ins by right-clicking any node and selecting New Window from Here.

Sample Scenario for Group Policy

To help you further grasp Group Policy processing, we have created a scenario with a few simple registry-based settings. Figure 7.26 shows this scenario, in which the Sanao Corporation has organized its resources into one Active Directory domain called `sanao.com` with two sites:

Boston (BOS) and London (LON). Each site has one or more domain controllers. There are four OUs: MFG, Users, Computers, and Servers. Two user accounts, Jack and Jill, are located in the Users OU. In addition, one security group called Assistants is also located in this OU. Jill is a member of this group. A Windows XP Professional computer named BosSanao100 is located logically in the Computers OU and physically in the Boston site. A server computer named LonSanao10 is located logically in the Servers OU and physically in the London site. Altogether, nine GPOs (GPO1 through GPO9) have been linked to these containers. These GPOs contain five settings called A through E. The GPOs differ from each other by specifying a value for certain settings—the value being the sequence number of the GPO.

In addition to creating the specified GPOs and specifying the settings shown in Table 7.11, the following was performed:

- GPO2 was marked with "No override" in order to ensure that every user logging on to a computer on that site would receive certain site-specific settings (such as IE proxy server settings).
- GPO5 was moved up on the GPO link list of the MFG OU properties so that it has higher priority over GPO4.
- The user administrator responsible for administering the Users OU blocked policy inheritance on the Group Policy tab of the Users OU properties.
- The Assistants security group was defined a Deny ACE for Apply Group Policy permission for GPO5.
- The Group Policy loopback processing mode was enabled and defined as "replace" for GPO6.

When users log on to these computers, they receive certain settings in their registry under `HKEY_CURRENT_USER\Software\Policies\Sanao`. Table 7.11 illustrates these effective settings. Let's walk through the GPO process in order to determine the final value for the settings when Jill logs on to the server computer LonSanao10.

1. Jill starts her computer.
2. Jill's computer determines which GPOs apply to the computer object. The applicable GPOs are GPO2, GPO3, Default Domain Policy, GPO4, GPO5, and GPO6. GPO6 contains the setting for loopback processing, and as a result user settings based on the location of her computer object are the ones that define the final results. The value for loopback processing is set in the registry.

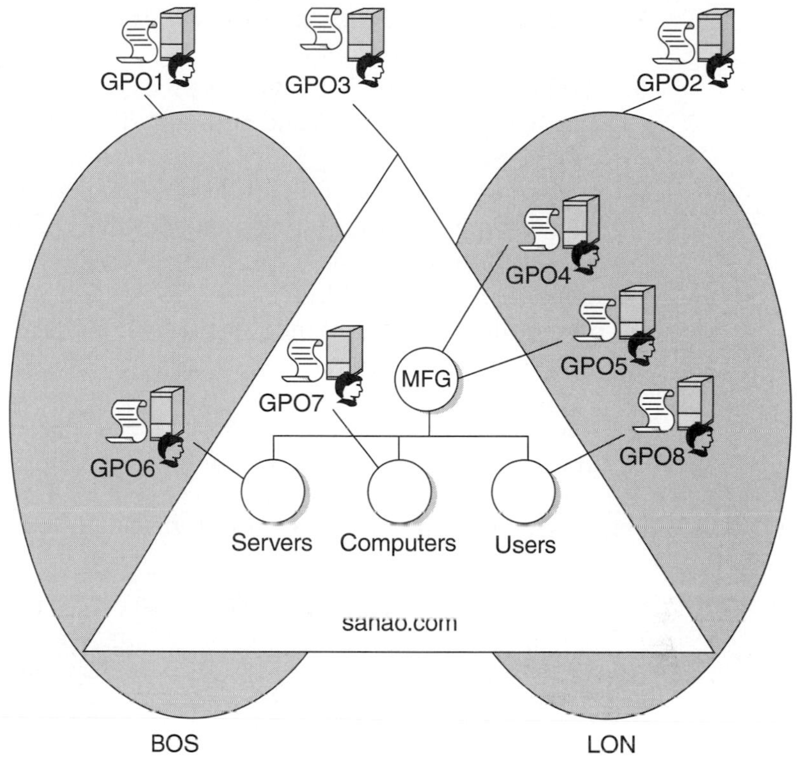

Figure 7.26 Sanao GPO infrastructure for the sample scenario

Settings are defined only in the user sections of the GPOs and, thus, no other value is entered into the registry.

3. Jill logs on to the computer.
4. Jill's computer determines which GPOs apply to the user object. Because the registry setting for loopback processing is set, the evaluation is done based on the location of Jill's computer object. As a result, the applicable GPOs are GPO2, GPO3, Default Domain Policy, GPO4, GPO5, and GPO6. GPO5 is not applied, because the Assistants group, of which Jill is a member, has a Deny ACE for the Apply Group Policy permission.
5. Based on this information, GPO2, linked to site LON, is processed, and consequently SettingB is set to the value 2.
6. Next, GPO3, linked to domain `sanao.com`, is processed. It defines the value 3 for SettingA, SettingC, and SettingE. These values are entered into the registry.

7. Default Domain Policy is processed. It doesn't contain any setting of interest for our scenario.
8. GPO4, linked to the MFG OU, is processed. It defines the value 4 for SettingA, SettingC, and SettingD. These values are entered into the registry.
9. As the last applicable GPO, GPO6 is processed. It defines the value 6 for SettingA, SettingC, and SettingE. These values are entered into the registry. The final values stored in the registry are as displayed in Table 7.11.
10. Jill's profile is loaded. Windows Explorer starts and Jill is able to start using the computer.

You can use the following instructions to create the simple ADM file to determine the effective settings in your environment. You would need

Table 7.11 Settings Used in Sample Scenario for Determining Effective Group Policy Settings

Settings	Values for Group Policy Settings on Boston (BOS) Site					Values for Group Policy Settings on London (LON) Site				
Setting Group Policy	A	B	C	D	E	A	B	C	D	E
GPO1	—	1	—	—	—	—	1	—	—	—
GPO2 No override	—	2	—	—	—	—	2	—	—	—
GPO3	3	—	3	—	3	3	—	3	—	3
GPO4	4	—	4	4	—	4	—	4	4	—
GPO5	5	—	5	—	—	5	—	5	—	—
GPO6 GP loopback processing mode: replace	6	—	—	6	6	6	—	—	6	6
GPO7	7	—	—	—	7	7	—	—	—	7
GPO8	—	—	8	—	—	—	—	8	—	—
	Jack logs on to workstation BosSanao100					Jill logs on to server LonSanao10				
Effective policy	—	—	8	—	—	6	2	4	6	6

at least three computers in order to run this scenario: two domain controllers and one member server. In addition, you would need to configure one Windows Server 2003 computer as a router or use a "real" router to create two subnets. You also want to create two sites, BOS and LON, and assign subnets for them. Alternatively, you could use an IP supernet and assign different computers to sites with IP subnets.

TIP You may want to refer to Chapter 5 for further instructions on sites and replication before trying this scenario.

To create and configure the GPOs, perform the following steps:

1. Start Notepad and type the following lines. Add the missing lines for settings C through E.

```
CLASS USER
CATEGORY !!_TestSettings
   KEYNAME " Software\Policies\Sanao"
   POLICY !!SettingA
      PART !!A                  NUMERIC REQUIRED SPIN 1
         DEFAULT 1
         MAX    10
         MIN    1
         VALUENAME "SettingA"
      END PART
   END POLICY

   POLICY !!SettingB
      PART !!B                  NUMERIC REQUIRED SPIN 1
         DEFAULT 1
         MAX    10
         MIN    1
         VALUENAME "SettingB"
      END PART
   END POLICY
*Repeat the same for Policies C through E
END CATEGORY    ; _TestSettings

[strings]
TestSettings=" TestSettings "
A="A"
SettingA="SettingA"
```

```
B="B"
SettingB="SettingB"
*Repeat the same for Policies C through E
```

2. Save the file as testsettings.adm in %SystemRoot%\inf on the domain controller.
3. Open the Active Directory Users and Computers or (Sites and Services) snap-in.
4. Right-click the Active Directory container into which you want to link the new GPO. Select Properties, and then select the Group Policy tab.
5. Click New and type the name for the new GPO.
6. Open the GPO for editing by clicking Edit, selecting the Administrative Templates node for User Configuration and right-clicking it, and selecting Add/Remove Templates.
7. Click Add and select testsettings.adm. Click Open, Close.
8. Open User Configuration\Administrative Templates\TestSettings. (You may have to use View, Filtering or View, Show Policies only in order to see the settings.)
9. Change the settings according to Table 7.11.
10. Repeat steps 3 through 9 for each GPO.
11. Replicate the changes to the other domain controller with Active Directory Sites and Services.
12. Try to log on as Jack or Jill and use rsop.msc or the Registry Editor to see the effective settings.

TIP You can find the .adm file as well as the script for creating the environment with the GPMC sample script CreateEnvironmentFromXML.wsf on the Web site for this book, `http://www.kouti.com`.

Managing Group Policies

Management of group policies involves the following specific tasks:

- Managing GPOs (creating, editing, and removing them)
- Managing GPO links
- Manipulating inheritance
- GPO operations (backup/export, restore, import, and copy)
- Reporting GPO settings

- Group Policy modeling (what-if analyses)
- Searching GPOs
- Delegating Group Policy management
- Scripting Group Policy management tasks
- Managing administrative template files

In this section we describe how to perform each of these management tasks with and without Group Policy Management Console installed. We have included Table 7.12 to provide a quick summary of the appropriate tools for each task.

Table 7.12 Group Policy Management Tools for Various GP Management Tasks in Different Windows Versions

Management Task	Windows 2000 SP4 w/o GPMC	Windows Server 2003 w/o GPMC	Windows 2000/ Server 2003 with GPMC
Creating GPOs	ADUC* ADSS*	ADUC ADSS	GPMC
Editing settings within a GPO	Group Policy snap-in	Group Policy Object Editor snap-in	Group Policy (Object Editor) snap-in
Linking GPOs to SOM	ADUC ADSS	ADUC ADSS	GPMC
Enforcing or blocking inheritance	ADUC ADSS	ADUC ADSS	GPMC
Filtering GPOs with permissions	ACL Editor	ACL Editor	GPMC ACL Editor within Group Policy Object Editor snap in
Filtering GPOs with WMI filters	N/A	Group Policy Object Editor snap-in	GPMC Group Policy Object Editor snap-in
GPO operations (backup, restore, import, copy)	N/A	N/A	GPMC

(continued)

* ADUC = Active Directory Users and Computers, ADSS = Active Directory Sites and Services.

Table 7.12 Group Policy Management Tools for Various GP Management Tasks in Different Windows Versions *(cont.)*

Management Task	Windows 2000 SP4 w/o GPMC	Windows Server 2003 w/o GPMC	Windows 2000/ Server 2003 with GPMC
Reporting GPO settings	N/A	N/A	GPMC
Analyzing Group Policy Results	N/A	Rsop.msc (logging mode)—only for Windows XP and Windows Server 2003	GPMC—Group Policy Results Rsop.msc (logging mode)
What-if analysis of GPOs	N/A	Rsop.msc (planning mode)—requires at least one Windows Server 2003 in the forest; also possible to analyze group policy on Windows 2000 computers	GPMC—Group Policy Modeling Rsop.msc (planning mode)
Searching GPOs	N/A	N/A	GPMC
Delegating Group Policy management	ADUC ADSS	ADUC ADSS	ADUC ADSS GPMC
Scripting GPO tasks	N/A	N/A	GPMC (32 sample scripts included)
Managing administrative template files	Text editor—e.g., Notepad	Text editor—e.g., Notepad	Text editor—e.g., Notepad

Group Policy Dialog Box

You can accomplish most Group Policy object management tasks through the Group Policy dialog box, shown in Figure 7.27. The buttons Add and Options are for managing links, whereas Edit and Properties are purely for managing GPOs. With New you can create a new GPO and link it to the current container. With Delete, you either remove the link between the current container and the GPO, or delete a GPO and its associated links.

Notice that there is no Save button for Group Policy—all changes are stored immediately when you click the OK or Apply button. However, they will be replicated to other domain controllers only through normal Active Directory replication.

Target Domain Controller for Group Policy Operations

By default, the MMC Group Policy snap-in is targeted at the operations master server that holds the PDC emulator role. This setup prevents two administrators from modifying settings on two domain controllers, and

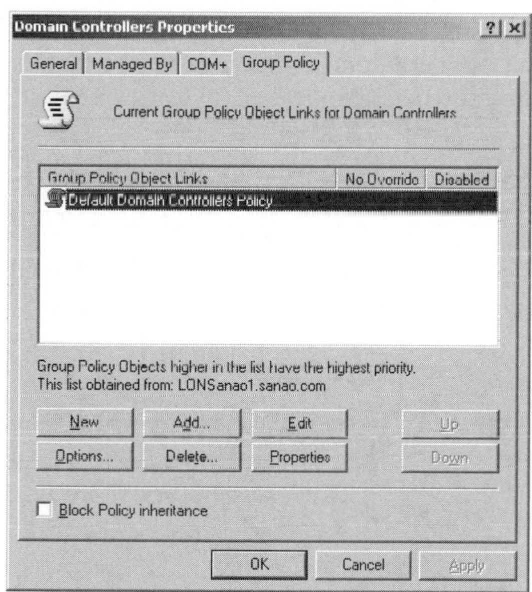

Figure 7.27 Without GPMC installed, you can perform most management tasks related to Group Policy objects in the Group Policy dialog box.

then one change overriding another later through replication. You can change this behavior by selecting View, DC Options while editing any Group Policy object.

As Figure 7.28 shows, the options for domain controller selection are in the most preferred order. If possible, you should always target the PDC emulator to prevent data loss. However, if the PDC emulator server is behind a slow WAN link, you might want to change the setting to use the same domain controller as your snap-in.

When using GPMC, you can target GPMC by right-clicking the domain object and selecting Change Domain Controller. A new option is to select any available domain controller running Windows Server 2003 or later.

TIP You can force your administrators to target the PDC role holder by setting User Configuration\Administrative Templates\System\Group Policy\Group Policy domain controller selection.

Creating GPOs

In order to create a new GPO, a user has to be a member of the Administrators or Group Policy Creator Owners groups, either directly or indirectly. The Domain Admins, Enterprise Admins, and Group Policy Creator Owners groups (and local system account) have the permission to create child objects in the `CN=Policies,CN=System, DC=`*`<domain>`* container, as Figure 7.29 shows. However, only the Administrators and Group Policy Creator Owners groups (and local system account) have the necessary NTFS permissions for SYSVOL.

The members of the Group Policy Creator Owners group cannot change the permissions for the Group Policy folders on the SYSVOL

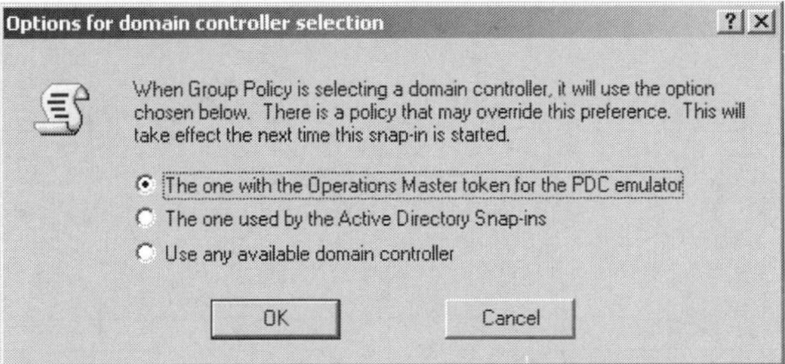

Figure 7.28 You can select the target domain controller for Group Policy operations by selecting DC Options from the View menu.

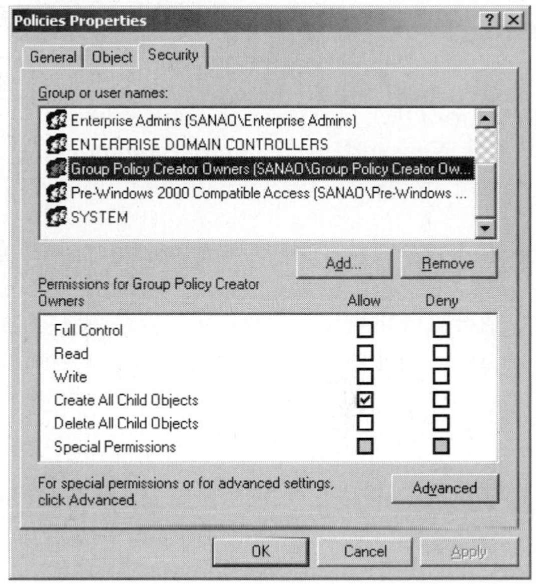

Figure 7.29 Group Policy Creator Owners has the Create All Child Objects ACE on the `CN=Policies, CN=System, DC=`*`<domain>`* container.

folder. Nor do the members of this group have permission to take the ownership of a GPO. However, all GPOs created by the members of this group have the user that created the GPO as the owner of the GPOs.

NOTE Since the Group Policy Creator Owners group is global by default, you cannot use it to include members from other domains for assigning the permission to create new GPOs. See the "Delegating Management of GPOs" section later in this chapter for another way to delegate this task.

Creating and Linking GPOs with GPMC

It is very easy to create new GPOs with GPMC. You can create a linked or an unlinked GPO. In order to create a linked GPO, you can right-click a container object and select "Create and Link a GPO here". Alternatively, you can first create an unlinked GPO by right-clicking the Group Policy Objects container and selecting New. After you have created the GPO, you link it to an AD container with drag-and-drop or by selecting the container, right-clicking it, and selecting Link an Existing GPO.

Creating and Linking GPOs without GPMC

To create a linked GPO, right-click the appropriate container (Site, Domain, or OU), and after selecting Properties, open the Group Policy tab. Click New and give a name to the new GPO.

There are two ways to create an unlinked GPO.

- Select any container that can host a GPO (i.e., Site, Domain, OU) in the Active Directory Users and Computers snap-in or in the Active Directory Sites and Services snap-in. Open properties for the container and navigate to the Group Policy tab. Click Add and select the All tab in the Add a Group Policy Object Link dialog box. Select the domain that you want to create the GPO in by selecting it in the "Look in" field. Right-click anywhere in the list and then click New (as shown in Figure 7.30) or click Create Group Policy on the toolbar. Type a name for the GPO. Click Cancel twice unless you want to edit the new GPO, in which case you have to link it to some container first or use a stand-alone MMC console.
- Open MMC. Add a new Group Policy snap-in and click Browse. On the All tab in the Browse for a Group Policy Object dialog box, select the domain that you want to create the GPO in by selecting

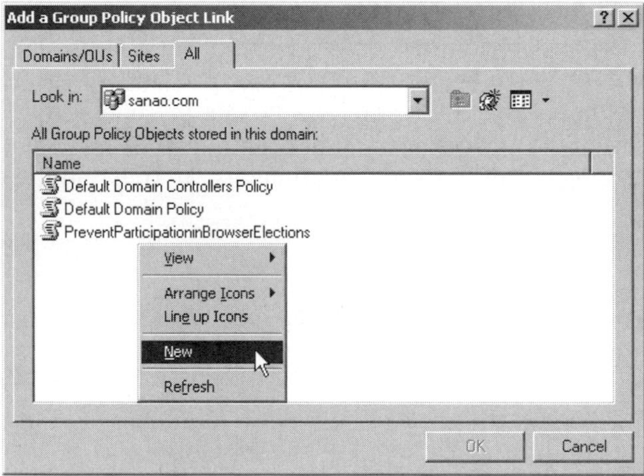

Figure 7.30 Creating an unlinked GPO is a rather complex operation without GPMC.

it in the "Look in" field. Right-click anywhere in the list and then click New or click Create Group Policy on the toolbar. Type a name for the GPO. Click Cancel twice unless you want to edit the new GPO, in which case you can simply select the new GPO, click OK, click Finish, and then click OK again.

Naming Convention for GPOs

Table 7.13 illustrates the naming convention for GPOs that Microsoft recommends using (and that we slightly modified). You can find more information in the User and Location Management Architecture Guide in the Account Management for Windows Server 2003 set of documents.

An example of using this naming convention is OU-C-R-WUS-1.1, which indicates that this is a GPO linked to an OU, which assigns WUS (Windows Update Services) settings to computers only, and is the revision to the original one.

In addition to the naming convention and the version number that the name contains, it is also important to assign ownership and responsibility of the GPOs. GPOs do not contain fields for such information, and thus you have to use other solutions for keeping track of changes.

Table 7.13 A Recommended Naming Convention for GPOs

Linked To	Target	PolicyType	Description	Version
Indicates whether the GPO is linked to a site (ST), domain (DO), or organizational unit (OU)	Indicates that the GPO contains policy settings that apply to computer objects (C), user objects (U), or all (A)	Indicates the type of policy settings contained within the GPO: Security (S), Application deployment (A), Registry (R), or policy settings that apply only to a specific group of users (G)	Indicates the main function and purpose of the GPO (free-format field)	Version number for the GPO e.g., v.1.5
(2 characters)	(1 character)	(1 character)	(200 characters)	(4–5 characters)

Editing GPOs

You can edit existing GPOs either with a stand-alone MMC console with the Group Policy snap-in added or with the default Group Policy Object Editor (or Group Policy for Windows 2000) console. You can access the latter from GPMC or through the Active Directory administration consoles. To edit a GPO, the user must have both Read and Write ACEs for that GPO.

By default, every Windows 2000/XP/Server 2003 computer has an MMC console for editing a Local Computer Policy, called gpedit.msc. There is no shortcut in the Start menu for it, but you could create one for it or you can start it by clicking the Start button, selecting Run, and typing "gpedit.msc". In addition, Windows 2000/XP/Server 2003 has one shortcut under Administrative Tools in the Start menu for editing security settings in the Local Computer Policy. The shortcut is called Local Security Policy, and it opens the security node of the Local Computer Policy. If the computer is a domain controller, it also has shortcuts for editing domain and domain controller security policies. Table 7.14 lists these MMC consoles.

NOTE Windows Server 2003 does not display Local Security Policy in the Start menu on domain controllers.

Table 7.14 Default Group Policy–Related MMC Consoles

Filename	Name Displayed in Start Menu	Available on Start Menu of Professional and Stand-alone or Member Servers	Available on Start Menu of Domain Controllers
gpedit.msc	N/A	No	No
secpol.msc	Local Security Policy	Yes	Yes for Windows 2000 No for Windows Server 2003
dompol.msc	Domain Security Policy	No	Yes
dcpol.msc	Domain Controller Security Policy	No	Yes

NOTE If a certain security setting has been defined in the GPOs in the domain and it affects Windows XP or Windows Server 2003, that setting is disabled in Local Security Policy (which you can edit with secpol.msc) or Local Computer Policy (which you can edit with gpedit.msc). This is also indicated with the icon that appears in the beginning of the row for an individual setting.

NOTE The consoles dompol.msc and dcpol.msc no longer work directly from the Run dialog in Windows Server 2003. See the properties of the icon in the Start menu to display the similar method for targeting the GPOE, as we explain next.

As displayed in Figure 7.31, you can create your own MMC console for editing Group Policy so that the focus of the saved console can be changed by starting the console from the command line or by clicking the Start button and selecting Run. You can start the Group Policy console with the following two command-line switches:

- `/gpcomputer:"machinename"`, where `machinename` can be a NetBIOS or DNS name, which opens the Local Computer Policy of the given computer

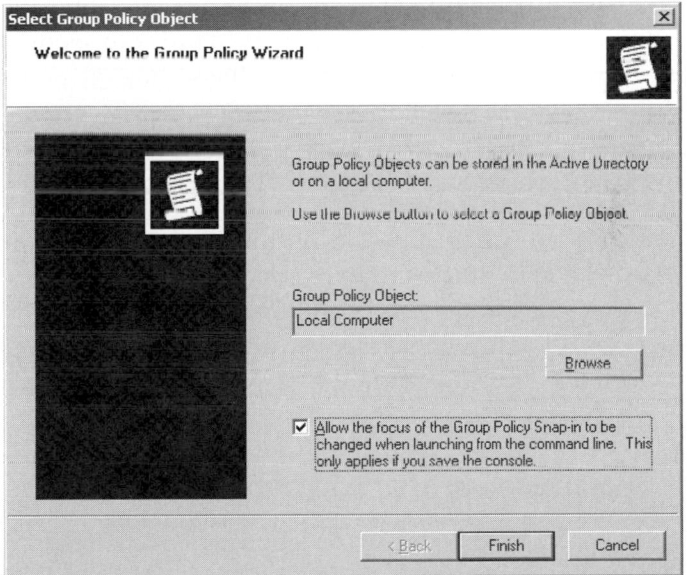

Figure 7.31 When you add the Group Policy snap-in to an MMC console, you can check the option to allow changing the focus of the saved console.

- `/gpobject:"ADSI path"`, where `ADSI path` could be `LDAP://CN={GUID of the target GPO},CN=Policies, CN=System,DC=Sanao,DC=com`, which opens the specified GPO for editing

MMC Extensions

MMC snap-ins can be extended to include the desired components. These components are called extensions. You can view them when using an MMC snap-in in author mode—for example, by starting gpedit.msc with the `/a` parameter. From the File (or Console, in Windows 2000) menu, select Add/Remove Snap-in and click the Extensions tab.

The Windows 2000 Group Policy snap-in has ten extensions, which all open by default whether all of them can be used or not. In addition, its Security Settings has two extensions: IP Security Policy Management and Public Key Policies. The Windows Server 2003 GPOE brings along one extension called Extended View, and its Security Settings has two new extensions called Software Restriction Policies and Wireless Network Policy Management. If you remove Extended View, the right window pane is displayed in the same way as in Windows 2000—that is, it doesn't have the Extended and Standard tabs on the bottom. The Extended tab is the default and a definite improvement over Windows 2000 (or standard view) since there is no longer the need to open the Explain tab of individual settings in order to see what a setting actually means. However, after you learn the settings at least almost by heart, the Extended tab becomes a nuisance.

Managing GPO Links

If you are using the Add button of the default Group Policy snap-in extension in the Active Directory Users and Computers or Active Directory Sites and Services snap-ins to create a new GPO, you always automatically associate this GPO with the current Active Directory container with a link. Either this link or parts of the newly created GPO can be disabled.

Disabling Parts of GPO or GPO Links

To speed up the startup or logon process, it might be beneficial to disable unused parts of a GPO, as shown in Figure 7.32. However, preferably use some other GPO than the Default Domain Controllers Policy for your experiments!

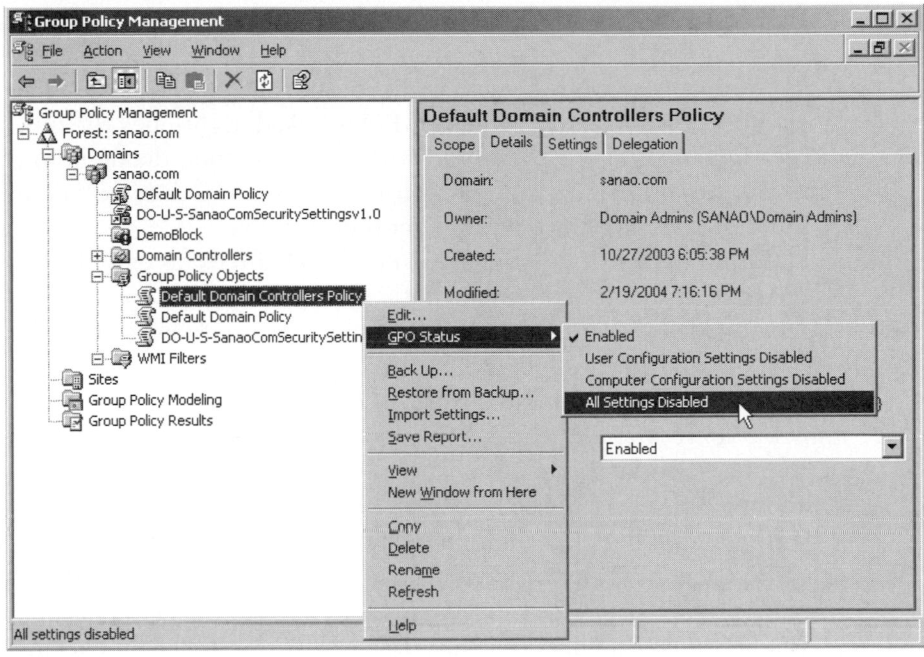

Figure 7.32 You can disable either the computer or user configuration settings (or even both) of a GPO from the context menu of a GPO

Especially when testing the effect of Group Policy settings, you may want to disable a GPO link temporarily. You do this by either double-clicking the Disabled column or clicking Options and selecting Disabled in the Group Policy dialog box.

If you are using GPMC, you can right-click the link and either select or deselect Link Enabled. In order to disable either the computer or user configuration settings, you can open the Details tab of a GPO or a GPO link. Alternatively, you can right-click a GPO under Group Policy Objects, click GPO status, and select the desired state for the GPO.

TIP To ensure that policies in a new GPO do not apply before you enable the link, you can force links to new GPOs to be disabled. The policy is located at User Configuration\Administrative Templates\System\Group Policy\Create new Group Policy Object links disabled by default.

Deleting GPOs and GPO Links

If you have GPMC installed, deleting a GPO is a very simple operation: locate the Group Policy Objects container in GPMC, right-click the

GPO, and select Delete. You are presented with a confirmation dialog before the GPO is permanently removed from Active Directory.

Removing a GPO link is no more difficult. Now you will have to locate the container into which a GPO is linked, right-click the link, and select Delete. You are presented with a confirmation dialog before the link is removed from Active Directory. The removal does not affect the GPO, nor does it remove links in another domain.

Without GPMC, deleting a linked GPO is almost as easy: Just locate the Active Directory container that a GPO is linked to, open the Group Policy dialog box, and click Delete. You are presented with two choices for deletion: You can delete only the link that associates the GPO with the container, or the link and the GPO. The former option removes the link but leaves the GPO unlinked or with its other existing links in Active Directory. The latter option removes the GPO and all links associated with it (see Figure 7.33).

If you want to delete an unlinked GPO without GPMC installed, you have to think in "Windows ways"; that is, in order to delete, you access the Add GPO dialog box from any container (Site, Domain, or OU). (This add/delete is like shutting down Windows 2000 by clicking the Start button and selecting Shutdown on the desktop.) Open the property dialog box for any container, click Add on the Group Policy tab, select the unlinked GPO on the All tab, right-click the unlinked GPO, and then click Delete (see Figure 7.34).

Group Policy Operations

One of the most welcome improvements that GPMC introduces is the capability to back up, restore, and transfer GPOs and their settings. We call these Group Policy operations and discuss next how you can perform the different operations.

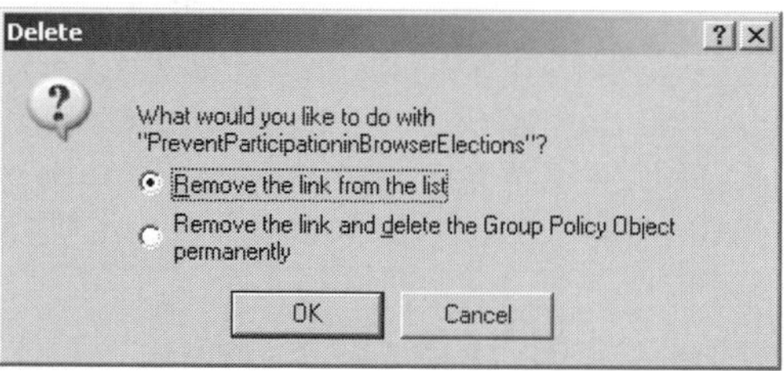

Figure 7.33 Deleting a GPO link enables you to delete the GPO as well.

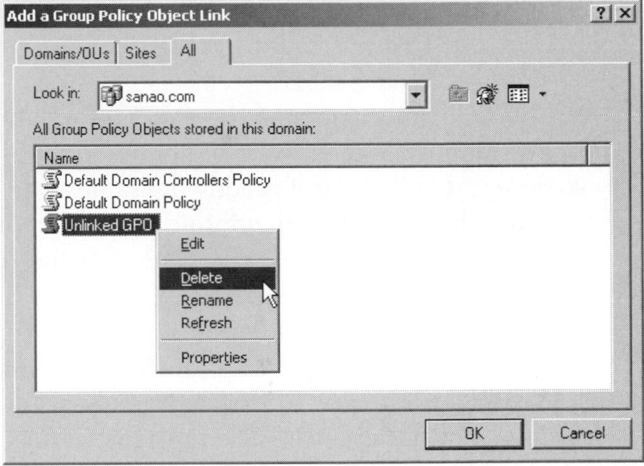

Figure 7.34 You delete an unlinked GPO from the Add a Group Policy Object Link dialog box.

Backing Up GPOs

You can back up GPOs individually, back up several of them, or back up all of them at one time. Backing up creates a folder structure in the file system, in a folder that you specify. It keeps track of the backups with manifest.xml files (one per backup location) stored in the root of the folder structure. This file contains the following:

- GUID and name for the GPO
- DNS name and GUID for the domain
- FQDN name for the domain controller where the backup was taken
- Backup date and time (stored in UTC time)
- GUID for the backup instance
- Description for the backup

These items are wrapped in <Backupinst> XML elements, which are created for each GPO that you back up at one time. A folder structure identified by the same GUID backup instance is created at the same time. There are three files in the root of this folder:

- Backup.xml. Contains the groups and file paths referenced in the GPO, Group Policy core settings (GUID, security descriptor,

options, user and machine version numbers, GUID for machine and user CSEs, a link to WMI filter, assigned IPSec filter), and settings for each CSE
- bkupinfo.xml. Contains the same information as the Backupinst element in the manifest.xml file
- gpreport.xml. Almost exactly the same as the XML report created from the Settings tab of the GPO, the only difference being <ReadTime>, which is the time that the backup or report was created

In addition to these three files, the folder DomainSysvol\GPO is created. This folder is a copy of the Group Policy Template of a GPO that we discussed in detail in the "Group Policy Objects" section earlier in this chapter. Figure 7.35 illustrates the folder structure.

In order to back up a GPO, you must have permission to read it and permission to write to the file system. And since every user in your forest has the Read permission (through the membership of Authenticated Users), they can also create backups of all the GPOs.

Without GPMC installed, the only supported way to back up Group Policy is to back up the entire Active Directory as part of the system state with the Windows 2000/Server 2003 Backup tool. The shortcoming of the system state is that it cannot be used partially. In other words, an individual GPO or even only all GPOs cannot be backed up or restored separately from the system state.

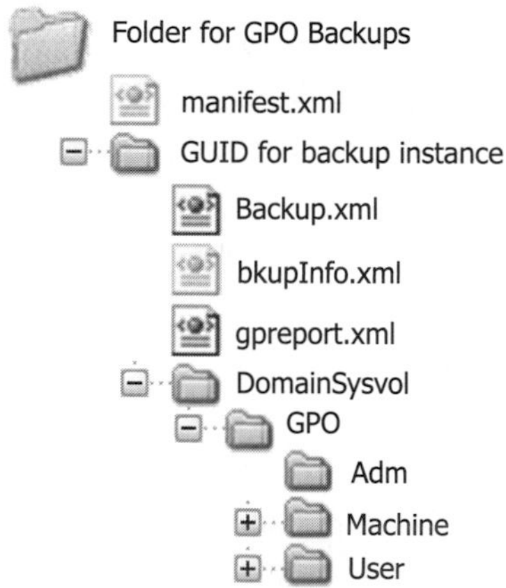

Figure 7.35 Folder structure for a GPO backup. Note that the manifest.xml and bkupInfo.xml files are hidden by default.

NOTE Prior to GPMC, a third-party backup application that supports backing up individual GPOs (e.g., Full Armor's FAZAM 2000) might have been a wise purchase. The so-called reduced functionality version of this FAZAM tool is included in the Windows 2000 Server Resource Kit, Supplement 1, in the apps folder of the Resource Kit setup CD. We discuss this as well as the other Resource Kit tools later in this chapter.

As you learned earlier, the instances for each GPO backup are stored in their own folders, and the manifest file keeps track of these folders. Consequently, GPMC enables storing several backups of the same GPO in the folder for basic versioning, as well as storing backups for different GPOs in the same folder. You can access the GPMC Manage Backups function by right-clicking either Domains or Group Policy Objects of a domain. When using the former method, you can manage GPO backups

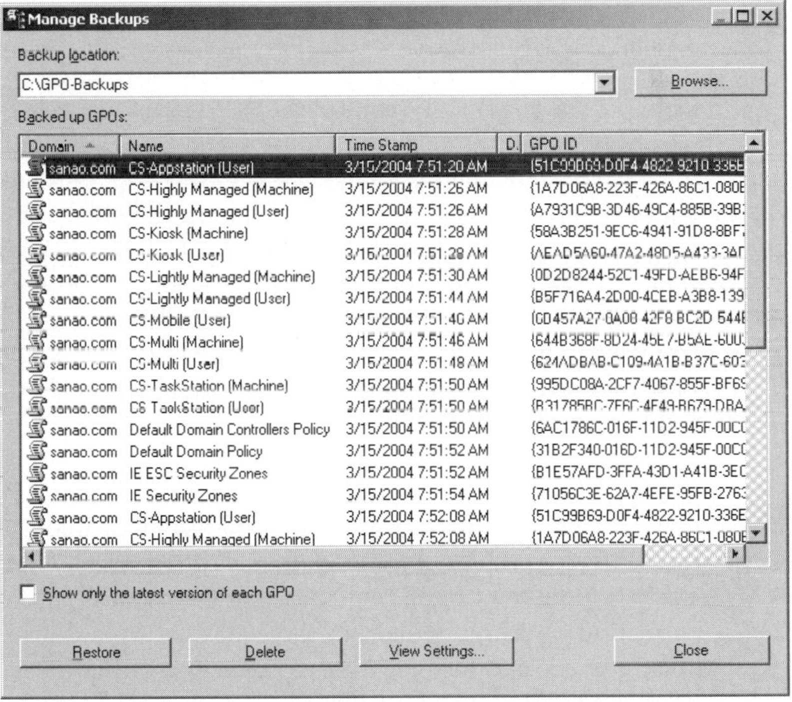

Figure 7.36 GPOs in Manage Backups are identified by domain, name, timestamp, description, and GUID. You can use the same dialog for restoring individual GPOs and accessing the reports for their settings.

for all domains, whereas with the latter method, you obviously see only GPOs for that domain. Figure 7.36 illustrates backup management for GPOs of one domain.

Restoring GPOs

You can restore the entire contents of one or more GPOs along with their settings with the GPMC restore function. Restore works for GPOs that were backed up in the same domain. In addition, the restored GPO retains its original GUID. Restoring a GPO does not restore its links to a site, domain(s), or OU(s), since the links are attributes of the site, domain, or OU. Nor does it restore WMI filters or IPSecurity policies.

In order to restore a GPO, you must have Write permission (edit settings, delete, modify security in the Delegation tab of a GPO in GPMC) on an existing GPO. If the GPO has been deleted, you must have permission to create new GPOs.

Copying GPOs

Copying a GPO enables you to use a GPO that you or someone else has prepared as the template for a new GPO. In order to copy GPOs, you must have simultaneous access to the source and destination domains. If you do not have this access, you can import the GPO settings.

If you copy a GPO within a domain, GPMC asks you whether you want to assign default permissions for the copied GPO or retain the permissions defined for the backed-up GPO. If you want to copy a GPO from another domain, the Cross-Domain Copying Wizard starts automatically. In addition to asking the same question, it also checks whether your source GPO contains references to any security principals (in user rights, restricted groups, system services, file system, registry or advanced folder redirection, or GPO DACL) or UNC paths (application management, scripts stored outside the GPO, or folder redirection). If those are found, you can create a *migration table* with the Migration Table Editor. The migration table maps the security principals and UNC paths in the source domain to those in the target domain. Figure 7.37 illustrates the options that you are presented with if the wizard finds that there is a need for using a migration table.

The migration table solves the problems associated with the security principals and file system paths. For example, permissions may have been assigned to domain local groups in the source domain that obviously cannot be used in the target domain even if a trust connects these

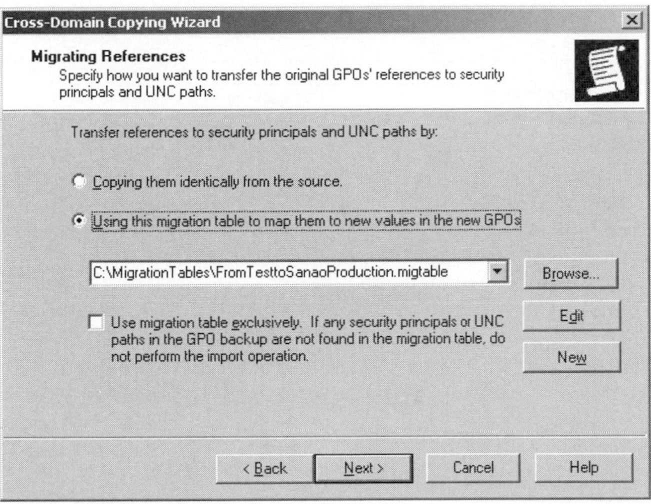

Figure 7.37 If the Cross-Domain Copying Wizard finds references to security principals and/or UNC paths, you can create a migration table in which the associations between those in the source and target GPOs are defined. You can also specify that the migration table be used exclusively.

domains. In addition, the application deployment file server might have a different name in the production domain from the one in the source domain.

TIP You can start the Migration Table Editor by right clicking the Domains or Group Policy Objects nodes in GPMC. Select Open Migration Table Editor. Alternatively, you can start it directly from %Program Files%\GPMC\mtedit.exe. To populate the table, use Populate from GPO or Populate from Backup in the Tools menu.

Migration tables are XML files with the extension .migtable. The file %ProgramFiles%\GPMC\ScriptsSampleMigrationTable.migtable, illustrated in Figure 7.38, contains all the different kinds of syntaxes that you can use in your own migration tables. After you have finished the file, you can validate it with Validate Table in the Tools menu.

When you copy GPOs across domains, assignments in IPSecurity policies and linked WMI filters are not copied. The Cross-Domain Copying Wizard displays a warning to you if there were any such policies or filters. Within a domain, the links are retained when copied.

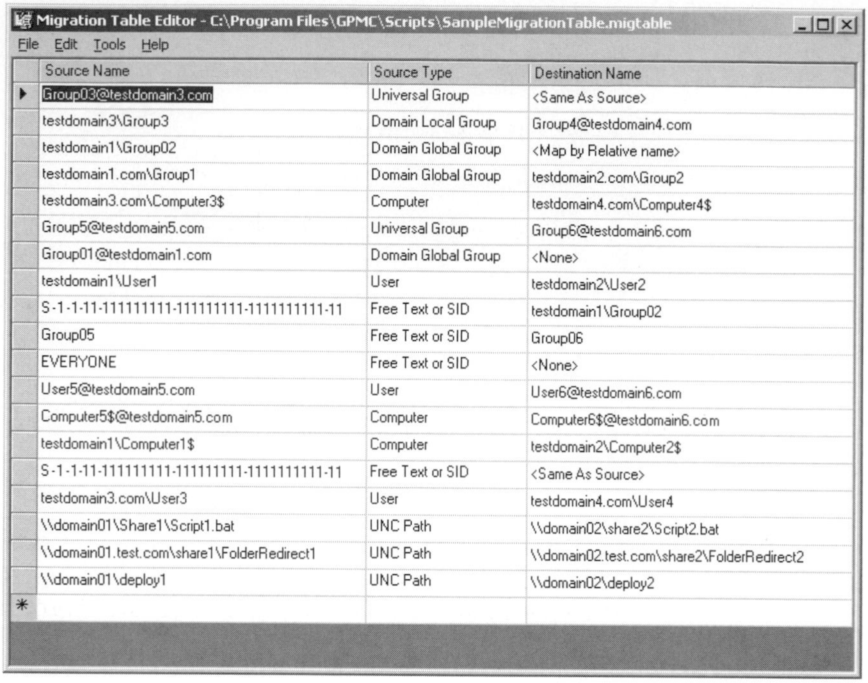

Migration Table Editor - C:\Program Files\GPMC\Scripts\SampleMigrationTable.migtable

File Edit Tools Help

Source Name	Source Type	Destination Name
Group03@testdomain3.com	Universal Group	<Same As Source>
testdomain3\Group3	Domain Local Group	Group4@testdomain4.com
testdomain1\Group02	Domain Global Group	<Map by Relative name>
testdomain1.com\Group1	Domain Global Group	testdomain2.com\Group2
testdomain3.com\Computer3$	Computer	testdomain4.com\Computer4$
Group5@testdomain5.com	Universal Group	Group6@testdomain6.com
Group01@testdomain1.com	Domain Global Group	<None>
testdomain1\User1	User	testdomain2\User2
S-1-1-11-111111111-111111111-1111111111-11	Free Text or SID	testdomain1\Group02
Group05	Free Text or SID	Group06
EVERYONE	Free Text or SID	<None>
User5@testdomain5.com	User	User6@testdomain6.com
Computer5$@testdomain5.com	Computer	Computer6$@testdomain6.com
testdomain1\Computer1$	Computer	testdomain2\Computer2$
S-1-1-11-111111111-111111111-1111111111-11	Free Text or SID	<Same As Source>
testdomain3.com\User3	User	testdomain4.com\User4
\\domain01\Share1\Script1.bat	UNC Path	\\domain02\share2\Script2.bat
\\domain01.test.com\share1\FolderRedirect1	UNC Path	\\domain02.test.com\share2\FolderRedirect2
\\domain01\deploy1	UNC Path	\\domain02\deploy2

Figure 7.38 The Migration Table Editor enables you to create a migration table file that converts references to security principals and UNC paths between the source and target domains.

In order to copy a GPO, you must have Read permission on the source and the permission to create new GPOs in the target.

Importing GPOs

If you don't have simultaneous access to the source GPO, you must use an import. Prior to the actual import, you must create a GPO. When the settings are imported, the existing settings are removed. However, the import does not modify the GUID, permissions, GPO links, or links to WMI filters. IPSecurity policy assignments are removed.

In order to import settings, you must have Write permission to the target GPO.

Managing WMI Filters

As you learned earlier, WMI filters are stored outside GPOs. Thus, managing them is separate from other GPO operations. You can export a

WMI filter to a .mof (Managed Object Format code) file and use this file later either to restore the WMI filter or to transfer it to another domain.

Scripts for GPO Operations

Table 7.15 lists the relevant GPMC sample scripts for automating GPO operation tasks.

Table 7.15 Relevant GPMC Sample Scripts for GPO Operations

Script	Function	Notes
Backup GPO.wsf	Backs up a GPO.	
BackupAll GPOs.wsf	Backs up all GPOs in a domain.	
CopyGPO.wsf	Creates a new GPO and copies settings from the source GPO.	
CreateMigration Table.wsf	Creates a migration table XML file.	
ImportGPO.wsf	Imports settings from the source GPO into the target GPO. If the target does not exist, it may be created with the `/CreateIfNeeded` parameter.	By default, uses the latest version of the source GPO. Use the backup instance GUID to specify an earlier version.
ImportAll GPOs.wsf	Imports settings for all GPOs in a backup location.	New GPOs are created if they do not exist. Settings in existing GPOs are overwritten.
RestoreGPO.wsf	Restores a backed-up GPO to the original domain where it was backed up.	By default, uses the latest version of the source GPO. If the original domain does not exist, the restore will fail.
RestoreAll GPOs.wsf	Restore the latest versions of each GPO.	
QueryBackup Location.wsf	Lists GPO backups in a certain backup location.	Use the `/verbose` parameter to see the instances/versions of each backed-up GPO.

TIP Since the scripts for backing up GPOs are available upon GPMC installation, you might as well make full use of them by backing up your GPOs regularly.

Restoring Default GPOs with Dcgpofix

Windows Server 2003 introduces a tool called dcgpofix for restoring the default GPOs (Default Domain Policy and Default Domain Controllers Policy, or either one of them). Dcgpofix is included in the %windir%\system32 folder of every Windows Server 2003 computer. Table 7.16 illustrates how the settings in different categories are restored.

You must be a domain or enterprise administrator to run dcgpofix.

NOTE This tool works only in Windows Server 2003.

Table 7.16 Restored Settings with the Command dcgpofix

Operation	Restored	Not Restored
Security settings	X	
Encrypting File System (EFS)	X	
Remote Installation Services (RIS)	X	
Software installation		X
Administrative templates		X
Scripts		X
Folder redirection		X
Internet Explorer maintenance		X
Security settings made by Exchange 2000 Setup		X
Settings migrated to default Group Policy during an upgrade from Windows NT to Windows 2000		X
Policy object changes made through Systems Management Server (SMS)		X

Reporting GPO Settings

It is very convenient to report settings included in a GPO with GPMC. You just open the Settings tab of a given GPO or GPO link.

TIP If you are using Windows Server 2003, you will receive an Internet Explorer Enhanced Security Configuration warning suggesting that you add the about:security_mmc.exe to the Trusted Sites zone. If you don't add it, you will not be able to hide and show setting categories.

You can store the reports in HTML or XML by right-clicking the GPO (or the report in the right pane) and selecting Save Report. Figure 7.39 has the Default Domain Policy settings displayed.

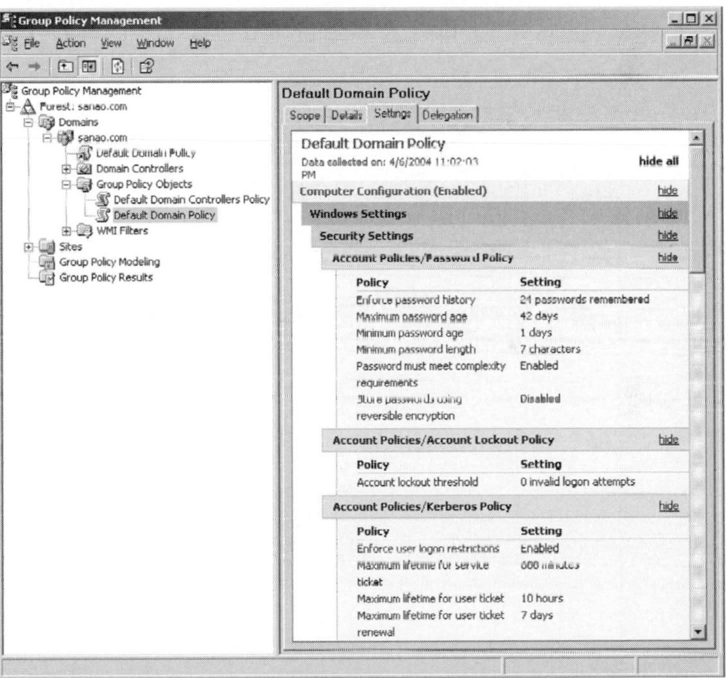

Figure 7.39 GPMC makes it easy to document GPO settings with its reporting feature.

Group Policy Analysis

As mentioned earlier, Windows XP introduced the RSoP console for displaying effective GP settings. When started with rsop.msc, the console runs an analysis for the current user using the current computer.

In Windows Server 2003, after the RSoP analysis is completed, you can right-click the top node and select Change Query. When you click Back, you will find out that there are two modes for the RSoP wizard: logging mode, which is on by default, and planning mode, with which you can perform what-if analysis. You can either find out which settings would apply to a certain user on a certain computer, or find out which settings would apply if a user and a computer were located in certain organizational units. In addition, rsop.msc also displays useful information for troubleshooting, as displayed in Figure 7.40. You can use the properties of the Computer and User Configuration nodes in order to access the Error Information tab, which has status information for each CSE that has settings to process. The properties of a GPO managed software application have a wealth of information on eight different tabs.

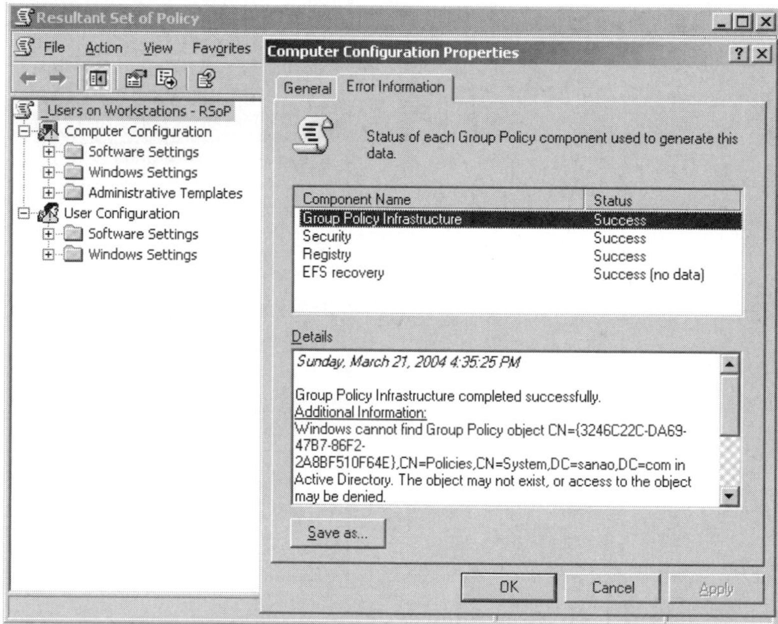

Figure 7.40 You can use rsop.msc for analyzing the effective settings. In addition, it can be useful in narrowing down problems associated with Group Policy processing.

TIP You also initiate RSoP in logging or planning mode in Active Directory Users and Computers by right-clicking a container, user, or computer object and selecting All Tasks.

NOTE RSoP analysis does not include Computer Configuration\Windows Settings\Security Settings\Account Policies\Kerberos Policy. Nor does it include Wireless and IPSec policies.

These two modes are integrated into the GPMC interface but with different names. Logging mode is called Group Policy Results, and planning mode is called Group Policy Modeling. In addition to incorporating this functionality into the same user interface, the primary advantage of using the GPMC versions of these tools is the capability to save the reports in HTML or XML files.

NOTE In Windows Server 2003, after you add the Resultant Set of Policy snap-in into a custom MMC console, you must select Generate RSoP Data from the Action menu. This starts the Resultant Set of Policy Wizard from the very beginning. In other words, you must select either logging or planning mode. In Windows XP, the wizard starts (with planning mode disabled) when you are adding the snap-in. In addition, refreshing the query is not available in Windows XP without creating a new RSoP console. In Windows Server 2003, you can right-click the query and select Refresh Query.

NOTE By default, analyzing computer settings is available only for administrators if used on Windows Server 2003 computer.

NOTE You can simulate slow link status, WMI filters, and loopback processing mode with Group Policy Modeling. The Local Computer Policy is not included in Group Policy Modeling.

Windows XP and Server 2003 also have RSoP integrated into the Help and Support Center. You can find this tool in Windows XP with the following steps: Start, Help and Support, Use Tools to view your computer information, Advanced System Information, View Group Policy settings applied. In Windows Server 2003, these are the steps: Start,

Help and Support, Tools, Help and Support Center Tools, Advanced System Information, View Group Policy settings applied. You can save the report to an HTML file in both operating systems. Unfortunately, the HTML formatting is not retained in the saved file.

NOTE In Windows XP the report is saved by default to C:\MyPolicy.htm, to which a nonadministrative user does not have Write permission by default. No error is displayed for the failure to write the file.

Searching GPOs

In a larger AD network, it might become necessary to find a GPO based on certain criteria. For example, you could use a search to locate the GPOs that have been filtered for a certain security group. GPMC allows you to search for a GPO based on the following criteria:

- GPO name (contains, does not contain, is exactly)
- GPO links (exist or do not exist)
- Security group (has or does not have explicit or effective permission)
- User Configuration (contains or does not contain folder redirection, IE branding, registry settings, scripts, and/or software installation)
- Computer Configuration (contains or does not contain EFS recovery, IP Security, disk quota, QoS packet scheduler, registry, scripts, security, software installation, and/or wireless policy settings)
- GUID

You access the search by right-clicking the forest or domain node. In Figure 7.41 we are looking for a GPO that contains security settings and for which Authenticated Users has effective permission.

Delegating Management of GPOs

Although you can delegate the administration of a specific OU with the Delegation of Control wizard, it does not imply that the members of the group to whom you delegated control could fully administer GPOs.

NOTE The only common task that can be delegated with the wizard in Windows 2000 is the ability to manage Group Policy links associated with a given container.

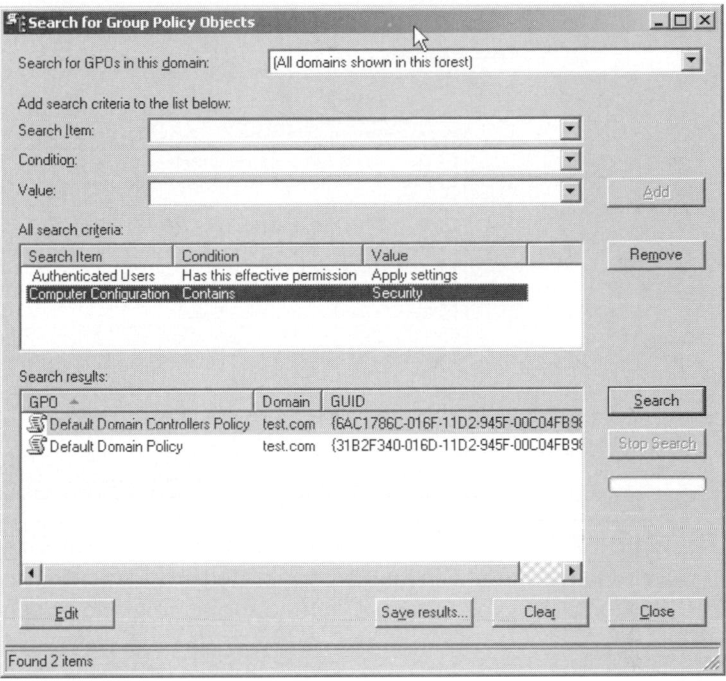

Figure 7.41 GPMC allows you to search for GPOs with versatile criteria.

In addition to delegating the permissions to link GPOs to a given container, the Delegation of Control wizard in Windows Server 2003 allows you to delegate RSoP Planning and Logging permissions, as displayed in Figure 7.42.

When you delegate to a user or group the ability to manage Group Policy links, the user or group gets Read and Write ACEs to the `gpLink` and `gpOptions` attributes. Table 7.17 lists the groups that have permission to link GPOs to different container objects.

If you want to enable the members of a certain group to edit a GPO, that group must have Read and Write permissions for the GPO. To modify the permissions, click Properties on the Group Policy tab and then select the Security tab. Add the necessary group and give it Read and Write allow ACEs. By default, Domain Admins and Enterprise Admins groups, along with System, have Write permission for new GPOs.

Once again, GPMC changes the way the delegation is done and displayed. You use the Add button on the Delegation tab of individual Active Directory containers for delegating three tasks. These tasks, along with the actual permissions they set, are listed in Table 7.18.

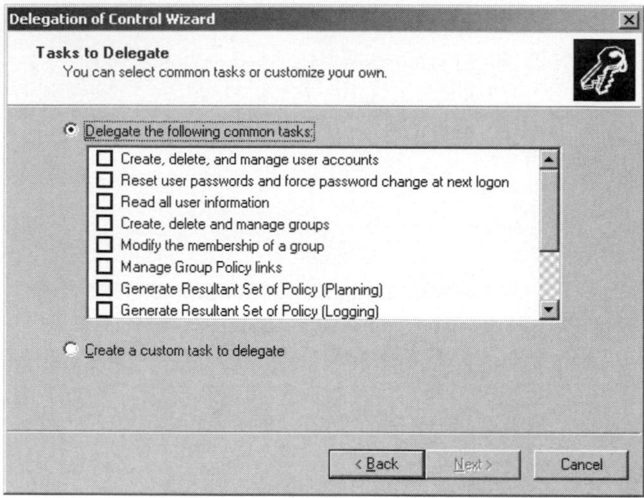

Figure 7.42 You can use the Delegation of Control wizard to delegate administration of GPO links associated with a container. In Windows Server 2003, you can also delegate planning and logging of RSoP tasks.

Table 7.17 Groups with Permissions to Link GPOs

Container	ACE Assigned Directly to the Container	Inherited ACE
Site	System	Enterprise Admins FRD (forest root domain) Domain Admins
Domain	Domain Admins Administrators System Enterprise Admins	
OU	System Domain Admins	Administrators Enterprise Admins

NOTE Generate Resultant Set of Policy (Planning) and Generate Resultant Set of Policy (Logging) are extended rights that are created when you run adprep/forestprep during the upgrading of AD2000, or when you create the forest root domain.

Table 7.18 Active Directory Container Permissions in GPMC

Permission in GPMC	Standard Permission	Special Permission(s)
Link GPOs		Read/Write gPLink Read/Write gPOptions
Perform Group Policy Modeling analyses	Generate Resultant Set of Policy (Planning)	
Read Group Policy Results data	Generate Resultant Set of Policy (Logging)	

When delegating these tasks, you can select whether the permissions apply to this container and all child containers or to this container only. You can access ACL Editor for seeing the actual permissions by clicking the Advanced button in the lower right-hand corner of the Delegation tab.

You use the Add button on the Delegation tab of Group Policy Objects in order to specify the users or groups who can create GPOs in the domain. The users or groups on this tab are assigned Create GroupPolicyContainer Objects in `CN=Policies, CN=System, DC=`*`<your domain>`*. In addition, they are assigned Read & Execute, List Folder Contents, and Read and Write standard NTFS permissions to the %windir%\sysvol\sysvol\<*yourdomain*>\Policies folder.

Each GPO (or a link with which it has been associated with an AD container) under Group Policy Objects also has the Delegation tab. You use it in the same way as for setting AD container permissions. Table 7.19 lists the permissions that are set with this tab.

As you learned earlier, a user (or a group that she is a member of) needs Read and Apply Group Policy permissions for that GPO in order to be affected by the settings in the GPO. You set the combination of these permissions with the Add button under the Security Filtering section on the Scope tab of a GPO or its link. You can also add/remove members to/from a group listed in this section with the Properties button.

Creating an MMC Console for a Delegated GPO

You can create an MMC console for editing the GPO that you just delegated. First start MMC, add the Group Policy snap-in, browse for the delegated GPO, and click Finish, Close, OK. If you want to restrict the user to a specific node, you can right-click the node and click New Window

Table 7.19 GPO Permissions in GPMC

Permission in GPMC	Standard ACL Permission	Special ACL Permission
Read	Read	
Read (from security filtering)	Read, Apply Group Policy	
Edit settings	Read, Create All Child Objects, Delete All Child Objects	Write All Properties
Edit, delete, and modify security	Read, Create All Child Objects, Delete All Child Objects	Write All Properties Modify Permissions Modify Owner
Custom	Any combination of permissions	Any combination of permissions

from Here. Close the original window (you might have to use the Window menu to make it visible). Then select Options from the Console menu. Finally, select User mode, limited access, single window, and save the console to an appropriate folder (e.g., C:\Documents and Settings\YourAdminUser\Desktop). Changing the mode restricts the user from seeing menus and modifying snap-ins or views.

TIP You can open the default administrative tools, the Active Directory Users and Computer snap-in, and the Active Directory Sites and Services snap-in in author mode by running dsa.msc and dssite.msc with the /a parameter. The author mode enables adding other snap-ins and manipulating windows within MMC. Right-clicking the icons on Start, Administrative Tools also displays Author on the context- sensitive menu for some consoles.

TIP You can prevent users from opening consoles in author mode with the policy User Configuration\Administrative Templates\Windows Components\Microsoft Management Console\Restrict users from entering author mode.

Another way to restrict the user is to modify the snap-in extensions that open when the user starts the console. There are ten extensions in Windows 2000, some of which are shown in Figure 7.43.

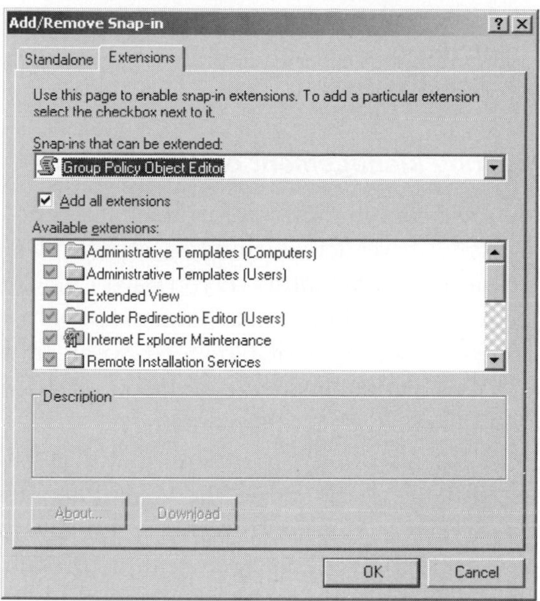

Figure 7.43 By default, all MMC snap-in extensions are added to the Group Policy snap-in. When delegating control of GPOs, you can select only some of the extensions.

TIP To ensure that the user will or won't be able to use specific MMC snap-ins, use the following policies: the policy User Configuration\Administrative Templates\Windows Components\Microsoft Management Console\Restrict users to the explicitly permitted list of snap-ins, and the 24 (or 12 in Windows 2000) policies under User Configuration\Administrative Templates\Windows Components\Microsoft Management Console\Restricted/Permitted snap-ins\Group Policy. Should you exclude yourself, seek help from Microsoft Knowledge Base article 263166.

Delegating Local Computer Policy

The only way to delegate control of a Local Computer Policy is to define NTFS permissions for the %SystemRoot%\System32\GroupPolicy folder. Because there is no Apply Group Policy ACE among the file system ACEs, every user who has Read permission for the folder will be affected by local Group Policy. If there is a conflicting setting in Active Directory, however, the setting in Active Directory wins. If you want to prevent the settings in the Local Computer Policy from applying to the members of a certain group, you can deny Read permission to the NTUser.pol file.

Delegating Management of WMI Filters

There are only two options for delegating the creation of the WMI filters: A security principal can have either Full Control or Creator Owner permission for WMI filters. If you have Full Control permission, you can create new WMI filters in the domain as well as manage the ones created by others. The holder of Creator Owner permission can only manage those filters that he or she created. You set these permissions on the Delegation tab of the WMI filters node.

You can also define permissions for individual WMI filters on the Delegation tab of the individual WMI filter. The holder of Full Control permission can define permissions, whereas the holder of the Edit permission can modify the selected filter through Write All Properties on the msWMI-Som object representing the WMI filter on `CN=SOM, CN=WMIPolicy,CN=System,DC=`<*domain*>.

In addition, Authenticated Users have permanent Read permission to all WMI filters through their Read All Properties ACL on `CN=SOM, CN=WMIPolicy,CN=System,DC=`<*domain*>.

Scripting Group Policy Management Tasks

As we have already illustrated on a few occasions, scripting GPO tasks is very easy, since GPMC includes 32 sample scripts, which can be found in the %programfiles%\gpmc\scripts folder after installing GPMC. For more information on sample scripts, see Using the Group Policy Management Interfaces, Group Policy Management Console Scripting Overview, Group Policy Management Console Scripting Samples in the GPMC online Help file (`%programfiles%\gpmc\scripts\gpmc.chm`). GPMC SDK documentation with definitions for all interfaces is also included in the Help file.

If you want to copy the scripts to another location that is different from the setup, you should also copy the Lib_CommonGPMCFunctions.js file, which many of the sample scripts depend on.

Managing Administrative Template Files

Understanding administrative template file management becomes crucial when a new version or service pack of either the server or client operating system becomes available. Usually, at least the primary system.adm file of the newer version includes new settings. These are obviously of no use until you decide to deploy any computers with the new version.

One option to deploy .adm files is to copy them directly to the %systemroot%\inf folder of the domain controller. However, the domain controller or its Group Policy Object Editor may not be capable of using all the functionality incorporated into the .adm file. This is the case, for example, if you want to manage all XP settings in AD2000. The Windows 2000 Group Policy snap-in is not capable of showing all settings, and its user interface is also more restricted. For example, you have to open the Explain tab in the properties of an individual setting in order to see the description.

The other option is to start an empty MMC console, add the Group Policy snap-in into it, and target it to any AD-based GPO. A timestamp comparison is performed on the source .adm files in the %systemroot%\inf folder of the client computer and the .adm files in the GPO. If the local files are newer, they are copied into the .adm folder of the target GPO. You can control this behavior with User Configuration\Administrative Templates\System\Group Policy\Turn off automatic update of ADM files.

NOTE See KB article 816662 for more information on managing administrative template files.

NOTE You should not modify the .adm files that ship with the operating system, because this will cause problems with the next version.

Managing User-Made Administrative Template Files

When you implement your own administrative template files, they must also be tested and distributed. When you create your own files, basic error checking is done for syntax errors. In Figure 7.44, the keyword SUPPORTED was in the wrong place, which caused an error to be displayed. Although there was an error, the administrative template appeared on the list of loaded files.

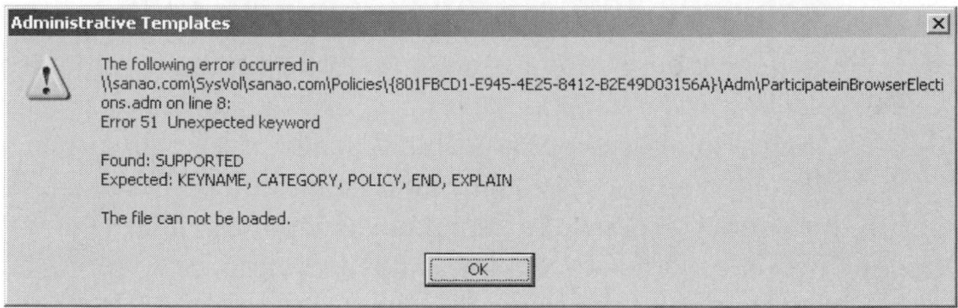

Figure 7.44 Administrative template file syntax is checked when the template file is loaded.

In order to update the new file, you must first unload the old version by removing it from the list of administrative files and then load the new version by adding it to the list.

Additional Tools

As you have seen, the number of tools for Group Policy has increased somewhat from Windows 2000 times. In addition to the tools included in the operating system and the Resource Kit Tools, at the time of writing, there are two tools available for download: Group Policy Inventory and Group Policy Common Scenarios.

Group Policy Inventory

Group Policy Inventory provides a GUI for RSoP or WMI queries that administrators run in order to collect information from a group of computers. You can store the query results to an XML or a tab-delimited text file for further analysis with, for example, Excel. Group Policy Inventory runs on Windows 2000, XP, and Server 2003 but requires at least .NET Framework 1.0 to be installed. Figure 7.45 illustrates two queries processed with Group Policy Inventory.

You must download Group Policy Inventory from the Microsoft Web site. When you run the setup file, it defaults to the C:\Program Files\Windows Resource Kits\Tools folder—in other words, the same folder where you would usually have the Resource Kit Tools installed. One of the three files installed, gpinventory.mht, contains simple instructions for using the tool.

You can specify the target computers by OU. Alternatively, you can type the names of the computers that you want to analyze into a text file, one per line, and import this file.

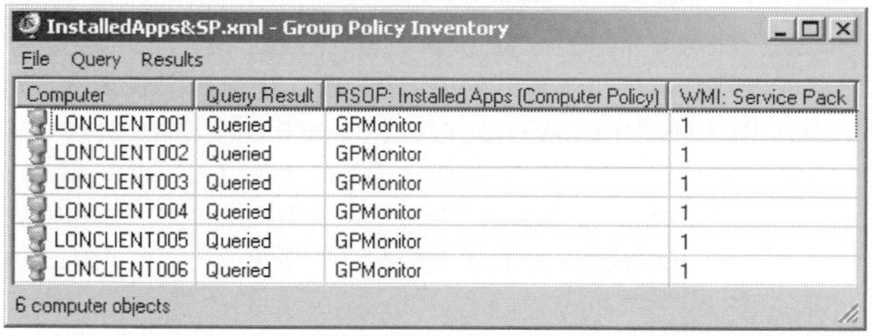

InstalledApps&SP.xml - Group Policy Inventory

File Query Results

Computer	Query Result	RSOP: Installed Apps (Computer Policy)	WMI: Service Pack
LONCLIENT001	Queried	GPMonitor	1
LONCLIENT002	Queried	GPMonitor	1
LONCLIENT003	Queried	GPMonitor	1
LONCLIENT004	Queried	GPMonitor	1
LONCLIENT005	Queried	GPMonitor	1
LONCLIENT006	Queried	GPMonitor	1

6 computer objects

Figure 7.45 The Group Policy Inventory tool provides a GUI for RSoP and WMI queries.

The tool loads the queries defined in the wmiqueries.xml file. This file contains initially 9 RSoP queries and 18 WMI queries, but you can append your own queries to this file.

You must have Generate Resultant Set of Policy (logging) permission on the target machines to run RSoP queries. In order to run WMI queries, you must be a member of the Administrators group of the target computer.

NOTE You can start the Group Policy Inventory tool from the command line. See gpinventory.mht for more information.

Group Policy Common Scenarios

Group Policy Common Scenarios Using GPMC is a toolset that you can download from the Microsoft Web site. It includes six usage scenarios, each with supporting GPOs. The settings in each GPO are documented and easily accessible in HTML files stored in the GPO-Reports folder.

You can import settings from any of the GPOs included in the Group Policy Common Scenarios one GPO at a time. Alternatively, you can create an OU structure and import the linked GPOs with the command CreateCommonScenarios.cmd, which is included in the package. This command uses the CreateEnvironmentFromXML.wsf script, which is one of the sample scripts included in GPMC. As a result, you get a new four-level OU structure with the top OU, CommonScenarios, under your domain node. In addition, the script creates 12 GPOs, imports their settings, and links them to the appropriate OUs.

NOTE The Windows 2000 version of this toolset includes various files, of which two command batch files, loadpol.bat and savepol.bat, are the most interesting. Although they are not supported for transferring GPOs from one domain to another, based on our experiments they work just fine. At the same time, these two tools can be used to back up GPOs. This functionality is now found in GPMC, and consequently we recommend that you use it.

In addition to 40 pages of documentation, settings for each scenario have been defined in a Microsoft Excel spreadsheet file.

Software Management with Group Policy

Group Policy can help you simplify the administration of software applications in your network. AD2003 brings along some additional functionality for 64-bit application compatibility.

Windows Installer

In the past, software applications were deployed and installed with various setup engines in Windows environments. Developers did not always follow the standards, especially the Windows logo requirements for applications (`http://www.microsoft.com/windowsserver2003/partners/isvs/cfw.mspx`). These requirements have to be fulfilled in order to get the application approved by a certifying company and, as a sign they have been fulfilled, a "Certified for Windows" sticker attached to the product box. Consequently, we have applications that store files in the wrong folders and settings in the wrong registry paths, unsuccessful uninstallation programs, DLL conflicts, and so on. Windows 2000/XP/Server 2003 include a new setup method that is enabled by the Windows Installer service. By including this service, the setup procedure has been standardized. Figure 7.46 illustrates the setup process.

The Microsoft Software Installer (MSI) database includes information stored on tables, based on which Windows Installer creates the actual setup script.

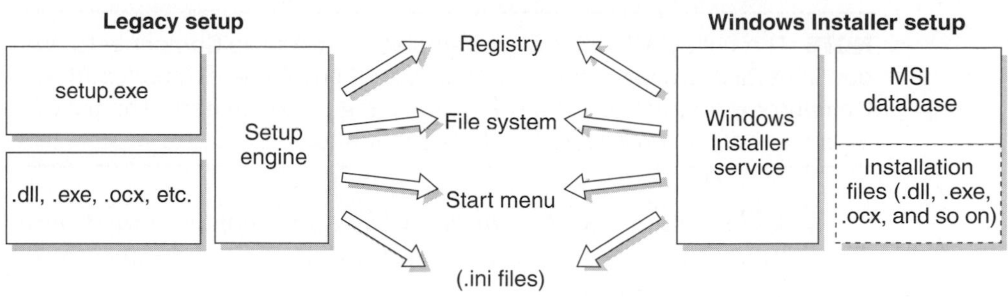

Figure 7.46 The applications are installed with a legacy setup or Windows Installer.

Using Windows Installer offers the following benefits to the Windows environment:

- *Rollback for the installation in case of an interrupted or failed process.* The computer (and especially the registry) is returned to the state it was in before the setup process was started.
- *Actual setup only on first use.* Only the shortcut may appear on the Start menu prior to first use.
- *Division of the setup into various components.* It is not necessary to install the whole application at once.
- *Option to store all files used during the setup in one .msi file.* The file may contain all .dll's, .exe's, and so on.
- *Merge modules.* These modules contain components used often in several packages.
- *Customizable installation packages.* You can customize a package to meet specific requirements with Windows Installer transform (.mst) files. For example, the Office 2003 Resource Kit includes the Custom Installation Wizard for creating .mst files.
- *Self-repairing applications.* If you start an application and Windows Installer finds a problem with, for example, one corrupted file, the file is replaced automatically by the Windows Installer service.
- *Setup with privileged rights.* The setup is performed in the security context of the system account, and, consequently, there is no need for an administrator to attend to the computer during setup if the user's privileges are insufficient for installing the application.

NOTE The policy Administrative Templates\Windows Components\Windows Installer\Always install with elevated privileges exists in both the Computer Configuration and the User Configuration folders. The policy is effective only if you enable it in both locations.

- *Additional information in the Add/Remove applet in the Control Panel.* For example, you can find the URL for the software vendor's support pages.

NOTE The Windows Installer service must be used to install a third-party application in order to display "Certified for Windows 2000/XP/Windows Server 2003" in the product documentation.

IF YOU KNOW NT If you try to install an MSI package into NT 4.0, the Windows Installer service is installed first, after which you must restart the computer and restart the setup. An example of this type of application is Office 2000.

The stages of the software installation process are as follows:

1. Copy files.
2. Create shortcuts.
3. Associate file types.
4. Register COM, COM+, and DCOM files.
5. Register the application for removal.

The Windows Installer service performs all these tasks as defined in the MSI databases in Windows Installer packages.

Creating Windows Installer Packages

The first stage of deploying software with Group Policy is to create a Windows Installer package. Various tools are available for this task. The Windows 2000 CD-ROM contains Veritas WinInstall LE in the Valueadd\3rdparty\Mgmt\Winstle folder.

TIP You can get the Windows Server 2003 version of this tool from OnDemand Software.

Other tools include the following:

- Microsoft Visual Studio Installer in Visual Studio 6 Enterprise Tools (`http://msdn.microsoft.com/vstudio`); Visual Studio .NET includes a Setup Project template to create .MSI files
- Wise for Windows Installer (`http://www.wisesolutions.com`)
- InstallShield AdminStudio (`http://www.installshield.com`)
- OnDemand Software WinInstall (`http://www.ondemandsoftware.com`)

Deploying Software with Group Policy

The next step is to store the installation package in a shared folder on a file server. You could use a Distributed File System (DFS) service to create a fault-tolerant and site-aware file distribution infrastructure. Then you have to choose whether to publish or assign the application. You also must decide whether to deploy the software for the computer or user.

Published versus Assigned Application

The two ways to deploy applications are as follows:

- The application is published to users so that it appears in the Add/Remove Programs applet in the Control Panel.
- An application is assigned to users or computers. If it is assigned in the Computer Configuration, it is installed when the computer starts. If it is assigned in the User Configuration, it appears in the Start menu after the user logs on, and the actual installation takes place when the user clicks the shortcut for the application, unless "Install this application at logon" is selected in the deployment options.

A published application can also be installed if the user opens a file with an extension that has been associated with a certain application. Table 7.20 compares these two methods of deploying applications.

TIP If you are deploying an application to users, you should use the new Windows Server 2003 feature, "Install this application at logon," for mobile users. This is in order to ensure that the application is already installed when the user is away from the office.

Table 7.20 Comparison of Published and Assigned Applications

	Published	Assigned to User	Assigned to Computer
When is the software available for installation?	When the next user to whom the GPO applies logs on	When the next user to whom the GPO applies logs on	The next time the computer to which the GPO applies is started
Who starts the installation?	User	User, or if "Install this application at logon" is checked, the setup is automatic	Automatic when the computer starts
Where or how is the installation started?	Add/Remove Programs in the Control Panel	By clicking the application icon in the Start menu	N/A
Is the installation started by opening an associated file?	Yes, if Auto-Install is selected	Yes	N/A
Removal from Add/Remove software?	Yes	Yes	No—only the local administrator can remove the application, but the user can repair it
What are the supported installation file types?	Windows Installer packages and .zap files	Windows Installer packages	Windows Installer packages

We list here the steps required to assign the Group Policy Monitor application, which we will discuss later in this chapter, to computers in an OU called `CN=GPMonitoredComputers,DC=sanao,DC=sanao`.

1. First, create a shared folder for the installation files—for example, D:\Apps—on the file server.
2. Copy the necessary files into the shared folder. In this case, the files are GPMON.cab and GPMonitor.msi.

3. Start Group Policy Management Console, right-click the GPMonitoredComputers OU, and select Create and Link a GPO Here.
4. Name the GPO appropriately—for example, OU-C-A-GP MonitorDeployment-v1.0.
5. Right-click the link to the GPO and select Edit in order to start the Group Policy Object Editor.
6. Open Computer Configuration\Software Settings\Software installation.
7. Right-click Software installation and select New, Package.
8. Type the UNC path to the installation source folder into the "File name" field—for example, \\lonsanao1\apps—and click Open.
9. Select GPMonitor.msi and click Open again.
10. Use the default deployment method (Assigned) and click OK.
11. That's all. Ensure that the client computer(s) are located in the OU that is the target for the GPO and restart them.

TIP In AD2000, you can use a script found in the "Improving Software Management in Your IT Infrastructure" chapter of the Change and Configuration Management Deployment Guide (`http://www.microsoft.com/windows2000/techinfo/reskit/deploy/CCM/`) for forcing the application assigned to the user to install completely at logon.

NOTE When you create an application package, corresponding packageRegistration objects are created in either the `CN=Packages,CN=Class Store,CN=Computer,CN={GUID for GPO},CN=Policies,CN=System,DC=`*`<domain>`* or `CN=Packages,CN=Class Store,CN=User,CN={GUID for GPO},CN=Policies,CN=System,DC=`*`<domain>`* containers.

Deploying Non-MSI Packages

To deploy an older application, you have two options: create an MSI file for the installation with one of the tools mentioned earlier, or create a .zap file that contains instructions so that Windows Installer can install the application. The contents for a sample .zap file for installing Excel 97 are as follows:

```
[Application]
FriendlyName = "Microsoft Excel 97"
SetupCommand = setup.exe
DisplayVersion = 8.0
Publisher = Microsoft
URL = http://www.microsoft.com/office
Architecture = Intel
```

Upgrading Applications

The applications that you deploy with Group Policy can be easily upgraded. For example, you can use Group Policy to deploy the current service pack to the Windows 2000 computers in your infrastructure, and when a new service pack is released, you can upgrade the computers with the new one. The example GPO in Figure 7.47 is used to install Windows XP Service Pack 1 and then upgrade it to Service Pack 2.

NOTE Using Group Policy to deploy service packs is no longer the only method available. You can use Microsoft Windows/Software Update Services (WUS/SUS) to deploy Windows 2000 SP4, Windows XP SP1, and other new service packs.

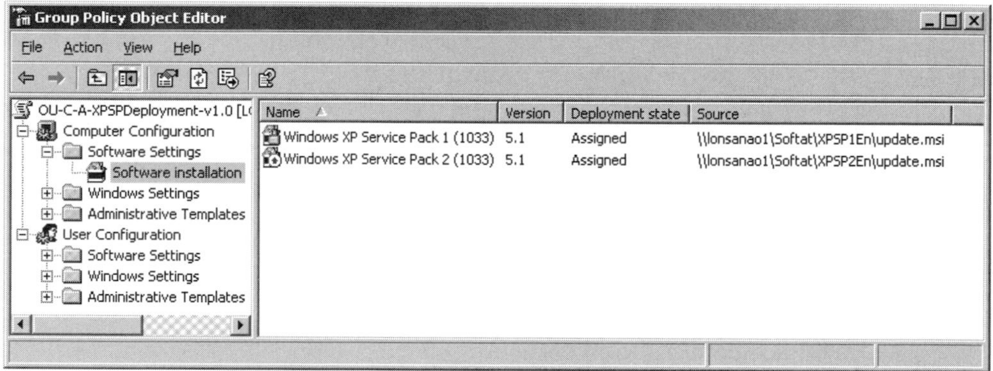

Figure 7.47 A GPO used to install and upgrade Windows XP service packs

Patching Applications

Software developers issue patches to their applications every now and then. As a result, maintaining an application includes the task of deploying these minor upgrades. You can redeploy an application that was deployed originally with Group Policy so that users who have it installed will receive the patched version automatically from the server. You can patch an application with a newer version by right-clicking an existing package and selecting All Tasks, Redeploy.

Removing Applications

The applications that were deployed with Group Policy can also be removed with Group Policy. The removal can be optional, in which case users can continue using the application that they installed earlier. However, new users can no longer install the application. The other option is to use mandated removal, in which case the application is removed from the computer when it is restarted or when the user next logs on.

NOTE Applications deployed with .zap files cannot be removed with Group Policy.

TIP Usually, if an application setup does not complete properly, Windows Installer retains the settings that existed prior to starting the setup. Should it fail, you can try using the Windows Installer Cleanup Utility, named msicuu, and as a last resort use the tool Windows Installer Zapper, msizap, for removing traces of the failed installation. See Windows Server 2003 online Help for more information on using these tools.

Troubleshooting Group Policy

Troubleshooting group policies has been drastically improved in Windows XP and Server 2003 over Windows 2000. The only graphical tools that Windows 2000 provides for expediting the effect of Group Policy settings are the Local Security Policy console and the Security Configuration and Analysis snap-in. With the former, you were able to see which security settings were in effect, although it did not give a clue as to where the settings came from. The Security Configuration and Analysis snap-in enables you to analyze your computer's security settings against settings stored in some of the security templates. The categories that this tool analyzes are as follows:

- Account policies
- Local policies
- Event log
- Restricted groups
- System services
- Registry
- File system

The GPMC console itself helps prevent administrators from missing the worst configuration problems because of its intuitive user interface. Should problems arise, the RSoP console or GPMC Group Policy Results gives very good indications as to where the problem might exist.

Logging Group Policy Events

Group Policy processing creates some events on the application log. You can see these events on the Policy Events tab of Group Policy Results after you have run the analysis for at least one scenario.

In order to gather additional Group Policy events in logs, you must edit the registry. No matter what you were used to before (RegEdit or RegEdt32), you will end up with the RegEdit UI in Windows XP/Server 2003. RegEdt32 was dropped in Windows XP, although there still is regedt32.exe in the %windir%\system32 folder. It is only a pointer to %windir%\regedit.exe.

NOTE In Windows NT 4.0/2000 we recommend using the registry editor RegEdt32 for the task rather than RegEdit because it had better support for different value types, such as `REG_MULTI_SZ` and `REG_EXPAND_SZ`, and for permissions. RegEdit was useful when you wanted to search for something in the registry. In Windows XP/Server 2003 the functionality of both tools is combined into RegEdit.

You can turn on the Verbose flag in the registry to generate more detailed information on Group Policy processing. Enabling this flag starts verbose logging in the application event log. The value is located under `HKEY_LOCAL_MACHINE\Software\Microsoft\WindowsNT\`

CurrentVersion\Diagnostics, and to turn on the logging, you create a value RunDiagnosticLoggingGroupPolicy of type REG_DWORD, and set its value to 1. Figure 7.48 illustrates an example event generated by turning this value on.

TIP The Diagnostics key does not exist by default. Thus, you must create it prior to creating the value RunDiagnosticLoggingGroupPolicy.

TIP Remember to remove the setting from the registry when it is no longer appropriate. If you leave it on, the application log will become full within a few hours because the default application log size is 512KB in Windows 2000 and Windows XP. For Windows Server 2003, the maximum size has been increased to 16,384KB.

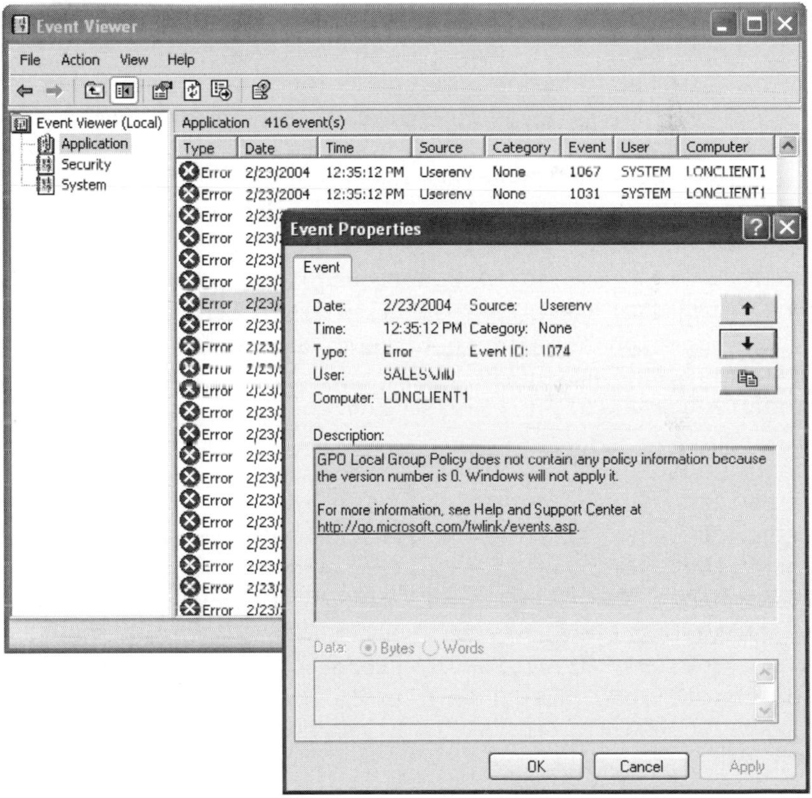

Figure 7.48 A sample event from an application log after the Verbose flag has been turned on

Another useful log, especially for in-depth understanding of Group Policy processing, is the Group Policy Processing Log. You can enable it by creating a `REG_DWORD` value called `UserEnvDebugLevel` under `HKLM\Software\Microsoft\Windows NT\CurrentVersion\Winlogon` and setting its value to 0x10002. After you have set the value, the log file %Systemroot%\Debug\userenv.log is created.

TIP Other possible values for `UserEnvDebugLevel` are 0x10001, which logs only errors and warnings, and 0x10000, which logs nothing (default behavior).

IF YOU KNOW NT In order to create a detailed NT 4.0 System Policy processing log for analysis or troubleshooting purposes, you'd have to use the Checked Build version of Windows NT 4.0 Workstation or Server.

The following is sample output for a Group Policy Processing Log (we have removed repetitive or nonsignificant lines):

```
USERENV(200.650) 01:40:59:650 ProcessGPOs:
USERENV(200.650) 01:40:59:650 ProcessGPOs:  Starting computer Group
Policy (Background) processing...
USERENV(200.650) 01:40:59:650 ProcessGPOs:
USERENV(200.650) 01:40:59:650 EnterCriticalPolicySection: Machine
critical section has been claimed.  Handle = 0x870
USERENV(200.650) 01:40:59:670 ProcessGPOs:  Machine role is 2.
USERENV(200.650) 01:40:59:719 PingComputer: Adapter speed 100000000
bps
USERENV(200.650) 01:40:59:758 PingComputer:  First time:  8
USERENV(200.650) 01:40:59:758 PingComputer:  Fast link.  Exiting.
USERENV(200.650) 01:41:25:013 ProcessGPOs: network name is 10.10.1.0
USERENV(200.650) 01:41:25:013 ProcessGPOs:  User name is:
CN=LONSANAO21,OU=GPMonitoredComputers,DC=sanao,DC=com, Domain name
is:  SANAO
USERENV(200.650) 01:41:25:013 ProcessGPOs: Domain controller is:
\\LONSanao1.sanao.com  Domain DN is sanao.com
USERENV(200.650) 01:41:25:022 ReadGPExtensions: Rsop entry point not
found for gptext.dll.
USERENV(200.650) 01:41:25:062 ReadExtStatus: Reading Previous Status
for extension {35378EAC-683F-11D2-A89A-00C04FBBCFA2}
USERENV(200.650) 01:41:25:062 ReadStatus: Read Extension's Previous
status successfully.
```

```
USERENV(200.650) 01:41:25:249 ProcessGPOs: Calling GetGPOInfo for
normal policy mode
USERENV(200.650) 01:41:25:249 GetGPOInfo:  ************************
USERENV(200.650) 01:41:25:249 GetGPOInfo:  Entering...
USERENV(200.650) 01:41:25:396 GetGPOInfo:  Server connection
established.
USERENV(200.650) 01:41:25:563 GetGPOInfo:  Bound successfully.
USERENV(200.650) 01:41:25:573 SearchDSObject:  Searching
<OU=GPMonitoredComputers,DC=sanao,DC=com>
USERENV(200.650) 01:41:25:573 SearchDSObject:  Found GPO(s):
<[LDAP://CN={BA2756CB-06A7-446A-A9B7-
2037C53745AD},CN=Policies,CN=System,DC=sanao,DC=com;0][LDAP://CN={08
B7C9EE-1684-48A6-93E4-
E8AF0149C1C2},CN=Policies,CN=System,DC=sanao,DC=com;0]>
USERENV(200.650) 01:41:25:573 ProcessGPO:  ========================
USERENV(200.650) 01:41:25:573 ProcessGPO:  Deferring search for
<LDAP://CN={BA2756CB-06A7-446A-A9B7-
2037C53745AD},CN=Policies,CN=System,DC=sanao,DC=com>
USERENV(200.650) 01:41:25:583 ProcessGPO:  ========================
USERENV(200.650) 01:41:25:583 ProcessGPO:  Deferring search for
<LDAP://CN={08B7C9EE-1684-48A6-93E4-
E8AF0149C1C2},CN=Policies,CN=System,DC=sanao,DC=com>
USERENV(200.650) 01:41:25:583 SearchDSObject:  Searching
<DC=sanao,DC=com>
USERENV(200.650) 01:41:25:583 SearchDSObject:  Found GPO(s):
<[LDAP://CN={31B2F340-016D-11D2-945F
00C04FB984F9},CN=Policies,CN=System,DC=sanao,DC=com;0]>
USERENV(200.650) 01:41:25:603 ProcessGPO:  ========================
USERENV(200.650) 01:41:25:603 ProcessGPO:  Deferring search for
<LDAP://CN={31B2F340-016D-11D2-945F-
00C04FB984F9},CN=Policies,CN=System,DC=sanao,DC=com>
USERENV(200.650) 01:41:25:721 SearchDSObject:  Searching
<CN=Default-First-Site-Name,CN=Sites,CN=Configuration,
DC=sanao,DC=com>
USERENV(200.650) 01:41:25:740 SearchDSObject:  No GPO(s) for this
object.
USERENV(200.650) 01:41:25:750 ProcessGPO:  ========================
USERENV(200.650) 01:41:25:750 ProcessGPO:  Searching <CN={31B2F340-
016D-11D2-945F-00C04FB984F9},CN=Policies,CN=System,DC=sanao,DC=com>
USERENV(200.650) 01:41:25:750 ProcessGPO:  Machine has access to
this GPO.
USERENV(200.650) 01:41:25:750 ProcessGPO:  GPO passes the filter
check.
USERENV(200.650) 01:41:25:750 ProcessGPO:  Found functionality
version of:  2
```

```
USERENV(200.650) 01:41:25:750 ProcessGPO:  Found file system path
of:  <\\sanao.com\sysvol\sanao.com\Policies\{31B2F340-016D-11D2-
945F-00C04FB984F9}>
USERENV(200.650) 01:41:25:957 ProcessGPO:  Found common name of:
<{31B2F340-016D-11D2-945F-00C04FB984F9}>
USERENV(200.650) 01:41:25:996 ProcessGPO:  Found display name of:
<Default Domain Policy>
USERENV(200.650) 01:41:26:006 ProcessGPO:  Found machine version of:
GPC is 3, GPT is 3
USERENV(200.650) 01:41:26:006 ProcessGPO:  Found flags of:  0
USERENV(200.650) 01:41:26:006 ProcessGPO:  Found extensions:
[{35378EAC-683F-11D2-A89A-00C04FBBCFA2}{53D6AB1B-2488-11D1-A28C-
00C04FB94F17}][{827D319E-6EAC-11D2-A4EA-00C04F79F83A}{803E14A0-B4FB-
11D0-A0D0-00A0C90F574B}][{B1BE8D72-6EAC-11D2-A4EA-00C04F79F83A}{53D6
AB1B-2488-11D1-A28C-00C04FB94F17}]
USERENV(200.650) 01:41:26:016 ProcessGPO:  ========================
USERENV(200.650) 01:41:26:016 ProcessGPO:  ========================
USERENV(200.650) 01:41:26:026 ProcessGPO:  Searching <CN={BA2756CB-
06A7-446A-A9B7-2037C53745AD},CN=Policies,CN=System,DC=sanao,DC=com>
USERENV(200.650) 01:41:26:035 ProcessGPO:  Machine has access to
this GPO.
USERENV(200.650) 01:41:26:045 ProcessGPO:  GPO passes the filter
check.
USERENV(200.650) 01:41:26:055 ProcessGPO:  Found functionality
version of:  2
USERENV(200.650) 01:41:26:065 ProcessGPO:  Found file system path
of:  <\\sanao.com\SysVol\sanao.com\Policies\{BA2756CB-06A7-446A-
A9B7-2037C53745AD}>
USERENV(200.650) 01:41:26:144 ProcessGPO:  Found common name of:
<{BA2756CB-06A7-446A-A9B7-2037C53745AD}>
USERENV(200.650) 01:41:26:153 ProcessGPO:  Found display name of:
<GPRefresh>
USERENV(200.650) 01:41:26:173 ProcessGPO:  Found machine version of:
GPC is 1, GPT is 1
USERENV(200.650) 01:41:26:183 ProcessGPO:  Found flags of:  0
USERENV(200.650) 01:41:26:193 ProcessGPO:  Found extensions:
[{35378EAC-683F-11D2-A89A-00C04FBBCFA2}{0F6B957D-509E-11D1-A7CC-
0000F87571E3}]
USERENV(200.650) 01:41:26:193 ProcessGPO:  ========================
USERENV(200.650) 01:41:26:203 ProcessGPO:  ========================
USERENV(200.650) 01:41:26:203 ProcessGPO:  Searching <CN={08B7C9EE-
1684-48A6-93E4-E8AF0149C1C2},CN=Policies,CN=System,DC=sanao,DC=com>
USERENV(200.650) 01:41:26:203 ProcessGPO:  Machine has access to
this GPO.
```

```
USERENV(200.650) 01:41:26:203 ProcessGPO:  GPO passes the filter
check.
USERENV(200.650) 01:41:26:203 ProcessGPO:  Found functionality
version of:  2
USERENV(200.650) 01:41:26:213 ProcessGPO:  Found file system path
of:  <\\sanao.com\SysVol\sanao.com\Policies\{08B7C9EE-1684-48A6-
93E4-E8AF0149C1C2}>
USERENV(200.650) 01:41:26:311 ProcessGPO:  Found common name of:
<{08B7C9EE-1684-48A6-93E4-E8AF0149C1C2}>
USERENV(200.650) 01:41:26:331 ProcessGPO:  Found display name of:
<OU-C-A-GPMonitorDeployment-v1.0>
USERENV(200.650) 01:41:26:331 ProcessGPO:  Found machine version of:
GPC is 5, GPT is 5
USERENV(200.650) 01:41:26:331 ProcessGPO:  Found flags of:  0
USERENV(200.650) 01:41:26:340 ProcessGPO:  Found extensions:
[{35378EAC-683F-11D2-A89A-00C04FBBCFA2}{0F6B957D-509E-11D1-A7CC-
0000F87571E3}][{C6DC5466-785A-11D2-84D0-00C04FB169F7}{942A8E4F-A261-
11D1-A760-00C04FB9603F}]
USERENV(200.650) 01:41:26:360 ProcessGPO:  ========================
USERENV(200.650) 01:41:26:370 GetGPOInfo:  GPO Local Group Policy
doesn't contain any data since the version number is 0.  It will be
skipped.
USERENV(200.650) 01:41:26:370 GetGPOInfo:  Leaving with 1
USERENV(200.650) 01:41:26:370 GetGPOInfo:  ************************
USERENV(200.650) 01:41:26:390 ProcessGPOs: Logging Data for Target
<LONSANAO21>.
USERENV(200.650) 01:41:26:419 ProcessGPOs: OpenThreadToken failed
with error 1008, assuming thread is not impersonating
USERENV(200.650) 01:41:26:429 ProcessGPOs: --------------------
USERENV(200.650) 01:41:26:429 ProcessGPOs: Processing extension
Registry
USERENV(200.650) 01:41:26:429 ReadStatus: Read Extension's Previous
status successfully.
USERENV(200.650) 01:41:26:429 CompareGPOLists:  The lists are the
same.
USERENV(200.650) 01:41:26:429 CheckGPOs: No GPO changes and no
security group membership change and extension Registry has
NoGPOChanges set.
USERENV(200.650) 01:41:26:429 ProcessGPOs: --------------------
```

As you can see, the first thing the engine does is check the speed of the connection. Next, the names of the computer, domain controller, and domain are determined. Then, an LDAP query can be done against the domain controller in order to find the applicable GPOs. The processing continues by checking if the GPO version numbers have changed and then determining which client-side extensions are needed to interpret the policies.

Detailed Logging

You can obtain more specific information for different Group Policy categories by enabling the logging in the registry. Table 7.21 lists the most common settings.

Table 7.21 Registry Values for Starting Detailed Logging

Key	Value	Type	Data	Log File	Purpose
`HKLM\Software\Microsoft\Windows NT\CurrentVersion\Winlogon`	`GPEdit-Debug-Level`	`REG_DWORD`	0x10002	%windir%\debug\usermode\gpedit.log	Troubleshooting GPO editing
`HKLM\Software\Microsoft\Windows NT\CurrentVersion\Winlogon`	`GPText-Debug-Level`	`REG_DWORD`	0x10002	%windir%\debug\usermode\gptext.log	Troubleshooting GPO editing
`HKLM\Software\Microsoft\Windows NT\CurrentVersion\Diagnostics`	`gpmgmt-trace-level`	`REG_DWORD`	1 (errors only) 2 (errors and verbose logging)	%temp%\gpmgmt.log	Troubleshooting GPMC
`HKLM\Software\Microsoft\Windows NT\CurrentVersion\Diagnostics`	`gpmgmt-logfile-only`	`REG_DWORD`	1	%temp%\gpmgmt.log	Troubleshooting GPMC
`HKLM\Software\Microsoft\Windows NT\CurrentVersion\Diagnostics`	`Fdeploy-Debug-Level`	`REG_DWORD`	0x0f	%windir%\debug\usermode\fdeploy.log	Troubleshooting folder redirection

Table 7.21 Registry Values for Starting Detailed Logging *(cont.)*

Key	Value	Type	Data	Log File	Purpose
HKLM\Software\ Microsoft\ WindowsNT\ CurrentVersion\ CurrentVersion\ Winlogon\ GpExtensions\ {827d319e-6eac-11d2-a4ea-00c04f79f83a}\	Exten-sion-Debug Level	REG_DWORD	0x2	%windir%\ security\ logs\ winlogon. log	Trouble-shooting security CSE
HKLM\ SOFTWARE\ Microsoft\ Windows NT\ CurrentVersion\ Diagnostics	App-mgmt-debug-level	REG_DWORD	0000009b	%windir%\ debug\ usermode\ appmgmt. log	Detailed software installa-tion logging
HKLM\ SOFTWARE\ Policies\ Microsoft\ Windows\ Installer	Debug-Log-ging	REG_DWORD REG_ STRING	00000003 "voice warm-up"	%windir%\ temp\ MSI*.log %temp%\ MSI*.log	Windows Installer trouble-shooting

Resource Kit Tools for Group Policy

Both the Windows 2000 Server and Professional Resource Kits include two tools for analyzing and troubleshooting Group Policy–related issues: Group Policy Results and Group Policy Verification Tool. You can find them in the Network Management Tool category. A third tool, Group Policy Migration, helps you to migrate NT 4.0 System Policy settings into Group Policy. It is located in the Deployment Tools category.

TIP You can also find some of these tools at `http://www.microsoft.com/windows2000/techinfo/reskit/tools/default.asp`

Group Policy Results was incorporated into Windows XP and is also integrated into Windows Server 2003. The new tools included in the Windows Server 2003 Resource Kit Tools are:

- ADM File Parser
- Group Policy Monitor
- Policy Spy

Group Policy Results

Group Policy Results (gpresult.exe) is a client-side analysis and troubleshooting tool that you can use to find, for example, the source of a client's Group Policy settings. For Windows XP and Server 2003, the tool has been vastly changed from Windows 2000 to incorporate RSoP data. Here is sample output of this tool (we have removed empty lines):

```
C:\>gpresult
Microsoft (R) Windows (R) XP Operating System Group Policy Result
tool v2.0
Copyright (C) Microsoft Corp. 1981-2001
Created On 3/23/2004 at 11:56:19 AM
RSOP results for SANAO\JackB on LONSANAO21 : Logging Mode
----------------------------------------------------------
OS Type:                       Microsoft Windows XP Professional
OS Configuration:              Member Workstation
OS Version:                    5.1.2600
Domain Name:                   SANAO
Domain Type:                   Windows 2000
Site Name:                     Default-First-Site-Name
Roaming Profile:
Local Profile:                 C:\Documents and Settings\JackB
Connected over a slow link?: No
COMPUTER SETTINGS
------------------
    CN=LONSANAO21,OU=GPMonitoredComputers,DC=sanao,DC=com
    Last time Group Policy was applied: 3/23/2004 at 11:56:02 AM
    Group Policy was applied from:      LONSanao1.sanao.com
    Group Policy slow link threshold:   500 kbps
    Applied Group Policy Objects
    -----------------------------
        OU-C-A-GPMonitorDeployment-v1.0
        GPRefresh
```

```
        Default Domain Policy
    The following GPOs were not applied because they were filtered out
    ---------------------------------------------------------------
        Local Group Policy
            Filtering:  Not Applied (Empty)
    The computer is a part of the following security groups:
    ---------------------------------------------------------
        BUILTIN\Administrators
        Everyone
        BUILTIN\Users
        LONSANAO21$
        Domain Computers
        NT AUTHORITY\NETWORK
        NT AUTHORITY\Authenticated Users
USER SETTINGS
--------------
    CN=Jack Brown,DC=sanao,DC=com
    Last time Group Policy was applied: 3/23/2004 at 11:55:19 AM
    Group Policy was applied from:      LONSanao1.sanao.com
    Group Policy slow link threshold:   500 kbps
    Applied Group Policy Objects
    -----------------------------
        Default Domain Policy
    The following GPOs were not applied because they were filtered out
    ---------------------------------------------------------------
        Local Group Policy
            Filtering:  Not Applied (Empty)
    The user is a part of the following security groups:
    -----------------------------------------------------
        Domain Users
        Everyone
        BUILTIN\Users
        LOCAL
        NT AUTHORITY\INTERACTIVE
        NT AUTHORITY\Authenticated Users
C:\>
```

The previous sample was run with no parameters. You can use /v for more detailed information and /z (or /s in Windows 2000) to see even the hex registry values. You can find further explanation of the output in the Resource Kit Help under "Interpreting GPResult Output."

NOTE Group Policy Results does not process the Local Computer Policy in Windows 2000. You must take this into consideration when you try to determine the effective policy settings.

Group Policy Verification Tool

Group Policy Verification Tool (gpotool.exe) is a server-side troubleshooting tool. You can use it to determine if the Group Policy components GPC and GPT are synchronized in a specific domain controller and among the domain controllers in the domain. The most valuable information the tool provides is an indication of whether all GPOs are synchronized. When everything has gone smoothly, the last line of the output is "Policies OK," as in the following sample:

```
C:\>gpotool
Validating DCs...
Available DCs:
LONSales1.sales.sanao.com
LONSALES2.sales.sanao.com
Searching for policies...
Found 2 policies
============================================================
Policy {31B2F340-016D-11D2-945F-00C04FB984F9}
Friendly name: Default Domain Policy
Policy OK
============================================================
Policy {6AC1786C-016F-11D2-945F-00C04FB984F9}
Friendly name: Default Domain Controllers Policy
Policy OK
============================================================
Policies OK
C:\>
```

In the preceding example, there were two domain controllers, and only the default policies (Default Domain Policy and Default Domain Controllers Policy) existed. In the next example, we add one GPO, called DO-U-R-SanaoGeneralGPOver1.0, with one computer setting. The output of the gpotool command is as follows:

```
C:\>gpotool
Validating DCs...
Available DCs:
```

```
LONSales1.sales.sanao.com
LONSALES2.sales.sanao.com
Searching for policies...
Found 3 policies
============================================================
Policy {31B2F340-016D-11D2-945F-00C04FB984F9}
Friendly name: Default Domain Policy
Policy OK
============================================================
Policy {5A59A545-E706-4DDB-94F4-EA77D0440C86}
Friendly name: DO-U-R-SanaoGeneralGPOver1.0
Error: Policy {5A59A545-E706-4DDB-94F4-EA77D0440C86}
       not found on DC LONSALES2.sales.sanao.com
Details:
------------------------------------------------------------
DC: LONSales1.sales.sanao.com
Friendly name: DO-U-R-SanaoGeneralGPOver1.0
Created: 3/22/2004 5:37:32 PM
Changed: 3/22/2004 5:37:33 PM
DS version:     0(user) 0(machine)
Sysvol version: 0(user) 0(machine)
Flags: 0 (user side enabled; machine side enabled)
User extensions: not found
Machine extensions: not found
Functionality version: 2
------------------------------------------------------------
------------------------------------------------------------
DC: LONSALES2.sales.sanao.com
Friendly name: (null)
Created: (null)
Changed: (null)
DS version: (null)
Sysvol version: (null)
Flags: (null)
User extensions: (null)
Machine extensions: (null)
Functionality version: (null)
------------------------------------------------------------
============================================================
Policy {6AC1786C-016F-11D2-945F-00C04FB984F9}
Friendly name: Default Domain Controllers Policy
Policy OK
============================================================
Errors found
C:\>
```

In the preceding example, the GPO had not yet replicated to domain controller LONSALES2. Thus, there was an error because the GPO did not exist yet on that domain controller. This can be interpreted from all fields having a NULL value.

As you may have noticed, gpotool only expands those GPOs that have errors. If you want to also analyze the processing and the contents of the GPOs with no errors, you can use the `/verbose` switch.

ADM File Parser

ADM File Parser (admX.exe) is a useful utility for analyzing administrative template files. You can use it to export the settings in an administrative template file into a text file, where individual settings are written on separate lines. The other way to use this tool is to compare two .adm files. For example, after you have copied the system.adm file from %systemroot%\inf on a Windows XP SP2 computer to C:\Data, you could use the following command to compare the settings contained in that file to those in Windows Server 2003:

```
C:\Data:\>"C:\Program Files\Microsoft\admX\admX.exe"
C:\WINDOWS\inf\system.adm /diff:C:\Data\system.adm
/output:C:\Data\DiffbetweenW2k3andWXPSP2System.admFull
          .txt /all
```

The output of the tool consists of the following fields:

- Computer/User Node
- Policy Path
- Symbolic Policy Name
- Full Policy Name
- Registry Settings
- Supported on
- Help/Explain Text

In order to install the ADM File Parser, you must first install Windows Server 2003 Resource Kit Tools. Only then can you start C:\Program Files\Windows Resource Kits\Tools\admx.msi. By default, the setup installs the executable, admX.exe, and the configuration file admX.exe.config into the C:\Program Files\Microsoft\admX folder. In the configuration file, there is a requirement for .NET Framework 1.0. Unless you have it installed (Windows Server 2003 and Windows XP SP2 include version 1.1), you can add the following line before the line reading </startup>:

```
<supportedRuntime version="v1.1.4322" />
```

In addition, the user running the tool must have the Write permission on the folder where he or she runs it. This is because the tool writes a log file called admX.log into that folder. If you want to use .adm files in a remote location, you must use a mapped drive letter since ADM File Parser does not support UNC paths.

NOTE ADM File Parser is a new tool for the Windows Server 2003 Resource Kit.

Group Policy Monitor

Group Policy Monitor installs a service (named Group Policy Monitor) that monitors GPOs when they are refreshed. The report for each GPO refresh is archived in RSoP file format into .cab files that are stored on a UNC path. You must configure a network share where the data is written. Figure 7.49 illustrates Group Policy refreshes in a small network.

In order to install Group Policy Monitor, you must first install Windows Server 2003 Resource Kit Tools. Then you will have C:\Program Files\Windows Resource Kits\Tools\gpmonitor.exe. You can execute this file and define that it is extracted into some folder—for example, C:\Program Files\Windows Resource Kits\Tools\GPMonitor. You will find in that folder the four files that are listed in Table 7.22.

In the lab environment, you can install GPMonitor into your own workstation and use the .adm file with the Local Computer Policy to configure the required settings.

You can start GPMonitor from Administrative Tools on the Start menu.

NOTE Group Policy Monitor is a new tool for the Windows Server 2003 Resource Kit.

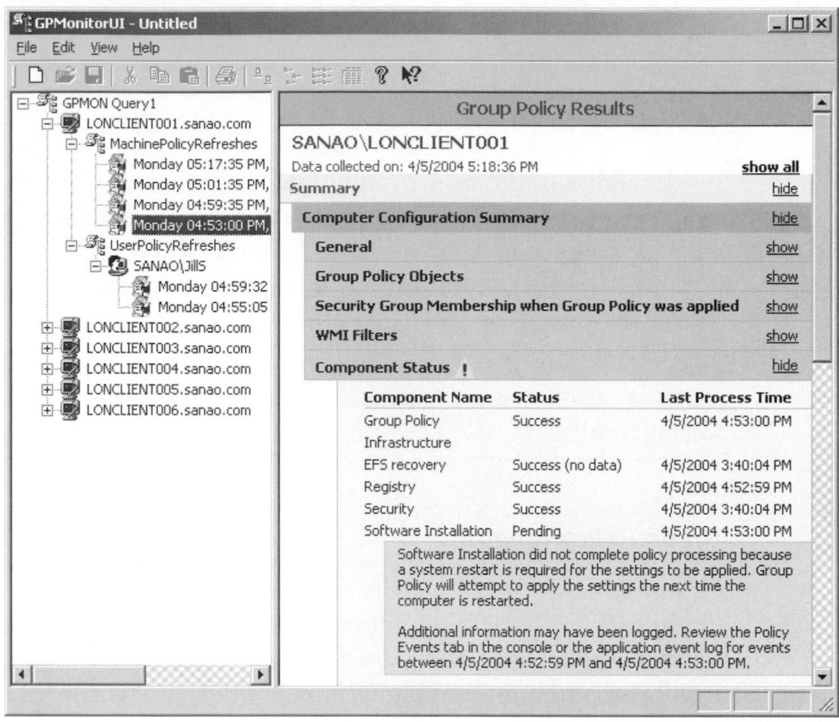

Figure 7.49 You can monitor Group Policy events for a group of computers with Group Policy Monitor.

Table 7.22 Files Included with Group Policy Monitor

File	Purpose	Notes
GPMON.cab GPMonitor.msi	Installation files for the service	Deployed to certain computers with Group Policy application deployment package assigned to computers; defaults to %windir%\system32\GPMON, where the main components GPMonSrv.exe and GPMonUI.exe are installed
GPMonitor.adm	Used as the administrative template of a GPO to define the GPMonitor settings	Defines the remote share for analysis files and the frequency of policy refreshes that are captured
GPMonitor.chm	Contains brief online help	

Policy Spy

Policy Spy (%ProgramFiles%\Windows Resource Kits\Tools\winpolicies.exe) is a very versatile tool for GP troubleshooting. Figure 7.50 illustrates the tool, which contains the following functionality:

- Initiating computer/user Group Policy processing (gpupdate/secedit)
- Pausing computer/user Group Policy processing for ten minutes
- Providing access to Event Viewer and primary troubleshooting files (appmgmt.log, gpedit.log, userenv.log, and fdeploy.log)
- Listing applying computer and user GPOs
- Dumping GP-related registry information
- Getting/setting three GP troubleshooting registry values

NOTE Policy Spy is a new tool for the Windows Server 2003 Resource Kit.

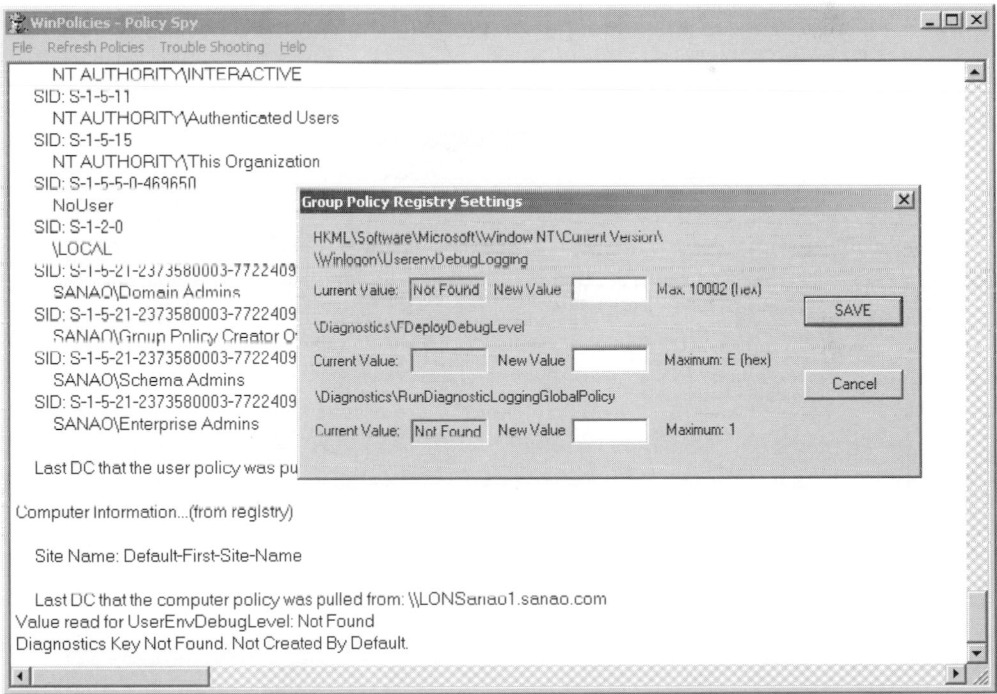

Figure 7.50 You can use Policy Spy to initiate various Group Policy actions or to dump/set information on Group Policy–related registry settings.

Replication Monitor

Replication Monitor is part of the Windows 2000/Server 2003 Resource Kit Support Tools. It has many capabilities for advanced analysis of replication issues. If you want to analyze GPOs on a domain controller within your Active Directory forest with this tool, you right-click the domain controller and select Show Group Policy Object Status from the context menu. Figure 7.51 displays sample output for this option. The Version column shows the GPC version, and the SysVol Version column shows the version of GPT. If they are not in sync for any GPO, a check mark is displayed in the Sync Status column.

Group Policy Migration

Because the location of the System Policy settings in the registry differs between Windows NT 4.0 and Windows 2000, a tool, gpolmig.exe, was created to migrate the settings from NT 4.0 System Policy files (ntconfig.pol) into the Windows 2000 GPO structure.

NOTE This tool is no longer included in the Windows Server 2003 Resource Kit Tools.

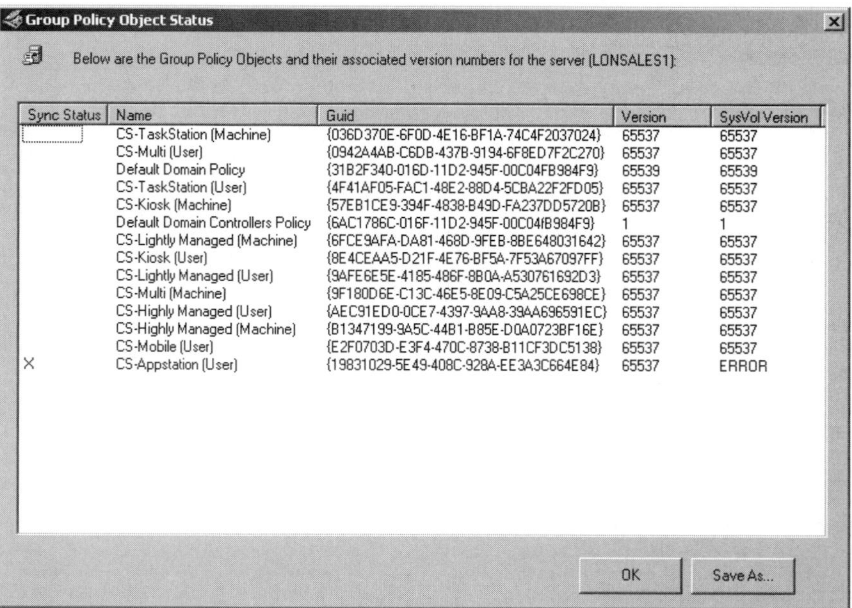

Figure 7.51 You can use Replication Monitor to display Group Policy Object status.

Group Policy Reference

The Windows 2000 Resource Kit Group Policy Reference (gp.chm) is an online Help file that contains all the same information as the Explain tabs for the Administrative Templates. In addition, the Reference contains hyperlinks and explanations for the security settings that are not available through the Group Policy dialog boxes.

NOTE The reference for security settings is incorporated into Windows Server 2003 online Help.

FAZAM 2000 RFV

The Windows 2000 Server Resource Kit Supplement 1 contains a third-party product called FAZAM 2000 RFV (Reduced Functionality Version). You could use this tool to analyze and report on group policies. In addition, it provides the capability to back up GPOs. However, most of the valuable functionality has been removed from this free version. The full version is only available at `http://www.fullarmor.com/` at a cost. Some of the most valuable additional functionality that the full version contains is versioning for GPOs and check-out/in for editing. Full Armor has also launched products called FAZAM GPAnywhere!, for managing Local Computer Policies for those computers that are not members of Active Directory, and FAZAM Auditing, for auditing Group Policy operations.

NOTE Group Policy Management Console contains all the functionality of FAZAM 2000 RFV.

Advanced Topics

In this last section, we discuss some topics that might be good for you to know, especially when you're troubleshooting or if you want to know Group Policy in more detail. First we present Group Policy–related registry settings that you can define centrally with Group Policy Administrative Templates. We also list the client-side extensions for Group Policy as well as registry values that they use, Group Policy History, and the storage for WMI filters and IPSec policies.

Registry-Based Settings for Group Policy Processing

For centrally managing Group Policy processing, there are 22 Group Policy–related registry settings for computer objects and 8 for user objects. You can locate the settings for both Computer and User Configurations in any GPO under Administrative Templates, System, Group Policy. Table 7.23 and Table 7.24 list each setting along with its purpose.

Table 7.23 Registry-Based Settings for Group Policy Processing for Computer Objects

Setting	Is Used to Define	Note
Turn off background refresh of Group Policy	Whether group policies can refresh periodically	Titled "Disable background refresh of Group Policy" in Windows 2000. Requires restart to take effect.
Apply Group Policy for computers asynchronously during start-up	Whether the logon dialog box is displayed before computer policies are completely processed	Only available in Windows 2000.
Apply Group Policy for users asynchronously during start-up	Whether the user sees and can use the shell (Windows Explorer by default) before user policies are completely processed	Only available in Windows 2000.
Group Policy refresh interval for computers	How often the computer policies are refreshed in the background for Windows 2000/XP workstations and servers that are not domain controllers	Default 90 minutes plus offset of 0 to 30 minutes. Default also applies if this policy is disabled. Available range for the interval is 0 to 64,800 minutes (45 days). If set to 0, the group policies are refreshed every 7 seconds. Available range for the offset is 0 to 1,440 minutes (24 hours). Ignored if "Turn off background refresh of Group Policy" is enabled.

Table 7.23 Registry-Based Settings for Group Policy Processing for Computer Objects (*cont.*)

Setting	Is Used to Define	Note
Group Policy refresh interval for domain controllers	How often the computer policies are refreshed in the background for Windows 2000/Server 2003 domain controllers	Default 5 minutes with zero offset. Default also applies if this policy is disabled. Available range for the interval is 0 to 64,800 minutes (45 days). If set to 0, the group policies are refreshed every 7 seconds. Available range for the offset is 0 to 1,440 minutes (24 hours). Ignored if set in Local Computer Policy or if "Turn off background refresh of Group Policy" is enabled.
User Group Policy loopback processing mode	Whether user policies based on the location of the computer object are in effect	Options: Replace and Merge. Both the computer and the user account must be in Active Directory.
Allow Cross-Forest User Policy and Roaming User Profiles	Whether policy based on the location of the user object in a trusted forest and the roaming profile, and the logon script defined per user object are processed when logging across forest trust. If not configured, these are not processed; the user receives a local profile, and she is presented with a roaming profile warning; two events are logged into the event log; and loopback processing will be applied in replace mode	Disabled same as Not configured. New for Windows 2000 SP4 and Windows Server 2003

(*continued*)

Table 7.23 Registry-Based Settings for Group Policy Processing for Computer Objects (*cont.*)

Setting	Is Used to Define	Note
Group Policy slow link detection	Threshold for determining if the connection to the authenticating domain controller is slow	Applies to computer policies. Default 500Kbps; enabled with value 0 disables slow link detection (i.e., all connections are considered fast). Available range is 0 to 4,294,967,196Kbps. See related settings in Computer Configuration\Administrative Templates\System\User Profiles.
Turn off Resultant Set of Policy logging	Whether RSoP logging is on to be used by MMC console rsop.msc	RSoP logging is on by default. Not available for Windows 2000.
Remove users ability to invoke machine policy refresh	Whether nonadministrators can initiate computer policy processing manually	Not available for Windows 2000. Only applies to Windows XP and Server 2003 computers. Requires restart to take effect.
Disallow Interactive Users from generating Resultant Set of Policy data	Whether interactive nonadministrators can view their own RSoP data with MMC console rsop.msc	Not available for Windows 2000. Only applies to Windows XP and Server 2003 computers.
Registry policy processing	When the policies changing registry settings are processed	Options for background and unchanged GPO.
Internet Explorer Maintenance policy processing	When the Internet Explorer Maintenance policies are processed	Options for slow link, background, and unchanged GPO.
Software Installation policy processing	When software is deployed	Options for slow link and unchanged GPO; does not work on Local Computer Policy.
Folder Redirection policy processing	When folder redirection policies are processed	Options for slow link and unchanged GPO.

Table 7.23 Registry-Based Settings for Group Policy Processing for Computer Objects (*cont.*)

Setting	Is Used to Define	Note
Scripts policy processing	When any Group Policy scripts are processed	Options for slow link, background, and unchanged GPO
Security policy processing	When security policies are processed	Options for background and unchanged GPO.
IP Security policy processing	When any Group Policy IPSec policies are processed	Options for slow link, background, and unchanged GPO.
Wireless policy processing	When wireless policies are processed	Options for slow link, background, and unchanged GPO.
EFS recovery policy processing	When EFS policies are processed	Options for slow link, background, and unchanged GPO.
Disk Quota policy processing	When disk quota policies are processed	Options for slow link, background, and unchanged GPO.
Always use local ADM files for Group Policy Object Editor	Whether .adm files in %systemroot%\inf are used	By default, the .adm files stored in the GPO are used. If enabled and if not all .adm files are available, some settings may not appear. New for Windows Server 2003 and only applies to Windows Server 2003 computers.

Client-Side Extensions

Client-side extensions (CSEs) are the components that actually process the Group Policy settings defined in the Local Computer Policy or in GPOs stored in the Active Directory. These CSEs are registered in the registry in `HKEY_LOCAL_MACHINE \SOFTWARE\Microsoft\Windows NT\CurrentVersion\Winlogon\GPExtensions`. Table 7.25 lists the GUIDs for different client-side extensions along with the names of the dynamic link library (DLL) files they use. The only Group Policy

Table 7.24 Registry-Based Settings for Group Policy Processing for User Objects

Setting	Is Used to Define	Note
Group Policy refresh interval for users	How often the user policies are refreshed in the background	Default 90 minutes plus offset of 0 to 30 minutes. Default also applies if this policy is disabled. Available range for the interval is 0 to 64,800 minutes (45 days). If set to 0, the group policies are refreshed every 7 seconds. Available range for the offset is 0 to 1,440 minutes (24 hours). Ignored if Computer Configuration\Administrative Templates\System\Group Policy\Turn off background refresh of Group Policy is enabled.
Group Policy slow link detection	Threshold for determining if the connection to the authenticating domain controller is slow	Applies to computer policies. Default 500Kbps; enabled with value 0 disables slow link detection (i.e., all connections are considered fast). Available range is 0 to 4,294,967,196Kbps.
Group Policy domain controller selection	Which domain controller the Group Policy snap-in focuses on (i.e., on which DC the changes are actually made)	Options for PDC, same as Active Directory snap-ins and any domain controller.
Create new Group Policy object links disabled by default	Whether links are created disabled	You can enable them later after you have configured GPOs and tested them.
Default name for new Group Policy objects	Default display name for new GPOs	Maximum length is 255 characters
Enforce Show Policies Only	Whether the user can deselect "Show Policies only" in the Group Policy snap-in	Determines if preferences can be displayed and configured.

Table 7.24 Registry-Based Settings for Group Policy Processing for User Objects (*cont.*)

Setting	Is Used to Define	Note
Disable automatic update of ADM files	Whether the system loads the most current .adm files from %SystemRoot%\inf	If enabled, you must manually update the .adm files if they are changed. You can achieve this through right-clicking Add/Remove Templates for Administrative Templates.
Disallow Interactive Users from generating Resultant Set of Policy data	Whether nonadministrators can view their own RSoP data with MMC console rsop.msc	Not available for Windows 2000. Applies only to Windows XP and Server 2003 computers

Table 7.25 Client-Side Extension GUIDs and DLLs as They Appear in the Registry (Sorted by GUIDs)

Client-Side Extension	GUID	DLL
Wireless Group Policy	0ACDD40C-75AC-47ab-BAA0-BF6DE7E7FE63	gptext.dll
Folder Redirection	25537BA6-77A8-11D2-9B6C-0000F8080861	fdeploy.dll
Registry Settings	35378EAC-683F-11D2-A89A-00C04FBBCFA2	userenv.dll
Microsoft Disk Quota	3610EDA5-77EF-11D2-8DC5-00C04FA31A66	dskquota.dll
QoS Packet Scheduler	426031c0-0b47-4852-b0ca-ac3d37bfcb39	gptext.dll
Scripts	42B5FAAE-6536-11D2-AE5A-0000F87571E3	gptext.dll
Security	827D319E-6EAC-11D2-A4EA-00C04F79F83A	scecli.dll
Internet Explorer Branding	A2E30F80-D7DE-11d2-BBDE-00C04F86AE3B	iedkcs32.dll
EFS Recovery	B1BE8D72-6EAC-11D2-A4EA-00C04F79F83A	scecli.dll

(continued)

Table 7.25 Client-Side Extension GUIDs and DLLs as They Appear in the Registry (Sorted by GUIDs) *(cont.)*

Client-Side Extension	GUID	DLL
Software Installation	c6dc5466-785a-11d2-84d0-00c04fb169f7	appmgmts.dll
IP Security	e437bc1c-aa7d-11d2-a382-00c04f991e27	gptext.dll

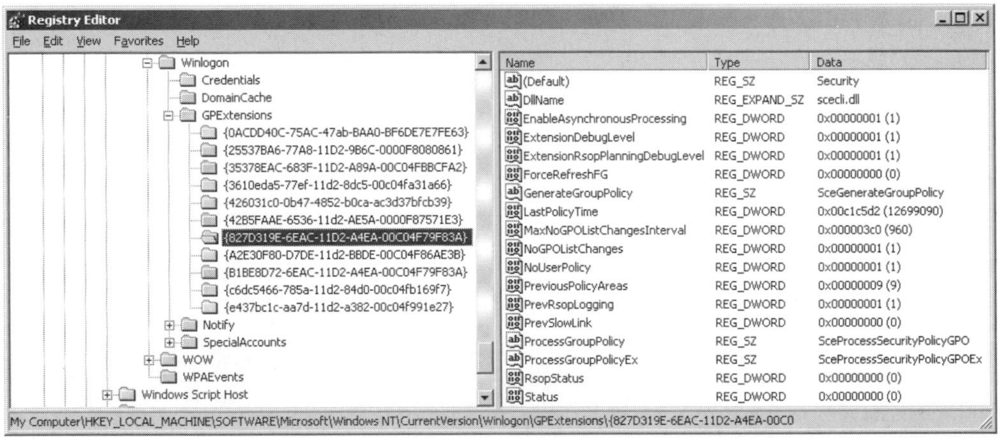

Figure 7.52 Client-side extensions are registered in the registry.

component that does not have a client-side extension is the Remote Installation Services (RIS). This is because the purpose of the RIS is to install the operating system, which obviously cannot have any DLLs before the installation is complete.

In Figure 7.52, notice that some of the registry settings that we introduced in the previous section are also defined per CSE.

Registry Settings for Group Policy History

As a result of Group Policy processing, certain settings for GPOs are written to the client's registry, forming what is called *Group Policy History*. These settings are organized by the client-side extension that processed them. You can find them under `HKEY_LOCAL_MACHINE\Software\Microsoft\Windows\CurrentVersion\Group Policy\History` for GPOs applied to the computer, and

Table 7.26 Group Policy History Registry Values

Value	Purpose
`DisplayName`	Name displayed in the Active Directory administration tools.
`DSPath`	LDAP path to the GPC. Not available for the Local Computer Policy.
`Extensions`	Bracket-separated ([]) list of GUIDs for client-side extensions that have settings defined in this GPO. Within each entry there are two or more GUIDs delimited with braces ({}). The first GUID in each entry contains the CSE that processes the GPO and applies them to the client. The other GUIDs identify MMC snap-ins and their extensions that are used to manage the settings for this CSE. If Disable Computer Configuration Settings is checked in the policy's properties, this property has no value.
`FileSysPath`	Path of the GPT for Active Directory–based GPO; %System Root%\system32\GroupPolicy for the Local Computer Policy.
`GPOLink`	Indicates what type of container this GPO is linked to: 0=unlinked, 1=local, 2=site, 3=domain, 4=OU.
`GPOName`	GUID of the GPO stored in Active Directory; Local Group Policy for the Local Computer Policy.
`Link`	Domain where this GPO resides; Local for the Local Computer Policy.
`IParam`	Used to perform various functions
`Options`	Indicates whether computer or user sections are disabled. If both are enabled, the value for this property is 0. If Disable User Configuration Settings is checked in the policy's properties, this property has the value 1, and if Disable Computer Configuration Settings is checked in the policy's properties, this property has the value 2. The value 3 means that both are disabled.
`Version`	Version number of the GPO that was last applied.

`HKEY_CURRENT_USER\Software\Microsoft\Windows\Current Version\Group Policy\History` for GPOs applied to the user. Under each of the GUIDs for installed CSEs there is a key for each GPO applied. These are given numbers starting from zero and incremented by one. The larger the number, the later in the processing cycle this GPO was processed (i.e., its priority would be higher). Table 7.26 lists these values and their purposes.

Table 7.27 Attributes of a WMI Filter

Value	Purpose
`msWMI-Author`	Displays the user principal name for the creator of the filter
`msWMI-ChangeDate`	As the name implies
`msWMI-CreationDate`	As the name implies
`msWMI-ID`	GUID for the filter
`msWMI-Name`	Name
`msWMI-Parm1`	Description
`msWMI-Parm2`	The actual WQL query

Storage of WMI Filters

WMI filters are stored as msWMI-Som objects in `CN=SOM,CN=WMI Policy,CN=System,DC=sanao,DC=com`. Table 7.27 lists the important attributes of WMI filter objects.

Storage of IPSec policies

When you open Computer Configuration\Windows Settings\Security Settings\IP Security Policies on Active Directory (`sanao.com`) in the Group Policy Object Editor, you see a list of IPSec policies that are stored as `ipsecPolicy` objects in `CN=IP Security,CN=System, DC=`*`<domain>`*. If you decide to assign one of these policies to the GPO, a link is created and stored as the `ipsecOwnersReference` attribute of the `ipsecPolicy` object in `CN=IPSEC,CN=Windows, CN=Microsoft,CN=Machine,CN={GUID for GPO},CN=Policies, CN=System,DC=`*`<domain>`*. You can link one IPSec policy to several GPOs by assigning the policy in that GPO.

`IpsecPolicy` objects in the System container are linked to `ipsecNFA` and `ipsecISAKMPPolicy` objects in the same container. `IpsecNFA` objects are linked to `ipsecNegotiationPolicy` and `ipsecFilter` objects.

Unfortunately, configuring IPSec policies is not much easier than trying to track associated items in Active Directory.

Conclusion

Group Policy is the main management infrastructure for administering resources in Active Directory. It is complex, but after you have mastered it and deployed Group Policy in your Active Directory network, you'll surely reap the benefits.

However, as you can see from the rather cumbersome and sometimes complicated ways of performing tasks, Windows 2000 and even Windows Server 2003 left plenty of room for improvement. The new Group Policy Management Console tool doesn't leave much for a wish list. Also, since it enables transferring GPOs and their settings between domains and even forests with such ease, you might want to create a test domain in which you can plan and evaluate your GPOs before bringing them into production.

PART III

Advanced Skills

CHAPTER 8

Active Directory Schema

This chapter describes the Active Directory data model and the way in which the rules of the schema enforce it. You can approach this chapter with the following three purposes:

- To understand better how Active Directory works behind the scenes
- To enhance administration by learning, for example, which attributes are indexed to make searches faster
- To learn the technical background to extend the schema of your forest and to prepare you for the next chapter about schema extensions

This chapter has the following sections:

- Overview of the Active Directory data model
- Schema in general
- Classes
- Attributes and syntaxes

Overview of the Active Directory Data Model

Active Directory uses the LDAP data model, which is derived from the X.500 data model, and, consequently, Active Directory implements many X.500 features. However, Active Directory is not a full X.500 directory service.

In this first section we introduce the Active Directory data model, including most notably classes and attributes, as well as their relationship to the normal user and other objects that you see in your domains.

Classes, Objects, and Attributes

As you know, information in Active Directory is represented as objects, and there is an object for each user, computer, printer, and so on. Objects of the same type belong to the same *class,* so all user objects belong to the class `user`, all computer objects to the class `computer`, and all printer objects to the class `printQueue`.

You also know that information in an object is stored as values of various *properties,* which the corresponding class supports. For example, a user may have a phone number and home folder, whereas a printer might have knowledge about supported forms or print speed. Because this chapter is about the inner architecture of Active Directory, we want to use the slightly fancier term *attribute* instead of *property.* You can use these two words interchangeably.

The *schema* dictates which object classes and attributes a given forest supports. The *base schema* that ships with Windows Server 2003 supports 191 object classes (142 in AD2000) and 1,070 attributes for those classes (863 in AD2000). The `user` class uses 257 attributes of the pool of 1,070 (207 in AD2000). Active Directory implements most of the X.500 standard classes, but not quite all. The classes that it does not implement are `alias` and `strongAuthenticationUser`.

NOTE The attribute pool is common to all classes. The `description` attribute, for example, may be used by several classes (actually, all classes use it).

Bringing in another fancy term, you could say that each object is an *instantiation* of the corresponding class. For example, the Jack Brown object is an instantiation of the `user` class. Just as the class contains a number of attributes, the instantiated object contains the values for those attributes. However, only some of the attributes for a class are *mandatory,* which means that they must contain a value (a *single-valued* attribute such as `homePhone`) or values (a *multivalued* attribute such as `otherHomePhone`). Most of the attributes for a given class are *optional;* that is, they may contain a value, but more often they don't. Figure 8.1 shows these relationships.

NOTE You can see only a small subset of object types in the Users and Computers snap-in and only a subset of attributes for each object.

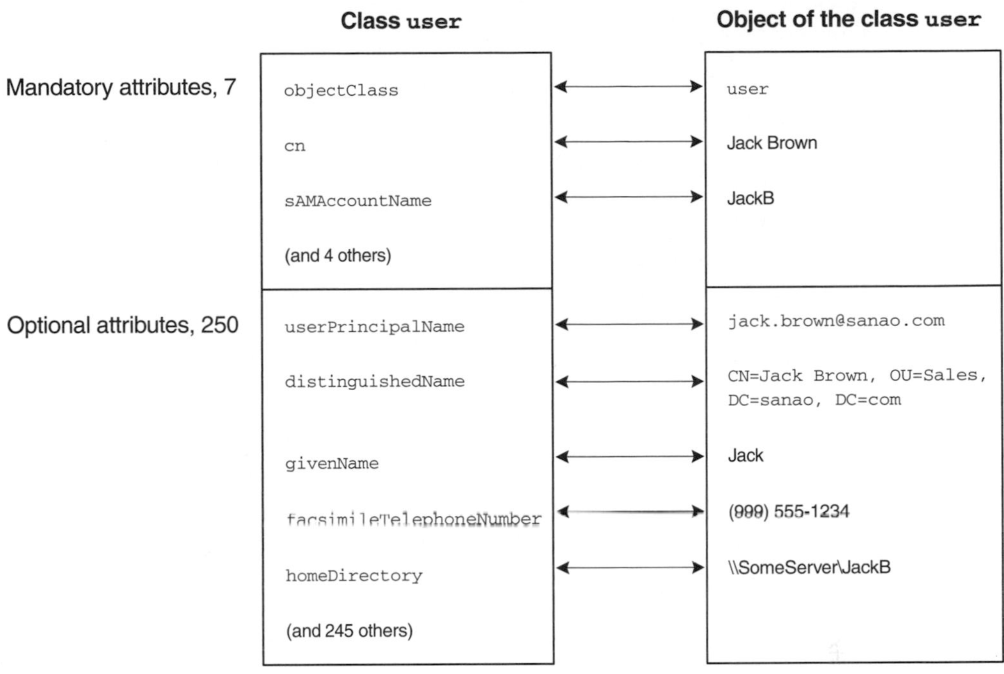

Figure 8.1 The class `user` defines 7 mandatory and 250 optional attributes for which any user object must *or* may contain values.

NOTE To create user objects with the Users and Computers snap-in, you must enter the user principal name (i.e., user logon name), even though it is just an optional attribute in the schema behind the scenes.

Each attribute has one of 23 *syntaxes,* such as `Integer` 14, `Unicode string` "abc", or `Generalized time` 04/26/2000 2:59:01 PM. We discuss syntaxes later in this chapter.

As you see in Figure 8.2, some of the classes (actually, most of them) are something other than the familiar users, groups, and computers.

Container and Leaf Objects

Active Directory objects of some classes are *container objects,* and the objects of the remaining classes are *leaf objects.* If you compare this to a file system, container objects correspond to folders and leaf objects correspond to files. We call these two types of classes *container classes* and *leaf classes.*

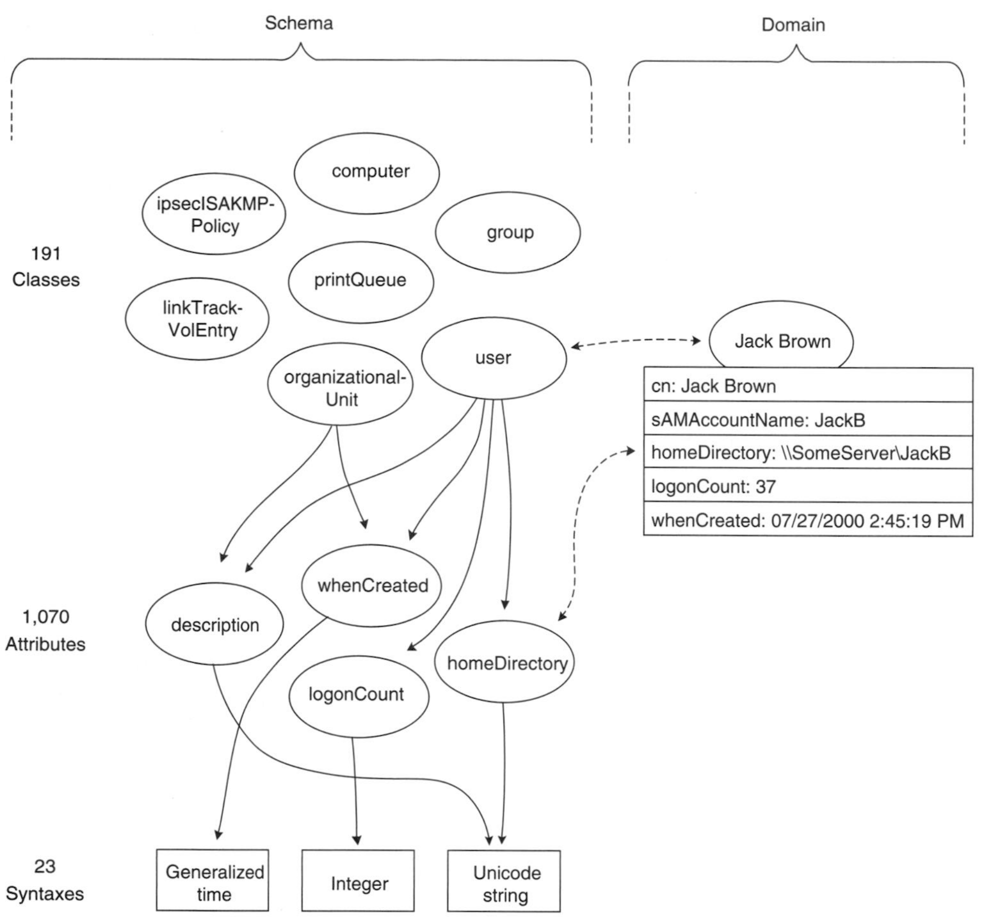

Figure 8.2 Each of the 191 classes uses a number of attributes, which in turn use a certain syntax.

One obvious example of a container class is `organizationalUnit`. There are also many others, however, because a total of 67 classes of the base schema are container classes and 124 are leaf classes (56 and 86 in AD2000). Interestingly, `user` is also a container class; `user` objects may contain `nTFRSSubscriptions` and `classStore` objects.

NOTE "Container" can also mean a specific class—one of the 67 container classes is called `container`. Two examples of this class are `CN=Users` and `CN=Computers`, which you see with the Users and Computers snap-in under any domain.

Even though the base schema contains 124 leaf classes, those classes are not doomed to "eternal leafhood." You can modify the schema to make a leaf class a possible superior (i.e., a parent) to some other class. When you do so, a former leaf class (except for schema objects) becomes a container class.

One difference in our file system analogy is that in Active Directory both containers and leafs contain data, whereas in a file system files contain data, but folders don't.

NOTE Just as there is a class called `container`, one of the 124 leaf classes is called `leaf`. You can make also that class a container, so one of your container classes could be called `leaf`.

Indexing and the Global Catalog

An Active Directory database can contain thousands or even millions of objects. Therefore, we obviously need *indexing* to locate the right object or objects fast. Of the base schema, 69 attributes are indexed (64 in AD2000), examples being `givenName`, `sn` (Surname) and `birthLocation`. Searching and retrieving objects via indexed attributes is naturally much faster and efficient than using nonindexed attributes.

The *global catalog* helps in making local searches in a multidomain forest. One hundred fifty-one attributes of the base schema are part of the global catalog (138 in AD2000), including `cn`, `userPrincipalName`, `givenName`, `sn` (Surname), and `printStaplingSupported`.

Schema

In this section we explain the role of the schema, its location, and its inspection. We also explain briefly the topics of subschema subentry and schema cache.

Role of the Schema

The schema contains rules for object instantiation—that is, it dictates which objects a directory can contain, their relationships, and their possible content. (This is true for other directory services as well as Active Directory.) In other words, the schema governs the structure and content of Active Directory with structure and content rules. Table 8.1 explains these uses of the schema.

Table 8.1 describes why the schema is necessary to maintain a directory. In addition, the schema contains information that helps to maintain the schema itself. This is described in Table 8.2. We explore the topics introduced in Table 8.1 and Table 8.2 in the later sections "Classes" and "Attributes and Syntaxes."

Table 8.1 Uses of the Schema

Category	Description
Structure rules	– Possible parent classes for each class (i.e., under what classes of objects each object can exist). For example, a user object may exist under the container types `organizationalUnit`, `domainDNS`, `builtinDomain`, `organization`, `container`, and `lostAndFound`.
Content rules	– The mandatory and optional attributes for each object class. – For each attribute there is a certain syntax and value range, as well as the choice between single-value and multivalue.
Miscellaneous	– Which attributes are indexed and which are stored in the global catalog. – The default security descriptor, category, and hiding value for each new object. – The name type (i.e., the naming attribute) of a class: CN, OU, or DC.

Table 8.2 Inside Uses of the Schema

Category	Description
Naming and identification	Various names and ID numbers for schema classes, attributes, and syntaxes
Schema class hierarchy	– Whether a class is *structural, abstract,* or *auxiliary* – The parent of a class in the inheritance chain – The auxiliary classes that give a class additional attributes
Protection	– Whether a class or attribute is *system-only* – The security descriptor for a class or attribute

Location of the Schema

Because everything in Active Directory is stored in objects, the schema is implemented as a number of objects. There is one object for each class in the schema (`classSchema` objects) and one for each attribute (`attributeSchema` objects). However, there are no objects for the syntaxes; they are hard-coded into Active Directory. This means that classes and attributes can be created and modified, but syntaxes cannot.

NOTE A directory service vendor could implement the schema as a long text file. Microsoft chose to implement the Active Directory schema as Active Directory objects. This enables administrators and applications to query the schema contents and add or modify classes and attributes using the same object manipulation techniques as would be used with any Active Directory objects.

Consequently, the location of the schema is the location of the schema objects.

The Physical Location of the Schema

As you learned in Chapter 5, every domain controller stores a full replica (or copy) of three partitions (or replication units): the schema, configuration, and domain partitions. Obviously, the schema (i.e., the schema objects) is physically located in the schema partition.

You also learned that the schema partition is replicated to every domain controller in a forest, so that all domain controllers contain identical information. Any changes to the schema would have to be initiated on the domain controller that holds the schema master role (as explained in Chapter 5).

Even though there are three separate partitions, their replicas in a given domain controller are stored in the same database table. That table resides in the Active Directory database file, which is called ntds.dit. The default location for the file is the folder C:\Winnt\NTDS.

There is another ntds.dit file, located in C:\Winnt\System32. That file serves as the initial database file and it is copied to C:\Winnt\NTDS (or whatever location you choose) during the DCPromo process.

NOTE You may also come up with a file schema.ini (in C:\Winnt\System32). Despite its name, it doesn't initialize the schema in any way. Instead, it contains the information for the initial objects in your tree—mostly for the domain and configuration partitions.

The Logical Location of the Schema

All the 1,261 schema objects (191 classes and 1,070 attributes) are located in the *Schema container*. That container is of class `dMD` (the letters stand for "directory management domain") and its distinguished name is `CN=Schema, CN=Configuration, DC=`*`forest_root_domain`*. Figure 8.3 shows the location of the Schema container in the directory tree.

NOTE Although there seems to be a `CN=Configuration` object under your root domain, you won't see it in the Users and Computers snap-in, even with Advanced Features turned on. That snap-in is meant to show contents of only domain partitions.

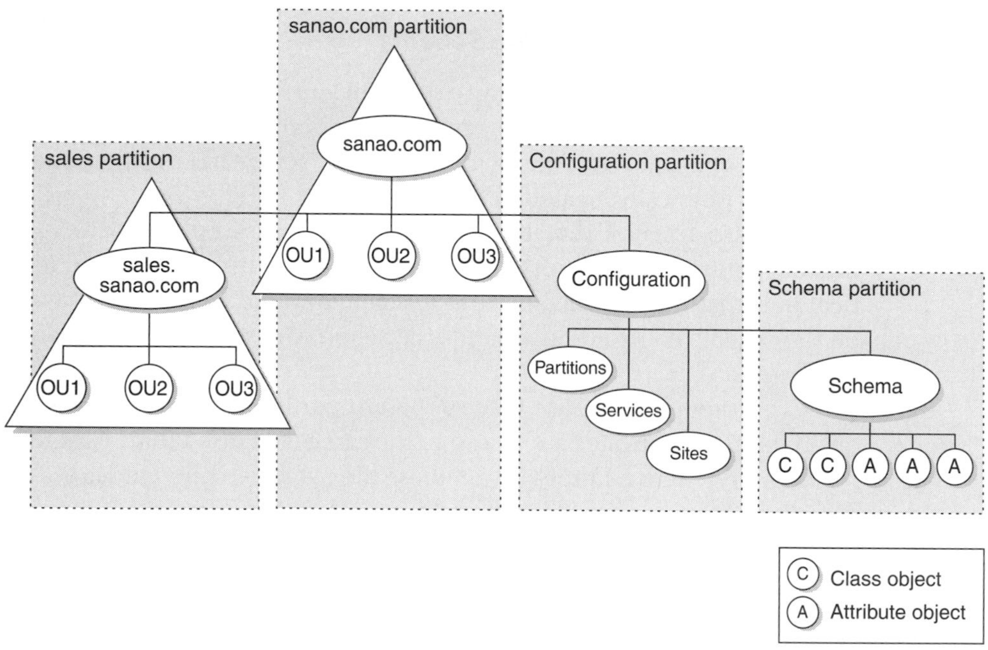

Figure 8.3 The Schema container is logically under the Configuration container, which in turn is under the forest root domain. Physically, however, the three are different partitions.

Inspecting the Schema with ADSI Edit

Now that you know that the schema is implemented as a number of objects and you know where to find them, we can start studying them in the user interface. The two main tools for the job are as follows:

- ADSI Edit, a general tool for viewing all the objects in Active Directory
- The Schema Manager snap-in, a specialized tool for viewing and managing the schema

We begin our discussion of these two tools with ADSI Edit. Because it is a general tool, it nicely shows you the general picture and the location of the schema objects, not just the schema contents.

NOTE There are other tools that you can use to view the schema. For example, Windows Support Tools contains LDP, which enables you to do various LDAP operations—among others, to view the schema.

We mentioned previously that with the Users and Computers snap-in you see only part of the objects and only part of the attributes of each object. With ADSI Edit you see all the objects and all of their attributes.

ADSI Edit is part of Windows Support Tools, which you have to install separately. Locate the folder Support\Tools on your Windows Server 2003 or Windows 2000 CD and run SupTools.MSI. After the installation, you will find the tool by clicking the Start button and then selecting All Programs, Windows Support Tools, Support Tools Help.

Figure 8.4 shows the screen that opens when you launch ADSI Edit. ADSI Edit shows container objects with yellow folder icons and leaf objects with white icons similar to the icons used for text documents in Windows Explorer. The left pane shows only container objects, and the right pane shows both container and leaf objects.

To familiarize yourself with ADSI Edit, it's a good idea to first check the properties (or attributes) of one of your users before you start to explore the schema objects.

Inspecting Attributes of Classes and Attributes

When you are ready to move to the schema objects, you can start inspecting their attributes. For example, you can check the attributes of the `user` class schema object (see Figure 8.5).

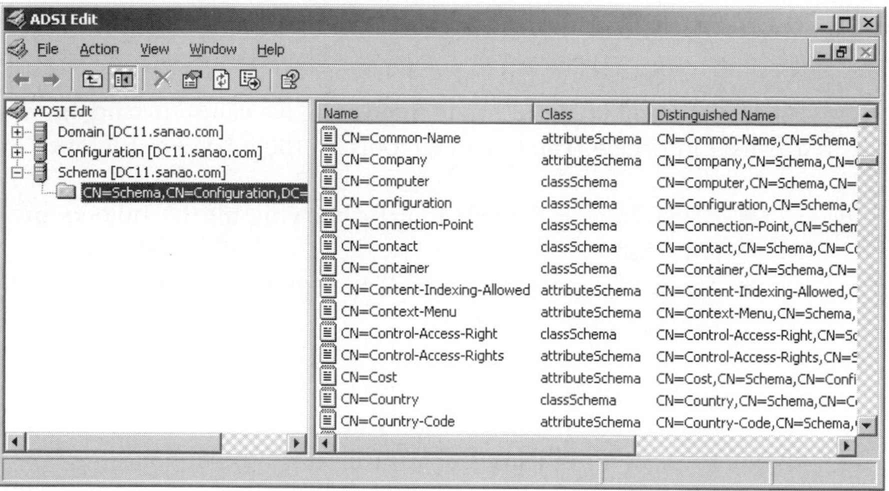

Figure 8.4 When you first start ADSI Edit, it shows three partitions (aka naming contexts). Under the Schema container you can see all the class and attribute objects.

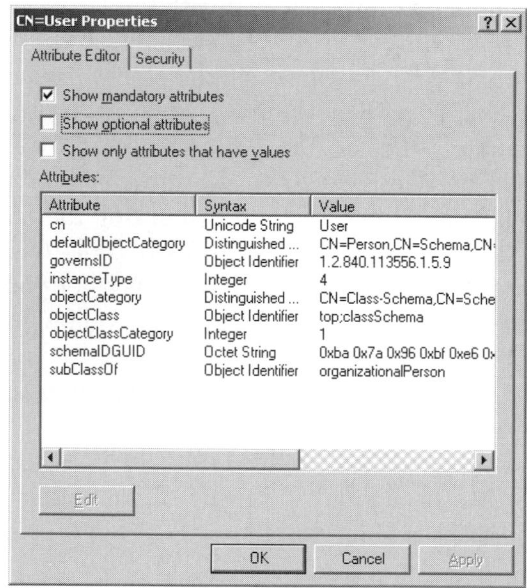

Figure 8.5 When you select Properties in the context menu of any object, ADSI Edit opens a dialog box that enables you to browse all the attributes of that object. By using the provided check boxes, you can choose to view mandatory attributes, or optional, or both.

WARNING ADSI Edit enables you to change the attribute values. When you study schema objects, be sure to click Cancel at the end. Do not click OK or Apply.

Note that because all objects contain attributes, `classSchema` and `attributeSchema` objects also contain attributes. For example, the object `CN=Jack Brown` has an attribute `givenName`, with the value "Jack." The schema contains the object `CN=Given-Name`, which in turn contains such attributes as `schemaIDGUID` and `attributeSyntax`.

We discuss the contents of `classSchema` objects a little later in the section "Classes" and `attributeSchema` objects in the section "Attributes and Syntaxes."

NOTE ADSI Edit displays all the attributes of a class or attribute object, but only some of them are meaningful to the schema. Most of the attributes are the same ones that all objects in Active Directory have, such as `uSNChanged`, which helps to track replication.

TIP `SchemaIDGUID` and some other attributes use `OctetString` syntax, which is about the same as binary. If you are using the Windows 2000 version of ADSI Edit and you want to see just the bytes without "0x"s, you can copy and paste the string to Notepad and then replace all "0x"s with nothing. The Windows Server 2003 version of ADSI Edit can display the hex data straight without "0x"s.

Various Attribute Names

You may have noticed that each attribute has two slightly different names. Table 8.3 summarizes the two naming conventions together with the administrative tool name.

NOTE Unlike the example in Table 8.3, the three attribute names may be quite different, such as "Surname" – "`sn`" – "Last Name" or "WWW-Page-Other" – "`url`" – "Web Page Address (Others)." This is the case especially with attributes that have long-established X.500 names.

Just as attributes do, classes have both common names and LDAP names. Usually, these two are quite similar, such as "Site-Link-Bridge" versus "`siteLinkBridge`."

Table 8.3 Various Attribute Names

Name	Example	Naming Convention	Where to Find
Common name	Facsimile-Telephone-Number	Each word starts with an uppercase letter; a hyphen occurs between words	The common name of the `attributeSchema` object.
LDAP name	`facsimile-Telephone-Number`	Name starts with a lowercase letter; each subsequent word starts with an uppercase letter; no hyphen between words	The `lDAPDisplayName` attribute of the `attributeSchema` object.
Name in admin tools	Fax Number	Any name that is descriptive and consistent	See the explanation in the text.

Sometimes the common name and LDAP name are the same, but they refer to different attributes. Table 8.4 gives two examples of this (using four attributes).

The attribute names that you see in administrative snap-ins, such as Users and Computers, are not usually stored in the schema. Instead, you find them under the DisplaySpecifiers container, which in turn is under the Configuration container. In this container, first locate the object with your locale identifier (e.g., 409 for "English (United States)"). Then open the properties for `CN=user-Display` and select the attribute `attributeDisplayNames`. It is a multivalued attribute that contains pairs of LDAP names and display names.

Table 8.4 Some Confusing Name Pairs

LDAP Name	Common Name
`info`	Comment
`comment`	User-Comment
`street`	Street-Address
`streetAddress`	Address

NOTE The list of name pairs is not likely to contain display names for all attributes. For names that are not on the list, each attribute schema object has an attribute `adminDisplayName`, which the administrative tools can use instead. In practice, for all but five base schema attributes, `adminDisplayName` is equal to the common name of the attribute.

NOTE In reality, the Users and Computers snap-in doesn't use all the display specifier attributes (even though it is suggested here and in Microsoft's documentation). For example, most of the field names in user properties (such as Description or Office) are hard-coded in the tool instead of readable from the `attributeDisplayNames` attribute.

We use mainly LDAP names in this book for three reasons:

- If you use ADSI scripts, you need LDAP names.
- If you use LDAP filters, you need LDAP names.
- The Schema Manager snap-in, Replication Monitor, LDIFDE, and many other administration tools use LDAP names.

Inspecting the Schema with the Schema Manager Snap-In

The Schema Manager snap-in (displayed as Active Directory Schema) is made specifically for viewing and managing the schema. Because Microsoft doesn't make it available to casual users, you have to take some extra steps to access it.

WARNING Just as with ADSI Edit, do not select OK or Apply in the Schema Manager snap-in dialog boxes. Always exit by clicking Cancel.

TIP If you want to run the Schema Manager snap-in in a workstation, you must first install the Admin Pak. Locate the file AdminPak.MSI in the I386 folder of a Windows Server 2003 or Windows 2000 Server CD. When you double-click that file, it will install the Admin Pak.

---

1. In the Run window (click the Start button and select Run) or at the command prompt, enter the command `regsvr32`

`schmmgmt.dll` and press Enter. You should get a message indicating that the registration was successful.

2. Start MMC (Microsoft Management Console) by typing "mmc" and press Enter (again, either in the Run window or at the command prompt).
3. In the File menu (or Console menu, if using Windows 2000), select Add/Remove Snap-in. In the dialog box that opens, click Add.
4. From the list of snap-ins, select Active Directory Schema, click Add, and click Close. Click OK to close the original dialog box.
5. To save what you just did, in the File menu select Save As, select the name and location of the .msc file that you want, and click Save. Next time you want to start the snap-in, double-click the .msc file you just saved.

Now you are ready to take a look at your schema from a slightly different view than what you saw with ADSI Edit. Figure 8.6 and Figure 8.7 illustrate this view.

Using the Schema Manager snap-in, you can also see the mandatory and optional attributes for any class, which would be quite cumbersome with ADSI Edit. Note that this time we don't mean the attributes of a `classSchema` object, such as `schemaIDGUID`, but the attributes that the instances of the class may use, such as `homeDirectory` or `givenName`.

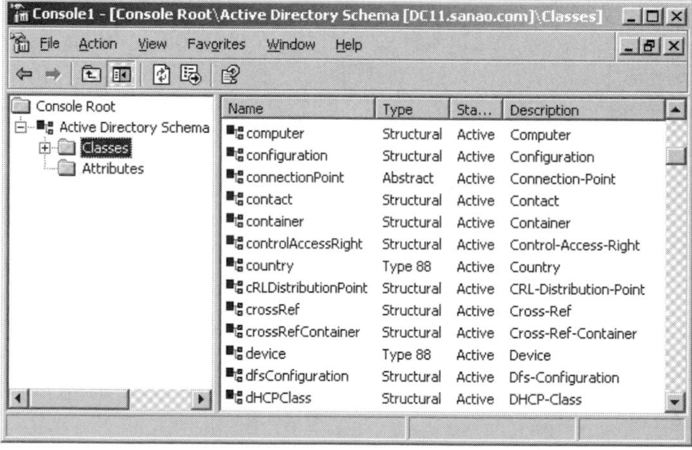

Figure 8.6 When you start the Schema Manager snap-in, it shows two containers: one for all the classes and one for the attributes. Unlike with ADSI Edit, the objects are listed by their LDAP names.

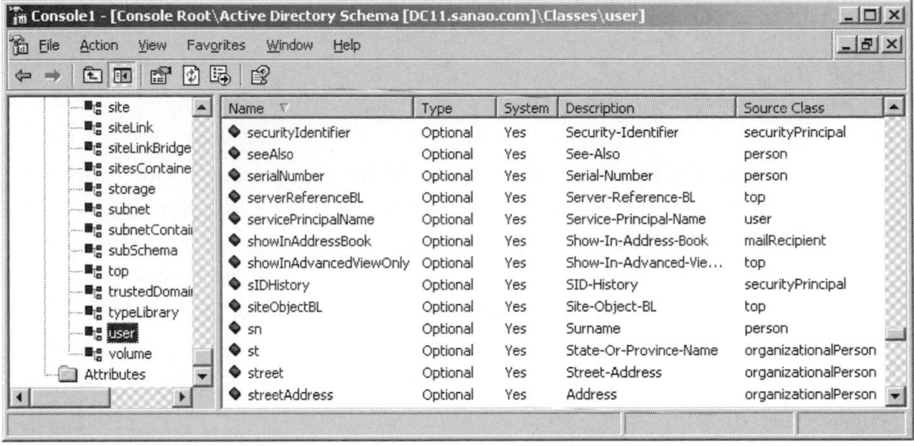

Figure 8.7 When you select a class in the left pane, the right pane shows the attributes for that class. Again, they are listed by their LDAP names. The text in the Description column is usually the same as the common name you can see with ADSI Edit.

In addition to the lists in the screen shots in Figure 8.6 and Figure 8.7, you can open a properties dialog box for any class or attribute. We show those dialog boxes and discuss them in the later sections "Classes" and "Attributes and Syntaxes."

NOTE You must select an attribute in the Attributes container to be able to open the properties dialog box for it. If you select the attribute from the list shown in Figure 8.7, you will see just two items, Refresh and Help, when you right-click the attribute.

Base Schema Versions

As you know, each forest has a certain schema, and that schema is common to the forest. If administrators, or the applications they install, modify the schema, the new extended schema will obviously be different than it was a minute ago. However, the base schema version does not change in the process.

The base schema version changes when the operating system is upgraded. Currently, there are the following base schema versions:

- Version 13, contained in Windows 2000
- Version 30 and its variations, contained in Windows Server 2003

The base schema version is recorded in the `objectVersion` attribute of the `CN=Schema, CN=Configuration, DC=<forest-name>` object.

You get version 30 by doing either of the following:

- Installing a new forest on a Windows Server 2003 computer.
- Running the command `adprep /forestprep` in an AD2000 forest. This command is about the first step on the path to an in-place upgrade of an AD2000 forest to AD2003. The command uses the SchUpgr.exe tool and a series of LDIF files (named SCH14.LDF through SCH30.LDF in the I386 folder of the installation CD) to modify the schema from version 13 to version 30.

We mentioned that version 30 has variations. There are two kinds of them:

- The base schema is slightly different in the forest functional levels Windows 2000 and Windows Server 2003. The version number, however, is 30 in both cases.
- The base schema is slightly different in an AD2003 forest that was upgraded from an AD2000 forest and in a forest that was installed to AD2003 from scratch (that is, on a Windows Server 2003 computer). The version number, however, is 30 in both cases.

We describe the differences of both variations in the following two sections, but before that, to sum up:

- The base schema of a from-scratch installed forest changes once, and this happens when you raise the forest functional level to Windows Server 2003 (only the GC attribute list changes).
- The base schema of an upgraded forest changes twice, (a) once when you run ADPrep (from version 13 to version 30) and (b) once when you raise the forest functional level to Windows Server 2003 (only the GC attribute list changes).

The Effect of Raising the Forest Functional Level

When the forest functional level is raised from Windows 2000 to Windows Server 2003, the number of attributes in the global catalog increases to the aforementioned 151. This is the only schema modification that takes place during the raise.

The case is different for an AD2003 forest that was installed from scratch on Windows Server 2003 and for an AD2003 forest that was upgraded from AD2000 (using the ADPrep command).

- *A forest installed from scratch* has 150 attributes in the global catalog, while still in the Windows 2000 forest functional level. During the raise, one attribute (`msDRM-IdentityCertificate`) is added, so the outcome is 151.
- *An upgraded forest* has 138 attributes in the global catalog, while still in the Windows 2000 forest functional level. These are the same attributes that existed in the global catalog in AD2000, which means that ADPrep doesn't add any attributes to the global catalog. This is a good thing, because adding an attribute would have caused a full replication (or "full sync") of all global catalog servers in the forest, causing possibly a massive load on the company WAN links. When the forest functional level is being raised, all domain controllers are running Windows Server 2003, so adding attributes is now a light operation (no full sync anymore). Thirteen attributes are added to get the count of 151. The attributes are `msDRM-IdentityCertificate`, `msDS-Entry-Time-To-Die`, `msDS-TrustForestTrustInfo`, `MSMQ-Multicast-Address`, `MSMQ-SecuredSource`, `printMemory`, `printRate`, `printRateUnit`, `securityIdentifier`, `trustAttributes`, `trustDirection`, `trustPartner`, and `trustType`.

The Effect of Upgrade versus From-Scratch Installation

In theory, the base schema is identical whether the AD2003 forest was created by upgrading from an AD2000 forest or installed to AD2003 from scratch (that is, on a Windows Server 2003 computer). In practice, however, there are some differences. We list the differences here, although the technical background for many of the topics appears only later in this chapter.

The differences that have some meaning are the following:

- The system ACL (SACL) part of the `defaultSecurity-Descriptor` attribute of the `domainDNS` class is different in the two cases, which means different auditing entries on objects, such as users, that reside in domains. In an upgraded forest, about all changes to objects would be audited, whereas in a from-scratch forest, only few changes would be audited. Note that in addition to the aforementioned auditing entries (visible in ACL Editor), there are auditing settings (visible in the Group Policy Object Editor). These are also different for upgraded and from-scratch forests, but this time the other way around. In an upgraded domain, very little is audited, but in a from-scratch domain, almost all successful operations are audited. Because both the SACL and auditing settings need to be "on" for object access to be audited, the result is that, by default, in neither a from-scratch nor an upgraded domain does an object modification end up in the event log. For more information on auditing, see Chapter 4.

- In a from-scratch forest, the `defaultSecurityDescriptor` attribute of the `rIDManager` class has the system ACL (SACL) part. This doesn't have an immediate effect, however, because the auditing entries here are a subset of the entries described in the previous bullet (which inherit also to the rIDManager object, located in the System container).
- In a from-scratch forest, the `systemFlags` attribute of the `applicationVersion` and `msDS-App-Configuration` classes is 0, which means that these two classes are not marked to be part of the base schema, leaving them slightly unprotected.

The differences that are more cosmetic (but listed here for completeness) are the following:

- `adminDescription` of `msDS-TombstoneQuotaFactor` is one word different.
- Six attributes have `description` set in the from-scratch version (which is the wrong place, since the text should be in the `adminDescription` attribute). The attributes are `entryTTL`, `msDS-NCReplCursors`, `msDS-NCReplInboundNeighbors`, `msDS-NCReplOutboundNeighbors`, `msDS-ReplAttributeMetaData`, and `msDS-ReplValueMetaData`.
- Three attributes are missing `showInAdvancedViewOnly = TRUE` in the from-scratch version. These are `msExchAssistantName`, `msExchHouseIdentifier`, and `msExchLabeledURI`.
- The `dynamicObject` class has `description` set in the from-scratch version (which is the wrong place, since the text should be in the `adminDescription` attribute).
- The `defaultSecurityDescriptor` attribute of the `samDomain` class is different in the two cases. This has no meaning, however,

because `samDomain` is an auxiliary class and therefore cannot have instances (as discussed later in the chapter).

- The `defaultSecurityDescriptor` attribute of the `site` class has an Enterprise Domain Controllers permission entry in a from-scratch forest, so each site object will have this entry. In an upgraded forest a similar entry exists in the Sites container, from where it is inherited to all sites. Therefore, the outcome is the same in both cases.

AD2003 Schema versus AD2000 Schema

The AD2000 base schema contains 142 classes and the AD2003 base schema 191 classes, which means 49 new classes. Of the 142 old classes, 52 have changed in AD2003, which leaves 90 unchanged classes.

Correspondingly, there are 863 attributes in the AD2000 base schema and 1,070 in the AD2003 base schema, meaning 207 new ones. Of the 863 old attributes, 53 have changed in AD2003, so 810 are unchanged.

Some of the old classes and attributes start with letters "ms" (that is, Microsoft), but most of them don't. In contrast, most of the new classes and attributes start with the letters "msDS" (Microsoft directory service) or "ms*SomethingElse*". As discussed in Chapter 9, new classes or attributes that are created should have the organization's name or acronym prepended in their names. Microsoft follows this convention in the base schema additions of AD2003. The exceptions to this are the new base schema classes and attributes that accommodate new RFCs, such as `carLicense` in RFC 2798.

Another change in names is the new convention that the LDAP name and common name should be the same. Consequently, most new LDAP names contain a hyphen, and most new common names start with a lowercase letter.

Schema Peculiarities

This section aims to be "gentle nagging" to Microsoft. We list some peculiarities, which are either bugs in the base schema, meaningless inconsistencies, or things that have a good explanation, but we just don't know it. If you are new to the schema, you may want to skip this section, or you may use it as an exercise: We don't explain the list items much, so as you read on in the chapter, you can relate the items to things you will learn. If you already know one or two things about it, you can just read the following list and wonder with us. The first four items are cosmetic.

- Two classes have `showInAdvancedViewOnly = FALSE`, while the remaining 189 have the value `TRUE`. Also, 51 attributes are not set to be `showInAdvancedViewOnly` (the value is either missing or `FALSE`).
- One class has `description` set, while the other 190 do not.
- The `AdminDisplayNames` of two classes are equal to their LDAP names, while with others they are equal to the common name. This also applies to five attributes out of 1,070.
- `DomainRelatedObject` seems to have a wrong `adminDescription`.
- `MsTAPI-RtConference` has `msTAPI-uid` as an `rdnattid` (that is, the "prefix attribute," such as `CN=`).
- Six classes have `objectClassCategory` zero, which corresponds to an 88-class. Perhaps these six follow an RFC that specifies such an `objectClassCategory`.
- Some base schema classes use `mustContain`, `mayContain`, and `possibleSuperiors`, instead of `systemMustContain`, `systemMayContain`, and `systemPossSuperiors`. This enables you to modify those classes in a way in which you cannot modify the remaining classes.
- In AD2000, `employeeNumber`, `employeeType`, `homePostalAddress`, and `userSMIMECertificate` were marked to belong to the base schema, but in AD2003 the marking indicates they would be schema extensions. In addition, there are a number of classes and attributes that in AD2000 were already marked as extensions, and consequently they miss the protection of base schema classes and attributes.

Dumping the Schema to a Spreadsheet

Although the two graphical tools we just described are nice to use to explore the schema, they both have one problem: You can see the attributes for only one `classSchema` or `attributeSchema` object at a time.

In this section we explain how you can dump all the information in your schema to a spreadsheet. It allows a broader view to the schema contents. Also, you can sort and filter the data, which gives you a better idea of how the various attributes are used. As you read on in this chapter, you can use the tables created here as a reference.

We use Excel in our explanation of how to dump the schema into a spreadsheet, but you can use other spreadsheet and database applications. First, you dump all your `classSchema` and `attributeSchema` objects into two text files, and then import those text files to Excel.

At a domain controller, you must type the following two commands at the command prompt (click the Start button and select Command Prompt) and press Enter after each command:

```
C:\>csvde -f classes.txt
    -d cn=schema,cn=configuration,dc=sanao,dc=com
    -r (objectCategory=classSchema)
C:\>csvde -f attributes.txt
    -d cn=schema,cn=configuration,dc=sanao,dc=com
    -r (objectCategory=attributeSchema)
```

You should see output like the following for each command:

```
Connecting to "(null)"
Logging in as current user using SSPI
Exporting directory to file classes.txt
Searching for entries...
Writing out entries
..........................................................
..........................................................
...............................
Export Completed. Post-processing in progress...
191 entries exported
The command has completed successfully
```

Each of the two commands specifics an output file, a base distinguished name from which to dump, and an LDAP filter.

NOTE You can use the CSVDE tool also on a workstation. See its online help for more information.

Next you must launch Excel and perform the following steps for both of your text files:

1. Select File, Open.
2. Select one of your newly created text files and click Open. A text import wizard should start up.
3. Specify that your data is delimited (instead of fixed width).

4. Specify that the delimiter is a comma.
5. Click Finish to complete the wizard. You should now have about 30 columns of data, one column for each attribute.
6. Click cell A2 to activate it. Choose Freeze Panes in the Window menu. Now your first row with the column labels (i.e., attribute names) stays visible, even if you scroll down the sheet.
7. Adjust the width of each column as you like. You can also double-click the right border of each column header (F, G, H, and so on) to autosize the columns. Note that some of the data values may be longer than the width of your screen. If you cannot resize a wide column by dragging its right border with a mouse, you can use the Format menu option Column, Width.
8. If they are present, remove the columns `uSNChanged`, `uSNCreated`, `whenChanged`, `whenCreated`, `instanceType`, `dITContentRules`, `extendedClassInfo`, `modifyTimeStamp`, and `extendedAttributeInfo`. You are not interested in them, because they don't define schema characteristics.
9. If you want, you can sort the columns to your taste and put the LDAP display name column to the left, for example. You can also sort the rows by the LDAP display name column to more easily locate a certain class (using the Sort feature in the Data menu of Excel).
10. Open the Data menu and select Filter, AutoFilter. This turns each column header into a drop-down list filter. When you open a list, you see all the distinct values for that column (i.e., attribute). If you select a value, your sheet will be filtered to show only the lines with that value.
11. Save the sheet in XLS format.

Figure 8.8 shows an Excel sheet that results from the preceding steps.

Schema References

In addition to dumping your own spreadsheets of schema information, as explained in the previous section, there are at least two ready schema references available on the Internet.

- The book's Web site at `http://www.kouti.com` includes an Excel file that contains several spreadsheets that list all schema-related information about the schema class and attribute objects.

	IDAPDisplayName	objectClass	cn	defaultHid	subClassOf	governsID	rDNAttID
21	computer	classSchema	Computer	FALSE	user	1.2.840.113556.1.3.30	cn
24	contact	classSchema	Contact	FALSE	organizationalP	1.2.840.113556.1.5.15	cn
30	crossRefContainer	classSchema	Cross-Ref-Container	FALSE	top	1.2.840.113556.1.5.7000.53	cn
42	domainDNS	classSchema	Domain-DNS	FALSE	domain	1.2.840.113556.1.5.67	dc
53	group	classSchema	Group	FALSE	top	1.2.840.113556.1.5.8	cn
58	inetOrgPerson	classSchema	inetOrgPerson	FALSE	user	2.16.840.1.113730.3.2.2	cn
76	locality	classSchema	Locality	FALSE	top	2.5.6.3	l
95	msMQ-Custom-Recip	classSchema	MSMQ-Custom-Recip	FALSE	top	1.2.840.113556.1.5.218	cn
99	mSMQQueue	classSchema	MSMQ-Queue	FALSE	top	1.2.840.113556.1.5.161	cn
101	mSMQSiteLink	classSchema	MSMQ-Site-Link	FALSE	top	1.2.840.113556.1.5.164	cn
140	organization	classSchema	Organization	FALSE	top	2.5.6.4	o
143	organizationalUnit	classSchema	Organizational-Unit	FALSE	top	2.5.6.5	ou
149	printQueue	classSchema	Print-Queue	FALSE	connectionPoin	1.2.840.113556.1.5.23	cn
181	siteLink	classSchema	Site-Link	FALSE	top	1.2.840.113556.1.5.147	cn
182	siteLinkBridge	classSchema	Site-Link-Bridge	FALSE	top	1.2.840.113556.1.5.148	cn
191	user	classSchema	User	FALSE	organizationalP	1.2.840.113556.1.5.9	cn
192	volume	classSchema	Volume	FALSE	connectionPoin	1.2.840.113556.1.5.36	cn

Figure 8.8 After you have all the class definitions in Excel, you can filter in just the classes you specify—for example, classes that have `defaultHiding-Value = FALSE`.

The file also contains some other spreadsheets that you can use as a reference, such as a list of all 257 user attributes, the correspondence to the Users and Computers snap-in field names, and about 20 other pieces of information about each attribute.

- Microsoft's Web site contains "Active Directory Schema Site," which documents all base schema classes and attributes. As of this writing, the address is `http://msdn.microsoft.com/library/default.asp?url=/library/en-us/adschema/adschema/active_directory_schema_site.asp`, but if this doesn't work, you can just search for the exact phrase "Active Directory Schema Site."

Subschema Subentry

Active Directory supports LDAPv3, which requires a directory service to expose its schema in a single `subSchema` object. Active Directory stores this object in the Schema container with the name `CN=Aggregate`.

The Aggregate object contains some multivalued attributes, which list the classes and attributes available in the schema. If you want to take a look, those attributes are as follows:

- `objectClasses`
- `attributeTypes`
- `extendedClassInfo`
- `extendedAttributeInfo`
- `dITContentRules`

In Chapter 10 and Chapter 11, we use the ADSI interface for directory access. When you specify a path such as `LDAP://sanao.com/schema` for ADSI, or just `LDAP://schema`, ADSI will expose the `subSchema` object as one container with 191 classes, 1,070 attributes, and 35 syntaxes under it. The properties for these "virtual objects" are more limited than those with the real Schema container, but they have some advantages for scripting.

NOTE Active Directory supports 23 syntaxes, as discussed later in this chapter. The ADSI interface is using 35 syntaxes because it must support other environments also—most notably, NetWare. The ADSI syntaxes are listed in Chapter 10.

Schema Cache

Because the schema guards the structure and content of Active Directory objects, it is needed every time any object (such as the user Jack Brown) is added or modified. Accessing the schema from the ntds.dit file would be too slow; therefore, every domain controller holds a copy of the schema in RAM. This copy is called the *schema cache.*

Internally the schema cache is not an identical copy of the bytes on disk; it is structured a little differently for easy and fast access.

Naturally the schema cache is built based on the information in the disk version each time the domain controller starts. If a change is made to the schema on the schema master, the change starts to replicate to other domain controllers, just as any change to Active Directory. In each domain controller, the change goes first to the schema on disk and then, after a five-minute delay, the schema cache is updated.

You cannot use most of the schema changes until they are in the schema cache of the domain controller you are using. Consequently, there is an additional five-minute wait after the possible replication latency from the schema master to your domain controller. During this waiting period, applications continue to use the old schema cache.

The five-minute delay here is for the same reason as with replication. After one change, usually more changes soon follow. Because each schema cache update consumes quite a few bytes of memory, it is more efficient to wait a little and make them all at once.

NOTE Contrary to what the February 2003 Platform SDK Documentation says, the five-minute period is counted from the first change, and it doesn't reset if there is another change one minute later. Therefore, that latter change has to wait only four minutes to get into the schema cache.

The extra memory consumption in schema reload is due to the fact that when a new schema version is reloaded in cache, the old schema cache stays in memory for all the threads that were already running. Once all the old threads have exited, the older schema cache copy is released from memory. This also means that if you test schema changes, you probably need to restart your admin tools, so that they start to use the new schema cache and therefore can see the changes.

Triggering the Schema Cache Update

If five minutes is too long for you to wait, you can trigger the cache update immediately with the Schema Manager snap-in. In the left pane, right-click the node Active Directory Schema and select Reload the Schema. There is also a programmatic way to trigger the schema cache update. You must write the value 1 to an attribute `schemaUpdateNow` residing in a special `rootDSE` virtual object. We cover this in later chapters:

- Chapter 9 contains an example of adding a new attribute and class to the schema and triggering the update using the LDIFDE tool.
- Chapter 10 describes the `rootDSE` object in more detail.
- Chapter 11 contains an example of adding a new attribute and class to the schema and triggering the update using the ADSI interface in a script.

Before we conclude our discussion about the schema in general, we'll mention the constructed attributes.

Constructed Attributes

Not all attributes for an object are stored in the directory database on disk. Instead, they are built from other attributes. Thirty-six of the 1,070 attributes in the base schema are constructed (22 in AD2000).

The 36 constructed attributes are as follows:

```
primaryGroupToken
allowedAttributes
allowedAttributesEffective
allowedChildClasses
allowedChildClassesEffective
aNR
attributeTypes
canonicalName
createTimeStamp
dITContentRules
entryTTL
extendedAttributeInfo
extendedClassInfo
fromEntry
modifyTimeStamp
msDS-Approx-Immed-
  Subordinates
msDS-Auxiliary-Classes
msDS-KeyVersionNumber
msDS-NCReplCursors
msDS-NCReplInboundNeighbors
msDS-NCReplOutboundNeighbors
msDS-QuotaEffective
msDS-QuotaUsed
msDS-ReplAttributeMetaData
msDS-ReplValueMetaData
msDS-TopQuotaUsage
msDS-User-Account-Control-
  Computed
objectClasses
parentGUID
possibleInferiors
sDRightsEffective
structuralObjectClass
subSchemaSubEntry
tokenGroups
tokenGroupsGlobalAndUniversal
tokenGroupsNoGCAcceptable
```

Classes

In the overview section of this chapter we introduced classes, and in the "Schema" section we mentioned that there is a class schema object for each class. In this section we examine classes and their schema objects in more detail.

Each class is defined by the attributes of its schema object. This means that examining classes actually means examining those attributes. Each `classSchema` object may contain at most 114 attributes (95 in AD2000). However, remember that many of these attributes are not related to defining the schema, but instead are "normal" attributes for any object. Examples of these normal attributes are `wWWHomePage` and `uSNChanged`. Here we discuss 36 attributes and omit 78 normal "uninteresting" attributes.

NOTE You could claim that some of the 36 attributes we address are also uninteresting. For example, they include 5 attributes that are not used at all. We include them so that you don't need to wonder what they are if you run into them with ADSI Edit or some other tool.

NOTE We list a few numbers of attributes in the text and in Table 8.5. The exact numbers are not important; we mention them to give you an idea of how many different kinds of attributes there are.

Classes can inherit from other classes attributes that their instances must and may contain. Of the 114 `classSchema` attributes, 24 are the class's own attributes and 90 are inherited from the `top` class. In the list of 36 attributes in Table 8.5, 22 are the class's own attributes and 14 are inherited attributes.

We have divided the 36 attributes into four categories. These categories resemble those listed in the "Role of the Schema" section earlier in this chapter (see Table 8.1 and Table 8.2).

- *Names and identifiers.* There are 14 of these attributes (plus 1 naming-type attribute). Fortunately, not all of them are used.
- *Structure and containment rules.* These 7 attributes define where in the tree each object may be created (or instantiated) and which attribute values it must and may contain.
- *Class inheritance.* A class may inherit containment from another class. The 4 attributes in this category define how this happens.
- *Miscellaneous.* The remaining 10 attributes provide some defaults, for example, to the objects that will be created to the corresponding class.

Table 8.5 lists the 36 attributes by their LDAP names. If the common name has no resemblance to the LDAP name, the common name appears in parentheses (such as "`distinguishedName` (Obj-Dist-Name)"). The Type column indicates whether the attribute is mandatory or optional. The Source Class column indicates either `classSchema` or `top`, the latter meaning the attribute was inherited from the `top` class. The Base Schema Classes column gives a summary of the kind of values the 191 classes have for the attributes in the table. Finally, the `user` Class Example column lists the values for the `user` class.

Table 8.5 Attributes of a `classSchema` Object

Name	Type	Source Class	Base Schema Classes (191)	`user` Class Example
Names and Identifiers				
`lDAPDisplayName`	O	`classS.`	All values are unique	`user`
`cn` (Common-Name)	M	`classS.`	All values are unique	User
`adminDisplayName`	O	`top`	189 are the same as `cn`, 2 are the same as `lDAP-DisplayName`	User
`name` (RDN)	O	`top`	Same as `cn`	User
`distinguishedName` (Obj-Dist-Name)	O	`top`	All values are unique	`CN=User, CN=Schema, CN= Configuration, DC=sanao, DC=com`
`canonicalName`	O	`top`	All values are unique	`sanao.com/ Configuration/ Schema/User`
`displayName`	O	`top`	Not used	—
`displayName Printable`	O	`top`	Not used	—
`classDisplayName`	O	`classS.`	Not used	—
`adminDescription`	O	`top`	165 are the same as `cn`, 2 are the same as `lDAPDisplay-Name`, 24 contain a real description, which, however, are too short to be helpful	User

Table 8.5 Attributes of a classSchema Object *(cont.)*

Name	Type	Source Class	Base Schema Classes (191)	user Class Example
description	O	top	Not used (although 1 contains a helpful description, the remaining 190 are <not set>)	—
governsID	M	classS.	163 are Microsoft IDs (1.2.840.113556), 18 are X.500 IDs (2.5), 8 are "ITU-T data – PSS" IDs (0.9.2342), 1 is a Mark Wahl ID (1.3.6.1.4.1.1466), and 1 is a Netscape ID (2.16.840.1. 113730)	1.2.840.113556. 1.5.9
schemaIDGUID	M	classS.	All values are unique	ba7a96bf e60dd011 a28500aa 003049e2
objectGUID	O	top	All values are unique	Such as 4856468b 62963047 8c32fcfe 70f6ca9b
rDNAttID	O	classS.	182 × cn, 4 × dc, 1 × c, 1 × 1, 1 × o, 1 × ou, 1 × msTAPI-uid	cn

(continued)

Table 8.5 Attributes of a `classSchema` Object *(cont.)*

Name	Type	Source Class	Base Schema Classes (191)	`user` Class Example
Structure and Containment Rules				
`mustContain`	O	`classS.`	4 are set; 187 are <not set>	— —
`systemMustContain`	O	`classS.`	74 are set; 117 are <not set>	—
`mayContain`	O	`classS.`	18 are set; 173 are <not set>	A list of 18 attributes
`systemMayContain`	O	`classS.`	143 are set; 48 are <not set>	A long list of attributes
`possSuperiors`	O	`classS.`	10 are set; 181 are <not set>	—
`systemPossSuperiors`	O	`classS.`	170 are set; 21 are <not set>	`builtinDomain` + `organizational-Unit` + `domainDNS`
`possibleInferiors`	O	`top`	67 are set (=container); 124 are not (=leaf)	`nTFRS-Subscriptions` + `classStore`
Class Inheritance				
`objectClassCategory`	M	`classS.`	169 are structural; 9 are abstract; 7 are auxiliary; 6 are 88-classes	1 (=structural)
`subClassOf`	M	`classS.`	122 are `top`; 69 are others	`organizational-Person`

Table 8.5 Attributes of a classSchema Object (*cont.*)

Name	Type	Source Class	Base Schema Classes (191)	user Class Example
auxiliaryClass	O	classS.	All are <not set>	—
systemAuxiliary-Class	O	classS.	7 are set; 184 are <not set>	security-Principal + mailRecipient
Miscellaneous				
nTSecurity-Descriptor	M	top	All are set	A DACL, SACL, and so on
isDefunct	O	classS.	All are <not set>	—
defaultObject-Category	M	classS.	Almost all are the same as the class distinguished name	CN=Person, CN=Schema, CN=Configuration, DC=sanao, DC=com
defaultHidingValue	O	classS.	174 are TRUE; 17 are FALSE	FALSE
defaultSecurity-Descriptor	O	classS.	187 are set; 4 are <not set>	Almost 1,000 characters long string, starting with D:(A;;RPWPCRCCDC
systemOnly	O	classS.	10 are TRUE; 181 are FALSE	FALSE
systemFlags	O	top	173 are "16", 3 are "134217744", 5 are "0", 10 are <not set>	16
objectClass	M	top	All are top + classSchema	top + classSchema

(*continued*)

Table 8.5 Attributes of a `classSchema` Object *(cont.)*

Name	Type	Source Class	Base Schema Classes (191)	user Class Example
objectCategory	M	top	All are CN=Class-Schema, CN=Schema, CN=Configuration, DC=sanao, DC=com	CN=Class-Schema, CN=Schema, CN=Configuration, DC=sanao, DC=com
schemaFlagsEx	O	classS.	Not used	—

In the remaining subsections, we examine each of the four categories.

Names and Identifiers

The various names and identifiers identify the classes by both people and Active Directory. This category of 15 attributes includes nine different names, two descriptions, and three identifiers. The fifteenth attribute (`rDNAttID`) is none of these, but we include it in this category because it is name-related.

Table 8.6 describes the 15 attributes. Fortunately, Active Directory doesn't use quite all of them, as indicated in the table. Consequently, we are left with "only" six different names and one description. Furthermore, `canonicalName`, `distinguishedName`, and RDN are redundant with `cn`, because you can derive them directly from `cn`. This leaves us with three "nonredundant" names (the first three in Table 8.6) and one description.

Object Identifiers

As you see in Table 8.6, one of the many identifiers for each class schema object is an *object identifier (OID)*. An OID consists of numbers that have dots in between them, such as 1.3.6.1.4.1.123123. The number is hierarchical, so the first number in an OID is the highest level of the tree.

Table 8.6 Name and Identifier Attributes of a `classSchema` Object

Name	Syntax*	Multi-valued	Description	`user` Class Example
`lDAPDisplay-Name`	`Unicode string`	No	Name to identify the class in ADSI scripts, LDAP filters, many low-level admin tools, and internally with all LDAP access.	`user`
`cn` (Common-Name)	`Unicode string`	No	Actual name of the class schema object.	User
`adminDisplay-Name`	`Unicode string`	No	Name that admin tools can use as their display name if there isn't a name in the `Display-Specifiers` container. If `adminDisplayName` is also not specified, the system will use `cn` instead.	User
`name` (RDN)	`Unicode string`	No	Same as `cn`.	User
`distinguished-Name` (Obj-Dist-Name)	`Distin-guished name`	No	"`cn` with a path," identifies the location of the object (which is always the Schema container).	`CN=User, CN=...`
`canonicalName`	`Unicode string`	Yes	"`cn` with a path," but using a different format from `distinguished Name`.	`sanao. com/ Configu-ration/ Schema/ User`
`displayName`	`Unicode string`	No	Not used.	—
`displayName-Printable`	`Print-able string`	No	Not used.	— *(continued)*

* We discuss the syntaxes in the "Attributes and Syntaxes" section.

Table 8.6 Name and Identifier Attributes of a `classSchema` Object *(cont.)*

Name	Syntax*	Multi-valued	Description	`user` Class Example
`classDisplay-Name`	Unicode string	Yes	Not used.	—
`admin-Description`	Unicode string	No	Descriptive text for the class for admin tools.	User
`description`	Unicode string	Yes	Not used.	—
`governsID`	OID string	No	Object ID (OID) of the class (see the next section, "Object Identifiers").	1.2.840.113556.1.5.9
`schemaIDGUID`	Octet string	No	128-bit unique GUID to identify the class.	ba7a96bf e60dd011 a28500aa 003049e2
`objectGUID`	Octet string	No	128-bit unique GUID to identify this class schema object (as well as any object in Active Directory).	Such as 4856468b 62963047 8c32fcfe 70f6ca9b
`rDNAttID`**	OID string	No	Whether the class prefix is `cn=`, `ou=`, `dc=`, `c=`, `l=`, `o=`, or `msTAPI-uid`. This attribute also specifies whether the naming attribute (i.e., RDN) of the instances of this class is `cn`, `ou`, or some of the other choices just listed.	`cn`

** The `rDNAttID` attribute choices `c`, `l`, and `o` are used by the `country`, `locality`, and `organization` classes, respectively. These classes exist in Active Directory, but are not used in any way. Consequently, you won't see them unless you install Microsoft Exchange 2000 or later, or some other software that would use them.

Anyone who "owns" a certain OID can allocate new child OIDs to it. For example, if you have the *base OID* (or *root OID*) 1.2.3, you could allocate to it OIDs such as 1.2.3.1, 1.2.3.77, and 1.2.3.77.4.3.2.1.

Just like IP addresses, OIDs are administered globally so that no two organizations in the world can have the same base OID. OIDs allow unique identification of all kinds of things—they are used to identify classes, attributes, and syntaxes in X.500 directories and variables in Simple Network Management Protocol (SNMP), among other things.

Microsoft uses the base OID 1.2.840.113556.1 in many Active Directory classes (and attributes). Table 8.7 describes the history of that OID.

NOTE All class schema objects and attribute schema objects of the Active Directory base schema don't use the OIDs in Table 8.7. Some use OIDs defined in X.500 or some other source, such as Netscape.

Another base OID that Microsoft owns is 1.3.6.1.4.1.311. Each numeric part has a name, so we can express this same base OID as `iso.org.dod.internet.private.enterprise.microsoft`. "Org" in the name indicates an "identified organization" that ISO acknowledges and "dod" indicates the US Department of Defense. These "private enterprise numbers" are currently assigned by the Internet Corporation for Assigned Names and Numbers (ICANN, `http://www.icann.org/`). In addition to assigning enterprise OID numbers, ICANN coordinates the assignment of Internet domain names and IP address numbers. You can see the current list of assigned private enterprise numbers at `http://www.iana.org/assignments/enterprise-numbers`.

Table 8.7 Microsoft Active Directory OIDs

Value	Owner
1	ISO, which issued 1.2 to ANSI
1.2	ANSI, which issued 1.2.840 to the USA
1.2.840	The USA, which issued 1.2.840.113556 to Microsoft
1.2.840.113556	Microsoft, which issued 1.2.840.113556.1 to Active Directory
1.2.840.113556.1	Active Directory, where class schema objects use either 1.2.840.113556.1.3 or 1.2.840.113556.1.5, and attribute schema objects use either 1.2.840.113556.1.2 or 1.2.840.113556.1.4

Recall that we discussed the X.500 standards in Chapter 1. OIDs have similar roots, since they were first defined in ITU-T X.208, which corresponds to ISO/IEC 8824. However, X.208 has been superseded by the ITU-T recommendation X.680 (07/2002): "Abstract Syntax Notation One (ASN.1): Specification of basic notation."

In addition to the OID notation, X.680 specifies the following base OIDs:

- 0: ITU-T assigned.
- 1: ISO assigned.
- 2: Joint ISO/ITU-T assigned. Active Directory contains some classes and attributes from X.500, and they use the base OIDs 2.5.6 and 2.5.4, respectively. There is also one "2.5.20" class ("X.500 schema object class") and six "2.5" attributes other than 2.5.4.

You can inspect various assigned OIDs at `http://www.alvestrand.no/domen/objectid/top.html`.

Obtaining a Base OID

If your organization needs to add classes or attributes to the schema, it must obtain a base OID. This need could rise from two situations.

- You need to modify the Active Directory schema of your organization.
- You sell applications to other organizations, and those applications need to modify the schema of the customer Active Directory.

Note that if you buy an application that will extend your schema, you don't need to obtain an OID. Instead, these schema extensions will use your application vendor's OIDs.

There are four ways to get a base OID.

- Run the OIDGEN utility included in the Windows 2000 Resource Kit (not available in the Windows Server 2003 Resource Kit). It generates one base OID for classes and another for attributes. A resulting OID could be 1.2.840.113556.1.4.7000.233.28688.28684.8.96821.760998.1196228.1142349. You can use these OIDs in your tests, but for a production network you should register a base OID, as explained in the next two choices.

- Apply for a free "private enterprise number" from ICANN using the form at `http://www.iana.org/cgi-bin/enterprise.pl`. You should receive a number (such as 1.3.6.1.4.1.123123, where 123123 is your company's number) in a few days by e-mail.
- Apply for a free base OID from Microsoft at `http://msdn.microsoft.com/certification/ad-registration.asp` or use the e-mail alias `schemreg@microsoft.com`. The OID you'll get is one such as 1.2.840.113556.1.6.123123 (where 123123 is your company's number). If you are an application vendor and want to apply for the "Certified for Windows" logo, you should also register your OID (regardless of where it was obtained from) with Microsoft at the aforementioned Web address or by e-mail.
- Apply for a base OID from another issuing authority, perhaps for a fee. Many countries have a country-specific organization to issue OIDs. For organizations in the United States, you can try ANSI and the Web page `http://www.ansi.org/other_services/registration_programs/reg_org.aspx?menuid=10`. It includes directions to obtain an "organization name" such as 2.16.840.1.123123, where 123123 is your company's number. The corresponding OID in text format is joint-iso-itu-t.country.us.organization.mycompany. As of this writing, the one-time fee for a permanent numeric OID is $1,000 US. (However, ANSI seems not to be very responsive. When writing the first edition of the book, we sent e-mail to three people whose e-mail addresses appeared on the ANSI Web page regarding OIDs, but we did not receive an answer from them in six months. When writing the second edition, we sent just one e-mail, but didn't receive any answer.) In other countries, you should contact a local name registration authority, a list of which you can try to find from the International Organization for Standardization (ISO/IEC) (`http://www.iso.ch/`).

Once you get the base OID, you should establish the policy regarding administration of the numbers in your organization, just as you probably have had to do with IP addresses. For example, you can dedicate the branch ".1" to new classes and ".2" to new attributes. Because OIDs are a general standard, you may also need the base OID for uses other than Active Directory.

Structure and Containment Rules

The main job of the schema is to establish the structure and content rules for Active Directory. This is done with the first six attributes described in Table 8.8. They consist of three pairs of a normal attribute and a system attribute (`mustContain` + `systemMustContain`, `mayContain` + `systemMayContain`, and `possSuperiors` + `systemPossSuperiors`).

When creating classes, administrators can set all six attributes. For existing classes, they can change only the three normal attributes, not their system counterparts. The base schema of AD2000 used only the three system attributes; it did not use their normal counterparts. This way, Active Directory could protect the base schema definitions. You could not remove base schema attributes from any base schema class, nor could you remove possible parent classes. AD2003 still uses mostly the three system attributes. For some reason, however, Microsoft chose to use also the normal counterparts for a few classes. Consequently, there is no protection for these definitions. For example, you can remove the attributes `carLicense`, `audio`, and `photo` from the `user` class.

NOTE Even if an attribute is not a system attribute, it doesn't mean that you can change it freely. There are other restrictions to modifying the schema, which we discuss in the next chapter.

Because all seven attributes here are multivalued and use the `OID string` syntax, Table 8.8 does not include this information. Table 8.8 indicates if each attribute is constructed and if only the system, but not an administrator, can alter the value.

NOTE If you compare the constructed `possibleInferiors` attribute to the attributes on which it is based, they seem not to match. The reason is that `possibleInferiors` accounts for the effect of inheritance, as discussed in the next subsection.

Figure 8.9 illustrates the role of the structure and containment attributes. The `systemMayContain` attribute of a `classSchema` object lists some of the attributes (inheritance may list more) that the instances of that class may contain (i.e., optional attributes). `SystemPossSuperiors`- specifies some of the possible parents that the instances may have, and `possibleInferiors` displays the list of possible children.

Table 8.8 Structure and Containment Attributes of a `classSchema` Object

Name	Con-structed	System Only	Description	`user` Class Example
`mustContain`	No	No	Admin-changeable list of mandatory attributes for the instances of this class	—
`systemMust-Contain`	No	Yes	Same as the previous, but only the Directory System Agent (DSA) can change the list after the class has been created	—
`mayContain`	No	No	Admin-changeable list of optional attributes for the instances of this class	A list of 18 attributes
`systemMay-Contain`	No	Yes	Same as the previous, but only the DSA can change the list after the class has been created	A long list of attributes
`poss-Superiors`	No	No	Admin-changeable list of possible parent containers for the instances of this class	—
`systemPoss-Superiors`	No	Yes	Same as the previous, but only the DSA can change the list after the class has been created	`builtin-Domain` + `organiza-tionalUnit` + `domainDNS`
`possible-Inferiors`	Yes*	Yes	List of the classes that an instance of this class can contain instances of (i.e., possible child object types)	`nTFRS-Subscrip-tions` + `classStore`

* `PossibleInferiors` is a constructed attribute. It is calculated from the attributes `possSuperiors` and `systemPossSuperiors` to sum up the effect, but the value is not stored in the schema on disk.

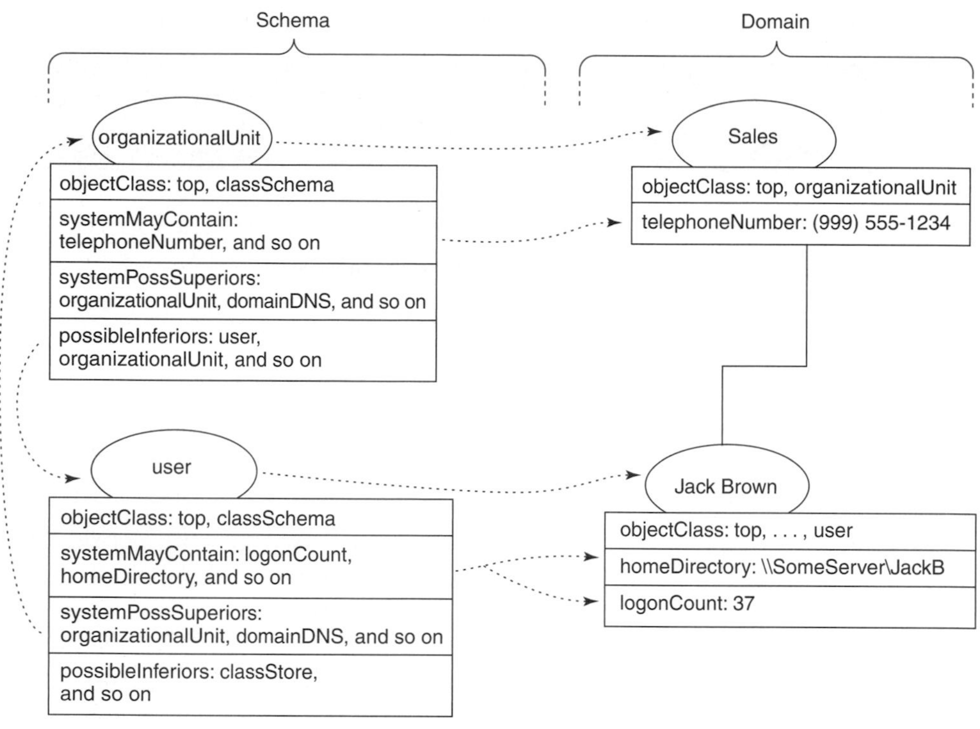

Figure 8.9 The main job of the schema is to establish the structure and content rules for Active Directory.

Four constructed attributes that are based on the attributes in Table 8.8 reside in the normal objects, such as users. Therefore, these attributes are not part of the schema, but still, you can study the schema by studying them.

- `AllowedChildClasses` contains the same information as `possibleInferiors` (mentioned in Table 8.8), but it resides in normal objects, such as the user Jack Brown.
- `AllowedChildClassesEffective` is the same as the previous, but it takes into account the permissions of the logged-on user (that is, the account whose credentials are used with the process that reads the value of this attribute).
- `AllowedAttributes` contains a list of all mandatory and optional attributes of an object. For example, with Jack Brown, this attribute contains a list of 257 attributes, the number of mandatory and optional attributes of any `user` class object.

- `AllowedAttributesEffective` is the same as the previous, but it takes into account the permissions of the logged-on user (that is, the account whose credentials are used with the process that reads the value of this attribute).

These four constructed attributes also take into account class inheritance. An application program can use the two "Effective" attributes to check what the user who is running it has permissions for. Based on this information, the application can, for example, show some edit fields as grayed to indicate a read-only attribute.

Class Inheritance

A class gets most of its characteristics from the corresponding class schema object. However, a class inherits some features from several class schema objects, using *class inheritance.* We can also say that a class is *derived* from another class.

In this section we explain how, by means of inheritance, the list of possible superiors, mandatory attributes, and optional attributes are built from the information in several objects.

Class inheritance makes defining new classes easier, because they can build on existing classes. There is no need to list all possible superiors and attributes from the ground up. Table 8.9 lists the four attributes relevant to class inheritance.

User Class Example

Figure 8.10 illustrates the way the three lists (possible superiors, mandatory attributes, and optional attributes) are built up for the `user` class. We picked the `user` class as an example because it is by far the most intuitive.

The inheritance chain in Figure 8.10 (`top` – `person` – `organizationalPerson` – `user`) has nothing to do with the hierarchy of the schema objects. They all exist as siblings in `CN=Schema, CN=Configuration, DC=sanao, DC=com`. Nor is there any connection with the normal directory hierarchy (domain – OU – user).

Figure 8.10 requires several explanatory comments.

- To save space, we abbreviated attribute names that start with "system"—`sMayContain` instead of `systemMayContain`, and so on.

Table 8.9 Class Inheritance Attributes of a `classSchema` Object

Name	Syntax	Multi-valued	Description	`user` Class Example
`objectClass-Category`	Enumer-ation	No	1 = Structural, 2 = Abstract, 3 = Auxiliary, 0 = 88-class.	1 (=structural)
`subClassOf`	OID string	No	The class from which this class inherits containment and structure attributes. The parent is called a *superclass* and the child a *subclass*.	`organizational-Person`
`auxiliaryClass`	OID string	Yes	Admin-changeable list of auxiliary classes from which this class inherits containment attributes.	—
`system-AuxiliaryClass`	OID string	Yes	Same as the previous, but only the Directory System Agent (DSA) can change the list.	`security-Principal` + `mailRecipient`

- In addition to the attributes shown in Figure 8.10, `mustContain` and `possSuperiors` also would inherit. This base schema example just doesn't happen to use them.
- `Top` has 87 optional attributes and `person` has 6 of its own. Still, the sum is 92 instead of 93 because there is 1 common attribute. For the same reason, the other sums may be a little less than you might expect.

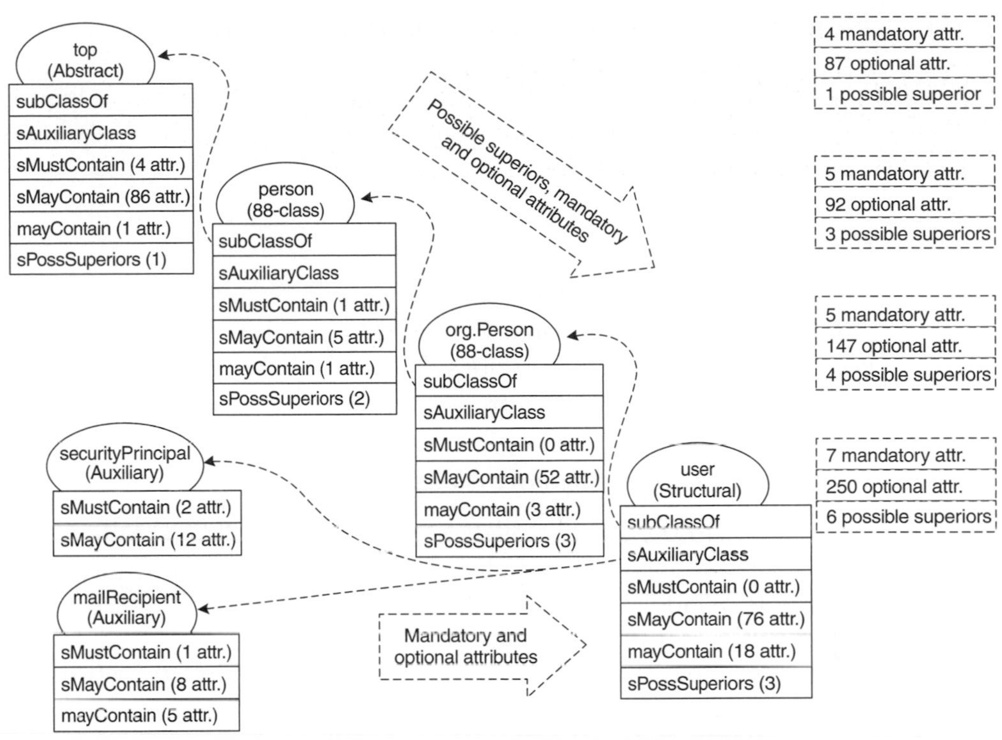

Figure 8.10 The list of possible superiors, mandatory attributes, and optional attributes for each class is the sum of its own list and the lists of all its superclasses. If the lists slightly overlap, however, the sum number on the right-hand side is a little less than a mathematical sum would be. Also, auxiliary classes may add attributes to the list of mandatory and optional attributes.

- The two auxiliary classes `securityPrincipal` and `mailRecipient` are also subclasses of `top`. To keep the figure simple, and because this relationship has no effect, Figure 8.10 does not show this relationship.
- In Figure 8.10, only the `user` class happens to use auxiliary classes. Any superclass could also use auxiliary classes, in which case those attribute lists would also affect the subclasses.
- We don't show it in Figure 8.10, but the inheritance chain actually goes on. The `user` class has the following three subclasses: `computer`, `inetOrgPerson`, and `msPKI-Key-Recovery-Agent`.

- We show LDAP names (such as `mailRecipient`) as object names, even though to be precise the object names should be common names (such as Mail-Recipient). LDAP names appear because in this book we systematically call classes and attributes by their LDAP names.

Class Categories

Each class in Figure 8.10 was marked to be in one of three categories: *structural, abstract*, or *auxiliary*. Active Directory classes belong to four categories, as Table 8.10 describes. Figure 8.11 shows three categories of classes and their relationships as superclasses and subclasses.

Dynamically Linked Auxiliary Classes

In Figure 8.10 the auxiliary classes were statically linked to the `user` class. As a new feature in AD2003 (and when the forest functional level is raised to Windows Server 2003), auxiliary classes can also be dynamically linked to individual instances of a class.

For example, an auxiliary class containing sales-related attributes can be linked to salespeople Jack and Jill instead of the `user` class when it would affect all users. Similarly, other auxiliary classes could be linked only to the users or other objects where they are needed. There is no performance saving, however, because even if the sales-related properties are statically linked to the `user` class (and therefore to every user object), it doesn't cost anything if their values are <not set>.

NOTE The feature is called dynamic linking, in contrast to static linking. In our opinion, there is nothing very dynamic here, and we would rather talk about per-instance linking in contrast to per-class linking.

To link an auxiliary class to an object, add the class's LDAP name or OID (that is, `governsID`) to the multivalued `objectClass` attribute of the target object. You can do this with ADSI Edit, script, LDIF file, LDP, or an application program. If the auxiliary class contains any mandatory attributes (that is, `mustContain` or `systemMustContain`), you must provide a value for them at the same time that you modify `objectClass`. We don't include a direct example of the linking process in the book, but you can easily do the trick by using other samples and information in Chapter 9 and Chapter 11.

Table 8.10 Class Categories

Category	Number of Classes in the Base Schema	Can Be Instantiated*	Purpose and Comments
Structural	169	Yes	– Structural classes are the normal ones, because you can actually create objects for these classes. – Structural classes are derived from abstract or other structural classes and they can include auxiliary classes.
Abstract	9	No	Abstract classes act as templates from which you can derive the actual structural classes or auxiliary and other abstract classes, if necessary.
Auxiliary	7	No	– Auxiliary classes just store lists of mandatory and optional attributes, which you can include in other classes. – An auxiliary class can be derived from another auxiliary class.
88-class	6	Yes	The 1993 version of X.500 introduced the three previous categories. Any class created before that time belongs to a generic 88-class, which refers to the year 1988, when the previous version of the standard was approved. You shouldn't create any 88-class classes.

* Remember that *instantiation* means creating an object of some class. For example, when you create user Jack Brown, you just made an instance (or object) of the class `user`.

Unfortunately, when you have created the link and then check the available attributes of the object with ADSI Edit, it doesn't show the ones that were received using the dynamically linked auxiliary class. Therefore, you need to enter the actual values with a script, LDIF file, LDP, or an application program.

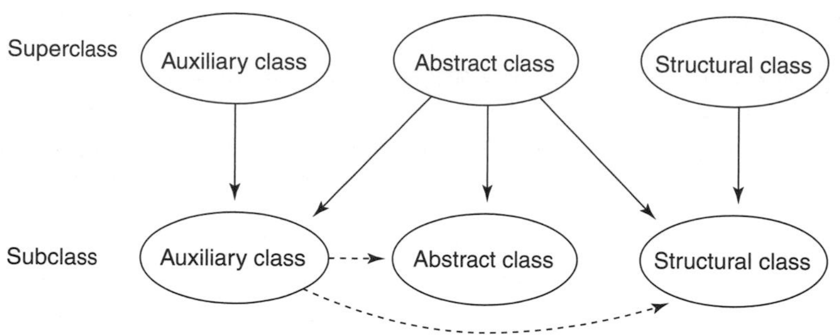

Figure 8.11 A class of any category can be inherited, or derived, from an abstract class. Only an auxiliary class can be inherited from another auxiliary class, and only a structural class can be inherited from another structural class. In addition, the attribute lists in auxiliary classes can be used in abstract and structural classes (indicated by the dashed arrows).

To later find out to which objects a certain auxiliary class is linked, you would use an LDAP filter such as `(objectClass=myAuxClass)`. The target objects also have the new attributes in their `allowed-AttributesEffective` list, so the administrator or application program can see what attributes are available.

If you later want to remove the link, first clear the values of all attributes listed in the auxiliary class, and then remove the class name from the `objectClass` list. If you dynamically add an auxiliary class that is a subclass of another auxiliary class, both auxiliary classes are added to the target object. However, removing the child auxiliary class does not remove its parent; each class must be explicitly removed.

You can also dynamically link an auxiliary class that is a subclass of another auxiliary class (that is, a superclass). In this case they both are linked to the target object. If you later remove the subclass, the superclass is not automatically removed.

ObjectClass versus StructuralObjectClass

As you know, each object belongs to some class—to be exact, it also belongs to all superclasses of the main class. For example, the object Jack Brown belongs to the classes `user`, `person`, `organizational-Person`, and `top`. This list is stored in the multivalued `objectClass` attribute. The four-class list is also the same inheritance chain that you saw in Figure 8.10.

NOTE Normally, you can forget the superclasses of the list and think of only the lowermost class. For example, you can use an LDAP filter (`objectClass=user`), and if you find Jack Brown with that filter, you think of him as a user object, not an organizationalPerson object or the top object.

The constructed attribute `structuralObjectClass` normally has the same contents as `objectClass`. The two become different if an auxiliary class is dynamically linked to an object, because the corresponding class name is stored in `objectClass`, but it won't appear in `structuralObjectClass`.

Because `structuralObjectClass` is constructed, it cannot be used in LDAP filters. For example, the filter (`structuralObjectClass=user`) doesn't work.

Miscellaneous Characteristics of Classes

As the last set of class characteristics, we discuss ten miscellaneous attributes. Three of them provide defaults for objects to be created and four are quite general attributes that any Active Directory object will have. See Table 8.11 for details.

Table 8.11 Miscellaneous Attributes of a `classSchema` Object

Name	Syntax	Multi-valued	Description	`user` Class Example
`nTSecurityDescriptor`	`NT security descriptor`	No	Security descriptor of the class schema object; allows Schema Admins to modify and other users to read schema objects.	A DACL, SACL, and so on
`isDefunct`	`Boolean`	No	If set to TRUE, the class is disabled.	—
`defaultObjectCategory`	`Distinguished name`	No	Default value for `objectCategory` attribute for each new instance of this class.	`CN=Person, CN=...`

(continued)

Table 8.11 Miscellaneous Attributes of a `classSchema` Object *(cont.)*

Name	Syntax	Multi-valued	Description	`user` Class Example
`default-Hiding-Value`	`Boolean`	No	(a) Default value for `showInAdvanced-ViewOnly` attribute for each new instance of this class. (b) If `defaultHiding-Value` is TRUE or <not set>, the corresponding class is not visible in the New context menu in a tool that honors this setting, such as the Users and Computers snap-in (even if Advanced Features is turned on).	FALSE
`default-Security-Descriptor`	`Unicode string`	No	Default value for the security descriptor for each new instance of this class, using Security Descriptor Definition Language (SDDL). The program that will create the instance can also specify a security descriptor to replace this default.	Long string, starting with `D:(A;;RPWPCR`
`systemOnly`	`Boolean`	No	If set to TRUE, only the Directory System Agent (DSA) can create and modify instances of this class.	FALSE

Table 8.11 Miscellaneous Attributes of a `classSchema` Object (*cont.*)

Name	Syntax	Multi-valued	Description	`user` Class Example
`system-Flags`	`Integer`	No	Fifth bit from the right (0x10) tells whether this class belongs to *category 1* (part of the base schema) or *category 2* (an extension).	16 (=0x10)
`object-Class`	`OID string`	Yes	Class of this class schema object itself, the value is obviously `class-Schema` for all class schema objects (plus the superclass `top`—see discussion about object categories later in this chapter).	`top` + `classSchema`
`object-Category`	`Distin-guished name`	No	Object category of this class schema object itself, the value is the distinguished name of the object `CN=Class-Schema` for all class schema objects.	`CN=Class-Schema, CN=Schema, CN=. . .`
`schema-FlagsEx`	`Integer`	No	Not used	—

Table 8.11 introduces the following four concepts:

- `showInAdvancedViewOnly`
- Category 1 and 2 schema objects
- `objectCategory`
- Security Descriptor Definition Language (SDDL)

ShowInAdvancedViewOnly

All Active Directory objects have a `showInAdvancedViewOnly` attribute, which is derived from the `top` class. If the value of this attribute is set to TRUE, an administrative snap-in or other program can choose not to show the object in the user interface. If the attribute value is FALSE or missing, an administrative snap-in or other program should show the object. Examples of programs that honor this attribute are the Users and Computers snap-in and the Windows shell.

Many objects are not interesting even to administrators, so setting this attribute helps to hide those objects. When you turn on Advanced Features in the Users and Computers snap-in, you make visible those objects that have the `showInAdvancedViewOnly` attribute set to TRUE.

NOTE `CN=Dfs-Configuration` has the value FALSE for this attribute. However, it doesn't show in the normal view of the Users and Computers snap-in, because the parent container, `CN=System`, has the value TRUE. Once you turn on Advanced Features, they will both show.

Category 1 and 2 Schema Objects

One bit in the `systemFlags` attribute tells whether the class belongs to category 1 or 2. *Category 1* classes and attributes are part of the base schema, and *category 2* schema objects are something that you or your application has added. In other words, category 2 schema objects are part of the schema extensions.

The reason for the two categories is that there can be (and there are) stricter rules for modifications of category 1 schema objects.

NOTE For some peculiar reason, 15 of the base schema classes are not marked to belong to category 1. Therefore, you could deactivate them, for example, even though you are not supposed to be able to do that for category 1 classes.

Object Category

You have seen the word "category" used in more than one context in this chapter. Here is one more: As you know, each object belongs to some class—to be exact, it also belongs to all superclasses of the main class. For example, the object Jack Brown belongs to the classes `user`, `person`, organizationalPerson, and top. To be able to contain this list, the objectClass attribute is multivalued.

Each object belongs also to some *object category*, as expressed with a single-valued attribute objectCategory. The object category is usually the same as the class, but it may be different, most likely one of the superclasses. For example, the objectCategory of most user class objects is person, which is two steps up in the class hierarchy.

As you can see in Table 8.11, the schema defines only the defaultObjectCategory of each class, but the actual objectCategory attribute is per object. Consequently, two objects of the same class could belong in theory to two categories. However, this would only make things more confusing when you used the category as a search criterion. Also, Active Directory doesn't allow changing the defaultObjectCategory of any base schema object or the objectCategory of any existing object, which fortunately makes this confusing situation difficult to achieve.

Using object categories in LDAP filters and queries has the following advantages over using object classes.

- ObjectCategory is an indexed attribute, whereas objectClass is not. Therefore, LDAP filters and queries that use objectCategory are much faster than those that use just objectClass.
- Objects of several classes can use the same category. If you use a filter or query objectCategory=person, you will get a list of all people, regardless of whether they are users, inetOrgPersons, or contacts. Apart from this "person = user + inetOrgPerson + contact," however, the base schema doesn't contain practical examples of several classes using the same object category.

Security Descriptor Definition Language

Microsoft uses Security Descriptor Definition Language (SDDL) whenever a security descriptor should be described in a string format. Two examples of this are as follows:

- The defaultSecurityDescriptor attribute, mentioned in Table 8.11
- Security templates, which are INF files in C:\Windows\Security\Templates

We explain SDDL briefly here by interpreting the `default-SecurityDescriptor` for the `group` class (i.e., for each new group that you create). We don't use the `user` class as an example, because the string would be ten times longer. For a detailed description of SDDL, refer to the Microsoft Platform SDK (software development kit) at `http://msdn.microsoft.com/library`.

The SDDL string for the `group` class is as follows:

```
D:
(A;;RPWPCRCCDCLCLORCWOWDSDDTSW;;;DA)
(A;;RPWPCRCCDCLCLORCWOWDSDDTSW;;;SY)
(A;;RPLCLORC;;;AU)
(A;;RPWPCRCCDCLCLORCWOWDSDDTSW;;;AO)
(A;;RPLCLORC;;;PS)
(OA;;CR;ab721a55-1e2f-11d0-9819-00aa0040529b;;AU)
(OA;;RP;46a9b11d-60ae-405a-b7e8-ff8a58d456d2;;
      S-1-5-32-560)
```

NOTE The string is divided here on eight lines to make it easier to read. In reality, it is one long string.

The SDDL string for the group class in AD2000 is the same, except the last line is missing. To interpret the string, you must be familiar with the contents of a security descriptor, as discussed in Chapter 4.

The `D:` in this string means that the subsequent data is a discretionary ACL. The owner, group, and system ACL are not included in this case.

The rest of the string consists of seven pairs of parentheses, each of which is one ACE. The ACE in turn consists mostly of two-letter acronyms specifying who has what permissions.

The semicolons divide each ACE into six fields:

- ACE type
- ACE flags
- Permissions
- Object GUID
- Inherit object GUID
- Account SID

Table 8.12 shows the interpretation of the seven ACEs. You can compare its elements to the SDDL string. Table 8.13 lists the SDDL

Table 8.12 Default ACEs for a Group Object

ACE Type	Permissions*	Object GUID	Account SID
Access allowed	Read Prop, Write Prop, Control Access, Create Child, Delete Child, List (Children), List Object, Read Control, Write Owner, Write DAC, (Standard) Delete, Delete Tree, Self (Write)		Domain Admins
Access allowed	Read Prop, Write Prop, Control Access, Create Child, Delete Child, List (Children), List Object, Read Control, Write Owner, Write DAC, (Standard) Delete, Delete Tree, Self (Write)		System
Access allowed	Read Prop, List (Children), List Object, Read Control		Authenticated Users
Access allowed	Read Prop, Write Prop, Control Access, Create Child, Delete Child, List (Children), List Object, Read Control, Write Owner, Write DAC, (Standard) Delete, Delete Tree, Self (Write)		Account Operators
Access allowed	Read Prop, List (Children), List Object, Read Control		(Personal) Self
Object access allowed	Control Access (i.e., extended rights)	Send to	Authenticated Users
Object access allowed	Read Prop	`tokenGroups-GlobalAnd-Universal`	Windows Authorization Access Group

* Domain Admins, System, and Account Operators have a list of 13 permissions. That list is the same as Full Control in the user interface. Authenticated Users and Self have a list of four permissions. The list is equal to the standard permission Read + special permission List Object.

Table 8.13 SDDL Permissions

AccessMask Bit Name	SDDL Acronym	SDDL Spelled-Out Name	Name In the User Interface
ADS_RIGHT_DS_CREATE_CHILD	CC	Create Child	Create All Child Objects*
ADS_RIGHT_DS_DELETE_CHILD	DC	Delete Child	Delete All Child Objects*
ADS_RIGHT_ACTRL_DS_LIST	LC	List Children	List Contents
ADS_RIGHT_DS_SELF	SW	Self Write	All Validated Writes*
ADS_RIGHT_DS_READ_PROP	RP	Read Prop	Read All Properties*
ADS_RIGHT_DS_WRITE_PROP	WP	Write Prop	Write All Properties*
ADS_RIGHT_DS_DELETE_TREE	DT	Delete Tree	Delete Subtree
ADS_RIGHT_DS_LIST_OBJECT	LO	List Object	List Object
ADS_RIGHT_DS_CONTROL_ACCESS	CR	Control Access	All Extended Rights*
ADS_RIGHT_DELETE	SD	Standard Delete	Delete
ADS_RIGHT_READ_CONTROL	RC	Read Control	Read Permissions
ADS_RIGHT_WRITE_DAC	WD	Write DAC	Modify Permissions
ADS_RIGHT_WRITE_OWNER	WO	Write Owner	Modify Owner

* In addition to the UI names listed in the table, these access mask bits can be used also for "partial" permissions. For example, the RP bit is used for both Read All Properties and Read a certain property.

acronyms, their spelled-out names, and their corresponding permission names in the user interface (i.e., in ACL Editor).

ClassSchema Object Property Pages

We conclude our discussion on classes by showing the Schema Manager snap-in property pages for a `classSchema` object. We picked (once again) the `user` class as an example.

We show three screen shots (Figures 8.12 through 8.14)—one for each property page. We exclude the Default Security tab because it is a normal ACL Editor screen corresponding to the `defaultSecurity-Descriptor` attribute. For each screen, we list the attributes that correspond to the fields in the screen.

In the course of this section we have discussed 38 attributes of a class. The Schema Manager snap-in screens in Figures 8.12 through 8.14 show the values for 16 of them (17 if you count the Default Security tab corresponding to the `defaultSecurityDescriptor` attribute). To see the remaining attributes, you need to use ADSI Edit.

Figure 8.12 shows the General tab. The corresponding attributes from top to bottom are as follows (the values are shown in parentheses):

- `lDAPDisplayName` ("user")
- `adminDescription` ("User")
- `cn` ("User")
- `governsID` ("1.2.840.113556.1.5.9")
- `objectClassCategory` ("Structural")
- `defaultObjectCategory` ("person")
- `showInAdvancedViewOnly` (Note that the Schema Manager snap-in shipping with Windows 2000 or Windows Server 2003 has a bug, so setting this check box doesn't have the desired effect. The check box should control `defaultHidingValue`, which in turn controls the `showInAdvancedViewOnly` attribute of the objects to be created. Currently, the check box controls `show-InAdvancedViewOnly`, which only dictates whether the schema object itself is visible in a nonadvanced view of an admin tool.)
- `isDefunct` ("checked", meaning the class is active and not defunct)

Figure 8.13 shows the Relationship tab. The corresponding attributes from top to bottom are as follows (the values are shown in parentheses):

- `subClassOf` ("organizationalPerson")
- `auxiliaryClass`, `systemAuxiliaryClass` ("mailRecipient, securityPrincipal")
- `possSuperiors`, `systemPossSuperiors` ("builtinDomain, domainDNS, organizationalUnit")

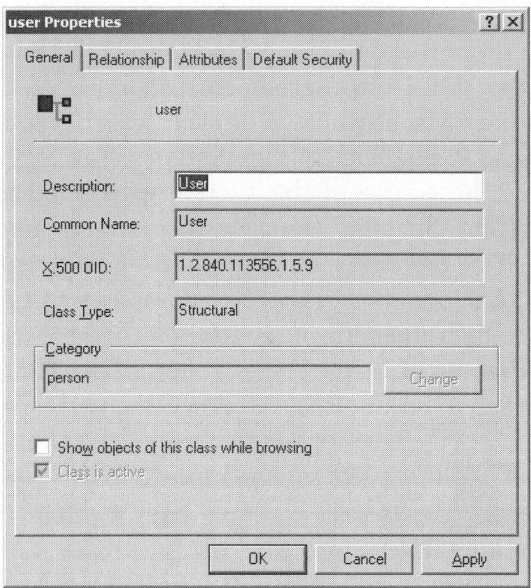

Figure 8.12 With the Schema Manager snap-in, you can see the attributes of various classes, such as the `user` class.

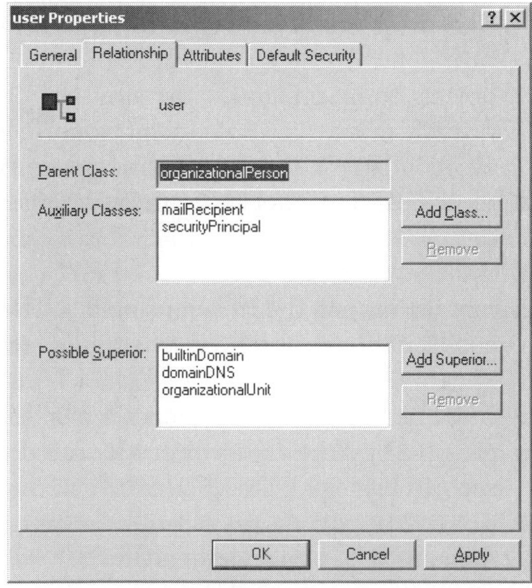

Figure 8.13 The Relationship tab shows both the inheritance hierarchy in the schema and the possible superiors in the normal directory tree.

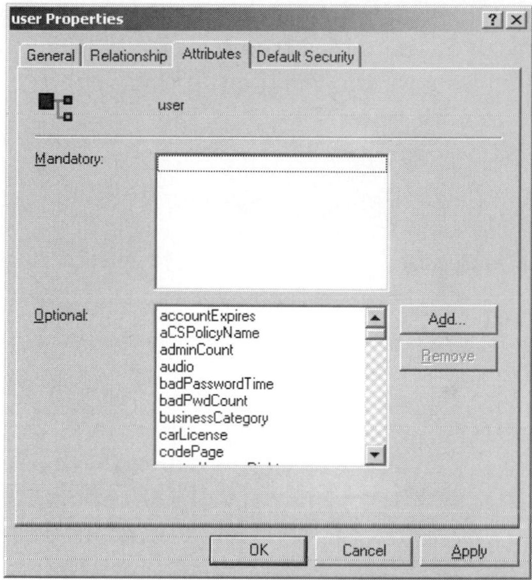

Figure 8.14 The Attributes tab lists the mandatory and optional attributes for the class, excluding inherited attributes.

Figure 8.14 shows the Attributes tab. The corresponding attributes from top to bottom are as follows (the values are shown in parentheses):

- `mustContain`, `systemMustContain` (empty list)
- `mayContain`, `systemMayContain` (a number of attributes)

Now that we have covered the different aspects of schema classes, we are ready to move on to the attributes and syntaxes. Attribute characteristics have something in common with class characteristics, but obviously there are also quite a few differences.

Attributes and Syntaxes

In this section we discuss the attributes that define the attributes in the schema.

As with classes, there is a schema object for each attribute, which means a total of 1,070 `attributeSchema` objects in the base schema (863 in AD2000). Each of these 1,070 attributes is characterized by the attributes of its schema object, and those `attributeSchema` objects themselves use 113 attributes out of the 1,070 (94 in AD2000). Figure 8.15 shows the relationship between the attribute schema objects and their attributes.

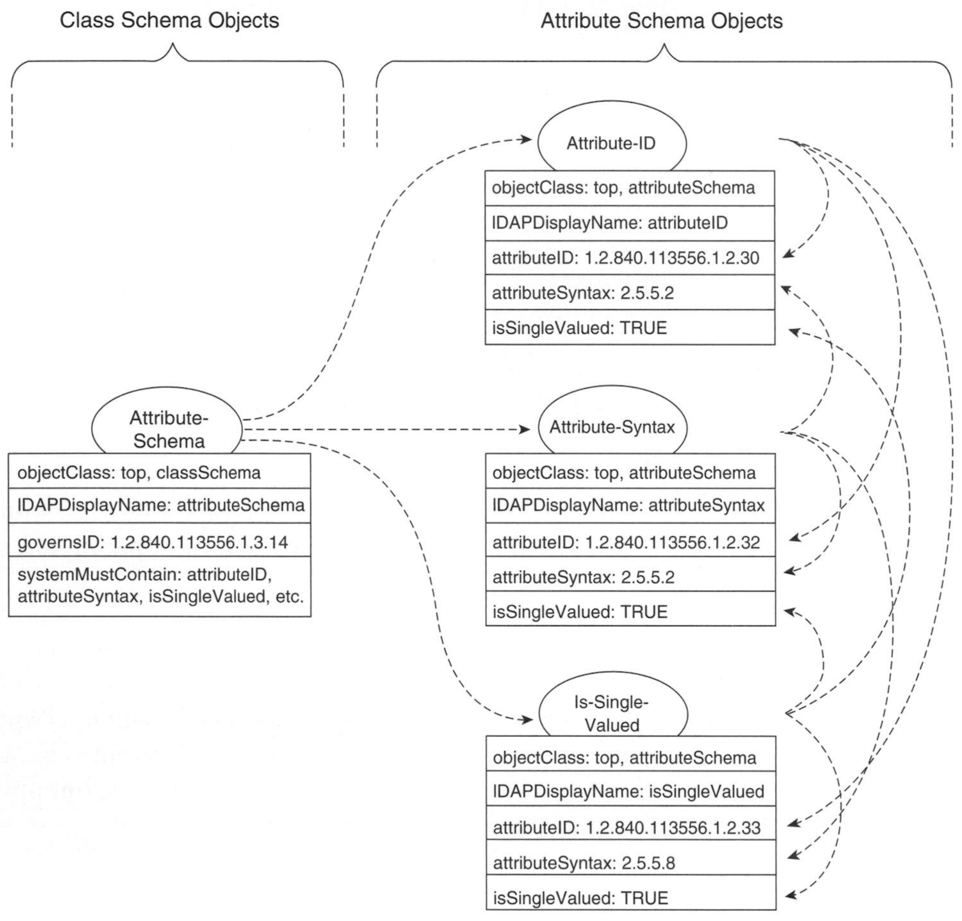

Figure 8.15 The `attributeSchema` class has 1,070 instances (i.e., `attributeSchema` objects) in the base schema. Each of these 1,070 objects defines the syntax and other aspects of one attribute. The definitions reside in the attributes of the objects, which means that the `attributeSchema` objects define attributes also for themselves. This figure shows three `attributeSchema` objects, which result in 3 x 3 arrows on the right side.

NOTE The other figures that we have included in this chapter show LDAP names as schema object names (although this is imprecise). In Figure 8.15 we show the common names (which is more correct), because we want to show the actual object name and the LDAP name attribute separately.

Of the 113 attributes that the `attributeSchema` class uses, it inherits 90 attributes from `top` and defines 23 on its own level. As with classes, most of the inherited attributes are quite general (after all, they apply to any Active Directory object). We cover 13 of the inherited attributes and 21 "own" attributes for a total of 34 attributes.

NOTE When discussing classes, we listed 14 inherited attributes and now 13. The list is the same except that `possibleInferiors` doesn't apply here. For example, the `homePhone` of a user cannot have child objects.

We divide the 34 attributes into four categories.

- *Names and identifiers.* You probably remember that `classSchema` objects have 14 various names, descriptions, and identifiers. `attributeSchema` objects have even more: 17 names, descriptions, and identifiers.
- *Syntax and content rules.* These 7 attributes define the kind of data the attribute accepts and the values that are possible for it.
- *Searches.* The 2 attributes in this category control things such as indexing of the attribute and whether it is part of the global catalog.
- *Miscellaneous.* There are 8 miscellaneous attributes.

Table 8.14 shows all 34 attributes listed by their LDAP names. If the common name is quite different from the LDAP name, it appears in parentheses. The four sections following Table 8.14 describe the attributes in more detail. The Type column indicates whether the attribute is mandatory or optional. The Source Class column contains either `attributeSchema` or `top`—the latter meaning the attribute was inherited from the `top` class. The Base Schema Attributes column indicates the kinds of values the 1,070 attribute objects have for the attributes in the table. Finally, the LDAP Display Name Attribute Example column lists the values for the `lDAPDisplayName` attribute.

Table 8.14 Attributes of an attributeSchema Object

Name	Type	Source Class	Base Schema Attributes (1,070)	LDAP Display Name Attribute Example
Names and Identifiers				
lDAPDisplayName	M	attr.S.	All values are unique	lDAPDisplay-Name
cn (Common-Name)	M	attr.S.	All values are unique	LDAP-Display-Name
adminDisplayName	O	top	1,065 are the same as cn, 4 are the same as lDAPDisplay-Name, 1 is roughly the same as cn	LDAP-Display-Name
name (RDN)	O	top	Same as cn	LDAP-Display-Name
distinguished-Name (Obj-Dist-Name)	O	top	All values are unique	CN=LDAP-Display-Name, CN=Schema, CN=Config-uration, DC=sanao, DC=com
canonicalName	O	top	All values are unique	sanao.com/Config-uration/Schema/LDAP-Display-Name
displayName	O	top	Not used	—
displayName-Printable	O	top	Not used	—
classDisplayName	O	attr.S.	Not used	—
adminDescription	O	top	964 are the same as cn, 102 contain a real description, 4 are the same as lDAPDisplayName	LDAP-Display-Name

Table 8.14 Attributes of an `attributeSchema` Object (*cont.*)

Name	Type	Source Class	Base Schema Attributes (1,070)	LDAP Display Name Attribute Example
`description`	O	`top`	Not used (although 6 contain a helpful description, the remaining 1,064 are <not set>)	—
`attributeID`	M	`attr.S.`	975 are Microsoft IDs (1.2.840.113556), 56 are X.500 IDs (2.5), 8 are Netscape IDs (2.16.840.1.113730), 27 are "ITU-T data – PSS" IDs (0.9.2342), 2 are RSADSI IDs (1.2.840.113549), 1 is a University of Michigan ID (1.3.6.1.4.1.250), and 1 is a Mark Wahl ID (1.3.6.1.4.1.1466)	1.2.840.113556.1.2.460
`schemaIDGUID`	M	`attr.S.`	All values are unique	9a7996bf e60dd011 a28500aa 003049e2
`objectGUID`	O	`top`	All values are unique	Such as 22a9624f 4b998f46 a658e3c2 7a357859
`attribute-SecurityGUID`	O	`attr.S.`	146 are set; 924 are <not set>	—
`mAPIID`	O	`attr.S.`	125 are unique values; 945 are <not set>	33137

(continued)

Table 8.14 Attributes of an `attributeSchema` Object (*cont.*)

Name	Type	Source Class	Base Schema Attributes (1,070)	LDAP Display Name Attribute Example
`linkID`	O	`attr.S.`	58 are unique values; 1,012 are <not set>	—
Syntax and Content Rules				
`attributeSyntax`	M	`attr.S.`	All are set to 1 of 15 values (ranging from 2.5.5.1 through 2.5.5.17)	2.5.5.12
`oMSyntax`	M	`attr.S.`	131 are set to "127"; 939 are set to 1 of 14 values (ranging from 1 through 66)	64
`oMObjectClass`	O	`attr.S.`	131 are set to 1 of 4 values; 939 are <not set>	—
`isSingleValued`	M	`attr.S.`	729 are TRUE; 341 are FALSE	TRUE
`rangeLower`	O	`attr.S.`	216 are set; 854 are <not set>	1
`rangeUpper`	O	`attr.S.`	231 are set; 839 are <not set>	256
`extendedChars-Allowed`	O	`attr.S.`	1 is TRUE, 1,069 are <not set>	—
Searches				
`searchFlags`	O	`attr.S.`	114 are nonzero; the remaining 956 are zero	9
`isMemberOf-Partial-AttributeSet`	O	`attr.S.`	151 are TRUE; 919 are <not set>	TRUE

Table 8.14 Attributes of an `attributeSchema` Object (*cont.*)

Name	Type	Source Class	Base Schema Attributes (1,070)	LDAP Display Name Attribute Example
Miscellaneous				
nTSecurity-Descriptor	M	top	All are set	A DACL, SACL, and so on
isDefunct	O	attr.S.	All are <not set>	—
systemOnly	O	attr.S.	117 are TRUE, 944 are FALSE, 9 are <not set>	FALSE
systemFlags	O	top	1,008 are set to a nonzero value, 22 are set to zero, 40 are <not set>	16
objectClass	M	top	All are top + attribute-Schema	top + attribute-Schema
objectCategory	M	top	All are CN=Attribute-Schema, CN=Schema, CN=Configuration, DC=sanao, DC=com	CN=Attribute-Schema, CN=Schema, CN=Config-uration, DC=sanao, DC=com
schemaFlagsEx	O	attr.S.	Not used	—
isEphemeral	O	attr.S.	Not used	—

NOTE As a detail, `lDAPDisplayName` is a mandatory attribute of an `attributeSchema` object, but it is only an optional attribute of a `classSchema` object.

Names and Identifiers

Most of the names, descriptions, and identifiers for attribute schema objects are exactly the same as the names, descriptions, and identifiers for class schema objects. Consequently, there is no need to repeat the descriptions of the following nine attributes:

- `lDAPDisplayName`
- `cn` (Common-Name)
- `adminDisplayName`
- `name` (RDN)
- `distinguishedName` (Obj-Dist-Name)
- `canonicalName`
- `adminDescription`
- `schemaIDGUID`
- `objectGUID`

Also, the following four attributes are not used, as they were not used with class schema objects:

- `displayName`
- `displayNamePrintable`
- `classDisplayName`
- `description` (well, six AD2003 base schema `attribute-Schema` objects have a description here, but it is in the wrong place)

This leaves us with four not-yet-familiar attributes. They are described in Table 8.15.

AD2003 contains a new, undocumented `msDS-IntId` attribute for internal use, which is present in category 2 attributes. Its purpose may be that because an OID can be reused in AD2003 (see Chapter 9), a new permanent ID was needed.

Table 8.15 Some Name and Identifier Attributes of an `attributeSchema` Object

Name	Syntax	Multi-valued	Description	LDAP Display Name Attribute Example
`attributeID`	`OID string`	No	Object ID (OID) of the attribute.	1.2.840.113556.1.2.460
`attribute-SecurityGUID`	`Octet string`	No	ID that links the attribute to belong to some property set; permissions may then be given for this property set (see Chapter 6).	—
`mAPIID`	`Integer`	No	Messaging API (MAPI) applications identify attributes with this ID. Note that only 125 attributes have the `mAPIID` attribute set.	33137
`linkID`	`Integer`	No	Some attributes form forward-back link pairs, as discussed in the "Linked Attributes" section.	—

Linked Attributes

When an attribute refers to another object in the directory, it is often beneficial that the target object has a reference back to the first object. An example is a user's membership in a group. The group has a `member` attribute, which includes the user (a forward link), and the user has a `memberOf` attribute, which includes the group (a back link). Figure 8.16 shows an example.

An even value in the `linkID` attribute denotes a forward link and a larger-by-1 odd value denotes a back link.

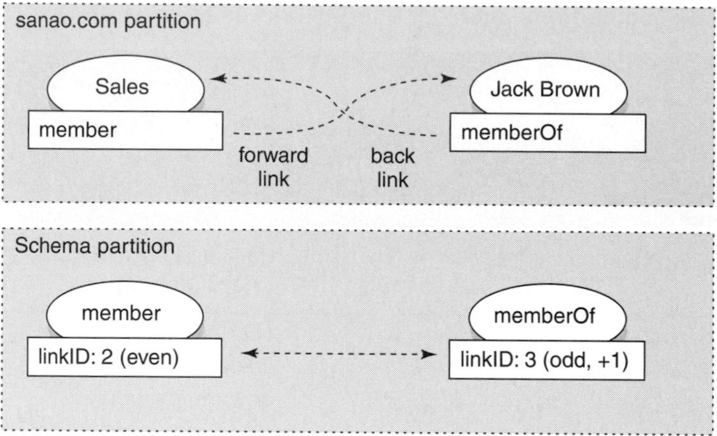

Figure 8.16 The `member` attribute is a forward link from a group object to a user object. The `memberOf` attribute is a back link from the user to the group. The relationship is defined in the corresponding `attributeSchema` objects.

The base schema of AD2000 contained 13 linked attribute pairs. The base schema of AD2003 contains the following 24 linked attribute pairs:

- `member` – `memberOf` (Is-Member-Of-DL)
- `manager` – `directReports` (Reports)
- `owner` – `ownerBL` (ms-Exch-Owner-BL)
- `siteObject` – `siteObjectBL`
- `nonSecurityMember` – `nonSecurityMemberBL`
- `queryPolicyObject` – `queryPolicyBL`
- `privilegeHolder` – `isPrivilegeHolder`
- `managedBy` – `managedObjects`
- `hasMasterNCs` – `masteredBy`
- `serverReference` – `serverReferenceBL`
- `bridgeheadTransportList` – `bridgeheadServerListBL`
- `netbootServer` – `netbootSCPBL`
- `frsComputerReference` – `frsComputerReferenceBL`
- `fRSMemberReference` – `fRSMemberReferenceBL`
- `msCOM-PartitionLink` – `msCOM-PartitionSetLink`
- `msCOM-UserPartitionSetLink` – `msCOM-UserLink`
- `msDS-NonMembers` – `msDS-NonMembersBL`
- `msDS-MembersForAzRole` – `msDS-MembersForAzRoleBL`

- msDS-OperationsForAzTask – msDS-OperationsForAzTaskBL
- msDS-TasksForAzTask – msDS-TasksForAzTaskBL
- msDS-OperationsForAzRole – msDS-OperationsForAzRoleBL
- msDS-TasksForAzRole – msDS-TasksForAzRoleBL
- msDS-hasMasterNCs – msDs-masteredBy
- msDS-ObjectReference – msDS-ObjectReferenceBL

NOTE If you count the attributes that have linkID defined, the number is not 2 x 24 = 48, but 58 instead. The reason is that the base schema includes 10 attributes that have linkID defined, but which are missing the corresponding back-link pair.

All back-link attributes, such as memberOf, are "system only"—that is, users or administrators cannot modify them. Active Directory is responsible for updating these attributes, maintaining *referential integrity* in the process. If either of the referenced objects is moved, Active Directory modifies the reference accordingly.

A forward-link attribute must use one of the following syntaxes: DN, DN with Unicode string, DN with binary, access point DN, and OR name. A back-link attribute must be of syntax DN.

Syntax and Content Rules

Seven attributeSchema attributes control the type of data and the values each attribute accepts. Table 8.16 describes these syntax and content attributes.

The data type is called syntax in this context and it is defined by three attributes: attributeSyntax, oMSyntax, and oMObjectClass. Naturally, the three attributes must be consistent, as you see in Tables 8.17 through 8.20, where we describe all the syntax choices.

Several attributes are necessary to express the syntax because more than one standard is involved. The first attribute (attributeSyntax) defines an X.500 syntax, and the two others a XOM syntax. "XOM" stands for "XAPIA X/Open Object Management," an interface for ASN.1 messaging defined by the X.400 API Association (XAPIA) and X/Open (a former vendor standards organization). Currently, "X/Open" is a trademark that belongs to the Open Group (http://www.opengroup.org/).

NOTE In "XAPIA," the *X* refers to X.400 and X.500 ITU-T standards, whereas in "X/Open," the *X* refers to UNIX.

NOTE The letters *XOM* can also stand for "X/Open OSI-Abstract-Data Manipulation."

Table 8.16 Syntax and Content Attributes of an `attributeSchema` Object

Name	Syntax	Multi-valued	Description	LDAP Display Name Attribute Example
`attribute-Syntax`	`OID string`	No	Identifies with an X.500 OID whether the value of this attribute is integer, string, or some other data format.	2.5.5.12
`oMSyntax`	`Integer`	No	About the same as `attributeSyntax` but expressed with a XOM code.	64
`oMObject-Class`	`Octet string`	No	If the XOM code is 127 (=object distinguished name), this attribute defines the "subsyntax."	—
`isSingle-Valued`	`Boolean`	No	Specifies whether the attribute is single- or multivalued.	TRUE
`rangeLower`	`Integer`	No	The lowest possible value for an integer attribute or the shortest possible value for a string attribute.	1

Table 8.16 Syntax and Content Attributes of an `attributeSchema` Object (*cont.*)

Name	Syntax	Multi-valued	Description	LDAP Display Name Attribute Example
`rangeUpper`	`Integer`	No	The largest possible value for an integer attribute or the longest possible value for a string attribute.	256
`extended-CharsAllowed`	`Boolean`	No	Specifies whether the attribute can contain extended characters; used only with the syntaxes `Teletex string`, `IA5 string`, `Numeric string`, and `Printable string`.	—

Syntax Choices

Active Directory supports 23 syntaxes, but it uses only 19 of them in the base schema. Because the syntax choices are hard-coded and don't appear as objects in Active Directory, you cannot add syntaxes.

We can divide the syntaxes into the following categories:

- Simple data types (4 syntaxes)
- String data types (10 syntaxes)
- Time data types (2 syntaxes), which are actually also strings
- Reference data types (7 syntaxes), which are various object references

Tables 8.17 through 8.20 describe the syntaxes of each category. Some syntaxes have two names, in which case we mention the second name in parentheses.

Table 8.17 Syntaxes for Simple Data Types

Syntax	attribute-Syntax	oMSyntax	Description	Count in Base Schema
Boolean	2.5.5.8	1	Values can be either TRUE or FALSE.	58
Integer	2.5.5.9	2	32-bit number.	193
Enumeration	2.5.5.9	10	32-bit number. Active Directory treats this as an integer.	6
Large integer (INTEGER8, Interval)	2.5.5.16	65	64-bit number.	72

Table 8.18 Syntaxes for String Data Types

Syntax	attribute-Syntax	oMSyntax	Description	Count in Base Schema
OID string	2.5.5.2	6	An object ID string (e.g., 2.5.5.2) consisting of digits (0–9) and dots	22
Case-sensitive string (case-exact string)	2.5.5.3	27	Case-sensitive* string, each character of which belongs to the General-String character set**	0
Case-ignore string (teletex)	2.5.5.4	20	Case-insensitive string, each character of which belongs to the teletex character set**	8

* Whether a string is case-sensitive or case-insensitive matters when you start to use LDAP filters to specify which values match certain criteria.

** Active Directory doesn't currently enforce General-String, teletex, Printable, or IA5 character sets, or the digit restriction. However, this may change, so you should use only valid characters.

Table 8.18 Syntaxes for String Data Types (*cont.*)

Syntax	attribute Syntax	oMSyntax	Description	Count in Base Schema
`Printable string`	2.5.5.5	19	Case-sensitive string, each character of which belongs to the `Printable` character set**	13
`IA5 string`	2.5.5.5	22	Case-sensitive string, each character of which belongs to the *International Alphabet* 5 (`IA5`) character set**	9
`Numeric string`	2.5.5.6	18	String, each character of which is a digit**	2
`Octet string`	2.5.5.10	4	Array of bytes (i.e., binary data)	138
`Unicode string (directory string)`	2.5.5.12	64	Normal case-insensitive string using any Unicode characters	394
`NT security descriptor`	2.5.5.15	66	An octet string that contains a Windows NT or later security descriptor (SD)	3
`SID string`	2.5.5.17	4	An octet string that contains a Windows NT or later security identifier (SID)	9

Table 8.19 Syntaxes for Time Data Types

Syntax	attribute-Syntax	oMSyntax	Description	Count in Base Schema
UTC time string	2.5.5.11	23	Time-string format defined by ASN.1 standards. See standards ISO 8601 and X.680 for more information.* UTC, or Coordinated Universal Time, is roughly the same as GMT, or Greenwich Mean Time. This syntax uses only two characters to represent the year.	4
Generalized time string	2.5.5.11	24	Time-string format defined by ASN.1 standards. See standards ISO 8601 and X.680 for more information.* This syntax uses four characters to represent the year.	8

* These two time formats are further described in Chapter 6 in the "Specifying Values" section.

All seven syntaxes in Table 8.20 have `oMSyntax = 127`, which means that they must have `oMObjectClass` also defined. The latter attribute distinguishes them, because some of them have identical `attributeSyntax` and `oMSyntax`. We list the `oMObjectClass` values in Table 8.21.

Table 8.20 Syntaxes for Reference Data Types

Syntax	attribute-Syntax	oMSyntax	Description	Count in Base Schema
DN (distinguished name or DN String)	2.5.5.1	127	Distinguished name of an object in the directory. If the target object is moved or renamed, Active Directory updates the DN attribute accordingly.	123
DN with binary (DN with octet string)	2.5.5.7	127	This syntax stores a distinguished name along with some binary data. Active Directory keeps the DN up-to-date. The format is B:*hex digit count*:*bytes as hex*:*DN* (e.g., B:6:F12A4B:*someDN*).	5
OR name	2.5.5.7	127	An X.400 syntax (related to e-mail addresses).	0
Replica link	2.5.5.10	127	Syntax that repsFrom and repsTo attributes use to control replication. The corresponding attributes contain things such as the up-to-date vector of a replication partition.	2

(continued)

Table 8.20 Syntaxes for Reference Data Types *(cont.)*

Syntax	attribute-Syntax	oMSyntax	Description	Count in Base Schema
`Presentation address`	2.5.5.13	127	OSI application entities use presentation addresses to address other application entities. See RFCs 1278 and 2252 and ISO DIS 7498-3 for more information.	1
`DN with Unicode string`	2.5.5.14	127	This syntax stores a distinguished name along with a string. Active Directory keeps the DN up-to-date. The format is `S:`*`character count`*`:`*`string`*`:` *`DN`*(e.g., `S:5:hello:`*`someDN`*).	0
`Access point DN`	2.5.5.14	127	An X.400 distinguished name.	0

Multivalued Attributes

In AD2000 each multivalued attribute could have up to 850 values, except for linked multivalued attributes, such as group members, which could have 5,000 values (i.e., group members). When one value was added, deleted, or modified, the whole attribute was replicated to other domain controllers. Therefore, it was not a good idea to make multivalued attributes too large.

All the aforesaid is true also for AD2003 until the forest functional level is raised to Windows Server 2003 (or Windows Server 2003 interim), after which the size limitations are removed and each value of a linked multivalued attribute is replicated separately. For example, a group can now have more than 5,000 members, and when one member

Table 8.21 `oMObjectClass` Values for "127" Syntaxes

Syntax	`attribute-Syntax`	`oMSyntax`	`oMObjectClass` (hexadecimal)
`DN`	2.5.5.1	127	2B0C0287731C00854A
`DN with binary (DN with octet string)`	2.5.5.7	127	2A864886F7140101010B
`OR name`	2.5.5.7	127	56060102050B1D
`Replica link`	2.5.5.10	127	2A864886F71401010106
`Presentation address`	2.5.5.13	127	2B0C0287731C00855C
`Access point DN`	2.5.5.14	127	2B0C0287731C00853E
`DN with Unicode string`	2.5.5.14	127	2A864886F7140101010C

is added, only this one membership is replicated instead of all 5,001 memberships.

If you want to put normal "application data" into a multivalued attribute, you should favor relatively small multivalued attributes for two reasons: (a) When you read the attribute, all values are normally returned together, and (b) nonlinked multivalued attributes are still replicated as one unit.

The values are returned in random order; if you write a program or script to read the values, you cannot depend on the order.

Even though returning all values of a multivalued attribute is the normal behavior, LDAP allows specifying the range of values. This is explained in Chapter 6.

Searches

Some attributes are indexed, which allows fast searches based on those attributes, and some attributes are part of the global catalog. The indexed and global catalog attributes are defined with two `attributeSchema` attributes, which are described in Table 8.22.

NOTE Indexing and global catalog membership are per-attribute settings, not per-class settings. In other words, if the `givenName` attribute is indexed, this will apply to any class that happens to use `givenName`.

Table 8.22 Search Attributes of an `attributeSchema` Object

Name	Syntax	Multi-valued	Description	LDAP Display Name Attribute Example
`SearchFlags`	`Enumeration`	No	The bits in this number define whether the corresponding attribute is indexed and how it is treated in searches. (Table 8.23 describes the bits.)	9
`isMemberOf-Partial-AttributeSet`	`Boolean`	No	If TRUE, the corresponding attribute is part of the global catalog and consequently is replicated to all global catalog servers.	TRUE

NOTE You might wonder how it is possible that the `member` attribute is part of the global catalog (`isMemberOfPartialAttributeSet` is TRUE), but only universal group members appear in the global catalog, whereas global and domain local group members don't. The answer is that Microsoft hard-coded this difference into Active Directory; that is, group membership doesn't care about the `isMemberOfPartial-AttributeSet` attribute.

`SearchFlags` is a *bitfield* attribute. It contains 32 bits, 6 of which have a meaning. Those 6 bits are the least significant ones, which means that they are the rightmost bits if you use Windows Calculator to convert a decimal number to binary. The bits are described in Table 8.23. The bit value "1" means "True"—that is, the setting is on.

If you specify an additional attribute to be indexed, the directory database usually grows less than 1 percent. Creating a tuple index, however, has a bigger impact on the database size; tuple indexing a single attribute can grow the database up to 20 percent. A tuple index enables

Table 8.23 `SearchFlags` Bits

Bit from Right	Hex Value	Description	Count in Base Schema
1	1	If set, the attribute is indexed. This allows fast searches on this attribute, as well as wildcards (*) in search strings.	69
2	2	If set, the attribute is indexed over container and attribute.	0
3	4	The attribute is part of the Ambiguous Name Resolution (ANR) set, which is explained in the "Ambiguous Name Resolution" section. This bit should be used in conjunction with the first bit.	9
4	8	The attribute is preserved when an object is changed to a tombstone (i.e., "deleted"). All attributes without this bit are deleted.	29
5	10	If set, the attribute is copied when duplicating a user with the Users and Computers snap-in.	33
6	20	If set, the attribute has a tuple index. It makes faster those searches that have a wildcard in the beginning of the specified string value. Examples are (sn=*son) and (sn=*der*).	0

users to use partial text strings in their searches, so the tuple index must include one entry for each substring of the attribute text values. And the longer the values, the more of these substrings there are.

Ambiguous Name Resolution

Ambiguous Name Resolution (ANR), which is mentioned in Table 8.23, needs a few words of explanation. ANR is an LDAP feature that allows using a simple LDAP filter instead of a complex filter in certain LDAP searches. You can use ANR manually with LDAP filters (discussed in Chapter 6). Also, when you perform a search with Windows Address Book, it will use ANR for you.

The following nine attributes are part of the ANR set in the AD2003 base schema (AD2000 didn't include `msDS-AdditionalSamAccountName`):

- `displayName`
- `givenName`
- `legacyExchangeDN`
- `msDS-AdditionalSamAccountName`
- `name` (RDN)
- `physicalDeliveryOfficeName` (user properties, General tab, Office)
- `proxyAddresses`
- `sAMAccountName` (user properties, Account tab, Pre-Windows 2000 name)
- `sn` (Surname)

ANR gives flexibility in two ways:

- Only a partial match is required from the beginning of the text. If you search for "Brown," you will get both "Brown" and "Brownfield."
- The search is performed on several attributes (those nine just listed). If you search for "Brown," it can be the starting part of not only the surname (last name), but also `displayName`, `sAMAccountName`, or any of the other six attributes.

If you search for two words, ANR works as just described, with one addition. It will also try if the words are "first name - last name" or "last name - first name." If you want to find Jack Brown, you can type either "jac bro" or "brow jack." The corresponding LDAP filters would be

```
(anr=jac bro)
(anr=brow jack)
```

It is possible to suppress the first name/last name functionality and/or the last name/first name functionality. You do this by modifying the same `dSHeuristics` attribute that is used to enable the List Object permission. We explained the procedure in Chapter 4 in the "Enabling and Using the List Object Permission" section.

Miscellaneous Characteristics for Attributes

Most of the miscellaneous `attributeSchema` attributes are also `classSchema` attributes. Because we described the `classSchema` attributes when discussing classes, there is no need to repeat the discussion of the following attributes:

- `nTSecurityDescriptor`
- `isDefunct`
- `objectClass`
- `objectCategory`
- `schemaFlagsEx`

One new attribute, `isEphemeral`, is not used, so we are left with only two attributes to address here: `systemOnly` and `systemFlags`. Although those two attributes also appeared in the discussion of classes, they have some new aspects. Table 8.24 describes the attributes `systemOnly` and `systemFlags`, and Table 8.25 continues the description of the `systemFlags`.

Table 8.24 Miscellaneous Attributes of an `attributeSchema` Object

Name	Syntax	Multi-valued	Description	LDAP Display Name Attribute Example
`systemOnly`	`Boolean`	No	If TRUE, you can set the value for the attribute only when creating an object. Afterward, only the DSA can change the value.	FALSE
`systemFlags`	`Integer`	No	The bits in this number define things such as whether the corresponding attribute is replicated or constructed. (Table 8.25 describes the bits.)	16

Table 8.25 `SystemFlags` Bits

Bit from Right	Hex Value	Description	Count in Base Schema
1	1	If set, the attribute is not replicated from one domain controller to another.	55
2	2	If set, the attribute must be in the global catalog. This setting overrides the one defined with `isMemberOfPartial-AttributeSet`.	46
3	4	If set, the attribute is constructed. It is built from other attributes and not stored in the schema on disk.	36
5	10	If set, the attribute belongs to category 1 (part of the base schema); otherwise, it belongs to category 2 (an extension).	1,007
28	800 0000	This is an undocumented bit used by the system.	21

NOTE For some peculiar reason, 63 of the base schema attributes and 15 of the classes are not marked to belong to category 1. Therefore, you could deactivate them, for example, even though you are not supposed to be able to do that for category 1 attributes or classes.

AttributeSchema Object Property Pages

There is only one property page for `attributeSchema` objects in the Schema Manager snap-in. Figure 8.17 shows the property page for the object `lDAPDisplayName`.

Of the 34 `attributeSchema` attributes that we have discussed in this section, Figure 8.17 shows the following 13, with the values in parentheses (we didn't count `showInAdvancedViewOnly`). To see all of the attributes, you need ADSI Edit.

- `lDAPDisplayName` ("lDAPDisplayName")
- `adminDescription` ("LDAP-Display-Name")
- `cn` ("LDAP-Display-Name")
- `attributeID` ("1.2.840.113556.1.2.460")

- `attributeSyntax`, `oMSyntax`, `oMObjectClass` ("Unicode String")
- `rangeLower` ("1")
- `rangeUpper` ("256")
- `isSingleValued` ("This attribute is single-valued.")
- `showInAdvancedViewOnly` (Note that even though checking the "Allow this attribute to be shown in advanced view" box sets this attribute to FALSE, it doesn't have any practical meaning. The same bug existed in the Windows 2000 version of Schema Manager, although the text was a little different.)
- `isDefunct` ("Attribute is active" checked)
- `searchFlags` ("Index this attribute in the Active Directory" checked, "ANR" not checked, "Attribute is copied when duplicating a user" not checked, "Index this attribute for containerized searches in the Active Directory" not checked)
- `isMemberOfPartialAttributeSet` ("Replicate this attribute to the Global Catalog" checked)

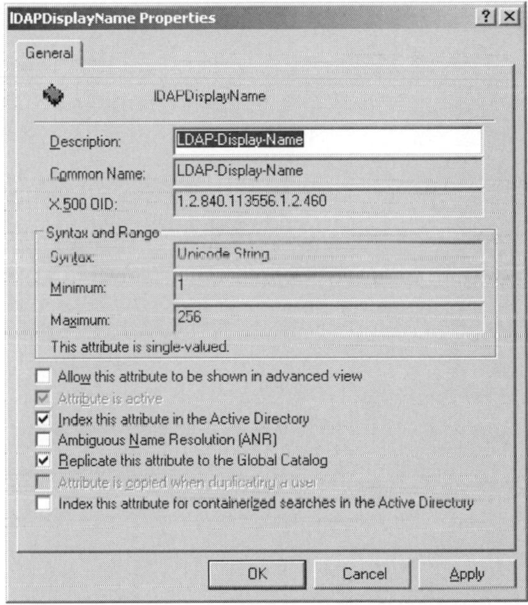

Figure 8.17 With the Schema Manager snap-in, you can see the attributes of various attributes, such as `lDAPDisplayName`.

Conclusion

In this chapter we discussed how the schema is built up from classes, attributes, and syntaxes. We also described the attributes of `classSchema` and `attributeSchema` objects.

We have examined the schema in detail thus far, but we have not made changes to it. In the next chapter we evaluate if we need to extend the schema, and if so, how to extend it.

CHAPTER 9

Extending the Schema

One of the advantages Windows 2000 and Windows Server 2003 have over the predecessor Windows NT is that Active Directory has an extensible schema. Even though the Active Directory base schema has quite a few classes and attributes, they cannot accommodate all data and anticipate every need that an organization may have. In this chapter we explain how to extend the schema by addressing the following topics:

- When and why to extend or modify the schema
- How to plan for various modifications
- How to perform modifications
- How to show the extensions in the user interface

These topics build on the knowledge that you gained in the preceding chapter.

In this chapter we talk about modifying the schema, and most of those modifications are extensions. The phrase "extending the schema" is well established to cover both extensions and other modifications. Therefore, we use the terms "extend" and "modify" somewhat interchangeably.

NOTE Even if you are not going to extend the schema, you should check the example in the "Bringing the Extensions to the User Interface" section later in this chapter. In that section, we demonstrate how to view logon counts and other information about users without extending the schema.

At the end of the chapter we show how to extend the `user` class. The example works as a summary of this chapter; however, it might be helpful to check the example first, and then read the chapter from the beginning with the example in mind as a point of reference.

When and Why to Modify

One reason to modify the schema is that the current schema doesn't contain the classes and attributes that would accommodate data that you as an administrator want to put in Active Directory. Another reason is that a directory-enabled application (DEA) wants to modify the schema to store its data in the directory.

Even though an extensible schema is a selling point for Active Directory, you obviously shouldn't modify the base schema unless necessary. You should first evaluate if the current schema would fill the need without modification. Unfortunately, the only way to do the evaluation is to examine the base schema and try to find out if a certain class or attribute would suit that need.

If you must modify the schema, you can modify some category 1 (base schema) classes and/or attributes, or you can create new (category 2) classes and/or attributes. There are two approaches to modifying or extending attributes.

- *Use an existing attribute unmodified.* Add an existing category 1 attribute to an existing or new class or classes.
- *Create a new attribute.* Create a new category 2 attribute and add it to an existing or new class or classes.

Note that neither approach includes modifying an existing attribute. We didn't include such an approach, because about all you can (or should) do to an existing attribute is to modify its indexing, ANR, and global catalog settings, or whether it is copied when a user is copied. None of the four options enables you to store any new kind of data in Active Directory—they are only for administrative tuning of Active Directory.

There are also two approaches to modifying or extending classes.

- *Modify (extend) an existing class.* Add category 1 and/or 2 attributes to the `mayContain` list of some category 1 class or classes and/or add new possible superiors for the class.
- *Create (and derive) a new subclass.* Create a new category 2 class using as a superclass a class that already has most of the attributes and possible superiors that you need. If none is suitable, you can derive from the `top` class (keeping in mind that from the `top` class alone you inherit 91 attributes to your new class). When you

create the class, add any appropriate category 1 and/or 2 attributes (to the `mayContain` list and/or the `mustContain` list) and possible superiors.

NOTE You cannot add `mustContain` attributes to an existing class (except when using dynamically linked auxiliary classes, as discussed in Chapter 8.) This would lead to an illegal situation, because you might already have a number of instances of that class, and those instances wouldn't have this new mandatory attribute set to any value.

Creating new attributes or classes requires more planning than just modifying existing ones. Once you create a new schema object, you cannot delete it, at least in AD2000 or AD2003 (a future version should support schema deletion). Consequently, the enterprise organization may be stuck with the extensions for some time. Further, if different departments all added something in addition to purchased applications, the number of attributes and classes in your directory would be much higher after a few years. When a directory accumulates a large number of category 2 classes and attributes, using and managing the directory and its schema is easier if they all are well documented and systematically named.

When adding new classes or attributes, you need to get all of their characteristics right, whereas if you modify an existing class or attribute, you need to focus on only some characteristics. Creating new attributes or classes seems less desirable than modifying existing ones, but it has one big advantage: The new attributes and classes are guaranteed to be for the exclusive use of your organization. Even though there are already 1,070 attributes in the base schema and you could imagine that there is an attribute for every need, how can you ever know which ones are safe to use? Microsoft doesn't offer a list to indicate "these 450 are OK to use," or anything similar. If you add some nice-sounding category 1 attribute to the `mayContain` list of a category 1 class, Microsoft might do the same in a future version of Active Directory, but for a different purpose. However, if you create a new category 2 attribute, it should be safe to use that attribute with a category 1 class and vice versa—using category 1 attributes in your new category 2 classes should also be fine. Not to mention that both the attribute and the class are category 2.

Guidelines

Based on the preceding discussion, we offer the following guidelines for schema modifications.

- Evaluate the need to change the schema.
- If you need to modify the schema, go ahead, but plan the modification thoroughly and put the plan on paper (or in an electronic file at least). You must plan the attribute values of each new and modified `classSchema` and `attributeSchema` object. You should also plan how to use class inheritance.
- If you are a software vendor, obtain a base OID that will be used when your application creates new classes and/or attributes in customer networks. Also obtain a base OID if you will create your own classes and/or attributes. For more information, see the "Obtaining a Base OID" section in Chapter 8.
- Document the modifications. This document is likely to be about the same as the documented plan we mentioned in the second point.
- If you are a software vendor and the modification will be applied in customer directories, give your customers the document. If you are the customer, require your vendor to provide you with the documentation.
- Consider not modifying category 1 classes, except for adding new attributes and possible superiors to some classes.
- Consider the impact that your modifications might have on other departments in the organization and on future modifications, whether they originate from manual modifications within the organization or from purchased applications.
- If you are a vendor of directory-enabled applications (that need to modify the schema of the customer directories), write a separate installation program for the schema modification. Include instructions that only the Schema Admins are able to run it as well as other information that a customer needs to perform a successful schema extension. This information is presented throughout the course of this chapter, especially in the "Order of Tasks" section.
- Put only one or two users in the Schema Admins group, which has a permission to modify the schema. Store the users' passwords in a safe and perhaps require them to use a smart card for logon. You could also remove all users from Schema Admins and add them

only when actually changing the schema (or when moving the schema master role to another domain controller).

- Establish a committee (or nominate a responsible person) to analyze and approve the applications to modify the schema (and probably also carry the modifications out).
- When the people on the committee in the previous point get a request for a modification, they should consider if the modification will fill one isolated need or if it could be used throughout the organization. Also, the committee should determine if they will consolidate multiple requests from different departments.
- Ensure that correct naming conventions and other design rules are used for the new schema objects, as explained later in this chapter.
- When you have a set of attributes that you may need to add to several classes, consider using an auxiliary class instead of adding attributes directly to a class.
- Don't create a subclass of the `user` class and start putting your users in that new class. User management is much simpler if they are all in the plain old `user` class.
- Consider if you can use existing attributes and perhaps add them to some additional classes (either new or existing), or if you need to create new attributes. For example, the `birthLocation` attribute is in the base schema, which you could add to the `user` class. However, that attribute accepts only binary data, so you might end up creating a new attribute that accepts text data.

Now we turn to consideration of the kind of data to put in Active Directory.

What Data to Put in Active Directory

Active Directory, as an information store, has the following characteristics.

- Because of intrasite and intersite replication, the data is highly available. There is fault tolerance, and a geographically spanned network has proximity of information.
- As a result of replication, the data in some domain controllers may be out-of-date at any given time (i.e., loose consistency).
- Active Directory hierarchies and permissions allow distributed management of the data. Permissions also allow control of which users see which objects and attributes.

- Active Directory is optimized for a high number of reads.
- Active Directory allows standards-based read and write access using the LDAP protocol.

Keep these characteristics in mind when you plan what data to put in Active Directory. In addition, there are the following three basic requirements for the data that will go in Active Directory.

- *"Globally" useful.* The data should be "globally" useful, because Active Directory provides an easy way to replicate data to different sites, as well as an efficient means to search, read, and modify the data. To be precise, your data doesn't have to be globally useful, but if it is not, it doesn't use this benefit of Active Directory, and it is replicated to several sites in vain (depending on the domain controller placement).
- *Not volatile (i.e., relatively static).* The data should not be volatile. Examples of volatile data are a single print job or e-mail message. If it would take one hour to replicate a change to all necessary domain controllers in a multisite network, there would be no sense in putting in data that would change every hour. Such data would be out-of-date most of the time. (However, AD2003 includes various techniques to store dynamic data. See the discussion in the next section.)
- *Relatively small.* The data items should be relatively small. Large, multivalued attributes would be costly to replicate among domain controllers and retrieve to clients. However, some clients are able to use the LDAP control that allows incremental reading of multivalued attributes. We cannot give you numbers, because they depend on physical network connections, among other things.

Especially the last two requirements are important because Active Directory data is replicated to several domain controllers, often on different sites. When you consider which attributes to put in the global catalog, the requirements are even more important. The level of importance increases further if you plan to store some data in the configuration partition instead of the domain partitions.

If you are a programmer, you should know some additional things about Active Directory. Active Directory is different from a relational database, such as SQL Server. A relational database allows joins with tables and views, but Active Directory does not. There is no distributed lock management in Active Directory, just the aforementioned loose consistency. Each object is a flat list of attributes, which has no substructure or nesting. Even though attributes can be multivalued, the multiple values are sets instead of vectors—you can never retrieve them in a particular order. You can perform complex queries, but there are only two bitwise operations available (implemented as LDAP extensions). Also, you cannot evaluate expressions in queries, which is quite different from SQL queries.

In addition, if your application must store several data elements in Active Directory, it is better to add one binary attribute that contains all of them than to add many individual attributes for the various needs of the application. In other words, Active Directory doesn't need to see the data structure of your application data. On the other hand, creating several smaller attributes may be better in terms of replication.

In summary:

- If your data is not globally useful, is volatile, or is too large, you should probably store it somewhere other than in Active Directory. Or, in the case of volatile data, consider the techniques introduced in AD2003 to store dynamic data (see the next section.) Some alternate locations are the file system, a database application such as SQL Server, and the registry. Another option is to use either an application partition, as explained in Chapter 6, or Active Directory Application Mode (ADAM), explained in the corresponding section later in this chapter.
- Or, if the data fills the criteria, you can store the data in Active Directory. First examine the existing classes and attributes to determine if some of them will fill the need.
- Or, if the existing classes and attributes are not enough, plan, implement, and document the necessary extensions to the schema.

Dynamic Objects in AD2003

Traditionally, directory services have stored static data for users and applications to utilize. Starting with AD2003, Active Directory supports also dynamic objects, as defined in RFC 2589 (see `http://www.ietf.org/rfc`). Microsoft was closely involved in writing the specification, because two of the three authors work for Microsoft.

Dynamic objects open new possibilities in application development. If an application is already using LDAP for its static, "globally interesting" data needs, it can now use the same LDAP, the same access control, and so on also for its dynamic data needs. Because domain controllers take care of deleting dynamic objects after a while, an application can let the directory service take care of its garbage collection.

The idea of a dynamic object is that when a client application creates one, a time-to-live (TTL) value is attached to the new object. The client application's responsibility is to refresh the TTL periodically by invoking the Refresh extended LDAP operation. If it doesn't do this, because it was closed, for example, the TTL will soon decrement to zero, and the server (that is, the domain controller) will delete the object. By performing the periodic refresh, the client application tells the server that the dynamic object is still valid and accurate.

When a domain controller deletes a dynamic object because of expiration, no tombstone is left behind. It is not needed, however, because each domain controller is responsible for deleting local dynamic objects when each one's TTL expires. The client application can also choose to delete the object, in which case a tombstone is left behind. Also other LDAP operations, such as search, modify, and modifyDN, are allowed.

A dynamic object can be of any normal class (even `user`, although it is not sensible), and it could represent practically anything. It could be a `person` object to represent a person who is currently online. When that person goes offline, the corresponding application either deletes the dynamic object or lets it expire and get deleted. Another example is a meeting object. It is created when the (online) meeting starts, and a certain participant (the meeting owner) or any participants can refresh the TTL while the meeting goes on. When there is no one left to refresh, the object is soon deleted.

Controlling the TTL

When a client creates a dynamic object, it can specify the TTL using the `entryTTL` attribute, with a value up to 31,557,600 seconds (that is, 365 days and 8 hours, corresponding to an average year length including the leap year). If a TTL is not specified, a per-forest default is used, which is by default 86,400 seconds (that is, 24 hours).

If the client requests a smaller-than-minimum TTL, the server will use the minimum instead. By default, this minimum is 900 seconds (that is, 15 minutes), again per-forest.

The two per-forest default values are stored in `CN=Directory Service, CN=Windows NT, CN=Services, CN=Configuration,`

DC=<forest_name>. Its multivalued attribute msDS-Other-Settings contains the following two values:

- DynamicObjectDefaultTTL=86400
- DynamicObjectMinTTL=900

You can modify the defaults either by modifying these values or by using the NTDSUtil tool and its menu choice Configurable Settings. Note that the Platform SDK documentation has the wrong value names. A long TTL would mean little refresh traffic; a short TTL would mean highly up-to-date dynamic data.

In the Active Directory implementation, entryTTL is a constructed attribute. Another attribute, msDS-Entry-Time-To-Die, contains the actual expiration moment in absolute time, such as "August 15, 2003, at 11:08:15 AM." Whenever the value of entryTTL is queried, the domain controller calculates how many seconds are left to that moment and returns the result.

The Refresh Request and Response

The client sends the periodic Refresh request as an extended LDAP operation that uses the OID 1.3.6.1.4.1.1466.101.119.1. This OID is also in the supportedExtension attribute of the rootDSE object of any Windows Server 2003 domain controller, so the client can first check that the server actually supports this feature.

In the Request packet, the client includes the distinguished name of the target object, as well as the requested new TTL value in seconds. In the response, the server sends back the TTL it actually chose to use, which may or may not be the same TTL that the client requested. The client must accept this returned value.

If the client requested a less than the previously discussed minimum TTL, the minimum is obviously used. If the client requested a value of over 24 hours, the RFC allows the server to decrease the value to a minimum of 86,400 seconds (that is, 24 hours). The latter would prevent clients from using unreasonably long TTLs. However, AD2003 seems to accept a value of 30,000,000 seconds (that is, about a year.)

Because of a network delay or outage, a Refresh request may get lost, and consequently the dynamic object may expire. The RFC requires the client to detect this and read the object.

Creating and Viewing Dynamic Objects

Typically, applications, not administrators, create dynamic objects. However, we introduce the process here so you can get a little acquainted with them.

A dynamic object is created instead of a static one when the `dynamicObject` auxiliary class is dynamically linked to the object at creation time (see Chapter 8 for dynamic linking of auxiliary classes). Afterward this is not possible, because a static object cannot be converted to dynamic, or vice versa. At the same time, the `entryTTL` attribute can be set.

Consequently, you can create a test dynamic object with an LDIF file, such as the following:

```
dn: CN=DynObject1, OU=Sales, DC=sanao, DC=com
changetype: add
objectClass: person
objectClass: dynamicObject
entryTTL: 1800
```

NOTE Typically, dynamic objects are created in application directory partitions, because in that case administrators and developers can control on which domain controllers they are replicated, regardless of the domain structure (see Chapter 5.) Here we create the test object in a normal domain partition, because this is just a small test. The configuration and schema partitions don't allow dynamic objects.

NOTE Active Directory doesn't quite follow RFC 2589. Because dynamic objects are not supported in the configuration and schema partitions, Active Directory should indicate this in the `dynamicSubtrees` attribute of the `rootDSE` object. Active Directory, however, doesn't contain the `dynamicSubtrees` attribute.

This creates the object, which has a lifetime of half an hour. You can see it right away in the Users and Computers snap-in only if you have Advanced Features turned on. Advanced Features is not required because of dynamicness, but because person objects are hidden by default.

To scan for all dynamic objects, including the one you just created, you can use a command such as this:

```
csvde -f dynObjects.txt -d dc=sanao,dc=com
   -r (objectClass=dynamicObject) -l entryTTL
```

The command lists all dynamic objects in the `sanao.com` domain and the remaining TTL value for each object (because `entryTTL` is an operational attribute, you won't get it unless you specifically request it). You could perform a corresponding query using the LDP tool.

NOTE As discussed in Chapter 8, ADSI Edit doesn't display the attributes that were received using dynamic linking. Therefore, you cannot use it to view the values of `entryTTL` or `msDS-Entry-Time-To-Die`.

You cannot create a static object as a child of a dynamic object.

Active Directory Application Mode

Active Directory Application Mode (ADAM) is somewhat of a light version of Active Directory. As the name implies, ADAM provides directory services for (directory-enabled) applications. You can also use the actual Active Directory for this, but using ADAM instead enables you to configure it more freely to the application's needs.

With ADAM, you don't have to approve application schema extensions that would otherwise have to be made to the enterprise Active Directory schema. Also, application vendors can sell their product to companies that haven't yet deployed Active Directory.

ADAM is an LDAP directory service, which you can install in a few minutes on any Windows Server 2003 (excluding the Web Edition) or Windows XP SP1 computer. The installation does not require reboot, and it is not related to the domain controller role. Prior to installation, you need to download an 8MB installation file at `http://www.microsoft.com/windowsserver2003/adam`.

ADAM runs as a user-mode service in a process called dsamain.exe. You can also have multiple instances (and consequently, multiple dsamain processes) in a single computer. Each instance has a name, such as SanaoHRApp, and a corresponding service name, such as ADAM_SanaoHRApp. Each instance has the schema and configuration partitions and an application partition to contain the actual data.

The regular Active Directory requires domain names that use the domain component prefix in distinguished names, such as `DC=sanao, DC=com`. With ADAM, you could name the application partition to be `CN=HRApp, O=Sanao, C=US`, for example.

Although ADAM is targeted to be maintained mostly with the application that a given instance was created for, ADAM includes the following administration tools:

- ADAM version of ADSI Edit
- ADAM version of NTDSUtil (divided in two parts: DSDBUtil and DSMGMT)
- ADAM version of DCDiag (called DSDiag)
- Normal versions of RepAdmin, LDP, LDIFDE, CSVDE, and DSACLS

The downloadable package contains release notes, an introductory white paper, a step-by-step reviewer's guide, and extensive information for a programmer.

Planning the Modifications

In planning modifications, you must consider the changes you could make, as well as gather and determine the necessary information relevant to each possible modification. Here we address the following operations:

- Creating a class
- Modifying a class
- Creating an attribute
- Modifying an attribute
- Deactivating a class
- Deactivating an attribute

Remember that creating or modifying a class or an attribute means creating or modifying the corresponding `classSchema` or `attribute-Schema` object.

Creating a Class

When we discussed `classSchema` objects in the previous chapter, we described 36 attributes for them. If you create a new `classSchema` object, you must define only 5 attributes and you may define 16 more. Table 9.1 lists these 21 attributes, with some guidelines. The remaining 15 attributes you cannot define, because they are one of the following:

- Not used
- Filled by the system
- Constructed attributes

The second column of Table 9.1 indicates whether you must or may specify a value for each attribute. Note that this is not the same as the attribute's being mandatory or optional. Some mandatory attributes are filled by the system and some attributes you need to assign a value, even though technically they are optional.

NOTE If you want to set an attribute that is marked as "system only" in Table 9.1, you must do this when you create the `classSchema` object. Afterward, you cannot change a system-only attribute.

TIP When generating the value for `defaultSecurityDescriptor`, you can probably do fine by taking a `defaultSecurityDescriptor` of one of the existing classes and modifying it to your needs. C programmers also have the option of generating the string with the `ConvertSecurityDescriptorToStringSecurityDescriptor` Win32 API function.

When a class is created, it must pass a series of *consistency checks*. Otherwise, Active Directory refuses to create the class schema object. Basically, the checks ensure that classes conform to certain requirements—for example, since the `governsID` should be unique, the checks verify that it really is unique. They also check that any attribute or class that is referred to in `mayContain` or `auxiliaryClass`, or any other attribute that refers to another attribute or class, exists and is the right type (e.g., an auxiliary really is an auxiliary).

Modifying a Class

When creating a new class, you could use 21 `classSchema` attributes. If you later modify the class, the number of possible attributes narrows to 10. The rest are either "system only" or the schema *safety checks* prevent the change. Table 9.2 lists the attributes that you can change.

NOTE In addition to the guidelines here, keep in mind also the guidelines for creating classes.

Table 9.1 Attributes of a New `classSchema` Object

Name	Must/ May	System Only	Guidelines
Names and Identifiers			
`cn` (Common-Name)/ `name` (RDN)	Must	`cn`: No/ `name`: Yes	Microsoft encourages you to set `cn` to be the same as `lDAP-DisplayName` (see the following guideline).
`lDAPDisplayName`	Must	No	Microsoft encourages you to use the following convention: The name consists of two parts that have a hyphen in between. The first part is your organization's name, acronym, or other string that uniquely identifies your organization. The second part names your class or attribute in any way you want, as long as it is descriptive. Obviously, the second part must be unique within the names containing your organization's first part. If you want to qualify for the Certified for Windows logo, you must follow this convention and also register the first part with Microsoft. Register at `http://msdn.microsoft.com/certification/ad-registration.asp` or use the e-mail alias `schemreg@microsoft.com`. The first part should start with a lowercase letter and the second part with an uppercase letter (e.g., `sanao-MyProductConfigInfo`).
`adminDisplayName`	May	No	Use any name you want, but usually it is best to define this to be the same as `cn`. Also, if you don't specify a name, the system will use `cn`.

Table 9.1 Attributes of a New `classSchema` Object (*cont.*)

Name	Must/ May	System Only	Guidelines
`adminDescription`	May	No	Use any description you want.
`governsID`	Must	Yes	Allocate an OID that is unique within all classes and attributes in the world from the "range" that was issued to your organization by an issuing authority. Microsoft recommends that you use only one category of your base OID for attributes and one for classes. For example, if your base OID is 1.3.6.1.4.1.123123, your classes could be 1.3.6.1.4.1.123123.1.x and attributes 1.3.6.1.4.1.123123.2.x. This way, replication among domain controllers is a little lighter.
`schemaIDGUID`	May	Yes	Active Directory generates this value if not specified. However, especially if you are an application vendor, you should provide a value so that your class will have the same value in all installations (this helps in tasks such as defining property sets and managing permissions programmatically). The value should be a 128-bit octet string that is unique within all classes and attributes in all directories in which this class will be used. To get a GUID, use UUIDGen or GUIDGen, which are part of the Platform SDK (see `http://msdn.microsoft.com/library`).
`rDNAttID`	May	Yes	Microsoft encourages you to use only "cn," which is also the default if you don't specify a value. You shouldn't use values other than "cn," "dc," "l," "o," "c," and "ou," because all LDAPv3 clients recognize them.

(continued)

Table 9.1 Attributes of a New `classSchema` Object *(cont.)*

Name	Must/ May	System Only	Guidelines
Structure and Containment Rules*			
`mustContain`	May	No	Include whichever mandatory attributes you want. Even though this attribute is not "system only," you cannot change the list.
`systemMustContain`	May	Yes	Include whichever mandatory attributes you want. You cannot change the list.
`mayContain`	May	No	Include whichever optional attributes you want.
`systemMayContain`	May	Yes	Include whichever optional attributes you want. You cannot change the list.
`possSuperiors`	May	No	Include whichever possible superiors (parents) you want. (See the end of this chapter for considerations of where in the directory to place the instances of new classes.)
`systemPoss-Superiors`	May	Yes	Include whichever possible superiors (parents) you want. You cannot change the list.
Class Inheritance			
`objectClass-Category`	Must	Yes	Specify structural, abstract, or auxiliary as you need, but don't create 88-classes.
`subClassOf`	Must	Yes	Specify `top` or some other existing class appropriate to your need (and inheritance plan).
`auxiliaryClass`	May	No	Include whichever auxiliary classes are appropriate according to your inheritance plan.

* We indicate in the table that you don't need to define the `mayContain`, `systemMayContain`, `mustContain`, and `systemMustContain` attributes. However, you cannot use the new class for anything unless you define at least one of them (except for the unlikely case that you want to make a new structural class that has only the 91 attributes that `top` already has).

Table 9.1 Attributes of a New `classSchema` Object *(cont.)*

Name	Must/ May	System Only	Guidelines
`system-AuxiliaryClass`	May	Yes	Include whichever auxiliary classes are appropriate according to your inheritance plan. You cannot change the list.
Miscellaneous			
`defaultObject-Category`	May	No	If you don't specify a value, this attribute defaults to the DN of the `classSchema` object itself (which is often fine). You can also specify a superclass if that is used in searches more frequently. If you inherit this new class from a category 1 class (other than `top`), specify the DN of that class for this attribute. This way, the instances of the new class are easier to find.
`default-HidingValue`	May	No	Set this value to TRUE if the instances of your new class should not be visible in the user interface (normal view of the Users and Computers snap in [without Advanced Features turned on] and the Windows shell).
`defaultSecurity-Descriptor`	May	No	Set a default if you want, using Security Descriptor Definition Language (SDDL).
`systemOnly`	May	Yes	Don't set this value. None of your classes should be "system only," because you couldn't use them.

The safety checks ensure that changes made by one application or user won't harm other applications and users.

As a safety check, Active Directory doesn't allow you to add or delete mandatory attributes of a class, either directly with `mustContain` or indirectly with inheritance/auxiliary. The reason is that there could

Table 9.2 `ClassSchema` Object Attributes That Can Be Changed

Name	Guidelines
cn (Common-Name)/ name (RDN)	See the guideline for lDAPDisplay-Name.
lDAPDisplayName	You shouldn't change this. However, if you accidentally create a class that is not quite what you want, you can rename the first class to something obsolete (cn and lDAPDisplayName) and create a new one. In addition to renaming, you should disable the erroneous class as described later in this chapter.
adminDisplayName	No guidelines.
adminDescription	No guidelines.
mayContain	If you want additional optional attributes, add them here directly or use an auxiliary class as a set of attributes.
possSuperiors	No guidelines.
auxiliaryClass	If you want additional optional attributes, add them directly to mayContain or add an auxiliary class as a set of attributes.
defaultObjectCategory	No guidelines.
defaultHidingValue	No guidelines.
defaultSecurityDescriptor	No guidelines.

already be a number of instances of that class that would suddenly become illegal because they didn't contain that mandatory attribute.

For category 1 classes (i.e., the base schema), Active Directory has the following additional restrictions as safety checks.

- You cannot change the lDAPDisplayName.
- You cannot change the defaultObjectCategory.
- You cannot change the objectCategory of any instance of a category 1 class.

NOTE Because 15 of the base schema classes don't have their system-Flags attribute set or the value is 0, they are not recognized as being in category 1. Consequently, you can do modifications such as changing their `lDAPDisplayName`.

TIP If you want to see which classes and attributes are without protection (not that you need that information for anything), you can use ADSI Edit to apply an LDAP filter `(!(systemFlags:1.2.840.113556.1.4.803:=16))` to the Schema container.

Creating an Attribute

When you are creating new `attributeSchema` objects, 13 of the 34 attributes that we discussed earlier are filled by the system, constructed, or not used. One attribute is discussed later when we cover deactivating attributes. Table 9.3 contains the remaining 20 attributes. You must use 5 of them and you may use 15 others. (Although to be exact, the list of 20 includes also a few that you can but should not use.)

Table 9.3 Attributes of a New `attributeSchema` Object

Name	Must/ May*	System Only	Guidelines
Names and Identifiers			
`cn` (Common-Name)/ `name` (RDN)	Must	No/Yes	Specify a name using the conventions we described when we covered creating classes in Table 9.1 (e.g., `sanao-MyProductUserData`).
`lDAPDisplayName`	Must	No	Specify a name identical to the `cn` (e.g., `sanao-MyProductUserData`).
`adminDisplayName`	May	No	Use any name you want, but usually it is best to define this to be the same as `cn`. Also, if you don't specify a name, the system uses `cn`.

(continued)

* As with classes, the division of whether you must or may define an attribute is not the same as the attribute's being mandatory or optional. Some mandatory attributes are filled by the system and some attributes you need to fill, even though technically they are optional.

Table 9.3 Attributes of a New `attributeSchema` Object *(cont.)*

Name	Must/ May*	System Only	Guidelines
`adminDescription`	May	No	Use any description you want.
`attributeID`	Must	Yes	Allocate an OID that is unique within all classes and attributes in the world, from the "range" that was issued to your organization by an issuing authority. Microsoft recommends that you use only one category of your base OID for attributes and one for classes. For example, if your base OID is 1.3.6.1.4.1.123123, your classes could be 1.3.6.1.4.1.123123.1.x and attributes 1.3.6.1.4.1.123123.2.x. This way, replication among domain controllers is a little lighter.
`schemaIDGUID`	May	Yes	Active Directory generates this value if not specified. However, especially if you are an application vendor, you should provide a value so that your class will have the same value in all installations (this helps in tasks such as managing permissions programmatically). The value should be a 128-bit octet string that is unique within all classes and attributes in all directories in which this class will be used. To get a GUID, use UUIDGen or GUIDGen, which are part of the Platform SDK (see `http://msdn.microsoft.com/library`).
`attribute-SecurityGUID`	May	No	If you want your new attribute to be part of some property set, store the `rightsGuid` of that property set to the `attribute-SecurityGUID` of your new attribute. (See Chapter 4 for more information on property sets.)

Table 9.3 Attributes of a New `attributeSchema` Object *(cont.)*

Name	Must/ May*	System Only	Guidelines
`mAPIID`	May	Yes	Don't set this value. You won't have MAPI applications that would identify your new attributes with this ID.
`linkID`	May	Yes	Set this value if you are creating a linked attribute. To avoid future problems, you should get nonallocated and registered values for this from Microsoft at `http://msdn.microsoft.com/certification/ADLinkID.asp`. For example, when you are upgrading a forest from AD2000 to AD2003, one of the new attributes wants to use `linkID` 1040. If your forest already contains another attribute with that `linkID`, the ADPrep tool cannot run, and your only choice is probably to install a new forest instead of upgrading.
Syntax and Content Rules			
`attributeSyntax`	Must	Yes	Set this according to the syntax you have chosen.
`oMSyntax`	Must	Yes	Set this according to the syntax you have chosen.
`oMObjectClass`	May	Yes	Set this according to the syntax you have chosen, when `oMSyntax` is 127. If you don't specify a value, Active Directory provides a default value that matches your chosen `attributeSyntax`. Remember, however, that one `attributeSyntax` may correspond to more than one `oMObjectClass` value, and if using the default, you cannot choose which one.
`isSingleValued`	May	Yes	Set this according to your needs. If you don't specify anything, the default is FALSE (i.e., multivalued).
`rangeLower`	May	No	Specify this if you want a lower limit. There is no default. *(continued)*

Table 9.3 Attributes of a New `attributeSchema` Object *(cont.)*

Name	Must/ May*	System Only	Guidelines
`rangeUpper`	May	No	Specify this if you want an upper limit. There is no default.
`extended-CharsAllowed`	May	No (was Yes in AD2000)	If you happen to use one of the syntaxes `Case-ignore string (teletex)`, `IA5 string`, `Numeric string`, or `Printable string`, you can set this value.
Searches			
`searchFlags`	May	No	Set this value if you want the new attribute to be indexed or part of the ANR set. You should index only attributes that have relatively unique values (such as last name). A Boolean attribute with TRUE/FALSE values is a bad choice for indexing. Also, multi-valued attributes are bad choices because they are not at all light to index. Note that indexing doesn't generate more data to be replicated, because indexes are created locally in each domain controller.
`isMemberOf-Partial-AttributeSet`	May	No	Set this to TRUE if you want your new attribute to be part of the global catalog. Unlike indexing an attribute, adding an attribute to the global catalog increases the amount of replication traffic in your enterprise WAN, because subsequent value changes to this attribute in any object must be replicated to all global catalog servers of the forest. Consequently, you should use this setting only for attributes that are relatively small, change quite seldom, and are probably of interest to most of the enterprise. See also the Warning in the text.

Table 9.3 Attributes of a New `attributeSchema` Object (*cont.*)

Name	Must/ May*	System Only	Guidelines
Miscellaneous			
`systemOnly`	May	Yes	You probably don't want to set this value. If you set it to TRUE, you can later give the corresponding attribute a value only when creating an instance. After that, you cannot change the value anymore.
`systemFlags`	May	Yes	Don't set this value. The bits in `systemFlags` are only for system use.

NOTE If you want to set an attribute that is marked as "system only" in Table 9.3, you must do this when you create the `attributeSchema` object. You cannot change a system-only attribute later.

WARNING In AD2000, adding a new attribute as part of the global catalog caused a full replication (or "full sync") of all partial replicas of all global catalog servers in the forest. For example, if you had a forest where the directory database on a global catalog server was 1GB larger than in a normal domain controller, the size of the partial replicas combined was 1GB (although the number varies in different domains). If your forest contained 25 global catalog servers, adding a new attribute to the global catalog would have generated about 25GB of replication in your LANs and WAN. This slight disadvantage was removed in AD2003. Already in AD2000, removing attributes from the global catalog didn't cause any replication. The global catalog servers removed the attributes locally from their databases.

When we discussed creating classes, we mentioned that a new class must pass some consistency checks. This is also true for new attributes. Two of these checks are not as evident as the rest.

- If `rangeLower` and `rangeUpper` are specified, `rangeUpper` must be larger than `rangeLower`.
- When you define link IDs, keep in mind that a back link must have a corresponding forward link.

Modifying an Attribute

Recall that when creating a new attributeSchema object, you can set 20 attributes. You can modify 9 of them, which we list in Table 9.4.

In addition, the following safety checks apply to category 1 (the base schema) attributes:

- You cannot change the lDAPDisplayName.
- You cannot change the rangeLower or rangeUpper.
- You cannot change the attributeSecurityGUID.

Table 9.4 AttributeSchema Object Attributes That Can Be Changed

Name	Guidelines
cn (Common-Name)/ name (RDN)	See the guideline for lDAPDisplayName.
lDAPDisplayName	You shouldn't change this. However, if you accidentally create an attribute that is not quite what you want, you can rename the first attribute to something obsolete (cn and lDAPDisplay-Name) and create a new one. In addition to renaming, you should disable the erroneous class as described later in this chapter.
adminDisplayName	No guidelines.
adminDescription	No guidelines.
attributeSecurityGUID	If you change an attribute to a new property set, it affects the permission of your Active Directory, so be very careful.
rangeLower	If you make a tighter range, you should first change the values of all instances to match the new limit.
rangeUpper	If you make a tighter range, you should first change the values of all instances to match the new limit.
searchFlags	If you index an attribute, the index will be built dynamically. If you choose not to index the attribute anymore, the index will be dropped from the database.
isMemberOfPartial-AttributeSet	Be sparing in what you store in the global catalog. See also the previous Warning.

Actually, the only sensible changes to any category 1 attribute would be the settings for indexing, global catalog membership, and perhaps ANR.

NOTE Because 62 of the base schema attributes don't have their `systemFlags` attribute set or the value is 0, they are not recognized as being in category 1. Consequently, you can perform modifications on them, such as changing their `lDAPDisplayName`.

Deactivating Classes and Attributes

When you decide that a class or an attribute is no longer necessary in your enterprise forest, you can deactivate it. This is also known as making it *defunct.* However, you cannot delete a class or attribute schema object.

Deactivating, rather than deleting, classes and attributes has two advantages.

- If the class or attribute were deleted, all the instances using it would have to be cleaned up from the forest in the deletion process. This would be a slow and difficult task, especially if your network spanned the globe.
- If you deactivate a class or an attribute by mistake and you need it later, you can resurrect it, and nothing is lost or corrupted in the process. Active Directory doesn't do any cleanup of the instances when a class or an attribute is deactivated.

Restrictions on Deactivation

The following are the restrictions on deactivating classes or attributes.

- You cannot deactivate any category 1 class or attribute, except those in which Microsoft did not include the `systemFlags` protection.
- You cannot deactivate a class if it is in use by any active (that is, nondefunct) class. In other words, the class to be deactivated cannot be a "source" of any inheritance/auxiliary relationships or possible superiors.
- You cannot deactivate an attribute if it is a member of any active class, either as a mandatory or an optional attribute, and either directly or through inheritance/auxiliary. This means that if you start "tearing down" some of your classes and attributes, you must deactivate the classes first and only then can you deactivate the attributes.

How to Deactivate

Before you deactivate an attribute that is indexed or part of the global catalog, you may want to remove indexing or the global catalog membership to save space in the Active Directory database. Of course, if you expect to delete all instances of the deactivated class soon, the storage would be of little concern. In this case you would also benefit from the attribute's being indexed and/or part of the global catalog; searching for instances to delete would be more efficient. An attribute cannot change after deactivation, so there will be no replication even if you don't remove the global catalog membership.

To deactivate a class or an attribute, set the `isDefunct` attribute of the corresponding schema object to TRUE. Another option is to use the Schema Manager snap-in and clear the check box "Class is active" that appears when you open the property page of a class or an attribute.

The order of events could be the following:

1. Deactivate the classes.
2. Deactivate the attributes.
3. Search for any instances you want to delete and delete them.

If you have any instances that you want to keep in the directory, but you don't need their deactivated attributes in the indexes or the global catalog, you can perform the following additional steps:

1. Reactivate each deactivated attribute that is indexed or part of the global catalog.
2. Remove the indexing and/or global catalog settings.
3. Deactivate the attributes once more.

How Deactivated Classes and Attributes Behave

After deactivation, the class or attribute behaves as if it still exists, or doesn't exist, depending on what you are trying to do. The class or attribute *seems not to exist* in the following cases. You will receive an error if you try to

- Create a new instance of the deactivated class
- Change an existing instance of the deactivated class

- Extend the schema by relying on the deactivated class or attribute (use the class in inheritance/auxiliary or possible superiors, or add the attribute as a new mandatory or optional attribute)

However, the class or attribute still *exists quite normally* for the following operations:

- Searching or viewing instances of the deactivated class or attribute
- Deleting an instance of the deactivated class
- Changing the deactivated class or attribute (i.e., the `classSchema` or `attributeSchema` object), starting with AD2003 (in AD2000 the only thing you can do to a class or an attribute is to activate it again; however, the Schema Manager that ships with Windows Server 2003 still claims that you can't make changes)
- Extending the schema and reusing in new classes or attributes some name or identifier of the deactivated class or attribute (such as `cn` or `linkID`); however, starting with AD2003, which has the Windows Server 2003 forest functional level, you can immediately after deactivation reuse the following names and identifiers: `lDAPDisplayName`, `governsID`, `attributeID`, `mAPIID`, and `schemaIDGUID` (except for the theoretical case where you would deactivate an attribute that is an rDNAttID of a class; such an attribute continues to use its `lDAPDisplayName`, `attributeID`, and `schemaIDGUID`)

NOTE ADSI Edit cannot show the contents of instances of deactivated classes, but LDP can.

NOTE Using class deactivation, you may end up with objects having mandatory attributes not set to a value. You can achieve this "illegal" situation in the following way: (a) Deactivate a class that has instances. (b) Create a new class with the same `lDAPDisplayName` and `governsID`, and add some mandatory attributes to the new class. (c) Now the old instances belong to the new class, which has some new mandatory attributes. However, the old instances probably won't have values for them.

NOTE Because a deactivated attribute can be a member of only a deactivated class, and you cannot create or modify the instances of that class, you obviously cannot create, modify, or even delete a value of a single deactivated attribute.

Because you can still see and delete all the instances of the deactivated classes and attributes, you can clean up the instances from your forest and be sure that no one can add new ones at the same time.

NOTE Because of the fact stated in the previous Note, if you have any instances that you want to keep in the directory, but you don't need their (soon-to-be) deactivated attributes at all, you must delete those attributes prior to deactivating the class.

NOTE Removing an auxiliary class from a structural class is somewhat similar to deactivating attributes. However, in this case the corresponding attributes become invisible, so you should first delete their values to save space in the directory database. For example, the `user` class of your forest is using the `sanaoHumanResources` auxiliary class, which contains the `salary` attribute. If you don't need the attributes (such as `salary`) of that auxiliary class anymore, you should first delete all their values, and after that remove `sanaoHumanResources` from the auxiliary class list of `user`. When you use this order of tasks, any salary data is removed from your directory database.

Reactivating Classes and Attributes

You can activate a deactivated class or attribute again—that is, make it nondefunct. To do this, either set the `isDefunct` attribute to FALSE or remove that attribute. Another way is to check the appropriate check box in the Schema Manager snap-in.

NOTE When you reactivate a class or an attribute, Active Directory performs the same checks as if you were creating the class or attribute. For example, the attributes in the `mayContain` list must exist and be nondefunct.

The Modification Process

Now that we have explained in theory how to modify the schema, it is time to put this into practice. In this section we discuss

- The order in which you should perform the various tasks
- The means and tools you have for the job
- Some additional issues related to schema modifications

Order of Tasks

You may want to add your own custom extensions to the schema, either for administrative purposes or for some in-house application, or you may have bought a commercial directory-enabled application (DEA) that you are about to install. In any case, when you want to add some classes and attributes to your schema, there is a preferred order in which to proceed.

NOTE A commercial DEA should have a separate installation program for any possible schema changes that it needs.

NOTE The text in this section is written from an administrator's point of view. If you are an application vendor, part of the discussion doesn't apply to you, except in the manner in which your customers will use your application.

We have divided the procedure into the following 15 steps.

1. *Assign responsibilities.* Decide who is responsible for the schema and its modifications, keeping in mind that the schema is an enterprisewide "asset." Do you have a schema team and do the same people who decide on the changes implement them? You also need someone to allocate OIDs in the organization, which is a similar process to allocating IP addresses in that OIDs must be unique and administered in an organized way. Because OIDs have uses outside Active Directory (e.g., SNMP management), the OID administrators might or might not be the same as the schema administrators.

2. *Obtain an OID.* If you haven't already done so, obtain a base OID from an issuing authority. From this base OID, you can create OIDs for all future classes and attributes. In the case of a commercial DEA, the OIDs of the application vendor are used, so the customer organization does not need its own.
3. *Plan the new classes and attributes.* We have described many attributes for the `classSchema` and `attributeSchema` objects. Either decide the value for each or decide not to assign a value. You should also have a strategy for the use of class inheritance and auxiliary classes. One of the guidelines at the beginning of this chapter recommends documenting all changes thoroughly. If you have a commercial DEA, evaluate the vendor's documentation to determine if you can employ those schema changes in your enterprise forest.
4. *Try the modifications in a test forest.* By following the remaining steps here, you should make any modifications first to a test forest (one domain controller in that forest is enough) that is separate from your production enterprise forest. You might make the changes to the test forest with the Schema Manager snap-in (and maybe with a little help from ADSI Edit). Then, using the LDIFDE tool, you could export the changes from the test forest and import them to your production forest. This way, the possibility of errors is minimized.
5. *Choose your schema master.* As you may recall from Chapter 5, one domain controller of your forest is holding the schema (operations) master role. All schema changes should be made on that domain controller. Unless you have already done so, choose your schema master according to the instructions in Chapter 5.
6. *"Unlock" Schema Admins.* If you normally don't have members in Schema Admins, add one now, or if the smart card for the Schema Admin logon is stored in a safe, get it now and log on.
7. *Enable schema modifications.* By default, schema modifications are not possible in any Windows 2000 domain controller, even in the schema master. If your schema master is running Windows 2000, you should enable the modifications on it. With a commercial DEA, the schema installation program may do this for you; otherwise, you have to do it manually (as described in the section that follows this list).
8. *Create the attributes.* Create the attributes you need. Naturally, you will use the values from the plan that you made earlier. With a commercial DEA, the schema installation program will do this.

9. *Create the classes.* Create the classes according to your plan. Now that your new attributes exist, you can also add them to your new classes. If you create classes that depend on each other (inheritance/auxiliary, possible superiors), you must first create the classes that others depend on. If you refer to the earlier attributes and classes with an OID, the five-minute wait before the schema cache update is not necessary. An OID refers to the disk version of the schema and, therefore, it doesn't matter if the schema cache is updated. If you use LDAP names instead of OIDs, you must either wait five minutes or update the schema cache manually. Note that if you use the Schema Manager snap-in, it shows LDAP names, but internally it uses OIDs. Again, with a commercial DEA, the schema installation program will do this.
10. *Check the changes.* If you made any errors, if there were other errors, or if the schema *concurrency control* kicks in, it is possible that some of your intended changes didn't complete. You should check that all the changes are OK by querying the modified schema objects and verifying that they exist and that their attribute values are what you specified. (We return to the topic of concurrency control in the "Some Gotchas in Changing the Schema" section later in this chapter.) A commercial DEA's schema installation program should perform the check (and fix anything that didn't pass in the first round).
11. *Disable schema modifications.* To prevent accidental changes, restore the protection that you removed four steps ago (if running Windows 2000). A commercial DEA's schema installation program may do this. However, it is a good idea to double-check it manually.
12. *Reestablish Schema Admin locks.* If you have a policy of doing so, remove again any members from Schema Admins and return the smart card for the Schema Admin logon to a safe.
13. *Don't boot the schema master.* There is no need to boot any servers after the schema changes.
14. *Perhaps force a schema update.* If you need to use the schema modifications to create new instances—for example, before the five-minute wait—you may update the schema cache. A commercial DEA's schema installation program may or may not do this, depending on how the vendor chose it to work.
15. *Perhaps trigger replication.* Schema changes are like any other Active Directory changes: They are normally replicated to other

domain controllers of the forest. If you need to create instances on a domain controller other than the schema master and you don't want to wait for normal replication, you could trigger it to happen sooner.

Enabling Schema Modifications

We mentioned in the previous list that you need to enable schema modifications on the schema master, if it is running Windows 2000, and also disable them after you have made the changes. There are two ways to do this.

- If you know how to use RegEdt32, start it and select the `HKEY_LOCAL_MACHINE` window. Next, locate the key `SYSTEM`, `CurrentControlSet`, `Services`, `NTDS`, `Parameters`. Under that key, add a value (if it doesn't exist already) named `Schema Update Allowed`, with the data type `REG_DWORD` and data "1" (without quotes). If the value already exists, change the data to "1". When you later disable schema changes, either change the data to "0" or remove the whole value (i.e., the parameter line).
- Start the Schema Manager snap-in and right-click the Active Directory Schema tree node in the left pane. Select Operations Masters from the context menu. The dialog box that opens includes a check box labeled "The Schema may be modified on this Domain Controller". By checking it, you actually turn on the aforementioned registry setting.

You could automate the registry change with the Resource Kit tool RegIni or use REG files with RegEdit. However, it is probably not a good idea to automate removal of such a protective setting.

The Means to Make Changes

There are several interactive and programmatic ways to change the schema:

- The Schema Manager snap-in
- ADSI Edit
- The LDIFDE utility and a text file in LDIF format
- The CSVDE utility and a text file in CSV (comma-separated values) format

- A script (e.g., in VBScript language) using the ADSI interface
- A schema installation program for some directory-enabled application (an EXE file)

Table 9.5 describes the pros and cons of each means.

Table 9.5 Means to Modify the Schema

Means	Description	Pros	Cons
The Schema Manager snap-in	The basic tool for managing the schema.	Specially made for manual simple schema changes.	Cannot set all the attributes you might want.
ADSI Edit	The tool to manage any attribute of any object in the directory.	Can set any attribute.	You must be careful to do things right.
LDIFDE	A command-line tool that exports objects to an LDIF format text file. LDIFDE can also add, modify, and delete objects based on an LDIF text file.	Can export changes from a test forest and import them in a production forest. The learning curve is not as steep as with scripts.	Not graphical or interactive.
CSVDE	A command-line tool that exports objects to a CSV format text file. CSVDE can also add objects based on a CSV text file.	Many spreadsheet, database, and other applications support CSV, so you can import and export Active Directory data to and from other applications.	Not graphical or interactive; can create objects but not change them; CSV format is not well suited for schema extensions.
Script*	A short text file containing script language (e.g., VBScript) that, by using ADSI operations, can modify the schema.	You can do just about anything you want. You can test the script in a lab network before deploying it to your production forest.	A learning curve in the beginning; possibility of bugs. *(continued)*

* See Chapter 11 for a sample script that creates an attribute and a class.

Table 9.5 Means to Modify the Schema (*cont.*)

Means	Description	Pros	Cons
An installation EXE file	Typically a software vendor might write a schema installation EXE file for its directory-enabled application.	Cannot be tampered with; can handle errors and provide feedback; also the pros of scripts.	The administrator of a customer cannot see in advance how the program will change his schema. The learning curve is steeper than with scripts and the possibility of bugs is greater.

The Schema Manager Snap-In

You can use the Schema Manager snap-in to create and modify both attributes and classes.

Creating and Modifying Attributes

We listed earlier 20 `attributeSchema` attributes that you might want to set when you create new `attributeSchema` objects. With the Schema Manager snap-in, you can set most of these attributes, but not quite all. Table 9.6 lists these attributes and specifies whether you can set them when creating an object or later. Table 9.6 also includes `isDefunct`, which you would set for an existing attribute.

NOTE Figure 9.3. contains the check box "Allow this attribute to be shown in advanced view". As discussed in Chapter 8, that check box is meaningless.

NOTE You cannot set the attributes `schemaIDGUID` or `linkID` at creation time. Because they are system-only (i.e., they cannot change afterward), if you need a value for any of them, you must use a means other than the Schema Manager snap-in to create the `attributeSchema` object.

To create a new attribute, right-click the Attributes container and select Create Attribute. A general warning will appear, as shown in

Table 9.6 The Schema Manager Snap-in and the Attributes of an `attributeSchema` Object

Attribute	Schema Manager Creation Time	Schema Manager Later	System Only	Name in the User Interface (Creation Time/Later)
cn (Common-Name)/ name (RDN)	Yes	No	No/Yes	Common Name
lDAPDisplayName	Yes	**No***	No	LDAP Display Name/—
adminDisplayName	No	No	No	—
adminDescription	Yes	Yes	No	Description
attributeID	Yes	No	Yes	Unique X500 Object ID/X.500 OID
schemaIDGUID	**No**	No	Yes	—
attribute-SecurityGUID	No	No	No	—
mAPIID	No	No	Yes	—
linkID	**No**	No	Yes	—
attributeSyntax	Yes	No	Yes	Syntax
oMSyntax	Yes	No	Yes	Syntax
oMObjectClass	Yes	No	Yes	Syntax
isSingleValued	Yes	No	Yes	Multi Valued/This attribute is . . .
rangeLower	Yes	Yes	No	Minimum
rangeUpper	Yes	Yes	No	Maximum
extendedChars-Allowed	No	No	No (was Yes in AD2000)	—
searchFlags	No	Yes	No	—/Index . . ., Ambiguous . . ., Attribute is copied . . ., Index . . .
isMemberOfPartial-AttributeSet	No	Yes	No	—/Replicate this attribute . . .
isDefunct	No	Yes	No	—/Attribute is active
systemOnly	No	No	Yes	—
systemFlags	No	No	Yes	—

* Bold "No" indicates what we consider a (perhaps slight) shortcoming of the tool.

Figure 9.1. When you click Continue, the dialog box shown in Figure 9.2 appears, where you can enter the attributes for the `attributeSchema` object.

Once you have created the attribute, you can open its property dialog box, as shown in Figure 9.3.

Creating and Modifying Classes

With new `classSchema` objects, there are 21 attributes that you might want to set. Table 9.7 lists these attributes and indicates whether you can

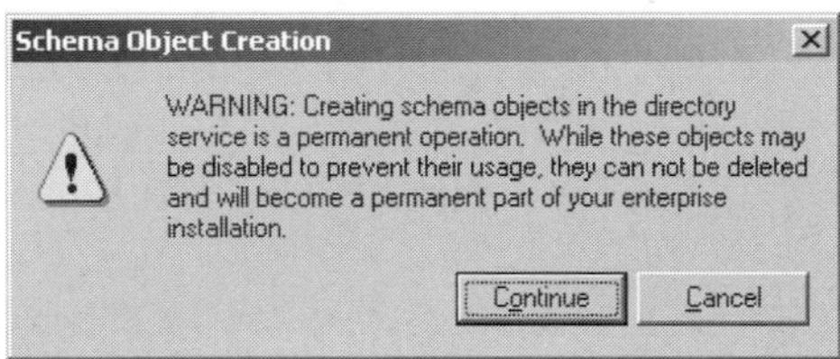

Figure 9.1 When you start creating schema objects, the snap-in warns that the operation is permanent.

Figure 9.2 To create a new `attributeSchema` object in your test forest, you can use the seven sample values shown here. Because `rangeLower` and `rangeUpper` are both 20, the octet string values that are later stored in this attribute must be exactly 20 bytes. The syntax choice corresponds to the `attributeSyntax`, `oMSyntax`, and `oMObjectClass` attributes.

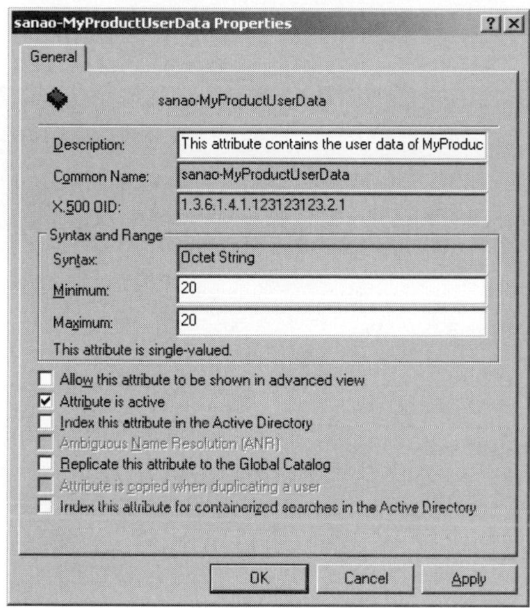

Figure 9.3 In the property dialog box, you can check what you just created and make some changes.

manage them with the Schema Manager snap-in at creation time or later. Table 9.7 also includes `isDefunct`, which you would set for an existing attribute.

When you create a `classSchema` object in the Classes container, you see the same warning as with attributes. After you dismiss the warning, you enter the `classSchema` attributes in a two-page wizard, as shown in Figure 9.4 and Figure 9.5.

Having created the object, you can see its attributes in four property pages. We show the first two in Figure 9.6 and Figure 9.7. The third property page has the same lists of mandatory and optional properties that you see in Figure 9.5 when creating the object. The only obvious difference is that you can no longer change the list for mandatory attributes. Remember that Active Directory doesn't allow this. The fourth property page is a normal ACL Editor screen.

ADSI Edit

To create a new attribute with ADSI Edit, you progress through a short wizard that prompts you for the values of the `cn`, `oMSyntax`, `lDAPDisplayName`, `isSingleValued`, `attributeSyntax`, and

Table 9.7 The Schema Manager Snap-in and the Attributes of a `classSchema` Object

Attribute	Schema Manager Creation Time	Schema Manager Later	System Only	Name in the User Interface (Creation Time/Later)
`cn` (Common-Name)/ `name` (RDN)	Yes	**No**[*]	No/Yes	Common Name
`lDAPDisplayName`	Yes	**No**	No	LDAP Display Name/—
`adminDisplayName`	No	No	No	—
`adminDescription`	Yes	Yes	No	Description
`governsID`	Yes	No	Yes	Unique X500 Object ID/X.500 OID
`schemaIDGUID`	**No**	No	Yes	—
`rDNAttID`	No	No	Yes	—
`mustContain`	Yes	No	No	Mandatory
`systemMustContain`	**No**	No	Yes	—
`mayContain`	Yes	Yes	No	Optional
`systemMayContain`	**No**	No	Yes	—
`possSuperiors`	No	Yes	No	—/Possible Superior
`systemPoss-Superiors`	**No**	No	Yes	—
`objectClass-Category`	Yes	No	Yes	Class Type
`subClassOf`	Yes	No	Yes	Parent Class
`auxiliaryClass`	No	Yes	No	—/Auxiliary Classes
`systemAuxiliary-Class`	**No**	No	Yes	—
`isDefunct`	No	Yes	No	Class is active
`defaultObject-Category`	No	Yes	No	—/Category
`defaultHiding-Value`	**No**	**No**	No	—
`defaultSecurity-Descriptor`	No	Yes	No	Default Security
`systemOnly`	No	No	Yes	—

[*] Bold "No" indicates a shortcoming, which may or may not affect you.

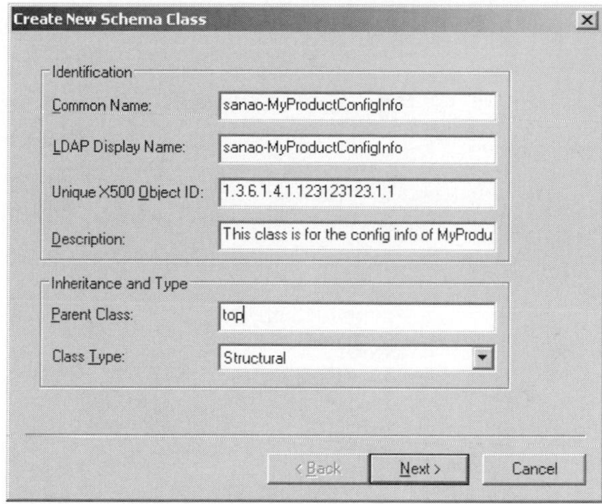

Figure 9.4 In the first page of the two-page wizard to create a new schema class, you enter the name and inheritance information.

`attributeID` attributes for the new attribute. If you need to enter other system-only attributes (which you cannot change later), you must click More Attributes.

Creating a new class is a similar procedure to creating an attribute. This time the wizard asks you to enter values for `cn`, `subClassOf`, and

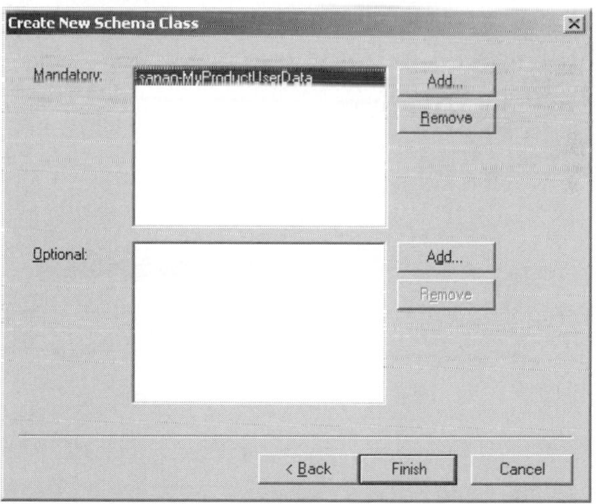

Figure 9.5 In the second page of the two-page wizard to create a new schema class, you can list mandatory and optional properties for the new class.

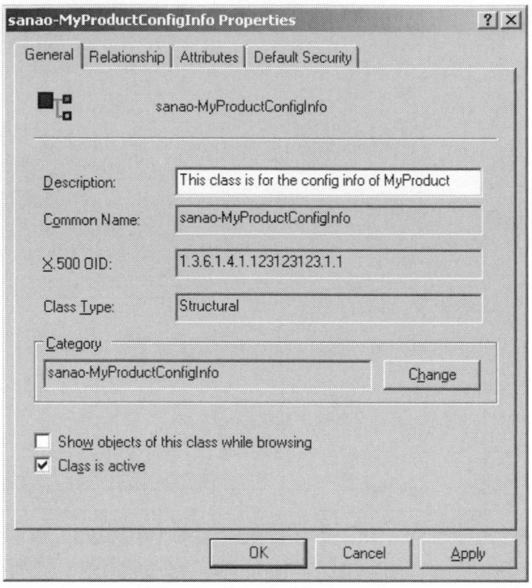

Figure 9.6 You can modify the description for the class, but unfortunately you cannot edit the `lDAPDisplayName` with the Schema Manager snap-in.

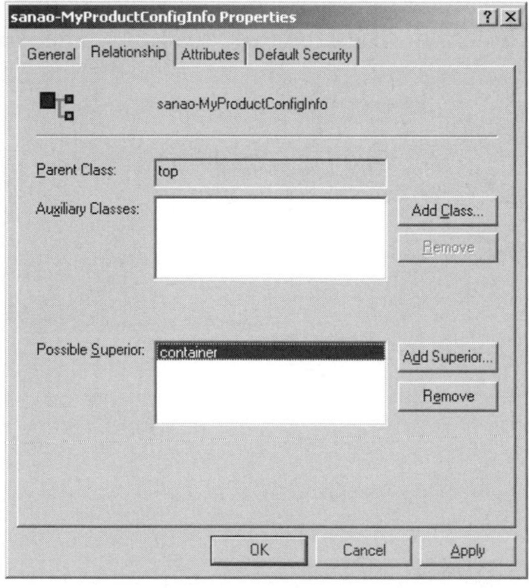

Figure 9.7 You must add at least one possible superior for a new class. Otherwise, you cannot use the class for anything (provided, of course, that it is a structural class).

governsID. You must click More Attributes to enter values of at least lDAPDisplayName and objectClassCategory.

WARNING Be sure to set objectClassCategory through More Attributes. Otherwise, you will get an 88-class, and you won't be able to fix the situation (except by deactivating the class and creating a new one). You may also want to set schemaIDGUID, mustContain, or any of the system-only attributes before you click Finish to create the class.

If you would like to try to create some new schema objects with ADSI Edit, you can use the sample values in the LDIFDE example in the next section.

LDIFDE

With LDIFDE you can create and modify any objects, so you can use it to create classSchema and attributeSchema objects. Recall that earlier in this chapter we introduced the following process as a preferred way to modify your schema (we'll now add more detail):

1. Use the Schema Manager snap-in and perhaps ADSI Edit to create your objects to a test forest.
2. Verify that all creations and changes are OK.
3. Use LDIFDE to export the creations and changes to a text file.
4. Edit the text file (or rather, a copy of it).
5. Use LDIFDE to test the edited text file in a second test forest.
6. Use LDIFDE to import the creations and changes from the text file into your production forest.

Now we explain how to export, edit, and import the text file.

If you type just "ldifde" and press Enter, you will get the online Help for the tool. To export the changes to a text file, use the following command:

```
C:\>ldifde -f myext.txt -d cn=schema,cn=configuration,
   dc=testsanao,dc=com -r (cn=sanao*)
```

This command writes all the schema objects that start with "sanao"—that is, those that you have created—to a text file called myext.txt.

NOTE There is an m parameter in LDIFDE to be used when you export and import objects from one Active Directory forest to another.

However, even if you use it, you still need to edit the file, so it doesn't actually save any work in this case.

Next you have to edit the text file with an ASCII text editor such as Notepad. First copy the file to myextmod.txt and then make the following changes to the latter file.

- Remove the lines that specify the following attributes (if they exist): `cn`, `instanceType`, `distinguishedName`, `name`, `objectCategory`, `objectGUID`, `uSNChanged`, `uSNCreated`, `whenChanged`, `whenCreated`, `objectClass: top`, `msDS-IntId`, and `systemOnly`. (`ObjectGUID` and `msDS-IntId` are actually the only attributes you must remove. Removal of the others makes the file a little cleaner.)
- Remove also the lines for `defaultObjectCategory`, `schemaIDGUID`, `rDNAttID`, `defaultSecurityDescriptor`, and `adminDisplayName`, unless you have a specific value stored in them. Note that the Schema Manager snap-in created a value for `defaultSecurityDescriptor`, which you may or may not want to use.
- If you were using the `testsanao.com` forest, change the distinguished names to `sanao.com`. Another method is to use the `c` parameter to replace the names when you later import the text file. (We show an example of this command line a little later in this chapter.)
- Order the lines so that the lines that create attribute objects appear before the lines that create class objects. Order also the lines for dependent class objects to follow the lines for the classes on which they depend.
- Because you now refer to the new attribute with an LDAP name instead of an OID, you must update the schema cache before you try to create the dependent class object. The update takes place when you insert the following lines in the correct position in your LDF file:

```
dn:
changetype: modify
add: schemaUpdateNow
schemaUpdateNow: 1
-
```

The empty distinguished name refers to the `rootDSE` virtual object. The hyphen in the last line designates the end of the attribute block.

The resulting file should look something like the following:

```
dn: CN=sanao-MyProductUserData, CN=Schema,
   CN=Configuration, DC=sanao, DC=com
changetype: add
attributeID: 1.3.6.1.4.1.123123123.2.1
attributeSyntax: 2.5.5.10
isSingleValued: TRUE
lDAPDisplayName: sanao-MyProductUserData
adminDescription: This attribute contains the user data
   of MyProduct
objectClass: attributeSchema
oMSyntax: 4
rangeLower: 20
rangeUpper: 20
showInAdvancedViewOnly: TRUE

dn:
changetype: modify
add: schemaUpdateNow
schemaUpdateNow: 1
-

dn: CN=sanao-MyProductConfigInfo, CN=Schema,
   CN=Configuration, DC=sanao, DC=com
changetype: add
governsID: 1.3.6.1.4.1.123123123.1.1
lDAPDisplayName: sanao-MyProductConfigInfo
adminDescription: This class is for the config info of
   MyProduct
mustContain: sanao-MyProductUserData
objectClass: classSchema
objectClassCategory: 1
possSuperiors: container
defaultHidingValue: TRUE
showInAdvancedViewOnly: TRUE
subClassOf: top
```

Binary values and some other attributes have a second colon, such as the following:

```
schemaIDGUID:: 8b9KkY41PES0YAF8iAA+4A==
```

In this case, the value is coded using the same *base64* representation that MIME attachments use in SMTP messaging.

Because you had to make a number of modifications, you should test your LDF file on another empty test forest. You cannot use the first test forest, because it already contains the new classes and attributes.

TIP If you want to clean up a one-server test forest, you can run DCPromo to demote the domain controller, and then run DCPromo again to build up a new forest.

TIP You can buy VMware or VirtualPC for your schema tests and development. You can install an Active Directory forest in one of them, make any changes you want, and then finally discard the changes without writing anything on disk.

Use the following command to import the text file to both the second test forest and your production forest:

```
C:\>ldifde -i -f myextmod.txt
```

If you didn't edit the forest name in your LDIF file (i.e., the test forest name is still there), you can use the following command instead when you import the file to your production forest:

```
C:\>ldifde -i -f myextmod.txt -c "DC=testsanao,DC=com"
    "DC=sanao,DC=com"
```

WARNING The first forest distinguished name after the c parameter is the one that you have in the LDIF file. For LDIFDE to work, the name on the command line must exactly match the name in the file. You must have identical lowercase/uppercase letters and spacing (i.e., if one name has a space after the comma, the other one must also have a space after the comma).

The output for either command should look like the following:

```
Connecting to "dc1.sanao.com"
Logging in as current user using SSPI
Importing directory from file "myextmod.txt"
Loading entries....
3 entries modified successfully.
The command has completed successfully
```

CSVDE

An LDIF file has a pair of an attribute name and a value on each line. A CSV file has a list of all attribute names on the first line and a list of values on another line, one line per object. This latter format is not practical for schema extensions, so we do not describe this option.

CSVDE is best suited for dumping an existing schema to a text file to be imported to a spreadsheet, as explained in Chapter 8.

An Installation EXE File

A commercial application vendor would probably choose to write an installation EXE file and ship it with its directory-enabled application. Although an EXE file doesn't show the customer administrator the changes that are going to happen to the schema, the EXE has the following advantages.

- Because it is a binary file, it is difficult to alter intentionally and impossible to alter unintentionally. If the file is corrupted by transmission, it is more likely to fail completely.
- The vendor can put more intelligence and interactivity into the program to adapt to various customers and error situations.
- LDIF uses base64 encoding for binary data, which is a somewhat awkward format for human beings. The programmer can handle various hexadecimal and Unicode data more easily when using the C language, for example, to write an EXE file.
- An EXE file can be digitally signed to prove its origin and to ensure that it hasn't been corrupted or infected by a virus.

Some Gotchas in Changing the Schema

We want to mention two minor issues before we conclude our discussion about the schema modification process. They are the replication of schema changes and the concurrency control.

Schema Replication

When you add a new class to the schema and then an instance (object) of that class, it is possible that the new instance reaches some other domain controller before the new class does.

We explained the situation in Chapter 5. We also described the following solution: If a domain controller receives an instance of an unknown class, it will abort processing the current replication data and write a "schema mismatch" message to the event log. Then it automatically resyncs the schema from the source domain controller and requests again the normal replication data. This time everything should go fine.

Concurrency Control

The schema has *concurrency control*—that is, only one schema object change can take place at a time. This prevents a situation in which two conflicting changes occur at the same time. Therefore, if two people or applications try to modify the schema simultaneously, some of the changes may not complete.

Because concurrency control controls each object change separately, it is possible that when two people try to make ten changes, eight of one person's changes and six of the other person's changes will complete. Consequently, to have all the changes in place, the former person should repeat two changes and the latter person should repeat four changes.

Any schema installation program, especially a commercial program, should accommodate concurrency control. If the installation program is run a second time, it should notice that some of the extensions are already in and gracefully add only the missing extensions.

Bringing the Extensions to the User Interface

Now that you have extended your Active Directory under the hood (i.e., added some attributes and classes to the schema), you are probably anxious to see the extensions in the user interface.

In this section we discuss three things about the instances of your new classes:

- Where to place them
- How to manage permissions for them
- How to create and display them, including their attributes

For brevity, we call the instances of your new classes "new objects."

Where to Place the New Objects

Depending on the intended purposes of the new objects, you can choose to place them in various places of a domain partition or sometimes in the configuration partition. You have the following five options:

- *Under the corresponding user objects*. If each new object directly relates to one user object, you should store the new objects under the corresponding user objects. This way, when you delegate administration of the user objects, the delegation applies also to these child objects. In addition, when you delete or move a user object, the child objects are deleted or moved with their parent.
- *Under other corresponding objects*. If each new object directly relates to some other object type, such as computer, you should store the new objects under these corresponding objects.
- *In any convenient OU*. If the new objects are not related to any specific objects in the domain, you can place them in any convenient OU. You would control their visibility to users, as well as delegate administration, using Active Directory permissions.
- *In the System container*. If you don't want the new objects to be part of the normal OU tree, you can store them in the System container, which exists in every domain. You should first create (using ADSI Edit, for example) a container that includes your organization's name and then store the new objects in this new container. This ensures that if you later buy a directory-enabled application, the objects it will create won't collide with the objects you are now creating. An example container would be `CN=Sanao Corp, CN=System, DC=sales, DC=sanao, DC=com`.
- *In the configuration partition*. You might want the new objects to be replicated to all domain controllers of your forest instead of just one domain. You can achieve this by placing the new objects in the configuration partition. Recall that the data in

Active Directory should be globally useful, relatively static, and small. Obviously, when you place the objects in the configuration partition, these requirements are even more important than in the single-domain case. Microsoft recommends storing the objects either in the Services container or in a site object. Again, the container you create for new objects should include your organization's name.

NOTE In the list of where to place new objects, we recommend in two situations that you create a container for the new objects and that it includes your organization's name. You might consider this for other situations as well (e.g., when creating child objects under a user object).

Managing Permissions

One important part of managing the new objects is to manage permissions for them. You can assign permissions either to individual attributes or to several attributes at once using property sets. We discuss both possibilities in the following two sections.

We use the `sanao-Class` class as an example. One of its mandatory attributes is `sanao-Attribute1` and one of its optional attributes is `sanao-Attribute2`. Remember that the second part of the names should be descriptive, but for this permission demonstration, we settle for the nondescriptive `Class` and `Attribute1/2`.

Managing Permissions for Individual Attributes

When you add attributes to either new or existing classes, those attributes automatically become visible on the property permission page of the ACL Editor, as Figure 9.8 illustrates. (You can hide some of the attributes from the list using DSSec.Dat, as described in Chapter 4.) Consequently, you can manage their per-attribute permissions as with any other attribute.

Using Property Sets

Now that you have new attributes, you can put them in a property set. This enables you to assign permissions for them as one entity. We show here an example of how to create a property set and put two attributes, `sanao-Attribute1` and `sanao-Attribute2`, in it. The set will apply to the instances of the `sanao-Class` class.

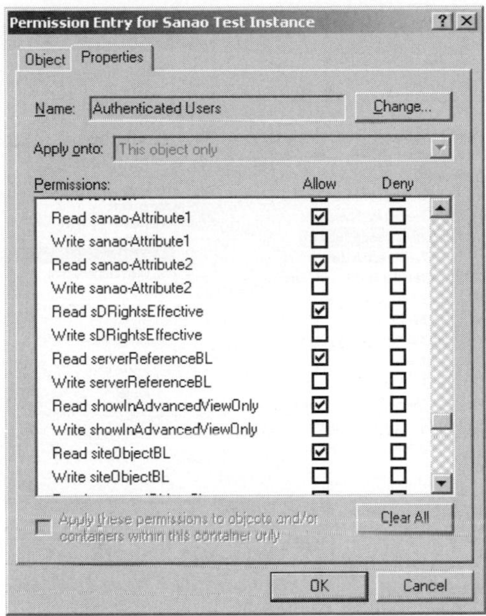

Figure 9.8 When you have two new attributes, `sanao-Attribute1` and `sanao-Attribute2`, in the `sanao-Class` class, the attributes automatically appear in the permission list.

First, use ADSI Edit to locate `CN=Extended Rights, CN=Configuration`, which resides in the configuration partition. Next, create a new `controlAccessRight` object in that container. Give the object a name (i.e., the `cn` attribute), such as Sanao Property Set. It is not necessary to set any other values yet. Figure 9.9 shows the ADSI Edit windows and the Create Object dialog box.

Now that you have the Sanao Property Set object, you need to set four attributes for it, as explained in the following list.

- *`AppliesTo`*. This attribute specifies the class or classes to which the property set applies. The value(s) must be the `schemaIDGUID` attribute of the corresponding `classSchema` object, although unfortunately in a different format. If `sanao-Class` has the `schemaIDGUID` of "73 a7 49 ad 86 05 e8 44 aa 46 a9 d3 bb e7 f9 bf," you must first remove the spaces to get "73a749ad-8605e844aa46a9d3bbe7f9bf." Next, you add three hyphens to get "73a749ad-8605-e844-aa46-a9d3bbe7f9bf." As the last step, you swap some bytes (remember that a byte corresponds to two hex

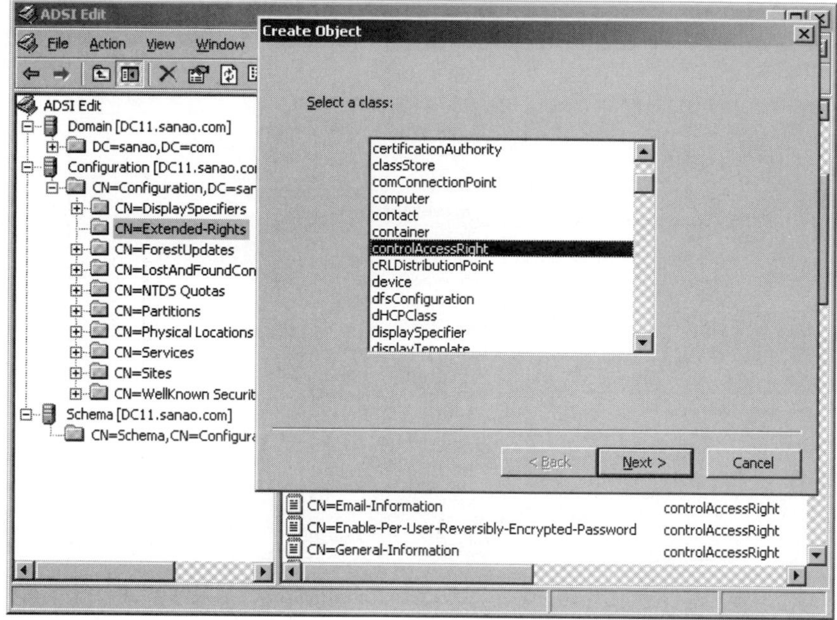

Figure 9.9 To create a new property set, begin by creating a `controlAccessRight` object. It will represent the property set.

characters). The first "word" up to a hyphen must be swapped—for example, you would replace 12345678 with 78563412. The two bytes in the second and third "words" must be swapped, such as 1234 to 3412. The result is "ad49a773-0586-44e8-aa46-a9d3bbe7f9bf," so now you (finally) have a GUID to store in the `appliesTo` attribute.

- *`DisplayName`*. This attribute specifies the text to show in the ACL Editor. You can enter "Sanao Properties" as the value.
- *`RightsGuid`*. This attribute serves as an identifier to which the attributes in the set will refer. You need a fresh GUID for this one, so you would run UUIDGen from the Platform SDK and get something like "55f648e1-f367-4ebb-9589-7e74fc2f8d84." If you haven't downloaded the Platform SDK, you can type any random hexadecimal characters to get a GUID. However, for production purposes, you must use UUIDGen or GUIDGen from the Platform SDK.
- *`ValidAccesses`*. This attribute specifies the possible permissions for the property set. The value 16 means that only Read is visible in the list, whereas the value 32 shows only Write. Normally, you

would define the value 48, which results in both Read and Write being visible. (The values correspond to `ADS_RIGHT_DS_READ_PROP` and `ADS_RIGHT_DS_WRITE_PROP`.)

After setting the four attribute values for the property set object, you must specify the attributes it should contain. You do this by setting the `attributeSecurityGUID` of each appropriate attribute to be the same as the `rightsGuid` of the property set object.

The value of our `rightsGuid` was "55f648e1-f367-4ebb-9589-7e74fc2f8d84." Unfortunately, `attributeSecurityGUID` uses the same format of GUIDs as `schemaIDGUID` did, which means that you must perform a reversed conversion process of what we described with the `appliesTo` attribute. The result is "e1 48 f6 55 67 f3 bb 4e 95 89 7e 74 fc 2f 8d 84." This is the value that you need to store in `attributeSecurityGUID` of each appropriate `attributeSchema` object.

At this point, you can try the new property set. Obviously, you need to create an instance of `sanao-Class` to be able to apply any permissions. You must create the test object with ADSI Edit, but after that you can use either ADSI Edit or the Users and Computers snap-in to see and modify the permissions.

Figure 9.10 shows the new property set. You will see the same two lines for Sanao Properties (Read and Write) if you click Advanced, click Edit, and click the Properties tab.

Creating and Displaying the Objects

Active Directory's architecture facilitates showing the new classes and attributes in various administrative tools as well as in the end-user interface. This architecture covers the following display elements:

- Property pages, which are different in admin tools (e.g., the Users and Computers snap-in) and end-user applications, including the Windows shell (My Network Places, Search Active Directory; and Start menu, Search)
- Property pages when multiple objects are selected in an admin tool
- Context menus, again different for administrators and end users
- Icons
- Customizing the list of attributes that can be selected to display in columns of the right-hand pane of the Users and Computers snap-in
- Creation wizards
- Class and attribute display names

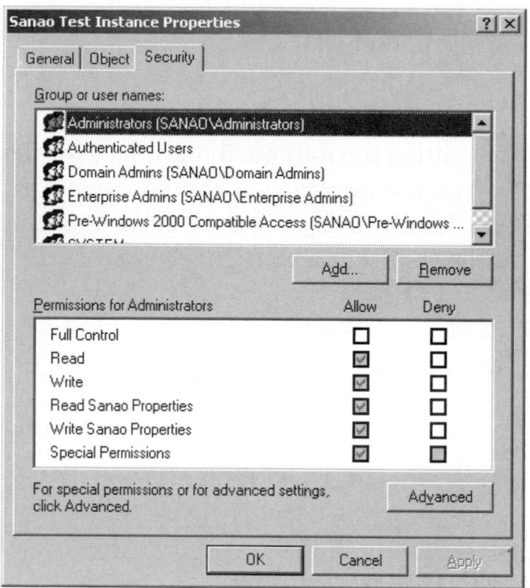

Figure 9.10 If you add a property set as a `controlAccessRight` object to the configuration partition, you can use the property set (such as Sanao Properties) to give permissions for applicable objects.

You can, of course, always use ADSI Edit to browse and manage any old and new classes and attributes. Using the listed display elements, however, facilitates building an easier user interface.

The good news is that the display elements are defined in Active Directory itself, which means that they are available to any user of the forest. The bad news is that the definitions in Active Directory refer to DLL and other files, which must be on any local computer where the new display elements are to be used. This brings up the question of distributing the files. The best choice probably is to prepare Windows Installer packages of the files and then distribute them using Group Policy.

Another piece of bad news is that adding display elements usually requires programming. Especially the property pages and creation wizards require that you create them as Component Object Model (COM) objects. Each COM object also needs to implement the appropriate COM interfaces, such as `IShellPropSheetExt` or `IContextMenu`.

NOTE Administration scripts are as far as we go toward programming in this book. Because you can write COM objects for property pages and creation wizards only with real programming languages, such as C++ (according to the Platform SDK documentation, Visual Basic is not an option), you need to turn elsewhere for that information.

Although you may not be a programmer, we briefly explain the display architecture here for two reasons.

- You wouldn't write COM objects, but you could buy an application that extends your displays, or your company might have an in-house developer to write those applications.
- Even without writing COM objects, you can still create some display elements. For example, at the end of this section we show how you can view logon counts and other information about your network users by adding an item to the context menu of users.

Display Specifiers

Each class that needs some of the display elements previously listed has a display specifier object to define the elements. You can use ADSI Edit to find these objects in the configuration container. First locate the DisplaySpecifiers container and then your locale identifier, such as 409 for English (United States). The common name for the container is similar to the following:

```
CN=409,CN=DisplaySpecifiers,CN=Configuration,DC=sanao,DC=com
```

Figure 9.11 shows some of the contents of the 409 container. As you can see, the display object names are the same as the class LDAP names, but "-Display" is appended. If a class doesn't have a display specifier, `CN=default-Display` is used.

NOTE As mentioned, the actual property or wizard pages must be implemented as COM objects. These objects are often stored in DLL files. Applications don't refer to various COM objects with their filenames, but use instead *class identifiers* (CLSIDs). Class identifiers are about the same as globally unique identifiers (GUIDs) or universally unique identifiers (UUIDs), and an example of all three is {6dfe648b-a212-11d0-bcd5-00c04fd8d5b6}. You can find in the registry all the class identifiers registered in your computer. You use RegEdit and locate the path `HKEY_CLASSES_ROOT, CLSID`. The class identifier keys in that location specify, among other things, the file that the COM object lives in.

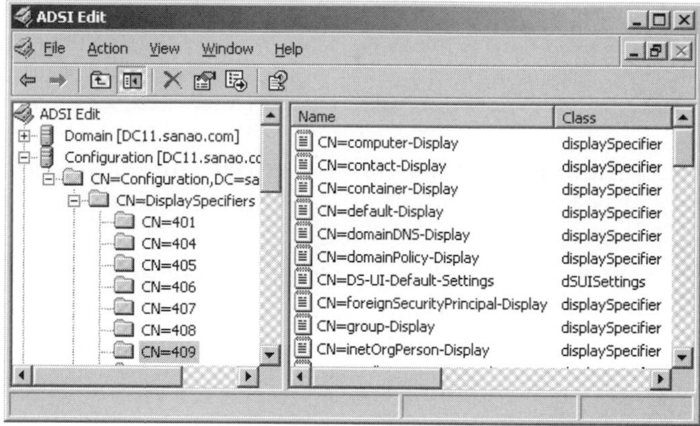

Figure 9.11 Each class that needs user interface elements has a corresponding object in the DisplaySpecifiers container. There can be separate display objects for each locale.

Table 9.8 describes the attributes that define the various display elements.

Table 9.8 Display Specifier Attributes

Attribute	Description
adminPropertyPages, shellPropertyPages	These two multivalued attributes define the COM objects that contain property pages for admin tools and the end-user Windows shell, respectively. Each element defines one COM object as follows: <order-number>, <CLSID>, [optional data]. The order numbers determine the position of each page, and they are not required to be consecutive. Each COM object may implement more than one property page.
adminMultiselect-PropertyPages	This multivalued attribute (introduced in Windows Server 2003) defines the COM objects that contain property pages for admin tools when multiple objects are selected. Each element defines one COM object as follows: <order-number>, <CLSID>. The order numbers determine the position of each page, and they are not required to be consecutive. Each COM object may implement more than one property page.

Table 9.8 Display Specifier Attributes (*cont.*)

Attribute	Description
adminContextMenu, shellContextMenu, contextMenu	These three multivalued attributes define the context menus for admin tools and the end-user Windows shell, or both, respectively. Each element defines either one COM object (as with property pages: `<order-number>, <CLSID>, [optional data]`) or an application. The syntax for the latter choice is `<order-number>, <context menu text>, <program name>`. The context menu text appears as the text in the context menu, and the program name defines which program is launched. If the full path hasn't been defined, the application must be in the search path of the computer where the new menu item is used. The LDAP path to the selected object and its class are passed as the first and second arguments for the program, respectively. The latter choice (an application instead of a COM object) allows using scripts also (see the next section for an example).
iconPath	This multivalued attribute defines the icons for the class. Each element uses either the syntax `<state>, <icon-file-name>` or `<state>, <module-file-name>, <resource-ID>`. The state is a value between 0 and 15, where 0 means "default" or "closed," 1 means "open," and 2 means "disabled." The icon or module file (usually an EXE or DLL file) must be in the search path of the local computer. `Resource-ID` is an index to the icon in the file.
creationWizard	This single-valued attribute defines the COM object that contains the pages for the creation wizard of an object class. The syntax is `<CLSID>`. Using this attribute completely replaces an existing wizard.
createWizardExt	This multivalued attribute defines the COM objects that contain additional pages for a creation wizard. The syntax is `<order-number>, <CLSID>`. Again, the order number determines the extension's position in the wizard. *(continued)*

Table 9.8 Display Specifier Attributes *(cont.)*

Attribute	Description
`createDialog`	This single-valued attribute allows modifying the formation of a user or contact's full name. If you type "Jack" for the first name and "Brown" for the last name, the full name is normally "Jack Brown." If you set `createDialog` to be `%<sn>, %<givenName>`, the full name will be "Brown, Jack." The third token you could use is `%<initials>`.
`classDisplayName`	This multivalued attribute defines the display name for the class to be used in admin tools and the end-user shell. If you add classes, you should include your organization's friendly identifier in the display name so that all people recognize its origin. For example, do not specify "App Xyz", but rather "Sanao App Zyx".
`attributeDisplayNames`	This multivalued attribute defines the display name for each attribute of the class. Each element contains a pair of `LDAP name, display name`, such as `samAccountName,Computer name (pre-Windows 2000)`. As with class display names, include your organization's friendly identifier to the display names of the attributes that you have created.
`extraColumns`	The Users and Computer snap-in allows the administrator to select which columns are visible in the right-hand pane by choosing View, Add/Remove Columns. The Windows Server 2003 version of the tool allows also customizing the list of where to choose from (if the schema also is upgraded to AD2003). The list can be defined using the multivalued `extraColumns` attribute on a given container display specifier, such as `organizationalUnit-Display` or `container-Display`. The syntax is `<ldapdisplayname-of-attribute>, <column header>, <default visibility>, <width>, <unused>`. The default visibility is 1 if the column is visible by default; otherwise, it is 0. The width is expressed in pixels, and the value -1 means that the column width is set to the width of the column header. Unused must be 0. Note that if you set this attribute for `organizational-Unit-Display`, for example, the hard-coded default list of 25 columns is replaced with your new

Table 9.8 Display Specifier Attributes *(cont.)*

Attribute	Description
	list (and not appended). Modifying the list in the `default-Display` object doesn't help, because it is used only if `organizationalUnit-Display` or `container-Display` wouldn't exist at all. You can, however, copy the list from `default-Display` to the display specifier you want, and then append some columns.
`treatAsLeaf`	If TRUE, this single-valued Boolean attribute defines that the corresponding class should be displayed as a leaf object in the user interface, even though it technically would be a container object. An example of this is the `user` class.

NOTE In reality, the Users and Computers snap-in doesn't use all the display specifier attributes (even though it is suggested here and in Microsoft's documentation). For example, most of the field names in user properties (such as Description or Office) are hard-coded in the snap-in, so the snap-in does not read them from the `attribute-DisplayNames` attribute.

As an example of a display specifier object, we used LDIFDE to dump the attributes of `computer-Display`. The appropriate lines of the dump are as follows:

```
dn: CN=computer-Display, CN=409, CN=DisplaySpecifiers,
  CN=Configuration, DC=sanao, DC=com
adminPropertyPages: 1,{6dfe6492-a212-11d0-bcd5-00c04fd8d5b6}
adminPropertyPages: 3,{77597368-7b15-11d0-a0c2-080036af3f03}
adminPropertyPages: 4,{6dfe648b-a212-11d0-bcd5-00c04fd8d5b6}
adminPropertyPages: 5,{6dfe6488-a212-11d0-bcd5-00c04fd8d5b6}
adminPropertyPages: 6,{4E40F770-369C-11d0-8922-00A024AB2DBB}
adminPropertyPages: 7,{B52C1E50-1DD2-11D1-BC43-00C04FC31FD3}
adminPropertyPages: 10,{0F65B1BF-740F-11d1-BBE6-0060081692B3}
shellPropertyPages: 1,{f5d121f4-c8ac-11d0-bcdb-00c04fd8d5b6}
shellPropertyPages: 2,{dde2c5e9-c8ae-11d0-bcdb-00c04fd8d5b6}
adminContextMenu: 1,{08eb4fa6-6ffd-11d1-b0e0-00c04fd8dca6}
contextMenu: 0,{62AE1F9A-126A-11D0-A14B-0800361B1103}
```

```
createWizardExt: 1,{D6D8C25A-4E83-11d2-8424-00C04FA372D4}
classDisplayName: Computer
attributeDisplayNames: samAccountName,Computer name
  (pre-Windows 2000)
attributeDisplayNames: operatingSystemVersion,Operating
  System Version
attributeDisplayNames: operatingSystem,Operating System
attributeDisplayNames: managedBy,Managed By
attributeDisplayNames: description,Description
attributeDisplayNames: cn,Name
treatAsLeaf: TRUE
```

Now that you know the attributes, you are ready to test changing a couple of them.

Testing to Change the Displays

If you have a test forest, you can test the following two things:

- Change the class display name
- Add an item to a context menu

If you locate the `computer-Display` object with ADSI Edit, you can see that the value for the `classDisplayName` attribute is "Computer." As an experiment, change this to "Television." If you now open up the Users and Computers snap-in, you will notice that the type of any computer object is shown as "Television."

NOTE Much of the information in the display specifiers is cached per process and per class (and for end-user information, per logon session). This means that if you already had the Users and Computers snap-in running, you might need to restart it to see the change.

Next we test adding a context menu item for user objects. To achieve this, we need to perform the following steps.

1. Add the two menu definitions to the `contextMenu` attribute of the `user-Display` object.
2. Create and test the first corresponding program (a batch file).

3. Create and test the second corresponding program (a VBScript file).

Adding the Menu Definitions

Locate the `user-Display` object with ADSI Edit and select the `contextMenu` attribute. Add to the attribute the following two values, but don't remove the existing values:

```
11, Test Item &1, c:\test\testitem.bat
12, Test Item &2, c:\test\testitem.vbs
```

We use numbers 11 and 12 to leave room in case a future version of Active Directory uses 1 and 2. (A proper way for a C programmer would be to list the existing values to find out which values are available.) The ampersand character (&) defines that the next character will be underlined, which allows you to use it as a hot key.

The result should look like the one in Figure 9.12, although the order of the values may vary.

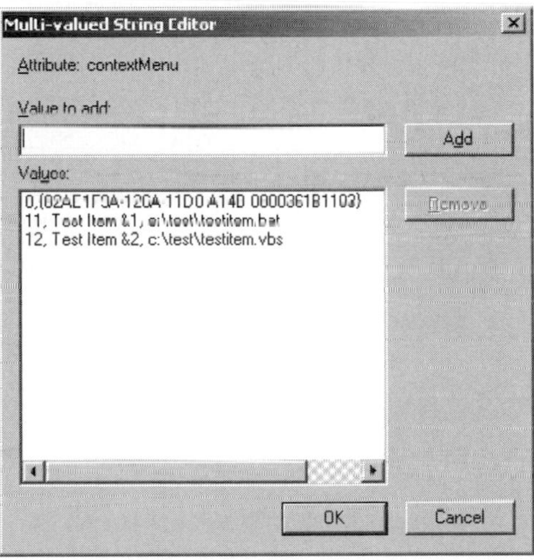

Figure 9.12 You can add context menu items to existing or new classes by adding the corresponding definitions as values in a display specifier object.

You would already see the new items in the context menu of any user, as shown in Figure 9.13. Selecting a new item would do nothing, however, because the corresponding program does not exist yet.

Creating and Testing a Batch File

Create the folder C:\Test. Using an ASCII text editor (i.e., Notepad), create the file C:\Test\TestItem.Bat and add the following lines:

```
@echo off
echo Name is: %1
echo Class is: %2
pause
```

Next, launch the Users and Computers snap-in and open any user's context menu. You should see the two new items you just added. When you select the first new item, a screen like the one shown in Figure 9.14 should appear.

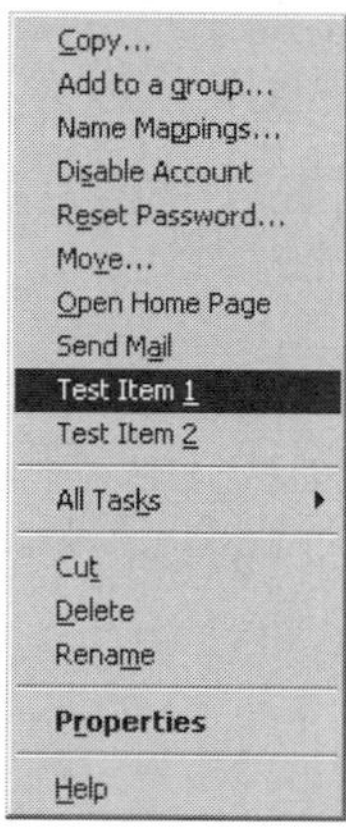

Figure 9.13 The new items appear in the context menu.

```
C:\WINDOWS\system32\cmd.exe
Name is: "LDAP://DC11.sanao.com/CN=Jill Green,OU=Sales,DC=sanao,DC=com"
Class is: user
Press any key to continue . . .
```

Figure 9.14 The LDAP path to the selected object and its class are passed to the launched program. This example doesn't use the two values, except for showing them to you.

We used a batch file as the first example to keep it simple but give you an idea of the process. In practice, however, if you are using batch files, your possibilities are limited.

Creating and Testing a VBScript Script

The Users and Computers snap-in doesn't show when a user has last logged on or if someone has tried wrong passwords for that user account (unless you install AcctInfo.dll from the Resource Kit). You can create a script to fill this need. Our example uses EditPlus (a shareware program from `http://www.editplus.com/`), but Notepad is also fine.

First create the file C:\Test\TestItem.VBS and add the lines shown in Figure 9.15. (You can also download the file from the book's Web site at `http://www.kouti.com/`.) Line 1 specifies that if a later line contains an error, continue with the next line instead of quitting the script right away. The most likely error source is that some attribute value is not set, in which case we just list all the others. Line 3 collects all arguments and line 4 creates a user COM object from the first (denoted by "0") argument. As you remember, the first argument is the LDAP path to the selected user.

Next the script retrieves each attribute and stores the values to six string variables, along with the description text. The last line (split across lines 13 and 14 with the underscore) pops up the result, putting a

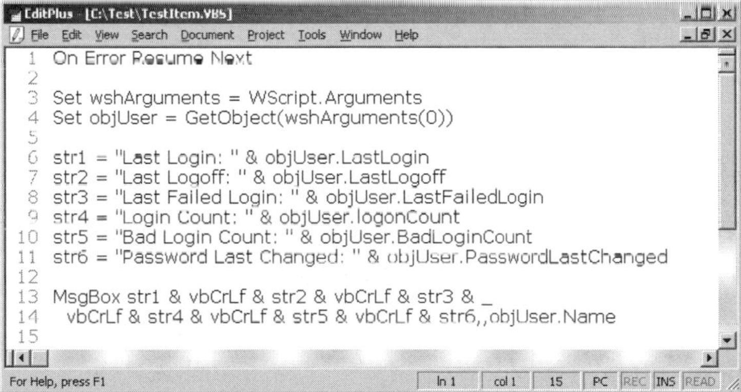

```
1  On Error Resume Next
2
3  Set wshArguments = WScript.Arguments
4  Set objUser = GetObject(wshArguments(0))
5
6  str1 = "Last Login: " & objUser.LastLogin
7  str2 = "Last Logoff: " & objUser.LastLogoff
8  str3 = "Last Failed Login: " & objUser.LastFailedLogin
9  str4 = "Login Count: " & objUser.logonCount
10 str5 = "Bad Login Count: " & objUser.BadLoginCount
11 str6 = "Password Last Changed: " & objUser.PasswordLastChanged
12
13 MsgBox str1 & vbCrLf & str2 & vbCrLf & str3 & _
14   vbCrLf & str4 & vbCrLf & str5 & vbCrLf & str6,,objUser.Name
15
```

Figure 9.15 TestItem.VBS. This script displays logon information about a user.

carriage return/linefeed (CrLf) between each attribute. It also puts the name property of the object in the caption text of the message box.

NOTE On line 9 of TestItem.VBS, "logonCount" starts with a lowercase letter, whereas "BadLoginCount" and others start with uppercase letters. The reason is that "logonCount" is an attribute LDAP name, but the others are ADSI property method names.

NOTE Actually, both "logonCount" and "LogonCount" would work. VBScript is not a case-sensitive language.

After saving the file, select your second menu item in the context menu of any of your users. A screen like the one in Figure 9.16 should appear. In this example, Jack has logged on 37 times. He has never tried to log on with a wrong password, nor has someone else tried to use his account. Consequently, the last failed logon time is A.D. 1601, when Henry IV (*le bon Henri*) still ruled France! The corresponding large integer attribute `badPasswordTime` has a value of zero, which indicates that ancient date. The time shows 3:00 AM instead of midnight, because the local time when running the script was 3 hours ahead GMT/UTC (2 hours for the time zone and another hour for daylight saving time).

A bad login count of zero indicates that there were no unsuccessful logon attempts after the last successful logon. Upon each successful logon, the bad login count is reset to zero.

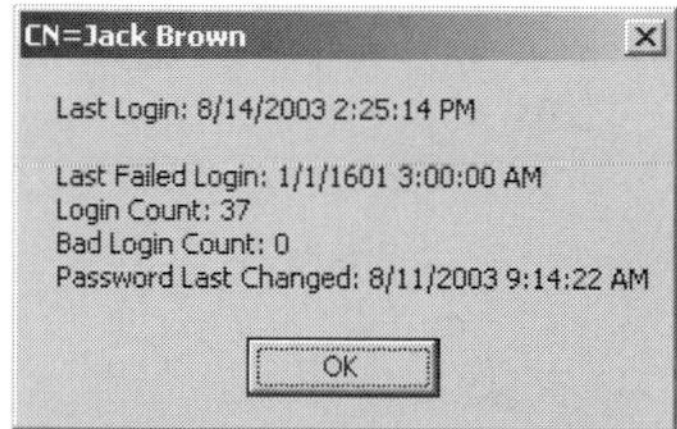

Figure 9.16 By adding a context menu item for user objects, you can display sometimes useful attributes that the Users and Computers snap-in doesn't show you.

WARNING In the example in Figure 9.16, all settings except `PasswordLastChanged` correspond to nonreplicating attributes. Therefore, each domain controller knows the values only for itself; you will get different results if you read the settings from different domain controllers.

NOTE As explained in Chapter 5, the old `lastLogon` attribute is not replicated among domain controllers, but AD2003 introduces a new attribute, `lastLogonTimestamp`, which is replicated (although only on weekly basis). We didn't include the new attribute in the TestItem. VBS script, because its value is a 64-bit large integer, which a VBScript script cannot display in a sensible date format. For more information on large-integer dates, see Chapter 10 and Chapter 11.

NOTE `LastLogoff` doesn't work. Therefore, the second line of the output is empty.

NOTE Microsoft uses "logons," but Novell uses "logins." Because ADSI is designed to work also with NetWare networks, Microsoft chose to use the name `LastLogin` instead of `LastLogon`.

NOTE If the default in your computer is CScript instead of WScript, you will see an extra character-based window when you select the menu item. We discuss this, as well as other aspects of scripting, in Chapter 10.

Extending the User Class

To summarize the discussion of extension and modification to the schema, we present an example of how to extend the `user` class.

You could use the `user` class extensions (i.e., new attributes) for at least two purposes:

- Human resources management for data such as the date each user started to work for your organization or the name of his or her previous employer
- IT management for data such as the primary workstation of each user

We use the first situation in this example. We will plan the extensions, implement them, and also show how to manage the values and permissions for the new attributes.

Planning the Extensions

We expect to have quite a few new human resources attributes for user objects. Therefore, it is convenient to first put the attributes into an auxiliary class and then add this auxiliary class to the `user` class. Figure 9.17

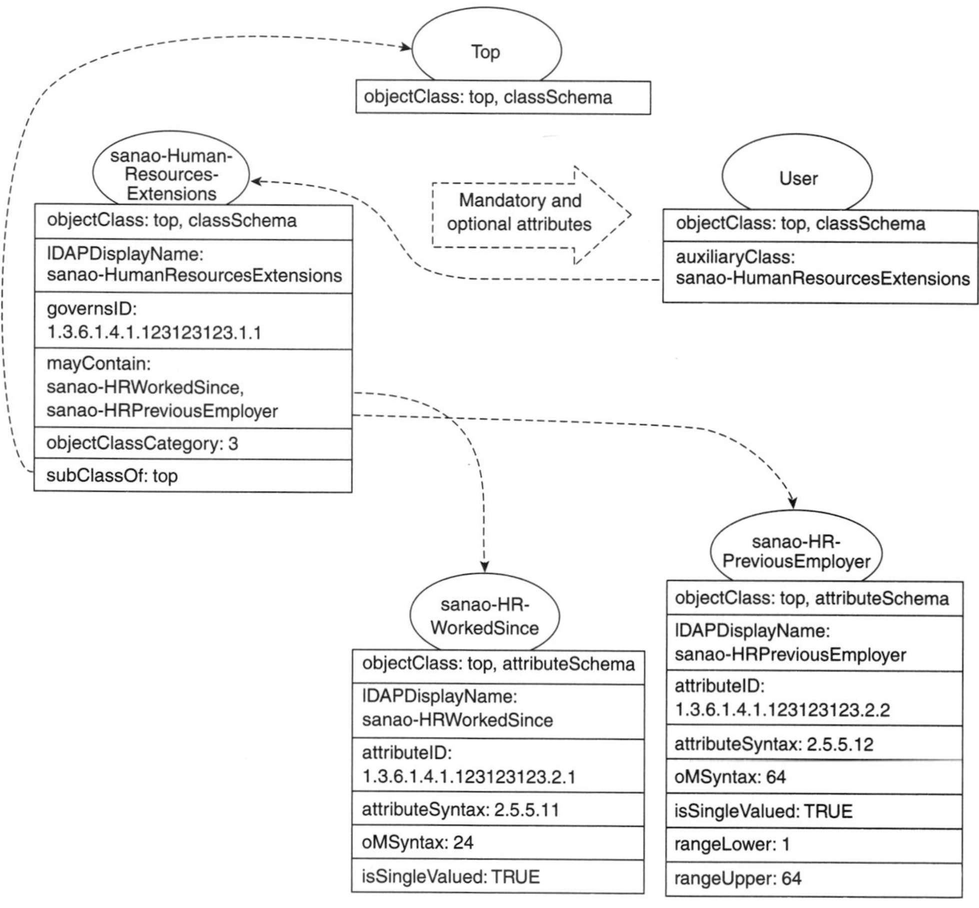

Figure 9.17 `ObjectClassCategory` 3 means that the new class on the left is auxiliary. It contains two optional attributes, which will be used in the `user` class through this auxiliary class.

shows the new auxiliary class as well as the two sample attributes it will contain.

We cannot add new mandatory attributes to an existing class, so both our new attributes are optional (i.e., `mayContain`).

Our company has a base OID "1.3.6.1.4.1.123123123." Below that base we have allocated "1" to human resources classes and "2" to human resources attributes.

The `sanao-HRWorkedSince` attribute uses the `Generalized time` syntax, whereas `sanao-HRPreviousEmployer` uses a normal `Unicode string` syntax. The latter attribute has a maximum length of 64 characters.

Implementing the Extensions

We use LDIFDE to create the three new schema objects and to extend the `user` class. It is a straightforward tool once we know the values for all needed attributes. Besides, an LDIF file allows us to list the extensions in an exact and compact way (both for the in-house document and this book). We don't want to repeat the numerous screen shots that you saw earlier in this chapter. The following 54 lines will do the trick:

```
dn: CN=sanao-HRWorkedSince, CN=Schema, CN=Configuration,
   DC=sanao, DC=com
changetype: add
objectClass: attributeSchema
lDAPDisplayName: sanao-HRWorkedSince
adminDescription: This attribute contains the date since
   when the employee has worked for the company.
attributeID: 1.3.6.1.4.1.123123123.2.1
attributeSyntax: 2.5.5.11
oMSyntax: 24
isSingleValued: TRUE
showInAdvancedViewOnly: TRUE

dn: CN=sanao-HRPreviousEmployer, CN=Schema,
   CN=Configuration, DC=sanao, DC=com
changetype: add
objectClass: attributeSchema
lDAPDisplayName: sanao-HRPreviousEmployer
adminDescription: This attribute contains the employee's
   previous employer.
attributeID: 1.3.6.1.4.1.123123123.2.2
attributeSyntax: 2.5.5.12
```

```
oMSyntax: 64
isSingleValued: TRUE
rangeLower: 1
rangeUpper: 64
showInAdvancedViewOnly: TRUE

dn:
changetype: modify
add: schemaUpdateNow
schemaUpdateNow: 1
-

dn: CN=sanao-HumanResourcesExtensions, CN=Schema,
  CN=Configuration, DC=sanao, DC=com
changetype: add
objectClass: classSchema
lDAPDisplayName: sanao-HumanResourcesExtensions
adminDescription: This auxiliary class contains the
  human-resources related attributes of the Sanao
  company.
governsID: 1.3.6.1.4.1.123123123.1.1
mayContain: sanao-HRWorkedSince
mayContain: sanao-HRPreviousEmployer
objectClassCategory: 3
subClassOf: top
defaultHidingValue: TRUE
showInAdvancedViewOnly: TRUE

dn:
changetype: modify
add: schemaUpdateNow
schemaUpdateNow: 1
-

dn: CN=User, CN=Schema, CN=Configuration, DC=sanao,
  DC=com
changetype: modify
add: auxiliaryClass
auxiliaryClass: sanao-HumanResourcesExtensions
-
```

We added `showInAdvancedViewOnly = TRUE` to each object to keep them hidden from normal administrative tools and the end-user interface. We did this because all the base schema objects should have the setting also. This is not part of the actual schema characteristics.

Managing the Attribute Values

Unfortunately the Users and Computers snap-in doesn't notice our new attributes and start magically showing them on one of the property pages. We would have to start writing a COM component (using the C language, for example) to implement a new property page.

We have two other choices to read and modify the values, although neither of them is particularly handy:

- Use ADSI Edit
- Use scripts

For the scripting option, you could create a new menu item for the `user` class, and when selecting that item on some user, you would see the current value and perhaps enter a new value. Another choice is to apply a script to a number of users, again either just displaying the current values or modifying them. You could have the values in a large Excel spreadsheet and write them to the new Active Directory attributes.

We demonstrate here the scripting option for a single user. Chapter 11 has examples of listing attribute values for a number of users and using an Excel spreadsheet as a means of input.

Adding a Script to the Context Menu

We explained earlier in this chapter how to add new menu items and use them. Here we briefly list the steps that apply to our user extension example.

1. Using ADSI Edit, locate the `user-Display` object (in `CN=409,CN=DisplaySpecifiers,CN=Configuration`).
2. Select the `adminContextMenu` attribute. Add to the attribute the value `2,S&anao Human Resources,c:\test\sanaohr.vbs`. Do not remove the existing values, and if number 2 is already in use, select a free number.
3. Create the file c:\test\sanaohr.vbs and add the lines shown in Figure 9.18.

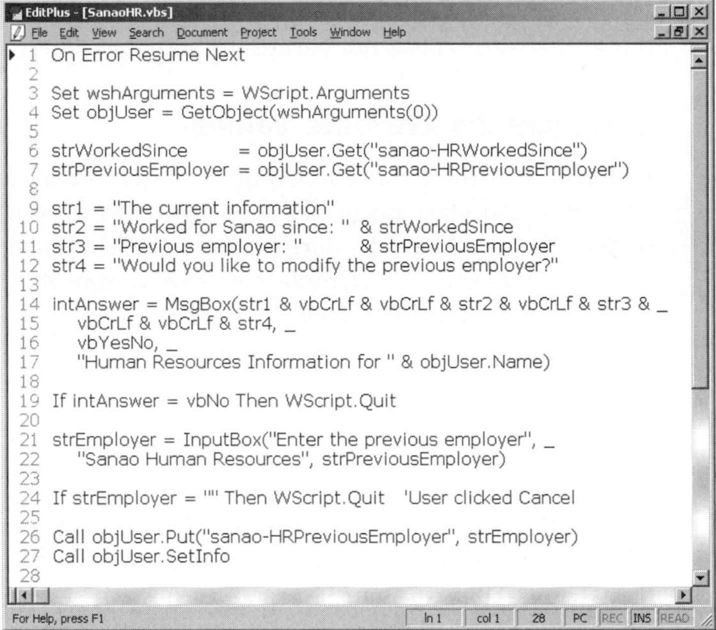


```
1  On Error Resume Next
2
3  Set wshArguments = WScript.Arguments
4  Set objUser = GetObject(wshArguments(0))
5
6  strWorkedSince       = objUser.Get("sanao-HRWorkedSince")
7  strPreviousEmployer = objUser.Get("sanao-HRPreviousEmployer")
8
9  str1 = "The current information"
10 str2 = "Worked for Sanao since: "  & strWorkedSince
11 str3 = "Previous employer: "        & strPreviousEmployer
12 str4 = "Would you like to modify the previous employer?"
13
14 intAnswer = MsgBox(str1 & vbCrLf & vbCrLf & str2 & vbCrLf & str3 & _
15     vbCrLf & vbCrLf & str4, _
16     vbYesNo, _
17     "Human Resources Information for " & objUser.Name)
18
19 If intAnswer = vbNo Then WScript.Quit
20
21 strEmployer = InputBox("Enter the previous employer", _
22     "Sanao Human Resources", strPreviousEmployer)
23
24 If strEmployer = "" Then WScript.Quit   'User clicked Cancel
25
26 Call objUser.Put("sanao-HRPreviousEmployer", strEmployer)
27 Call objUser.SetInfo
28
```


Figure 9.18 SanaoHR.VBS

On lines 6 and 7 of Figure 9.18 we read the current values for the two human resources attributes. On line 14 we use the `MsgBox` function to display the results. Line 16 specifies that there are Yes and No buttons instead of the default OK button.

If the user clicks No, the script will terminate on line 19. If she clicks Yes, we use the `InputBox` function to ask for a new value for one of the attributes. Finally, on lines 26 and 27 we store the new value back to Active Directory.

After saving the file, you can select the menu item Sanao Human Resources in the context menu of any of your users. A screen like the one in Figure 9.19 should appear. If the user clicks Yes, he will see the dialog box shown in Figure 9.20.

Searching on the New Attributes

The new attributes will show in the Find dialog box of My Network Places if you only add a display name for each of the attributes.

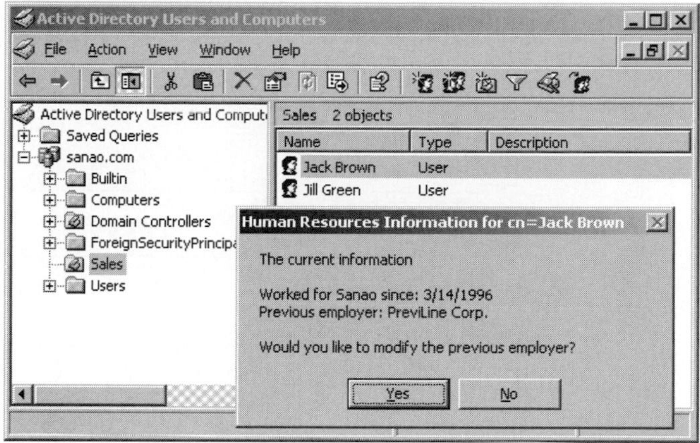

Figure 9.19 When you select Sanao Human Resources in the context menu of Jack Brown, you see the contents of our two new attributes.

As with adding menu items, you need to modify the attributes of the `user-Display` object. Add the following two new values to the `attributeDisplayNames` attribute:

```
sanao-HRWorkedSince,Sanao HR Worked Since
sanao-HRPreviousEmployer,Sanao HR Prev. Employer
```

Next, open My Network Places and click Search Active Directory in the list of common tasks (in the left-hand pane). The new attributes are available in the Advanced tab, as shown in Figure 9.21. If you use Windows 2000, you may need to log off and on again to see the new attributes.

It is not practical to use the Find dialog box with date attributes. With the fields shown in Figure 9.21 you cannot choose to find "all users that have joined our company since 1996." However, you can find those

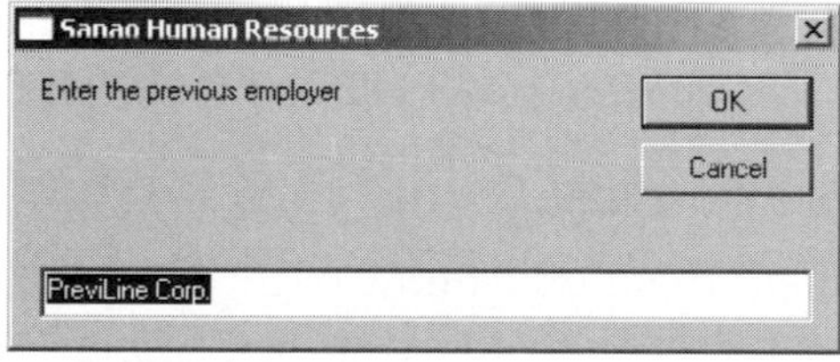

Figure 9.20 You can enter a new value for one of the attributes. We show the existing value as a default.

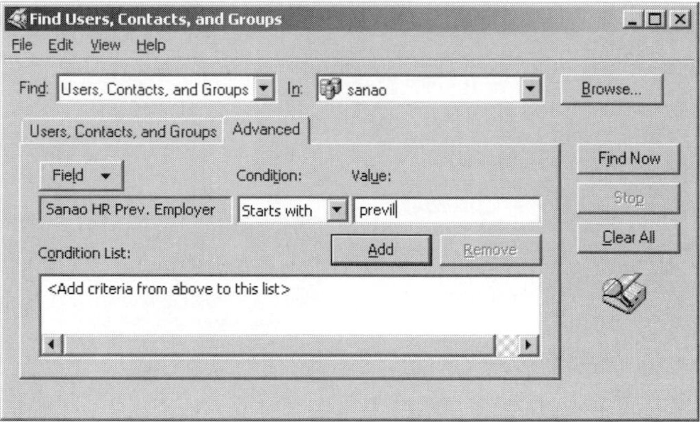

Figure 9.21 You can use the Find dialog box to list all users who have a certain previous employer. Note that the In box contains Entire Directory by default. It refers to the global catalog, but because our sanao attributes are not in the global catalog, you must change to a domain name instead of using Entire Directory.

users with an LDAP query, which you can enter if you select Custom Search, Advanced. (LDAP queries are discussed in Chapter 6.)

Managing the Attribute Permissions

The new attributes will automatically show in the ACL Editor, as explained earlier in this chapter. You can also create a property set to assign permissions to several attributes at once. Creating a property set requires quite a few steps, as described earlier in this chapter. We won't repeat the steps here.

Conclusion

Schema modifications should not be taken lightly, but they are also not forbidden. If you feel that the base schema doesn't serve all your needs, you must evaluate which changes are necessary, plan them carefully, and implement them efficiently. In this chapter, you learned guidelines and saw examples of how to do so.

CHAPTER 10

Administration Scripts: Concepts

We discuss administration scripts in two chapters. This chapter covers the concepts; the next is full of examples and explanations of how they work. We also include more concepts in the next chapter so as not to pack too much background theory in this chapter.

If you want to learn to speak a new language, you first need some basic vocabulary, grammar, and so forth. After a while you will learn more effectively—and more entertainingly—if you read some good novels in that language or travel to a country where the people speak that language. This chapter gives you the basic "vocabulary and grammar" of scripts, and the next will increase your skills. These two chapters will be useful if you are in one of the following three situations.

- You want to learn to write scripts to enhance administration and save work.
- You want to learn to read scripts. If you download scripts from the Internet or get them from other sources, you'll want to check what they do before you use them in your organization.
- You want to learn more about Active Directory architecture. Outputs of many of the examples in the next chapter provide architectural information about Active Directory and you can run those scripts without knowing what they do on each line. You should, of course, read the description first to check that that script isn't going to modify your Active Directory in any way. For instance, one example extends your schema (although we do include safety mechanisms in that script).

This first chapter covers the following topics:

- Getting started (i.e., how to download everything you need and how to use the Windows Script Host environment)
- The basics of the VBScript language
- ADSI concepts
- Additional scripting techniques, such as how to input and output information and how to debug scripts

You can download the scripts presented in the two chapters from `http://www.kouti.com/`.

Getting Started

You have probably written and/or used batch files, which contain command-line commands. As you know, they are a convenient way to automate administrative tasks.

Scripts are like "super batch files." They are usually more powerful and versatile than batch files; however, because they are a step toward real programming, there is a steeper learning curve than with batch files. Fortunately, you don't have to be a rocket scientist to use scripts. If you read this chapter and practice a little, you should be able to create quite useful administration scripts.

This chapter has another goal that is perhaps even more important than the goal of teaching you how to write scripts: This chapter aims to teach you how to *read* scripts. Quite a few scripts are available from Microsoft and on the Internet. Depending on the source, you might want to read through a downloaded script to learn what it does before you apply it in your enterprise.

You can use scripts at least for the following administrative tasks:

- To manage Active Directory objects
- To manage servers and services, such as Internet Information Server (IIS)
- To manage user workstations
- To create logon scripts for users and/or workstations

In this book we cover the first item in the list and give brief examples of the second one.

The Script Execution Environment

The following list contains three things that make up the environment to run Active Directory scripts, and the fourth item in the list could be beneficial.

- *Windows Script Host (WSH)* is a generic environment included in Windows 2000 and later (and also Windows 98) for running scripts written in various languages.
- *VBScript* is the language interpreter for the VBScript language. It is included in WSH.
- *Active Directory Service Interfaces (ADSI)* is the programmatic interface to Active Directory.
- *ActiveX Data Objects (ADO)* is a programmatic interface to any database or data source that has implemented an OLE DB provider, such as SQL Server, Oracle database server, or Active Directory.

Figure 10.1 shows a WSH script that uses the VBScript language and uses ADSI to access Active Directory.

All four items in the previous list are purely Microsoft technologies. We discuss WSH in this section, focus on VBScript and ADSI in later sections of this chapter, and present ADO in the next chapter. The four technologies make a good team, but there are alternatives (except for ADO). We list some choices along with their pros and cons in the following three sections.

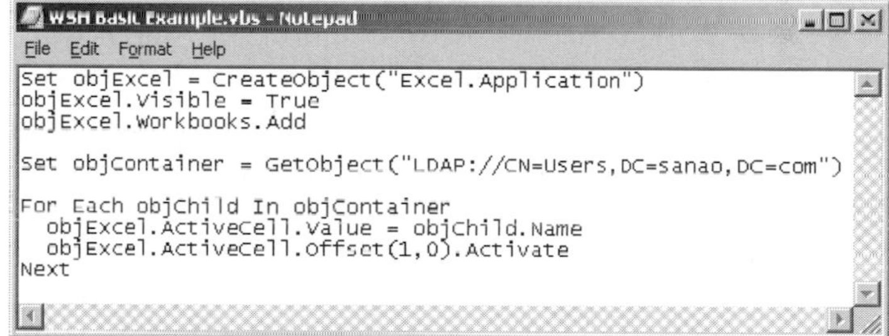

Figure 10.1 You can use Notepad to write a script that contains lines in the VBScript language. The WSH environment enables you to run this sample script, so it can open Excel, use ADSI to bind to the `CN=Users` container in a given domain, and write the names of all child objects in an Excel spreadsheet.

The WSH Environment

Windows Script Host, or WSH, is a generic environment for running scripts written in various languages. It includes VBScript and JScript, but the architecture enables vendors to create and install other languages as well. Windows Server 2003 and Windows XP include WSH 5.6, Windows 2000 includes WSH 2.0, and Windows 98 includes WSH 1.0. You can download WSH 1.0 for Windows 95/NT from `http://msdn.microsoft.com/scripting`. The version number jumped from 2.0 to 5.6 because it was aligned with the VBScript version number.

The WSH environment has the following advantages.

- In general, scripts are easier to learn to write than real programs, and they are more powerful than batch files.
- You can call and use any services based on Component Object Model (COM). This opens up a world in which you can interact with Active Directory via ADSI, with databases via ADO, with Office applications via their COM support, and with the local file system and the registry via WSH COM components. You can also do messaging via Collaborative Data Objects (CDOs), or do anything for which some vendor has written a COM component. For example, you could write a WSH script that displays the correct numbers for the next week's lottery, if you can find a vendor that is selling a COM component for that.
- WSH is included in the operating system. It is present in all the Windows 2000 and later computers of your company, meaning that they are ready to execute any WSH script (including malicious scripts, such as LOVE-LETTER-FOR-YOU.TXT.vbs).
- WSH is widely accepted and used, and it has broad support from Microsoft and other vendors.
- WSH takes only a few megabytes of a computer's RAM.
- You can run scripts both on the command line and in the graphical user interface.
- Starting from version 5.6, WSH includes an integrated method for running a script in a computer other than your local computer. You can also start a script to run simultaneously in several computers. You can check the progress of a running remote script, and you can see whether it ran successfully or terminated with an error code. In addition to running scripts remotely, you can have a script running on your workstation manage a server or another workstation if the COM component that you are calling from the

script supports remote access. For example, ADSI supports remote access.

- If you prefer, in WSH you can use the JScript language instead of VBScript. You can also download, buy, and install other languages that vendors have made for WSH.

The disadvantages of the WSH environment are as follows.

- In general, scripts are less powerful than real programs, and they are harder to learn and write than batch files.
- You cannot create full-fledged interactive programs that use the graphical user interface. You can display and input text in graphical pop-up messages, but you cannot go any further.
- WSH is not an *integrated development environment (IDE)*, which would contain features such as an intelligent editor, debugging support, and integrated Help files.
- There are some features in ADSI that you can access only with compiled programming languages and not with a scripting environment. An example of this is the `IDirectorySearch` interface; fortunately, you can pretty much achieve its functionality by using ADO.

In addition to, or instead of, WSH, you can use the following solutions for administrative tasks:

- *Visual Basic.* You can buy this development environment separately from Microsoft. Visual Basic enables you to write real programs that are compiled to binary EXE files (or DLL and OCX files, if needed). The programming language is a superset of VBScript. Compared to WSH scripts, Visual Basic applications may include an interactive graphical user interface, but learning to write those applications takes more time than learning to write scripts. Typical users of Visual Basic are in-house programmers who develop solutions for their own company. Commercial vendors may also use it, and sometimes administrators use it.
- *C/C++ compiler (and others such as C#).* C and C++ are (much) harder to learn than Visual Basic, but many professional developers prefer these languages because of their greater versatility and power.
- *Visual Basic for Applications (VBA).* Excel and other Microsoft Office applications, as well as some third-party applications, use

VBA. The language is almost the same as VBScript. You need to learn the object model of the hosting application, such as Excel, but once you do, you can integrate your scripting solutions to that application. If you write something with VBA, it is called a "macro" instead of a "script." However, in this book we tend to call these macros "scripts."

- *Active Server Pages (ASP) scripts in IIS.* You can write and run ASP scripts for your IIS Web server. Those scripts can be integrated with Active Directory via ADSI, and they can be used by administrators and end users.
- *Commercial scripting and management environments.* These include WinBatch (`http://www.windowware.com/`) and XLNT (`http://www.advsyscon.com/`).
- *Batch files.* You can do amazing things with plain old batch files that use standard command-line commands or other suitable EXE file commands acquired separately (including the ones in Windows Support Tools and Resource Kit).

Note that apart from VBA, commercial scripting environments, and batch files, the other items in the list are probably off-limits for an administrator. He could learn any of the others, but it would probably be an inappropriate way to spend his working hours. In a large company, in-house developers may be able to spend more time on learning the more difficult but powerful alternatives.

In conclusion, because WSH is the most natural choice to cover, we focus on it in this book.

NOTE Batch files and scripts are executed "sequentially." When we launch one, the processing begins from line 1. After that, the processing continues to line 2, line 3, and so on, unless there are some *conditional* or *loop statements* to control the flow. In contrast, normal Windows programs written in Visual Basic or C/C++ are written to react to various events, such as user actions.

The VBScript Language

WSH includes two scripting languages, VBScript and JScript, either of which you could use in your administrative scripts.

Windows Server 2003 includes version 5.6 of both languages (as does Windows XP) and Windows 2000 included version 5.1. The examples in this book don't require the new features of version 5.6. JScript 5.6 mostly conforms to ECMAScript Edition 3 (ECMA 262 language specification), a standard scripting language for the Web. It is not entirely compliant to maintain backward compatibility with older JScript versions.

VBScript is considered the easier of the two languages, and because administrators cannot dedicate their lives to learning a programming language, VBScript should be a better choice for them. JScript is more C-like, and while it has some fancier features, it is also more difficult to learn. Consequently, we use VBScript in this book for administrators.

The ADSI Interface

Active Directory Service Interfaces, or ADSI, is the programmatic interface to Active Directory, as well as to Windows NT and NetWare 3, 4, and later versions. Windows 2000 and later include ADSI, and you can download it for Windows 95/98/NT from `http://www.microsoft.com/adsi`. Also, if you install the Directory Service Client (DSClient) on Windows 95/NT, you will get ADSI. ADSI offers almost the full range of access to Active Directory from your scripts. The following alternatives provide some of the functionality of ADSI.

- You can call NET commands from your WSH scripts, such as `NET USER Jack /add`. They are somewhat easier than pure ADSI, but you will have access only to some of the user properties (those that existed already in Windows NT).
- You can call the DSAdd command from your WSH script, as well as other DS commands introduced in Windows Server 2003. Unlike the old NET commands, DS commands enable you to access most practical user properties. A sample DS command is `dsadd user "CN=Jack Brown, OU=Boston, DC=Sanao, DC=Com" -samid JackB -pwd *`
- There is an LDAP C API that gives you access to Active Directory. However, as the name implies, you must use the C language, so WSH wouldn't be an option. Even for C programmers, Microsoft recommends ADSI.
- Windows Server 2003 includes a new System.DirectoryServices (SDS) interface, which is on top of ADSI. SDS is intended for application programmers who want to access Active Directory from the .NET programming environment, but it is not targeted for scripters.

- Windows Management Instrumentation (WMI) is a COM interface that enables you to access (among many other targets) Active Directory. WMI is more difficult than ADSI, but a person who already knows WMI for other purposes can leverage this knowledge for Active Directory scripts.
- ADO is a way to read (but not write) Active Directory information.

Clearly, ADSI is the best choice.

Launching WSH Scripts

There are various ways to launch WSH scripts on the command line or through the graphical user interface. Before we get into that, however, we'll say a few words about the different script file types.

Script File Types

As a default, WSH interprets the following file types as executables:

- *VBS:* The file contains VBScript.
- *JS:* The file contains JScript.
- *WSF:* The file contains either VBScript or JScript, along with some Extensible Markup Language (XML) tags.
- *WSH:* The file contains settings for a script, along with the actual script filename (VBS, JS, or WSF).

To launch a script via one of these four file types, use any of the traditional ways to launch a file.

- Double-click the file with your mouse.
- While the file is selected in the graphical user interface, press Enter.
- Type the filename on the command line (specify the path if the file is not in the current folder or search path).
- Click the Start button, select Run, type the filename (and maybe the path), and press Enter.
- Drag and drop with a mouse another file over the script file. In this case, the dropped file (or files) will be an argument for the script.

WScript versus CScript

You run a WSH script in either the graphical environment ("WScript") or the command window ("CScript"). The differences are explained in Table 10.1.

You choose WScript or CScript by typing the corresponding word in front of the script filename. If you don't specify the choice in the launch command, there is a per-computer default, as explained in the next section.

The following lines are some examples of possible commands:

```
hello
c:\test\hello
cscript hello.vbs
cscript c:\test\hello.vbs
wscript hello.vbs
wscript c:\test\hello.vbs
```

NOTE When typing just the script filename (and maybe the path), you can drop the file extension, but you cannot drop the file extension when you also type `wscript` or `cscript`.

Table 10.1 WScript and CScript Comparison

Feature	WScript	CScript
The process that is executing the script and that you will also see in the Task Manager process list	wscript.exe	cscript.exe
An extra (black) command window appears if you start the script from the graphical environment	No	Yes
Errors show as	Graphical dialog box (pop-up)	Line or lines in the command window
Script output that is using the `WScript.Echo` method appears as	Graphical dialog box (pop-up)	Line or lines in the command window

NOTE If you type just `hello`, and you have both Hello.VBS and Hello.WSH, the former takes precedence.

Testing with a Small Script

To test a small script on your own, you can launch Notepad and type the following line:

```
WScript.Echo "Hello, world"
```

Save this line to a file called Hello.VBS (case is not important) and try to start your script in various ways. Figure 10.2 and Figure 10.3 show examples of the WScript and CScript output, respectively.

NOTE If you launch the CScript example in Figure 10.3 from the graphical environment (for example, by clicking the Start button, selecting Run, and typing the script filename), you will see the command window with the output for less than half a second. The same applies to any error messages. Consequently, you probably want to use the actual command window (i.e., cmd.exe).

The choice between the two environments depends on your needs. WScript is perhaps better suited to "end user–like" scripts, and CScript is better suited to serious administrative tasks. If you print a list of 100 users, for example, you don't want that many pop-up messages, but rather a 100-line list in a command window.

Figure 10.2 Hello.VBS launched with WScript

Figure 10.3 Hello.VBS launched with CScript

You can also redirect the CScript output to a file with the following command (note that you need to include `cscript` on the line in this case):

```
cscript hello.vbs >results.txt
```

For many scripts, it doesn't matter which environment you use.

TIP As you write more scripts, you also tend to make their names longer in order to make them easy to find. If you don't want to type a script's long name when starting it at the command line, you can use the `CompletionChar` feature. Depending on your operating system version, the feature may already be enabled. If not, start RegEdt32 and select either the `HKEY_LOCAL_MACHINE` or `HKEY_CURRENT_USER` window (depending on whether you want the feature for the computer or for the user). Next, locate the `CompletionChar` parameter in the key `Software`, `Microsoft`, `Command Processor`, and change the value to 9. The value 9 is the ASCII value for the Tab character, which means that now you need to type only a few characters from the beginning of the script name and then press Tab. This will autocomplete the name, or if there are several matches, it will cycle through several names.

Next we look at how you can change the default for WScript/CScript and control the other aspects of script execution.

Controlling WSH Scripts

You can store some per-computer, per-user, and per-script settings. Before we discuss them, however, we'll explain the command-line options.

Command-Line Options

If you have used commands on the command line, you have noticed that command options are often preceded by a slash—for example, `dir /p`. With WSH we must have a way to separate the options for the script host from the options for the script. You separate them by using two slashes for the script host options. The command would be something like this:

```
cscript //hostopt1 //hostopt2 scriptname scriptopt1 scriptopt2
```

Actually, you can also use just one slash for the host options, as long as these options appear before the script name on the command line. Because Microsoft always uses two slashes in its documentation and Help files, we use that convention as well.

There are 13 host options for `cscript` and `wscript`, and we describe them in Table 10.2.

NOTE The script options could be whatever your script happens to use.

Table 10.2 Host Options for CScript and WScript

Option	Description
`//T:n`	Timeout. The option specifies how many seconds (`n`) the script is allowed to run. If `n` is zero or the option is omitted, there is no time limit.
`//Nologo`	By default there is a two-line Microsoft copyright notice at the beginning of the `cscript` output. This option omits those two lines.
`//Logo`	This option is the opposite of the `//Nologo` option. Once you change the default setting to "no logo," you can use this option (but you probably don't want to).
`//S`	Save. When used with `//T`, `//Nologo`, or `//Logo`, this option saves the timeout or logo visibility as a per-user setting.
`//B`	Batch mode. This option suppresses any script error messages or other output from showing on the screen, either on the command line or in pop-up windows.
`//I`	Interactive. This option is the opposite of `//B`. Note that in the previous version of WSH you could make the batch mode the default. Now the interactive mode is always the default, so this `//I` option is obsolete.
`//H:cscript`	Host. This option changes the default environment to CScript.
`//H:wscript`	Host. This option changes the default environment to WScript (which is also the initial default).
`//U*`	Unicode. If you redirect the script input or output when using CScript, this option assumes that that I/O is using Unicode, instead of the traditional PC-ASCII character set.

* The last five options (`//U`, `//X`, `//D`, `//E`, and `//Job`) were introduced in WSH 2.0 and don't exist in WSH 1.0.

Table 10.2 Host Options for CScript and WScript *(cont.)*

Option	Description
`//X`	"Execute script in debugger." This option opens your script in the Script Debugger, placing the debugging cursor over the first script line.
`//D`	"Enable Active Debugging." This option starts running your script, but if there is an error, your script will open in the Script Debugger, and the debugging cursor will be on the line that contains the error. Unfortunately, you receive no indication of what the error was.
`//E:engine`	With this option, you can specify a certain engine to process your script. Two examples are VBScript and JScript. Normally the file type (VBS or JS) specifies the engine, so there is no need to specify it using this option.
`//Job:name`	If you include several script jobs in one WSF file, you can use this option to specify which job to run. The online Help for WSH 2.0 explains how to do this.

WARNING You can use the `//S` option with any other option and you will always get the message "Command line options are saved." However, only the timeout and logo settings are actually saved. For the other options, the message is erroneous.

Even though you can use the host options with `wscript`, you would normally use them with `cscript`. Also, three of the options (`//Nologo`, `//Logo`, and `//U`) are meaningful only with `cscript`.

NOTE As mentioned, you can launch a script by just typing its name. If you want to specify host options, however, you must first type `cscript` (or sometimes `wscript`).

Script Settings

Some of the command-line options described in the previous section are used to make a default setting. Apart from that, any command-line options are in effect only for one invocation of a script.

Unless you change them, some settings remain in effect permanently. Table 10.3 lists these settings and also indicates where they are stored and how to change them. You are already familiar with the actual settings, because they are the same ones you saw with command-line options.

You don't need the following information to run scripts, but if you are interested, you can examine the HKEY_CLASSES_ROOT contents by performing the following steps:

1. Locate the key .VBS (note the dot as the first character). It has a reference to the key VBSFile.
2. Locate the key VBSFile, ScriptEngine. It has a reference to the key VBScript.
3. Locate the key VBScript. It has a reference to the key {B54F3741-5B07-11cf-A4B0-00AA004A55E8.}.
4. Locate the long key name from the previous step under the CLSID key (they are sorted alphabetically).

Table 10.3 WSH Script Settings

Type	Settings	Stored In	How to Change
Per-computer	WScript or CScript as the default	Registry HKEY_CLASSES_ROOT	cscript //H:cscript or cscript //H:wscript.
Per-user	Logo or no logo, timeout	Registry HKEY_CURRENT_USER, Software, Microsoft, Windows Script Host, Settings	Start wscript.exe to open a settings page or use the command-line host options with //S.
Per-script*	Logo or no logo, timeout	Text file <script name>.WSH	Right-click a script file, select Properties, and select the Script tab.
Per-instance (or per a time a script is run)	Logo or no logo, timeout, and others	Nowhere	Use the options described in Table 10.2.

* The per-script and per-user settings are the same. If you use both, the per-script settings take precedence.

5. Once you find the key, you will see the `InprocServer32` key, which has a reference to vbscript.dll.

This way, you have found the file (vbscript.dll) that actually interprets your VBScript file and carries out the operations defined in that script.

Table 10.3 briefly mentions how to change the various settings. Now we will elaborate on these procedures with a few examples.

You can use the following commands to change the default environment to either CScript or WScript:

```
cscript //H:cscript
cscript //H:wscript
```

Or, if you like, you can use the following two commands:

```
wscript //H:cscript
wscript //H:wscript
```

NOTE If you launch a script using a WSH file, it will use WScript, even though your default environment is CScript.

To open the per-user settings page (see Figure 10.4), use this command:

```
wscript
```

Another way to set the two per-user settings is to use commands such as the following:

```
cscript //nologo //s
cscript //t:15 //s
```

As mentioned in Table 10.3, to see the per-script settings, right-click a script file, select Properties, and select the Script tab. That property page is similar to the per-user page shown in Figure 10.4.

When you click OK to save the per-script settings, a file with a WSH extension is created with the same name and in the same folder as the script. See Figure 10.5 for an example.

NOTE If you are using WSH 1.0 (e.g., with Windows NT), you can also add a third setting in the `Options` section: `BatchMode=1`. This setting corresponds to the `//B` command-line option.

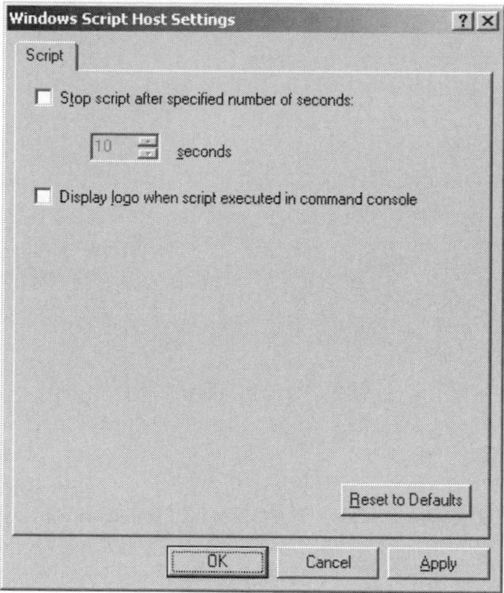

Figure 10.4 If you type the command `wscript`, a settings page with two general per-user settings will appear.

Killing a Script

Sometimes a script goes into an *infinite loop,* which means that it will never stop (unless you have specified a timeout, of course). The script could also spend more time on some operation than you are willing to wait. It is possible to kill a script without harming your system in any way.

WARNING There is a theoretical possibility that the script that seems to be in an infinite loop is just in the middle of some Active Directory batch update, in which case killing the script would cause part of the update not to take place. It shouldn't cause any other damage, though, if you happen to kill a script at such a moment.

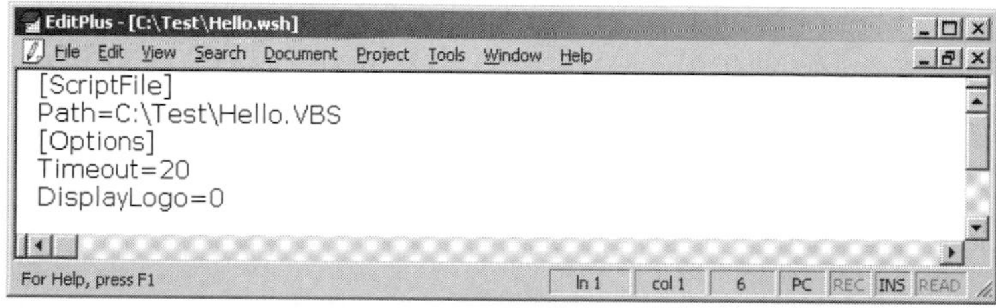

Figure 10.5 The per-script settings are stored in a WSH file.

The following factors affect how a running script is visible in the user interface:

- Whether the script is running in WScript or CScript
- Whether the script was started from the command line or from the graphical environment
- Whether the script is doing any input or output

Depending on these three factors, you may see your script in the Windows taskbar or in the Applications tab of the Task Manager (press Shift-Ctrl-Esc to launch the Task Manager). If so, you can just select Close or End Task and that may kill your script. The taskbar Close operation probably closes just one pop-up message of your script, but the End Task operation of the Task Manager should kill the whole script, at least if you wait a few seconds. If the script is running in a command window (i.e., CScript), pressing Ctrl-C should kill the script.

To check if those operations helped, and possibly to finish the job, you can perform the following steps:

1. Select the Processes tab of the Task Manager.
2. Click the Image Name column to sort the processes alphabetically.
3. Locate any cscript.exe and wscript.exe processes, select one, and click End Process. Then select the next process, click End Process, and so on.

TIP You can use the Task Manager to see the amount of I/O that each process is doing. While in the Processes tab, select View, Select Columns and check I/O Reads and I/O Writes. The numbers in these new columns may help you deduce whether a script is actually doing something or has just "hung."

Being able to kill a script requires appropriate privileges. If you start a script with the Task Scheduler service that is running with the credentials of LocalSystem, you cannot kill that script later, even though you are an administrator.

WARNING Be careful not to kill the wrong process.

Setting Up the Development Environment

Although the minimum requirements for writing scripts are Notepad and quick fingers, your work will be easier with the following extra tools:

- An effective and convenient editor
- Windows Script 5.6 Documentation (includes documentation for VBScript and WSH, among others)
- ADSI documentation

Getting a Script Editor

An editor that is made especially for writing scripts or programs has the following advantages over Notepad.

- It shows you line and column numbers. If you try to run a script, but WSH tells you that there is an error on line 137, you can easily locate the problem line (although also with the Windows Server 2003 version of Notepad you can turn on the status bar, which shows the current line number).
- It has *syntax highlighting*, which means that you will see the reserved keywords, comments, strings, and function names all in different colors. This is a tremendous improvement over a black-and-white view. Colors help you quickly to notice typing errors and they make any script much more readable.

Of course, if a company is trying to sell an editor to replace Notepad, it has probably included various other enhancements in its product. One such editor is EditPlus (`http://www.editplus.com/`), a shareware program from ES-Computing. Figure 10.6 shows a basic view of the program.

We use EditPlus for our examples in this and the next chapter—not because of color highlighting, but because of the line numbers. As we explain each code example, you can easily locate the corresponding line of the script. EditPlus also provides us with nice frames around the examples. Note that after Figure 10.6 we have stripped away the toolbars, status bars, and rulers to save some space in the examples.

Other script editors include Primal*script* (`http://www.sapien.com/`), UltraEdit (`http://www.ultraedit.com/`), VBScript Editor (`http://www.koala.it/Eng/script.htm`), and WinEdit (`http://www.winedit.com/`).

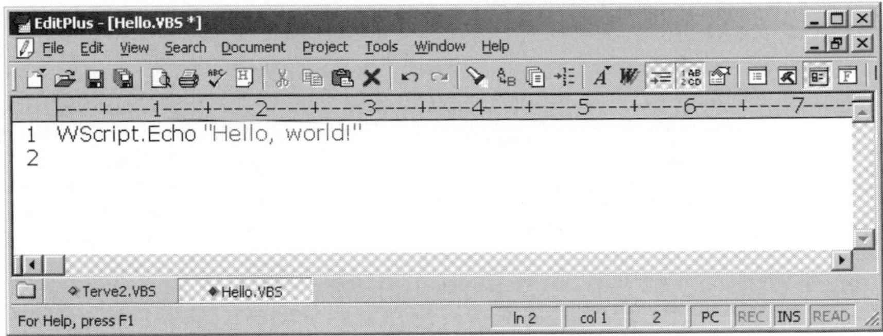

Figure 10.6 EditPlus is made for scripting, programming, and HTML editing.

TIP You can make EditPlus or any other editor the default editor instead of Notepad, at least for VBS files. To do this, open any folder in Windows Explorer, select the Tools menu, select Folder Options, select the File Types tab, locate and select the extension VBS, click Advanced, select the action Edit on the list, and click the Edit button. Now you should see the text that defines the editor application. Using the Browse button, change the path to your favorite editor to replace Notepad. Finally, click OK a few times to save your changes. Now you can right-click any VBS file with your mouse and when you select Edit from the context menu, your script opens in your favorite editor.

Getting the Documentation

Even though WSH (including VBScript) and ADSI are part of Windows 2000 and later, you need to download the documentation separately. As of this writing, the starting point for the download is the Microsoft Scripting Technologies site (`http://msdn.microsoft.com/scripting`).

There you can download a 1,395KB scrdoc56en.exe file, which includes the documentation for WSH 5.6 and VBScript 5.6, among others. When you download and run the file, it will install the documentation for WSH and VBScript into your Start menu (click the Start button and select All Programs, Microsoft Windows Script). Figure 10.7 shows the opening page of the documentation file.

The old Help file (from 1999) for ADSI is available from Microsoft at `http://www.microsoft.com/ntserver/downloads/bin/nts/adsi25.chm`. There you can download a 1.5MB ADSI25.CHM

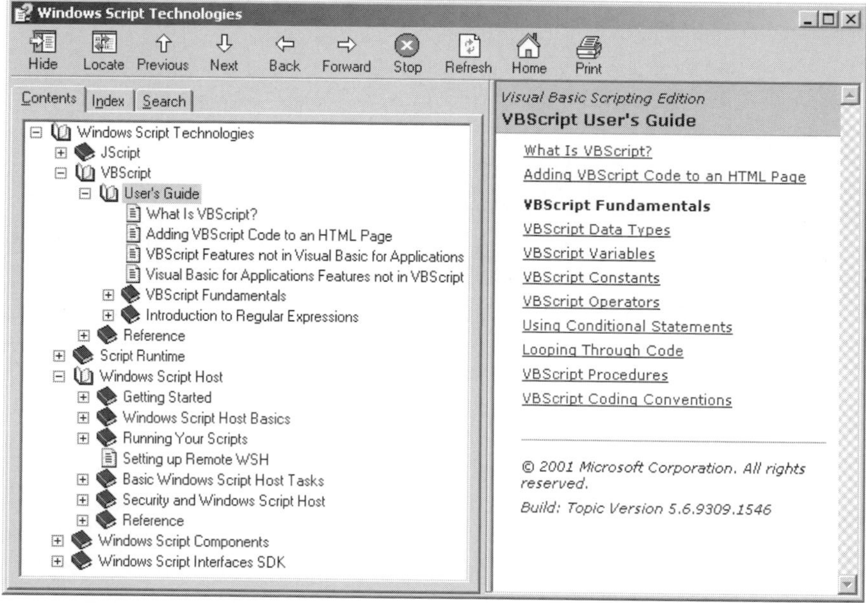

Figure 10.7 The Windows Script documentation file is created in the compiled HTML (CHM) format. The navigation tree contains both user's guides and references for the VBScript language and WSH.

file and place it in any convenient folder on your hard disk. This Help file more or less fulfills its purpose, but it's not quite current anymore. However, it is easy to get.

Another old Help file—from 2001—is NetDir.CHM. It seems not to be available at Microsoft's Web site anymore, but you may find it on the Internet using a search engine. The file is relatively current and less than 3MB in size.

The current documentation is included in the Platform SDK and it is continuously updated. You can access the Platform SDK online at the MSDN Library address `http://msdn.microsoft.com/library`, in the branch Networking and Directory Services. To download the Platform SDK Core SDK, go to `http://www.microsoft.com/msdownload/platformsdk/sdkupdate`. Another option is to buy the Platform SDK CD for the cost of shipping and handling at `https://qmedia.e-storefront.com/showcontent.asp?contentname=PlatformSDKHome`.

A new option is to use the 3.1MB file ADAM-SDK.CHM, which is available for download at `http://www.microsoft.com/windows`

server2003/adam. As of this writing, the file is dated May 2003, so it is even newer than the downloadable Platform SDK (dated February 2003).

Sources of Additional Information

This chapter and the next chapter give you a good basis for reading, using, and writing scripts to administer Active Directory. The information in these two chapters alone may even suffice for your purposes. However, if you want to keep up with new developments, learn additional aspects of scripting, and see more sample scripts than fit on these pages, you can use the Web and Internet news areas to update your knowledge. The following list contains some Web sites for you to visit:

- http://www.kouti.com/ (this book's Web pages)
- http://msdn.microsoft.com/scripting (Microsoft Scripting Technologies)
- http://www.microsoft.com/technet/scriptcenter (Microsoft TechNet Script Center, a large collection of sample scripts and some scripting tools)
- http://www.microsoft.com/adsi (Microsoft's Active Directory Service Interfaces Overview)
- http://msdn.microsoft.com/library (Microsoft's MSDN Library documentation, including the Platform SDK)
- http://www.15seconds.com/ (15 Seconds)
- http://communities.msn.com/windowsscript (Windows-Script community site)
- http://cwashington.netreach.net/ (Win32 Scripting)
- http://www.win2000mag.com/ (*Windows 2000 Magazine*, formerly *Windows NT Magazine*)
- http://www.win32scripting.com/ (*Windows Scripting Solutions*, from the publisher of *Windows 2000 Magazine*)

Microsoft has a news server at nntp://news.microsoft.com. It contains, among others, the following scripting newsgroups:

- microsoft.public.scripting.wsh
- microsoft.public.scripting.vbscript
- microsoft.public.adsi.general

You can also access any developer-related Microsoft public newsgroups with a browser at the address http://msdn.microsoft.com/newsgroups.

Obviously, we can list only a few Internet resources out of the many available. You can use a search engine to find more sites if you feel the need.

VBScript Language

Batch files are often just a series of commands that you have typed in a text file (of type BAT or CMD) so that you don't have to type the same series again and again.

With scripts, you use a programming language and that enables you to use the following programming constructs:

- Constants and variables of different data types
- Arrays
- Objects
- Operators
- Conditional statements to control program flow
- Looping statements to control program flow
- VBScript functions
- Procedures and functions

NOTE A batch file isn't necessarily just a series of commands; some of the items on the list are available also in the batch language.

In this section we explain the basic features and use of the VBScript language. At the same time we give some general guidelines for programming. If you are anxious to learn about ADSI, you may skip this section. Learning and understanding ADSI doesn't require you to know the information presented this section. To make good use of ADSI in scripts, however, you must be conversant with some aspects of VBScript.

By no means can we cover VBScript fully here. We try to offer enough information for you to gain an elementary understanding of it, while keeping the section to a reasonable length. The documentation that you downloaded includes the language reference with a complete list of all keywords, functions, and so on. The file also lists how VBScript is different from VBA, both of which are subsets of Visual Basic.

Dissecting a Sample Script

We start exploring VBScript by introducing and explaining a short sample script. It contains the most basic features of the language. After the first sample, we show two other scripts that do about the same things as the first one but in fewer lines.

The script first asks for your height in feet and in inches. Then it calculates your height in centimeters and displays it. Figure 10.8 shows the input box for the first question (feet). The input box for the second question (inches) looks nearly the same, so we don't show it separately. Figure 10.9 shows the script output.

The First Sample (Normal)

Now that you have seen how the script works, we show the contents of the script source (see Figure 10.10). This first version represents the typical style of scripting.

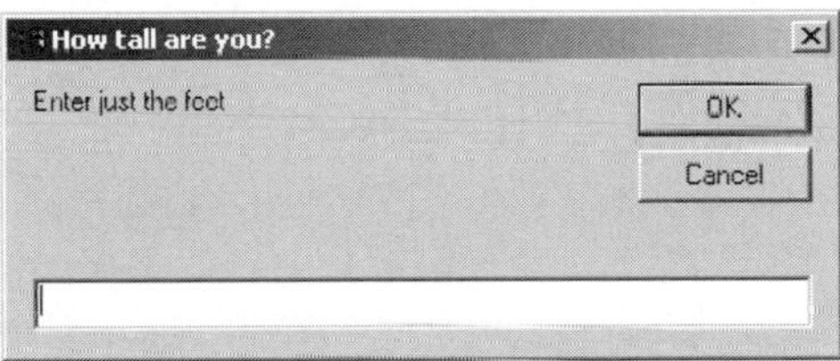

Figure 10.8 Using VBScript, you can ask the user for script input.

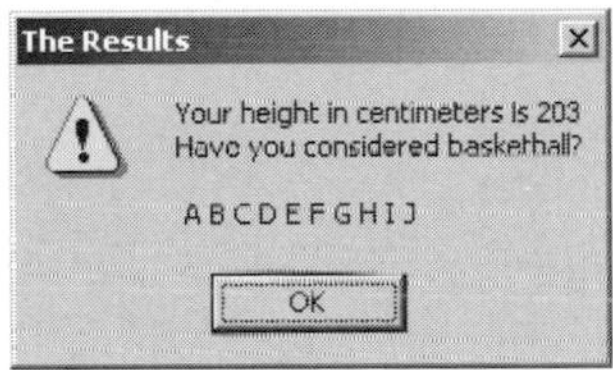

Figure 10.9 In VBScript, a script can display a message box to show some text, warnings, or results.

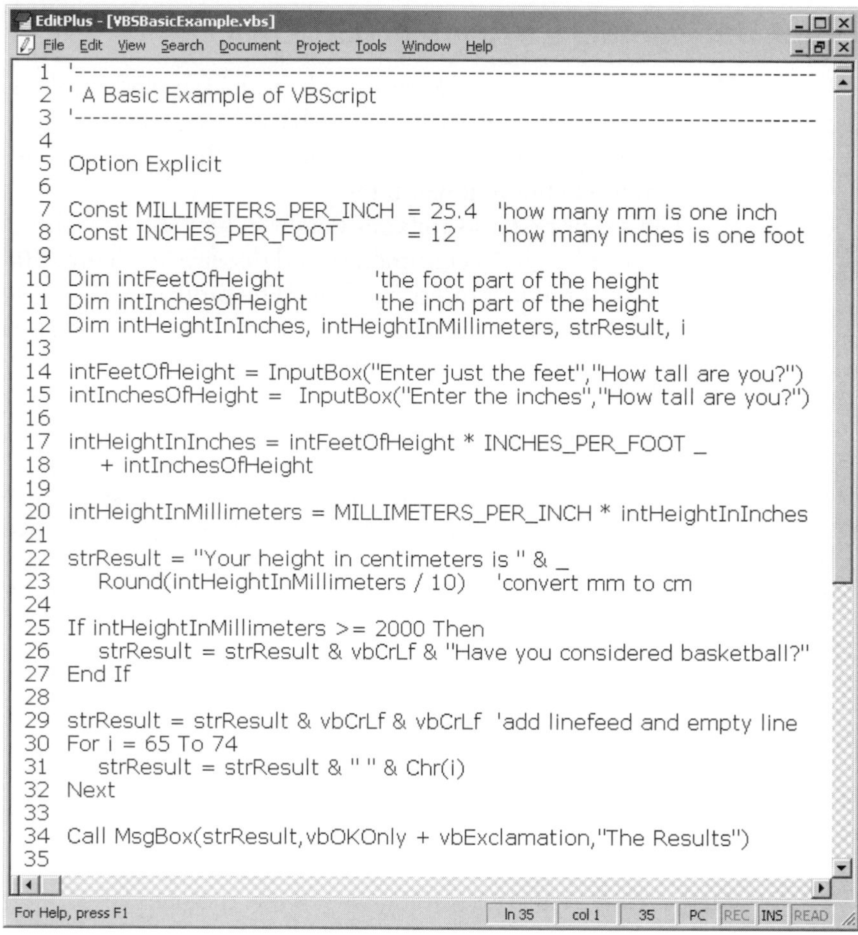

```
 1 '--------------------------------------------------------------------------------
 2 ' A Basic Example of VBScript
 3 '--------------------------------------------------------------------------------
 4
 5 Option Explicit
 6
 7 Const MILLIMETERS_PER_INCH = 25.4  'how many mm is one inch
 8 Const INCHES_PER_FOOT      = 12    'how many inches is one foot
 9
10 Dim intFeetOfHeight           'the foot part of the height
11 Dim intInchesOfHeight         'the inch part of the height
12 Dim intHeightInInches, intHeightInMillimeters, strResult, i
13
14 intFeetOfHeight = InputBox("Enter just the feet","How tall are you?")
15 intInchesOfHeight =  InputBox("Enter the inches","How tall are you?")
16
17 intHeightInInches = intFeetOfHeight * INCHES_PER_FOOT _
18    + intInchesOfHeight
19
20 intHeightInMillimeters = MILLIMETERS_PER_INCH * intHeightInInches
21
22 strResult = "Your height in centimeters is " & _
23    Round(intHeightInMillimeters / 10)   'convert mm to cm
24
25 If intHeightInMillimeters >= 2000 Then
26    strResult = strResult & vbCrLf & "Have you considered basketball?"
27 End If
28
29 strResult = strResult & vbCrLf & vbCrLf  'add linefeed and empty line
30 For i = 65 To 74
31    strResult = strResult & " " & Chr(i)
32 Next
33
34 Call MsgBox(strResult,vbOKOnly + vbExclamation,"The Results")
35
```

Figure 10.10 The contents of our basic example script

To write a VBScript:

- You should write *comment lines* at the beginning of the script to explain what the script does. Each comment line starts with an apostrophe ('). Our example in Figure 10.10 has only three comment lines (lines 1 through 3), but you are encouraged to write several lines, particularly for more complex scripts.
- You can add *comments at the end of any line* in the script (e.g., lines 7 and 8 in the sample). Again, the apostrophe indicates the beginning of comment text. Comments help other people understand quickly what the script does, as well as how and why it does

it. Comments will help you also, when after a couple of years you try to remember what the script does. It is not necessary to comment on every line, however—some lines are self-explanatory.

- You can use *empty lines* to make the script easier to read (e.g., lines 6, 9, and 13 in our example).
- *Constants* are known values that do not change as the script runs. When you define them with the `Const` keyword, their values cannot change. The formulas that calculate inches and millimeters (lines 17 and 20) are descriptive when you use names (such as `INCHES_PER_FOOT`) instead of just 12. By convention, names of constants are all uppercase letters.
- *Variables* can change their values, so the script can calculate the height in millimeters and store the answer in the corresponding variable. You use variables to store numbers, strings, and other kinds of data that the script needs.
- Using good and descriptive *constant and variable names* helps in understanding what the script does. The three-letter prefix of the name indicates the data type to be used with the variable: "int" stands for integer and "str" stands for string. The Help file has a list of recommended prefixes.
- Using `Option Explicit` in the beginning forces you to *declare* each variable with the `Dim` keyword (short for "dimension"). Although this may seem to be unnecessary extra work, it is actually a good thing. Without `Option Explicit` you could mistype a variable name and not notice it. Everything would seem to work, so such bugs could be hard to locate and fix. You can list several variable names in one `Dim` line.
- VBScript language is *not case-sensitive,* which means that instead of `Dim` you can also use `dim`, `DIM`, or `DiM`. Likewise, `intMyVar` and `Intmyvar` are the same variable.
- You must use a *decimal point* in decimal numbers (line 7), even though your regional options might define another decimal symbol.
- You must put any *string values in quotation marks* (e.g., line 22).
- Your script may use VBScript *functions*, such as `InputBox` to ask for user input, `Round` to get rid of too many decimals in the number, and `MsgBox` to display some output to the user.
- Each function may require some number of *arguments*. In our example, `InputBox` is using two arguments separated with a comma (e.g., line 14). `Round` takes just one argument (line 23), and `MsgBox` takes three arguments separated by commas (line 34).

- Each *function returns one value,* which you typically store in a variable (e.g., in the `InputBox` lines 14 and 15 of our example). `MsgBox` would also return a value to tell you whether the user clicked OK, Cancel, or some other button. Because we don't need the return value, we just use the `Call` statement to call the function.
- Many arguments are *optional,* which means that they have a default value and you can just omit them. For example, `InputBox` could take seven arguments, but we need only the first two, leaving the remaining five to their default values. If you omit an argument from the middle, you must insert a comma to indicate this.
- You can use various *control statements* to control the program flow. The `If` statement in the sample script has two parts—the conditional and consequence clauses. The conditional clause on line 25 (`If intHeightInMillimeters >= 2000 Then`) is evaluated first, and if true, the consequence clause on line 26 is executed. The lines in the `For` statement (line 30) are carried out a certain number of times.
- You should *indent the lines* inside `If` and `For` statements to enhance readability.
- You can use *operators,* such as an asterisk (*) to multiply, a plus sign (+) to add, a slash (/) to divide, and an ampersand (&) to concatenate two strings into one.
- Note that when forming the `strResult` string (line 22), you actually concatenate a string with a number. They are two *different data types.* Some other programming language would generate a "type mismatch" error, but VBScript changes the number 200 to a string 200, so the concatenation succeeds.
- Sometimes the automatic conversion doesn't work, so you have to use a *conversion function* (such as `CStr`) to convert a number to a string, for example.
- You can *cut long lines* by typing an underscore (_) and continuing the line on the next physical line (lines 17 and 18). This way, the lines are nicely visible in the editor window.
- You can also put *two short script lines together* with a colon between them. We don't use this in the sample script, however.
- In addition to two of our own constants, the script contains some *intrinsic constants.* `VbCrLf` (standing for carriage return/linefeed) equals the characters that cause the output to scroll to the beginning of the next line. `VbOKOnly` (line 34) corresponds to the value 0, which causes `MsgBox` to show just the OK button and no other buttons, such as Cancel. `VbExclamation` equals 48,

which causes `MsgBox` to show an exclamation mark. Again, a script is more readable when it says "vbExclamation" instead of just "48."

NOTE The term "carriage return/linefeed" was born back in the 1970s, when computer terminals printed all output on paper. The terminals had a carriage with a device (ball, cylinder, or row of rods) that contained all necessary characters (just like the old IBM typewriters). Once the carriage neared the right edge of the paper, it needed to return to the left edge. Linefeed rolled the paper up one line.

The Second Sample (Short)

Next, we write the same sample in 10 lines (see Figure 10.11) instead of 34. To be able to shorten the script

- We drop out all comments.
- We drop out the `For` loop, which adds the letters A–J to the output.
- We drop out `Option Explicit` as well as all `Const` and `Dim` statements.
- We do not store the user input to a variable first, but instead place the `InputBox` functions directly in the formula.
- We do not calculate intermediate results, such as `intHeightInInches`.

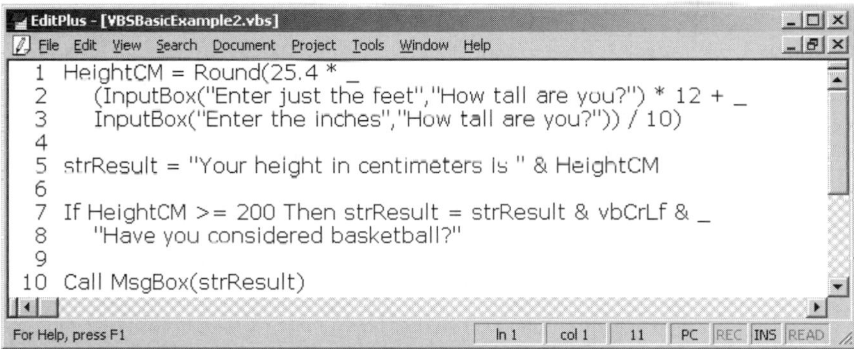

Figure 10.11 The contents of a shorter version of the sample script in Figure 10.10

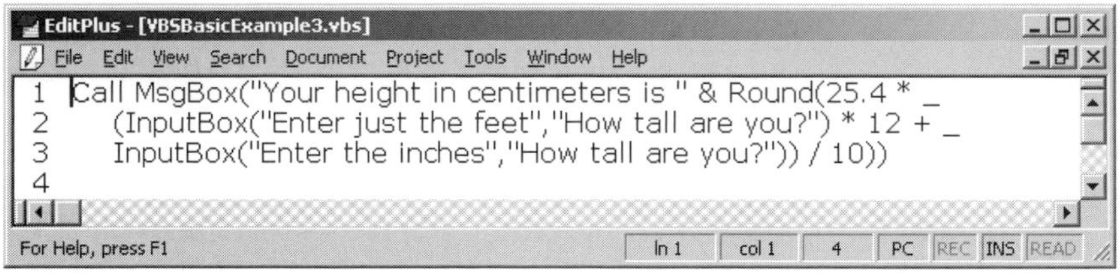

Figure 10.12 The contents of the shortest version (just one line) of the VBScript sample in Figure 10.10

Although 10 lines may seem better than 34 lines, shorter is not always better. A shorter script is usually less readable. We show it here so you can see some possibilities. We consider the longer sample better in many regards.

The Third Sample (Very Short)

If we don't need the comment "Have you considered basketball?" (lines 7 and 8 of Figure 10.11), we do not need intermediate results. In this case, we can squeeze everything into one line (which we cut into three to fit it on a book page). Figure 10.12 shows the result.

Notice that the return values of `InputBox` can be used directly as arguments for `MsgBox`.

ADSI Concepts

In this section we explain the general concepts of ADSI. We also show some small code fragments to demonstrate the concepts. However, we leave most of the code details to the next chapter, which is full of ADSI examples and explanations.

ADSI provides access from a number of programming environments to a number of directory services (see Figure 10.13). Because ADSI is implemented as COM objects, any programming environment that understands COM will understand ADSI.

There are two kinds of COM clients:

- Automation clients (that use *late binding*), such as WSH + VBScript and WSH + JScript
- Nonautomation clients (that use *early binding*), such as Visual Basic, VBA, and C/C++

Using ADSI differs depending on which client type is in use. Because this chapter is about scripting, we discuss ADSI from the automation client's point of view. Our examples will use late binding, but we don't discuss what late binding or early binding actually means in the background. We introduced the terms so that when you see one of them in the documentation, you'll know if it is related to scripting.

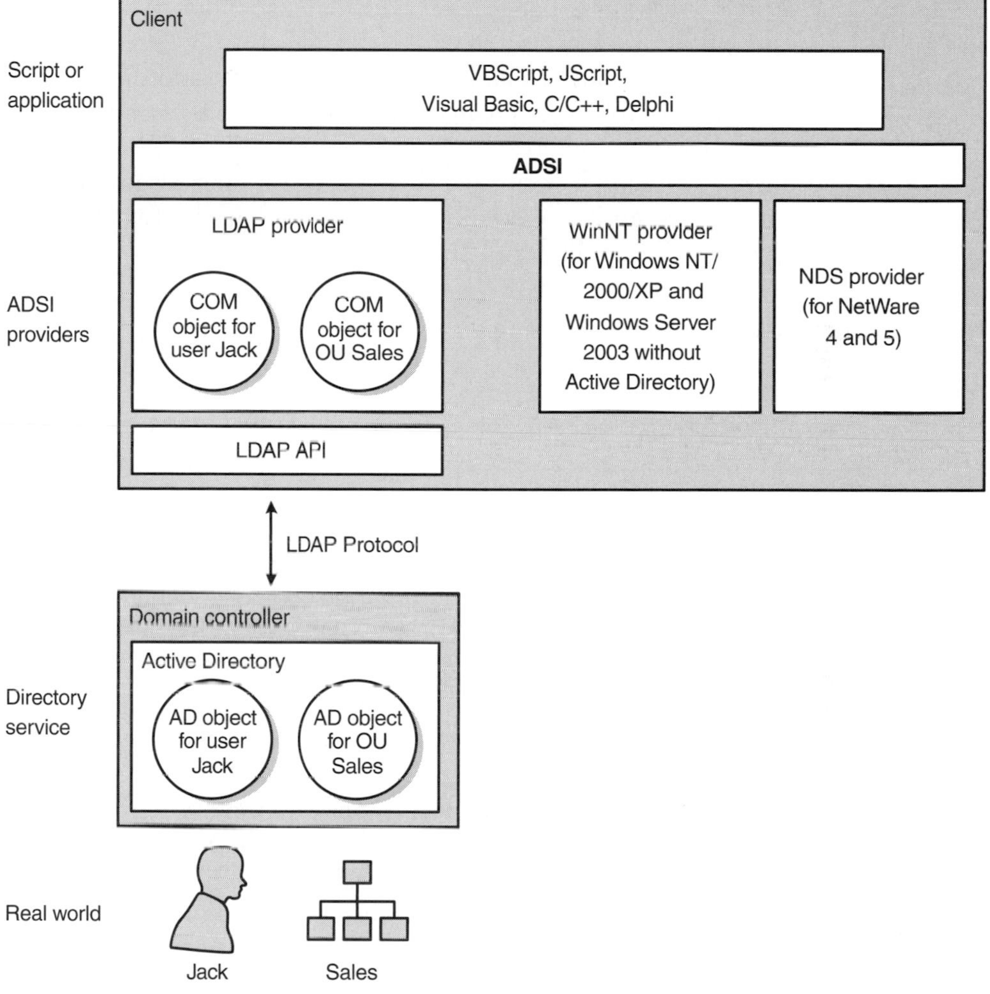

Figure 10.13 Active Directory objects abstract real-world users and resources. ADSI COM objects in turn abstract Active Directory objects. When your script manipulates the COM objects, it eventually affects the corresponding Active Directory objects.

In addition to early-binding fashion, you can use Visual Basic and VBA also in late-binding fashion. Consequently, the information and sample scripts of this chapter and the next chapter apply also to these two environments. Because of language differences, however, you must modify any sample script in the following ways to make it work in Visual Basic.

- Change any `WScript.Echo` output method to `Debug.Print` (or, if you want to compile an EXE file, use other suitable means for output, such as `MsgBox`).
- When you declare variables in `Dim` statements, add the data type of each variable (e.g., change `Dim i` to `Dim i As Integer`).

To make the sample scripts work in VBA, you must also replace the `WScript.Echo` output method. If you're working in Excel, for example, you can dump the script output into Excel spreadsheet cells.

TIP If you like VBA's integrated development environment, you can use it instead of WSH for your administrative script. The best platform application in this case is probably Excel.

NOTE The term "automation" comes from "OLE automation." OLE stands for "Object Linking and Embedding" and it is a Microsoft technology that facilitates cooperation among applications. An automation client can also be called an "OLE automation controller" and ADSI (or any other COM component) would be an "OLE automation server."

Even though ADSI stands for "Active Directory Service Interfaces," it supports different directory services by using the following providers:

- *LDAP.* This provider supports Active Directory and any other LDAP directory service from vendors such as Netscape and Novell. You can access also Exchange 5.5 with the LDAP provider.
- *WinNT.* This provider supports not only Windows NT, but also Windows 2000 and Windows XP workstations and standalone/member servers that don't contain Active Directory. In addition, you can manage on Windows 2000 and later domain controllers some server services, such as file shares and print queues, using the WinNT provider.

- *NDS*. This provider supports Novell NDS, which is included in NetWare 4, 5, and beyond.
- *NWCOMPAT*. This provider supports NetWare 3, which stores users and groups in a place called "the Bindery."

The four providers match four identically named namespaces. Even though ADSI is an interface common to all of them, the features (which object types are supported and in which way) are somewhat different in each namespace. Also, the naming conventions to address an object, such as a certain user account, are somewhat different in different namespaces.

NOTE Some of the ADSI features support only NDS, and because this book is about Active Directory, we don't discuss those features.

In addition to the four system providers on the list, any vendor can write a provider for its directory service. Microsoft has written a provider for IIS and Novell has written a provider for NDS to replace the one that Microsoft is shipping with ADSI.

NOTE The term *directory service* is used quite loosely with ADSI. To be exact, Windows NT, NetWare 3, and IIS don't include a true directory service.

Basic ADSI

This section lists some typical operations that you would do with ADSI and shows some fragments of scripts to demonstrate some of these operations.

ADSI Operations

A typical flow of events consists of the following steps:

1. Bind to an Active Directory container object or directly to some target object.
2. If bound to a container, list all or certain child objects in that container.
3. Read or write properties of the target object or listed child objects.

Some other ADSI operations that you can perform on Active Directory objects include the following:

- Create, delete, move, and rename objects.
- Manage the schema.
- List and manage permissions (ACLs) for Active Directory objects.

The sample script in the next section demonstrates the first three operations (bind, list, and read).

A Sample ADSI Script

The script in Figure 10.14 demonstrates the basic operation of ADSI. It lists all the user objects in the `CN=Users` container along with the descriptions of the users. If you run the script, you will see the output shown in Figure 10.15. As you see, our test forest `sanao.com` has only the predefined users in `CN=Users`.

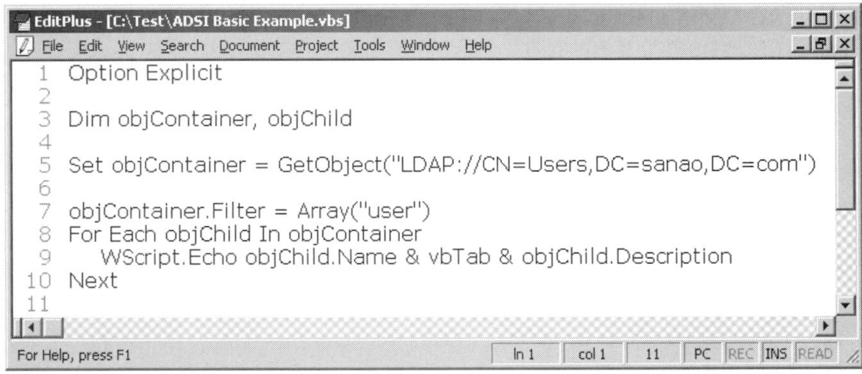

Figure 10.14 A basic example of ADSI

```
Command Prompt
C:\Test>"ADSI Basic Example.vbs"
CN=Administrator        Built-in account for administering the computer/domain
CN=Guest        Built-in account for guest access to the computer/domain
CN=krbtgt       Key Distribution Center Service Account

C:\Test>_
```

Figure 10.15 The output of the example of ADSI in Figure 10.14

On line 3 of Figure 10.14 we declare two object variables. Later in the script we will need one for the target container and another for the child objects. On line 5 we bind to a certain object in Active Directory. As a result, we get an instance of an object variable (`objContainer`) in our script that we can use from that point on. The *binding string* in quotation marks specifies the provider/namespace (`LDAP:`), two slashes, and the distinguished name of an object. Because we bound to a container object, we can list its child objects. On line 7 we define a filter for the container that includes only those children whose LDAP class name is `user`.

Now we are ready to list the names and descriptions of all child objects. We use a `For Each . . . Next` loop that browses through the contents. Within each cycle, we print out one username along with the user's description.

NOTE This note may sound a little confusing, but if you apply the sample script shown in Figure 10.14 to some container that contains computer objects, those objects are listed as well. The reason is that in the schema the `computer` class is a subclass of the `user` class and the filter will also include all subclasses.

LDAP Binding Strings

When you bind to a container or some other object, you need to specify the target with a *binding string*, which is synonymous with *ADSI path* or `ADsPath`.

As mentioned previously, a binding string is (normally) the text `LDAP://` concatenated with the distinguished name of the target object. An example of this is as follows:

```
LDAP://CN=Guest,CN=Users,DC=sanao,DC=com
```

NOTE The binding strings for namespaces other than LDAP, such as WinNT, are somewhat different. We discuss here only the LDAP version. In the next chapter we present examples of WinNT binding strings.

You could also include the target server name and, if needed, a TCP/IP *port number*. An example of this longer path is as follows:

```
LDAP://dc1.sanao.com:389/CN=Guest,CN=Users,DC=sanao,DC=com
```

In the binding string, "389" is the standard LDAP port number. You don't usually need to include it. If you omit the port number, the default "389" is used.

In most of the examples in this chapter and the next chapter, we don't specify the server name either. We just let ADSI pick a domain controller for us. When using this *serverless binding,* ADSI selects a domain controller of the default domain, which is the domain of the user whose credentials are being used (normally the logged-on user). A hard-coded server name might point to a domain controller that is on another site for some user running the script, or a domain controller that is not on when some user is running the script. Therefore, it is better to use serverless binding.

Instead of 389, we could sometimes use the port 3268, which is the default port for the global catalog. However, instead of changing the port, we can change the first letters to "GC"; that is, we use the following binding string:

```
GC://CN=Guest,CN=Users,DC=sanao,DC=com
```

All the binding examples you have seen use the credentials of the logged-on user. In the next chapter we show how you can bind with some alternative credentials. However, binding with credentials is not usually necessary.

The distinguished name can be replaced with some other provider-specific path. An example of this is to bind using the `objectGUID` attribute of an object. The path would look like the following:

```
LDAP://<GUID=a434e4ee3da56b4a81a282fcb79e1748>
```

When you use `objectGUID` attributes instead of distinguished names, your script will still work even if the object name is changed. However, you'll lose the descriptiveness of the names.

Using rootDSE

The examples you have seen so far include a domain name in the binding string. In other words, the domain name is hard-coded in the script. This presents a slight disadvantage, because if you want to execute the scripts in another domain, you need to change all the domain names. By adding one line to each script, you can remove the hard-coded domain name and use `rootDSE` instead.

The root of the directory information tree in every LDAPv3 directory server (i.e., domain controller in Active Directory) is called `rootDSE`. It is a virtual object that is not part of any partition (i.e., naming context) and it includes 22 attributes (or 19 if the server is running Windows 2000) that provide information about the directory server and directory. DSE stands for "DSA-Specific Entry." DSA, in turn, stands for "Directory System Agent." DSA is an X.500 term for a directory server, which in Active Directory is the same as a domain controller.

The attributes that are most interesting for our scripts are the distinguished names for the default domain, the root domain, the Schema container, and the Configuration container. The corresponding attribute names are as follows:

- `defaultNamingContext`
- `rootDomainNamingContext`
- `schemaNamingContext`
- `configurationNamingContext`

With these four attributes, you can access every object in Active Directory without knowing the domain or forest name at the time you write the script. The following lines show how to bind to the user Guest in the default domain:

```
Set objDSE = GetObject("LDAP://rootDSE")
Set objUser = GetObject("LDAP://CN=Guest,CN=Users," & _
    objDSE.Get("defaultNamingContext"))
```

NOTE To be exact, the "default domain" means the domain that the domain controller belongs to. However, because you don't specify a domain controller, ADSI will find a domain controller from the domain of the user whose credentials are being used (normally the logged-on user). In other words, `defaultNamingContext` refers to the user's domain.

The other 18 attributes of `rootDSE` are as follows:

- `currentTime`
- `subschemaSubentry`
- `dsServiceName`
- `namingContexts`
- `supportedControl`
- `supportedLDAPVersion`

- `supportedLDAPPolicies`
- `highestCommittedUSN`
- `supportedSASLMechanisms`
- `dnsHostName`
- `ldapServiceName`
- `serverName`
- `supportedCapabilities`
- `isSynchronized`
- `isGlobalCatalogReady`
- `domainFunctionality`
- `forestFunctionality`
- `domainControllerFunctionality`

We do not discuss these attributes here, but we provide the names in case you encounter them or find a use for them. Most of the attributes are described in the ADSI documentation.

Basic COM

COM is a standard mechanism that, among other things, enables you to control binary components from text-based scripts. These components are called *COM objects,* and using them gives your scripts tremendous power to do a variety of things.

As you know, you can enhance your batch files by calling appropriate EXE files. They enable you to do tasks that a basic batch file couldn't accomplish. This same principle applies to scripts and binary COM objects—in this case, however, the ways in which a text file can interact with the binary component are more versatile than with the batch files.

A COM object is an entity that often represents something concrete. In the case of ADSI, COM objects mostly represent Active Directory objects, as you saw in Figure 10.13 about ADSI.

A COM object has one or more *interfaces* that enable you to interact with the object. An interface is likely to have *methods;* each time you call a method, it invokes an operation for the interface to perform. An interface also has *properties,* which store some values about the COM object just as Active Directory attributes store values about an Active Directory object. You read and write COM property values using *property methods.* In addition, the normal methods may return values.

Figure 10.13 shows the ADSI COM object for OU Sales. That object could have (or one of its interfaces could have, to be exact) a property `FaxNumber`, a property method `FaxNumber`, and a method `Delete`. If the name of the COM object in a script were `objOU`, you could read and display the `FaxNumber` property using the `FaxNumber` property method with the following script line:

```
WScript.Echo objOU.FaxNumber
```

As you can see, in VBScript you refer to a property method or method with the following syntax:

```
object_name.property_method_or_method_name
```

NOTE The property names and property method names are the same in VBScript, which usually makes things quite easy. If you used the C language, you would need to read the `FaxNumber` property with the `get_FaxNumber` property method.

NOTE `Echo` is a method of the `WScript` COM object.

You write to a property with a command such as the following:

```
objOU.FaxNumber = "555-3159"
```

Finally, you call the `Delete` method with one of the following commands:

```
Call objOU.Delete("user", "CN=Jack")
objOU.Delete "user", "CN=Jack"
```

NOTE From here on we use mostly the first version of the two commands (the one with `Call` and parentheses), because it is more in line with the next command, where a method returns a value. We like to have parentheses around the arguments in both commands. However, when you read the ADSI documentation and some other sources, you often see the latter version (without `Call` or parentheses). We may also use the latter version when there are no arguments for the method.

If the same method returns a value, you use a command like the following:

```
ret = objOU.Delete("user", "CN=Jack")
```

Because ADSI uses COM technology, it has objects and properties, and as you already know, Active Directory is full of objects and properties. In the next section we examine the relationship between the two.

The Property Cache

The ADSI documentation talks about an attribute when it means a phone number in Active Directory and about a property when it means the same phone number in ADSI. We follow the same convention in this chapter (and the next), even though we may have used the two terms interchangeably in other chapters.

A script does not read and write attributes of Active Directory objects directly, but it goes through the *property cache.* The benefit of the property cache is that if you read five attributes, this doesn't generate five small separate network requests and replies; instead, it generates one larger request. The latter choice is more efficient in terms of speed and network utilization.

There are ADSI methods that you use to read and write attributes between Active Directory and the property cache, as well as methods you use between the property cache and the script variables. Figure 10.16 shows the principle of the property cache along with the ADSI method names.

NOTE You might wonder why if there are `Get` and `GetInfo`, there aren't also `Put` and `PutInfo`, instead of the current `Put` and `SetInfo`. One answer could be the following: `Get` and `Put` are traditional statements for I/O in the Microsoft Basic language (and others) and they existed back in the 1970s. `GetInfo` and `SetInfo` are traditional function names that appeared in 1988 to enable programmers to read and write user and group properties in OS/2 LAN Manager, which is the ancestor of Windows NT.

Technically, the property cache is common to all objects, but you can think of it as a per-object instance.

As you can see in Figure 10.16, there are reads and writes

- Between the property cache and Active Directory
- Between your script and the property cache

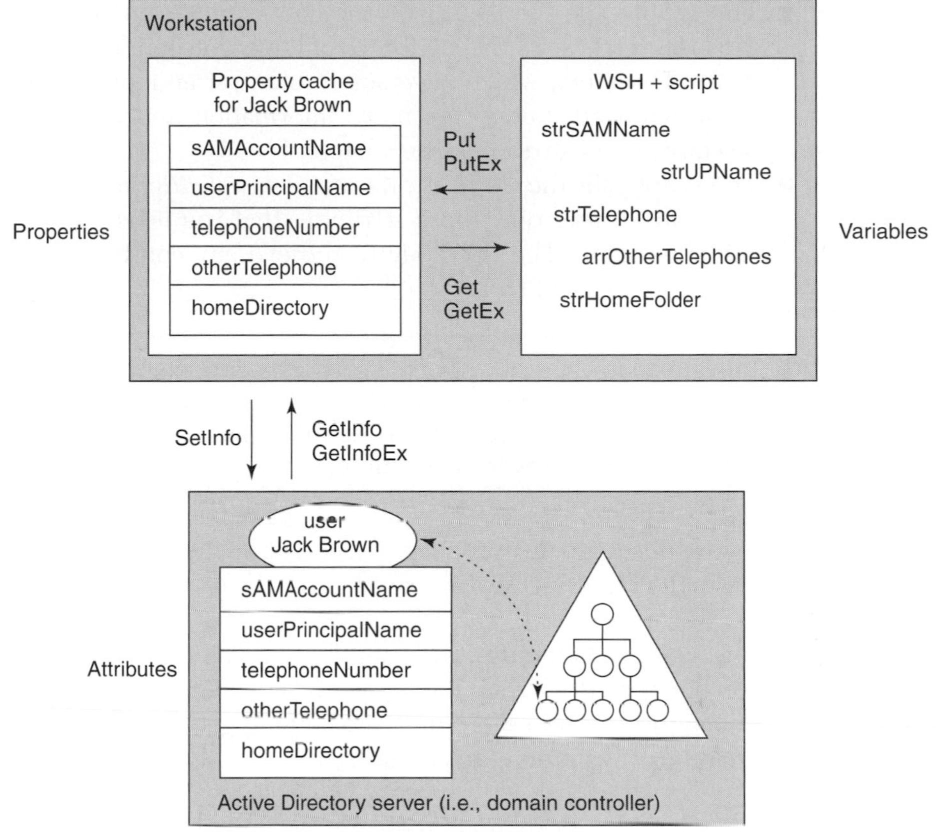

Figure 10.16 When your script reads attributes of an object in Active Directory, those attributes first go to the property cache in your workstation. After that they can be stored in the variables of the script.

Between the Property Cache and Active Directory

The property cache for a certain object gets attributes from Active Directory in one of the following three ways.

- The script calls the `Get` or `GetEx` methods, and the property cache for that object is empty. This will invoke an *implicit* `GetInfo` method. Therefore, you don't normally need to use `GetInfo` explicitly in your scripts. However, if you want to *refresh* the non-empty property cache (i.e., retrieve the new and changed attributes from Active Directory), you must call `GetInfo` explicitly.

- The script calls the `GetInfo` method *explicitly* in your script. This will retrieve all the attributes of the corresponding object in Active Directory, which have some value set and which are not constructed attributes (for more information and a list of the 36 constructed attributes, see Chapter 8).
- The script calls the `GetInfoEx` method *explicitly* in your script. This will retrieve only those attributes that you listed as method call arguments. The only way to retrieve any constructed attributes is to use `GetInfoEx`.

NOTE Performance is usually not an issue with scripting, but if you are concerned about it, you could retrieve with `GetInfoEx` only those attributes that you need instead of letting the implicit `GetInfo` retrieve all 30 attributes (or whatever the count is).

The properties in the property cache get written back to Active Directory in the following way.

- The script calls the `SetInfo` method *explicitly* in your script. If you don't call `SetInfo`, it is like writing text into Notepad but not saving the text to a file. Similarly, nothing gets written to Active Directory if you forget to call `SetInfo`.

NOTE Methods (except property methods) bypass the property cache. If you delete an object in an OU with `objOU.Delete` or set a user's password with `objUser.SetPassword`, you don't need to use `SetInfo` after those methods.

Between Your Script and the Property Cache

This part is a little tricky because there are several ways to read and write properties and because there are special considerations associated with some attributes.

Figure 10.16 shows that you read properties from the property cache with the `Get` and `GetEx` methods and write them with the `Put` and `PutEx` methods. This is actually a simplification. Table 10.4 offers a fuller picture (we don't cover `GetEx` and `PutEx` yet).

Table 10.4 Ways to Read and Write the Property Cache

Way	Read and Write Code Examples	Description

A. Explicit `Get/Put` methods with attribute LDAP names	`strLastName = objUser.Get("sn")`
	
	`Call objUser.Put("sn", strLastName)`
		This choice enables you to read and write "any" property of any object using the LDAP name of the corresponding attribute as an argument. We put "any" in quotation marks because there are some exceptions and special considerations with some attributes (explained in the text).

B. Dynamic property methods (i.e., attribute LDAP names without `Get/Put`)	`strLastName = objUser.sn`
	
	`objUser.sn = strLastName`
		When a new object is fetched in the property cache, ADSI lists all attributes of the corresponding class and dynamically creates a new property method for each of them. Choice B uses attribute LDAP names, as does choice A, but this time you don't see any `Get` or `Put`. (The differences between choices A and B are explained in the text.)

C. Static property methods	`strLastName = objUser.LastName`
	
	`objUser.LastName = strLastName`
		You can access some properties of some classes with static property methods. For example, with the `user` class, you can access 36 out of 257 properties this way. (See the section "The IADsUser Interface" later in this chapter.)

D. Property cache interfaces	`Set objPropEntry = objUser.Item("sn")`, and so on	ADSI includes *property cache interfaces,* which help in listing, reading, and writing the properties in the property cache. Just as with `Get/Put`, you can use these interfaces to any Active Directory object class. (See Chapter 11 for more information and examples.)

NOTE A static property method sometimes modifies the value to a different format before returning it, instead of returning the raw value. For example, many dates are expressed as `large integers` in Active Directory. If you retrieve the property with `Get`, you will get that `large integer` value, but if you retrieve the value with a static property method, it will be converted to a date string.

Choices A and B in Table 10.4 are fairly equivalent, but there are two differences.

- When a value is not in the property cache, choice A will return an error ("property not found"), whereas choice B will return a `vbEmpty` "value." Consequently, choice B is easier to use because it avoids the extra hassle of error checking.
- Because the attribute names are not arguments in choice B, you cannot use string variables for them. When we show examples of displaying user properties in the next chapter, you will see how handy it is to use string variables with choice A.

When we later read and write properties, we use mostly choice A. We like to see (and also show you) the explicit `Get/Put` methods along with the attribute LDAP names. This way you will know each time that we are referring to a certain LDAP name and not just some new mysterious ADSI method name. At the same time, we admit that the script lines using choice B would look a little easier.

However, we use choice B when we specifically want to avoid getting those "property not found" errors.

In the next chapter, we show how to apply choices A, C, and D to list all properties of the user Guest.

- The property cache interfaces example (choice D) finds about 30 properties in the cache and lists those property names along with their values.
- The `Get/Put` example (choice A) lists all 257 property names of the `user` class and values for those that Guest has a value for.
- The static property method example (choice C) lists those of the 36 properties that have a value, which results in a list of about 20 properties.

Table 10.4 mentions that there are exceptions and special considerations with some attributes.

- You are naturally subject to normal Active Directory access control when you try to read or write any property value. Normally your scripts run with the privileges of your logged-on user account.
- As noted earlier, constructed attributes will be missing from the property cache unless you specifically retrieve them using the `GetInfoEx` method. And if they are missing from the property cache, you will get a "property not found" error when you try to read them with the `Get` method or some static property method.
- Multivalued properties require special handling, as explained in the next section.
- Properties that use normal data types (integer, string, date, or Boolean) are easy to read and handle in VBScript. `DN with binary`, `DN with Unicode string`, `NT security descriptor`, and `large integer`, as well as binary data types, are more difficult and require special handling.

Handling Special Data Types

VBScript is not well suited for some special data types. The following list briefly describes how to handle these special data types.

- `DN with binary` and `DN with Unicode` string both consist of two components, as explained in Chapter 8. ADSI has two special interfaces, `IADsDNWithBinary` and `IADsDNWithString`, that help to get access to the DN component and the binary or string component of the property. Both data types are extremely rare—refer to the ADSI documentation for more information if you need either data type.
- There is an interface called `IADsSecurityDescriptor` for accessing NT security descriptor properties (which contain the access permissions for Active Directory objects). We explain how to use it in the next chapter.
- Because VBScript doesn't understand 64-bit `large integers`, you can access the high and low 32 bits of any `large integer` single-valued property using the `IADsLargeInteger` interface. You could use the parts separately and try to figure out what they mean, or you could count the total value with the formula `HighPart * 2^32 + LowPart`. However, if the resulting number were too large for VBScript's 32-bit integers, it would be converted to a floating-point number. The result could be

"3.26074403172981E+17," where "E+17" would mean that you should move the decimal point 17 spaces to the right. Because there are "only" 14 decimals in the number, you would need to add three zeros—the resulting number could be wrong by several hundreds. With some extra work you can handle `large integer` properties, perhaps losing some accuracy. (Chapter 11 has examples of handling `large integers` when listing user properties.)

- Properties with binary values will give you some headaches. ADSI returns their values as arrays of bytes, but VBScript is not very good at handling them. We show one tricky but effective way in the next chapter.

NOTE The previous list mentions that you can access single-valued `large integer` properties. The `IADsLargeInteger` interface seems not to work with multivalued properties, but fortunately there is only one such attribute in the base schema.

Single-Valued and Multivalued Properties

The `Get` method is meant for single-valued properties and `GetEx` is meant for multivalued properties. However, you can use either method for either type of property, as Table 10.5 describes.

Table 10.5 `Get` versus `GetEx`

	Single-Valued	Multivalued*
`Get`	Returns a normal data type value (e.g., string).	If there is only one value, returns a normal data type value (e.g., string); if there are multiple values, returns an array of normal data type values (e.g., strings).
`GetEx`	Returns an array of normal data type values (e.g., strings); however, there is only one element in the array.	Returns an array of normal data type values (e.g., strings).

* When you retrieve the values of a multivalued property, they are not in any particular order in the array. You cannot rely on them to be in the same order as you stored them. This is a feature of Active Directory and not ADSI.

Given this flexibility, you can use one of three "strategies" with `Get` and `GetEx`:

- *Always use* `Get`. This choice is possible, but more difficult, because for multivalued attributes you would need to examine each time whether you received an array or not.
- *Use* `Get` *with single-valued and* `GetEx` *with multivalued.* This choice is normally the best. It is easy to handle the normal data types for single-valued properties, and arrays for multivalued.
- *Always use* `GetEx`. For example, if you list all 257 user attributes, it is probably easier to always use `GetEx` than to figure out when to use `Get` and when to use `GetEx`. We show an example of this when we list user properties in the next chapter.

When your script is writing properties, `Put` is meant for single-valued, and `PutEx` for multivalued properties. Again, you could use either method for either type of property.

Before we compare `Put` and `PutEx`, Table 10.6 describes the four modes of the `PutEx` method. The method includes an additional argument that enables you to specify the mode. Consequently, `PutEx` takes three arguments:

- The mode as a value between 1 and 4
- The attribute LDAP name
- An array of values to be added or removed

For example, to delete two home phone numbers, you would use a line like the following (divided into two lines):

```
Call objUser.PutEx(ADS_PROPERTY_DELETE, "otherHomePhone", _
    Array("111-1111","444-4444"))
```

In Table 10.7, we describe how `Put` and `PutEx` work with single-valued and multivalued properties. The result of the table is that you only need to use `PutEx` if you need one of the `append`, `delete`, or `clear` modes.

Table 10.6 The Four Modes of `PutEx`

Mode	Value	Description
`ADS_PROPERTY_UPDATE`	2	The values you specify are stored in the property and they replace any previous values. If you had a list of five phone numbers and updated them with a list of two, only those two would remain.
`ADS_PROPERTY_APPEND`	3	The values you specify are stored in the property with the existing values. You could append two phone numbers to a list of five, resulting in a total of seven numbers.
`ADS_PROPERTY_DELETE`	4	The values you specify are removed from the property. You could delete two of five phone numbers, resulting in three numbers.
`ADS_PROPERTY_CLEAR`	1	All the values are cleared from the property. If you later tried to read the property with `Get`, you would get the "property not found" error. You can include any array of values as an argument, or rather, use the `vbEmpty` constant.

Table 10.7 `Put` versus `PutEx`

	Single-Valued	Multivalued
`Put`	Writes a normal data type value (e.g., string).	Works almost like `PutEx` in `update` mode. If there is only one value, you can use either a normal data type or an array. If there are multiple values, you must use an array.
`PutEx`	Works like `Put`, but you must use the `update` mode and store the value to be written in a one-element array.*	Allows you to use any of the four modes (`update`, `append`, `delete`, and `clear`). You must always use an array, even if there is only one value.

* You can use `PutEx` for a single-valued property also in the `clear` mode to put it in a "not set" state.

ADSI Interfaces

As with COM in general, ADSI interfaces enable you to interact with ADSI objects, because each interface has properties and/or methods to use. An ADSI provider, such as the LDAP provider, is responsible for implementing most of the ADSI objects and interfaces. Some of them are implemented also by the *router* component, which corresponds to the file activeds.dll.

The ADSI documentation lists 65 interfaces. Almost all of their names start with "IADs" and each is meant to give access to something. For example, `IADsLargeInteger` gives access to the high part and low part of a 64-bit number, `IADsUser` gives access to user objects, and so forth.

Some interfaces are meant to give access to only one object class—for example, `IADsUser` is meant just for user objects. Some other interfaces are meant to give access to any object class, such as `IADs` and `IADsPropertyList`.

All access capabilities that ADSI offers are implemented as various interfaces. Many of the interfaces give access to Active Directory, but some of them give access to other services, such as file shares and print queues.

Even though there is the class `user` in Active Directory and the corresponding interface `IADsUser` in ADSI, it doesn't follow that there is an interface for each Active Directory class. Fewer than ten ADSI interfaces correspond to Active Directory classes.

One interface, called merely `IADs`, contains the familiar methods `Get`, `GetEx`, `Put`, `PutEx`, `GetInfo`, `GetInfoEx`, and `SetInfo`. You can use this generic interface with any Active Directory objects, so it doesn't matter that only some classes have their own interfaces dedicated. Even when you are managing user objects, you will use `IADs` instead of `IADsUser` when you use any of the methods just listed.

This raises the following question: What do we need `IADsUser` for if `IADs` alone would be enough? The answer is twofold.

- A dedicated interface may add some useful methods, such as `SetPassword` to set a user's password in a secure manner.
- A dedicated interface may add some static property methods, such as those 36 for `IADsUser`. Static property methods exist mainly for the `user` class, so we get back to the topic in the section "The IADsUser Interface."

In Visual Basic you would define two object variables as follows:

```
Dim objUser As IADsUser
Dim objGroup As IADsGroup
```

Even when specifying that `objUser` is using the `IADsUser` interface, you can use in addition the properties and methods of the `IADs` interface. The reason is that `IADsUser` and the other per-class interfaces inherit the features of `IADs`.

Interestingly, in VBScript you don't need to (and cannot) specify which interfaces you will use. You can just use them. A VBScript equivalent for the previous lines is as follows:

```
Dim objUser
Dim objGroup
```

This is easier, but it doesn't mean that you can forget the existence of interfaces. When you read the ADSI documentation, you still need to locate either the `IADsUser` or `IADsGroup` part to see what methods and properties there are.

NOTE One consequence of not specifying the interface is that you can use `IADsUser` properties and methods also for classes other than `user`. However, if `IADsUser` contains the `Lastname` static property method, there is not much point in trying to read the last name of an OU.

NOTE The official convention of expressing a certain method of a certain interface is to use two colons between them. An example is `IADsUser::SetPassword`. We don't use this convention in this book, because with VBScript it is not important in which interface each method is implemented.

The List of ADSI Interfaces

Of the 65 interfaces, almost all are *dual interfaces,* which means that they can be used from both automation clients (e.g., VBScript) and nonautomation clients (e.g., C/C++).

When you read the documentation for the dual interfaces, you will see references to `IUnknown` methods and `IDispatch` methods. You cannot call these methods from VBScript scripts. However, `IDispatch` methods are made for automation clients, but they are called automatically behind the scenes.

A couple of interfaces can be used only from nonautomation clients. Some interfaces are obsolete or meant to be used only with Novell NDS. Therefore, we are left with 45 interfaces, which we list in Table 10.8 (divided into categories).

Table 10.8 Relevant ADSI Interfaces

Category	`IADs` Interfaces*	Description
Core	`IADs`, `Container`, `Namespaces`, `OpenDSObject`	These interfaces provide the common features to manage any Active Directory object, such as the familiar `GetInfo` and `SetInfo` methods.
Persistent object**	`Collection`, `Computer`, `Domain`, `FileService`, `FileShare`, `Group`, `Locality`, `Members`, `O`, `OU`, `PrintJob`, `PrintQueue`, `Service`, `User`	These interfaces enable you to browse and modify Active Directory objects and some server services, such as file shares and print queues.
Dynamic object	`ComputerOperations`, `FileServiceOperations`, `PrintJobOperations`, `PrintQueueOperations`, `Resource`, `ServiceOperations`, `Session`	These interfaces enable you to browse and manage current user sessions to a server, current open files, and other dynamic server services.
Schema**	`Class`, `Property`, `Syntax`	These interfaces enable you to browse and modify the classes and attributes of your Active Directory and browse the syntaxes.
Property cache**	`PropertyEntry`, `PropertyList`, `PropertyValue`, `PropertyValue2`	These interfaces enable you to browse and modify properties in the property cache.

(continued)

* We left "IADs" out of every name to save space. An exception is the first interface, because its name is just `IADs`.

** We present examples of many of the interfaces in the next chapter. Specifically, we cover the following interface categories: persistent objects, schema, property cache, and security.

Table 10.8 Relevant ADSI Interfaces *(cont.)*

Category	`IADs` Interfaces*	Description
Data type	`DNWithBinary`, `DNWithString`, `LargeInteger`	These interfaces enable you to access some special data types.
Security**	`AccessControlEntry`, `AccessControlList`, `SecurityDescriptor`	These interfaces enable you to browse and modify the ACLs of Active Directory objects.
Extension	`Extension`	This interface enables organizations (e.g., independent software vendors [ISVs]) to add new properties and methods to existing ADSI interfaces.
Utility	`ADSystemInfo`, `DeleteOps`, `NameTranslate`, `ObjectOptions`, `PathName`, `WinNTSystemInfo`	These interfaces provide additional helper functions.

In the following four sections we describe these four interfaces:

- `IADs`
- `IADsContainer`
- `IADsUser`
- `IADsGroup`

The discussions of these interfaces, which are relatively brief, give you an idea of what you can do with them. Because they are the most basic interfaces, they appear frequently in the examples of the next chapter.

The IADs Interface

As mentioned previously, you can use the methods and properties of `IADs` to manage any Active Directory object, and those features are also inherited to the class-specific interfaces, such as `IADsUser` and `IADsGroup`.

The `IADs` interface has the following methods: `Get`, `GetEx`, `Put`, `PutEx`, `GetInfo`, `GetInfoEx`, and `SetInfo`. (The section of this chapter titled "The Property Cache" provides descriptions of these methods.)

Table 10.9 Properties of the `IADs` Interface

Property	Description
`ADsPath`	This property contains the `ADsPath`, which is the binding string to the target object. With the LDAP provider, this is normally in the form `LDAP://distinguished name`.
`Class`	This property contains the LDAP name of the schema class of the target object.
`GUID`	This property contains the `objectGUID` of the target object. Of the two GUID formats, this property uses the format without curly braces or dashes.
`Name`	This property contains the RDN (i.e., naming attribute) of the target object.
`Parent`	This property contains the `ADsPath` to the parent container of the target object. Note that even though it would seem that you could build up an `ADsPath` to an object from its `Parent` and `Name` properties, you shouldn't do this, because it is not guaranteed to work always.
`Schema`	This property contains the `ADsPath` to the schema class object of the target object.

The `IADs` interface has six properties, which are listed in Table 10.9. Their contents vary slightly depending on the namespace, so we explain them from the LDAP namespace's point of view. All six properties are read-only and return a string.

The script in Figure 10.17 displays the values of all six properties for the user Guest. When you execute the script, you will see the output shown in Figure 10.18.

The IADsContainer Interface

The `IADsContainer` interface contains properties and methods that are meaningful with container objects, such as browsing, creating, and deleting child objects. Table 10.10 lists three properties and Table 10.11 lists five methods for the interface.

The following lines demonstrate the use of `GetObject` (on the second line), which is described in Table 10.11:

```
Set objContainer = _
    GetObject("LDAP://CN=Users,DC=sanao,DC=com")
Set objUser = objContainer.GetObject("user", "CN=Guest")
WScript.Echo objUser.Name & vbTab & objUser.Description
```

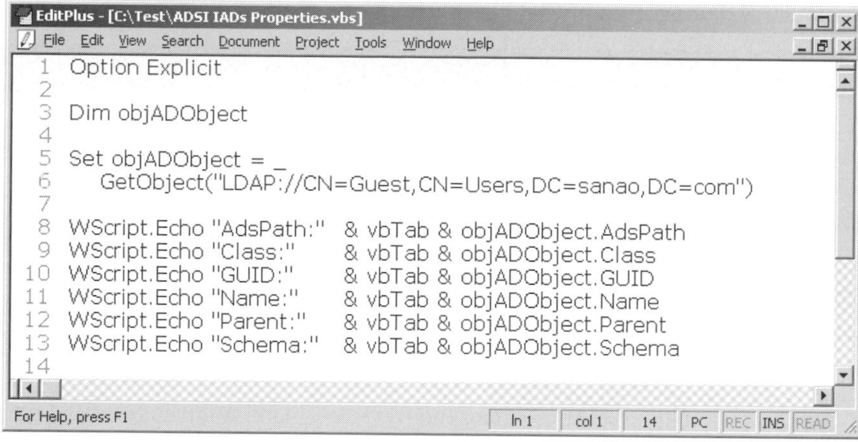

Figure 10.17 The properties of the IADs interface enable you to display six basic values for any Active Directory object.

Normally you would combine the first two lines and use the traditional `GetObject` to create the `objUser` variable. However, this longer form can be handy if, for example, you need to access several objects in one container.

If you want to move Jack from Sales to Users, use the `MoveHere` method as follows:

```
Set objContainer = _
    GetObject("LDAP://CN=Users,DC=sanao,DC=com")
Set objUser = _
    objContainer.MoveHere( _
    "LDAP://CN=Jack,OU=Sales,DC=sanao,DC=com", "CN=Jack")
```

If you would also like to rename Jack, change the last argument (`"CN=Jack"`) to the new name—for example, `"CN=Jill"`. If the

```
Command Prompt
C:\Test>"ADSI IADs Properties.vbs"
AdsPath:        LDAP://CN=Guest,CN=Users,DC=sanao,DC=com
Class:  user
GUID:   b424e3ef3ca56b4a80a272fcb79e1748
Name:   CN=Guest
Parent: LDAP://CN=Users,DC=sanao,DC=com
Schema: LDAP://schema/user

C:\Test>_
```

Figure 10.18 Output from the script in Figure 10.17

Table 10.10 Properties of the `IADsContainer` Interface

Property	Description
`Count`	This read-only property is not implemented in Microsoft's LDAP provider (for performance reasons). Otherwise, it would give the number (perhaps filtered) of child objects in the container.
`Filter`	This property is an array, where each element is an LDAP class name. When you list the contents of the target container, only the objects that match the filter (including any subclasses) are returned. (For an example of the `Filter` property, see the basic ADSI example in Figure 10.14.)
`Hints`	This property is an array, where each element is an LDAP attribute name. When you list the contents of the target container, only the specified attributes for each object are retrieved to the property cache, possibly optimizing the network traffic and speed. The `Hints` property wasn't supported in the Windows 2000 version of the ADSI LDAP provider. The current documentation suggests that it is now supported. However, it seems not to work.

Table 10.11 Methods of the `IADsContainer` Interface

Method	Description
`GetObject`	This method creates a new object variable for the specified object in the target container. After that, you can access the child object directly.
`Create*`	This method creates the specified object in the target container.
`Delete*`	This method deletes the specified object from the target container.
`CopyHere`	This method copies the specified object to the target container. You cannot use this method with Active Directory.
`MoveHere`	This method moves the specified object to the target container. You can also use this method to rename an object without moving it.

* Examples of these methods appear in Chapter 11.

source and target containers are the same, the object is just renamed, not moved.

If you don't need an object variable for the moved object, you can ignore the returned value and put a `Call` instead. The replaced second line (divided into lines 2, 3, and 4) would be the following:

```
Call objContainer.MoveHere( _
    "LDAP://CN=Jack,OU=Sales,DC=sanao,DC=com", "CN=Jack")
```

The IADsUser Interface

The `IADsUser` interface offers three methods and a number of static property methods to help you manage user objects.

In the discussion of reading and writing the property cache (earlier in this chapter), we listed the following syntax choices to read the last name of a user:

```
A: strLastName = objUser.Get("sn")
B: strLastName = objUser.sn
C: strLastName = objUser.LastName
D: Set objPropEntry = objUser.Item("sn"), etc.
```

Choices A (explicit `Get/Put`) and B (dynamic property methods) are about equivalent and they both use the attribute LDAP name to retrieve the value. Choice C (static property method) uses something other than an LDAP name. Choice D uses the property cache interfaces, which we explain in Chapter 11.

Now it's time to compare choice A/B to choice C. We use the `user` class as an example because of the following reason: Choice C requires a per-class ADSI interface. `IADsUser` is the most common per-class interface to use, and that interface is the most comprehensive in the number of static property methods.

Table 10.12 lists the 36 `IADsUser` static property methods that correspond to attributes in Active Directory (excluding the ones that apply only to NetWare). Note that these 36 property methods are not the same as the most common attributes. You see only 22 of them in the Users and Computers snap-in.

Table 10.12 Static Property Methods of the `IADsUser` Interface

Property Method	Attribute LDAP Name	Syntax	Visible in Users and Computers Snap-In
`Account-Expiration-Date`	`accountExpires`	Large integer	Yes
`BadLoginCount`	`badPwdCount`	Integer	No
`Department`	`department`	Unicode string	Yes
`Description`	`description`	Unicode string	Yes
`Division`	`division`	Unicode string	No
`EmailAddress`	`mail`	Unicode string	Yes
`EmployeeID`	`employeeID`	Unicode string	No
`FaxNumber`	`facsimile-TelephoneNumber`	Unicode string	Yes
`FirstName`	`givenName`	Unicode string	Yes
`FullName`	`displayName`	Unicode string	Yes
`HomeDirectory`	`homeDirectory`	Unicode string	Yes
`HomePage`	`wWWHomePage`	Unicode string	Yes
`LastFailedLogin`	`badPasswordTime`	Large integer	No
`LastLogin`	`lastLogon`	Large integer	No
`LastLogoff`	`lastLogoff*`	Large integer	No
`LastName`	`sn`	Unicode string	Yes
`LoginHours`	`logonHours`	Octet string	Yes
`LoginScript`	`scriptPath`	Unicode string	Yes
`Login-Workstations`	`user-Workstations`	Unicode string	Yes
`Manager`	`manager`	DN	Yes
`MaxStorage`	`maxStorage`	Large integer	No
`NamePrefix`	`personalTitle`	Unicode string	No
`NameSuffix`	`generation-Qualifier`	Unicode string	No

(continued)

* `LastLogoff` isn't maintained in Windows 2000 or Windows Server 2003.

Table 10.12 Static Property Methods of the `IADsUser` Interface *(cont.)*

Property Method	Attribute LDAP Name	Syntax	Visible in Users and Computers Snap-In
`Office-Locations`	`physical-Delivery-OfficeName`	`Unicode string`	Yes
`OtherName`	`middleName`	`Unicode string`	No
`PasswordLast-Changed`	`pwdLastSet`	`Large integer`	No
`Picture`	`thumbnailPhoto`	`Octet string`	No
`PostalAddresses`	`postalAddress`	`Unicode string`	No
`PostalCodes`	`postalCode`	`Unicode string`	Yes
`Profile`	`profilePath`	`Unicode string`	Yes
`SeeAlso`	`seeAlso`	`DN`	No
`TelephoneHome`	`homePhone`	`Unicode string`	Yes
`TelephoneMobile`	`mobile`	`Unicode string`	Yes
`TelephoneNumber`	`telephoneNumber`	`Unicode string`	Yes
`TelephonePager`	`pager`	`Unicode string`	Yes
`Title`	`title`	`Unicode string`	Yes

In addition to the 36 static property methods in Table 10.12, there are two yes/no-type static property methods that correspond to individual bits in the `userAccountControl` attribute:

- `AccountDisabled`
- `PasswordRequired`

NOTE There is also a third similar yes/no property method: `IsAccountLocked`. You can use it with Windows Server 2003 and Windows NT, but it doesn't work with Windows 2000 Active Directory and the ADSI LDAP provider. The reason is that in Active Directory this setting changed to be in the `lockoutTime` attribute, but the Windows 2000 version of the property method tries to read it from the `userAccountControl` attribute.

With choices A and B you would get the "raw" value of an attribute, as you would with most choice C static property methods. However, some static property methods may return a "better" value than just the attribute value in Active Directory. For example, `userWorkstations` is a single-valued attribute, which could contain the string "PC25, PC37,PC38." When you retrieve it with the `LoginWorkstations` static property method, the string has been modified to a multivalued property containing three values: "PC25," "PC37," and "PC38."

Using static property methods (i.e., choice C) has the following advantages.

- When you use the two static property methods that correspond to the bits in `userAccountControl`, you don't have to do bitwise arithmetic in your script.
- Some of the static property method names are more descriptive than the LDAP names (such as `LastName` versus `sn`). Therefore, it may be more comfortable for you to use the static property method names.
- `LastLogin`, `LastFailedLogin`, and the other dates in Table 10.12 are stored as `large integers` in Active Directory. If you use choices A or B to read the `badPasswordTime` property, you get a 64-bit number (in two parts) telling you how many 0.1 micro-second intervals (i.e., 1/10,000,000 seconds) have passed since the beginning of the seventeenth century (i.e., January 1, 1601). It would be very difficult to convert this to a meaningful date in your script (although you can use the RepAdmin tool manually, as shown in Chapter 11). Using the corresponding `LastFailed-Login` property method would give you a meaningful date and time string right away, including the time zone correction.

NOTE When reading attributes with date syntaxes using choices A or B, you will get UTC times (about the same as GMT). Active Directory stores times in UTC, regardless of whether the syntax is `UTC time string` or `generalized time string`.

Static property methods have the following disadvantages.

- There are only 36 + 2 of them. For example, there is a static property method for `HomeDirectory` but not one for `HomeDrive`. Also, 14 of those attributes that correspond to static property methods are not found in the Users and Computers snap-in (as listed in Table 10.12); therefore, it is likely that you will never use them.

- You cannot use a variable as the attribute name to browse through all static property methods in a single loop, as you could when using choice A (i.e., `objUser.Get("attrLDAPname")`).
- You may still have to do bitwise arithmetic, because `userAccountControl` contains other settings than just those two.
- The behavior is not always consistent. If you are reading `PostalAddresses`, which is multivalued, you will get an error, a string, or an array, depending on whether there are zero, one, or multiple values defined. With `LoginWorkstations`, you will get an error or an array but not a string. Similarly, a single-valued `EmployeeID` returns an empty string if it is not set, but `FaxNumber` returns a "property not found" error.

Consequently, you must use choices A or B anyway for some of the properties. As mentioned previously, for consistency we use only choice A in this book, unless there is a specific advantage to using a property method (choice B dynamic or choice C static).

`IADsUser` also has three normal methods, which are listed in Table 10.13.

Table 10.13 Methods of the `IADsUser` Interface

Method	Description
`Groups`	This method returns a collection of groups to which the user belongs. They are managed by the `IADsMembers` interface, which works much like `IADsContainer`. You can set a filter and list all members in a `For Each . . . Next` loop. However, all the members in the collection belong to the class `group`, so the filter is obsolete.
`SetPassword`	This method sets the user's password. In Active Directory this happens primarily using a 128-bit SSL connection and secondarily with the secure Kerberos protocol. If neither option is possible, the legacy `NetUserSetInfo` API call is used.
`ChangePassword`	This method changes the user's password as long as you are able to enter the old password as an argument.

Table 10.14 Methods of the `IADsGroup` Interface

Method	Description
`Members`	This method returns a collection of objects that are the members of this group. They are managed by the `IADsMembers` interface. You can set a filter* and list all members in a `For Each . . . Next` loop. Because the members could be users, contacts, computers, or other groups, you can narrow the list with a filter. You can also use the `Count` property to get the number of members.
`IsMember`	This method returns True or False, depending on whether a given object is a member in the target group.
`Add`	This method adds a given object to the target group.
`Remove`	This method removes a given object from the target group.

* You would do this using the `Filter` property, but it seems not to work with `IADsMembers` in Windows 2000 or Windows Server 2003.

The following lines demonstrate the `Groups` method:

```
Set objUser = _
    GetObject("LDAP://CN=Administrator,CN=Users,DC=sanao,DC=com")
For Each objChild In objUser.Groups
    WScript.Echo objChild.Name & vbTab & objChild.Description
Next
```

The IADsGroup Interface

The `IADsGroup` interface provides some methods that help in managing group memberships. It has one static property method, `Description`, which corresponds to the `description` attribute in Active Directory. Table 10.14 describes the normal methods.

WARNING If you have an AD2000 forest or an AD2003 forest running on the Windows 2000 functional level, you should take into account the following warning: All members of a group are stored as one multivalued attribute. Because Active Directory replication is attribute-based (in the mentioned cases), changing the membership on two domain controllers at the same time results in the loss of one of the changes. Therefore, you should make a habit of modifying group memberships on only one domain controller, which could be the PDC emulator, for example. In this case, the `ADsPath` would be `"LDAP://dc1.sanao.com/CN=SomeGroup, CN=Users, DC=sanao, DC=com"`.

NOTE The `Members` method normally returns an empty list for Domain Users, because the method lists only members that are stored in the `members` attribute. This attribute doesn't include users that have the group as their primary group, and Domain Users is by default the *primary group* for every user. The primary group membership is stored in the `primaryGroupID` attribute of each user.

The following lines demonstrate how you can list the members of Domain Admins:

```
Set objGroup = _
    GetObject("LDAP://CN=Domain Admins,CN=Users,DC=sanao,DC=com")
WScript.Echo objGroup.Members.Count
For Each objChild In objGroup.Members
    WScript.Echo objChild.Name
Next
```

ADSI Syntaxes

Chapter 8 lists 23 syntaxes (or data types) that Active Directory supports. They are mapped to 20 LDAP types, which in turn are mapped to 13 ADSI data types, or `AdsTypes`, in the ADSI LDAP provider. Finally, the 13 `ADsTypes` are mapped to 6 OLE automation data types (see Figure 10.19).

In Figure 10.19, `large integer` is an example to show values for various data type identifiers. As you can see, `large integer` has quite a few identifiers, as do the other 22 syntaxes. (See Chapter 8 for some of the identifiers.)

NOTE There are more than 40 LDAP types (e.g., `LDAPTYPE_AUDIO` and `LDAPTYPE_TELEXNUMBER`), but Active Directory uses only 20. There are also 28 `ADsTypes`, but again, only 13 are used in Active Directory.

You are probably happy to hear that for scripting, it is quite sufficient if you just know the list of `ADsTypes` and how they correspond to Active

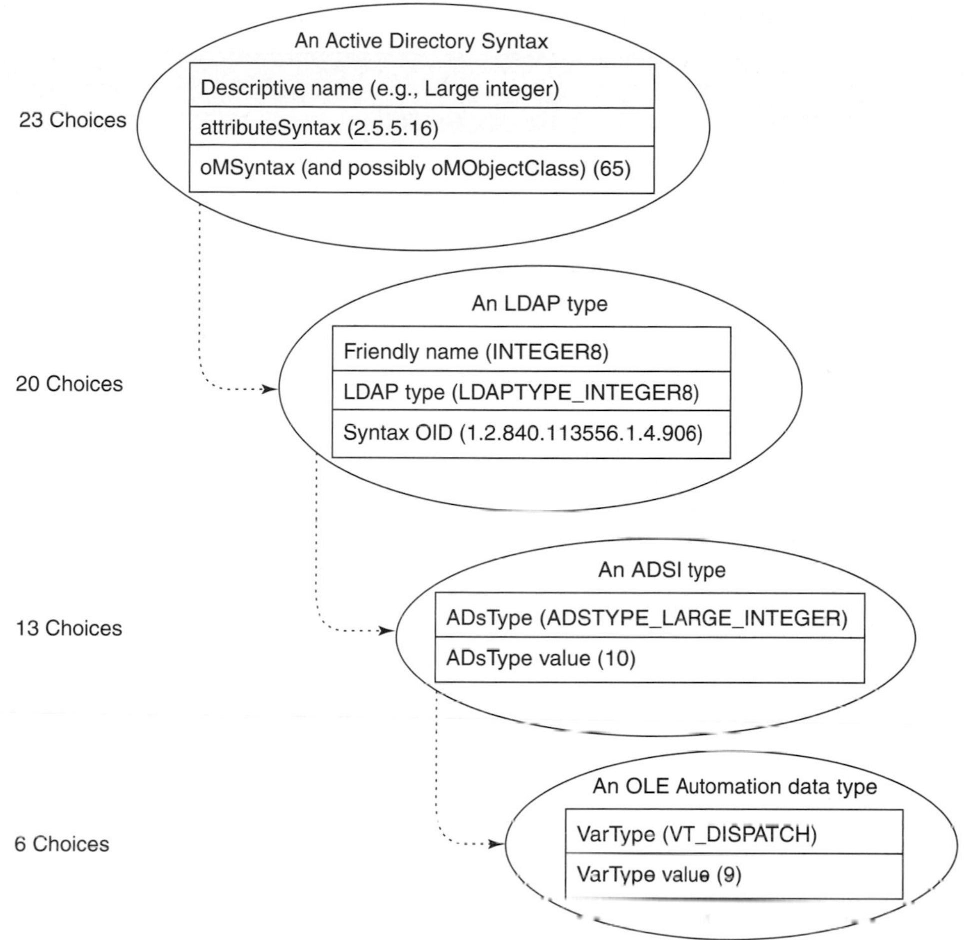

Figure 10.19 Twenty-three Active Directory syntaxes map to 20 LDAP types, which map to 13 ADSI types, which map to 6 OLE automation data types. Example values for each identifier appear in parentheses, using the `large integer` syntax as an example.

Directory syntaxes. Table 10.15 lists the 23 Active Directory syntaxes and how they map to the 20 LDAP types and 13 ADSI types. Table 10.15 also shows how many attributes of the base schema use each of the syntaxes.

Table 10.16 shows which Active Directory syntaxes map to which OLE automation data type. This information is not essential to write a script, but it may help you to understand how your script handles various types of data.

Table 10.15 Syntaxes and Data Types

Descriptive Name	Count in Schema	LDAP-Type Friendly Name	ADsType	ADsType Value
DN (aka distinguished name)	123	DN	ADSTYPE_DN_STRING	1
Case-sensitive string	0	CaseExact-String	ADSTYPE_CASE_EXACT_STRING	2
Unicode string	394	Directory-String	ADSTYPE_CASE_IGNORE_STRING	3
OID string	22	OID	ADSTYPE_CASE_IGNORE_STRING	3
Case-ignore string (teletex)	8	CaseIgnore-String	ADSTYPE_CASE_IGNORE_STRING	3
IA5 string	9	IA5String	ADSTYPE_CASE_IGNORE_STRING	3
Presentation address	1	Presentation-Address	ADSTYPE_CASE_IGNORE_STRING	3
OR name	0	ORName	ADSTYPE_CASE_IGNORE_STRING	3
Access point DN	0	Access-PointDN	ADSTYPE_CASE_IGNORE_STRING	3
Printable string	13	Printable-String	ADSTYPE_PRINTABLE_STRING	4
Numeric string	2	Numeric-String	ADSTYPE_NUMERIC_STRING	5
Boolean	58	Boolean	ADSTYPE_BOOLEAN	6
Integer	193	INTEGER	ADSTYPE_INTEGER	7
Enumeration	6	INTEGER	ADSTYPE_INTEGER	7
Octet string	138	Octet-String	ADSTYPE_OCTET_STRING	8

Table 10.15 Syntaxes and Data Types *(cont.)*

Descriptive Name	Count in Schema	LDAP-Type Friendly Name	ADsType	ADsType Value
SID string	9	Octet-String	ADSTYPE_OCTET_STRING	8
Replica link	2	Octet-String	ADSTYPE_OCTET_STRING	8
Generalized time string	8	Generalized-Time	ADSTYPE_UTC_TIME	9
UTC time string	4	UTCTime	ADSTYPE_UTC_TIME	9
Large integer	72	INTEGER8	ADSTYPE_LARGE_INTEGER	10
NT security descriptor	3	Object-Security-Descriptor	ADSTYPE_NT_SECURITY_DESCRIPTOR	25
DN with binary (aka DN with octet string)	5	DNWith-Binary	ADSTYPE_DN_WITH_BINARY	27
DN with Unicode string	0	DNWith-String	ADSTYPE_DN_WITH_STRING	28

Table 10.16 OLE Automation Data Types and Corresponding Active Directory Syntaxes

VarType	Value	Comment	Active Directory Syntaxes
VT_I4	3	4-byte (32-bit) signed integer	Integer, Enumeration
VT_DATE	7	Date	Generalized time string, UTC time string
VT_BSTR	8	OLE automation string	DN, Case-sensitive string (aka case-exact string), Unicode string (aka directory string), Case-ignore string (teletex), Printable string, Numeric string, Presentation address, Access point DN, OID string, IA5 string, OR name
VT_DISPATCH	9	IDispatch	Large integer (aka INTEGER8), NT security descriptor, DN with binary, DN with Unicode string
VT_BOOL	11	Boolean	Boolean
VT_VARIANT	12	VARIANT	Octet string, SID string, Replica link

* VT_DISPATCH is the type that handles the four syntaxes that have dedicated ADSI interfaces to give you access to the corresponding data. For more information, see the "Handling Special Data Types" section.

Additional Techniques

It is good to be aware of the following additional scripting techniques:

- Ways to input and output information
- Using executables (such as the NET commands) from scripts
- Using COM components
- Using the Win32 API
- Debugging scripts

- Encoding scripts
- Including script lines from another file

We describe the techniques in the following sections and present many examples of the first three list items in Chapter 11.

Ways to Input and Output Information

As mentioned, WSH scripts cannot be very interactive. There are still several ways to input information to your scripts and output information from your scripts.

The methods to input information are as follows:

- Use the `InputBox` function of VBScript to prompt the user to enter text in a pop-up window.
- Use command-line options (arguments).
- Read a text file or an Excel spreadsheet.
- Read standard input (likely to be redirected from a text file).
- Read another source of information, such as Active Directory or a database.

The ways to output information are as follows:

- Use the `MsgBox` function of VBScript to display a pop-up window.
- Use the `WScript.Echo` method to display a pop-up window or lines of output in the command window, depending on whether WScript or CScript is used.
- Use the `WScript.Popup` method to display a pop-up window.
- Write to a text file or an Excel spreadsheet.
- Write to standard output to display lines of output in the command window (equal to `WScript.Echo` used with CScript).
- Write to another destination, such as Active Directory or a database.

Using Executables from Scripts

You can start applications from your WSH scripts. These applications may be graphical or command-line tools, including any Windows operating system "DOS" commands (DIR, COPY, and so on), NET commands (e.g., NET USER), and the DS commands (e.g., DSAdd). You can probably solve your administrative scripting tasks without these commands, but you should keep in mind that they are available.

Using COM Components

To write scripts that interact with Active Directory, you will use ADSI and often also ADO. In addition, you could use, among others, the following COM components in your scripts.

- *VBScript* includes `FileSystemObject`, which enables you to browse and manipulate drives, folders, and files. One thing you cannot do, however, is manage file and folder permissions. There is also an `Err` object, which you can use in error handling of the scripts.
- *WSH* includes 15 objects, such as `WScript`, `WshArguments`, `WshNetwork`, `WshShell`, and `WshRemote`. They enable you to perform such operations as using command-line arguments and environment variables, modifying the registry, and creating network mappings and desktop shortcuts.
- *Microsoft Office* components enable you to control the Office applications. For example, you can write and read information to and from Excel sheets.
- *The ADSI Resource Kit* includes the components ADsEncode.dll, ADsError.dll, ADsFactr.dll, ADsFSMO.dll, ADsLocator.dll, ADsRAS.dll, ADsSecurity.dll, and ADsVersion.dll. These eight components provide additional functions to manage Active Directory and other things. For example, ADsFSMO enables you to list the operations master role owners, and ADsSecurity enables you to manage file and folder permissions. As of this writing, you can download the ADSI Resource Kit at the address `http://www.microsoft.com/ntserver/nts/downloads/other/ADSI25/default.asp` by clicking the link "Download the SDK for ADSI 2.5." You could say that the files are included in the SDK as samples. There are also some sample scripts that demonstrate use of the functions and some brief documentation. Of the eight components, ADsSecurity is relatively popular. Because standard WSH + VBScript + ADSI doesn't enable you to manage file and folder permissions, ADsSecurity fills a specific need in scripting.
- *IADsTools* includes well over 100 functions to access and manage Active Directory. Most of the functions are site- and replication-related—the Replication Monitor utility uses them. IADsTools.dll and the documentation in IADsTools.doc are included in Windows Support Tools (which you can install from the Windows Server 2003 CD-ROM).

- *Homemade components* enable your scripts to do "anything." You just need a developer in your organization who can write these components.
- *Purchased components* could be shrink-wrapped products or custom-made products for you. Just like homemade components, purchased components could do "anything."
- *Windows Management Instrumentation (WMI)* is a COM interface that enables you to manage the operating system, services, and devices in Windows 2000 and later computers (and other Windows computers if you download WMI for them). WMI is quite extensive—it includes providers for Active Directory, Windows Installer, performance counters, registry, SNMP, event log, Win32 API, and Windows Driver Model (WDM). You could use WMI to manage Active Directory; however, WMI is beyond the scope of this book. For more information, see the documentation at `http://msdn.microsoft.com/library` and browse to Setup and System Administration, Windows Management Instrumentation (WMI).

Using the Win32 API

Without learning WMI, you can call at least some Win32 APIs (application program interfaces) from your scripts. You use the same RunDLL32 command that you can use on the command line.

You can try the following command either on the command line or in the Run window (click the Start button and select Run):

```
rundll32.exe user32.dll,LockWorkStation
```

NOTE The last word (`LockWorkStation`) is case-sensitive.

The command calls the `LockWorkStation` API function, which locks your computer. To do the same in your script, use the following lines:

```
Set WshShell = CreateObject("WScript.Shell")
WshShell.Run "rundll32.exe user32.dll,LockWorkStation"
```

Unfortunately, there are two difficulties in using the Win32 API.

- You need to study a huge amount of information (available at `http://msdn.microsoft.com/library`) to find the right function.

- Most of the functions require passing parameters and you can pass only some of the data types on the RunDLL32 command line.

You may occasionally see an example of Win32 API usage (such as the one here); otherwise, using those functions is not a viable option in scripts.

Debugging Scripts

Recall that there is no integrated development environment for WSH scripts. Despite this shortcoming, you have two satisfactory means to debug your scripts: extra output commands or the Microsoft Script Debugger.

Debugging with Extra Output Commands

You can add output commands in appropriate places within your script. The output commands could print just "Here we are" or "Next we'll try to create the user." You could also include some variable values in the output to help you determine what is going on in your script at that moment.

You could prefix each script line containing an output command with `If DebugIsOn Then`. This way, you could easily turn on or off debug printing by setting the value of `DebugIsOn` to either 1 or 0 (using the `Const` keyword) in the beginning of the script.

Microsoft Script Debugger

Microsoft has made a debugger to be used when you debug scripts in HTML or ASP files, which execute in Internet Explorer or Internet Information Server, respectively. This Script Debugger also works to some degree with WSH scripts.

Windows 2000 includes a version of the Script Debugger, which is dated May 1997, but Windows Server 2003 seems not to include one. You can download a newer version from `http://www.microsoft.com`, by searching for the word "scd10en.exe". This way, you should find the download page for "Script Debugger for Windows NT 4.0, 2000, and XP." However, that downloadable version is not much newer (it is dated October 1997).

NOTE Because the Script Debugger program was made for a different environment, it has features that are not meaningful with WSH scripts.

Also, it is quite possible that the Script Debugger itself halts when you try to start it, or stops responding later, so that you need to kill it with the Task Manager.

TIP If the Script Debugger starts without your script in it, you can try to fix this by logging off and on again.

You can launch the Script Debugger with either the `//X` or `//D` host options.

- The `//X` option opens your script in the Script Debugger and places the debugging cursor over the first script line.
- The `//D` option starts running your script. If there is an error, however, your script opens in the Script Debugger and the debugging cursor will be on the line that contains the error. Unfortunately, you don't receive information that would identify the error.

The corresponding two example commands are as follows:

```
cscript //x myscript.vbs
cscript //d myscript.vbs
```

Figure 10.20 shows the Script Debugger when it was launched using the `//X` option with our earlier VBS basic example.

Figure 10.20 requires some explanation.

- The arrow symbol on the left indicates the line where the debugging cursor currently is. You have executed the script up to this line (excluding the line where the debugging cursor is).
- You can execute the line (and advance to the next line) by pressing F8.
- You can move the normal "vertical line" text cursor to any line and insert a *breakpoint* on that line by pressing F9. The line will turn dark red and a ball will appear on the left. The `If` statement in the figure is an example of this.
- When you press F5, the script starts executing from the line where the debugging cursor is. It will continue executing until the script ends, until there is a line with an error, or until there is a line where you have set a breakpoint.

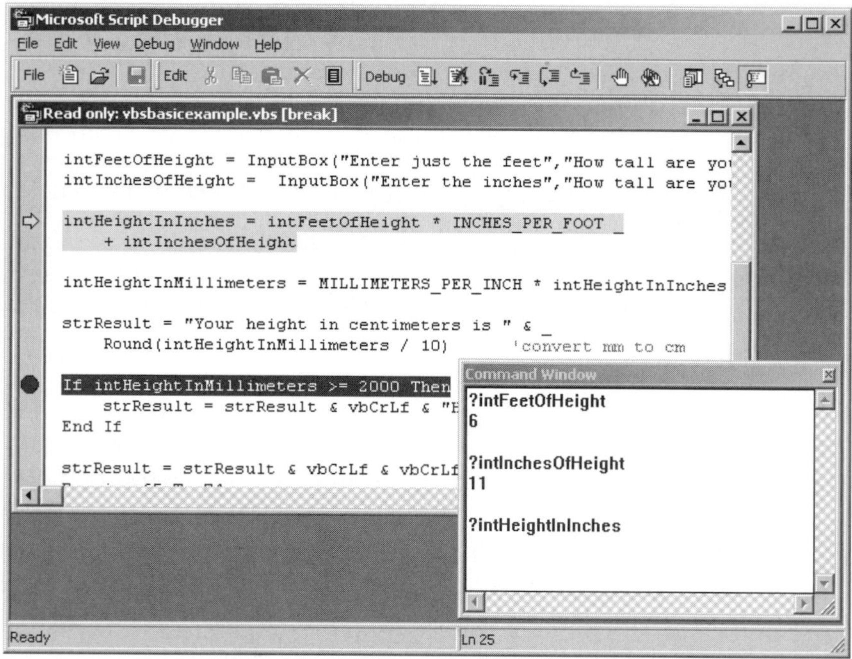

Figure 10.20 Our earlier basic example script (in Figure 10.10) shown in the Script Debugger.

- You can use the Command Window to query the current value (or set a new value) for any variable. In the figure there is no value for `intHeightInInches` yet, because the line where it would get a value is the next one to be executed.
- You can use the Call Stack window (not visible in Figure 10.20) to track the chain of procedure/function calls. This is useful if one procedure (or subprogram) in your script calls another, which calls another, and so on.

NOTE You cannot edit the contents of a WSH script with the Script Debugger.

NOTE In more complex scripts, a certain part of the script might not be used for a long time and sudden bugs could arise once the functions in that part are used.

Encoding Scripts

You can use Microsoft Script Encoder to protect the contents of your scripts. After you download sce10en.exe at `http://msdn.microsoft.com/scripting` and install it, you have the screnc command available. A sample command is as follows:

```
screnc MyScript.vbs MyScript.vbe
```

The command leaves the .vbs file intact, but creates an encrypted .vbe file. The contents of the latter file look like "+MdbWU,x!:4", but you can run it as any .vbs file.

Microsoft warns that this encryption doesn't protect against serious cracking, but it prevents the users in your organization from inspecting or modifying the scripts. The encryption may also be adequate for commercial use, but only if the script buyers trust the vendor enough so that the buyers are willing to run scripts whose contents they cannot check for Trojan horses or similar threats.

Including Script Lines from Another File

You may have script lines that you would like to reuse in other script files. Of course, you could copy and paste the lines from one file to another, but if you later wanted to modify the lines, you would have to do this in (at least) two files. The solution is to have the lines in only one file and use some special XML tags to include them in others.

The lines to include could be a series of *constant definitions*. (They could also be some *functions* or *subprograms*, which we address in the next chapter.)

Figure 10.21 shows a "huge" number of constant definitions that you would like to include in many of your scripts. As you can see, the file to be included is just like any script. However, the receiving file is a little different. It must use the file extension "WSF" instead of "VBS," and some XML tags must be in the beginning of the file and their closing pairs must be at the end of the file (see Figure 10.22).

Lines 1 through 3 in Figure 10.22 contain the required XML tags, and lines 14 through 16 contain the corresponding closing tags. The file to be included is specified on line 3 and the reference can be either an absolute or a relative path to the file. Lines 4 through 13 are normal VBScript lines.

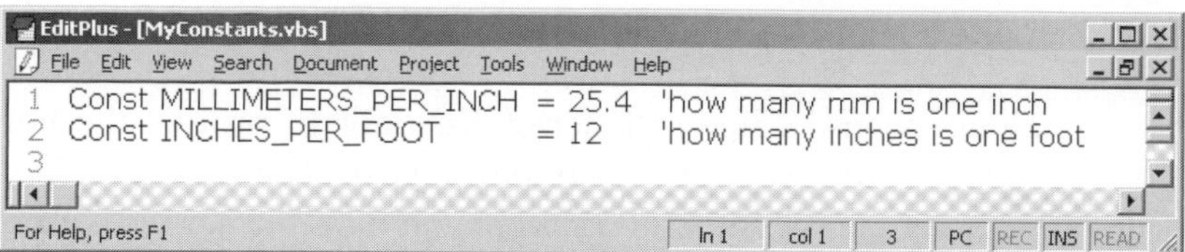

Figure 10.21 The same constant definitions are typically needed in many scripts. You can gather all constant definitions in a single file and include that file in your scripts, as shown in Figure 10.22. The figure shows only two definitions—it is not useful to show a 200-line file here.

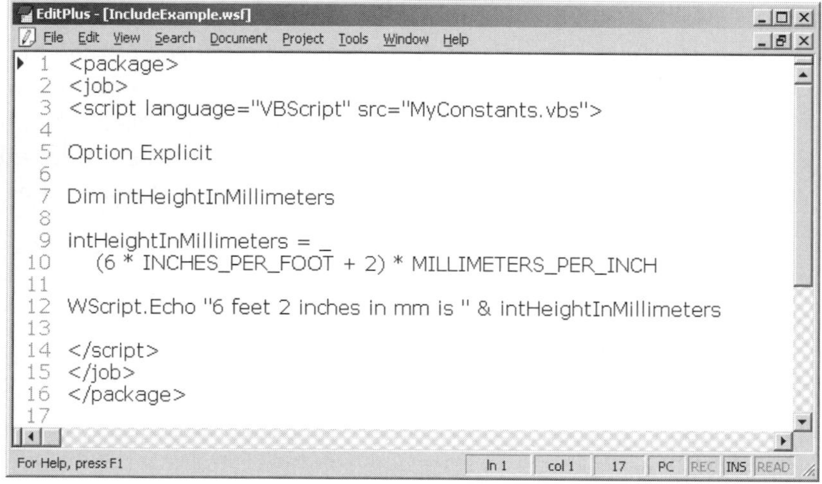

Figure 10.22 By using the XML tags shown in the figure, you can include another script file (see line 3). The result is the same as if the lines of the included file were directly in the receiving file.

NOTE You'll see tens of constant definitions in the various ADSI examples in the next chapter. We have gathered all the definitions in one file that you can download from `http://www.kouti.com/`.

Conclusion

This chapter presented the ADSI concepts and explained how to set up a script-writing environment. Now you are ready to explore and test-run the sample scripts.

CHAPTER 11

Administration Scripts: Examples

This chapter is the second of the two scripting chapters. The first scripting chapter presented the concepts, and this chapter focuses on providing practical examples. In addition, this chapter presents a few more concepts so as not to pack too much background theory into the previous chapter. Also, any concepts in this chapter are explained with immediate examples.

You may recall from the introduction to the previous chapter that these two chapters will be useful to people in one of three situations.

- You want to learn to write scripts to enhance administration and save work.
- You want to learn to read scripts. If you download scripts from the Internet or get them from other sources, you'll want to check what they do before you use them in your organization.
- You want to learn more about Active Directory architecture. Outputs of many of the examples in this chapter provide architectural information about Active Directory and you can run those scripts without knowing what they do on each line. You should, of course, read the description first to check that a script isn't going to modify your Active Directory in any way. For example, one script extends your schema (although we do include safety mechanisms in that script).

Let the journey begin.

ADSI Examples

Now that you know the concepts of scripting and ADSI, the best way to continue learning is to see examples of various tasks. Therefore, in this chapter we show a number of sample scripts.

We have divided the sample scripts into the following categories:

- User management
- Schema access
- Configuration information
- Access control lists
- OU, group, and computer management
- ADSI without Active Directory
- Additional techniques
- Using ADO

NOTE Several of the samples in the user management category apply to any class. All you need to do is change the binding string to point to some other object.

The scripts also include more programming techniques than the category name suggests. Some scripts may prompt for user input with the `InputBox` function, some may accept command-line arguments, and some may use Excel spreadsheets for input or output. When you build your own administration scripts, you can pick up these various techniques from different samples and combine them to create a solution that serves you best.

TIP To find all scripts that use Excel, for example, you can use the Search feature of Windows. Once you have downloaded the samples from `http://www.kouti.com/` and placed them in a folder on your local hard drive, right-click the folder and select Search. If you type "excel" in the "A word or phrase in the file" field, you will get a list of all scripts that somehow use Excel. Instead of the Search feature, you can use the command-line commands Find, FindStr, and QGrep.

We use the following principles with the sample scripts.

- When a section covers a sample script, the script name (although without a number) is the section heading, including the extension .vbs or .xls.
- Most of the sample script filenames start with "ADSI," "WSH," "ADO," or some other prefix to indicate the main technology in the sample.
- We show the script numbers when we list the scripts of each section. It helps you to match them to the script files that you can download from `http://www.kouti.com`. These script file numbers do not match any figure numbers in this chapter.
- To save space, we don't do error checking in the scripts. We discuss error checking in one special example toward the end of the chapter.
- Also to save space, we use comments sparingly, but after each sample we explain how it works. We encourage you to use plentiful comments in your own scripts.
- We explain the first scripts thoroughly, and as the chapter proceeds, our explanations become shorter. Also, if a later script uses a technique that we have explained with an earlier script, we don't repeat the explanation.
- We may hard-code a script to display information only of the Guest account, for example. Depending on your needs, you can apply various input techniques to apply the script to one object or a number of objects.
- When reading or writing Active Directory attributes (or rather, property cache properties), we mostly use explicit `Get` and `Put` methods. For example, we use `objUser.Get("givenName")` instead of `objUser.givenName`. Although the latter format may be shorter and simpler, we consider the former format clearer—it emphasizes that now we are using an Active Directory attribute's LDAP name instead of an ADSI interface method or some other new mysterious function name.

We show the examples as screen shots in EditPlus if they fit nicely on one page. Longer, multipage examples appear as multiple screen shots or are included in the normal text, but in a different font.

NOTE The sample scripts use quite a few constant definitions to specify various values. We have gathered them all in one file, which you can download from `http://www.kouti.com/`.

TIP The third field in the EditPlus status bar indicates the length of the script in lines. If you see only 14 lines in a figure, but the third field in the EditPlus status bar indicates that the total length is 112 lines, you will know that you are looking at only part of the script.

NOTE The output of several sample scripts is tens or hundreds of lines long. Therefore, we show only some lines, if any. We have manipulated the output so that it seems complete, but lines are still missing.

User Management

This section includes the following sample scripts:

- CH11-01 ADSI List the Users of One Container.vbs
- CH11-02 ADSI List the Users of One Container to Excel.vbs
- CH11-03 ADSI List the Property Cache Contents.vbs
- CH11-04 ADSI List User Properties with Get.vbs
- CH11-05 ADSI List User Properties with Methods.vbs
- CH11-06 ADSI List the Account Options of a User.vbs
- CH11-07 ADSI Create a User with Minimum Attributes.vbs
- CH11-08 ADSI Create a User with More Attributes.vbs
- CH11-09 BAT Create a User with a Batch File.bat
- CH11-10 WSH Create a Home Folder for a User - ver 1.vbs
- CH11-11 WSH Create a Home Folder for a User - ver 2.vbs
- CH11-12 Read User Information from Excel.xls
- CH11-13 Read User Information from Standard Input.xls

The first two examples list all the users in one container, and the next three list the properties of one user with three different approaches. The rest of the examples do just what their names imply.

In addition to this user management section, two user management scripts appear later in the chapter.

- In the "Additional Techniques" section we show how to list users of several containers.
- In the "Using ADO" section we add a home folder for users that don't yet have one.

The other examples are normal WSH scripts, but number 12 is written in VBA to run as an Excel macro.

List the Users of One Container.vbs

This sample script asks you to enter a container name and then lists all users, along with their descriptions, in that container. The sample is quite similar to the basic ADSI example that you saw in the previous chapter (in Figure 10.14). Now it just has a few more bells and whistles.

Figure 11.1 shows the input box for the distinguished name of the container. Figure 11.2 shows the script's contents.

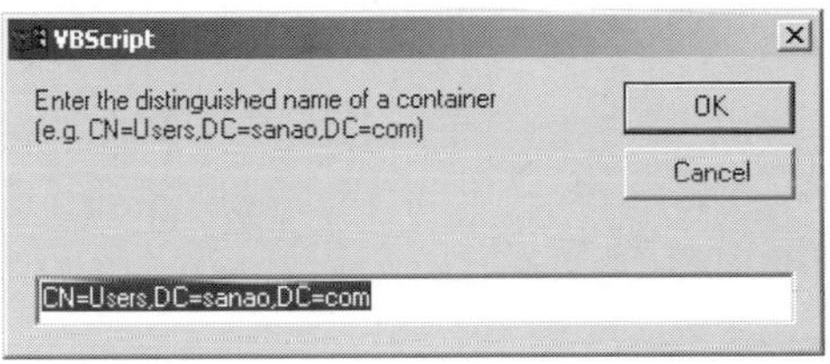

Figure 11.1 The input box for "ADSI List the Users of One Container.vbs"

```
Option Explicit

Dim objDSE, strDefaultDN, strDN, objContainer, objChild

Set objDSE = GetObject("LDAP://rootDSE")
strDefaultDN = "CN=Users," & objDSE.Get("defaultNamingContext")

strDN = InputBox("Enter the distinguished name of a container" & _
   vbCrLf & "(e.g. " & strDefaultDN & ")", , strDefaultDN)

If strDN = "" Then WScript.Quit(1)     'user clicked Cancel

Set objContainer = GetObject("LDAP://" & strDN)

objContainer.Filter = Array("user")
For Each objChild In objContainer
   WScript.Echo objChild.Name & vbTab & objChild.Description
Next
```

Figure 11.2 The contents of "ADSI List the Users of One Container.vbs"

On line 5 in Figure 11.2 we bind to the `rootDSE` object, so that we can read the default domain of the logged-on user. This way, we get a default for the distinguished name.

On line 8 we ask the user to enter a container name and on line 9 we add a second line to the prompt text (see Figure 11.1). We don't specify a title for the input box, so we have two commas before we put the default name as an argument. The entered text you saw in the input box was provided by this default.

On line 11 we will quit the script if the user clicks Cancel. The number 1 as an argument returns an *error level,* which any possible calling application or batch file may use to recognize that there was an error.

On line 13 we finally bind to the chosen container, which is something that we could have done on line 1 if we had hard-coded it (and if there weren't any `Option Explicit` and `Dim` statements).

On line 15 we set a filter for the `user` class and then browse through all appropriate child objects of that container and display their names and descriptions.

NOTE As we mentioned in the basic ADSI example (see Chapter 10, the Note after Figure 10.15), the filter for the `user` class accepts also its subclasses, such as `computer`. It is not a bug in your script if you see some computer objects on your output list.

On line 17 we use `objChild.Description` instead of `objChild.Get("Description")`. This way, we don't run into the "property not found" error.

List the Users of One Container to Excel.vbs

Like the script in the previous example, this script displays the usernames and descriptions of one container. The only difference is that this time we dump the information into an Excel spreadsheet instead of the command-line window. To save space, we also removed the lines to create a default DN.

Figure 11.3 shows the script result when you choose to list the contents of the `CN=Users` container with the default objects. Figure 11.4 shows the script's contents.

On lines 7 through 9 in Figure 11.4 we instantiate a COM object for Excel, which also starts the application (it must be installed in your computer), makes the application visible, and creates a workbook with an empty spreadsheet.

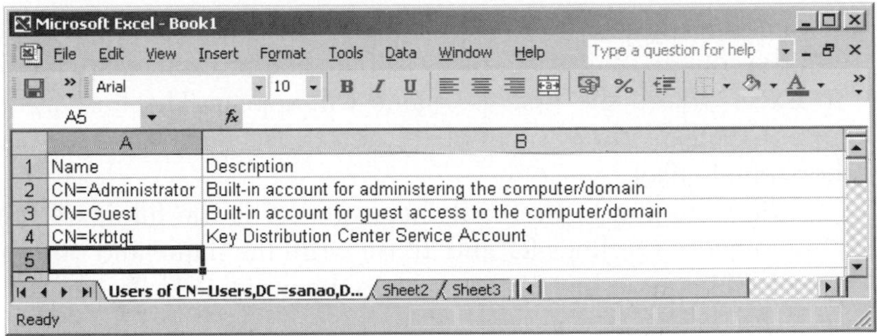

Figure 11.3 The output of "ADSI List the Users of One Container to Excel.vbs"

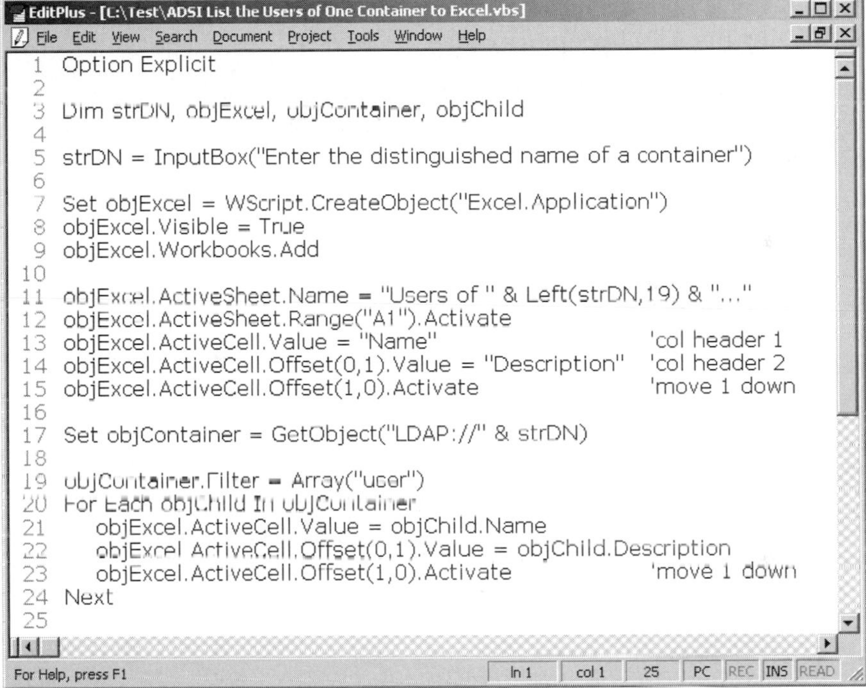

Figure 11.4 The contents of "ADSI List the Users of One Container to Excel.vbs"

On line 11 we define a name for the spreadsheet. We need to cut the distinguished name, because Excel allows only 31 letters for the spreadsheet name. Note that if the DN is short, we needlessly truncate it and append the ellipses, but we didn't want to add extra lines that would have taken care of this.

On line 12 we move to the upper-left corner, on lines 13 and 14 we put the column headers in place, and on line 15 we move to the next line in Excel, where the first username will appear. The first argument in `Offset` means the vertical offset, and the second argument means the horizontal offset.

After binding to the container and setting the filter, we browse all child objects. On lines 21 and 22 we write the name and description to Excel cells and on line 23 we move to the next line in Excel.

List the Property Cache Contents.vbs

In this sample we take one object, the user Guest, and list all the properties and their values that he has in his property cache. We do this by using the ADSI property cache interfaces.

TIP You can use this script for any object class by just changing the target object to bind to.

Figure 11.5 shows some lines of the script's output. As you see, each property name is on its own line in column 1. The number in parentheses is the `ADsType` (integer, string, and so on) of the property, as discussed in the previous chapter. In column 26 (i.e., character position 26 from the left) we have all the values, and in the case of multivalued attributes, each consequent value appears on a new line. You can see that Guest is a member not only of the `user` class, but also of any of the `user` superclasses (`organizationalPerson`, `person`, and `top`).

The property cache and, therefore, the script's output don't contain constructed attributes. We would need to use `GetInfoEx` for them, but we don't (until the next example).

TIP You can use RepAdmin (part of the Support Tools) to see what date/time a large integer value corresponds to. For example, the output in Figure 11.5 indicates that Guest's password was last changed at the time "1.27115703873392E+17." To convert this value, first divide it by 10,000,000, so you get 12711570387. Then use the command `repadmin /showtime 12711570387`, which gives you the result `03-10-25 15:46.27 UTC`. The tool also shows the local time, but we didn't include it in the book, because it depends on your time zone setting.

```
D:\WINDOWS\System32\cmd.exe

C:\Test>"ADSI List the Property Cache Contents.vbs"
Number of properties in the property cache: 29

objectClass (3)          top
                         person
                         organizationalPerson
                         user
cn (3)                   Guest
distinguishedName (1)    CN=Guest,CN=Users,DC=sanao,DC=com
whenCreated (9)          8/26/2003 9:45:05 AM
whenChanged (9)          10/26/2003 3:46:49 PM
uSNCreated (10)          8195
uSNChanged (10)          16725
name (3)                 Guest
objectGUID (8)           some octet string
userAccountControl (7)   66082
pwdLastSet (10)          1.27115703873392E+17
accountExpires (10)      9.22337203255981E+18
sAMAccountName (3)       Guest
objectCategory (1)       CN=Person,CN=Schema,CN=Configuration,DC=sanao,DC=com
nTSecurityDescriptor (25) some security descriptor

C:\Test>_
```

Figure 11.5 Some lines of output of "ADSI List the Property Cache Contents.vbs." Because the original output is tens of lines long, we display only selected lines.

WARNING Some of the attributes that this script displays are nonreplicating (such as `lastLogon` or `badPwdCount`). Therefore, each domain controller knows the values only for itself; you will get different results if you read the settings from different domain controllers. To get exact answers, query all domain controllers and pick the latest value or sum the values, depending on the attribute.

Property Cache Interfaces

Before we show the script, we need to explain how the property cache interfaces work. There are four property cache interfaces, which are illustrated in Figure 11.6.

- `IADsProperyList` has a property method to indicate how many properties there are in the cache. It also enables you to browse through the properties in the cache, perhaps skipping some of them. The `Item` method (and also `Next` or `GetPropertyItem`) retrieves one property from the list to a property entry object. You can select the property either by name (e.g., `.Item("givenName")`) or by index number (e.g., `.Item(2)`).
- `IADsPropertyEntry` enables you to see the name and `ADsType` of the property, as well as browse the values. You can also modify all of these if you are writing some properties to the property cache.

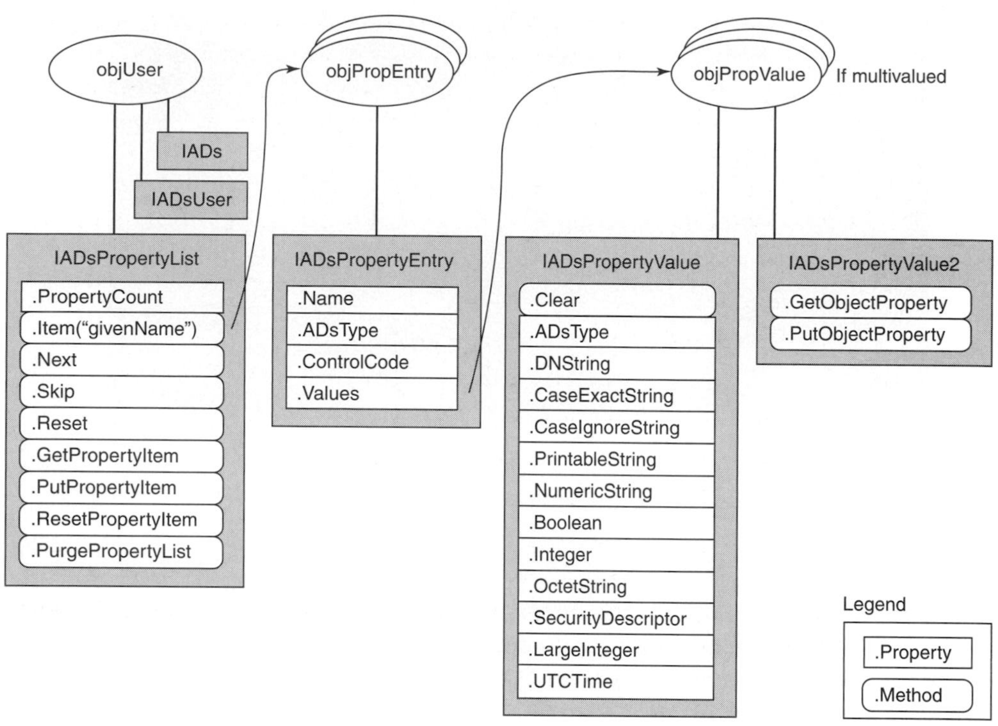

Figure 11.6 To list everything in one user's property cache, you use the `IADsPropertyList` interface. It enables you to browse through the properties in the cache and access each entry with `IADsPropertyEntry`. That interface in turn enables browsing through the values of that property.

- `IADsPropertyValue` and `IADsPropertyValue2` enable you to read and write individual values. The former uses the `ADsType` as a property and the latter uses the `ADsType` as an argument to the `GetObjectProperty` method.

The following two lines show an example of `IADsPropertyValue` and `IADsPropertyValue2`, respectively:

```
strSomething = objPropValue.CaseIgnoreString
strSomething = _
  objPropValue.GetObjectProperty(ADSTYPE_CASE_IGNORE_STRING)
```

The latter example looks more difficult, but it is better for our sample script, as you will soon see.

NOTE We have drawn several `objPropEntry` and `objPropValue` variables in Figure 11.6. In practice, however, there is usually only one of each and they represent different entries or values one at a time.

NOTE You don't create a new object for `IADsPropertyList`, but you use that interface with the original object, such as `objUser`.

Now it is finally time to show the sample script.

The List the Property Cache Contents Sample Script

We show the script in two parts. Figure 11.7 shows part A and Figure 11.8 shows part B.

Later in the script we need to recognize octet strings, large integers, and security descriptors in order to handle them differently. Consequently, we included the constant definitions for them on lines 3 through 5. We copied and pasted the constant names and values from the ADSI documentation and added the keyword `Const` to each line.

After binding to Guest with the help of `rootDSE` we need to call `GetInfo` on line 13. Otherwise, we wouldn't have anything to list in the property cache.

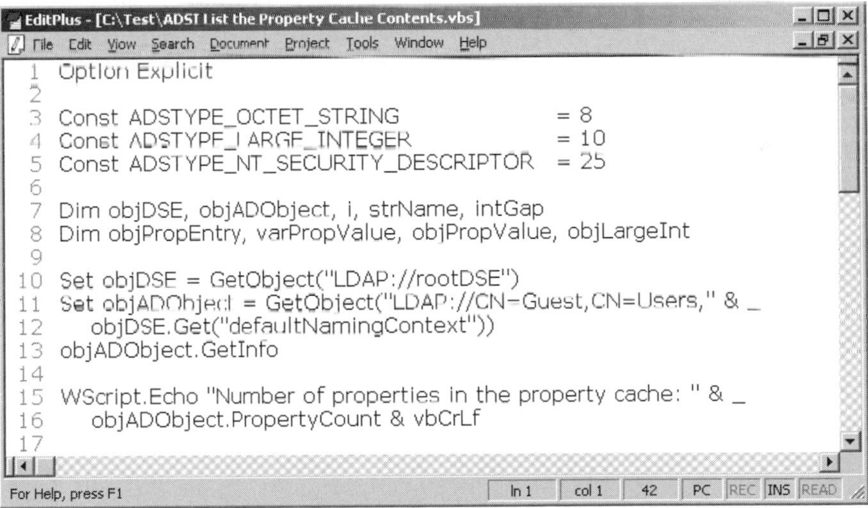

EditPlus - [C:\Test\ADSI List the Property Cache Contents.vbs]
File Edit View Search Document Project Tools Window Help
1 Option Explicit
2
3 Const ADSTYPE_OCTET_STRING = 8
4 Const ADSTYPE_LARGE_INTEGER = 10
5 Const ADSTYPE_NT_SECURITY_DESCRIPTOR = 25
6
7 Dim objDSE, objADObject, i, strName, intGap
8 Dim objPropEntry, varPropValue, objPropValue, objLargeInt
9
10 Set objDSE = GetObject("LDAP://rootDSE")
11 Set objADObject = GetObject("LDAP://CN=Guest,CN=Users," & _
12 objDSE.Get("defaultNamingContext"))
13 objADObject.GetInfo
14
15 WScript.Echo "Number of properties in the property cache: " & _
16 objADObject.PropertyCount & vbCrLf
17
For Help, press F1
ln 1
col 1
42
PC
REC
INS
READ

Figure 11.7 Part A of "ADSI List the Property Cache Contents.vbs"

On lines 15 and 16 we use the `IADsPropertyList` interface to display the number of properties in the cache. Note that the host object (`objADObject`) is not a new object, but rather it is the existing object that represents Guest.

We use a `For ... Next` loop (lines 18 through 41 in Figure 11.8) to browse through the whole property list (i.e., property cache). Because the indexing starts from 0, we must go on only until `count - 1`.

On line 19 we use the index number (0, 1, 2, and so on) to retrieve a property entry and create an object for it. On line 20 we read the name and `ADsType` (which we display in parentheses in the script's output) of the property. We store them in a string that we print later on line 38.

On lines 21 through 40 we have a `For Each ... Next` loop that browses through all values of a single property. If the syntax (i.e., `ADsType`) is either a `security descriptor` or an `octet string`, we don't retrieve the actual value, because it would be too complicated for this example.

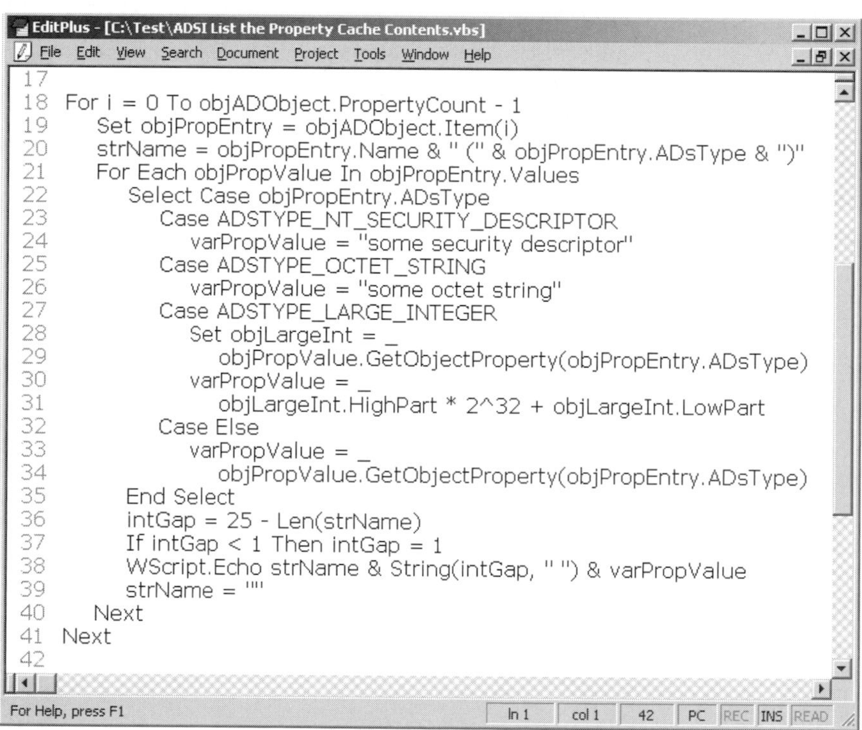


```
17
18 For i = 0 To objADObject.PropertyCount - 1
19    Set objPropEntry = objADObject.Item(i)
20    strName = objPropEntry.Name & " (" & objPropEntry.ADsType & ")"
21    For Each objPropValue In objPropEntry.Values
22       Select Case objPropEntry.ADsType
23          Case ADSTYPE_NT_SECURITY_DESCRIPTOR
24             varPropValue = "some security descriptor"
25          Case ADSTYPE_OCTET_STRING
26             varPropValue = "some octet string"
27          Case ADSTYPE_LARGE_INTEGER
28             Set objLargeInt = _
29                objPropValue.GetObjectProperty(objPropEntry.ADsType)
30             varPropValue = _
31                objLargeInt.HighPart * 2^32 + objLargeInt.LowPart
32          Case Else
33             varPropValue = _
34                objPropValue.GetObjectProperty(objPropEntry.ADsType)
35       End Select
36       intGap = 25 - Len(strName)
37       If intGap < 1 Then intGap = 1
38       WScript.Echo strName & String(intGap, " ") & varPropValue
39       strName = ""
40    Next
41 Next
42
```


Figure 11.8 Part B of "ADSI List the Property Cache Contents.vbs"

In the case of a `large integer` (lines 27 through 31), we retrieve the value to an object variable (`objLargeInt`). Then we use that variable to access the upper 32 bits and the lower 32 bits of the value. We get the result with the formula on line 31. However, if the high part is not zero, the result is too large for a VBScript integer, in which case the result will be converted to a floating-point number, losing some accuracy.

All other data types are easy, so we can just retrieve the value using the `ADsType` number as an argument (lines 33 and 34).

NOTE We use the `IADsPropertyValue2` method's `GetObjectProperty` on line 34. This way, we can specify the ADsType number as an argument. The clumsier choice would be to use `IADsPropertyValue` and lines such as `varPropValue = objPropValue.CaseIgnoreString`, because in the latter case we would need to use a different line for each `ADsType` (lengthening the `Select Case` statement quite a bit).

Line 36 calculates the space required after the property name to align all the values to column 26 onscreen. The next line makes sure that the result is not negative or zero.

Finally, on line 38 we display the property name (and `ADsType`), a proper number of spaces, and the actual value. On line 39 we clear the property name part so that any additional values of the same property will have just the value on each line.

List User Properties with Get.vbs

As in the previous example, this one lists the properties of Guest and their values. This time we retrieve all 257 mandatory and optional attribute names from the schema (assuming we have the AD2003 base schema with no extensions) and try to access them all with `Get` or `GetEx`.

TIP You can also use this script for any object class by just changing the target object to bind to.

Figure 11.9 shows some lines of the script's output. On each line we have the attribute number (1 through 257), attribute LDAP name, syntax in parentheses, and the value aligned to column 41. In a case of multiple values, each one is on a new line. Because only some of the optional attributes have a value, quite a few show just `<not set>`.

```
Command Prompt
C:\Test>"ADSI List User Properties with Get.vbs"
1: cn (DirectoryString)                       Guest
6: objectSid (OctetString)                    ???
7: sAMAccountName (DirectoryString)           Guest
8: accountExpires (INTEGER8)                  9,22337203255981E+18
16: allowedChildClasses (OID)                 nTFRSSubscriptions
                                              classStore
27: canonicalName (DirectoryString)           sanao.com/Users/Guest
46: distinguishedName (DN)                    CN=Guest,CN=Users,DC=sanao,DC=com
98: memberOf (DN)                             CN=Guests,CN=Builtin,DC=sanao,DC=com
149: name (DirectoryString)                   Guest
155: objectGUID (OctetString)                 ???
174: physicalDeliveryOfficeName (DirectoryString) <not set>
176: postalAddress (DirectoryString)          <not set>
177: postalCode (DirectoryString)             <not set>
178: postOfficeBox (DirectoryString)          <not set>
188: pwdLastSet (INTEGER8)                    1,27115703873392E+17
213: street (DirectoryString)                 <not set>
214: streetAddress (DirectoryString)          <not set>
234: userAccountControl (INTEGER)             66082
245: uSNChanged (INTEGER8)                    16757
246: uSNCreated (INTEGER8)                    8195
253: whenChanged (GeneralizedTime)           10/26/2003 3:46:49 PM
254: whenCreated (GeneralizedTime)           8/26/2003 9:45:05 AM

C:\Test>_
```

Figure 11.9 Some lines of output of “ADSI List User Properties with Get.vbs”. The original output is over 1,000 lines long, so we selected only some lines to show.

Attribute 8, `accountExpires`, specifies the date and time when the account expires. It is expressed as 1/10,000,000 seconds since the beginning of the year 1601. New users that are created to a domain get by default the value 9,223,372,036,854,775,807, which is equal to $2^{63} - 1$. It is the largest value that a 64-bit integer value can represent (when half of the values are reserved for negative numbers). This special value means that those accounts never expire. The `accountExpires` value of Guest is roughly the same, and Guest never expires either.

If you run the script yourself, you will get more than 1,000 lines of output. The attribute `AllowedAttributes` alone produces over 200 lines (which shouldn’t surprise you, because it lists all 257 attribute names of the `user` class). You can use one of the following command lines to handle the long output:

```
ListUsers.vbs >result.txt
ListUsers.vbs | find /i "integer)"
ListUsers.vbs | find /v "not set"
```

The first command redirects the output to a text file, the second command shows only the lines with integer syntax, and the last command shows all lines except those that include the text “not set”.

We show the script in six parts (Figures 11.10 through 11.15). Figure 11.10 shows part A.

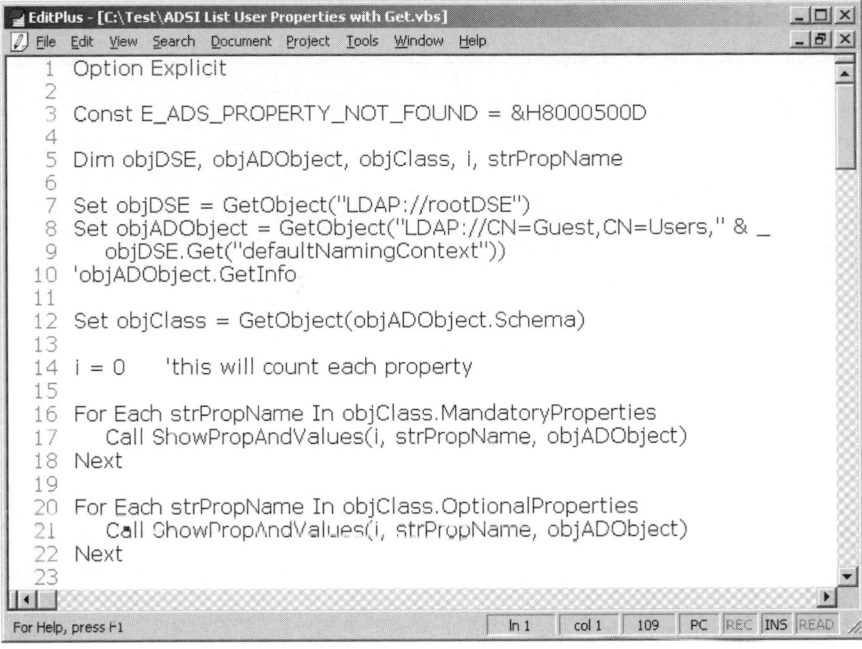
EditPlus - [C:\Test\ADSI List User Properties with Get.vbs]
File Edit View Search Document Project Tools Window Help
1 Option Explicit
2
3 Const E_ADS_PROPERTY_NOT_FOUND = &H8000500D
4
5 Dim objDSE, objADObject, objClass, i, strPropName
6
7 Set objDSE = GetObject("LDAP://rootDSE")
8 Set objADObject = GetObject("LDAP://CN=Guest,CN=Users," & _
9 objDSE.Get("defaultNamingContext"))
10 'objADObject.GetInfo
11
12 Set objClass = GetObject(objADObject.Schema)
13
14 i = 0 'this will count each property
15
16 For Each strPropName In objClass.MandatoryProperties
17 Call ShowPropAndValues(i, strPropName, objADObject)
18 Next
19
20 For Each strPropName In objClass.OptionalProperties
21 Call ShowPropAndValues(i, strPropName, objADObject)
22 Next
23
For Help, press F1
ln 1
col 1
109
PC
REC
INS
READ

Figure 11.10 Part A of "ADSI List User Properties with Get.vbs"

Later in the script we need to recognize which attributes don't have values in the property cache, so we include the error constant for that on line 3. The characters "&H" mean that the number is in hexadecimal format.

On line 10 we have the `GetInfo` call, but unlike in the previous example, it is now "commented out." In that example we needed to call it explicitly, but now an implicit call (with the first property access) is enough.

On line 12 we bind to the `user` class of the schema, so that we can list the names of all mandatory and optional attributes on lines 16 and 20. We discuss schema access further in the appropriate examples later in the chapter.

As we browse through all mandatory and optional attribute names, we call the subprogram (or procedure) `ShowPropAndValues`. We also pass three variables as arguments to the subprogram.

NOTE The subprograms (`Sub`) and functions (`Function`) can be at the beginning, middle, or end of the script. In our examples we put them at the end.

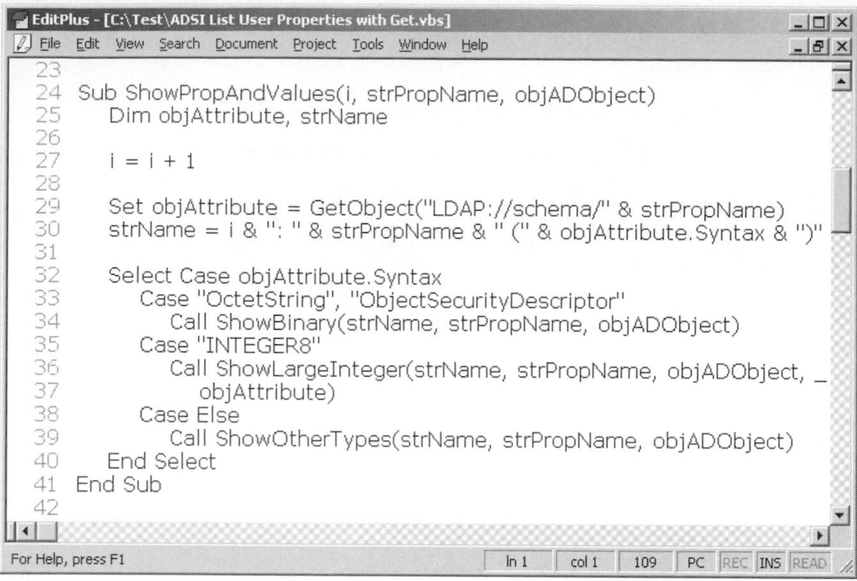

EditPlus - [C:\Test\ADSI List User Properties with Get.vbs]

```
23
24 Sub ShowPropAndValues(i, strPropName, objADObject)
25    Dim objAttribute, strName
26
27    i = i + 1
28
29    Set objAttribute = GetObject("LDAP://schema/" & strPropName)
30    strName = i & ": " & strPropName & " (" & objAttribute.Syntax & ")"
31
32    Select Case objAttribute.Syntax
33       Case "OctetString", "ObjectSecurityDescriptor"
34          Call ShowBinary(strName, strPropName, objADObject)
35       Case "INTEGER8"
36          Call ShowLargeInteger(strName, strPropName, objADObject, _
37             objAttribute)
38       Case Else
39          Call ShowOtherTypes(strName, strPropName, objADObject)
40    End Select
41 End Sub
42
```

Figure 11.11 Part B of "ADSI List User Properties with Get.vbs"

Figure 11.11 shows part B of the script, which is the `ShowPropAndValues` subprogram.

On line 25 we declare two variables for the subprogram, which means that they are valid only in this subprogram. In this case, their *scope* is said to be *procedure level.*

NOTE Another choice is to declare all variables to be *script level* by adding the `Dim` statements to the beginning of the script outside any subprograms. We could also use these script-level variables to pass any information between subprograms, so we wouldn't need any arguments. This may be easier in short scripts, but as your scripts get longer, procedure-level variables and passing values in arguments helps you to avoid nasty bugs.

In order to handle various property values, we need to know the syntax of each attribute and whether it is multivalued. On line 29 we bind to the attribute in the schema to get this information.

On line 30 we store the name and syntax of the attribute to later display them.

We have three more subprograms, `ShowBinary`, `ShowLargeInteger`, and `ShowOtherTypes`, to retrieve and handle the attributes of various syntaxes. Based on the syntax, we call one of these subprograms on line 34, 36, or 39.

Figure 11.12 shows part C of the script, which is the `ShowBinary` subprogram.

It is quite expected that some attribute values won't be in the property cache, and we don't want the whole script to stop running in this case. We need to take error control into our own hands with the `On Error` statement on line 46. It defines that if there is an error on some line, the script just continues running from the next line.

NOTE In theory, you can put the `On Error` statement just once in the beginning of the script. However, in practice it doesn't always work unless you put it in each subprogram that needs the feature.

WARNING The `On Error` statement hides also other errors besides ADSI-related ones. For example, it nullifies the effect of `Option Explicit` so you don't get any warning when you use undeclared variables.

In the case of an error, the `Number` property of the `Err` object contains the error code. Because that property is the default property of `Err`, we can use just "Err" instead of "Err.Number."

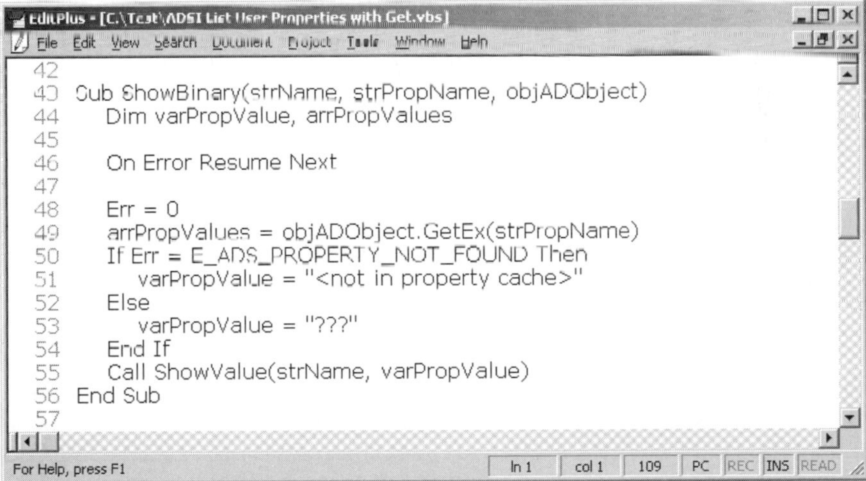

EditPlus - [C:\Test\ADSI List User Properties with Get.vbs]
File Edit View Search Document Project Tools Window Help
42
43 Sub ShowBinary(strName, strPropName, objADObject)
44 Dim varPropValue, arrPropValues
45
46 On Error Resume Next
47
48 Err = 0
49 arrPropValues = objADObject.GetEx(strPropName)
50 If Err = E_ADS_PROPERTY_NOT_FOUND Then
51 varPropValue = "<not in property cache>"
52 Else
53 varPropValue = "???"
54 End If
55 Call ShowValue(strName, varPropValue)
56 End Sub
57
For Help, press F1
ln 1 col 1 109 PC REC INS READ

Figure 11.12 Part C of "ADSI List User Properties with Get.vbs"

To detect an error, we perform the following steps:

1. On line 48 we set Err to 0.
2. On line 49 we try the possibly failing operation.
3. On line 50 we test if Err now contains the error code.

The error we may get just indicates that the property value is not in the property cache. We don't know if there is a value in Active Directory or not. Therefore, on line 51 we don't display <not set>, but only <not in property cache>. Even if there is a value, we are not interested enough in the value to add the extra lines that would retrieve and show it.

On line 55 we call the last subprogram that will show the property name and "value."

Figure 11.13 displays part D of the script, which contains the ShowLargeInteger subprogram.

The IADsLargeInteger interface could retrieve also multivalued properties, but there is only one such property in the base schema, and the user class doesn't use that property. Therefore, we don't add lines to handle this nonexisting situation, and just state this on line 64. Actually,

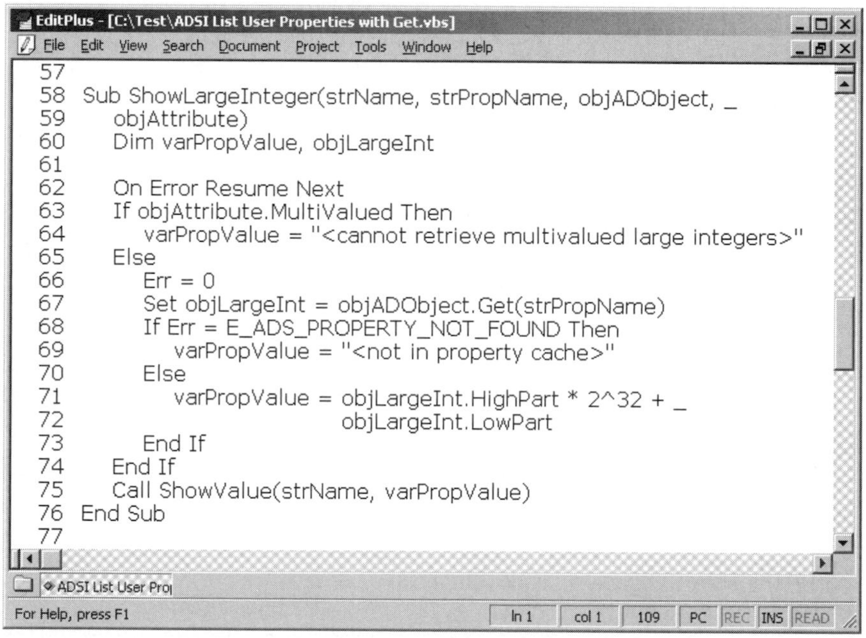

```
57
58 Sub ShowLargeInteger(strName, strPropName, objADObject, _
59    objAttribute)
60    Dim varPropValue, objLargeInt
61
62    On Error Resume Next
63    If objAttribute.MultiValued Then
64       varPropValue = "<cannot retrieve multivalued large integers>"
65    Else
66       Err = 0
67       Set objLargeInt = objADObject.Get(strPropName)
68       If Err = E_ADS_PROPERTY_NOT_FOUND Then
69          varPropValue = "<not in property cache>"
70       Else
71          varPropValue = objLargeInt.HighPart * 2^32 + _
72                         objLargeInt.LowPart
73       End If
74    End If
75    Call ShowValue(strName, varPropValue)
76 End Sub
77
```


Figure 11.13 Part D of "ADSI List User Properties with Get.vbs"

we should never get to line 64, so you would see the text only when you look at the script contents, not when you are running the script.

With single-valued attributes, we do the same error handling as in the previous subprogram, only this time we need to access the property with the `IADsLargeInteger` interface. We explained the procedure in the previous example involving property cache contents.

Figure 11.14 displays part E of the script. It contains a subprogram that handles all other data types.

This subprogram has a few additions, compared to the previous subprograms. On line 84 we use `GetEx`, which works with both single-valued and multivalued properties.

Lines 85 through 90 contain an extra step. If the property was not in the cache yet on line 84, we try to read it again from Active Directory with `GetInfoEx`. The result is that we will also get all constructed attributes. For `GetInfoEx` to work, we need to put the property name in an array (line 86) and add an extra 0 as a second argument. It is not used for anything, but it must be there.

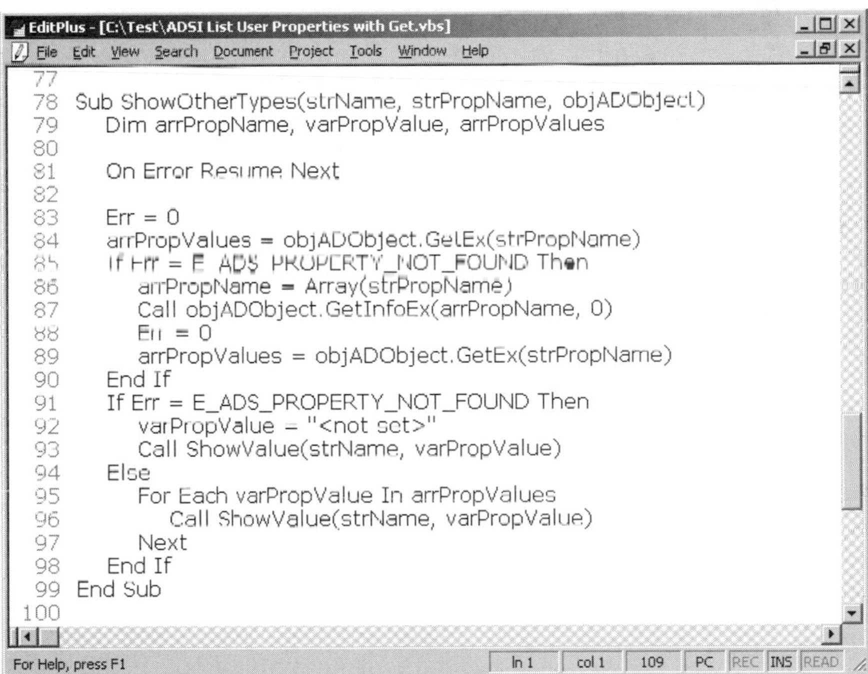

```
 77
 78 Sub ShowOtherTypes(strName, strPropName, objADObject)
 79    Dim arrPropName, varPropValue, arrPropValues
 80
 81    On Error Resume Next
 82
 83    Err = 0
 84    arrPropValues = objADObject.GetEx(strPropName)
 85    If Err = E_ADS_PROPERTY_NOT_FOUND Then
 86       arrPropName = Array(strPropName)
 87       Call objADObject.GetInfoEx(arrPropName, 0)
 88       Err = 0
 89       arrPropValues = objADObject.GetEx(strPropName)
 90    End If
 91    If Err = E_ADS_PROPERTY_NOT_FOUND Then
 92       varPropValue = "<not set>"
 93       Call ShowValue(strName, varPropValue)
 94    Else
 95       For Each varPropValue In arrPropValues
 96          Call ShowValue(strName, varPropValue)
 97       Next
 98    End If
 99 End Sub
100
```

Figure 11.14 Part E of "ADSI List User Properties with Get.vbs"

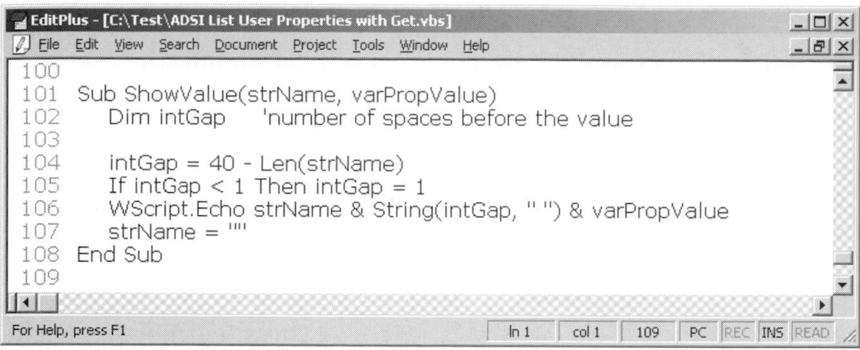

Figure 11.15 Part F of "ADSI List User Properties with Get.vbs"

If we still have an error on line 91, this time we know that the attribute really doesn't exist and we can display `<not set>` instead of the previous `<not in property cache>` text.

Because we used `GetEx`, whether there is a single value or multiple values they will always be in an array. As a result, we need to browse through this array on lines 95 through 97.

Figure 11.15 shows the last part of the script (part F), which is the subprogram that displays any results onscreen.

This part works in the same way as the display part of the previous example. On line 104 we count the number of spaces between the property name and value to align the values. On line 107 we clear the property name so that additional lines of multivalued properties will show just the value.

In this example, we used the explicit `Get` method and put the attribute LDAP name as an argument. This enabled us to get a list of 257 attribute names and feed them one at a time to be that argument. If we used the other syntax (e.g., `objUser.givenName`), we would have needed to include 257 such lines to our script. Additionally, that version would have worked only with user objects (and any subclasses). The current script will work with any object class.

List User Properties with Methods.vbs

In this example, we list the properties and values of user Guest for the third time. Now we use the static property methods of the `IADsUser` interface. This has the following implications:

- This script works sensibly only for user objects.
- We need to hard-code the static property method names into the script.
- We will get roughly 40 properties at the most.

Figure 11.16 shows the script's output. In this script, we don't align all the values to a certain column. We just put a tab character before each colon, so there is some aligning effect.

Many properties are missing from the output, because the corresponding attributes are not set in Active Directory and those static property methods return an error. However, some static property methods, such as `EmployeeID`, return an empty string in this case; therefore, they show in the output, although without a value.

NOTE The first property of the output in Figure 11.16 doesn't mean that the Guest account expired in 1970. The attribute value in the background is 9,223,372,036,854,775,807, which indicates that the account never expires (see the previous sample script). When the `AccountExpirationDate` static property method converts the value to a meaningful date, it converts that special value to 1/1/1970, which is the origin of date values in the C language. With normal expiration dates, the method shows the normal date.

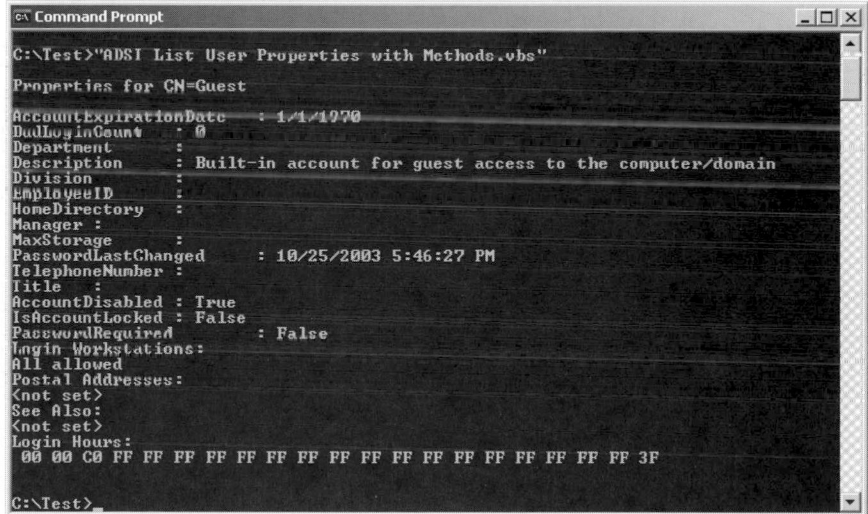

Figure 11.16 Output of "ADSI List User Properties with Methods.vbs." In contrast with the two previous examples, this figure shows all the lines of the script's output.

We show the script in five parts (Figures 11.17 through 11.21). Figure 11.17 shows part A.

Part A doesn't introduce anything new. Note that when we print the object name on line 14, that `Name` property is one of the general properties in the `IADs` interface.

Figure 11.18 shows part B of the script. It lists all the property methods that we can handle, each on one line.

We have a tab character before each colon in Figure 11.18, but we don't use the `vbTab` constant. Instead we just pressed the Tab key in the editor. This is a "quick and dirty" solution, but it makes the script look cleaner as long as the editor supports this feature.

NOTE The `description` attribute is defined in the schema to be multivalued, but the corresponding static property value exposes it as single-valued.

Figure 11.19 shows part C of the script, which handles `LoginWorkstations`.

In contrast with `Description`, `LoginWorkstations` is single-valued in the schema, but the static property method exposes it as multivalued.

If the corresponding property (`userWorkstations`) is not in the cache, it means that there are no workstation restrictions (line 59). Otherwise, there is an array of names, which we display on lines 61 through 63.

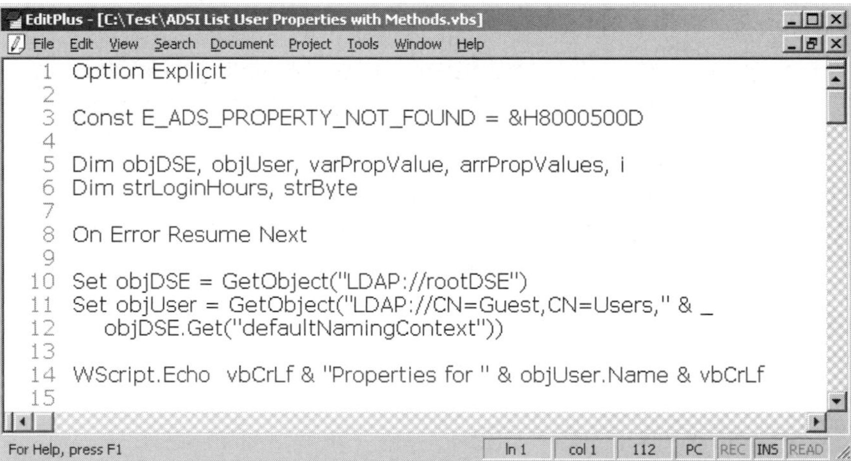

Figure 11.17 Part A of "ADSI List User Properties with Methods.vbs"

```
WScript.Echo "AccountExpirationDate : " & _
    objUser.AccountExpirationDate
WScript.Echo "BadLoginCount    : " & objUser.BadLoginCount
WScript.Echo "Department     : " & objUser.Department
WScript.Echo "Description : " & objUser.Description
WScript.Echo "Division : " & objUser.Division
WScript.Echo "EmailAddress  : " & objUser.EmailAddress
WScript.Echo "EmployeeID    : " & objUser.EmployeeID
WScript.Echo "FaxNumber : " & objUser.FaxNumber
WScript.Echo "FirstName   : " & objUser.FirstName
WScript.Echo "FullName    : " & objUser.FullName
WScript.Echo "HomeDirectory     : " & objUser.HomeDirectory
WScript.Echo "HomePage  : " & objUser.HomePage
WScript.Echo "Languages  : " & objUser.Languages
WScript.Echo "LastFailedLogin   : " & objUser.LastFailedLogin
WScript.Echo "LastLogin    : " & objUser.LastLogin
WScript.Echo "LastLogoff  : " & objUser.LastLogoff
WScript.Echo "LastName    : " & objUser.LastName
WScript.Echo "LoginScript : " & objUser.LoginScript
WScript.Echo "Manager : " & objUser.Manager
WScript.Echo "MaxStorage : " & objUser.MaxStorage
WScript.Echo "NamePrefix : " & objUser.NamePrefix
WScript.Echo "NameSuffix : " & objUser.NameSuffix
WScript.Echo "OfficeLocations    : " & objUser.OfficeLocations
WScript.Echo "OtherName : " & objUser.OtherName
WScript.Echo "PasswordLastChanged  : " & _
    objUser.PasswordLastChanged
WScript.Echo "Picture    : " & objUser.Picture
WScript.Echo "PostalCodes    : " & objUser.PostalCodes
WScript.Echo "Profile    : " & objUser.Profile
WScript.Echo "TelephoneHome   : " & objUser.TelephoneHome
WScript.Echo "TelephoneMobile : " & objUser.TelephoneMobile
WScript.Echo "TelephoneNumber    : " & objUser.TelephoneNumber
WScript.Echo "TelephonePager   : " & objUser.TelephonePager
WScript.Echo "Title   : " & objUser.Title
WScript.Echo "AccountDisabled  : " & objUser.AccountDisabled
WScript.Echo "IsAccountLocked  : " & objUser.IsAccountLocked
WScript.Echo "PasswordRequired    : " & objUser.PasswordRequired
```

Figure 11.18 Part B of "ADSI List User Properties with Methods.vbs"

Figure 11.20 shows part D of the script, which handles `PostalAddresses` and `SeeAlso`.

Whereas `LoginWorkstations` may return an error or an array, `PostalAddresses` and `SeeAlso` may return one of three things:

- `PostalAddresses`: 1) An error, 2) a string, or 3) an array
- `SeeAlso`: 1) `vbEmpty` (different from an empty string), 2) a string, or 3) an array

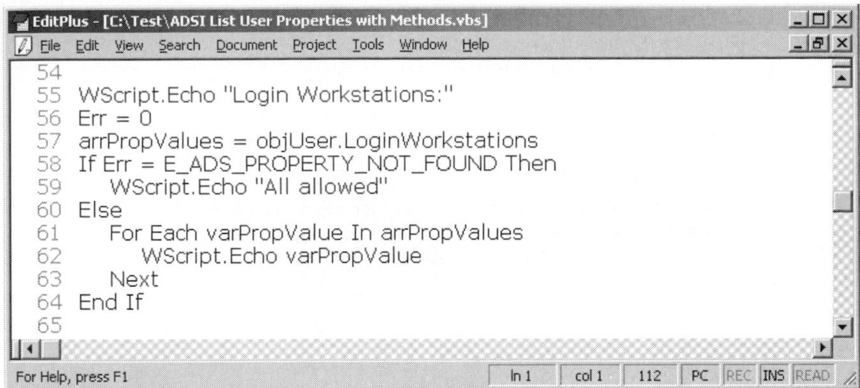

```
WScript.Echo "Login Workstations:"
Err = 0
arrPropValues = objUser.LoginWorkstations
If Err = E_ADS_PROPERTY_NOT_FOUND Then
   WScript.Echo "All allowed"
Else
   For Each varPropValue In arrPropValues
      WScript.Echo varPropValue
   Next
End If
```

Figure 11.19 Part C of "ADSI List User Properties with Methods.vbs"

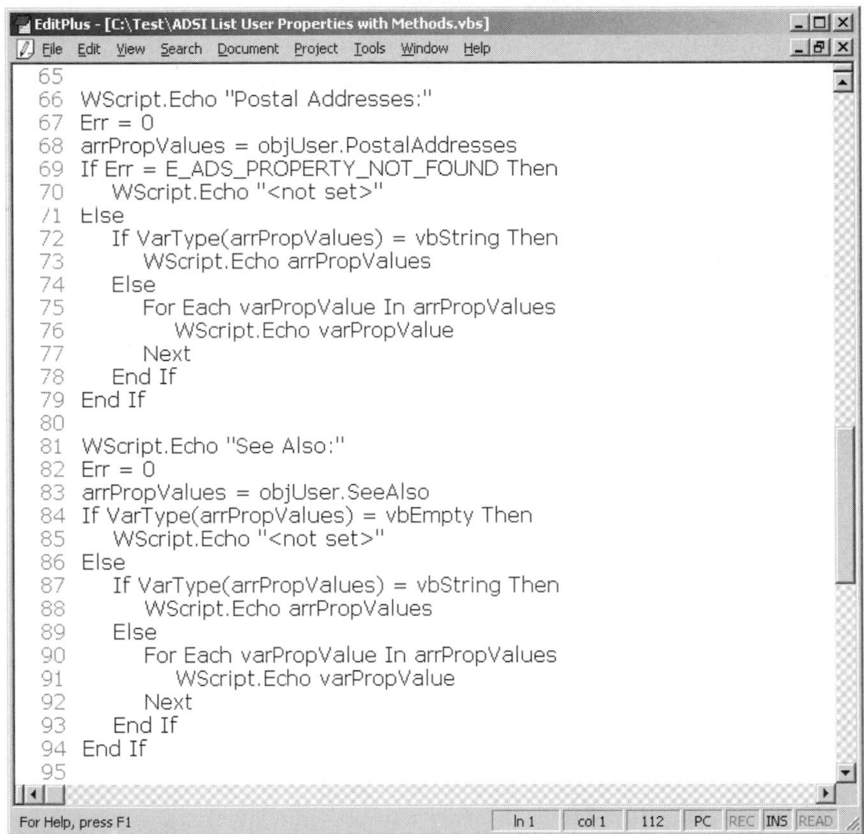

```
WScript.Echo "Postal Addresses:"
Err = 0
arrPropValues = objUser.PostalAddresses
If Err = E_ADS_PROPERTY_NOT_FOUND Then
   WScript.Echo "<not set>"
Else
   If VarType(arrPropValues) = vbString Then
      WScript.Echo arrPropValues
   Else
      For Each varPropValue In arrPropValues
         WScript.Echo varPropValue
      Next
   End If
End If

WScript.Echo "See Also:"
Err = 0
arrPropValues = objUser.SeeAlso
If VarType(arrPropValues) = vbEmpty Then
   WScript.Echo "<not set>"
Else
   If VarType(arrPropValues) = vbString Then
      WScript.Echo arrPropValues
   Else
      For Each varPropValue In arrPropValues
         WScript.Echo varPropValue
      Next
   End If
End If
```

Figure 11.20 Part D of "ADSI List User Properties with Methods.vbs"

Consequently, we need to adapt to these various possibilities on the lines shown in Figure 11.20.

NOTE You will probably never use `PostalAddresses` and `SeeAlso`, but we show the lines so that you can learn the different techniques to retrieve various values. Because Microsoft hasn't been very consistent with these static property methods, it offers a nice way to demonstrate all possible variations.

Figure 11.21 shows part E of the script, which is the last part. It displays the allowed logon hours.

Because each day has 24 hours, we need the bits of 3 bytes (3 × 8 = 24) to store the permit/deny settings for one day. For the whole week, we need 21 bytes (3 × 7 = 21).

Each permitted hour of the week is represented by bit "1" and each denied hour is represented by bit "0." If all times are permitted, that would mean 21 times hexadecimal "FF" bytes. Also, if the property is not set, all times are permitted.

The first 3 bytes correspond to Sunday, the next 3 to Monday, and so on.

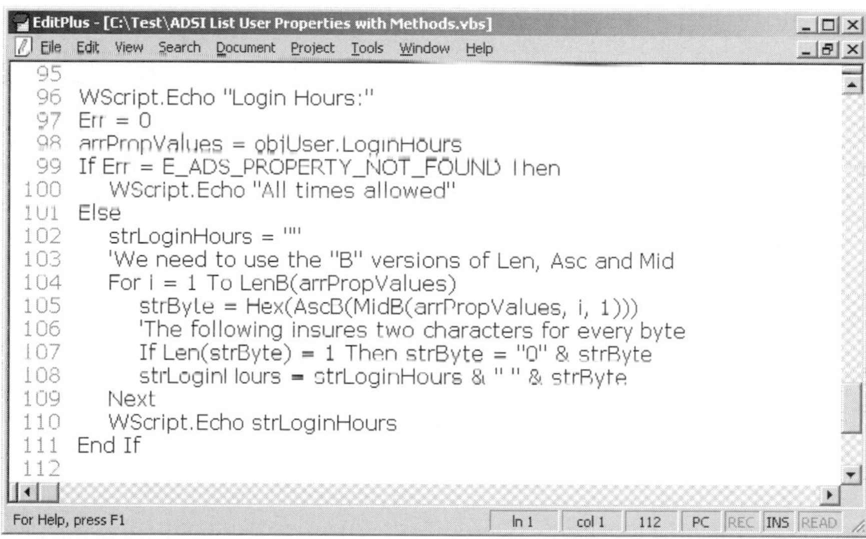
EditPlus - [C:\Test\ADSI List User Properties with Methods.vbs]
File Edit View Search Document Project Tools Window Help
WScript.Echo "Login Hours:"
Err = 0
arrPropValues = objUser.LoginHours
If Err = E_ADS_PROPERTY_NOT_FOUND Then
WScript.Echo "All times allowed"
Else
strLoginHours = ""
'We need to use the "B" versions of Len, Asc and Mid
For i = 1 To LenB(arrPropValues)
strByte = Hex(AscB(MidB(arrPropValues, i, 1)))
'The following insures two characters for every byte
If Len(strByte) = 1 Then strByte = "0" & strByte
strLoginHours = strLoginHours & " " & strByte
Next
WScript.Echo strLoginHours
End If
For Help, press F1
ln 1
col 1
112
PC
REC
INS
READ

Figure 11.21 Part E of "ADSI List User Properties with Methods.vbs"

The 21 bytes are returned in a binary array `arrPropValues`. We browse through the array from the start up to its length (i.e., `LenB`) and convert each byte to a hexadecimal number.

VBScript is not well suited to handling binary data types, but we are still able to read the value properly. We need to use the binary versions (or "B" versions) of the functions `Len`, `Mid`, and `Asc`, and the resulting line 105 looks a little complicated.

TIP If you need to manage complicated binary data in your scripts, you can find some tips at `http://www.pstruh.cz/tips/detpg_binarytostring.htm`. This Web page also contains a shareware COM component, ScriptUtilities, that among other things includes functions to handle binary data.

The bits of the `logonHours` attribute are stored in UTC/GMT time. When you define the permitted logon hours in the Users and Computers snap-in, the tool will take into account your time zone, but not any daylight saving time setting. For example, if you deny Sunday from a user, and you are in a time zone UTC + 2 and have DST + 1 also on, the tool will make a 2-hour correction instead of the 3-hour correction.

WARNING When you retrieve the permitted logon hours with `LoginHours`, that static property method doesn't use any time zone correction, so you should do this in your script. Guest in our sample domain is not allowed to log on on Sundays (for a time zone UTC + 2). You can see this restriction when you look at the script output in Figure 11.16. The first three bytes (i.e., Sunday) are "almost zero." However, in the output there are bytes "C0" and "3F." They are in binary "1100 0000" and "0011 1111," meaning a 2-hour difference.

List the Account Options of a User.vbs

There is one user attribute, `userAccountControl`, that is a 32-bit number. It contains a number of account options, one in each bit of the number. In this script we explore those options. There are also account options that are stored in other attributes, as explained in this section.

Figure 11.22 shows the script's output. First we display the three settings that the `IADsUser` static property methods can provide us. Note that in Windows 2000, the third method (`IsAccountLocked`) does not work, but in Windows Server 2003, it does work.

```
Command Prompt

C:\Test>"ADSI List the Account Options of a User.vbs"

Account Options for CN=Guest

=== With Property Methods ===

AccountDisabled : True
PasswordRequired        : False
IsAccountLocked : False

=== With userAccountControl ===

UserAccountControl value is 66082 (hex 10222)

Account locked out       : False

User must change password at next logon: False
User cannot change password       : Determined by Change Password ACEs
Password never expires   : True
Store password using reversible encryption       : False
Account is disabled      : True
Smart card is required for interactive logon     : False
Account is trusted for delegation        : False
Account is sensitive and cannot be delegated     : False
Use DES encryption types for this account        : False
Do not require Kerberos pre-authentication       : False

Password not required    : True
Password expired         : False
The Delegation Tab: Use any authentication protocol      : False
MNS_LOGON_ACCOUNT        : False
Not used: Logon script required : False
Not used: Home folder required  : False
Not used: Account locked out    : False
Not used: UF_PASSWD_CANT_CHANGE : False

C:\Test>_
```

Figure 11.22 The output of "ADSI List the Account Options of a User.vbs"

Then we display the `userAccountControl` attribute value, both in decimal (here "66082") and hexadecimal (here "10222"). If you enter one of these values in Windows Calculator and convert it to binary (in Scientific view), you will get a result of "1 0000 0010 0010 0010." As you probably know, each hex character corresponds to 4 bits.

The next 11 lines mimic the Users and Computers snap-in, using the same text labels and order that appear in the Account tab of a user object. The one exception is that if your domain is on the Windows Server 2003 functional level, the "Account is trusted for delegation" setting would appear on the Delegation tab instead of the Account tab.

The last eight lines are not visible in the snap-in (except the one in the Delegation tab), and of them Active Directory doesn't use the last four lines. The requirement for logon script and home folder was used over ten years ago in LAN Manager. `UF_PASSWD_CANT_CHANGE` was still used in Windows NT, but now in Active Directory the ACL in the user object determines if the user can change his password.

"Account locked out" appears twice in the output. The first occurrence displays the actual value from the `lockoutTime` attribute. The second occurrence is listed as "Not used," because it corresponds to the

UF_LOCKOUT bit in userAccountControl, but that is not used in Active Directory anymore.

NOTE Even though you cannot set "Password not required" with the Users and Computers snap-in, you can do so with the command NET USER JackB /passwordreq:no. The name "JackB" here is the pre–Windows 2000 name of the user.

WARNING You can also use the command NET USER JackB /passwordchg:no to state "User cannot change password." In Windows 2000 this command, however, changes JackB's ACEs more than needed by removing other permissions from the list in addition to the one it should remove. This may or may not harm you, but you are better off using just the graphical tool for this setting.

We show the script in three parts (Figures 11.23 through 11.25). Figure 11.23 displays part A.

Twenty-one of the possible 32 bits in userAccountControl are defined and they are listed in Figure 11.23 as constant definitions. The constant names and values are copied from the ADSI documentation. They also appear in the file lmaccess.h, which is part of the Platform SDK. "UF" stands for "user flags." Each hexadecimal value corresponds to 1 bit. If you want to find out which bit, you can again use Windows Calculator.

The 5 bits on lines 21 through 25 are not actual account options, but they indicate the account type. Each account should be one of the five types and consequently have one of the bits set. Line 27 contains a VBScript error code definition, which we need later in the script.

Figure 11.24 shows part B of the script.

There is no bit in userAccountControl that indicates whether or not the account is locked. This is defined in the lockoutTime attribute instead. If the attribute value is not set (corresponding to line 40) or equals 0, the account is not locked out. If the value is nonzero, the account is locked, as we test on line 43. Because the attribute is a large integer, we need line 38 to retrieve it in an object variable. We also need to include the error handling, because if the attribute value is not set, it will cause a VBScript error.

If the value of the pwdLastSet attribute is 0, the user must change his or her password at the next logon. This attribute is also a large

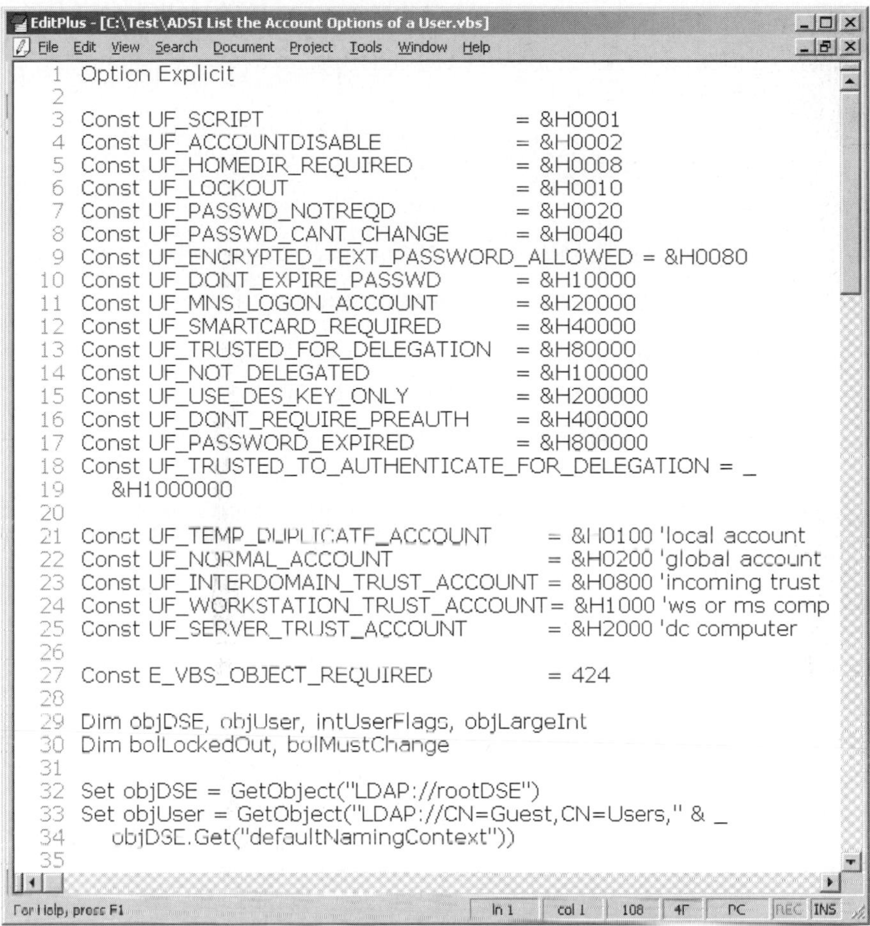

```
EditPlus - [C:\Test\ADSI List the Account Options of a User.vbs]
File Edit View Search Document Project Tools Window Help
 1 Option Explicit
 2
 3 Const UF_SCRIPT                          = &H0001
 4 Const UF_ACCOUNTDISABLE                  = &H0002
 5 Const UF_HOMEDIR_REQUIRED                = &H0008
 6 Const UF_LOCKOUT                         = &H0010
 7 Const UF_PASSWD_NOTREQD                  = &H0020
 8 Const UF_PASSWD_CANT_CHANGE              = &H0040
 9 Const UF_ENCRYPTED_TEXT_PASSWORD_ALLOWED = &H0080
10 Const UF_DONT_EXPIRE_PASSWD              = &H10000
11 Const UF_MNS_LOGON_ACCOUNT               = &H20000
12 Const UF_SMARTCARD_REQUIRED              = &H40000
13 Const UF_TRUSTED_FOR_DELEGATION          = &H80000
14 Const UF_NOT_DELEGATED                   = &H100000
15 Const UF_USE_DES_KEY_ONLY                = &H200000
16 Const UF_DONT_REQUIRE_PREAUTH            = &H400000
17 Const UF_PASSWORD_EXPIRED                = &H800000
18 Const UF_TRUSTED_TO_AUTHENTICATE_FOR_DELEGATION = _
19    &H1000000
20
21 Const UF_TEMP_DUPLICATE_ACCOUNT          = &H0100 'local account
22 Const UF_NORMAL_ACCOUNT                  = &H0200 'global account
23 Const UF_INTERDOMAIN_TRUST_ACCOUNT = &H0800 'incoming trust
24 Const UF_WORKSTATION_TRUST_ACCOUNT= &H1000 'ws or ms comp
25 Const UF_SERVER_TRUST_ACCOUNT            = &H2000 'dc computer
26
27 Const E_VBS_OBJECT_REQUIRED              = 424
28
29 Dim objDSE, objUser, intUserFlags, objLargeInt
30 Dim bolLockedOut, bolMustChange
31
32 Set objDSE = GetObject("LDAP://rootDSE")
33 Set objUser = GetObject("LDAP://CN=Guest,CN=Users," & _
34    objDSE.Get("defaultNamingContext"))
35
For Help, press F1   In 1   col 1   108   4F   PC   REC   INS
```

Figure 11.23 Part A of "ADSI List the Account Options of a User.vbs"

`integer`, so we need lines 47 through 49 to check if this setting is on and store the result in the Boolean variable `bolMustChange`.

On line 61 we retrieve the value of `userAccountControl`, and on lines 63 and 64 we display it in decimal and hexadecimal. We would display it also in binary if there were a function for it in VBScript.

Figure 11.25 displays the last part of the script (part C). It shows the value of each setting.

Each of the `UF` constants has 1 bit set (i.e., "1") and all other bits not set (i.e., "0"). To find out if the corresponding setting is on in `userAccountControl`, we need to do a bitwise logical `And` operation

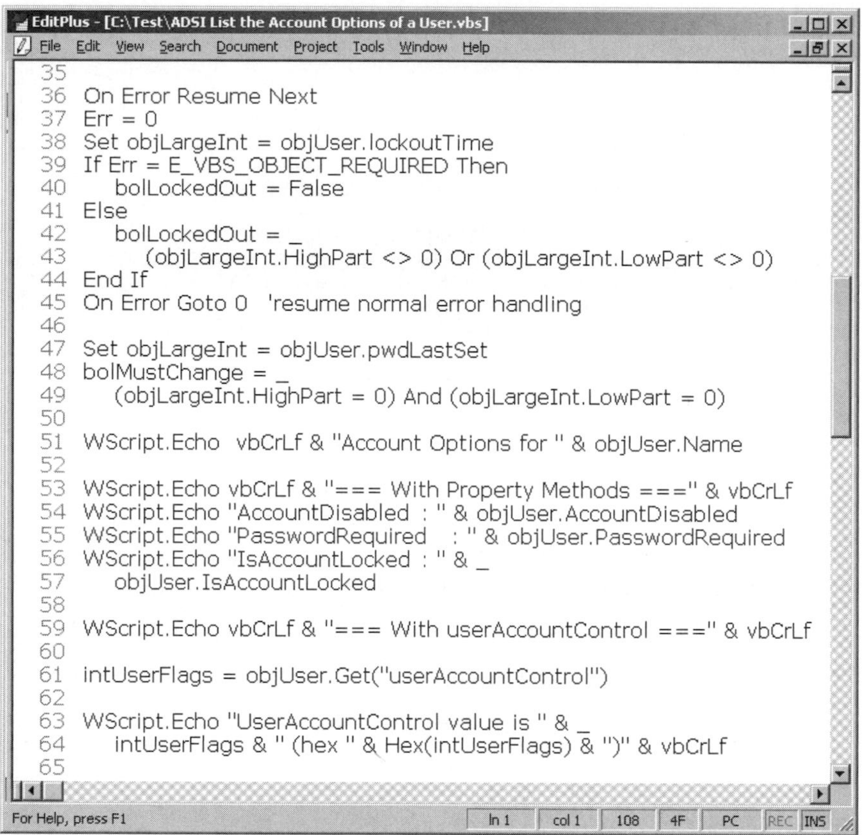

EditPlus - [C:\Test\ADSI List the Account Options of a User.vbs]

```
35
36 On Error Resume Next
37 Err = 0
38 Set objLargeInt = objUser.lockoutTime
39 If Err = E_VBS_OBJECT_REQUIRED Then
40    bolLockedOut = False
41 Else
42    bolLockedOut = _
43       (objLargeInt.HighPart <> 0) Or (objLargeInt.LowPart <> 0)
44 End If
45 On Error Goto 0  'resume normal error handling
46
47 Set objLargeInt = objUser.pwdLastSet
48 bolMustChange = _
49    (objLargeInt.HighPart = 0) And (objLargeInt.LowPart = 0)
50
51 WScript.Echo  vbCrLf & "Account Options for " & objUser.Name
52
53 WScript.Echo vbCrLf & "=== With Property Methods ===" & vbCrLf
54 WScript.Echo "AccountDisabled : " & objUser.AccountDisabled
55 WScript.Echo "PasswordRequired   : " & objUser.PasswordRequired
56 WScript.Echo "IsAccountLocked : " & _
57    objUser.IsAccountLocked
58
59 WScript.Echo vbCrLf & "=== With userAccountControl ===" & vbCrLf
60
61 intUserFlags = objUser.Get("userAccountControl")
62
63 WScript.Echo "UserAccountControl value is " & _
64    intUserFlags & " (hex " & Hex(intUserFlags) & ")" & vbCrLf
65
```

For Help, press F1 | ln 1 | col 1 | 108 | 4F | PC | REC | INS

Figure 11.24 Part B of "ADSI List the Account Options of a User.vbs"

between the two (see Figure 11.25). If the result is zero, the setting is off, and if the result is nonzero, the setting is on.

For example, if `userAccountControl` (stored in `intUserFlags`) is "1 0000 0010 0010 0000" and `UF_DONT_EXPIRE_PASSWD` is "&H10000" or binary "1 0000 0000 0000 0000," the `And` between those two is "1 0000 0000 0000 0000," meaning that the setting is on.

Line 73 performs this check for the "Password never expires" setting and the consequent lines for all other settings. On lines 66 and 69 we can use the results that we calculated in part B.

Whether a user can change his password or not is determined by the access control ACEs in the user object. We don't start to inspect them here, so on line 71 we just state this.

EditPlus - [C:\Test\ADSI List the Account Options of a User.vbs]

```
WScript.Echo "Account locked out  : " & bolLockedOut
WScript.Echo ""
WScript.Echo "User must change password at next logon: " & _
   bolMustChange
WScript.Echo "User cannot change password   : " & _
   "Determined by Change Password ACEs"
WScript.Echo "Password never expires    : " & _
   ((intUserFlags And UF_DONT_EXPIRE_PASSWD) <> 0)
WScript.Echo "Store password using reversible encryption : " & _
   ((intUserFlags And _
   UF_ENCRYPTED_TEXT_PASSWORD_ALLOWED) <> 0)
WScript.Echo "Account is disabled  : " & _
   ((intUserFlags And UF_ACCOUNTDISABLE) <> 0)
WScript.Echo "Smart card is required for interactive logon : " & _
   ((intUserFlags And UF_SMARTCARD_REQUIRED) <> 0)
WScript.Echo "Account is trusted for delegation    : " & _
   ((intUserFlags And UF_TRUSTED_FOR_DELEGATION) <> 0)
WScript.Echo "Account is sensitive and cannot be delegated  : " & _
   ((intUserFlags And UF_NOT_DELEGATED) <> 0)
WScript.Echo "Use DES encryption types for this account   : " & _
   ((intUserFlags And UF_USE_DES_KEY_ONLY) <> 0)
WScript.Echo "Do not require Kerberos pre-authentication : " & _
   ((intUserFlags And UF_DONT_REQUIRE_PREAUTH) <> 0)
WScript.Echo ""
WScript.Echo "Password not required  : " & _
   ((intUserFlags And UF_PASSWD_NOTREQD) <> 0)
WScript.Echo "Password expired: " & _
   ((intUserFlags And UF_PASSWORD_EXPIRED) <> 0)
WScript.Echo _
   "The Delegation Tab: Use any authentication protocol  : " & _
   ((intUserFlags And _
   UF_TRUSTED_TO_AUTHENTICATE_FOR_DELEGATION) <> 0)
WScript.Echo "MNS_LOGON_ACCOUNT    : " &
   ((intUserFlags And UF_MNS_LOGON_ACCOUNT) <> 0)
WScript.Echo "Not used: Logon script required : " & _
   ((intUserFlags And UF_SCRIPT) <> 0)
WScript.Echo "Not used: Home folder required : " & _
   ((intUserFlags And UF_HOMEDIR_REQUIRED) <> 0)
WScript.Echo "Not used: Account locked out    : " & _
   ((intUserFlags And UF_LOCKOUT) <> 0)
WScript.Echo "Not used: UF_PASSWD_CANT_CHANGE   : " & _
   ((intUserFlags And UF_PASSWD_CANT_CHANGE) <> 0)
```

For Help, press F1 | ln 1 | col 1 | 108 | 4F | PC | REC | INS

Figure 11.25 Part C of "ADSI List the Account Options of a User.vbs"

Create a User with Minimum Attributes.vbs

So far we haven't made any changes in our Active Directory—we have just listed objects and their properties. In this example, we create 1 user or 100 users, but we use only the more or less mandatory attributes (not quite the same as what the schema lists as mandatory attributes).

We could, of course, add some output to indicate that the "command completed successfully," but at present, this script doesn't display anything.

Figure 11.26 shows the script's contents.

We put the actual creation as a subprogram (lines 13 through 27) so that you can call it either one time or several times. Currently, lines 7 through 11 are commented out, but if you uncomment them, they will create users Uu00, Uu01, Uu02, and so on, up to Uu99.

Now the usernames are hard-coded in the script, but you could use a command-line argument or an input box to get the names, as shown in earlier examples. A couple of examples later, we also show how to read the usernames from Excel (see the "Read User Information from Excel.xls" section).

We need to bind to the container where the user will appear, and we do this on lines 16 and 17. Next, on line 19 we use the `Create` method of `IADsContainer` to create a class `user` object with a common name `CN=whatever`.

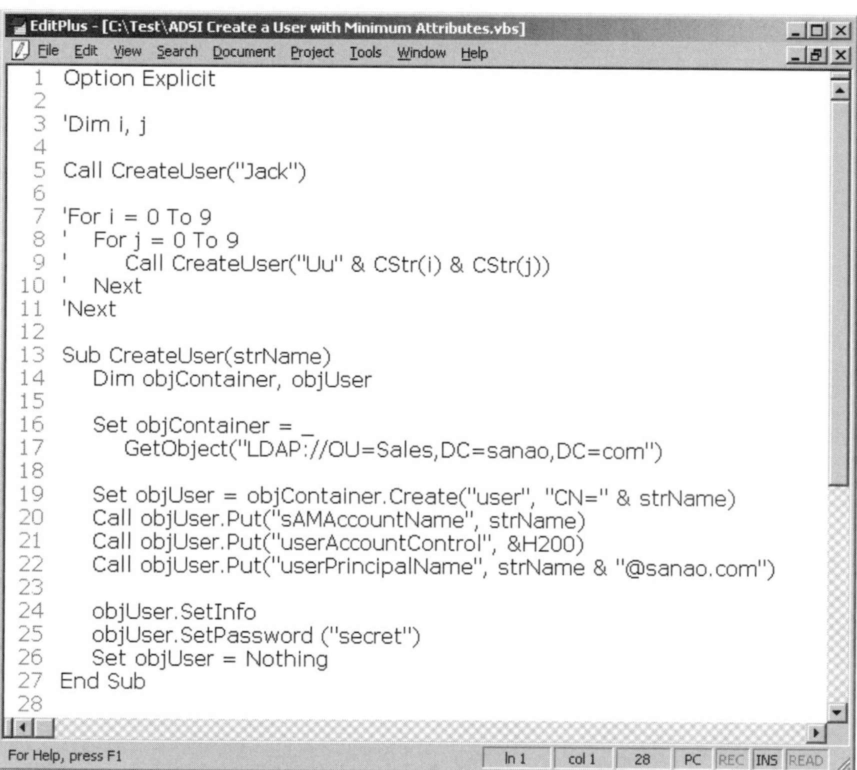


```
1  Option Explicit
2
3  'Dim i, j
4
5  Call CreateUser("Jack")
6
7  'For i = 0 To 9
8  '   For j = 0 To 9
9  '      Call CreateUser("Uu" & CStr(i) & CStr(j))
10 '   Next
11 'Next
12
13 Sub CreateUser(strName)
14    Dim objContainer, objUser
15
16    Set objContainer = _
17       GetObject("LDAP://OU=Sales,DC=sanao,DC=com")
18
19    Set objUser = objContainer.Create("user", "CN=" & strName)
20    Call objUser.Put("sAMAccountName", strName)
21    Call objUser.Put("userAccountControl", &H200)
22    Call objUser.Put("userPrincipalName", strName & "@sanao.com")
23
24    objUser.SetInfo
25    objUser.SetPassword ("secret")
26    Set objUser = Nothing
27 End Sub
28
```

Figure 11.26 Contents of "ADSI Create a User with Minimum Attributes.vbs"

Before we write this from the property cache back to Active Directory with the `SetInfo` method (line 24), we need to set some attributes. `SAMAccountName` on line 20 is a mandatory attribute. `UserAccountControl` and `userPrincipalName` are not mandatory in the schema, but we want to set them anyway.

`SAMAccountName` corresponds to the pre–Windows 2000 logon name. With Windows 2000, you must provide one, but with Windows Server 2003, if you don't provide any, a random name is generated. You shouldn't rely on this, because the random name is quite difficult for the user to use (although she could use only the UPN). The pre–Windows 2000 logon name is used also here and there in other places, such as the user's profile folder and the user's directory object quota definition.

The ADSI default for `userAccountControl` is hexadecimal "222" (password not required, account disabled), but the Users and Computers snap-in default for `userAccountControl` is hexadecimal "200" (password required, account enabled). With the setting on line 21, we are using the same value as the latter default.

We want to set the UPN because the graphical tool also requires it and we want to ensure that all users can log on with a UPN.

TIP If you don't want to hard-code your enterprise name (such as `sanao.com`), you can read the value from the `dnsRoot` attribute of the object `CN=Enterprise Configuration, CN=Partitions, CN=Configuration, DC=`*`<yourforestname>`*`, DC=com`. If you want to use other UPN suffixes (defined in the Domains and Trusts snap-in), you can use the `uPNSuffixes` attribute of the object `CN=Partitions, CN=Configuration, DC=`*`<yourforestname>`*`, DC=com`.

NOTE If you run the script in a domain that has a password policy of a minimum password length and/or a requirement of complex passwords, you will get the error "The server is unwilling to process the request." The next example, for creating a user with more attributes, presents a solution.

After you have called `SetInfo` on line 24, you can set the password with the `SetPassword` method on the next line.

On line 26 we release the object that we have used. This also releases any memory it has used. This is actually not needed, because when our script completes, all variables are released anyway and so is all memory. We put line 26 there to symbolize that now we are done with the object. Another reason is that we wanted to tell you about it because the Nothing line appears in many sample scripts that you run into in various sources.

Create a User with More Attributes.vbs

In this example, we expand the user creation process by including many more attributes, as is likely the need in the real world. Of course, we cannot know which of the 257 attributes you are going to use, so we've picked the most representative attributes to demonstrate various techniques and because you are more likely to use them as the remaining attributes.

As with the previous example, the creation process is a subprogram and the username is hard-coded. Again, you can use command-line arguments, input boxes, or Excel to get the usernames.

We show the script in three parts (Figures 11.27 through 11.29). Part A is in Figure 11.27.

The first part is almost similar to the previous "minimum attributes" example. In addition, on lines 3 through 6 we define four user flags, which we are going to use later. We assign the user a common name, "lastname firstname," but later on line 58 we assign the `displayName` as "firstname lastname." Whether you will do the same obviously depends on how your e-mail application and other applications use either the common name or the display name.

On line 21 we generate a SAM name like "JackB." After writing the creation and first settings back to Active Directory (line 28), we need to (or at least it is very preferable to) refresh the property cache on line 30 to also get all predefined or default values.

On lines 23 and 24 we set three user flags by summing up three individual flag values and writing the result in the `userAccountControl` attribute.

- The first "normal account" flag specifies that the user will be a normal "global" user account in contrast to a "local" user account. The latter account type could be used in Windows NT, but now, user accounts are always global. Actually, even if you don't specify the "normal account" flag, it will appear in the created user account.
- The second user flag specifies that a password is not required for this user. Without this setting, it would not be possible to create a user account in a domain where password policy requires a mini-

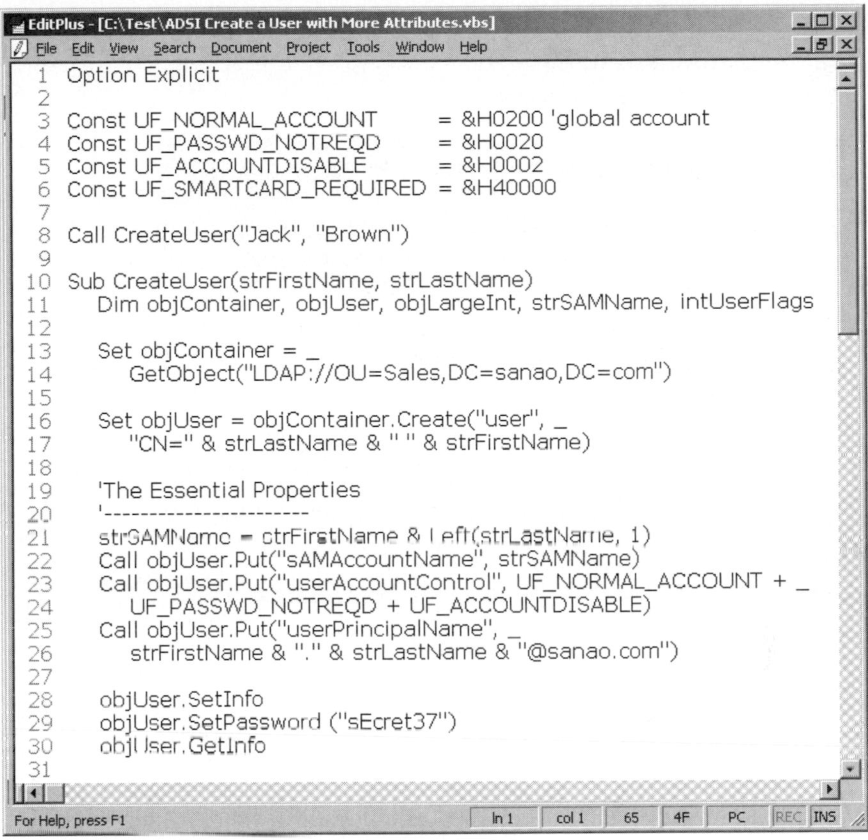


```
1  Option Explicit
2
3  Const UF_NORMAL_ACCOUNT      = &H0200 'global account
4  Const UF_PASSWD_NOTREQD      = &H0020
5  Const UF_ACCOUNTDISABLE      = &H0002
6  Const UF_SMARTCARD_REQUIRED = &H40000
7
8  Call CreateUser("Jack", "Brown")
9
10 Sub CreateUser(strFirstName, strLastName)
11    Dim objContainer, objUser, objLargeInt, strSAMName, intUserFlags
12
13    Set objContainer = _
14       GetObject("LDAP://OU=Sales,DC=sanao,DC=com")
15
16    Set objUser = objContainer.Create("user", _
17       "CN=" & strLastName & " " & strFirstName)
18
19    'The Essential Properties
20    '------------------------
21    strSAMName = strFirstName & Left(strLastName, 1)
22    Call objUser.Put("sAMAccountName", strSAMName)
23    Call objUser.Put("userAccountControl", UF_NORMAL_ACCOUNT + _
24       UF_PASSWD_NOTREQD + UF_ACCOUNTDISABLE)
25    Call objUser.Put("userPrincipalName", _
26       strFirstName & "." & strLastName & "@sanao.com")
27
28    objUser.SetInfo
29    objUser.SetPassword ("sEcret37")
30    objUser.GetInfo
31
```

Figure 11.27 Part A of "ADSI Create a User with More Attributes.vbs"

mum password length and/or complex passwords (we would get the error "The server is unwilling to process the request"). Later in the script, we reverse the setting (line 49), so the user is actually required to have a password.

- The third user flag causes the user account to be disabled. We can later enable it, once we first set a password for it (on line 29). This is just a precaution that if—for some reason—the script were not able to set a password, there wouldn't be an enabled user account without a password.

Figure 11.28 shows part B of the script, which sets the rest of the significant properties (for a description of the differences between significant and informational properties, see Chapter 3).

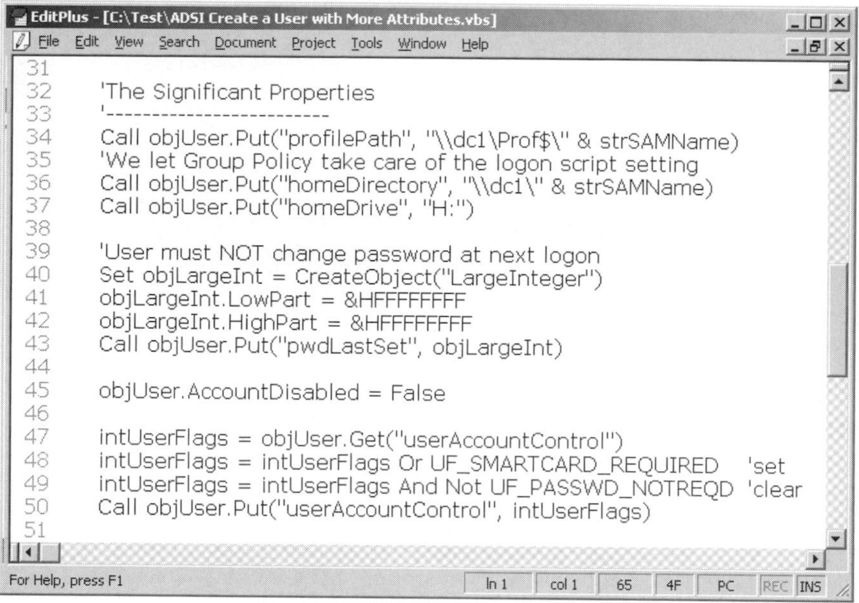

Figure 11.28 Part B of "ADSI Create a User with More Attributes.vbs"

On lines 34 through 37 we set the usual paths, but we leave the logon script name to be defined in Group Policy. Because the `Prof$` share name has a dollar sign as the last character, that share is hidden so that our users don't mess with the files and folders in that share.

In this example, we don't want to require the user to change her password at the next logon, so we need to write the value of –1 to `pwdLastSet`. In hexadecimal, that value is all Fs. On lines 40 through 43 we set the appropriate value to this `large integer` property.

NOTE `PwdLastSet` normally indicates when the user changed her password the last time. If you later write 0 to it to indicate that the user must again change her password at the next logon, or if you set it back to –1 to relieve the user from having to change her password at the next logon, the actual last change time is lost. When you write –1 to this attribute, what actually gets stored is the current date and time.

Originally we created the user account as a disabled account, but because on line 29 we set a password for it, now on line 45 it is safe to enable the account. Because there is a corresponding static propery method (`AccountDisabled`), we don't have to manipulate a single bit of `userAccountControl` (as we do on the consequent lines 47 through 50).

On line 48 we turn on the smart card requirement by using the `Or` operator. Before that, we needed to read the current property into a variable so that the `Or` operator will change just 1 bit. Next, on line 49 we clear a `userAccountControl` bit, replacing `Or` with `And` and adding a `Not` in front of the flag constant. This removes the "password not required" setting, so a password is required from now on.

Figure 11.29 shows the third and last part of the script (part C). It sets all the desired informational properties.

We don't need to use `PutEx` even for multivalued attributes, such as the one on line 60, because we don't need to use any special flags (`append` and so on).

Note that we store the first letter of the firstname and lastname (such as "JB" for "Jack Brown") in the `initials` attribute, whereas the Users and Computers snap-in uses that attribute to store the middle name initial.

In this example, we defined a home folder and roaming profile folder path for the user but didn't create either one. After the next example, we present two short sample scripts that address creating a home folder. We don't need to worry about the roaming profile folder, because the user's workstation creates it automatically when the user logs on for the first time.

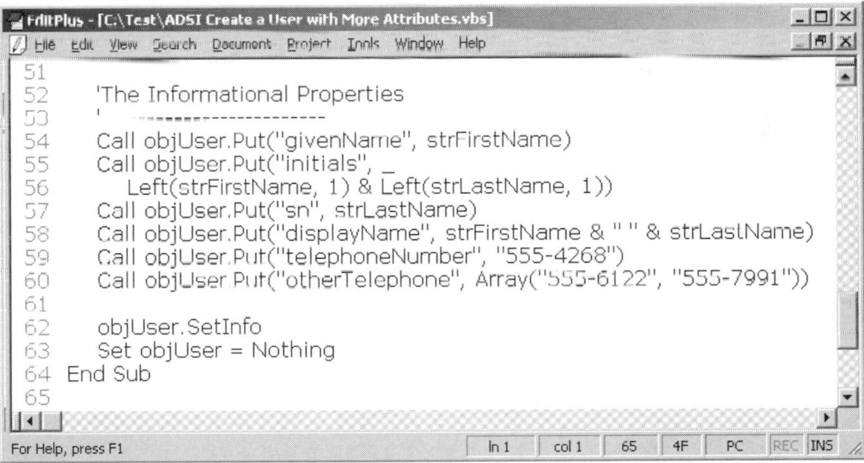

Figure 11.29 Part C of "ADSI Create a User with More Attributes.vbs"

Create a User with a Batch File.bat

Our next three examples use some traditional command-line commands instead of pure scripting. For a comparison to WSH + VBScript, we first want to show a batch file that creates a user.

The motivation behind this comparison is the fact that sometimes you have to use traditional commands in your scripts, and sometimes you don't have to, but if you do so, it is somewhat easier to get the job done. You get the most obvious benefits of using commands in the scripts when managing folders and their permissions. For a comparison, see the "pure WSH + VBScript + ADSI" approach discussed in the "Add ACEs to a Folder.vbs" section.

This example of creating a user is much shorter and simpler than a WSH script. Figure 11.30 shows the batch file.

You would launch the batch file with a command like the following (with a shortened filename):

```
createuser Jack Brown
```

The arguments `Jack` and `Brown` will replace `%1` and `%2` in the batch file when it runs. Lines 6 through 9 add the user, line 12 creates a home folder, and line 15 grants the user the Change permission for the new

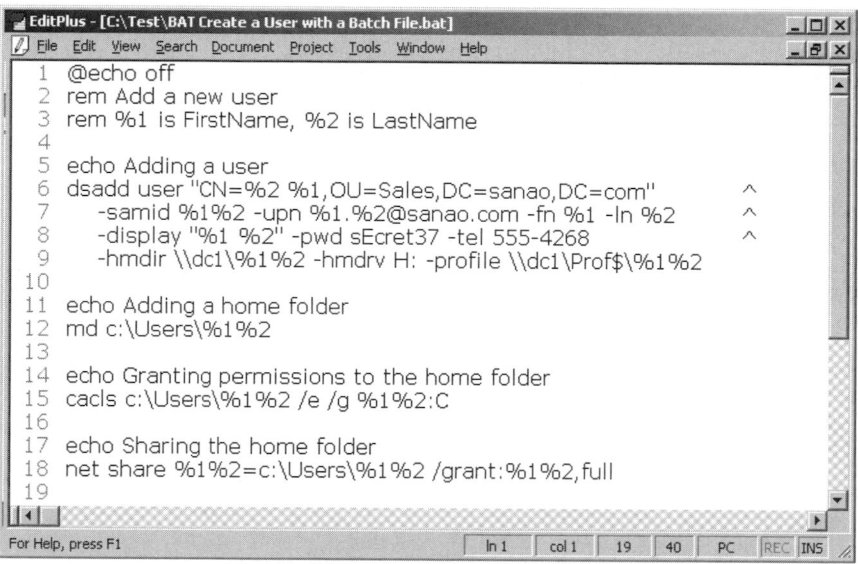

Figure 11.30 The batch file "BAT Create a User with a Batch File.bat"

folder. The /e option means "edit"—that is, previous permissions are not removed. Finally, on line 18 the new home folder is shared with the same sharename as the user's username, and the user is given full control for the share.

The DSAdd command was introduced in Windows Server 2003, but the other commands were available already in Windows NT (and Windows 2000). The carets (^) on lines 6 through 8 indicate that the command continues on the next line.

TIP You can get help with the commands `DSADD USER /?` and `CACLS /?`.

WARNING CACLS has a potential problem. It doesn't understand permission inheritance available in Windows 2000 and later, so in some cases the tool blocks permission inheritance without asking or warning you. Such cases are if you use CACLS to assign permission without the /e option (i.e., replace all permissions) or replace certain permissions with the /p option. Also, in Windows 2000 prior to Service Pack 2, CACLS may order ACEs incorrectly, and when you open such a permission list in ACL Editor, you'll receive a warning: "The permissions on *folder* are incorrectly ordered, which may cause some entries to be ineffective."

NOTE Other command-line tools for permission management are XCACLS in the Windows Resource Kit and FILEDACLS.PL in the Windows 2000 Resource Kit Supplement 1.

Create a Home Folder for a User - Ver 1.vbs

This sample script creates a home folder for a user, grants some permissions for it, and shares the folder. We use the same commands as in the previous batch example, and the script launches the commands with the `Run` method of the `WshShell` object. That method allows us to start new programs, such as Notepad, or some command-line command. Figure 11.31 shows the script.

In order to be able to use the `WshShell` object, we need to instantiate one on line 11. Then we need three commands for our home folder task, so we store them in a three-element array on lines 15 through 18. Finally, on lines 20 through 22 we run each command as a hidden window and wait for each command to complete before moving to the next one.

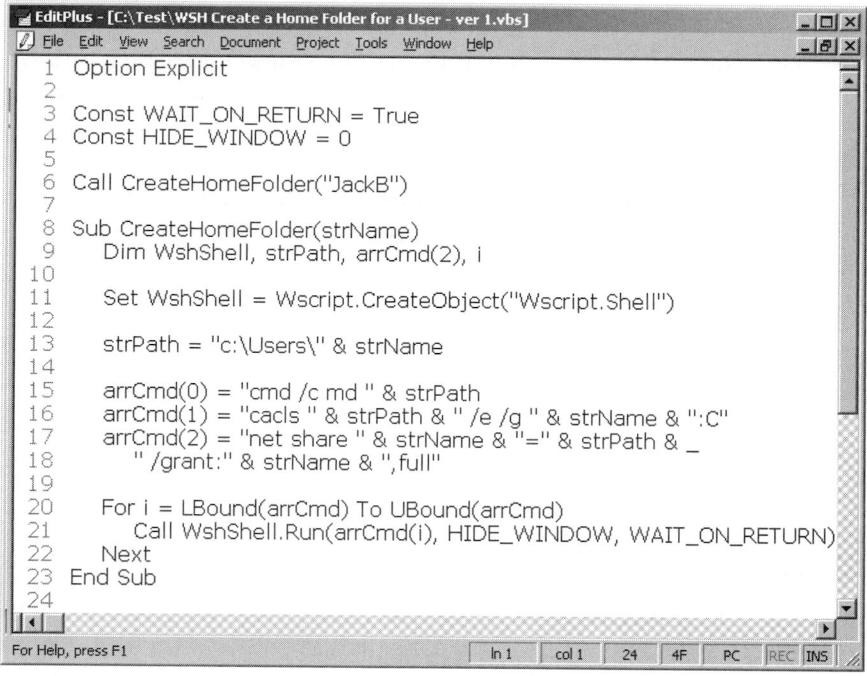

```
Option Explicit

Const WAIT_ON_RETURN = True
Const HIDE_WINDOW = 0

Call CreateHomeFolder("JackB")

Sub CreateHomeFolder(strName)
   Dim WshShell, strPath, arrCmd(2), i

   Set WshShell = Wscript.CreateObject("Wscript.Shell")

   strPath = "c:\Users\" & strName

   arrCmd(0) = "cmd /c md " & strPath
   arrCmd(1) = "cacls " & strPath & " /e /g " & strName & ":C"
   arrCmd(2) = "net share " & strName & "=" & strPath & _
      " /grant:" & strName & ",full"

   For i = LBound(arrCmd) To UBound(arrCmd)
      Call WshShell.Run(arrCmd(i), HIDE_WINDOW, WAIT_ON_RETURN)
   Next
End Sub
```

Figure 11.31 WSH Create a Home Folder for a User - ver 1.vbs

The MD command that we use to create the folder is implemented in CMD.EXE and there is no MD.EXE. Therefore we need `CMD /C` on that command line.

NOTE If you have a need to use the CACLS command without the `/e` ("edit") option (i.e., to remove all previous ACEs), the script would want confirmation (i.e., "are you sure, yes/no") and would halt to ask for it. In this case, you should remove the `HIDE_WINDOW` setting (but keep the comma) so you can answer "yes" when you are prompted for it.

TIP If you want to automate pressing the *y* key, you can create a small file with just that letter and the word "Enter" in it, and use the file as input. In this case you would need to append "<yourfilename.txt" at the end of the CACLS command.

The script in its current form must be run locally on the server where the home folder is created. If you want to run it from another computer, you can use a UNC path (such as \\dc1\users\JackB) instead of a local path (such as c:\Users\JackB) in the MD and CACLS commands. Unfortunately, NET SHARE doesn't work this way, but if you have the Windows NT Server Resource Kit, you can use RMTSHARE from the kit. For some reason, the later Resource Kits don't include it.

See also the CACLS warning in the "Create a User with a Batch File.bat" section.

Create a Home Folder for a User - Ver 2.vbs

This second version does the same things as the first, but this time the folder creation and sharing is done using COM components (WSH and ADSI). We have also enhanced the script so that you can run it from any workstation. Figure 11.32 shows the script's contents.

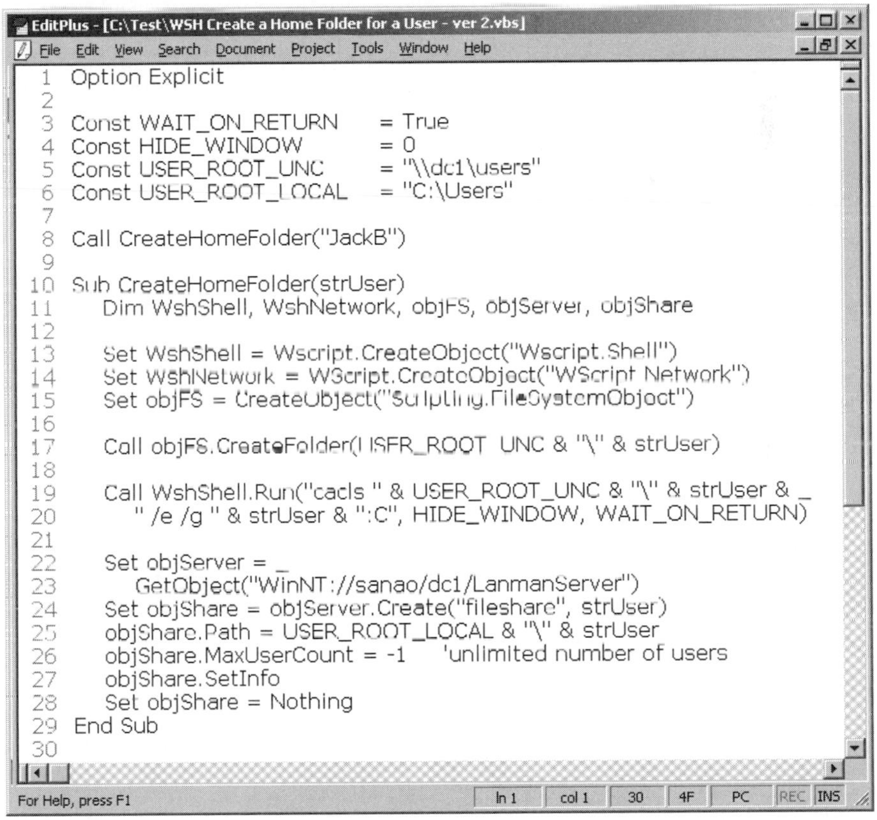
EditPlus - [C:\Test\WSH Create a Home Folder for a User - ver 2.vbs]
File Edit View Search Document Project Tools Window Help
Option Explicit
Const WAIT_ON_RETURN = True
Const HIDE_WINDOW = 0
Const USER_ROOT_UNC = "\\dc1\users"
Const USER_ROOT_LOCAL = "C:\Users"
Call CreateHomeFolder("JackB")
Sub CreateHomeFolder(strUser)
Dim WshShell, WshNetwork, objFS, objServer, objShare
Set WshShell = Wscript.CreateObject("Wscript.Shell")
Set WshNetwork = WScript.CreateObject("WScript.Network")
Set objFS = CreateObject("Scripting.FileSystemObject")
Call objFS.CreateFolder(USER_ROOT_UNC & "\" & strUser)
Call WshShell.Run("cacls " & USER_ROOT_UNC & "\" & strUser & _
" /e /g " & strUser & ":C", HIDE_WINDOW, WAIT_ON_RETURN)
Set objServer = _
GetObject("WinNT://sanao/dc1/LanmanServer")
Set objShare = objServer.Create("fileshare", strUser)
objShare.Path = USER_ROOT_LOCAL & "\" & strUser
objShare.MaxUserCount = -1 'unlimited number of users
objShare.SetInfo
Set objShare = Nothing
End Sub
For Help, press F1
ln 1 col 1 30 4F PC REC INS

Figure 11.32 WSH Create a Home Folder for a User - ver 2.vbs

We still grant permissions with the CACLS command. Later in the "Access Control Lists" section we present a script that modifies folder permissions using the `ADsSecurityUtility` interface. However, that choice is much more laborious than CACLS.

We want to create a constant for the root of all home folders, as both a UNC path and a local path. Note that we need to know the local path for the share, even though we would run the script on another computer.

On lines 13 through 15 we need to create three objects that we can use on the later lines. On line 17 we use the `CreateFolder` method of `FileSystemObject` to create the home folder. On lines 19 and 20 we use the CACLS command to apply the permissions. The CACLS command is similar to the one in the previous example, except that now we use a UNC path for the script to work remotely.

On lines 22 and 23 we use the WinNT provider for the first time in this chapter. We need it because even though we are using ADSI, we are not using Active Directory now. The file shares are owned by the server service (or `LanmanServer`), and therefore we need to bind to that service on the right server. In the binding string, we have the domain NetBIOS name, server name, and `LanmanServer` as the service name.

By using the `objServer` service object ("Server" here doesn't refer to a server machine), we create a file share with the user's name (line 24) and use the object that was also created to set the path and save the changes.

In Windows 2000, without the `MaxUserCount` setting on line 26, only one user at a time could connect to the share. This might not be a problem with a home folder share, but we wanted to show you the setting—you will need it when you create normal shares in Windows 2000. Or because the default in Windows Server 2003 is "unlimited", you might want to set the limit to 1.

NOTE When you create a share in Windows 2000 using either the graphical user interface or the `NET SHARE` command, the default share permission is Everyone:Full Control. In Windows Server 2003, the default changed to Everyone:Read. However, when you create a share using ADSI (as here on lines 22 through 27), the default is still Everyone: Full Control. To modify the share permissions, use the `IADsSecurity-Utility` interface, available in Windows XP and Windows Server 2003, and described in the "Add ACEs to a Folder.vbs" section.

If you combine this last example with the "Create a User with More Attributes" example, you will have a complete script to create user accounts.

See also the CACLS warning in the "Create a User with a Batch File.bat" section.

Read User Information from Excel.xls

In an earlier example, we dumped usernames into Excel by controlling Excel from outside using the WSH + VBScript environment. Now we use Excel VBA inside Excel to retrieve a number of usernames from an Excel spreadsheet.

Figure 11.33 shows how the first name and last name of each user would be stored in a spreadsheet.

To get to the script part (or macro, in other words) you must select the Tools menu, Macro, Visual Basic Editor, or just press Alt-F11. The Visual Basic environment opens, even though you must remember that it is not a real Visual Basic environment (despite the title). If you already have a script file, you'll see something similar to the screen in Figure 11.34. If you don't, you need to select the Insert menu, Module and start typing in the lines.

This script is different from WSH + VBScript in two ways.

- We don't have any main program—just subprograms. The subprograms that don't have any arguments appear in Excel's Macro dialog box (select the Tools menu, Macro, Macros), so you can run them manually

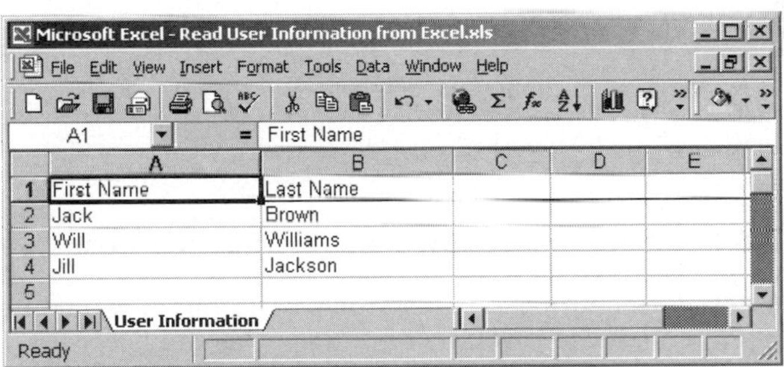

Figure 11.33 The input data of "Read User Information from Excel.xls"

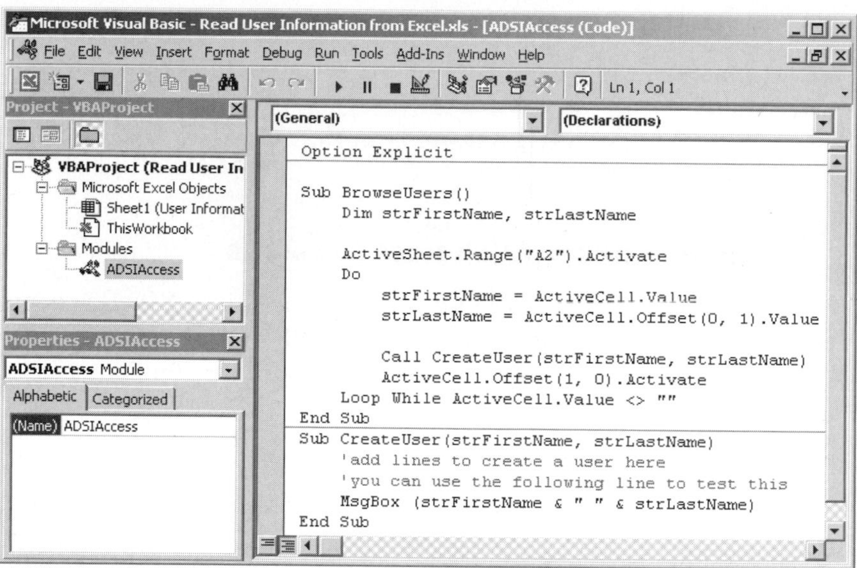

Figure 11.34 Read User Information from Excel.xls

- Because we are already inside Excel, we don't need to add lines `WScript.CreateObject("Excel.Application")`, and so on. Also, we don't need to refer to Excel elements via an Excel object, but we can do this directly.

In the script we first activate cell A2 and then read the names from that line. Next we call a subprogram to create a user (a fake one, in this case) and then move to the next line. These lines will be repeated (or looped) as long as we don't run into an empty cell, which indicates the end of the list.

To replace the fake `CreateUser` subprogram with a real one, you can take the real `CreateUser` subprogram from the "Create a User with More Attributes.vbs" sample.

Read User Information from Standard Input.vbs

A program (including a WSH script) running in the command window can read from *standard input* and write to *standard output* and/or *standard error output*. Standard input typically means your keystrokes, while the two latter options typically show as lines of output in the command window.

About Standard I/O

Standard I/O features become useful when you start redirecting the standard I/O to or from text files. You redirect standard input to be read from a text file with the less-than sign (<). An example command is as follows:

```
someprogram <myinput.txt
```

You could redirect standard output when you want to capture program output to a text file. This is useful at least in two cases. In the first case, a program could output some list that you want to capture in a file. In the second case, you want to schedule a program to be run as a background process at night, and by capturing the output in a file, you could see the next morning what it did. By saving the output (and probably the error output) to a text file, you would have log files of the otherwise mysterious events of the night.

The redirection character for standard output is the greater-than sign (>). When you add 2, you will capture the error output as well. An example command is as follows:

```
listusers >userlist.txt 2>possibleerrors.txt
```

NOTE Some programs also use standard output for errors, and some may use error output for output other than errors. Therefore, you may have to experiment with a program before you learn what is output where. Or you can just capture both, as shown in the previous command example.

Sometimes you would like to append new output to an existing file and not destroy the old lines. This is possible by adding another greater-than sign using a command such as this:

```
listusers >>moreuserlist.txt 2>>morepossibleerrors.txt
```

You can redirect the output of one command to the input of another command by using the pipe sign (|). A sample command is as follows:

```
someprogram | anotherprogram
```

Because you already know how to output from a script (i.e., use `WScript.Echo`), you probably don't need to use standard output inside your scripts. Therefore, our next sample script shows only the input part.

TIP In Windows Server 2003, you can also redirect output to the Windows Clipboard by using the `clip` command. First type a command such as `dir | clip` and then paste the result in any graphical application, such as Notepad.

The Read User Information from Standard Input Sample Script

Our previous sample script read user information from an Excel spreadsheet. Now we do the same with a text file. Figure 11.35 shows the contents of the sample text file.

To use the input data with our script, you would use the following command (we have somewhat shortened the script name):

```
cscript ReadUserInfo.vbs <UserInfo.txt
```

NOTE You must use "cscript" at the beginning of the command line, even if CScript is your default environment.

The script lines are shown in Figure 11.36.

We read standard input just as we would read a file—as a result, we name the variable `objFile`. On line 5 we create this `objFile` by associating it with the `StdIn` property of `WScript`.

On lines 7 through 10 we have a loop that goes on as long as we haven't reached the end of the text stream. On line 8 we read a line of input and use the `Split` function to separate the tab-separated elements. Each line element is stored in an element of the `arrInfo` array,

Figure 11.35 The input data from "Read User Information from Standard Input.vbs"

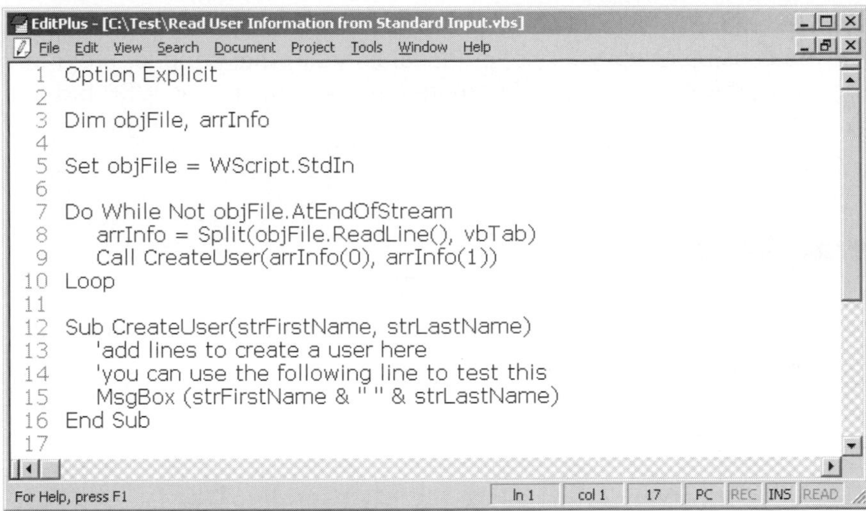

Figure 11.36 Read User Information from Standard Input.vbs

so we can pass them on to the subprogram as each user's first name and last name.

We could, of course, read the input from a named file, but the beauty of standard input is the fact that we don't need to include any file or folder names in the script. Of course, we must include the filename on the command line, but that choice is often easier than including it in the script lines.

If you would rather have the filename inside your script and forget standard input, you can do so by replacing line 5 with the following three lines:

```
Const ForReading = 1
Set objFS = CreateObject("Scripting.FileSystemObject")
Set objFile = objFS.OpenTextFile("C:\Test\UserInfo.txt", _
    ForReading)
```

The lines use the VBScript `FileSystemObject` functionality to open and read the input file. We have included the folder name (C:\Test) on the last line, but you can omit it if the file is in your current folder.

NOTE The example presented here accessed the standard input of the script itself. A new feature of WSH 5.6 enables you to also access the standard input and output of another script or program. This is possible when your script launches that other script or program with the `Exec` method. For more information, see the WSH 5.6 documentation.

Schema Access

Before we show any schema access script samples, we describe some schema access concepts.

Concepts

There are two ways to access the schema with ADSI:

- Using the real schema objects
- Using the abstract schema objects that ADSI creates based on the schema definition in the `subSchema` object (`CN=Aggregate, CN=Schema, CN=Configuration, DC=sanao, DC=com`)

We introduced the latter concept in Chapter 8. We compare the two choices in Table 11.1.

NOTE We identify the real schema objects with their common names, but we identify the abstract schema objects with the LDAP names of the class or attribute.

While the abstract schema objects contain only a subset of all the schema information, they have the following advantages over the real schema objects.

- The `ADsPaths` (i.e., the binding strings) are easier because they are shorter and use LDAP names, and you don't have to specify a forest name if you don't want to.
- The abstract schema objects combine information from several real schema objects and show it in an easier form. For example, they indicate with a True or False value whether or not each class is a container. If you were using the real schema objects, you would need to browse through all other classes and check if the first class was a possible superior in any of them.

Table 11.1 The Two Ways to Access the Schema with ADSI

Feature	Real Schema Objects	Abstract Schema Objects
ADsPath to schema root	`LDAP://CN=Schema, CN=Configuration, DC=sanao, DC=com`	`LDAP://schema` (or `LDAP://sanao.com/schema` or `LDAP://dc1.sanao.com/schema`)
ADsPath to `user` class	`LDAP://CN=User, CN=Schema, CN=Configuration, DC=sanao, DC=com`	`LDAP://schema/user`
ADsPath to `givenName` attribute	`LDAP://CN=Given-Name, CN=Schema, CN=Configuration, DC=sanao, DC=com`	`LDAP://schema/givenName`
Class name of class	`classSchema`	Class
Class name of attribute	`attributeSchema`	Property
Class name of syntax	Not available	Syntax
Allows schema extensions and modifications	Yes, create and modify objects just as any Active Directory objects	No
Available schema object properties	All	Only some

We discussed the attributes of the real `classSchema` and `attributeSchema` objects in Chapter 8. In the next subsection, we briefly list the properties of the abstract schema objects.

Properties of the Abstract Schema Objects

You access the abstract `class`, `property`, and `syntax` schema objects with the interfaces `IADsClass`, `IADsProperty`, and `IADsSyntax`, respectively. The interfaces have a number of read/write properties, but because the `subSchema` is read-only, you should only read the interface properties.

Table 11.2 lists the properties for abstract schema classes.

Table 11.2 Relevant Properties of the Abstract Schema Classes (`IADsClass` Interface)

Property	Description
`Container`	True if some other class has this class as a possible superior; otherwise, False
`Containment`	An array of LDAP names for the classes that can be children of this class
`PossibleSuperiors`	An array of LDAP names for the classes that can be parents of this class
`MandatoryProperties`	An array of LDAP names for the mandatory attributes of this class
`OptionalProperties`	An array of LDAP names for the optional attributes of this class
`NamingProperties`	An array of LDAP names for the naming attributes of this class (i.e., "cn," "ou," and so on)
`OID`	The object ID of this class
`Auxiliary`	True if this in an auxiliary class; otherwise, False
`Abstract`	True if this in an abstract class; otherwise, False
`DerivedFrom`	The LDAP name of the superclass (`subClassOf`) of this class
`AuxDerivedFrom`	An array of LDAP names for the auxiliary classes of this class

WARNING If there is only one element in the array—for example, with the `Containment` property—the property method returns a string instead of an array. This makes writing scripts a little harder, because you first need to check the data type and then handle it accordingly.

Table 11.3 lists the properties for abstract schema properties.

We don't have a table of abstract syntax objects, because `IADsSyntax` has just one property. `OleAutoDataType` indicates which OLE automation data type the syntax maps to.

Table 11.3 Properties of the Abstract Schema Properties (`IADsProperty` Interface)

Property	Description
`Syntax`	The LDAP-type friendly name of the property (see the "ADSI Syntaxes" section in Chapter 10)
`MultiValued`	True or False depending on whether or not the property is multivalued
`MinRange`	Possible minimum for the value(s)
`MaxRange`	Possible maximum for the value(s)
`OID`	The object ID of this attribute

Retrieving the Path to an Abstract Schema Class Object

In Chapter 10 we introduced the `Schema` and `Class` properties of the `IADs` interface. For example, for user objects, they contain the values `LDAP://schema/user` and `user`, respectively.

With the help of these two properties (or just one), we can bind to the abstract schema class object that corresponds to any object, such as Jack. We would use the following line to do this:

```
Set objClass = GetObject(objADObject.Schema)
```

Now that you have an understanding of schema access concepts, it is time to move on to the sample scripts.

Schema Sample Scripts

We present the following sample scripts (and a section on ANR, non-replicated, and constructed attributes) for schema access:

- CH11-14 ADSI List All Abstract Schema Objects.vbs
- CH11-15 ADSI List the Member Attributes of a Given Class.vbs
- CH11-16 ADSI List the Member Attributes of a Given Class to Excel.vbs
- CH11-17 ADSI Show Property Properties.vbs
- CH11-18 ADSI Container or Leaf.vbs

- CH11-19 ADSI List All Real Schema Objects.vbs
- CH11-20 ADSI List Indexed Attributes.vbs
- List ANR, nonreplicated, and constructed attributes
- CH11-21 ADSI List Global Catalog Attributes.vbs
- CH11-22 ADSI List All classSchemas to Excel.vbs
- CH11-23 ADSI List All attributeSchemas to Excel.vbs
- CH11-24 ADSI Create an Attribute and a Class.vbs

Examples 14 through 18 use the abstract schema, and the rest use the real schema objects.

List All Abstract Schema Objects.vbs

Our first schema sample script reads the abstract schema and lists all 191 classes, 1,070 properties, and 35 syntaxes. As with any command-line output, you can redirect the output to a text file using the greater-than sign (>).

Figure 11.37 shows part of the output of the script. We show only the beginning of each category. Figure 11.38 shows the entire script.

We could have used just one short `For` loop instead of three, but this way we could order and number the output and also print some extra fields, depending on the schema object type.

List the Member Attributes of a Given Class.vbs

This example takes a class LDAP name as a command-line argument and then lists all mandatory and optional property names of that class.

Figure 11.39 shows the beginning of the output of the script when the `user` class is specified. Again, you can redirect this to a text file using

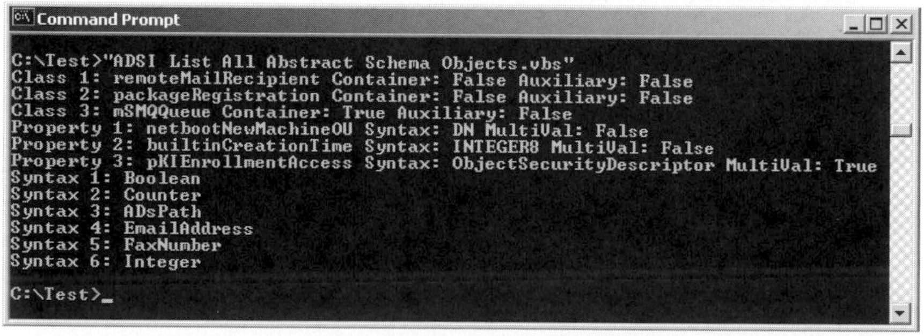

```
Command Prompt
C:\Test>"ADSI List All Abstract Schema Objects.vbs"
Class 1: remoteMailRecipient Container: False Auxiliary: False
Class 2: packageRegistration Container: False Auxiliary: False
Class 3: mSMQQueue Container: True Auxiliary: False
Property 1: netbootNewMachineOU Syntax: DN MultiVal: False
Property 2: builtinCreationTime Syntax: INTEGER8 MultiVal: False
Property 3: pKIEnrollmentAccess Syntax: ObjectSecurityDescriptor MultiVal: True
Syntax 1: Boolean
Syntax 2: Counter
Syntax 3: ADsPath
Syntax 4: EmailAddress
Syntax 5: FaxNumber
Syntax 6: Integer

C:\Test>_
```

Figure 11.37 Some lines of the output of "ADSI List All Abstract Schema Objects.vbs"

```
Option Explicit

Dim objSchema, objChild, i

Set objSchema = GetObject("LDAP://schema")

i = 0
For Each objChild In objSchema
   If objChild.Class = "Class" Then
      i = i + 1
      WScript.Echo "Class " & i & ": " & objChild.Name & _
         " Container: " & objChild.Container  & _
         " Auxiliary: " & objChild.Auxiliary
   End If
Next

i = 0
For Each objChild In objSchema
   If objChild.Class = "Property" Then
      i - i + 1
      WScript.Echo "Property " & i & ": " & objChild.Name & _
         " Syntax: " & objChild.Syntax  & _
         " MultiVal: " & objChild.MultiValued
   End If
Next

i = 0
For Each objChild In objSchema
   If objChild.Class = "Syntax" Then
      i = i + 1
      WScript.Echo "Syntax " & i & ": " & objChild.Name
   End If
Next
```

Figure 11.38 ADSI List All Abstract Schema Objects.vbs

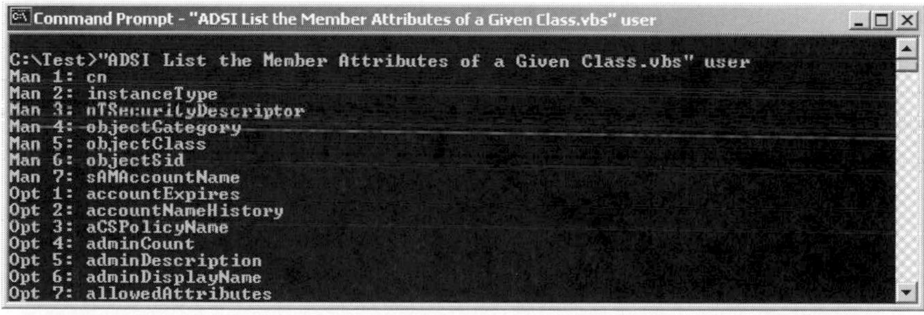
Command Prompt - "ADSI List the Member Attributes of a Given Class.vbs" user
C:\Test>"ADSI List the Member Attributes of a Given Class.vbs" user
Man 1: cn
Man 2: instanceType
Man 3: nTSecurityDescriptor
Man 4: objectCategory
Man 5: objectClass
Man 6: objectSid
Man 7: sAMAccountName
Opt 1: accountExpires
Opt 2: accountNameHistory
Opt 3: aCSPolicyName
Opt 4: adminCount
Opt 5: adminDescription
Opt 6: adminDisplayName
Opt 7: allowedAttributes

Figure 11.39 Some lines of output of "ADSI List the Member Attributes of a Given Class.vbs"

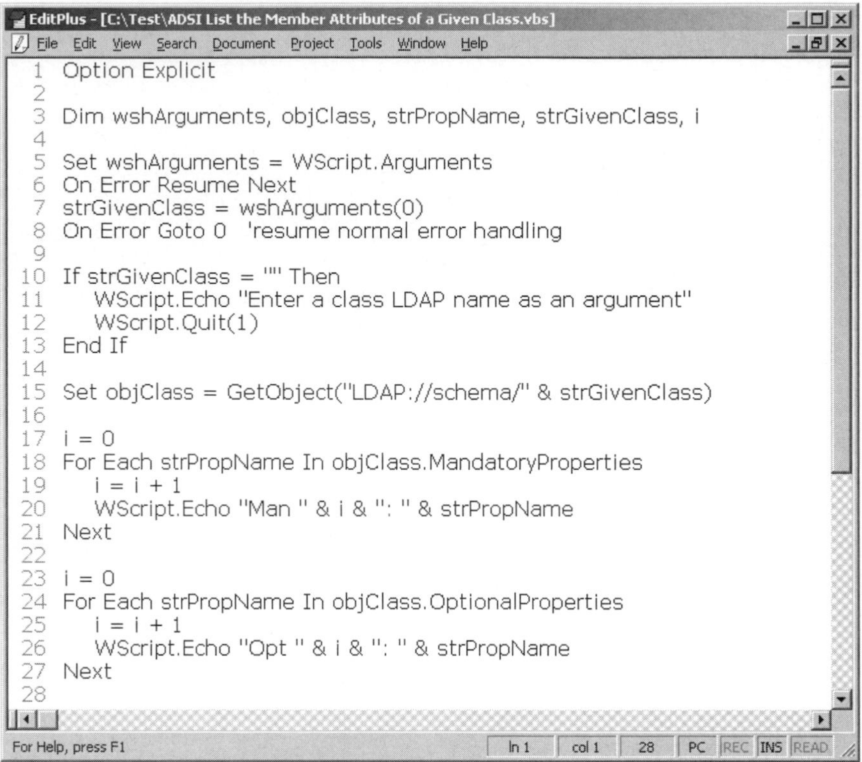

EditPlus - [C:\Test\ADSI List the Member Attributes of a Given Class.vbs]
File Edit View Search Document Project Tools Window Help
Option Explicit

Dim wshArguments, objClass, strPropName, strGivenClass, i

Set wshArguments = WScript.Arguments
On Error Resume Next
strGivenClass = wshArguments(0)
On Error Goto 0 'resume normal error handling

If strGivenClass = "" Then
WScript.Echo "Enter a class LDAP name as an argument"
WScript.Quit(1)
End If

Set objClass = GetObject("LDAP://schema/" & strGivenClass)

i = 0
For Each strPropName In objClass.MandatoryProperties
i = i + 1
WScript.Echo "Man " & i & ": " & strPropName
Next

i = 0
For Each strPropName In objClass.OptionalProperties
i = i + 1
WScript.Echo "Opt " & i & ": " & strPropName
Next
For Help, press F1
ln 1
col 1
28
PC
REC
INS
READ

Figure 11.40 ADSI List the Member Attributes of a Given Class.vbs

the greater-than sign (>). Figure 11.40 shows the script's contents. As you can see, we use the abstract schema.

NOTE You cannot bind to the real `classSchema` object `CN=User` and use `objClass.Get("mustContain")` or `mayContain` in a similar way. The reason is that the mandatory and optional properties of the `user` class are the sum of the `mustContain`, `systemMustContain`, `mayContain`, and `systemMayContain` attributes not only from the `user` class, but also from all of its superclasses and auxiliary classes. The `mustContain` and `mayContain` attributes are not even set for the `user` class.

List the Member Attributes of a Given Class to Excel.vbs

This next example extends the previous one. We now ask the class name in an input box and dump the attribute names into Excel. Because Excel

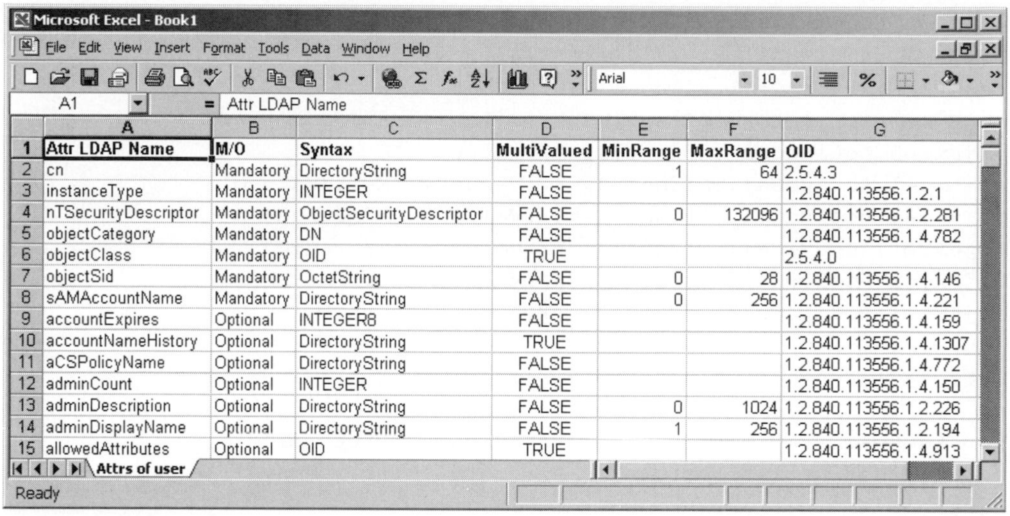

Attr LDAP Name	M/O	Syntax	MultiValued	MinRange	MaxRange	OID
cn	Mandatory	DirectoryString	FALSE	1	64	2.5.4.3
instanceType	Mandatory	INTEGER	FALSE			1.2.840.113556.1.2.1
nTSecurityDescriptor	Mandatory	ObjectSecurityDescriptor	FALSE	0	132096	1.2.840.113556.1.2.281
objectCategory	Mandatory	DN	FALSE			1.2.840.113556.1.4.782
objectClass	Mandatory	OID	TRUE			2.5.4.0
objectSid	Mandatory	OctetString	FALSE	0	28	1.2.840.113556.1.4.146
sAMAccountName	Mandatory	DirectoryString	FALSE	0	256	1.2.840.113556.1.4.221
accountExpires	Optional	INTEGER8	FALSE			1.2.840.113556.1.4.159
accountNameHistory	Optional	DirectoryString	TRUE			1.2.840.113556.1.4.1307
aCSPolicyName	Optional	DirectoryString	FALSE			1.2.840.113556.1.4.772
adminCount	Optional	INTEGER	FALSE			1.2.840.113556.1.4.150
adminDescription	Optional	DirectoryString	FALSE	0	1024	1.2.840.113556.1.2.226
adminDisplayName	Optional	DirectoryString	FALSE	1	256	1.2.840.113556.1.2.194
allowedAttributes	Optional	OID	TRUE			1.2.840.113556.1.4.913

Figure 11.41 Some lines of output of "ADSI List the Member Attributes of a Given Class to Excel.vbs." The column widths were adjusted and the headers were bolded manually.

is well suited for tables, we can also write other attribute information besides just the name there. Figure 11.41 shows the beginning of the output of the script.

When you start to manage objects of some particular class, you can first dump all its attributes into Excel, so you'll get a nice documentation of the attributes you can start playing with.

Next, we show the script's contents.

```
Option Explicit

Dim objExcel, objClass, strPropName, strGivenClass, strSheetName

strGivenClass = InputBox("Enter a class LDAP name")

Set objExcel = WScript.CreateObject("Excel.Application")
objExcel.Visible = True
objExcel.Workbooks.Add

strSheetName = "Attrs of " & strGivenClass
If Len(strSheetName) > 31 Then _
   strSheetName = Left(strSheetName,28) & "..."
```

```
objExcel.ActiveSheet.Name = strSheetName
objExcel.ActiveSheet.Range("A1").Activate
objExcel.ActiveCell.Value = "Attr LDAP Name"
objExcel.ActiveCell.Offset(0, 1).Value = "M/O"
objExcel.ActiveCell.Offset(0, 2).Value = "Syntax"
objExcel.ActiveCell.Offset(0, 3).Value = "MultiValued"
objExcel.ActiveCell.Offset(0, 4).Value = "MinRange"
objExcel.ActiveCell.Offset(0, 5).Value = "MaxRange"
objExcel.ActiveCell.Offset(0, 6).Value = "OID"
objExcel.ActiveCell.Offset(1, 0).Activate

Set objClass = GetObject("LDAP://schema/" & strGivenClass)

For Each strPropName In objClass.MandatoryProperties
   Call ShowAttrAndFeatures("Mandatory", strPropName)
Next

For Each strPropName In objClass.OptionalProperties
   Call ShowAttrAndFeatures("Optional", strPropName)
Next

Sub ShowAttrAndFeatures(strManOrOpt, strPropName)
   Dim objAttribute

   On Error Resume Next

   Set objAttribute = GetObject("LDAP://schema/" & strPropName)

   objExcel.ActiveCell.Value = strPropName
      objExcel.ActiveCell.Offset(0, 1).Value = strManOrOpt
   With objAttribute
      objExcel.ActiveCell.Offset(0, 2).Value = .Syntax
      objExcel.ActiveCell.Offset(0, 3).Value = .MultiValued
      objExcel.ActiveCell.Offset(0, 4).Value = .MinRange
      objExcel.ActiveCell.Offset(0, 5).Value = .MaxRange
      objExcel.ActiveCell.Offset(0, 6).Value = .OID
   End With
   objExcel.ActiveCell.Offset(1, 0).Activate
End Sub
```

The `With` statement is something that we now use for the first time. Instead of `objAttribute.Syntax`, we can write just `.Syntax` while we are inside the `With` statement.

TIP Another way to get data into Excel is to first print it onscreen with `WScript.Echo`, then redirect the output to a text file with the greater-than sign (>), and finally import the text file into Excel. If you print several properties on each line, you can put tabs in between them so that the data will import nicely into Excel.

Show Property Properties.vbs

This example is a subset of the previous one. It takes one attribute LDAP name as a command-line argument and then shows its properties. It doesn't introduce any new techniques, but it is a handy, small script if you quickly want to check some properties. Figure 11.42 shows the output of the script. Figure 11.43 shows the script's contents.

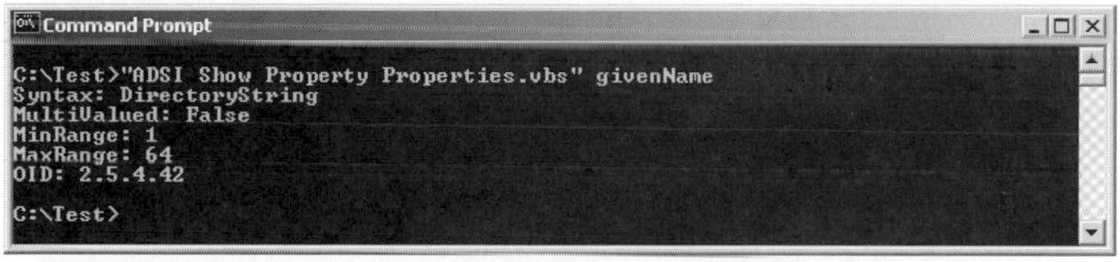

```
C:\Test>"ADSI Show Property Properties.vbs" givenName
Syntax: DirectoryString
MultiValued: False
MinRange: 1
MaxRange: 64
OID: 2.5.4.42

C:\Test>
```

Figure 11.42 The output of "ADSI Show Property Properties.vbs"

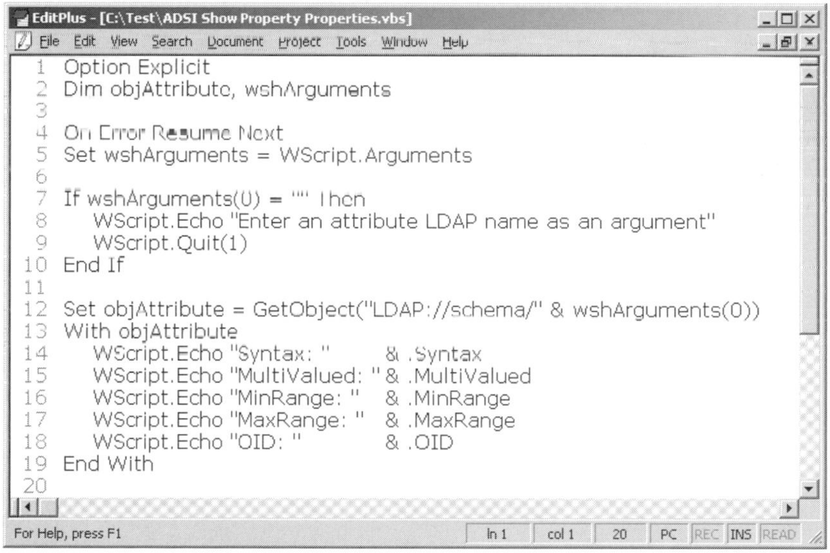

```
Option Explicit
Dim objAttribute, wshArguments

On Error Resume Next
Set wshArguments = WScript.Arguments

If wshArguments(0) = "" Then
   WScript.Echo "Enter an attribute LDAP name as an argument"
   WScript.Quit(1)
End If

Set objAttribute = GetObject("LDAP://schema/" & wshArguments(0))
With objAttribute
   WScript.Echo "Syntax: "       & .Syntax
   WScript.Echo "MultiValued: " & .MultiValued
   WScript.Echo "MinRange: "    & .MinRange
   WScript.Echo "MaxRange: "    & .MaxRange
   WScript.Echo "OID: "         & .OID
End With
```

Figure 11.43 ADSI Show Property Properties.vbs

Container or Leaf.vbs

This is our last example that uses the abstract schema. The script binds to a container (CN=Users) and lists the names of all child objects and whether they are containers or leafs. Figure 11.44 shows some lines of the output. Figure 11.45 shows the script's contents.

The Schema property contains a string such as LDAP://schema/user, which binds to the abstract schema class object of the hosting object.

NOTE By default, there are no leaf objects in the CN=Users container, because users and groups are containers. If you want to check that the script really works, you can add one contact object to that container.

```
E:\WINNT\SYSTEM32\cmd.exe

C:\Test>"ADSI Container or Leaf.vbs"
Cont: CN=Administrator
Cont: CN=Cert Publishers
Cont: CN=Domain Admins
Cont: CN=Domain Guests
Cont: CN=Domain Users
Cont: CN=Enterprise Admins
Cont: CN=Guest
Cont: CN=Schema Admins
Leaf: CN=Carl Contact

C:\Test>_
```

Figure 11.44 Some lines of output of "ADSI Container or Leaf.vbs"

EditPlus - [C:\Test\ADSI Container or Leaf.vbs]

```
Option Explicit

Dim objDSE, objContainer, objChild, objClass

Set objDSE = GetObject("LDAP://rootDSE")
Set objContainer = GetObject("LDAP://CN=Users," & _
   objDSE.Get("defaultNamingContext"))

For Each objChild In objContainer
   Set objClass = GetObject(objChild.Schema)
   If objClass.Container Then
      WScript.Echo "Cont: " + objChild.Name
   Else
      WScript.Echo "Leaf: " + objChild.Name
   End If
Next

```

Figure 11.45 ADSI Container or Leaf.vbs

NOTE If we wanted to make the script three times longer, we could have added lines to check the `treatAsLeaf` attribute of the corresponding display specifier object. It would specify that even though `user` and `group` are technically containers, the Users and Computers snap-in should treat them as leaf objects.

List All Real Schema Objects.vbs

With this example, we begin using the real schema objects instead of the abstract schema. The sample script reads the schema container and lists all 191 classes and 1,070 attributes. This time we don't list syntaxes, because they don't exist as objects in the real schema.

Figure 11.46 shows part of the output of the script. We show only the beginning of each category. After classes and attributes we list the `subSchema` object named `Aggregate`. It is the single object that contains the abstract schema definitions.

Figure 11.47 shows the script's contents.

We could also use just one loop instead of three, but this way we were able to sort the objects by their class.

If you want, you can add `objChild.Get("lDAPDisplayName")` to the output line, because the `Name` property method retrieves only the common name this time. We implement this in the next example. However, the `subSchema` object doesn't have an LDAP display name, so you will get an error in that case.

List Indexed Attributes.vbs

The abstract schema doesn't know whether an attribute is indexed, so we need to use the real `attributeSchema` objects and their `searchFlags` attribute. This script browses through all those objects and checks if one certain bit of `searchFlags` is set.

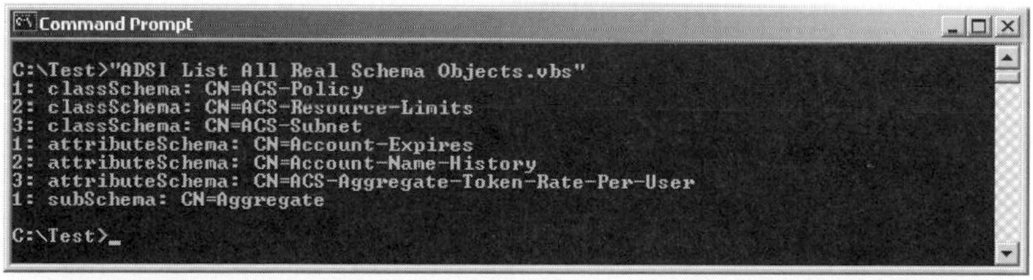

```
Command Prompt
C:\Test>"ADSI List All Real Schema Objects.vbs"
1: classSchema: CN=ACS-Policy
2: classSchema: CN=ACS-Resource-Limits
3: classSchema: CN=ACS-Subnet
1: attributeSchema: CN=Account-Expires
2: attributeSchema: CN=Account-Name-History
3: attributeSchema: CN=ACS-Aggregate-Token-Rate-Per-User
1: subSchema: CN=Aggregate

C:\Test>_
```

Figure 11.46 Some lines of output of "ADSI List All Real Schema Objects.vbs"

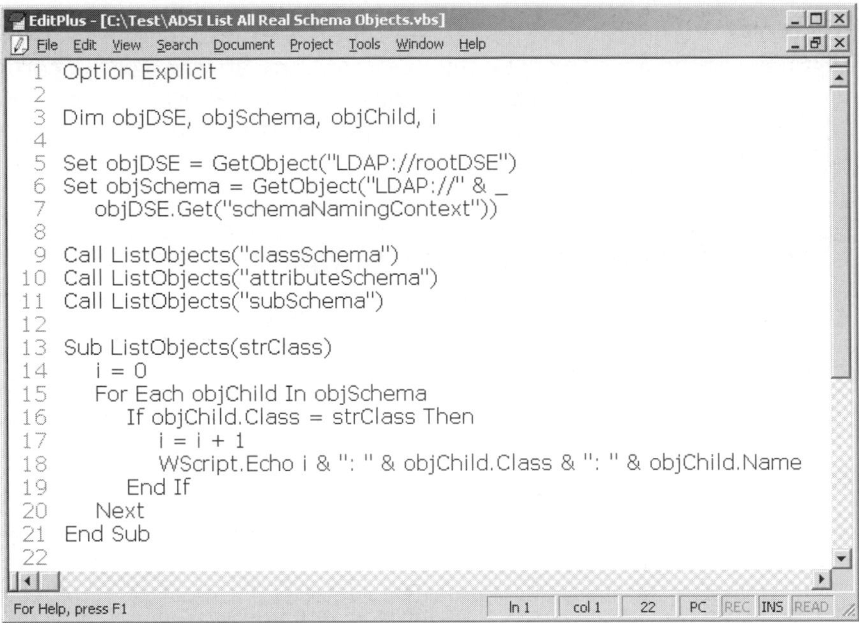


```
Option Explicit

Dim objDSE, objSchema, objChild, i

Set objDSE = GetObject("LDAP://rootDSE")
Set objSchema = GetObject("LDAP://" & _
   objDSE.Get("schemaNamingContext"))

Call ListObjects("classSchema")
Call ListObjects("attributeSchema")
Call ListObjects("subSchema")

Sub ListObjects(strClass)
   i = 0
   For Each objChild In objSchema
      If objChild.Class = strClass Then
         i = i + 1
         WScript.Echo i & ": " & objChild.Class & ": " & objChild.Name
      End If
   Next
End Sub
```

Figure 11.47 ADSI List All Real Schema Objects.vbs

Figure 11.48 shows the first few lines of the output of the script. Figure 11.49 shows the script's contents.

You can modify this script for other purposes, as described in the next subsection.

NOTE The base schema has the `searchFlags` attribute set for all `attributeSchema` objects, but if there are any new attributes in your test forest, they might not. The sample script won't work in this case, unless you either add at least the `On Error Resume Next` statement or modify the script as described in the next example.

```
Command Prompt
C:\Test>"ADSI List Indexed Attributes.vbs"
Attr 1: SearchFlags 1: CN=Alt-Security-Identities (altSecurityIdentities)
Attr 2: SearchFlags 1: CN=Birth-Location (birthLocation)
Attr 3: SearchFlags 1: CN=COM-ClassID (cOMClassID)
Attr 4: SearchFlags 1: CN=Common-Name (cn)
Attr 5: SearchFlags 1: CN=dhcp-Type (dhcpType)
Attr 6: SearchFlags 5: CN=Display-Name (displayName)

C:\Test>_
```

Figure 11.48 Some lines of output of "ADSI List Indexed Attributes.vbs"

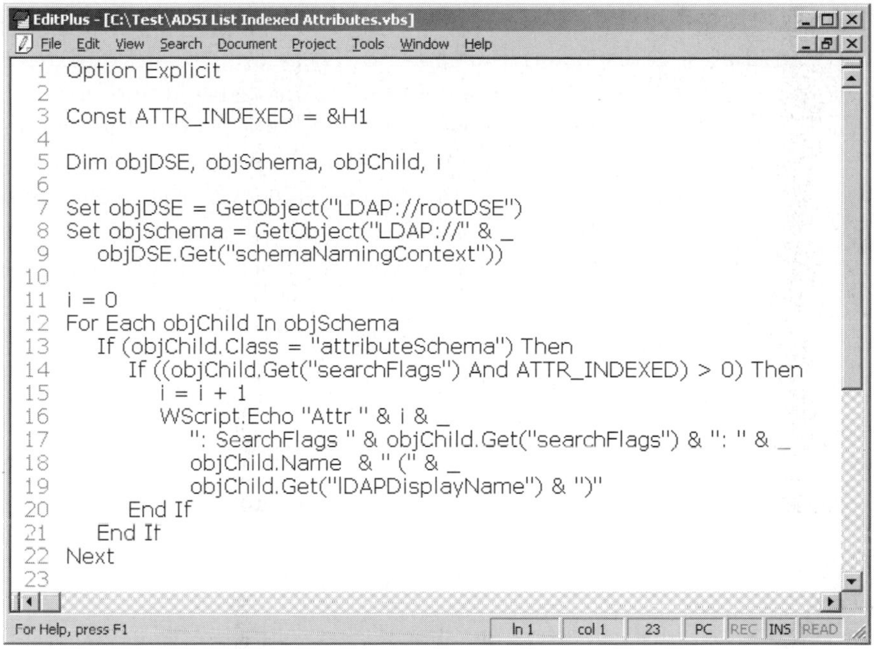

EditPlus - [C:\Test\ADSI List Indexed Attributes.vbs]

File Edit View Search Document Project Tools Window Help

```
Option Explicit

Const ATTR_INDEXED = &H1

Dim objDSE, objSchema, objChild, i

Set objDSE = GetObject("LDAP://rootDSE")
Set objSchema = GetObject("LDAP://" & _
   objDSE.Get("schemaNamingContext"))

i = 0
For Each objChild In objSchema
   If (objChild.Class = "attributeSchema") Then
      If ((objChild.Get("searchFlags") And ATTR_INDEXED) > 0) Then
         i = i + 1
         WScript.Echo "Attr " & i & _
            ": SearchFlags " & objChild.Get("searchFlags") & ": " & _
            objChild.Name  & " (" & _
            objChild.Get("lDAPDisplayName") & ")"
      End If
   End If
Next
```

For Help, press F1 | ln 1 | col 1 | 23 | PC | REC | INS | READ

Figure 11.49 ADSI List Indexed Attributes.vbs

List ANR, Nonreplicated, and Constructed Attributes

Now that you have a script that scans the `searchFlags` attribute for one certain flag, you can also use it to scan other search flags as well as system flags.

To scan other search flags, just replace `ATTR_INDEXED` with one of the following constants:

```
Const ATTR_PART_OF_ANR_SET = &H4
Const ATTR_SURVIVE_DELETION = &H8
Const ATTR_COPY_WITH_USER = &H10
```

If you replace the `searchFlags` attribute with `systemFlags`, you can use the following constants:

```
Const ATTR_NOT_REPLICATED = &H1
Const ATTR_MUST_BE_IN_GC  = &H2
Const ATTR_IS_CONSTRUCTED = &H4
Const ATTR_IS_BASE_SCHEMA = &H10
```

For more information on these flags, see Chapter 8.

The `systemFlags` attribute is not defined for 40 base schema attributes, as discussed in Chapter 8. Therefore, you need to modify the script a little so that you don't get the "property not found" error.

The easiest way to avoid the error is to remove the explicit `Get` method from the `If` statement and use a dynamic property method instead. When you retrieve an attribute value with the `.LDAPname` syntax instead of `.Get("LDAPname")`, you will get `vbEmpty` when the attribute is not set. It is equal to 0 in the `If` statement evaluation, so you don't need any extra lines for error checking.

The resulting line looks like the following:

```
If ((objChild.systemFlags And ATTR_NOT_REPLICATED) > 0) Then
```

Obviously, you can use the same syntax for `searchFlags` if some of the new `attributeSchema` objects don't have that attribute set.

List Global Catalog Attributes.vbs

This script lists all attributes that are part of the global catalog.

The global catalog setting is in the `isMemberOfPartialAttributeSet` attribute, which is usually present only on those attributes that are part of the global catalog. To avoid dealing with the "property not found" error, we use the same approach as in the previous example. We retrieve the value with the `.LDAPname` syntax instead of `.Get("LDAPname")`.

Figure 11.50 shows the first few lines of the output of the script. Figure 11.51 shows the script's contents.

A missing attribute causes a `vbEmpty` situation, which the `If` statement considers to be False. Therefore, we can directly use `objChild.isMemberOfPartialAttributeSet` in the `If` statement (see line 12).

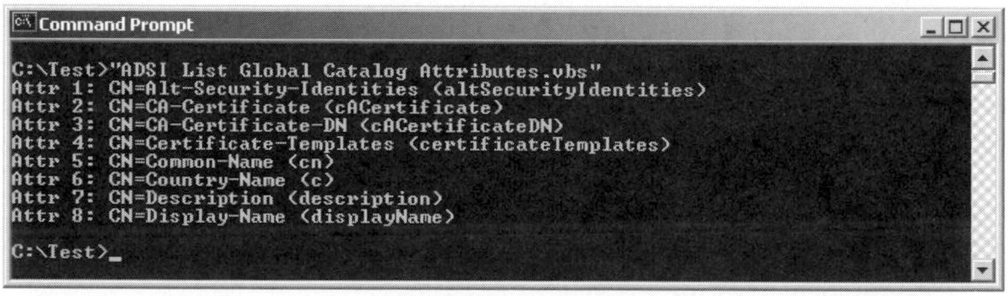

```
Command Prompt
C:\Test>"ADSI List Global Catalog Attributes.vbs"
Attr 1: CN=Alt-Security-Identities (altSecurityIdentities)
Attr 2: CN=CA-Certificate (cACertificate)
Attr 3: CN=CA-Certificate-DN (cACertificateDN)
Attr 4: CN=Certificate-Templates (certificateTemplates)
Attr 5: CN=Common-Name (cn)
Attr 6: CN=Country-Name (c)
Attr 7: CN=Description (description)
Attr 8: CN=Display-Name (displayName)

C:\Test>_
```

Figure 11.50 Some lines of output of "ADSI List Global Catalog Attributes.vbs"

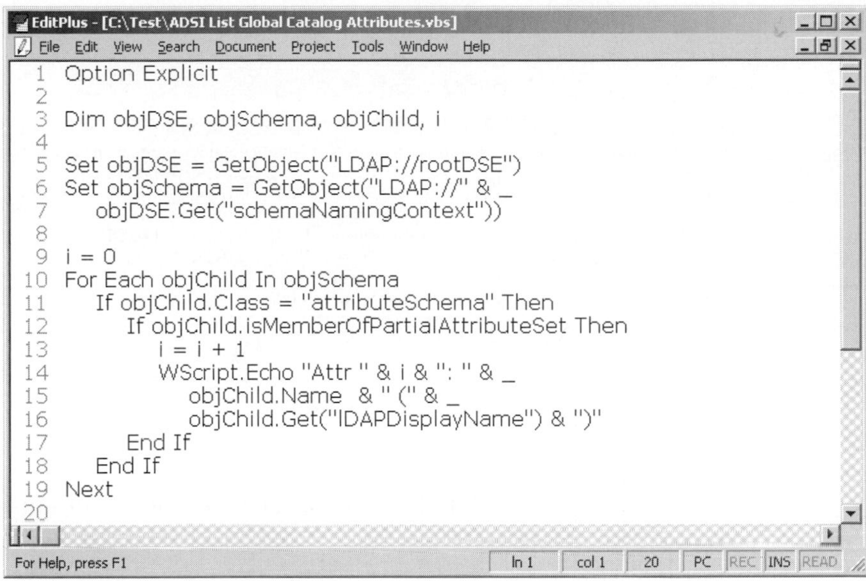

EditPlus - [C:\Test\ADSI List Global Catalog Attributes.vbs]
File Edit View Search Document Project Tools Window Help
Option Explicit

Dim objDSE, objSchema, objChild, i

Set objDSE = GetObject("LDAP://rootDSE")
Set objSchema = GetObject("LDAP://" & _
objDSE.Get("schemaNamingContext"))

i = 0
For Each objChild In objSchema
If objChild.Class = "attributeSchema" Then
If objChild.isMemberOfPartialAttributeSet Then
i = i + 1
WScript.Echo "Attr " & i & ": " & _
objChild.Name & " (" & _
objChild.Get("lDAPDisplayName") & ")"
End If
End If
Next
For Help, press F1
ln 1
col 1
20
PC
REC
INS
READ

Figure 11.51 ADSI List Global Catalog Attributes.vbs

List All classSchemas to Excel.vbs

This script dumps all `classSchema` objects into Excel and includes all their attributes that are easy to read. In other words, it doesn't include any multivalued, binary, or constructed attributes. We also omitted the attributes that `classSchema` objects don't use, such as `displayName`.

First we list the attribute names in a table using the same order and categories that we introduced in Chapter 8. Then we browse through the Schema container, picking up all `classSchema` objects and reading the listed attributes.

Figure 11.52 shows the resulting Excel spreadsheet. We have manually chosen Freeze Panes and bolded the first line. We haven't adjusted the column widths yet.

If you are interested in the attributes we didn't include, you have two options.

- Enhance this script with the reading techniques that we showed when reading user information earlier in this chapter (see the "List User Properties with Get.vbs" section).
- Use the script "List User Properties with Get.vbs", but replace the target object `CN=Guest` with a `classSchema` object such as

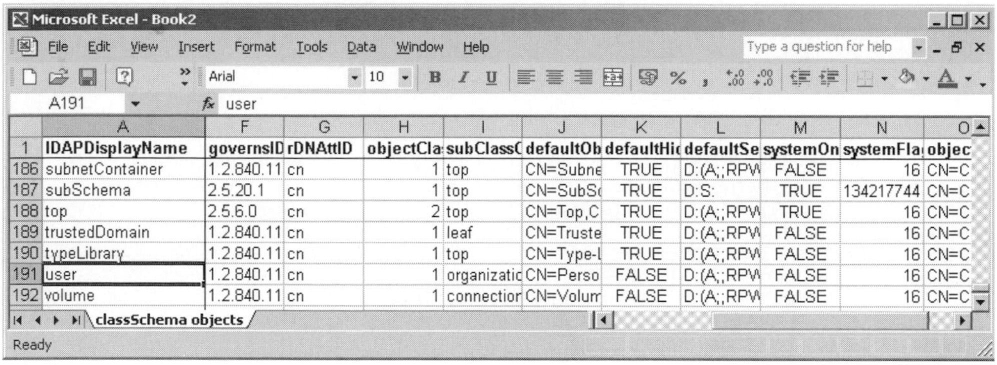
Microsoft Excel - Book2
File Edit View Insert Format Tools Data Window Help
Type a question for help
Arial
10
A191
user
A F G H I J K L M N O
1 lDAPDisplayName governsID rDNAttID objectCla subClassC defaultOb defaultHi defaultSe systemOn systemFla objec
186 subnetContainer 1.2.840.11 cn 1 top CN=Subne TRUE D:(A;;RPW FALSE 16 CN=C
187 subSchema 2.5.20.1 cn 1 top CN=SubS TRUE D:S: TRUE 134217744 CN=C
188 top 2.5.6.0 cn 2 top CN=Top,C TRUE D:(A;;RPW TRUE 16 CN=C
189 trustedDomain 1.2.840.11 cn 1 leaf CN=Truste TRUE D:(A;;RPW FALSE 16 CN=C
190 typeLibrary 1.2.840.11 cn 1 top CN=Type-l TRUE D:(A;;RPW FALSE 16 CN=C
191 user 1.2.840.11 cn 1 organizatic CN=Perso FALSE D:(A;;RPW FALSE 16 CN=C
192 volume 1.2.840.11 cn 1 connectior CN=Volum FALSE D:(A;;RPW FALSE 16 CN=C
classSchema objects
Ready

Figure 11.52 The output of "ADSI List All classSchemas to Excel.vbs"

`CN=User`. That modified script lists all constructed and multivalued attributes, but not any binary attributes (i.e., the two GUID attributes).

The script is as follows:

```
Option Explicit

Dim objExcel, objDSE, objSchema, objChild, i, varValue
Dim arrParamList(14)

'Names and Identifiers
arrParamList(0) = "lDAPDisplayName"
arrParamList(1) = "cn"
arrParamList(2) = "adminDisplayName"
arrParamList(3) = "distinguishedName"
arrParamList(4) = "adminDescription"
arrParamList(5) = "governsID"
arrParamList(6) = "rDNAttID"
'Structure and Containment Rules: None
'Class Inheritance
arrParamList(7) = "objectClassCategory"
arrParamList(8) = "subClassOf"
'Miscellaneous
arrParamList(9) = "defaultObjectCategory"
arrParamList(10) = "defaultHidingValue"
arrParamList(11) = "defaultSecurityDescriptor"
arrParamList(12) = "systemOnly"
arrParamList(13) = "systemFlags"
```

```
arrParamList(14) = "objectCategory"

Set objExcel = WScript.CreateObject("Excel.Application")
objExcel.Visible = True
objExcel.Workbooks.Add
objExcel.ActiveSheet.Name = "classSchema objects"

objExcel.ActiveSheet.Range("A1").Activate
For i = LBound(arrParamList) To UBound(arrParamList)
   objExcel.ActiveCell.Offset(0,i).Value = arrParamList(i)
Next
objExcel.ActiveCell.Offset(1,0).Activate   'Move to next line

Set objDSE = GetObject("LDAP://rootDSE")
Set objSchema = GetObject("LDAP://" & _
   objDSE.Get("schemaNamingContext"))

On Error Resume Next
For Each objChild In objSchema
   If objChild.Class = "classSchema" Then
      For i = LBound(arrParamList) To UBound(arrParamList)
         varValue = objChild.Get(arrParamList(i))
         If Err <> 0 Then   'property not found or some other error
            Err.Clear
            varValue = ""
         End If
         objExcel.ActiveCell.Offset(0,i).Value = varValue
      Next
      objExcel.ActiveCell.Offset(1,0).Activate   'Move to next line
   End If
Next
```

In previous examples, we cleared the error code with a line `Err = 0`, but this time we used a cooler way: `Err.Clear`.

List All attributeSchemas to Excel.vbs

This script is identical to the previous one, except that now we pick up `attributeSchema` objects and the list of their attributes is naturally slightly different.

Figure 11.53 shows the resulting Excel spreadsheet. Again, we have manually chosen Freeze Panes and bolded the first line. We haven't adjusted the column widths yet.

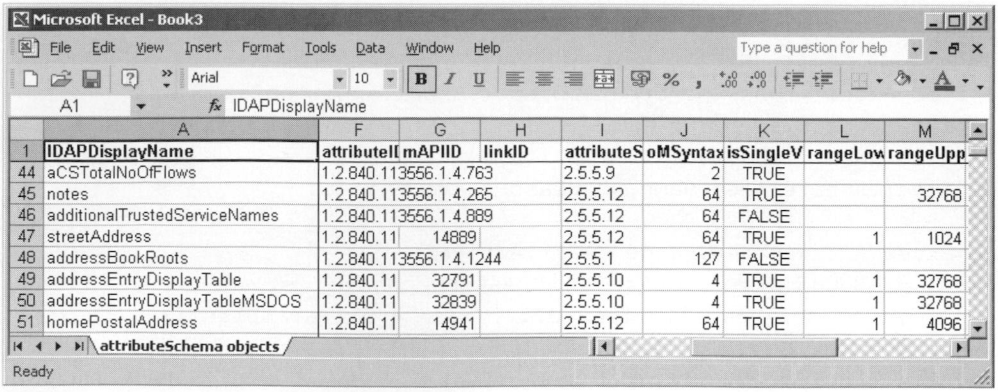

Microsoft Excel - Book3

A1 | IDAPDisplayName

	A	F	G	H	I	J	K	L	M
1	lDAPDisplayName	attributeI	mAPIID	linkID	attributeS	oMSyntax	isSingleV	rangeLow	rangeUpp
44	aCSTotalNoOfFlows	1.2.840.113556.1.4.763			2.5.5.9	2	TRUE		
45	notes	1.2.840.113556.1.4.265			2.5.5.12	64	TRUE		32768
46	additionalTrustedServiceNames	1.2.840.113556.1.4.889			2.5.5.12	64	FALSE		
47	streetAddress	1.2.840.11	14889		2.5.5.12	64	TRUE	1	1024
48	addressBookRoots	1.2.840.113556.1.4.1244			2.5.5.1	127	FALSE		
49	addressEntryDisplayTable	1.2.840.11	32791		2.5.5.10	4	TRUE	1	32768
50	addressEntryDisplayTableMSDOS	1.2.840.11	32839		2.5.5.10	4	TRUE	1	32768
51	homePostalAddress	1.2.840.11	14941		2.5.5.12	64	TRUE	1	4096

attributeSchema objects

Ready

Figure 11.53 Output of "ADSI List All attributeSchemas to Excel.vbs"

The script is as follows:

```
Option Explicit

Dim objExcel, objDSE, objSchema, objChild, i, varValue
Dim arrParamList(18)

'Names and Identifiers
arrParamList(0) = "lDAPDisplayName"
arrParamList(1) = "cn"
arrParamList(2) = "adminDisplayName"
arrParamList(3) = "distinguishedName"
arrParamList(4) = "adminDescription"
arrParamList(5) = "attributeID"
arrParamList(6) = "mAPIID"
arrParamList(7) = "linkID"
'Syntax and Content Rules
arrParamList(8) = "attributeSyntax"
arrParamList(9) = "oMSyntax"
arrParamList(10) = "isSingleValued"
arrParamList(11) = "rangeLower"
arrParamList(12) = "rangeUpper"
arrParamList(13) = "extendedCharsAllowed"
'Searches
arrParamList(14) = "searchFlags"
arrParamList(15) = "isMemberofPartialAttributeSet"
'Miscellaneous
arrParamList(16) = "systemOnly"
```

```
arrParamList(17) = "systemFlags"
arrParamList(18) = "objectCategory"

Set objExcel = WScript.CreateObject("Excel.Application")
objExcel.Visible = True
objExcel.Workbooks.Add
objExcel.ActiveSheet.Name = "attributeSchema objects"

objExcel.ActiveSheet.Range("A1").Activate
For i = LBound(arrParamList) To UBound(arrParamList)
   objExcel.ActiveCell.Offset(0,i).Value = arrParamList(i)
Next
objExcel.ActiveCell.Offset(1,0).Activate   'Move to next line

Set objDSE = GetObject("LDAP://rootDSE")
Set objSchema = GetObject("LDAP://" & _
   objDSE.Get("schemaNamingContext"))

On Error Resume Next
For Each objChild In objSchema
   If objChild.Class = "attributeSchema" Then
      For i = LBound(arrParamList) To UBound(arrParamList)
         varValue = objChild.Get(arrParamList(i))
         If Err <> 0 Then   'property not found or some other error
            Err.Clear
            varValue = ""
         End If
         objExcel.ActiveCell.Offset(0,i).Value = varValue
      Next
      objExcel.ActiveCell.Offset(1,0).Activate   'Move to next line
   End If
Next
```

Because this script and the previous one perform similar actions (but for different data), we could have combined the two and used a subprogram to perform the action. However, we preferred to use two short, independent scripts.

Create an Attribute and a Class.vbs

In our last schema example, we create one `attributeSchema` and one `classSchema` object. We use the same values for the object attributes that we had in Chapter 9.

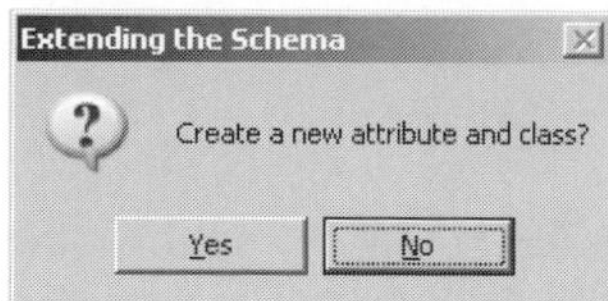

Figure 11.54 The confirmation message box of "ADSI Create an Attribute and a Class.vbs." Note that we have set "No" as the default.

Because schema extensions are something that we don't want to accidentally create, we have a confirmation box at the beginning of the script (see Figure 11.54). For the same reason, we don't take the forest name from `rootDSE`. You have to edit the forest name manually for each forest that you are going to use this script in. Without these precautions, you might just double-click the script and it would create an attribute and a class for you.

There is also one new element in the binding string. We want to specify the server, because any schema changes are possible only on the schema master. With the serverless binding strings we have used so far, you probably bind to a domain controller that is not the schema master and some of your change operations might fail.

If you try to modify the schema on a domain controller that is not the schema master, that wrong domain controller will forward your request to the schema master. Consequently, the modify operation may very well succeed. However, this doesn't apply to the part when the script updates the schema cache using `rootDSE`. As a result, any subsequent modify operations in the same script may fail. The easiest way to ensure that the script works is to specify the schema master in all the binding strings of the script.

The script is as follows:

```
Option Explicit

Dim intYesNo, objSchema, objAttr, objClass, objDSE

intYesNo =  MsgBox("Create a new attribute and class?", _
   vbYesNo + vbQuestion +vbDefaultButton2, _
   "Extending the Schema")
If intYesNo = vbNo Then
   WScript.Quit(0)  'no error so no errorlevel
End If
```

```
Set objSchema = GetObject("LDAP://dc1.sanao.com/" & _
   "CN=Schema,CN=Configuration,DC=sanao,DC=com")

On Error Resume Next

Set objAttr = objSchema.Create("attributeSchema", _
   "CN=sanao-MyProductUserData")

Call objAttr.Put("lDAPDisplayName", _
   "sanao-MyProductUserData")
Call objAttr.Put("adminDescription", _
   "This attribute contains the user data of MyProduct")
Call objAttr.Put("attributeID", "1.3.6.1.4.1.123123123.2.1")
Call objAttr.Put("attributeSyntax", "2.5.5.10")
Call objAttr.Put("oMSyntax", 4)
Call objAttr.Put("isSingleValued", True)
Call objAttr.Put("rangeLower", 20)
Call objAttr.Put("rangeUpper", 20)
Call objAttr.Put("showInAdvancedViewOnly", True)
Call objAttr.Put("searchFlags", 0)

Err.Clear
objAttr.SetInfo  'write the new attribute to the server
Call CheckIfError("create the attribute")
WScript.Echo "Created the attribute"

'Err.Clear
'Set objDSE = GetObject("LDAP://dc1.sanao.com/rootDSE")
'Call objDSE.Put("schemaUpdateNow", 1) 'trigger schema cache update
'objDSE.SetInfo
'Call CheckIfError("trigger schema cache update")
'WScript.Echo "Updated the schema cache"

Set objClass = objSchema.Create("classSchema", _
   "CN=sanao-MyProductConfigInfo")

Call objClass.Put("lDAPDisplayName", _
   "sanao-MyProductConfigInfo")
Call objClass.Put("governsID", "1.3.6.1.4.1.123123123.1.1")
Call objClass.Put("mustContain", _
   Array("1.3.6.1.4.1.123123123.2.1"))
'Call objClass.Put("mustContain", _
'   Array("sanao-MyProductUserData"))
Call objClass.Put("possSuperiors", Array("container"))
```

```
Call objClass.Put("objectClassCategory", 1)     'Structural
Call objClass.Put("subClassOf", "top")
Call objClass.Put("defaultHidingValue", True)
Call objClass.Put("showInAdvancedViewOnly", True)

Err.Clear
objClass.SetInfo 'write the new class to the server
Call CheckIfError("create the class")
WScript.Echo "Created the class"

Err.Clear
Set objDSE = GetObject("LDAP://dc1.sanao.com/rootDSE")
Call objDSE.Put("schemaUpdateNow", 1)   'trigger schema cache update
objDSE.SetInfo
Call CheckIfError("trigger schema cache update")
WScript.Echo "Updated the schema cache"

Sub CheckIfError(strAttemptedOperation)
   If Err <> 0 Then
      MsgBox "Couldn't " & strAttemptedOperation & vbCrLf & _
         "Error code " & Hex(Err), _
         vbOKOnly + vbCritical, "Error"
      WScript.Quit(1)   'there was an error so we set the errorlevel
   End If
End Sub
```

Note that the `showInAdvancedViewOnly` attribute is not part of the schema definition, nor do we need to add `searchFlags = 0`. However, we included them to be consistent with the base schema objects.

We wouldn't have to use arrays for the two multivalued attributes (because we include only one value), but we wanted to emphasize their nature with the `Array` keyword.

Between adding the attribute and class, we have six lines that are commented out. If you uncommented them, they would trigger the schema cache update. The reason we don't need them is that we add the attribute to the `mustContain` list of the class using the `attributeID`. If we wanted to use the attribute LDAP name (the two next commented lines), we would need the schema cache update first.

Anyway, we trigger the schema cache update at the end of the script. It saves us the five-minute waiting period, so we can start creating instances of this new class right away (e.g., using ADSI Edit). The main reason, however, for triggering the update is that we want to demonstrate how you can do it.

An alternative way to trigger the schema cache update is to use the `IADsADSystemInfo` interface. The following two lines do the trick:

```
Set objSystemInfo = CreateObject("ADSystemInfo")
Call objSystemInfo.RefreshSchemaCache
```

If all goes well when the script runs, you will see the output shown in Figure 11.55. If all doesn't go well, you will see an error box like the one in Figure 11.56 and the script will quit.

Some other errors that are quite possible with this script are as follows:

```
Const ERROR_DS_NO_ATTRIBUTE_OR_VALUE = &H8007200A
Const ERROR_DS_UNWILLING_TO_PERFORM = &H80072035
```

You will get the former error, for example, if you try to use an attribute name in the `mustContain` assignment and you haven't updated the schema cache. The latter error occurs if you haven't allowed schema changes on the schema master (as described in Chapter 9).

Figure 11.55 Output of "ADSI Create an Attribute and a Class.vbs" if all goes well

Figure 11.56 Error box of "ADSI Create an Attribute and a Class.vbs." The error code in the figure means `ERROR_OBJECT_ALREADY_EXISTS`. If you run the script several times without changing the object names and identifiers each time, you will see this error.

Configuration Information

The sample scripts in this section mostly access the configuration partition of Active Directory, but some of the examples also do other things. The section presents the following examples:

- CH11-25 ADSI List the Supported Namespaces.vbs
- CH11-26 ADSI List Attribute Display Names.vbs
- CH11-27 ADSI List the DC GUIDs.vbs
- CH11-28 ADSI List the rootDSE Property Cache.vbs
- CH11-29 ADSI List the GPO GUIDs.vbs
- CH11-30 ADSI List the Operations Masters.vbs
- CH11-31 ADSI List the Operations Masters with ADsFSMO.vbs
- CH11-32 ADSI List ADSystemInfo.vbs

All the examples just list information, because you probably don't want to make any changes to the information using scripts. If you do, you already know how to create objects of any class and modify their attributes.

List the Supported Namespaces.vbs

We start the configuration category with a short sample script that lists the ADSI namespaces that are currently installed on your computer. The script uses a special binding string, `ADS:`, to do this. The script's output appears in Figure 11.57 and the script's contents are in Figure 11.58.

Because the IIS namespace is also on the output list in Figure 11.57, the script was run on a computer that had the IIS service running.

```
Command Prompt
C:\Test>"ADSI List the Supported Namespaces.vbs"
WinNT:
NWCOMPAT:
NDS:
LDAP:
IIS:

C:\Test>_
```

Figure 11.57 Output of "ADSI List the Supported Namespaces.vbs"

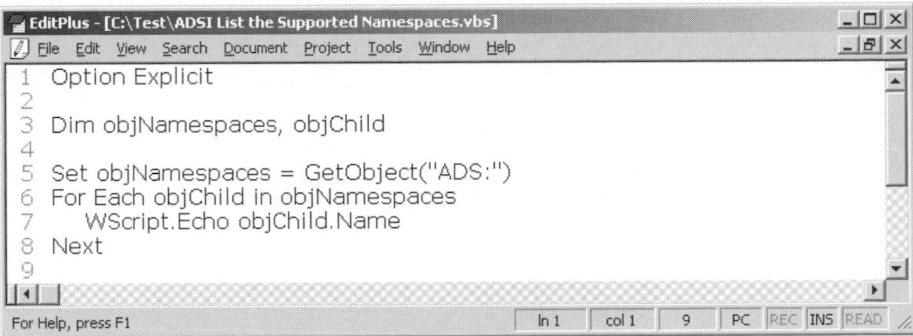

Figure 11.58 ADSI List the Supported Namespaces.vbs

List Attribute Display Names.vbs

This sample takes a class LDAP name as a command-line argument and lists all attribute display names versus their LDAP names. The information is read from the `attributeDisplayNames` attribute that resides in the display specifier object of the class.

If you want to manage objects of a certain class with ADSI or LDAP filters, you can first use this script to list the attribute names that correspond to the names that you see in the user interface.

Figure 11.59 shows the first lines of output for the user class. Figure 11.60 shows the script's contents.

`AttributeDisplayNames` is a multivalued attribute, where each value consists of a `display name, LDAP name` pair. As we browse through the values in the `For` loop, the `Split` function splits the value, using the comma character as a separator.

```
Command Prompt

C:\Test>"ADSI List Attribute Display Names.vbs" user
Web Page Address        wWWHomePage
Logon Name      userPrincipalName
Logon Workstations      userWorkstations
Display Name    displayName
Web Page Address (Others)       url
Job Title       title
Telex Number (Others)   telexNumber
Telephone Number        telephoneNumber
Street Address  streetAddress
State/Province  st
Last Name       sn
Logon Name (pre-Windows 2000)   samAccountName

C:\Test>_
```

Figure 11.59 Some lines of output of "ADSI List Attribute Display Names.vbs"

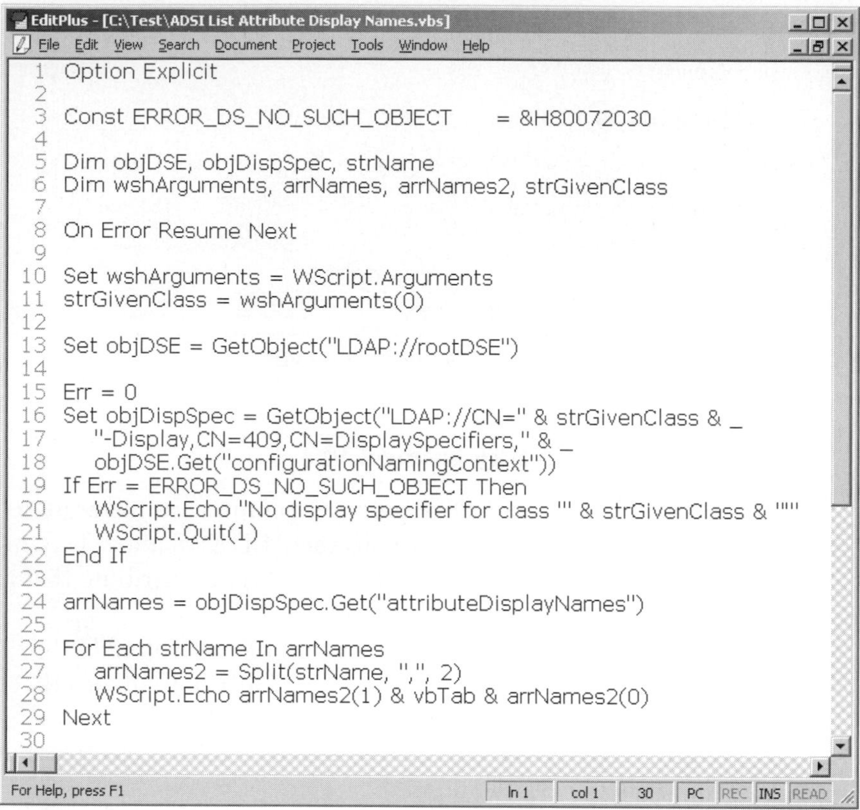

```
Option Explicit

Const ERROR_DS_NO_SUCH_OBJECT     = &H80072030

Dim objDSE, objDispSpec, strName
Dim wshArguments, arrNames, arrNames2, strGivenClass

On Error Resume Next

Set wshArguments = WScript.Arguments
strGivenClass = wshArguments(0)

Set objDSE = GetObject("LDAP://rootDSE")

Err = 0
Set objDispSpec = GetObject("LDAP://CN=" & strGivenClass & _
   "-Display,CN=409,CN=DisplaySpecifiers," & _
   objDSE.Get("configurationNamingContext"))
If Err = ERROR_DS_NO_SUCH_OBJECT Then
   WScript.Echo "No display specifier for class '" & strGivenClass & "'"
   WScript.Quit(1)
End If

arrNames = objDispSpec.Get("attributeDisplayNames")

For Each strName In arrNames
   arrNames2 = Split(strName, ",", 2)
   WScript.Echo arrNames2(1) & vbTab & arrNames2(0)
Next

```

Figure 11.60 ADSI List Attribute Display Names.vbs

List the DC GUIDs.vbs

This script reads the Sites container in the configuration partition and lists three things about each domain controller in the forest:

- The domain controller name (i.e., the common name of the server object)
- The DC GUID (i.e., the `objectGUID` attribute of the NTDS Settings object under the server object)
- The site name

Figure 11.61 shows the script's output.

You can use the script if you want to document the replica ring of one of your Active Directory sites. The GUIDs listed determine the order of the domain controllers in the ring. The easiest way to get the

```
C:\Test>"ADSI List the DC GUIDs.vbs"
CN=BOSSALES1 6f9092ef369beb4590714dfaee357c21 CN=Default-First-Site-Name
CN=BOSSALES2 b7ef457ff8ab93449f2a3a736e2a98eb CN=Default-First-Site-Name
CN=BOSSANA01 c5ccf9a2cb309c489ef69d0c27b3f675 CN=Default-First-Site-Name
CN=BOSSANA02 636d3c023da3a64b92ec7e2c06965e1d CN=Default-First-Site-Name
CN=BOSSANA03 6f606c1087960d489035295b90681a23 CN=Default-First-Site-Name
CN=BOSSANA04 12c3dd185037034bba8ac1f95dfaf8eb CN=Default-First-Site-Name
CN=BOSSANA05 48b6597ae112bf44883b6d531393594a CN=Default-First-Site-Name
CN=BOSSANA06 a6e61913d72a234c8e5737a5850dcbd1 CN=Default-First-Site-Name
CN=BOSSANA07 fb8b1bd46d640843a266360be9e6e1ea CN=Default-First-Site-Name

C:\Test>_
```

Figure 11.61 Output of “ADSI List the DC GUIDs.vbs”

correct ring order is to first redirect the output to a text file, such as dcguids1.txt, then delete lines containing other sites, and finally use the following command:

```
sort /+14 <dcguids1.txt >dcguids2.txt
```

This command reads the file, sorts it based on column 14, and outputs the result to dcguids2.txt.

To refresh your memory, Figure 11.62 shows the Sites and Services snap-in. You can refer to it when you read through the script in Figure 11.63.

Because the NTDS Settings objects are quite deep in the hierarchy, we need several nested `For` loops and `If` statements to reach them. Even though the `objectGUID` attribute is binary, it is easy to retrieve. The `Guid` property method of the `IADs` interface returns it in a nice text format.

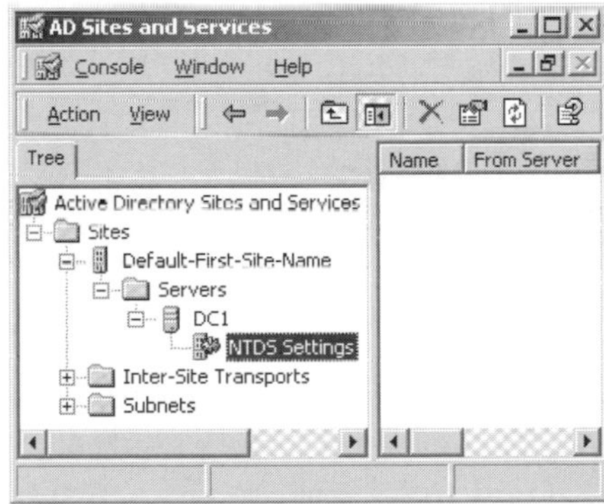

Figure 11.62 The Sites and Services snap-in. The sample forest in the figure has just one domain controller: DC1.

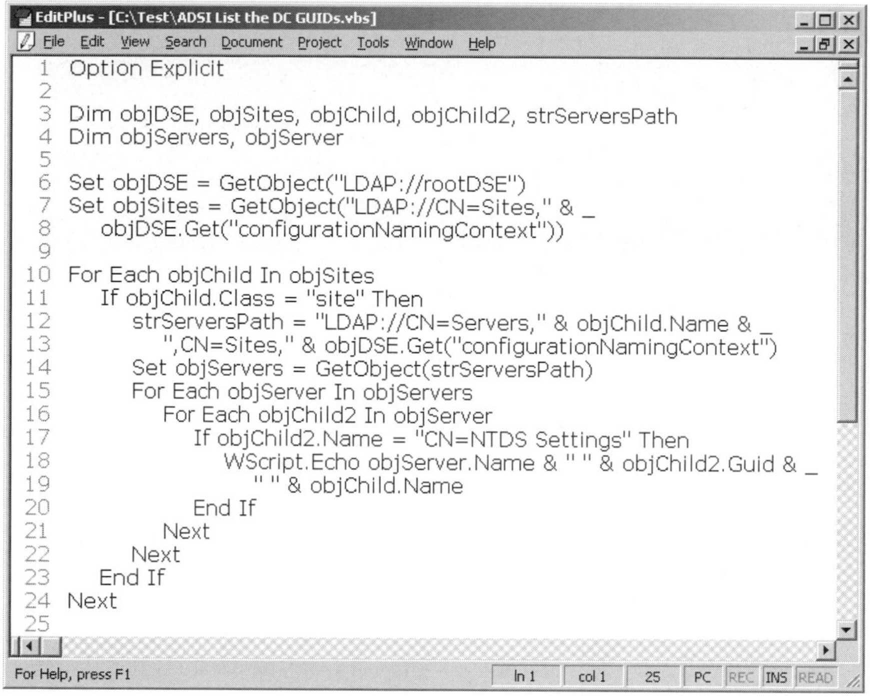

```
Option Explicit

Dim objDSE, objSites, objChild, objChild2, strServersPath
Dim objServers, objServer

Set objDSE = GetObject("LDAP://rootDSE")
Set objSites = GetObject("LDAP://CN=Sites," & _
   objDSE.Get("configurationNamingContext"))

For Each objChild In objSites
   If objChild.Class = "site" Then
      strServersPath = "LDAP://CN=Servers," & objChild.Name & _
         ",CN=Sites," & objDSE.Get("configurationNamingContext")
      Set objServers = GetObject(strServersPath)
      For Each objServer In objServers
         For Each objChild2 In objServer
            If objChild2.Name = "CN=NTDS Settings" Then
               WScript.Echo objServer.Name & " " & objChild2.Guid & _
                  " " & objChild.Name
            End If
         Next
      Next
   End If
Next
```

Figure 11.63 ADSI List the DC GUIDs.vbs

List the rootDSE Property Cache.vbs

So far we have used some of the `rootDSE` information to bind to objects without hard-coding the domain name. This script reads and displays everything that is in its property cache. Figure 11.64 shows most properties of the output. Figure 11.65 shows the script's contents.

We explained `rootDSE` at the end of Chapter 10.

List the GPO GUIDs.vbs

You can use this sample script to list all Group Policy objects (GPOs) that exist in your domain. The listed GUIDs are used as folder names when GPOs are stored in Active Directory and the file system. Figure 11.66 shows the script's output for a domain that has only the two default GPOs. Figure 11.67 shows the script's contents.

The GUID is easy to retrieve because instead of a binary attribute, it is the common name of the object in this case.

```
C:\Test>"ADSI List the rootDSE Property Cache.vbs"
currentTime (3)          20031103153427.0Z
subschemaSubentry (3)    CN=Aggregate,CN=Schema,CN=Configuration,DC=sanao,DC=com

dsServiceName (3)        CN=NTDS Settings,CN=DC1,CN=Servers,CN=Default-First-Sit
e-Name,CN=Sites,CN=Configuration,DC=sanao,DC=com
namingContexts (3)       DC=sanao,DC=com
                         CN=Configuration,DC=sanao,DC=com
                         CN=Schema,CN=Configuration,DC=sanao,DC=com
                         DC=DomainDnsZones,DC=sanao,DC=com
                         DC=ForestDnsZones,DC=sanao,DC=com
defaultNamingContext (3) DC=sanao,DC=com
schemaNamingContext (3)  CN=Schema,CN=Configuration,DC=sanao,DC=com
configurationNamingContext (3) CN=Configuration,DC=sanao,DC=com
rootDomainNamingContext (3) DC=sanao,DC=com
supportedLDAPVersion (3) 3
                         2
highestCommittedUSN (3)  24599
supportedSASLMechanisms (3) GSSAPI
                         GSS-SPNEGO
                         EXTERNAL
                         DIGEST-MD5
dnsHostName (3)          DC1.sanao.com
ldapServiceName (3)      sanao.com:DC1$@SANAO.COM
serverName (3)           CN=DC1,CN=Servers,CN=Default-First-Site-Name,CN=Sites,C
N=Configuration,DC=sanao,DC=com
supportedCapabilities (3) 1.2.840.113556.1.4.800
                         1.2.840.113556.1.4.1670
                         1.2.840.113556.1.4.1791
isSynchronized (3)       TRUE
isGlobalCatalogReady (3) TRUE
domainFunctionality (3)  2
forestFunctionality (3)  2
domainControllerFunctionality (3) 2

C:\Test>_
```

Figure 11.64 Most properties of the output of "ADSI List the rootDSE Property Cache.vbs"

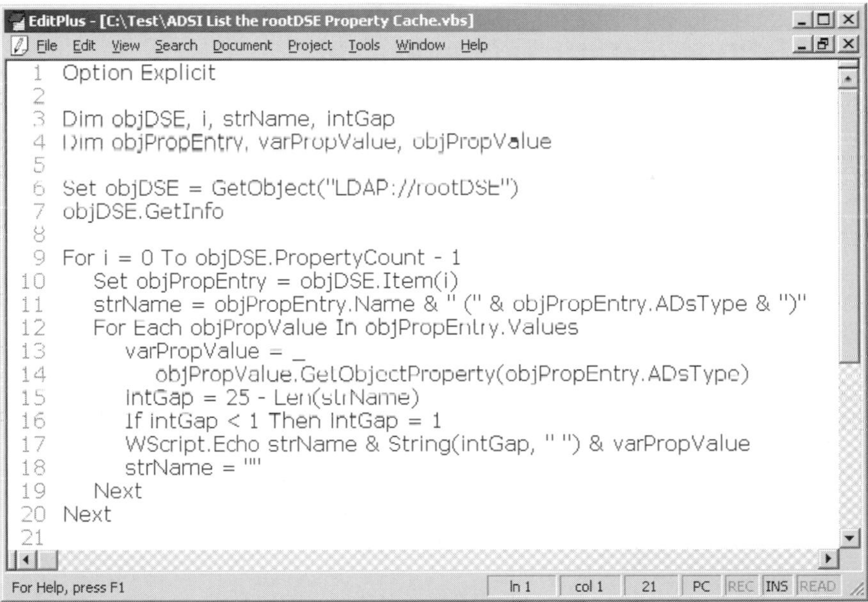

```
Option Explicit

Dim objDSE, i, strName, intGap
Dim objPropEntry, varPropValue, objPropValue

Set objDSE = GetObject("LDAP://rootDSE")
objDSE.GetInfo

For i = 0 To objDSE.PropertyCount - 1
    Set objPropEntry = objDSE.Item(i)
    strName = objPropEntry.Name & " (" & objPropEntry.ADsType & ")"
    For Each objPropValue In objPropEntry.Values
        varPropValue = _
            objPropValue.GetObjectProperty(objPropEntry.ADsType)
        intGap = 25 - Len(strName)
        If intGap < 1 Then intGap = 1
        WScript.Echo strName & String(intGap, " ") & varPropValue
        strName = ""
    Next
Next
```

Figure 11.65 ADSI List the rootDSE Property Cache.vbs

```
C:\Test>"ADSI List the GPO GUIDs.vbs"
CN={31B2F340-016D-11D2-945F-00C04FB984F9} - Default Domain Policy
CN={6AC1786C-016F-11D2-945F-00C04fB984F9} - Default Domain Controllers Policy

C:\Test>
```

Figure 11.66 Output of "ADSI List the GPO GUIDs.vbs"

```
Option Explicit

Dim objDSE, objChild, objPolicies

Set objDSE = GetObject("LDAP://rootDSE")
Set objPolicies = GetObject("LDAP://CN=Policies,CN=System," & _
   objDSE.Get("defaultNamingContext"))

For Each objChild In objPolicies
   If objChild.Class = "groupPolicyContainer" Then
      WScript.Echo objChild.Name & " - " & objChild.Get("displayName")
   End If
Next

```

Figure 11.67 ADSI List the GPO GUIDs.vbs

List the Operations Masters.vbs

In Chapter 5 we listed the objects that contain an `fSMORoleOwner` attribute that points to the NTDS Settings object of each role owner. This script reads those attributes and displays the five role owners. You can enter the domain name into an input box that has your default domain as a default.

Figure 11.68 shows the script's output. As you see, all five roles are in the same domain controller in this case.

```
C:\Test>"ADSI List the Operations Masters.vbs"

== PER-FOREST ==
Schema Master:          dc1.sanao.com
Domain Naming Master:   dc1.sanao.com

== PER-DOMAIN ==
RID Master:             dc1.sanao.com
PDC Master:             dc1.sanao.com
Infrastructure Master:  dc1.sanao.com

C:\Test>_
```

Figure 11.68 Output of "ADSI List the Operations Masters.vbs"

The script is as follows:

```
Option Explicit

Dim objDSE, strDefaultDom, strDom
Dim objSchema, objPartitions, objRID, objDom, objInfra

Set objDSE = GetObject("LDAP://rootDSE")
strDefaultDom = objDSE.Get("defaultNamingContext")

strDom =  InputBox("Enter the distinguished name of a domain" & _
   vbCrLf & "(e.g. " & strDefaultDom & ")", , strDefaultDom)

If strDom = "" Then WScript.Quit(1)  'user clicked Cancel

'Get the objects that have a pointer to each operations master
Set objSchema = GetObject("LDAP://" & _
   objDSE.Get("schemaNamingContext"))
Set objPartitions = GetObject("LDAP://CN=Partitions," & _
   objDSE.Get("configurationNamingContext"))
Set objRID = GetObject("LDAP://CN=RID Manager$,CN=System," & _
   strDom)
Set objDom = GetObject("LDAP://" & strDom)
Set objInfra = GetObject("LDAP://CN=Infrastructure," & strDom)

WScript.Echo vbCrLf & "== PER-FOREST =="
Call ShowFSMO("Schema", objSchema)
Call ShowFSMO("Domain Naming", objPartitions)
WScript.Echo vbCrLf & "== PER-DOMAIN =="
Call ShowFSMO("RID", objRID)
Call ShowFSMO("PDC", objDom)
Call ShowFSMO("Infrastructure", objInfra)

Sub ShowFSMO(strName, objPointerObj)
   Dim objNTDS, objDC, intGap

   Set objNTDS = GetObject("LDAP://" & _
      objPointerObj.Get("fSMORoleOwner"))  'pointer to CN=NTDS
                                           'Settings
   Set objDC = GetObject(objNTDS.Parent)  'server object

   intGap = 14 - Len(strName)
   WScript.Echo strName & " Master: " & String(intGap, " ") & _
      objDC.dnsHostName
End Sub
```

This is the first example in which we pass an object variable as an argument to a subprogram. In the variable name `objPointerObj`, the first "obj" means that the variable is a VBScript object. The second "Obj" means that this is an Active Directory pointer object.

Changing an Operations Master

We explained in Chapter 5 how to manually transfer or seize an operations master role to another domain controller. There shouldn't be a great need to script either of these tasks, because they are quite infrequent. However, we introduce the principles briefly.

To initiate a role transfer (i.e., in cooperation with the previous role owner), you must write the value 1 to the appropriate operational attribute of `rootDSE`. As a result, an atomic transfer of the role occurs, including the synchronization of any vital configuration information. The five attributes that correspond to the transfers of the five roles are as follows: `becomeSchemaMaster`, `becomeDomainMaster`, `becomeRidMaster`, `becomePdc`, and `becomeInfrastructureMaster`. For example, executing the following lines transfers the infrastructure master to `dc2.sanao.com`.

```
Set objDSE = GetObject("LDAP://dc2.sanao.com/rootDSE")
Call objDSE.Put("becomeInfrastructureMaster", 1)
objDSE.SetInfo
```

If you need a role-transferring script in practice, you can use the preceding lines and incorporate error checking from the "Create an Attribute and a Class.vbs" section. You can also add lines from this section to list the new role owner.

Of the five listed attributes, `becomePdc` requires special handling—otherwise you get the "server is unwilling to perform" error (corresponding to the error code "80072035"). Special handling means that instead of the value 1, you must provide the domain SID in binary format, so the lines are the following:

```
Set objDSE = GetObject("LDAP://dc2.sanao.com/rootDSE")
Set objDomain = GetObject("LDAP://DC=sanao,DC=com")
Call objDSE.Put("becomeInfrastructureMaster", _
    objDomain.objectSid)
objDSE.SetInfo
```

To initiate a role seizure (i.e., when the previous role owner has failed), you must write a pointer to a new domain controller in the `fSMORoleOwner` attribute of the appropriate object. For information on which objects to use and what to put in `fSMORoleOwner`, refer to the listing script in this section.

WARNING Performing a role seizure in a wrong way can corrupt your forest. Before attempting a seizure, be sure to throroughly understand the information on role seizures presented in Chapter 5.

List the Operations Masters with ADsFSMO.vbs

One of the components in the ADSI Resource Kit is ADsFSMO. We can use it to list the same operations master roles that we listed in the previous example.

To use the component, you must perform the following two steps:

1. Locate the file adsfsmo.dll in your Platform SDK folder (perhaps C:\Program Files\Microsoft\ADSI Resource Kit, Samples and Utilities\ResourceKit). You can either leave the file where it is or copy it to some other folder, such as C:\Winnt\System32.
2. Register the component with the command `regsvr32 adsfsmo.dll`. If the DLL file is not in the current folder, you must include the location in the command. You should see a pop-up message indicating that "DllRegisterServer in adsfsmo.dll succeeded."

Now you are ready to use the component in the script shown in Figure 11.69.

First we create the ADsFSMO object, and then we connect to some domain controller. This determines the domain for which we query the operations master roles.

Because the component knows right away the role owners of each operations master, all we need to do is list them.

NOTE Even though this operations master script is easier and shorter than the former operations master script, we wanted to include the former one too, because it is much more educational.

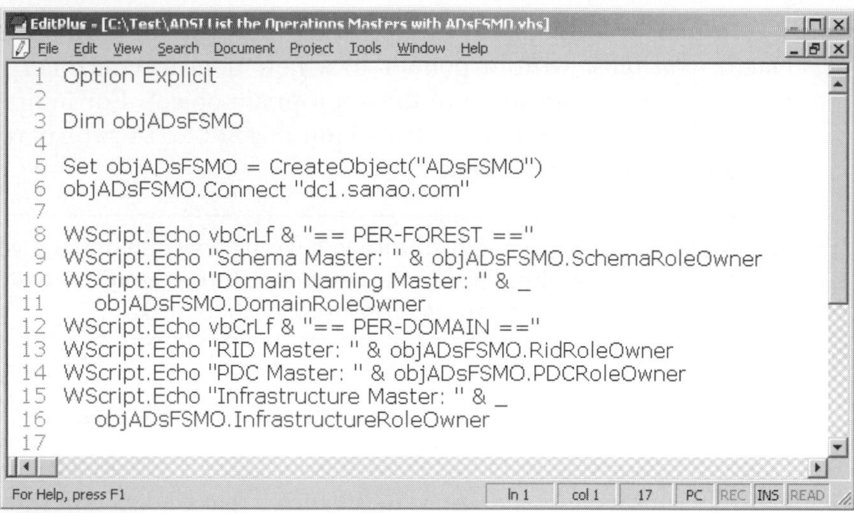

```
Option Explicit

Dim objADsFSMO

Set objADsFSMO = CreateObject("ADsFSMO")
objADsFSMO.Connect "dc1.sanao.com"

WScript.Echo vbCrLf & "== PER-FOREST =="
WScript.Echo "Schema Master: " & objADsFSMO.SchemaRoleOwner
WScript.Echo "Domain Naming Master: " & _
   objADsFSMO.DomainRoleOwner
WScript.Echo vbCrLf & "== PER-DOMAIN =="
WScript.Echo "RID Master: " & objADsFSMO.RidRoleOwner
WScript.Echo "PDC Master: " & objADsFSMO.PDCRoleOwner
WScript.Echo "Infrastructure Master: " & _
   objADsFSMO.InfrastructureRoleOwner
```

Figure 11.69 ADSI List the Operations Masters with ADsFSMO.vbs

List ADSystemInfo.vbs

ADSI includes an `ADSystemInfo` interface, which shows you some general configuration information. The output of this information is in Figure 11.70 and the script's contents are in Figure 11.71.

The `ADSystemInfo` interface includes also the method `Refresh-SchemaCache`, which we explained in the "Create an Attribute and a Class.vbs" example.

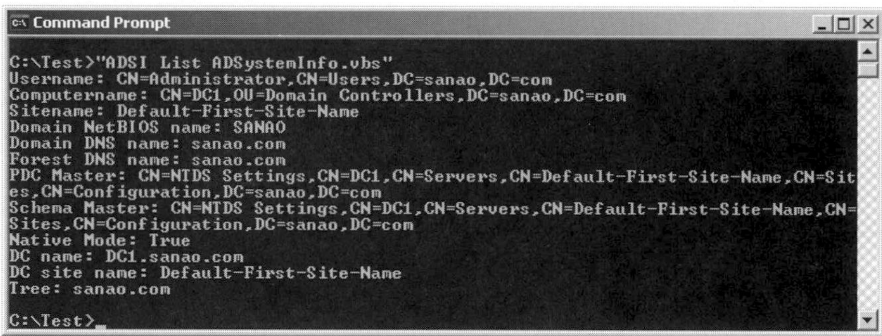

```
C:\Test>"ADSI List ADSystemInfo.vbs"
Username: CN=Administrator,CN=Users,DC=sanao,DC=com
Computername: CN=DC1,OU=Domain Controllers,DC=sanao,DC=com
Sitename: Default-First-Site-Name
Domain NetBIOS name: SANAO
Domain DNS name: sanao.com
Forest DNS name: sanao.com
PDC Master: CN=NTDS Settings,CN=DC1,CN=Servers,CN=Default-First-Site-Name,CN=Sit
es,CN=Configuration,DC=sanao,DC=com
Schema Master: CN=NTDS Settings,CN=DC1,CN=Servers,CN=Default-First-Site-Name,CN=
Sites,CN=Configuration,DC=sanao,DC=com
Native Mode: True
DC name: DC1.sanao.com
DC site name: Default-First-Site-Name
Tree: sanao.com

C:\Test>
```

Figure 11.70 Output of "ADSI List ADSystemInfo.vbs"

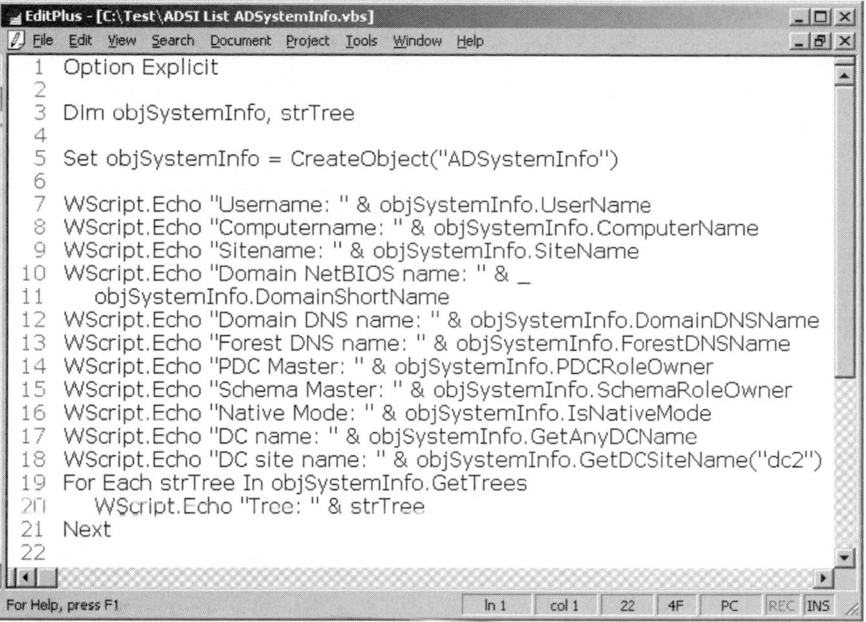

Figure 11.71 ADSI List ADSystemInfo.vbs

Access Control Lists

ADSI enables you to list and modify the access control lists (that is, permissions) of Active Directory objects by using three security interfaces In this section, we first explain the interfaces and then show the sample scripts.

The Windows XP and Windows Server 2003 versions of ADSI include also a fourth security interface, called `IADsSecurityUtility`, which you can use to manipulate the access control lists of NTFS files and folders, file shares, and registry keys. As the last example (the "Add ACEs to a Folder.vbs" section), we show how to use the fourth interface to modify NTFS folder permissions.

Security Interfaces

Active Directory uses security descriptors, ACLs, and ACEs to control who has access to each object and what kind of access he has. We explain them all in detail at the end of Chapter 4, so you might want to refresh your memory by reading those pages again.

The three security interfaces are as follows:

- `IADsSecurityDescriptor` gives you access to the fields of a security descriptor, the most interesting one being the discretionary ACL.
- `IADsAccessControlList` gives you access to ACLs, whether they are discretionary or system ACLs. This interface enables you to enumerate all ACEs.
- `IADsAccessControlEntry` gives you access to the fields of an individual ACE.

Figure 11.72 shows how the interfaces work.

NOTE We have drawn several `objACE` variables in Figure 11.72. Depending on the script, however, there is perhaps only one of them to represent different entries one at a time.

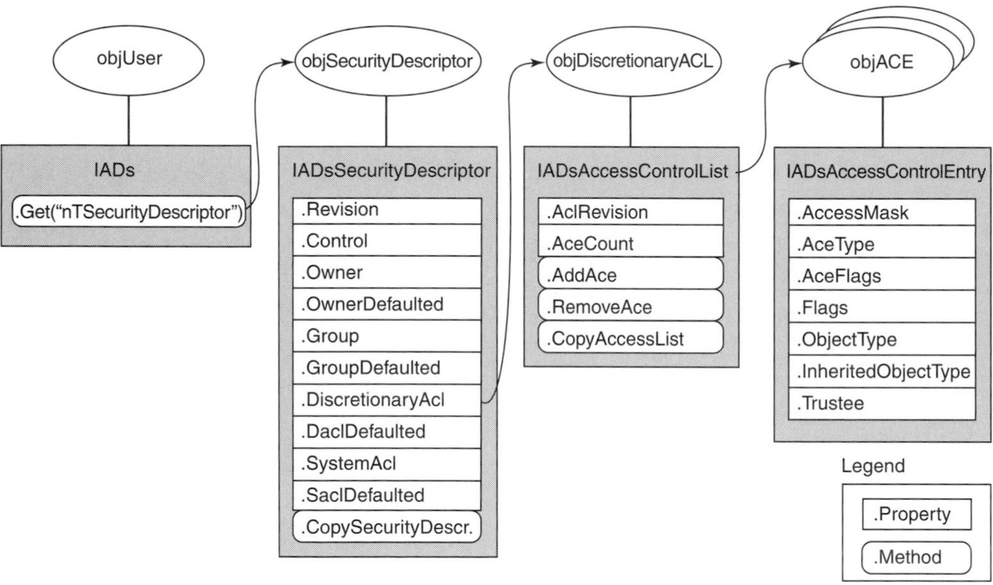

Figure 11.72 By reading the `nTSecurityDescriptor` attribute of an Active Directory object, you can create an object variable to be used with the `IADsSecurityDescriptor` interface. This way, you will get your hands on the discretionary ACL and the individual ACEs.

The Access Control List Sample Scripts

We present the following examples in this section:

- CH11-33 ADSI List ACEs - Short.vbs
- CH11-34 ADSI List ACEs to Excel - Short.vbs
- CH11-35 ADSI List Binary GUIDs.vbs
- CH11-36 ADSI List ACEs - Long.vbs
- CH11-37 ADSI Add ACEs.vbs
- CH11-38 ADSI Add ACEs to a Folder.vbs

We start with a short example as an introduction and then present a long script that is probably more useful in practice.

List ACEs - Short.vbs

We start with a short script that lists all (discretionary) ACEs of a given Active Directory object. You can enter the object name into an input box.

Figure 11.73 shows part of the script's output for the `CN=Users` container. We interpret something of the output with the next sample, where we have the same output in Excel. Here we just say that the access mask "&HF01FF" is the same as Full Control.

Figure 11.74 shows the script's contents.

If you like to see only some of the ACEs, you can put an `If` statement inside the loop to filter out unwanted ACEs.

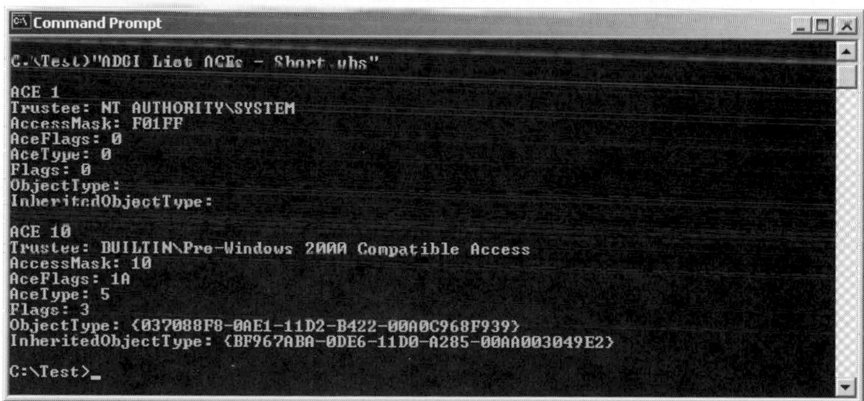

Figure 11.73 Output of "ADSI List ACEs - Short.vbs"

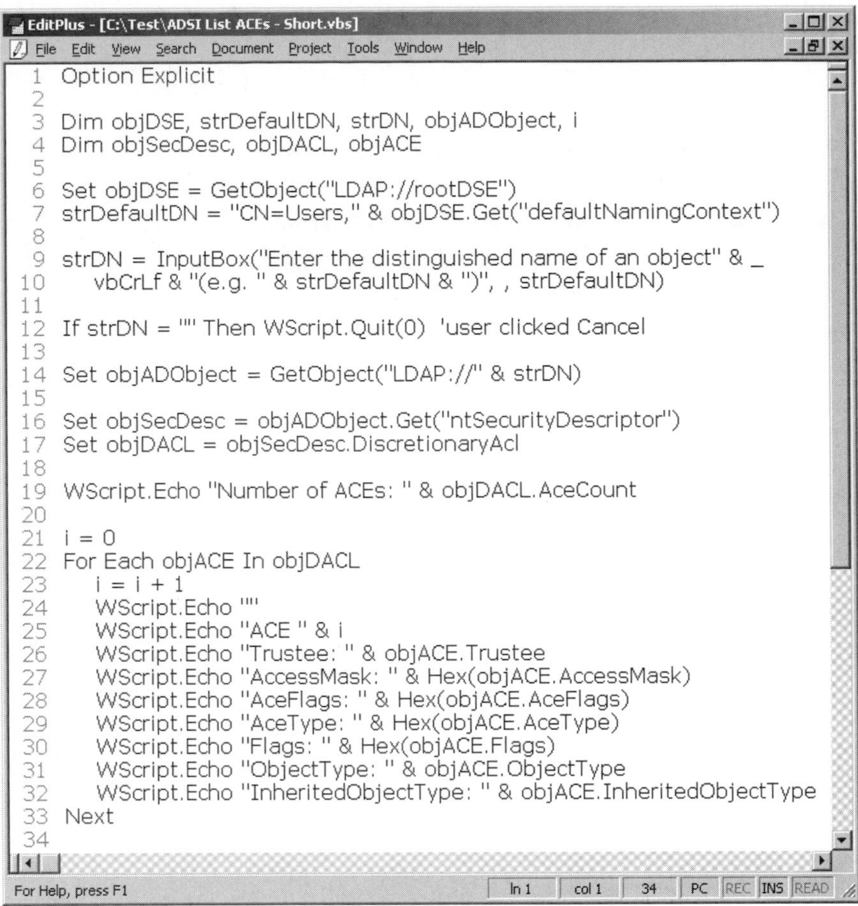

```
Option Explicit

Dim objDSE, strDefaultDN, strDN, objADObject, i
Dim objSecDesc, objDACL, objACE

Set objDSE = GetObject("LDAP://rootDSE")
strDefaultDN = "CN=Users," & objDSE.Get("defaultNamingContext")

strDN = InputBox("Enter the distinguished name of an object" & _
   vbCrLf & "(e.g. " & strDefaultDN & ")", , strDefaultDN)

If strDN = "" Then WScript.Quit(0)  'user clicked Cancel

Set objADObject = GetObject("LDAP://" & strDN)

Set objSecDesc = objADObject.Get("ntSecurityDescriptor")
Set objDACL = objSecDesc.DiscretionaryAcl

WScript.Echo "Number of ACEs: " & objDACL.AceCount

i = 0
For Each objACE In objDACL
   i = i + 1
   WScript.Echo ""
   WScript.Echo "ACE " & i
   WScript.Echo "Trustee: " & objACE.Trustee
   WScript.Echo "AccessMask: " & Hex(objACE.AccessMask)
   WScript.Echo "AceFlags: " & Hex(objACE.AceFlags)
   WScript.Echo "AceType: " & Hex(objACE.AceType)
   WScript.Echo "Flags: " & Hex(objACE.Flags)
   WScript.Echo "ObjectType: " & objACE.ObjectType
   WScript.Echo "InheritedObjectType: " & objACE.InheritedObjectType
Next
```

Figure 11.74 ADSI List ACEs - Short.vbs

List ACEs to Excel - Short.vbs

This script is nearly identical to the previous one, except this time we dump the ACEs into Excel. You have the knowledge to write this script on your own based on the samples we have provided so far, but we wanted to show a complete script because the output format is so nice.

Figure 11.75 shows the resulting spreadsheet for the `CN=Users` container.

We are not going to repeat the ten-page discussion that we presented about the access control architecture in Chapter 4. However, we will provide you with some short comments on the output.

Microsoft Excel - Book4

A1 Trustee

	A	B	C	D	E	F	G
1	Trustee	AccessMa	AceFlags	AceType	Flags	ObjectType	InheritedObjectType
2	NT AUTHORITY\SYSTEM	F01FF	0	0	0		
3	SANAO\Domain Admins	E01BF	0	0	0		
4	BUILTIN\Account Operators	3	0	5	1	{BF967ABA-0DE6-11D0-A285-00AA0	
5	BUILTIN\Account Operators	3	0	5	1	{BF967A9C-0DE6-11D0-A285-00AA0	
6	BUILTIN\Print Operators	3	0	5	1	{BF967AA8-0DE6-11D0-A285-00AA0	
7	NT AUTHORITY\Authenticated Users	20094	0	0	0		
8	BUILTIN\Account Operators	3	0	5	1	{4828CC14-1437-45BC-9B07-AD6F0	
9	BUILTIN\Administrators	F01BD	12	0	0		
10	SANAO\Enterprise Admins	F01FF	12	0	0		
11	BUILTIN\Pre-Windows 2000 Compatil	4	12	0	0		
12	BUILTIN\Pre-Windows 2000 Compatil	10	1A	5	3	{037088F8-0	{BF967ABA-0DE6-11D
13	BUILTIN\Pre-Windows 2000 Compatil	10	1A	5	3	{59BA2F42-7	{BF967ABA-0DE6-11D
14	BUILTIN\Pre-Windows 2000 Compatil	10	1A	5	3	{BC0AC240-7	{BF967ABA-0DE6-11D
15	BUILTIN\Pre-Windows 2000 Compatil	10	1A	5	3	{4C164200-2	{BF967ABA-0DE6-11D
16	BUILTIN\Pre-Windows 2000 Compatil	10	1A	5	3	{5F202010-79	{BF967ABA-0DE6-11D
17	BUILTIN\Pre-Windows 2000 Compatil	20094	1A	5	2		{BF967A9C-0DE6-11D
18	BUILTIN\Pre-Windows 2000 Compatil	20094	1A	5	2		{BF967ABA-0DE6-11D
19	BUILTIN\Pre-Windows 2000 Compatil	10	1A	5	3	{037088F8-0	{4828CC14-1437-45BC-
20	BUILTIN\Pre-Windows 2000 Compatil	10	1A	5	3	{59BA2F42-7	{4828CC14-1437-45BC-
21	BUILTIN\Pre-Windows 2000 Compatil	10	1A	5	3	{BC0AC240-7	{4828CC14-1437-45BC-
22	BUILTIN\Pre-Windows 2000 Compatil	10	1A	5	3	{4C164200-2	{4828CC14-1437-45BC-
23	BUILTIN\Pre-Windows 2000 Compatil	10	1A	5	3	{5F202010-79	{4828CC14-1437-45BC-
24	BUILTIN\Pre-Windows 2000 Compatil	20094	1A	5	2		{4828CC14-1437-45BC-
25	NT AUTHORITY\ENTERPRISE DOM	10	1A	5	3	{B7C69E6D-2	{BF967ABA-0DE6-11D
26	NT AUTHORITY\ENTERPRISE DOM	10	1A	5	3	{B7C69E6D-2	{BF967A9C-0DE6-11D
27	NT AUTHORITY\ENTERPRISE DOM	10	1A	5	3	{B7C69E6D-2	{BF967A86-0DE6-11D0

ACEs

Ready

Figure 11.75 Output of "ADSI List ACEs to Excel - Short.vbs"

- AccessMask "F01FF" (hex) is the same as Full Control, and "20094" (hex) is the same as Read + List Object.
- AceFlags "12" (hex) means that the ACE was inherited from above and it applies to "This object and all child objects."
- The GUIDs starting with "BF967ABA" refer to the user objects (i.e., those ACEs somehow apply to user objects).

You can open up the list of permission entries for `CN=Users` (i.e., ACL Editor) using the Users and Computers snap-in. This way, you can compare those entries to the ones shown here.

NOTE If you compare what you see in ACL Editor to the output in Figure 11.75, you'll notice that the script lists ten ACEs (or five ACEs in AD2000) that are not visible in the user interface of the snap-in (lines 12 through 16 and 19 through 23 in the Excel spreadsheet). Those ten/five ACEs are read permissions to various property sets applying to user and inetOrgPerson objects, but because line 18 is a read permission to all user properties and line 24 is a read permission to all inetOrgPerson properties, those first ten or five are redundant. It is logical that the user interface doesn't show them, but it is a slight bug that those redundant ACEs are part of the default permissions.

The script is as follows:

```
Option Explicit

Dim objDSE, strDefaultDN, strDN, objADObject, i
Dim objSecDesc, objDACL, objACE, objExcel

Set objDSE = GetObject("LDAP://rootDSE")
strDefaultDN = "CN=Users," & objDSE.Get("defaultNamingContext")

strDN = InputBox("Enter the distinguished name of an object" & _
   vbCrLf & "(e.g. " & strDefaultDN & ")", , strDefaultDN)

If strDN = "" Then WScript.Quit(0)  'user clicked Cancel

Set objADObject = GetObject("LDAP://" & strDN)

Set objSecDesc = objADObject.Get("ntSecurityDescriptor")
Set objDACL = objSecDesc.DiscretionaryAcl

Set objExcel = WScript.CreateObject("Excel.Application")
objExcel.Visible = True
objExcel.Workbooks.Add
objExcel.ActiveSheet.Name = "ACEs"

objExcel.ActiveSheet.Range("A1").Activate
objExcel.ActiveCell.Value = "Trustee"
objExcel.ActiveCell.Offset(0,1).Value = "AccessMask"
objExcel.ActiveCell.Offset(0,2).Value = "AceFlags"
objExcel.ActiveCell.Offset(0,3).Value = "AceType"
objExcel.ActiveCell.Offset(0,4).Value = "Flags"
objExcel.ActiveCell.Offset(0,5).Value = "ObjectType"
objExcel.ActiveCell.Offset(0,6).Value = "InheritedObjectType"
objExcel.ActiveCell.Offset(1,0).Activate  'goto next line
```

```
i = 0
For Each objACE In objDACL
    objExcel.ActiveCell.Value = objACE.Trustee
    objExcel.ActiveCell.Offset(0,1).Value = Hex(objACE.AccessMask)
    objExcel.ActiveCell.Offset(0,2).Value = Hex(objACE.AceFlags)
    objExcel.ActiveCell.Offset(0,3).Value = Hex(objACE.AceType)
    objExcel.ActiveCell.Offset(0,4).Value = Hex(objACE.Flags)
    objExcel.ActiveCell.Offset(0,5).Value = objACE.ObjectType
    objExcel.ActiveCell.Offset(0,6).Value = _
        objACE.InheritedObjectType
    objExcel.ActiveCell.Offset(1,0).Activate  'goto next line
Next
```

The script should be self-explanatory.

List Binary GUIDs.vbs

This example shows how to list values of binary GUIDs. We have placed this sample in the middle of the access control samples because you mainly need to access binary GUIDs when listing or modifying ACLs.

GUIDs in ACEs and the `rightsGuid` attribute use the string representation of GUIDs. The binary format in turn is in use with `objectGUID`, `schemaIDGUID`, and `attributeSecurityGUID`.

Figure 11.76 shows some lines of the output of the script when it displays the `schemaIDGUID` for all classes and attributes.

The script shows `schemaIDGUID` for the `user` class to be the following:

```
BA7A96BFE60DD011A28500AA003049E2
```

```
Command Prompt
C:\Test>"ADSI List Binary GUIDs.vbs"
1 CN=account: account: 6AA42826ADA6E04AB8542B12D9FE6F9E
2 CN=Account-Expires: accountExpires: 157996BFE60DD011A28500AA003049E2
3 CN=Account-Name-History: accountNameHistory: EC5219037233BD21190CC00C04FD91AB1
4 CN=ACS-Aggregate-Token-Rate-Per-User: aCSAggregateTokenRatePerUser: 7D12567F01
53D111A9C50000F80367C1
5 CN=ACS-Allocable-RSVP-Bandwidth: aCSAllocableRSVPBandwidth: 8312567F0153D111A9
C50000F80367C1
6 CN=ACS-Cache-Timeout: aCSCacheTimeout: A155B31CD056D111A9C60000F80367C1
1226 CN=User: user: BA7A96BFE60DD011A28500AA003049E2

C:\Test>
```

Figure 11.76 Some lines of output of "ADSI List Binary GUIDs.vbs"

If we need to compare this to a string format GUID used in ACEs, we must first convert it. As we add curly braces and some hyphens, we get the following:

```
{BA7A96BF-E60D-D011-A285-00AA003049E2}
```

Then we swap bytes 1, 2, 3, and 4 to be 4, 3, 2, and 1 (and also bytes 5, 6, 7, and 8) to get the final result:

```
{BF967ABA-0DE6-11D0-A285-00AA003049E2}
```

Our next sample script (List ACEs - Long.vbs) is a complete solution and in it we include lines to automate this conversion process.

NOTE The `Guid` property method of the `IADs` interfaces returns the `objectGUID` for any Active Directory object. Note that even though the value is of the string data type, there are no hyphens or curly braces and the bytes are in the same order as in binary GUIDs.

Figure 11.77 shows the script's contents.

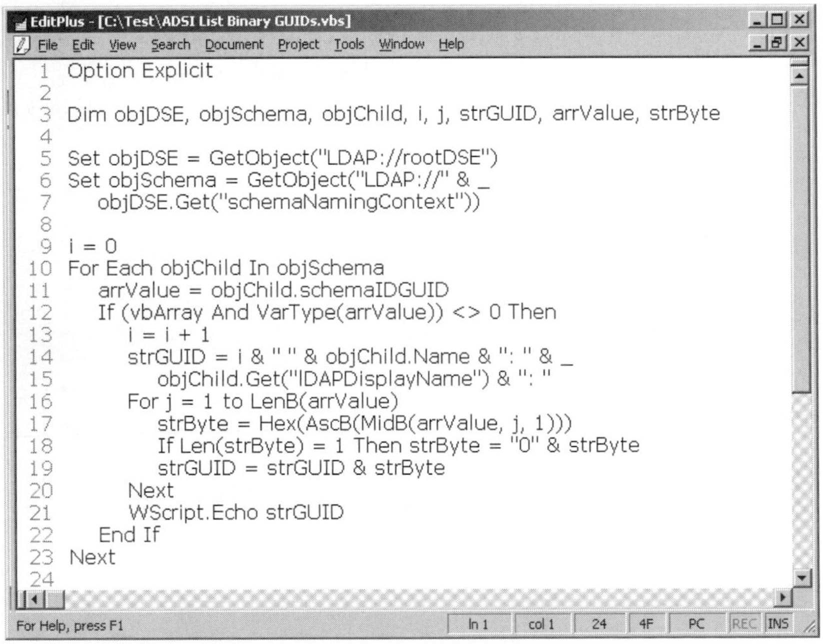
EditPlus - [C:\Test\ADSI List Binary GUIDs.vbs]
File Edit View Search Document Project Tools Window Help
Option Explicit
Dim objDSE, objSchema, objChild, i, j, strGUID, arrValue, strByte
Set objDSE = GetObject("LDAP://rootDSE")
Set objSchema = GetObject("LDAP://" & _
objDSE.Get("schemaNamingContext"))
i = 0
For Each objChild In objSchema
arrValue = objChild.schemaIDGUID
If (vbArray And VarType(arrValue)) <> 0 Then
i = i + 1
strGUID = i & " " & objChild.Name & ": " & _
objChild.Get("lDAPDisplayName") & ": "
For j = 1 to LenB(arrValue)
strByte = Hex(AscB(MidB(arrValue, j, 1)))
If Len(strByte) = 1 Then strByte = "0" & strByte
strGUID = strGUID & strByte
Next
WScript.Echo strGUID
End If
Next
For Help, press F1
In 1
col 1
24
4F
PC
REC
INS

Figure 11.77 ADSI List Binary GUIDs.vbs

If an attribute has no value, `objChild.schemaIDGUID` returns a `vbEmpty` variable. The `VarType` check on line 12 filters out these entries, so that we examine GUIDs only when they exist. There is actually only one object, `CN=Aggregate`, that doesn't have this attribute set. Lines 16 through 20 handle the binary value in a similar way to the "ADSI List User Properties with Methods.vbs" sample.

List ACEs - Long.vbs

In two earlier examples, you saw all the ACEs, but the contents were just hex numbers. In this script, we interpret the numbers and display the results in (more or less) plain English.

Unfortunately, interpreting the numbers makes the script quite long. We need to define all the bit values and bit names for the ACE fields, and that alone takes 80 lines, which is about one-third of the total length of 250 lines.

We define all ACE "constants" in arrays and use `For` loops to go through them. This approach makes the script slightly more cryptic, but the alternative would have been a 30 percent longer script (320 lines).

NOTE The array approach works only when you go through all values. If you need to use certain values, it is better to have traditional constant definitions, such as `Const ADS_RIGHTS_DS_WRITE_PROP = &H20`.

NOTE In the constant definitions (such as `ADS_RIGHTS_DS_WRITE_PROP`) permissions are called "rights."

Figure 11.78 shows part of the script's output for the `CN=Users` container. The access mask "&HF01FF" contains 13 set bits and now you see which 13 permissions they correspond to. As we mentioned earlier, this list of 13 permissions is the same as Full Control.

NOTE Be careful if you run this script in a production environment. The script doesn't make any changes, but it uses a considerable amount of CPU time on a domain controller when it compares over and over again which GUID corresponds to which class, attribute, property set, or extended right.

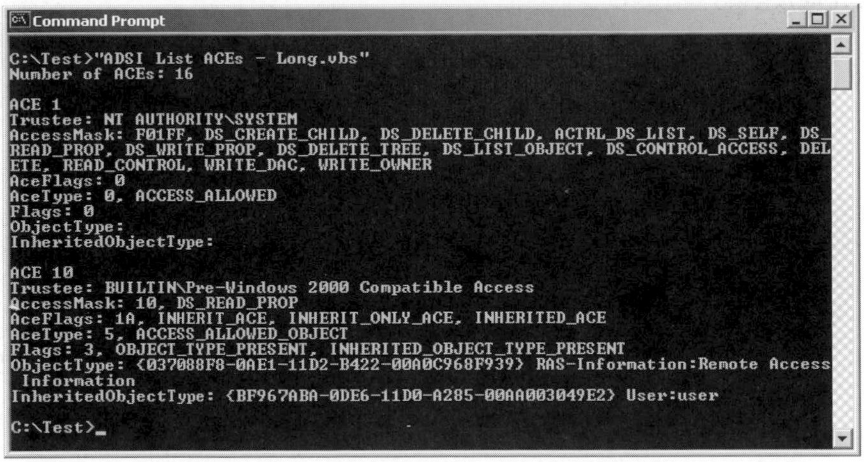

```
C:\Test>"ADSI List ACEs - Long.vbs"
Number of ACEs: 16

ACE 1
Trustee: NT AUTHORITY\SYSTEM
AccessMask: F01FF, DS_CREATE_CHILD, DS_DELETE_CHILD, ACTRL_DS_LIST, DS_SELF, DS_
READ_PROP, DS_WRITE_PROP, DS_DELETE_TREE, DS_LIST_OBJECT, DS_CONTROL_ACCESS, DEL
ETE, READ_CONTROL, WRITE_DAC, WRITE_OWNER
AceFlags: 0
AceType: 0, ACCESS_ALLOWED
Flags: 0
ObjectType:
InheritedObjectType:

ACE 10
Trustee: BUILTIN\Pre-Windows 2000 Compatible Access
AccessMask: 10, DS_READ_PROP
AceFlags: 1A, INHERIT_ACE, INHERIT_ONLY_ACE, INHERITED_ACE
AceType: 5, ACCESS_ALLOWED_OBJECT
Flags: 3, OBJECT_TYPE_PRESENT, INHERITED_OBJECT_TYPE_PRESENT
ObjectType: {037088F8-0AE1-11D2-B422-00A0C968F939} RAS-Information:Remote Access
 Information
InheritedObjectType: {BF967ABA-0DE6-11D0-A285-00AA003049E2} User:user

C:\Test>_
```

Figure 11.78 Part of the output of "ADSI List ACEs - Long.vbs"

It would seem that ACE flags and flags are not interpreted for ACE 1. However, because the value for both is "0," it means that they have no bits (and, consequently, no flags) set, so there is nothing to interpret. An ACE flag "0" means that the ACE was not inherited and it does not inherit. On the other hand, ACE 10 has the value "1A," which means that it is inherited and it inherits to children.

ACE type "0" we have interpreted. It is not a bitfield like the others, so the value "0" means something (it means "access allowed").

The script is as follows:

```
Option Explicit

'AccessMask Bits
'Constants would be like ADS_RIGHT_DS_CREATE_CHILD
Dim arrADSRights(18,1)   '19 value pairs, name and bit in each
arrADSRights(0,0) = "DS_CREATE_CHILD"
arrADSRights(0,1) = &H1
arrADSRights(1,0) = "DS_DELETE_CHILD"
arrADSRights(1,1) = &H2
arrADSRights(2,0) = "ACTRL_DS_LIST"
arrADSRights(2,1) = &H4
arrADSRights(3,0) = "DS_SELF"
arrADSRights(3,1) = &H8
arrADSRights(4,0) = "DS_READ_PROP"
arrADSRights(4,1) = &H10
arrADSRights(5,0) = "DS_WRITE_PROP"
```

```
arrADSRights(5,1) = &H20
arrADSRights(6,0) = "DS_DELETE_TREE"
arrADSRights(6,1) = &H40
arrADSRights(7,0) = "DS_LIST_OBJECT"
arrADSRights(7,1) = &H80
arrADSRights(8,0) = "DS_CONTROL_ACCESS"
arrADSRights(8,1) = &H100
arrADSRights(9,0) = "DELETE"
arrADSRights(9,1) = &H10000
arrADSRights(10,0) = "READ_CONTROL"
arrADSRights(10,1) = &H20000
arrADSRights(11,0) = "WRITE_DAC"
arrADSRights(11,1) = &H40000
arrADSRights(12,0) = "WRITE_OWNER"
arrADSRights(12,1) = &H80000
arrADSRights(13,0) = "SYNCHRONIZE"
arrADSRights(13,1) = &H100000
arrADSRights(14,0) = "ACCESS_SYSTEM_SECURITY"
arrADSRights(14,1) = &H1000000
arrADSRights(15,0) = "GENERIC_ALL"
arrADSRights(15,1) = &H10000000
arrADSRights(16,0) = "GENERIC_EXECUTE"
arrADSRights(16,1) = &H20000000
arrADSRights(17,0) = "GENERIC_WRITE"
arrADSRights(17,1) = &H40000000
arrADSRights(18,0) = "GENERIC_READ"
arrADSRights(18,1) = &H80000000

'AceFlags Bits
'Constants would be like ADS_ACEFLAG_INHERIT_ACE
Dim arrADSACEFlags(5,1)  '6 value pairs, name and bit in each
arrADSACEFlags(0,0) = "INHERIT_ACE"
arrADSACEFlags(0,1) = &H2
arrADSACEFlags(1,0) = "NO_PROPAGATE_INHERIT_ACE"
arrADSACEFlags(1,1) = &H4
arrADSACEFlags(2,0) = "INHERIT_ONLY_ACE"
arrADSACEFlags(2,1) = &H8
arrADSACEFlags(3,0) = "INHERITED_ACE"
arrADSACEFlags(3,1) = &H10
arrADSACEFlags(4,0) = "SUCCESSFUL_ACCESS"
arrADSACEFlags(4,1) = &H40
arrADSACEFlags(5,0) = "FAILED_ACCESS"
arrADSACEFlags(5,1) = &H80
```

```
'AceTypes
'Constants would be like ADS_ACETYPE_ACCESS_ALLOWED
Dim arrADSACETypes(5,1)  '6 value pairs, name and value in each
arrADSACETypes(0,0) = "ACCESS_ALLOWED"
arrADSACETypes(0,1) = 0
arrADSACETypes(1,0) = "ACCESS_DENIED"
arrADSACETypes(1,1) = &H1
arrADSACETypes(2,0) = "SYSTEM_AUDIT"
arrADSACETypes(2,1) = &H2
arrADSACETypes(3,0) = "ACCESS_ALLOWED_OBJECT"
arrADSACETypes(3,1) = &H5
arrADSACETypes(4,0) = "ACCESS_DENIED_OBJECT"
arrADSACETypes(4,1) = &H6
arrADSACETypes(5,0) = "SYSTEM_AUDIT_OBJECT"
arrADSACETypes(5,1) = &H7

'Flags Bits
'Constants would be like ADS_FLAG_OBJECT_TYPE_PRESENT
Dim arrADSFlags(1,1)  '2 value pairs, name and bit in each
arrADSFlags(0,0) = "OBJECT_TYPE_PRESENT"
arrADSFlags(0,1) = &H1
arrADSFlags(1,0) = "INHERITED_OBJECT_TYPE_PRESENT"
arrADSFlags(1,1) = &H2

Dim objDSE, strDefaultDN, strDN, objADObject, i
Dim objSecDesc, objDACL, objACE

'===The Main Program===

Set objDSE = GetObject("LDAP://rootDSE")
strDefaultDN = "CN=Users," & objDSE.Get("defaultNamingContext")

strDN =   InputBox("Enter the distinguished name of an object" & _
   vbCrLf & "(e.g. " & strDefaultDN & ")", , strDefaultDN)

If strDN = "" Then WScript.Quit(0)  'user clicked Cancel

Set objADObject = GetObject("LDAP://" & strDN)

Set objSecDesc = objADObject.Get("ntSecurityDescriptor")
Set objDACL = objSecDesc.DiscretionaryAcl

WScript.Echo "Number of ACEs: " & objDACL.AceCount
```

```
i = 0
For Each objACE In objDACL
   i = i + 1
   WScript.Echo ""
   WScript.Echo "ACE " & i
   WScript.Echo "Trustee: " & objACE.Trustee
   WScript.Echo GetStringBits("AccessMask", _
      objACE.AccessMask, arrADSRights)
   WScript.Echo GetStringBits("AceFlags", _
      objACE.AceFlags, arrADSACEFlags)
   WScript.Echo GetStringAceType(objACE.AceType)
   WScript.Echo GetStringBits("Flags", _
      objACE.Flags, arrADSFlags)
   WScript.Echo GetObjectType(objACE.ObjectType)
   WScript.Echo GetInheritedObjectType(objACE.InheritedObjectType)
Next

'===End of the Main Program===
'=============================

Function GetStringBits(strName, intBitfield, arrBits)
   Dim strOut, i

   strOut = strName & ": " & Hex(intBitfield)

   For i = LBound(arrBits) To UBound(arrBits)
      If intBitfield And arrBits(i,1) Then
         strOut = strOut & ", " & arrBits(i,0)
      End If
   Next

   GetStringBits = strOut
End Function

'=============================

Function GetStringAceType(intACEType)
   Dim strOut, i

   strOut = "unknown ACE type"
   For i = LBound(arrADSACETypes) To UBound(arrADSACETypes)
      If intACEType = arrADSACETypes(i,1) Then
         strOut = arrADSACETypes(i,0)
      End If
   Next
```

```
    GetStringAceType = "AceType: " & Hex(intACEType) & ", " & strOut
End Function

'==============================

Function GetObjectType(strGUID)
    GetObjectType = "ObjectType: " & _
        strGUID & " " & MapGUIDToMatchingName(strGUID)
End Function

'==============================

Function GetInheritedObjectType(strGUID)
    GetInheritedObjectType = "InheritedObjectType: " & _
        strGUID & " " & MapGUIDToMatchingName(strGUID)
End Function

'==============================

Function MapGUIDToMatchingName(strGUIDAsString)
    Dim strOut, objExtRights, objChild, objSchema

    If strGUIDAsString = "" Then Exit Function

    strOut = ""

    Set objExtRights = GetObject("LDAP://CN=Extended-Rights," & _
        objDSE.Get("configurationNamingContext"))

    For Each objChild In objExtRights
        'Actually all should be of the same class
        If objChild.Class = "controlAccessRight" Then
            If UCase("{" & objChild.Get("rightsGuid") & "}") = _
                UCase(strGUIDAsString) Then
                strOut = objChild.Get("cn") & ":" & _
                    objChild.Get("displayName")
                Exit For
            End If
        End If
    Next

    If strOut = "" Then  'Didn't find a match in extended rights
        Set objSchema = GetObject("LDAP://" & _
            objDSE.Get("schemaNamingContext"))
```

```
        For Each objChild In objSchema
            If objChild.Class = "classSchema" Or _
               objChild.Class = "attributeSchema" Then
                If UCase(GetSchemaIDGUID(objChild)) = _
                    UCase(strGUIDAsString) Then
                    strOut = objChild.Get("cn") & ":" & _
                        objChild.Get("lDAPDisplayName")
                    Exit For
                End If
            End If
        Next
    End If

    MapGUIDToMatchingName = strOut
End Function

'================================

Function GetSchemaIDGUID(objSchemaObj)
    Dim arrValue, i, strByte, strGUID

    arrValue = objSchemaObj.Get("schemaIDGUID")
    strGUID = ""
    For i = 1 to LenB(arrValue)
        strByte = Hex(AscB(MidB(arrValue, i, 1)))
        If Len(strByte) = 1 Then strByte = "0" & strByte
        strGUID = strGUID & strByte
    Next
    GetSchemaIDGUID = GuidBinFormatToStrFormat(strGUID)
End Function

'================================

Function GUIDBinFormatToStrFormat(strGUIDBin)
    Dim i, strDest
    Dim arrBytes(16)       'We will use elements 1 to 16 but not 0

    For i = 1 To 16   'A GUID has 16 bytes
        arrBytes(i) = Mid(strGUIDBin, 2 * i - 1, 2)
    Next

    strDest = "{"
    For i = 1 To 4 : strDest = strDest & arrBytes(5 - i) : Next
    strDest = strDest & "-"
```

```
    For i = 1 To 2 : strDest = strDest & arrBytes(7 - i) : Next
    strDest = strDest & "-"
    For i = 1 To 2 : strDest = strDest & arrBytes(9 - i) : Next
    strDest = strDest & "-"
    For i = 1 To 2 : strDest = strDest & arrBytes(8 + i) : Next
    strDest = strDest & "-"
    For i = 1 To 6 : strDest = strDest & arrBytes(10 + i) : Next
    strDest = strDest & "}"

    GuidBinFormatToStrFormat = strDest
End Function
```

As with previous examples, if you like to see only some of the ACEs, you can put various `If` statements inside the loop to filter out unwanted ACEs.

The `GetStringBits` function can handle all ACE fields that are bitfields. ACE type is not a bitfield, so it needs a separate function.

In `MapGUIDToMatchingName` we find the extended right name (including property sets) that corresponds to the GUID in the ACE. If there is no match, we next check all the `classSchema` and `attributeSchema` objects and compare the GUID to their `schemaIDGUID` attribute.

The latter comparison requires converting the binary GUID to a string format. In `GetSchemaIDGUID` we convert the binary attribute to a string value and then in `GUIDBinFormatToStrFormat` we finally convert it to a string format.

NOTE ACEs contain both "ACE flags" (containing mainly inheritance information) and "flags" (indicating whether ObjectType or InheritedObjectType is present). Don't get confused.

Using Regular Expressions to Convert the GUID

VBScript includes a feature called *regular expressions* (regexp), which should be familiar to anyone who has used UNIX sed (streaming editor). Regular expressions enable you to perform complex search/replace functions and other string manipulation. Therefore, we could use them to convert the GUID format.

The following lines show `GUIDBinFormatToStrFormat` implemented using regular expressions:

```
Function GUIDBinFormatToStrFormat(strGUIDBin)
    Dim objRegExp, strRearranged

    Set objRegExp = New RegExp

    objRegExp.Pattern = _
        "(.{2})(.{2})(.{2})(.{2})(.{2})(.{2})(.{2})(.{2})(.{16})"
    strRearranged = objRegExp.Replace(strGUIDBin, _
        "$4$3$2$1$6$5$8$7$9")

    objRegExp.Pattern = "(.{8})(.{4})(.{4})(.{4})(.{12})"
    GUIDBinFormatToStrFormat = objRegExp.Replace(strRearranged, _
        "{$1-$2-$3-$4-$5}")
End Function
```

Each `(.{2})` means "take two characters and remember them for later use." This means that we first chop the 32 hex characters to 2+2+2+2+2+2+2+2+9 characters and then rearrange the chops again as 4-3-2-1-6-5-8-7-9. After rearranging, we chop the result again so that we can add curly braces and hyphens. If we tried both steps together, we would get ten chops, but VBScript regular expressions support only nine chops ($1–$9).

This latter implementation uses fewer script lines, but it is 30 percent slower, so we opted to use a traditional approach in our long script. However, we wanted to introduce regular expressions to you.

Add ACEs.vbs

This script demonstrates how to add new ACEs to Active Directory objects. The script shows the order of events and the appropriate lines that will get the job done. However, we don't explain which ACE flags and other settings you should use in various scenarios. There are two reasons for this.

- We already explained the ACE contents thoroughly in Chapter 4.
- There is an easy way to get the right ACE contents for any scenario you could imagine, as explained in the next subsection.

After presenting the sample script, we have two subsections at the end of this section about how to use trustees and how to use the generic permissions.

Knowing What to Add

To find out which inheritance and other flags and settings you should apply to your various ACEs you can take the following steps:

1. Create a test target object and a test user, who will become the trustee in the ACE.
2. Using ACL Editor in the Users and Computers snap-in (or perhaps the Delegation of Control wizard), add any necessary ACEs to your test trustee and for your test target object.
3. List the ACEs using the "List ACEs - Long.vbs" script presented earlier in this section and redirect the output to a text file with the greater-than sign (>).
4. Open the text file in Notepad and remove ACEs other than those to your test trustee.

Now you have an exact documentation of what settings you need to put in your ADSI script. For example, you might notice that you need to apply `INHERIT_ACE` and `NO_PROPAGATE_INHERIT_ACE` together if you want to apply the ACE to children in this container only.

NOTE The "List ACEs - Long.vbs" script lists both the hex values and their interpretations, such as that the value "20094" would correspond to four different permissions (i.e., access mask bits). If you are a little lazy, you can just use the number "20094" (and use the "List ACEs - Short.vbs" script) without even knowing which permissions it contains. A more descriptive way, however, is to use the actual constants, such as `ACTRL_DS_LIST + DS_READ_PROP + DS_LIST_OBJECT + READ_CONTROL`.

The Add ACEs Sample Script

We have about 40 lines of constant definitions in the script, because we want to define all access mask, ACE flag, ACE type, and flag constants, whether we use them or not (because you may want to use any of them in your scripts).

For your convenience, we have also added the `schemaIDGUIDs` for the `user`, `group`, `computer`, `contact`, `organizationalUnit`, and `printQueue` classes.

We create an OU ACEDemo for which the ACEs will be added. As a trustee, we use RedBaron (`Red.Baron@sanao.com`), which must be created manually beforehand. The reason that we create the OU automatically, but not the user, is that we want to delete the OU between each run of the script and this way clean the table for the next test.

We add the following three ACEs:

- ACE 1: Write all properties of this OU.
- ACE 2: Full Control to user objects in the subtree. With this ACE, we define the `user` class in the `InheritedObjectType`, because `user` is where the permissions will be inherited.
- ACE 3: Create/delete user objects in the subtree. With this ACE, we define the `user` class in the `ObjectType`, because user is the target of the permission.

The last two ACEs are the same ones that the Delegation of Control wizard adds if you select the "Create, delete and manage user accounts" option.

Both ACEs 2 and 3 use the ACE flag "inherit ACE." ACE 2 also uses "inherit only," because we don't want Full Control to apply to the OU itself.

Here is the script:

```
Option Explicit

'AccessMask
Const ADS_RIGHT_DS_CREATE_CHILD              = &H1
Const ADS_RIGHT_DS_DELETE_CHILD              = &H2
Const ADS_RIGHT_ACTRL_DS_LIST                = &H4
Const ADS_RIGHT_DS_SELF                      = &H8
Const ADS_RIGHT_DS_READ_PROP                 = &H10
Const ADS_RIGHT_DS_WRITE_PROP                = &H20
Const ADS_RIGHT_DS_DELETE_TREE               = &H40
Const ADS_RIGHT_DS_LIST_OBJECT               = &H80
Const ADS_RIGHT_DS_CONTROL_ACCESS             = &H100
Const ADS_RIGHT_DELETE                       = &H10000
Const ADS_RIGHT_READ_CONTROL                 = &H20000
Const ADS_RIGHT_WRITE_DAC                    = &H40000
Const ADS_RIGHT_WRITE_OWNER                  = &H80000
Const ADS_RIGHT_SYNCHRONIZE                  = &H100000
Const ADS_RIGHT_ACCESS_SYSTEM_SECURITY = &H1000000
Const ADS_RIGHT_GENERIC_ALL                  = &H10000000
Const ADS_RIGHT_GENERIC_EXECUTE              = &H20000000
Const ADS_RIGHT_GENERIC_WRITE                = &H40000000
```

```
Const ADS_RIGHT_GENERIC_READ           = &H80000000

Const ADS_RIGHT_FULL_CONTROL           = &HF01FF

'ACE flags
Const ADS_ACEFLAG_INHERIT_ACE              = &H2
Const ADS_ACEFLAG_NO_PROPAGATE_INHERIT_ACE = &H4
Const ADS_ACEFLAG_INHERIT_ONLY_ACE         = &H8
Const ADS_ACEFLAG_INHERITED_ACE            = &H10
Const ADS_ACEFLAG_SUCCESSFUL_ACCESS        = &H40
Const ADS_ACEFLAG_FAILED_ACCESS            = &H80

'ACE types
Const ADS_ACETYPE_ACCESS_ALLOWED           = 0
Const ADS_ACETYPE_ACCESS_DENIED            = &H1
Const ADS_ACETYPE_SYSTEM_AUDIT             = &H2
Const ADS_ACETYPE_ACCESS_ALLOWED_OBJECT    = &H5
Const ADS_ACETYPE_ACCESS_DENIED_OBJECT     = &H6
Const ADS_ACETYPE_SYSTEM_AUDIT_OBJECT      = &H7

'Flags
Const ADS_FLAG_OBJECT_TYPE_PRESENT             = &H1
Const ADS_FLAG_INHERITED_OBJECT_TYPE_PRESENT = &H2

'Some schemaIDGUIDs
Const SCHEMAIDGUID_USER     = _
    "{BF967ABA-0DE6-11D0-A285-00AA003049E2}"
Const SCHEMAIDGUID_GROUP    = _
    "{BF967A9C-0DE6-11D0-A285-00AA003049E2}"
Const SCHEMAIDGUID_COMPUTER = _
    "{BF967A86-0DE6-11D0-A285-00AA003049E2}"
Const SCHEMAIDGUID_CONTACT  = _
    "{5CB41ED0-0E4C-11D0-A286-00AA003049E2}"
Const SCHEMAIDGUID_OU       = _
    "{BF967AA5-0DE6-11D0-A285-00AA003049E2}"
Const SCHEMAIDGUID_PRINTER  = _
    "{BF967AA8-0DE6-11D0-A285-00AA003049E2}"

Dim objDSE, objDom, objOU, objSecDesc, objDACL
Dim objACE1, objACE2, objACE3

'======================
```

```
'Create the OU
'-------------
Set objDSE = GetObject("LDAP://rootDSE")
Set objDom = GetObject("LDAP://" &
objDSE.Get("defaultNamingContext"))
Set objOU = objDom.Create("organizationalUnit", "OU=ACEDemo")
objOU.SetInfo

'Create the first ACE - write all properties of the OU
'-----------------------------------------------------
Set objACE1 = CreateObject("AccessControlEntry")
objACE1.Trustee     = "Red.Baron@sanao.com"
objACE1.AccessMask  = ADS_RIGHT_DS_WRITE_PROP
objACE1.AceFlags    = 0  'no inheritance from up or to below
objACE1.AceType     = ADS_ACETYPE_ACCESS_ALLOWED
objACE1.Flags       = 0  'no object types present
'objACE1.ObjectType = not used
'objACE1.InheritedObjectType = not used

'Create the second ACE - Full Control to user objects in the subtree
'-------------------------------------------------------------------
Set objACE2 = CreateObject("AccessControlEntry")
objACE2.Trustee     = "Red.Baron@sanao.com"
objACE2.AccessMask  = ADS_RIGHT_FULL_CONTROL  'all 13 bits
objACE2.AceFlags    = ADS_ACEFLAG_INHERIT_ACE + _
                      ADS_ACEFLAG_INHERIT_ONLY_ACE
objACE2.AceType     = ADS_ACETYPE_ACCESS_ALLOWED_OBJECT
objACE2.Flags       = ADS_FLAG_INHERITED_OBJECT_TYPE_PRESENT
'objACE2.ObjectType = not used
objACE2.InheritedObjectType = SCHEMAIDGUID_USER

'Create the third ACE - Create/Delete user objects in the subtree
'----------------------------------------------------------------
Set objACE3 = CreateObject("AccessControlEntry")
objACE3.Trustee    = "Red.Baron@sanao.com"
objACE3.AccessMask = ADS_RIGHT_DS_CREATE_CHILD + _
                     ADS_RIGHT_DS_DELETE_CHILD
objACE3.AceFlags   = ADS_ACEFLAG_INHERIT_ACE
objACE3.AceType    = ADS_ACETYPE_ACCESS_ALLOWED_OBJECT
objACE3.Flags      = ADS_FLAG_OBJECT_TYPE_PRESENT
objACE3.ObjectType = SCHEMAIDGUID_USER
'objACE3.InheritedObjectType = not used
```

```
'Add the ACEs
'------------
Set objSecDesc = objOU.Get("ntSecurityDescriptor")
Set objDACL = objSecDesc.DiscretionaryAcl

Call objDACL.AddAce(objACE1)
Call objDACL.AddAce(objACE2)
Call objDACL.AddAce(objACE3)

objSecDesc.DiscretionaryAcl = objDACL
Call objOU.Put("ntSecurityDescriptor", objSecDesc)
objOU.SetInfo

WScript.Echo "Number of ACEs after: " & objDACL.AceCount
```

We could have used just one `objACE` variable if we had arranged the lines a little differently. However, we wanted to get the "Add the ACEs" lines together, so that you could see in a compact way how we first retrieve the current discretionary ACL from `nTSecurityDescriptor`, add the ACEs to the list, and then put the new list back.

The order of the ACEs in an ACL is important, because the same ACEs may have a different effect, depending on the order. We explain this in the next subsection.

Order of ACEs

When a securable object (such as an Active Directory object or a file) is opened, Windows must evaluate the ACEs in the object's DACL to determine whether or not to allow access. Windows starts from the beginning of the list and goes on through the ACEs as long as needed to find enough permissions to either grant or deny the access. Also, if the list runs out before enough permissions are found, Windows will deny the access.

If a certain access-denied ACE applies to Jack, he will be denied access if the ACE is at the beginning of the list. On the other hand, if the ACE is at the end of the list, Jack might be allowed access (depending on whether there are appropriate access-allowed ACEs for him).

Because the effect of ACEs in a DACL depends on the order, Microsoft has defined a preferred order for the ACEs. All inherited ACEs should be after noninherited ACEs, and within these categories all access-allowed ACEs should be after access-denied ACEs. The following hierarchical list illustrates the preferred order:

```
Noninherited ACEs
   Access-denied ACEs
      ACEs with ACE type ADS_ACETYPE_ACCESS_DENIED
      ACEs with ACE type ADS_ACETYPE_ACCESS_DENIED_OBJECT
   Access-allowed ACEs
      ACEs with ACE type ADS_ACETYPE_ACCESS_ALLOWED
      ACEs with ACE type ADS_ACETYPE_ACCESS_ALLOWED_OBJECT
Inherited ACEs
   Access-denied ACEs
      ACEs with ACE type ADS_ACETYPE_ACCESS_DENIED
      ACEs with ACE type ADS_ACETYPE_ACCESS_DENIED_OBJECT
   Access-allowed ACEs
      ACEs with ACE type ADS_ACETYPE_ACCESS_ALLOWED
      ACEs with ACE type ADS_ACETYPE_ACCESS_ALLOWED_OBJECT
```

Remember from Chapter 4 that the ACE types that end with "_OBJECT" indicate that either ObjectType or InheritedObjectType is not empty, so the corresponding ACE is for some particular object class, property, property set, or extended right.

If the order of the access-denied ACEs is not correct when you open the ACL Editor, you will see the error message shown in Figure 11.79.

The `AddAce` method doesn't allow you to specify where in the list the new ACE will go. The three levels of hierarchies in the preceding list will be handled as follows:

- *Noninherited versus inherited.* You shouldn't add any inherited ACEs, because they will appear automatically where and when appropriate. As you add noninherited ACEs with the method, it

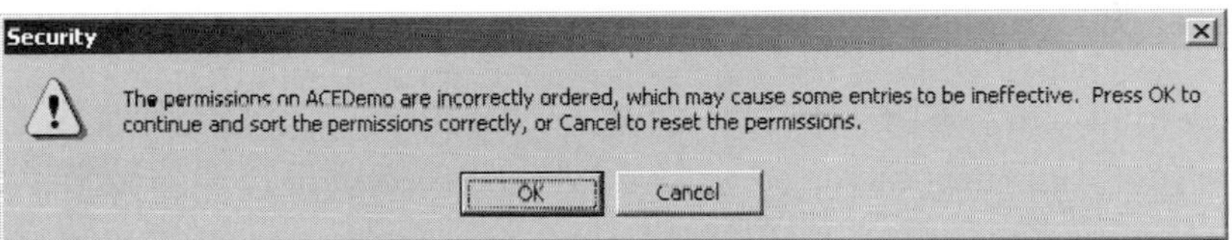

Figure 11.79 In Windows 2000, if you add access-denied ACEs with the `AddAce` method, you will get the error shown in this figure once you go to the security page of the object. If you click OK on the error message and then click OK on the security page, the ACL Editor will sort the ACEs in the correct order. Note that the Apply button is grayed out in that case, which might lead you to think that there is nothing to be saved if you click OK. However, the reordering will take place when you click OK.

will automatically place them before any inherited ACEs. Consequently, the outcome is just right.

- *Access denied versus access allowed.* If you add an access-denied ACE, in Windows Server 2003 the `AddAce` method puts the ACE at the beginning of the list as it should. In Windows 2000, however, the ACE is likely to go in the wrong place, and you will run into the situation displayed in Figure 11.79. If you need to add access-denied ACEs in Windows 2000, you can use the `ReorderDacl` subprogram listed in Microsoft Knowledge Base article Q279682. That subprogram divides the ACEs in an ACL into five pools and rebuilds the ACL in the correct order.
- *Apply to the object versus apply to the "subobject."* The `AddAce` method doesn't perform the preferred ordering in this case. However, you don't get any error message when opening the ACL Editor. Also, the wrong order is not likely to hurt you—even some Active Directory default permissions use a different ACE order than this third level of the hierarchy indicates.

Defining Trustees

You already know that trustees can be users, security groups, computers, or well-known security principals. In Table 11.4 we list the name formats that you can use in the `Trustee` property of the `IADsAccessControlEntry` interface. Note that you cannot use the common name, such as `CN=Red Baron`.

Using the Generic Permissions

We listed 19 access mask bits as constants in the script. Active Directory uses the first 13 of them; therefore, we discussed those 13 in Chapter 4. We called those 13 permissions "special permissions," and you probably remember that there were also standard permissions, each of which mapped to a certain set of special permissions.

The generic permissions discussed here are like standard permissions, because they also map to a set of certain special permissions. The only difference is that the generic permissions are used in the programming interface and the standard permissions are used in the user interface. And as you would guess, the list of generic permissions is not the same as the list of standard permissions.

Table 11.4 Name Formats to Use in the `Trustee` Property

Name Format	Examples
SAM name (pre–Windows 2000 name)*	RedBaron Authenticated Users Users
SAM name with domain** NetBIOS name	SANAO\RedBaron NT AUTHORITY\Authenticated Users BUILTIN\Users
User principal name	`red.baron@sanao.com`
Distinguished name***	`CN=Red Baron, CN=Users, DC=sanao, DC=com`
SID (string representation)	S-1-5-21-1718597718-1078345429-1030254238-1143 (same as RedBaron) S-1-5-11 (same as Authenticated Users) S-1-5-32-545 (same as Users)

* Computers have a dollar sign ($) as the last character in the SAM name. If you have a computer named DC1, you must use the name DC1$ in the `Trustee` property.

** Whether the "domain" name is SANAO, NT AUTHORITY, or BUILTIN depends on in which category the corresponding SID belongs. See the discussion of SIDs in Chapter 4.

*** Not in Windows 2000.

Even though Active Directory doesn't use the remaining 6 permissions (of the 19) in ACEs, the 6 include the 4 generic permissions, which you can use when setting permissions programmatically.

NOTE Don't use the remaining two permissions (i.e., `ADS_RIGHT_SYNCHRONIZE` and `ADS_RIGHT_ACCESS_SYSTEM_SECURITY`).

Each generic permission maps to some of those first 13 permissions. If you give someone the `ADS_RIGHT_GENERIC_ALL` permission, he will actually get all the 13 permissions, meaning that he just got Full Control. Table 11.5 lists the generic permission mappings.

NOTE When you read ACEs, you never see generic permissions. Even if you wrote them, they were converted to corresponding permissions from the set of the first 13.

Table 11.5 Generic Permission Mappings to Special Permissions

Generic Right	Maps to Access Mask	Access Mask Contains	Maps to the User Interface*
`ADS_RIGHT_GENERIC_ALL`	F01FF (13 are set)	All 13	Full Control
`ADS_RIGHT_GENERIC_EXECUTE`	20004 (2 are set)	`ACTRL_DS_LIST`, `READ_CONTROL`	List Contents, Read Permissions
`ADS_RIGHT_GENERIC_WRITE`	20028 (3 are set)	`DS_SELF`, `DS_WRITE_PROP`, `READ_CONTROL`	Write, Read Permissions
`ADS_RIGHT_GENERIC_READ`	20094 (4 are set)	`ACTRL_DS_LIST`, `DS_READ_PROP`, `DS_LIST_OBJECT`, `READ_CONTROL`	Read, List Object

* We have both standard permissions and special permissions in this column. For example, Write is a standard permission, but Read Permissions is a special permission.

As you can see in Table 11.5, the generic write and read are not quite the same as the standard permissions Write and Read in the graphical user interface (i.e., ACL Editor). Both these generic permissions map to one more special permission than their standard permission counterparts.

We explained in Chapter 4 that in a prerelease version of Windows 2000, the standard permission Read corresponded to four special permissions, but in the final release, List Object was dropped out, so Read now corresponds to three special permissions. As you see in Table 11.5, the generic read permission is equal to standard Read + special List Object. Consequently, the generic read permission is the same as the prerelease definition of the standard permission Read.

Now that we have added ACEs to an Active Directory object, we will show the same process for a folder on disk.

Add ACEs to a Folder.vbs

Adding ACEs to a folder is quite similar to adding ACEs to an Active Directory object. There are, however, the following differences.

- You read and write security descriptors with the `IADsSecurityUtility` interface, instead of the three interfaces that were used when accessing the permissions of Active Directory objects.

- The meanings of access mask bits, as well as of the other flags in the ACEs, are somewhat different. Also, if some meaning is the same, it may have a different constant name, because these constants are defined in two different header files (WinNT.h versus IADs.h).

The following sample script creates a folder and adds one ACE for it. The ACE grants Modify permissions, which apply to the whole subtree. The script wouldn't be that long if we hadn't added all the constant definitions for the ACE contents.

```
Option Explicit

'AccessMask
Const FILE_READ_DATA              = &H1      'file & pipe
Const FILE_LIST_DIRECTORY         = &H1      'folder
Const FILE_WRITE_DATA             = &H2      'file & pipe
Const FILE_ADD_FILE               = &H2      'folder
Const FILE_APPEND_DATA            = &H4      'file
Const FILE_ADD_SUBDIRECTORY       = &H4      'folder
Const FILE_CREATE_PIPE_INSTANCE = &H4      'named pipe
Const FILE_READ_EA                = &H8      'file & folder
Const FILE_WRITE_EA               = &H10     'file & folder
Const FILE_EXECUTE                = &H20     'file
Const FILE_TRAVERSE               = &H20     'folder
Const FILE_DELETE_CHILD           = &H40     'folder
Const FILE_READ_ATTRIBUTES        = &H80     'all
Const FILE_WRITE_ATTRIBUTES       = &H100    'all
Const DELETE                      = &H10000
Const READ_CONTROL                = &H20000
Const WRITE_DAC                   = &H40000
Const WRITE_OWNER                 = &H80000
Const SYNCHRONIZE                 = &H100000
Const ACCESS_SYSTEM_SECURITY      = &H1000000
Const GENERIC_ALL                 = &H10000000
Const GENERIC_EXECUTE             = &H20000000
Const GENERIC_WRITE               = &H40000000
Const GENERIC_READ                = &H80000000

Const FULL_CONTROL = &H1F01FF   '14 permissions
Const MODIFY = &H1301BF   '11 permissions
```

```
'ACE flags
Const OBJECT_INHERIT_ACE                  = &H1
Const CONTAINER_INHERIT_ACE               = &H2
Const NO_PROPAGATE_INHERIT_ACE            = &H4
Const INHERIT_ONLY_ACE                    = &H8
Const INHERITED_ACE                       = &H10
Const SUCCESSFUL_ACCESS_ACE_FLAG          = &H40
Const FAILED_ACCESS_ACE_FLAG              = &H80

'ACE types
Const ACCESS_ALLOWED_ACE_TYPE             = &H0
Const ACCESS_DENIED_ACE_TYPE              = &H1
Const SYSTEM_AUDIT_ACE_TYPE               = &H2
Const SYSTEM_ALARM_ACE_TYPE               = &H3
Const ACCESS_ALLOWED_COMPOUND_ACE_TYPE    = &H4
Const ACCESS_ALLOWED_OBJECT_ACE_TYPE      = &H5
Const ACCESS_DENIED_OBJECT_ACE_TYPE       = &H6
Const SYSTEM_AUDIT_OBJECT_ACE_TYPE        = &H7
Const SYSTEM_ALARM_OBJECT_ACE_TYPE        = &H8

'Flags
Const ADS_OBJECT_TYPE_PRESENT             = &H1
Const ADS_INHERITED_OBJECT_TYPE_PRESENT = &H2

'IADsSecurityUtility ADS_PATHTYPE_ENUM
Const ADS_PATH_FILE             = 1
Const ADS_PATH_FILESHARE        = 2
Const ADS_PATH_REGISTRY         = 3

'IADsSecurityUtility ADS_SD_FORMAT_ENUM
Const ADS_SD_FORMAT_IID         = 1
Const ADS_SD_FORMAT_RAW         = 2
Const ADS_SD_FORMAT_HEXSTRING   = 3

Dim objFS, objSecDesc, objDACL, objACE, objADsSec

'Create the Folder
'----------------------------
Set objFS = CreateObject("Scripting.FileSystemObject")
Call objFS.CreateFolder("D:\ACEDemo")
```

```
'Create the ACE - modify permission for a subtree
'-------------------------------------------------------------
Set objACE = CreateObject("AccessControlEntry")
objACE.Trustee      = "Red.Baron@sanao.com"
objACE.AccessMask   = MODIFY
objACE.AceFlags     = OBJECT_INHERIT_ACE + _
                      CONTAINER_INHERIT_ACE
objACE.AceType      = ACCESS_ALLOWED_ACE_TYPE

'Add the ACE
'-----------------
Set objADsSec = CreateObject("ADsSecurityUtility ")

Set objSecDesc = objADsSec.GetSecurityDescriptor("D:\ACEDemo", _
    ADS_PATH_FILE, ADS_SD_FORMAT_IID)
Set objDACL = objSecDesc.DiscretionaryAcl

Call objDACL.AddAce(objACE)
objSecDesc.DiscretionaryAcl = objDACL
Call objADsSec.SetSecurityDescriptor("C:\ACEDemo", _
    ADS_PATH_FILE, objSecDesc, ADS_SD_FORMAT_IID)
```

Windows 2000 doesn't contain the `IADsSecurityUtility` interface, so in that environment you must use the ADsSecurity component, which is part of the ADSI Resource Kit. This requires slight changes to the script presented here, and that script version is available at `http://www.kouti.com`. The `AddAce` method of the ADsSecurity component doesn't order the access-denied ACEs to exist before any access-allowed ACEs. Consequently, if you check the permissions with the ACL Editor after having added access-denied ACEs, you will get the ACE-ordering error message that we discussed in the "Order of ACEs" section (see Figure 11.79). If you need to add such ACEs, you can use the `ReorderDacl` subprogram listed in Microsoft Knowledge Base article Q279682.

TIP The preceding sample script assumes that you have permission to read and write the entire security descriptor. If this is not the case, you can use the `SecurityMask` property that only the discretionary ACL (or DACL), for example, is read and written. For more information, see the Platform SDK documentation.

OU, Group, and Computer Management

In this section, we show how to manage OUs, groups, and computer objects. With OUs, we use just a few line clips instead of complete, independent scripts. With groups, we show two complete scripts and one clip, and with computers, we show a full, working script. We present the following independent scripts in this section:

- CH11-39 ADSI Create a Group.vbs
- CH11-40 ADSI Add Users of One OU to a Group.vbs
- CH11-41 ADSI Create a Computer Object.vbs

We start with managing OUs.

OU Management

In this section, we'll cover the following OU management tasks:

- Creating an OU
- Deleting an OU
- Moving users of one OU to another
- Deleting objects of one OU

We've already shown how to list users of one OU in the "User Management" section.

Creating an OU

You create an OU just like any other object by using the `Create` method of `IADsContainer`. The following lines create an OU under a domain root:

```
Set objContainer = GetObject("LDAP://DC=sanao,DC=com")
Set objOU = objContainer.Create("organizationalUnit",
   "OU=Sales")
objOU.SetInfo
```

As usual, you need to call `SetInfo` to save the new object to Active Directory.

Deleting an OU

There are two ways to delete an OU (or any other Active Directory object): (a) Bind to the parent container and then use the `Delete` method of the `IADsContainer` interface, or (b) bind to the object itself and use the `DeleteObject` method of the `IADsDeleteOps` interface.

In choice "a" the object to be deleted must be empty of any child objects. You would use lines such as the following:

```
Set objContainer = GetObject("LDAP://DC=sanao,DC=com")
Call objContainer.Delete("organizationalUnit", "OU=Sales")
```

Choice "b" deletes an entire nonempty tree, so you must be careful when using it. See the following lines:

```
Set objObject = GetObject("LDAP:// OU=Sales,DC=sanao,DC=com")
Call objObject.DeleteObject(0)
```

According to the Platform SDK documentation, the 0 argument in `DeleteObject` has no meaning. It is just reserved for future use.

Note that with either choice, you don't need to call `SetInfo`.

Moving Users of One OU to Another

The third `IADsContainer` method that you might use is `MoveHere`. The following lines show how you can move all users (and computers) of one container to another:

```
Set objSourceContainer = GetObject("LDAP://OU=RD,DC=sanao,DC=com")
Set objTargetContainer = _
    GetObject("LDAP://OU=Sales,DC=sanao,DC=com")

objSourceContainer.Filter = Array("user")
For Each objUser in objSourceContainer
    Call objTargetContainer.MoveHere(objUser.ADsPath, objUser.Name)
Next
```

NOTE As we mentioned earlier, the `user` filter also includes `computer` class objects, because `computer` is a subclass of `user`.

Deleting Objects of One OU

If you want to delete all objects in one container, you can use the following lines:

```
Set objContainer = GetObject("LDAP://OU=Sales,DC=sanao,DC=com")
For Each objADObject in objContainer
   Call objContainer.Delete(objADObject.Class, objADObject.Name)
Next
```

Usually there are no child objects in the user objects, but if there are, you can use the `DeleteObject` method instead of the `Delete` method. See the code lines in the "Deleting an OU" section.

Needless to say, you should be careful with a script like this.

Group Management

Next, we'll cover the following group management tasks:

- Creating a group
- Deleting a group
- Adding users of one OU to a group

In addition, in Chapter 10 we showed how to list members of a group or groups of a user.

Create a Group.vbs

When you create a group in Windows 2000, you must specify `sAMAccountName`, just as when you create a user. When you create a group in Windows Server 2003, you could omit `sAMAccountName`, in which case a random name is generated. A better practice, however, is to specify a name. You may also define the `groupType` attribute, which defines both group scope (global, universal, or local) and type (security or distribution).

`SAMAccountName` corresponds to the pre–Windows 2000 logon name. With Windows 2000, you must provide one, but with Windows Server 2003, if you don't provide any, a random name is generated. You shouldn't rely on this, because the random name is quite difficult for the user to use (although she could use only the UPN).

The lines shown in Figure 11.80 create a group.

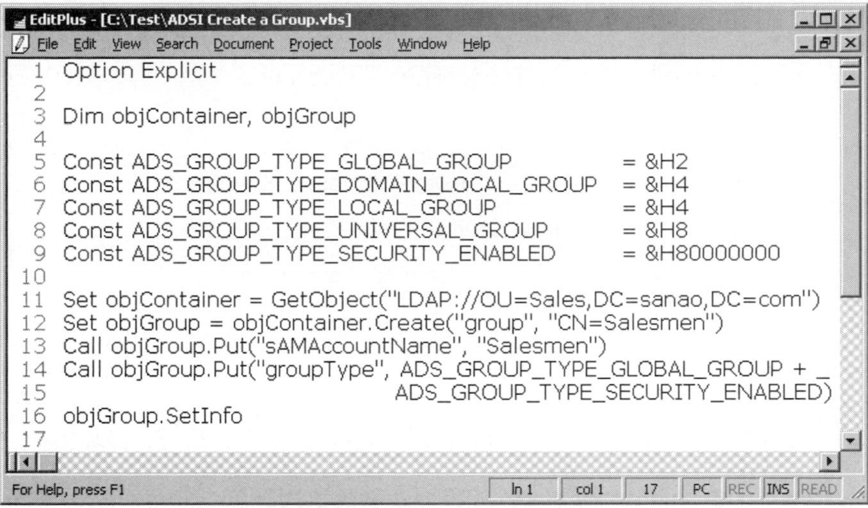

Figure 11.80 ADSI Create a Group.vbs

If you don't specify `groupType`, the default is scope "global" and type "security," which is actually what we just specified in the example. However, we wanted to include setting the `groupType` to show you how to do it.

There is no flag for distribution groups. If you want a distribution group, you just don't include the "security enabled" flag, but you do include some scope flag so that the default doesn't kick in.

Deleting a Group

You delete a group just as you would delete any other object type. The following lines delete a group:

```
Set objContainer = GetObject("LDAP://OU=Sales,DC=sanao,DC=com")
Call objContainer.Delete("group", "CN=Salesmen")
```

You don't need to remove any members from a group before you delete it.

Add Users of One OU to a Group.vbs

As you know, you cannot give permissions to an OU. Therefore, you may want to have a security group that has all the users of an OU as members.

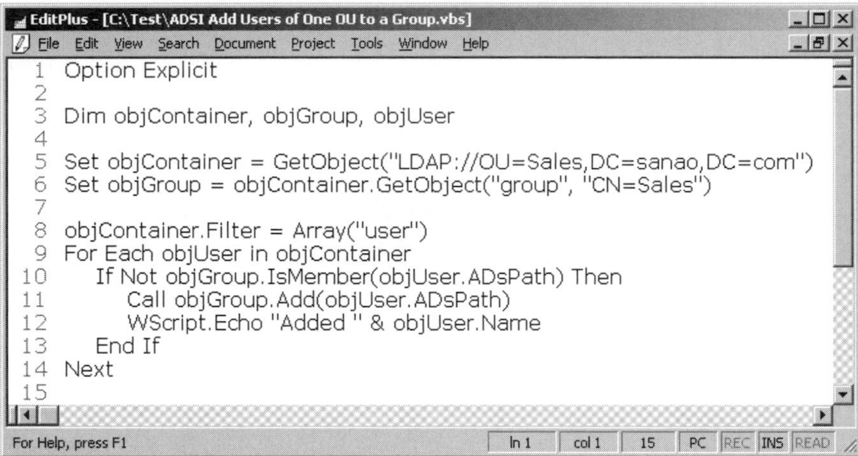

EditPlus - [C:\Test\ADSI Add Users of One OU to a Group.vbs]
File Edit View Search Document Project Tools Window Help
Option Explicit

Dim objContainer, objGroup, objUser

Set objContainer = GetObject("LDAP://OU=Sales,DC=sanao,DC=com")
Set objGroup = objContainer.GetObject("group", "CN=Sales")

objContainer.Filter = Array("user")
For Each objUser in objContainer
   If Not objGroup.IsMember(objUser.ADsPath) Then
      Call objGroup.Add(objUser.ADsPath)
      WScript.Echo "Added " & objUser.Name
   End If
Next
For Help, press F1
ln 1
col 1
15
PC
REC
INS
READ

Figure 11.81 ADSI Add Users of One OU to a Group.vbs

The little script in Figure 11.81 browses through the users of `OU=Sales` and adds them to the group `CN=Sales`, unless they are already members.

If you need to remove group members, the `Remove` method works like the `Add` method. There is one argument, which is the ADSI path.

Create a Computer Object.vbs

You saw earlier that you could create an OU with just two lines of code (`Create` and `SetInfo`). Creating a computer object requires over 100 lines, because you need to specify a number of settings that ADSI doesn't specify for you.

- As with users and groups, you need to specify the SAM name. It should be the same as the common name, but with a dollar sign ($) appended as the last character.
- You need to specify that the account type of the object is `UF_WORKSTATION_TRUST_ACCOUNT` (workstation or member server account) instead of `UF_NORMAL_ACCOUNT` (user account).
- You must enable the account.
- You must not require a password.
- You could set the initial password to "computername$". However, the script works also with an empty password.
- You must give the following eight permissions for the computer object to the user or group that will join the computer to a domain:

Write Account Restrictions, Write Logon Information, Write Description, Write Display Name, Write Pre-Windows 2000 Computer Name, Validated write to service principal name, Validated write to DNS host name, and a special permission combination "List Contents + List Object + Read All Properties + Read Permissions + Delete + Delete Subtree + All Extended Rights." If an administrator will perform the join, then these eight permissions are not needed (because an administrator will have all the necessary permissions by inheritance). Note that the computer object creation sample script in Microsoft Knowledge Base article 315273 grants just Full Control to the user or group. This is different than if the Users and Computers snap-in was used, but the resulting script becomes much shorter this way.

NOTE The previous list contains the settings that the Users and Computers snap-in applies when you create a computer object. We haven't tested whether or not you could skip some of them, but obviously the safest path is to create similar settings to the snap-in's.

The following is the script that does all the listed things and creates a computer called PC17:

```
Option Explicit

Const UF_ACCOUNTDISABLE                    = &H0002
Const UF_PASSWD_NOTREQD                    = &H0020
Const UF_WORKSTATION_TRUST_ACCOUNT         = &H1000 'ws or ms computer

Const ADS_RIGHT_ACTRL_DS_LIST              = &H4
Const ADS_RIGHT_DS_SELF                    = &H8
Const ADS_RIGHT_DS_READ_PROP               = &H10
Const ADS_RIGHT_DS_WRITE_PROP              = &H20
Const ADS_RIGHT_DS_DELETE_TREE             = &H40
Const ADS_RIGHT_DS_LIST_OBJECT             = &H80
Const ADS_RIGHT_DS_CONTROL_ACCESS          = &H100
Const ADS_RIGHT_DELETE                     = &H10000
Const ADS_RIGHT_READ_CONTROL               = &H20000

Const ADS_ACETYPE_ACCESS_ALLOWED           = 0
Const ADS_ACETYPE_ACCESS_ALLOWED_OBJECT = &H5
Const ADS_FLAG_OBJECT_TYPE_PRESENT         = &H1
```

```
' Property set rightsGuids
Const GUID_ACCOUNT_RESTRICTIONS = _
    "{4C164200-20C0-11D0-A768-00AA006E0529}"
Const GUID_LOGON_INFORMATION    = _
    "{5F202010-79A5-11D0-9020-00C04FC2D4CF}"

' Attribute schemaIDGUIDs
Const GUID_VALIDATED_SPN        = _
    "{F3A64788-5306-11D1-A9C5-0000F80367C1}"
Const GUID_VALIDATED_DNSHOST    = _
    "{72E39547-7B18-11D1-ADEF-00C04FD8D5CD}"
Const GUID_DESCRIPTION          = _
    "{BF967950-0DE6-11D0-A285-00AA003049E2}"
Const GUID_DISPLAY_NAME         = _
    "{BF967953-0DE6-11D0-A285-00AA003049E2}"
Const GUID_SAM_ACCOUNT_NAME     = _
    "{3E0ABFD0-126A-11D0-A060-00AA006C33ED}"

Call CreateComputer("PC17", "Red.Baron@sanao.com")

'===================================

Sub CreateComputer(strComputerName, strWhoCanJoin)
    Dim objDSE, objComputersContainer, objComputer, objSecDesc
    Dim objDACL, objACE1, objACE2, objACE3, objACE4
    Dim objACE5, objACE6, objACE7, objACE8

    Set objDSE = GetObject("LDAP://rootDSE")
    Set objComputersContainer = GetObject("LDAP://CN=Computers," & _
        objDSE.Get("defaultNamingContext"))

    Set objComputer = objComputersContainer.Create("computer", _
        "CN=" & strComputerName)
    Call objComputer.Put("sAMAccountName", strComputerName & "$")
    Call objComputer.Put("userAccountControl", _
        UF_PASSWD_NOTREQD _
        Or UF_WORKSTATION_TRUST_ACCOUNT _
        ) 'Or UF_ACCOUNTDISABLE   We want to enable, not disable

    objComputer.SetInfo

    Set objACE1 = CreateObject("AccessControlEntry")
    objACE1.Trustee      = strWhoCanJoin
```

```
objACE1.AccessMask   = ADS_RIGHT_DS_WRITE_PROP
objACE1.AceFlags     = 0 'no inheritance from up or to below
objACE1.AceType      = ADS_ACETYPE_ACCESS_ALLOWED_OBJECT
objACE1.Flags        = ADS_FLAG_OBJECT_TYPE_PRESENT
objACE1.ObjectType   = GUID_ACCOUNT_RESTRICTIONS
'objACE1.InheritedObjectType = not used

Set objACE2 = CreateObject("AccessControlEntry")
objACE2.Trustee      = strWhoCanJoin
objACE2.AccessMask   = ADS_RIGHT_DS_WRITE_PROP
objACE2.AceFlags     = 0 'no inheritance from up or to below
objACE2.AceType      = ADS_ACETYPE_ACCESS_ALLOWED_OBJECT
objACE2.Flags        = ADS_FLAG_OBJECT_TYPE_PRESENT
objACE2.ObjectType   = GUID_LOGON_INFORMATION
'objACE2.InheritedObjectType = not used

Set objACE3 = CreateObject("AccessControlEntry")
objACE3.Trustee      = strWhoCanJoin
objACE3.AccessMask   = ADS_RIGHT_DS_WRITE_PROP
objACE3.AceFlags     = 0 'no inheritance from up or to below
objACE3.AceType      = ADS_ACETYPE_ACCESS_ALLOWED_OBJECT
objACE3.Flags        = ADS_FLAG_OBJECT_TYPE_PRESENT
objACE3.ObjectType   = GUID_DESCRIPTION
'objACE3.InheritedObjectType = not used

Set objACE4 = CreateObject("AccessControlEntry")
objACE4.Trustee      = strWhoCanJoin
objACE4.AccessMask   = ADS_RIGHT_DS_WRITE_PROP
objACE4.AceFlags     = 0 'no inheritance from up or to below
objACE4.AceType      = ADS_ACETYPE_ACCESS_ALLOWED_OBJECT
objACE4.Flags        = ADS_FLAG_OBJECT_TYPE_PRESENT
objACE4.ObjectType   = GUID_DISPLAY_NAME
'objACE4.InheritedObjectType = not used

Set objACE5 = CreateObject("AccessControlEntry")
objACE5.Trustee      = strWhoCanJoin
objACE5.AccessMask   = ADS_RIGHT_DS_WRITE_PROP
objACE5.AceFlags     = 0 'no inheritance from up or to below
objACE5.AceType      = ADS_ACETYPE_ACCESS_ALLOWED_OBJECT
objACE5.Flags        = ADS_FLAG_OBJECT_TYPE_PRESENT
objACE5.ObjectType   = GUID_SAM_ACCOUNT_NAME
'objACE5.InheritedObjectType = not used
```

```
Set objACE6 = CreateObject("AccessControlEntry")
objACE6.Trustee      = strWhoCanJoin
objACE6.AccessMask   = ADS_RIGHT_DS_SELF
objACE6.AceFlags     = 0 'no inheritance from up or to below
objACE6.AceType      = ADS_ACETYPE_ACCESS_ALLOWED_OBJECT
objACE6.Flags        = ADS_FLAG_OBJECT_TYPE_PRESENT
objACE6.ObjectType   = GUID_VALIDATED_SPN
'objACE6.InheritedObjectType = not used

Set objACE7 = CreateObject("AccessControlEntry")
objACE7.Trustee      = strWhoCanJoin
objACE7.AccessMask   = ADS_RIGHT_DS_SELF
objACE7.AceFlags     = 0 'no inheritance from up or to below
objACE7.AceType      = ADS_ACETYPE_ACCESS_ALLOWED_OBJECT
objACE7.Flags        = ADS_FLAG_OBJECT_TYPE_PRESENT
objACE7.ObjectType   = GUID_VALIDATED_DNSHOST
'objACE7.InheritedObjectType = not used

Set objACE8 = CreateObject("AccessControlEntry")
objACE8.Trustee      = strWhoCanJoin
objACE8.AccessMask   = _
    ADS_RIGHT_ACTRL_DS_LIST + _
    ADS_RIGHT_DS_LIST_OBJECT + _
    ADS_RIGHT_DS_READ_PROP + _
    ADS_RIGHT_READ_CONTROL + _
    ADS_RIGHT_DELETE + _
    ADS_RIGHT_DS_DELETE_TREE + _
    ADS_RIGHT_DS_CONTROL_ACCESS
objACE8.AceFlags     = 0 'no inheritance from up or to below
objACE8.AceType      = ADS_ACETYPE_ACCESS_ALLOWED
objACE8.Flags        = 0
'objACE8.ObjectType = not used
'objACE8.InheritedObjectType = not used

Set objSecDesc = objComputer.Get("ntSecurityDescriptor")
Set objDACL = objSecDesc.DiscretionaryAcl

Call objDACL.AddAce(objACE1)
Call objDACL.AddAce(objACE2)
Call objDACL.AddAce(objACE3)
Call objDACL.AddAce(objACE4)
Call objDACL.AddAce(objACE5)
Call objDACL.AddAce(objACE6)
```

```
    Call objDACL.AddAce(objACE7)
    Call objDACL.AddAce(objACE8)

    objSecDesc.DiscretionaryAcl = objDACL
    Call objComputer.Put("ntSecurityDescriptor", objSecDesc)
    objComputer.SetInfo

    WScript.Echo "Created computer " & strComputerName
End Sub
```

The script is implemented as a subprogram so that you can easily adapt it to create several computer accounts. Currently, the script creates computer objects always in `CN=Computers`, but you can change this if you'd like.

ADSI without Active Directory

Recall from Chapter 10 that even though the WinNT provider is primarily for Windows NT, you could use it also with Windows 2000 and later computers for the following tasks:

- Managing some server services, such as file shares, print queues, user sessions, and so on (even on domain controllers)
- Managing users and groups of Windows 2000 and later workstations and stand-alone/member servers

We don't cover the preceding tasks extensively in this Active Directory book, but we do give you the following short examples to provide you with a taste of these functions:

- CH11-42 ADSI List Services.vbs
- CH11-43 ADSI List Shares.vbs
- CH11-44 ADSI Create a Share.vbs
- CH11-45 ADSI List WinNT Properties of User Class.vbs
- CH11-46 ADSI Create a User in a Workstation.vbs

You can apply the "List Services.vbs" script also to list users, groups, and print queues.

When we create a share, we also publish it in Active Directory, so we do use Active Directory a little.

List Services.vbs

This script lists the Win32 services in a computer, whether they are running or not. The script has the lines shown in Figure 11.82.

We read the local computer name from the WSH Network object. We also need to add `,computer` to the binding string so that ADSI knows to find a computer DC1 instead of a domain DC1.

Because the same computer container also contains the users, groups, and print queues of the computer, we need to apply a filter to include just the services. With Active Directory, the filter used to refer to a class LDAP name, but this time "service" in the filter is an "internal ADSI class name."

In the `For` loop, we browse through all services and list a number of properties for each service. Note that the `Status` property is from a

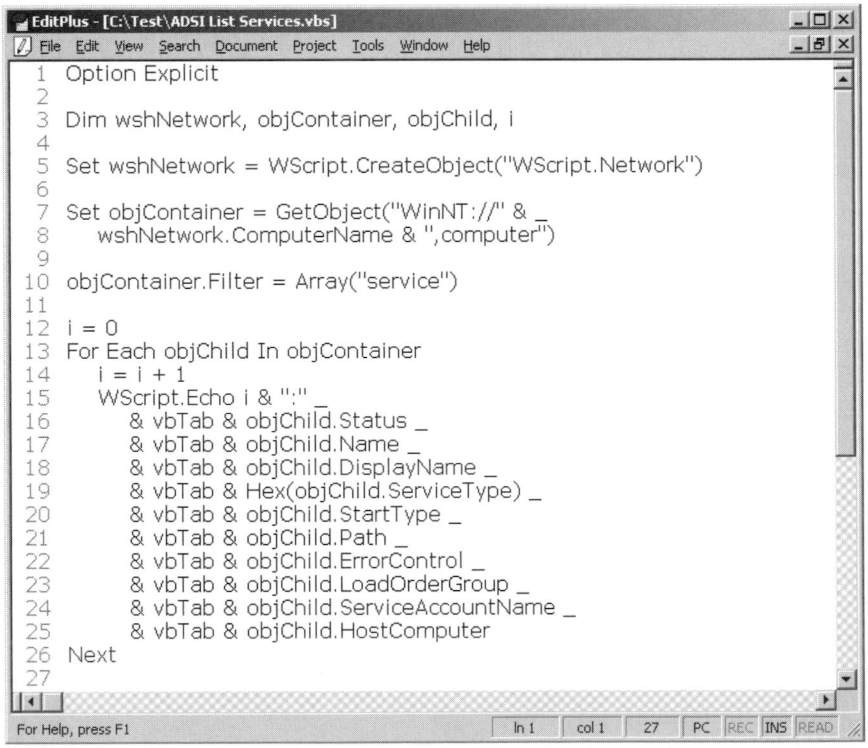

EditPlus - [C:\Test\ADSI List Services.vbs]

```
Option Explicit

Dim wshNetwork, objContainer, objChild, i

Set wshNetwork = WScript.CreateObject("WScript.Network")

Set objContainer = GetObject("WinNT://" & _
   wshNetwork.ComputerName & ",computer")

objContainer.Filter = Array("service")

i = 0
For Each objChild In objContainer
   i = i + 1
   WScript.Echo i & ":" _
      & vbTab & objChild.Status _
      & vbTab & objChild.Name _
      & vbTab & objChild.DisplayName _
      & vbTab & Hex(objChild.ServiceType) _
      & vbTab & objChild.StartType _
      & vbTab & objChild.Path _
      & vbTab & objChild.ErrorControl _
      & vbTab & objChild.LoadOrderGroup _
      & vbTab & objChild.ServiceAccountName _
      & vbTab & objChild.HostComputer
Next
```

Figure 11.82 ADSI List Services.vbs

dynamic ADSI interface, `IADsServiceOperations`, while the remaining properties are from a persistent ADSI interface, `IADsService`. (We listed the persistent and dynamic ADSI interfaces in Chapter 10.)

Because each line of output contains 11 elements, it is pretty ugly to read. However, because of the tab characters between the elements, it is easy to redirect the output to a text file and open it in Excel. Figure 11.83 shows the first lines of the output.

Column B contains the status code of each service. The value "4" means "running" and the value "1" means "stopped," as you can see from the following constants:

```
Const ADS_SERVICE_STOPPED            = 1
Const ADS_SERVICE_START_PENDING      = 2
Const ADS_SERVICE_STOP_PENDING       = 3
Const ADS_SERVICE_RUNNING            = 4
Const ADS_SERVICE_CONTINUE_PENDING   = 5
Const ADS_SERVICE_PAUSE_PENDING      = 6
Const ADS_SERVICE_PAUSED             = 7
Const ADS_SERVICE_ERROR              = 8
```

If you already know how services are defined in Windows NT, Windows 2000, or later, the output looks pretty familiar. Explaining all the options is outside the scope of this book, but we cannot resist the temptation to give a few hints.

- Column E contains the service type as a hexadecimal number, because the type is a bitfield. "&H10" means that the service is running in its own process, such as Distributed File System is running in Dfssvc.exe.

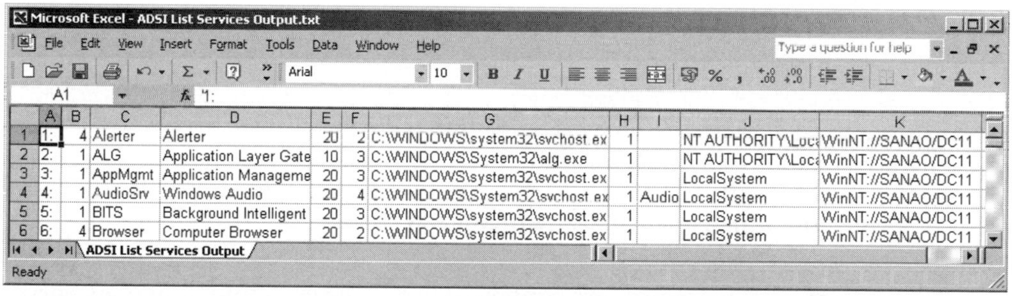

Microsoft Excel - ADSI List Services Output.txt

	A	B	C	D	E	F	G	H	I	J	K
1	1:	4	Alerter	Alerter	20	2	C:\WINDOWS\system32\svchost.ex	1		NT AUTHORITY\Loc	WinNT://SANAO/DC11
2	2:	1	ALG	Application Layer Gate	10	3	C:\WINDOWS\System32\alg.exe	1		NT AUTHORITY\Loc	WinNT://SANAO/DC11
3	3:	1	AppMgmt	Application Manageme	20	3	C:\WINDOWS\system32\svchost.ex	1		LocalSystem	WinNT://SANAO/DC11
4	4:	1	AudioSrv	Windows Audio	20	4	C:\WINDOWS\System32\svchost.ex	1	Audio	LocalSystem	WinNT://SANAO/DC11
5	5:	1	BITS	Background Intelligent	20	3	C:\WINDOWS\system32\svchost.ex	1		LocalSystem	WinNT://SANAO/DC11
6	6:	4	Browser	Computer Browser	20	2	C:\WINDOWS\system32\svchost.ex	1		LocalSystem	WinNT://SANAO/DC11

Figure 11.83 Part of the output of "ADSI List Services.vbs"

- Service type "&H20" means that the service is running in a process with other services, such as Alerter, and many others are running in services.exe.
- Column F contains the start type, and the value "2" means "Automatic," whereas the value "3" means "Manual" (or "Load on Demand").
- Column K contains the name of the computer that contains the service as an ADSI path (e.g., WinNT://SANAO/DC1).

You can list the services and processes of a computer in the following ways.

- To see all running processes, start the Task Manager by simultaneously pressing Ctrl-Shift-Esc. Then choose the Processes tab.
- To see all running services, start Command Prompt (click the Start button and select Command Prompt), type "NET START", and press Enter.

You can see more information on each service in two places: (a) the Services snap-in (click Start, Administrative Tools, Services) and (b) the System Information applet (click Start, Run, type "msinfo32", and press Enter).

List Users, Groups, and Print Queues

You can also use the previous script to list users, groups, and print queues. Just replace the `service` filter with `user`, `group`, or `printQueue`, respectively.

Obviously, you also need to change which properties you read from these other "classes."

List Shares.vbs

Our next example lists the file shares of a computer. The script has the lines shown in Figure 11.84.

This script is similar to the previous one in many ways, but there are also the following differences between them.

- The file shares are contained not in the computer, but in its Server service. However, that is only a display name. The internal name of the service is `lanmanserver` and that is the name we need to

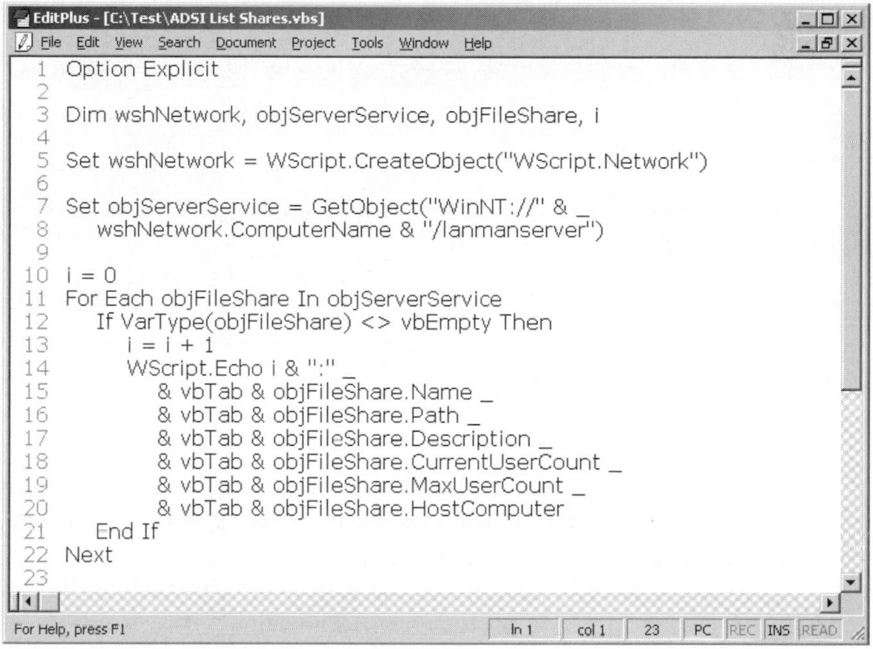

```
Option Explicit

Dim wshNetwork, objServerService, objFileShare, i

Set wshNetwork = WScript.CreateObject("WScript.Network")

Set objServerService = GetObject("WinNT://" & _
   wshNetwork.ComputerName & "/lanmanserver")

i = 0
For Each objFileShare In objServerService
   If VarType(objFileShare) <> vbEmpty Then
      i = i + 1
      WScript.Echo i & ":" _
         & vbTab & objFileShare.Name _
         & vbTab & objFileShare.Path _
         & vbTab & objFileShare.Description _
         & vbTab & objFileShare.CurrentUserCount _
         & vbTab & objFileShare.MaxUserCount _
         & vbTab & objFileShare.HostComputer
   End If
Next
```

Figure 11.84 ADSI List Shares.vbs

append to the binding string (internal service names are the same as their key names in the registry). "Lanman" refers to LAN Manager, which we have already mentioned in this book several times.

- Now that we append `/lanmanserver` to the binding string, our target is not a computer anymore and, consequently, the text `,computer` doesn't work. ADSI will still find the target computer, but you must wait 20 seconds, because ADSI first tries if the name is a domain name. If you don't want to wait, you can hard-code the domain name (in NetBIOS format) to your binding string. You could also use the `UserDomain` property of the WSH Network object. However, this method works only if the user logged on to the same domain that the computer is a member of.
- We don't need the filter anymore, because `lanmanserver` contains only shares.

When we browse the children of `lanmanserver`, we get all the file shares as object variables. However, for some reason after the file shares we get one extra `vbEmpty` when running the script on a Windows 2000 server (but not on a Windows 2000 workstation or Windows Server

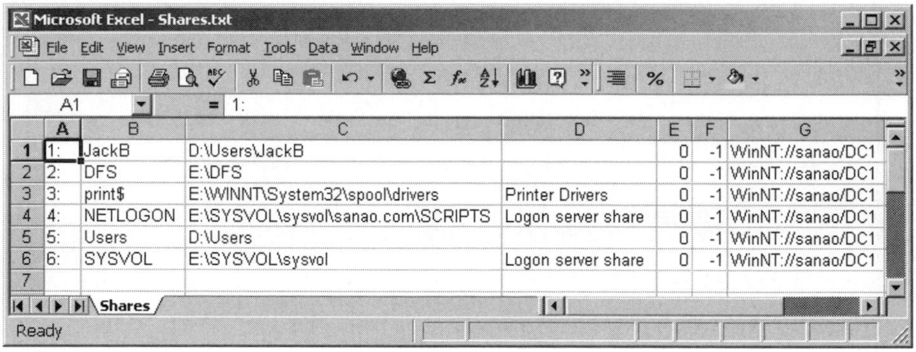

Microsoft Excel - Shares.txt

	A	B	C	D	E	F	G
1	1:	JackB	D:\Users\JackB		0	-1	WinNT://sanao/DC1
2	2:	DFS	E:\DFS		0	-1	WinNT://sanao/DC1
3	3:	print$	E:\WINNT\System32\spool\drivers	Printer Drivers	0	-1	WinNT://sanao/DC1
4	4:	NETLOGON	E:\SYSVOL\sysvol\sanao.com\SCRIPTS	Logon server share	0	-1	WinNT://sanao/DC1
5	5:	Users	D:\Users		0	-1	WinNT://sanao/DC1
6	6:	SYSVOL	E:\SYSVOL\sysvol	Logon server share	0	-1	WinNT://sanao/DC1
7							

Figure 11.85 Output of "ADSI List Shares.vbs"

2003). Therefore, we have included the `If VarType(objFileShare) <> vbEmpty` statement. You can remove this `If` statement if you won't run the script on Windows 2000 server.

Again, it is best to redirect the output to a text file and open it in Excel. Figure 11.85 shows the result. The value "–1" in column F means that there is no limit on how many users may connect to the share at the same time.

NOTE The `IADsFileShare` interface, which we use in this script, returns only those file shares (normal or hidden) that are defined in the `lanmanserver` key of the registry. Consequently, the shares that the Server service creates each time it is started are not listed. These automatically created shares include IPC$, ADMIN$, C$, D$, and so on. You can see them with the NET SHARE command.

Create a Share.vbs

The script shown in Figure 11.86 creates a new folder and shares it. At the end we include lines that publish the new share in Active Directory.

You probably want to change the target container `CN=Users` to something else. We are using it so that this demo script will work in any domain (except in those domains where the default Users container is redirected to somewhere else). In Windows 2000 without the `MaxUserCount` setting on line 18, only one user at a time could connect to the share. In Windows Server 2003, the default max user count is unlimited, so in that case you don't need line 18.

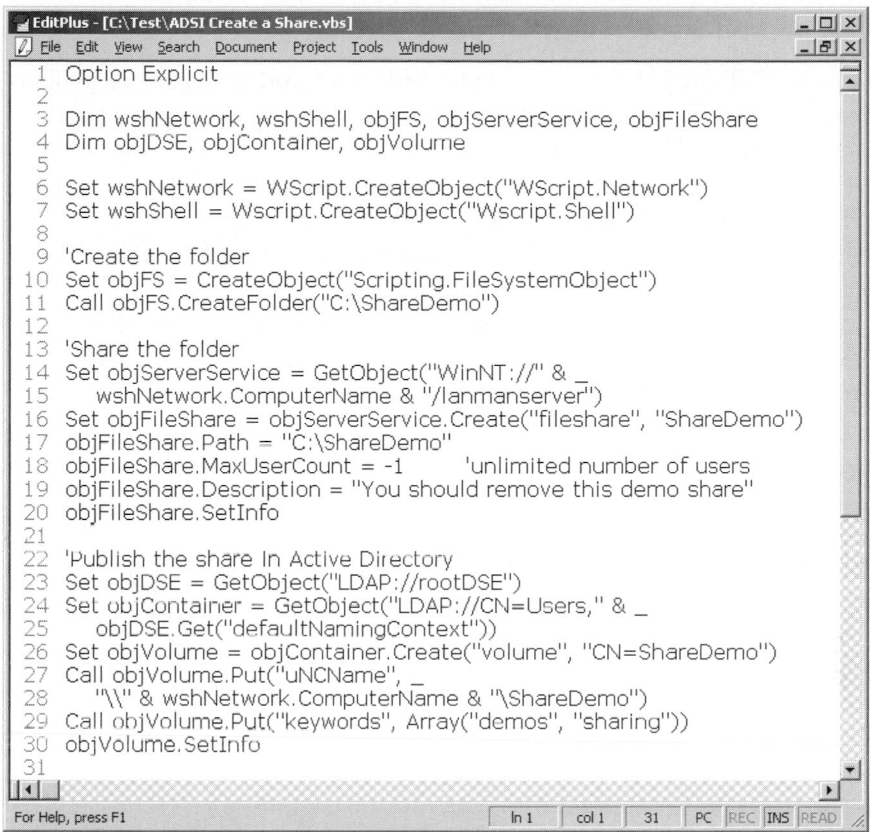

```
Option Explicit

Dim wshNetwork, wshShell, objFS, objServerService, objFileShare
Dim objDSE, objContainer, objVolume

Set wshNetwork = WScript.CreateObject("WScript.Network")
Set wshShell = Wscript.CreateObject("Wscript.Shell")

'Create the folder
Set objFS = CreateObject("Scripting.FileSystemObject")
Call objFS.CreateFolder("C:\ShareDemo")

'Share the folder
Set objServerService = GetObject("WinNT://" & _
   wshNetwork.ComputerName & "/lanmanserver")
Set objFileShare = objServerService.Create("fileshare", "ShareDemo")
objFileShare.Path = "C:\ShareDemo"
objFileShare.MaxUserCount = -1       'unlimited number of users
objFileShare.Description = "You should remove this demo share"
objFileShare.SetInfo

'Publish the share in Active Directory
Set objDSE = GetObject("LDAP://rootDSE")
Set objContainer = GetObject("LDAP://CN=Users," & _
   objDSE.Get("defaultNamingContext"))
Set objVolume = objContainer.Create("volume", "CN=ShareDemo")
Call objVolume.Put("uNCName", _
   "\\" & wshNetwork.ComputerName & "\ShareDemo")
Call objVolume.Put("keywords", Array("demos", "sharing"))
objVolume.SetInfo
```

Figure 11.86 ADSI Create a Share.vbs

Note that the published share in Active Directory refers to a UNC path (\\server\ShareDemo) instead of a physical path (such as C:\ShareDemo).

NOTE Normally you don't need to set any file share permissions, because NTFS permissions are enough. The default share permissions for a new share created with ADSI are Everyone:Full Control, in both Windows 2000 and Windows Server 2003. If you want to modify the default, you can use the `IADsSecurityUtility` interface that we discussed in the "Add ACEs to a Folder.vbs" section. ADSI doesn't allow you to manage the caching settings of file shares. For this task, you can use the NET SHARE command and call it from a script using the `Run` method, as we demonstrated in the example "Create a Home Folder for a User - ver 1.vbs" earlier in this chapter.

List WinNT Properties of User Class.vbs

The WinNT provider has somewhat different and many fewer properties for user objects than LDAP. WinNT has only 25 user properties, whereas Active Directory has over 200.

Even though there is no real schema in Windows 2000 workstations, Windows XP, or Windows NT, the WinNT provider exposes a fake schema. You can read it just like the abstract schema of LDAP to find out which classes and properties are supported.

The script in Figure 11.87 reads the fake schema and lists all optional properties of the `user` "class." We didn't include lines for mandatory properties, because there wouldn't be any.

NOTE If your test computer is a domain controller, you can still run this script, even though it is meant for workstations and stand-alone/member servers.

Unlike with the LDAP provider, we now have to include a domain or computer name in the path, so the path becomes something like `WinNT://pc17/schema/user` instead of just `WinNT://schema/user`.

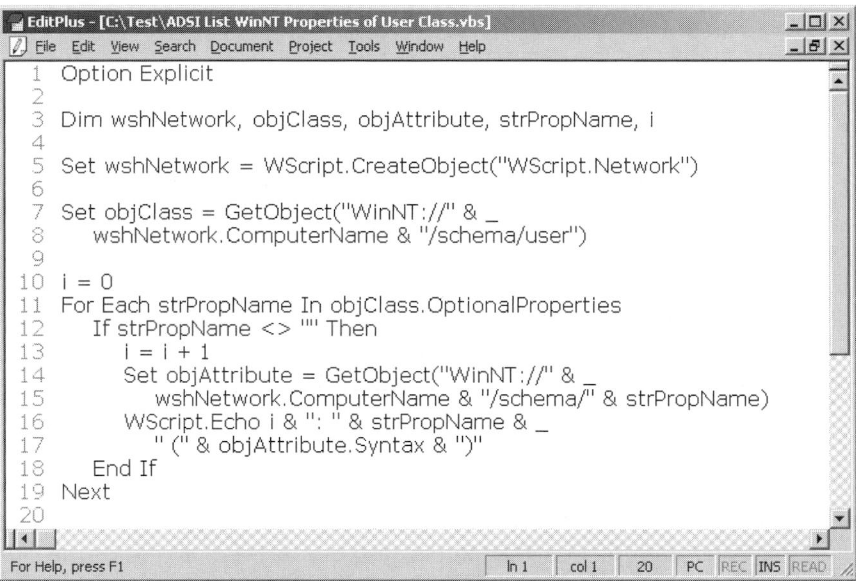
EditPlus - [C:\Test\ADSI List WinNT Properties of User Class.vbs]
File Edit View Search Document Project Tools Window Help
Option Explicit
Dim wshNetwork, objClass, objAttribute, strPropName, i
Set wshNetwork = WScript.CreateObject("WScript.Network")
Set objClass = GetObject("WinNT://" & _
wshNetwork.ComputerName & "/schema/user")
i = 0
For Each strPropName In objClass.OptionalProperties
If strPropName <> "" Then
i = i + 1
Set objAttribute = GetObject("WinNT://" & _
wshNetwork.ComputerName & "/schema/" & strPropName)
WScript.Echo i & ": " & strPropName & _
" (" & objAttribute.Syntax & ")"
End If
Next
For Help, press F1
ln 1
col 1
20
PC
REC
INS
READ

Figure 11.87 ADSI List WinNT Properties of User Class.vbs

In Windows 2000, the list of optional properties includes one empty name, and that is why we have one extra `If` statement inside the `For` loop. In Windows Server 2003, you can remove the `If` statement.

Figure 11.88 shows most of the output of the script. We dropped four lines out (password minimum length and so on), because they are actually per-domain (or per-computer) settings instead of per-user. The `PasswordAge` property indicates how old the user password is in seconds.

NOTE In addition to the properties shown in Figure 11.88, you can use the following `IADsUser` static property methods: `AccountDisabled`, `IsAccountLocked`, `PasswordRequired`, and `PasswordExpiration-Date`. The fake schema doesn't list them.

NOTE `UserFlags` in Figure 11.88 corresponds to `userAccount-Control` with the LDAP provider. Both have the same bits, except that `UserFlags` doesn't support the smart card requirement and some other new settings. Also, `UserFlags` uses `UF_PASSWD_CANT_CHANGE`, while `userAccountControl` does not (because Active Directory implements that feature using ACLs).

Create a User in a Workstation.vbs

Now that you know which properties you can use with WinNT users, we'll show how to create a user. The lines in Figure 11.89 create the user

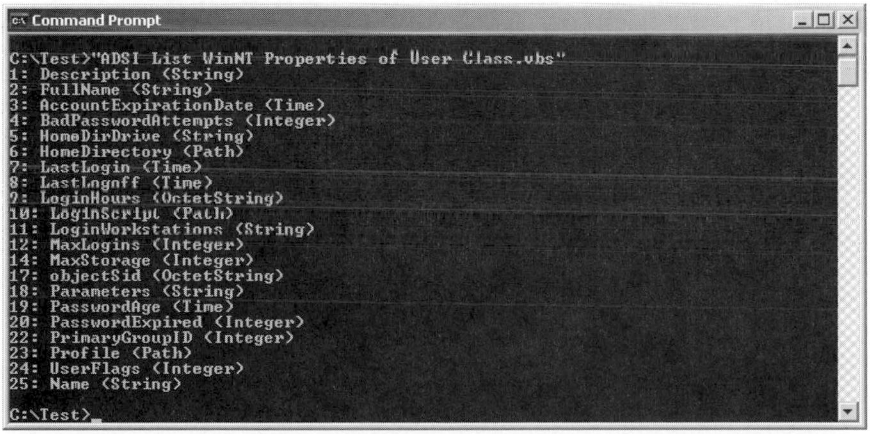

```
Command Prompt
C:\Test>"ADSI List WinNT Properties of User Class.vbs"
1: Description (String)
2: FullName (String)
3: AccountExpirationDate (Time)
4: BadPasswordAttempts (Integer)
5: HomeDirDrive (String)
6: HomeDirectory (Path)
7: LastLogin (Time)
8: LastLogoff (Time)
9: LoginHours (OctetString)
10: LoginScript (Path)
11: LoginWorkstations (String)
12: MaxLogins (Integer)
14: MaxStorage (Integer)
17: objectSid (OctetString)
18: Parameters (String)
19: PasswordAge (Time)
20: PasswordExpired (Integer)
22: PrimaryGroupID (Integer)
23: Profile (Path)
24: UserFlags (Integer)
25: Name (String)

C:\Test>_
```

Figure 11.88 Most of the output of "ADSI List WinNT Properties of User Class.vbs"

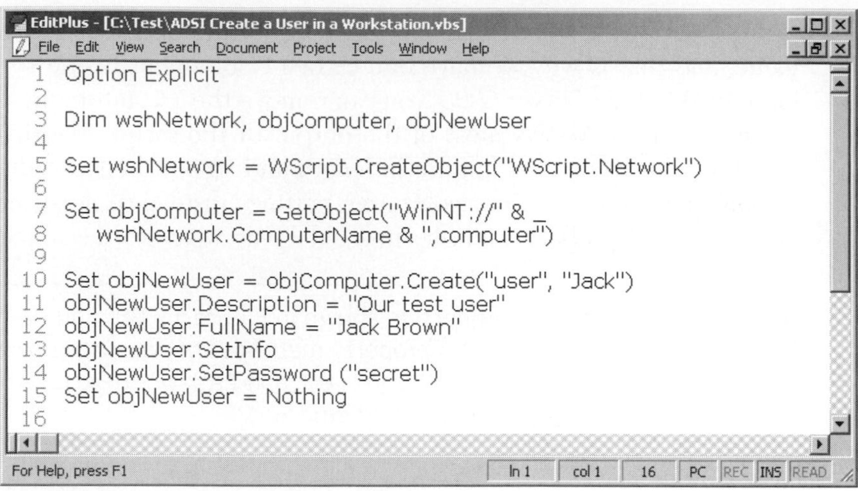

```
Option Explicit

Dim wshNetwork, objComputer, objNewUser

Set wshNetwork = WScript.CreateObject("WScript.Network")

Set objComputer = GetObject("WinNT://" & _
   wshNetwork.ComputerName & ",computer")

Set objNewUser = objComputer.Create("user", "Jack")
objNewUser.Description = "Our test user"
objNewUser.FullName = "Jack Brown"
objNewUser.SetInfo
objNewUser.SetPassword ("secret")
Set objNewUser = Nothing
```

Figure 11.89 ADSI Create a User in a Workstation.vbs

Jack on the local computer. Note that the name to be created is just "Jack," not "CN=Jack."

This time we don't use the explicit `Put` method, because there are no attribute LDAP names that we would want to emphasize. You can choose whether or not to use explicit `Get` and `Put` except with the four static property methods we listed in the previous section. Because they are already methods, you cannot put them inside a `Put`.

Additional Techniques

In this section, we briefly explain some additional techniques that you can use in your scripts. The techniques are as follows:

- Binding with credentials
- Binding with WKGUIDs and binding rename-safely to other objects
- Binding to the global catalog
- Listing objects of a subtree
- Error checking
- Scripts as command-line tools

We show some example lines of each technique. In addition, we present the following complete scripts in this section:

- CH11-47 ADSI Bind to a WKGUID.vbs
- CH11-48 ADSI List WKGUIDs.vbs
- CH11-49 ADSI List the Users of a Subtree.vbs
- CH11-50 VBS Error Checking.vbs
- CH11-51 CmdTool.vbs

We start by explaining how to bind with credentials.

Binding with Credentials

So far, all the scripts we have shown have used the credentials of the logged-on user, because it is usually most convenient to log on as an administrator and then run any appropriate scripts.

Occasionally there may be a need to run a script with alternate credentials. One way is, of course, to use the `RunAs` feature of Windows 2000 and later, but ADSI also allows specifying the credentials.

When you bind without credentials (the traditional way), you use the following lines:

```
Set objDSE = GetObject("LDAP://rootDSE")
Set objContainer = GetObject("LDAP://CN=Users," & _
    objDSE.Get("defaultNamingContext"))
```

When credentials are added to the picture, you must use `OpenDSObject` instead of `GetObject`. In this case, you use the following lines:

```
Const ADS_SECURE_AUTHENTICATION = 1
Set objDSE = GetObject("LDAP://rootDSE")
Set objLDAP = GetObject("LDAP:")
Set objUser = objLDAP.OpenDSObject( _
  "LDAP://CN=Guest,CN=Users," & _
  objDSE.Get("defaultNamingContext"), _
  "red.baron@sanao.com", "somesecret", _
  ADS_SECURE_AUTHENTICATION)
```

You need one extra step, because you first need to bind to the LDAP namespace ("LDAP:") and only then can you call `OpenDSObject`. In addition to the same `ADsPath` as with `GetObject`, there are three other arguments: username, password, and authentication method.

The following usernames are valid:

- UPN (user principal name), such as red.baron@sanao.com
- SAM name, such as "RedBaron"
- SAM name with domain NetBIOS name, such as "SANAO\RedBaron"
- Distinguished name, such as CN=Red Baron, CN=Users, DC=sanao, DC=com

If you use a constant vbNullString as both the username and password, you will authenticate with the credentials of the logged-on user, so the result is actually the same as if you used plain old GetObject.

For the authentication method, you can use the following constants:

```
Const ADS_SECURE_AUTHENTICATION   = &H1
Const ADS_USE_ENCRYPTION          = &H2
Const ADS_USE_SSL                 = &H2
Const ADS_READONLY_SERVER         = &H4
Const ADS_PROMPT_CREDENTIALS      = &H8
Const ADS_NO_AUTHENTICATION       = &H10
Const ADS_FAST_BIND               = &H20
Const ADS_USE_SIGNING             = &H40
Const ADS_USE_SEALING             = &H80
Const ADS_USE_DELEGATION          = &H100
Const ADS_SERVER_BIND             = &H200
```

Some of the authentication methods can (or must) be used together using the "+" operator. For example, the sealing option requires also the secure authentication option. ADS_SECURE_AUTHENTICATION, which we showed in the example, means a normal authentication that any Windows 2000 or later does when a user logs on to Active Directory. The underlying protocol would be Kerberos (or NTLM, if there were Windows NT computers involved).

Using the option ADS_NO_AUTHENTICATION would result in using the anonymous access option, or "null session." In this case, the username and password must be empty strings—that is, two consecutive quotation marks (""). Note that we cannot use vbNullString with ADS_NO_AUTHENTICATION, even though we are talking about a null session.

NOTE Whether anonymous access is allowed at all and what an anonymous logon may do is explained in Chapter 4.

For information about the other authentication options, refer to the ADSI documentation.

ADSI caches the credentials supplied in `OpenDSObject`, so you need to define the password only in the first call. In subsequent calls, you can use just `vbNullString` instead of the real password. However, this works only if the following conditions are true:

- You use exactly the same username in all `OpenDSObject` calls.
- You use serverless binding or specify the same server name in all `OpenDSObject` calls.
- You keep the session open by keeping at least one object in use all the time from one of the `OpenDSObject` calls.

Needless to say, you should avoid storing administrative passwords in your clear-text scripts. You should at least download Microsoft Script Encoder and use it to encode those scripts.

Binding with WKGUIDs

WKGUID means a GUID for a well-known object. ADSI has a special syntax that specifies how you can use WKGUIDs in your scripts.

The reason behind WKGUIDs is that if you bind to `CN=Users`, for example, your script is not *rename-safe*. It works only if that container is still using its default name. If you use the WKGUID for `CN=Users`, the script will always work because the corresponding GUID will always be the same.

NOTE Active Directory doesn't allow you just to change the name of `CN=Users`. You must use a special `redirusr` command, as discussed in Chapter 3.

The syntax for using a WKGUID is as follows:

```
Set objContainer = _
    GetObject("LDAP://<WKGUID=someGUID,parentContainerDN>")
```

WKGUIDs don't use any curly braces or hyphens, even though you use them as strings inside the binding string. They just have 32 hexadecimal characters, which results in a 128-bit value.

In this section, we first show a script that binds using a WKGUID and then we explain how to create new WKGUIDs.

Bind to a WKGUID.vbs

The following lines show a script that binds to `CN=Users` using a WKGUID and lists all objects in that container:

```
Option Explicit

Const GUID_USERS_CONTAINER                  = "a9d1ca15768811d1aded00c04fd8d5cd"
Const GUID_COMPUTRS_CONTAINER               = "aa312825768811d1aded00c04fd8d5cd"
Const GUID_SYSTEMS_CONTAINER                = "ab1d30f3768811d1aded00c04fd8d5cd"
Const GUID_DOMAIN_CONTROLLERS_CONTAINER = "a361b2ffffd211d1aa4b00c04fd7d83a"
Const GUID_INFRASTRUCTURE_CONTAINER         = "2fbac1870ade11d297c400c04fd8d5cd"
Const GUID_DELETED_OBJECTS_CONTAINER        = "18e2ea80684f11d2b9aa00c04f79f805"
Const GUID_LOSTANDFOUND_CONTAINER           = "ab8153b7768811d1aded00c04fd8d5cd"
Const GUID_FOREIGNSECURITYPRINCIPALS_CONTAINER = _
    "22b70c67d56e4efb91e9300fca3dc1aa"
Const GUID_PROGRAM_DATA_CONTAINER           = "09460c08ae1e4a4ea0f64aee7daa1e5a"
Const GUID_MICROSOFT_PROGRAM_DATA_CONTAINER = _
    "f4be92a4c777485e878e9421d53087db"
Const GUID_NTDS_QUOTAS_CONTAINER            = "6227f0af1fc2410d8e3bb10615bb5b0f"

Dim objContainer, objChild, strContainerDN

Set objContainer = GetObject("LDAP://<WKGUID=" & GUID_USERS_CONTAINER & _
    ",DC=sanao,DC=com>")
strContainerDN = objContainer.Get("distinguishedName")
Set objContainer = GetObject("LDAP://" & strContainerDN)

For Each objChild In objContainer
   WScript.Echo objChild.Name & vbTab & objChild.Description
Next
```

We didn't use `rootDSE` this time so that you could better see how the binding string is formed.

If you right away start to use an object that was bound with a GUID, you will have only part of the properties and interfaces available. Therefore, we get the distinguished name of the container and perform a second bind right after the first one. Without the second bind, you would see only the child object names in the list and not their other attributes, such as descriptions.

NOTE We use `objChild.Description` instead of `objChild.Get ("Description")` to avoid "property not found" errors.

We took the WKGUID names and values from the NtDsAPI.h file, which is part of the Platform SDK. Note that `GUID_SYSTEMS_CONTAINER` refers to `CN=System` despite the extra "S" and that the `GUID_INFRASTRUCTURE_CONTAINER` name is a little misleading because `CN=Infrastructure` is a leaf object.

NOTE `GUID_LOSTANDFOUND_CONTAINER` and `GUID_DELETED_OBJECTS_CONTAINER` can also be used in the Configuration container—not that you are likely to do so.

List WKGUIDs.vbs

WKGUIDs are not the same as `objectGUIDs` of the corresponding containers. Instead, the values are stored in the `wellKnownObjects` attribute of the parent container. That attribute uses the `DN with binary` data type, which is so exotic that even ADSI Edit cannot show the contents to you. It shows, however, ten semicolons, which indicate that there are 11 (invisible) values.

To see the values, you can use LDIFDE with the following command:

```
ldifde -f wellKnownObjects.txt -p base -l wellKnownObjects
```

The `-p base` option specifies that we don't want any child objects, and the `-l` option lists the attributes that we are interested in. Because there is no search root defined with the `-d` option, the command will use the default of the root of the domain of the logged-on user. Figure 11.90 shows the resulting file.

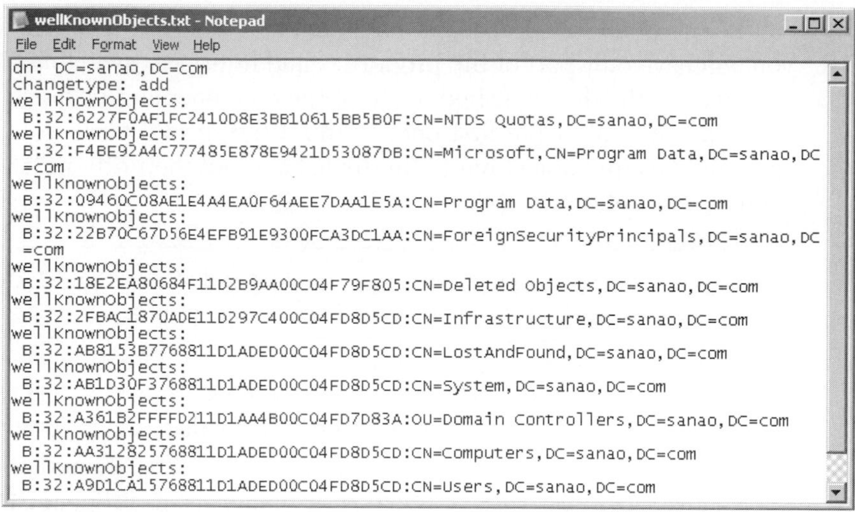
```
dn: DC=sanao,DC=com
changetype: add
wellKnownObjects:
 B:32:6227F0AF1FC2410D8E3BB10615BB5B0F:CN=NTDS Quotas,DC=sanao,DC=com
wellKnownObjects:
 B:32:F4BE92A4C777485E878E9421D53087DB:CN=Microsoft,CN=Program Data,DC=sanao,DC
 =com
wellKnownObjects:
 B:32:09460C08AE1E4A4EA0F64AEE7DAA1E5A:CN=Program Data,DC=sanao,DC=com
wellKnownObjects:
 B:32:22B70C67D56E4EFB91E9300FCA3DC1AA:CN=ForeignSecurityPrincipals,DC=sanao,DC
 =com
wellKnownObjects:
 B:32:18E2EA80684F11D2B9AA00C04F79F805:CN=Deleted Objects,DC=sanao,DC=com
wellKnownObjects:
 B:32:2FBAC1870ADE11D297C400C04FD8D5CD:CN=Infrastructure,DC=sanao,DC=com
wellKnownObjects:
 B:32:AB8153B7768811D1ADED00C04FD8D5CD:CN=LostAndFound,DC=sanao,DC=com
wellKnownObjects:
 B:32:AB1D30F3768811D1ADED00C04FD8D5CD:CN=System,DC=sanao,DC=com
wellKnownObjects:
 B:32:A361B2FFFFD211D1AA4B00C04FD7D83A:OU=Domain Controllers,DC=sanao,DC=com
wellKnownObjects:
 B:32:AA312825768811D1ADED00C04FD8D5CD:CN=Computers,DC=sanao,DC=com
wellKnownObjects:
 B:32:A9D1CA15768811D1ADED00C04FD8D5CD:CN=Users,DC=sanao,DC=com
```

Figure 11.90 Each domain object contains a `wellKnownObjects` attribute, which lists the default object distinguished names and corresponding GUID values.

The benefit of using `DN with binary` is that should an object name change, Active Directory will update the distinguished name part of the value pair and, consequently, the name will always be current.

To list WKGUIDs with a script, you need to use the `IADsDNWith-Binary` interface to handle this special data type. Also, you need to handle the binary value as shown in the "List User Properties with Methods.vbs" section earlier in this chapter.

The following lines show the script contents.

```
Option Explicit

Dim objDSE, objDom, arrValues, objVal
Dim strGUID, strByte, binVal, i

Set objDSE = GetObject("LDAP://rootDSE")
Set objDom = GetObject("LDAP://" & _
    objDSE.Get("defaultNamingContext"))

arrValues = objDom.GetEx("wellKnownObjects")
For Each objVal In arrValues
    strGUID = ""
    binVal = objVal.BinaryValue
    For i = 1 To LenB(binVal)
```

```
        strByte = Hex(AscB(MidB(binVal, i, 1)))
        If Len(strByte) = 1 Then strByte = "0" & strByte
        strGUID = strGUID & strByte
    Next

    WScript.Echo strGUID & "   " & objVal.DNString
Next
```

Figure 11.91 shows the script output.

Rename-Safe Binding to Other Objects

The `wellKnownObjects` attribute is "system only," which means that even administrators cannot modify it. There is also an `otherWell-KnownObjects` attribute, which works like `wellKnownObjects`. This other attribute is not "system only"; therefore, it allows administrators and developers to specify new rename-safe objects in addition to the few default ones.

Handling `DN with binary` attributes with VBScript is not straightforward. ADSI does contain an interface `IADsDNWithBinary`, but the binary component is returned as a byte array, which is somewhat laborious to digest in VBScript. LDIFDE is much more straightforward, so it is best to use LDIFDE when you want to create a new WKGUID.

To create your own WKGUID for `OU=Sales` (in the domain root), perform the following steps:

1. Run UUIDGen from the Platform SDK to generate a new GUID. You will get a GUID such as "aa63b9fc-e8bb-4e8a-b235 cf3556517d32."
2. Because that GUID is using the string representation of a GUID (even though curly braces are missing), swap some bytes

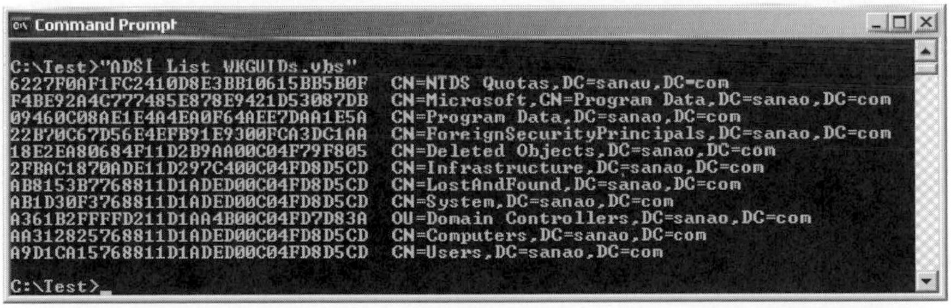

```
Command Prompt
C:\Test>"ADSI List WKGUIDs.vbs"
6227F0AF1FC2410D8E3BB10615BB5B0F  CN=NTDS Quotas,DC=sanao,DC=com
F4BE92A4C777485E878E9421D53087DB  CN=Microsoft,CN=Program Data,DC=sanao,DC=com
09460C08AE1E4A4EA0F64AEE7DAA1E5A  CN=Program Data,DC=sanao,DC=com
22B70C67D56E4EFB91E9300FCA3DC1AA  CN=ForeignSecurityPrincipals,DC=sanao,DC=com
18E2EA80684F11D2B9AA00C04F79F805  CN=Deleted Objects,DC=sanao,DC=com
2FBAC1870ADE11D297C400C04FD8D5CD  CN=Infrastructure,DC=sanao,DC=com
AB8153B7768811D1ADED00C04FD8D5CD  CN=LostAndFound,DC=sanao,DC=com
AB1D30F3768811D1ADED00C04FD8D5CD  CN=System,DC=sanao,DC=com
A361B2FFFFD211D1AA4B00C04FD7D83A  OU=Domain Controllers,DC=sanao,DC=com
AA312825768811D1ADED00C04FD8D5CD  CN=Computers,DC=sanao,DC=com
A9D1CA15768811D1ADED00C04FD8D5CD  CN=Users,DC=sanao,DC=com

C:\Test>_
```

Figure 11.91 Each domain object in AD2003 has a list of 11 well-known objects.

to get a binary representation (even though WKGUIDs are strings). We explained in the example "List Binary GUIDs.vbs" how you need to swap bytes 1-2-3-4 to 4-3-2-1, 5-6 to 6-5, and 7-8 to 8-7. When you also remove the hyphens, you will get "fcb963aabbe88a4eb235cf3556517d32."

3. Create an LDIF file that specifies that you want to add one new value to the `otherWellKnownObjects` attribute of the `DC=sanao,DC=com` object. The file should look like the one in Figure 11.92.
4. Import the LDIF file with the following command:

```
ldifde -i -f addotherwk.ldf
```

Now you have a new WKGUID, and you could use the following line to bind to `OU=Sales`:

```
Set objOU = _
    GetObject("LDAP://<WKGUID=FCB963AABBE88A4EB235CF3556517D32" & _
    ",DC=sanao,DC=com>")
```

If you later use LDIFDE to export the contents of `otherWell-KnownObjects`, you will get a text file similar to the one you just saw about `wellKnownObjects`.

NOTE If the common name of your object contains characters other than "safe UTF8 characters," LDIFDE will show the name in base64 encoding, as RFC 2849 mandates. An example of an "unsafe" character is the European "ä" (a-umlaut). Also, if you delete the target object, it will get a distinguished name with some special characters, and again base64 encoding kicks in. Base64 encoding looks like this: QjozMjpGQ0I5.

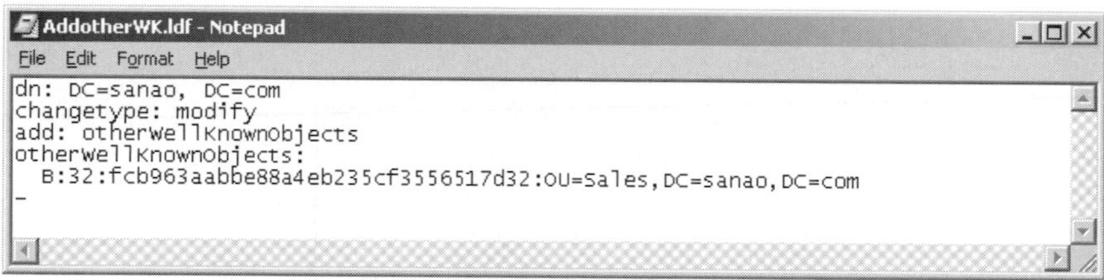

Figure 11.92 This LDIF file modifies the domain object by adding a new value to the `otherWellKnownObjects` attribute.

Binding to the Global Catalog

You can replace "LDAP:" with "GC:" in a binding string, in which case you bind to the global catalog in a global catalog server. Just as with the LDAP choice, you can either specify a server name or do a serverless binding.

As you probably know, the global catalog has the following characteristics and they naturally apply also when you use it with ADSI:

- The global catalog is read-only. You cannot create or modify objects.
- The global catalog contains all the objects of a forest. You can search the whole enterprise forest using a single server.
- The global catalog contains only part of the attributes (in the base schema of AD2003, 150 out of 1,070).

The first and third items in the list limit your options, but the second item is an advantage. You can bind to objects in other domains and still communicate with a server that is located on your local site—provided, of course, that you have designated a global catalog server for each location.

NOTE We don't show a sample script of binding to the global catalog (using a path such as `GC://CN=Users, DC=sanao, DC=com`), because the only difference from using "LDAP:" is a couple of letters.

You get the biggest benefits from binding to the global catalog when you perform searches. However, when using VBScript, searches require ADO and therefore we show any related examples in the ADO section later in this chapter.

When you later perform ADO searches, binding to any "GC:" container enables you to enumerate all the objects in the tree below that target of binding. For example:

- If you bind to the root domain of a domain tree, you can enumerate all the objects in the domain tree.
- If you bind to any domain, you can enumerate not only all objects in that domain, but also all objects in its child domains.

NOTE There is also an option to bind to just "GC:" without any distinguished name, but that option is for C programmers. You don't need it in your VBScript scripts.

NOTE We explained in Chapter 6 that when searching the global catalog, you can use `DC=com` or just an empty string as the DN of the base object. This includes several domain trees of a forest in a query. Unfortunately, this option seems not to work with ADSI/ADO scripts, so you can search only one domain tree at a time.

List the Users of a Subtree.vbs

So far when we have enumerated children of a container, we have done so for a single container only. In this example script, we show how it is also possible to include the whole subtree in the enumeration.

In the sample script, we use *recursion*. This means that we perform the enumeration of a single container in a subprogram, and each time our enumeration notices an OU or another container, the subprogram will call itself to enumerate that target also.

If we have a domain where we have added a couple of users in the `CN=Users` container and two more in `OU=Sales`, our script would produce the output shown in Figure 11.93. The script's contents are shown in Figure 11.94.

We start the recursion by calling the `ListUsers` subprogram the first time. After that, we call the same subprogram from itself every time we find an OU or another container.

Error Checking.vbs

We have occasionally done some error checking in the scripts of this chapter. In those cases, we have wanted to react to some expected situations and not to actual unexpected errors. Consequently, the error code we may have received is not an indication of a traditional error. Instead, the error code has told us, for example, that a certain attribute is not set.

```
Command Prompt
C:\Test>"ADSI List the Users of a Subtree.vbs"
CN=Helen Randell        CN=Helen Randell,OU=Sales,DC=sanao,DC=com
CN=Tim Carson   CN=Tim Carson,OU=Sales,DC=sanao,DC=com
CN=Administrator        CN=Administrator,CN=Users,DC=sanao,DC=com
CN=Guest        CN=Guest,CN=Users,DC=sanao,DC=com
CN=IUSR_DC1     CN=IUSR_DC1,CN=Users,DC=sanao,DC=com
CN=IWAM_DC1     CN=IWAM_DC1,CN=Users,DC=sanao,DC=com
CN=Jack Brown   CN=Jack Brown,CN=Users,DC=sanao,DC=com
CN=Jill Green   CN=Jill Green,CN=Users,DC=sanao,DC=com
CN=krbtgt       CN=krbtgt,CN=Users,DC=sanao,DC=com

C:\Test>_
```

Figure 11.93 Output of "ADSI List the Users of a Subtree.vbs"

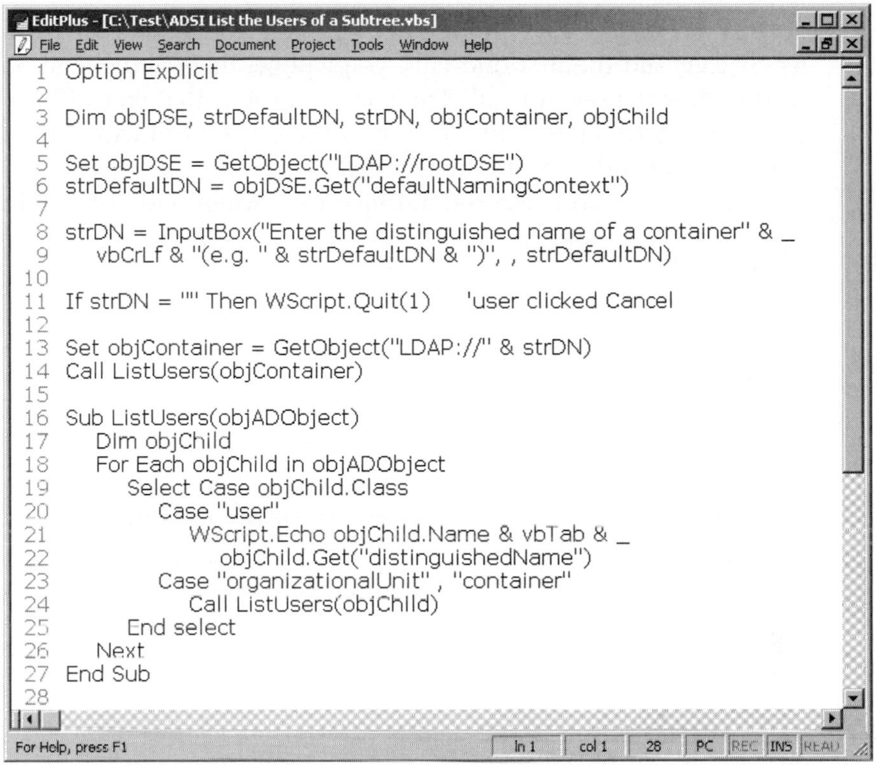

```
Option Explicit

Dim objDSE, strDefaultDN, strDN, objContainer, objChild

Set objDSE = GetObject("LDAP://rootDSE")
strDefaultDN = objDSE.Get("defaultNamingContext")

strDN = InputBox("Enter the distinguished name of a container" & _
   vbCrLf & "(e.g. " & strDefaultDN & ")", , strDefaultDN)

If strDN = "" Then WScript.Quit(1)     'user clicked Cancel

Set objContainer = GetObject("LDAP://" & strDN)
Call ListUsers(objContainer)

Sub ListUsers(objADObject)
   Dim objChild
   For Each objChild in objADObject
      Select Case objChild.Class
         Case "user"
            WScript.Echo objChild.Name & vbTab & _
               objChild.Get("distinguishedName")
         Case "organizationalUnit" , "container"
            Call ListUsers(objChild)
      End select
   Next
End Sub
```

Figure 11.94 ADSI List the Users of a Subtree.vbs

If you want to write complete scripts, you should prepare for unexpected real errors. The need for error checking increases if other people in various environments will run your scripts.

In this section, we say a few words about error mechanics, introduce the various error categories, and finally give an example of an error-checking script.

Error Mechanics

As we explained in the example “List User Properties with Get.vbs,” VBScript has an `Err` object that has a `Number` property. Because `Number` is the default property of `Err`, you can refer to it with just `Err` instead of `Err.Number`. You can clear a possible old error code with `Err.Clear` (or `Err = 0`) and then retrieve the new error code by reading the value of `Err` (`.Number`).

A successful ADSI call doesn't clear the error code. If you make two ADSI calls and the first one fails, you will get its error code also if you read it after the second call. The consequence is that you will probably get confused trying to find an error in the second call without knowing that the error code is from the first call.

Any error code is cleared automatically when one of the following statements is executed:

- `On Error Resume Next`
- `Exit Sub`
- `Exit Function`

However, it may be easier to add some extra `Err.Clear` lines than to try to remember when it was already called automatically.

Normally any error will terminate the script execution, but you can take error handling into your own hands by adding an `On Error Resume Next` statement to either the beginning of the script or some other location, such as the beginning of a subprogram. You can reverse the effect by adding an `On Error Goto 0` statement.

NOTE If you handle errors yourself, perhaps the biggest drawback to this is that you don't see the line number where the error occurred anymore.

NOTE Depending on your needs, you may do perfectly fine by relying on the default error handling of VBScript.

Error Categories

Your ADSI VBScript script could run into the following kinds of errors:

- VBScript syntax errors (or compilation errors), such as "Expected identifier." These errors are easy to notice and locate because the script doesn't run at all. It just displays the error message and the line it appears on. Using `On Error Resume Next` won't hide these errors.
- VBScript runtime errors, such as code "438" (decimal): "Object doesn't support this property or method."

- Generic COM errors, such as code "80004001" (hex): `E_NOTIMPL` ("Not implemented").
- Generic ADSI errors, such as code "8000500D" (hex): `E_ADS_PROPERTY_NOT_FOUND`.
- Standard Win32 errors, such as code "80072030" (hex): `ERROR_DS_NO_SUCH_OBJECT`. You can get some help on the error by taking the last four digits (2030), converting them to decimal (8240), and then typing "NET HELPMSG 8240" (without quotes) on the command line. That command has been around since the 1988 launch of LAN Manager. This category includes the traditional errors dating back to MS-DOS, such as code "5": "Access denied." Only this time it is "80070005." The LDAP provider maps also any LDAP errors to this "8007" format. The example in the beginning of the paragraph is the same as the LDAP error `LDAP_NO_SUCH_OBJECT`.

Of course, your script may also have errors that don't produce error codes or messages, but are just logical errors in what the script is doing.

Though there are quite a few possible error sources, try not to fall into despair. You can find more information about the two VBScript error categories in the VBScript documentation and more information about the three last categories in the ADSI documentation.

The first category and partly the second category are something that you don't want to prepare for in your scripts. They are just plain programming errors and there is no point in writing code in your script to test whether you forgot to declare some variable, for example.

The Error-Checking Sample Script

This sample script checks for errors after each ADSI operation. It doesn't have any fancy logic to evaluate if it continues running after some corrective action. It just displays the error code and quits.

You might wonder why you should write lines for this, because VBScript would do this automatically for you. Well, there are two reasons.

- You can give better feedback to the user by handling the errors yourself.
- For the functionality of your script, you may be forced to use `On Error Resume Next`. This means that you should probably also handle the unexpected (real) errors.

However, we don't want to tell you that you must write your scripts like this. We just want to demonstrate the option.

The following lines show the sample script. They create user Jack in OU=Sales.

```
Option Explicit

Const ERROR_OBJECT_ALREADY_EXISTS = &H80071392
Const ERROR_DS_NO_SUCH_OBJECT     = &H80072030

Dim strName, objContainer, objNewUser

On Error Resume Next

strName = "Jack"

Err.Clear
Set objContainer = _
    GetObject("LDAP://OU=Sales,DC=sanao,DC=com")
Call CheckIfError("Bind to OU=Sales")

Err.Clear
Set objNewUser = objContainer.Create("user", "CN=" & strName)
objNewUser.sAMAccountName = strName
objNewUser.userAccountControl = &H200
objNewUser.userPrincipalName = strName & "@sanao.com"
objNewUser.SetInfo
Call CheckIfError("Create user " & strName)

Err.Clear
WScript.Echo "Last name " & objNewUser.Get("sn")
Call CheckIfError("Read the last name of " & strName)

Err.Clear
objNewUser.SetPassword ("secret")
Call CheckIfError("Set password for user " & strName)

Sub CheckIfError(strOperation)
    Dim strMessage, intErrCode

    If Err = 0 Then Exit Sub

    strMessage = "Attempted operation: " & strOperation & vbCrLf
```

```
    Select Case Err
        Case ERROR_OBJECT_ALREADY_EXISTS
            strMessage = strMessage & _
                "Unfortunately the object already exists."
        Case ERROR_DS_NO_SUCH_OBJECT
            strMessage = strMessage & _
                "Unfortunately couldn't find that object."
        Case Else
            strMessage = strMessage & _
                "Error code: " & Hex(Err) & " (hex)" & vbCrLf & _
                Err.Description
            If (Err And &HFFFF0000) = &H80070000 Then
                intErrCode = (Err And 65535)  '65535 = &HFFFF
                strMessage = strMessage & vbCrLf & _
                    "You can get more help on the error by typing" & _
                    vbCrLf & _
                    "on the command line: NET HELPMSG " & intErrCode
            End If
    End Select

    MsgBox strMessage & vbCrLf & vbCrLf & _
        "Click OK to terminate the script.", _
        vbOKOnly + vbCritical, "Error"

    WScript.Quit(1) 'there was an error so we set the errorlevel
End Sub
```

We call `Err.Clear` before each ADSI operation to make sure that there is no previous error code. Immediately after each operation, we call the subprogram `CheckIfError` and pass the operation description as a text argument.

If there was no error, we immediately return from the subprogram. Otherwise, we build an error message string, which reports the attempted operation and what went wrong. After the user clicks OK, we terminate the script with an error level set.

Setting the error level is useful for the following reason: If the script was launched from another application or batch file, that other party will know about the error if it only checks the error level.

NOTE It wouldn't make much difference if we omitted the `Err.Clear` calls. Because we quit in case of an error, it is highly unlikely that any old error code was already there. Anyway, we play it safe and use plenty of `Err.Clear` calls. This way, we make sure that the correct error code and operation name appear in the message box.

We expect that a couple of errors are more likely to occur than any others, so we want to dedicate a `Case` option to handle these particular errors. Another reason for this dedication is that Win32 errors (i.e., "8007xxxx") don't include `Err.Description` texts, so this way we can type our own error description. Figure 11.95 shows one of the error messages that we created.

We handle all other errors in the `Case Else` option. We include the error code (in hexadecimal because the ADSI documentation lists them in that format) and a possible error description. Figure 11.96 shows one such error.

NOTE The VBScript documentation lists errors as decimal values, so if you get any of those errors, you need to convert them back to decimal before looking them up in the documentation.

In the last `If` statement, we check if the error code is of type "8007xxxx." These errors don't have a built-in error description, but you

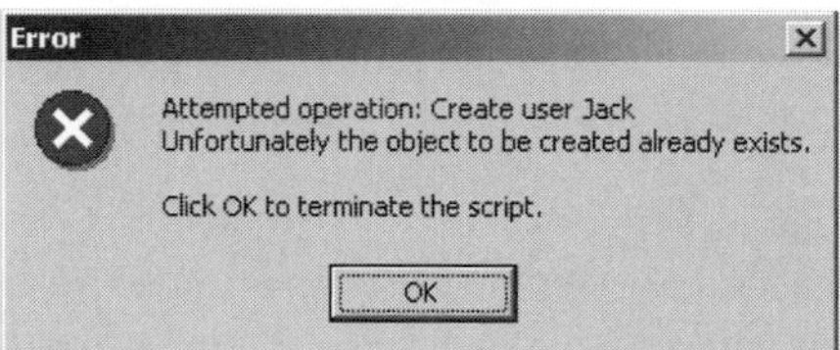

Figure 11.95 In case of ADSI error "80071392," we build a description text for it and display the bad news to the user.

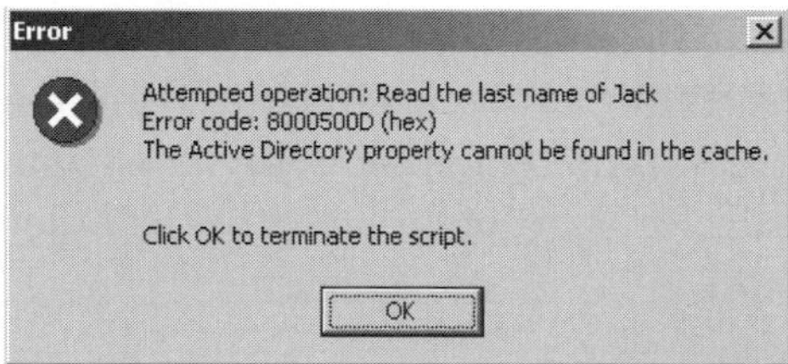

Figure 11.96 For most errors, we display the error code (line 2) and "built-in" description (line 3).

Figure 11.97 In case of "8007xxxx" errors, we want to give a hint about the command that offers the error description.

can get it with the command `NET HELPMSG errnumber`. Therefore, we want to give a hint of that in the message, including the right decimal value to enter. Figure 11.97 shows the resulting message box. If you type the suggested command, you will see that the description is as follows: "A referral was returned from the server." This description means that you specified an unknown forest name in the binding string.

It would be logical to use "&HFFFF" in the latter `And` expression to get the lower 16 bits (or four digits) of the error code. However, it doesn't give the desired result, so we use "65535" instead.

Scripts as Command-Line Tools

Most traditional command-line commands and tools enable you to specify options that determine which kind of operation or operations should be performed this time. For example, you can use the `/S` option with XCOPY to specify that you want to copy the subfolders also.

You can do the same with your scripts by examining the command-line options (i.e., arguments) and changing the script behavior accordingly. There are two slightly different approaches.

- The script has one basic purpose (e.g., XCOPY's basic purpose is to copy files), and the options somewhat adjust how the mission is accomplished.
- The script includes various functions that are related to some degree. By specifying an option, you choose which function should be performed. For example, the Resource Kit includes REG.EXE, which you can use to manipulate the registry. You can use it with options such as `REG QUERY`, `REG ADD`, and `REG SAVE` to perform the functions you want.

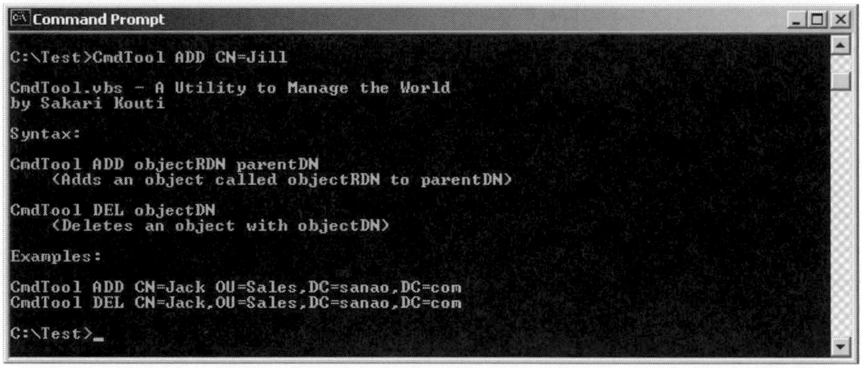

```
C:\Test>CmdTool ADD CN=Jill

CmdTool.vbs - A Utility to Manage the World
by Sakari Kouti

Syntax:

CmdTool ADD objectRDN parentDN
    <Adds an object called objectRDN to parentDN>

CmdTool DEL objectDN
    <Deletes an object with objectDN>

Examples:

CmdTool ADD CN=Jack OU=Sales,DC=sanao,DC=com
CmdTool DEL CN=Jack,OU=Sales,DC=sanao,DC=com

C:\Test>_
```

Figure 11.98 If used with the "ADD" option, the tool requires two more arguments. However, the user entered only one (`CN=Jill`), so the script just shows the help screen and terminates.

In this section, we show a sample script that is a skeleton of the latter case. It doesn't do anything yet, but once you add your own functions, you will have a command-line tool ready for use.

NOTE If you want to implement the former case (the one with one basic purpose and modifying options) with five options that the user can specify in random order, you can use the `<named>` element of WSH 5.6. This feature mostly automates the handling of named command-line arguments, such as `/username:Jack`, and allows you to enter them in random order. For more information, see the Windows Script documentation.

CmdTool.vbs

The help screen of the sample script is displayed in Figure 11.98. The script shows the help screen because the user entered one argument too few.

The script is as follows:

```
Option Explicit

Const ERROR_NOT_CSCRIPT     = 1   'wrong WSH environment
Const ERROR_NO_OPTIONS      = 2   'wrong number of options or
                                  'requested help
Const ERROR_COULDNT_ADD     = 3
Const ERROR_COULDNT_DELETE = 4
```

```
Dim objArguments, intResult
Dim strObjectDN, strObjectRDN, strParentDN

Call CheckWSHEnvironment   'we want CScript and not WScript

Set objArguments = WScript.Arguments
If objArguments.Count < 1 Then Call ShowHelp

Select Case UCase(objArguments.Item(0))
   Case "?", "/?", "H", "/H", "HELP"
      Call ShowHelp
   Case "ADD"
      If objArguments.Count <> 3 Then ShowHelp
      strObjectRDN = objArguments.Item(1)
      strParentDN = objArguments.Item(2)
      intResult = AddObject(strObjectRDN, strParentDN)
   Case "DEL"
      If objArguments.Count <> 2 Then ShowHelp
      strObjectDN = objArguments.Item(1)
      intResult = DeleteObject(strObjectDN)
    Case Else
      Call ShowHelp
End Select
WScript.Quit(intResult)   'the program end

'==========================

Function AddObject(strObjectRDN, strParentDN)
   WScript.Echo "Object RDN: " & strObjectRDN
   WScript.Echo "Parent DN: " & strParentDN
   AddObject = 0  'and not ERROR_COULDNT_ADD
End Function

'==========================

Function DeleteObject(strObjectDN)
   WScript.Echo "Object DN: " & strObjectDN
   DeleteObject = 0  'and not ERROR_COULDNT_DELETE
End Function

'==========================

Sub CheckWSHEnvironment()
   Dim strScriptHostName
```

```
    strScriptHostName = WScript.FullName
    strScriptHostName = Right(strScriptHostName,  _
        Len(strScriptHostName) _
        - InStrRev(strScriptHostName,"\"))
    If UCase(strScriptHostName) <> "CSCRIPT.EXE" Then
        MsgBox "You should run this script in the CScript" & vbCrLf & _
            "command line environment. Either type CSCRIPT" & vbCrLf & _
            "before the script name or change CScript as" & vbCrLf & _
            "the default environment with the command" & vbCrLf & _
            "CSCRIPT //H:CSCRIPT", _
            vbOKOnly + vbCritical, "Error"
        WScript.Quit(ERROR_NOT_CSCRIPT)
    End If
End Sub

'=========================

Sub ShowHelp()
    WScript.Echo _
        vbCrLf & _
        "CmdTool.vbs - A Utility to Manage the World" & vbCrLf & _
        "by Sakari Kouti" & vbCrLf & _
        vbCrLf & _
        "Syntax:" & vbCrLf & _
        vbCrLf & _
        "CmdTool ADD objectRDN parentDN" & vbCrLf & _
        "    (Adds an object called objectRDN to parentDN)" & vbCrLf & _
        vbCrLf & _
        "CmdTool DEL objectDN" & vbCrLf & _
        "    (Deletes an object with objectDN)" & vbCrLf & _
        vbCrLf & _
        "Examples:" & vbCrLf & _
        vbCrLf & _
        "CmdTool ADD CN=Jack OU=Sales,DC=sanao,DC=com" & vbCrLf & _
        "CmdTool DEL CN=Jack,OU=Sales,DC=sanao,DC=com"
    WScript.Quit(ERROR_NO_OPTIONS)
End Sub
```

First we check that we are running the script in the CScript environment instead of WScript. This is not that important if we just add or delete an object, but because this is a skeleton, you could use the script for displaying a long list, in which case WScript would mean tens or hundreds of message boxes.

NOTE Of course, we could add the environment check to all our sample scripts, but we don't want to repeat the same 20 lines in all scripts.

We implement the help screen as a subprogram, so that we can call it from here and there if we find anything wrong with the arguments.

We define a number of error constants and return them outside the script to indicate what went wrong, if anything. Because this is a command-line tool, chances are that you are calling it from a batch file (or another script), and returning a descriptive value from the script enables the calling application to know what happened.

The main program includes a `Select` statement and almost nothing else. It is then up to that `Select` statement to call the appropriate function based on the command-line option.

The next (and last) section in the chapter describes how to use ADO to enhance Active Directory searches.

Using ADO

ActiveX Data Objects (ADO) is a programmatic interface to any database or data source that has implemented an *OLE-DB provider*—that is, a driver component between ADO and the data source. Examples of such data sources are SQL Server, Oracle database server, and Active Directory.

In this section, we describe ADO concepts and then provide a few examples of how you can use ADO in your administration scripts. Note that you can use ADO in one script either together with ADSI or in place of ADSI.

We offer the following examples in this section:

- CH11-52 ADO Basic Example.vbs
- CH11-53 ADO Basic Example with SQL.vbs
- CH11-54 ADO Modifying Objects.vbs
- CH11-55 ADO List Objects That Have Blocked ACL Inheritance.vbs

We also describe how you can pass partition boundaries by using the global catalog or turning on referral chasing.

ADO Concepts

ADO is a COM-based programming interface that Microsoft has designed to be used with relational databases, such as SQL Server, but also with other data sources, such as other databases and Active Directory (or rather, any LDAP directory).

Figure 11.99 presents the ADO architecture and how it relates to ADSI. As you can see from the figure, you can use ADSI in your script or ADO, or both. Whether you choose to use just ADO for some script or to complement ADSI with ADO depends on what you are doing with your script.

One analogy for ADSI versus ADO is that using ADSI is like opening a Web page by typing its URL (Uniform Resource Locator) and using ADO is like searching Web pages using a search engine.

ADSI versus ADO

In Table 11.6 we compare ADSI and ADO, so you can see the different nature of ADO as well as its pros and cons.

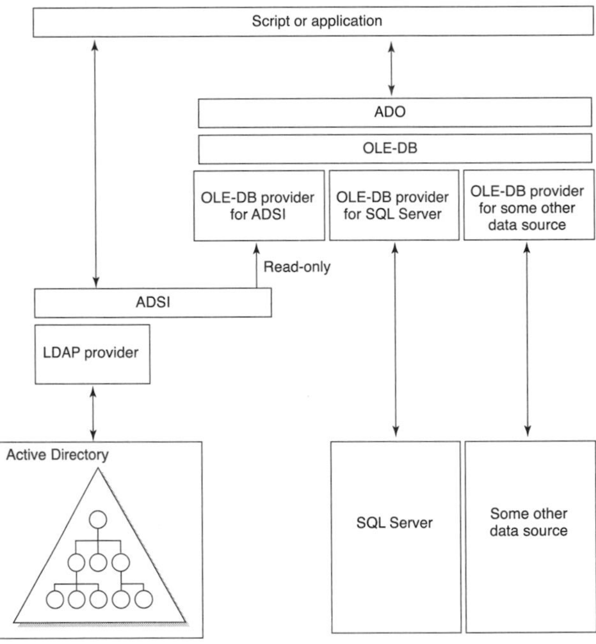

Figure 11.99 ADO is another COM-based programming interface that can be used on top of ADSI. However, this provider is read-only, so you cannot change any Active Directory data using ADO.

Table 11.6 ADSI and ADO Comparison

Feature	ADSI	ADO	ADO Pro/Con
Binding	To one object based on its name and path in the directory	Cannot bind; instead returns a set of all objects that match the search criteria (zero, one, or several objects)	+ –
Enumerating objects	Need to use recursion if you want to enumerate from several containers	Easily from several containers	+
Filtering of objects	Limited to class name	Full power of LDAP search filters and some other search settings	+
Reading other domains	Can do with default settings	Requires nondefault settings	–
Available attributes	All	Only those that were listed in the search	–
Authentication	Use the credentials of the logged-on user or specify others	Use the credentials of the logged-on user or specify others	
Can modify object	Yes	No	–

You could use ADO for two slightly different purposes, or should we say, usage philosophies:

- *Searching.* For example, you could use ADO to locate a certain user or if you don't remember which objects have the `fSMORoleOwner` attribute.
- *Filtering.* For example, if you want to copy a file to every user's home folder, you could use ADO to filter all those user objects from different OUs that have a home folder attribute set. Then you would perform the copy operation on all found users. You could also print out a report of all those users that don't have their phone number set and ask someone to fill in the missing phone numbers.

The latter purpose is probably more common in administration.

NOTE It doesn't really hurt that ADO over ADSI is read-only. You could use ADO to retrieve the distinguished names or ADSI paths of 137 particular users, bind to each one using ADSI, and then modify the objects. We show an example of this later.

ADO Mechanics

ADO has an object model that includes among others *connection*, *command*, and *recordset* objects. These three objects have certain properties and methods.

There are at least three ways to use various properties and methods when reading Active Directory with these objects. Also, you could specify many settings either as properties before calling a method or as arguments in the method call. This introduces variety to the scripts that you will see if you read scripts from different sources.

Because you need only one way to access Active Directory with ADO, we present only one in this book. Also, we are not very interested in all possible options and settings, so we explain only those relevant when working with Active Directory (most of them appear later in this section, however).

The three objects we mentioned work as follows:

- A *connection object* represents a connection from your script to a data source, such as Active Directory. Using this object, we can specify a username and password (although usually we don't) and open the connection.
- A *command object* represents a search command, and by specifying this object's properties, we can specify what kind of query we want to perform. We perform the query with the `Execute` method.
- A *recordset object* represents the returned data. You can think of it as a two-dimensional array, where each row corresponds to one returned Active Directory object and each column to one attribute.

Next, we show the first example and continue the discussion based on it.

Basic Example.vbs

This script picks up all users and contacts in your default domain (no matter what container they are in) that have a last name starting with A.

Then it lists the distinguished names of all those people. Figure 11.100 shows the script's output and Figure 11.101 displays the script's contents.

On lines 7 through 9 we create a connection object, and then tell it to use the OLE-DB provider for ADSI and open the connection.

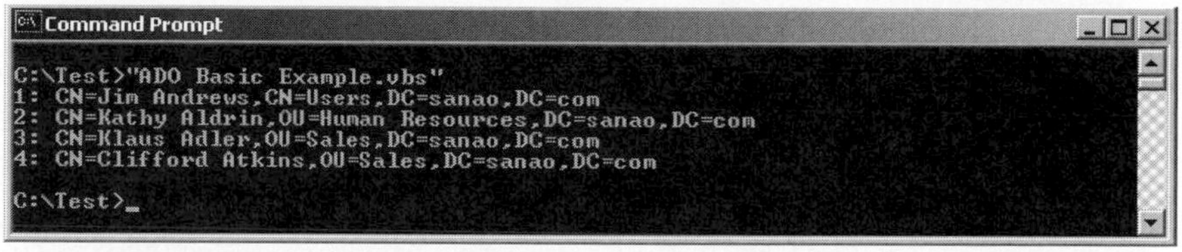

```
Command Prompt
C:\Test>"ADO Basic Example.vbs"
1: CN=Jim Andrews,CN=Users,DC=sanao,DC=com
2: CN=Kathy Aldrin,OU=Human Resources,DC=sanao,DC=com
3: CN=Klaus Adler,OU=Sales,DC=sanao,DC=com
4: CN=Clifford Atkins,OU=Sales,DC=sanao,DC=com

C:\Test>_
```

Figure 11.100 Output of "ADO Basic Example.vbs"

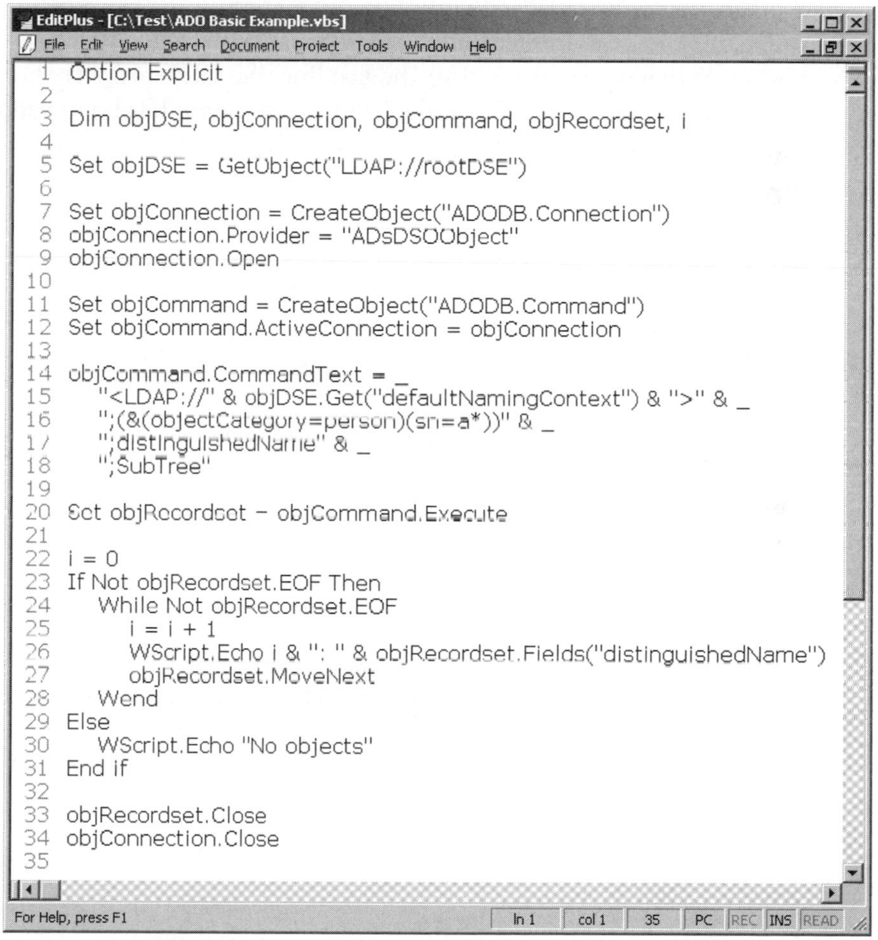

```
EditPlus - [C:\Test\ADO Basic Example.vbs]
File Edit View Search Document Project Tools Window Help
1  Option Explicit
2
3  Dim objDSE, objConnection, objCommand, objRecordset, i
4
5  Set objDSE = GetObject("LDAP://rootDSE")
6
7  Set objConnection = CreateObject("ADODB.Connection")
8  objConnection.Provider = "ADsDSOObject"
9  objConnection.Open
10
11 Set objCommand = CreateObject("ADODB.Command")
12 Set objCommand.ActiveConnection = objConnection
13
14 objCommand.CommandText = _
15    "<LDAP://" & objDSE.Get("defaultNamingContext") & ">" & _
16    ";(&(objectCategory=person)(sn=a*))" & _
17    ";distinguishedName" & _
18    ";SubTree"
19
20 Set objRecordset = objCommand.Execute
21
22 i = 0
23 If Not objRecordset.EOF Then
24    While Not objRecordset.EOF
25       i = i + 1
26       WScript.Echo i & ": " & objRecordset.Fields("distinguishedName")
27       objRecordset.MoveNext
28    Wend
29 Else
30    WScript.Echo "No objects"
31 End if
32
33 objRecordset.Close
34 objConnection.Close
35
For Help, press F1    ln 1   col 1   35   PC   REC   INS   READ
```

Figure 11.101 ADO Basic Example.vbs

Because we didn't specify a username or password, the connection is made with the logged-on user's credentials.

On lines 11 and 12 we create a command object and tell it to use our just-opened connection.

On lines 14 through 18 we have the LDAP search string, which specifies what objects and attributes should be read from Active Directory. We describe the string contents in the next subsection.

Now we are ready to perform the query. We do it on line 20, and on the same line we get the read data in a recordset.

A recordset has a *cursor,* which specifies the line (or *record*) that we can currently read. Because we want to read every line, we start from the beginning of the recordset, and with each loop, we read one line and then move the cursor to the next line.

We could first call the method `objRecordset.MoveFirst` to move the cursor to the first line, but because it is already there, we don't bother. When the cursor is after the last line, the EOF property becomes True. EOF stands for "end of file," and the acronym has been used with computers since the 1960s. It was chosen also for ADO, even though we don't have a "file" this time.

NOTE For the purposes of this book and the skills it covers, it's quite sufficient to read the recordset just from the beginning to the end. If you get more into ADO programming, you can start learning how to move around the recordset, perhaps with help from bookmarks.

On line 23, we first test that EOF is not already True. This would indicate that the query didn't return any objects from Active Directory, as we display on line 30.

Usually the recordset contains data, so we can browse through it on lines 24 through 28. We can read the attribute value from the recordset by specifying the attribute LDAP name as an argument to `Fields`.

NOTE We could also read the value using an index number instead of an attribute name. The first retrieved attribute would be `objRecordset.Fields(0)`, the next one would use index "1," and so on. However, Microsoft is not committed to this syntax in the long run and they recommend using the attribute names.

The LDAP Search String

When you study the script, you'll notice that lines 1 through 14 are always the same, no matter what you search. The same goes for lines 19 through 34, perhaps with some slight variance around line 26. Therefore, lines 15 through 18 contain the "beef" of the script—they define what the search is actually like. The rest is just mandatory dressing.

Lines 15 through 18 contain an LDAP search string. It consists of four parts separated by semicolons. The string has the following syntax:

```
<LDAP-path-to-base-object>;LDAP-filter;list-of-attributes;scope
```

These four parts correspond to the four main parameters of an LDAP search, which are described in Table 6.9 in Chapter 6. We show a brief summary in Table 11.7.

NOTE Because the essence of an ADO query is in the LDAP search string, you could say that in the case of Active Directory, ADO is just a wrapper that enables you to perform LDAP queries in a script.

Table 11.7 The LDAP Search String Contents

Part	Example	Comments
LDAP path to base object	`LDAP://DC=sanao,DC=com`	The ADSI path (i.e., LDAP path) to the base object of the query.
LDAP filter	`(&(objectCategory=person)(sn=a*))`	Specifies the criteria that each object must meet to be included in the search result set.
List of attributes	`distinguishedName, givenName, sn`	The list of attribute LDAP names that are to be returned in the query.
Scope	`SubTree`	The value is `Base`, `OneLevel`, or `SubTree`; if you omit this fourth part, `SubTree` is the default.

NOTE By default, even with the `SubTree` keyword, the scope of the query doesn't cross partition (or naming context) boundaries, such as from one domain to another. Later, in the "Multipartition Queries" section, we explain how to reach multiple partitions in one query.

When you use with ADO an LDAP search string, it is called the *LDAP dialect*. Another dialect you could use is the *SQL dialect*, which we introduce next.

Basic Example with SQL.vbs

The Structured Query Language, or SQL (pronounced "sequel"), is used to read, write, and manage data in relational databases, such as SQL Server. Because the roots of ADO are in databases, Microsoft implemented also the SQL dialect to the OLE-DB provider for ADSI.

If you don't already know how to use SQL, you shouldn't learn it just because of ADO. We do not teach SQL in this book, but we present the previous script modified to use the SQL dialect, so that if you do know SQL, you can easily catch on from this example.

The only thing that has changed from the previous example is the "beef" part of the script. Therefore, we show only lines 14 through 18 in Figure 11.102. You can see the familiar elements in a different order and with different surroundings. Note that the strings on lines 15 through 17 have a space as the last character so that there is a space before the first word on the next line. Note also that there is an apostrophe (`'`) at the end of line 16 between the quotation marks.

You cannot specify the search scope with this dialect, so the default `SubTree` is used unless you change it with the command object parameters, as described later.

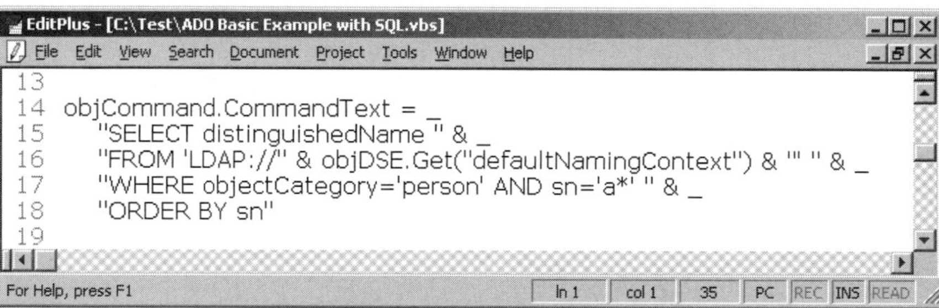

Figure 11.102 Part of the script lines of "ADO Basic Example with SQL.vbs." The lines not shown are identical to the previous example.

There is also one new element. We now sort by the last name (`sn`). When using the LDAP dialect, you can define the sort order with those command object parameters that we describe later. You must use indexed attributes for sorting; otherwise, it doesn't work.

Modifying Objects.vbs

An easy way to circumvent the read-only restriction of ADO over ADSI is to get just the object names with ADO, bind to each one using ADSI, and finally modify them as needed. This script demonstrates the technique. It finds all users of the domain that don't have a home folder set and sets this attribute for them.

We show the contents in two parts: part A in Figure 11.103 and part B in Figure 11.104. The latter part handles the returned set of users.

Once again, the only changed lines are the LDAP search string on lines 15 through 19. The best way to filter user objects is to use both the conditions on line 16. The first attribute is indexed, which makes it efficient, and if it alone would also return contact objects, the latter condition makes sure that only user objects are returned. In addition, as you know, if we used only the latter condition, we would get all computer objects.

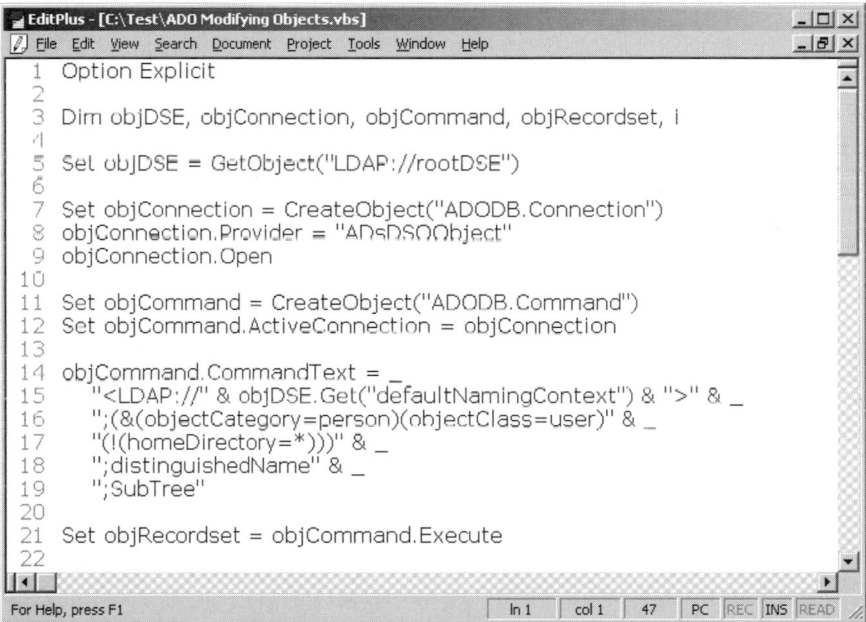

Figure 11.103 Part A of "ADO Modifying Objects.vbs"

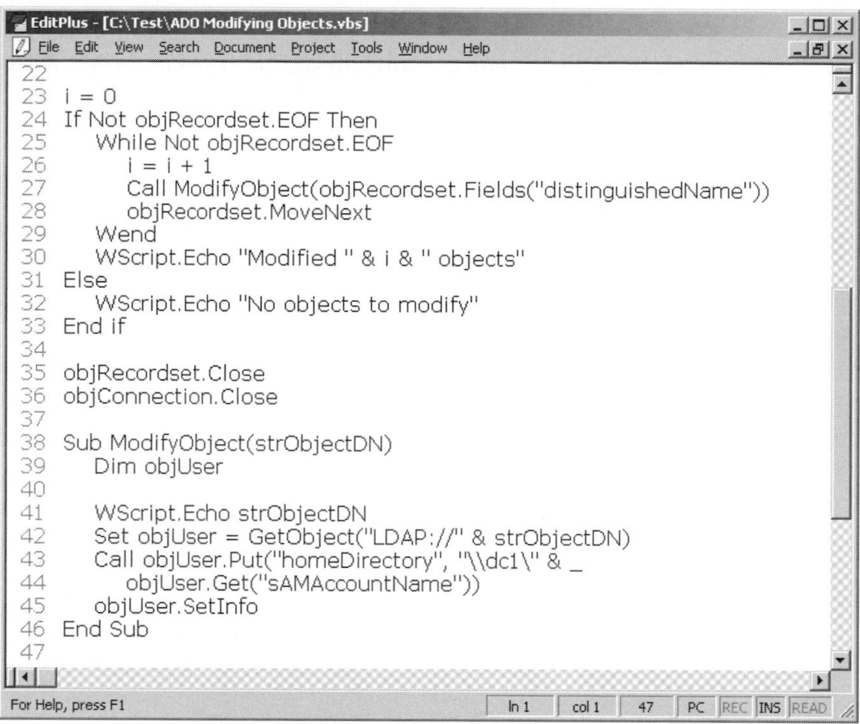


```
22
23 i = 0
24 If Not objRecordset.EOF Then
25    While Not objRecordset.EOF
26       i = i + 1
27       Call ModifyObject(objRecordset.Fields("distinguishedName"))
28       objRecordset.MoveNext
29    Wend
30    WScript.Echo "Modified " & i & " objects"
31 Else
32    WScript.Echo "No objects to modify"
33 End if
34
35 objRecordset.Close
36 objConnection.Close
37
38 Sub ModifyObject(strObjectDN)
39    Dim objUser
40
41    WScript.Echo strObjectDN
42    Set objUser = GetObject("LDAP://" & strObjectDN)
43    Call objUser.Put("homeDirectory", "\\dc1\" & _
44       objUser.Get("sAMAccountName"))
45    objUser.SetInfo
46 End Sub
47
```

Figure 11.104 Part B of "ADO Modifying Objects.vbs"

The `=*` on line 17 means "attribute value exists," and the exclamation point in the beginning negates the effect.

We browse through the recordset in a loop in Figure 11.104 (lines 25 through 29), where we just call a subprogram, passing the distinguished name as an argument. On lines 42 through 45 of this subprogram, we bind to one user and set her home folder.

We also want the script to report on which users it is changing and how many users there are. These output commands are on lines 30, 32, and 41.

NOTE Now we retrieve the distinguished names and add `LDAP://` on line 42. Another approach would be to retrieve the `ADsPath` properties, which already contain the `LDAP://`. However, we wanted to avoid retrieving the same seven characters for each user over the network, although we admit that this is not a big deal.

Multipartition Queries

All the ADO examples so far have used the `SubTree` scope, but as we mentioned, they were still limited to a single partition only (or naming context).

There are two ways to include several partitions, such as several domains or the configuration and schema partitions, in one query:

- Use the global catalog
- Turn on referral chasing

We discuss both options in the following subsections.

Using the Global Catalog

You can direct a search to the global catalog by specifying "GC:" instead of "LDAP:" in the base object path.

Using the global catalog is easy, because all you need to do is change a couple of letters. It is also efficient in terms of network utilization and search performance, as long as you have a decent communication link to the nearest global catalog server.

An obvious limitation to this approach is that you can search on and retrieve only those attributes that are part of the global catalog.

A `SubTree` query to the global catalog will automatically include any child domains, and if targeted to the forest root domain, the query will include the configuration partition, which in turn will include the schema partition. Figure 11.105 should help you visualize the tree and the partitions.

Next we describe the other option: referral chasing.

Referral Chasing

By default, referral chasing is off, which means that an LDAP query (wrapped in ADO) is limited to only one partition. In addition, that one partition must exist on the domain controller that you are communicating with. This results in two limitations.

- Even though the configuration and schema partitions are on your server, they are not included if you target the read to the domain partition.
- If you want to read just one domain, but that domain is not the home domain of your domain controller, you need to specify in

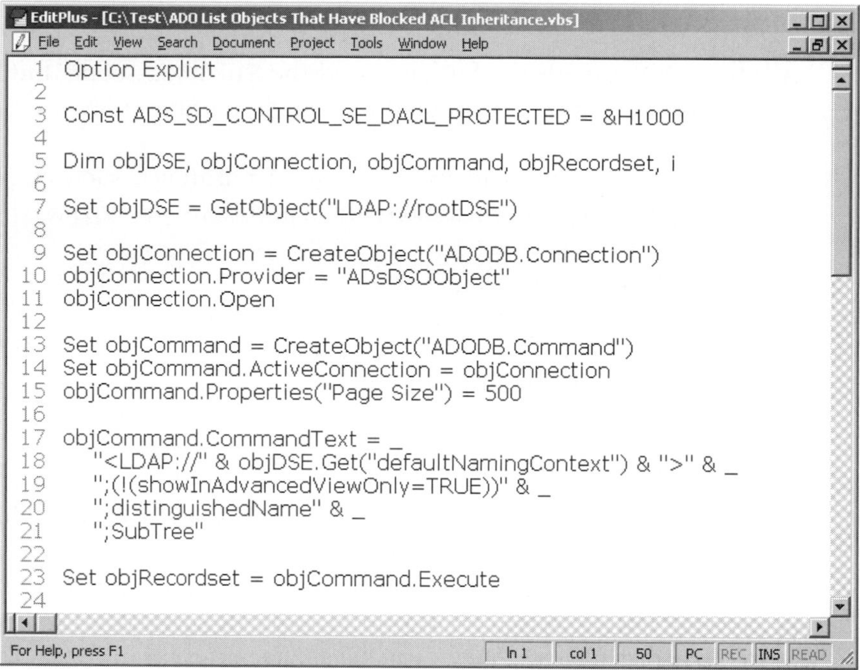

Figure 11.105 Configuration, schema, and every child domain are independent partitions, but together they form a logical tree where each one is a child to another.

the LDAP path a domain controller name that is a member of the wanted domain.

You can turn on referral chasing with one of the command object parameters. When you do this, the WLDAP32.DLL component of your computer starts chasing referrals for you. If a server doesn't contain the requested object, the server returns a *referral* to the client that points to another server, so WLDAP32.DLL can contact that server to get the needed information.

This description of referrals suggests that the configuration and schema partitions should be included, because they already are on the first domain controller. However, as stated earlier, they are not included, because they are different partitions.

WARNING Using referral chasing in a large network could mean that your computer starts gathering the information from ten domain controllers all over the world. Consider using the global catalog instead.

To turn on referral chasing, you could add the following lines to your script:

```
Const  ADS_CHASE_REFERRALS_NEVER          = 0
Const  ADS_CHASE_REFERRALS_SUBORDINATE    = &H20
Const  ADS_CHASE_REFERRALS_EXTERNAL       = &H40
Const  ADS_CHASE_REFERRALS_ALWAYS         = &H60   '&H20 + &H40
objCommand.Properties("Chase referrals") = _
    ADS_CHASE_REFERRALS_ALWAYS
```

As we mentioned, the default is `Never`, so there is no point in adding that choice to your script (unless you explicitly want to show that `Never` is in use). We explain the other choices in the following list:

- *`Subordinate`*. Specifying this option includes those other partitions that have the base object's distinguished name as part of their distinguished name. In other words, it will include all child domains (not just immediate), and if the base object is the forest root domain, it will include also the configuration and schema partitions.
- *`External`*. Specifying this option returns referrals to objects in other directory trees as well as the other domain trees in the forest.
- *`Always`*. Specifying this option includes both `Subordinate` and `External`.

NOTE If your default domain controller belongs to `sanao.com` and you specify an LDAP path `LDAP://DC=sales,DC=sanao,DC=com`, your query won't return any objects with the `Subordinate` option. You need to use `External` instead, which may seem a little confusing.

Referrals are returned based on `crossRef` objects, which reside in the `CN=Partitions` container of the configuration partition. If you are interested, you can check them with ADSI Edit. Notice in particular the attributes `dnsRoot`, `nCName`, and `trustParent`.

Additional Settings

You can specify some settings with either the connection object or command object properties, as explained in the next two subsections.

The Connection Object Properties

Before opening the connection, you can specify a username and password with the following properties:

```
objConnection.Properties("User ID") = _
    "CN=Jack Brown,OU=Sales,DC=sanao,DC=com"
objConnection.Properties("Password") = "somesecret"
objConnection.Properties("Encrypt Password") = True
```

In addition, you can use the `ADSI Flag` property to specify any of the authentication flags that we listed in the discussion about binding to ADSI with credentials (such as `ADS_SECURE_AUTHENTICATION`).

Search Options as Command Object Parameters

You can specify a number of search options as command object properties. Even though they are properties of an ADO object, they are actually general LDAP search options. Table 11.8 explains these options.

Table 11.8 Search Options

Option	Default	Description
`Asynchronous`	False	Setting this option to True specifies that control should return to the program after the first row of the search results is available (instead of waiting for all rows or at least the first page). This option has no meaning in VBScript scripts.
`Deref Aliases`	0	If Active Directory supported alias objects, you could use this option to specify that when the base object of a search (or some of its subordinates) is an alias, it will be dereferenced to get the target object.
`Size Limit`	0 (i.e., no limit)	Setting this option specifies how many objects you want back. Unlike the later `Page Size` option, this one doesn't return more than the specified number of objects. If you sort the returned objects based on some attribute, you may want to retrieve only the first ones on the list.

Table 11.8 Search Options *(cont.)*

Option	Default	Description
`Server Time Limit`	0 (i.e., no limit)	Setting this option specifies the number of seconds the server should use to fulfill your query. Unlike the later `Time limit` option, this one will fail if the specified time is not enough.
`Column Names only`	False	Setting this option to True returns only the attribute names and not their values. In LDAP searches, you could use this option to determine which attributes are present, but in ADO scripts, you probably don't have any use for it.
`SearchScope`	2 (i.e., `SubTree`)	This option has the same three choices as the fourth part of an LDAP search string (`Base`, `OneLevel`, and `SubTree`).
`Timeout`	0 (i.e., no timeout)	Setting this option specifies how many seconds the client is willing to wait for the query results.
`Page Size`	0 (i.e., no size)	With the default value "0" there is no paging, which means that if a query contains 15,000 objects, the server sends them all to the client. By specifying the page size (i.e., the number of objects returned in one chunk), you can lessen the burden of your client, the network, and the server. You don't have to add lines to the script to read the next page. ADSI takes care of this automatically when the objects of the previous page run out.
`Time limit`	0 (i.e., no limit)	Like `Page Size`, this option turns on paging. However, instead of the number of objects, this one specifies how many seconds the server can spend gathering the objects. After the time is up, it must return the objects found so far to the client.
`Chase referrals`	0 (i.e., never chase)	We described this option in the "Referral Chasing" subsection.
`Sort On`	(none)	If you specify an attribute LDAP name, the returned objects are sorted on this attribute. However, the attribute must be indexed in Active Directory for this option to work. Note that for some reason you cannot sort on the `objectCategory` attribute, even though it is an indexed attribute. If you try, no records are returned. *(continued)*

Table 11.8 Search Options *(cont.)*

Option	Default	Description
`Cache Results`	True	The default setting True means that the results are cached on the client. This is beneficial if you want to move back and forth in the recordset. If you just browse through the set once, the default setting only consumes more memory.

For example, to set the `Page Size` to 500, you would use the following line:

```
objCommand.Properties("Page Size") = 500
```

NOTE It is a good idea to set a `Page Size` for all your ADO scripts to avoid overloading the client, network, or server.

You can use the following constants for `SearchScope`:

```
Const ADS_SCOPE_BASE     = 0
Const ADS_SCOPE_ONELEVEL = 1
Const ADS_SCOPE_SUBTREE  = 2
```

Before we conclude our ADO discussion, we present one more example.

List Objects That Have Blocked ACL Inheritance.vbs

This last example lists all (visible) objects of the default domain that have blocked inheritance of ACEs. You might want to list these objects, because they are exceptions to the general access control strategy. However, if blocking the inheritance means that your permissions are also blocked, you obviously won't get a complete list.

Because the search is based on one bit in the `nTSecurityDescriptor`, we cannot use an LDAP filter for the job. Instead, we need to read all the objects and then inspect them individually.

We use the LDAP filter just to narrow the field a little by excluding all those objects that are set to "show in advanced view only." They are likely to be system objects, which we don't manage.

We show the script in two parts. Figure 11.106 displays part A and Figure 11.107 shows part B.

On line 15 we set the `Page Size`, because we recommended that you should always set it.

On line 19 is the LDAP filter. We must use "not true" instead of "false," because many objects are missing that attribute. Without this syntax, we wouldn't get those objects.

In the subprogram (lines 38 through 49 in Figure 11.107), we bind to the given object and read the `Control` property of its security descriptor. If that integer property has a certain bit set, it means that the corresponding object won't inherit any ACEs from above.

Note that we pass the value of the `i` variable as an argument and then change the value in the subprogram. By default, the argument was passed "by ref," which means that the changed value can get back to the

```
1  Option Explicit
2
3  Const ADS_SD_CONTROL_SE_DACL_PROTECTED = &H1000
4
5  Dim objDSE, objConnection, objCommand, objRecordset, i
6
7  Set objDSE = GetObject("LDAP://rootDSE")
8
9  Set objConnection = CreateObject("ADODB.Connection")
10 objConnection.Provider = "ADsDSOObject"
11 objConnection.Open
12
13 Set objCommand = CreateObject("ADODB.Command")
14 Set objCommand.ActiveConnection = objConnection
15 objCommand.Properties("Page Size") = 500
16
17 objCommand.CommandText = _
18    "<LDAP://" & objDSE.Get("defaultNamingContext") & ">" & _
19    ";(!(showInAdvancedViewOnly=TRUE))" & _
20    ";distinguishedName" & _
21    ";SubTree"
22
23 Set objRecordset = objCommand.Execute
24
```

Figure 11.106 Part A of "ADO List Objects That Have Blocked ACL Inheritance.vbs"

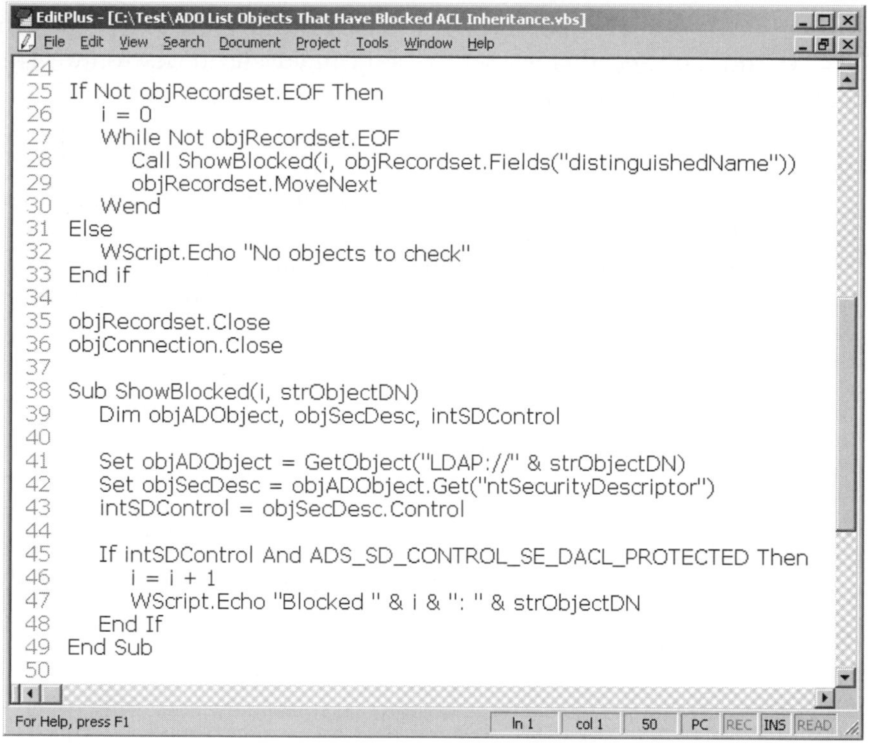
EditPlus - [C:\Test\ADO List Objects That Have Blocked ACL Inheritance.vbs]
File Edit View Search Document Project Tools Window Help
If Not objRecordset.EOF Then
i = 0
While Not objRecordset.EOF
Call ShowBlocked(i, objRecordset.Fields("distinguishedName"))
objRecordset.MoveNext
Wend
Else
WScript.Echo "No objects to check"
End if
objRecordset.Close
objConnection.Close
Sub ShowBlocked(i, strObjectDN)
Dim objADObject, objSecDesc, intSDControl
Set objADObject = GetObject("LDAP://" & strObjectDN)
Set objSecDesc = objADObject.Get("ntSecurityDescriptor")
intSDControl = objSecDesc.Control
If intSDControl And ADS_SD_CONTROL_SE_DACL_PROTECTED Then
i = i + 1
WScript.Echo "Blocked " & i & ": " & strObjectDN
End If
End Sub
For Help, press F1
ln 1
col 1
50
PC
REC
INS
READ

Figure 11.107 Part B of "ADO List Objects That Have Blocked ACL Inheritance.vbs"

calling program. This way, the incremented value is available in the next call. We could also have not passed it as an argument, which would have given us the same result.

Conclusion

After having read this chapter and studied some or all of the sample scripts, you should have sound knowledge and skills to administer your Active Directory network with scripts. At the same time, you have probably also learned quite a few things about the Active Directory architecture.

Bibliography

Books

Arkills, Brian. *LDAP Directories Explained: An Introduction and Analysis.* Boston: Addison-Wesley, 2003.

Howard, Michael, with Marc Levy and Richard Waymire. *Designing Secure Web-Based Applications for Microsoft Windows 2000.* Redmond, Wash.: Microsoft Press, 2000.

Howes, Timothy A., Mark C. Smith, and Gordon S. Good. *Understanding and Deploying LDAP Directory Services.* Indianapolis: New Riders Publishing, 1999.

Iseminger, David. *Active Directory Developer's Reference Library.* Redmond, Wash.: Microsoft Press, 2000.

Iseminger, David. *Active Directory Services for Microsoft Windows 2000 Technical Reference.* Redmond, Wash.: Microsoft Press, 2000.

Lissoir, Alain. *Understanding Windows Management Instrumentation (WMI) Scripting.* Burlington, Mass.: Digital Press, 2003.

Liu, Cricket, Matt Larson, and Robbie Allen. *DNS on Windows Server 2003.* Sebastopol, Calif.: O'Reilly, 2003.

Microsoft Consulting Services. *Building Enterprise Active Directory Services—Notes from the Field.* Redmond, Wash.: Microsoft Press, 2000.

Microsoft Windows 2000 Server Resource Kit. Redmond, Wash.: Microsoft Press, 2000.

Microsoft Windows Server 2003 Deployment Kit. Redmond, Wash.: Microsoft Press, 2003.

Web Sites

Active Directory Schema Site. http://msdn.microsoft.com/library/en-us/adschema/adschema/active_directory_schema.asp?frame=true

Active Directory Technology Center. http://www.microsoft.com/ad/

Group Policy Technology Center. http://www.microsoft.com/gp/

Platform SDK—Active Directory. http://msdn.microsoft.com/library/en-us/ad/ad/active_directory.asp?frame=true

Windows 2000 pages. http://www.microsoft.com/windows2000/

Windows Server 2003 pages. http://www.microsoft.com/windowsserver2003/

Windows Server 2003 Technical Reference. http://go.microsoft.com/fwlink/?LinkId=21711

Index